12/12/88

To The Women's Center
of Contra Costa College.

From,
Cecelia
Mendoza

ALSO BY SHERE HITE

The Hite Report: A Nationwide Study of Female Sexuality

The Hite Report on Male Sexuality

Women and Love

THE HITE REPORT

Women and Love

A Cultural Revolution
in Progress

SHERE HITE

ALFRED A. KNOPF

New York

"Perhaps the greatest problem which any historian has to tackle is neither the cataclysm of (violent) revolution nor the decay of empire but the process by which ideas become social attitudes."—J.H. PLUMB

"The current political goals of the women's movement . . . are neither to participate as equals in man's world, not to restore to women's realm and values their dignity and worth. Conceptions such as these are superseded in the present will to extirpate gender and sex altogether and with them all forms of domination. To aim at this . . . is a program that penetrates both to the core of self and to the heart . . . of the male domain, for it will require a restructuring of all social institutions." —JOAN KELLY

"Celie's quest is not so much to straighten out her relationship with her Mister, but to develop her relationship with the universe." —ALICE WALKER

"Anyone who wants to work on women has to completely break with Freud."—SIMONE DE BEAUVOIR

Contents

Preface   *x x i i i*

Acknowledgments   *x x v*

Philosophical Reflections on the Hite Reports, by Joseph P. Fell   *x x v i i*

*Quantifying the Emotions: Methodological Observations on the Hite
Report Trilogy, by Gladys Engel Lang*   *x x i x*

*The Hite Reports: Charting an Ideological Revolution in Progress,
by Naomi Weisstein*   *x x x i i i*

PART I The Emotional Contract: Emotional Life in
Marriages and Love Relationships with Men

What happens to love?   *3*

1   The Major Problems in Love Relationships   *5*

Men's emotional withholding and distancing: reluctance to
talk about personal thoughts and feelings   *5*

Lack of emotional support from men: not being listened to,
heard or "seen"   *11*

Listening with enthusiasm vs. listening "patiently": Do
men feel women have anything important to say?   *14*

Emotional indifference   *17*

Most men assume they have a right to emotional support
from women, that women should be loving and caring   *22*

How lonely can you be in a love relationship?   *23*

Men's distancing: part of an ideology   *24*

Emotional withholding: power and control
in relationships   *25*

Emotional and psychological harassment of women   *26*

Gender insults, condescending and trivializing attitudes,
slights, and put-downs   *26*

Hidden gender bias in language   *32*

Male nagging?   *39*

Emotional violence   *39*

After twenty years of the women's movement, do women
feel they are seen as equals in their relationships?   *40*

Loving one who loves you, yet believes you are inferior (or
"less rational," more "intuitive")   *43*

2   Fighting and Arguing in Relationships: What Do
    They Mean?   *45*

Typical fights   *45*

"If a woman doesn't bring it up, nobody will": the role
society gives women in fights   *47*

The riddle of male passivity in fights with women   *55*

"I feel fine. Why are you complaining?": men's patterns
during fights   *56*

Unfair fighting   *59*

"Don't make your bed a battleground": But is having sex
really making up?   *61*

Can fighting help?   *62*

Productive fighting: techniques for staying close   *62*

The intimidation of women through physical violence   *65*

Much, perhaps most, fighting represents women standing
up for their dignity, trying to make a relationship work   *70*

3   The Ideology Behind the System—Women's Giving,
Men's "Being"   75

The emotional contract   75

   What is emotional equality?   76

Women: the ones who try to "make it work"   77

Men assume they will "star" in relationships   79

   What does *being* loved feel like? Do men love women—or
just need them?   83

   Are men more emotionally dependent than women?   85

   Men's value system makes love less important—although
most men expect to receive love and nurturing
from women   86

   Men's emotional demands on women   88

Women are questioning the emotional arrangements in
their lives   89

   Women's emotional "duty"   90

   Can we continue to be nurturing, or should women
become more "like men"?   93

Loving men under the current system: What happens?   95

   Struggling to maintain identity and dignity, while
still loving   96

   Disappearing slowly like the Cheshire cat:
women's identity   102

   Women's anger—but do women have a right to anger,
since "good" women are loving?   109

   Feeling insecure and depressed: Are we too "obsessed
with love," or are men often treating us outrageously?   111

   Isn't women's anger logical? Women have a right to
be angry   114

   Men should not fear women's anger; they should
welcome it   117

Do women "love too much"? Or do men love too little?   117

   Is it women's values which should change—or men's?   118

A new view of "female psychology": goodbye to Freud and
assorted others   118

   Standard theories of women's psychology are wrong   121

Men's double message to women, not women's "lack of
self-esteem," makes women feel insecure   121

A note on the popular epithet, "Women lack self-esteem"   122

Wondering whether to leave: Is the love we want only
a dream?   123

Giving up on love: leaving the system behind emotionally
and intellectually   124

Relationships: Are they still the center of most
women's lives?   130

Women are changing the emotional structure of their lives
from what it has been for generations   131

Conclusion to Part I: A Conflict of Two Cultures: Women's
View of Love as Part of a Separate Culture and Value System   132

The "male" ideology and the slow erosion of love   133
The emotional contract: injustice built into the system   134
"Women's" culture and "men's" culture: two worlds   136

The two cultures: a historical tradition or a
biological given?   136

"Men are the reality, women are the role"   137
What is the "male" ideology and why does it make it so
hard for men to love?   138

Hierarchy: the essence of the "male" ideology   139

The psychology of being "male": "someone has to be
on top"   140

Why are most men confused when they fall in love?   141
What are the values of "women's" culture?   142

Women's thinking about relationships is leading women
to ask deeper questions about the nature of society   144

Women are faced with a historic choice   145

Could the "female" or "love" value system (the family
value system) disappear?   146

Seeing the world through new eyes: the
"Other" transformed   146

PART II Being Single: Women and Autonomy

Being single; feeling free—or emotional confusion and
relationship burnout? 151

    To define one's own life 151

4   Four Single Women Describe Their Lives 153

5   Dating Men: Fun or Russian Roulette? 172

The agonizing moment of starting a new relationship:
Should you have sex? Will he "trash" you later? 172

    Was it a "one-night stand," or did he change his mind? 174

    "The happy story of one woman's revenge ... ." 175

    The latest in "lines" men love to use 177

    "Nobody dates anymore, they just sleep together"
    (. . . *still*, since AIDS?) 180

    "Birth control? condoms? He's never even asked!" 181

    The double standard lives 183

    Do men have a right to push for casual sex? What gives
    them this right? 184

    When does date pressure become rape? 186

Does having intercourse with a man "mean" anything? If
you do have "sex," what can you "expect"? 188

    "After the first time we made love, he said, 'Let's not
    get serious.' " 189

    2,500 college men vote on whether to continue the
    double standard 190

    "Having sex shifts the power thing: When you meet
    the next night, you are no longer just two equals
    having dinner." 190

Using boys as "toys": Do women like sex "for fun"? 192

    Women describe their sexual adventures 192

    Most women want sex with feelings and love, most of
    the time 195

    Flirting and using men: female "conquests" 198

A new virginity and celibacy 202

    What does "virginity" mean? 205

Did women have more "power" before the "sexual
revolution" by remaining "virgins" while single,
"withholding" sex?   205

Is looking for lots of "sex" "natural"? Are women
"brainwashed"—or are men "dehumanized"?   207

Was the "sexual revolution" wrong? or is it the "male"
ideology and its double standard that make it wrong?   208

   Where did the double standard come from? Adam and
   Eve as early propaganda   209

   Does the new religious revival movement challenge the
   double standard?   210

What is sexuality? Creating a new vision of sexuality   211

   What was women's sexuality originally like?   211

   Can women, even now, define sex on their own terms?   213

   Continuing controversies over the nature of
   female orgasm   213

   But—do men really enjoy their definition of sexuality
   so fully?   217

   Toward a new sexuality: reintegrating sexuality
   and spirituality   219

6   Inside Dating Relationships: How Are Women Feeling?   222

Emotional uncertainty in relationships   222

   Is it "a relationship" or isn't it?   226

   Men's fear of commitments   230

   The "playboy generation" and the ideology of "freedom":
   Why are so many men so ambivalent about love
   and commitments?   237

   Pretending not to care: Should women be as "cool"
   as men?   238

   Should a woman be monogamous if a man doesn't make
   a commitment?   242

Power and games of strategy   244

   Edith Bunker and the Mme de Pompadour school
   of thought   244

   Breaking the spell of the singles game   246

   Do most single women want monogamous relationships?   250

To believe in love, no matter what the cost: Does love have
to be so difficult?   258

"Love is a battlefield"   *258*

How many compromises should a woman make?   *259*

Men's patterns in single relationships   *260*

Women's growing disrespect for men with
these behaviors   *265*

A new analysis of "male" psychology   *266*

7 Loving Men Who Are "Bad for You": The Myth of
   Female Masochism   *267*

"Do you sometimes think you pick the wrong men?"   *267*

What does "wrong" mean?   *270*

Great loves, painful love affairs   *274*

How much unhappiness do women put up with, and
why? Why do women stay in difficult relationships?   *280*

Most women do leave unhappy and
exploitative relationships   *281*

Is it worth having a less intense relationship, just to avoid
the pain of volatile ups and downs?   *285*

Practicality versus the soul: Must every relationship end
with the "perfectly adjusted heterosexual couple"?   *286*

Instead of being called "masochists," why aren't women
admired for their loyalty?   *287*

Is following an impractical "great love" a mistake?   *288*

Is there a "true masochism"? Unanswered questions
about passion   *289*

Sexual passion: a desire for "submission"?   *291*

8 Single Women Debate Whether to Marry   *293*

Pressures on women to marry—still   *293*

Do women have the freedom *not* to marry?   *293*

Most women are not married for large parts of their lives:
being single is "normal"   *295*

Mixed feelings about marriage   *297*

Women who don't want to marry   *299*

Women who do want to marry: What are their reasons?   *302*

Loving one person: emotional security   *302*

Wanting children   *302*

Social pressure: "Why aren't you married yet?"   *304*

Thirty and not married: the terror . . .   *306*

Family pressures   *310*

Reproductive time pressures   *310*

Struggling against the stereotypes   *312*

Is it better to marry the "wrong" man or to stay "single forever"?   *314*

Feeling embarrassed to admit you want marriage: the new pressure to be "independent"   *315*

Being ideologically "correct"   *316*

Do women still have the "right" to be financially "dependent"?   *317*

"Women are fed up with having 'equal rights'—it means you have to do everything!"   *318*

What does it mean to be "independent"?   *322*

Conclusion to Part II: Being unattached and independent: calling your life your own   *323*

In celebration of life on our own   *323*

Why women like being single   *323*

Having children on your own: woman/child as a family unit   *326*

"Older" single women: happy or alone?   *328*

Our right to ourselves   *336*

Most women love to spend time alone   *336*

PART III Marriage and the Nature of Love

The beauty of marriage   *343*

The feminist critique of marriage   *344*

9   Ten Women Describe Their Marriages   *346*

10   Extramarital Sex and Affairs   *395*

Are most women monogamous?   *395*

Why do women have affairs?   *396*

Double lives: What do they mean? 409

The chronology of alienation 409

How do women feel about their husbands' affairs? 412

Men's reactions to their wives' affairs 417

Being "the other woman" 423

Whatever happened to "the other man"? 430

11 Finances and Housework 431

Finances: Who earns the money and how is it split? 431

70 percent of women now earn money: What is the effect
on marriage? 431

How do women feel about being financially dependent on
their husbands? 432

Money-sharing arrangements of those with
double incomes 443

Housework: Are women still doing the housework? even
though most women work outside the home? 449

Are changing finances changing the shape of marriage? 457

12 Women's Feelings About Divorce 459

Women initiate most divorces 459

What are divorces like for women? 460

The process of divorce and the courts 465

The economics of divorce and the "feminization of
poverty": facing poverty but leaving anyway 467

13 What Is the Purpose of Being Married, According to
Married Women 469

The basic pleasures and benefits women find in marriage 469

Companionship, "belonging somewhere," and security 469

Economic cooperation 473

The physical warmth of marriage—for some 475

Having children 478

Social acceptability/social approval 484

Love: What kind of love do most women want in
their marriages? 485

14   What Is Love—Passion or Caring?   *488*

Women, both single and married, debate the nature of love   *488*

How does it feel to be passionately "in love"?   *489*

Many women don't like—or no longer trust—their
passionate feelings   *491*

    Being "in love" is impractical and painful   *491*

    Is being "in love" a delusion, a psychological problem?
    just lust?   *496*

What is passionate love? How does it fit into life?   *499*

    "If I can't have passion, I'd rather not bother." Are single
    women more likely to prefer being "in love"?   *500*

Women who believe in love as caring   *501*

    Does the emotional contract make it necessary for women
    to "play it safe" in relationships?   *506*

    Is caring always "love" or is it sometimes just "liking"? Is
    there anything wrong with this?   *506*

    When is "caring" just following social pressures to "take
    care of others"?   *510*

"Is the normal course of relationships that passion just dies
after a while?"   *510*

    The checkmate pattern: male emotional
    distance/harassment, followed by female sexual lack
    of interest   *511*

Married women who *are* in love with their husbands   *515*

Which kinds of love work best in marriage?   *519*

    New emotional arrangements within marriage   *521*

    Is it possible to love and not love totally?   *523*

Conclusion to Part III: Marriage—A Promise of Home   *524*

Are married women happy, or not going after their dreams?   *524*

    "I'm not really happy but I'm not unhappy either."   *524*

Double lives: leaving a marriage emotionally   *526*

    Are "home-base" marriages the answer?   *530*

    Redefining marriage: progress or cop-out? Does
    "liberation" mean rejecting marriage?   *530*

Was there marriage before patriarchy?   *531*

    Marriage as longing for home   *532*

Is the "age of the family" over? 533

"The family is the basis of our society; without it, the society will crumble." 533

"The family would lose its central personality—the mother . . ." 535

Longing for love 536

PART IV Women Loving Women

Listening on another frequency 541

15 Seven Women Describe Loving Women 543

16 Are Love Relationships Between Women Different? 573

Another way of life 573

What is love? 574

Pleasures of relationships: What are the parts of love relationships between women that women most enjoy? 579

Problems between women in love relationships 585

Is love between women more equal? Do women treat each other with more respect? Is emotional giving and sharing more reciprocal? 588

Fighting 591

Are women in gay relationships monogamous? 597

"We're wife and wife" 604

Fear of non-lasting relationships 604

Do gay relationships last? Does gay marriage work? 604

Breaking up: Is it harder for gay women? 605

Gay women and money 611

How do most gay women handle finances in their relationships? share money and expenses? 611

Do gay women have money—or are most poor? 613

Being single and gay 614

Do gay women like being single? 614

Coming out is hard to do—but most women sound very happy about it 617

Women over forty: becoming gay for the first time 621

Once gay, always gay? Once straight, always straight?   *628*

    Being gay: a political choice, or a biological given?   *635*

    Is gay love more "politically correct" love? more chic? (Is
    there such a thing as "heterosexual oppression"?)   *637*

Loving women: Does this "make" you gay?   *638*

    Where is the dividing line between gay and straight
    affection for a friend?   *638*

    Gay women describe their love for their best friends   *639*

    When is love for another woman "gay," and when is
    it friendship?   *641*

    Fear of loving and desiring another woman: Do some
    heterosexual women love their women friends more than
    they love men?   *643*

    Being woman-identified: a valid alternative   *643*

Another world, another culture   *644*

PART V To Transform the Culture with Our Values

The Other transformed   *649*

    Women's thinking about relationships is causing them to
    question the whole system   *649*

    Women's dissatisfaction: driving social change   *650*

    "I don't just want equality—I want something better"   *651*

    Women as a force in history   *652*

17 Loving Men at This Time in History   *654*

Where is love?   *654*

Can women change relationships?   *659*

    Old-style relationships   *660*

    "New model" relationships: changing the
    emotional contract   *664*

    Couples involved in change (20 percent succeed)   *665*

    Marriage and living with "younger men"   *677*

Men's resistance to change   *681*

    Why is it so hard for men to change?   *686*

    What should a woman do if a man won't change
    the relationship?   *686*

To appease men or confront them: a political question 687

How many women find it necessary to leave, or be
prepared to leave, to make their demands for
change heard? 687

Risking losing all love by insisting on real love 688

Is it *women's* responsibility to help men change? 689

Should women take a mass vacation from trying to
understand men? 691

The gradual wearing down of an identity: a betrayal
of yourself? 692

"Women haven't yet begun to fight for their rights in
personal relationships" 692

A long goodbye to the "male" ideology 693

The "male" ideology and the psychology of a culture 696

Hierarchy: "human nature" or an
ideological construction? 697

How big a part of the "male" ideology is seeing women
as second-class? 699

Men's fear of being "in love" 701

Change is a Catch-22 for men 702

The current state of world affairs: the connection between
"male pride," hierarchical social structure, and
international terrorism 702

Origins of "male" domination 704

How angry could women get? 706

Do almost all women feel generalized repressed anger at
men and "male" society for dominating them? 706

"Kept waiting for too long?" 707

18 Friendships Between Women: Another Culture, Another
Way of Life 709

Women love their friendships with other women 709

Why are women so happy with their women friends? 715

Emotional empathy and subtle communication
between women 715

The importance of women's friendships 719

Women speak more freely with each other 719

Women's friendships: often emotionally closer than love
relationships with men   *720*

Talking about men: are women "using" their friends, or
trying to understand another culture?   *721*

Breaking up with a friend   *723*

Women and power   *726*

We may love our women friends, but do we take
them seriously?   *726*

Fear of the power of the "male" system   *728*

Noble thoughts and extreme transcendence—men only?   *730*

Solidarity among women   *731*

Can women be power centers in society now? Can we
trust each other enough? Will we stand up for each other?   *731*

Being proud of each other and supporting each other: the
key to changing our status   *733*

19 To Make a World in Which More Love Can Flourish   *736*

A renaissance of human nature and the spirit   *736*

The twenty-first century—now?   *737*

Could the values of "female" culture serve as a framework
for a revolutionary philosophical transformation?   *741*

"Women's" culture: a different tradition   *742*

Theoretical debates over "women's" culture   *748*

How would this transformation in culture occur? How does
change happen?   *754*

Are revolutions about changing thinking, or
taking power?   *754*

Will non-violent resistance work?   *757*

Are we pacifists by choice—or are we *afraid* to fight?   *758*

A militaristic strategy?   *759*

Women's honor—our own code   *760*

Ideological revolution   *761*

A new philosophy   *763*

Not "the human condition"—not forever . .   *764*

A new spirit: the "other" now as seer   *765*

Appendixes 767

    Essay on the Methodology of the Hite Reports 769

    Questionnaire 787

    Statistical Data 801

Bibliography and Additional Reading 905

Preface

Women are suffering a lot of pain in their love relationships with men. Why?

We have known about this problem for a long time, but—strangely—no one has ever asked a large number of women what is really going on, how *they* describe what is happening.*

Are women really "neurotics" who "love too much" or "can't get it together"? Do they need to "shape up"?

Here 4,500 women have poured out their stories, the real truth of what is going on emotionally inside their relationships, things that go on in private that they may not want to tell anyone who knows them. But here, through the privacy of an anonymous essay questionnaire, women of all ages and backgrounds, with many different points of view, speak freely about their relationships, no matter how revealing or damaging what they say may be. This is a great act of sharing, which allows us to develop a new perspective on the situation we find ourselves in, to think what to do about it.

The inner debate that is documented here is part of a great change women are making in their lives and in the world right now. The new definitions women are giving to relationships completely turn around ideas of what has been accepted for so long as "female psychology."

This book is a journey into ourselves, remembering the most deeply we have ever been in love, how it feels; asking who we love now or if we don't, what it "means"; and answering the questions why things don't always work out, where we can go from here—and a celebration of each other and the greatness of women.

With my personal thanks to all the women who have contributed to this book, for what it has meant to me and my life.

Shere Hite

---

*This includes psychologists such as Freud as well as feminist writers. Women here are revising psychological theory of the last hundred years, challenging Freud and others in the largest sample of its kind. This is an unfinished revolution, the beginning of larger changes yet to come.

Acknowledgments

The author wishes to thank the many people who have been of help over the years of research involved in this project. Those who were kind enough to read this manuscript and offer helpful criticism include Frank Sommers, Barbara Ehrenreich, Peter Gay, Eric Foner, Jessie Bernard, and Albert Ellis. Their insights were invaluable and undoubtedly saved me from many pitfalls.

Not only for this, the last volume of the Hite Reports, but during all three reports, there have been those who have been intellectually supportive. They include Barbara Seaman, Leah Schaefer, Shirley Zussman, William Granzig, Mary Calderone, John Money, Bob Gottlieb, Janet Wolfe, Naomi Weisstein, Jesse Lemisch, Martha Kaplan, and Howard Wilson. Regina Ryan was the principal editor of the first volume, and has also worked importantly on the later two volumes. Lindy Hess worked with great skill on the first Hite Report, and also added her considerable talents to part of the editing of this volume. Anya Schiffren was also extensively involved in editing of this volume.

Particular credit should be given to those who, with great patience and intelligence, spent long hours working with me making the data manageable. They include Susan Rolnick, Rose Sabunjian, Barrie Sternberg, Audrey Fishburn, Annick Delorme, David Jones, Lin Crouch, Kate Colleran, and Micka Menos.

Two of my friends who were very close to me and involved in the manuscript have died during the course of this work, and I would like to commemorate them here: Gudula Lorez, the feminist publisher and translator of my works into German; and my oldest and deepest friend, Julian Prose, born Eros Gyulya, earlier in his life a member of the Hungarian Parliament.

Also, without the support of my remarkable women friends, most of whom I first met during the early days of the women's movement, this work would not have remained the great pleasure and excitement that it continues to be and always was. For being there, I would like to thank Joyce Gold, Syd Beiner, Catharine di Maria, Rikke Andersen, Calla Fricke, Margaret Civan, Tere Tereba, and Sarosh Roshan.

My editor, Bob Gottlieb, was an important force in the creation of this trilogy. His faith and commitment from the very beginning, through all three books, and in the case of this volume, when the work was barely conceptualized, meant more to me than I can ever say. Through the early and middle stages of this manuscript, when the argument was not as yet totally crystalized, he continued to believe in the importance of what was being documented, and provided brilliant editorial and conceptual clarity at many crucial points along the way. Corona Machemer is the editor responsible for much of whatever elegance of style and presentation can be found in these pages, and for many profound and subtle touches throughout.

My brilliant and inspiring husband, Friedrich Höricke, has been so understanding and supportive during the final stages of this work that I have grown to admire him even more than I already did. He fills my life with music and poetry, more every day—so many kinds of beauty.

To all these, and to my darling Rusty, my winged deer, I send my thanks—which is hardly an adequate word for how deeply I feel a closeness to all of them.

Philosophical Reflections
on the Hite Reports

As a philosopher I believe that the task of ethics or moral philosophy is to determine what the real and pressing needs of human beings are and then to determine how these needs can be fairly and justly met. The first requirement for moral philosophy is thus actual knowledge of human needs, knowledge which, historically, has not been easy to obtain. The Hite Reports are concrete empirical studies in which thousands of individual human beings, women and men, express some of their deepest needs and satisfactions and frustrations in their relationships with each other. This is powerful and profoundly moving material. It is powerful because the Hite Reports are a medium that has made it possible for a large number of human beings to speak openly and candidly about needs the expression of which society has tended to censor or limit, and the satisfaction of which society has often condemned and punished. It is profoundly moving in the way that all human revelations of deep and persistent but frustrated needs are moving. It's not too strong to say that I find in the Hite Reports a massive cry of the human heart, a cry for the open recognition of the fundamental needs so eloquently revealed.

This open recognition is a historical and moral necessity. We find ourselves in the midst of a vital struggle to revise a long history of repression of the distinctively human need to be able to express our needs, together with unjust condemnation of our attempts to fulfill them. The historical and moral importance of the Hite Reports lies precisely in their challenge to this history of repression and suppression, which has kept us ignorant of each other's deepest feelings. Nothing is more tragic than human beings misusing the brief time they are allowed on this earth by suppressing their own needs, by failing to recognize each other's needs and so failing to fulfill each other.

Responsible and moral treatment of each other and of ourselves requires knowledge of others and self-knowledge. We must know what each other's deep, often unexpressed needs are if we are to treat each other humanly, responsibly, justly, lovingly. And I must know that others have deep-seated needs like mine if I'm not to mis-know myself and so condemn myself as a freak or a misfit or a depraved animal. The Hite Reports are essays in knowledge of others and also in knowledge of ourselves. In them we have a classic example of how science and morality can go hand in hand: they offer a knowledge of human beings directed at a future in which we may better fulfill each other because we better understand each other.

JOSEPH P. FELL
Presidential Professor of Philosophy
Bucknell University

Quantifying the Emotions: Methodological Observations on the Hite Report Trilogy*

Quantification and analysis of attitudes and emotions is one of the most difficult tasks faced by social scientists—and one rarely attempted, almost never on such a large scale as in Hite's work. It has been one of Hite's contributions to devise an excellent methodology for studying the attitudes and emotions of a large population, while at the same time retaining a rich qualitative base: extensive data in people's own words about their deepest feelings.

When analyzing emotions and attitudes in depth, it has been customary in the social/psychological sciences to use extremely small samples; indeed, Freud based whole books on a handful of subjects. Thus for Hite to have used the small samples typical of psychological studies would have been quite legitimate. However, she also took on the more difficult goal of trying to develop a larger and more representative sample, while still retaining the in-depth qualities of smaller studies. She does the latter by allowing thousands of people to speak freely instead of forcing them to choose from preselected categories—in essence, predefining them and prepackaging them, as with so many studies. It is a method that is hard on the researcher, requiring analysis of thousands of individual replies to hundreds of open-ended questions, an analysis that involves many steps.

Hite's work has been erroneously criticized by some members of the popular press as being "unscientific" because her respondents, though numerous, are not a "random sample." However, scientists and scholars in the field of method-

*See also Essay on the Methodology of the Hite Reports, page 769.

ology and opinion sampling know that for many kinds of studies, and Hite's is one of them, a very large non-random sample generating rich data is preferable to a randomly chosen sample. A "random sample" does not guarantee representativeness; frequently, in practice, there is a problem of "who didn't respond." In this kind of sampling, to be perfectly mathematically "representative," all of those chosen must respond. However, in most cases, no such perfection is achieved. Thus, to put it bluntly, there *are* almost no "random samples."* As John L. Sullivan, the noted research theorist, puts it, "Most of the work in the social sciences is not based on random samples; in fact, many if not most of the articles in psychology journals are based on data from college students, and then generalized. . . . Interestingly, these small and non-representative samples have not been criticized in the same way Hite's larger and more representative sample has been." Hite's large and rich sample of 15,000 is an excellent achievement in itself. Moreover, Hite has matched her sample carefully to the U.S. population at large; the demographic breakdown of the sample population corresponds quite closely to that of the general U.S. population.

Another hallmark of Hite's methodology is the anonymity guaranteed participants. It is this which makes it possible for her respondents to speak so freely about their most private feelings and thoughts, and ensures that they do not feel they must hold back any of the truth about these very personal matters for fear of being ridiculed, judged, or simply "known." It is in fact because the respondents are guaranteed anonymity that one can be confident of the accuracy of Hite's findings. And indeed studies in three other countries testing the findings of the first Hite Report have replicated her basic results.

As Robert L. Emerson of UCLA explains, "Hite's methodology is perfectly suited to her aims . . . the distinctive quality of her data is exactly that it allows men and women to talk about the subjective meaning and experience of a variety of personal matters. The purpose of her research is then to describe and categorize the varieties of such experience . . . so that the whole range of such experiences can be described . . . [and she] has more than fulfilled this goal." Hite is straightforward about her procedures and has done as much and more than other researchers to explain her methods. She makes absolutely clear what she is doing methodologically—in fact, her degree of clarity is not frequently achieved in social science research.

There is a growing literature advocating the use of methods similar to Hite's in the social sciences. Feminist scholars in particular have developed a sophisticated critique of standard research theory, demonstrating its many built-in biases and distortions (see, for example, the anthology edited by Sandra Harding and Merrill Hintikka, *Discovering Reality*). Hite's work can thus be seen

---

*Therefore most survey research today tries to match its samples demographically to the general population in other ways, by, for example, weighting responses to conform to the population profile, as Hite does.

as part of this general rethinking, one of the first studies, in fact, to put new theories into practice.

Nancy Tuana of the University of Texas at Dallas writes: "For centuries, through the guise of science, men have been constructing theories of woman's nature. Although women have been the object of study, our experiences and feelings have not been taken seriously. Shere Hite's work provides a model of a methodology that is based on women's experience. Hite has rejected the silencing of women by recognizing that a theory about women's ways of loving must be rooted in our efforts to give voice to our own experiences. Her work will be valued not only for the insights she provides, but also for her revolutionary approach." And Barbara Ehrenreich, whose background is in the biological sciences, notes that "Tables, graphs, correlation coefficients, etc., do not, in and of themselves make a study 'scientific.' In fact, I would say that any study of human behavior that does not include—and highlight—the element of subjective experience is, in a fundamental sense, unscientific. This was what was wrong with the Kinsey Report and Masters and Johnson's work, and what makes the Hite Reports so ground-breaking: at last we know something about love as women and men experience it and that is the most important thing we can know about it."

In summary, as a scientist and as a human being who obviously cares very much about her subjects, Shere Hite presents in the Hite Reports a deeply penetrating portrait of our culture, based on empirical data, giving us insights into who we are and where we are going. This work is an enormous contribution.

GLADYS ENGEL LANG
Professor of Communications,
    Political Science and Sociology
University of Washington, Seattle

The Hite Reports:
Charting an Ideological Revolution in Progress

This book is the final volume in a series of three books dealing with private life and gender definition in the United States, one which combines philosophical discussion with impressive empirical research. Published internationally with widespread influence, these books comprise complex and fascinating portraits of a crucial fifteen-year period in American culture—a period in which society came into an extraordinary confrontation with the traditional ideas of home and family.

This confrontation is examined in the Hite Reports by looking at what really is there—i.e., documentation consisting of the responses of thousands of people to anonymous, open-ended questionnaires—rather than at what reigning theory tells us should be there, and by a debate carried on sometimes among the participants, sometimes between Hite and the participants, a debate based on a coherent theoretical perspective. Perhaps we will look back and say that what is documented here is the ideological revolution of the end of the twentieth century.

The Hite Report on female sexuality:
The redefinition of sexuality: sex is cultural

Hite began this project in 1971 when, on leave of absence from graduate school, she became involved with the feminist movement, and taking seriously the idea that the personal is the political, undertook a major effort to find out what really happens in women's sexual lives.

From 1972–76 she distributed a lengthy essay questionnaire to women all over the country; in 1976, on publication of the findings from the responses of 3,500 women, she explained her goals: "The purpose of this project is to let *women* define their own sexuality—instead of doctors or other (usually male) authorities. Women are the real experts on their own sexuality; they know how they feel and what they experience, without needing anyone to tell them. This is not to say that Masters and Johnson's and Kinsey's work is not invaluable—it is. However, their work continued to view sex through certain cultural blinders which kept them from understanding the whole truth about female sexuality. In this study, for the first time, women themselves speak out about how they feel about sex, how they define their own sexuality, and what sexuality means to them." Hite's background in social and cultural history helped her to provide a cultural framework for this discussion, to see female sexuality for what it is, rather than how it fit into the prevalent patriarchal ideology.

Hite's basic finding was that 70 percent of women do not have orgasms from intercourse, but *do* have them from more direct clitoral stimulation. This testimony from thousands of women blew the lid off the question of female orgasm. Masters and Johnson had brought up the importance of the clitoris, but had emphasized that women should get enough clitoral stimulation from simple thrusting during intercourse to lead to orgasm; if they did not, they had a "sexual dysfunction." Kinsey had hinted at this issue by noting briefly that women like cuddling and that they have their highest rate of orgasm during masturbation, but he did not define masturbation beyond a few sentences, nor did he come to the logical conclusion implied, or reach the new understanding of women's sexuality that Hite formulated.

Ann Koedt had first questioned whether women have orgasms during intercourse and suggested that the issue involved a patriarchal definition of female sexuality in her ground breaking 1968 essay "The Myth of the Vaginal Orgasm."

Following publication of Hite's work, one commentator placed the discussion in historical perspective: "Ann Koedt's . . . 'The Myth of the Vaginal Orgasm' and Shere Hite's *The Hite Report* . . . are unique discussions of female sexuality because they treat sexuality as the unity of both human biology and psychology imbedded in a political formation. Advancing from the personal 'sharing of experiences,' Koedt and Hite both revealed how men have constructed sexuality to their advantage. In particular, Hite illustrated that within the dominant pattern of heterosexual interaction male pleasure is primary. The importance of her work lies in the fact that Hite clearly views sexual patterns as social constructions. Her book not only sheds light on contemporary sexual practice, but works to direct the creation of noninstitutionalized sexuality."[*]

Hite's documentation with such a large sample of exactly how women do

*Rhonda Gottlieb, "The Political Economy of Sexuality" in *Review of Radical Political Economics* 16 (1): 143–65.

have orgasm easily—during self-stimulation—and that they do not usually have orgasms during simple intercourse without additional stimulation, as well as her declaration that there was nothing "wrong" with this, that if the majority of women said this, it must be "normal" for women—no matter what "professional sexologists" said—was, after an initial period of shock among some in the sex research community, accepted widely, and eventually Hite received the distinguished service award from the American Association of Sex Educators, Counselors and Therapists.

Hite's finding that women could easily reach orgasm with clitoral stimulation (although society had said women had a "problem" having orgasms) also raised a further question—i.e., is sex as we know it (the basic set of physical activities with its focus on coitus) a social or a biological phenomenon? Hite had raised this question in the sense that she showed that for the majority of women, intercourse itself doesn't necessarily lead to orgasm, although clitoral stimulation does. Therefore we are forced to ask ourselves whether sex was "created" for pleasure and intimacy, or simply for reproduction. If the former, then the fact that the kind of stimulation the majority of women need for orgasm should be included in the definition of sex forces us to consider redesigning sex.

If women had been compelled to hide how they could easily reach orgasm during masturbation, then the definition of sex, it follows, is sexist and culturally linked. Hite, again, writing in 1976: "Our whole society's definition of sex is sexist—sex for the overwhelming majority of people consists of foreplay, eventually followed by vaginal penetration and then by intercourse, ending eventually in male orgasm. This is a sexist definition of sex, oriented around male orgasm and the needs of reproduction. This definition is *cultural*, not biological."

In other words, Hite's study showed that sex is part of the whole cultural picture; a woman's place in sex mirrors her place in the rest of society. Although until that time, female sexuality had been seen essentially as a response to male sexuality, this was not a scientific or objective summation of the facts. It was a view of female sexuality through a certain ideological perspective.

Thus, *The Hite Report* linked the definition of sex as we know it to a particular society and historical cultural tradition, saying sex as we know it is *created* by our social system; it is a social institution.

While it is currently fashionable in academic circles to credit French philosopher Michel Foucault with the discovery that sex is cultural, that the way sexuality is defined is tied to a certain historical time and place, certain social structures, in fact, the idea grew out of early feminist discussions which were widely circulated both in the U.S. and France. *The Hite Report* contains the earliest full-scale statement of the clear connection between sexuality, its formation, shaping and definition, and the society that channels it in certain directions.

Carrying these thoughts further, into an "un-definition" of sexuality, the first Hite Report continued, "Touching friends and sitting together intimately should be possible. . . . Intense physical contact should be possible in many varied ways. In short, our whole idea of sex must be reevaluated."

Not the least of the contributions of the first Hite Report was the presenting of women's own voices on this topic for the first time—as Hite said, "The statements women sent were full of beautifully written, moving descriptions of their feelings—an anonymous and powerful, deep communication, almost a soul to soul communication, from the women who answered to all the women of the world. Receiving these replies was one of the most emotionally fulfilling experiences of my life—and it is this I want to share with other women who read the book."

The Hite Report on Male Sexuality: ### toward a new definition of masculinity

The second Hite Report, *The Hite Report on Male Sexuality*, was the first study of how men feel about themselves, their relationships and their sexuality: no such book had ever been done, certainly none using a data base approaching Hite's in size and representativeness. Although comparisons are often made with Kinsey, in fact Kinsey measured the frequency of sexual behaviors, not attitudes or feelings about sex, and he was dealing only with sexuality, not love or relationships.

Here also, Hite followed the format of anonymous essay questionnaires, asking men questions not only about sexuality, but also about love—about how it feels to fall in love for the first time, about their feelings concerning growing up with their fathers, their current relationships with women, their marriages, and what they would like to change about their sexuality and their lives if they could.

All told, *The Hite Report* on men presents a staggering picture of men, told in men's own words. The heart of this book is about ideology, that is, about why people behave as they do—and specifically, about the patriarchal ideology and how it permeates men's behaviors in every area, including sexuality, which is supposedly biologically determined. In other words, what we call "sex"—as stated in the first Hite Report—comes down to a reflection of attitudes and values (i.e., an ideology) that extend through large segments of the overall society. These sexual behaviors are socially created, not just biological; further, this socially directed institution of sex does not equally value the needs and possibilities of women and men.

In effect, with this volume, Hite was beginning a re-evaluation of "male psychology" and "male sexuality," which are so intimately linked—something rarely done,* since the assumption has been that the psychology of men is

---

*Psychologists earlier in the century such as Karen Horney and Beatrice Hinkle commented and wrote on these issues.

human psychology itself, that the way men are is "natural": not a socially constructed set of behaviors and perceptions, but "biological human nature in action."

To understand "male sexuality" it is necessary to understand the culture and what it informs men "male sexuality" and "masculinity" are—the whole context in which men are taught to see/express their "sexuality," and, especially, to see their emotional world. Men are offered a very limited repertoire of admissible (or at least publicly admissible) emotions; if a man feels other emotions, he must hide them. Therefore, most men, if asked on the street for their opinion, are quick to say, "Well, I don't think I'm a typical male." And they are probably right; there *are* almost no "typical males," since few humans could live with the limited set of feelings they are "permitted." Furthermore, not being allowed to express their emotions, not even (in a way) being allowed to *feel* all the things humans feel, makes men confused and uncomfortable when asked to talk about their "feelings," and this, in turn, causes deep problems for them in their relationships with women.

While in this book Hite has sympathetically pointed out the difficulties for many men—the awkwardness of some male rituals, how many men are stuck in these ritual patterns, this system, and suffering from it—possibly all this was a shock to men, since they are not used to seeing themselves as the object of studies, not to mention a study done by a woman. Perhaps because it is so shocking for men to be treated as a specific group, rather than as a universal standard, the second Hite Report received dismayed and sometimes even lunatic reactions from some male critics.

Hite, in effect, was receiving criticism for her bold dissection of the current socio-sexual system: by daring to claim that socialization pressures the male to adapt and perform in a particular sexual manner, she challenged the usual and highly touted idea that male physiology and evolutionary processes create and control male sexuality. As a result, she was subject to a deeply entrenched prejudice based upon her sex and the topic of her study. In effect, male critics attacked her expertise and her commentary on a matter which men consider to be extremely personal and important to their sense of being male. In other words, she was viewed as treading on sacred ground, an area which so greatly forms the male ego.

Again, in this volume, Hite stressed the cultural relativism of sexuality. In a section on the politics of intercourse, she argued that a man's "sexual drive" is not a biological imperative, but that our society's definition of sex is culturally created: if you can show that there are cultural pressures on people to behave in a certain way, then you cannot make the assumption that the behavior is a biological given.

But what we know as "male sexuality," Hite explains, is not only a socially constructed but also a very limited version of what male sexuality might be. Just as men are offered a very narrow range of emotions by the culture, also their sexuality is narrowly defined and subtlety inhibited. As she states in the preface to that work, society tells men to "define love as sex, and sex as penetration and ejaculation within a woman . . . [therefore] it is not simply by looking at the small details of men's sexual lives and understanding how they may hurt or give pleasure that will change our idea of what male sexuality is—discussing them rationally as if more "pleasure" were the aim—because that is not the definition of male sexuality—male sexuality is not based on simple pleasure. Male sexuality, and masculinity, is based on a larger ideology; [*in fact, "sex" in general*] *is not so much about pleasure as it is about a certain emotional symbolism that is a part of that ideology, a ritual drama re-enacted over and over.*"*

Hite, in essence, is appealing for a redefinition of masculinity, for men to stop and look at what it is they are doing with their lives. This is a book full of possibilities for the future.

Women and Love:
redefining the nature of emotional life

I have always felt that "love," perhaps because it is considered to be the center, if not the totality of a woman's life, is a risky business, and one to which feminists should address much energy and ingenuity. When I was in graduate school in the early 60s, I was appalled by the abuse that my female colleagues sustained in the pursuit and achievement of love. Indeed, I organized a "syndicate" (modeled after Milo Minderbinder's in Joseph Heller's *Catch-22*) to resist such abuse, collectively taking the initiative in dating and blacklisting men who mistreated members of the syndicate. The outrage which resulted from these efforts convinced me that I was tampering with what men considered their sacred rights. I continued this work later, when, as a member of the Chicago West Side Group, I led a drive to organize women in singles bars to rationalize and dignify the pursuit of love. But although the members of the group had previously demonstrated extraordinary courage, facing police, tear gas, going to jail in draft resistance demonstrations, when it came to the singles bars, their courage faltered. The project was abandoned because only two of us would regularly show up for planned actions at the bars, no matter how many had promised to come. At an early meeting of feminists from across the country in 1968, I spoke of the need for a task force of feminists to fight the oppression and dehumanization of women that went along with our pursuit and achievement of love.

But the politics of heterosexual love and romance have never been fully explored nor documented on a large scale. In the first Hite Report, in 1976, Hite had announced her intention of studying women's feelings about love, asking women to define the nature of love†—because "it is in the emotional dynamics of love relationships, and in the psychological assumptions, that stereotypes

---

The Hite Report on Male Sexuality (New York: Alfred A. Knopf, 1981), p. xvii.
†See *The Hite Report* (New York: Macmillan, 1976), Chapter 6.

about women remain most deeply embedded."* And also, women have been defined by the society for a very long time in terms of "love"—i.e., told that they must raise a family, be loved by a man, married, or face being an "outcast."

Much of this feeling, that women's basic function in life is to be loving and nurturing, still remains; it has not been fully accepted that women are complete above and beyond their biological capabilities, or ability to take care of, "service" others. This does not mean, of course, that it is "wrong" to be nurturing; the question here is whether all of the nurturing of society is supposed to be done by women.

In particular, there is a bias against women that often comes out in personal relationships—i.e., that men express by their behavior, actions and statements to women in private. Love between women and men is an area that needs to be analyzed more deeply than it has been. As Carol Gilligan has pointed out, "Among the most pressing items on the agenda for research on adult development is the need to delineate *in women's own terms* the experience of their adult life."†

Several earlier works broached these issues. Simone de Beauvoir's *The Second Sex* opened up some of the deeper areas of women's concerns about love, bringing out poignantly the mixed sense that love is great and yet somehow involves pain and humiliation for women—so that, according to de Beauvoir at the time, we finally may come to learn to love humiliation in love. In the 1970s Kate Millett's *Sexual Politics* shook the world with its statements about love between women and men, exposing the violence in much of men's writing about women they love, or supposedly love. Ti-Grace Atkinson, in *Amazon Odyssey*, coined the phrase, "Scratch his love, and you'll find your fear." Shulamith Firestone and Laura X also presented interesting theoretical statements, and additional work was done by Elaine Walster-Hatfield and Dorothy Tennov.

However, after the early 70s, issues of love between women and men did not receive as much attention as issues of sexuality (notable exceptions were Jessie Bernard, Letty Cottin Pogrebin, Barbara Ehrenreich and Andrea Dworkin). Indeed, in a strange sort of reverse Victorianism, theorizing and writing about sex became more acceptable than writing about love, and some interesting theoretical works were produced by Alison Jaggar, Catherine Stimpson, and a group of women editing *Powers of Desire*. But feminists rarely confronted the politics of heterosexual love head-on. Rather, two trends, both of which skirted the issue, arose. One went off men entirely, embarking on a stunningly

---

*This explains the explosion of popular psychology books in which the subject of relationships between women and men is now being talked about: as women become more and more unafraid of the social system and of men, more independent financially and ideologically, yet find themselves in love with or living with men who still express (perhaps unconsciously) old stereotypes about women's "nature"—expecting women will be loving, take second place emotionally in relationships, not being angry when the man does not reciprocate with this emotional support—women wonder what to do about the situation, whether to leave or stay, what to think.

†Carol Gilligan, *In a Different Voice* (Cambridge: Harvard University Press, 1982), pp. 172–73.

revolutionary exploration of how women can love women without reservation. However, a sectarian part of this trend claimed that women still attached to males were "consorting with the enemy," thereby dismissing millions of women who had associations with men either by choice or circumstance. The other trend was of the position that "Men are changing, so why talk about it? There *is* no problem—a smart woman should be able to find herself one of the 'new men' out there."

Thus heterosexual love relationships became almost a taboo subject in feminist circles, not politically "correct" or "relevant." And yet this is one of the most important political topics there is, if one takes seriously the original slogan of the women's movement, that is, "the personal is political."

Academic psychological studies in recent years have come to focus on gender issues, but have also shied away from the study of love and emotion, perhaps since they are not easily quantified, and therefore the work might not be considered "scientific" by colleagues. Studying love, in other words, is difficult, and could easily leave one open to attack—as Elaine Walster-Hatfield found in 1972 when, after obtaining a government grant to study love, she was berated publicly by Senator William Proxmire, who thought the taxpayers' money was being wasted on such a frivolous topic, and as a result lost her grant. Nevertheless, in recent years, Pepper Schwartz and Phillip Blumstein of the University of Washington have published in this area, as have philosophers such as Joseph Fell, Irving Singer and Emilie Rorty.

In *Women and Love*, Hite and the 4,500 women participating begin the process of re-naming what is going on in personal life, re-seeing the emotions involved and the patterns of behavior, debating with each other the definition of love and various emotions felt for another—not only for men but also for women.

What do women say here about love, and what is going on in their lives? Basically, whether married or single, most say they do not feel emotionally satisfied in their relationships with men, often finding themselves frustrated, alienated, distanced and unable to break through to a man who doesn't see what is missing. Many women leave these relationships, while others stay, but often stay physically only, looking elsewhere for their primary emotional connection—often with women friends. The frustration women feel in these situations, in fact, the tragic aspect of many relationships—is staggering and profoundly moving.

We know that the home has been women's ghetto, and were surprised when we first began to hear of the incidence of physical violence in these private settings. Now we see here something harder to pinpoint, that is the terrible emotional draining of women that has been and is going on in relationships, the subtle ways women are badgered emotionally in private (even just by "standard" and "acceptable" usage of language which inherently puts women down)—and still expected to provide loving and nurturing.

Love relationships take place in private, there is no one to witness what goes on there, to name what is happening; each individual has to name it for herself, by herself—amidst the confusion of also loving and perhaps being loved—and doubt that she is ever right in her naming. (If a relationship is painful, a woman may feel she cannot or "should" not complain, lest she be seen as having "problems.") So, many of these things are not said in daily life—in fact, some of the voices we hear here seem almost to be voices from hidden bedrooms, sobs never before heard by anyone—or voices surfacing finally after months and years of numbness, of having almost forgotten how to speak because of the futility of it, since one's own "voice" was never heard. And yet there is also in these voices a great strength and determination to be heard, to speak, to no longer remain silent or be told what "reality" is.

The documentation women give here of their inner emotional lives should finally provide much of the material necessary to replace the Freudian-descended systems of "women's psychology."

Was Freud wrong about women? Yes, indeed, as I first argued in 1968:[*] Personality theory in general, whether Freudian or not, has missed the central importance of social expectation and culture in determining what we do and how we feel, and thus is largely irrelevant to an understanding of our lives and our behavior. As I showed, Freudians and others can neither predict what we do, nor seriously explain what we have done. Nonetheless, the idea of women's inherent "passivity" or "masochism" has remained a bedrock of the cultural myth about women, a myth strengthened by the cultural recidivism of the current era. Here this myth is annihilated by a large body of proof and documentation.

What women say in *Women and Love* supersedes Freud and many other current schools of therapy, none of which are based on large data bases, and especially not on what *women* say. This book shows the fallacy of many of the stereotypes placed on women ("defining" women) by, as Hite describes it, "Freudian Mysticism—i.e., that particular brand of mystifying women Freud had which was a retort to the feminism of the 1900s; women are not 'dissatisfied,' he said, because of their secondary social status, or because they are in fact overworked; women are 'dissatisfied' for neurotic personal reasons." Hite goes on: "This line of 'thinking' continues today in abstruse academic theory and in popular advice books which tell women they 'love too much' and should change their 'crippled,' 'neurotic' patterns of behavior. But women are confronted by very real, negative situations in their lives. The question for any group in this situation is, what to do about it. Women are trying to get men

[*]An early version of this argument appeared in "Psychology Constructs the Female," published as a pamphlet in 1968 (Boston: New England Free Press); it was then reprinted as " 'Kinder, Kuche, Kirche' as Scientific Law: Psychology Constructs the Female" in Robin Morgan's *Sisterhood is Powerful: An Anthology of Writings From the Women's Liberation Movement* (New York: Random House, 1970, pp. 205–20); and was later revised and updated as "Psychology Constructs the Female; or the Fantasy Life of the Male Psychologist—With Some Attention to the Fantasies of His Friends, the Male Biologist and the Male Anthropologist" (*Social Education*, April 1971, pp. 363–73).

to see personal relationships differently, to change their values, but when they don't, women now feel forced either to leave, or if they stay, to become less committed emotionally—they feel psychologically divided and frequently confused and depressed. Freud may have, with his sample of three women, documented this stage of the process, but it was not correct to build an entire 'theory of women' or 'psychology of women' around it. What we are documenting here, by listening to women, is the *whole* panorama, and not forgetting the cultural milieu in which we are living."

Some readers may be surprised by the small focus on class analysis here, since it has become so prominent in some feminist scholarship. Hite's data (as seen in particular in the statistical appendixes), simply do not warrant such a breakdown. How women are "seen" by the culture transcends class: almost all women are expected to be "loving" and not "bitchy," no matter what their class, education or socioeconomic group. Indeed, class analysis has never struck me as appropriate in an understanding of women's oppression. Rather I have always suspected that it is a scam whose aim is to keep women in the place assigned to them by Marxists.* Interestingly, however, an important part of what Hite has done in her work is to involve a great number of people in significant discussions and in the political process of defining their own lives and the culture.

Hite's theoretical framework for understanding what is happening today in personal relationships and in the culture is neither Freudian or Marxist, but builds on feminist analyses of patriarchy. As she says in Part V of this volume, Freud eventually came to believe that aggression was inherent in biology, and could not be eradicated from society in order to make a better society; Marx, however, declared that aggression was caused by the economic system, a system which should be changed; Hite, like many feminists, believes that the society we have, with so much emphasis on aggression and competition, is not necessary—we simply don't have to live this way—and what is needed to change it is a complete understanding and revision of the ideological system at hand. It is to this that her books are dedicated.

We seem to be living in a time of a radical shift: we are in the midst of a very real revolution. Despite the cultural backlash, despite the media blitz and the mocking of feminism, what the modern women's movement started continues its explosive growth. Women all over the United States have come to some very important conclusions; indeed, their whole perspective on the world seems to be changing. What we see in *Women and Love* is women defining themselves emotionally, defining themselves on their own terms, leaving behind a "male" view of the world, saying goodbye to an allegiance to "male" cultural values which define women as second-class emotionally or any other

---

*Naomi Weisstein, Virginia Blaisdell, and Jesse Lemisch, *The Godfathers: Freudians, Marxists and the Scientific and Political Protection Societies* (New Haven: Belladonna Publishing, 1981).

way, and which insist that competition and aggression are the basic realities of "human nature."

Women are finding new strength in their women friends, and women as lovers—although women's friendships may have been even stronger in Victorian society, when friends walking arm in arm or holding hands was commonplace, as was writing passionately affectionate letters to one's friends, and although in general women have throughout history taken strength from each other.* In fact here, a significant number of previously married women over forty are finding love with another woman to be a new and satisfying way of life.

The debate here is in part about what "women's revolution" will mean to the society: if we change our status, will the whole society be changed thereby, transformed? Will women's consciousness change the culture, or will women be totally assimilated into "male" ways of thinking and perceiving the world? Women here, while taking on some "male" ways of dealing with the world, seem quite clearly to be rejecting the "male" value system, and taking a new path—although where that new path will lead is as yet unclear.

In other words, women are leaving "home" and creating a new culture—radically altering the psychological structure of their lives, leaving behind an authoritarian allegiance to "male" dominance and to the acceptance of male definitions of who women are. Hite calls this, "Seeing the world through new eyes: if women have been the 'Other,' in the famous phrase of Simone de Beauvoir, now the 'Other' have turned that role to advantage, 'Seeing' in a new way. From our role as 'outsider,' we have found we are able to see and analyze what is going on much more clearly than those at its center. Women are changing the role of 'Other' from outsider to that of Seer, inventing a new analysis of culture."

Here then, is a massive wealth of data on women's inner world, and the current struggle in personal life against ideology—deeply perceptive theoretical treatises, juxtaposed with rich, personal and subjective material from 4,500 women about their personal private thoughts. This volume is a scholarly landmark, ahead of its time, and an invaluable contribution to the transformation of our culture currently going on.

NAOMI WEISSTEIN
Professor of Psychology
SUNY, Buffalo

*While it is likely that for most times and places, women have had close friendships with each other, in the twentieth century before the second wave of feminism, intense friendships between women became socially unacceptable, deemed sick and abnormal by the early sexologists and other patriarchal enthusiasts. In her brilliant book, *Surpassing the Love of Men: Romantic Friendships and Love Between Women from the Renaissance to the Present* (New York: William Morrow, 1981), Lillian Faderman documents the passionate attachments between women that were the social norm throughout the seventeenth, eighteenth, and nineteenth centuries, and which we see women re-claiming here.

The Emotional Contract:

Emotional Life in Marriages and

Love Relationships with Men

What Happens to Love?

"Initially, being in love is fun but something happens and it becomes frustrating, painful, and disappointing. What is the thing that happens?"

"I try to open him up. I want to talk about our relationship, feelings and problems, and develop solutions or compromises. He is quiet, so I have to initiate it and drag it out of him. I usually work the hardest to resolve the problem. Sometimes, when he finds it hard to express himself, he withdraws. Without communicating, how can you solve anything?"

"Although I find that I'm funny, sarcastic, and energetic when in mixed groups, 'the life of the party'—when my boyfriend's there . . . boom. I'm very quiet. Almost like I don't want to steal his 'spotlight.' Am I alone in this?"

"My father was somewhat affectionate, as much as he knew how to be—you know, that masculine way, by being insulting."

"When I was three or four, my mother was already teaching me to *see* dust and other people's feelings. ('Don't bother your father, he's tired.') Men don't learn the same sensitivity."

"Generally I like least about men their tendency to bottle up their thoughts and emotions so that you have to use all your energy trying to get them to speak out and share their inner selves."

"I don't know if my short relationships with men are at all typical. The main thing that struck me was that there was virtually no discussion of anyone's feelings. Most men seem to see women as women, never as people. Things that I kept finding myself doing/feeling around men: Feeling like they were the important ones. Feeling too big, in all ways. Too tall, too large, said too much, felt too much, occupied more space than I had a right to. Wanting to please them. Wanting to appear femininely pretty."

"I was so hurt by the emotional abuse that I can't even talk about it now. Funny how feminists always get excited about physical abuse. Me too. If he'd ever hit me I would have walked out forever. Emotionally is something different . . . but the sick cycle of lashing out and then being repentant, and of finally in the end giving the emotional 'gifts,' is the same. It is sick, sick, sick, but when you are in the middle of it, it is hard to see, hard to get the perspective. You keep giving, simply the fact that you have invested so much makes it harder to give up."

Most people live their "real" lives in an emotional world—a world of feelings and beliefs. These interior lives are more real to them, more present with them, than politics or the day's news. There is great beauty in sharing these worlds with another. As one woman puts it, "The times you feel really alive are times like when you are in love, or there is something very real and intense, when a contract between a deep part of yourself and another being is made real."

Why do things so often change or go less "right" after the first weeks of happiness? Why is "love the greatest blessing, and the scourge of the earth"? Is it the normal course of relationships that passion and even closeness just die after a while? Here women describe what it is that they believe is going wrong between people who truly do love each other—a chain of events so common that one often hears cynicism expressed over the possibility of two people ever living happily together.

Ninety-eight percent of the women in this study say they want to make basic changes in their relationships and marriages, improve the emotional relationships they have with men.* How do women analyze the issues—what do women say are the main problems in relationships?

---

*A 1986 study by *Woman's Day* magazine found similar dissatisfaction; four out of five women asked said they would not marry the same men again, if they had it to do over. Also, large sales of "advice books" for women seem to indicate that this is an area women are intensely interested in.

1

The Major Problems in Love Relationships

Men's Emotional Withholding and Distancing: Reluctance to Talk About Personal Thoughts and Feelings

"What is the biggest problem in your current relationship? How would you like to change the relationship, if you would? Could it be better? How?"

98 percent of the women in this study say they would like more verbal closeness with the men they love; they want the men in their lives to talk more about their own personal thoughts, feelings, plans, and questions, and to ask them about theirs:

"The biggest problem? Not being able to tell him or explain to him what the problem is when I am angry or have other negative feelings. His background is such that he learned to repress his feelings, feels that they are a sign of weakness. I have had to learn to swallow my anger (when I can) or have him treat me as a child (when I can't). He has occasionally apologized for this in a roundabout manner."

"It could be better if he would open up and talk to me more. He keeps things bottled up."

"Our biggest problem is not being able to talk. He talks *at* me, and what he says is law. I don't seem to be allowed an opinion. We don't have fights—he makes statements, and the discussion doesn't go any further. He expounds, I clam up, bang the door to the bedroom, and fall silent. Very frustrating on both sides."

"Our problem is lack of open communication because of my husband's fear of exposing himself to himself, let alone to me."

"I need more feedback—verbal or non-verbal—from him. It is difficult to tell whether I'm irritating or satisfying him."

"His refusal to really share himself with me is a problem. I would like him to be more spontaneous, to talk deeply about his feelings, fears, or whatever. His ego doesn't permit it. I've yearned for sharing, but only get it with other friends. It could be better if he'd be more of a companion, talk more, have a sense of humor, and not consider his work so blastedly important."

"He closes me off from him when he most needs support. Sometimes I feel like an outsider looking in."

"When I try to tell him my feelings or needs, he always says it's bullshit."

"I would like for us to be able to say what is on our minds. My clue that something is bothering him is when he grinds his teeth when he sleeps."

"I do more of the talking than he does. I would like more intimate talk, I wish he would tell me what he wants to happen in the future, but he doesn't talk to me. There seems to be a gap between us that grows as time goes on. Sometimes I feel like I can't share certain things with him because of what he might say or do. But I would love for both of us to share everything with each other. I don't know if that is possible or not."

83 percent of women say they initiate most deep talks—and try very hard to draw men out:

"I push the discussions on feelings, but he'll talk about his work. I cannot get him to think about the future or to dream. I wish he had a dream—even if it didn't match mine."

"I have to ask how he feels, he doesn't volunteer it."

"I always tell him that anything he wants to tell me he should. He never tells me when he's down or depressed. He says he doesn't want to bother anyone with his problems. I tell him that is what I'm there for—the bad times as well as the good."

"He's often silent for hours while we are alone, which gets on my nerves. I would like him to talk more about feelings—reactions—problems—but he's just not interested. But he will only talk to me if he sees I'm desperate and I start to cry . . ."

"My lover and I seldom talk intimately. If we do, I do most of the talking. I think women have a knack for doing the deep talking. I wish more men would."

"I love to share every part of myself. I don't know how much more my boyfriend wants to know. I ask him quite often if he wants to ask me anything about me, but he doesn't seem to."

"We don't talk much. I refuse to detail the weather after thirty-one years—the only subject he seems to want to discuss."

"I talk more than he does. I seem to have more questions. I would like for him to talk more about his feelings, I think he would feel better if he could."

"He refuses to let anyone inside his shell even on a conversational level."

"We do not talk about feelings as much as I need in order to keep a relationship alive. I am hoping this will correct itself given some time and lots of energy. I would not only like more intimate conversation, but I would like him to initiate it."

"I would love to be able to really talk about everything—we have our moments but they're few and far between. I have to be very careful about what I say and how I say it."

Some women say men believe not talking about "feelings" is part of being "male"; "real men do not talk about "soap opera" topics (which are for women)—real men are supposed to be only "rational," "logical," "scientific," and "objective": *

"I think there is heavy conditioning for men—most are taught that they are not supposed to be affected by falling in love. Many of them hold such things as a job more important. A lot of them are more interested in 'security'—'having a wife,' i.e., somebody at home to count on—than in actually having a love relationship. I think many men don't know *how* to have one. Women, I've noticed, usually want to talk things out more."

"He criticizes the fact that my emotions are so strong and so important to me. I criticize him for being overly rational. The objective and subjective must be balanced—he tends to ignore the subjective because it ruins his neat calculations. If you ignore the subjective, you ignore 50 percent of the facts, and so have little chance of coming up with a useful conclusion. He thinks I allow our boys to express too much of their negative feelings. I believe a person should go ahead and feel what they feel, allow an emotion to run its course. It's not necessary to have hysterics all the time and we don't exaggerate our feelings, but neither is it good to pretend you don't feel strong feelings, as long as you don't inflict them unnecessarily on the people around you."

71 percent of women say the men in their lives are afraid of emotion:

"He has real difficulty with emotion. All emotion embarrasses him. Rage scares the hell out of him. He'd like everything to be on a nice even keel at all

*See *The Hite Report on Male Sexuality,* (New York: Alfred A. Knopf, 1981), Chapter 1.

times. Even passion in bed scares him. I'm always looking for the hidden significance of everything he says, and so I can never be happy—he says. Is he happy? He says he is, and I honestly think he believes it. But as afraid of emotion as he is, I don't think he could stand being really happy."

"My grievance with men is that they seem to be afraid to fall in love. They don't let themselves go as much as I do."

Or that they are too unemotional and "logical" (their own "logic," that is):

"My husband is practical and sensible. He does not show his emotions. And sometimes I wonder if he has any emotions at all. This has hurt me deeply . . . especially over the recent illnesses and deaths of my mom and dad."

"Men are afraid of intimacy and equate it with loss, not merger of self. They are too logical, or detached."

This can put women in an awkward position:

"I *always* have to initiate talking things over when something has upset me. I don't like the 'bad guy' that this makes out of me because my husband is of the type that lets things pass—they're always *my* problems."

63 percent of women meet with great resistance when they try to push their husband or lover to talk about feelings:

"By far I'm the talker. I initiate all discussions, fights, all talk on any level. I find it easy to talk about any subject, and I do. But he has enormous difficulty. Mostly, when things get too close to home he says, 'I'll have to think about that.' Translated, that means I can't deal with that and I don't want to try."

"It is not easy for us to talk. I am always the one to start talking about our feelings, reactions, or intimate talk. He gets very upset if I bring up our problems and he just won't talk quietly and easily with me. He always gets irritated."

"It's extremely easy for me to talk about anything and everything. Him— nothing. He never talks, I even start conversations—they go nowhere. I encourage talking, he watches TV. Fights never get resolved. I simply learn to get over it, because I hate the children to see me unhappy, and besides, when we aren't getting along, he takes it out on the children. This is not fair."

Sometimes trying to get a lover or husband to open up can even lead to a violent reaction:

"My lover lost his job (due to the company closing), had the wheels stolen off his Corvette, and learned his father was dying, all in a four-month period.

He was on the edge. I tried to push him to reveal his feelings and he struck out in violence instead and slapped me."

"I think it is his fear of intimacy that causes him to get cold or aggressive and violent even when we are closest. But it's taken me a long time to understand this. I would prefer anything more regular and secure and less rejecting. But I'm even getting used to accepting these negative bits of acknowledgment."

One woman writes letters when communication is blocked:

"It is not always easy to talk—but it is the path to understanding and mutual forgiveness. We love each other very much—and if we quit talking, we wouldn't know each other—then how could we love each other? I often initiate particularly deep psychological or philosophical discussions—but he is good about making the first move to talk when we have had a volatile argument. I really respect his courage in trying to reopen the lines of communication. Sometimes if I am deeply hurt, I cannot talk without crying—sometimes then I'll write him a letter and leave it in his room—then we'll talk after he reads it. All this pain is worth it—we each have a true friend."

52 percent of women doubt men's true desire for deeper communication:

"I would like to have my husband know what is inside me, but I don't think men ever try to get that deep."

"Personally, what I least like is their tendency to hide troubles from me, with the attitude that 'what she doesn't know won't hurt her, or for that matter, *me* as much.' "

"Most men do not seem to be able to adequately communicate in a relationship. There is no real gut-level honesty or disclosure of feelings."

71 percent of women in long marriages who had originally tried to draw their husbands out finally gave up:

"I'm willing to talk about anything—if he'd listen and not fall asleep or get uncomfortable and move away. But he's very insecure talking about himself and his feelings. I tried a long time—and finally don't do it anymore. I would share every part of me if someone would just listen and accept what they hear but my husband does not. We are two different people, but he does not want to hear about those differences."

"There is just no communication. He refuses counseling. It will never be better, I've given up."

"I feel that he should understand me more after being together for seven years. He can't clarify his feelings—it's like pulling teeth. We'll have a conversation and four days later he'll have a comment on it. We've tried to work it out, but that is the way he is. I'm resigned to it, sometimes I'll even joke about it. That doesn't mean I like it!"

"He will do anything, such as crossword puzzles or watch TV, except consider what he wants out of life and how he could set about getting it. I find that so desperately frustrating because I believe we could actually have what's called happiness together if he would just insist on going out for it. I have tried everything I am capable of and it is useless. He will either break through or we will both not get what we want."

Women explain why talking and listening, sharing thoughts, is important to them:

"I really treasure the intimacy that develops, the freedom to 'compare notes' with another consciousness. I believe that the accuracy of what a person says is not the issue; what *is,* is that this is what the person saying it feels, and for this reason it is precious."

"I've been the happiest when we have talked and I have felt truly understood and accepted."

But only 17 percent of women say the communication in their relationship is good, makes them happy, adds to their life:

"This relationship is important to me because of the capacity for understanding—here's a person to whom I can say anything. I can ask him any question and he will answer with candor. He listens and cares about what I think, feel, and do. I know this because of living with another man for eighteen years who never heard, cared, or felt about my innermost thoughts. The more intimately we relate on an intellectual and emotional level, the more intense the passion and sexual intimacy becomes on the physical level. We don't have children together, but he is close to my daughters."

"We go through cycles of talking about intimate matters. Very intense. I don't think either of us can live with the intensity full-time, so we don't do it all the time. We went through extensive and intense therapy together, bared our souls. It was passionate, loving, gay, joyous, freeing. Everything it should have been."

"It's very easy to talk with each other. We're usually very honest and everything gets out in the open. We share our dreams and aspirations, and he's one of the few males I know who has little trouble showing or talking about his feelings or what's bothering him. I can't imagine a closer, deeper relationship than the one I have with my husband. It very much fulfills me."

"He is very easy to talk with. There are times when I talk more and times when he talks more, depending on our moods. We have a lot of intimate talk. We enjoy sharing our thoughts with each other. I feel extremely close to him and he feels the same way with me. That is one of the nicest things we have going for us. I feel like I can share anything with him. When we discuss things that one of us doesn't understand, we keep talking and asking questions. Our relationship is too important to have misunderstandings between us."

One woman reports on a specific incident:

"After we had only lived together a few months, he and I both thought his parents were coming for an afternoon visit. But, uninvited, on the first day of my vacation they came and parked a camper behind our house to stay for an indeterminate number of days. His father poked around in my friend's tool shop and our laundry room uninvited and started fixing things uninvited. I felt a tremendous invasion of privacy when it became apparent they were staying as long as they wanted—and my friend didn't have the courage to deal with this intrusion. I felt my home was no longer my home—his parents seemed to view it as their son's home and me as a temporary visitor. I told my friend his failure to set his parents straight was upsetting me—and that I felt sad—that I wanted to go to some man who would welcome me. This upset him. On the third day of their visit, I became very upset (triggered by a problem connected with my job) and just left—for a long drive—I told him I'd be coming back, that I just needed to drive and think. While I was sobbing and driving, he told his parents it would be better if they left. They had already been there three days. I came home later that afternoon and he and I really talked."

One couple has a special system to ensure they have private times for themselves, just to talk and cuddle:

"Daily life is good. Most important, we have at least two or three 'horizontals' (lying down holding each other, talking) a day. We like to look at each other."

Lack of Emotional Support from Men: Not Being Listened to, Heard, or "Seen"

"What does your partner do that makes you maddest?"

The most frequently expressed reply (77 percent) is "He doesn't listen."

"Whistle and sing and slam doors when I try discussion."
"When I get upset (mad), he tells me to 'calm down.' "
"Not answer my questions or have no comment on something I've said."
"Not listen to me when I speak."

"Cuts me short when I ask questions."

"Teases when I'm trying to discuss something serious."

"When I get on him about something, he says I nag him, and puts his fingers in his ears, so he blots out my voice. This gets me mad! It doesn't last long, though. We usually end up laughing at ourselves."

"Patronizes or humors me."

"My partner stops talking. Ignores or grunts in reply and can be like this for days, if he's in a mood."

"He hides behind a silent wall."

"I would get terribly angry when we were discussing something important and he would continue eating or taking notes for school or doing some silly task around the house. He was, in fact, telling me that his particular activity was more important than what I had to say."

"Sometimes he walks into another room while we're talking—I told him that upsets me and he's recently stopped."

"Our 'talking' is always him telling me how it is, and me being expected to listen and take it in, and not have a viewpoint of my own."

"He's more interested in doing the talking than listening to what I have to say. I would say he talks more, though he would deny that and make a remark about how I talk too much. I would like the equality of our conversations to improve—but wouldn't bank on it. Instead, I hope to find other people to carry on conversations with."

"The worst thing he does is ignore me, be silent for hours when I try to talk. Dump all his baseball and football equipment all over the floor when he comes in, watch TV when he comes back from work—dumb shows (that I'm starting to get addicted to)—for a long time in his dirty clothes. Go out 'just to go to the corner store' and come back two hours later."

41 percent of women say men give non-verbal cues that they are not listening:

"I'd like to talk more, but I feel like I bore him when I talk too much."

"He won't let me talk about anything and so I finally explode and say all the wrong things in front of anybody, mostly the children. I talk and he does nothing. He doesn't listen. He has a short attention span and no desire to change."

59 percent report that men interrupt:

"The one thing that men constantly do that irritates the hell out of me is they always interrupt women. In a group of men, I get interrupted nine times out of ten. Men assume women's contributions to conversation to be meaningless and not worth listening to. One guy I knew was so bad he'd ask me a question and interrupt my answer to ask me another question or answer his question himself."

"As far as who talks more, not only what is said but how much and by whom it's said, all men talk and interrupt conversation more than women. I deliberately make a point of saying 'fair share,' and taking the lead and directing the conversation when I'm talking to men. As a result of my anger and frequent turnoff, my lover is far more conscious and sensitive to it now than most men (and women), and makes an honest attempt at listening more. He has no choice!"

84 percent say men often seem not to really hear:

"I'll tell him something and a few days later he says, 'You never told me that.'"

"He does not hear what I'm saying, he hears what he wants. I feel I read my lover well, like a boring novel. He could never understand most parts of me because he's never given his emotions a chance to mature."

"If I'm really pouring my heart out to him, sometimes I think he only half listens. He doesn't hear me. It doesn't sink in."

Some don't want to hear:

"There are parts of me that I cannot share with him fully . . . mainly my profession and the work that I do. His attitude toward my work is generally good, but he feels insecure, defensive, and often disagreeable when I try to discuss various career options open to me, etc. One of my husband's 'rules' is that one does not make a decision except on one's own when it concerns one's profession. This also tends to cut down on the conversation that either one has about his or her business."

47 percent of women say men often make a habit of negating or looking for a way to "one-up" whatever they say, rather than just listening with empathy or seriously involving themselves in the issues:

"When I explain my feelings, he nearly always says he doesn't understand why I think like that. He often tells me I'm wrong. 'You shouldn't feel like that.'"

"He puts a big emphasis on 'getting along,' which translated means, 'Why do you make trouble by asking so many questions?'"

41 percent of women report that men even tell them not to feel what they are feeling:

"It used to be, no matter what I said, he behaved as if I were wrong. He said if the way I felt about something bothered me, then I should change the way I felt about it. He's developing to the point now that he knows my feelings are important to me and he no longer behaves as if they are symptoms of mental aberration."

"He is always interposing how *he* would feel—and I'm supposed to feel the same way, the implication goes. (Because that is the logical, reasonable way—*his* way!)"

66 percent of women say they are often expected to agree with men in "conversation"; any other behavior in women is seen as aggressive and disagreeable, unnecessarily rude and "unpleasant":

"Quite often I've felt treated as if I was misbehaving somehow if I didn't agree with a lover, or remarked on something he did or didn't do. My opinions just weren't as valid somehow."

"It's like we are rivals or competitors somehow if I try to express myself."

Listening with enthusiasm vs. listening "patiently": Do men feel women have anything important to say?

69 percent of women say men generally don't listen or ask, draw them out about their activities or opinions:

"My husband is into sports. I was to take him to the bowling alley the night of the championship. I came home late, just after he had called someone else to drive him. When I pulled up to the house, I tried to explain why I was late, but he said he didn't want to know. He called me from bowling to apologize. When he called, I asked him if he had seen the mail. He said yes, so I asked him if he saw my grade report from school. He said no. So I told him I got an A in a subject. He said, just an A? I hung up the phone and went to school. When I came home, I sat and waited for him, he came in and all he said was hi—we won the championship—what is the baseball score?—turn on the basketball game! I got mad and started screaming about how all he cared about is sports."

"The worst thing he has ever done is to show a lack of interest in my poetry, my short stories. They express who I am at my deepest core and yet I had to beg him to read them—which he finally did, a year later. I feel cheated because I was into his music, his songwriting from the start, and am very supportive."

83 percent of the women in this study remark on the fact that men only seem to listen to what they say, or be interested, in the beginning of a relationship:

"When we were first in love, I used to talk to him about so many things, and he would listen—or I thought he listened; maybe he was just enthralled with my presence. Later I noticed when I spoke, he would walk out of the room, look preoccupied, or totally neglect to answer me, even when I ended my thought with a question. That hurt."

Most women say they can talk easily and intimately with their women friends—often noting how much easier it is to talk to other women than to men:

"I can't imagine talking to my husband the way I talk to my best friend. He's not interested in the same things that she and I are. We talk about very personal issues, past and present experiences, hopes for the future. He couldn't handle it. However, I think the right kind of husband for me would be right in there with me. If I ever marry again, I'll have me a man I can talk to. I tell my young daughters to look out for that."

"My husband doesn't seem interested in finding out what I think about anything. If he and I could only relate verbally the way I do with my best friend, 80 percent of our problems would be solved. When I try to tell him this, he has no idea what I'm talking about. Maybe if he did I wouldn't need the affairs."

"My friends are genuinely interested in how I feel. We take turns talking and listening. My husband only wants a 'good listener.' Once I start to speak up and express opinions, he is uncomfortable."

"Conversation with women I know is less game-oriented, more in the interest of furthering the knowledge of a situation, whatever the topic is."

"Men have a hard time discussing and listening to me. They have no interest in how I feel and what I need. From women you get understanding, support, and caring on a level that truly meets needs."

"It's easier to talk to women because they do not doubt your credibility— they are not looking at you through sexist stereotype glasses—thinking of words like 'complaining,' 'nagging,' 'she needs a good fuck,' etc."

Living with a cheering section vs. living with a critic*

74 percent of women say, as we have seen, that they feel they lack "credibility" with men they love:

"To live with a man is to be constantly disagreed with, day and night, to constantly have one's credibility called into question—either I'm not important enough to hear, or he has a different ('right') interpretation, or it's my period or something . . ."

*Courtesy Lindy Hess.

*One young woman (like many others; see Part V) comments on the relief she
feels relating to other women, since she does not continually have to defend or
prove what she is trying to say:*

"My most important relationships with women are with an aunt and a
girlfriend. They are both very kind and considerate and like me. I do not always
feel I have to be working around them—they listen to my feelings and thoughts
and do not continually negate what I say."

*Regarding being negated, some women suggest this might be part of the
competition theme in men's cultural training to be "male":*

"Some men look for ways to disagree and 'one-up' women in conversation,
negating whatever they say, rather than listening with their hearts. They often
miss the point. Why? To avoid discussing it?"

"The other day, I went to the supermarket. I had the 'nerve' to ask the man
working there where a certain soup was. He said they didn't carry it. I said,
'But yes you do, I have bought it here before.' Since I 'dared' to contradict him,
he became very rude and walked over to complain about me to another clerk.
When I finally asked would he hurry up and find out when they would be
getting it in, he started shouting at me: 'I told you we don't have it. What *are*
you, a crazy lady? Go on, get out, don't come here anymore.' "

––––––––––––––

An unfortunate current in our society trains men not to trust women, to deny
women's credibility. Simone de Beauvoir referred to this in her famous work,
The Second Sex, when she described men's view of women as "the other."* A
stereotype that repeatedly surfaces when women talk about their problems with
men is the subliminal implication on the part of some men that "all women are
slightly crazy" or "neurotic" (see also Chapter 3). One woman has interiorized
some of this feeling: "There are some parts of me I can't share with my
husband—parts that are too 'crazy' or parts of my woman self, the ways I feel
insulted and oppressed as a woman that a man can never understand. He
understands a good-sized portion of that, I'll give him credit, but sometimes he
thinks I'm 'paranoid.' "

Do men take women seriously? Are men *interested* in who women are?

Many men don't pick up on the subjects women initiate, personal or otherwise.
As one woman puts it, "I can have limited serious talks with my husband—I

*Simone de Beauvoir, *The Second Sex* (New York: Alfred A. Knopf, 1953).

can even laugh—so long as *he* feels like it and the subject is correct by his standards. It is not spontaneous."

Women are often greeted with silence when they offer their comments, even in small talk such as the following conversation, overheard on the street:

Woman: That's a pretty dog.

Man: No response.

Woman: Well, it's got a pretty coat . . .

Man: Silence.

Unfortunately, women's perceptions are frequently not acknowledged as being equal; how women see things is "by definition" not as valid, so women's opinions are not listened to, have less credibility. It's as if some men feel women could have nothing interesting or important to say. Men generally do not seem to seek out women's opinions, and when women offer them, they frequently do not seem to matter or be taken seriously.

There are many subtle ways in which men repress women in their relationships, let women know that their role is to be supportive while the man talks about his interests, and that it will be considered rude or aggressive if the woman counters with her own information or opinions—rather than considered interesting.

Emotional indifference

When asked, "How do you feel about the statement 'You don't try hard enough to find out what is inside of me'?" 76 percent of women say that their husband or lover rarely tries to draw them out or get them to speak about their thoughts and feelings the way women do (or try to do) for men:*

"He doesn't care enough to find out what's inside of me. He's too busy with his own problems."

"In my relationship I don't think he's really that interested."

"My husband definitely doesn't make the same efforts as I do to know what's inside me. I don't like it, but I accept that as being his way."

"I used to say that to my ex-husband, but he wasn't capable of such talk. Now I'm glad that my present partner doesn't try. I have more privacy to go and come as I please and think what I wish."

"I love being delved into in a loving manner, having a really intimate relationship. My husband has never asked me any intimate questions. He doesn't want to hear the answers. It doesn't bother me that my husband doesn't want to be intimate in that way. I can do that kind of relating with other people.

*This question was added to the second edition of the questionnaire at the suggestion of a woman answering the original.

Why would I want him to know my inner self if he doesn't want to? Especially if I know he couldn't appreciate it?"

"I often wish my lover would make the effort to find out about things he knows I'm carrying around inside."

Most women think of this as an individual man's problem, rather than a larger social one (in which the society encourages men not to take women seriously)— and cite individual and personal reasons from the man's childhood or past to explain why he doesn't talk and listen easily:

"He finds it very difficult to talk about his personal feelings, and intimidates me into not talking either. He also finds it very difficult to accept my affection. Knowing his background, I can understand why he is so cold and detached, but when I am in need of his loving I become angry that his need to be unemotional is more important than my need to have an outward show of love. Why do I always have to be the one that is understanding?"

"It is easy for me to talk but hard for him. There are areas we no longer raise to discussion. When I talk, I can see he can't wait for the end of the conversation! I think he was brought up to avoid and inhibit and ignore unpleasantness and issues; and being an only child, he didn't get the give-and-take and fractiousness that comes with living in a larger family. His parents, for instance, have been married about fifty-five years and have never had a heated discussion. Their way of handling disagreement is to clam up and mope. I've made him sound sullen and withdrawn. In all fairness, he expresses himself effectively with actions. He spent his Christmas bonus on jewelry for me. When given an automatic garage door opener as a present, he installed it on my side of the garage."

"My husband grew up in a very non-emotional family and it took a long time for me to make him understand that it's a good thing to let people (especially the ones you love) know how you feel."

Women sometimes use the idea that "one person can't fill all your needs" as a justification for a severe and even paralyzing lack of closeness in their relationships:

"The best way to make a love relationship work is to realize that the other person has needs you can't fill, be it in sports or in some other interest. I can always talk to my women friends, if I want to discuss what I think about things, which he doesn't really enjoy."

"I share everything that I want to share with him. When our interests differ, I have friends to share those things with. I wouldn't expect one person to fill all my intimate needs, although for a long time I hoped to find that one person. I think I was looking for myself."

This lack of communication means that many women do not feel known or understood by their husbands or lovers—they are not really "seen":

"He does not understand my feelings. He does not know me, although I've given him many chances to—he just doesn't seem to want to understand my feelings. And he will never suggest a solution or some action to make things better."

"I get mixed feelings about his understanding of me. Sometimes I think he knows what's going on, other times I think he is totally confused."

"The worst thing my partner has ever done to me is to misread my feelings and actions when I feel that after twelve years he should know me better."

"My deepest needs are satisfied with other women. He could know me absolutely intimately, because God knows I've said the words, used every word I know. But he chooses not to. Other women, my friends, are more giving."

"The relationship did not fill my deepest needs for closeness, that's why I'm no longer in it. I did share every part of myself with him but it was never mutual. I wasn't accepted or understood. I don't think he knew me very well at all. He was incapable of understanding. It got impossible to talk because everything turned out to be a sore subject. He refused to communicate on any deep level or get a third party (a counselor) to help us. I would have liked (and still would, but it's not possible anymore) more intimate talk about feelings, reactions, and problems, but he would clam up and refuse."

"I'm not important enough for him to know me. He doesn't care."

One woman takes all the responsibility on herself:

"I don't think anyone has the right to expect the other to be a mind reader. If I want him to do something or say something or understand something, I make sure my expectation is clearly stated, just as I would with the children."

32 percent of women feel apologetic and guilty for their desire for more expression:

"Sometimes he feels I invade or demand too much."

"When I feel insecure, I need to talk about things a lot. It sometimes worries me that I say the same things over and over."

"I can be an emotional drain on my husband if I really open up."

Most girls had the same feeling of distance with their fathers; their fathers did not talk to them or ask them about their feelings or inner thoughts either:

"My father seemed to have a sense of responsibility for providing materially for the family, but he didn't seem to have a capacity to provide mentally or emotionally. I never knew what to say to him, I was always a little afraid of him. I remember that I really wanted to talk to him, really badly, but I just couldn't find words. Sometimes we would ride to church and back in almost complete silence. I guess he didn't know what to say to me either."

"I tried to talk to him, but he never seemed to hear what I was saying. But I was always going places with my father. Now that I think of it, that must have been his way of showing affection, letting me tag along."

"He'll always be the biggest mystery and the biggest complexity of my life. He was a human being who could not reach out to other human beings. He just didn't have it, he didn't know how. I think that he was probably a person imprisoned emotionally. He was only affectionate when he was very drunk and only by pulling me near him to kiss him. We talked very seldom. I just didn't interact with him."

Some women say that if communication is a problem, it is a sign of someone not caring; loving behavior would include times to talk and open up:

"I think each is responsible for letting the other know about pertinent things 'inside,' but additionally, loving partners do ask how the other is from time to time, which is a way of saying, 'I care and I am ready to listen to what's going on with you.' "

"Two people should want to listen with their hearts. It isn't hard to know what's inside someone. I feel it's written on a person's face, in their tone and daily patterns."

In 47 percent of relationships, the only way to get real verbal communication is eventually to have a fight:

"There was a time when I welcomed a fight for clearing the air and to get the machine of communication cranked up again."

Some say that having sex will often loosen up some communication:

"Right now I think sex is more important to me than to him because it plays the part of being a catalyst for communication. This is very important."

Many men feel that having sex in itself serves as communication; * *but most women say a lack of talk usually detaches sex from its moorings, from any meaning:*

"My husband thought having sex was synonymous with 'getting along.' If we talked, my husband was always right. Being affectionate meant groping."

"My husband thinks he knows me, but he has shut so much of me out that I now feel like a prostitute when I have sex with him."

---

*See The Hite Report on Male Sexuality, Chapter 2.

One woman plaintively explains how the man's non-verbal style can involve her in endless guessing games about where the relationship is or is not going, about what the man's expectation or point of view is:

"I don't seem to be able to forecast how seriously men are willing to take the relationship—and I don't seem able to control or help control the course of the relationship so that I don't get burned. I've learned how not to view most relationships as having to be serious to be worthwhile—but my feeling that sex needs some kind of commitment behind it does not seem to be the same feeling that most men have. I have trouble with the hot/cold mind games and forever trying to figure out how the man feels because I don't seem to get involved with the verbal, expressive type."

A few women describe a deep closeness they cannot explain, which is not based on verbal communication, that <u>almost</u> makes up for lack of talking:

"I don't feel the need to share everything I think or feel. The 'deep need for closeness' I have is more of a spiritual nature."

"If I had to pick someone to love it would be him. I'd like to share more with him if and when he will let me. I've been with many men in my years and he's the hardest to crack with feelings, yet there is a softness, a caring about him I have never felt with anyone else. I would have to say, I have it all with him, except the words that mean so much. Sometimes I want to scream."

76 percent of women feel that this treatment of them—men not listening, not taking what they say seriously, not drawing them out to say more—is maddeningly unfair, because most women do provide these services so congenially and unobtrusively for men:

"It seems if I'm attentive and at his disposal everything runs smoother. But every time an important decision is made, he makes it. You don't question his decisions."

"If I could change one thing—it would be to get him to be more expressive of his emotions, his wants, needs. I most criticize him for not telling me what he wants or how he feels. He denies he feels things when his non-verbals indicate he does feel them. I guess showing him true things, trying to get him to talk, is another service I am providing."

In fact, most men, according to women, are hardly aware that the woman is providing any services or "giving" anything; they seem to have the impression that this is "natural" behavior on the part of women, something women automatically do for men, whose opinions always deserve to be heard and discussed.

Most women say they would very much enjoy being drawn out by their husbands or lovers—but all too often their opinions about things somehow do not seem to matter.

Men, the great majority of women (82 percent) believe, often don't realize how much they depend on and use women's emotional support and concerned listening:

"I think men fear women's dependency without realizing how much more dependent they usually are. Men usually have only one person with whom they talk; women have many. I usually feel like I'm giving more support than I'm getting."

"There have been times when my partner has made me feel as if I am responsible for his mental and emotional health, as I am his only outlet. It makes me feel uncomfortable. A person can't expect one other person to be his entire support system."

"My father has no idea, doesn't understand, how much of his own life rests on my mother's existence. Now that she is ill, he may not know what to do. It is significant that he doesn't visit her very often in the hospital, he just seems to drift around the apartment in a state of disorientation."

Most men assume they have a right to emotional support from women, that women should be loving and caring

According to women, many men's unconscious assumptions about women categorize them as "love givers" (or if they are "bad women," as "withholders"). But most men have very little idea that they think of women in this way. And men need women's love, since they cannot get this quality of emotionality from most other men; however, by not reciprocating, they can almost "suck women dry," so that women in many marriages and relationships gradually stop giving love and sympathetic understanding or attention.

Men are often surprised and bewildered when this happens, since they have no conception that by not providing emotional support to their wives or lovers they are causing a fatal rift in the relationship—after all, they feel, emotional nurturing is not what men are "supposed" to do. But to give "love" is women's "nature"—just the way women (good women) are—nurturing. Many men do not understand that being equal with a woman now means being emotionally supportive and verbally sharing, having an interchange about life. Such men are surprised when women are slowly angered and eventually begin to lose interest in sex, frequently "complain" or finally leave them.

How Lonely Can You Be in a Love Relationship?

Not being able to talk to their husbands or lovers about their deeper thoughts and feelings makes many women feel very lonely.

Strangely enough, the most common answer to the question "When were you the loneliest?" refers to a time in life when one "should" be closest: Most women (82 percent) say they are loneliest when married to someone with whom they cannot talk:

"I remember crying over problems with my husband. Why? Because he could never—I could never reach him. I could never really communicate with him, never really share with him. I had two nervous breakdowns during the course of my marriage and felt very bad during the period following my divorce. But I was the loneliest *during* the marriage, when my husband didn't share my life. I was lonely because he was with me but I just couldn't reach him."

"Even though I am married, I have always been lonely once the children were in bed."

"I was the loneliest when I was first married. I was terrified to be a mother and I sensed at the time that I would be doing it alone, not physically alone but emotionally alone."

"The loneliness comes from knowing you can't contact another person's feelings or actions, no matter how hard you try."

"I felt loneliest when I was married. I felt my husband rejected the inner me—the self that I feel is the essence of me. He wanted me to be a lawyer like him, have his materialistic values. I often—especially at the end of the marriage—cried myself to sleep after having sex with him. We never made love, it was just screwing."

"When I was married, it was devastatingly lonely—I wanted to die—it was just so awful being in love with someone who so obviously didn't love me back, who never talked to me or consulted me, etc."

"The loneliest was when I was married to my second husband—I cried a lot, and thought about suicide many times when I felt trapped and scared. At the same time, my husband slept the sleep of the blessed. That feeling of despair . . . knowing that that marriage was rotten, knowing that the person I was trying to be at home was not me . . . knowing that nothing . . . would ever get better. I contemplated suicide because no good wife and mother walked out on her family."

"I was loneliest just before I left home after twenty-eight years of marriage and tried to find a life for myself. The sexual neglect, the loss of self-esteem, often made me weep. The nights of insomnia, wondering why, as I was the primary wage earner (he loafed for several years after retirement from the Navy), I was so worthless."

"I cried out of frustration in my relationship with my husband when I repeatedly was unable to get him to respond to my emotional needs. After a few years, I was very depressed, everything felt like alienation, and the future looked like a black void. It was horrible."

"When I was raising four small children I felt very isolated. My husband had no idea of my loneliness because he was so engrossed in his work. We had little in-depth communication, which resulted in terrible loneliness. But I never considered suicide because of the four children whom I adored."

"I was the loneliest in my failing marriage (until I found other black feminists to relate to). I felt unworthy. I was nothing. That was my experience during my marriage. Isn't it fortunate that we can choose to grow from these debilitating experiences?"

Some women express a similar loneliness in a non-married relationship, but this is much more rare:

"During the last relationship I had with a man I spent moments so lonely I sometimes wondered if everyone else had disappeared off the face of the earth. I spent many nights crying. I cried, I think, because the whole situation was on his terms, and because I knew from the start I was a convenience."

"I've been lonely when my current relationship was having problems. I felt depressed and nervous and afraid."

Very few women answered this question by saying that they were loneliest when they had *no* relationship. Although they could feel lonely then, this is a different type of being alone, sometimes exhilarating, sometimes full of the excitement and the suspense of an open future, etc. The harshest loneliness is being with someone with whom you cannot make contact.

Men's Distancing: Part of an Ideology

Why do many men do such a good job of conversational distancing when women are trying to talk to them? Why do so many dislike talking intimately? On one level, as pointed out, there is the "male" role and the idea that "mushy talk" is too "feminine" (for soap operas). These men see women's behavior and expression of feelings as embarrassing or "weak."

But on another level, could there be an element of men unconsciously wanting to remind women to "know their place," to keep a certain distance appropriate between two non-equals? Is it that men are taught to fear any "feminine" traits in themselves to such a degree that perhaps they grow to feel that talking easily, as with an equal, with a woman would mean loss of status for them? Is good communication a form of equality with women which many men are not yet ready to participate in?

Emotional withholding: power and control in relationships

Do men always *want* to be understood? Or is not sharing their thoughts a way of keeping a woman beneath them? As one woman puts it, "I've heard it said that 'communication happens only between equals' and since it's practically gospel that good relationships have good communication, then . . . maybe men don't see us as equals. Or they don't want to be equals."

We usually don't want to see (it is not very pleasant to think about) non-communication or distancing types of behavior as expressing attitudes of inequality or superiority, as signs of a man not wanting to fraternize (sororize?) with someone of lower status. This is too painful. And yet, many men seem to be asserting superiority by their silences and testy conversational style with women. Thus, not talking to a woman on an equal level can be a way for a man to dominate a relationship. (In the same way, an employer may not bare his or her soul to an employee, and for the same reason.)

Most men also display this non-communicative style with their male associates and friends—perhaps also as part of a game of dominance: if you tell too much, the other man may "have something on you"; if you are too "emotional," he may think you are "weak." Thus it is obvious why most men, as documented in *The Hite Report on Male Sexuality,* turn to women, not to men, as their "best friends" when they want someone they can really talk to.

On the other hand, it could be argued that, if men are silent, they are not trying to dominate women; rather, they are trapped in their own silence (and their own pain), unable to talk or communicate about feelings, since this is such forbidden behavior for men. Even the brief style of most men's statements in *The Hite Report on Male Sexuality* could be said to demonstrate their fear.

But can men understand *themselves* if they don't talk about their inner lives with anyone on an ongoing basis? Women frequently use discussions with friends as a way of figuring out how they feel about something that has happened; if men don't talk with someone in the same way, then can they stay in touch with their deeper feelings?

Men's inability to listen to women also carries a poignant loss—that is, many men never really know the women they may be in love with. The women are never really "seen" for themselves, but rather through the reverse telescope of men's view of "women" and "who women are."*

But whether a man is trapped in his own silence and really longs to speak, or couldn't care less and is showing his disdain for women by not bothering to communicate, the effect on a woman (or anyone) is likely to be the same: it tends to silence that person too.

Emotional and Psychological Harassment of Women

Gender insults, condescending and trivializing attitudes, slights, and put-downs

79 percent of women report painful and infuriating attitudes on the part of men in their love relationships:

"He interrupted me on the phone to tell me I was crazy and stupid to suggest what I was saying. (Meanwhile, my son kept interrupting me too till I said 'hold on' and asked him to please be quiet.) I was very insulted by what my husband said. Even if it was a far-out idea, it was 'mine own.' "

"He uses his tone of voice to make me feel inefficient and dumb."

"He degrades me in front of his kids, calling me on the carpet for all I haven't done, etc."

"I will ask two or three questions at once—example: 'Do you want milk, or coffee?' and he will answer, 'Yes,' or he will say, 'No, no, yes.' He feels I should ask them one at a time. 'Do you want coffee?' (wait for a reply). 'Do you want soda?' (wait for a reply). 'Do you want milk?' (wait for a reply). Since I ask multiple questions often and he answers with a yes or a no instead of stating his choice it always annoys me."

"The put-downs and demeaning which my father subjected me to were awful—always in the context of 'joking.' Now when my husband sinks to laughing at me he really gets a strong reaction!"

"The worst thing I have done to him is not to tell him years ago how devastated I was by his put-downs, caustic remarks, and insensitive rudeness.

*A good example of this is how female orgasm was studied by male researchers for over fifty years: they only looked for it to occur as a consequence of the same stimulation as male orgasm. Assuming this, they would ask, "Why don't women have orgasm more easily during coitus?" Out of this question grew various fallacious "theories" about women's sexuality, such as that women have more psychological "hang-ups" about sex, etc. See *The Hite Report: A Nationwide Study of Female Sexuality* (MacMillan: New York), 1976.

It was a mistake to let him think that behavior was acceptable to me. I shouldn't have harbored my anger all those years."

"I'd rather not ever ask anything of a man, including his company, if he—when he gives me cause for anguish and I complain about it—takes on an air of a long-suffering, beleaguered man—leaving me to feel and look to onlookers like a 'bitch on wheels.' I'd rather just be happy with my friends—I don't need to be made to feel guilty every minute of the day—because, unfortunately, unless I do just what he wants, he behaves in such a way that I finally have to 'bring it up,' i.e., 'complain,' and then the cycle I just described starts. So I never win, but just wind up feeling smaller and smaller. So I'd rather be alone—at least that way I don't have to be put down."

91 percent report subtle (or not so subtle) forms of condescension—signals that speak volumes:

"What drives me craziest is his sometimes 'know-it-all' attitude, his desire to dominate (although I'm not sure he's aware of it)."

"He acts arrogant, like he knows EVERYTHING. He has a huge ego for someone who is aware of the corruption of the ego. He can be one pain-in-the-ass know-it-all. Sometimes when he acts like that I take him down a peg or two and he thanks me later."

"I have sometimes been mortified and angered by possessive gestures (hand on the shoulder, a certain sort of smile) from men with whom I was not even in a 'relationship.' "

"When men assume that a woman is nearing her period or needs sex if she gets upset about something, totally disregarding the issues and being narrow-minded, it really gets me mad!"

"What bothers me is when he gets paternalistic—when he starts giving me advice for my own good. A lot of that is stuff he picked up from his father. He recognizes it when his father does it, but he has a harder time seeing it in himself."

"We've had a running series of fights in the last few years over the fact that I will not be put down anymore. It usually happens at the end of dinner, but it can happen after we've been with people. I'm just not going to be shut up or talked down to anymore. My husband blames my behavior on the menopause! We have fought a lot recently over this."

61 percent of women say their husbands' or male friends' reactions are often abrasive and imply that they see much of what women do or say as trivial, unimportant:

"I thought we were close friends and trusted him with confidences I usually reserve for women friends. He used the information against me, and then later couldn't understand why I was upset. He became scornful of me, trivialized my feelings and everything that's important to me. I tried using his techniques on him to get him to see what he was doing, and it put him on very shaky emotional ground, but he didn't learn from it. I told one friend, who listened and felt angry along with me. She hates him too."

"He takes things too lightly that I consider important. When I try to get him to see their importance, he changes the subject."

"The one thing I hate most in an argument is when a man says (and many do), 'I'm sorry *you* feel that way.'"

"My husband never saw me as an equal and treated me as an inferior. From the beginning, he constantly stood me up ('something came up'), refused or ignored small requests, called me stupid if I didn't agree with his point of view on any issue. In later years, when I returned to college, he realized that others respected me, and began to see me through their eyes. His changed attitude toward me merely angered me then—too little too late."

Or a little "odd":

"When I feel forced to justify my idiosyncratic feelings about my garden and my sleep habits, I always say that I like doing everything, I just don't like to stop. If I am sleeping, I like to sleep longer. If I am reading a book, I don't want to go to sleep. If I am sewing something, or weeding the garden or taking a walk, I cannot easily switch activities. I like to immerse myself in whatever I do. Why does he challenge me about this and make me feel it's odd?"

84 percent of women describe a frequent attitude of ridicule and condescension in men's tone—as if women are "cute," entertaining, or funny—"woman as clown"; some men do not feel comfortable with women who are serious:*

"Men have tended to treat me with amused indulgence, like a pet or child they enjoy. I don't mind this most of the time, but I find that if something really bugs me, or if something is very important to me, I have to practically hit them over the head with a two-by-four to get my point across! Then I have the additional problem that they think I'm funny when I'm mad! This has applied to men at work, and bosses too."

"Most men think I'm an airhead and aren't interested in any opinion I might have. I might add that I am not an airhead at all, but an extremely intelligent woman. I really resent this! Women need support and understanding from men, not bigotry."

*Talented as they are and were, Lucille Ball and Gracie Allen portrayed these "acceptable" stereotypes.

Also frequently seen, including on television, is the strange "male" attitude of seeing the woman-as-easily-upset (or "watch out or she'll get hysterical"): *

"My family thinks I'm crazy, that I don't really know what I'm talking about. They never listen."

"How do most men feel about the women's movement? The same way they feel about God and the Ten Commandments. They wholeheartedly believe in the main issue and the concept in general, but if you make specific points, they fire you a small smile and wish you would return to bed . . . and shut up!" If I get mad about their attitudes, they accuse me of over-reacting—and then I get really worked up, and they call me hysterical!"

55 percent of women report that men they know often negate or ridicule, make fun of things they say—trying to put them on the defensive, or reduce any authority that appears in their speech, manner, or statements:

"When we have a disagreement, he ridicules and belittles me into being quiet. He has this need to always be right, which certainly does not solve anything."

"His word is the law. He does ask my opinion on some issues, but then tells me how wrong I am and why his opinion is by far the correct one."

"There was a time when he would scold and lecture me like a child. I kept after him about it and now it has stopped."

"If I have both hands full and/or am struggling with something, he'll tweak my breast and laugh before helping me."

56 percent talk of being undermined:

"I had to deal with a young theater manager who felt women could never compare with men in expertise in any field. He especially hated us community women who had kept the struggling theater afloat by fund-raising and ticket sales for six years previous to his being hired. He wanted to disband the Women's Guild. It became evident that he had some kind of mother complex and was most threatened by women who were at least fifteen years his senior. He totally undermined projects I was doing by his obstructive behavior. I documented his obstruction item by item and took it to the artistic director, his boss, not once but upon every occasion. He finally resigned when he realized the artistic director believed the truth of my accusations. I was very

---

*One sees the stereotype of woman as obsessed by fear, hysterical, most exaggerated in the horror-film genre.

angry, as were a great many of the women I worked with. It was, of course, a prime example of the kind of injustice I most deeply bridle at, largely due to the early experience in my family, where I learned that women are not as valued as men."

"My husband would make my life harder, but never in ways I could really 'catch' him, so he always looked like a 'good guy.' For example, I was hosting a barbecue for about forty of my colleagues—it was an important occasion to me. While I was out of the house, one colleague phoned to inquire whether he still needed to bring his extra skewers—my husband said 'no,' leaving me without an adequate number to serve everybody. To this day, I don't know whether he really didn't know I was short (but why didn't he tell the man to bring them anyway, if he wasn't sure?) or if it was some subtle way of getting back at me for being so 'overly preoccupied' with 'fussing' over my 'party.' Such great emotional support—ha-ha—reflects the way things were with us."

One woman (representing 67 percent of mothers) complains that, particularly in front of their children, her husband does not back her up, undercutting her authority:

"He makes me maddest when he puts me down, particularly in front of my child. This is not a good example of the way a woman should be treated. I used to put up with it because I was afraid of his temper tantrums, but I'm not letting myself be emotionally blackmailed anymore. I don't let a single time go by. He's beginning to try to behave himself!"

As another woman points out, men with these demeaning attitudes are not treating women they love with even the courtesy they would show a business associate:

"I sometimes think it gives some men a sense of power to treat women with less courtesy and consideration than they would a business acquaintance. I have been privileged to know a handful of men who valued me highly and treated me well; they were also the best lovers. But I've known several that have placed their relationships with me well below their other interests, treating me in a very cavalier fashion. Whenever I would indicate that I was about to call it quits, they would suddenly reverse this attitude, take me more seriously. I've known men to cry, hit the bottle quite irrationally, when I told them I was breaking off a relationship. If they had treated me with more respect in the first place, the breakup might not have come at all."

37 percent of women say that in mixed groups, with men and women present, the men often bond together and stick up for one another's point of view, not supporting their wives or lovers in front of other men:

"What I dislike most is their gender loyalty and absolute inability to confront another man. I've found this true particularly in regard to sexism. I've never heard a man criticize another man for . . . saying something sexist, even when I knew that they *knew* it was sexist. They would, at best, do it indirectly, such as, in their next sentence, use the word 'woman' (but never tell their associate that 'girl' is inappropriate for anyone over twelve)."

"My husband does not realize how much he hurt me by not being loyal to me during a recent incident. I fell out with our dentist and complained against him to the Dentists' Association, because of unprofessional conduct. The authorities agreed with me and allowed me to have free corrective treatment from another dentist. Two months later, my husband had a bad toothache, so he went to my former dentist. When the dentist told my husband he would not treat him, my husband tried to persuade him, saying that after all he was a totally different patient from his wife! The dentist pointed out his notion of loyalties by declaring he would never treat anyone related to that woman again, she had cost him far too much money.

"My husband claimed that I had just no idea how bad a toothache could be. He did find another dentist that same afternoon and thinks me completely unreasonable because I am still waiting for him to understand that the dentist episode demonstrates why I do not believe that he loves me or that we have a relationship."

49 percent of women report a strange tunnel vision on the part of men who seem not to be aware of insults or the hurts they cause (perhaps they are not aware of their own unconscious assumptions about women's "otherness" or inferiority):

"He insulted me very badly and then didn't know what he said to hurt my feelings."

"I told him he hurt me a lot when he didn't remember to ask me how my job interview went. Instead of apologizing, he said 'Oh—' and then started talking about something else, and then telling me how he missed me, he loved me and everything. I felt like saying, 'If you really loved me, you would ask me about my job interview.' (He still hadn't asked me to tell him about it.) So I just felt withdrawn and got kind of quiet. Then he asked me why I was so silent, was I tired?"

"Many men consciously enjoy putting women down—many others don't realize that they do it unconsciously very often—or as 'teasing.' They're hell-bent on winning all the time."

———————

Many women also report that men who have these subtle ways of putting them down frequently seem not to be aware of what they are doing, and are surprised if they receive any negative reaction, often accusing the woman of being "overly sensitive" (or "bitchy"). For example, it was common for men in *The Hite Report* on men to remark that their wives' request for a divorce had come "out of the blue," or been a "sudden surprise": "I didn't have any idea something like that was coming." And yet, women are trying to tell men every day "what the problem is."

Hidden gender bias in language

Sometimes men's belief in male superiority—and female inferiority—is directly, verbally stated; more frequently, patterns of speech, special inflections, or special phrases indicate these attitudes.

The vast majority of women (92 percent) say men use special phrases or patterns of speech which indicate condescending, judgmental attitudes toward them:

"I'm certain my husband thought he was superior in *every* way. He especially thought he knew more than I did on any subject. I remember one time I was discussing mortgages with a girlfriend. I had been working in a bank for five years and she had been working in one for eight years. My husband kept contradicting both of us because a man he worked with had just bought a house. He was using secondhand information against thirteen combined years of banking experience and he was wrong, because I checked the next day. His tone of voice during this discussion was extremely superior and I'm sure we would have had a huge fight if my girlfriend hadn't been there."

"He complains that taking a long time to get ready to go out must be in the female genes."

"My father would put me down, saying that I couldn't even make an apple pie, he'd bet. He said that one afternoon, shortly after I had just finished baking an apple pie, it was on the counter behind him. But I was so far gone in those days that do you know I believed him? I agreed that I couldn't make a pie, because he said so, even though I'd just made one! Other times he would cut me down for something and then say, in an oozily sentimental and awful way, 'Oh, Beckie, I love you so much,' and hold his arms out for an embrace. Like an automaton, my ego freshly destroyed, I would oblige and let my enemy embrace me and think that I loved him."

"I am most angry when he cuts me down either by words or action—even when I suspect it's the classic bully's way of trying to build up his own esteem by hurting someone else. When I try to discuss a difference I feel strongly about, he refuses. I withdraw from arguments."

"We bicker almost constantly about the annoying habit he has of the constant 'put-down.' He can make me feel more useless than anyone I know."

"I hate it when men refuse to admit to a mistake, or say that they simply 'don't know.' It's as if they think their penises will fall off if they do. And then, if I, a woman, turn out to be wrong in something, I'd damn well better own up to it and apologize and be more careful in the future. Men's insistence that they 'know' when they don't can cause them, and me, serious problems. If you don't know how to fix the car—even though a 'man' 'should' know—don't fool around with it, saying you know what you're doing, and *really* screw it up! If you don't know what a woman wants in bed—and how can you possibly, since every woman is an entity unto herself, with her own ideas and feelings?—don't assume you must know and try to fake it. You'll only be keeping up the pattern of lies that has caused us all so much unhappiness."

"The young man I was in love with was pretty respectful, but if I started talking geology (my major), he'd say, 'Quit showing off.' And if I ventured into a foreign language, he would correct my pronunciation."

"He criticizes my age when I'm tired. Says I'm no fun."

Teasing is a common form of emotional harassment:

"He made some bitchy remark which I hated, then when I got mad, he gave me the 'I was only kidding' line."

One woman is trying to convince herself that "teasing" should not annoy her:

"I sometimes take teasing too seriously and am trying to learn to tease back. He is emotionally supportive when I need it—but I have to learn to really let him know when I need it. I have to learn to ask for explanations if I can see that I am interpreting things in a different way than intended. My habit or pattern is to take everything negatively about myself, so I am trying to relearn how to hear things about myself. I am glad that I am friends with someone who is willing to be patient and understanding."

This woman seems to be taking all the blame on herself—even expecting herself to "realize" she might be "interpreting things in a different way than intended." But how can one know how something is intended, if one has misunderstood, unless one is told? Is it her responsibility to somehow figure it out by herself? Many of men's "teasing" put-downs represent a failure to see women as equals—but most men seem unaware of this as yet.

Emotional harassment or a put-down can be a pattern in a relationship—but even more importantly, it is a pattern in society, a pattern which is socially acceptable. Therefore, it can happen at any moment, when a woman is least expecting it—a kind of emotional terrorism. (Unfortunately, "teasing" is also one of the few ways women are allowed to express anger at men, so that one finds it a common pattern on TV sitcoms, such as *The Jeffersons;* the result is a bantering to see who can ridicule the other's remark first.) Men may feel much more social credibility when "teasing" women, since this has been legitimized by society's seeing women as less, or "foolish," for a very long time. A notorious example of this "accepted" teasing or poking fun at women was White House chief of staff Donald Regan's statement in 1986 that women would not really be interested in the problems of South Africa, for they are more interested in diamond bracelets.

Adjectives typically used for women and not men: subliminal messages

91 percent of women say men frequently use stereotypical words that diminish or demean them, words that are especially used to characterize women:

> pushy
> demanding
> complaining
> neurotic
> behaving like a prima donna
> narcissistic
> vain
> bitchy
> self-indulgent, indulging yourself
>   ("You are indulging in your own ———.")
> hysterical
> screaming
> irrational
> petty
> needing reassurance
> overly emotional
> aggressive
> too sensitive

One of the most frustrating aspects of the stereotyped put-downs women live with is that they frequently crop up in conversation "in passing." They are so enmeshed in the larger conversation that it would seem disruptive and "out of proportion" to stop the discussion to point them out. Women often find such built-in, loaded words offensive, but not to such an extent that they want to risk being called "obnoxious" or "aggressive" by making an issue out of them. On the other hand, this leaves the woman to swallow the thing said, and even worse, to seem to be condoning both it and the assumptions (hardly noticed by the speaker) it embodies.

These comments can be subtle and almost "unretortable," according to most women:

"My boyfriend often says that I am too 'fat' and that I should lose weight. He is always finding fault in everything I do. I know I should lose weight, but I don't like him telling me to. But I can't disagree with him, he's right."

"I hate it when men say something to the effect of 'Isn't that just like a woman,' or 'All women are like that.' I feel we deserve to be judged on a one-to-one basis, not as part of a vague mob. It is the main thing I am trying to correct in my attitude toward men. Whenever I catch myself saying, 'You men are all alike,' I stop and try to see the man as himself, not as a group. Also I hate it when a man I like calls me his 'old lady,' 'broad,' or 'the little woman.' "

Even more subtle may be the put-downs contained in what is *not* said. For example, the way the language celebrates masculinity—with the traditional cry of delight on the birth of a male child, "It's a *boy!*" There is no equivalent cry of delight when it is a girl, although many people are thrilled to have girls. However, the fact that one phrase is standard, and no equivalent other phrase is, carries a significant message to women and men every time they hear it, whether they recognize it or not: boys are more valuable than girls.

95 percent of women say this atmosphere—"men are more important," "men are the ones who matter"—is still all around us even now, twenty years into the current women's movement:

"Men in relationships I have seen always wanted to control or at least feel their own power—and it seeps in no matter how subtle it is. The hardest part is, just like sexism has poisoned us all in very subtle ways, it can be tedious and troublesome to remember that everyone else is wrong about a very important part of your nature—sort of like keeping the ghosts out by locking the door and then finding they still get in through the cracks."

"In retrospect, the biggest problem in our marriage revolved around my husband's paternalistic belief that he was 'taking care of' 'poor (me),' a belief in which I colluded. With our breakup and property settlement, it became clear that, to a large extent, I was taking care of him. I had colluded in a myth and accepted a 'bum rap,' an inaccurate evaluation of me. He most criticized 'evidence' of my dependency. He also said I was a good work partner but a 'drudge'—no fun. 'White man's burden' might be a phrase to suggest the paternalism and put-downs which were involved."

Value judgments built into words used to describe women

Many particularly ideologically laden words and phrases relate to the supposedly "dependent" nature of women in relationships. "Being left" almost always refers to a woman "being left"—with the implication that now the woman is sad and alone, rejected. It is usually assumed, when marriages break up, that it was the man who wanted to leave, although according to this study, it is usually women who decide to do so. "Deserted" and "abandoned" are other words with similar connotations applied almost exclusively to women. It does not fit in with beliefs about men's superior status to think that women could be the less "needy" ones.

Another related stereotype is the idea that women have difficulty accepting men's departures because they fear "being left"; this is said to be a woman's "syndrome," part of women's "psychology," its origin existing in women's "nature," i.e., women are biologically dependent on men because of becoming pregnant and needing men to stay and protect them and their babies. (But in other societies women bond together, or the clan takes care of mother and child.) In fact, needing men's support is not something which grows out of women's "innate" or "biological" psychology. Rather, in our society, it is more likely that women have sometimes felt uncomfortable about men's departures because of economic dependence—and because of men's non-communicative attitudes, which leave women feeling emotionally uneasy, unclear about what will happen next.

Many, perhaps most, people display a subtle gender bias in their choice of the adjectives they apply to behavior, depending on whether it is a man or a woman's behavior they are describing: people may watch a man do exactly the same thing they watch a woman do—argue with a taxi driver over the fare, for example—and characterize what they have seen in a totally different way. The man may be seen as "righteous," as not a fool, not letting himself be taken; the woman may be seen as argumentative, loud, "bitchy," aggressive, and so on.

Commonly used words relating to sexuality are also laden with judgments about women. Men are not "promiscuous," they are "sowing their oats," or "studs," etc. One woman says poignantly, "I remember my father calling my mother a whore because she wasn't tidy enough in the kitchen." Also relevant here is the phrase, "Treat her like a lady"—which implies that, at any moment, if the woman doesn't behave "right," she can be turned against, treated without respect, called the opposite, "a bitch."

Or consider the common use of diminutives when referring to women, and the tendency to see women's achievements as "good" rather than "great" (women are "brilliant," but almost never "geniuses"). Women can be counselors or advice-givers, but not philosophers. People belittle women also by using their first names, though they have just been introduced, or worse, by calling them "dear" and "honey," even when they are complete strangers. In a similar situation, a man would probably be addressed as "Mr. Smith"; at least, he would never be called "dear."

Even compliments can refer to women's lesser status. Most women like to hear things such as "I think you're beautiful. You're so pretty . . ." And men too like to hear, "You're so handsome, so attractive . . ." And yet, as one woman puts it, "The thing I like least about men is that they judge you like you're a goddam cow at the county fair. I wonder how they would feel if we started judging them like that, telling them to their faces how we rated their looks! They say things like that about me and other women as we pass by on the street all the time. What gives them the right to be the judges, anyway???"

Everyday language as a tool of ideology: emotional aggression against women

Names—what things are called, which feelings are given "reality" by having words that refer to them (and which are not)—are among the most powerful tools of a society for carrying on and reinforcing its ideology. In the case of gender, words embedded in the language act as hidden, subliminal attacks and value judgments, often leading to irrational interpretations of behavior.

The language that exists dictates, in a way, what "reality" will consist of, what parts of oneself one can let exist, tell others about. For this reason, in many parts of this book, we are trying to find new terms for women's experiences which may have been misnamed, inadequately named, or negatively named. For example, terming women "emotionally needy" or "overly emotional"— with "male" behavior considered to be the norm—is not an objective description of women's qualities. To reverse the point of view, one might call "male" behavior "emotionally repressed," and "female" behavior "gloriously expressive." But in our society, non-communicative "male" behavior is more generally seen as something like "heroically in control."

The frequent use of words and phrases with built-in gender insults for women (words that have special meaning when used for/about women) creates an atmosphere of emotional intimidation, which weighs just as heavily on women as economic intimidation has. Through using this vocabulary, subtly, often unconsciously, and in a socially acceptable way, many men bully women emotionally, and thus control relationships. The implied threat often is that if the woman "complains" too much, or wants a better relationship (is "demanding" or "nagging")—she will be unlovable and therefore a man will leave her.

Verbal clichés and assumptions: being "insisting" and being "demanding"

Gender-biased remarks—such as the statement often made to women: "I think you've got a complex," as a retort to any "complaint" a woman might have about a man's treatment of her—are so intertwined with the language we use to discuss our emotional relationships with one another, and to describe our feelings, that even in the midst of "trying to talk," a woman can find herself being unconsciously (?) put down by the "caring" or even "solicitous" (condescending) responses of others, especially of men. For example, the word "sensitive," with its two meanings, illustrates the sexism of words as they are often applied to women's behavior: to be "sensitive" to the world and others is good, but to be a "sensitive" woman (i.e., a woman who is always having her feelings hurt) is bad.

Another frequent retort made by men, referred to over and over by women in this study, occurs when a woman has just described her injured feelings in a relationship and the reply is: "I'm sorry you feel that way." This, rather than opening up the topic for discussion and serious consideration, places the burden for the "feelings" on the other person, and no responsibility on the person spoken to for trying to understand those feelings. In other words, the man has no emotional responsibility in the relationship. Do men who say things like this realize they are being emotionally destructive? Or do they simply believe they are right, that women *are* too "emotionally demanding" and "difficult," and that it is the proper role of men to make sure women don't "go too far" and "dominate" a relationship? In any case, men often use this and similar statements to end a conversation, turn a cold shoulder, rather than examine in more depth what a woman is trying to express. It is a form of emotional violence—the cutting off of communication—and is very harmful to relationships.

Many women, of course, have interiorized second-class values about themselves and each other, such as in the put-down of herself contained in one woman's response to being asked if she can talk easily to her husband: "If I want to whine, moan and groan, and be dramatic, I'd best talk to a woman friend. My husband comes from a place of analyzing and being rational. I need a little drama." In this book itself, one could characterize what women are saying about their relationships as "Women often *complain* that . . ." rather than "Women often *report* that . . ." The gender-biased choice of verbs is one we might all make unconsciously, not realizing the implications.

Male nagging?

Several women point out that, in fact, the "male" behavior of emotionally harassing and subtly belittling women—even though it has no name—is no different from what some men refer to in women as "bitchy" or "nagging" behavior.

67 percent of women assert that men do much more complaining than women (although stereotypes have it the other way around):

"I really do believe that men are far superior to women in the bitching, complaining, whining, and nagging department. Women will never be able to catch up!"

"In daily life he criticizes me for trivial things, cupboards and doors left open, etc. He will also criticize me if he doesn't like what I'm wearing. I only get compliments from others. I'm certainly not a sloppy housekeeper. In fact, I'm just the opposite. So why do little things like this bother him? He does little things too but I don't criticize him because it makes him angry and I don't like him angry. So I just close the cupboards, close the drawers, switch off the lights, pick up after him, etc., etc., and say nothing."

"Men think they are so mature, but deep down they are such babies. They expect to be catered to. They whine and complain about everything—expect the world to owe them a living."

Emotional violence

There are more extreme cases of emotional harassment which amount to emotional violence (for which the perpetrator need never answer, will never be called to justice):

"My ex-husband destroyed my confidence in myself. I remember once he wanted me to make a soup like his mother, so I spent all afternoon shopping and preparing it from scratch. Then he came home, and when he tasted it, he said that I put too much paprika in it and flushed the whole thing down the toilet and then slapped me. You can't just start living again after many experiences like that."

"In my sixth month of my first pregnancy I was spotting and the doctor put me to bed. That night my husband insisted on having intercourse. The next day I went to the hospital and gave birth to my first child prematurely, who weighed only one pound fourteen ounces, but who survived. I'm sure I would have given birth [prematurely] anyway, but I felt very hurt by that for a long time."

"We had been going together for six months, and told each other how much we loved each other. Then I realized I was pregnant, and bought one of those home tests. I was nervous about taking it, and before doing it, I told him. I said, 'You won't believe this, darling, but I think I'm pregnant.' After a while he said, 'How can I be sure it's mine?'"

"Years ago, when I was pregnant with my second baby, we had gone to a dance. I was sick, exhausted, and a number of other things, and had gone only because I didn't want to be a party pooper and spoil his fun. I made the best of a totally miserable evening, but by 1:30 a.m. I had had it and told him that I wasn't feeling well, had not been all evening (he didn't even notice), and could we please leave now. He agreed and I got my coat and stood by the door while he table-hopped and said goodbye for another forty-five minutes. I finally left without him, in tears. This leads to the worst thing that I ever did to him . . . I took the car out of the parking lot, and by this time I was furious. He was leaving the building as I drove down the street, so I swerved the car to run him over, just missing him. I drove like a maniac for three blocks, then parked the car and got hold of myself. I almost left him that night when I got home. I started to pack and we had a terrible argument. I didn't leave him, and now I'm glad I didn't. It was uncharacteristic of him to be so thoughtless, and uncharacteristic of me to react the way I did."

"I was very hurt that he just left without a word. I thought we should have been able to talk about it. I thought he knew me well enough to know I would not create a scene. He was my first real love and everything was so good. It has taken me a long time to put myself back together, and to accept the fact that I will never see him again."

After Twenty Years of the Women's Movement, Do Women Feel They Are Seen as Equals in Their Relationships?

Despite the rhetoric of the "sexual revolution" that insists women and men are now equal, we have seen women say here that subtle but extremely painful (and powerful) forms of discrimination are still built into the very structure of relationships, lodged in the smallest wedges of daily interaction. This puts women in the position of having continually to fight for their rights, or try to ignore these subtle cues, discount their reality—"he doesn't mean it," "he doesn't realize what he is saying or what it implies," etc.

78 percent of women say ruefully that still, all too often in love relationships they have to fight for their rights and respect:

"He feels superior to me even though I'm sure he'd deny it. But little things tell me he thinks he's pretty damn good and I ain't shit."

"In language I'm equal. In actuality, he often does things to demonstrate that I am inferior. For instance, promises made to me are not as binding as promises made to men. And there are times when I am simply left out of decisions, decisions that will impact on my life."

"We say we see each other as equal, but sometimes my husband will say to me, 'Some things are hard to explain to a woman.' He says we can't grasp things the same as a man."

"I don't honestly think any middle-aged man, brought up typically in the thirties and forties, considers women as complete equals. Perhaps they have come to it intellectually, but it's still a 'man's world,' imprinted on them subtly."

"He thinks he treats me as an equal and is surprised when I point out ways that he patronizes me. The burden of proof is always on me."

"Usually he treats me equal. But when it comes to my car, all of a sudden I'm a 'dumb blonde.' I know very little about cars, but I'm very anxious to learn about mine. He always decides where car repairs are to be done on my car. I often remind him it's my car and I'll do what I want with it."

"He gives lip service to consulting me about decisions but really has already thought through the problem and decided by himself."

"I never was an equal. No money, no clout. Even when I was handling the checking account and doing a damn fine job, he swept in one day and took it back. As for major decisions, I knew of them and discussed them, but we both knew he would do as he pleased."

"I love the way he treats me during lovemaking. But otherwise he is a bit of a MCP."

47 percent of women say, "He acts superior—but I know he doesn't really mean it," denying the reality of these parts of their lovers' and husbands' behavior:

"He doesn't always treat me as an equal—but he doesn't mean it—it's not serious, he knows better."

"Sometimes he kids me and says, 'The only mistake women make is thinking they're real people.' I know it's only a joke, so I'm good-natured about it. If I thought he was serious, I'd really be pissed."

"My husband does see me as an equal, yet there are times when he seems to treat me as an inferior and act superior. I don't think he would mean to, though—it's just when he's tense about other things and overworked."

And as always, others offer psychological explanations, so that they can deny the reality of their lovers' attitudes—and what they may mean about the status of women:

"We are about equally dependent on each other, but he puts on a bigger show of independence. He had a very strong mother and three sisters and has a need to assert his independence from time to time or he feels female-dominated."

"I think in my case there has been schizoid perception by the men. On the one hand they see me as lesser as a woman, but on the other, they know *I* am not their inferior—in fact, I think one of my difficulties has been being involved with men who are not my equal and that the men recognized this before *I* did."

One man, as 26 percent of women's partners, is making an important effort to buck the trend:

"There are occasions when it is evident that the old male cultural values surface. But he wants to be rid of them and tries hard when they are pointed out in a reasonable way. He sometimes treats me like I am his child, but I'm quick to let him know those occasions. So he tries to stop and the times are fewer and fewer."

But most women say men seem still to fear any approach toward equality, seeing it as a threat to their "dominance," rather than envisioning a new relationship:

"Even though he earns more than twice what I do and he is more intellectual, he feels I am a threat and a challenge to him all the time."

"At first he was superior (in his eyes). As I succeeded in my career, he saw me as a threat, competition—he began playing bizarre tricks on me. I think he was very jealous of me."

There are also some very happy answers; 19 percent of women describe real and equal emotional relationships with the men they love:

"Being with him is a feeling of happiness. I can be free to be myself—be crazy or dumb or intelligent and/or anything—I feel free. I do enjoy his company and we get along. He is special to me and I feel free and not dominated or put down by him."

"He always asks how I am, and wants to know little details of my day, tells me what happened to him at work, we trade funny stories. I especially like it when he comes and sits and talks to me while I am taking a long bath. There I can unwind and think out loud about whatever's on my mind. We keep each other up to date that way."

"My husband sees me as more of an equal than I do. He consults with me and respects my decisions and actions and never questions my role as a mother or as a professional or student."

"My husband depends on me as a good friend. He seeks my advice for his personal and professional problems and we talk before making plans. I treat him with the same respect—that's equality at work."

Loving One Who Loves You, Yet Believes You Are Inferior (or "Less Rational," More "Intuitive")

Each day many women in their own private relationships with a lover or husband endure the sum of his (unconscious) built-up attitudes toward women—attitudes which he usually also has in his personal life, whether he means to or not. A man may think a woman is exceptional—but even that thought still places her in a category which is not quite the regular, top-notch "human" group. As we have seen, the slights that result from these attitudes can be verbal, the repetition of clichés and phrases about women: "just like a woman," "don't be girlish," "there she goes, overly emotional again," and so on. And they can be conveyed without a word—by his not listening (although he would pay close attention to whatever his "boss" or male peers might say); or by his sitting down and dominating the living room (picking without a thought the best chair, waiting for her to offer him a drink—but not offering her a similar courtesy when she is at his house). Or by his habit of relating his ideas ad infinitum without really caring for feedback from her; or by his discussing world affairs or sports, but withholding personal doubts and introspective thoughts.

Emotional harassment and put-downs of women (those many small layers of habit, verbal and non-verbal cues—no *one* of which one would want to start a fight about, or if one did, one might be called "hysterical") are more or less a pattern in society—and in many women's personal love relationships, so that a remark can be made at any moment, when a woman is least expecting it. This amounts to a kind of emotional terrorism.

Women are blackmailed into silence by the labels which wait for them if they do "complain" (i.e., women are "nagging" or "difficult"). Thus, an individual woman, no matter how strong or aware, living with these stereotypes over a period of time, can find her will steadily, slowly eroded, her self-esteem becoming something to be fought for, piece by piece, day by day, in an unending, uphill battle. Popular magazines say it is *her* problem, not men's or the society's problem.

Gender-biased attitudes are particularly harmful in a deep, intimate personal relationship. If the butcher or a salesperson makes a demeaning remark (which, as every woman knows, can always happen), it is one thing: something unpleasant, but something one can overlook as coming from a prejudiced person. But if the person one loves, is closest to, and depends on for one's most intimate contact with humanity makes such a remark—that is another matter. And this seems to be, in case after case, exactly what is happening. It is possible that many men have no idea what they are doing. Most do seem to be quite unaware of the residual stereotypes they hold. They think, "Oh, this is just Mary, she is like that. She had a childhood that . . ." Or, "She is a specialist with children, who cannot understand all that I, having been in the world so long, can know . . ." and so on.

If these attitudes were blatantly expressed they would be easier to fight. But the subtle distancing and harassment that have been accepted for millennia not as "put-downs" but as just describing "how women are," are very difficult to deal with, and their effects are insidious.

What is the answer then? For women to keep putting in disproportionate amounts of time in relationships with men to explain all of this (over and over), and also to rebuild their own damaged self-esteem? Or are women giving up some of their belief in the importance of love, deciding to stop investing so much energy in "love," adopting a "male" point of view, placing love second after work or career? Women could easily decide to take this route as the path of least resistance, unless equality, openness, and emotional support become traits men choose to develop in themselves—so that women can share a highly developed inner emotional world with men, without winding up feeling burned out and terribly lonely.

Fighting and Arguing in Relationships: What Do They Mean?

Typical Fights

Describe the biggest or most recent fight you had with your husband or lover:

"My lover came to visit me uninvited, then sat listening to me talking with a girlfriend I hadn't seen in several months. He made no effort to join in the conversation, although I did say a few things to him. After five hours he left, and later called to break up with me, saying he'd never had such a cold reception in his life."

"He criticized me indirectly and then would not admit that he was actually criticizing me. When I got mad about it, he said I was being 'unreasonable.' I was furious. I feel he should admit what he is doing and not be devious."

"We are both short on cash. We went to Burger King and he ordered a bunch of stuff, and I ordered just a little bit. Then he said, 'Is that all you want? We could have gone to my house to get something if I'd known you only wanted a little bit—I'm spending my money needlessly.' "

"He was lying on the bed watching TV while I got stuck cleaning up the huge mess after a party we had. We had a big fight—it was his party too!"

"My husband was out of town and I was driving to work. The highway was two lanes only. Two cars came over the hill racing side by side. To avoid a head-on collision I drove off the road. I managed to keep my car out of a ditch, but it scraped some cedar bushes, stuck in one, and hung on the ledge. A truck had to come pull me out backwards. Luckily the car wasn't so damaged that

I couldn't get to work. I was shook up but alive. When I told my husband he got angry that I let the cars force me off the road! He didn't seem to care how *I* was. I still can't believe it!"

"We were in bed. It was his birthday and I had put a lot of energy into making it a great day. It was late, about 1:30 a.m., and we both had to get up for work early. We were making love—or leading up to it anyway. It was very nice, very passionate, and I was quite lost in it. All of a sudden he said, 'Holy shit, I have to be at work at seven-thirty tomorrow instead of eight!!' He stopped what we were doing, reset the alarm, kissed me good night, and turned over to go to sleep. I felt hurt, I felt like he hadn't even been feeling what we were doing if he was thinking about the time. It felt like a slap in the face. He could not understand why I was so upset. I grabbed my pillow and stomped out and went to sleep in the next room. This led to a ridiculous argument the next morning."

"The worst thing he has ever done is to stay out all night once when I was pregnant and vulnerable and not call me to say where he was. This he did in pursuit (with a fellow electrician) of some strippers to perform at an electricians' party—which incensed me because I had assumed that my husband was more enlightened than to do something adolescent and macho like that. Then, after our big fight, he had the lack of grace to go to the damn party (which he really did not enjoy) to prove to his fellow union members that he was not pussy-whipped! This disappointed me greatly and it hurt me to see him subscribe to those traditional male values of thinking of certain 'types' of women as objects for entertainment."

"I told him I hadn't had a vacation in three years, nor even been out of the city in seven years! and that I was feeling very harassed and frantic with work, and just overwhelmed with things that had been happening in my family, various crises to deal with, also my job was overworking me . . . I shed a tear or two, as I was letting all of this out just before we drifted off to sleep. The next morning, I woke to hear him telling me that he had been thinking about me, that this just couldn't go on, and how about making this Sunday at least a one-day vacation? We would go to the beach and windsurf or just do whatever we wanted, just the two of us. I was so touched and thrilled. I was really looking forward to it. But later in the week, he started saying things like, well, there's no point in going if the weather isn't good, I hear it's going to rain, and so on. I asked him if I should really cancel work plans. His answer was vague, but I still was looking forward to the possibility of taking off together. Then on Saturday he didn't mention it at all . . . Later I heard he went to the beach with his best friend on Sunday, then he called in the evening as if nothing had happened! I didn't want to cause a 'scene,' and so I was just tight-lipped (after working all day again) and didn't tell him I was angry. Now I'm supposed to see him tomorrow. I don't know what will happen."

"If a Woman Doesn't Bring It Up, Nobody Will": the Role Society Gives Women in Fights

"He never apologizes, he just makes fun of me if I complain or get upset about anything. If I really insist, he just walks out. This puts me in an impossible position—what do I do, leave him? If I don't want to leave him, do I have to swallow my pride and never complain? This hurts my dignity, and affects my ability to handle the rest of my life well. (I work, etc.) Then I feel too upset or bothered by my unreleased or un-talked-about feelings with him to focus clearly on what I am doing. But if I let it out and scream, he looks at me like I am a 'nagging bitch' and still won't discuss the topic. So I am at a loss as to what to do. I don't know how to relate to him and still keep my sanity—but I don't want to lose him either."

Many arguments are "started" by women who are not getting enough communication or two-way interchange, or who are being emotionally harassed or sabotaged by their husbands/lovers:

"I don't really like fighting, but I will resort to it when I get mad enough. It is usually triggered by him making sarcastic remarks to me about me. Nobody wins, but I usually wind up feeling bad about it. Sometimes we are able to end it with humor."

"It seems like my problems and ideas are never taken as seriously—or at least as seriously as I take his. I try to listen to him, to empathize with him—but when I talk about my plans, instead of listening he changes the subject. Then if I complain, instead of apologizing, he mimics me! He says things like 'Oh, boo-hoo-hoo, poor little girl.' I'd like to see how he would take it if *I* did such a thing to him! I try to control my anger, but sometimes I really let it all out."

"When I point out that I am tired of having to be the one to remember things and remind him about them, that I keep lists and he doesn't—for example, thank-you notes, invitation responses, repairs, etc.—he never says I'm right, he always snarls. So I am doubly overworked: I have to remember his part of the family chores and suffer emotional abuse for the service of reminding him. There is no way to remind him in a way that does not offend him. This offends *me.*"

"I didn't argue with him for a long time because I was keeping the peace. But that just encourages a person to act worse. I think we fight more now than we ever have. In the beginning he wanted me to go along with him, I wasn't to argue. So he didn't try to see my side, and the old conflicts were never resolved. I'm not trying to resolve them anymore. I just decided when I turned forty that there were certain behaviors toward me I wasn't going to put up with anymore in anybody. And I don't."

"We always fight about what I consider a constant, negative put-down of a role I refuse to play."

"We argued until both decided that to ignore was easier. Most of the arguments were over the kids. Example: one day I corrected and reprimanded a four-year-old at about one in the afternoon. I had smacked his fanny, gently, and set him in a chair for some quiet time. At five-thirty the father walked in the door. The kid had seen the approach of the car and ran to his bedroom, flailing himself across the bed with tears and sobs authentic enough to melt paint. The father said, 'WHAT DID YOU DO TO THAT CHILD?' . . . not 'Hello, why is he crying?' I never abused the kids, the corrections and disciplines were prompt, brief, and followed with a lot of love. A smack on the bottom was rare, but when required administered with love. I was to blame for everything, and I accepted this until I had an affair and realized that I wasn't to blame for *EVERYTHING*. I returned to college, obtained a degree, studied myself, developed myself."

72 percent of women say they are the ones to "bring up issues" that need talking about—and that all too often this turns into fights:

"It's always me who has the gripe, me who wants to make the point. There's never any resolution of our bickering, I guess the reason is I don't want to make such a scene that I scare him off, and lose the relationship entirely, so when things happen, I try to overlook them—but I find myself taking swipes at him, jabs, almost like I can't help myself. Sometimes they're about little issues, often not even related to the latest upsetting (to me) 'incident.' I'm never quite sure if he's aware how these incidents upset me, and I try to figure out if things I do upset him, but he just doesn't tell me either. Is he thinking, 'Take it like a man,' don't complain? Sometimes I think he does things like not showing interest that day, going off with his friends, because of something I did which he interpreted negatively. But I don't want to make an issue out of them, usually, and so I just let it go. Maybe if we would fight more dramatically, there would be a resolution, not this permanent, constant feeling of uncertainty. I keep waiting for 'it' to end. But it never does. I guess unless we change our way of relating, this will be our permanent 'thing,' and 'it' will never end—that is, there will never be a resolution. What I want to know is, can we go on like this indefinitely, or will the relationship break down because of it?"

"Until he 'resigns himself' to a talk, I meet with resistance all the way. Like, I am talking and talking and getting little um-hmms and suddenly he looks up at me and says, 'Would you like to talk?' . . . I scream, 'That is what I have been doing!' Our talks are wonderful things, I often wish they didn't have to end, that we didn't have to stop and go to sleep or do chores or go get the kids or whatever it is. I initiate the 'talk-over,' and am insulting and ugly until he finally starts talking and things begin to be productive, constructive. Then we get to calmness and acceptance."

"I always initiate talking about the problem. I think of what I'm going to say umpteen times, and then finally spit it out because I can't stand the silence anymore."

88 percent of women say the men in their lives seem to prefer to avoid "talking things over"—which only makes a fight inevitable:

"When I'm trying to talk something out, I hate men who rush you through the problem (because you're not supposed to be upset, men think it's weakness to be upset), i.e., so they'll say, at the slightest beginning of a conversation or of bringing up a subject, 'What's the problem?' with that tone of voice like 'You wouldn't start complaining on me, now, would you???'—almost a threat, or trying to minimize or trivialize what you were about to say. It makes it very difficult."

"Usually it goes like this: He thinks everything is fine—so why do *I* feel miserable? Because everything is fine as long as I support him, I am there for him. But when I feel emotionally or verbally 'unheard,' and then complain—and finally scream and shout—then *I* am to blame because, after all, *he* was happy before *I* brought it up."

76 percent of women say men do not take the initiative in solving personal problems:

"He usually will not admit that a problem exists! The loneliest times were when we had argued until the wee hours of the morning, and the problems were not only unresolved but seemed worse than when we started, he fell asleep in mid-argument, leaving me all alone in the dark, cold night."

"If I bring up something he did that hurt me, he yells, 'That's a lie!' and leaves. Making up? He just goes on as though nothing was said. Why can't he face our agreements and disagreements more realistically in daily life, before it gets to a fight?"

"I have screamed in utter frustration at someone I wanted to remain close to when they have refused to try to understand my needs and feelings. Sometimes that's the only way someone will believe how bad I feel. They don't seem to 'hear' me otherwise."

Not only will a woman bring up her own problems or grievances, but if a man seems unhappy, many women will try to find out why he is unhappy (part of women's "emotional housework"*):

"I usually ask what is bothering my husband. I wish he would open up but he has the tendency to deny that he is upset. But he's improved."

"He is quiet when he is upset, so I have to initiate his talking to me, telling me what is wrong, and draw it out of him."

Women often have a feeling they are the "bad guy" for bringing up problems —but they say if they don't bring them up, no one else will, and so they feel forced into the position of the stereotypical "nagging woman":

"It's always, *I* have all these problems, and he's perfectly O.K. He can't believe that any of my behavior is a reaction to things he does/that he did. He just thinks it's 'just how I am'—I've tried logic and everything."

"I always initiate talking things over when something has upset me. I don't like the 'bad guy' that this makes out of me because my husband is of the type that lets things pass—they're always 'my' problems."

"I hate confrontation, but hate not being understood more. Therefore, when I am unhappy about something, I will eventually express it in as honest a way as I can. This usually is productive and leaves me feeling better afterwards. I feel very close when we resolve something which has been eating away at me. I'm getting better at being clear-minded during arguments. Emotion used to take over, because I so rarely expressed dissatisfaction—I felt that my suffering was O.K. and that I couldn't make life uncomfortable for anyone else. Now if I'm unhappy, I'm willing to upset someone else."

81 percent of women—harking back to the training that a woman, a nice woman, is not supposed to be angry—say they feel guilty for arguing, whether they bring up the complaint or the man does; they feel guilty—whether wrong or right—for disturbing the peace:

"I don't like to fight. Ever since childhood some people can make me feel guilty when there is tension, etc. My mother is one and my husband is now the other. I almost always end up apologizing."

"If I lose my temper, I feel like it is the end of the world, I am the one who has caused it . . . But my children have learned how to fight and quarrel—and then be friends. I have to learn from them."

---

*This term was coined by Gudula Lorez, German feminist publisher, referring to the emotional work women do for men. Trying to draw men out, keep the emotional lines open, is a real and undervalued service women provide for men much of the time.

"He usually wins. I usually feel guilty because somehow I've been inconsiderate and have injured him."

39 percent of women are at times afraid to even bring up what is bothering them:

"In past relationships, old conflicts kept going, as I was too withdrawn and scared to assert myself, or confront the problem, out of fear of losing the relationship. This is not the situation now and I hope I don't ever get into that terrible circle of anger and resentment again."

"I'm very dependent emotionally on my husband and when I'm angry I try to keep it to myself. To have him angry with me removes the basis of my world."

"I do find it very difficult during sex to tell him if he is doing something wrong—even if what he is doing is physically hurting me. For example, I seem to have very sensitive tissue near my clitoris. When he is rubbing it, I say over and over, silently, to myself, 'Please stop, that hurts.' But I find it almost impossible to say it out loud to him, unless it becomes *very* painful, and then I feel terrible to have to possibly hurt his feelings."

Others feel they usually can't "win" in fights, and are very frustrated during and after:

"Deep inside me I tend to operate from a position of 'You're O.K., I'm *not* O.K.' In a fight I give in to my anxieties and let others win, even if I feel my cause is just. Fighting is a skill I need to learn. I dread fighting, I don't know how to do it effectively, I usually wind up feeling impotent, shamed, frustrated, confused. I want to be able to fight back effectively when I feel I'm being manipulated or used. I often feel that my partner has made himself righteous at my expense. For example, when I act sophisticated, he accuses me of being a snob; when I act less sophisticated, then he says I'm an embarrassment and hold him back socially! Or if I'm more inhibited, he says I'm a prude or not sophisticated enough; if I'm less inhibited, then I'm dirty, disgusting, disgraceful."

"About fighting, I wish that in general I had the stamina, guts, and skill to not get pushed around by men! I generally lose arguments and smolder with resentment."

But still others have learned some helpful strategies:

"It used to make me physically ill to fight—like coming down with a virus. Now, since I've become more self-assured, I settle into a fight to make my case clear, state my position and stick to it. I feel more offensive and less defensive. I usually win."

"I go to great lengths to avoid fighting or emotional confrontations. I especially remember about a year ago when I was to meet my lawyer, my husband, and his lawyer and wanted to clarify some points in the separation agreement. I'd never met his lawyer and wanted to impress the man, so, quite spontaneously, I bought a red hat an hour or so before the meeting and wore it. Under the red hat I felt somewhat protected since hardly anyone wears hats, and it set me apart as 'different.' Explaining this to my psychiatrist a few days later, he asked, 'Why?' I said because I didn't want to lose my cool during the meeting. The psychiatrist said sarcastically (to get a reaction from me—he did not), 'It was very important to remain cool and distant about something so unimportant as ending a twenty-year marriage?' Yes, it was very important even in that event not to show my vulnerability. P.S.: The ploy worked, I got all my concessions."

61 percent of women say that no matter how hard they try, issues are not resolved:

"I hate our arguing. My whole world seems turned upside down when there is tension. I'm normally a happy person, but get very down then. I usually initiate talking over the problem—but it never gets resolved. It's always the same problem—my need for him to be tender and loving."

"I think fighting is vital to a relationship—if both people keep to the issues. I feel good being honest and open about my needs, but usually I am not heard. Nothing is ever accomplished by our quarrels. We fight about the very same issue once every three or four months. Nobody wins, though I get it off my chest. The fights are ended with his going into his room and hiding, usually with the promise to 'think about it.' This issue never has (and probably never will) be resolved."

"I am inclined to start an argument. My husband will avoid it if he can. He always wins, because he never changes his mind. I feel more furious when it's over than I did when it started, because I can never gain any ground with him. He is very, very opinionated and his mind cannot be changed through logic, proof that he is mistaken, tears, shrieking, or anything else. Seldom is anything resolved. We don't talk anything over after a fight, just drift back together. I try to find out how he feels but to no avail."

"I hate fighting. It makes me feel miserable. No one wins. I feel furious during and defeated afterwards. Arguments in our relationship never seemed to get resolved. They just cropped up again later. I usually ended up saying I was sorry just to keep the peace. If we tried to talk the problem over, it usually ended up in another fight, so eventually all the fighting was ended by ending the relationship."

"The pattern was that I'd get irritated, shout, he'd shout back. I'd cry, he'd stomp out of the house. I'd calm down, and when he came back in, we'd go on as if nothing happened. There was never any catharsis or meeting of the minds."

"Our problems were never resolved. I would initiate talking something over, he would say anything he thought you wanted to hear to get it over with."

"My ex-husband had an uncontrolled temper and resorted to very abusive language. If he didn't get his way, he became physically violent. I was usually terrified when he exploded and nothing was ever resolved."

"We don't have fights—he makes statements and the discussion doesn't go any further. He expounds, I clam up, bang the door to the bedroom and fall silent. Very frustrating on both sides."

"I don't like fighting, it's usually about money and then everything I've done all my life. I get very angry and defend myself more than I used to. After, I feel angry and depressed."

"The pattern usually is, I feel I have a legitimate grievance to air, but he is not one to readily admit that he is wrong, and will not usually apologize. He says he is just not that kind of person and can't change—and that I knew that when I married him. After the 'talk,' the problem gets modified for a while, then he slips back to too cool, distant behavior and I stew and then we have a discussion again when I can't take it much longer. I (and my husband will agree—but not change) think that I do most of the 'giving' and the fussing and the little loving things. He does not give of himself that much to make me feel loved. I may have unreal expectations of what a marriage *can* be, but in the affection department, he just does not reciprocate."

"I hate fighting with my husband because he gets too emotional. I think a fight ought to clear the air, but he gets mean. I used to let him win every time because I was afraid of his temper. Now I never let him win. I make my point and stick to it. But it still doesn't resolve anything, so then he accuses me of not letting him express his feelings! I still don't give up my point. However, I end the fight by getting us to agree on something—anything. The moon is made of green cheese! I try to make him laugh."

"All the time, I am hoping he will say something that will release me from the pain. Even as I say the things that hurt I am picturing the releasing tender words."

For couples who successfully talk things over, see Chapter 17.

89 percent of women say men do not really hear what they are saying during fights; "They hear what they want to hear." Most women say men seem to feel that reasons other than those the woman is stating are causing her "problem," and that "they know these reasons better," since the woman herself is not "rational" enough to know:

"His opinion is that I'm criticizing him whenever I try to bring up anything that's bothering me, or that he has done to hurt me. He tells me I am just making trouble. He doesn't really listen to what I am saying. I usually have tried to tell him all this calmly before, and got no response, so now I am yelling it and he tells me I am attacking him. I can't win."

"It's usually something that's been building up, he just doesn't want to deal with it, and finally I can't stand it any longer. So there is a big scene. It really hurts me when he refuses to discuss the issue, and just ridicules me, saying, 'You must have your period, you're hysterical.' Even if I *did* have my period (it *does* make me dramatic at times), it doesn't mean that what I am saying isn't true and isn't a problem, something that should be dealt with."

73 percent of women say they are almost always the ones to say they are sorry after a fight, who try to talk things over; although the man often makes an overture in terms of a kiss or a hug, most men do not readily say they are sorry or want to talk:

"Most of our arguments usually end up with us just not talking for a while, or one of us falling asleep. When one of us says they are sorry, it is usually me. Either that or neither one of us says it. Most of the time after a fight, I want to make up. I want to be held close, and know that even though we may not agree, he still loves me."

"The person I lived with never said, 'I'm sorry.' He'd choke first. I would always try to work it out. He'd never hear what I said. He'd always interrupt when I would be talking. He'd turn things around to suit himself. Things were never settled."

"Our conflicts end either by my saying I'm sorry or by my not speaking to my husband for days until I can put the problem aside somehow. My husband has never said he is sorry."

"How do arguments usually get resolved? When he makes me so miserable I say I'm sorry because he makes sure I'm sorry. I feel defeated."

"If anyone is to say they are sorry, I do. He has never said he was sorry about being wrong. He's only sorry he made me cry! I must 'make up.'"

"In my marriage, I was the initiator, the maker-upper, etc. This only served to put my husband in a superior, self-righteous position—in his eyes."

But 12 percent of women say the man in their life does the apologizing:

"I won't make up. He causes the problem, so he can make up first. I always respond."

"He often initiates making up—and tells me he doesn't want to lose my love. (This is the exact opposite of my unhappy marriage, in which I always apologized.)"

"Conflicts and arguments are usually resolved immediately, we don't let anything fester. He usually says he's sorry first, because I am stubborn and don't like to admit that I am wrong. We make up right after."

One man wrote a very touching and amusing letter, describing his own analysis of his fighting habits: *

"The more mad at me she gets, the more superior I feel. I just sit, stoically, waiting for it to end. While sitting there, with her screaming or waiting for me to 'say something' (which I won't), or to apologize, I am thinking, 'Why is she doing this to *me?*' Of course she says that she was the one whose feelings were hurt first, but I don't honestly feel responsible. She shouldn't have got them hurt, I didn't mean it, after all. Why is she being so difficult? She should stop behaving this way. If she loved me, she wouldn't act this way. She doesn't respect me.

"Sometimes she really gets mad and demands more than monosyllabic grunts. My usual response, if pressed, would be to say, 'I need time' or 'Give me space' or 'Leave me alone, I've gotta think about it'—meanwhile thinking how noble I am, to put up with all of this. I'm a martyr and a saint. But really, if I am honest with myself, this is a passive-aggressive attitude, full of anger. Where do these attitudes come from? I don't know. I see them on TV commercials in which little boys have to be catered to by their mothers—who are idiots, naturally—with the little boys being smarter than them, etc.

"But it's a great pleasure to withdraw into monosyllables—feeling like a wounded hero, for two or three days at a time even! Sulking—what an impediment to figuring things out! I guess, in our fights, we were always just missing each other. Why didn't I just say, 'This troubles me, and here's why . . .'? instead of sulking or thinking myself superior and waiting for her to get over 'her problem'?

"I guess it's pretty clear that in this pattern I and probably other men too are avoiding any responsibility for what goes on. What is needed is greater assertion and autonomy in men—real male pride, men taking responsibility for an honest interaction with women—not just being passive and yet seeming superior. Not making it like 'Your job is to run circles around me, try to figure out what I want when I speak in only monosyllables, and satisfy my every unstated requirement.' "

The Riddle of Male Passivity in Fights with Women

Most women say men in their lives seem extremely reluctant to discuss areas of difference, and that this attitude finally leads to "confrontation"—which both people like even less. Then the woman, who most often "brought up the issue" may be accused of being a troublemaker.

*This is one of the letters received in response to *The Hite Report on Male Sexuality.*

There is a sort of passivity in this kind of "masculinity," a "what can *I* do about *your* problem?" attitude. Women then can wind up feeling quite guilty, since they are supposed (by role) to be the peacemakers in life, and also are supposedly responsible for being loving, keeping the relationship running smoothly. In fact, men "win" either way, emotionally, because if the man loses the argument, the woman was "giving him a hard time"; if he wins, the woman was "irrational" and "hysterical," as everyone knows women are—and so, no matter what, the woman is the guilty party.

"I feel fine. Why are you complaining?": men's patterns during fights

Many women describe a kind of silent withdrawal on the part of men during arguments:

"I do most of the talking, screaming, yowling, and crying during the fight. He just sits there. He is very unemotional and not good at expressing himself."

"Male nagging is silent. Silent sulking, or silent, arrogant disapproval."

"His expression seems to say, 'Why are you behaving this way? Making a scene. I have no idea what you expect me to do about it.' "

"The usual pattern is, he makes me furious, I sound off, he says nothing, finally I demand that he say something, he says, 'What do you want me to say?' which makes me more furious because I still don't know what he is thinking about whatever I'm so upset about."

"He has a classic pose. He sits immobile, looking 'above it all'—the Mussolini pose, I call it. Aloof, while I try to get through to him. What really infuriates me is that he comes off looking like he is the one with 'good manners,' while I'm making a fool of myself, becoming emotionally out of control and hysterical."

Seventy-six percent of women say that most men show very little emotion, effort, or empathy in trying to understand them during a fight. Most say that if a silent hostility ensues after they have "brought up something," it is very easy to wind up shouting, in an (unconscious) effort to finally really be *heard*.

As one woman describes this wrenchingly sad situation in her mother's case, "My mom tried to argue but my dad would never respond, which to me at that time made her look foolish. My father's attitude toward Mom was to not get as 'worked up' as her, because he was 'above it.' He looked superior to me. Mother's attitude: 'Work around him in order to get what you want from him.' "

In other words, shouting, getting "worked up" in a fury of powerlessness over a man's refusal to discuss something, take one's feelings seriously, only leads most women to finally be called "irrational" or "hysterical"—two gender-biased words which are still remarkably current, according to women in this study. Used either as a put-down—i.e., "You're being hysterical"—or as a patronizing way of "calming her down"—i.e., "Now, now, don't get hysterical"—such words only make matters worse. Are men aware of their own hostility at these times?

As one woman reports what goes on in her relationship, "His attitude when I am upset is usually 'I feel fine. Why are you complaining?'—or, if I keep on, and really get upset, he will say, 'You're causing scenes.' Or he'll say, 'Why do you have to insist on making your point?' to which I say, 'I'm not "insisting"—I'm trying to talk to you!' "

On the other hand, negative or "emotional" behaviors common to men are not named, have no common-usage phrases, so that there are gaps, missing elements in the language. For example, the male equivalent of a "nagging woman," standing with her hand on her hip shouting at a man, seems to be (according to women here): "He looked at her with arrogant disdain." Why is there no word or phrase for men's characteristic silent withdrawal?

In the previous chapter, we saw that the language has many built-in statements and phrases which represent subliminal sexist psychological attacks on women. (One can even find them used in supposedly objective, "scientific" journals.) Men often feel free to use this vocabulary with impunity, believing absolutely that what they are saying is true, not realizing the self-serving and sexist nature of the clichés. Especially do they use such language, evidently, in situations in which a woman is angry or upset, most probably because of the stereotypes present in our society about women: women are illogical, overly emotional, tend to "nag," and you have to keep them under control or they will be impossible, will "pussy-whip" you, will become shrewish (i.e., independent and demanding of respect) as in Shakespeare's *Taming of the Shrew* (still studied in many high school and college English classes with no mention of its sexist implications).

In other words, men's passivity and silence, interspersed with references to women's "hysterical" or "out of control" behavior during fights, are provocative and inflammatory. Since the man is refusing to discuss the issue, even when a woman is quite upset about it, he is denying her any recourse: his withdrawal (and, frequently, his condescending attitude) is making a very clear statement. It is saying that she must either accept matters as they are or leave. Since he refuses to negotiate or compromise, talk about it, "She can yell all she wants, but it's not my problem," as one woman quotes her brother saying about his wife.

Another problem with male patterns of fighting, according to 48 percent of the women in this study, is the tendency for men to become competitive, rather than to listen and empathize. As one woman describes this, "It seems I never get anywhere by bringing things up that hurt me, because if I tell him he hurt my feelings, like by something he said, he will only respond with some accusation that now I have hurt his feelings *too*, by saying this, criticizing him (that's what he calls it). The other day, after he had been two hours late to pick me up and I complained, he said, 'What about *my* feelings?! You should apologize to *me* for criticizing and attacking me!' Then he went into a silent pout all the way to Long Island, throwing me nasty, stony glances and basically refusing to look at me. He gets me so mad. And it's all so unnecessary. Why is he like that?" In other words, if the woman states a grievance, the man may declare he has a worse grievance against the woman.

Perhaps some men carry over the "rules" of competition from work to their emotional relationships. Women who fall in love, and expect that the man, in love too, will give emotionally in the same way that they believe in, are often surprised when the man becomes competitive. Is this competitiveness in emotionally tense situations brought about by men's training to be competitive in all situations, to win no matter what—or by men's desire to avoid becoming "womanly" or "feminine," "overly emotional"? Most men think the point of the argument is to win, and especially to make sure "the woman doesn't get the upper hand." (See pages 138–9, "The 'male' ideology.") They do not see the discussion as an effort to struggle through together, to come to a better understanding of each other.

One woman speculates on why so many men seem to love winning psychological struggles:

"Men's attitude is something like 'Women are always screaming at you, they're always bugging you, they never let you do what you want to do.' But men love to aggravate the situation—i.e., withhold their feelings and thoughts. The more the woman needs to discuss something with them, the more they won't. I've seen this pattern over and over again with my brother and his wife, and myself and my boyfriend. So finally the woman is screaming (me), and the guy thinks it's funny. Why? Are they putting something over on their mothers, thinking how clever they are to get away with it?

"Like, my younger brother (age seventeen) asked our mother at the dinner table whether anal penetration of a girl wasn't O.K., right? because 'it's birth control, after all'—ha-ha. This, after pretending to ask her a serious question about whether she thought it was O.K. He really got her, right at the dinner table. She didn't know what to say, and everybody laughed. Why do men like to 'get' women like that? They say women are always nagging them, etc., when it's really men who tell women what to do. Isn't this just a form of woman hatred? Baiting women? Or is it that since women bring up men, and therefore have the power, absolute power over them, men resent women so? That's what some people say. But women are brought up by women too, and they don't want to 'get one over' on women—i.e., prove how stupid women are."

Unfair Fighting

The worst kind of fighting is unfair fighting, dirty fighting—in which the idea isn't to air grievances and reach an understanding, but just to wound the other person as deeply as possible:

"Lying, while fighting, is dumb; like, out of anger he lied and told me he'd been seeing another girl and had screwed her. I asked her name. He had to think a long time. A few months later I gently nudged her name into a conversation. He said, 'Who the hell is that? I've never heard of her!' Dummy! I feel lost when we fight. Very empty."

"I hate to fight, it leaves too many scars. People usually end up saying a lot of things they don't really mean. Like, if I say he hurt my feelings by not calling, he says things like 'You might ask yourself why I don't call . . .' and so on, implying some vague nasty thing. So my husband usually won. If he thought he was losing—he'd change the rules! I was hurt; paralyzed; speechless. A no-win situation."

The most complete and utter alienation is eventually reached by couples who fight, with no one saying they are sorry afterwards, and one or both pretending it just hasn't happened; 53 percent of women say this is what happens in their relationships:

"He usually initiates the making-up process while I haven't even begun to say what's bothering me, or I have but he's shot down everything I have to say. I go along with the peace initiative but not with joy or energy. He usually wins in the sense that we do what he wants to do, keep sleeping together, stay together."

"In silence, we go to separate rooms—we don't say: sorry—we tacitly agree to drop the issue."

"I always walk away from a fight—nothing gets solved and it's tense for a few days—but you never forget."

"Most of our big fights are about drinking or money. I hate fighting. I don't know who wins because the argument just quiets down. Sometimes we talk about it but not to a great extent because he can't express himself. I feel hurt when we fight. I think to myself, 'What's the purpose of it all? It's just not worth it. Life's too short.' Or 'Why the hell am I here?' "

"I dislike his defensiveness—always having to be right—always arguing louder or saying, 'You're wrong'—period—and I'm supposed to accept that!"

"It's not very often the word 'sorry' is said after a fight. We do not make up, we just get on with what we were doing. I do not believe in making up by sex."

"I hate fighting, yelling, or swearing at anyone! If he'd be more rational we could discuss it, but no. He shrieks! We make up in bed, usually, and then, if I try to discuss anything, he just huffs and puffs and goes to sleep. He won't concede to anything."

Not having a way to resolve differences, grievances, is very serious, and can lead a woman (or a man) to leave a marriage—first emotionally, then, later, possibly physically:

"Fighting just keeps increasing the rift in our marriage. Just makes me want to get up and run and not look back. We have broken up a few times after periods of such fierce arguing, him leaving was the only solution. He returns but the problems remain."

"We used to argue a lot—now there's more of an indifference-type atmosphere. It's as if we're roommates with children in common and not much else. The love died long ago."

"The best way to make it work for thirty years? Give in and give in and give in. He has to win and I have to apologize. There's no other way to do it. He never wants to talk things over. It's his way, and his way only."

After thirty-eight years of unresolved fights and arguments, one woman exclaims:

"The old ones never got resolved. They just got coded down so they didn't take long to review before embarking on all the new ones. You always run through the whole tape first. I used to think it was like pulling a garbage truck around all the time. There was no way to get rid of it. It was tied tightly to each of us through the whole thirty-eight years and if I saw him today it would still be there. Thank the Goddess he's on the other side of the continent."

Many women point out how important it is to them to try to resolve the problem or conflict that day—not letting time pass during which the hurt can solidify:

"I never like us to go to bed without making up our quarrel. I feel miserable and unhappy, it makes me cry. It's so good to be friends again."

"I like to talk about a problem when it happens—so there are no straws to break the camel's back."

"I initiate talking it over—he'd prefer to leave it alone for a while—I like to talk about it right away. We usually hold each other closely after, rarely do we have sex after. I usually feel drained, sore, and empty."

"Don't make your bed a battleground": But is having sex really making up?

"This is an odd observation: Back when we had a sex life, he got turned on by fighting. The more vicious it was, the more turned on he got. This is the kind of fight that turns me *off*. He seemed to like the excitement of it. I noticed that his mother is also the most loving just after she's reduced everybody to rubble. I have no idea what this means, but I instinctively will not let myself be touched by anyone who's just humiliated me."

But, as one woman says, "Women are often admonished not to take their fights to bed with them. If a woman does go to bed with a man who refuses to discuss something with her that matters to her, doesn't try to understand, isn't going to bed with him capitulating?"

Most women in this study say they like to talk about problems and misunderstandings as soon as possible, so no buildup occurs. However, as most women indicate, many men would rather leave the discussion for another time, or avoid these "talks" altogether. Therefore, it often happens that a couple arrives at bedtime with tension hanging in the air—or, at least, one person's feelings hurt. Should women "take these fights to bed" and "withhold sex"—or be able to put them aside and "not let fighting interfere with lovemaking"?

Often if a woman feels she can't get something resolved, she doesn't feel like having sex later—she feels disregarded as a person. However, in this situation a woman may be accused of "withholding sex" to "manipulate" the man. In fact, many articles in popular magazines by various counselors and psychologists use these terms and imply that this is a "bad habit" women have. But to put women down for feeling alienated, and to imply they should not connect sex and feelings so deeply, is to pressure them to accede to the "male" value system, to give up their own integrity.

A woman can find herself in the position of not wanting sex because of unresolved quarrels once or twice in a relationship—or again and again until it becomes a pattern. Even if the disagreements are small, still, the failures to resolve them can mount up, and a woman may feel less and less like sex. This becomes "ammunition" for some men to put the woman down even more. Yet it is a valid way in which a woman is asserting her own dignity and rights, trying to be heard, to get a resolution, so that she can continue the relationship as her full self, not as a non-person who has to fantasize to get aroused, lubricated enough to have intercourse.

Can Fighting Help?

Productive fighting: techniques for staying close

Most women say the best kind of fighting ends in a resolution in which each person comes to understand the other's point of view:

"Often in arguments, I feel unable to get him to understand my point of view. 'Winning' for me would involve both of us understanding the other's viewpoint. Afterwards, if this worked, I would feel very relieved, as one feels when a burden has been removed."

"We have unbelievably upsetting discussions about uncomfortable emotional subjects. But my husband will more often than not end up understanding what is going on. I feel very close when we resolve something which has been eating away at me."

"We don't fight. We resolve the problem. It feels great. Years ago we used to fight because I wanted to get every place on time, and we were always late because of him. We solved the problem by deciding that for movies, plays, and concerts, we would be on time, because it's important. For dinner, gatherings, and parties we are more lax about arrival time. Now he only feels pressured when it is important."

"After a fight we both sit down and talk things out. We will then come to an understanding and cuddle up in each other's arms and fall asleep or make love."

"Conflicts get resolved by talking about them, and thinking about what was happening at the time. We both apologize. He usually starts talking about it first."

"At first, I usually say I'm sorry, even if the problem was his. Then when we are feeling better, he'll say he's sorry too and the real explanation for things gets uncovered."

Sometimes disagreements or small hurt feelings can turn major because of an underlying fear on the part of one or both people that the other doesn't really love them, "hates" them, is going to reject them. If you really love someone, perhaps you always live with this worry and it is frightening:

"He stalked through the house breaking pottery he had made. He was totally 'out of control' and I let him rage awhile and then held him and told him how glad I was he finally 'let go.' His biggest fear was that I really didn't like him. He always said that first when we fought through these conflicts. I was really overwhelmed, sad and angry, but on some level knew he had to get a lot of stuff out."

Some are learning to disagree politely—quite an art:

"To talk very openly is the best approach that I have found to resolving problems. Of course, the partner has to be talking just as openly in order for things to work. And just as important—is to listen openly."

"I have a tendency to express all my feelings, down to the slightest irritation. My partner has a tendency not to express any of his negative feelings. We have been very good for each other in that because he is generally always so nice and polite to me, I have learned not to blurt out the first bitchy thing that comes into my mind. When I am annoyed, I stop and think whether I am actually angry enough that a confrontation is in order. Usually I'm not; he has learned that it is all right to express his anger, that I may initially respond with anger myself but it is possible to calm down and discuss the problem. We are now generally able to discuss everything."

"We recently returned from spending several days at my parents' house. I guess being there stirs up the old sexual 'shoulds'—nice-girls-don't type of feelings. I was feeling very vulnerable and trying to talk to him about it. I interpreted his reaction as being: 'Oh, no, now she's not going to want to have sex for a month!' I went nuts—a throwback to earlier sexual problems. We talked later and he was accurately able to assess my feelings—a real step in the right direction for us, as I'm usually the one doing the analyzing. I was thrilled."

Two women take the lighthearted approach to fights:

"We rarely fight, when we do it is usually small disagreements. When I am tired or preoccupied or just have a different opinion, my wonderful husband will know when to say, 'You need a hug,' and that is exactly what I need—not ugliness for my ugliness. And when he is being unreasonable because he feels crummy it's O.K. We love each other, we apologize to one another, we're both wrong at times."

"When he doesn't let me know what his plans are, forgets to phone, I get so mad. Or we fight because he's too slow doing something, I'm too defensive, he's not phoned or come home for hours, I made plans without checking with him, etc., etc. No one 'wins' exactly. He usually starts laughing in the middle because he really hates fighting. Fortunately they are usually short fights and then they're over. We rarely fight about something for longer than twenty minutes. I cannot function normally when we fight. I get really carried away in the heat of the moment. This must be why my partner ends up laughing. I probably look like a maniac."

A few couples have their own ingenious institutions for clearing up feelings after fighting; one has a special "friendship" song and pipe: *

"I think what makes our relationship work is the fact that we never create any barriers between us. Even though an issue may appear trivial, it's not if it creates a distance. There is nothing taboo—we talk about whatever is on our minds. The other thing that's very important is our arguments have two parts. First we resolve whatever the issue was that caused the fight. Then we work to make sure that each of us feels good again, better about the other person. We cuddle, smoke an imaginary peace pipe, sing our original 'friendship' song. We rate our feelings on a percentage scale and keep this up (this is the exhausting part of our relationship!) until we each are 100 percent. It sounds silly but what it does is help us get back our good feelings. And once a fight is over, we don't have to deal with it again—even the bitterness and remorse are gone."

Another has made a promise to talk until "clear":

"We don't have any problems now, although we still and always will fight, as we think this is part of growth. Up until fifteen years ago, our problem was that my husband had a great fear of being close and losing himself, and I was passive and bewildered. Now I know exactly what I have a right to do and what not. Blocks do not build up; that is because we have one commitment: that if there is difficulty between us we will *talk*—like in gestalt therapy, until we 'clear' (feel good about ourselves and the other, and our bodies feel good and energetic). We also have an agreement to take turns being responsible every other day for the daily consideration of feelings. Implicit in this is that we are equal, that we can say anything we want. We do not tell the other what to do, nor do we interrupt when one is talking, but truly listen."

Another has a religious method:

"We made a point right at the start of our relationship to humble ourselves before each other and the Lord whenever we started arguing. Otherwise anger can lead to bitterness which may never go away. It's hard to stay mad for long when the other person is being humble and asking you to be the same. I've forgotten a lot of past upsets that way, and after it's all over, there's a lot of relief and very little resentment."

*See also Part V.

Others learn how to fight more constructively through counseling which they attend together:

"I always hated fighting and so for the first five months of our marriage we were in counseling together to learn how to fight more constructively. At first I felt horrible during and after our fights, but now I feel fine about them. We don't fight too often and when we do it's pretty minor stuff."

The Intimidation of Women Through Physical Violence

"The battering process begins with your mind, your mind is battered. First, you lose your self-esteem."
—*Statement of a woman beaten several times by her husband*

"Did a husband or lover ever strike you or beat you up? Why? How did you feel?"

The majority (61 percent) of women in this study say they have never been struck or beaten, and many emphasize that they would not tolerate it:

"A lover has never struck me. I would not allow it. If it happened, I'd have him beaten better by someone much more vicious and strong."

"If one did, I would walk out immediately. I lived with that with my parents and it is something I will not tolerate. I deserve better treatment than that—every woman does."

"So help me God, if any guy ever hit me, he'd be put in jail so fast his head would spin!"

27 percent say they have been hit or beaten by a husband or lover once; some were angry, some felt ashamed and degraded:

"My husband beat me once when he was jealous. I left him for a while. I felt degraded."

"My husband hit me once. I was afraid but prepared to run. My dog interrupted it before it got serious."

"Once, in the street—a slap in the face. It made me very angry. It was about an unimportant thing. I felt it was an attack on my personality."

"Once. I wanted to kill him. I felt very cheap and degraded."

"It was about five years ago. I still don't know why he did it. I felt ashamed of him and didn't want anyone to know. I felt disappointed—betrayed. Disgraced. It also made me confused and puzzled."

"He hit me once when I had just come home from the hospital with a four-day-old baby (his) and wouldn't drop what I was doing to fix him a cold drink. I picked up the cast-iron frying pan and told him he would be wearing it for a necklace if he hit me again. He believed me."

"The time I was beaten was pretty dramatic. It was a big goodbye scene, not just to the relationship, but this guy was quitting his education, job, etc., and I tried to stop him, finally, by physically blocking the door. He had no tolerance for that and got me out of the way and made sure I wouldn't follow. I can't say I hated him, even when I was beaten."

"The worst thing is when he spat in my face and shoved me around in the street and hit me because I wanted to leave with another guy. The worst thing I did, I guess, is tell him about my affair; he cried, it's the first time I saw him cry."

"Last year, after all these years of holding in my true feelings and always pampering his ego and going along with his desires (but him never with mine), my anger was triggered to the point that it never has been. I really exploded and told him I was tired of being his mother, tired of never being able to express my desires, and tired of not being able to wear what I wanted without being laughed at—and just plain tired of not being able to be me! Of course this made him very angry and he told me to get out. I started to leave the room to pack a bag and he shoved me down on the floor. I tried three times to make a move and he shoved me down each time. That was absolutely the worst time of my marriage. I had bruises on my chest. He felt very badly about doing this afterward and he did go to see our minister to talk about this problem of his—anger and abusing me.

"I had been wanting us to go to a marriage counselor for years but he never would. I also talked with the minister and we each took a certain test. Afterward the minister told me my test showed I was all right in my thinking but that my husband really needed help. My husband will not talk to the minister again, nor will he talk with anyone else. He said he doesn't want to get another person involved in our problem—that we will solve it ourselves. We've tried to solve this ourselves for years. He has said he isn't going to someone who is going to tell him he is a jerk. I asked him why he thought they would tell him that and he said, 'Because I am a jerk.' "

Is "once" enough to remind the person, serve as a warning, and thus keep her in line?

"Yes, once—I felt very afraid, unable to defend myself. Probably that's why to this day I always walk away from a fight."

Only a minority say that they broke up then and there and never saw the person again:

"One boyfriend hit me, knocked me down, and then kicked me because I didn't want to go somewhere with him after we had made plans to. I felt like that was the last straw. I broke up with him permanently. I don't have to take that. I am worth more to myself than that. There is no reason good enough to cause physical damage to another."

"Yes—because he thought I was rude to his mother. I broke off the relationship immediately."

12 percent say they have been or are being beaten on a more frequent basis:

"I was beaten up quite a few times in the past, and I could honestly say that I did not know exactly what for. It was basically when my boyfriend got drunk or mad, he took his frustrations out on the closest living thing around, which was me. I began to actually think that I was to blame. I lost a lot of self-esteem."

"My present lover has hit me and beat me. The first time I was in shock for days. I felt like a worm of society, a dog to be kicked, that no one respected me, that I was owned by a woman-hating society. He was trying to knock some sense into me, he said, because he was jealous (ha). Then I learned to know him, I learned strategy. I have always fought, with my brothers and sisters, growing up, life is not soft feathers. I think I like to fight with my lover now, we do not hurt one another."

"My ex-husband used to slap me about. That was just after Vietnam, and for a while I told myself he didn't really know what he was doing. I actually felt virtuous for taking it, for 'understanding.' Of course, the thrill of that wore thin, and eventually I got to feeling very small, frightened, vulnerable, worthless. Then I got angry. Then I grew to genuinely hate him for all his cruelty. I don't think it was actually me my ex-husband hated. I think it was life and women in general. He had always hated his mother and grandmother (by whom he was raised) and he always had contempt for female 'frailty.' I think his violence was directed at me only because I was handy."

"One man hit me, not too hard, on a number of occasions. Every time I see him now (four years later) he still apologizes and is so upset about it."

"My husband has beaten me off and on for as long as I know, up to almost two years ago. He beats me in fits of rage, or bad moods. His father beat his mother. I felt hate. I could have killed him easily and felt nothing. Then he'd be contrite, make up, but I never forgot. I knew I didn't deserve that. Yet I felt powerless to leave him and felt he was sick. Women don't leave the people they love because they're sick! I persuaded him to go to a psychiatrist but it didn't last. The beatings have stopped because he knows now I *would* leave him. My lover did that for me, made me see I could function without my husband."

Significantly, only 1 percent of these women say that they called the police or anyone to help. Nor do they mention why they didn't call the police, or if it even occurred to them, in most cases. Do we think that this would be an act of disloyalty or "unloving" behavior? Are we afraid of reprisals? Do we think we should try to understand? Not make trouble? Not ruin his reputation publicly? Or is it because we doubt they would help? One woman says, "The police came, but pretty much laughed at me, told him they understood what his problem was, and left." In many cities, this situation is improving, as police take special courses to change their attitudes in cases of domestic violence, and women are added to that part of the police force.

A small number of women say that they fought back:

"I hated my ex when we were married. I once kneed him in the groin because he tried to choke me."

"When my ex-husband would slap and beat me, I'd hit him back, but I always got it worse in the end. He would twist my arms behind my back till I fell to the ground, then grab me by the neck. This happened when he would accuse me of even 'looking' at other men (always his fantasy)."

1 percent say that they struck the man first:

"My husband struck me twice—right after I struck him first. I can't say I had it coming, but I certainly provoked it. The other times, he just held me down so I couldn't continue to hit him. How did I feel? Surprised perhaps, but I didn't feel it wasn't justified. I didn't do anything since it was a response to my violence."

"A couple of times my present lover has hit me, when I've really provoked him. I have always hit him first."

Or both fought, as one woman describes:

"When we argued about breaking up, I bent one of the metal fixtures in his trailer. He then got angry and told me to leave. He threw me out of his trailer without any shoes. He ordered me to get out, and when I wouldn't leave the grounds, he threw rocks at me. I hated him for throwing rocks at me. I felt like a dog and didn't know where to go. He embarrassed me in front of the neighbors when he started throwing those rocks. I was very angry.

"I do not believe in physically hitting anyone, though I did hit him. Of course, I couldn't hit him as hard as he returned the hit. I felt very bad after we physically fought. When he threw me out without any shoes, throwing rocks at me, telling me to get out, I cried and begged him to [let me] stay, as

I was left helpless in a strange city. I was very surprised at myself when I hit him, as I usually have a lot of self-control. I became very scared after, cowering and running away from him, knowing that he would hit me back."

3 percent say they have hit or been violent with a man, but were not hit back:

"He refused to communicate at a vital time and I kicked him in the balls. This event has not reoccurred since then."

"I became violent toward the man who left me for a girlfriend—I kicked him and threw him to the ground. I was amazed at my strength during this rage, and my potential for violence given the right provocation. He was not violent toward me, except to use force to subdue me."

_____

Although when the high incidence of domestic violence became an issue in the media in the United States during the early 1980s, a cry was heard from some corners that wives were beating husbands too, subsequent studies (several) showed without a doubt that the number of such incidents is minuscule, compared to the incidence of wife battering by husbands.

Many others (57 percent) have experienced the threat of violence; some women live with violence always present as a possibility:

"He was furious and slammed out of the house. He frightens me when he's like that. I know it's going to continue when he returns from work."

"He has raised his hand to me in a playful manner, but I will not play that way. Still, I wonder if it affects me, unconsciously."

"We share the same bed, unless there has been a fight and I fear violence. Then I sleep in another room."

"He has an unfair advantage during conflicts: he gets more emotionally out of control, walks out, throws things, calls me horrendous names, and I don't do any of those things. He's never struck me, but the melodramatics often have the effect of whipping me into line."

"My husband can become a violent person when angered. He resorts to verbal violence and on to physical violence to the point of pushing and shoving. I dislike this sort of behavior and tend to try to avoid topics that will cause it."

Younger women in relationships still find physical violence; they are not statistical exceptions—as this statement by a twenty-one-year-old woman demonstrates:

"I was in love with George, a twenty-five-year-old chemistry graduate. The relationship lasted for seven months. I was happy for the first two months, but

I cried myself to sleep over our problems many times, when I knew the feeling of being 'in love' was dwindling—he began not to treat me with respect, he played games. I wanted our relationship to have back the magic of when we first discovered each other.

"During one fight, he did hit me and almost choked me to death. During the choking he squeezed me with his arms around my waist and stomach. He was drunk when he did this, and said he did these things because he thought I was going to leave him. On the other hand, he told me later he couldn't remember striking me, just the reason he was upset."

What is the effect of being hit or beaten, even if only once? And of staying in the kind of relationship that this implies? Many women have mentioned feeling degraded, that somehow they were guilty, had to be ashamed of what had happened, couldn't tell their friends—because they would somehow be seen as "less," have less status in the eyes of others—and so women who are beaten feel very isolated and alone.

One woman only in her late twenties, coming out of a long marriage which involved physical violence, describes her state of mind:

"I entered therapy when I almost had a breakdown before the divorce. I continued in therapy until a year after the divorce. The therapy helped me to find myself. I had been so restricted and so dominated, so devoid of any kind of feeling after all the physical and emotional violence, that I could not express any kind of feeling, no anger, no crying, nothing. It helped me tremendously to discover myself. And to realize that I had done everything I could to save my marriage and it was O.K. to get a divorce. I felt like a failure but I felt very relieved when everything was over—like a different person. I was very angry with my husband once I stopped being numb, but I never told anyone about the violence while it was happening, only at the end my therapist."

Much, Perhaps Most, Fighting Represents Women Standing Up for Their Dignity, Trying to Make a Relationship Work

Many women feel that the men they live with, by not treating them with respect and equality, more or less force them to "complain," stand up for their rights—or become submissive and resentful.

Much of the arguing and bickering that goes on in relationships—and which can kill love—is a sign that a woman is trying to reformulate a relationship, struggling to achieve real understanding and emotional equality, to "make it work." Of course, fighting can be about other things, unique things, but the patterns described in this chapter stand out so clearly that they seem to be classic between the genders. These patterns have not been noted in the psychological literature generally, or integrated into theory, perhaps due to lack of large-scale documentation such as that given here; furthermore, these questions have not been formulated in the same way previously.*

Although it might have been thought that extramarital affairs and so on would have been the major source of conflict in relationships, leading to fighting and breakups, this is not the case. It is the subtle, constant, and continuous buildup of slights and condescensions that lead to the "complaining," and often the complete alienation of a woman from the man she once loved.

Ironically, although women are seen as "troublemakers" by men for frequently bringing up "complaints" and "hurt feelings," in fact, women are making it possible for relationships to survive, by doing just this—bringing up the issues, doing the "emotional housework"† that needs to be done to keep the couple alive. At a later point in many relationships, women frequently give up and don't even try to discuss things anymore—just going their own way, either emotionally or finally leaving the relationship altogether.

"It's usually the woman's fault if there are fights—you know, women get 'bitchy' and 'nag,' and men can't take it"

Although most women know there is "something wrong," many don't perceive that they are actually being abused psychologically. Many tend to blame themselves. Why not? After all, the general social atmosphere usually blames the woman, and many women themselves often feel like they are in a fog, constantly questioning what they are thinking and seeing since their perceptions are rarely validated. And if a woman is angry with a man, she is likely to be told she is mentally unbalanced.

Emotional harassment is much more common in relationships than those suffering these kinds of slights usually think; since the slights often are inflicted

---

*This is an example of what feminist social scientists who specialize in methodology mean when they write that the ideology of a culture influences formulation of questions and choice of questions so subtly that people may leave out the most obvious questions, only because the society has not thought that way before, their minds are not "set" in that direction. So much of social science research only reiterates the "biases" of the status quo, because the biases are built into the way the questions are formulated. See Sandra Harding and Merill B. Hintikha, eds., *Discovering Reality: Feminist Perspectives on Epistemology, Metaphysics, Methodology and Philosophy of Science* (Holland: D. Rudel Publishing, 1983).
†See page 50.

in private, women frequently think their situation is unusual, even that their dilemma (not knowing how to stop it) is a secret shame. But fully 71 percent of the women in this study report experiencing such slights on at least a daily basis. The most common way of "dealing" with the problem is to try to hide it from outsiders, so that nobody will know—because it is not so much the bully who is to blame, according to this social "reasoning," as the woman herself, who is somehow "weak" and "deserves it." She may especially blame herself for staying with a man who does not always respect her, criticizing herself for accepting his love in other ways, sex with him, etc.

For example, while many women become quite irritated with men when they make condescending remarks (and if she complains, he will often laugh and say he was "only teasing"), women often give up trying to get men to stop. They may rationalize to themselves, first thinking, "Well, it is a loving relationship otherwise, and I don't want to disrupt it by 'complaining' about this little thing." But eventually, most women become more and more irritated, as aggression unchecked only becomes worse.

The general tacit social perception that women have less right to their perceptions, their selfhood, than men do, and the oblique ways that men have of telling women in private conversations that they are not interested in hearing what they have to say, put women in the position of having to stand up for their rights, on a daily, personal, ongoing basis—or trying to somehow ignore or consider "not serious" or "not real" the constant subliminal information they receive about their status. This second choice tends to create a kind of sharp personality, a taking on of "male" "in control" values—and a dislike for women who do not do the same. It is perhaps one of the severest forms of emotional repression created by this cycle, in which the "victim," by taking on the values of those in power, loses touch with the fact that she is still in her situation. And can she be "herself"?

The phrase "lack of communication" is often used as a catchall for these problems in relationships, but is too general to be accurate or helpful. Many men are not aware of the specific dynamics women are discussing here, of their own attitudes, or of women's feelings about these "small" issues—what the bickering is really about. All too often, any given issue seems "petty" to them—which only makes women angrier, because this attitude in itself is another sign of the same condescension, of not bothering to hear what the woman is saying.

The emotional stereotypes, the beliefs most men hold (including in a relationship with a woman they love), are that women are less, less important, less credible, less serious, less "right." When women try to "bring up" the symptoms of these issues and talk about them, men often react by "complaining" that the woman is "complaining," and do not listen seriously (who likes to listen to criticism anyway?). But this only causes another round of the escalating vicious circle, as the woman feels even more that she has no credibility or that her feelings are not heard or important to the man. Often men do not realize that a divorce or an affair is coming.

As one woman describes her increasing alienation, "For example, he doesn't care if I climax or not, but only is interested in his own ability to be satisfied, mostly because he is not knowledgeable and he doesn't want to become knowledgeable. This would make him look like less of a man to himself, I suppose. So I think he is a chickenshit and a bore and I've told him so. I suppose trying to be honest is the worst thing I ever did to him, yelling at him. (He loves it too, though, because then he looks like the knight in white armor and I look like the whore/screamer.) I finally explode and say all the wrong things in front of anybody, mostly the children. I talk and he does nothing. He doesn't listen. He has a short attention span and no desire to change. I would have shared all of myself if only I were loved, but I've tried and been rejected for it. It is hard to share with a person who just doesn't talk to you."

The pattern of alienation

Many women know they are not getting equal emotional support, esteem, or respect in their relationships. And yet it can be difficult to describe definitively to a man just how he is projecting diminishing attitudes. Some of the ways this happens are so subtle in their expression that, while a woman may wind up feeling frustrated and on the defensive, she can find it almost impossible to say just why: pointing to the subtle thing said or done would look petty, like overreacting. But taken all together, it is no surprise when even one of these incidents can set off a major fight—or, more typically, another round of alienation which never gets resolved. These little incidents cut away at the relationship, making women angry and finally causing love to dwindle down to a mere modest toleration.

Does fighting, bringing up the issues, work? Do women change their relationships this way?

Most women wind up screaming or shouting at men from time to time because they so often feel they can't be heard, that men don't hear them. Since women generally have such low credibility in the culture, men often do not hear them objectively, justly.

Do men make an effort to understand women, to talk with them? Not usually, according to the women in this study—and the statistics on the number of women taking tranquilizers and consulting psychologists also attest to the fact that women are having a rough time constructing mutually satisfying personal relationships.

Negotiating for respect and understanding in a relationship is important, something which possibly could be accomplished with grace and good humor. But if men are satisfied with the status quo in relationships, and women are not, what should women do? What should a woman do when there are frequent subtle indications of condescension toward her because of her gender, and mentioning these to a man once or twice does not suffice to change his attitude?

The issues women are bringing up may appear on the surface to be "petty," but the pattern of condescension that is provoking women is so widespread that women are forced to fight back, even on this level. And yet, individual fighting back doesn't always work, because most men don't understand what it is women are trying to point out to them. Perhaps it will be necessary for women to change the status of women as a whole before gaining enough respect and dignity to make it possible for their love relationships to survive.

The Ideology Behind the System— Women's Giving, Men's "Being"

The Emotional Contract

What most women are trying to describe here is an entrenched, largely unrecognized system of emotional discrimination—a system whose subterranean roots are entwined so deeply in the psyche of the culture that it underlies our entire social structure. As many women point out, the incidents that upset them can be small—and yet these incidents are troubling because they reflect an overall attitude, are part of a fabric of denial of women as complete human beings.

How does one begin to name and demonstrate a pattern that has had no name for so long—these subtle interactions and subliminal messages that are much more deadly to love than arguing over money or children?

The emotional contract in relationships hasn't really been looked at yet, as we are doing here: it is the core of a relationship—the implicit understanding between two people about how each should behave in a relationship, how each expects the other to express her or his emotions, how each interprets the emotional outcries and silences of the other. These tender and often brief moments are the lifeblood of the emotional closeness between two people, and small misunderstandings can lead to a chain reaction, ending empathy between the two—even though they may remain "married" or "together." But this emotional interaction is troubled by an unclear, demeaning, and gender-oriented set of subliminal attitudes, assumptions interwoven into our ideas of who men and women are. We believe that women are "loving and giving" and men are "doers," that one has more rights than the other.

Thus the emotional contract contains psychological stereotypes which put women at a disadvantage, and give men preferential treatment, superior psychological status that is built into the system, into the tiniest crevices of our minds. It is the fundamental cause of the problems between women and men in love relationships.

What is emotional equality?

One woman describes what it isn't:

"Men have all these power behaviors—you know, like turning their backs on you, and walking off, shutting the door, or 'going out for a walk' when you are trying to tell them something, or bring up something. They think they have the right not to listen, they don't have to be bothered with *'your* problem.' They do just as they please, no matter how much we (I or my girlfriends) talk or plead or shout or reason—they just show contempt for who we are, basically.

"Like today, R. just turned his back on me while I was talking to him, thinking that would be the end of it. Was he surprised when I grabbed him by the arm and jerked him around! I could tell he wanted to really hit me, but he didn't. Then he said something like 'You can't make me do anything you want. I don't take orders from you.' I suppose that refers to the chores I asked him to do. He could help me a *little*—like maybe screw in a light bulb without being asked. If I ask him, he says, 'Oh, I didn't notice it.' I can't believe it. Incredibly juvenile. Men can get away with it, because they run things. Or they think they can. But if women would stick together and not put up with this stuff, we could change it. If England could run the whole world for a time, and David could beat Goliath, we as women can get ourselves out of this hole and end the stupidity of the whole male thing."

———————

The signs of this unequal emotional "contract"—the unspoken assumptions, the word choices—are thrown at women every day, as we have seen, in a thousand ways. Indeed, these patterns are so subtle and accepted, coloring everything, that they make discussion of the "problem" almost impossible, and arguments seem circular. As one woman puts it, "There are no words, to begin with, and when you *do* use words, they are viewed by men through a reversing telescope (when they are heard at all)—taking what I said for something totally NOT what I meant."

Another woman describes this dilemma in a typical "non-conversation" about an issue she is trying to discuss: "If we go out, we always end up going out with his friends and not mine. If I tell him this, he says, that's not true, my friends are just around more. I say, so why don't you make an effort to get to know my friends better—they're important to me. Him, totally missing my point: well, you know how it is when I hang out with the boys. How do I explain to him that it bothers me that I can't explain to him *why* it bothers me that his friends are more important than my friends—or that he seems to be saying that his friends are BETTER than my friends. That's it—he really thinks his friends are better! But I can't tell him that, because then he'll say, no they're not, I don't think that. And then we're at a dead end."

Lack of emotional equality is the fundamental stumbling block to love in relationships. Furthermore, the underlying inequalities are so taken for granted—often not even consciously noticed, built into the culture—that women can become angry without knowing exactly why. As one young woman says, "I wonder if our relationship could get better, because I resent him and don't know why. I feel on the defensive a lot."

It is our purpose here to unravel some of the traditional assumptions in relationships, to see more clearly what is going on.

Women: the Ones Who Try to "Make It Work"

Almost every woman says she feels she is trying harder to make relationships work than the man is:

"The biggest problem is that when there is a problem, I have to do most of the solving. It's part of his nature to be too laid back. I am always aware of our relationship, always defining it; when I want to change something, I work on it."

"I work more at keeping us together—being lively and exciting, planning things to do, trying to understand and hear how he feels. It takes a lot of energy."

"I always felt I tried harder to work at getting to the real issues that were causing problems, and that my partners weren't doing their part so we could get on with enjoying the good parts."

"Most men aren't willing to see through the changes in their women, and hang in there and grow from the experience and maybe learn something. When the going gets tough, they give up sooner, whereas the women (most) are more willing to stick through the tough times and weird changes their husbands go through, always trying to make things better."

96 percent of women say they are giving more emotional support than they are getting from men (although they get it from their women friends; see Part V):

"Men are lucky. Their lovers cushion them emotionally and generally mother them, so they can be hard and competitive in the outside world."

"I sometimes think I give too much love. You might say I love right down to my bootstraps. Unfortunately, the men in my life were better at taking my love than giving any in return."

"Men are not taught the skills and attitudes that make a good spouse, lover, or (by my definition) friend. When I was three or four, my mother was already teaching me to see dust and other people's feelings. ('Don't bother your father, he's tired.') It is generally agreed that even big strong men need to be mothered a little, but who mothers the mothers?"

"Most men—while they take love seriously—expect more love from the woman. I don't think there's a difference in emotional needs, but men expect and demand more nurturance (and women give it)."

"I don't believe men are capable of loving me as much as I am them, because so many have been raised to believe they and what they want are more important than women, children, and nature."

"Men grow up with a different set of expectations for their emotional lives—that they will be served and loved, without much emotional expenditure on their part. They only must make money."

"He doesn't realize—perhaps even now—that he needs to spend time and thought and energy on the relationship. He realizes that to some degree now but not sufficiently, I think. It's always left up to the woman—still too much of the time. Therapy has helped, though."

"My husband and I could have had a great friendship if he had wanted 'all of it' and was willing to work for it. But he just wanted a good relationship when he desired it, similar to his television set—on and off at the touch of a finger."

Some women wonder, with frustration, if they can ever do enough emotionally to satisfy men:

"I finally broke up with my husband because I was beginning to grow, and he wanted me to stay quiet and let him 'rule the roost.' Devastating. It was so unnecessary, it's still sad to think about. But I was stifled! I have some regrets I didn't try harder with him, but everything I didn't try I tried the next go-around, and it still didn't work. I'm wondering if you can ever do enough in a relationship with a man."

"I give and give and give. Being always the peacemaker sometimes gets to me. I get angry that he doesn't care enough to try to work things out—he'd rather ride his anger than let his love help our reconciliation happen. I get tired of that, and angry, cold."

"I somehow feel a heavy responsibility for so much of his life, added onto an immense feeling of responsibility I already feel for my own. Sometimes, however, I manage to feel very happy."

"I have given heart and soul of everything I am and have. Somehow it is taken leaving me with nothing and lonely and hurt and he is still requesting more of me. *I* am tired, so tired."

Yet 84 percent of women say they believe that having loving relationships is one of the most important parts of life:

"I never have enough time to do all the things I want. I always have to choose between spending time with the children, making love with my husband, watching television (to relax me when I've been putting out a lot), writing letters to my family. Sometimes I get very frustrated, with all the demands on me, but really, much as I would like a little time to dawdle in the shower, etc., I want to spend time with those I love above all else. This is really the point of life—to see them happy, and feel us being together."

"Nothing else we do in this world can matter as much as loving people and being loved. I care deeply about the people in my life, I want to be there for them, notice when something goes wrong."

"My job is only secondary in importance to me; people and human relationships are the most important. If anything happened to my relationship with J. or my son, I would be a basket case. If I couldn't get my business going faster, I'd be frustrated but it wouldn't be the end of everything."

"I'm a romantic, being in love and growing together is the main thing for me. I believe that, most of all, I need someone to love me and to love them back."

The kind of love most are referring to is long-term warmth, giving to those one cares about:

"I'm very concerned with my loved ones. Being there when they want to talk, sharing their joys and sadnesses—these are the things that make me happy."

"I think sharing your life with one person you love is the most important part of life. It is the most satisfying, it goes deeper and beyond everything else."

Men Assume They Will "Star" in Relationships

How do women describe the basic role men assume they will play in relationships as their part of the emotional contract?

95 percent of women say men assume they will take first place:

"Generally men are quite entranced with themselves, they live their lives as though they were starring in them. (Not to condemn an entire gender; I didn't intend to make such a rash generalization.) But anyway, many men will never take the time and effort to find out what's inside their mates. Co-stars."

"He loves me very much and says he is very happy. I love him but am not always happy. I have this idea that we should share more as a family. He is more self-centered in daily life. I don't have as strong a sense of my rights as he does. He says he doesn't stand in the way of my going out and doing things, meetings, etc., and some days I believe it. I blame my wishy-washiness on myself and the feeling that I have to ask permission even for my own freedom."

"He's not an insensitive pig but his dreams are often so strong as to fade out mine."

"Damn straight men think they're more important! They've been conditioned to expect female energies to be focused on them since birth. Their needs, emotional or otherwise, come first."

"In my experience, men expect everything—including relationships—to be done their way. There's no expectation that they should be making space for other people's needs. At least that's the way it is with him."

"My overall grievance with men I have had relationships with is that they all seem to be self-centered. Most don't think of how their actions affect the people they live with. They automatically think of themselves first."

"The problem is, so many men think so much of themselves, as if they are better than women. Many are spoiled, especially by women who are condescending to themselves and other women by treating men as if they are gods."

"Some men see women as a vast vat of affection for the preening male."

As seen in Chapter 1, most women say that men put themselves first (act like stars), even just in conversation:

"Men are glad of a listening ear for their own worries (and accomplishments) but rarely want to hear about mine. On the average worldwide, women work harder than men, have less free time, and end up poorer. Men are selfish—even in conversation."

Or in territoriality, whether psychological or physical:

"It's really true that men never think about women's space. I have had so many boyfriends who'd borrow something, like a typewriter, and instead of putting it back on the desk and plugging it in the wall, would leave it in the middle of the floor, or men who don't pick up after themselves or who read my letters. It's all part of that invasive thing, claiming territory. When they stay over, it's always apparent, trail of socks, books, dishes, etc. When I go to their house, I fold my clothes and put them in a corner, help clean up after dinner—it's just a different attitude."

"When he's asleep, I would never wake him up just because I want to make love or talk—I know he needs to sleep regularly to work and be happy. But I have to keep asking him not to wake me up (and then he pouts later) if I am tireder than he is and need to sleep later, or *I* stayed up late cleaning up or working around the house. It seems like he has the right to set his schedule, but he also has the right (he thinks) to set mine."

76 percent say men expect women to be at their disposal, "at the ready," at all times:

"My husband used to call me at work and interrupt me. If I was on the phone with one of my customers, he would want me to drop the customer so I could talk to him. If I was in a meeting, he would leave messages for me. I had a territory with several hundred customers and I had to spend a lot of time in the field. If he called for me when I was out, when I returned his call he would ask me where I had been, who I was with, etc., etc. It would drive me crazy. I felt like I was a little kid checking in with my dad."

"The area I think is the most telling for male/female relationships is something about who's waiting for whom, and how important is it that they're waiting. I seem to be always waiting for him—I come home from work or from picking up our son, and then I am supposed to fix dinner and wait for him to arrive. I don't mind, if I know *when* he will arrive. But just waiting . . . Also, I used to have to wait for him to call me for dates. Somehow it was important for him that he be in control, and I be the one who would be there waiting."

"What I find so difficult in my relationship and I've told it to many friends: How can I have an individual life—going out with girlfriends, having my personal activities—and still coordinate this with my boyfriend's life? He doesn't hesitate to have his own life, and *he* doesn't feel guilty. But me, I feel sort of paralyzed—I have to stay at home and wait, wait until he gets back. Boy. Have I ever waited after that guy!"

"The main theme of our arguments was always him going to too many meetings—two to three nights a week and going for a beer afterwards. Coming home late. And me waiting."

"I really burn when he's inconsiderate. He's learned that he better phone if he's making plans or going to be late."

"I keep telling him that if he is going to call me, call me when you say you are going to."

Another way the attention of the relationship is focused on the man is—ironically—that when the woman brings up unmet needs of her own, such as communication (see Chapter 1), the discussion may gradually center on why the man is not comfortable talking, etc. The woman is thus involved in "helping" the man discover and understand himself, develop new skills—while her original need is not being addressed:

"The biggest problem in my relationship is that I am a very verbal person, it is easy for me to talk, but he cannot express his inner feelings. Our relationship would grow one hundred percent if he would only tell me what he is feeling about us today—tomorrow is another day. I'm not asking for a commitment of forever. He's a loner. After spending the weekend (nights) with him and maybe a Sunday, he is exhausted from so much social life. He's drained. He needs time to himself, which I find hard to understand, but give him the time. At times I feel I'm putting him out to be with me on a Friday or Saturday night, yet it seems we both expect it. He told me he would like more time to himself but it would not be fair to either one of us. All I can do is be patient and give him the time he so needs. Also the time to trust me, as he feels I will hurt him."

Most women/girls under age twenty-five are still receiving subliminal messages that the father is the center of the family, the head of the household, and that most of the emotional energy should be focused on him:

"When I got home from school in the afternoons, my mother and I would talk about what happened that day, fix something in the kitchen, hang out. When we heard the car pull in the drive, that meant my father was home from work, and the tone would change. My mother would become distant, and prepare to greet him. The rest of the evening, she and I would remain distant, not really talking to one another, as if somehow that would be intrusive on him, would offend his sense of being given most of the attention. It was never anything explicit, just a feeling in the air."

"I learned from my mother that the proper attitude toward my father was to defer to him and give his opinions the most time and attention."

Sixty-five percent of women now under age twenty-five, who grew up during the period encompassed by the recent women's movement, still report that they were raised with this picture of home life, that the mother was providing more services for the father than vice versa, working around his needs, with the father seeming to expect it.

Many women complain about the constant reinforcement in men of their superior social status—especially by women who give men's opinions exaggerated importance:

"I dislike the fact that the male figure is catered to and given the utmost respect as the dominant sex. I hate it when women subordinate themselves to men."

"My mother is much more loving and kind to my brother than she ever was to me. She prefers him. Many times she won't send me a birthday or Christmas present because she says she wanted to get him something really special. She just gave him several thousand dollars to pay his debts and sent me one thousand! I just always knew that boys were more special. People rejoice over the birth of a son in a way they don't do with a daughter."

"The thing I dislike about some women is their willingness to let men run the world both at work and at home, and the subservience they show to men's ideas, rather than a willingness to form and to express their own. It is depressing to see some young women still doing this; I had hoped for more from the younger generation!"

Is it that many women believe that men deserve more authority and respect—or that they know that most men have more power and money, and therefore feel they *must* respond to them as if they are more important?

What does *being* loved feel like? Do men love women—or just need them?

When asked, "Do you love your partner as much as he/she loves you? More? Is the way your partner loves you satisfying to you? Do you feel loved?" most women say that they feel loved most frequently when their lover or husband seems to *need* them—although this is not the optimum way they would like to be loved.

How do women describe the feeling of *being* loved? Perhaps with all the emphasis on women being "loving" and "giving," never being the "star" (don't be too "pushy," "a prima donna"), it can feel more comfortable to a woman to love than to be loved. As one woman puts it, "Right now, loving someone is easier than being loved, because my opinion of myself, unconsciously, is still rather low."*

Perhaps many women don't really know what it feels like to be loved, since most women (84 percent) describe the men they live with as loving them in terms of needing them:†

"I think that he may love me more than I do him. Or maybe it's actually that he is more dependent on me than I am on him."

---

*However, many women say *being* loved is more satisfying to them: "I would choose, if I had to choose, being loved. I always give love; being loved is more unusual, more wonderful."
†Of course, as definitions of love go, this is not such a bad one—but how many women are loved for themselves, for their personalities or individual character?

"I felt that he loved what I did for him and was dependent on what I did for him, not that he loved me. He couldn't even see me."

"The way my partner loved me made me feel insecure—totally unsatisfying. Sometimes I felt loved, other times I felt like a convenience—used. Now that we are apart, I feel more independent, he feels depressed."

"In the beginning of our marriage I loved him very much more and it was frightening to be so dependent upon a person. Now I don't think he realizes it, but it almost seems as if he needs me more. Men do not particularly want to learn how to cook, clean the bathrooms, or wash the clothes, whereas women have learned how to go out into a man's working world and can make a passable wage, so that she does not need him for security to the degree that she used to in past years. Men can only function well in the working world, and still remain very dependent upon women for their creature comforts."

"I think I love him more. But that is his loss, because I think then I have more love within my own heart. I think my husband needs me more. He needs me to keep a level head. I am the one who keeps this house together."

"We need each other in different ways. He is more dependent than I. He would be quite content to be with me twenty-four hours a day; I would be totally stifled by this. But I need to know he is there, I just need a lot more time to myself than he does."

In other words, many women point out that, in general, men do not usually love women so much as need them:

"Men like the security of home and a woman to fulfill their needs, but when they leave the house they want to feel like a bachelor."

"Love is important to men, but I think it is more a dependency than true sharing love. Usually it is relegated to the parts of their lives that require 'mothering.' "

"I think love is a pretty calculated, rational act for most men. It plays the part of getting them some security—i.e., marriage or a live-in companion, steady girlfriend, etc. Only certain poets, I think, lose their head over someone (maybe I'm wrong?)."

"It plays a part in their lives when they really want to settle down and they've had all their fun with other women—then they start looking for a serious relationship. If they're ready for it, it gives them a good base for everything else they do and need."

One woman says she feels most men judge love selfishly—"rationally," in terms of their needs, comfort, etc.—rather than by the sheer depth of their feelings; in other words, it is more a question of how well the woman treats them than a true sensation of love for a particular woman:

"I think men judge love selfishly, like how good they feel in the presence of the particular woman, while the woman tends to try to understand the man, once in love, no matter what."

Are men more emotionally dependent than women?

Surprisingly, the overwhelming number of women (87 percent) say that men are far more emotionally dependent on women than vice versa after the first few months of a relationship, especially in marriage:

"Men fear women's dependency without realizing how much more dependent they usually are. Men frequently have only one person with whom they talk; women usually have many. I usually feel like I'm giving more support than I'm getting."

"Men's lovers cushion them emotionally, and generally mother them, so that men can be hard and competitive in the outside world."

"Women may appear more dependent but they are truly more capable and better able to adjust to changes and giving."

"A man *needs* a woman more than loves her—whether it is for sex or for wifely duties."

"We're raised to be nurturers, and they're raised to be nurtured. So men are more dependent just by draining us, even though on the surface, it seems like the opposite; in fact, men like to make the woman feel that it's she who's doing the clinging, when it's really he."

77 percent of women married over three years say that the men turn to them to be taken care of emotionally, assuming the role of dependent—contrary to the stereotype of the woman being emotionally insecure and "taken care of" by the man:

"I was most deeply in love with my husband when we were married. It felt exciting, bells rang, and I felt very mature. He was older and could take care of me, I thought. As time went on, I found *I* was the caretaker."

"If a man is very emotionally dependent on me, to some extent I feel that I'm being pushed into a mother role, not being allowed to be a friend and lover. This is partly because I feel that my father put all women in his life, including me, into a mother role. I react by drawing back. Then I try to see if the man is really just being a friend and opening up to me or if his dependency is too much. If it is too much, I begin to demand more time for myself and to make him do stuff alone and make his own decisions."

"Possibly men take love more seriously at the beginning, but (here is my rotten experience affecting my opinion) I think many men are looking for mothers, maids, babysitters, available fucks, and someone lucky enough to be chosen to bear their children."

The love they receive isn't satisfying to 64 percent of women:

"He may love me more, but it's not satisfying. I don't feel loved."

"I try to treat him as he wants to be treated, but he doesn't really appreciate it. Then when he doesn't return it, I ache inside. I know he loves me, but I wish he could express it differently."

"I believe my partner is afraid to love—that requires a commitment he can't give. His wall gets higher and higher—but he clings tighter and tighter."

Are men giving love or demanding attention by saying how much they love and need a woman in some of the relationships we have seen?

23 percent of women feel loved as an individual*, "seen," understood—besides being needed—and are very happy:*

"He truly made me happiest of any person in my life. I felt totally accepted and admired and respected. He showed me in little ways every few days."

"His love is expressed with supportive compliments, sex, and having a good time. I feel that there is someone there who cares about me and who would help me if I needed it, or listen to me if I needed someone to talk to."

Men's value system makes love less important— although most men expect to receive love and nurturing from women

74 percent of women say that most men do not put love relationships first in their lives:

"Men take love as a secondary factor in their lives—their careers are more important and the area they can get most admiration."

"Men do not take love and falling in love seriously, except on TV. Women are on the edge of men's lives, in a supportive role, not as partners. Men see women as sources of food and sex."

"Men like to play knights rescuing the princess or saving the queen from the men whose asses they just want a good excuse to stomp anyway. Maybe we're just status symbols or good-luck charms. Maybe they're into idol worship and simply are looking for someone beautiful enough to glorify."

"Men are taught that love, although it may be great, is really of second-rate importance in their lives. How many men would tell their bosses they don't want to go out for drinks after work because they can't wait to get home to their loving wives? If anything of that sort was said it would be with a snicker and a snort and an 'if you know what I mean' remark."

"Women seem to build their life around a man, and men build their life."

"Falling in love doesn't play as strong a part in their lives as it does in women's. Men's work plays a stronger part—and themselves. They are conditioned to consider themselves more."

"Men are confused now by having to be lovable when their entire socialization consists of toughening them for the work world."

"All men take seriously is men and man's power. About love, men commonly hold two views. Either they are threatened by it or they think it's silly."

One woman points out, sympathetically:

"Men do not think of a career as optional, and that makes very heavy competition for first-place priority."

57 percent of women mention that men sometimes seem afraid of falling in love—or that when these feelings come to men, they seem very confused: *

"They love to fall in love, until things start getting real serious, then they get scared. The women I know seem to fall much harder than the men they become involved with."

"I think they take love seriously but are culturally programmed to suppress this. It plays an important *unconscious* part in their life. I think the denial of the importance of love causes tremendous stress and confusion in men."

"Most men are afraid to let go in love, because love is a form of expression and men have been raised to not show their emotions. Many want the kind of love that is there when they need it, no matter whether they work to keep it alive or not. It depends on the man and how deep his understanding of himself is."

"Men do fall in love but I think they are afraid to admit it. Like it is a weakness or something. They like to hide it because it isn't macho to have feelings. Both my husband and my lover have trouble in these areas, but my lover will express himself in private."

*In *The Hite Report on Male Sexuality,* men discuss this confusion in various ways; basically it seems clear that being "in love" goes against "male" training to be in control at all times.

"Love relationships do not seem to be the final part of the puzzle for men that they are for women—like they could take it or leave it. Their career, schoolwork, or sports career takes precedence. Men seem to be able to control their emotions like a switch—now it's time to train for football season—so no matter what we had, I have to do that instead. I think a woman often 'needs' to be in love to feel complete more than a man does."

One woman points out that another reason men avoid love may be economics:

"I think men take love seriously, but fear it, because they assume they will have the responsibility for providing financial support."

———————————

But is this still generally true? After all, most women now have jobs too. And, as women earlier in this chapter point out, it is not only their work that men think is more important than relationships, but also themselves and their own thoughts and desires, who they are and what they want.

62 percent of women, however, point out that love is important to men, even if not in first place, because it is the only time they do get to be emotional and affectionate:

"Men I have known, both as lovers and friends, said that love is enormously important in their lives, because it is absolutely necessary for their emotional well-being."

"I think they take love *more* seriously. It finally gives a man a chance to let his guard down and be honest with someone."

Men's emotional demands on women

Many women feel very confused by all of this—reality turns out not to be what it is said to be. Most women say that, after the first six months of a relationship, especially a marriage, men seem to be more emotionally dependent on them than vice versa—contrary to stereotypes which label women as "dependent" and "clinging."

This also represents a profound irony; that is, that men—no matter what negative behaviors they may display to women (we have seen that it is common for men to be emotionally withholding, condescending, and harassing)—still, at the same time, turn to women for love and emotional understanding, support. In other words, men harass women, but want and expect their love. Why? Because, despite "manliness," men need emotional support as much as women do. And yet, what effect does this have on women and their perception of men?

Women Are Questioning the Emotional Arrangements in Their Lives

79 percent of women are now questioning intensely whether they should put so much energy into love relationships, or give them the highest priority in their lives; * *89 percent feel a conflict between men's demands on them to be loving— i.e., their "duty" to be loving and giving ("endlessly . . .")—and their own need to be themselves:*

"I am afraid I cannot love, that I don't love, and that since love is the most important feeling in the world to have, no matter how great my garden is or how slender and healthy I get, I will never be able to be a whole person. I feel happiest when I am working in my garden, or other alone times. And that is the problem because I am not living alone, I am a mother of two children and living with a man for fifteen years. I don't like my alone times to end until I am ready and when I can slip easily into family life. If someone comes to get me at the garden, if a creative time of writing, sewing, yoga is interrupted, I almost want to shout at them."

"I wish that I didn't spend so much mental energy thinking about relation-ships (friendships). I am a good student but too often my work gets put aside because I am focusing on the people in my life. I feel like I can't help it. People are so important to me. My work always comes second. I wish that I could find a balance. I still value love relationships highly but I am consciously trying to switch my priorities."

"During a relationship, so much time is spent on learning about the other person and just enjoying the feelings that it puts a stop on every other part of life. Too much time and effort is wasted (?) on just *being* with this other person—at least that's how it's always been for me. In school I never put enough thought into what it was that I wanted to *do* in life (except being a wife and mother)."

"He demands my total involvement. If I gaze out the window of the plane to study the cloud formations, he has to keep intruding on thoughts, to be the total center of my attention all the time. He phones from work several times a day, and pouts when I am in conference and cannot talk. The way to solve my dilemma would be to change the dead-bolt lock on the door. Oh, I'm oversimplifying . . . This man is mid-forties but his insecurities and needs will consume me if I don't try to find answers."

"In both my relationships I've become far too involved in making rela-tionships work that should have worked on their energy or I should have let go down the drain. I had a lot of trouble doing anything good or useful for

*For each year of data received, the number of replies questioning this idea grew.

myself dating them, and this affected all my relationships with other peo-
.ple."

———————

Many women feel a great conflict between having a relationship and still taking
time for themselves, their own thoughts, or a job that they take seriously. Over
half worry that they spend too much energy on relationships.

Women don't want love to be a conflict, don't want to be forced into a
choice between being themselves and loving a man—but all too many women
say that this is the very position they are in. They must choose between leaving,
fighting for their rights, or losing some of the relationship—over and over
again, every day.

Women's emotional "duty"

*The "male" ideology pressures women to love in a "helpmate," self-denying sort
of way; the "rules of the game" say that women should not put themselves
first—a good woman should always put her husband and family first; the most
important thing in the world for a woman should be loving and giving to
family*—more important than career, work, or self:*

"A woman's primary concern should be her family—not herself or her
career. To childless women I say: Don't get pregnant unless you're prepared
for total sacrifice to your child. A woman should commit herself totally to
bringing up her child, to be with that child twenty-four hours a day to meet
its needs until it is capable of caring for itself."

"My mother certainly did show me how to be 'feminine.' Don't be tough,
don't be strong, be 'nice,' polite, passive, assume you are wrong and everyone
else is right. Always put others' needs before your own. Oh, and it's an absolute
duty to be as pretty as possible."

———————

Women are almost not allowed *not* to love by the traditional ideology, which
defines women solely in terms of their love relationships with men—or lack of
them. As one woman puts it, "A woman, to be a real woman, should love
someone, have a love relationship—and also have children to love. She will be
very lonely and empty without these things. Her nature requires them."†

---

*Why does one have to be "first" and the other "second"? See pages 138–9. "The 'male' ideology."
†This is of course the premise of Richard Strauss's opera *Die Frau ohne Schatten*—i.e., that women become
neurotic if they cannot have children. (Men don't.) This theme appears in various psychological theories,
plays, and homilies, although there is no evidence that it is true.

47 percent of women describe rather intense childhood training to be giving to the extreme—supportive of others, not dynamic, not starring in their own lives—passive:

"I was trained to be submissive, with a very heavy church background. Having no ability to make rational decisions, I asked God for a verse of what to do after college, looked in the Bible, and it said, 'Leave your country and your relatives and go into the land which I will show you.' So I left. I was shocked to discover that I loved being away from home in college. Because of my mother's constantly telling me what a wonderful and close family we had, I had thought going away to school would be difficult. I did not miss being yelled at at all. My dependence was nonexistent!"

"Femininity in the South where I was growing up meant being sweet and nice and ladylike. I was not expected to be smart. I found myself years later still playing dumb so that some man could feel smart."

"My father was very domineering. He kept us children at the supper table with long lectures, we were not allowed to express ourselves at all. Many times I would try and my father would scare me by 'blowing up' and yelling. I would leave the table crying and confused emotionally. I learned to be a 'good girl.' To me this meant you obeyed the 'authorities,' you didn't talk back, you were quiet and respectful, you stayed at home and followed your parents' wishes."

"As a child, I was told to love my mother and do everything she said. If my mother and I began to have a fight, my father would stop it by saying, 'Not now, girls.' My mother gave me double messages about my father. She threw herself away for him—even to the point of saying or implying that she only had children for him—not for herself or because we were wanted. I was given the idea that being a good girl meant not disturbing anyone, being quiet. The idea was that children are to be seen and not heard . . . except that it was better if I wasn't even seen."

"Everybody always told me to be a good girl. They rarely told me I *was* a good girl. They expected good behavior and good grades. I did those things but never got recognized for them. I guess I'm still trying, because I'm still doing what people expect."

"I think I was a fairly inert person most of my life—that is, I learned as a child to survive by being repressed, withdrawn. It would make me very happy to change myself and become more active."

"Femininity" is also described frequently as having the same characteristics:

"Define femininity? Submissiveness, agreeableness, smiling a lot, weakness."

One woman tells poignantly how she habitually represses her own opinions, focusing her energy and support on the other person—a pattern which is interiorized by not a few women:

"I am so repressed I feel myself not wanting to upset even my therapist by too disturbing a sharing of feelings. I follow a pattern of observation and accommodation with people—I watch the other person's behavior and reactions, and then accommodate myself to them."

Women who feel they are not loving—a small minority—describe themselves in very negative ways indeed:

"I am quite hard and calculating, never let my feelings go."

"I don't think I am good at giving love. I can be a real coldhearted bitch at times."

But most women now are resisting this ideology; only 26 percent of women say that real love is essentially giving to the point of selflessness. In fact, many women state that too much "selflessness" is dangerous, "martyr-ish," and speak in favor of "selfishness" in love:

"Being in love is mutual selfishness, but of the best kind. For without taking, being yourself, you create a burden on the other person to feel grateful, and also to relate only to your love for them, not to *you*—which makes the relationship shaky. Women have been told to be selfless in their love; men have not. Therefore what winds up happening in all too many relationships is that the woman is being walked all over; both should try looking at it in the opposite way."

56 percent of women speak of the fine but very important line between giving and being used:

"I was the most giving and understanding with a man for five years. I tried to rationalize his actions, letting him hurt me instead of facing what was happening."

"I like giving—until I get too drained."

"I have trouble being me while in a long-term relationship. I am not assertive enough and end up doing things that leave me bankrupt. There is a confusion as to how much energy to give the other person and how much to save for myself."

Can we continue to be nurturing, or should women become more "like men"?

Many women believe that women should stop giving so much, should learn to be more "like men" emotionally. As one woman puts it, with naive charm, "Love is a problem because we women have the very bad habit of getting emotionally involved. It is unfortunate that we do this and men do not seem to!"

34 percent of women think the solution to women's "being used" is to accept "male" behavior patterns and try to adopt them ourselves—to be less "emotional," less focused on love as a basic means of fulfillment:

"If I could change one thing about all the relationships that I have had, I would make myself less emotional, less involved, less concerned about them."

"I try to avoid acting like a silly female in relationships. It's time women stopped being so emotional."

"My family used to call me 'blubber baby' because I would cry if my pet turtle died, or anything. They said, don't be a baby, etc., so I learned to be strong. Today I feel I can handle my relationships quite well, and I don't let myself get too carried away—and end up crying, like some of my friends."

"Love with a man seems like the most important thing in the world when it's going on because of the strength of your feelings. But it really isn't. Family, friends, and work are more important in the long run. Falling in love can disrupt those important things and it's important to resolve it somehow so you can be free of the tension and upset, and go about your business."

"I do not like being in love because it acts as a compulsion, always wanting to be with the other—never feeling strong and independent. I much prefer varied, loving relationships. I love myself, and whatever anyone else thinks is far less important than it used to be in my life. Most love stories seem extremely romanticized and unrealistic to me. I like stories of strong, brave women who have many loving companions. There are not many of these stories published."

Some women envy men's ability to live without worrying so much about other people's feelings:

"I envy their sense of control over their own lives—they go ahead and do what they want without worrying so much about it."

Still, 42 percent of women take the opposite point of view and assert that men or women who call women "too emotional," or too interested in love, are wrong, and only reflect their own problems and biases:

"I don't think I should listen to people who try to repress my emotions (don't be loud, be a 'good girl,' etc.) because they can't express their own emotions. But my grievance would be with myself, not with them. I think that I should like myself more, respect myself, and not allow others to push me down."

In fact, most women do not want to give up women's traditional involvement with feelings—even though they also agree that giving all one's love to a man is wrong at this point in time; still, they don't want to give up on love and take on "male" values:

"It is actually a big burden having to worry about the other person's feelings. But it is worth the trouble—it is so great to be able to really talk about things, know there is one person who can talk in depth to you, to whom you can tell anything, and they'll understand what it's all about, *really.*"

But another woman—perhaps inwardly wishing that men would be more loving, but having decided that this is an impossible dream, at least in her lifetime!—is in favor of at least beating men at their own competitive, use-or-be-used game:

"All this equality shit is bullshit. Every man you meet still tries to hump you every way he can. It's about time we humped them back."

Are women nurturing and loving because they/we want to be, or because we have been brought up to be?

Aren't the values women have been discussing here just part of a system that has been forced on women? Aren't all people "naturally" aggressive, power-driven and self-interested—"like men"? If women are "not like that," isn't it simply because these traits have been repressed in us? (Or because we have special hormones related to child-bearing that make us "nurturing" by "nature"?)

The fact is that we don't know what traits are inborn in people—if any. Although anthropologists for several decades carefully compiled the Human Area Files (extensive cross-indexed lists of behavior of all the extant "primitive tribes" around the world), it is now clear that many of the questions they asked were severely culturally biased. For example, questions regarding sexual behavior were posed as if "sex" were always and everywhere defined as "coitus" (intercourse); therefore relatively few or no questions were asked that left open other possibilities such as masturbation, just touching and petting, or same-sex relations—questions like "What do you do physically to give yourself pleasure? Do you touch yourself? When you are with others or another? How do you like to be touched or close to others/another? Is dancing sexual to you?" and so on. In consequence, the Files tell us over and over what was said when people were asked about coitus—and not much else.* Similarly, "male" and "female" characteristics (and this applies to much of primate research too) are described with the gender-biased vocabulary and its attendant value judgments seen in Chapter 3.

A further problem with the Human Area Files is that almost all of these so-called "primitive" cultures had already come into contact with "Western culture," through trading, industrialization, etc. And, recently, anthropologists have been making the point that these are not "primitive" cultures anyway; that they have long traditions of their own. Just because their societies didn't turn out to be like ours does not make them "primitive."

The battles rage on in almost every academic discipline over these issues, and the debates still are not unbiased. For there is a strange dichotomy at work when human males and females are discussed, i.e., it is commonly implied that women have been "brainwashed" to have their characteristics, to be "nice"—but it is rare to hear it said that men are "brainwashed" to be "aggressive" and "competitive." It is assumed that men's traits are either "naturally" male, the product of male hormones; or that men have the "natural," unbrainwashed set of characteristics that women too would have if they were not so "repressed." And yet, we cannot assume that "male" traits are "natural" either, since in fact men are encouraged every day in myriad ways to be "strong," "aggressive," "combative," and so on. Why not imagine, just for the exercise of it, that it is women who have the "natural" traits, and men who have been artificially pumped up with ideas, propaganda about their behavior—made to think they should be "tough" and want to "dominate"? There is just as much evidence that this is the case. Actually, the fact is that as a civilization, we can *choose* the characteristics we want to encourage. "Human nature" seems to be infinitely malleable.

Loving Men Under the Current System: What Happens?

Women's belief that in a relationship, people should nurture each other, share feelings, and attune themselves to, be sensitive to, the emotional states of the

---

*Although some anthropologists, especially female anthropologists in the last ten years, have begun radically to change the approach taken.

other is good. The problem is that most men are not prepared to do this in return, and often in fact look down on women, withhold an emotional connection and harass them—at the same time that they are demanding their love! (See Chapters 1 and 2.) In this unequal situation, giving can be draining, confusing, exhausting and infuriating.

How are women, questioning as they are all the traditional pre-set definitions of "loving," finding that this unequal emotional "contract" affects them when they live with a man? Can we live with someone who holds the attitudes of the "male" ideology, "understand," and be impervious to it? Can we still love and be happy?

Struggling to maintain identity and dignity, while still loving

> *"Even though my husband has hurt me emotionally and physically, I can't seem to find the strength or desire to break free—a little voice in the back of my mind keeps saying, 'Please love me, I'll be good, I'll be good . . .'"*

What effect does constant emotional harassment or emotional withholding (sometimes added to economic dependence) have on women?

Too much giving without an equal exchange can make women feel emotionally needy and insecure, psychologically on the defensive:

"I just never felt secure in any relationship I ever had. Therapy helped some (at least I talked about it), but it didn't help me become any more secure. When I'm with a man, I just start feeling doubtful of myself."

Psychological harassment and emotional deprivation, lack of communication, have been shown in many experiments (not gender-related in particular) to cause a feeling of unworthiness, a habit of being self-effacing; in short, men's emotional distance mixed with emotional demands and harrassment leaves many women feeling psychologically needy and frustrated:

"I have been most passionate when my husband shares his life, thoughts, dreams, feelings, with me. Most of the time I just feel left out—not his best friend. I feel insecure and a fear of abandonment. Even though my husband says we'll talk each day, he just talks two minutes before he falls asleeps, about himself. I want to talk about *us*. I can't get into his head. I don't feel accepted or understood."

"He hates my crying so much, it makes him feel helpless. He tells me I am too sensitive, and sometimes he is afraid to say things because I am so sensitive."

"I'm a very affectionate person, I need lots and lots of love that most men I've been with do not want to give. I get afraid of clinging, many times it has had disastrous effects."

"I think women need more love than men. I don't understand it, we are all human and we all need love. But men are more involved in activities such as fishing, sports, working on cars, etc."

"I always felt I tried harder than the men I was involved with. Once the newness of the living situation settled down, they usually found other interests. As a result, I felt insecure, so I worked harder, clung more, and they tried to get away more, so it seemed."

"Once, I was totally consumed, I lost all rationality and objectivity. I became very insecure—how could I be prettier, sexier, more appealing to him? I could never be perfect enough for him—not that he required it, but emotionally he was aloof, and found it difficult to show affection. Somehow I thought that I could help him warm up. He didn't. My insecurity became overwhelming—I felt I was making myself too available and vulnerable and broke it off."

Sometimes men aggravate the situation, behave provocatively:

"Last night I asked my husband to clarify a statement he made the night before. We were discussing my insecure feelings and he said of all the women he has come in contact with, probably 95 percent did not desire his body. I asked him if he would tell me who were the 5 percent who indicated to him that they wanted to have sex with him. (I'd like to know who the competition is.) He got angry and said he didn't really mean it, that it was just a general statement. When I tried to pin him down, he punched his fist through the wall in the family room.

"My depressed moods and anxiety are usually triggered by something he says or does that hurts me. But this makes me miserable because my husband doesn't like being near me when I'm upset, yet he's the one I need most. His not wanting to be around me is what has caused our problems. After he comforts me I'm relieved but unsure of his show of affection. Is it genuine or just to make me feel better? Then we call a truce. He insists that we stop talking about it or go for a walk."

"About the radio in his car, I have the feeling he puts the music on to stop us from talking. So I ask him to shut it off. (I also find it egotistical.) He says no, shut up, whose car is it anyway? And I insist that I'll get out of the car if he continues. I really have to yell loudly so he can finally realize that I'm not

kidding. I have to cry, make a fit, feel all fucked up! Finally he understands—
but he does it all over again the next time."

*Many women in these situations eventually come to feel that they need approval
frequently or constantly; many express a fear of not being lovable enough, of
being left:* *

"I did and I do worry. I've been hurt so much I almost expect to be deserted
now. People don't grow tired of me . . . just fed up."

"I guess it's fear. Fear of him leaving me. If I could change the situation
in some way, I would like to become more 'self-assured.' "

"I'm afraid my boyfriend will leave me because he will get tired of me. That
he will find someone he loves better and that he will never come back to me."

"Right now I'm in the process of losing the 'nagging fear' of my husband
leaving me. With our counseling I'm hoping I will become secure enough to
lose any vestige of this fear that comes back to haunt me. But then the experience of extramarital stuff is recent. I guess I'm not really too afraid he will stop
loving me. I think my fear is that he will find someone else, someone newer,
more romantically exciting, a greater love. But I'm working at not allowing
that fear to control me and at becoming secure in myself so it won't matter so
much if it does happen. I don't worry because I'm getting older—that wouldn't
count (if he left me because of his age and his infirmity and his not wanting
to 'miss opportunities' in life). Or he might desert me if I started an extramarital
affair again myself."

"That fear of losing him used to cause me cold-sweat nightmares. It doesn't
anymore. That doesn't mean I'm absolutely sure he'll always stick by me. It
means that his staying isn't as important to me as it once was. I'll survive if I'm
deserted. But I'm sure that many women fear desertion—women aren't allowed to grow old, and men have the power in this world to define what is
valuable. Because women are defined by their relationships to men, we are more
vulnerable to desertion than men. And more frightened by it. I used to be too.
But now I don't worry. If he leaves, he leaves."

*There is a well-known adage that women should not "cling"—implying that
women are by "nature" too needful of affection and attention:*

"In the past I've had to watch myself for clinginess. It seems obvious that
men don't want a clingy woman."

"I'm quite afraid of clinging. Men I know aren't the type to be tied down.
I don't feel too emotionally dependent—but I fear getting that way. I don't
think men in my age group like women's dependency."

---

*"Did you ever have a nagging fear of losing someone's love or being deserted? That the other person
would grow tired of you?"

But some women say these attitudes are a conscious power play on the part of men:

"Men try to make women feel like they are 'clinging' to get the upper hand. Men are really the more dependent, they *want* to keep us clinging, while complaining."

One woman has a completely different attitude:

"I was never afraid he would desert me—who the hell would ever take *him?*"

Gradually a woman, trying harder and harder to make things work, to please a man, to back him emotionally, can lose her own self-esteem and self-confidence:

"When he notices that I exist, calls me by my name, introduces me to his friends as his wife, touches me or puts his arm around me when we're with other people, I feel so happy—when I am made to feel loved, respected, and a person of worth, not someone you had to take with you because everyone else brought their wife.

"But I watch him talk to other women about things he doesn't talk to me about, smiling at them with obvious enjoyment—when he doesn't smile at me ever, even when he greets me. He answers other people's questions graciously, but if I ask him to explain something, he tells me I wouldn't understand, or is indignant that I would have to 'question' a statement or decision.

"At this point, I doubt that he loves me or wants me. I do not like the way I look. I do not consider myself very feminine. I fear for myself when my husband stares at young, pretty girls. Sex between us is physical, no talking. It is probably the only time during the marriage when his attention is centered totally on me. I try to wear more feminine nightgowns and do things to please him."

One woman who feels very trapped describes an inertia, almost a kind of paralysis, that seems to have overtaken her—or at least a feeling that perhaps there is nothing "out there" worth trying for that is better:

"It's hard to stop loving someone. My husband has hurt me deeply, but I can't seem to make myself leave. I am a very average middle-class housewife. Not unattractive but not a raving beauty. A little overweight. I'm thirty-eight. My work is my home. My husband and children seem to dictate my life. Lots of family responsibilities. My daughter is my one true complete love. I love my sons, but my daughter has my soul. She is my link to myself.

"My husband doesn't seem interested in finding out what I think about anything. If he and I could only relate verbally the way I do with my best friend, 80 percent of our problems would be solved. When I try to tell him this, he has no idea of what I'm talking about. Maybe if he did I wouldn't need the affairs. He is also very unliberated and wants my daughter brought up in the traditional female role. I want her to grow up to be what *she* wants to be, with the option of marriage if she chooses. We fight over this frequently.

"My husband has hit me. I wanted to kill him. I never hated him as much as I did then.

"My lovers I have met when I've been out alone for a night on the town. (I have always had on my wedding ring—it doesn't seem to be a deterrent.) Two of my lovers are married, including my ten-year affair. They're safer, no complications, no commitments. Mostly fun and games.

"I figure I work about 100 hours a week for $20. My husband works, then gives me his pay, less money for himself. I handle all the bill paying, groceries, etc. If there is anything left after bills, groceries, etc., I give myself an allowance. My husband does none of the household chores, believing it's my job. I have a friend whose husband helps with dishes, laundry, kids, even though she isn't employed outside the home either. I envy that. They seem much more loving because of the sharing.

"I'm not sure if I'll ever have the kind of love relationship with a man that I desire. No one as of this date has ever made me feel that alive, that excited, or that loved. I'm still looking. The closest I have ever felt to a perfect love was the love I feel for my daughter. I hope my daughter and I will be the best of friends and that she can always come to me. I don't want to be just her mother, I want to be her best friend. (She's only three.)

"I have become very disillusioned with love relationships. I could easily have a rewarding life without one, maybe just a casual lover now and then. If I had the choice, I would choose children and career, not necessarily marriage. I'd like to know if all I'm feeling is normal."

Women often give individual reasons from their childhoods for why they feel so "emotionally needy," not taking into account that their feelings may be valid, logical reactions to concrete messages they are getting in their relationships and from society, bombarding them from every direction:

"I know I have an excessive need for love and affection. You have only to look at my childhood to see why. However, I don't apologize for it. I just want to find a man who has the same needs. I can find women who need love and friendship. Why not men?"

"I went into therapy to figure out why my relationships weren't working. I decided that I never learned how to deal with anger, and I got into a martyr role as a way of dealing with angry feelings. I learned that from my mother."*

*It is important to note how many people come out of therapy with the belief their problems were caused by their mothers; this reflects a bias on the part of some psychological theory which does not expect as

"There came a time (about two years ago) when I realized that the pain of my romances was essentially the same pain and conflict I experienced in dealing with my mother and that I was using romance as a way of dealing with my mother, of trying to be separate—individual."

———————

But the situations described here involve large *social* issues; they are not something one person can or should have to fight alone. Although it is productive to understand one's own personal history and personality, to come away from "therapy" without it having been acknowledged that the culture has a strong hand in *creating* these situations is extremely unfortunate. After all, women will have to continue dealing with society's messages about women's status and "characteristics"; what tools would a therapy which does not acknowledge the existence of this gender bias in the culture give to a woman to help her go on with her life?*

Even worse, some schools of therapy seem to blame women as a general principle by labeling their *socially* created problems with gender-biased and blaming phrases, such as "masochistic," "dependent," and so on—completely ignoring the concrete phenomenon of most women's economic dependency during most of the twentieth century (encouraged by the culture) and the effects this has had on women's (and men's) "psychologies."

What one woman says is much more to the point about why women are sensitive as to whether they are loved—if you include the social context as part of an overall atmosphere of less-love-for-women:†

"Of course women need more love and affection—but only because they aren't getting enough to begin with."

Some types of therapy and psychoanalysis also seem to believe that women have no right to "complain"—that a woman's "complaining" is a sign of a woman having a problem (rather than the society having a problem: i.e., trying to discover whether there is a reality in the woman's relationship causing this; this means, again, that women have no right to name things):

"In early marriage I felt ganged up against by the man/woman therapy team trying to help J. and me solve our problems. It always seemed that I was neurotic and he was not. Fine help. Finally I met up with a Jungian analyst

———————

much "mothering" from men, or blame them as often. See page 118 for the implications of findings of this study for the psychology of women—and men.
*Only a smug "Don't bug me, don't bring your troubles to me; go get therapy" attitude—because this will fit women into the "male" world?
†As a comedienne on the Johnny Carson show said, "My ex-boyfriend and I had one thing in common—we both loved him and hated me!"

who was very helpful in getting me to sort out my relationship with my parents, but he also as much as turned to J. and said, 'You are suffering from the existential alienation of modern man,' and to me said, 'You are neurotic.' I ultimately quit, and not until I discovered feminism and consciousness raising did I begin to sort out my feelings about therapy, aided by Chesler's *Women and Madness* and others. I learned a lot but it *did not help me at all.*"

However, some forms of counseling are more progressive. Another woman describes a very good experience she had with an unusual therapist, who did not deny the reality of gender bias against women in society, and took her anger against "male" society into realistic account:

"Therapy can be wonderful—with the right therapist. At the point when I was in despair after the breakup of my affair after my marriage, I needed a therapist—and after trying two I didn't like, I found one who proved just right. I knew he would be right when he suggested at the initial session that if I really would prefer a woman therapist, he'd help me find one.

"We worked together for nearly three years—I say 'worked together' very much on purpose, for I felt very much an equal in the relationship—perhaps the only relationship with any man in which I've really felt equal. My initial 'love relationship problem' faded, and most of the therapy delved into the causes for my tendency toward depressions—which basically has to do with my frequent feeling of helplessness to be equal to men in the world as it exists. This starting from the birth of my brother and being reinforced at every point in my life. I could never be outstanding enough in anything I did to be taken as seriously as men were—it is a fight I will fight all the rest of my life.

"Therapy helped me understand that this is the structure of our social milieu, and that I do not lack something essential. Thanks to the therapy, and to my own strengths, I understand now that I don't have to be perfect and invulnerable. I see some of my hang-ups and realize that I'll never get over some of them. I know that, as a woman playwright, in a world where men pull the puppet and purse strings, I will have to work twice as hard as men and there will be a lot of unfairness and enormous frustrations. I won't like it one bit, but mostly I won't think my failures are because there is something inherently wrong with *me*. Therapy went a long way beyond curing a 'broken heart.'"

Disappearing slowly like the Cheshire cat: women's identity

Too much giving without receiving, non-reciprocal giving, or constantly being belittled by someone one loves, can eventually threaten one's personality and identity—or at least one's ability to express that identity.

One young woman describes the feeling she had in her first serious relationship of her self gradually disappearing, like the Cheshire cat, while she watched:

"When I fell in love, I wasn't really happy. I felt myself becoming less and less my own self and more and more and more a part of him. The relationship lasted about a year, and I finally got up the courage to break it off. We did see each other as friends after that, but I didn't want to be enveloped. I couldn't seem to stop it from happening as long as we were together."

Another woman, in the process of a divorce after many years, describes a similar feeling, and the choices she is faced with:

"I have been very lonely in the presence of my husband while being ignored. It's understandable to be lonely when you're alone, but the loneliness you can feel with someone you care for is pretty dismal. I still share my feelings and thoughts with him, but he chooses to ignore most of them and gives very little credibility to the others. More intimate talk or meaningful talk on any important subject would have been helpful—it might have saved our marriage.

"Now I am faced with either giving up my 'self' or building a shell around it or getting out of the marriage. It's sad, I don't hate him, I just can't make that big a sacrifice for him. If I give up my self I am also giving a real poor role model to my children, and neither he nor myself is getting anything positive out of our life together."

Another young woman, now a reporter, describes her earlier marriage, in which she even "forgot" how to drive:

"It's amazing how the human soul can be transformed through certain pressures. He was very conservative, from a very religious family, and I wanted to please him. I forgot how to drive, I would never consider going out alone—even though I had been a completely independent woman before, when I was in college. It was like being in shackles—traipsing around after someone, trying to be brave and get it together. But after a while, I realized that every day would be like this, there would never be a resolution, and that's when I decided to leave. I was trying but he wasn't. I was always supposed to follow and repress myself, and he would lead. I loved him, but I couldn't do it—after two years I was a wreck."

Other women have had similar experiences:

"I think I was given all these crossed messages, and so ended up being 'nothing' because that was safer. It wasn't just my parents giving me crazy directions about how to be—it was all reinforced by friends, classmates, teachers, and eventually men. Don't be muscular. Don't be loud. Don't be 'selfish,' 'opinionated,' don't be anything masculine, which means don't think at all. Don't be smart, men don't like that, etc."

"I have to work with myself in order to give the other person the attention they need without taking away from the attention I give myself."

"He seems to be so well adjusted without working at it, whereas for me, it has been a long struggle to even begin to feel 'normal.' "

"I feel that my husband stifles me. I cannot really be myself when I am with him. I am very careful about what I do and say."

"My love relationship does not make me feel good. It puts a drain on me, trying very hard to be myself, and still please him—which is impossible. He wants to change me to be someone else."

"I value love relationships but I wish that I didn't spend so much mental energy thinking about relationships and friendships. I am consciously trying to switch my priorities."

The problem is caused by the definition of love which means not only giving, but giving all of one's self, in the cultural context we now know:

"My definition of love is caring about someone in every way more than you care about yourself—a total giving of yourself to the other person."

The lack of reciprocity of this giving in many female-male relationships or marriages causes many women to have to struggle not to lose their own selves or identities:

"The worst part of my marriage of seven years was the criticism, abuse, put-downs, the blocks to progress by my husband. We weren't moving as a couple—seemed to spin in circles—as if in a whirlpool—being pulled down with constant struggles to surface for air—to let be free. Being the one to always give in to his unreasonable demands; having him make things harder than they had to be—the list could go on and on. We lived separate lives eventually."

Another woman describes the total repression of her own feelings during her marriage, so that eventually she lost touch with herself and had to go into therapy to learn to express herself again:

"We were married eighteen years. Finally he became too violent and I left. I felt like a failure but I also felt very relieved—I was like a different person. I was very angry with my husband. Immediately after we got married (I was seventeen), I felt I was not free to express my feelings anymore and I just responded to him. It all started when we had been married for three weeks and my husband walked out. I went and talked to the chaplain about it. When he came back and found out what I had done, he knocked me around and made me go back and tell the chaplain everything was O.K. He always won because he would never let me say anything. Lots of times I was scared during the arguments, and angry that I couldn't say anything. The arguments would end when he was through talking. We didn't talk over problems, he stated his position and that was that.

"I entered therapy when I almost had a breakdown before the divorce. I continued in therapy until a year after the divorce. The therapy helped me to find myself."

If a woman is economically dependent, this can greatly increase her chances of becoming psychologically self-denying or overly accommodating:

"I stayed in the marriage because of the kids and he was a good provider. I thought there was no way I could ever make money. My self-image was that the only job I was qualified for was that of dishwasher in a hotel basement. That's the image he reinforced through years and years of marriage. When I did run away once, he threatened me that if I ever left him, he'd prove me insane and I'd never see my children. I was terrified. He kept me feeling crazy all the time. No woman should be financially dependent. It throws the power all his way."

But in the context of our society, this economic factor need not even be present for a woman to feel afraid to leave a "bad" relationship. Remarkably, on the other hand, some women who *are* economically dependent manage not to feel pressured by this—perhaps they have savings or skills so that the possibility of divorce does not frighten them. Of course, theoretically, if women's home skills were valued* more, economic dependence "should" not be a cause for a feeling of inequality. However, the fact is that when the man earns all the money, he becomes, in a way, the woman's employer whom she may have to please. See Chapter 10 for women's feelings on this.

One unspoken rule in many families seems to be that the woman/wife/mother who is financially dependent can "ask for things"—but not "just for herself," they must be for the good of the family or the children:

"Mom is sometimes subservient to Dad, sometimes domineering. She tells him what to do, and if he's indifferent enough, he'll do as she says. She is subservient in that she never asks him for something just for her (like to go out to dinner, or out for any reason. They haven't been out in years.). If Dad comes home late and Mom is tired, she still makes him an elaborate meal. She'll

---

*The international British-based women's group Wages for Housework has for years been advocating that women receive actual financial payment for their work, to avoid these problems.

complain behind his back—but she does it. Mom works in the home part-time as a secretary, full-time as a homemaker."

Another woman only began to worry about the joyless atmosphere of her marriage when she thought about its possible effect on her new child—not on herself!

"When my daughter was born, I began to reassess the kind of home life I had versus the kind I wanted for this beautiful child. I wanted a loving, laughing, happy family for her, an environment of intellectual stimulation, rich experiences, and joy. We didn't have that, by a long shot."

One woman describes the painful process of watching a friend she loves let herself be drained hollow by her relationship with her husband and children:

"Her husband is her financial prop. Although he is not supposed to live at home he stays there, occasionally overnight. Her two children are grown up and still think they should be fed, watered, sheltered, financed. They are beautiful but a bloody, fat drag. I love her and want to be supportive but I can see they are draining her down to her hollow teeth."

Many note this process in past relationships of their own:

"Love for a man has meant 98 percent hurt up to now. Maybe I have behaved as a masochist, maybe I confuse the Christian notion of 'love thy neighbor' sometimes with the social notion of love between man and woman. But I've given so many times and been hurt that now I have to hold back or lose some of myself."

"It took me altogether seventeen years to find myself one day sitting in the sun, realizing that I was doing just that—sitting in the sun—without any real awareness of myself. I mean, I used to remain aware that I had placed myself in the sun, as well as sitting in the sun accepting the warmth that I was meant to enjoy.

"I think I would claim this as the event that took me the most courage to get through, because I did become aware of what was happening to me after five years and then set about quite purposefully to become a person who will be able to meet death as an appropriate conclusion. Sounds morbid, it probably was. But things were so bad that on contemplating suicide I felt I could not even use that solution because there was nothing left of me that could be killed off. I was simply floating."

One young woman is consciously making an attempt to retain her right to selfhood within her new marriage:

"I maintain a lot of my singleness in my relationship with my husband. Perhaps because of these years of solitude, I have recognized in me a need for space to myself. I need time alone at home, and we have integrated this into the scheme of things. It is sometimes a simple matter of knowing what you want and feeling you have the right to ask for it. We unfortunately have very few role models to look to."

89 percent of women also point out that their life disappears because this conflict in the relationship happens in a context of overwork—there is too much to do, between an outside job, running a home, working on the relationship, possibly having children to look after; women are bombarded with multitudes of conflicting pressures of things to do and take care of—and their life can disappear in the process:

"Women are overworked to begin with. Then their husbands resent it when their wives are not ready to give them attention, be with them, have sex with them, when the husbands wants, on his time schedule. They cannot understand why the woman is so tired! Or the husband resents the fact that she has so much more to attend to than he does and doesn't feel very romantic by the time bedtime arrives. But it is not only that now women have jobs and families and the overload is too great, which is what we hear all the time (women *could* handle all these things, although it is not fair), but the real problem on top of all this is the constant unstated demand for attention made by men, the assumption that women should be 'there for them' if they love them—women should never be focusing on themselves (so in a relationship, she keeps on feeling more drained, rather than refreshed). This is what makes women say, 'You can never do anything right. There is too much expected of women.' Men's constant, silent, unconscious demand for emotional energy and attention makes women exhausted and drained. Perhaps it is easier to be a single mother!"

Everyone needs time for themselves—but it is something women (especially those with children) almost never get; the well-known lack of "space" is still a problem:*

"The girls just got through nursing school and my husband has been involved with a new business. I loved working but feel a need to stop for

*What Virginia Woolf wrote about in the 1920s with *A Room of One's Own.*

refueling. I've supported all these people financially and emotionally for the past six years and now feel the need to give something to myself."

"I work two full-time jobs and go to school. A luxury I love is to lock the door, take the phone off the hook, and stay in bed all day reading and napping. These are my 'lost weekends,' but I think of them as well spent rather than wasted!"

"My only grievance in this relationship has been my own personal problem—that I like my personal space and time and need to be left alone sometimes."

"On fleeting occasions I need more space. We've worked very long and hard on this issue for both of us. We've finally reached a marvelous point where we can understand the other's needs. With that possible, we can take our space whenever we need it!"

74 percent of women describe having no psychological "space"; most say that not only is there pressure on them to be "loving" and emotionally "there" in a relationship, but there is also pressure to always be positive and nice, love everybody in general—woman as "service" person:

"Until recently in my love relationships I would only express my opinions if they were in agreement with my partner. I was afraid if I expressed any negative feelings about life, I was letting him down. I thought I was supposed to be happy and optimistic."

"I am always smiling and cheerful, qualities that have earned me the nickname Sunshine. I try not to let things bother me and find pleasure in small things."

"Women are constantly told they should 'Smile!' or 'Be nice.' I think it's sickening."

Eighty-nine percent of women say they do not have time for themselves. This is not only a question of hours in the day, but also a question of mental space: women are brought up to or want to constantly "see dust," to "see" other people's feelings—not to rest until those they love are happy and tranquil, etc. This can leave little time or emotional energy for focusing on one's *own* thoughts, priorities, and endeavors.

One woman celebrates her divorce, because now she can be herself all *the time, not just when she goes out to work, returning to a secondary, non-respected role at home:*

"I am forty-eight, now single, developing the person—and the lifestyle—that I had wanted for many years. I'm graying, aging fast, yet feel more alive and vital and youthful than I did at twenty-nine, when a big thrill was stirring up a batch of peanut-butter cookies.

"My greatest achievement has been becoming the person I tried to be for thirty years of marriage, where I was one person (or becoming that person) in the business world and became a nonentity when I went home. It took a lot of courage, supportive friends, and a long time to save the bucks to do it, before I finally moved out and can be 'me' twenty-four hours a day. This 'me' is not a selfishly designed person only for her own satisfaction and gratification. But she is a person of *self-worth*. This is the biggest achievement of my life— realizing that I can be someone I like all the time."

But 74 percent of married women have a strong sense of themselves as someone above and beyond the family unit:

"I love my husband, I would never hurt him and I would never leave him—but if he left me, I would survive and go on. I would never be that heartbroken. I think I'd feel relief because he prevents me from total involvement with my career."

"It took years and years to decide that I was dying inside and that no matter how complicated it was going to be, no matter how hard, no matter how much security I had to give up—I had to get out. I wanted it. I was so glad! The relief and freedom far outweighed any feelings of failure I had. I hated him for things he did, then I'd forget and forgive, then hate again. Swinging back and forth. I was so very, very relieved and at thirty-nine I felt like I was just starting my life."

Women's anger—but do women have a right to anger, since "good" women are loving?

On top of the difficulties women encounter in their daily lives, women are told they are not supposed to get angry about any of it. According to the traditional ideology, women should be kind and loving at all times, never angry or threatening, "complaining"—in fact, women really have no right to anger. When men are angry, they are considered "righteous"; when women are angry, they are frequently seen as "bitchy," "out of control," or "tough."*

81 percent of women say men tell them or imply to them that there is "something wrong with them" when they are not "loving" and "giving";

---

*And yet images of Athena's wrath, as the wrath of many of the gods/goddesses in the Greek pantheon, are portrayed as "righteous," logical emotions provoked by just causes. The images portrayed are heroic *and* feminine.

*anger, they say, is "unfeminine," unbecoming in women (not "ladylike") and
never justified—and, most men take on the part of the innocent, unfortunate,
beleaguered husband or boyfriend if the woman shows anger, especially in
public:*

"I hate it when my husband says I shouldn't feel a certain emotion—mainly
anger. God—it's what I feel, that's my prerogative!"

"On every occasion when I have become angry with a man, I've been made
to feel that it was a totally unfeminine thing to do—the fierceness of my passion
seems to have stunned them. (Too much has been repressed, so that the fierceness is truly out of proportion to the matter at hand.)"

"Did you ever notice—if we scream, we are 'bitches.' If men scream, they
have a just cause, we 'drove them to it,' they have to get control back into the
situation, regain order—like an army sergeant."

"I hated him for cheating and lying. It made me feel crazy. But he had that
'Mr. Nice Guy' image and people thought *I* was a bitch to live with. I tried
to leave a couple of times, but somehow always wound up thinking I must be
the cause of the problems, and stayed and tried harder!"

"I suppose yelling at him in front of other people is the worst thing I did
to him. He loved it, though, 'cause then he looks like the knight in white armor
and I look like the whore."

"My anger at my father poisons our relationship sometimes, he says. But
I consider it a hidden source of strength, in the sense that women often don't
make a necessary change in their lives until they get darned pissed! 'Ladies
don't get angry.' An angry woman terrifies men! Now, I'm hardly a raging
maniac, in fact I'm rather mild and unassertive at times. I *have* been called
opinionated, though. Maybe unresolved anger poisons me from within. But I
still need that anger. I don't know what for, but I'll keep it. Maybe it's still with
me because I've never explored the depths of it, which in therapy could be a
good idea."

To be angry or to be loving? You can't win either way!

It is deemed improper for women to say negative things, especially to men, but,
in a sense, to anyone. Even if anger is justified, the social atmosphere implies
that women should confine themselves to acting hurt or victimized, and wait
for someone else to take up their cause (a knight in shining armor)—never go
out and fight and be angry themselves.

Women are not supposed to fight back or take revenge, even psychologically. They are supposed to be "nice" and "loving," no matter what—an almost
victim-like psychology?—and to turn the other cheek. While boys are taught
in schoolyards to fight back, to compete in athletics, to use a team for support,
and so on, girls are taught (or do we ourselves determine?) to be compassionate

and understanding, never thinking in terms of fighting back or being "selfish." We are taught always to question our motives, to give the other person the "benefit of the doubt."

Men's double message to women

But there is a Catch-22: this still doesn't gain men's automatic respect. At the same time that most men enjoy and exploit (or use without thinking) women's emotional support, women's skill at listening and drawing them out ("emotional housework"), many men still look down on the "loving nature" of women, thinking of it as "weak," even slightly "stupid," seeing the woman as an emotional pushover. So—if a woman fights back, she is often labeled "aggressive" or "unfeminine"; if she always turns the other cheek, and acts understanding no matter what, she is likely to be thought "weak," "passive," and eventually seen as "wimpy." If she is not "loving," she is rejected; if she *is* loving, she may not be taken seriously.

Feeling insecure and depressed: Are we "too obsessed with love," or are men often treating us outrageously?

Turning anger against oneself: depression

Women describe how they have turned their anger on themselves, looking for the cause of problems rather than wanting to see men who hurt them as an enemy (because men are too strong?):

"I never hated a lover. When we would be at a point in an argument where it could come to my feeling like hitting or hurting them, I'd hurt myself instead."

"I don't ever get jealous or angry, I do something even worse. I turn on myself—for not being better, not being as good as, etc., etc."

"A woman acquaintance told me when her husband does something nasty to her, she automatically assumes she must deserve it."

"I grew to hate my husband, although the hate was usually hidden by feelings of false sympathy. I never acted violently or screamed, even though he was domineering and chauvinistic. I got very depressed, later angry, and eventually divorced him."

"Oddly, when we broke up, I felt like a failure. As if, had I been a good enough wife, he wouldn't have been the way he was. I hated him. I think the reason was that I never had a chance to confront him with the way he treated me. He just abused me and I never fought back (literally or figuratively). That's why I ended up in a suicidal depression."

"I think due to repressed anger for years at my husband—or at least at my role in the marriage—I'm now dealing with heavy depression."

"As an adult, I have had long periods of depression over relationships—a year, a couple of months. I don't know how I managed to survive. Sometimes I would get out of it eventually by becoming sexually attracted to another man. That would make me feel alive again. I cried a lot and felt that I didn't deserve to be alive, there was no point to it, things would never get better, no one would ever love me, I always did everything . . . everything was my fault. I realize now that a lot of the depression was anger turned upon myself. It is always easier for me to take things out on myself rather than to fight against the person who hurts me. I would not stand up for myself for fear of losing their love."

"Did you ever grow to hate a lover? seek revenge?"

The great majority of women, even when profoundly angry, say they would never get revenge, that it is better to try to understand and forget it:

"The man I have actually hated the most is, I suppose, my husband. But it's only been the concomitant of love and frustration. I remained angry about some issues for years—especially the issue of his not treating me as a peer, an equal. I was and have been depressed—sometimes badly—but revenge doesn't seem to be in my makeup, although I have certainly had revengeful thoughts. Perhaps my withdrawal in some ways—sexually, for instance, in degree of interest—has been a type of unconscious punishment. But vengeance is not my style. I can't consciously do vengeful things even when I have vengeful thoughts. Either enlightened self-interest prevents it, or my parents' and the church's training or both."

"I hated one boss I had—he was insecure, and so scapegoated me and demeaned me. I got depressed—but no revenge."

"If I have ever hurt anyone in the past, I would be sorry that I did. I may think of doing things, but I always turn the other cheek."

"I have never purposely hurt someone. If I did, I would regret it. I just become angry and depressed."

"I really feel revenge is not the way—it would dehumanize me. I don't want to ever be as inhuman as your average American male. God, am I angry when I admit it."

"I hated my first husband, and still do, because he never used contraceptives at all—just told me I wouldn't get pregnant if he pulled out. I was fifteen and believed him. I hate him for getting me pregnant, for not holding a job while we were married, for leaving our baby, for gossiping about me, for moving in with one of my so-called friends, and for just generally being an asshole. I've never gotten 'revenge,' or seen justice done—except in my blood-soaked fantasies."

"I still hate him because of how he made me think about myself, and finally how he used my body. It took some distance to become angry. I really did nothing about it, and sometimes the anger comes back very strongly. I merely content myself with hoping things go badly for him."

Many women even feel guilty for having broken up with men they didn't love:

"I have hurt some men by ending relationships or not being what they wanted, not being able to give them what they said they needed."

"I feel I unintentionally hurt people, when they begin to feel too intense for me and I cannot return the same."

Or for no longer loving:

"My present husband—I will probably hurt him when I leave him. He loves me—but it is the wrong way to love. He'd be happier with someone more docile."

"I think I very much hurt my husband in the course of falling out of love with him. He had, in fact, hurt me deeply earlier, when I had a hysterectomy due to a positive Pap smear—by reacting not to my needs for assurance and comfort but to his own fears about death and about being left alone with small children to care for. I do not remember wishing him any revenge—just feeling deeply hurt."

Only a few women have actually taken revenge:

"When I fucked a lover's friend I got revenge—in my head. He only found out years after, when it no longer mattered."

"I tried to destroy his reputation. Some people were talking about how trustworthy he was and I immediately told them that he should not be trusted further than he could be thrown. I guess I felt it was un-Christian to humiliate him. But I couldn't begin to catalogue the harm this man did to me."

"There was one guy I started to make out with. He wanted to 'go all the way' and I tried to stop him, but he persisted, so I kneed him right in the balls. The 'revenge' felt very good! I don't have any regrets either!"

"I felt tremendously rejected by my husband when I was married. No matter how I looked (I am told I am very sexy and pretty) he acted as if I wasn't good enough. He said I didn't have Raquel Welch's legs. He looked at women in *Playboy*, *Penthouse*, and *Hustler* magazines. Anyway, nearly a year after I left him, I became involved with another man, and I made clear to my ex-husband that this new man was one thousand times better in bed than he was (which was true). You should have seen his face!"

"I had a boyfriend for four years who drove me crazy with his not making a commitment, not keeping appointments, telling me how much he loved me but just never really asking about *me*, listening to me, etc. During fights he became barbaric, just shouted back the meanest things he could think of. I believe in fair fighting: the point is to get to a new understanding, not to gash each other. He, obviously, thought the idea was to win by crushing the enemy into submission—which only enraged me all the more. Finally, after three years, I caught on to his strategy and decided to try playing by his rules! During an argument, in the midst of everything, out of nowhere, I blurted out, 'And you're a lousy lover.' Silence. He became immediately contrite, and asked in a small voice, 'Am I? I'm not, am I?' The truth is, he wasn't for a minute—but I just stood there. I never told him I didn't mean it. Then all he wanted was to make up and make love. After that, I found I could cut off his nastiness (saying things to me like 'You're a horrible person, none of your friends like you,' etc.) by a direct attack against him. But even though this worked, it did not satisfy *me*—I wanted to be close and for us to love one another. So after a while, I broke it off."

Women are much more likely to leave, as a final way of showing their anger and disappointment, than to fight. In addition, it is not clear which kinds of fighting in such a situation lead to winning. See Part V.

Isn't women's anger logical? Women have a right to be angry

"Why did I leave my husband? Because I had too much anger pent up against him, and men. I am very angry at the way men look at me and treat me. This colors everything I feel about them, so I think I shouldn't try another relationship with one of them—at least not now."

If we are in a culture in which men are suppressing us, and yet demanding our love, it is illogical *not* to be angry. Indeed, it could even be said that women as a group would have to be "abnormal" if they were *not* angry, living with the amount of woman baiting and repression we have seen in a society in which men are born with the right to "keep women in check." (This does not mean that an individual woman, feeling all this, may not also at the same time be very much in love with an individual man.)

Are we afraid of where our anger may lead us?

One woman makes an excellent point about where we __should__ direct our anger, and why we don't:

"Depression is, for me, taking out my anger on myself because it's too scary to face up to the real person who is making me angry. If you have been taught by your parents that you are worthless, it is then easier to consider self-destructive acts and behavior than to fight back against the people who you think are better than you. You don't know that you have any rights."

Anger against men is forbidden

Anger unexpressed can become a fog which pervades everything, leading to a perpetual low-level anxiety. Indeed, women's frustration and/or anger is responsible in large part for much of the psychological counseling, tranquilizers, and so on women use.* And yet, it is considered almost treasonous for a woman to say she is angry with men or with "male" culture—either for personal reasons or for larger social reasons (i.e., because men still do not share their social and political power equally with women).

In fact, anger against men is the most *verboten* feeling a woman can have. A woman who says she is angry at men, or, even more, at "male" culture or the "male" system, is frequently labeled a "crazy lady," a "man-hater," or "hysterical," "needing a psychologist," and so on. To be seen as freaks, being made outcasts or pariahs, is the unspoken threat to which so many women react by saying—as one sees frequently in magazine articles, etc., when women worry they cannot keep up with all that is expected of them, i.e., maintain their looks, make men desire them and now, earn money too—that they fear their

---

*Statistically, in the United States twice as many women go to psychiatrists, psychologists, and counselors as men; this figure has not changed since the 1950s, despite monumental feminist works, including "Psychology Constructs the Female" by Naomi Weisstein, works by Shulamith Firestone, and *Women and Madness* by Phyllis Chesler.

In the 1880s, Freud gave his fiancée cocaine for her "nerves." Perhaps it was Freud himself, or her position in the general society with its limitations for her, that gave her "nerves." Also, in Spanish culture women are well known for having *"nervios"*; in our own, as noted, women are by far the largest consumers of tranquilizers, so that it could be said that a large percentage of the female population is chemically pacified.

fate will be to become a "bag lady." Even though we joke about this, it is significant: we wonder if there is really a place in society for us, especially as older women. We cannot afford *psychologically* to be mad at men, because we fear we may wind up as outcasts.

Women's way of fighting: non-violent resistance

While the initial impulse might be to say, well, why don't women get even with men? revolt?—the matter is more complicated than that. Women don't take violent revenge on individual men (or society) because not to do so is in accord with their most basic values.

Most women, as we have seen, do not believe in fighting back on men's terms (although they could—i.e., be cold and distant, less interested in "hearing" and understanding the other person, or on a larger level, undertake terroristic actions to influence government policy, etc.); most feel it would be unethical to fight men "male" style, beneath them. Instead, most prefer a stance of non-violent resistance, for which they deserve respect. However, some would not give women credit but put women down as not "smart," as too "stupid" to fight and get their own way—saying that women are "peaceful" only because they are afraid or have been "brainwashed" not to fight back. But women do fight back in arguments, and stand up for themselves, as seen; and increasingly they fight back by leaving unsatisfying relationships: 90 percent of the high number of divorces in the United States are initiated and carried through by women.

Is not fighting a basic "female" value because this is what women have been taught?* Or because women believe in these values? Women have tried, during the last ten to twenty years, to take on new values, i.e., women have experimented with not connecting love and sex, with repressing their emotions, and with taking jobs out of the home. The only values of the recent years of experimentation they seem to have taken firmly to heart are those of independence defined as having jobs, incomes of their own (see Chapter 10), and as being able to express oneself, be complete, a person in one's own right, not only as attached to a man. But women seem to have firmly rejected the "male" culture's belief in expressing less love in personal life. And when they fail to convince men they love to join them in *their* value system, they are likely to begin expressing nurturing and enthusiasm for their work and for their friends—nurturing and enthusiasm that were once reserved for their husbands and families.

*And taught by whom? taught by a "social structure" which would deform them? or by an historic tradition handed down by their mothers, aunts, grandmothers, and so on? This poses interesting questions not yet adequately addressed in the literature.

Men should not fear women's anger; they should welcome it

Men should not fear women's anger. After all, it is right to express anger at injustice. If we state clearly what the problems are, then we have a chance to think clearly about strategies for change. For men to simply ignore the problem of the status of women in society, and/or problems in relationships, or think of them as "women's issues" and turn their attention to other matters, rather than making an effort to do something about the situation, will only make the problem worse. This is the same phenomenon as seen in Chapter 2 writ large: women "bring up issues," and men fall silent, hoping the "problem" will go away—which only makes women angrier and the problem worse. It could be said that women's so-called passive nature is just a screen for women's fury* —which is channeled in the wrong direction (against women) but could turn to become a positive force for society.

But it is not only anger women are expressing here: what we hear woman after woman describe is a mixture of anger and sadness: anger and frustration at not being able to get through to a man with their love, their hearts, their *selves;* and sadness that most men just will not see what is happening, so that women watch as the love fades and the dreams slowly die.

Do Women "Love Too Much"? Or Do Men Love Too Little?

Women's belief in giving and nurturing is very controversial. Women have been criticized in recent years, first by some in the women's movement and later by "advice books," for being "too loving," too giving, too nurturing, obsessed with "romance." The theory has been that women rely too much on love for their fulfillment in life, that women "cling" because they are brought up to be psychologically "dependent," even that women are "crippled" psychologically (!). If women would only give up these behaviors and stop loving "too much," be more "like men," they would find that they would be happier, they wouldn't have so many problems with love.

Women have a lot to say about this, and in fact are in the midst of an important, historic debate within themselves about it, as we see throughout this book. In particular, individual women everywhere now are engaged in redefin-

---

*As the acceptance of Freudian "explanations" of women's nature at the turn of the century was a way of "explaining away" the women's movement of that time, according to Shulamith Firestone in *The Dialectic of Sex.*

ing love for themselves. What they are struggling with is one of the most important issues of our times: how to love, how to restore feeling and emotionality to life, while not letting oneself be done in by those who would take advantage of a person who is less aggressive, more nurturing and giving.

Many women in this study express anger at the ridicule so often addressed to them for their interest in love: instead of women loving less, women ask, why can't men love more, be more emotionally supportive and involved? Why must it always be *women* who change? And what kinds of love are we talking about anyway?

Is it women's values which should change— or men's?

There are many assumptions about acceptable behavior in the traditional emotional contract. The one most frequently noted is that women's role is to be loving and "mothering," non-"demanding." Less frequently noted is the role that the ideology gives to men: that of being "dominant," of "starring" in relationships, and of being the active "doers" in charge of the world. These assumptions are built into the culture—into language and psychological theories and philosophy—and are based on an underlying set of beliefs which we call here the "male" ideology.

If women want to love men, but men have little practice in loving in the sense that women mean (nor are most men busily engaged in trying to cultivate these characteristics in themselves), then women's desire to have equal, noncompetitive, nurturing relationships puts women in an awkward position. The advice that is often being offered to them now as to how to relieve their "discomfort" is to stop loving so much.

Should women stop loving "too much" (if you can't beat 'em, join 'em)—or do women now expect men to change and become more loving?

A New View of "Female Psychology": Goodbye to Freud and Assorted Others

If women feel "needy" and "insecure," looking for reassurances that men love them, it is said that this is a sign of women's "biological" character or of some innate fear of "being left," resulting from the fact that they get pregnant and "must" have a man to take care of them at this vulnerable time.* But are not

---

*This is often "supported" on "biological" grounds: that is, since women become pregnant and need men to take care of them, they are somehow hormonally, psychologically disposed to being "dependent" on men. Logic of nature is "unarguable" according to its adherents. However, one could argue that if society

women's feelings a logical reaction to the fact that many men are treating women as if they indeed do *not* love them, no matter what they say—at least not according to women's definition of love?

If a woman complains of bad treatment from a man (and it is always part-time bad treatment, not full-time, which adds to the confusion), she is apt to be told she is a "masochist," and she must "like it"—i.e., "if you don't like it, why do you stay and take it?" But this is "blaming the victim": for a social structure in which women have been brought up and are still brought up to make love the wellspring of their identity in life, to then put down women for being "too focused on love," "obsessed with love," and so on is astonishing. Women are being blamed for doing what the social situation asks of them.

And women do this in the confusing context of having to love individually those of a "superior" group socially: men. In other words, women are told to focus love on a group—men—whose status is "above" their own. Being told they should love people of a "superior" group automatically proposes that women be "martyrs," in that they must give to those who do not give as much back, those who do not spend time changing society to make women's status equal.

This makes the labeling of women as "masochistic" particularly ironic and even sadistic: women are told to love men, who (as a group) are "above" them, then told to endure men's condescending or superior behavior (because men "don't mean it," and "really love you")—and when women do this, and still keep on loving, they are rewarded by being called "masochistic"! And so women are told it is their own fault if their status in society doesn't change: "Why don't you change it if you don't like it?," they are taunted, aggressively. These are baiting remarks.

Perhaps another way to look at women's and men's situation would be in terms of a family in which there are two young children who have a fight. One hits the other, who begins crying. Now the family has the option of labeling the second one a "crybaby" or the first one "mean" and "aggressive."

In our society/family, men are constantly being psychologically aggressive with women, but rarely are men called to account for this: instead, society criticizes women for being "too emotional," too easily upset, too needful of reassurances of love, too obsessed with "romance." People rarely think to criticize the man involved, to try to get him to change, because our mind-set is focused on women as "the problem child," the "problem gender." And so women live with the frustration of an unfair social setup, finding that they can only really talk to one another about it.

---

were constructed differently (as it has been in many times and places), maternal clans, mothers, uncles and brothers, female lovers and friends, could protect pregnant women, and later the baby, as they have done and do in some societies—and to a great extent, even in our own.

Culture creates psychology*

The standard understanding of women's psychology is thus inaccurate, and standard judgments of women by the "male" system are wrong—or lacking in subtlety, to say the least. Certainly the 4,500 women here express better than Freud who women are.†

The "male" ideological structure (since it is the dominant ideology) extends into the farthest recesses of the psyches of both women and men, as seen here and in the previous study on men. Women who want to love are all too often forced into compromise after compromise with a culture that sees them as emotionally inferior or "different." Furthermore they must overlook this time and again, appear not to see how they come second, how their thoughts and points of view are disregarded—or even receive no attention at all, being perceived by men as less important than work, friends, football on TV, and so on. For their patience, they are frequently seen as "wimps" or "martyrs," as "non-assertive," "easy," and so on.

A woman faced with a daily lack of communication and lack of respect often feels a loss of dignity: she is placed in a position of having to choose either leaving the relationship and being "alone" (but is one more alone?) or staying and living with this pattern of subtle belittling and condescension. The outward symptom of her inner struggle to maintain dignity and self-respect is usually bickering and small daily hostilities, silences—or feeling emotionally "insecure." But although bickering can be "normal" in human relationships, in our world it is more frequent and bitter than need be, because female-male relationships are "political"—i.e., the stereotyped way of seeing female psychology is to see women as "emotionally unstable" or "irrational" and to give women less credibility, place them constantly on the defensive and in a secondary role.

How does the psychological position women are put in by "male" behavior patterns seen in this section relate to so-called normal behavior? By the terms of traditional "social science," if the majority of people display certain feelings, this makes those feelings "normal behavior" in that group, and therefore "how

---

*Bruno Bettelheim, in his writing on concentration camps during World War II, showed clearly that psychology can change within days of a person's being placed in a totally new environment with a totally new set of rules—i.e., people who were proud became humble and fearful, and so on. Thus, while childhood upbringing is important, even more important is the constant cultural messages we are all receiving all the time about "who we are."
†Women's behavior in love relationships has long been interpreted by "studies" done from a "male" ideological perspective. As Simone de Beauvoir explained in 1984, "Although I admire Freud . . . I find that in the case of women, as he said himself, there's a dark continent; he understood nothing of what women want. Anyone who wants to work on women has to break completely with Freud. (Interview by Helene Wenzel, published in The Women's Review of Books, July 1985.)

people/women are"—i.e., if women love "men who hurt them," women are "masochists."

And yet, if one takes a historical and philosophical perspective, one can see these behaviors quite another way—i.e., as logical responses to the specific cultural setup. Indeed, if we are to lift ourselves out of the forest, to see our alternatives, to understand, have visions and make plans, we must take this broader perspective, see the current situation between women and men as only the creation of the larger overall ideology or set of beliefs—the "male ideology." (We will discuss this belief system in more detail in Part V.)

Standard theories of women's psychology are wrong

Women's statements and descriptions of their experiences here have clear and pressing implications: changes in the way women are seen should be immediate. Women must no longer be "defined" and "judged" through the lens of a culture which for centuries has barely seen them as "second-class" psychologically, certainly as less than the standard of "normality." Data must be looked at from a new standpoint. The myriad findings and statements here from women's testimony (and there are other women scholars engaged in this work) present the field of psychology with a wealth of basic new information— information which must be seen in terms of a new philosophy. Psychology currently has little vocabulary which can encompass the real form of women's thinking and psychology: it is, in general, very unfamiliar with women's culture, and should begin immediately to try to familiarize itself with the literature of this different cultural perspective.

Men's double message to women, not women's "lack of self-esteem," makes women feel "insecure"

The "psychology of women," women's "human nature," is not inherently passive, "martyrish," "masochistic," complaining, and so on—but these characteristics, when they occur, are usually part of the logical reaction of an individual to the subliminal attacks of the "male" ideology.

If men withhold equal companionship with women, distance themselves emotionally (the one less vulnerable has more power . . .); and if men aggressively harass and trivialize women in relationships, and then turn to those same women looking for love, affection, and understanding, believing that the women should "be there" for them (as well as provide domestic services such as cooking and housekeeping)—what effect must this have on women?

What effect would such contradictory behavior have on anyone? That is, how *should* we react to being with someone who, on the one hand, frequently acts emotionally distant and inaccessible, even ridiculing you or not listening—and then, on the other, at times turns to you expecting love and affection, saying he loves you?

If a woman loves a man, and he says he loves her (even though exhibiting the two-sided behavior just described), she may feel off balance and disoriented—though probably she will want to stay and "make it work." But which is the "real" other person? she may wonder. The one who loves her, or the one who is distant and ridiculing? How can she break through that distance when it occurs to the "good parts"? So she tries to "bring up the issues," and keeps on trying, but often goes through an agony of frustration at the cruelty and emotional coldness she encounters along the way.

A note on the popular epithet, "Women lack self-esteem"

Do women, as is so often heard, have "low self-esteem"—or is this to "blame the victim"?

In fact, women are doing quite well, considering all the propaganda coming their way that they aren't worth as much as men. But there is great social pressure on women to prove this "self-esteem" by becoming as aggressive and aloof as many men. One woman's statement portrays this new equation of aggressiveness with having a sense of self: "It seems to me that many women—myself included—don't have the sense of self that men are trained to have. Men don't have to feel badly if they hurt someone; they are supposed to beat up other people, in a way—even their mothers probably told them, 'Go back to the schoolyard and beat him up, whoever gives you a hard time,' and are always pushed to win in all competitions. This makes for the difference in women's rules and men's rules."

But do women really undervalue themselves as much as is popularly suggested—or is it just that women refuse to behave aggressively and give up their beliefs in nurturing and loving as the right and proper ways to be, still hoping that men will join their system, and learn how to be more nurturing too?

Most women do, as we have seen, try harder to make relationships work; indeed, they stay even in the face of the most adverse circumstances. Then they may be put down for this! (They are also put down for leaving.) But isn't this loyalty admirable? Isn't this what men should be doing too—i.e., putting more effort into understanding and caring for the other person, even when the other seems to be going through some sort of unintelligible hard time? Trying to draw that person out, helping, "being there" emotionally, listening, and giving feedback are what one needs then in a friend—and in those one loves.

It is "blaming the victim" for a society that has brought up and still brings up women to focus on love as their basic goal and self-definition, their basic identity (especially with women still under economic pressure), to then put women down for being "too focused on love," "obsessed with love," and so on. This is even more pointedly true when, as in our culture, women are told to focus that love on a group—men—whose status is "above" their own.

What women are going to do about this situation of unequal relationships is the subject of most women's daily inner struggles with how to deal with men and love—as we are seeing here. This is a political struggle. Women, as they are now more and more clearly seeing and naming their situation, are pitting themselves against the entire "male" system—even while still loving men: they are on the threshold of deciding whether to "give up on love" and take on "male" values or to rework their own system, with its greater focus on human warmth and understanding, and try to infuse the culture with its spirit—i.e., change the world.

Wondering Whether to Leave: Is the Love We Want Only a Dream?

"What is there to do? Last night, whilst I was out, my 'friend' (my lover) called, very distressed apparently about the distance that has developed between us. I am distressed too. But the closeness of the relationship would only be possible for me if he was to change. If I would try to carry the relationship, accepting him as he is, I would explode with indignation, take revenge on him for everything that I had accepted in demure affection for the sake of the truly wonderful moments we are able to share. That way I would eventually kill the potential of these moments happening between us. Then I would have to withdraw because there would be nothing to stay for. So, to preserve what I love I must withdraw now.

"I must withdraw for the sake of my belief in a real—or what I call real—relationship, because I must grow more and more to become myself to be able to respond to other people with all my potential, if I want to have a chance to meet the person with equality—if ever I should meet the person with whom it is possible to fulfill my belief. I believe you have to learn to treasure all you have and not go beyond the line of what you honestly can treasure. If that means that I have to live more remote from another human being than I wish to do, then that is the better pain to take into the future."

Giving up on love: leaving the system behind emotionally and intellectually

"Every time we make up, the relationship that's left is a smaller island than what we had before, because the thing we fought about was never resolved. So we make up, but it's becoming a smaller and smaller thing that we have together. You see what I mean?"

Although, as seen, 84 percent of women say that they believe love relationships should *come first in life, 74 percent also say that their current relationship is* not *the center of their lives—that they have given up on trying to make their own current relationship/marriage their primary focus:*

"This relationship has been peripheral for four to five years because he refuses to accept changes in me as I grow. I would leave it if I earned more money."

"This relationship helps to sustain me and gives me strength to cope with daily life. I wouldn't say it's the center of my life. I am the center of my life. I'd leave if I were financially independent."

"There was a time in my life, as recently as five years ago, when I would just drop anything for the man in my life at the time. I would put female friendship 'on hold,' participate in his interests rather than mine, see his friends, etc. I don't do that anymore. The relationships I have now are more a *part* of my life than my entire life."

"My marriage relationship is very important to me, but not the center. I'm not sure why. I do like the companionship my husband offers. But if the children were grown and I was offered a grand job somewhere away from home, I might very well take it."

"My life is padded by the relationship, it is not my life."

"Men are very important, but no man can be the sole purpose in my life anymore. I can no longer value myself only through a man's eyes. I like me, I love people and doubt I'd be as content if I didn't love these men—but my children come first, then my career, and finally love."

"The way I wish to share my life at this point is with total lovingness, but not directed toward a man. I have learned after a few 'love affairs' that I have too much in me to play games."

"Love is really important only if it's deep and if they are in love back and you share things. Otherwise, you can turn to completely new interests and find other parts of life fulfilling."

"I've always put love relationships first, which is why I got myself into so much trouble. Now I've decided to give up on them and focus on other stuff, so there will be somebody there (MYSELF) when or if the right one comes along."

Some women express great disappointment and anger:

"I have given up on love relationships. I basically believe in love, but men have lied so much to me that I feel it's best I live my own life."

"I decided somewhere along the way that love relationships aren't worth the trouble. I have a fling now and then, but make a point of never getting too serious."

"I decided that I was brought up in a dream world when it comes to love relationships. They are great but not what I base my life on."

"After being dumped time after time, I just felt it wasn't worth the time and energy anymore, when I was always the one getting hurt."

"My own development is now much more important to me than worrying about developing a relationship. I feel like I have always done my part and more in developing relationships, but it has not been reciprocal and I'm not willing to carry someone else's load. If I socialize with a man, he will have to work to keep the relationship up as much as me—and if it would be a lot of work, I would probably bow out and put my energies to something that showed better results. I am not dependent on having a relationship and therefore I'm not willing to deplete myself to hold one together."

Only 19 percent of women say that their relationship actually does come first in their lives:

"When my husband suffered a stroke, the reality of his mortality (and my own) really hit me between the eyes. I know I'd get along if he died, but a big part of me would die with him. My work and my children are important, but not as important to me as he is."

"Our relationship is very much the center of my life—although it is lacking a lot of little things. If I wasn't with him, I don't know what I'd *do*. If he walked out on me and never wanted to see me, I would beg or do anything to get him back."

"My whole life revolves around this man and my children. My job is eight hours. He's twenty-four hours in my mind. He makes the world go around. Get upset with him, my job does not go well. That's hard, as I work with the public. I have not let anyone this close to me for a long time. He can make my day, or he can turn it all very dark by what he says."

"My relationship with my husband is central to my life. I think I have been able to take risks with other people, especially with other men, because I feel a basic sense of security at home."

And one woman says interestingly—and unusually:

"This relationship is central to my growth as a woman."

*In fact, 34 percent of women now say that they believe that love relationships
need not be "number one" in life for happiness—and some question whether a
relationship is necessary at all:*

"After my husband left, I made a commitment to myself not to get emotionally involved for a while, feeling a need to tune back into myself, get to know
myself again. I love a good love affair but can live without it."

"A love relationship is a wonderful thing when it exists, and we are richer
for having it. But right now, truly alone for the first time in years (as my
younger daughter has also 'left the nest'), I feel more a complete person than
ever before."

"A love relationship is not all that important if it is not with the 'right'
person. Life can be satisfying and rewarding without a man—especially a man
I don't respect."

"My work is by far the single most important thing in my life. And I think
that's good. No one should have the kind of power over someone that I let my
husband have over me."

"Relationships are nice, but work and my life come first. It is one year now
since I have had a relationship. I am taking care of my needs, not catering to
someone else's. I don't think one needs a steady love relationship to have a
rewarding life."

"Love is very important to me, but not the most important thing in my life.
Having another person in my life makes me feel wonderful, but I am complete
as is."

*26 percent of women are trying to look with more interest at other parts of life,
and not to focus so strongly on men and love relationships:*

"I still think that what I want most out of life is a 'happy ever after' with
another person. But I accept the notion that it might never happen, and I now
put a commitment into other aspects of my life that went before entirely into
agonizing over relationships."

"After this marriage, I've decided to look around at what else life has to
offer. I've missed out on a lot because I've wrapped myself up too much in my
love life."

"There is a great freedom in being uninvolved sexually—a great sense of
power or personal achievement not to continue in behaviors that everyone
takes for granted, but which actually lead to such misery. I am unattached and
am liking this situation better with each passing year."

One young woman in college explains how she came to this conclusion:

"When I lived with George I already had a good job, my working was essential (someone had to buy groceries). He did some cooking but rarely cleaned up around the apartment (though he always thought he was a firm believer in equal rights). He never really did treat me as an equal, full-blown human being—contrary to his claims of Mr. Equality. There were several times he would treat me as an inferior, even with my knowledge and accomplishments—like he did make a lot of decisions on his own, then wouldn't tell me what was going on. I would find out either accidentally or through the grapevine. He did act superior quite often.

"Once I let myself be partially financially dependent on him when we lived together; this did turn into an immense problem because he couldn't be trusted to pay rent without bouncing a check or borrowing more money from me. He didn't know how to manage money. Now I feel I should've always trusted myself—I was doing just fine before him. It affected the relationship in a straining way for both of us and caused tension to mount.

"Finally, I had to change my priorities about the relationship. At first, school and George were both #1 in my life. I didn't realize my priorities should be different until he mentioned that school was #1 and always had been for him. I decided then that I would always have school, if not George. After that, I put my college education first."

14 percent of women are against making a relationship with a man the center of their lives, as a matter of principle:

"This relationship is important to me but not the center of my life. I don't think it is positive to have a relationship as the central feature of one's life. I've done this in the past, and when they end it can be devastating. I'm working on making a better relationship with myself—balancing my needs with the needs of others. Sometimes relationships in my past became abusive to the point where the drain was so great that I could never imagine how to recoup the energy."

"Most of the time I think romance is bullshit and only keeps women down. It's like a pressure center that you want to keep pressing. It's based in escape from reality."

Sometimes women are apologetic for making love "too important":

"I am afraid that the relationship I have with my love controls a large part of my life. It is too important, but I can't seem to help that.

"I tend to want a new relationship soon or right away after breaking up with someone. I feel this is a problem, needing to have a man in order to feel normal, secure; not being able to accept the love of friends as enough reassurance that I am good and lovable. But I would like to find a man to fall in love with who could respect and appreciate me."

The issue of the importance of love relationships is clearly quite complex—not something one can always decide on a purely "logical" basis:

"I feel secure in the knowledge that I can function without a relationship, but I feel hungry for attention and affection when by myself."

"I separated, eagerly seeking myself. Since the divorce, I have had a deep depression. I am now somewhat frustrated and lonely, glad for strong friendships."

"Most of my life I just believed that a girl should be with someone. That was how you got your identity—so-and-so's girlfriend. Now I don't know—being so attached to someone, overwhelmingly so, seems to work out just the opposite of how it should."

Some women say that although they want to accept the idea that friendship and time for oneself are just as important as love relationships with men, they can't:

"I love that warm feeling when they hold you, the admiration, appreciation. From women you get understanding—but it's not enough."

But a large number of women, 59 percent, are very consciously thinking through and rejecting the male-love-self-esteem-and-approval ideas they had before:

"It used to be I just felt I should have boyfriends—and never questioned this continuing search for them. I wasted so many years of my life trying to get a boyfriend and feeling inadequate about not having one. I hope I can help my sister avoid spending too much time worrying about this too."

"I find when I'm with someone, I get used to walking down the street with the 'protection' of a man. When I realize that, I get angry with myself. Being with a man protects you from the hassles you get being alone—but I get angry (not only at myself) at society for perpetuating this situation."

"I cannot reiterate enough how good it was for me to enter into a period of celibacy to find myself. Now I do not in any way feel desperate—though I am delighted to be in a loving relationship with my lover. Any woman who begins to feel desperate should forget about men for a while—live alone, get to know herself, develop her sense of self."

"I have made a conscious choice to overcome my need of romantic emotional involvement. I am presently on a long sabbatical from social and sexual relations with men. I decided that there was something drastically wrong with relationships and that I would stand on neutral ground and try to figure it out . . . I think I have not known what I am or my capability, and I have sought affirmation from sources outside myself, especially in the emotional realm where men are concerned. I believe my friendships are better."

"Men don't really have anything that we absolutely need. But we have been made psychologically dependent on them. That psychological dependence can be overcome, but not easily. There are many things that women offer that men (at this point in time) can't give me. Empathy is one of them. Women seem to understand where I'm coming from. There is an unspoken knowledge of something only women understand. I can't really explain it."

"Love is a problem for most women because they put so much energy into it and get so little in return. I used to feel emotionally dependent on men. Now I don't really care about men, but my relationships with women still take on this 'clinging' quality. At least with women it is better received."

"Being single, you have the opportunity to, in fact, change the world—as male thinking patterns are quite stuck and it is difficult to debrief yourself while involved with them. You have no one controlling or discounting you as a single—hopefully, anyway. Your life is more flexible. The disadvantages, I think, mainly rest in one's security and affirmation needs.

"At their present stage of development, women are more defined by love relationships than men. Women want to be substantiated because this is an area of poverty for women—they don't usually substantiate themselves adequately, so they look for affirmation from the power group. On the other hand, men need women as a buffer to the awful world they have made—and in that respect, need women more. They cannot get very good caring from other men and they like to have us as satellites revolving round them to supply their wants."

As we will see, especially in Part III, many women lead double lives. In order to be themselves in marriage or love relationships, they find they must develop *two* selves—one for their husband or lover, to make the man in their life happy and keep the peace, take care of their family, and the other to express and stay in touch with other parts of themselves. As so many women have been saying in various ways, "It is easy for me to *act* loving, and take care of others. The difficulty comes in being able to be loving and keep something of myself at the same time."

For a long time now, women have been partitioning off different aspects of themselves to buy time in their relationships—but women are growing increasingly frustrated and dissatisfied with the kind of life this creates. And, with growing economic independence, many are thinking hard about what they want for their future.

Relationships: Are they still the center of most women's lives?

What women are saying here contrasts strikingly with the results of studies of twenty-five years ago,* in which women definitely saw their relationships *as* their lives—i.e., the famous study wherein, when women and men were asked to draw a circle symbolizing their relationship and then another circle designating themselves, women's drawings looked like this:

And men's like this:

SELF   RELATIONSHIP

SELF   RELATIONSHIP

That is, women almost always drew themselves inside or partially inside the larger circle of the relationship, while men drew two equal and non-touching circles. Many psychological studies of women done between 1950 and 1975 showed the same result: women then placed their love relationships at the center of their lives, defining themselves as a part of a relationship, a subsidiary of it, or at least peripheral.

Thus, what we are seeing here is a new phenomenon, a new definition by women of themselves. Many women are coming to the conclusion that they can no longer emotionally afford to put love relationships first in their lives—although this is not what they would want, and, indeed, most feel they are being forced to come to this decision.

Women are leaving relationships with men emotionally—while still sometimes trying to make it all work—not because they want to separate themselves, but because they find themselves mentally arriving at a new place, on a different wavelength from the men they live with. They may still truly love a man, but see him as if from another star, another planet. Even if they wish to stay, if they have tried and thought and thought about the relationship, wondering how to break through—don't get through, they feel alienated. How can they help it? They cannot will themselves not to know what they do now know, all that they have learned in their weeks and months of trying to understand what is interfering with their love relationships.

*See *Sociometry and the Science of Man*, ed. J.L. Moreno. (Beacon, NY: Beacon House, 1956), and also *Sociometry, A Journal of Interpersonal Relations*, vols. 15–18 (Beacon, NY: Beacon House). This journal later became the *American Sociological Association Journal of Personality and Social Development*.

Women Are Changing the Emotional Structure of Their Lives from What It Has Been for Generations

Women are in the midst of a dramatic shift. While most women say that, *theoretically,* love should be the most important part of life, most women (both married and single) also say that *their* love relationship is not the center of *their* life. The majority of women also say that they are still hoping they will have a greater, deeper, better love "yet to come." And so it seems that women now are very ambivalent: most want a deep love relationship and think it should be the most important thing in life; however, most have found it almost impossible to get love to work the way they *want.* Most women find they have to face a daily stream of identity-challenging behaviors from the men in their lives; increasingly they are solving this dilemma by reordering their priorities and making love with men less important than before.

If women say they can no longer emotionally afford to put love relationships with men first in their lives, does this mean that women, in "giving up on love," are taking on "male" values? Have we decided that the "male" model is right in its tradition of making love only part of life, less important than work, career, identity, pride in "being a man"? Or are women keeping their belief in love, just putting their hopes for this with men away for a while, protecting themselves until such time as the men in their lives can relate as equals to them?

Many women are creating a third alternative: they say love can continue to be the basis of one's value system, but its object can be changed. Many women are diversifying their love, still believing in love, but finding other objects to exchange it with, such as friends, children, lovers—even embellishing their work, and the people they come in contact with, with more caring and loving. Though women may be sad not to have the degree of closeness and intimacy with men that they would like, and some are giving up on *ever* having it, and look back with deep regret and longing, many also definitely relish this new diversity, with its new opportunities.

CONCLUSION

A Conflict of Two Cultures:
Women's View of Love
as Part of a Separate Culture
and Value System

Love is eroded and lost so frequently, after the first beautiful feelings. Why?

Reading what women have said in these three chapters—despite the sense of humor and strength in so many of their statements—leaves one with a very poignant feeling; why does it often have to be so hard? Many women say they are emotionally worn out from all of this—but almost all still want to try, to keep searching, to make it work. Is this because love is a basic human hunger? Or are women brought up to focus so much on men's love as "their destiny" that no matter what their experiences with men, they still believe they must find a way for this dream to work? That other dreams are not as valid?

It is ironic that the place women are going for love, to get love, is the very place from which getting it is hardest, according to women—because of the way men in this culture are conditioned, what "masculinity" means. As woman after woman struggles to draw a man out, to develop emotional companionship, she finds that for every two steps forward, she goes one step back. Although sometimes, while lying in bed at night, she and her husband or lover may break through and talk, the next day the atmosphere often returns to a silent ambiguity.

But it is not women or the dream that is wrong; it is the cultural context which makes love and relationships with women such a threatening and confusing area for men.

The "Male" Ideology* and the
Slow Erosion of Love

Over and over, women of all ages express their increasing emotional frustration and gradual disillusionment with their personal relationships with men:

"I am fighting with him all the time to preserve our relationship. He is happier when I never bring anything up. But if I don't, *I* feel unhappy, because emotional issues are never discussed—and I feel isolated, at a distance, alone. If we can't really be together, I'd rather leave the relationship. He probably doesn't realize this, because when I try to discuss things, he acts very put upon and martyred, or bitchy—certainly he shows no serious attempt to listen (although I am always there for him). He just seems to want to get any discussion over as quickly as possible, saying as little as possible. But later, when he's ready to cuddle in bed and have sex, he doesn't expect me to be distant because of his previous attitude. He doesn't realize it's all connected for me—wanting to have sex is, for me, connected to our warmth and closeness."

"If I tell him there's something he is doing that's bothering me, he'll say, 'Well, that's just the way I am.' But if he doesn't like something about *me*, I'm supposed to change. Then I worry about it a lot, trying to figure out if he's right, if there's something wrong with me. I spend a lot of energy trying to keep track of the relationship—knowing what kind of a mood he's in, asking him how he is feeling, keep things going, in touch. I know he loves me, but he just doesn't seem to have the same needs—he'll rarely ask me about the same things. When I try to explain this, he doesn't understand what 'the problem' is."

"To me, being involved with another person means asking them about things they have expressed concern over, giving them a chance to talk about things they are wondering about, being *with* them emotionally, to toss around whatever's on their mind that day, if they're worried or if they're excited about something. My friends and I do this all the time, but my husband never seems to do this with me. When I ask him, finally, to ask me how I'm feeling about something I've told him about, it is like pulling teeth to get him to do it even a little bit. And he never brings up the things later that I said were on my mind. It's so frustrating. He often tells me he loves me, and I believe he does, but why isn't he more interested in what's on my mind?"

This study shows widespread dissatisfaction among women about their love relationships. Most women are not in love relationships they consider to be

*In this book, the "male" ideology (as "women's" culture) always refers to an historically built-up cultural system—not to biological or innate characteristics which every man must have.

anywhere near what they would like. Ninety-five percent of the married women in this study want to make basic changes in their marriages, and 84 percent of single women say that love relationships with men are more often than not filled with anxiety, fear of being "un-cool" (by wanting commitment), and so on. Woman after woman says she is putting enormous amounts of energy into trying to make her relationship work—but that the man doesn't seem to be putting in the same effort. This makes women even more alienated, frustrated, and often angry.

Many women lie in bed at night, knowing things could be so much better, wondering how to reach the man sleeping next to them, or wondering why a man they love doesn't call—or how to get out of a relationship although they can't really explain just why they don't like it. So many women lie there thinking, "It's too bad that things are like this. . . . Why can't they change?"

Women have been "complaining" about love relationships for some time, at least since Freud, but these complaints have rarely been taken seriously. What women say is going on has rarely been given full credibility, instead being discounted all too often as "women bitching and moaning" and so on. Society blames women's feelings of frustration with men on women's "psychology"—not on the fact that most women have a legitimate complaint, i.e., that they live with discrimination, even in love relationships.

It is usually implied that if a woman is having problems, the problem is with the *woman*—with her outdated values, "demanding" behaviors, "neediness," upbringing, "dependency," and so forth. Women daily hear themselves referred to as "messed up," "masochistic," or "neurotic" if they step the least bit out of line, and some part of them wonders if it could be true. They wonder, "Do I send out vibrations that attract the 'wrong men,' " or they fault themselves for not recognizing or disengaging quickly enough from "destructive" relationships. Alternately, women worry that they may not be patient *enough*, understanding enough, expect too much, are too "idealistic." But are women really doing something wrong?

The Emotional Contract: Injustice Built into the System

We have seen women here paint a picture of widespread gender stereotyping and condescension to women—even in their most intimate moments with men they love, which makes the impact even more devastating. The dynamics of this situation in personal life have been only cloudily seen up to now, perhaps for lack of the kind of massive documentation provided here—documentation that is an indictment of the traditional gender system with its unfair emotional "contract." That contract (the still-not-eradicated psychological counterpart of the centuries-long legal domination of women by men) exploits women emotionally while not even acknowledging that this is going on, insisting that women who "complain" have "complexes," not real problems created by a real social ideology which is negative to women. There is not "something wrong" with women—women don't have a "problem," a "bad attitude"—but there *is* a problem in the society: that is, the attitudes of the dominant "male"-oriented viewpoint (especially as sanctified by much "psychological theory") toward women as a class.

Women are engaged in profound questioning about how they can go on living with this situation, what to do about it. Their choices seem to be: leave the relationship/marriage, keep struggling to "get him to see," or tune out, become less emotionally involved, i.e., take on "male" values in love relationships.

If women have different beliefs about what a relationship should be, are operating on different premises and define their priorities differently from most men, then it is obvious that a struggle is likely to ensue eventually in most relationships. We have heard women state that most men don't believe in such behaviors as empathic listening: trying to understand without judging and being emotionally supportive are basic to what having a relationship means; at least they do not offer these things. Instead, most women say men seem rather to think of a relationship in terms of "being there," with the man "of course" psychologically dominant (although most men would be quick to say that they do not *intend* to dominate women they love). Listening empathically, drawing the woman out, supporting her projects are not first priorities in most men's definition of relationships. Though both women and men at least do agree that physical affection is a number-one priority, in most other ways their value-systems differ. (In Part II we will see another manifestation of these differences: most women say that men do not connect sex with love relationships the way women want to, and also that men do not see why having a fight should get "in the way" of having sex.)

Most women are surprised when men don't respond with fairness in a relationship, follow the general rules of give and take, and most are even more surprised when a man begins to use a relationship for his own emotional support, not seeing (even when it is pointed out to him) that he is getting this but not giving it back. The problem is that many men have a double standard for their behavior with women and their behavior with the rest of society: since women are "less" or the "other," the same rules, many men unconsciously believe, do not apply. And as the pattern of men's unwitting gestures of inequality, followed by women's "bringing up the issues," which in turn is often greeted with gender-stereotyped remarks, continues, women become more and more dissatisfied, and begin to disrespect men, since it is difficult to respect someone who is unfair.

Why is this so? Why do men and women have such different ideas about relationships? Why does men's value system see love as something a "real man" wouldn't take as seriously as his job, his "honor as a man," and so on?

"Women's" Culture and "Men's" Culture: Two Worlds

Women and men really live in two different worlds, with two interlocking sets of values. In the personal sphere, these values work out to mean that women nourish men, while men believe they have no duty to nourish but only to *be*, to achieve. Men generally expect the world to want and value them for *themselves* and for their work.

These semi-articulated beliefs (seen not as "beliefs" but as "how things are") have been built into theories of behavior, psychology, "human nature," religion, etc., over several thousand years, until they seem "obvious"—and trying to find the language for unraveling the assumptions is like Alice trying to walk through the Looking Glass.

Historically, the situation is now volatile: with most women working outside the home as well as in, the two value systems are in conflict, as men apply the values of competing and winning to relationships (in and out of marriage)* and women wonder whether (as with the idea of wearing male-type business suits) they should adopt "male" values in love too, give love a lesser place in their world than they often want to do (for example, not "insist" on connecting sex with love). The weight of society is on the side of women adopting "male" values, since these form the dominant culture: men are the "standard of reality," the reality-testing point.

In other words, the problems between women and men in personal relationships have not been overcome because there is a cultural conflict going on.

The two cultures:† a historical tradition or a biological given?

If women have a separate "sub"-culture, is it based on biological difference, or historical tradition?

---

*Karl Marx predicted that in a capitalist society the values of the marketplace would eventually penetrate everything, even personal life.
†For other discussions of whether or not there are "two cultures," or depictions of "woman's voice," see the works of Jesse Bernard, Joan Scott, Mary Daly, Carroll Smith-Rosenberg, Carol Gilligan, Elizabeth Petroff, and others included in the bibliography. Certainly a well-developed "female" culture and value-system is implicit in what the majority of women are saying in this study, and in women's and men's statements in the two previous Hite Reports.

There is no need to posit a biological difference between "male" and "female" "human nature" to explain the two different value-systems defined by women here and by men in *The Hite Report* on men, nor does the existence of these double cultures in any way prove that they are inevitable/or a product of "nature." In fact, they are not biological; they are historical: two separate historical traditions that have grown up over centuries. We have very little information regarding ideologies which preceded our own in history, but we do have enough to know that there *were* different ideologies: Adam and Eve were the first ideological lesson for the West in the version of gender differentiation which grew out of the Indo-European frame of reference as it came to the Mediterranean basin.*

That these two cultures are in conflict now, and how this conflict will be resolved, how the transformation will be made to a new world-view is one of the momentous questions of our time.

"Men are the reality, women are the role"†

As the song from *My Fair Lady* says, "Why can't a woman be more like a man?" So *we* might ask—"Why can't a man be more like a woman??"

Men, it seems don't want to be "like women." The general presumption is that women, to "gain equality," should try to learn from men, drop their "old values" and become more "like men."‡

The emotional contract reflects this general presumption of men's psychological superiority: men have the edge in psychological power and status in relationships just as they have higher status in the outside "work" world. Men are seen by the society as somehow more "legitimate" and psychologically "right." Men's opinions and actions are given much more credibility than women's, which are more likely to be criticized or scrutinized. In other words, the culture considers whatever men do the "norm," a somehow unquestionable "reality," while seeing what women do as a "role," and one with inferior characteristics, at that.

Women's value system, always "second-best," is currently under very strong attack. There is great pressure on women to "realize" that "men are better," more "normal," for women to throw off their "old-fashioned" values

*See Elaine Pagels, *Adam, Eve and the Serpent* (New York: Random House, 1988); also Marija Gimbutas, *Goddesses and Gods of Old Europe* (Los Angeles: University of California Press, 1982).

†This is true even in language, where "man" stands for "men and women" in many "humanistic" book titles and television "educational" programs; and "he" is the "correct" pronoun to use when discussing behavior in the abstract. All this has been shown to have a profound effect on kindergarten girls and boys. It also has a profound effect on personal relationships between women and men.

‡Doesn't this sound something like the nineteenth-century presumption that the West would "civilize" the natives in various colonies, expecting the "natives" to drop their own "superstitions" and become "rational," like us?

about love, "grow up," become more like men in their view of the world. (At the same time, men still expect women to be supportive, loving, and nurturing of them.)

The reality is, in fact, that both systems have important values—there is not one "reality" and another group of people who need to stop thinking the way they do and get in touch with "reality." And "women's" system of values (belief in nurturing, putting relationships first in life) has been providing most of the love and emotional support the "male system" has been running on.

Part of many men's disdain for "women's" value system comes out of the belief that "men are the reality, women are the role"—i.e., a woman without role training (or, for some, hormones) would just "naturally" be like a man. But this contains the assumption that men are not just as heavily laced with role training, and that their beliefs and behavior patterns are not just as much culturally or historically fabricated. And even for many of those who agree that men's behaviors might be culturally produced or emphasized, the assumption is still that men's characteristics are superior. But men's "psychology" or value system is just as much arbitrarily fashioned as "women's"—whether through history or a long ideological legacy and "role-indoctrination." Men's way of life is not "natural" or somehow "right," the bottom line of "reality" for measuring the behavior of the whole world. In fact, now, in the late twentieth century, if we want to invigorate our "system" and have it continue, we may well have to reassess what it is that our culture and political tradition are all about, what they stand for—and whether we are being true to the best parts of them.

If most women are put on the defensive in their private lives about their values and behavior (and this has been increasing during the last twenty years), what should women do? Argue back all the time? How can a woman feel good about herself in a relationship if she is fighting an endless inner war between who she is and her loved one's perception of who she is? Love relationships with men can be emotionally dangerous for women, since our philosophy makes it hard to stop giving, even when it has become more than we can afford.

What Is the "Male" Ideology* and Why Does It Make It So Hard for Men to Love?

What is behind the "male" system that makes men emotionally distant—at the same time that it makes them need love desperately, precisely *because* of this emotional isolation, *because* they are so cut off from their feelings? Many men

*It is important to point out here that this ideology is not something a man is automatically part of just because he is anatomically male. The "male" we refer to in the phrase "male" ideology is cultural: men who adopt the cultural style of masculinity as domination. See also Part V.

are wracked and torn over how to relate to women they love, in deep anguish over their personal lives and love relationships.

Obviously, men want love; they look to women for love, are angry if women are not "loving," and 90 percent get married by the age of twenty-seven. Rarely are men the ones to bring up divorce. Men want a home, and warmth, just as women do. But they also have deeply ambiguous feelings: real closeness is a threatening state of emotionality that most can't afford. Men learn that a "real man" never completely lets his guard down, or loses control of a situation; a man must continually assert his "independence" or "dominance." Real closeness is forbidden for men because it makes them vulnerable.

It is often said, "It's the mothers' fault if men are macho—they bring up boys that way." But this is an aggressive remark, simplistic, and not really to the point at all; after all, the fathers, by the example of not being home, or by their emotional distance when home, also "bring up the boys." The real problem is the ideology with which we live, the entire system which teaches men that to be "real men" they must follow "male" codes, other male examples—not create their own way.

The basic tenets of the "male" ideology are only beginning to be understood—since for many centuries male behavior and personality, and male-designed religious and state systems, were thought to grow out of "human nature," rather than being part of a belief structure which one could stand back from and analyze.

Hierarchy: the essence of the "male" ideology

One of the earliest and still repeated stories, by which the hierarchical system of unquestioning obedience to authority is explained to Jews and Christians—by which it is ordained that one must not put personal feelings of love before duty and obedience to the rules of this hierarchy—is the biblical tale of Abraham taking his son up on the mountain, where God has commanded that he kill/"sacrifice" his son—with no explanation given. The message is: obey and don't ask questions. As a reward for their obedience to this hierarchy, men in other parts of the scriptures are promised rulership over women, children, and "nature"; women are told, "Wives, be obedient to your husbands."

Even today, men are told in one "nature" special after another on television, and in many biology textbooks, that they have a "natural" tendency (right?) to be "dominant," to rule—as part of a "natural instinct." The assumption that men are more important than women, that they have more right to be "in charge," that their thoughts are more "rational," "clear," and "objective," underlies much of the culture. In other words, the "male" ideology is still all around us, and still tells men that if they follow the expected patterns of behavior of the "male" hierarchical system (show "loyalty"), they will have all

the "natural" rights of men to be dominant over women, children, and the
planet. Thus the concept of "male pride."

The conceptualization of democratic government, as its ideas were developed during the Enlightenment and the French and American Revolutions,
was in part a reaction against this hierarchical view of unthinking obedience
to a ruler who was king because of his lineage and "the right of God." Men
should no longer be *told* what they should do: now *all* men were thought
"educable," able to think for themselves. Still, this new system of equal rights
and dignity for "all" was only for men.*

The psychology of being "male": "someone has to be on top"

According to the "male" ideology, hierarchy and fighting for "dominance" are
part of "nature"; therefore there can be no such thing as equality—"someone
has to be on top." For this reason, the very idea of equality with women is
interpreted unconsciously by many men to mean a challenge to their "dominance." A man should "keep a woman in line," keep her from her propensity
to try to "run things." It is a mental construct that sees women as "the other,"†
and makes men apply different "rules" in their relationships with other men
than in their relationships with women.

But if women want equality, of course, they *have* to "challenge" "male"
dominance—and do so daily, as seen in Chapter 2. But if most men do not
believe that there is such a thing as equality (since in a hierarchy someone has
to be "on top"), it seems to them that what women are "demanding" is "dominance" or "power." And if men cannot understand equality, perhaps women
in frustration will have to wind up doing this.

The "male" ideology, based on dominance, and the "female" belief in love
and nurturing thus create a tragic pattern in many individual lives—a man
being "full of his rights," condescending (even unconsciously), while a woman
is trying to "talk," understand, explain, draw the man out, and somehow "make

---

*As Mary Midgley describes it, "Essentially, much of today's trouble (women's rebellion) is a nemesis
for the vast ambitions of the Enlightenment. Many of those who proclaimed . . . high ideals of human
freedom and equality instinctively protected themselves from disturbance by tacitly applying these ideals
only to a limited group—namely, white males. This protective habit went so deep that remarks on its
inconsistency tended simply not to register; they sounded frivolous and unreal . . . And the issue does
indeed centre in the United States, whose founders, by giving it a constitution devoted to Enlightenment
ideals, loaded it far more openly than other nations with a painful choice between profound change and
rampant hypocrisy" (*Times Literary Supplement*, August, 1983).

"Freedom" in the "male" code, as noted in Chapter 5, means that a "real" man should be "independent," should not be "told what to do"—especially by a female. Surely, Thomas Paine in the eighteenth
century could not have had in mind the propping up of the modern "macho" personality when he exalted
the "Rights of Man." And yet, this "democratic" language is what is being used today to make some men's
insistence on being dominant sound righteous.

†The famous phrase and theory of Simone de Beauvoir.

it all work." Often the two remain locked in this struggle throughout the relationship, at an unclear, basically undefined, and therefore inescapable impasse.

Why are many men so confused when they fall in love?

In *The Hite Report on Male Sexuality*, many men describe being brought up to avoid discussing their emotional lives, and their surprise and emotional confusion when (usually in their teens or twenties) they do fall in love. Many picture a really "masculine" man as being in control of his emotions, rational and "objective" above all else—to the extent that they actually feel uncomfortable being "in love." There is an inherent contradiction for them between staying in control of their feelings and loving another person—which they fear may make them "weak," "soft," and vulnerable. Although men often enjoy being "in love" temporarily, basically many are uncomfortable and say that the sooner their less rational feelings are "gotten rid of," the better.

Thus men's ambivalence about love involves not only a desire for "freedom," as will be discussed in Chapter 5, but also grows out of a fear of their own feelings flooding over them—a fear that is often reinforced by parental injunction. Thus boys are often advised by their fathers (or even mothers): "Don't marry the first girl who comes along just because of your feelings. Others will come along later." Or: "Make the right decision, son. Don't let your feelings (sexual) carry you away," implying that it's "just sex," that a boy may let his first sexual feelings make him think he is in love. (Isn't he?) Or another frequent piece of advice reported by men: "Success is much more important. (There will always be women.)"

In other words, the ideology of masculinity deeply affects men's ability to love and be close. If a "real" man should be a tough, rugged, independent loner (like the Marlboro man), how can a man accept a relationship or marriage without feeling split: if a man "should" be independent, but is not (in fact, is married, in love, or in a relationship), how can he not feel constantly torn between his feelings of love for his wife/lover and his concern that he should be asserting his dignity as a "man," his independence? He may see the relationship as a constant test or threat to his "dominance" (only by having "dominance" in a love relationship can a "man" retain his masculinity . . .); a man should not become a "wimp" or be "dominated by a woman" if he falls in love. As one woman puts it, "Most single men appear to have deep fears about loving women. They fear that loving is not 'macho.' They can let a woman love *them*, but try to keep their own feelings in check, hold back. It's a wonder they don't all get sick more than they already do."

For all these reasons, perhaps the deepest love a man feels for a woman can also bring out his deepest hate or fear, because his love is threatening to his ideal of autonomy—perhaps he doesn't want to feel that connectedness, even if it feels *good*. A man may feel very conflicted if he interprets his feelings as dependency, neediness—even "weakness." In fact, according to *The Hite Report* on men, most men say they did not marry the women they most deeply loved.

Thus, many men are trapped, tragically, in a kind of permanent isolation and aloneness by a system which offers them "dominance" (and says their only alternative is not equality, but "submission"!) in exchange for holding back their feelings, keeping their emotional lives in check, suffering loneliness as they attempt to judge every situation "rationally"—and wind up with no one to whom they can talk, really talk, about their feelings. Eventually, they often lose the women in their lives, too, who come to resent them and withdraw emotionally and sexually.

What Are the Values of "Women's" Culture?

"When I'm in love, I feel like I'm part of them—
and they're part of me. If they're upset about something
or if I do something they're upset about, it bothers me
terribly until we can talk about it and resolve it."

Women's philosophy and "sub"-culture have been forged over the centuries by women's personal thoughts, their discussions with other women about their relationships, families, and inner feelings of love—and in their practical experience of what it takes to make a family function emotionally. Its values include working together with others (rather than emphasizing competition), valuing friendship, listening with empathy, not being judgmental, trying to bring out the best in others, nurture, not dominate.

One woman describes the qualities in "women's" "weltanschauung," way of looking at life, that she admires:

"I admire the quiet work of women, their defense of interpersonal peace—doing decent things when they don't get much credit for doing anything. I want to see women move into the world and rebuild the bridge between private spheres and public works, which was destroyed by industrialization. How about the hundreds of women going to graduate school in chemistry? Right on! I'd like to see private morality extended to the earth; I hope that women retain some of the knowledge they gained raising children and shoring up civilized human relationships when they are out in the dogfight."

Another describes the qualities in her sister that make her feel close, qualities she would also like to find in a man in a love relationship:

"The closest I feel to anyone is my sister—she's who I turn to in time of trouble. She doesn't try to solve my problems, just helps me sort them out and solve them myself. There is nothing I can't share with her, nor she with me. I feel good when we're together. I like best her total lack of making judgments about anyone or anything and the fact that she'll listen to anything I want to talk about."

And one woman says what almost all women say: how much easier it is to talk to other women (see Chapter 18):

"I am nineteen, white, a college student in Des Moines, Iowa. I am creative, angry, sensual, intelligent, and a great cook. I value love, respect, gentleness. Right now there are two people that I am closest to, one a woman, and one a man. The man is my lover, and although I am living with him and try to talk to him about everything, he doesn't understand some things very well. The woman is my very best friend, and we talk about everything."

When asked what women contribute to the world, most women say that women are givers—women take care of humanity:

"Women in general care about others and work to make life better. They give of themselves."

"What things about women do I admire? Their marvelous humanity, their genuine caring about people, their nurturing, sharing, generosity, willingness to give of themselves."

Women's descriptions of themselves frequently reflect characteristics of being a giving person, supportive:

"I derive much happiness from doing nice things for other people. It gives me a sense of purpose and makes me feel needed and wanted."

"I am a mother and a wife. I like to cook, garden, and enjoy nature. I have a deep concern for the welfare of others. I am creative and active. I love animals. I am a family person—all that I do is for my family and with my family. I want to go through life helping as many people as I can in a quiet way. What makes me happiest is watching my daughter grow and develop, and seeing and feeling the love within our little family unit. I feel the greatest love for my husband when he's holding our child."

Are women "better"?

By stressing the positive, nurturing qualities that women believe in, and that they are asking men to consider taking on, are we falling into the trap of saying that women's moral sense is superior to men's? No, we are not saying that women are, or have been, perfect, "saints" who love everyone, without a vicious bone in their bodies. However, the nurturing qualities that women have developed in the home may be more appropriate, in fact the needed antidote for the emphasis on aggression that has come to characterize the dominant "male" system.

Although we are not saying that women are inherently "better" than men, women do have a right to be proud of their values and their philosophy—which they have worked very hard to refine. In this study, women are seen subscribing to a belief in the importance of caring about the feelings of others, a philosophical system based on the primacy of human relationships and cooperation. This is not dissimilar to what women seem to have said in psychologist Carol Gilligan's study, *In a Different Voice*, in which attachment and bonding emerge as the basis of women's moral sense. Women should be respected for this system, not put on the defensive.

Women have worked out their philosophy in the area of love and family relationships because this has been the traditional area of women's primary concern: if men have been urged to go out and succeed in the world, women have been urged to succeed in personal relationships and having a family. Women's speculations are no less dense or profound because they are focused on love or relationships, instead of "abstract" discussions of "politics." The moral and strategy issues are essentially the same.

Women's thinking about relationships is leading women to ask deeper questions about the nature of society

Women at this time in history are thus staging a very complex debate over whether or not they will continue to define love as their primary focus or their primary role in their lives in the future, how they should deal with 'male' attitudes and the compromises they are often expected to make, whether men should learn to change their focus to be more involved with love, or whether women should find other parts of life more interesting, stop being "overly concerned" with men and love, and see the rest of life as more important.

Women are Faced with a Historic Choice

Women are under great pressure now to give up their traditional values, as redefined over recent years, and to take on "male" values, not be "overly focused on love." But most women, after the attempts of the last ten to twenty years to "have sex like men" (not connect sex to emotions or a "relationship") and to "feel less," "love less," have not found these ways of life satisfying. Most women feel uncomfortable taking on these values; they feel they cannot live this way and maintain their own integrity, be true to themselves.

Moreover, even when women, despite their preference for their own value-system, accede to the pressure to take on "male" values, and *do* act in a "male" style (stop nurturing), men often berate them for it. So women are caught in a no-win situation: no matter what they do, they are put down. This has made many women do a lot of thinking about what can be done to change things.

As women run up against the male gender system time and time again in their relationships, trying to break through, make real contact, they begin to ask themselves deeper questions about the "male" system and why men behave as they do. In other words, the pain in their personal lives with men they love leads many women to think about *why* love is so difficult—and then to ask themselves a whole spectrum of questions.*

As women try to figure out relationships, they often start by questioning themselves, asking themselves if *they* are doing anything wrong; then they may try to figure out the psychological make-up of the men in their lives—a man's individual psychological background. This often then leads a woman to look at the structure of her lover's family, his parents' relationship—and finally, to look at the overall social structure, the whole system and how *it* got that way. Asking themselves so many questions about themselves and the men in their lives thus leads women to think deeply about the whole culture—and, frustrated with their relationships with men, often also to become angry and frustrated with the society itself.

It is not simply by chance that we look at the basic values of our society here through the lens of personal relationships.† Rather, it is in fact essential to look at the fundamental beliefs of our society as they exist within individuals, and in relationships between two people, because it is individuals and these very relationships that form the building blocks of our social system: the way we form relationships with others IS the social structure. It is the way we build

*Women's re-thinking now is going on at the same time as women are also drastically changing their economic situation. Within the last ten years, the number of women taking jobs and starting businesses has escalated so rapidly that in fact women as a group are no longer dependent on men: although most women still have relatively low salaries (and day care is expensive), more women than ever have enough resources to make it on their own, even if only minimally. The consequences of this large-scale change will obviously be enormous and are as yet only in the beginning stages. See also Chapter 11.

†Men's view of these relationships can be found in *The Hite Report on Male Sexuality*.

governments, corporations, the structure of work and home—everything. Without examining these basic beliefs and conflicts about how relationships are made, what they are at the deepest level, we cannot possibly unravel what is going on with our society on a "macro" level, eg., in domestic politics or international relations.

As women struggle with men to change the whole aura and understanding of relationships, they are pitting themselves against the entire "male" system. The result of this struggle will determine the values and direction of the culture for the foreseeable future.

Could the "female" or "love" value system (the family value system) disappear?

If women give up love as a basic value (since women have carried this "home" or "love" value system more than men), will love/family disappear as a way of life? And are millions of women now waging an inner struggle over whether they should do just that—urged on by the constant attack on and ridicule of "women's values," plus the fact that continuing these loving (defined as "giving") patterns, being "givers," doesn't "get them anywhere"? Almost all the "liberal" media are urging women to stop being so "feminine," to get "smart," be more aggressive, be more like men. If they were to do so, this could mean the complete victory of the "male" ideology. But will men like this victory? Will it be good for the society—or will life become harsher, more unfriendly, and the world a less hospitable place in which to live?

This is the point of the revolution we are at now, a turning point, in effect: Will women go along with the "male" emotional value system, making competition and coldness (staying "in control") their watchwords, since they are so ridiculed for being too "emotional"? Or will women, somehow, manage to keep their tradition of nurturing and warmth alive, even "underground," as a secondary culture, living bi-culturally: acting one way when they go to work, and another at home? Or will the set of values women have carried for so long be lost altogether? Do we care?

Seeing the world through new eyes: the "Other" transformed

Some women are beginning to express a new choice—to say that the choice is not simply between taking on "male" values and keeping "female" values, but that a third choice is for women to keep their own value system of believing in caring and nurturing as a way of life, but to change its focus. While most women still believe in loving and giving as a primary value system, something they admire in others too, many now question whether the best, the most important, expression of this loving and giving is or should be "being there" for a man.

Some women, while keeping their belief in love, are diversifying it, shifting its focus away from individual men who still don't see them as equals, and applying its emotional strength to a whole spectrum of relationships, even to work and politics. There is a difference between giving up on love relationships with men for the moment, while still keeping our belief in love, trust, and kindness as a basic way of life—and giving up on love by adopting cooler, more distant "male" values and behaviors.

As women, will we take with us our belief in love, giving, and understanding as we are more and more involved in the running of the "outside" world?

This is a turning point for the culture, a historical moment. Most of the pressure is (as always) on women to change. Will men see that a new direction is possible for them? Will women push for their own beliefs, their own value system, or will we decide that changing the society or even our own relationship is too difficult, and settle back into the "male" superstructure?

In effect, to reassess one's idea of love and how one expresses it, how one defines it and whom one should choose to love, is to call for a complete reevaluation of the culture and its world view. All of these issues are interconnected: by working on/improving/solving some of our problems in "love"— its meaning, and especially seeing how it is often destroyed by the emphasis for men on competition and "winning"—by taking these issues seriously, we can solve some of our political and economic problems as well, and create a more positive framework for society.

Being Single:
Women and Autonomy

Being Single: Feeling Free—or Emotional Confusion and Relationship Burnout?

> *"I like being single. Being single you have time to putter, ponder, read, take classes, go to movies—you see more of the world, instead of having to learn about another person. You can be closer with friends. Sure, it's got its ups and downs—but as they say, 'No pain, no gain—no guts, no glory!'"*
>
> *"My experience of being single and having relationships is that first I am consumed twenty-four hours a day. This goes on for about three months of agonizing and craziness, with intense emotional involvement. Then I have something like a nervous breakdown and we break up. Then I talk to great girlfriends on the phone about it all until I am myself again. Until the next time."*

To define one's own life

Women of all ages enjoy being on their own. Most like having a wide circle of friends and open avenues to meeting and relating to others, taking any job they want, and following a multitude of interests. On the other hand, in a couple, one may relate more narrowly, and there is often not time for all one's friends. Women like being in charge of their lives—whether this includes deciding to marry or remain "single."

But most single women describe disturbingly rough and upsetting relation-ships with men, emotional rollar-coaster rides, with men first very nice, then very rude. Often the agonies women go through in single love affairs are even harsher than the difficulties seen in marriages and long-term relationships. The emotional contract (see Part I) is just as evident here, but somehow worse, exaggerated by the "marketplace" atmosphere prevalent in the "singles" world.

One woman, after going through a few of these up and down relationships, describes her state of mind:

"Despite all the pain of my past love relationships, I keep trying again and again after rests and periods of never wanting to love anyone anymore in life!—just lying back, regrouping, being celibate for about a year, trying to think about me and my part in relationships. Many times I wonder, why do I have to do all the compromising, adjusting, changing, growing, etc.? My friendships are often more rewarding and enduring. My love relationships have all consisted of me having to be, in some ways, not on an equal level—sometimes even subservient, to keep the peace. My relationships were full of double standards on roles, in sex, etc., and full of contradictions. Contradictions between what a man says and wants you to believe, and his actions. But falling in love must be important. You can't control it, or can you?"

Most women love the feeling of being single, calling their lives their own—but cannot simply enjoy that feeling, that state, because hovering over the whole subject of "being single" is the feeling that being "single" *must* be transitory, that no woman would want to remain "single forever"—that this would leave one an outcast (especially "after a certain age"!), that it would mean one was "undesirable."

Most women do not believe this anymore, on one level—and yet the pres-sures are so great that the fears remain, ready to pop up at any time, no matter how strongly one fights against them, as we see women doing here.

In fact, single women are in the midst of some of the most profound changes and inner debates of the moment. Conflicting pressures are coming at them from all sides—pressures to act in all kinds of ways. Which to choose? *Which is the way that one really feels?* Which will make one happy? These are the questions we see women confronting: women are struggling against the weight of the society—while at the same time wondering sometimes if what the society says they should want is in fact what they do want; one needn't rebel just for the sake of rebelling, after all. How is it possible to know what is *oneself?* Women here are facing such complex questions as these, making choices in their lives in the midst of one of the most confusing yet exciting revolutions in history. Their choices deserve to be listened to with great attention.

4

Four Single Women
Describe Their Lives

1

I'm twenty and recently gave birth to a baby which I decided to give up for adoption. This has been my greatest achievement and biggest emotional upset. It was my greatest achievement because I made my decision after much thought, I weighed both sides (keeping her or adopting). It was hell, but I made the decision on my own and I'm very proud of the way I handled the situation. Giving up my baby was the hardest thing I ever had to do. It took a lot of heartache and thought.

I was in an all-girls Catholic school before, and then I lived with my sister while I was pregnant. I was closest to my boyfriend during the pregnancy. He was with me for the birthing and greatly supported me during my depression afterwards, while I was making my decision. We became so close during the pregnancy. Now we're in the process of splitting up because we need our independence for a while. I like how good and sincere he is to me. He hasn't cheated on me in three years. I admire him because he has a very good heart, he's a wonderful person. We just can't seem to be ourselves with each other. Neither of us is as happy as we could be. I feel we started too young and now I just want to be free for a while. I still feel a lot for him, but we need to have our own breathing spaces for a while.

Falling in love is important to me, but not now. It's hard work and my energy has to be in other places. But, in the future, it will be important. The biggest problem in our relationship, at least for me, was a feeling of being closed in, not being able to be fully myself. I wanted to be free to meet other men, have sex with them, without feeling guilty or unloyal. Another problem was that he worked a great deal and I only saw him in the evening. There wasn't a whole hell of a lot to do except go to dinner or have sex. I just became bored and began not to enjoy sex as much.

In the beginning sex was excellent. He would talk very tenderly and intimately to me—in Italian!—very romantic, exciting, and sexy. I loved it. I would orgasm every time, during intercourse, oral sex, masturbating together. Toward the end, we just began going through the motions and sex wasn't as fulfilling anymore. We became so different from how we had been. It just got to the point that I didn't care to have sex anymore, since I wasn't emotionally satisfied. Then he'd criticize me for not being loving and affectionate, and I'd criticize him for always being horny and wanting sex and not fully understanding how I felt.

It was easy for us to talk after I gave birth. He saw me in such a raw physical and emotional state that after that anything was easy. [But] after the adoption, we began to fall back into our old ways.

The worst thing he ever did to me was messing around with other girls while I was pregnant. He never had intercourse, but he'd just sort of brag about all these girls that were attracted to him. I was bummed out because I felt he wanted to get me down. When he would talk about other girls a great deal, I felt as if he was comparing me to them—he always made them sound so much better than me. I knew he was kidding and I'd tell him how mad it got me, and to quit it, but he'd always do it again.

He allowed one girl to give him a head job, but since I was pregnant at the time, he couldn't go through with it. He was always very honest and told me anytime something happened. I definitely want my partner (if I am in a serious relationship) to be monogamous. It hurts a great deal to know your partner is enjoying someone else when he should be enjoying you. You feel so betrayed and mistrustful and that is too much negative energy to have in a relationship. If my partner is monogamous, I know he's putting his energy into helping the relationship grow and not squandering it on outside activities.

The worst thing I did to him was having a small affair with a scuba master on a diving trip. He was very hurt and betrayed by that, and I understood why.

But usually we never fought. We would talk about how we felt and try to resolve it by compromising or being more aware of our actions. We felt it was a waste of energy to fight. It is too hard to see the issue when you're angry. We always resolved things very calmly. We enjoyed working together, helping each other do the dishes, cook, fix the garden, do work around the house. I'd say my boyfriend saw me as an equal. He admired me. I never felt myself as being different from him because he was male. Only when it came to physical things, he's stronger, can easily get jobs in landscaping, carpentry, any type of labor, things of that nature. Most guys I know feel the women's movement is great. It definitely makes a woman more interesting. They understand women have many needs to fulfill and that the movement is aiding in that growth.

I was the happiest, when I thought back on my stay in the hospital, during and after the birth, how wonderful my boyfriend had been. He was with me through it all and supportive of me during that whole time. I realized what a beautiful person he was and was so happy that fate threw us together and that he touched my life in such a special way.

Even though I wanted my independence and to split, I hate the thought of him getting involved with others. We're still close and it would hurt me to know. I'm not depressed or anything, it will just be difficult to go on without him, missing out on his life, his accomplishments, his downfalls. But our relationship is very special. It's an intuitive feeling I have—our initial meeting was fateful, its circumstances special, somehow meaningful, important. We have to go our separate ways for a while, but when we have matured, we'll be ready to develop a stronger relationship together. This is my gut feeling—that inevitably we'll get back together. (Part of me fears that he will get completely over me and find someone else that he'll love and care for more than me.)

I loved my child the most and that love for her made it terribly difficult for me to give her up. Even though I didn't see her or have her for long, my love was strong and still is and always will be. We are spiritually bonded by that love and I look forward to the day when we will be reunited.

My mother has no idea we've split up and I'm not really sure if my father takes much of an interest in it at all. If my mother finds out, she'll keep hounding me why, because she can't understand my logic. She really likes him a lot, she knows he's a "good catch" and she won't be able to comprehend why I "gave him up."

I'm definitely not out for another relationship. This will be my time to work on me, get my act on the road and start working toward my goal. I can't let things interfere. I don't feel there's any pressure on me now to get married. I plan to have a career, probably get married later and have children—not in the near future, though.

I like to go places alone. In my generation, it's no big deal being single. I feel that things in my age group are so different as compared to the over-thirty group. They seem to be more paranoid and have hang-ups. Right now, I'm kind of scared to go out there and relate sexually again. I've been out of it so long.

I admire men who are confident, sure of themselves, men from the sixties—they are laid back. That's the kind of man I like, one who doesn't act male. I dislike men who act macho, who stare at you and expect you to melt from their glance, who are chauvinists and treat "their women" with no respect. I can't stand stuck-up and conceited guys. I love to wound their ego once in a while because they disgust me so much, they need it too—brings them back to earth.

I'm in favor of the women's movement and I can't understand why all the necessary states never ratified the ERA. It's crazy and kind of discouraging to think that some people can't accept women as being equal. I can't believe our country hasn't evolved enough to realize that women are a great asset. Also, in the future, there shouldn't be a distinction between a mother's role and a father's role, that's what has separated the sexes up till now. If both partners take an equal position in parenting, the child will grow up seeing everyone as a person, not whether they are male or female.

So far in my life, *I* made myself feel the most alive, the most me. Others helped, but I was the one that allowed myself to feel like that. Most of the type of things I want are yet to come. I'm still young and have a lot to learn. I know it's in my hands to determine how I want something to work out. I'm in control of my life.

2

I am from Haiti. I came to this country, learned English almost all by myself. I was proud putting myself to school. I am thirty-seven years old—female, never lived with anyone, has ten-year-old daughter (planned).

First, I would like to express my gratitude at someone giving me a chance to write about my life story. I have been wanting to talk to someone. But it seems only way to have someone listen to you, is to have psychiatrist. There are not many people who are willing to listen without criticizing or giving advice unless of course you go to psychiatrist. (But I have never been able to afford one.)

I have a job (registered nurse) which pays enough to be financially independent. I do not have husband (never married). I don't have any kin folks who bothers me (other than my daughter). My parents are dead so I have no worry of parents been getting sick or become my dependent. I do not have as much complaint as most of women do, especially so called housewives do. But I am terribly lonely sometimes. I think I am dying inside. I need a man to love and be loved, but I don't think I find him soon enough.

I remember being extremely happy when I was in love (infatuated). They were all one sided love. Breaking up, twice being rejected by a boyfriend has been most upsetting to my life. I guess it was the feeling of failure. I was not used to face failures. I did well at school. I did not know I could fail myself falling in love with wrong type of men. I was upset when I discovered there are some things you do not get. It doesn't matter how hard you try, "one's heart cannot be won."

Quite often love is so called chemistry. It just happens. I learnt from taking care of children. You just look at a person and fall in love just like magic. I fell in love with a two-year-old girl. I was working in house, for her mother, as maid. She was not pretty, but she was my baby. We missed each other when we were apart. Since then I don't blame my ex-boyfriends for not loving me.

He was not in love with me. It also can happen even when you know the person for a long time. One day he becomes someone special. I wish to know everything about him. Want to be near him all the time. But basically loving is caring. You care about the particular person, worry about his well being.

(I was better mother before I became real mother myself. I planned to have my baby. But as soon as I became mother I became a plain human being with a lot of faults. I was much idealistic and patient with children when I was single.)

I met a wonderful man three months ago. I wish to live with him, but I am waiting for him to make decision. I love him for being tender hearted, he is kind. I can trust him that he would never hurt me or anyone on intention. I can believe that he is one woman man. He does not seem to need (or appear to) sex often but when he does make love to me it is intense and very satisfactory. To me he is my kind of lover. I am surprised that he makes me orgasm every time. I enjoy companionship just being with him. We could discuss about money freely, I hope our relationship is heading toward something solid, but I also want him to be sure that is what he wants to do, if we ever decide to have permanent arrangement.

He is younger than me (ten years younger), more enthusiastic about simple things in life, e.g. going places, seeing places. I like his attitude toward life. He does not have bitterness toward life nor toward people. It is very refreshing to be with someone so naive. What I don't like at the moment is that he is not very happy about his job. He might be going through the period of "Who am I? What I am going to do with my life?" etc.

I love him but I don't think I am in love. I am very happy thinking about him and wish he is also happy about himself. I don't know if he loves me, or if he does, how much. I believe he doesn't know himself at the moment. He seems very happy when we are together. He is in terrible mood when our parting is near. (We have 1500 miles between us.)

I would not give up present job until I am sure of his feelings toward me. If I move in with my boyfriend, I must work full time. His income is not enough to support two. (I was always financially independent, not make so much but enough.)

We are having difficult time telling our feelings at the moment. I think it might change after he gets divorce. I feel that he may feel he has no right to tell me loving words until he gets divorced.

To my life, I cannot decide which is most important. My work is my self-respect. My daughter is my responsibility and my life, until I met him. He is my inspiration. I weigh three of them evenly.

I planned to get pregnant to have a child. I wanted to fill the void I had inside me. I wanted to satisfy my deprived childhood by giving the childhood to a baby. It worked. I grew up at the same time my baby did.

I seem to be good with giving love, reassuring people, occasionally I have difficulty understanding motive of why people do certain things. I'd like to give what I would like to get. But some people are taker. I learnt to select people who I love. I try to avoid "taker." My daughter is very affectionate. She shows me her affection when I want to shut myself from world. So I can't help but return her affection.

I don't like to be single. But I'd rather be single than being with someone I don't love or respect. Advantage is to be able to make decision alone. Disadvantage is not to have anyone who makes decision for me. It gets tiresome to make decisions sometimes. Sometimes I like to do what my loved one wants to do.

I do feel I am a failure not being married. I feel inadequate, being neglected, being deprived of something everyone should have. It may be due to growing up feeling lonely, left home early. I wish very much to have a warm loving "home life."

I was quite serious with two men at separate times. They turned cool after awhile. I decided I did not wish to live with someone who is not warm and affectionate. On the process of wondering what happened to the wonderful relationship, I cried a lot, worried, depressed. But when I finally realized, "hey he is not worth crying" then I felt better. I wanted to talk to someone. But most of so called friends who came to me when they had problems did not want to listen. They tried to shut me up. I did have one friend who listened to me and reassured me. I am very grateful to her. I never forgot her effort to comfort me.

I got over by rebuilding self-esteem. "I am worth someone better than him." I actually felt good after I said "goodbye" to him. The second man was harder to give up since I had a child by him. We had fairly good communication all along. It took four years to give him up in my mind. I was not interested in any other man for four years. My work was great support. I concentrated in work. Put all my mind into work and worked harder.

I love being in love. I think it is great privilege to be in love. I am grateful to mighty power for giving me the opportunity. I feel more confident when I am in love. It gives me good feeling. I feel pretty inside.

I once wanted my (previous) lover to know everything about me. But he was not interested. I would tell if my present boyfriend wants to know about me. I won't tell him unless he asks. We (or he) needs some time before our relationship becomes a deep one, where I want it to be (share every thought— not only hope but fear). He verbalizes males being superior, but I think he just says it to make him feel better. I was in love with a man who is deep down "women-hater." Trying to help him was like trying to help alcoholic who want you but don't want to help himself. I gradually lost my self-esteem. Our relationship ended. My ex-boyfriend tried to slap my face. It was half joke as he said himself. But I got angry and upset. He reminded me of my father who was violent at times, when he had drink. I told him never to try again or else I would walk out immediately. He was surprised by my statement, he never tried again.

My mother and father relationship was very sad one. I decided to be independent when I grow up so I don't have to stay married if I did not like the husband. My mother's father forced my mother to marry my father. Arranged the marriage. My mother never liked or loved my father. I felt she loved me when she tried to provide things which other kids had. There were not enough food for lunch sometimes. But somehow she borrowed the money, brought lunch to school by lunch time. She tried to cook special meal on special occasions (holidays, birthdays). I know she borrowed money from someone.

My father did not know how to be affectionate. We kids always avoided him since he came home drunk and nagged everyone. He was also ashamed of his poor education (3rd grade). It angered him when we knew so much about everything. I was afraid of him. He was often violent. Authorities did not pay attention to family quarrels in those days. I felt we had no one to get help. When I was five years old, I thought about killing him, sacrifice myself so the rest of family can live in peace. I did not have courage to commit actual murder.

My mother seemed given up about life. She seldom talked. Did not care about anything. She was very much withdrawn in the last five to seven years of her life. She died at age forty-two. Now I feel sorry for my father (he is dead now). I feel he is also a victim of time. He was very macho but sad thing was that he did not have quality to be a real macho (size—he was small—no education, financial support). He did not know how to be tender and understanding.

As a child, I was the least attractive kid in the neighborhood. I never had clothes that fit. I seldom smiled. We had chickens, I used to get scared of the rooster. When I was about ten years old, I learned about my body. One night I woke up with a powerful, tremendous, bright and beautiful feeling. I had my hands (one holding another) on my private area. Some force has taken over me! I had no control over what's happening. I never thought such pleasure existed in this world.

By age nineteen, I had urge to do two to three times a day. But I had guilt feeling. I pray to not want to do so. I asked God for forgiveness every time I masturbated until recently.

When I was in fourth grade, a female teacher attempted to explain about menstruation. She got embarrassed and quit. I learned from books. I knew it would come one day. But what I didn't know was that we could not control the flow of blood. I thought I could expel the blood just like urination. When it just came out, could not control it, I was angry at world. I thought that was disgrace (as much as women kneeling—scrubbing floors).

I left home when I feared my safety. My mother was dead. My father began to show interest in me. It made me sick since I did not feel any affection toward my father. I still avoid men who remind me of my father. Did not date until age of twenty-four.

• • •

My current man is just what I always wanted. He performs intercourse just the way I always wanted. I always reach orgasm which is really a surprise to me. (He was very nervous at the first time.) The worst is that he is not quite confident about his ability, also worried about the size of his penis (medium—or average rather). His unfaithful ex-wife is to blame for his insecurity. I hope to rebuild his confidence if our relationship lasts. He seems shy to talk about sex. He has not asked me much personal questions.

It is good to let males know about clitoral stimulation. But I don't want clitoral stimulation neither before, during nor after intercourse. I do enjoy cunnilingus if it is done with steady rhythm. The man who I had relationship in last ten years did not communicate much when it came to sex. Once I tried to tell him how I wanted (faster, with steady rhythm, not to change the pattern or position once I was on the way toward climax). He was hurt. He said, "Well, doing it fast is not the way to do it." He refused to learn.

My friendship with girls are all precious. It continues even when they get divorce, remarry. (I have given up looking for male friends for just friendship. They seem to always want to make love to me which I don't.) I like my special girlfriend's positive attitude toward life. She is friendly with people. She believes in people (which I lack). She has quick temper sometimes. But she is not afraid to make apology when she was wrong. She does not pretend to know when she doesn't. She does not hesitate to admire others. She is a good listener as well as being a great talker. She understands her husband. She thinks she is lucky to have someone as a friend. I think I am lucky to have her as a friend.

Women seem to have less self-esteem than men, need a lot of reassurance. Less conceited than men in general. Sometimes women take criticism too personally, but they listen better, want to do something about it.

Women are used to listen to others, know people sometimes want to talk, want someone to listen to them, know you don't have to do anything—basic need is just listen to. Men might think they have to do something about it if someone comes to them and talks about one's problem.

Men and women both I admire who is unique. Whose idea and clothing are not same as others. I like person who feels secure even if he or she is not in the crowd.

When I was younger my choice in life was passionate relationship. I am older, mature and wiser now. I go for stable relationship. If two people have the same idea, it'll be possible to improve the quality to relationship which lead the life to a more rewarding one. I think to find the person who could bring out the best of myself.

3

I am forty-eight, divorced, no children, working in a profession (a second career) which gives me much satisfaction. I was married for almost twenty years, but the five years since my separation have been the happiest of my life. I have been able to be myself. The happiest times were spent with my last two lovers. They were both extremely intelligent, warm, loving, sensitive, and witty men and both were superb lovers. I am lucky to be considered by others to be a beautiful woman still. (Most people I meet tell me I look thirty-five.) I have many friends, and have a reputation of being an expert in my field—so, all in all, I have been very lucky. My hobbies? I love doing puzzles—word puzzles, mathematical puzzles, logic puzzles, and jigsaw puzzles!

I am still not recovered from my last lover's leaving. We were together for two years, and I have been celibate for eight months now since he left, although I have been dating some. We were an impossible match from the beginning, but shared a very deep love in spite of a sixteen-year difference in our ages, different class backgrounds, and some personal problems on his part at the time. I knew he would have to leave, because he wanted and needed things in life that I couldn't give him—marriage and children, for instance. We are in touch by letter and still love each other. We will never regain the relationship we had, but we will always remain loving friends.

We haven't entirely broken off the relationship. He has gone back to his home state, but we are corresponding. Our letters are very much love letters. I liked best his sensuousness, his humor, and his respect and love for me. The worst times occurred when, in the throes of a depressed period, he would ignore me for several days in a row. We were happy and unhappy in cycles, and my happiness depended on his moods. We also enjoyed sharing intellectual ideas, philosophical, political, artistic, and literary interests, and conversations. We seldom agreed with each other in any of these, but it was stimulating!

In intimate moments my lover was always sensitive, sensuous, gentle, and very loving. He truly enjoyed making love and liked to savor it. He delighted in helping me achieve orgasm, either before or after his own—he always left that up to me. A day never went by without him telling me he loved me, that I was beautiful, and not only during lovemaking. He always made me feel desirable and very feminine. He was one of those rare men who could share an intimate physical moment without immediately pressing it to the point of intercourse every time.

He criticized me for not being involved enough in political movements. I criticized him for his anger at the world and his attempts to find solutions in drink. (He no longer does this, and I admire him for being strong enough to rid himself of this dependency.) In the early stages of our relationship, he would frequently blame me and my friends for all the ills of society that he identified with. This was clearly a class war and, I thought, extremely unfair. As he got to know me better, this ceased.

Our love, when things were going well, was ideal. I am looking for the same type of love again and am not willing to settle for less. He has, I'm afraid, shown me what equality in a love relationship is like, that it is, indeed, possible, and he has possibly ruined me for other men. I compare my new male friends with him and find the love they offer lacking: too much domination, too strong a desire to "look after" me, to take me over and rule me. To me, this is not love, this is the exertion of power.

As much as I loved him, my work was always important too. We both understood that sometimes work had to take precedence over one of us. But when I think of the things I gave up for him (other friends, outside activities), I can see that, in the end, the relationship was more important than almost anything else. We needed each other for different reasons, perhaps, but we each fulfilled something in the other.

We shared all the practical arrangements and split expenses down the middle. There was no formal agreement on how to divide the chores but, since I hate cleaning, he did that and, since he hated shopping, I did that. We took turns cooking. Otherwise, he pitched in and did whatever was necessary without being asked. We both worked and each of us retained complete control over our own paychecks. We kept a record of what we spent on our shared living expenses and at the end of each week would total what each had spent and settle the account equitably.

We were both definitely faithful and I like it that way.

While there were many very close and intimate moments with him, there were two that stand out as very special:

1) He had fallen asleep while watching television. When I saw this, I got up and quietly put on a very sexy outfit that he had never seen before—black silk short pants and camisole, black stockings, garters, and high-heeled black shoes. I then climbed back into bed and began making love to him. As he slowly awoke, he saw me astride him, and the ecstatic expression on his face was one I will never forget. He later said he thought he had "died and gone to heaven." We continued then to make love and it was the gentlest, most tender, and most passionate lovemaking of all our time together.

2) I had just received news by phone that my father had contracted cancer. When I hung up the phone and told him, he immediately, without a word, got up and came to me, knelt by my chair and put his arms around me. I cried in his arms uncontrollably and unashamedly while he held me in what must have been a most uncomfortable position (for him) for about ten minutes. I have always been most grateful to him for that act of emotional support and I loved him even more for it.

. . . .

I *say* I'm looking for my next love now. But am I? I have been dating, but I haven't been giving anyone much of a chance—I dismiss men for rather trivial reasons, so I guess I am shying away from love. Loving someone is always a risk and I suspect that I am not willing to place myself at a risk for a while. A few years ago, after the breakup of a love affair, I would rush right out and replace my lover with someone new. This time I have not entered into a new relationship. It's as if I'm in a resting period. Still, I'm keeping my eyes peeled for a man who will awaken my interest once more.

Anyway, as I've become older, I've experienced less and less dependency on love. I have a stronger sense of myself now than I had even just five or six years ago. I'm more self-sufficient, more self-aware, and am less willing to settle for an inadequate love. The rewards aren't worth the grief.

Of course, meeting someone is extremely difficult in the city where I live now. In the city I lived in before, single people met each other freely in bistros, bars, restaurants, theaters—everywhere people gather. Now, I find myself in a very closed society where single people are not welcome, and where single women are treated with little respect by men in public places. And of the men I do meet, few have the wit and imagination or even the education, in many cases, that I require. Single women here agree that the men are scared to death of accomplished, intelligent, independent women.

.   .   .

I was married for almost twenty years. I didn't like it. I suppose the best part was the early years, the sharing in building something together. I was the major breadwinner for the first three years while he earned his Ph.D. But as he became more involved in his career, I became increasingly lonely, ignored, and felt unloved, undervalued. I had not expected this; I had expected companionship at the very least.

My reasons for getting married were a mixture of social expectation and romanticism. I remember feeling that I had better get married before it was too late (at twenty-three!) and I did think I loved him. After an eight-month engagement, I wasn't so sure, but, since I had given my word, I felt I had to go through with it. So I did marry him and regretted it for twenty years. I did neither of us a favor, and I don't think I will do it again.

When I left home to get married, although I felt a measure of independence in doing this, it really wasn't, it was merely the traditional act of a father handing his daughter over to the care of another man. My husband, an extremely intelligent man, married me, he said, because of my intelligence, and then proceeded to treat me as if I had none. I almost came to believe I couldn't look after myself or do anything of real importance.

My husband saw me as an inferior from the beginning. He constantly stood me up ("something came up"), refused or ignored small requests, called me stupid if I didn't agree with his point of view on any issue. In later years, when

I returned to university, he realized that others respected me. He began to see me through their eyes and his changed attitude toward me merely angered me then—too little, too late. Twenty years of an emotionally exhausting effort trying to reach him had been too much.

I was financially dependent on him for two years while I returned to university to train for my present profession. I didn't like the feeling but that was not his fault, for he was always generous in giving me a large enough allowance that I didn't have to ask him for any money for personal expenses. The fact that I had worked to support him in his studies for the first three years of our marriage made it easier to bear than it might have been otherwise.

I felt a great sense of relief when we separated. I was fed up and couldn't wait to get out. My husband didn't contest my leaving; he was actually support-ive, resigning himself to the inevitability of our separation. The divorce, when it came four and a half years later, was an anticlimax, like adding a period to the end of a sentence.

My greatest achievement to date was finding the courage to break away from the marriage and to strike out on my own. It wasn't easy for me to do this, for I had been thoroughly indoctrinated in my youth to think that a woman needed a man to look after her. It took many long miserable years before I was able to leave. Other achievements, academic or professional, pale in comparison with this one personal act of independence.

. . .

I have changed dramatically over the past five years. Now in a new career in which I am respected, and after having looked after myself for five years, I would never, ever again, allow a man to take over my life as my husband had.

My first important love affair after I left my husband was with a man on whom I depended emotionally but in no other way. He was a wonderful loving man, and with him I regained much of the self-confidence I had lost with my husband. I also regained the belief in my desirability as a woman and in my own femininity. The end of this relationship was very painful for me, but I entered another shortly after that, not "in love," but with a true warm caring for the man.

One of my lovers, after my separation from my husband, encouraged me to see other men and I occasionally did so if attracted strongly enough. Since the affairs generally occurred when we were not getting along too well, I suppose there was a bit of an "I'll show you" attitude involved, but also a reaffirmation of my desirability as well as some excitement. I was never really happy with these encounters but I've never been ashamed of them either. Because I found that these forays did nothing to destroy my love for him, I can understand that a man could indulge himself briefly with another woman without it destroying his love for me. (It would matter to me how often it happened, though.) With a man who feels very strongly about monogamy, I don't even entertain the idea of an outside affair.

Then my career took me away to a city where I met my important love—the man I've described, who was sixteen years younger. He needed me in a way I had never experienced before. I feel that I grew as a person during this relationship; I stopped considering only myself and gave more than I ever had before. Now, since circumstances forced him to move away, however, I have changed again. I feel less open to men, less interested in their advances. It's as though I'm afraid to try again. I have hurt one man in this period when I turned down his proposal of marriage, but he was the type of man who would have wanted to take me over, to take care of me, who would have wanted me to give up my hard-won independence.

Perhaps the greatest problem that faces me is the way to meet men that are appropriate for me. Bars frequently mean that I meet alcoholics, though why this should necessarily be so puzzles me; after all, men have met me in bars, and I am not an alcoholic. In any case, alcoholics have frequently, in spite of their addiction, turned out to be sweet, lovable men. I sometimes wonder if men who have all the gentle qualities are so buffeted by the world that they are forced to seek refuge in drink. The warmth and sensitivity, combined with intelligence, that I respond to seems to place a great burden on the men I have loved.

I have turned down three proposals of marriage in the past five years. But then, none of these had the qualities that make me love a man. When I am in love, I feel extreme ecstasy, exhilaration about everything in life, a new spring in my step. One of the proposals was from a man who insisted on paying for everything when we were out together. He said he could afford to take me out to dinner twice a month; other evenings had to be spent at home. When I pointed out that we could go out twice as often if I were to pay my own way, he absolutely refused. My argument was that if my pleasure depended on his finances, he was exerting a form of control over me. He could not understand my attitude. He proposed marriage a short time later, saying he wanted to take care of me and that I could quit working. He knew (or should have known by that time) how much enjoyment and fulfillment I got from my profession and I was angered that he thought he had the right to take control of me and my life.

I feel so claustrophobic with men who believe a man must protect and look after a woman. Another rather dear man would warn me of traffic before I stepped into the street, of barriers on the sidewalk so I wouldn't trip over them, checked my operation of my own coffee maker to see if I was operating it correctly, the list could go on and on. I began to feel that he thought I was an idiot who couldn't handle the simplest things without his assistance and guidance. He also seemed to expect me to account to him for every minute of my day. I felt suffocated and when his behavior didn't modify even after I discussed this with him, I broke off the relationship.

I have found that very few men believe in total equality. Whenever a man begins to expect me to cater to his wishes while ignoring mine, I quickly lose interest in him. I am always honest, I tell men that they'll understand me if they'll take the trouble to listen to me. In fact, most never bothered to really listen when I tried to tell them about myself. I merely represented some sort of image to them. I have been fortunate, though, in having known three men who did make the necessary effort to get behind my appearance to my thoughts and feelings. I shall always be grateful for the feeling of having been appreciated for myself alone that these men gave me.

. . .

My sex life has been very good in the past five years, especially with my two most important, long-term lovers. With them, sex was wonderful. They both understood affection. In intercourse, they were considerate, and, since I achieve orgasm only with a vibrator, the vibrator was included in our lovemaking. Yes, they knew I masturbated; they insisted on knowing.

Other, shorter-lived relationships have been disappointing. Most men either don't know how women orgasm or they don't care. If, after two or three lovemaking sessions, the man has not expressed any interest in my orgasm, I open up the subject. I am constantly amazed at how little men know and am angered that they haven't bothered to find out. If a man expresses an interest in learning, I'll help him, but, otherwise, I end the relationship. When I do end it, he never seems to understand why.

My (younger) lover and I read *The Hite Report* together. The section on how women achieve orgasm was a revelation for me, for it made me realize how normal I was. Men have a way of making you think you're abnormal or even frigid if you don't orgasm as a result of their thrusting. But another important section was the final chapter, where women insisted that intercourse was still pleasurable even without orgasm, and that they were happy to engage in it because they loved their men. I was relieved to come upon this chapter because I was afraid that a man, in reading this book, would get the impression that women didn't want them or need them. With women's increased independence today, too many men already fear this to be true. I hope that this chapter will help men know that they are still needed and wanted by women. However, I do wish more of the men I meet would read this book!

How I hated sex with my husband! It was so boring and always left me feeling used. My first orgasm with a partner occurred with my first lover *after* I had left my marriage. (I was forty-three years old!) My lover asked me how I achieved orgasm, and when I told him I used a vibrator (I was ashamed to tell him), he insisted on using it and we included it in every lovemaking session thereafter.

Unfortunately, it appears that most men feel lessened somehow when I mention the vibrator. I don't pursue the subject when I sense this. They don't remain as lovers of mine very long, though. I quickly tire of looking out for their orgasms when they obviously don't care about mine. I feel sorry for them and their lack of ego strength. This selfishness shows up in other ways too, so I am seldom sorry to get rid of them. I can *almost* achieve orgasm during coitus.

I feel as if I am on the brink, but I do need the vibrator to come to full satisfaction. Using it during coitus is lovely.

One thing that has always amazed me is how a man can ignore you or treat you shabbily and then expect you to respond to him with love when he wants sex. It seems that the quality (or lack of it) of the relationship is not important to men, only the sex is. This is not true for me; if the relationship is not good, neither is the sex. Affection is terribly important—touching, caressing, holding, snuggling, and yes, even flirting. Many men can't or won't include these acts of affection in their daily existence with a woman.

I remember one incident with my second, young lover, who was very good at including all of the acts of affection mentioned above: after we had experienced an especially passionate session of lovemaking late at night, I told him that I had been feeling sexy all day long and had been thinking about making love to him all throughout the day. He said, "You should have told me," meaning that we could have made love earlier. I explained that it was precisely that anticipation and the buildup from small acts of affection that had led to the high level of passion we had shared. That appeared to be a new idea to him. Whatever happened to the idea of titillation, of romantic anticipation and even flirting which can make love so wonderful? For me, sex isn't nearly so good when it is viewed as instant gratification, as a down-to-earth act of reality.

. . .

I am very much a feminist and always have been, long before the term reached the public eye. I agree with just about everything the women's liberation movement has advocated. Though I sometimes have felt a bit embarrassed by the stridency of some feminists, I realize that it has been necessary in order for the public to be made aware of the issues.

Although I held all the views espoused by the movement, I needed the movement to assist me in freely expressing them and in taking a strong stance where my rights were concerned. Certainly, improved working conditions and salaries for women helped to give me the courage to break out of a suffocating marriage and to strike out on my own. I have also been able to relate better to other women and they to me: no longer eyeing me as a possible threat in terms of her man (this *is* how women related to each other!), a woman can now be an open, honest friend. As for men, I no longer feel that I must settle for the role of ornament or bedmate, without the more important role of equal and respected partner. More and more men are adjusting to this new expectation on the part of women, and some of them even admit to preferring it!

From a man I want loving, affection, his ability to make me exult in my femininity, sharing of emotion and respect—and the sexual excitement he can stir up in me! Women friends generally treat me with more respect, and I don't feel I have to prove that I deserve it as I do with men. I also prefer working with women. I find that working with men involves a lot of strutting and swaggering on their part while they jostle for position. With women, we just get down to business and get the job done.

I admire the devotion that women can give to other people and the care, intelligence, and organization they can bring to their work. They can humanize an otherwise sterile workplace. The things I dislike are the willingness to let men run them, both at work and at home, and the subservience that they show to men's ideas rather than the willingness to form and to express their own. It is depressing to see young women still doing this; I had hoped for more from the younger generation.

I revel in my femininity! I love being a woman. I have always spent a lot of time on my appearance. Men have told me that I am beautiful, so it must be true. I generally feel, though, that I am not, I always wish that I could look better. Beauty, however, is not what makes a woman "feminine." What does "feminine" mean? If it means being weak, frilly, gentle, and subservient, then I am not at all feminine. I am gratified that I am considered intelligent and good at my chosen profession, but I also am glad of a man who stimulates my sexual desires, who puts his arms around me and makes me feel loved and secure.

Sometimes I wonder about my life. I have often observed that other women, less well endowed physically, have managed to establish long-lasting relationships with men, usually in marriage. Does their experience with men differ from mine, or do they remain in unsatisfactory relationships because they fear they might not find another man? Are they truly satisfied with their situations? I'd like some feedback on these questions. What are the experiences of other women?

.   .   .

Now, being single, I have total privacy, absolute freedom to come and go as I please, no one to try to dominate me or bend me to his will. There are, of course, lonely times, but I feel that I have been very lucky throughout my life: good childhood home, supportive parents, and education. I have been fortunate in having known some fine men (even my husband, who, though the personal relationship was very bad, was a good man in his own way) and haven't been forced to settle for poverty in love.

But I haven't found all that I want, not yet. I want what I was able to find with my two important lovers but with the stability and long-term commitment that these relationships lacked. I hope I will find this someday. Somehow, though, I doubt that I ever will.

4

My divorce is a month away—finally! I have two children. I am very happy. What makes me happiest? Wow! My work, my lovers, music, traveling, my children, and my family. My goal? To become totally autonomous.

What I'm looking forward to most? Discovering the world out there and joining it.

Currently I go out with several men who are married but whom I see as frequently as possible. One is of four years', another three, and the third of two years' duration. I love them because of many reasons, our mutual love of the same things, our laughter, their interest in how I feel, their always being there to listen, their attentiveness, desire to make me happy, their experience at lovemaking, and my lack of inhibitions with them. They are delightful people to be with and a constant source of joy. I feel very lucky to have found three such men and hope to find more.

In each case, much as I love them, I would not want to spend my life (what remains) with any one man—no more than I'd have steak every day. I may enjoy it but everything becomes boring or loses its appeal somewhat if overdone. If I have my way, we'll be close forever, but I guess, too, I want some "free space" for just me.

I've been married eighteen years but this is the last. It's been awful. The financial security was the best part. Being in a relationship out of habit that long has meant nothing—I originally thought it would be different. I feel no shame over the breakup of my marriage. I feel very relieved and delightfully free.

With my three lovers, I have been very warm and caring and they have too, with a great deal of fun and laughter. We don't talk about love except when it is said as an exclamation, because we are enjoying each other that moment so much. They say all the lovely things like "wonderful," "beautiful," "fun," etc.—that they want to have sex with me, can't see me or think of me without wanting more—all kinds of things—we laugh and joke a lot and they talk tenderly to me. Two of them sing tender songs. I feel very warm and loved and lucky and I want to return all those feelings to them.

The worst they have done to me, all of them, is make promises not kept. I think this is conditioning in men—they feel they should promise things they think will make me feel good, knowing it'll never happen. I've begun to point this out recently, and while they are initially embarrassed, they finally laugh and agree that I'm right. I prefer honesty to false, pretty promises.

I used to believe in monogamy. I began having "extramarital affairs" only after marriage became unbearable. As for how many—three constants for two to four years, and five or six very brief ones each year. The reason during the marriage was to find love and caring and respect from a man. Now I am not monogamous for a different reason—the reason is that I enjoy different things about different people. The effect is wonderful for me—I've never enjoyed life more. My affairs never affected the marriage, it was dead by then. As for my partners, one knows and it's no problem, the other two know I'm not monogamous and as they are a little possessive, feel uncomfortable. It affected our relationships for a while, as they were also friends, and became angry and jealous of each other. However, as I expected no exclusivity from them, they have adjusted, although their friendship—which was superficial, it seems—is over. I guess they feel they are competing now, though it's not true and I've assured them of that.

I am certain one of the men was very hurt when he learned about the other. At the time, I felt, since I loved them both, I wouldn't give up either and it could be kept secret. Naturally, that didn't work out. I'm sorry for the hurt I caused, but now he has slowly resumed our former relationship. I believe (since neither wants to talk about the other) that they know I love them both and see both of them, but they convince themselves the other may be out of the picture—I hope this doesn't cause another hurtful situation for either, but I've been honest now and love them equally, so I guess if it happens again it will not be my fault.

They are married and also see other women, I'm sure. It's fine with me and I wouldn't want the responsibility that would go along with being exclusive. The only difficulty is we have to be discreet and hide the affairs, like we can't join mutual friends for dinner or at a bar. I sometimes resent this. But we find enough time and places to enjoy together in public and private so that it's no real problem.

Sex with my lovers is great! I enjoy it very much. The worst thing about sex with two of them—and my biggest complaint about men in general—is that after their orgasms, it's over. They sleep or leave too abruptly. Granted, they bring me to orgasm several times first, but a half hour of tenderness could be nice after we are finished with sex. Maybe it's not fair to accuse both of them of this as a constant occurrence, I've also had sex or played around in bed with each of them for twelve to an all-time exhaustion of fifteen hours without cessation—I could hardly call that abrupt! They've had orgasms, rested and played around and repeated over and over. However, I do hate it when they are abrupt. On the other hand, the third partner will wrap me in a tight embrace which feels lovely—but eventually it annoys me, as I can't sleep.

In my marriage, sex became a bore to be avoided and strictly for his pleasure. He used sex as a means of control—to please him was my only means of affecting him. Our marriage was a legalized prostitution—part of the problems leading to divorce. My soon-to-be-ex wanted to be the sole economic provider with all the controls that allowed.

My lovers see me as an equal. My husband always treated me as inferior, made all major decisions himself, and acted far superior. He always had very derogatory things to say about the women's movement too, and at one point recently when I was expressing my rights as an individual, he concluded with "You libbers are all alike and you're all lesbians." Obviously it must have threatened his masculinity a great deal to face a world wherein women are equal.

It hurts if someone cares so little that they are disinterested in who you are. In my current relationships they do care who I am and what I feel and "what is inside of me"—we talk about feelings all the time, but then, that is probably why I love them and always will. There are some things they really don't want to hear, and if a man wants and asks for reassurance that he is the "best," is it really to anyone's advantage to get into a conversation about his being best at this, second best at that, etc.? If that's manipulative, then I guess I am.

I am "older" now, in my forties, and it feels great to give up all the values society forced on me, and have the maturity to form my own value system and believe in it no matter how non-conformist it seems to others. As I approach middle age, for the first time in my life I'm finally free to be me. I finally like myself and have self-confidence and a great interest in other people. A description of myself? Why does that feel immediately that I should be careful not to sound boastful? O.K., honestly . . . I'm more attractive than most, in great physical shape, healthy, intelligent, a good, dry sense of humor, an excellent mother, most enjoy meeting new people and getting to know them, enjoy life enormously, am kind, interested in people's feelings, have a good laugh but I can be very moody at times too—and last, but not least, I'm very sexy (sensual is a better word).

"Free at last, free at last!" Martin Luther King summed up my feelings best with that quote. The divorce is all very ugly now, as it reaches the end. I cried five years ago, a lot. I talked to friends constantly as the marriage was breaking up, I needed their support. It took me a long time to make the decision originally, about five years. Now I feel happier than I ever have. The experience is painful, and eventually a lot of wasted time and energy gets put into bad feelings. I would never remarry because of it—but it did teach me that I can be independent and love it. I guess I feel hatred toward the man I'm divorcing—but for things he has done, I'm not sure it's hatred for him as a person. I'd just like to have him out of my life for good and forget him and all he's done.

I answered this questionnaire because of several reasons—an obvious need for men and women to communicate somehow. Also to "talk to" a lot of women out there who are locked into degrading, loveless marriages. While it's not easy to get out of them, there is a world out here with some very lovely men and no matter how difficult it seems, we can make it. If women enter marriages because of love, that being their real choice, then that is probably ideal. But let's have that *choice* by being independent and happy on our own first. If we don't need a man for basic survival or for our source of value ("If he thinks I'm O.K., then I guess I am."), then we can need a man for all the right reasons—love and friendship of another human being.

The women's movement caused me to totally stop competing with other women, being jealous of them and trying to find things wrong with them. We're all in this together and have no time to waste fighting each other.

5

Dating Men: Fun or Russian Roulette?

The Agonizing Moment of Starting a New Relationship: Should You Have Sex? Will He "Trash" You Later?

"I sometimes feel like I would rather they slit my throat than make me tenth in their starting lineup or a notch in their belt. Since I would never do such a thing to any man, even if I disliked him, I can't see why they would ever do it to me. I wish they would give me the courtesy up front of telling me what they want or expect from me, and give me the chance to decide if I can live with it. Sometimes I feel as if one more time being left up the river will do me in. Several times I have been hurt when I allowed my feelings to grow and was led into a relationship believing that I meant something to him, and then found out he was seeing how far he could go.

"From time to time I angrily ask myself where are the men that are so affectionate and caring that I read about in magazines, and never meet? I have gotten to a point many times when I will burst into tears, the ache will be so great to be needed, to be loved. I can't seem to find a man interested in more than sex with me. I don't know if it's unhealthy. After a good cry I find it a little easier to go on, but it scares me. Sometimes I think I must send out vibrations that say, 'Calling all rats, calling all rats!' I may be impossible and intolerant sometimes, but it can't be all my fault!"

The situation before knowing if a relationship IS a "relationship" (and if so, which kind) is hardest—the time they feel most vulnerable, according to 94 percent of women:

"I don't seem to be able to forecast how seriously they are willing to take the relationship—and I don't seem able to control the course of things, either, so that I don't get burned. I've learned not to view most relationships as having to be serious to be worthwhile—but my feeling that sex needs some kind of commitment behind it does not seem to be the same feeling that most men have. I have trouble with the hot-cold mind games and I get tired of forever trying to figure out how the man feels."

"Right now we are going out but we haven't had sex yet—I still feel like I have a little power. You know, he is pursuing me. Before we actually have sex, I have the most power. After sex—why is it?—I always feel sort of like conquered territory."

Many women point out that if there are no shared assumptions about the ground rules, then misconceptions of the "meaning" of being "in bed together" can be shockingly different:

"There aren't that many rules—so it's hard to know if one is going the right direction, behaving morally, 'normally,' etc."

"You have to choose someone who has the same ideas about how to run a relationship; whether to be monogamous, how often to see each other, what you do together. Otherwise, it's a mess."

56 percent of single women complain that many men seem to think that they are always "available," "on the make"; a woman can't even be friendly with a man without the possibility of being spoken to sexually:

"Most men regard a friendly gesture from a woman as a flirtation, an invitation to have an intimate relationship! Most are confused by an offer of platonic friendship from a woman."

"They still think we all want them. They see us as sex objects even though we're working—they don't understand we want to be valued as individuals just like they do. They don't understand why pornography and sexist jokes hurt— they think our disgust is because we don't like sex!"

One woman labels them "hit and run" men:

"A lot of men are having a difficult time with maintaining stability in their relations with women. They like to hit and run, hit and run. They are fearful, very fearful. Avoid commitment!! Many I have known couldn't even bring themselves to say the word, I swear."

85 percent of single women say most men still see sex as a sport or have a "shopping" attitude toward women; "conquest" as a way to prove "masculinity" is alive and well:

"I hate being single—too many guys try to pick you up and like you for your looks—not you. It's boring, nothing is solid."

"Most of the men I know here at college are too arrogant, too 'macho,' too interested in screwing for the sake of screwing—doesn't matter who it is or if you care about her or what. Just fuck, fuck, fuck . . . that's the only goal for most guys I know."

"Usually after the second or third experience . . . the relationship breaks apart. The guy resorts to typical American chauvinist behavior and decides he doesn't respect me because I was 'too easy.' Of course, it's O.K. for him to have been too easy for me, and it's O.K. that he put an unfair amount of pressure on me to have sex in the first place."

Has this pattern changed with the AIDS epidemic, or the possibility of contracting AIDS? Not according to 1987 replies, although some men are starting to complain about the price of condoms.

Was it a "one-night stand," or did he change his mind?

80 percent of single women say they have had sex with a man and then never heard from him again; they feel cheap, used, and angry:

"I've had sexual intercourse with men who don't have much to do with me after that. I feel used, cheated, and immensely angry. Therefore, now I find sexual intercourse difficult to handle. When I'm not involved sexually with a man, life can be more satisfying and rewarding."

"The idea of a 'one-night stand' conquest sort of thing is really old-fashioned. It's only happened to me once, last month. One of my friends said, 'Oh, don't take it so seriously. He just changed his mind. Everybody can change their mind.' (I've done this—I've changed my mind after having sex with them once.) But this guy didn't change his mind. I think he was dishonest from the first, he just wanted to get me in bed, that was all he ever wanted—to 'get' me. It wasn't even the sexual pleasure, I bet. Anyway, if he did change his mind, he didn't have to be so rude about it. There should be some kind of protocol—like send the person flowers or a message, you found your long-lost ex-girlfriend, etc. Don't just never call."

"Last Saturday night I wound up with a man after an unusually pleasant intellectual conversation. I suggested he come home with me, which he seemed glad to do. We hugged a lot, kissed a lot, cuddled each other (I put my diaphragm in when we got home), he fucked me, and afterwards confessed to having a vasectomy and said it seemed too presumptuous to mention it earlier . . . (just like always, better late than never). It's Thursday and I give up hoping to hear from him."

It is not so much that women always want to have sex with a relationship, but just they want to feel good about the sex they do have—that it is their decision, that they are not pressured into it, that it is something they truly want to do—and something the man won't trash them for afterwards:

"If I do have sex with a man and I didn't want to, but was pressured, I feel used, dirty, guilty, and down on myself. On the other hand, some of the happiest moments I have experienced with another person were when we were in bed together. I often felt safe, secure, natural, and cut off from all the responsibilities of life. These persons were not necessarily those I was in love with or even loved . . ."

Several women are embarrassed to tell anyone when they have sex with someone who doesn't call again:

"He was large, fascinating, unpredictable, manipulating, almost sadistic and not only toward myself. A parasite, a user of other people. Lazy, a gossip and a lion. After a brief fling, I avoided him like poison, never admitted to anybody that I ever went to bed with him, and am angry only at myself for being so foolish."

"I'm basically shy. I have sex when I am in a relationship that looks serious. When the relationship goes nowhere, I regret giving my body to the man."

"The happy story of one woman's revenge . . ."

One woman in her early twenties tells "the happy story of one woman's revenge over the mean one-night stand"—which she calls "A Major Victory for Womankind":

"I went out with Sam twice about two months ago. The reason I went out with him in the first place was he kept telling me how beautiful I was, and I was a real sucker for it—oh, you have such beautiful legs, such beautiful eyes. . . . I should have known.

"Anyway, I totally disregarded all my natural instincts and went out with him. The first time, I didn't sleep with him. But the second night I stupidly did, and he never called me again. That was awful, the first time it's ever happened to me. I didn't expect it. He had said he wasn't into one-night stands, so I was really hurt and mystified. I kept thinking to myself, 'Why did he bother?' I went around asking all my men friends if they had ever done that, and asking my women friends if it had ever happened to them, reading stupid *Cosmo* articles on what to do when he doesn't call up. One of my friends said she bet if you'd questioned him, he would have justified himself, he wouldn't even have admitted being a fraud. Like he would have said, 'Well, how was I to know I'd change my mind? I thought she'd be different than she was,' or something like that.

"Then one day I ran into him on the street, and like an idiot, invited him to a party I was giving. I didn't tell anyone except my best friend I'd invited him—because I knew everybody would pounce on me for being a masochist. I hoped he wouldn't show up, so nobody would ever know I'd broken down and invited him. But he showed up, and I ignored him. Then we were in the kitchen and he tried to kiss me. I looked at him, and said, 'Sam? Why on earth would I want to kiss you? The last time I slept with you, you didn't even call me again. So why would I want to do that?' And he said, 'You're making me feel guilty!'

"So anyway, after the party, we went with some people to a coffee shop and he kept touching me and stuff, acting like I was his date. When we all left, he started kissing me on the street. I was real uninterested, but he said to me anyway, 'Do you want to make love now?' This guy is so persistent—if you say no, he just asks you again! Ten times, until he sort of wears you down—that is what happened last time. And I said, 'Of course not. For what? You know how I feel, I've already told you. This is ridiculous.' So he just ignored that and said, 'Don't you want to come to my place?' I said, 'NO!' He then said, 'Can I walk you upstairs?' (to my apartment). I thought to myself, 'If he wants to be such an idiot, let him; in fact, I'll bring him upstairs, then I'll throw him out of my house.' I thought it would be fun to get my revenge. I was definitely into being a fifties cock tease and then leaving him with aching balls.

"So I brought him upstairs, and we had this vague conversation which ended up really boring, I was yawning, etc. So I walked him out to the hallway, by the elevator. But he wouldn't get in it. He kissed me good night, then started getting more and more passionate. We were standing by the door, in the hallway, and he undid my dress in back and then started touching me. He kept saying, 'God, you're so adventurous—I can't believe we're doing this . . .' and then finally he put his hand in my underwear and I thought, 'Good! Maybe he'll actually do some decent foreplay for a while, and then I can have an orgasm and throw him out!' This I could handle! I thought, 'What the hell, I haven't had sex in a long time, I might as well take advantage of it.' But as soon as I had just started enjoying that, I looked down and suddenly he was unzipping his pants and pulling his dick out, trying to get me to touch it by moving my hand. I was squirming away. Then he started trying to get his dick in me—without even making sure I was wet first. He just played with me long enough to get me wet enough for him to get inside me (he thought), and then he tried to do it—really horrible. *Then* he says, 'Do you have birth control?' (I had my period anyway.)

"Then he just barely puts it in, he's just getting the tip in there, and I say, '*Stop right now!*' He immediately jumps back two feet and says, 'Why??!' (We're standing there, my dress is all undone, his pants are down on the floor around his ankles, etc.) I say, 'Look, Sam, I told you that it really bothered me when you didn't call me last time, and to be honest, I was a little mystified, because why did you go to all that trouble—dressing up, taking me out to dinner and driving me places. Why didn't you just stay home and jerk off? I mean, making interesting conversation and all that . . .' He said, 'Oh, it was no trouble making interesting conversation . . .'!!! He didn't say, 'I enjoyed being with you, or I enjoyed our evening,' he just said, 'It was easy making conversation!' And then he said (God, this is really heavy), 'No, really, I like being in love, I'd like to be in love; with my first girlfriend, we fell in love in a matter of weeks, and then we went out for years'—sort of implying to me, like, 'I haven't fallen in love with you yet, so therefore I couldn't fall in love with you—you're in a different category.'

"He was trying to prove he was a good guy by showing me he believed in love. Then he repeated, 'I don't like one-night stands.' I said, 'Sam, when I slept with you, that is what you said to me, that you don't believe in one-night stands . . . That's why I slept with you in the first place, because I thought you wanted a relationship, but you obviously didn't, so *forget it!* I'm just a body to you, you didn't even care about me (not that you have to, because you don't even know me), but don't try to pretend it's anything different!' So that was how it ended, with him being like stunned. But he got himself back together enough, as he was leaving, to mutter a few more times, 'You're such an adventuress . . .'

"So we did have a date for dinner this Saturday. I have no idea if I will hear from him or not.

"P.S. Now it's next week, and I never heard from him."

The latest in "lines" men love to use*

"He said, 'What do you mean you're going home without sleeping with me?! You put on your come-fuck-me pumps and your tight jeans and spend

*These "lines" were collected from college students across the United States by the author, from 1982 to 1987, during lectures at over thirty colleges and universities in twenty states.

all evening looking at me with your please-take-me-to-bed eyes and you wait till now to change your mind???' "

"Would you like some affection?"

"It's the will of God."

"I bought you a beer."

"We've been friends so long—we know almost everything about each other. What difference would it make, except to heighten our friendship?"

"If we sleep together we can get rid of this sexual tension in our friendship."

"I just want to hold you all night."

"Let's merge."

"Do you have your diaphragm in?"

"He said, 'What do you mean you're going home? What a tease!' I said, 'If I stay, I'm a slut.' He didn't contest my remark and I went home."

"I'm x years old. I can't believe I'm x years old and *still* a virgin!"

"Usually the first person I see in the morning is me—in the mirror. How would you feel if I said that I'd like tomorrow to be different?"

"Should I call you or nudge you tomorrow?"

"So . . . uh . . . how do you like your eggs?"

"Do you wanna come upstairs and tuck me in?"

"I've never done this before, I knew you were the one."

"My balls hurt."

"So . . . are you game?"

"I just want to make you feel good."

"I just want to show you how much I love you."

"If there is a nuclear war tomorrow, you will die without ever having had sex with me."

"There's a rumor around school that you are a lesbian."

"If you love me, prove it."

"Well???" (tacky)

"Want to watch the sunrise?" (mushy)

"Do you wanna be called for breakfast, or should I just blow in your ear?"

"I think you're beautiful . . . I'd love to make love. (However, truly, I only say this when I feel it's true.)"

"But it'll be so good . . ."

"The way I see it is that our sex life is only so long, so we may as well live it up now."

"Do you want to exchange massages?"

"But I could teach you so much . . ."

"I've been taking all these women's studies courses and I'm so confused about my sexuality."

"Nice dress. Can I talk you out of it?"

"Are you on the pill?"

"Want to come up and see my rock collection?" (told to me by a geology major)

"I like your legs . . . I'd like them better up in the air."

"You know you want it."

"Do you want to get a pizza and then fuck?" (She slaps him.) "What's the matter, you don't like pizza?" (actually overheard in a bar)

"I could tell you I really like you for your intelligence, your wit, and your personality. But I'm honest . . . Let's have sex."

"I'm collecting pubic hairs. May I have one of yours?"

"I'm gay but I'm not sure. I guess I'm questioning. Do you think you could help?"

"May I examine your private parts?"

"Would you like to come back to my place for a drink and a fuck, or don't you drink?"

"Want to dance? No? Well, I guess a blow job's out of the question."

"If you loved me you would."

"What do you think about two people who are close friends? I mean, do you think they can have sex and it won't affect their friendship?"

"If you don't, I'll tell everyone that you did."

"Do you want to dance?" "No." "Do you want to have sex?" "No." "Neither do I, let's get it over with."

He: "Can I buy you a drink?" She: "No, but I'll take the two dollars."

"Personally, my favorite 'line' is 'I love you.' Maybe it's not a line because I always mean it."

"You need it."

"I've never been in love like this before. You're so special, not like the rest."

The famous "I'll still respect you in the morning!"

"Oh, come on . . . You want it just as much as I do."

"Let's go up to my room and smoke some pot." (passé)

"Let's get away from the crowd."

"Will you rub my back?"

"Wanna see my marble collection?"

"Ever heard the *1812* overture in CD [compact disc]?"

"I'm not wearing underwear."

"I think I'm in love—but you'll do for tonight."

"My roommate's gone for the weekend. I'll move the beds together if you'll keep me company."

"Could you do me a favor? I'm curious as to how you kiss."

"I've been stuck on the farm for a month—can you help me out?"

"My zipper is reaching a critical mass."

"Nobody dates anymore, they just sleep together" (. . . *still*, since AIDS?)

According to 85 percent of single women, most men expect sex on the "first date." 76 percent of women say they do usually have it then—although 65 percent say they would frequently rather wait, even if they are excited and *physically* want sex. But most don't feel they have much freedom to choose: if a woman doesn't go along with sex, a man may accuse her of "playing games." On the other hand, if she does have sex, he may imply she is "easy," and feel she is not a woman he can "trust," fall in love with, or take seriously—so she can't win, in either case.

Most men in *The Hite Report* on men say they don't like one-night stands, but clearly this does not mean they do not wind up having them. If most think they are "not that kind of guy," most also feel they have a right (that there is pressure on them, in fact) to "try the woman out," see how far things can go—to find out if the *woman* is a one-night stand. As one woman puts it, "It's not *their* fault if *we* turn out to be one-night stands!"

41 percent of women married during the last ten years say that one of the worst things about being single is having to be constantly wary of being "taken"; most are delighted to no longer have to play the "stupid games" they encountered so often while single:

"I've been married for six months, and I like it. I love no longer having to worry about the stupid games played between single males and females. Getting rid of the anxieties resulting from these games has gone a long way toward making me a calmer person. The best parts of being married are the moments of very deep feeling for the other person. You can enjoy and allow yourself to have these feelings, because you know he won't be gone tomorrow."

"Until I married this year, my sex life was very, very sporadic. A lot of one-

and two-night stands; men frequently got it on with me once and then wouldn't give me the time of day—it was a repeating pattern. (Occasionally there were guys who were more interested in me, and I'd reverse the role and not want to repeat a bedroom scene.) And I had a couple of short-lived boy-friend relationships, never more than three months maximum. I enjoyed the periods of no sex—they were the most emotionally stable and productive periods in my life."

A forty-seven-year-old recently widowed woman comments on suddenly being thrown into the singles dating scene; casual sex is something men may want, she says, but she does not:

"As a forty-seven-year-old widow, I think it is impossible to be honest with men in a dating situation. If I were introduced to some nice middle-aged man, I could not possibly be honest enough with him to say on the first date that I was interested only in a committed relationship, that I chose for a variety of reasons not to be sexually intimate with him outside of such a relationship. Even if he himself were seeking a wife and generally viewed sexual promiscuity as a bad thing, he would not react positively to my honesty. I think the sexual revolution which has freed women to have casual sex has also freed them from the option of not having casual sex, and I think that is unfortunate.

"So many of today's divorced men figure if there is no sex forthcoming by the second or third date there is absolutely no reason to continue the relation-ship. I am very confident of my value as a friend, support, sexual partner, and intellectual companion; I'd make some lonely man an awfully good wife, but I don't get the chance to prove myself in *my* arena until I prove myself in *theirs*. Not only do I view casual sex as immoral, I also would probably not be very good or responsive, and so would fail their test if only given one chance anyway! Discouraging situation!"

"Birth control? condoms? He's never even asked!"

91 percent of single women in this study say men rarely ask about birth-control measures before intercourse, although in 1987 15 percent of men were offering condoms, presumably because of AIDS; if asked later, men say they assumed the woman was "protected"—and that "if she had AIDS, she would have said so: *

"There is a man in my hometown who thinks he's tough and cool. He got a fifteen-year-old girl pregnant and dumped her. She had a baby and he's never even seen it."

---

*But do the same men know if *they* have AIDS?

Despite the spread of AIDS, most men do not clearly state, while kissing and moving toward "sex," that they have a condom and plan to use it. Even fewer realize or acknowledge that they should use the condom during fellatio, and often pressure women for fellatio before intercourse—or "if there isn't going to be intercourse, could you just suck me?"

According to 87 percent of girls age nineteen or younger, most teenage boys don't use condoms—even now, with fear of AIDS a consideration.* If a teenage girl does use birth control, the boy may think that she *expected* to have sex, that she "does it all the time" and is "knowledgeable." Thus she may be considered "easy" or a "whore" by the boy because she is prepared and thus "experienced." This is especially likely to be true if she offers him a condom or uses a diaphragm, which makes her seem much more "knowledgeable." Hence, if she doesn't want to add chemicals to her body, she is likely to go without. In many areas of the country, moreover, if a girl tries to get the pill or a diaphragm, her parents may find out because she still goes to the family doctor.

If a single woman becomes pregnant, and decides to go for an abortion, she will most likely go alone. If she does, she may be shouted at by picketers who call her a "murderess" for "killing her baby"—whereas nobody is shouting anything at the boy (who definitely had an orgasm, even if she didn't). On the other hand, if she decides to keep the baby, she is often told she is "manipulating" the boy—or, as a final twist, not living up to her full potential as a modern woman who "should" be thinking of a career! She can't win; it is always her fault, her responsibility, not the boy/man's.

Once again, responsibility for worrying about protection from AIDS seems to be falling to women—and, as one woman puts it, "I'd almost not have sex than deal with it—I mean, bringing it up, feeling weird, not trusting each other. I guess among my friends (I'm twenty-four) there is a surprising apathy about it all. Well, most people are going with one person. And, then, there is automatic amnesty for everyone you've ever slept with before, right? I know it's not logical, but that's the way it is on an emotional level—pretty lame, huh? But the whole idea of no exchange of body fluids is just too strict—nobody is that hard-line about it."

*The best way to avoid AIDS during coitus, for both parties, is to use a latex condom. However, this leaves a small possibility (statistically less) of contracting it during oral sex, especially fellatio. Although fellatio to orgasm would be the most likely to be unsafe, fellatio only for stimulation might produce pre-ejaculatory fluid, the drop of fluid that appears at the tip of the penis long before ejaculation. Ingestion of this could also be unsafe. Since there is often blood near the surface of the gums around the teeth, the virus could enter the body this way. Similarly, a man might contract the virus during cunnilingus. Will people prefer to wear protection, even during these activities, or take their chances?

"Unwed fathers"

The problem of teenage pregnancy is almost never addressed adequately, at its source: that is, the idea that is taught to boys that when they first have intercourse, they will become "a man." A shift in what the culture tells boys is "male sexuality" is necessary to reduce teenage pregnancies—that is, why can't boys enjoy affection and oral sex?

Although girls are often blamed for becoming pregnant ("she should have used birth control"), or one hears "their" situation "explained" ("she wanted to be loved," "she came from a bad family background and wanted a family," and so on—giving a victim-like aura to the girl), rarely are books or television documentaries devoted to the "unwed fathers" or the psychological debility evidenced by their having fathered a child and then walked away, or their failure to have used birth control.

If men/boys were not taught that sex means "penetration/intercourse" and that everything else is "teenage stuff," "second best"; and if boys were not taught that as men they "can't help" wanting/needing intercourse, that they are overcome by their "hormones," and that this means they are "real men"; and if boys were not taught that birth control is the woman's responsibility ("if she gets pregnant, it's her own fault"—"she tricked me"); and if girls were not taught to be always loving and giving, and especially that they should not disagree with or challenge men, who are "smarter" and more desirable—*then*, would there be so many pregnancies, teenage or otherwise, for which the father decided he would rather not be responsible, either financially* or emotionally and morally, by maintaining a relationship with the child, if not the mother?

The double standard lives

Most women under twenty-five say men/boys still look down on and may trash women who have had "too much" sexual experience:

"When I lost my virginity, he was surprised. He said he thought any woman as passionate as I must have had some previous experience. He didn't believe passion would be natural in a virgin. It never crossed my mind that my 'passion' could be held against me."

"I am very much in love with a man whom I see very rarely because we attend different universities. Our only problem is with our sex life. I am much

---

*Female "single heads-of-households" (single mothers with children) are now the largest group in the country below the poverty level.

more sexually experienced than he is. This bothers him very much, for moral reasons, and he does not like to be reminded of my sexual liaisons. He is very gentle and passionate, we have a good sense of humor in bed. But it is rare that he succeeds in bringing me to orgasm, somehow he just lacks that special 'something' to bring me to ecstasy. I have not told him that I am dissatisfied, because I am afraid it will damage that famous male ego and just remind him, in a negative way, of my past experiences."

"I'm a recently separated woman of twenty-two, with one child. My goals at this time are to go back to school and obtain a degree in mathematics. I'm very secure about my sexuality and haven't any guilt about sex. I'm able to give freely and also like and demand satisfaction. But men seem intimidated by my sexual prowess. It seems I'm the woman who satisfies fantasies but is not to be taken home to Mama. Since I was a teenager experimenting with sex, my main problem has been with men's madonna/whore stereotypes. I enjoy sex and giving a man sexual satisfaction, but I'm torn between being myself and being what everyone expects of me."

Do men have a right to push for casual sex?*
What gives them this right?

Many women feel great pain because of men's attitudes

One woman, after trying various relationships, in none of which she was treated very well, feels a kind of despair/outrage, and asks, at age thirty-four, what is it all about?:

"My sex life is a joke. The men who are interested in me seem to be only interested in something very casual, or a one-night stand. I come off feeling worse than if I had no sex at all. The saying 'I feel so cheap' sounds silly and dumb, but that's exactly how I feel. I have reached a point where I need a deep lasting relationship, even if it isn't a marriage. I can't give temporary love anymore. I think I must be sending out the wrong 'signals,' but I haven't figured out what the right 'signals' are yet.

"Whenever a man doesn't inform me that it is just for fun and not a serious thing, and I start falling in love, they get very upset and leave. This has happened two or three times. If they had told me up front their intentions, of course I wouldn't have let them go as far as they did, and then I wouldn't have felt so used.

"Why don't they want to settle down? Of my lovers so far, the ones in their

---

*Although there is widespread discussion of AIDS, men's pressuring of women for sex has not noticeably lessened.

forties either 'have had all the children they want' or they cringed at the thought of children at all. Of the ones who were young, they didn't want to have children 'yet'; they weren't ready (some thought in maybe fifteen years!). There must be some father types out there somewhere, but I haven't found one yet. I feel cheated as a woman, but I am not in favor of getting pregnant without a man wanting the baby too.

"I'm not sure, maybe I just don't know how to make a relationship work, or maybe my problem is I'm *too* loving. Do I end up smothering the person I love? The more I love someone, the faster they seem to flee! I have of late been very cautious about showing love to men. I am trying to evaluate myself to attempt to arrive at a state where I can love a man without burying him in my love, a state where he can feel comfortable and I can feel secure."

The game now: "to see how much humiliation will she take, and still have sex"

Most women say that men are generally loving and affectionate before sex. How can a women tell—if she wants to have sex only if this will *not* be a one- or two-night stand—whether he feels any real emotion or just the emotion of wanting to have sex? This can be very confusing, and can lead women (especially young girls with little affection from their families who are much in need of affection and attention) into one blind alley after another, feeling emotionally devastated. Especially the first year at college or away from home can be very lonely for people; demeaning or shabby treatment by men can dangerously increase a young woman's sense of isolation.

Since the "sexual revolution," and the widespread acceptance of the idea that "now women can have sex without marriage," women have been in a very difficult position. If a woman likes a man, she often feels she must go ahead and have sex to *see* whether a relationship will develop. As one woman puts it, "It's impossible to tell at first if he likes *you*, or just the idea of sex. So, to find a relationship, you have to put yourself on the line and go ahead and have sex." But according to single women in this study, only one out of five experiences is loving or at least respectful. The same woman concludes, "There is a terrible feeling of being ripped off, demeaned, when he is nasty later—but what other choice is there except to throw yourself into all these situations, and keep on trying?"

Do men have a right to push for one-night stands/casual sex, not knowing if they have any other interest in the person? What gives them this right? "Nature"? Society? While there is an enormous amount of social pressure on boys and men to "have sex" to be "masculine," and sex is the basic means men are given by the "male" ideology to experience their dominance of women, shouldn't more individual men begin to question these pressures—to ask themselves what "sex" means to *them*, and to think for themselves?

92 percent of single women express outrage at this constant pressure from men: *

"Pressure to have sex has been a big problem for women since the phony 'sexual liberation' of the sixties, which made us 'free' to do whatever a man wanted us to do. They all had the gall to assume that now that the moral constraints didn't forbid our having sex, of course we wanted to 'do it' with them, whenever they asked for it, and AIDS hasn't stopped this attitude one bit. As a teenager, I did it to be hip, to be shocking, to be mature, and convinced myself I was 'horny'—when all I was hungry for was love and acceptance. With long-term relationships I did the same thing, to be a loving and sexy girlfriend, to make him feel like a big man so he'd love me and stay with me."

"I often feel pressured into sex by my lover. Also pressured into liking sex—being told that what feels good to him ought to be my primary satisfaction. I pressure myself. I often try to make my vagina please me, but without real confidence that it can. I do it to end the tension of his wanting sex, to maintain the relationship despite my doubts, to justify my anger against him. The pressure to be open to whatever feels good to the man is sometimes overwhelming. One feels that they set the pattern, that if anal sex is a turn-on, a tight fit feels good, it's full speed ahead and damn the rectal fissures."

"As soon as he said he wanted to, we got birth control and did it, though I'd rather have waited, making more sure of my feelings for him. But in this day and age, he was such a prince to go out with me a whole month before asking for sex, how could I refuse? I didn't want to lose him."

When does date pressure become rape?

Date rape is extremely widespread, but as yet mostly unacknowledged by society:

"Often when I have sex I am sort of 'wheedled' into it. Several times I just had sex so the guy would leave me alone."

"When I was a junior in high school, I ran around with strangers more than I do now, and a few times ended up in cars and things with an older man/boy who would ignore my non-verbal refusals."

"One guy I felt real excited about. I made a date with him, thinking we would get together to drink and talk, walk around a little. It turned out he assumed I would come up to his place. I still wanted to give him the benefit of the doubt, not thinking he could possibly try to push anything *that* fast. I was disappointed in his apartment when one move led to another—just like all

*How much has changed since *The Hite Report* was published in 1976? Certainly the chapter on the sexual revolution seems to be as pertinent today as it was ten years ago. Women in that earlier study, of all ages, were angry at the pressure put on them to "have sex" and the cheapening and vulgarizing of sex in the media, which often implies that women are there to be "taken," they "really want it too," are ready for sex at all times. The only difference now is that things seem to have gotten worse.

the other guys—sitting me on the couch, giving me a drink, taking off my shoes, giving me a pillow, lying next to me, holding my hand, then pressing himself to me. I could have gotten up at any stage, but it is just like paralysis, they always accuse you of making a scene over 'nothing' if you get up at any one of the little stages, and then if you get up after one of the big stages, they claim you are a cock teaser, why did you go so far? and now just to leave them there like this . . . ? Anyway, I got into that old college thing and just lay there not believing the pumping away that he did. I just wished it were over so I could get away, but I was unable to tell him."

And "real" rapes, which are still increasing, remind women constantly that they are targets for men's aggression:

"The rape was a biggie—it happened fourteen months ago, and I'm still waiting to go to trial. It was all the Police Department–related crap that was the worst. The actual rape wasn't as bad as a time I felt really strongly for a guy, then found out I was only a cunt to him. And that's the truth."

"I think the most traumatic thing in my life was being raped as a nineteen-year-old virgin. It took years and years to get through that one. After the initial details were dealt with, I figured the excuse of virginity wouldn't hold up any longer and I had no way now to say no to all the creeps who wanted to sleep with me. Maybe that was the worst outcome of being raped. The other worst was disillusionment with men. I was nineteen and he was a familiar person on campus and in his forties, I think, but someone whom I *knew* had fatherly feelings for me that couldn't possibly be sexual because he was so much older, you know? Once all that happened, I had a well-founded paranoia about men but continued to get myself into situations where the only way out was to say okay and then resolve never to see *that* person again."

"When I was raped, during the middle I thought, 'This is just like some fantasy.' This messed me up, because it was like a fantasy and I came. But all I felt was fear and disgust for the creep. It was so horrible, yet I had this nagging feeling that I'd asked for it. It was just like all men say—you wanted it—you liked it. But even though I had an orgasm, I didn't like it and I didn't want it."

One woman expresses feelings of justified anger, in response to "How do you define femininity?"

"As I grew older, into an adult, being female meant feeling like a hole, feeling defined as a hole. I loved my vagina, my clitoris, but I hated what they seemed to mean to men. I hated the advantage their convexity seemed to give them in their own eyes. Conquest. Or rejection of an inferior grade of cunt, not pretty enough, not smooth enough, not feminine enough. Rigorous standards. (I didn't realize then that they were going through much the same hell with their own standards for being male, but then, if they succeeded they would be superior to all women, so that didn't move me to much sympathy.) Love, love, love, the arts of loving men, being seen as a big vat of affection for the preening male. Not being respected. Being made fun of for the very things they would punish you for *not* having—vanity, breasts, bottoms, high heels. The constant undermining of dignity. That's my experience of femininity."

Another woman, age twenty-six, says, laughingly—but in part seriously—about men and the whole situation:

"I am so overwhelmed by all of it—I just want to be sixty-five and live in a cabin in New Hampshire with cats and warm cocoa and not have them [men] come around!"

Does Having Intercourse with a Man "Mean" Anything? If You Do Have "Sex," What Can You "Expect"?

Whether and when to have sex with a man is clearly an area of tremendous anxiety and questioning for women of all ages. Since the "sexual revolution" did away with the "rules" for non-married "dating" (i.e., first you "go steady," then get "pinned," then "engaged," with a certain level of physical intimacy being acceptable at each stage), what to do *when* has become a guessing game. And what has made this guessing game more like Russian roulette than normal human interchange (with all the normal misunderstandings that go with it) is the continuing presence of the full-blown (but denied) double standard: while most men constantly encourage women to have sex with them, they often do not respect or take those women seriously after they do have sex, unless the woman has "held out" for quite a long time. How to tell one man's honesty from another's lines before sex is almost impossible.

In a way, this has been the most difficult and complicated part of this book to research and write, because it deals with an area that is in great flux. Within the last twenty years, we have seen the conflicting countercurrents of the "sexual revolution," the women's movement, and the "return to traditional values." Young girls and women in college, especially, have been in the midst of these controversies—and the almost unbelievable confusion they have engendered. There was and still is extraordinary pressure on girls, in high school and even grade school—from boys and other girls—to be "sexy"; but if they are, they will still get a "reputation." Women now have to live through the most extreme changes, some growing up with a strict code of "nice girls don't" from their parents, then suddenly being told at school in their teens or their twenties, "Everybody does. What's wrong with you?" to then finding out with a rude shock that one can still lose the respect of a man one deeply loves by having a sexual relationship with him (and perhaps lose one's own respect for him after seeing *his* attitude).

"After the first time we made love, he said, 'Let's not get serious.'"

The unspoken rule is: "Just because you had sex together one time doesn't mean anything, it doesn't imply you will see each other again, or try to have a relationship—not to mention love each other." "Women shouldn't tie men down," men must be "free," has become the unquestioned motto of the singles world. Therefore, polite, "proper" behavior after sex is not to say you want the person for your "very own," or even care "too much" about seeing him again—but to imply you are open but not "overly" interested, somehow indicating that you consider that you are both still "free," acting nonchalant—but "warm," not "threatening"! Like, "that was nice" but you have no "expectations."

And if a woman does manage all this (having to take his feelings and reactions more into consideration than her own, not having the luxury of defining the situation or behaving in a way consistent with *her* feelings), she may then be rewarded, not with gaining a friend or lover, but by a reproach or a condescending attitude, implying she is not a very serious person, she is "too casual," probably "does it with everybody," and so on.

Thus, these ongoing decisions about whether to have sex require a lot of energy and thought on the part of women, and involve women in much more intense speculations over the "meanings" of relationships than men usually have to worry about. Women still also have to look out for their "reputations," unbelievable as this may seem after all the rhetoric of the "sexual revolution." Yes, the double standard is still going strong—and worst of all, most younger men still have not learned to question it.

Some college males have what is called, at some schools, the "three-date-rule": that is, if by the third date you haven't made a home run, you've struck out and should move on. On the other hand, many women at those same schools say that even if they have sex by the third date, the man will still move on—because now he has "scored," so why stay? This is a kind of culturally created war between the sexes: he is taught to get "points" by "making it," while she doesn't want to be "had" but wants to share closeness and/or sex and so goes, with trepidation, into having sex, wondering if she will be trashed later.

The unspoken assertion is, "If we have sex, it doesn't mean anything and shouldn't lead you to 'expect' anything—so I might call you again and I might not, but let's not worry about that now, let the future happen when it happens.

If you can't, there's something wrong with you." Isn't this pure market psychology applied to the bedroom?

2,500 college men vote on whether to continue the double standard

Between 1983 and 1987, over 2,500 college males were asked the following series of questions by the author, with the following responses:

1. Do you believe the double standard is fair? *No, according to 92 percent of men.*

2. If you met a woman you liked and wanted to date, but then found out she had had sex with ten to twenty men during the preceding year, would you still like her and take her seriously? *Most men were quite doubtful they could take her seriously; only 35 percent could.*

3. If one of your best male friends had sex with ten to twenty women in one year, would you stop taking him seriously and see it as a character flaw? *Definitely not—according to 95 percent of the men.*

4. Isn't this a double standard? And to equalize it, what should be done? Do you believe (a) men should stop being so "promiscuous" or (b) women should have as much sex as men do, with no negative feedback?

Most men found this a very difficult choice, but could see the logic of the question; the majority, approximately two-thirds, voted for (b), preferring giving women "equal rights" to changing their own view regarding sex. But many men also commented that of course the woman they would marry would probably not be one of those women who had chosen to have sex with that many men!

"Having sex shifts the power thing: When you meet the next night, you are no longer just two equals having dinner."

Ironically, having sex can often increase the emotional distance between a man and a woman, with the level of fear and distrust escalating around the time of first sex. As seen, women are often in a no-win position: the simple fact of having sex with a man means the man may trust (respect?) the woman less for a while—because of lingering feelings that "she probably does it with everybody," and therefore "I could never trust her"—and so on. So, sadly, the two become less close instead of more; indeed sex even increases the chances of not seeing each other again.

Even if a woman who goes to bed with a man ("has sex") tells him she loves him, this often does not convince him—or it confuses him. He has been told—subliminally or otherwise—that you can't trust sexual women, and so, although he probably was anxious to have sex, her having it and thus showing her affection is still not enough to make him trust and believe in her. To "prove" to a man she loves him, something else is necessary—often some form of self-sacrifice. The fact that women have to "prove" themselves and their love at all demonstrates psychological discrimination.

And yet a woman can't ask a man on the first date what his goals are—or can she? How much of what is going on—men being sexually aggressive and provocative, without any clarification beforehand (in the current cultural context)—should women go along with? Do women have to go along with the (still current) playboy mentality and its double standard? Must they accept "male" rules about when sex happens, and what it consists of?

Ninety-two percent of the women in this study are quite irritated that the game ("sport"?) of "trying to get a girl," seduce a woman, just for the "score" of it, is still going on. There is very little honesty which can be expected before sex, they say—and they are growing more and more tired of the constant pressure, the constant possibility that all the friendliness is just a lie to trap them into sex, which is then followed by coldness or ridicule. In short, men's lack of respect is making women lose respect for men. But while some women are still reluctant to tell their friends about how a man behaved, thinking it would reflect badly on them, many others are not; and almost all, as seen here, *believe* men's behavior speaks badly of *men*.

Having fun with attention from men

On the other hand, there are things that women find a lot of fun in dating men; many women say that having a man treat you "special" is one of the great treats in life, something to look forward to after a hard day at work; perhaps these things are underestimated:

"To be honest, even though men make me mad and I think their attitudes to women are stupid, I get a lot of attention from men that I can't get from women. Women friends don't admire my looks and brains like men do. Also I like the way a man holds me and caresses me and kisses me and desires me. However, when I need to talk and express myself, I go to a woman. She is usually more understanding, sympathetic, and emotionally supportive. Men have a hard time discussing things with me and listening to me. They have no interest in how I feel and what I need. Still, I need their warm embraces, sweet words, and admiring looks. Am I beyond hope?"

"I'm just wondering about myself, because it's so hard for me this summer—you know, when I get depressed or something, I've noticed my impulse is to call somebody up and go out for a date, right? And be flirtatious—and now I guess I can't do that, because my fiancé is out of town and I just have to wait it out. So I'm just kind of working. I wonder if it'll change me, trying not to be flirtatious."

"I love it when he treats me very lovingly, and tells me I am beautiful and very sexy. When he treats me this way, I feel that there is nothing else in existence at that moment but him and me! It's as if we're entirely alone with our love and feelings, just the two of us."

"Actually, there is nothing like those special little moments of flattery that a man can give you, making you feel adored, that you are the most desirable, the most beautiful, or the mother of his children, or whatever—but just to make you feel really needed and wanted. Nothing can feel quite as good as when he takes you in his arms and tells you all these things."

"It's so much fun when we're going to go out. I spend time getting dressed, then he comes to pick me up, or I'm in a taxi going to meet him. I know it will be fun, I know he'll tell me how great I look, and he'll look great, and it will be so exciting being together, just enjoying each other, seeing a movie, touching during ordinary things, like stopping for a drink. And then when we 'decide' to go back to his apartment . . . which is always messy with very dirty sheets, because he never changes them or makes his bed—but I find this lascivious-looking bed very sexy too—I love it!'"

Using Boys as "Toys":* Do Women Like Sex "for Fun"?

Since the "sexual revolution," don't women like sex "just for fun" too? Some do. While most women say they definitely prefer sex with feeling, most women at some point or other in their lives also like to play around.

Women describe their sexual adventures

13 percent of single women say they like casual sex, or even one-night stands:

"One thing I love sometimes is sex with different men. Why? The desire to experiment! All men have a different touch."

*This refers to a belt worn by Madonna, the rock singer, labeled "Boy-Toy."

"I've learned no one person can fulfill all of my needs. Monogamy is a romantic idea. I don't know if I could ever be completely monogamous. If you are in a relationship, sex outside of it is O.K. as long as the partner never finds out—especially if things aren't going too well and you need some tender loving care and shoring up."

"I felt the most passionate when I 'fell in lust' with a man I met in Paris, a brief interlude, a true Parisian *coup de foudre.* I met my lover in a café and spent the next three days (nights) with him, playing 'musical hotel rooms.' He was the sort of marvelous continental man—tall, Ivy League, sophisticated, handsome—that, in theory, I'd always been attracted to—for example, Cary Grant. The affair ended when he left for London. We parted at a Métro station in a blinding rainstorm. The Arc de Triomphe was against the night sky. I never saw him again. I never regretted it either. But I think I could use another Paris adventure!"

"I must admit there are times when I desire a one-night stand! Sometimes I succeed, sometimes it isn't worth the hassle."

"I lived with a man for six years, we broke up five years ago. For two years afterward I was celibate—didn't even masturbate. Then one day I got curious about sex again. This time I tried a new (for me) approach: casual sex—i.e., mainly picking men up in bars, 'cause that's where it was most likely to happen. I've been living this way for about a year and I like it. I like it better than waiting around for someone special, not getting any loving or affection. You have to be careful about disease, but sex with strangers is fun because it allows me freedom of expression. Since they don't know me, they don't know what to expect. This freedom allowed me to 'discover' masturbating during coitus. Now, if I take a man home and he's a creep who won't go down on me, or whatever, or if he really seems nice but I don't want to feel resentful if he comes without me, *I* make sure I get off! That has taken quite a strain off things for me."

"I have had sex with three people, once, when I went to an orgy. Many of my female friends recoiled in horror when I told them. I think I'm pretty loose, in fact. I like being nude with other people, I like sex and I like my body."

"At twenty-four I had my first 'affair.' It was fantastic, intense. I was drunk when I picked the guy up. I had been very frustrated sexually. It was fantastic— it was a summer night and there was a huge rainstorm. His windows were open and it was raining on us while we were making love. I found him so special, his long green slanted eyes. I didn't really have an orgasm, or get that aroused, but the next day we just sat facing each other, looking into each other's eyes—it was exciting. I never saw him again, however, because I told my boyfriend, who was extremely jealous. I dreamed about him for months."

"Sex life? I don't have a sex life except sometimes I fool around with some friends (my girlfriends' boyfriends)—but nothing that could upset my girl-friends."

"If it's short and sweet, I still get a good feeling out of it—it boosts my ego. I feel very sexy—exotic—desirable."

"I'm a single, twenty-six-year-old M.D.—really horny, and find there are lots of cute men around. So many that I don't know if I could ever be monogamous. I guess what I feel right now is the desire to experiment! Explore men's bodies! I like their chests and tummies and flanks. . . ."

"When I was having affairs, I picked men who were interested in one thing, sex for the night. They were perfect for me."

Or, as one woman puts it, mysteriously:

"I would truly like to know if more people than myself can feel ultimate physical contact even though the person is a total stranger?"

Many other women (53 percent) fantasize about a very free sexual life—but also worry about these thoughts, fearing becoming "too sexual":

"If I were free, I'd have sex every night with a different lover."

"Sometimes, I picture myself living alone and being very sexy and free and receiving lots of men in my bed; a pretty marginal but exciting life, with a career. And other times, I see myself with one man, lots of children, and occasionally extramarital affairs. My aunt told me recently that my mother was so screwed up and neurotic, she never loved my father, but married him out of fear of being a whore. Lately, since my boyfriend's been gone on his trip, I've had a few one-night stands. I find that I love to give love sexually—I may be very vain and fascist—but I love men finding me beautiful and being excited by me—and I love the closeness we can attain sexually. But I have to say that I've been drunk every time, really—I worry that I could so easily be a whore."

These are fantasies that women are still not supposed to have—though the majority of women's fantasies, based on *Hite Report* research, do contain visions of strangers, anonymous sex, multiple partners, and so on. However, fantasy is not reality, and women's fantasies are a topic which has not been sufficiently analyzed, so simple analogies cannot be drawn.

One young woman is quite repentant for the "horrible sins" she committed once while away from home:

"The biggest crisis I ever had was when I was in Europe, staying with a strange family for a month when I was sixteen. I didn't speak the language well, although my high school report card said I did. I was very homesick and lost. I felt that I couldn't communicate with anyone. I started coming on to all the guys because I knew that would make me popular, desirable, and would also give me something to do. (I felt that my host family didn't really want me and that the daughter who was my age resented me.) I left them one month later, probably with the misconception that Americans are all loose, because I slept with about nine guys (lost my virginity to a guy I knew only about one hour) and kissed at least fifteen others. I didn't think about what I had done. If I did I would have gone nuts.

"To this day I believe I did all that because I was psychologically unstable. The whole time I was there I felt it wasn't me but rather someone else. After all, would I have sex without birth control about fifteen times with various strange men? Hardly. I must have been someone else.

"I finally came to grips with the whole thing and now I can go through whole weeks without looking in the mirror and seeing a terrible person, a slut. I can accept what I did and have a relationship with a guy and even be sexual without thinking I'm terrible."

Most women want sex with feelings and love, most of the time

Many single women say they have tried experimenting with having sex with various lovers, not making "love" a prerequisite—but that eventually, usually before too long, they got tired of it, it seemed pointless; 62 percent of single women say they do not like sleeping with a series of men, going from man to man:

"I tried being promiscuous, but I wasn't able to keep it up because it seems so purposeless. Sometimes I can enjoy it as a gift to me but I hate hate hate a trail of different men."

"I hate going to bed with a lot of different men. It's no fun. Sex for me with the same person seems to get better and better. To have sex with someone just one time makes me want more. I do better without any than just once. Having sex just one time psychologically really messes me up too, I feel worse usually."

"My sex life is the pits. I don't like sex just once with everybody in town. I do better with no sex at all. I haven't found the right person yet. It does get lonely sometimes—but I try not to let it bother me."

"Last year in high school, I slept with a few guys who were in the circle of people I spent time with, and it was horrible. I knew they were into the 'let's fool around but still stay friends' school of sex. Of course, they never really were *friends* to begin with and I lost all feelings and respect for them when they wanted casual superficial sex with no obligations. I have some sort of friendship with one of them now. I did it by forgetting we had ever slept together. Not a good environment to come of age in. All the sex you could want but no relationships."

24 percent of women say they feel—on some very deep level—that it is wrong for them to have sex without marriage or deep love:

"I was probably the most passionate with my boyfriend, because I felt it was O.K. to be passionate with someone I was somewhat committed to. A sense of guilt sometimes attends me when I am truly passionate with someone I really don't know and am merely attracted to."

"I feel like a low-down floozy if I jump from guy to guy. I like a steady relationship."

"My sex life sucked when I was single. I always felt like a whore."

One woman in her early twenties explains her worries about her right to have sex when it is not with the "right" man:

"I have experienced wanting to have sex with someone I didn't like or knew wasn't good for me. I wanted to say no because I didn't think that the whole affair was wise, but when he touched me I was 'gone'! I was wanting it but there was this sense of anxiety or unwillingness. I think men have described one-night stands in similar terms, but it's socially condoned for men—'boys will be boys.' "

Men generally do not connect sex and feelings the way women do, according to most single women participating; or as one woman says, the feelings of many men don't last longer than it takes them to "come":

"In my experience most men just want to fuck. This society seems to create an unreal sexual need in men. Most can separate love and sex easily."

"Most of the women I know (including myself) have had troublesome relationships with men at one time or another. We fall in love with the wrong men, take love more seriously than they do. Women connect sexual expression and love. We take it as a genuine reflection of our feelings. It is hard to realize that the other half of the species doesn't. Especially, I think most women feel an emotional attachment from the expression of their feelings (love?) through sex. Most get involved sexually as an expression of their commitment to their partner, but often he isn't having sex for the same reason. This is what creates the bad emotional trips for us."

83 percent of women say they prefer sex in the context of emotional involvement, sex with feelings:

"I have many offers but I don't want just sex. I like it to be 'making love.' It has to be someone important. I can have 'sex' by myself. I do enjoy dating, but sometimes I feel pressured, though."

"I love sex—but I refuse to have sex without a good relationship anymore. I can jog and have more enjoyment than when sex is performed without emotion."

"Meaningless sex is worse than no sex. Perhaps a less satisfactory sexual partner is preferable to loneliness, but it should at least be someone who offers warmth and friendship."

"Some of the times I have had sex with people who didn't care for me or relate to me, were probably some of the loneliest moments of my life."

"The best thing about sex is the feeling of oneness and the excitement. The worst thing is the vulnerability, the possibility that it won't be valued or appreciated—that the man won't respect you later."

"Sex always seems to be lacking. I think it is because it has been too casual. The intercourse itself is wonderful, I love it. I usually orgasm if I'm aroused enough, which is about eighty percent of the time. But it is hard to share this part of me with someone I feel is not going to be around. That's probably the worst thing about a man, the feeling if after it's over he hasn't gotten anything special out of it other than relief. The best part is when you can wake up and he is still there and still prepared to enjoy. A rare treat."

"Many women are disappointed that the man does not really care for her as a human being; he wants her body to masturbate into. I know, I've been one of them."

"I think emotion and sex are much more connected in a woman's mind—or maybe it's society's persistent 'good girls don't' attitude that does not allow women to be sexually free without being labeled a tramp. This college is very conservative and close-knit—men here are hailed as studs with far more acclaim than a woman with a similar sexual record! None of my friends have sex with people they do not have a strong emotional feeling toward—whether it is love or just strong affection."

Although most single women want to have sex with feelings, this does not imply that they are all looking for marriage:

"I have my doubts about marriage. Emotionally, I could see marriage, but intellectually the idea turns me off. For me, the optimum relationship is a monogamous one wherein we both maintain separate homes, but spend a lot of time together eating, talking, and making love. I love my privacy."

"As a single person, I am seeing a married man. I am not 'going' with him. I see him when we are both available. I do not telephone him. He contacts me. When he does, I am sometimes available, other times I am not. What is it like? It's like getting sexual needs met. We are very giving in bed and lovemaking is satisfying. He is someone, additionally, that I like just as a person. I see other men, because of course this relationship lacks other components that are important, and equity between the two of us is just not possible due to the fact that he is married."

"Biggest problem? I'd say that perhaps Michael doesn't know how ambivalent I am sometimes. I feel that I dove headfirst into this relationship, and I'm sometimes uneasy about it. The best way for me to feel better about it is for me to maintain my independence and freedom, and I retreat a bit if I feel it's getting too heavy."

In short, women sometimes like sex for fun; it is the games and trashy, double-standard attitudes surrounding it that hurt them and make them distrust men:

"I think the worst thing about sex as a single woman is the games that have to be played to have sex. But as far as the actual sexual act, I can't think of a 'worst thing' about it!"

With the negative sexual stereotypes relating to women being "whores" (or "too free," etc.) if they like sex for itself with no emotional ties, it is not always possible for women to enjoy such experiences, or have them at all. In particular, men's attitudes during sex or while with a woman may make it impossible for the woman to behave "naturally." (This is not to say, by any means, that "promiscuity" is women's—or men's—"natural" state, and that it is only society that keeps them in check;* just that an experimental attitude may be appropriate for parts of a person's life.)

Women have the right to desire sex, and their sexual feelings are varied and diverse. But the undercurrents still "remind" us that a woman who has "indiscriminate" sex is not quite respectable—even though men are allowed and encouraged to "sow their wild oats."

Flirting and using men: female "conquests"

Flirting, having fun with men—some women enjoy "conquering" men in this way, that is, making men fall in love with them, chase them, show need or desire. This can be very gratifying to some women, a kind of turning the tables on men's superior status.

*Some Darwinians claim that the "primeval horde" must have been "promiscuous," in order to further "natural selection." However, this is a subject of debate in anthropology and paleo-anthropology/ archaeology fossil studies, as there is as yet no hard evidence of the nature of the early "family." This was the subject of a panel organized by Shere Hite and Robert Carneiro for the 1985 annual meeting of the American Association for the Advancement of Science: *Controversies over the Nature of the Early Family.* Abstracts are available from the American Association for the Advancement of Science, in Washington, D.C.

In most women's minds, the culmination of the flirtation, the "conquest," is the emotional victory—when she gets him to <u>want</u> her, not when she gets him into bed:

"I feel the most power *before* we have sex, when we're kissing and making out—in fact, it's a real ego trip."

"I started dating at thirteen, I was always interested in boys. It was because I was flattered—I wasn't used to being liked. (My parents didn't like me.) I always dated a lot of boys, I loved catching them, it was exciting."

"When I'm swooning in his arms and I know that he is dying to have me—then, that's when I feel the most ecstasy."

"I enjoy bartending. You know, sort of an ego trip, wearing skimpy clothes and turning all the guys on."

"With men, most of the time, I felt during sex like I was being 'hip.' I liked getting the attention, even though I knew it wasn't really me they were responding to—just my body or my availability. I didn't care. I don't get much love or attention in this life!"

Is there something wrong with flirtation?

Some feminists have pointed out that make-up and "feminine wiles" can be *symbolic* of a system in which women have *had* to please and attract men. But one woman believes there are two sides to the issue: "I think 'femininity' was created by women as a means to subdue the male and get what she desired. It is an expression of victimization, being at the mercy of men; since they controlled the power, it was a means by which women could (at least attempt) to control the man. Aware of men's need for sex, women probably devised 'feminine wiles' to obtain power over their own lives. We still see it today and it will probably exist as long as women are at the mercy of men. But I do not always consider dressing up, doing one's hair, make-up, etc., necessarily being defined as powerless, it is just what it is . . . a desire to present oneself to the world looking good and a creative expression of one's own individuality."

In fact, this is a very complicated issue, not as simple as early feminist theory would make it, nor as simple as some socialist theory.

Is there such a thing as sexual power?

Most girls learn about their heterosexual power as young girls or teenagers:

"I can be very seductive and I know that. I think it's learned. I think you learn it when you're a little girl when you sit on daddy's lap and you were so cute, and people reinforced you for that, so all of a sudden you find yourself doing the same thing with a boy, being cute, and then later on, you find that being feminine really has some payoffs to it. Yeah, I know how to use that to my advantage, and when I really want sex, I can get that across—and use it for what I want too."

"For a long time during high school, I thought I'd like to pose for sex magazines. It seemed glamorous but sleazy. I knew that when I used my sexiness I was in power. Boys could hardly resist. I became an expert flirt. A 'prick tease.' "

"They tell me my father was affectionate when I was a baby—I didn't sleep well and he stayed up and held me. But when I started puberty, I think I made my father uncomfortable. I was and am considered 'sexy.' Whatever that means—I think it's when I discovered that sexiness is where a woman's power lies. I think it was the time of the total break between us—all he did throughout high school was criticize me and complain about me. We argued about what time I should get in at night, my hair, my clothes, my laziness, my grades—he simply made fun of me constantly."

"My mother wanted a little doll. (She still calls me 'Bettie.') She dressed me up until I was five, she gave me dolls and permed my hair. But I now believe that I got a negative view of women from my father and brothers—so negative that I simply decided not to be one. I think I learned that everything she did was 'silly.' We had totally divided roles. I did dishes and helped with dinner. (I vowed I'd never wait on anyone for the rest of my life.) I did laundry and ironing—many fierce arguments. I cleaned bedrooms and bathrooms and floors and vacuumed. My brothers mowed the lawn and washed cars, repaired things and made things out of wood. My room was painted pink even though I wanted blue.

"I saw a movie at a drive-in with my parents that had a stripper in it when I was six or seven and became preoccupied with the 'sexiness' feeling I got. I would put five layers of clothes on and take them off while parading up and down in my room (locked my door). My mother caught me once in my slip—she wasn't sensitive about it. I don't know what she thought. She wouldn't go away. I liked the sexy feeling but I knew it was a secret thing and was vaguely 'wrong.'

"In high school, I was determined to 'get' guys. At first I was amazed that boys found me attractive—many boys. It went to my head, I think. I was silly and cute and could do some art work. I didn't do very well academically. I had several 'best friends' but lost them due to boy conflicts.

"I started drinking at seventeen, so I was catapulted into another peer group. I loved being friends with girls, though, and miss it—we had 'total trust' and talked about everything. But I was moody, rebellious, antagonistic, fearful, angry, mixed up, a 'tough guy,' silly, reclusive (really, I'm amazed at this description). I'm O.K. now. I wanted to be a hermit when I grew up. My parents were of the 'where did we go wrong' school."

In these stories, we see how men's/the culture's definitions of sexuality can be projected onto women and then internalized, at least on some level, as was well described by Karen Horney, the famous rival of Freud.*

While a conscious attempt should be made by men to reexamine their definitions of sexuality, heterosexuality, and the double standard, all displays of sensuality and sexuality by girls and women should not be declared somehow off limits, something women have no right to—because they only relate to what men will think of them.

Flirtation has been declared off-limits by the women's movement, because it is seen to imply women's subservience, women's position in the "male" system, i.e., having to "catch that man." And indeed, this has often been the reality. However, flirtation can also be fun (and give one temporary power). Consider, for example, the implications of the coquettish personal style (which was at one time called being a "femme fatale") of Marlene Dietrich; today we see it in Madonna and other female rock stars, or perhaps in Joan Collins of "Dynasty." Flirtation as a style has for years now been called a "dying gasp of the old"—and yet, is it? The assumption behind this statement is that "naturally" women would not (nor would men) want to flirt or try to fascinate others with their "charms" in a new and "equal" society.

But to erase beautiful clothes, witty style, and sexual intrigue from our existence—as the Chinese did during their cultural revolution, making women and men wear uniforms, with no make-up, short haircuts, all looking the same—would this only impoverish our lives? Such a narrow view, in the end, usually becomes dictatorial and has not brought equality. Since the beginning of classical civilization (and even before—elaborate beaded costumes have been found in graves 20,000 years old), women *and* men have used artistry to decorate or make statements with their personal appearance. After all, men dressed in a more "feminine " way in Roman times, and again particularly in the seventeenth and eighteenth centuries with laces, perfumes, silk stockings, and flowing garments.

While at this time in history, adorning oneself *may* symbolize being "male-identified," trying to eradicate class and gender differences by a code of allowable dress ("regulation uniform"), though it reflects a noble goal—to make everyone "equal"—has not worked; being more severe-looking has not made women as powerful as men. And indeed, the way to equality may be just the opposite: let women retain all styles of dress as one of their options—and encourage men to take these options for themselves too. "Femininity" is a style that has existed for centuries, and is a style which both women and men can continue to enjoy using. In other words, let everyone have as many choices as

*Marcia Westhatt, *The Sexualization of Girls* (New York: Oxford University Press, 1986).

possible—*more* choices—and thus perhaps make us a society of *individuals*, without one rigidly enforced "ideology."

A New Virginity and Celibacy

Are these women withdrawing from "sex," or from the "male" value system?

While some women are trying out casual sex, others are feeling such revulsion against non-loving, "out to get something" sexual behavior on the part of men (*or* women) that they prefer to remain celibate, to have more time for themselves, to avoid frequent chances of feeling "used" or "taken."

27 percent of women say they feel that so much "sex" is just not worth it, and prefer to disassociate themselves from the constant pressure and climate of having to have sex:

"I'm not sure how often I like to have sex. Sexual intercourse is not that important to me anymore. I satisfy myself more than any man has in the past, so I really don't need a man sexually. Men I've known seem to just want sex, so I wind up feeling used and angry. Men now play less of a role in my life. Sex is very much overemphasized, I don't think people are being honest concerning sexuality. They are on the bandwagon, saying sex is 'cool,' the more the better. I can take sex or leave it."

"I go long periods without sex. Every once in a while I will make out with a guy I meet at a dance, but intercourse has been difficult for me to handle emotionally, as the guys usually don't want to have much to do with me after one time in bed."

Celibacy ("no intercourse") was chosen by 33 percent of single women in this study, for a period of at least six months after they had been sexual earlier in their lives; almost all praise it because of the chance it gives them NOT to be *sexually involved—to take an emotional break, to focus their energy and attention on other things:*

"For a period of three years, I chose to be celibate. This was a good time in my life. I was in school and very busy with my work. I was sick of men, I'd had enough of their shit forever. Being single, you have the clarity of self

*Of course, celibacy is possible in marriage, too. See Part III.

to do unusual and imaginative things! Disadvantages: loneliness, too many men trying to pick you up."

"People tend *not* to believe I can exist outside a sexual relationship, and keep mentally popping me into bed with anyone, male or female, that I seem close to. I suppose they would think something was wrong with me if they knew the truth—that celibacy is my normal state."

"If I am not in an intimate relationship, I have no sex life. I enjoy these periods of celibacy, it makes me feel more powerful."

"I have experienced celibacy by choice for about six months. I could focus on my own growth and really reassess what I wanted and expected to have in a relationship with a man. I have previously gone for a couple of years without a sexual relationship. Sometimes I got lonely but it was also good for me to develop my independence and talents. I certainly didn't look upon it as an in-between time, it was what I needed."

"I like being single because my fear of men and uneasiness with them is so great. Also, being single fits my fiercely independent spirit. I am very attractive and invariably get comments like 'Why is such a pretty girl not married?' etc., ad nauseam. That angers me. Most people probably assume something is wrong with me."

"I cannot reiterate enough how good it was for me to enter into a period of celibacy to find myself. Before, I was feeling desperate about my relationships with men. Any woman who begins to feel desperate has no self-respect. She should forget about men for a while—live alone, get to know herself."

"I was celibate for a year. I am convinced that period of sexual self-identity and acquiring self-respect after an affair with a married man was essential to preparing for my current relationship. I think celibacy is really good to get a perspective on what you want and deserve."

Celibacy is easier, it seems, when one is not dating; trying to see men and limit physical involvement to "making out"—is infinitely harder:

"It's either 'all or nothing' when I go out with a guy, even though I don't like it. Once when I was protesting that he was pressuring me too much, he implied there was something wrong with me, that I saw him and men and sex as 'the enemy.' He said he was just trying to please me, make me feel good— why was I resisting? He wouldn't understand, no matter what I said. It's happened other times too. It's so frustrating."

Is it realistic to ask if there can be a return to including "making out" as one option, a possibility, rather than always having to "have sex" (intercourse) or nothing? Perhaps with the growing fear of AIDS, this will become a more interesting possibility for men. Women in *The Hite Report* on female sexuality often expressed an interest in making this an option.

11 percent of the women in this study have remained virgins and never had sex (coitus)—almost miraculously considering the pressures of the last few years (a few cite religious reasons for this preference):

"I have always been celibate. Officially that makes me a 'virgin,' but since I learned to have orgasms (by myself) I have experienced myself as celibate rather than 'virgin.' The vibrator is a wonderful invention, as is running water. Being 'single' is the way I have lived. What is lacking in intensity allows space and clarity—an ink-and-brush drawing of an iris, as compared with Van Gogh's vivid oil painting. I daydream of having someone to snuggle up to, then the daydreams dissolve into imagined quarrels, misunderstandings, hurt feelings, and so on."

"I am a virgin, but other sexual activity could be a part of my life. It is very difficult for me to meet someone I like and am attracted to and have respect for, who won't pressure me. If it was easy, I'd be in a relationship now. I feel disheartened. I enjoy being single, but I would be happier in a relationship."

"I don't mind saying that at twenty-two years old I'm still a virgin. I want the first time I make love to be with someone I really, really love—and that opportunity just hasn't presented itself yet."

"I'm still a virgin. It's not because I haven't been asked. The man I just broke off with was terrific, and great as far as sex was concerned. We indulged in foreplay and he was content with that, he never made me feel guilty about my decision of wanting to wait till I was married. One reason he was so patient was because he had intentions of marrying me."

"I have never had sex. I plan to save it for marriage. I am a twenty-one-year-old student in Louisiana, white. I got this questionnaire from our Bible training center. I live with my parents and commute thirty miles each day to college. In high school, I didn't get asked out by guys because although I am attractive, I was a 'nice' girl. Guys take that to mean 'no good time.' I never felt pressure to conform, however, because people liked and accepted me the way I was. It helped that my best friend was also a Christian, so we gave each other support. She and I are still best friends."

Some fundamentalist religious groups have instituted activities through which a woman can become a "Born-Again Virgin"—that is, the woman, in a sort of group meeting, "confesses" her past and promises never again to have intercourse until marriage. But really, what seems to be in most women's minds when they consider stopping sexual relationships is not so much a return to shame about their own sexuality as emotional frustration and a feeling that men rarely know how to have a sexual relationship with a loving attitude. For this reason, they find, out of respect for themselves, they are happier staying away from sex.

What does "virginity" mean?

One woman says virginity and purity are spiritual and not physical matters, and warns women not against giving away their bodies but against giving away their hearts and minds too easily:

"I am twenty-three, a graduate student, single, and into all forms of art and media. In dealings with men, I find putting up a front works beautifully. Men still have internalized the woman as 'object of desire' that should be conquered. Keeping one step sideways of their gaze encourages pursuit, heightens the desire, the theater. If you're ready to throw it all away too soon, it's underselling yourself. Funny, but I don't mean sexually either! Which was the commodity not long ago. When I say giving yourself away I mean psychologically, emotionally, and intellectually as well as/or sexually."

Virginity can be a state of mind, a way of life one passes into and out of, but always connected with a woman's owning herself—not saving herself to be "owned" by someone else. Diana/Artemis in classical times was known as the "virgin goddess." This did not mean she was not sexual, or did not have sex with men, but that she was never *owned.* For some women in this study, this concept seems to be returning: to have sex, but not to be owned, to return oneself *to* oneself—remaining true to oneself, never being possessed.

Did women have more "power" before the "sexual revolution" by remaining "virgins" while single, "withholding" sex?

One woman, age sixty-five, expresses the standard of sexual behavior for women as it was in the 1950s before the "sexual revolution":

"When I was a young girl the saying was: 'If you let a man have his way, he got what he wanted and he will leave.' I think a girl should make a man wait for sex."

A woman in her early twenties expresses the order of the day sexually when she was in college:

"I slept with lots of boys when I went to school. It was because of the times. My boyfriend I liked most would say, 'I want you to sleep with other men.' Can you believe it? I felt obliged to. It was also a bit of revenge—boys do it, why can't I? Well, I'd say now: because I didn't really want to. But any other attempt at a relationship didn't work and I didn't know what else to do. Plus, in some ways it was fun and defiant."

But the same young woman adds:

"I wish I was a virgin now, sort of. I almost feel like one."

Ever since the "sexual revolution," women have been expected to have sex before marriage. With the end of the double standard, it was said, women would be able to have sex as often as they wanted to, without being considered "bad girls." In fact, as seen here, what happened was that women were now expected to have sex whenever *men* wanted, while at the same time still being looked down on for being "loose," "free," "available"; in short, women were seen as being "not quite top of the line" by many men when they did, often under pressure, have sex freely. (As one woman in college puts it, "Men look down on you if you're 'too sexy' or 'too free,' but they won't relate to you, will find you 'ridiculous' and 'disturbed,' if you won't.")

Some people believe that the answer to this Catch-22 for single women is a return to virginity before marriage. (Women are "the guardians of morality" anyway . . .) But can we go back? If one just says, "Women can say no," this puts the problem back on women, and also forces women to choose between expressing themselves and defending themselves. No one thinks of a campaign advising men, "You can come by yourself, you can masturbate—you don't have to have intercourse for orgasm."

If men assume, are taught, that they should try to have sex without commitment, then the idea is: "How can they best 'get away with it'?" Boys and men will often even boast that they are "only male, after all," "out for what they can get." The nastiness of some aspects of the sexual situation consists in the arrogance and haughtiness with which men/boys can so easily dispose of women after having "had" them sexually—with a feeling of utter self-righteousness and justification (this is "natural" animal behavior after all, etc.).

If the problem is put back on women—return to "virginity," "women can say no"—then men are tacitly encouraged, given the right, which they always had, to have sex wherever they can find it, to pressure women into having it, because "men are men" and "they can't help it"—and the underlying message to men that if they don't try for it, they had better worry about their "masculinity," they are not "real men," is perpetuated.

Women's training to be loving and giving (see Part I) makes dating very lopsided in terms of the needs of the two parties. Alienated, unscrupulous men and boys who want to feel very "masculine," who have been taught that their "hormones" propel them to have intercourse with women, and that this makes them "real men," take advantage of women's desire to love and be giving, to push for sex.

Some men say, "Well, don't women enjoy sex too, just as much as men? Therefore, the man is not taking advantage of the woman, he is giving her something she needs as much as he does—even if temporarily." But while sometimes women are at a point in their lives when they enjoy experimenting and having "adventures," it is quite clear that most women, for most of their lives, prefer sex in a context of feelings and respect.

Women should not have to choose between being sexual and not being sexual; nor should women have to define their sexuality under such pressure and negativity from men. Instead women and men should challenge the reigning ideology—i.e., the version of the "male" culture which decrees that "boys will be boys," closing a blind eye to many boys' "hit and run" or "shopping" attitudes toward girls—the same "male" culture which looks down on teenage girls for getting abortions, but does not think that the missing boys who probably pushed for intercourse are also "villains"/victims, now set up for emotional confusion and alienation too. Sex is not bad; treating another person with disrespect is.

Is Looking for Lots of "Sex" "Natural"? Are Women "Brainwashed"—or Are Men "Dehumanized"?

Is monogamous love, and/or a desire for marriage, a "natural" tendency which men have been taught to repress? Or are multiple sexual relationships "natural," and do women typically avoid them only because they are brought up to be prudes and "good girls"? (Or because people call them "sluts" otherwise?)

The presumption, as we noted in the conclusion to Part I, is usually that what men do, think, or feel is "natural," that if only women would give up their "hang-ups," they would naturally be "like men" too. The assumption since the "sexual revolution" has therefore almost universally been that women would—and should—change their values and sexual behavior to be more like men, i.e., to have sex more outside of marriage and have it not mean so much. This thinking assumes that the "male" system is biologically ordained, and the "female" system is "acculturated"—that women are "held back" because of the fear of getting pregnant and other historical reasons.

But is there any logical reason for believing that "promiscuity" is "natural"? (After all, men are *taught* to "go after sex.") Even if it might be "natural" (to start with that as an *assumption*), to value "having sex" over having a very emotional love (and wanting to be monogamous) is not a belief system most women want to take on. Most women would say here that it is men who should change and begin to understand the connection of sex with feelings, understand that the body and spirit may not be as separate after all.

Was the "Sexual Revolution" Wrong?* or Is It the "Male" Ideology and Its Double Standard That Make It Wrong?

Are boys alienated from themselves by being taught to see girls as "scores"? By the playboy mentality?

It is the "male" ideology that tells boys that a boy becomes a man when he first "has" a woman—i.e., has intercourse/penetrates a woman—and that a man stays more of a man the more often he continues to do so. Other aspects of this "male" credo include "the more sex, the better," "shopping around is natural," "nature made men to disseminate their semen to the widest possible sample" (as in *The King and I:* "Bee must go from blossom to blossom," etc.). The corollary to this kind of attitude (wherein "getting some"—i.e., penetration—is still "scoring," "getting it over on so-and-so," having her") is the idea that all women "want a man," need to "catch a man," "trap" one into marriage. So there is a built-in, never acknowledged game going on: he trying to "get some," she trying to "get him to care"—and he fleeing as if "caring" were a fate worse than death.

The "male" philosophy has tended to see sex as a simple biological pleasure,

*There is a great deal of confusion about the difference between the "sexual revolution" and "women's liberation." Many people seem to believe that "women's liberation" led to the current "freedom" about women's sexuality, and the pressure to have sex at every turn. However, it was the "sexual revolution" which said that now women could have "free sex" without marriage, supposedly with no recriminations.

While some parts of the "women's movement" did believe that the "sexual revolution" was a step forward for women, most see the whole question another way. The core issues of "women's liberation" have always had a different focus from those of the "sexual revolution." While the "sexual revolution" was in favor of "free sex" and an end to legal marriage, the women's movement was a much broader social force asking questions about women's status, male power, and its origins, and calling for equal economic and educational opportunities for women.

On the other hand, *Re-Making Love* by Barbara Ehrenreich, Betsy Hess, and Gloria Jacobs (New York: Doubleday, 1986) reminds us how much women have done to claim their rights to their/our own bodies.

indeed, to endorse this view of it. Men have put an enormous amount of pressure on women to have "sex." Women find this pressure and this philosophy, for the most part, mechanical and insensitive, making erotic and sensual interaction almost impossible. Men have called women who say "no" to sex when there are no feelings involved "hung up" or "Victorian" (1960s) or "anti-male," "man haters" (1970s and 1980s). Even in "serious" academic journals, these theories have consistently been proposed or assumed—i.e., that women historically have been "brainwashed" to be "good girls" and for this reason are afraid to like sex, especially sex without love—"the way men (in their more grown-up way?) do." Rather than seeing women's philosophy as just as valid as their own, a topic for research or philosophical debate between two equal, differing cultural perspectives, requiring thought and analysis, many men ridicule women's point of view as nonsense, both personally and in articles. Whether the prospect of getting AIDS will change this behavior has yet to be seen; 1987 research for this study shows a surprising apathy with regard to changing behavior—although everyone agrees they "ought to."

Where did the double standard come from?
Adam and Eve as early propaganda

Why does the "male" ideology have to make such an extreme fetish of gender division? Many theorists have pointed to the obvious: that only through controlling women's sexuality and reproduction can men have inheritance pass through them—i.e., have a male-dominated society. Without strict rules and regulations regarding gender behavior (especially for women), men could not be sure that the children women were bearing were their own, claim them as their legal property, have rights over them. This is why such continuous cultural reinforcement of "what sexuality is" is necessary. (Is it possible that gender division has not always been the fundamental principle of society—or that the genders were not always defined in the ways they are now?)

But there is another way of looking at the Adam and Eve story than that usually seen by historians. Could it be that one of its messages—a message now unseen, but clear to those of early times—was exactly this: *to focus attention on gender division as the fundamental principle of a new social order* and to establish the basic "personality traits" of these two "original beings" as the prototypes for future society? These personality traits may not have been standard for the two genders at that time. Certainly Adam and Eve are the earliest symbol known of the double standard and negative attitudes toward women in Western thought.*

And symbols and pictures of Adam and Eve continue to be used in advertis-

---

*Other creation stories, with some similar themes, are found in surrounding cultures around 3000 B.C., such as in Sumerian texts, etc.; some may be older.

ing and design, appearing constantly all around us, reminding us of Eve's "wickedness," that she caused our "downfall," our being expelled from the Garden of Eden. Women were supposedly responsible for "original sin," and we are still being reminded of our "basic natures"—thus making us try even harder to be "good," show we are "trustworthy," so as to be accepted by the society, be loved. It is no surprise that something as old in Western tradition, in patriarchal tradition, as the dichotomy between "bad" women and "good" women* has not been ended by the mere twenty years of women's challenging male domination. Or even by the last hundred years since the end of women's legal ownership by husbands and fathers, since the dichotomy—and there is, of course, no such dichotomy for men—has ancient roots entwined in the foundations of our culture.

Does the new religious revival movement challenge the double standard?

Has the religious revival movement made any change in the widespread male acceptance of the double standard? Not really. The movement puts great pressure on women to "realize" their natural desire for children, to be mothers, and to put the needs of the children and family/father *first*. Women who are not married or mothers are asked to reexamine their reasons and listen carefully to those who know better about what is "right" in life. In addition, the religious version of the "male" ideology usually expects women to make sacrifices in marriage and love relationships that men are almost never asked to make.

There are, in fact, two sides to the double standard: the playboy version— "all women are for sex, let's take them"; and the religious version—"all women should be in the home, mothers." In other words, the double standard is part of the "male" ideology, which is so enmeshed in all aspects of our lives. This is why the double standard did not disappear with the "sexual revolution," and why it has not yet disappeared even with the strides made by the women's movement.†

Moreover, while it certainly does not endorse the "playboy" mentality, the "born again" movement has produced very little propaganda exhorting boys not to see girls either as "targets" from which to get sex or as "mothers"—i.e., service people—especially compared to the amount of propaganda directed at

*See Professor Wendy Doniger O'Flaherty's work for the documentation of this split in classical Indian culture, in the Rig Vedas; that culture, like ours, was also based in large part on the ideology and social structure of Indo-European tribes; indeed we have an extremely important common cultural heritage, which is, however, generally unmentioned.

†Of course, not all men agree with the playboy game plan regarding sex, or with the religious revival movement's version of the proper way of life for women either. There is a vigorous minority of men of every political persuasion who do not see themselves in either the men-are-beasts-who-want-women's-bodies idea of who men are, or the men-marry-mothers-only school of thought. Some of these interesting men appear in *The Hite Report* on men.

women stressing the values of motherhood and subordination to one's family. And most parts of the revivalist religious movement also clearly state that although husband and wife are a team, in the final analysis the man must lead—in traditional, patriarchal fashion. As Jerry Falwell put it in 1986 on television, "The man is the spiritual fountainhead of the family—the leader." In other words, the "good old days" are simply the old, unequal, oppressed days women have been struggling to get choices out of, to escape from.

Still, the atmosphere in a family-oriented philosophy, even a hierarchically organized one, can be felt as an improvement for a woman emerging from the singles arena of the "sexual revolution," wherein sex is seen as a biological urge not to be denied or interfered with by interpersonal relationships or ethical codes. Thus it is no surprise that much of the conservative religious movement's backbone is made up of women or that it is driven largely by women's energy—women's donated office work, organizing abilities, church attendance, fund-raising activities. Many women like the church because it supports them in their struggle to continue the home-family value system*—i.e., it supports them as long as they stay in the home (or at most combine home with career only after children are in school; women with young children who want to work are sometimes made to feel ashamed of "shirking their responsibility"). But there is something appealing about the desire, at least on the part of some men, to continue a tradition of "family" values—i.e., humane values. If only these men could learn not to make those values conditional on women's secondary status, on women's subservience—and their own dominance.

What Is Sexuality?
Creating a New Vision of Sexuality

What was women's sexuality originally like?

What would women's sexuality be like without a society to shape it? Do we know? Women in the first *Hite Report* asserted that women have a right to "undefine" sexuality, to redesign it individually; that we have a complete right to say "no" to sex; and that we may not really know yet what "female sexuality" is.

Is sex basically "intercourse"—or an individual vocabulary of activities? *The Hite Report* in 1976 argued for undefining sexuality†—both the physical "acts"

---

*See Part I.

†In other words, *The Hite Report* stated that what we think of as "sex" is not a biological given, but a historically and culturally created phenomenon. Much ridicule was heaped on this idea by parts of the popular press at the time—and again when it was reiterated in *The Hite Report on Male Sexuality* in 1981.

that we define as "sex" and the cultural atmosphere surrounding "sex." Sex could become an individual vocabulary of activities, chosen to show how we want to express ourselves at a given time, with a specific feeling and meaning—an individual choice of activities, not always necessarily "foreplay" followed by "vaginal penetration" (why not call it "penile covering"?) and intercourse, ending with male orgasm.

The Judeo-Christian tradition has had a very narrow idea of what "sexuality" should be, mostly relating to reproductive activity. It spelled out, both in the Bible and in rabbinical and papal encyclicals, how often one should have coitus, with whom, when, and so on—thus certainly giving the impression that coitus is the central act of "sex," and that it is, furthermore, the central connecting point, the nexus, between the two genders—their most important relationship. Interestingly, the Bible does not speak of female orgasm, only male orgasm. Is this because it is only male orgasm which is necessary for pregnancy and reproduction?

Undefining sex: sex should become a more individual vocabulary

While women, as documented over and over in *The Hite Report*, may love having intercourse with men they want to have intercourse with, orgasm or no orgasm—the idea that one *must* have intercourse, that this *must* be one of the activities when you caress a person, does not make for spontaneous expression or freedom of desire, an open way of translating feelings into actions. And as long as the "male" ideology persists, and sees women as "scores" or mothers, the atmosphere around physical pleasure will not change. We will not be free to discover and feel, design new types of sexuality that celebrate the richness of the whole spectrum of what "female sexuality" and "male sexuality" can be all about.

We still haven't undefined sex enough to permit an individual redefinition of sexuality—or is it that we haven't changed social conditions enough yet to allow ourselves to feel free enough to do this?

As this was summed up in the *Hite Report* on female sexuality: "Although we tend to think of 'sex' as one set pattern, one group of activities (in essence,

---

Michel Foucault took up this theme, that sexuality is historically and culturally formulated, in his 1978 and 1982 works, *The History of Sexuality, vols. I and II.* It is interesting to note that while *The Hite Report* was ridiculed for this thesis (both here and in France) in 1976–77, Foucault's work in 1978 and later was accepted. Was this because it was published later and the climate of opinion had changed, or because—as women assert throughout this book—women's ideas and thoughts are not always taken so seriously? Scholars citing Foucault as the originator of this thesis should be careful to note accurately the earlier statement of this theory in *The Hite Report*, and should also be aware of Foucault's exposure to feminist intellectual debate in France during those years.

reproductive activity), there is no need to limit ourselves in this way. . . . Our definition of sex belongs to a world view that is past—or passing. Sexuality, and sexual relations, no longer define the important property right they once did; children are no longer central to the power either of the state or the individual. Although all of our social institutions are still totally based on hierarchical and patriarchal forms, patriarchy as a form is really dead, as is the sexuality that defined it. We are currently in a period of transition, although it is unclear as yet to what. . . .*

Can women, even now, define sex on their own terms?

If understanding our own bodies well enough to know how we have orgasms and not be inhibited from telling this to men is a "sexual revolution"—and in fact, it is a profound change from the days in which, after sex, a woman would go into the bathroom and close the door and masturbate—still, the fact is that almost every man with whom a woman has sex continues to expect that sex will center on intercourse/penetration—almost as his automatic "right." Although many men now understand most women's need for clitoral stimulation, still, generally most men continue to see "penetration" and intercourse/coitus as the only "real" definitions of sex. This is not to say that women don't enjoy these activities, but that the focus on these activities, their glorification over all others by the society, is as much a matter of ideology as of physical desire.

Continuing controversies over the nature of female orgasm

But haven't women made profound changes in their sexuality over the past years? In terms of the stimulation for orgasm, yes, to some extent. The idea that most women need some form of clitoral or exterior (non-vaginal) stimulation in order to orgasm, as documented in *The Hite Report* (1976), has now been accepted by women (and by gynecologists and counselors) on a large scale—both in the United States and in many other countries.

As early as the 1950s questions were raised about whether vaginal intercourse alone leads to orgasm for most women, in particular by Albert Ellis in his essay, "Is the Vaginal Orgasm a Myth?"† Another pioneer was Anne Koedt, who, in 1970, wrote "The Myth of the Vaginal Orgasm," an essay

---

The Hite Report (New York: Dell, 1977), p. 527.
†Albert Ellis and A. P. Pillay, eds., "*Sex, Society and the Individual*," *International Journal of Sexology* (1953): pp. 337–49.

which was later published in the anthology *Radical Feminism.* * In Germany, in 1975, Alice Schwarzer published *Der Kleine Unterschied,* † also attacking the idea that women should be expected to orgasm from simple vaginal penetration.

In 1973, Dr. Leah Schaefer published, as part of an earlier Ph.D. thesis done at Columbia with Margaret Mead and others, in-depth interviews with thirty women about their sexual feelings which demonstrated that it was more "normal" for women not to orgasm from simple coitus than "abnormal." In a psychological study published in 1972, Seymour Fisher,‡ although not describing this as "normal," stated that two-thirds of the women in his study said they could not orgasm during coitus per se (although they could in other ways), while one-third of them could. Dr. Fisher tried to connect this "ability" to orgasm with whether or not the women had been encouraged to achieve in general by their fathers—since, among all the variables, this was the only correlation he found. Finally, in *The New Sex Therapy,* § in 1974, Helen Singer Kaplan also questioned whether it is correct to label the large number of women who do not orgasm from coitus alone (but do orgasm in other ways) "abnormal."

The Hite Report, in research extending from 1971 to 1976 and including 3,500 women, found that two-thirds of women do not orgasm from intercourse but orgasm easily in other ways—and went on to call into question, on the basis of women's statements, the definition of "sex" our culture has considered a biological given. *The Hite Report* also documented the many ways women have of reaching orgasm easily during self-stimulation (masturbation), saying that these stimulations should be included as part of what we call "sex," and considered as important and exciting as the activities which lead to male orgasms.

It is astonishing to see that even today Masters and Johnson classify women who can orgasm easily in other ways, but do not orgasm during simple "vaginal penetration," as having a "sexual dysfunction." Although they state that they believe clitoral stimulation is important for women's orgasms, they believe a "normal" woman should get enough "indirect" clitoral stimulation from simple intercourse (coitus) to lead to orgasm. They do not believe manual stimulation should be "necessary." ‖ They say this in the face of the evidence in *The Hite Report* ** and other studies, evidence that intercourse alone is not enough

*See Anne Koedt in Ellen Levine and Anita Rapone, eds., *Radical Feminism* (New York: Quadrangle, 1973).
†Leah Cahan/Schaefer, *Women and Sex: Sexual Experiences and Reactions of a Group of Thirty Women as Told to a Female Psychotherapist* (New York: Pantheon, 1973).
‡Seymour Fisher, *The Female Orgasm* (New York: Basic Books, 1972).
§Helen Singer Kaplan, *The New Sex Therapy* (Boston: Little, Brown, 1971).
‖In 1986, Masters and Johnson published *The Art of Human Loving,* reiterating their earlier position, although they have done no survey work to back up their claims.
**This study has been replicated in Norway, Sweden, and Brazil, with the findings regarding orgasm being basically the same. A similar study was undertaken in England, also based on *The Hite Report* questionnaire, with the same basic findings.

stimulation for most women to orgasm. In fact, there is no point in labeling women "normal" or "abnormal," depending on whether they orgasm from "vaginal stimulation" or "clitoral stimulation."

It is interesting to speculate as to why Kinsey did not go into this subject, since it has been "common knowledge" for so long that "women have a problem" having orgasms during "sex"—i.e., intercourse/coitus—and that women could orgasm much more easily from clitoral stimulation or masturbation. However, aside from two or three oblique sentences, Kinsey does not address the topic. In private correspondence, however, it is said that he did discuss this matter, and that he believed clitoral stimulation by hand or mouth to be by far the easiest way for women to orgasm.* In other words, "Although the 'problem' had been known for some time, it was not until research was done for *The Hite Report*, and given a culturally related analysis that the ideological misunderstanding of female sexuality was made clear, on the basis of scientific evidence," as Dr. William Granzig, past president of the American Association of Sex Educators, Counselors and Therapists, has put it.

The most advanced information presented recently has been the anatomical drawings by illustrator Suzanne Gage which show the interior clitoral system in detail. One can begin to understand the anatomy of female sexuality much more fully through these drawings, which Freud would surely have appreciated; as he said, perhaps all his theories on female sexuality would turn out to be inaccurate, since the interior anatomy of women's sexual organs was not known at the time he was writing. We are still learning about this interior anatomy, especially the structures beneath the skin. The Gage drawings are available in *A New View of a Woman's Body*, the best source for information at present.

One woman, age twenty-six, explains the struggle taking place in her relationship right now over redefining the feeling around sexuality:

"My anger with him began very quickly with the first intercourse. First, I was resistant to sex at that moment, and felt that he ignored this in his typically male intense desire to complete the act, as if that would couple us even without my cooperation. Then I disliked the crudeness of fucking, his absorption in the act, my lack of pleasure or orgasm, and the fact that he fell asleep on top of me and was quite satisfied with himself. I feel that fucking is much more pleasurable for him than for me, that the whole system is geared toward the pretense that fucking is the epitome of sexuality. So I feel our most obvious problem is sex.

"I've told him that I don't usually orgasm from intercourse and that when I do, it's less intense and satisfying than a clitoral orgasm. I've been telling him

*See also James Jones' forthcoming biography of Kinsey, done through use (among other sources) of the archives of the Kinsey Institute in Bloomington, Indiana.

this for almost two years. He keeps trying to think of it as a temporary condition—because otherwise, he says, it ruins something for him. He always dreamed of finding a woman who would respond to him, to his penis. He says this is something that takes away the whole pornographic, sadistic image of the man as taking, and makes him a giver.

"He has never really accepted my clitoris as the source of complete satisfaction for me, despite whatever wonderful sensations I get from my vagina. It's hard for me to enjoy my sexuality when he considers it a sad joke on men. It's funny, because I really understand Freud now. It must have been sad for this phallocentric Victorian male to realize that his penis counted only for him—he wanted it to be the ultimate sexual tool. Reaching outward, transforming. It even made my brother, who is eighteen, sad to realize that his penis couldn't give a woman as much pleasure as it could give him. I mean genuinely sad— like, what's the use?

"What I keep trying to tell my lover is that it wouldn't matter to me—that I'd be more than happy to give in that way—if he would accept *my* sexuality as it is. I've never felt accepted by him for what feels best to me; we are always at cross-purposes and trying to accomplish the impossible. But then what makes me mad is that in the process he's getting off and I'm not. I feel guilty for not coming from fucking. I'm afraid he's going to leave me for someone who'll pretend to come from fucking, who'll lie, or who doesn't know any better. He feels guilty for wanting the turn-on of a woman who really loves fucking. The funny thing is that what turns me on most about fucking is how good it feels to him. I feel sad sometimes that we're in such a quandary.

"The simplest way for me to come is through manual stimulation (I hate that phrase) either by myself or by a partner who knows how good it feels to me. It doesn't feel good as a sort of half-ass compensation program. It isn't hard to do, just natural. But he has never learned to touch me properly, so it has become another reminder that I'm sort of the impotent one in our bed—the one who has to have 'extra' stimulation.

"For a long time, no amount of attention paid to my clitoris after intercourse (before intercourse, it was always curtailed by his eagerness to begin fucking) could make up for the intensity with which he pursued vaginal stimulation. Obviously, this was much more fun for him. I began to feel that my having a vagina was for the male's pleasure, not mine. It was partly an 'if you won't play by my rules, I'll take my football and go home' reaction, but it was worsened by his assumption that the vagina was for both of us, that vaginal and clitoral stimulation were interchangeable feelings, that the clitoris was for starting or finishing real sex, not for sex.

"It makes me angry that with a man I love I have to go through the unpleasantness of birth control, bladder infections, vaginal infections, long periods of sex that I'm supposed to pretend are as great for me as for him. I think fucking ought to be seen as women fucking men, but that seems to go against the grain of male pride. They seem to want to 'justify' it by insisting that it is as good for us as it is for them. Even though a woman sleeping with a man is dependent on him for her pleasure in cunnilingus and manual sex, it is somehow unallowable to admit that he is dependent upon her for his pleasure in fucking. We are always kept in debt.

"I also had a great deal of pain through the first months of our relationship. We had a lot of sex, and I was constantly sore, developing a raw vagina, vaginal fungus, and bladder infection (which have finally healed). My lover was ignorant about the vulnerability of my membranes as opposed to his; it seems to scare him to think it.

"I really wonder whether there are women that have the sense of actively fucking the man with their vaginas or something like that. I'd like to ask women how they live with men, how they enjoy sex, until I get some real answers. I've talked about not coming from intercourse with two or three women—that it makes me mad that men can have such reliable pleasure from sex and we can't. Usually from women I get the feeling that it's just one of those things they've learned to live with. Yet one woman I talked to apparently has a great deal of mutuality in her sex with her boyfriend, and feels free not to have sex with him, depending on their emotional situation. Another woman I talked to had given up on men as lovers, though she occasionally has a one-night stand—that is, she's given up on men emotionally, which to me means that at some level she must be pretty pissed off."

Of course, another way to look at our question, "What can sexuality/pleasure be like for women?" is to look at sex as it is understood/defined/created by women together in lesbian relationships. See Part IV.

But—do men really enjoy their definition of sexuality so fully?*

Although it seems so obvious, do we know what "male sexuality" really is? After all, it is impossible for us to know exactly how much of what we see men do is "natural" "male sexuality" and how much is learned or reinforced behavior.

The current definition of "male sexuality" (as a driving desire for "penetration") is quite clearly culturally exaggerated. "Male sexuality" certainly comprises a much larger, more varied group of physical feelings—as men describe them in *The Hite Report* on men. We hardly know what "male sexuality" is, because it has been so narrowly channeled by the culture.

Surprisingly, when looked at more closely, the definition of "sexuality" put

---

*Men are encouraged to define themselves in great part by their sexual "abilities" or lack of same: "impotent," meaning "lack of erection," can also apply to a man's whole being!

forth by the "male" ideology is actually quite negative. This is surprising because it is often thought that men are very "pro-sex," while women are "anti-sex." In fact, women are more pro-sensuality, most women think in terms of a much broader concept of sexuality than the reproductive model we have come to believe is "natural"—while the basic "male" ideology refers to sexuality as a "body function," an instinct, an "animal feeling" of pleasure—the "opposite" of spiritual feeling. In this value system, "animal feeling" is somehow not respectable, something "without soul" (animals in early Christian tradition did not have "souls")—brute "bestial behavior." While the point here is certainly not to say that sex must always be "sweet," not passionate, the idea of sexuality as completely cut off from feeling—sex as something "subhuman" that animals (who have no feelings?) do and therefore not part of our humanity, part of a whole person—is a rather strange definition of sexuality, and probably not the most erotic one we could espouse.

"For men—to be penetrated not only physically but emotionally . . ."

A part of the double standard not frequently cited is what may be an alienating pressure on *men* to have frequent sex, and to think and see the world in mostly compartmentalized sexual terms. In fact, the "male" ideology (and the life cycle it creates) robs men of the chance to enjoy love, by warning them against "confusing" a passionate attraction with "love," warning them against real closeness, saying "you can't trust women," "don't let your sex drive confuse you," and so on—stating that a "real man" should be "independent," remain "free" and unmarried for as long as possible, watch out for being "tied down." "Real men" should go after/want to have sex with as many women as possible, as often as possible. "Real men" don't fall head over heels in love. The result of all this training of men to control their feelings is that many men become alienated from their deeper feelings.

The re-invention of "male sexuality" was discussed in *The Hite Report on Male Sexuality*, with many men seeming to feel on a gut level that somehow they were missing out—that no matter how much sex they had, they were left feeling unsatisfied on some level. And yet our culture's lessons to men have been so strong that few men have been able to go past them, to create their own personal sexuality or to transcend the double standard. But a new sexuality and identity is certainly possible for men.

This is by no means to downgrade men's traditional "lust," but to redefine it: "Passion is one of the most beautiful parts of all sensuality—the desire to possess, to take, to ravish and be ravished, to penetrate and be penetrated. But is physical love real love? While love is caring, love is also passion and desire, the desire to belong to, mingle with, be inside of another. Part of love is a sheer physical feeling—a desire not only to have orgasm and 'sex,' but to lie close while sleeping together, to inhale the breath of the other, to press chests (and souls) together, so tightly, as tightly as possible; to lie feeling the other breathe as they sleep, their breath grazing your cheek and mingling with your own breath; to smell their body, caress their mouth with your tongue as if it were your own mouth, know the smell and taste of their genitals—to feel with your finger inside them, to caress the opening of their buttocks. What is love? Love is talking and understanding and counting on and being counted on, but love is also the deepest intermingling of bodies. In a way, body memory of a loved one is stronger and lasts longer than all the other memories."*

Toward a new sexuality: reintegrating sexuality and spirituality

In traditional Western ("male") philosophy and religion, the body has been seen as separate from the mind, soul, and, in consequence, "sex" has likewise been presented as without context (except that of conquest or reproduction?), its meaning removed from mutual expression of feelings, cut off from the rest of life.

For most women, however, this body/mind split hardly exists; for them the body and spirit are united and sex is inseparable from emotion. As one woman describes love, "Love is a longed-for feeling of unity, bliss, fulfillment. A strong feeling you feel for someone right from the beginning—a feeling of well-being all over. Sexual passion and the desire for a relationship are indistinguishable." And another: "I usually feel the closest after we make love, because it is an expression of all the wonderful and closest feelings I have toward her. When we make love, I feel as though we are a total entity—I can't tell where she leaves off and where I begin. It seems to be a 'complete' feeling, capturing my emotions, my intellect, and my physical awareness."

Thus most women feel that passion includes not only the body but also the mind and the emotions; when they speak here about a "passionate connection," they are not referring to just a feeling of lust. As one woman puts it, "There are more passionate and less passionate relationships. The passion is involved in every part of knowing the person, not just the sex." And many women, referring to a deeply passionate attraction when speaking of "falling in love," also include transcendent or spiritual feelings.

To try to downgrade this to "mere" lust is again a problem of language, reflecting the philosophical biases of Western history. The phrases we have to work with in English are "lust," "loving," "caring," and being "in love." But

The Hite Report on Male Sexuality (New York: Ballantine, 1982), pp. 610–11.

love as sexual desire, love as caring—are these really the categories women feel? Or are many women here describing passion as an intensity of the mind and body felt all at the same time in a kind of ecstatic mingling?

Some feminist philosophers* have questioned whether the mind/body split has ever existed for women. Certainly, the evidence of this study is that the majority of women—although, of course, they know the difference—do not feel such a split. Women often see and feel things "holistically"—i.e., as wholes, rather than dualistically, as the "male" ideology does. And this is in spite of the fact that images reinforcing the "male" ideology's separation of sexual and motherly love are all around us, reflected particularly in the Eve/Mary split— the "good" woman and "bad" woman of the Judeo-Christian tradition;† "good women" are mothers, asexual (like Mary, who bore a child without having sex), and "bad women" are sexual and pleasure-seeking (those who "eat the apple of carnal knowledge" and "lead men astray"). Such stereotypes pervade popular slogans and motifs, and indeed women and even girls in high school, as seen in this study, are still continuously having to fight their effects, as boys treat them with disrespect during and after sex. And though girls and women themselves may interiorize these images, and face a split identity, wondering which "type" they are before they are even old enough to know that they need not choose between preexisting stereotypes, women continue to resist abandoning their own definition of passion.

As seen in the conclusion to Part I, the "male" ideology implicitly holds that the way men do things is somehow "reality," "the real world," whereas how women do things is a "role." So, in this way of thinking, if women connect sex and feelings, this is a "role" they have been taught, one they should drop, not a "reality" or part of "nature." "Natural sex" is what men do—i.e., see no need to connect sex with emotional life. In fact, however, most people (men as well as women) probably experience a passionate attraction to someone, falling "in love," as both physical and emotional—although men in particular (but women, too, since the "sexual revolution") are encouraged to label these feelings "only physical," "just sex." But almost all women continue to hold that these early feelings of attraction include both physical and emotional elements, that there is no way to separate them. This leads to the situation in which a woman, after a short time with a man, may say she is ready for an emotional relationship—whereas the man usually takes much longer to reach this conclusion.

Is women's connection of sex and feeling a "moralistic" holdover that keeps us from our "true hedonism," if not "repressed" by culture and religion? Or is it that the mind/body split in the area of love and sex has never fit human

---

*See Alisson Jaggar, *Feminist Politics and Human Nature* (Roman and Allantold, 1983), and unpublished papers presented before the Society of Women in Philosophy.
†During the Middle Ages, perhaps as many "bad women" as Jews during World War II were exterminated, in a concrete attempt to "cleanse" the world of "wicked women."

feelings or human experience? After all, men also say that sex is much better when you love someone (see *The Hite Report* on men)—although they would still feel comfortable having sex without feelings more often than women.

Actually, in the earliest civilizations, before the "Garden of Eden," sexuality may have been not only an individual behavior but also part of spirituality, religion, sometimes even part of religious rites; then reproduction and the feelings leading up to reproduction were seen, rightly, as part of the mystery of rebirth of life. Even in Greek times, the remnants or descendants of this early religion, the "Mysteries," included sexual/religious rites. In other words, some of the meanings of sexuality were probably once religious, related to the worship of reproduction, the sacredness of the re-creation of life.* Thus seen, women's resistance to separating sex and feelings may have an entirely different cast to it, as something with roots in the distant past—in a different philosophy. And it may presage a very different future.

*See Marija Gimbutas, *Goddesses and Gods of Old Europe* (Los Angeles: University of California Press, 1982). See also Colin Renfrew, ed., *The Monolithic Monuments of Western Europe* (London: Thames and Hudson, 1981).

Inside Dating Relationships: How Are Women Feeling?

Emotional Uncertainty in Relationships

One woman describes her feelings of frustration, confusion, and love, all mixed together, as she experiences a great deal of ambiguity in the man she loves:

"I have a constant feeling of never being satisfied for some reason. Either he's not calling, or when he's calling, it's not romantic, and so on. . . . When I try to talk to him, really talk to him, I feel like I just can't get through—except sometimes, when *he* wants to talk, he'll say the loveliest things. Other times, he just won't respond and/or doesn't want to make love, and I never know why.

"It seems to revolve around a constant question of should I be asking myself, 'Is everything all right in terms of him (does he still love me)?' or 'Is everything all right in terms of *me*? How am *I*?' If I am unhappy a lot, and he won't talk to me about the problems or resolve the issues, should I say, 'Well, everything is really O.K. because he's O.K. and he's still there and still loves me'? Or should I say, 'This relationship is terrible and I will leave it because he is not making me happy'? Loving him makes it difficult to leave him.

"Should I want to help him open up more, or should I worry about myself and break up with him? Or maybe I should become pregnant and solve the whole question of what will become of us (I'm sure he'd never want me to have an abortion).

"But he keeps saying these condescending remarks, like, I was a little girl or something. I found myself trying to write him a note to explain my feelings to him the other day. I wrote it late one night. The next morning I looked at it and it started out, 'I know that you think of me as complicated and crazy, but I just want to explain to you . . .' I couldn't believe I had written that, and just put myself down! What a macho view he has, like *Gaslight*, the movie, to imply there is anything wrong with my thinking! You know, the movie with Ingrid Bergman and Charles Boyer made a long time ago, where he tries to convince her she is losing her mind, by making the lights flicker and claiming they are not, that it's all in her mind? The idea is that men are the norm, I guess, and women are the deviants. But it starts subtly—I would have been outraged three months ago if anyone had implied I was 'complicated and crazy'—but it happens gradually, you lose your self-esteem and belief in yourself gradually. Now all that seems apparent to me is that I want to be alone and strong again. I say that now, but . . .

"The problem is that first he says he's vulnerable and in love—then later he denies it or doesn't act like it, acts cold. I ask myself, 'Is the goal this man at any cost?' It's almost as if someone is egging me on to go into the deep end of the pool—and then when I get there (with my emotions) and really fall in love, trust him, he says, 'What? Why me?' I've been so scared all the way, thinking to myself, no matter what happened, giving him the benefit of the doubt, 'Let me trust, let me trust,' not letting myself believe the negative signals, thinking he was just insecure or reacting to something I had done in my *own* effort to seem invulnerable—I've always been so afraid, wondering, 'Will somebody stay?' A relationship like ours where there is no commitment yet means anybody can pull out whenever they want—but I have tried not to believe that would be the case, to believe we are building something more valuable, more permanent, even though he has not said so.

"Maybe this whole relationship has been a big mistake on my part. I feel less strong. Instead of working on my career, I am obsessed with our phone calls and meetings. I feel weak. Why does love have to make you feel weak? Does it? It all turns into a game of strategy. It always feels like he is in control. But who knows, maybe he feels like *I* am in control, he feels just as vulnerable as I do. Oh, here I go again obsessing about this relationship. I am so angry at myself that I have lost myself in this love affair.

"How to judge the situation is so hard: is he afraid to love, or does he really not love *me*? It's all so one-sided, I feel sometimes. Then sometimes I think he loves me, but he would never marry me—you know the way I mean? And *if* he loves me, why does he leave me so often? Does he really have to spend so much time at work? If we were married, it would give me a base to know he really did care and love me in some special way; just the way we are, although he calls me every day, I always wonder and feel very insecure. Everything seems to be on his terms—he tells me when he can come and see me; I tried doing the same thing to him and being busy at work a lot, but it didn't bother him at all, it just hurt me because I missed him.

"Why do I want somebody who is not making me happy? His low and trivializing opinion of women comes out in bits and snatches. But other times are really great, and he can be so charming and so much fun, and then say some really beautiful things. He's not that great in bed, however, I must admit.

"My mother has counseled me the following way: She said, when I complained I couldn't get through to him about what was bothering me about the relationship, 'It is easy to speak with a friend, but not with a man. With a man, you become silent. You have to find your own liberty inside—and then you can be with a man. No matter how free and strong you are, when you are with a man, you start thinking how *he* feels, lose any self, any center. You feel he's not completely yours—especially if you are creative. You want to be comforted by a man. Men want a woman who looks good, is brilliant, but still will be dominated.' I couldn't believe she told me these things. I guess, as Laurence Olivier once remarked in one of his films, 'No matter what they tell you, you really *are* on your own out there. Completely and totally alone.' I guess this is why people become mediocre—safety in following the flock.

"Anyway, there's something about the setup with men that's so unfair. It's O.K. if *men* bring up commitment, but not if we do. So—life isn't fair, love relationships with men aren't fair—but I still want one! But how do I get him??? Do I have to play a game and wait for him? Should I appear strong and independent, or do I have to seem to *need* him??? I feel so depressed, but there's no reason! I'm starting to be insecure, and worse, to show him my insecurities. It's not knowing what's going to happen with us, and I really care."

77 percent of women say that they often feel they are put in awkward situations emotionally, by men's on-again, off-again behavior; most wonder how to deal with this, what "strategy" to employ so as not to come out feeling "used," "taken advantage of," or otherwise "fucked over":

"I can't tell him that I want to be with him all the time, and marry him, because that way I lose power. I can't tell you why, but I just know it in my bones. He has to be the pursuer, he has to *want* me—I can't *seem* to want him or I will lose him. It's crazy, but that's just the way it is."

"I always feel like I lose something when I make the gestures with men—calling them, telling them how much I like them, etc. When you try to play fair with men, they think you are weak and stupid. So I finally give in and use power tactics, but I don't respect them anymore, or want them. But they want me."

"What we do is always in *his* control—whether we go out to eat, when he is in town, when he has time, whether we have dinner alone or with his friends, when he calls me, and so on . . . ."

"What drives me crazy in the relationship is NOT KNOWING . . . not knowing if he really loves me, if he wants to marry me eventually, if he is just going along to see if we get along O.K. before he brings it up, or is he just taking me for a joyride for however long it lasts . . . ???"

"I seem to have a problem with low self-esteem when I am in a relationship with a man. And it's *my* fault for being in that relationship in the first place—*my* psychological hang-up. (But I know it's one that society encourages enormously.) Something about the dynamics of it makes him come out on top every time. I have to accept his coldness (i.e., his domination), his draining my emotional energy to keep on giving him love when he leaves me so insecure—or leave."

In answers to all kinds of questions, women make statements which imply that they feel somehow men are emotionally in control—of relationships and of the "singles" situation in general:

"Men have baffled me most of my life and I have cried myself to sleep in utter despair over some of my relationships with them. I consider all of my relationships (love) before the one with my husband to have been pretty awful. They followed the distinct pattern of first my being chosen by them and feeling flattered, then very little communication, with me in the passive, pleasing role and them playing the role of themselves."

"I usually feel that the other person has the upper hand, emotionally, in a relationship."

"I fear his leaving me, I fear he will grow tired of me . . . I hate feeling this way. It confronts my integrity."

"I do feel at the mercy of the other person to accept or reject me. Being beautiful and seductive helps, but it can also threaten. I have pretended a lot and nearly all the time when I am in love—until the man declares himself I am unable to show him I care. The man has to go after me all the way. I feel very shy and I pretend I am indifferent when it is all the contrary, fear and terror of rejection. It works when men are really interested, which is not that often."

"My greatest fear was always of half losing him, having him walk in and out of my life entirely on his own time schedule."

"If men could just stop not showing up for dates, a simple thing, trust could be more readily built. I don't think I ever made plans with a woman in which she just simply did not show up, or telephone or anything. Even telephoning with an excuse that is a lie would show some measure of caring, not leaving one stranded or on hold and unable to make alternative plans. If you or anyone can tell me why men don't show up as planned, life would be much calmer."

"Love is a problem for women because they get too involved and too dependent. They want security and a commitment, and men do not—that's where the problems are for a lot of women, including myself at times."

"The existence of this relationship is completely dependent on whether he wants it or not—'cause I do."

Is it "a relationship" or isn't it?

Many single women describe very vague or ambivalent behavior on the part of men:

"The first weekend he did not show up or telephone; after several days passed I wrote him. I suggested sarcastically that perhaps I was 'confused' about the date we had planned. I made it clear that I expected to hear from him to resolve what happened. He did, after receiving my letter, telephone me. He explained that something was wrong with the car. Further, he said it is his way to not always let the other know that something came up. I told him his behavior was unacceptable—it sends a message that I'm not important. I thought he understood.

"But then just this weekend, he was due and did not show up again. I won't be calling or writing this time to find out what happened. If he wants me as a friend, he must deal with this. If he does not address the issue, he stands to lose me. This not doing what he says he will do is what he does that makes me angriest. It sends a message that I am not important—and is very destructive and debilitating to our relationship. I am honest with men. I abhor game playing. I don't do it and expect them not to do it either. Why is he doing this??? He is ruining the relationship, as far as I am concerned."

"When I first got out of my marriage, I was extremely open and sharing, and had high sexual desire. I started seeing and having sex with a new man. However, about three weeks into the relationship he informed me that he couldn't handle the physical intimacy of sex—it made him feel closed in and suffocating. So we agreed to have a platonic relationship, but he said there was still a possibility of our eventually having a primary relationship. So we continued our phone conversations and seeing each other occasionally without sex.

"Last weekend I saw him. We went boat riding, grocery shopping, and then to his home, he was fixing dinner for me. At this point, he grabbed me and kissed me. I was standing in the dark watching lightning bugs out the window when he came up behind me and put his arms around me and started caressing me, then turned me around and kissed me a couple of times. Later when we were cooking dinner he put his arms around me again and really started kissing and caressing me. We both were very aroused. We turned off dinner and had sex. Then we ate dinner and went to bed. (I was very careful to sleep on my side of the bed and not touch him. I have a healthy respect for his need to have his space, and I don't invade it unless he invites me to do so.)

"I asked him the next morning if he had any regrets and he said no, and we sat and drank coffee for an hour before I left. When I left, he kissed me again. This was Sunday morning and now it's Thursday night. I don't know if he's made up his mind that he can't handle being with me—that he really doesn't want sex and doesn't know how to tell me—or that he does care for me and is afraid of that. I am beginning to feel less open and sharing. Relationships are so screwed up."

57 percent of single women say most men do not end relationships gracefully; quite a few say they have been "dumped" by men abruptly with no explanation:

"He just stopped calling, and when I called him he wasn't really interested in getting together. I hurt a lot—the last time we were together everything was great and I don't understand the change. I feel betrayed—I really thought he was a 'nice' person. There was so much good about the relationship, I don't know why he gave it up. I know he got a lot out of it. Now I wish I could tell him exactly how I feel but I can't ever get a phone call from him and, like I said, I tried calling him. It was a very intense four months (to the day) and it was great—great fun too. Just a crummy way to end it."

"I have been dumped many times. I have never had any warning or any choice in the matter, and that's what's made me maddest. No one ever says, 'We have this/these problem(s) and we're going to have to work this out or it's the end.' No one ever says, 'Hey, we've had some fun, but it's over now and let's say goodbye.' They just stand me up and don't return my phone calls, or call me."

One describes how her boyfriend just started to date someone else:

"It was horrible. He didn't say anything about breaking up; he just started dating someone else. When I found out about it and questioned him, he said it was 'nothing' and that he still loved me, for me to 'hang in there,' yet he would spend the night with her. I left town.

"I did not feel I had a choice about whether or not to leave. I figured if he loved me, he'd come after me (he didn't), and if he didn't love me, I was better off away. I still loved him for many months (and still do, a little) after I left—I was devastated, felt like I hadn't been 'enough': good-looking enough, funny enough, cute enough. I hated him but I loved him—during those months, if he had 'come back' (like he'd done many times before), I probably would have taken him back. Thank the Lord, he didn't, so after six months, when he finally did, I had created a new life with new friends and new things to do, so that I could take him or leave him. That's where we are now. He definitely has a way with women but I think I have him figured out now.

"Just a week ago we were at a party (not together) and I was talking to this other guy. Robert came over and said, 'My place . . . fireplace . . . bottle of wine . . . later.' Six months ago I would have thought that meant something, but that night I just looked at the other guy and said, 'Don't pay attention to him. He says that to all the girls.' Frankly, I wish he'd leave me alone for six more months until I really get on top of things. Moving away was the best thing I ever did."

Another was asked to have an abortion by her boyfriend, who then left her:

"When I was twenty-one, I was really in love with this guy (I guess you could call it my first 'real love'). I ended up pregnant. I wanted to have the baby and get married to him and live 'happily ever after.' When I told him about it, he told me (not asked me, but told me) that he would have nothing to do with me again unless I had an abortion. He was so cold and unfeeling about the whole thing. He had no job and no money; I had no money at the time either. So he called his father and got the money. He took me to the local doctor, whom I had heard from other friends was a 'butcher.' He was the cheapest one around, and did the abortions right in his office. He drove me to the doctor, went in and paid for it, then told me he'd be back in an hour to pick me up. I was scared shitless. He couldn't even sit there with me and wait, he just took off. It was one of the most painful and degrading things I have ever done in my life. I did it for him, just so he would still go out with me, because I loved him so.

"After that incident, he took up with another girl. I had no one to talk to about it. In fact, the same day I had the operation he told me that I had to go back to work (even though I took the whole day off). He said that if I went back to work and 'acted normal,' no one would know what happened. I never told anyone about this for three years. Then I finally broke down and told my mother. I really do think that incident has left me emotionally scarred. I still run into Roger now and then; in fact, I took him back after several of his 'flings' with other women.

"It's strange, because after all this time I honestly think I still care for him—even though I am now married to a wonderful man, whom I truly love. I guess some men just don't give a damn about women and women's emotions or feelings. Roger is one of them."

One woman describes the pain of being unjustly accused and mistrusted—the man's suspicions and unilateral decisions ruined a very deep love on her part:

"My response to him was deeper than to anyone else, even though it was not a satisfactory relationship and it ended in disaster. I felt at that time that he was a person of some emotional, ethical substance. I liked especially our periods of lengthy touching and caressing, that he was a verbal person. He liked to talk. Unfortunately, this man was having a series of personal problems which caused him to be very suspicious.

"What happened was, in the midst of our beautiful romance, he suddenly accused me of giving him a venereal disease. I hadn't slept with anyone else— simple as that. It was the furthest thing from my mind. I thought we were too close for that.

"It was like experiencing someone's death, I imagine, only worse. One minute you're something special and the next minute you'll never see him again because he has totally rejected you (for false reasons). He decided he couldn't trust me. I was innocent of his accusations and was unable to rationalize with him. About eight months later, I contacted him in order to vent my fury and hurt at being so heartlessly treated. After his initial anger and embarrassment at my disrupting his domestic situation (in the meantime, he had apparently sought solace from a former girlfriend, whom he had since impregnated and married), he pursued me in order to rekindle the relationship!

"I began to think he had some serious psychological problems. He wanted my relationship back, but with his wife and baby. He saw it as perfectly fine to have both her and me: he said his wife wouldn't ask about a relationship. My opinion of him fell. I developed some creative outlets, just existed as best I could through this.

"When I saw him months later and he had resolved his distrust of me, I was torn in my emotional feelings and became involved with him very briefly again. It was a no-win situation, and I felt cheap and degraded. I did not like it on those grounds. I could see no way it could ever be anything special. I felt like an animal in a trap who had to chew its own paw off to survive. I severed all ties with him and have never seen him since.

"If I had not had other bad experiences with men in my life, perhaps this wouldn't have been so devastating, but it was a strong attachment and was an absurd, tragic, and preventable outcome. I was totally disgusted and disillusioned about relationships with males by then.

"I had a very long period of recovery after that, five to six years. I surely would not have minded being dead. I muddled along, psychologically damaged. I don't want to give in to letting these experiences wreck my life, I thought. Creative endeavors helped me; in fact, one of these efforts developed to the point where I am now earning my living with it. Once I stopped putting my energy into relationships I was able to develop my creative instincts and skills."

Women in such ambiguous relationships easily wind up feeling emotionally needy, vulnerable, insecure, and depressed for reasons similar to those we saw in Chapter 3. The patterns of the dominant culture's attitudes toward women play themselves out in myriad ways, but they frequently tend to put women in the position of questioning what is going on, questioning their own perception of reality. Women frequently wonder why they feel so uneasy, uncertain, and "unsatisfied"—in fact, women wonder so much, searching themselves psychologically and the men they are with, that, finally, women have begun to question and analyze men's behavior, and through it, the larger patterns of the culture—saying there is something wrong, not with them, but with the whole "male" way of doing things in relationships.

Men's fear of commitments

82 percent of single women say that most men they know want to avoid commitments:

"One guy said to me, 'I only want to see you once every two weeks. If you can't relate to that, it's your problem.' I think that after four months, you should be able to see someone more than once a week without being made to feel like you're proposing marriage!"

"He said if I needed commitment, I had a problem. I should overcome my 'need.'"

"After two years together, a man I loved dearly would say to me, 'Why can't you just be happy just in the present, why are you always worrying about the future?'—as if there was something wrong with me. We were in our thirties, and if we were going to have children, we should have talked about it—or if he didn't want them, he should have said so and offered me the choice of staying with him or leaving. But he never wanted to discuss it at all, he just wanted us to keep on having a good time—and, I suppose, staying the same age forever—or should I say, juvenile? Personally, I think growing up is fun—now that I have finally left him and done it."

"I'm sympathetic to a point . . . One part of me is sympathetic, but another part says, 'He's just got classic male cold feet. He's afraid to get married.' At first he said, 'I love you, I love you, I want to marry you!' But when I finally said yes, then *he* wanted to wait, he wasn't sure, he didn't show up the day we were supposed to go pick out the ring, he forgot my Christmas present . . . The chase—men are used to it—but once they 'catch' someone, they don't know what to do. And his best friend is now advising him not to 'rush into anything.' How can I respect him when he's acting like this? I guess getting married is an identity crisis for men, a conversion from being a boy to being a man and it's frightening."

"I've always put love relationships first in my life. The problem is, most men don't seem to take love too seriously—it plays a minor role in their lives. Single men are afraid of commitment for fear of losing their independence. Usually, as the relationship progresses, we go in two different directions: I want commitment and they don't. So I guess I pick the wrong men."

"Men fall in love and court you and then it starts getting serious and they back off. Why?"

"I seem to pick men who want *me* to make a total commitment, but they are not sure they want to make it themselves."

"Sometimes he seems to love me and like me, other times he doesn't, or he acts cold or distracted. He refuses to talk about our future, even though we have been going out for ten months—or whether we have a future. He just changes the subject if I bring it up. I don't know what to do or think. I really like him, so I'll try to stick it out. But I feel out of touch and out of control a lot of the time."

"I used to get involved with men who were 'free spirits'—non-commitment types. I was often hurt and left feeling there was something wrong with me when these relationships ended—like I was too dependent, too emotionally demanding. I now realize I was, but also that these men are afraid of intimacy. My present lover is not like this at all."

"I'm attracted to men that are ambivalent toward me. I seem to keep going through the same thing—I want to be serious, they don't."

"Men seem to be partially committed."

"I feel that most men get you in a position where they know you feel strongly for them, then are afraid of being married again and having it turn out as a failure, so they back off. I cannot figure that out. A man just will not let himself follow his feelings."

"He was so smart and thinking about going on to business school—he played Varsity soccer—had very clear ideas about where he wanted the future to take him. It lasted for four months—actually a long time here—until he got into an 'I'm a senior and need to find myself' frame of mind. He was the first man I had sex with. He broke up with me one morning after he had stayed over. I didn't even see it coming. Maybe my overexuberance frightened him. I've never since or before felt such a sense of self-loathing and rejection."

"I know many men who take falling in love with women very seriously. I also know many who do not. The ones who do care seem highly sensitive, more intense, gentler, nurturing sorts of people, softer, kinder. The second 'type' somehow seems too much into self-control (into self, period), into male games, male bonding, establishing territories, remaining as emotionally non-committal as possible—as if their commitment to *any* woman is a gift from God, and since God isn't giving any gifts lately, their commitment isn't going to be one of them."

"We went out together off and on for three years. I guess you could say that I tried to 'pressure' him into marrying me. He always had one excuse after another why he wouldn't. I got pregnant (not intentionally). He told me to have an abortion or else he would never see me again. I did, and felt so immoral and degraded. I needed someone to talk over my fears with. He wouldn't listen, wouldn't discuss it. He decided he needed to date other women so he could find out 'where his head was at.' I put up with this for the three years. He was always taking off to 'find himself.' Finally I got sick of it and refused to see him. He then asked me to marry him. I refused, because it was a one-sided relationship. He was not there when I needed him and I had a hell of a time even trying to communicate with him. I cut it off, even though it hurt tremendously. I still see him now and then, and still care about him."

65 percent of single women describe men's attitudes toward marriage as somewhere in the "playboy generation":

"Most single men think marriage is a dread disease which cuts off multiple sexual experiences. They avoid commitment, but not before they get you into bed. As for trusting women, they consider that a contradiction in terms."

"Most men today like to be single and play around. They find it hard to accept the idea of marriage. Some want to avoid commitment, but still get married—without a commitment involved! They know it is easy to get divorced."

"Most guys are afraid, what if this girl isn't the one, what if in six months I see someone else I want more?"

"The men of today (I think) are scared to commit themselves. Also, from what I've experienced in a commitment-type relationship, they want you to be a hundred percent devoted while they play the field. It's like having your cake and eating it too!"

"They don't want commitment. They want to check out how many girls they can lure into their web."

"They say that men want to get married, but I just don't see it."

"Our times reward the single man and encourage him to keep his 'freedom.' He's supposed to be the sexy swinger out having a good time. Keeping his options open. There is less value placed on the family man—he's the dull guy who watches TV every night and spends his weekends mowing the lawn. Which is not true anyway."

A young graduate student, age twenty-four ("in the ranks of those who have no real direction," as she says), describes being in love with another extremely ambivalent student:

"I am very much in love right now. The happiest I have ever been was just last month when he first asked if I ever thought of spending the rest of our lives together, because he had and he liked the idea. Then within ten days of discussing marriage like this, he told me the relationship was over. He told me we were through because he wanted another woman. Then the next time I saw him, he asked my forgiveness and told me he realized he wanted to be with me after all. Vacillation!

"We have been together five months. Considering that I had chosen to remain a virgin until about eight months ago, I sure have changed! I was by no means celibate before, but this really is my first love and my first affair. Actually, I felt pressured into my first sexual experience with him, in a way. Although I was ready and eager to 'mess around,' I didn't want total intimacy that soon. But now I love our intimacy together—which can mean sex, or our philosophic ponderings (that is what you get with two grad students), or playing with his cats. During these times he gets quiet and soft. He will tell me he wants me, he feels warmly toward me, at peace with me. He uses 'sex talk,' tells me I feel good, taste good, am beautiful. I feel desirable and very at home.

"I am jealous to an extent. I can tolerate, even appreciate other loves in his life if I am feeling secure in ours. That is very changeable. I feel most jealous of his insistence on dependence (methinks he doth protest too much). I can cope with the other women, the fifty-to-sixty-hour workweek, his golf, his bridge clubs. But I must admit I did check up on him, drive by his apartment, to see if he really was there or at work or out with someone else.

"The relationship is close to being the center of my life, but I try to keep it from that extreme as I cannot count on his commitment. I am supposed to leave here in a matter of months. Because he is not willing to commit, I will not toss aside my degree and my job search to wait for him. If he wants me to stay, I will (I could stay and finish my thesis), but I will not unless it is clear he wants me to.

"I like what we have and dream of more. I have the patience to wait, I think it is worth the investment. But I don't know if he thinks so much of us, and it frustrates me not to know what the future holds, but my commitment and love for him gives me the stamina to keep hanging on in the face of all this. I feel more passionate toward him than I ever have, and the passion is something deeper, stronger, more all-encompassing than just physical.

"But lots of my nights lately have been spent crying on an old teddy bear who shares my bed when no one else does."

In single women's descriptions of their relationships, doubts about the future are expressed more often than not:

"The fun times, the love I feel from him are best. Least I like the insecure feeling that I don't know what will happen with us."

"The thing I like best is knowing that he is there. We share so much, and it is great to know that I have this person who is close and means so much to me. The thing I like least is a bit of uncertainty—the fact that he might meet someone else tomorrow and then it will be over for us, he might just drop me. I wish sometimes I had more security in the relationship. But I'm happy for the most part."

58 percent are living with constant ambiguity, wondering what will happen:

"He's making me wait, and wait. I'd like to know if we're ever going to amount to something, because if I've been wasting my time for the past three years waiting for him, I'd like to know so I could get on with my life. But I'd never consider him wasted time. He is wonderful."

"Sometimes I look at friends who are getting married and get jealous because he hasn't asked me yet."

Women often feel they are in a sort of half-of-a-relationship—something that at the drop of a hat may end, so that "You are never sure if you will spend Christmas or the holidays together, or how to plan."

Sometimes men seem to enjoy creating or heightening the uncertainty, dramatizing their lack of commitment in a "prima donna" (or "primus homo"?) manner:

"Some days he called and was very attentive and loving and wanted to see me. Other times, if I called him, he would make fun of me or ridicule me, or be noncommittal. I don't think it was that he was busy or had someone there, I think he just enjoyed displaying his power. He knew I would put up with his moods, do anything to please—just as his previous girlfriend and his mother had always done."

This suspense often drains a lot of women's energy and can, understandably, lead to a lot of unnecessary tenseness and uneasiness, leaving them prone to flare-ups.

Another woman puzzles over whether there is a connection between her striving to have a perfect, absolute love and finding only men who do not want to remain in a relationship:

"You find these men who are just not there, they are enigmas, they disappear—you cannot reach for the absolute, it seems. It would be wonderful, you feel the moon and the stars with them, but just as you are reaching for it, they evaporate. (Do they realize what they are missing? Are they afraid?) Everybody tells me I am crazy, that I reach for a lost star and so on. But I know it is possible. It's like there are two categories of men—boring and interesting. But those who are interesting just go away."

Another woman thinks men's reluctance to commit themselves might be economic:

"I think both men and women are a little leery these days of marriage, considering the statistics that one out of two marriages ends in divorce. If men seem to avoid marriage and commitment more, it may be because the man is still the one in our society to carry the financial burden should the marriage end."

―――――――――――

But is this still true, now that most women are employed outside the home? Indeed, more and more women are providing the major economic support, or certainly paying their own way in marriages; And, in the case of divorce, women actually wind up bearing most of the expense of child rearing. Logically, then, it should be women who think twice about marriage, more so than men. Why should men assume women are a financial liability now that over half of married women work outside the home?

One woman—who had been through two long-term relationships waiting for a man to make up his mind regarding whether they had a future or not, "whether she was finally acceptable or not"—came to this point of view:

"I don't particularly care what men in the world think or want. I'm tired of trying to make relationships work with their egotistical little selves! If I am single all my life, it's better than focusing on one of those warped mentalities and trying to deal with it."

Another woman jokes about men who are "so busy avoiding commitment" that they don't even notice that the woman doesn't want one:

"Single men always think that every woman that goes out with them wants to marry them, while they are trying to avoid commitment. Even when you don't want this commitment, they're busy avoiding it because they think you want it!"

One young woman suddenly found herself an "unwed mother," due to the ambivalence of the father over whether he wanted to make a commitment:

"My mate and I were to be married (long-planned), but when my pregnancy, two weeks before the wedding date, became known, he left. He was not able to talk to me about it at all, just suddenly I was alone carrying the child. It was difficult and took all my courage to be strong and do what was good in the face of my own personal hardship and fears, because after he left me (us), I had no home. It was hard to deal with.

"The most solid thing during that time was the child I carried, even though it was also the most frightening, overwhelming aspect. I have been wondering if I ever will put that much energy and attention into a relationship with a man now. I saw a psychologist, but it was no help, really.

"I got over it by moving eight-hundred miles distant. Now I am a new mother with a six-month-old daughter and I love her dearly. I live in a beautiful woods. I am self-employed and earned about $2,000 last year. What helped me most was the birth of my daughter and the tremendous love and energy I put out to her. I did talk with friends some, and cry when I was alone. I concluded that within me is the right answer for solving problems—if I'd pay better attention and quit feeling sorry for myself.

"I've no interest in men right now since my mate left me. No sex life. I am not one to 'have sex' for the sake of it. I like to be in a love relationship, but that doesn't come often in one's life. Sometimes I feel envious of another person's life who seems to have everything working out so nicely. Maybe I pick quitters. Men who are afraid to face themselves?

"There is an advantage to being without my mate—that is that I'm no longer getting psychological abuse. At times he would go days without talking with me. I am really glad I am single, and I am glad it happened before the birth of my child. Still, I get lonely. I do not party or go out—no money to do so anyway. Many people think 'you need a man,' but some respect what it takes to be a single parent in this situation.

"I don't hate my ex-mate. I feel a lot of anger at times, and a lot of compassion at others: he ran from our relationship because of my pregnancy. He has multiple problems to work through before he can live with someone.

"He came to see our daughter when she was four months old. Now he comes to visit her when he can. He wants to reestablish our sexual relationship as lovers. I do not. He was always unable to accept my love. He tried to see ulterior motives as to why I would do such and such, rather than seeing/ accepting/receiving it as an expression of love to him. He distrusts love.

"In a relationship, it seems like I give and give and give, and being always the peacemaker sometimes gets to me. I get angry that the other person doesn't care enough to try to work things out—that they'd rather ride on their anger. Also, many men have trouble with being shown affection, being told you love them. They get defensive and feel you're 'dependent.' I have been emotionally dependent when going through personal crisis or change, but so have others gone through these times, and clung to me—and I was glad to be there and to have that strength to give them. I did not feel threatened. In my experience most men just want to fuck. This society seems to create unreal sexual need in men.

"Years ago, under pressure from a man, I had an abortion. It felt horrible. Very, very, very distressing. Eventually I had two. After the second one, I fell into a deep depression of self-hate, self-distrust, and an ongoing chronic depression. I asked the clinic for the remains—and buried them in the woods.

"The person to whom I feel closest now is my daughter. I am in love with her. I love her dearly. This relationship is by far the most fulfilling and happiest thing in my life. My only worries are my financial situation, we have no home to settle in."

The "playboy generation" and the ideology of "freedom": Why are men so ambivalent about love and commitments?

Many single men in *The Hite Report* on men said that their basic reason for ambivalence about commitments to women (not to jobs or careers) is that they want to be "free" and "independent." Many believe that a "real man" should be "independent" and "free";* love, marriage, and children are responsibilities which "tie a man down." This definition of "freedom" and "independence" is pointedly focused on freedom from *women;* as one woman quotes her boyfriend saying, "Thank goodness my brother got out of my mother's clutches."

"Freedom" can have many definitions: it can mean freedom to be, to define, make, quest for truth, explore science—or it can be psychological independence, or political freedom. But a major part of what we hear men speak of as freedom here is not "freedom of speech," but freedom from any constraint whatsoever—i.e., a "real man" doesn't "answer to" anybody. This is the version of masculinity which proclaims that men have the right to be dominant, no one should "tell a man what to do"—especially a woman.

Men are not reluctant to make commitments at work, to their jobs or careers; in fact, they usually welcome the chance. Why don't many men feel this way about relationships with women? Why does popular male sentiment hold that marriage is a "trap" to be avoided? Why do so many single men, when they are taking wild advantage of women justify it as their "right" under the name of "freedom"?

The underlying assumptions of the emotional contract, as worked out in non-married relationships or in the "singles" pool, amount to a setup: women are pressured by society to get married,† but men are taught that they should keep their "freedom." This is a recipe for humiliating treatment of one group by the other: if women want relationships, feeling, and commitment, this puts women at a psychological disadvantage with a male population which has been brought up to see women, as one young man in *The Hite Report* on men put it, as "traps and burdens, but the best that is available for avoiding loneliness."

Thus, the "male" ideology of "freedom" and "independence" is in direct conflict with women's upbringing to make love the most important thing in life.

*Surely, the eighteenth-century Enlightenment philosophers, such as Diderot, or the heroes (male and female) of the French Revolution could not have had in mind the propping up of the modern "macho" personality when they proclaimed "freedom for all men." And yet, this "democratic" language is what is being used today to make some men's insistence on being dominant sound righteous and noble. Here we see that theories of male personality/psychology follow the same lines as "male" political theory.
†See Chapter 8 for women's feelings about this subject.

Pretending not to care: Should women be as "cool" as men?

"Have you ever pretended to a man that he was less important to you than he was? put up a front?"

62 percent of women say they have done this—and that it was not pleasant:

"It's the old playing-hard-to-get theory we've been raised with. Usually I put up a front because I found that if I really showed them how much I cared or 'loved' them, their actions toward me were not as attentive. If I acted like I didn't care as much and let them make the moves, they seemed to be more interested. It worked temporarily, but the relationships never worked because it's a stupid, dishonest game."

"If you tell a man you love him . . . oh, disaster, disaster, disaster. Will he feel tied down? Yes. Absolutely."

"I have pretended that I was just a friend when I really cared much more than that. I did this because I thought he would be too threatened by my expression of love for him. I was afraid to rush ahead in the relationship too fast. I felt anger because of this, like I was holding myself back."

"I have often pretended to care less than I did, but eventually one has to decide which way the relationship is to go."

"Part of my problem is that I'm so afraid of losing love once I've found it that I try too hard and have the opposite effect of what I intended. It scares them off. Once I'm into a relationship I can usually flaw it by pushing for intimacy too fast. I'm working on that."

"I never let him know anything he did bothered me—even when he walked into a bar I was in and began to make out with someone else. I let him make all the moves first—never called him or made demands on his time. The last thing I wanted to be accused of was tying him down or being possessive. I didn't want him to think he had me in a position of being dominated. For a while it did work and I got a lot of his attention. But once I started to sleep with him it did not work as well. I couldn't understand why he did not seem to care about me very much."

"I did it because he felt that he was in such a power position. He felt I loved him more than he loved me, so he had the upper hand. I had to show him that I still had control of my life."

"I've pretended I didn't care as much for a man as I did, and it did work. Some men are frightened if you care too much. I don't like this kind of game playing, though. If a man is afraid of feelings, this is the kind of man no woman really wants. Life is too short. Find a man who *wants* you to love him. I'd rather be alone than to have to pretend."

"I sometimes wonder if I am too honest with men. I wonder if it is the right thing to do. I don't know. I just have to find someone who likes me as an honest person. I'm scared that if he really knows how I feel, he'll turn colder. If I act like I don't care as much, he'll keep wanting me."

In the same vein, when asked to comment on the remark "She was afraid that if she showed a man she loved him, he would consider her inferior and leave her," 94 percent of women say most men seem to think that women are desperate for men and that women will do anything to keep them.

The great majority of women in this study, especially single women, say that acting "insecure" or "clinging" is definitely "against the rules." One has to make every effort *not* to be perceived as "one of those women who cling" or "are overly emotional and needy," etc. To put it in the colloquial, "A cool girlfriend doesn't want to tie a man down." She should "give him his freedom," his "space." Women are seen by men as needing men more than vice versa—the same psychological power imbalance documented in Part I. But women, too, want freedom—although they don't see why love, commitment, and freedom are so contradictory.

74 percent of women answer yes when asked, "Are you afraid of clinging?* Making someone feel tied down?"

"I don't want to cling to anyone. I think one of the best gifts you can give another person is their freedom."

"He likes to have his freedom, so I let him be alone a lot, and occasionally he'll feel like seeing me. He likes the laid-back approach."

"I often do feel emotionally dependent when I'm involved with someone, but I just can't help it. No matter how strong I am in my career and other parts of my life, I suffer from emotional dependency. I think men are terrified of women's dependency. It makes them nervous. I don't think they know how to handle it or even want to bother trying. I don't think you should tell a man you love him until you're reasonably sure he feels the same way. And if he does, I don't see any reason why that would make him

---

*Even the nature of this question shows the culture's bias: it implies that women *do* have this tendency, that there *is* such a phenomenon. And yet, as women feel annoyed by this constant cultural message, "Don't cling," it was important to ask the question in just this way, with all the bias of the culture in it, to hear women's responses to the culture.

feel tied down. But if you think you're in love and he's not sure, telling him could ruin everything."

"There are times I've said 'I love you' to a man, and he'll immediately tighten up, because they interpret 'I love you' as meaning 'protect me,' 'take care of me.' They get scared. My brothers used to talk around the house about how if a woman got too dependent, you just had to get out, so I never wanted to be that way, to be clinging."

"I am very afraid of clinging. I sure do not plan to or desire to. I pride myself on my independence and do not care to usurp anyone else's. I have been involved with men who feel I am clinging. I don't know if they are paranoid or if I really, unbeknownst to myself, am. I believe love is a freeing thing and should not threaten someone, but I have observed that many people react to another loving them as tying them down."

Only a few women disagree:

"I used to think a relationship should be 'free,' but now I think the reassurance of 'tying each other down' is nice for both of us."

"I used to be afraid to tell a man 'I love you,' that he'd feel tied down and oppressed. This is stupid, of course. Another example of how the sexual revolution has added yet another fetter on women. What's wrong with admitting that one is emotionally dependent, that someone matters to you? We all are."

Although women are so often put down for wanting too much affection (being too "needy"), 61 percent of single women here deny that deep needs for affection are "unhealthy," stating that, in fact, they are a necessary and good part of life:

"My love of affection is not excessive. The more affection I have, the healthier, more human I am."

"If I have a problem—in my life or work—I crave affection. I sometimes just feel I need someone to tell me everything will be O.K. That doesn't strike me as neurotic."

"I not only crave but need affection all the time. That is the key to my sexual drive! I think it's healthy to have great needs for love, affection, and a little dependency."

"We all have a physical need for touch (watch children and animals!), as well as an emotional need to be known and cared about. Those needs become 'excessive' from long denial, and in the beginning of a relationship one may need a few weeks or months of remedial pampering. I have sometimes worried that a man, not understanding that this 'excessive' stage is usually temporary, might panic and run. So I never let it all out."

But some women are defensive:

"I think my unhealthy needs for love in past relationships, my wanting to be dependent, have someone 'take care of me,' created unhealthy relationships with the men I've been involved with. But some affection is necessary: I have always felt a need to be held, and I still miss that immensely, along with the stroking, kissing, and soothing. I don't know if that's 'unhealthy,' but I feel an intense need for it."

One woman points out that it is a "male" cultural value to ridicule people—women or men—for needing affection, being emotional, equating this with "weakness":

"I always think the definition of an 'excessive need for affection' is made by someone who either has no need for it at all or who is fearful of it in themselves. I used to think I was excessive in this need, until I met my husband, who also has a great need for affection."

Using "women's" value system, the opposite assertion could be made; women are not too emotional but many men *are too* unemotional, *especially in personal situations:*

"The culture has damaged men's ability to be in touch with their feelings, own them, and consider them when they behave. So men tend to be dysfunctional in relationships when they do not acknowledge desires to give and receive affection."

Where did the perception come from that women want to "tie men down"? And what does it mean, exactly? That a woman shouldn't expect or ask for a monogamous relationship? That she shouldn't ask for "forever"? The implication here is that women want these things more than men, that women need men more than vice versa, that men are more desirable.

Most women in this study—specifically single women, but even married women—have a great fear of making a man feel "tied down," of appearing too demanding, seeming "too available," or needful of love. Why is this? Because, having second-class status, women know from experience that their love and desire will all too often be seen as an expression of a lack in them—as a kind of "social climbing"—rather than a simple expression of pleasure. This is a barbaric situation.

In fact, the reality of a relationship is much more likely to be that the woman will turn out to *be* the one "tied down." For one thing, if a couple has children, it is the woman who will usually stay home. Traditionally, in marriage, since the man was supposed to earn all the money, he was in that sense "tied down" to making a living—but then, most women now work outside the home too. What is it then that men are "tied down" to?

Almost all studies show that men after marriage are much more content and live longer than unmarried men. So why the stereotype that women have to chase men to get them to marry them? Because of women's low status.

As seen in Part I, much of the so-called neediness on women's part is caused by male behavior which subtly, on a daily basis, puts down and demeans women—so quietly and softly that women can hardly struggle against it without being accused of being "too sensitive." Equality, emotional equality, would put an end to this endless struggling. In short, the ideology that says that women are *by nature* too emotionally demanding, too needy of love, always wanting a commitment—with men at the same time expecting women to give *them* all these things (commitment, love, nurturing, affection, etc.)—is a blatant form of the psychological power imbalance in the larger society, *not* a reflection of "innate" biological or psychological dispositions or tendencies. As one woman puts it, "We try to retain our pride by not clinging. But we don't have the power or status to command real respect." However, women, as seen here, are in the process of changing this; *how* is a large part of the debate women are having in this book.

Should a woman be monogamous if a man doesn't make a commitment?

"The boy disease:* being in a relationship but pretending you're not"

Most women prefer to be monogamous in relationships, but 22 percent follow a policy of "if we are not thinking about a future together, and even if we are having sex, I will also date others who may want a future":

"My last boyfriend (before my husband) made it clear that he was a loner and had no intentions of ever getting married, that there was no future with him. I was just lucky enough to also be dating my husband-to-be at the time. Fortunately, I didn't wait and stay 'faithful,' hoping for the first guy to change. In the midst of going with them both, I broke up with the first one, and John and I got engaged."

"I learned I'm wrong to put my life on hold when I'm in love. I used to date only one guy at a time, but I couldn't stand the endless waiting every week to see if we were still going out or what, did we have a date for Saturday night

---

*Name created by Anya Schiffren, writer.

or not? I found that waiting like that only made me more 'in love' with the guy, usually the *wrong* guy, it would turn out. I decided I hadn't promised anything, so I might as well keep looking around. It was the smartest move I ever made."

"I am single. Most men my age (thirty-three) who are not married are very wary of committed relationships, which they perceive to be T-R-A-P-S! Also, most married men I know—although they seem to need the domestic stability and the 'caretaking' that marriage gives—still act as though they are single, and don't hesitate to get involved with a single woman (especially attractive, self-sufficient ones). So meanwhile, while I wait to find a good relationship that works for me, I have lots of friends, and right now I am sexually involved with three male people."

One woman who declared her freedom to date others describes her lover's reaction in a letter she wrote him:

"You said you weren't ready to marry yet, but you loved me and were thinking about it. I said, O.K., but now after a year of waiting for you to make up your mind, I'm going to date other men too because in my life I want a marriage sooner or later. Then when I did go out with other men, you acted like I was unfaithful, a whore who should feel guilty and ashamed! I 'understood' and empathized with what you were feeling, that you were feeling hurt, and let you treat me terribly."

Should a woman be monogamous with a man who can't decide whether he wants to make a commitment or not? Is her only choice either to break up with him or to continue to accept the situation on his terms? Most women do not relish the thought of having more than one sexual relationship at a time, if they are in love with someone (enough in love to want a commitment from that person), and AIDS makes it all even more of a problem. One way to avoid the dilemma of being put on hold is for a woman, if she wants a permanent commitment, to set a certain date for herself; if by that date the man has not made up his mind, she can inform him that she will now no longer be exclusive with him and tell him why. As one woman puts it, "Mark your calendar, and tell the person—and then make yourself leave after enough time has passed."

Simultaneous sexual relationships

The prevalence of the "freedom" philosophy in men means that multiple sexual relationships are almost inevitable. As mentioned, if a woman has sex with a man because she likes him and wants a relationship, then he doesn't call her again and she goes out with another, giving up on the first, has sex (not wanting to imply she doesn't trust the new man), and then the first calls back and she sees him again, and so on—simultaneous relationships become inevitable. A woman may be very uncomfortable having multiple sexual relationships, but it is very common. Seventy-two percent of single women say they often wind up having "casual sex" even though they don't mean to. The possibility of AIDS has not significantly changed this; the thinking is just, "How can I get him to wear a condom without causing a fight?"

In other words, the "sexual revolution's" insistence that sex happen right away more or less decrees that single people will live at times with more than one sexual relationship going on simultaneously. To put it another way, there is an automatic anti-monogamy component in many men's ambivalent attitudes and continuing belief that "getting a woman," "making a score," is a basic goal.

In the past, a woman could date several men (and vice versa) without sex being really expected, at least for a while, so that there was time to get to know the other person. Now, sex is expected so soon after meeting that if a woman wants to get to know several men, to look around, she has to either (1) date and have sex with several men at one time or (2) date, have sex with, and break up with/stop seeing quite a string of men, one after the other ("serial monogamy"). Both of these situations can be very stressful—because, as seen earlier, while the thrill of sex and being desired may carry most women for a time, after a while most find it emotionally involving to have sex. Therefore, a break-up—no matter who wants it—is emotionally taxing; on the other hand, having sex with more than one man is usually emotionally confusing.

It is a strange society in which in order to get to know someone of the opposite sex, one is required to have sex.

Power and Games of Strategy

Edith Bunker and the Mme de Pompadour School of Thought

> "It's like he has _all_ the power, she has to give every-
> thing, including her body, her heart—it's all a gamble.
> He can have it all and then decide . . ."

One woman describes her desire for more power:

"I don't like to admit this, but I am envious of women who have the seduction power to take a man who is very sexy or socially powerful or both and manipulate him. Relationships that seem this way to me: Natacha Rambova and Valentino, Bathsheba and David, Wallis Simpson and the Duke of Windsor, Lady Hamilton and Lord Nelson, Cleopatra and Antony/Ceasar, Marion Davies and W.R. Hearst, Madame de Maintenon and Louis XIV, and Amelia Folsom and Brigham Young. How are these better than my relationships? (1) The men are more prestigious, and (2) when there is a conflict, these women manage to be the fucker rather than the sucker."

Perhaps Pompadour, the eighteenth-century courtsan who gained power at the French court, would have said: "If men are not giving to you and respecting you as an equal, use them and their own weaknesses to gain what you want: quit trying to be so idealistic. Start strategizing how to get the most out of men as they are."

Are we too "good"? Are we inhibited from using all the strategies we *know* to fight back? Remember Edith Bunker in "All in the Family," who was constantly being walked on by Archie? On the rare occasions in which she would rebel, audiences cheered her on—because her situation was instinctively felt to be unfair. To see that personality arise and use all its resources, rather than being meek and letting itself be walked on, was refreshing. If men are in power in relationships and the world (and men exploit that power and flaunt it in the most flagrant ways), so what? We *could* be "realistic" and devise more hard-edged strategies to deal with it—instead of sticking to our "nice-girls-are-loving-and-understanding, never-evil-and-mean," belief system. But we may be unwilling to compromise our values, lose the integrity of our beliefs. Are we faced with a choice between continuing to be perceived as "wimpy," second class—and becoming as calculating and ruthless as some forms of "male" behavior?

Classically, one way of "handling men" and men's power over women has been for women to "use" men. This could include such things as mothers' traditional advice to daughters to "marry a good provider" (since the women would not be able to have the education or job training to make a living themselves, not to mention job opportunities). At some earlier times in history—or even with Marilyn Monroe and Jane Russell in *Gentlemen Prefer Blondes* in the 1950s*—a rather playful attitude has been taken to male power: women could use and manipulate men to get what they wanted. Some would say, "And what's so wrong with that? It doesn't hurt men, since they are enjoying the process too, and it doesn't hurt women . . ."

Of course, the idealism of many women and of the feminist movement is to state that this unequal balance of power and subsequent need for "strategy" and "war games" can be ended, and that love and relationships can become more real and much closer. But at this stage, many women are still living with

*Or Madonna's take-off of this in the 1980s.

the choice of either using games of strategy and manipulation or possibly being "victims" themselves—poor and single with children to support. (Although this does not automatically make one a "victim.")

As we saw a few pages back, if a woman wants to marry a man in the age of the "playboy philosophy," and the man is ambivalent, the woman does have a choice of employing tactics. Perhaps here Mme de Pompadour might advise: "If you are with a man who won't marry you, you either break up or get pregnant." This is at least an alternative, these kinds of hard-headed options, to living by the "woman-must-be-loving-no-matter-what" ideology, any planning for her own well-being considered "cold," "bitchy," "manipulative," or "calculating." (Although in men, it would be considered "smart," "realistic," and so on.)

What should a woman do when she finds herself in a non-committed relationship and she loves the man? Should she manipulate him into marrying her? Should she be idealistic and stick to the principles of fair play, or give in and go along with the realpolitik of sexual politics—of which we know the rules only too well?

One woman offers her hard-core analysis:

"I think love is a problem for women because they need to please too much. They criticize themselves too much, and others not nearly enough. They eat a lot of shit because they are lousy at intrigue and vengeance. When they win at love, it's because they have undergone an incredible amount of self-development and are therefore 'attractive.' They lose because they don't have the political skills or self-respect to keep themselves from being ripped off."

Breaking the spell of the singles game

*"Love relationships with men aren't fair, but so
what, I still want one. I just want to know what I have
to do to get one to work."*

Several women offer their advice on dealing with single men's assumptions about commitment:

"If you feel strongly, even quickly, that this is the one—then speak your mind right away, if you want a serious relationship, or to get married. Let him start thinking about it . . . In my experience, this avoids a lot of shock and unexpected conversations later."

"If you see there's months of trouble ahead, even if you love him, leave him if he won't make a decision. One week of pain, or a month, and then you're fine."

"When I was in the 'market' I 'laid it on the line' as to how I felt. Then I watched the reaction—over a period of weeks. I was serious, and expected him to be, and to take me seriously. I felt he needed the information of what I was looking for, and wouldn't give me anything close to accurate feedback if I were less than straightforward and honest with him. There are plenty of fish in the sea, as they say, and I have never felt 'at the mercy of' any of them. I just kept looking if I didn't get the response I needed within a reasonable amount of time."

"I believe you have to draw a line. If you want marriage or a definite commitment, before too long draw a line—say you will leave after that time—because if not, you will be having constant small fights and bickering, and you will lose the relationship anyway."

One woman tells the story of how she got married:

"He wanted me to live with him, and I loved him, so I told him I would, but only for three months, because I didn't like the idea of not making a commitment one way or the other eventually. I had been through all that before with my former boyfriend. After three months, we should make up our minds to either get married or leave each other, because otherwise I should get over him and find someone who does want to settle down with me. So I gave him three months, and after that, I told him I would leave, no matter how much I loved him, because I wanted marriage and a real commitment, if I was going to give him all my love.

"Three months was approaching, and nothing was happening. I felt tense, but I didn't want to start fights about it—or about little things, because I was so tense. So I marked my calendar and just kept real cool. A couple of days before the three months were up, I mentioned it, but nothing came of it. So, the next weekend, on Friday, I packed all my things and put them in a suitcase, then I put the suitcase under the bed, and left a note on the bed saying I had left and the reason and that I loved him, and where I had gone. All weekend I was crying, dying inside, waiting—finally on Monday he called! We got married right away and have been married ever since and very happy too."

Should a woman bring up commitment—and if so, when? There seems to be a pattern in many single relationships: first, there is the positive, "in love" stage, which lasts perhaps two weeks to two months, followed by a decline. This decline often happens because "real life" sets in (the daily struggle to keep afloat financially and the many responsibilities of life)—and while dealing with these realities, the patterns described in Part I can set in, and get in the way of love continuing: the woman may (of necessity) begin "bringing up" relationship issues such as seen in Chapter 2; the man may react by feeling that he is "inadequate" or a "villain," that he is "not right" for the woman. ("Why is she complaining all the time?") And so on. Meanwhile, the woman may be becoming, as we have seen, more and more nervous as the relationship continues, wondering if there *will* be a commitment or not, further escalating the atmosphere.

For these reasons, some women feel that it is best to "catch" the commitment during the "in love" period in the beginning, or at least to state that this is what one is looking for—rather than have this come as a surprise to the man later. If the woman waits to have the man bring up these topics, especially with the "playboy generation's" reticence about commitments (although there are men of all ages who are not of this "generation"), she may start to bring up other arguments, simply because of the tension of wondering whether there is a commitment or not.

One woman offers another suggestion: the two should agree in advance whether they 1) are "going out together" in order to decide whether this would eventually be a good relationship for marriage, or 2) are just friends who have no intention of marriage, are just keeping each other company. If this basic clarification is not made, the "relationship" can become a form of tyranny, in which one is totally at the mercy of the other (the one who wants more). Another woman suggests there should be a time-frame agreed upon by both people as to how long they will try to work it out before deciding whether to make a commitment, or perhaps separate as lovers.

Another way of taking power back is to think of relationships as this woman suggests:

"It was such a surprise to me to realize one day how differently I could see things. I mean, I had always thought I was pretty cool, talented, intelligent, etc. But one day I was talking to a friend of mine, and I realized my approach to a relationship (like with a lover) is to sort of think, 'How can I get somebody to like me enough to want to stay with me?' Or, 'Who will like me, what man will like me and accept me? How long will it take them to figure out that I'm not worth enough to stay?' Why don't I think, instead, so that I could pick out a better relationship for myself, 'Here is what I would like: I would like a relationship or to live with somebody for two years. *I would like that person to give me two of the following three things . . .*' and then list on a piece of paper the qualities I would like that person to have—why don't I think like that? Instead, I'm just feeling like someone has to pick *me*. I should believe in myself more. I can't believe I didn't even notice how I was putting myself down without even being aware of it."

Do women really want marriage more than men?

Lurking all through these pages about men lacking commitment, and so on, is the assumption that women want commitment and marriage, even to be "taken care of" more than men do.

All these behaviors and assumptions on the part of men—that women are "out to get them," "tie them down," that men should try to avoid entangling "commitments" to women—add up to another version of the emotional distancing and distrust of women seen in Part I in the emotional contract and in the general "male" ideology, and they tend to evoke similar feelings in women, as those discussed in Chapter 3. For example, 56 percent of single women here say that in order not to appear in the least bit like "losers" in what men perceive to be women's big "manhunt," women must be sure never to appear to care for or need someone "too much."

On the other hand, by now there has been a lot of discussion in the society about marriage's possible bad effects on women; in fact, marriage has been called a prison for women, unequal, exploitative. Why do women still want it? Women discuss this question in Chapter 7; often it is men's practice of keeping women off balance in non-married relationships that makes women finally see marriage as a better relationship—or feel they want to "get the whole thing over," go along with social pressures, and also create, finally, some sort of reasonably solid arrangement in their lives.

Should women embrace the "male" idea of freedom?

> *"We were raised to look for the Great Love. But now we have to learn new rules, 'men's rules' at that— play around, don't get attached. It doesn't feel natural."*

Should women adopt the "male" model of controlling emotions, or the "male" model of "freedom" from "commitment," as the standard for sexual relationships? Or does society lose something through women's jettisoning of their own values, shunning them, since the dominant ideology labels them "silly" and "Victorian," etc.?

Since the "sexual revolution," women in "dating" situations are being pressured more and more to accept "male" rules. Many have been trying to adjust to "male" patterns in relationships, since the "sexual revolution" decreed women's value system to be a "hang-up," but this has been a severe culture shock for most women.

Do most single women want monogamous relationships?

84 percent of single women believe that if they are in a relationship, ideally it should be monogamous; in fact, 77 percent of single women in relationships are monogamous, a higher figure than among married women (although, of course, relationships tend to be shorter):

"I've never cheated on a lover. When I'm having a serious relationship, sex with anyone else is unthought of. It would destroy the special precious meaning of our love."

"I am not cheating on my boyfriend. I am very fulfilled by him. He has been faithful to me, and I would be extremely hurt if he cheated on me. I want to be satisfied by only him."

"I firmly believe in monogamy, and I *am* monogamous. I love my boyfriend—and I have learned that sleeping with someone else while in a relationship never works. I did in the past have sex outside of relationships, and it has always been a mistake."

However, 43 percent of single women report relationships in which the man is non-monogamous:

"A boyfriend who was living with me told me about an 'affair' he'd had with someone else. I flipped! I did not like hearing about this! But I didn't feel I had the right to complain—it's hard for me to explain why. I definitely can't deal with someone having sex with someone else when they're in a relationship with me."

One woman, living with her boyfriend in college, accepts his non-monogamy (although it hurts her), while she waits for him to decide whether he wants to make a commitment:

"I am a student, supporting myself with a scholarship, proud to say that I'm from the Midwest! I have a very good, stable relationship with a young man in my class. We live together (unofficially) and plan to become engaged and eventually married when we all grow up and get jobs.

"My idyllic (now and then) relationship has gone on for one year. He is happy, although the job hunt is getting him down. I kind of wish he would tell me he loves me more often, but I know he does, which is almost as good.

"He still has a tendency to want to date other people. He says he knows he can't find anyone else to love like he loves me, but he is scared of marriage and wants to prove he's not tied down. He never went out behind my back, and he hurt my feelings *really* badly when he first asked if he could date others.

"The biggest fight we ever had was when I was swamped with work and felt he was not supporting me. He was dating other women, griping a *lot* about the job interviews he had, and worrying about whether he would graduate. Finally he accused me of picking a fight, saying, 'I don't have time for this!' I blew up and started screaming at him that I was drowning in work, while he was taking only one class and spending a lot of time with his frat brothers, and giving me no support, emotionally or financially. Things got better after that, although I still pay all the rent (I have more money than he does). But when he gets a job our financial situation will change considerably.

"I like our daily life and the dull things we do, like grocery shopping or going to the zoo. He is great fun, special occasions are fun, and we are very comfortable together. We are both pretty conservative and hold family-oriented values. We also have a very active and—shall I say?—creative sex life. He makes me feel incredibly sexy and desirable, special. He is kind of teasing and playful in bed and I am uninhibited with him.

"The biggest problem we have is that we can't make any plans beyond graduation. I want him to admit we can stay together even if we have to move, and propose to me. (He thinks it is his place to propose, and would get flustered if I proposed to him.) I am frustrated by the fact that he is scared to get tied down before he has a career. He says that because he sees me as an equal, he doesn't want to hear any talk of my moving out to wherever he may be if he gets a job elsewhere."

Another woman describes quite a fight she had with her boyfriend when he was seeing another woman:

"My most recent fight was the biggest I have ever had. It was over my boyfriend's infidelity. I went through a long period of feeling depressed, weepy, and letting all that tension build up, and then one afternoon I drank a little wine, and when he came back, I sat through the obligatory silence whilst he read the paper. Then a stream of words and tears flooded out and I ran out of the room screaming, 'You bastard, I hate you!' I ran to my room and there was nothing stopping me—I ripped pictures off the wall, tore books off shelves, turned my craziest music on at full volume. I was so hysterical that I totally destroyed my room in search of drugs!!! Hearing the hysterical chaos, he came downstairs—and some very bitter words were exchanged. I was out of my mind—my face had swollen to twice the size and I'd consumed more alcohol and was clutching my 'death drugs.'

"Then two male friends of ours turned up and talked to him. He said things like 'Well, you've got to let them scream sometimes.' Crazy stupid analogies that they just listened to. Then they all left. I lay on the bed exhausted, a dreadful mess. I had a shocking headache. Then I experienced an amazing surge of strength—what a fool I had been! I didn't care it was him that was going out; he would see the rest of me—the strong one. I quickly got changed, made some attempt to patch up my face and went to join them in the pub. I put on the biggest confidence act ever—even when I had to sit next to him and the woman who was my 'replacement.' Then I said to his friend, 'Come on, this pub is driving me crazy. Let's go somewhere else.' And off we went. Later on we met up with him and her again—the replacement—when they came to the disco where we were.

"I danced with his friend all evening intimately. Within the space of two hours, there was a complete role reversal. He was now the jealous passive person. I was conscious of his hurt and jealousy and I was enjoying it so much. I wanted him to be the one who was hurt—he did silly things like ask for certain records, our songs. I never took any notice. Nigel (his friend) and I came back home together. Then he turned up about one A.M.—he wasn't going to sleep with his new girlfriend after all. . . . Anyway, I was still happy and confident and I didn't give a fuck!! To cut a long story short, two hours later, about three in the morning, he came into my room almost crying. How stupid he'd been. I was the only woman he could ever love and even would I marry him! During this emotional onslaught, I kept my new hardened face and just looked him in the eye, never altering my expression. When he'd finished, I said, 'I'm tired now and I'm going to sleep,' and turned off the light. Our relationship was definitely improved as a result of this—I've never been the passive urchin since."

23 percent of single women in relationships of more than four months do not believe in or do not practice monogamy:

"I'm twenty-four and in two relationships. One has been going for one year and the other for five years (they live in different cities). I live with one—which makes the situation difficult sometimes. We have no children. The basis of both is friendship, with sexual intimacy being very important. I was not strongly attracted to the man I live with at first, but gradually his kindness, respect, and honesty won my love. Very simple. I like being part of a couple—life is certainly easier (social life, that is).

"I do not believe in monogamy as a thing which *should* be, like a rule—but I do find two relationships very difficult emotionally at times, so I think maybe monogamy makes life easier. Still, everyone should have the choice. I have been with this lover for a year. The only other times I have had outside sex were when I was overseas. The man I live with knows about these times but not the steady relationship. My affair has not directly affected our relationship because he doesn't know—but I think it has made me less relaxed when I am with him. Both relationships are very serious. I get the same out of one as the other—neither is inferior.

"Although I believe my lover should be free to do as he wants, I am quite glad that he hasn't fucked anyone else. I don't think I would mind too much—but it's hard to know until it happens. My other love has recently had a one-night stand with a girl from work and I am trying to get used to the idea, although I feel jealous."

"I'm not sure if I could ever be monogamous for any length of time. As soon as a relationship becomes dissatisfying, I will usually start dating again—but I try to be honest about it. In my last relationship, my lover knew of it, but didn't know how often. We had an agreement—as long as he was my 'main man,' it was O.K. Not great, but O.K."

"I travel a lot and have lovers in several places. They are aware of the existence of the others. Most of these have been going on for over a year. Sexual activity and daily companionship are high among the reasons for these relationships. My partners and I are pleased with these arrangements because they allow us to enjoy each other while still living an independent life."

"I have three lovers. Each of them is very different, and our times together are different. Sometimes it's hard to 'shift gears' between them! I wouldn't want to have a long-term, monogamous involvement with any one of them, they're not right for me that way."

Some are the "other woman" for men who have other "real" relationships:

"He hasn't told his girlfriend of two years he's seeing me—so I'm not expecting it. He acts very warm and loving, though I know he doesn't love me. I don't want him to love me. He tells me that I'm sexually desirable and a very good lover. He talks tenderly and we can just hold each other for hours. It's really nice."

"Right now I am involved in a relationship with my ex-boyfriend, who happens to be living with his present girlfriend. I have known him for nine years, and I have been seeing him again now for two years. His girlfriend probably has some idea, but does not broach the subject with him. At first the idea of being the 'other woman' seemed very exciting to me—like those shows on TV where the mistress is portrayed like the desirable one and the wife more of a nag. But now, two years later, the affair has lost much of its romance. I cannot call him at home. (She would be there.) He cannot call me from home. (My number would appear on the bill.)

"The relationship is played totally by his rules—when he can see me, when she is out of town, etc. The funny thing is that I am still in love with him. But I could never see a future in us. My feeling is that if he can cheat on his girlfriend to see me, why couldn't he cheat on me, too, sometime in the future? I would ideally love to remain *friends* with him, but his girlfriend would remain jealous, and any relationships I might have would feel the same way. Why can't men and women have friendships? That's my big question lately! And if we happen to go to bed together? Well, I would not want her to get all freaked out about it. After all, he would be sharing his entire life with her, his family, friends, innermost thoughts, day-to-day activities, while we would be having just brief encounters between friends. But being that life is not like that, I think the affair is over. I think I may always be in love with him, but I have to put him and my love for him out of the picture, and move on."

One woman, obviously deeply in love, is trying to live in a non-monogamous way, because she theoretically believes in "non-possessive" (non-monogamous) relationships:

"I tend toward being relatively monogamous, but I am working against this, and am in several relationships right now. First, there is the man I love, and there is a younger man also, and an older one. My love has other lovers too. All I want is to know what's going on. Sneakiness makes me uneasy. I hate it when he lies or sneaks around about another woman, because I'm trying to deal with those issues and feelings consciously, and it undermines my efforts. We usually fight about jealousy in one form or another. Nobody wins. I mostly feel scared, sometimes angry or hurt. Afterwards, regretful, afraid I've gone too far, said too much. How does he deal with the argument? He leaves, goddammit! I usually initiate peace overtures, etc.

"Our most frequent arguments are around the question of including someone else, maybe as a lover to one of us. This is very hard to pull off without hurting. We have such deep training to be monogamous and insecure. I'm still trying to learn. I had an abortion while carrying his baby, which I wanted. I'm really still not through the abortion, though it happened almost four years ago. Later, he told me he'd made a woman I hate pregnant (a lie to upset me) after inviting that same woman to come traveling with us and our other friends, and repeatedly lying about small things having to do with her.

"I have hurt him also. Last year I went off to live and work alone, without him. I was being single to clear the circuits, get back in touch with myself and what I wanted, how I wanted things to be. Although I feel we love each other equally, I am less frightened by the love and more expressive of it. Sometimes I feel less loved. I think I need him more than he needs me. I do not know; who can read another's heart truly? He doesn't talk much about love or loving. I have to read his actions and his touch, which is hard."

Another woman, not finding one "right man," decided to relate to more than one, finding some good parts in each:

"Loving a man is full of special problems: if a woman shows she loves a man, he might fear he is obligated to commitment on a long-term basis. Additionally, he might feel, if he is very macho-traditional, that in loving a woman, he shows himself as inferior to men who do not love anyone. Men tend to be dysfunctional in relationships. The culture has damaged their ability to be in touch with their feelings.

"So—what can I say? I am currently relating to three men. The alternative seems to be being a couple with someone who is less than I want. I am black and I prefer to relate to black men, although I have dated white men. The first is Andy, who lives in another state. Then there is Tony, who is married and spends 80 percent of his time on his business. David lives with another woman, and ours is a recent relationship, mostly sex. Of these three men, I love most Andy.

"I like these relationships and their diversity, but they certainly do not fill my deepest needs for closeness. I would like more talk about us, as two people relating. I would like to be in a committed long-term relationship with a man eventually. I could get that with a woman, but I want it with a man. I want more (from men)—friendship, reliability, and support when I feel down. Why are men so unreliable for emotional support? I guess it comes out of some basic fears and insecurities they have. So my real question is, why the hell don't they work on these issues???!

"All three of these lovers do tend to see me as an equal—probably because I am not exclusively involved with them. In other words, if I were only seeing one of them exclusively, the dynamics might shift."

4 percent of single women have "open" relationships:

"I have had three affairs with other men while I have been with my present lover. They were all very short-term (a day to a month long). I told my lover all about them. He is curious, because he has never had sex with another woman. He would like to, though. He accepts it and knows that I will accept his affairs in the future. We have an open relationship."

"It is mutually agreed that we can both see other people. I don't, as it isn't comfortable for me to juggle more than one man at a time in my life, and I feel it isn't fair to keep them hanging and eventually let someone down. I *did not mind* when he started to date others, as I knew before I got involved that he would, and I accepted that. However, he feels guilty and then gets angry.

"I have a girlfriend who is also having this problem with the current love of her life. He hates it when she doesn't see anyone but him and he dates around. He hates it that she accepts his dating, he can't stand her 'singleness of purpose.' He then tries to ease his conscience by pushing her to date. Then he wants to murder her for being unfaithful and running around! What do men want?"

Another woman comments wryly:

"The people I have seen who were best at keeping lovers faithful seemed to know some sort of cult-leader brainwashing technique. They are able to make the partner feel in some subtle way that they would be worthless on their own. I can't figure out how they do this exactly but I am both appalled and envious."

A "blond ex-punk-rocker" (as she describes herself) tells about a devastating three-way relationship she was involved in, and how she got out of it, with the help of a therapist:

"I have left the man—it's a relief and also awful. I felt guilt and sadness that it didn't work. I missed him. I was miserable for weeks and doubted my wisdom—acted like a fool, wrote letters that I either never sent or if I did would like to blow the mailbox up. I said the nastiest things. I cried for days and walked around with a lump in my throat—listened to Emmylou Harris records—got drunk—hated myself, wondered what's wrong with me. I went to a psychotherapist. Maybe I was so 'needy' that I accepted someone I shouldn't have. It took me weeks to at least breathe again. I think I feel good now, it's been on and off—but basically for two months I'm better. I still think of him and feel sadness and I hope he never calls me.

"It involved a triangle. My lover had his other woman and me. He always came over and we dated regularly, slept together, and she knew about it and all that—but I always felt insecure. It was an emotional edge-of-my-chair feeling all the time. I was so insecure that eventually he did grow tired of me. I ate away at the whole thing.

"I don't like feeling that the things I share with a man are the same things he shares with someone else. He is special to me and I want to be special to him—with no other lovers. This attitude seems to be disappearing. During the affair, I tried to do what intellectually I knew made sense—but emotionally I was still monogamous. I wanted to feel love—I felt love when making love—but I can't or don't enjoy separating love from sex. It's better for me and happier if I feel some true empathy, affection, and concern from the other person.

"It was so sexually intense, I feel I learned how to make love for the first time in my life. We were really compatible. He knew just what to do. He had the touch. He was passionate, romantic, and affectionate. He cared so much whether I had an orgasm. (I had more orgasms with him in one and a half years than I had in my entire life before him—usually with oral sex—I may have used them all up!) I didn't even know I was capable of always having them—he just knew how to be gentle. He was perfect—too bad he was also living with someone else. He also drank.

"My therapist encouraged me to take a good cold look at what kind of men I was choosing—I mean, even though he lived with another woman, he wanted to have us both. I finally thought that my relationship with him was just a symptom of all kinds of problems I'd never resolved. I felt I needed to improve my self-confidence and begin to have an image of myself as a working, contributing person. My therapist helped me plan to go to school again. I still saw the man off and on.

"I've had four abortions. That's hard to say. I usually lie about it. I never felt I could support a child, I thought it wouldn't be fair to do that to a child. I did feel bad when I met my brother's kids—I never knew how wonderful babies can be. I'll never have another abortion. The clinic I went to was so good, I had supportive experiences. I went to two of the abortions alone. I never told anyone about them. I paid for them myself, the last one with student insurance. One was the result of a one-night stand. I'm fertile, I guess.

"My best relationship so far was with my 'shrink.' She really cares. She's totally authentic and honest. I love her. She taught me so much. She became my friend and spent time playing tennis with me, it was a laugh. She helped me learn to draw. She supported me when I wanted to move. She wouldn't let me give up. I relied on her. She never acted like *she'd* 'made it,' she only used her learning to inspire mine. In a year, I gained so much self-confidence by knowing her. I have lots more to learn, but I have so much more hope now.

"I even see my mother differently—despite her problems, my mother can be funny and talkative. She was a teacher, worked for twenty-five years, was very well liked. She was a good role model for a certain kind of strength—it was confusing, though, because later she'd drink and lose her power and our respect. I am just like her in many ways, it drives me crazy sometimes. She has a good sense of humor—very silly, I like that. I drink and it's similar sometimes. I don't want to end like her. It's a waste. I am small, blond, spiked hair, and am interested in punk music and art, also love classics. I hope I do have a daughter sometime and I hope I'll be tolerant if she comes home with a bald head and a Hollywood push-up bra, or whatever.

"I would like to have a lover again, maybe next year. I can't put the brain through anything new now. I still like being in love. It's thrilling. But I guess relationships are tough endeavors and shouldn't be taken up lightly. Now that I know all the feelings that happen within a relationship, and that they are normal and to be expected, I'm more ready for an important one."

To Believe in Love, No Matter What the Cost: Does Love Have to Be So Difficult?

Reading what women have said in these chapters—despite the sense of humor and strength in so many of their statements—leaves one with a very poignant feeling: why does it often have to be so hard? Many women say they are emotionally worn out from all of this—but almost all still want to try, to keep searching, to make it work. Is this because love is a basic human hunger? Or are women brought up to focus so much on men's love as "their destiny" that no matter what their experiences with men, they still believe they must find a way for this dream to work? That other dreams are not as valid?*

It is ironic that the place women are going for love, to get love, is the very place from which it is hardest to get, according to women—because of the way men in this culture are conditioned, what "masculinity means." This is very sad, as woman after woman struggles to draw a man out, to develop emotional companionship to go along with more or less instant physical intimacy. Most find the going difficult. For every two steps forward, they go one step back. Although while lying in bed together at night, they may break through and talk, the next day the atmosphere is often changed back to a silent ambiguity.

"Love is a battlefield"†

Women are having to live with men who have grown up with images of the Marlboro man (the idealized "loner") and single male movie heroes, men who don't want to commit themselves and who believe in "freedom"—freedom from relationships with women. Thus, when most men are *in* relationships, they act ambivalent. This puts women emotionally on the defensive. The rules are: "don't cling," "don't ask for monogamy," "there is something wrong with you if you feel insecure," etc.

Women are defined by the "male" ideology as needing men more than men need women. This puts women in a vulnerable position psychologically with men—women must "catch" men, not seem too "needy" of a relationship, not "complain" about men's lack of emotional support or condescension, bad manners, and so on.

---

*Also, of course, there is great pressure on women—a feeling (after age twenty-eight or so) that this is the only basic way to fit into society; most women feel that there will be no place for them in society after their twenties if they don't "find someone" and get married. See Chapter 8.
†As the hit rock video by Pat Benatar says.

There is an undercurrent in most dating relationships of this unstated imbalance of power status between women and men—i.e., the so-called desirability of females vs. the desirability of males. The suspense in a relationship for a woman hovers around the question "Is it love, or is he just using you?" Women have a realistic fear of being tricked—then being left, to end up feeling taken, yet emotionally open and still loving. Meeting men and having sex/ friendships with men becomes a minefield, often filled with traumas, perhaps also with some pleasant surprises, but almost always involving the terror of never knowing what to expect next. Indeed, women often want to get married sometimes just to escape all the put-downs, the endless "looking" and "trying out," the doubts and fears of single life. In fact, it is the "male" ideology and double standard that make it dangerous to "fall in love," not women's "need" to know someone for a long time and "learn to care" as the only way to have a good experience.

How many compromises should a woman make?

One woman offers her thoughts about what is going on in the whole singles area:

"In a desperation to get the supposed security of having a man, single women may hurt their own self-esteem. They cater to what they feel the man wants, while completely ignoring their own needs, which are reasonable and correct. For example, they are having sex with men after just a date, hoping the man will love and be close to them, marry them, and it doesn't even work. The tragedy is how much women are hurt along the way. Women are answering to men's needs, believing that men's ideology about marriage and love is correct, not being true to themselves. They're afraid to be rejected if they state their real hopes and dreams—and try to be 'loose' the way the 'male' culture is. But they should have more belief in themselves. Their ideas have dignity and depth and profundity. *Women* should set the standards, and not listen to 'male' standards."

Many women are really torn over whether they are making the right choices, whether they have the "right" feelings about love, whether they are assessing clearly what is happening in their lives: "Sometimes I'm depressed or sad for a short while after leaving a lover. The first few times, I thought I might die, but I guess I'm getting used to it. It seems the older I get, the easier the break-ups become. I'm not sure how great that is, and it depresses me, all this long string of love affairs—even if some of them are 'good friends' later. What does it mean?"

Many women's relationships are miserable, even degrading (though no one wants to say so)—and many men treat women condescendingly—so casually that they may drop a woman at any time, proposition another, talk of love but never feel obliged to discuss the pros and cons of commitment or their plans for the future. There is very little idea of team sharing; the "lone hero" version of the "male" ideology does not stop to consider women as having equal rights. Hence, women's pride can be whittled away at during the course of their relationships with men.

Women frequently feel they are being "fucked over," not only physically but also emotionally, by men who reflect the values of a culture which is trying to persuade women to take on the "male" ideology (even though it does not value sex and love in the way most women feel they should be valued), and even though it tends to see many of women's beliefs as laughable or "psychologically defective."

Many women still take all this, even though they know what is going on, because they feel they have no choice: feel every woman "has" to get married eventually; and also, being asked out by men, paid attention to by men, it is natural that a woman would eventually fall in love with one—and then the cycle begins.

All of this can lead to what one woman described as "relationship burnout": "I do believe love involves problems for many women. Just by the mere fact that loving requires a tremendous amount of work and energy—on an ongoing basis. This could lead to 'relationship burnout.' (I just made up this term!)"

Men's patterns in single relationships

> *"You want to forget the feeling of being so hurt and just go on—like in a break up—but is life serious? Does one event imply thinking about it, and changing your view of life? Or can you just forget and cover everything over?"*

The whole scenario—a woman feeling, when meeting someone or starting a relationship, that if she doesn't sleep with him relatively quickly, he may never call her again; but if she does sleep with him, he may not take her seriously or treat her respectfully and may never call again anyway—puts women in an impossible position. Even worse, it never allows a woman to be the "judge" of a relationship: women hardly have a chance to think about what they actually feel, because they are so busy having to deal with the man's prejudices, stereotypes, and possible condescending remarks. She has to judge situations in an atmosphere which makes the man a possible adversary: he trying to "get" something, she wondering if she is being "had" or not.

The "male" pattern of no-holds-barred competition and aggression has become much harsher during recent years in the "singles world," and that pressure on single women to try to appease men and fit in with their system has become stronger. Women in the "singles scene" often rightly feel anxiety about whether men will drop or dump them—the man first acting loving, then leaving and acting unfriendly, then later returning to act loving again (meanwhile hotly denying any wrongdoing, and wondering why she is "so unstable and frequently demanding to know if he loves her or if he is only there for sex"). How can women love men in this atmosphere?

Men's trashy behavior and bad manners

Men's casual treatment of women in single relationships seems to be becoming more hostile and confrontational; the wild impoliteness of many men in the "dating scene" documented here seems to represent an enormous increase over previous years. The rudeness at times amounts to a flagrant show of male power and contempt: since a woman is so "powerless," it cannot hurt a man to be rude to her or treat her callously.

In the world of non-committed, fluctuating relationships, men's leaving immediately after sex, not calling, calling at random times, keeping unpredictable schedules, but still expecting the woman to be available, are all standard behaviors—so that a woman often finds it hard to enjoy a relationship—or even to know *if* she is in a relationship or what the status is. The attitude of "I deserve a woman to love me and be nice to me, but I don't have to be nice back" has become very widespread. As one woman asks, "Are they afraid and nervous, or did someone tell them it's macho to be mean?" Many men seem to have leaped mentally from the 1950s attitude that women who are not playing the role of mothers/Marys are "bad girls" to a post- "sexual revolution" attitude that since most women now have sex before marriage, and furthermore work outside the home, most women are "bad girls" who deserve to be treated roughly, or however one wants—"they deserve what they get" because they gave up being put on pedestals when they went out into the "male world." Chivalry, they say, was extra-special treatment (naturally they do not usually recognize the special treatment women give men—i.e., listening to men's opinions as if they are more important, being there emotionally for them, etc.); in some instances, as we have seen, they do not even treat women they have slept with with the same amount of respect and politeness that they would a business associate.

Emotional violence

Many men have a pattern of giving a woman a lot of attention until she is interested and involved, has come to trust them and enjoy them—then changing, coming and going (both physically and emotionally) casually, irregularly (having established their territory?). If a woman "complains" (see Chapter 2), she may be reminded by the man, "I'm happy, why are you making waves?", with an undertone of "Now, don't start being a neurotic, clinging woman on me. I thought you were different." Thus, men's behavior, while provoking a realistic response in women, i.e., women are wondering what is going on and trying to find out—comes off seeming "neutral": the man is "not doing anything." In these situations, men often then accuse women of "attacking them for no reason." In fact, the man is practicing a form of passive aggression.

Do men go through this process of flirtation, seduction, saying "beautiful things" only for "conquest"? No, it is also because they want the adulation, the affection, and the understanding that women give.

It is hardly surprising that many women feel very angry and unsettled about these situations. While they may know that in fact it is the whole weight of the system against them that they are feeling, and that the system is unjust to do this—still, for an individual who has just been called names or had all her assumptions challenged by her "boyfriend," this knowledge is not too helpful.

Nor is it perhaps surprising that, by contrast with single life now, men's commitment in marriage can look more civilized to single women than what they are experiencing. As one woman puts it, "It's all a jungle—but maybe at least if you're married, it's a private jungle."*

Men's manipulation of power in relationships: the emotional contract writ large

The psychological imbalance many men set up in single relationships often leads women to wind up asking themselves, "Is everything all right with him? Does he still love me? What is his mood today?"—not "Is everything all right with me? How am I? Do I want this kind of relationship?" After all, women are used to men's setting the rules, declaring what reality is, with women being expected to make the adjustments in *their* lives. Even if they realize how outrageous the situation is, they still feel they should stay, due to the heavy social pressure to "have a man."

Ironically, in non-married relationships, it often seems now that men are even *more* in charge, have more power, than they do in marriage (ironically, since feminists fought against men's ownership of women in marriage). This is because in single relationships, in addition to the usual subtle gender put-downs, emotional harassment, and not being listened to seen in Part I, the man here has the ace in the hole of total privatization of the relationship: his staying or leaving will never be judged publicly—as it will be if he divorces. So he feels

*To look at it more cynically, "male" culture has caused the harassment of women sexually with the "sexual revolution," putting women down for being "too sexual" outside of marriage at the same time that it urges women to be sexual (on male terms)—then offered "protection" inside marriage if women give up this idea of "freedom"—like a "Mafia" shakedown.

no responsibility to "the relationship," and comes and goes at the drop of a hat.*
The ideology of "freedom" and "independence" can even make him a hero if
he leaves: he is seen as questing after his inner needs and existential self (she
was trying to "tie him down"). To depart mysteriously or agitatedly, with no
explanation, may make him a "rebel without a cause," even more interesting.
And, outsiders usually assume that it was the woman who was "impossible to
live with," or is to be "pitied" for being "deserted" or "dumped," etc., rarely
that she asked him to leave, etc.

This is the emotional contract writ large: men have more power and status
than women, and instead of trying to equalize that imbalance and make equality
(and thus love) more possible in personal relationships, many are doing just the
opposite, i.e., taking every opportunity to remind women of the "male" need
for "freedom." These are controlling and dominating behaviors; men have been
warned all their lives never to "let a woman get the upper hand" or "she'll take
advantage of you!" Men "must" assert dominance in every instance, "show her
who's boss."

Disoriented and confused about this, unprepared for the kind of guerrilla
warfare that goes on (especially when a couple is supposed to be "in love"),
wondering why it feels to them like the man they love is using them for target
practice, many single women suffer enormously. The privatized nature of the
relationship adds to this: whatever goes on is seen only by the couple, and so even
when men behave despicably, commit gross injustices, no one bears witness, and
a woman's own perception of what is happening is usually challenged by the
man, who says she is "over-reacting." A great amount of emotional violence
against women is done by men, but rarely "seen," almost never castigated by the
larger society. And whatever men do, when the break-up comes, it almost always
still seems as if the man somehow "won"—that it was brought on, caused
somehow, by the woman (she was "too obsessed with love," she "picked the
wrong man"). Most men are never reproached for their behavior by anyone but
the woman herself, and most men who do these things do not seem to feel guilty.

Are "great men" great in the way they treat women in their personal lives?:

> *"He's a fine person; it's just the macho part
> that's bad."*

Can a man be deeply in love with a woman and still see her as "less"? Is this
illogical? If a man is a "great man," a "fine man" at work and in the community,

*This is not an argument against "freedom," but, whether a man or woman leaves, it should be done
in a reasonable context; a man should not try to find the most humiliating and inconsiderate behavior
possible, as many women describe here.

does this mean he won't be condescending to a woman at home? It is, unfortunately, possible for a man to be creative, a genius, a mastermind in business, or a kind and generous teacher—and still be a "pig" in his personal relationships with women because men have a double standard for their lives. As one woman puts it, "He treated me so terribly—but deep down, I think he's really a great person—so interesting, so talented, so knowledgeable."

What gives rise to this dichotomy? *Is* he really a "great guy"? Maybe—with other "guys." But many men are brought up to believe that women are so lowly that being with a woman brings out "another them," their worst side. (Are they basically "racist"—i.e., genderist—without realizing it?) This can happen especially where love and romance are concerned, since this is where all a man's values and beliefs about women are really put to the test.

Love, even falling in love, does not make women and men automatically equal—unfortunately. Even most "good men" look down on women, have certain "special" expectations of women's behavior—conscious or unconscious. Most men assume they can touch women, that they can speak about "personal things" to women, and that women will offer them comfort and solace, reassurance. Men look to women, almost all women, to be a kind of emotional cushion or pillow for them—without imagining that they have to give this support back equally. And men generally would never expect these comforts from other men; certainly they would never think of touching other men with the same ease. Yet, men do not see how this is taking advantage of women. As one woman says, "Men apply a double standard of legitimacy to their male friends and business associates, and to women—especially women they love. They definitely accord men more rights and respect."

This is confusing for many women: if they *know* the man loves them, they therefore can't understand when he behaves arrogantly and inconsiderately. A man can be deeply in love with a woman—and still emotionally stereotype her and disrespect her. And this includes fine, humanitarian, brilliant, and sensitive men. Of course, this does not make it right.

Isn't this a paradox? If a man were "great," wouldn't he be above shallow stereotypes and hurtful assumptions and prejudices? It seems very hard for many men to see this in themselves. Perhaps seeing some of the examples and patterns in this book will make it easier.

Women who fall in love, and expect that the man, seeming to be in love too, will see them as equals and give emotionally, "play fair" emotionally—are often surprised when the man becomes competitive. This is what one woman referred to, after hearing story after story from her unmarried friends, when she called them "innocent people walking into dark alleys."

Although some men may protest that their being in love means the woman actually has power over them, still, the man has all the resources of a society that puts men first behind him to support him in his sense of dignity and self-esteem, no matter what happens in the relationship; on the other hand, rejection for the woman from a man carries the whole weight of society behind it—she is an "unacceptable woman."

On another level, if a man can be "in love" with a woman, deeply, and still treat her with disrespect, even be macho and cruel—does a woman want a man like this? But what if *most* men are like this? (And most men *are* brought up to see women as "second," "different" fundamentally, more emotional, not as "rational," etc.) Should a woman take a man she loves and who loves her, and try to fight it through with him, to get him to see her as an equal, change his thinking, learn about emotional sharing, etc.? Or is this a job which may never succeed, and which may take up more of her time and energy than it should?

Women's growing disrespect for men with these behaviors

Perhaps women have great courage in not being afraid to keep on trying to love in the face of all of this. But at the same time, more and more women are becoming exasperated with men's behavior, often losing their respect for men. In fact, women are becoming increasingly restive, increasingly concerned with changing this situation, perhaps leaving. Individual women everywhere are asking, why does it have to be like this? *Does* it have to be like this? What is behind this system? Isn't another system possible?

Actually, single women are doing quite well, despite all these circumstances. They very much enjoy their lives in general, being on their own—their work, their friends, even some of the playing around with men. Even when hurt and upset, they often display a marvelous sense of humor in the face of it all—mixed with wrath.

In fact, it is just this thinking going on in women's lives, combined with women's growing economic self-sufficiency and their happiness with friends, that is creating the new philosophical outlook, the new vision of what life can be, that is beginning to emerge, as woman after woman comes to the conclusion that there is something wrong with the system, not with her. On another level, women are coming to see that it is not even so much a problem with the individual men they know, but that somehow men too are caught up in an unreasonable set of beliefs which twists their lives and causes them to behave in truncated and distorted fashions. This system grasps men so tightly that many become lonely and desperate, finally losing "control": it is almost always men who are reported to have committed violent crimes. It is likely that women do not become violent because their system, "women's" culture, allows for talking things out. But men feel they have no place to turn, that they are not allowed any place to turn—except perhaps to sex, through which they can at least get physical affection. (Thus rape is often a way for men to try to make a statement to themselves about themselves and the attention they are angry they are not receiving.) The "male" system hurts men and closes them off from others, and yet men continue to believe in it, to defend its "values" no matter what. Why?

A new analysis of "male" psychology

Does the great amount of emotional violence by men in relationships with women imply a sort of vague unrest men feel with their lives *in general*? Are men the "winners" in the system of "male dominance" that they are supposed to be? What we see men expressing here (against women, where it is easiest) is a kind of fury, a nervousness that might indicate a feeling on men's part that things are not in fact going well, that men are not getting the rewards they were meant to get. Perhaps men are finding their world now somewhat frightening and unsatisfying, particularly with jobs often scarce and the future uncertain in a world where one is now expected to change jobs or careers several times in a lifetime. Even the once guaranteed love from women may be taken away, as men are expected to see women as equals, to "watch every little thing one says around them." Maybe men can no longer expect women to "be there," "be nice," ready to be caretakers, to make a home, etc. No longer is there a promise that there will be someone there, someone at "home" waiting. It is possible that how men treat women is a stage on which men are acting out their general feelings about life, themselves, and the future.

As Jacob Bronowski has stated, "Perhaps we have dehumanized ourselves and others with World War II and the bomb."* "Masculinity" has undergone a great change since World War II, a toughening. Is it possible that the collective male psyche in America somehow felt uncomfortable with war, with learning to believe it was right to kill—and so dealt with its guilt by glorifying it, glorifying the tough, brutal loner, the jungle fighter—the man who could "take it," "do what he had to do"—as a way of absorbing the shock of collective responsibility for the violence and death which was the price of victory? This style has remained popular; yet, not all men "buy into" this brutalized idea of masculinity. What makes them different, what keeps them safe from this desensitizing process?

*Public Television series, "The Ascent of Man," with Professor Jacob Bronowski host.

Loving Men Who Are "Bad for You": The Myth of Female Masochism

"Do You Sometimes Think You Pick the Wrong Men?"

The overwhelming majority of single women, 88 percent, say they sometimes think they pick the "wrong men"; almost every woman thinks that this is her own unique problem, and wonders if she has a hidden neurotic, masochistic side to herself:

"I almost always pick the wrong guys—and get hurt."

"I sometimes think I pick the wrong lovers. They usually aren't ready to settle down, while I am. In the beginning it's great, but as soon as he realizes I'm serious and I realize he's not, we've got problems."

"I think I pick the wrong men. The only common denominator is that they all have had less education than me—not that formal education means smartness. Or maybe it's that I fall for a flattering line?"

"I had a history of going out with weak men, which I finally stopped doing. It was too twisted. Being a strong person, it was tough to find anyone who was as strong. I finally realized, better to be single than stuck with a wimp."

"I seem to pick ones that are reaching for help—and then find that they need a shrink, or a boot in the ass, more than a lover."

"I like bad boys—not too tame."

"I pick lovers who are sexy, excellent lovers but they always have too many hang-ups and problems."

"Men that seem strong, but are really weaker than me—men who were not able to be there for me due to their own emotional problems."

"I do pick the wrong kind of men—so far, mainly losers, barren personalities, and egotists, and bores!"

"Unobtainable ones that deep down I know I can never possess."

"Usually men who don't want to get involved in anything and don't care about pleasing me, just showing off."

"I pick guys who are bound to hurt me—dishonest, macho."

"Selfish, good-looking ones."

"Possibly too domineering, like my father."

"I don't know what healthy security in a relationship is like. I see it, but I don't know how to choose the type that would be good for me."

"Users."

"I did at one time pick all the jerks to be my lovers. It seems there are more of them now than ever."

"I choose men who care for me a great deal, but not enough to make a commitment."

"I seem to pick the ones who have been hurt too many times."

"Boys."

"I pick intense, brilliant men. That works out right (for the attraction) and wrong (for the long haul). It's O.K. at first—then I feel trapped and lonely."

"I tend to be attracted to very gentle men. Sometimes they are weak morally or emotionally, not always."

"I pick the ones who make it the hardest for me, 'cause I like struggle. Anyone who is too nice to me turns me off! Loving, yes?"

"I seem to pick flakes with no goals."

"The men I have picked so far have all turned out wrong for me. But I've thought about it and come to the conclusion that I did not deliberately set out to have a negative experience with any of them. They all had some good qualities that in the beginning outweighed the bad ones. Then the bad ones took over."

"Men like my mother—injured emotionally—like me."

"I tend to fall for effeminate, even homosexual, men. My first two lovers ended up loving each other."

"My love relationships have always been with men that I have disliked as people, but became emotionally involved with anyway. I seem to fall for men who are chauvinistic and not at all what I would want in a man if I were rational at the time."

"The first I picked for glamour. All I got was housework and a lot of nights alone."

"Men who treat me like a body instead of a spirit."

"I mainly pick men just interested in a sexual relationship. I want it to go further, they don't. But I do have some good male friends."

"I always pick men who in some way are rejecting or abandoning me."

"A lot of style, attractive. I can't seem to find stable ones who have style and attraction."

"The ones that I pick are insensitive to my needs, but I continue to pick the same type."

"I have picked violent men and male chauvinists before, and my lover is not like that. Or is he? He likes to have one woman for sex and excitement and then another woman he keeps for his wife."

"I definitely pick the wrong men—men who are authoritarian, discounting of women, successful (monetarily) like my father."

"For years, I picked momma's boys so I would be in control of not getting hurt."

"Sometimes I do think I choose the wrong lovers. Very often, I have wound up with married men, finding out about it only afterwards. I'm not really sure why this occurs. Could it be that married men feel more comfortable and are more sociable around women, and are more attractive? A psychologist would probably say that by dating men already attached, I am looking for a relationship without the room to decide whether or not I want to make a commitment. I don't think that is the case, though."

"I am very attracted to the rebel type, non-conformist, who always ends up hurting me."

"I first went into therapy to try to work through why I keep repeating the pattern of attracting 'losers' and getting hurt and all bummed out. I'd fall madly in love and I wouldn't give up. I would feel desperate, like if I didn't get this guy my world would crumble, that it just *had* to work out . . . and it never would. I wish I could have been more secure in loving myself, and not wasted my time on these people. By the way, I don't think therapy helped me come up with any conclusions—I just eventually met my husband."

Sometimes women say the "new sensitivity" in men turns out to be more byronesque and self-involved than empathic or egalitarian—i.e., some men are now becoming more sensitive and in tune with their own feelings, but not women's:

"I have, in the past, been attracted to what Bertrand Russell calls the 'Byronic unhappier.' The kind of man who is moody, sensitive, needy. Luckily I have found out they aren't good for me. I can't rescue them; they rarely want to be rescued. They have to do it for themselves."

"I did pick wrong men. I wanted gentle men; instead I picked meek, selfish, unfeeling men, sensitive to their own feelings but insensitive to others."

"I thought he was a 'liberated man,' he looked sweet and sensitive as well as extremely sexy—a long-haired hippie type. He turned out to be on a tremendous ego trip—he loved manipulating several women at once. It ended badly—he wanted me to go to bed with other men, and watch. I did not. For months and months I alternated between anger and depression. I have never since then become dependent on a man for my identity or life."

The few "no" answers look like this:

"I pick men who are kind, loving, and have a good sense of humor and self-confidence without being egotistical."

"I pick the right lovers. Communicative, gentle, honest, sexy, healthy, hardworking, intelligent. And they love me."

"I pick caring, sharing, strong, ambitious, well-bred men. I feel that if they had sisters, they'll probably have more insight into female feelings also."

"The shy types, with a good sense of humor, easygoing, and open-minded."

"Men that care for my moods and respect me. Cute men, sexy and funny."

"I picked the right man. I know there's no Mr. Perfect. I did real well! The man I picked is loving, faithful, caring, fun, bright, and I could go on."

Several women say they never feel they pick, but rather that the men pick them:

"I usually pick from men that pick me first, which doesn't make sense. I think my whole life is making the best of what comes along."

"I was brought up to believe the boys or men do the picking, and if you like them, fine. I feel at this time I should more actively choose a partner."

"I don't think women 'pick' as much as men do. Women are chosen, and then they either accept or reject the men, depending on how needy they are. I think I have been repeatedly chosen by men who are not my equal."

"I would go out with the boys who fancied me rather than choosing the ones I liked—that was safer, and I could always finish with them when I was fed up or someone else was interested. It was a very passive existence, but I could control it without getting my feelings hurt."

What does "wrong" mean?

Does "wrong" mean non-committed? Inconsiderate? That the woman winds up being hurt?

One woman points out that a man being "wrong"—meaning he does not make her "happy" and is not stable—does not always mean that he is "wrong" for her in other ways:

"I pick the right ones for growth and learning always. I used to be afraid to allow myself to fall for the ones who really turned me on deeply; but now I know that's where my best growth and learning came from, so I take a deep breath and go for it."

Others also see the issue as more complex:

"I think my friends would say that I do pick the 'wrong' men, but who are they to judge and on what basis are they judging? I choose men who have certain qualities of personality and character and, while some may not have been considered 'stable' by average standards, each has given me something precious and important."

"I don't think I ever picked the wrong men, I just think they turned out a lot different than I expected. Through each experience, I learned something, so I never regretted it too much."

"I've made a few mistakes, but the ones that have counted have been great. Of course, things didn't always work out, but they were good people to relate to. If they were the wrong men, I don't think I could have loved them."

"I have risked adventurers, neurotics, unreliable liars, handsome married actors, young Africans telling me various stories to make me pay their taxi or anything else they might want. Well, these men might seem like 'wrong' men to most people, but they are never boring."

"I never have picked 'wrong' men—some proved incompatible, but none were abusive. There are other reasons to love someone than that you settle down together. It depends on what you want."

"Even though none have worked out yet, they are not 'wrong.' I am not quite sure yet what I am looking for. I want to try various possibilities to find out."

Another adds that she doesn't like either tame men or macho men:

"What do I like about men? I like the wildness inside them. I don't like the meanness, or when they get tame. And of course, the patriarchal mind-set of kill or control—but that's in women, too, though I'd call it a 'male' attitude. I like men when they have courage and strength, gentleness and warmth, sexiness, intelligence, humor, good humor, playfulness, generosity of spirit. I dislike selfishness, self-centeredness, cruelty, uncaring, meanness, bullying, sex hating, life hating, narrow-mindedness, those who manipulate women or make my friends feel bad. I hate it if they put women at odds with each other."

Many women have quite a few unhappy relationships before finding or developing a good relationship; an unhappy relationship, or a series of "wrong men" by no means dooms one to a lifetime of them:

"This was an almost constant pattern in about 90 percent of my relationships prior to meeting my husband (and it was absolutely exhausting). I had to do all the emotional, mental, and often financial footwork. I felt terrible separation anxiety, like a total love junkie. I was often insanely jealous of other women; even seeing lovers speaking to other women was enough to turn my stomach and pour me right into a fit of anxiety. This doesn't occur any longer. My relationships then did not work, because I was constantly betraying myself and not setting my real boundaries and limits. Prior to my current relationship, I never allowed myself to set my own limits, edges, as to what was O.K. and what was not for me."

But—do women really "pick the wrong men," or are there very few men "out there" who can relate equally to women?

"It is very, very difficult to meet someone special. Worthwhile men are about one in ten thousand, if that. I'm talking about a developed person, an independent thinker, a man of knowing and ethics. Very rare."

"I have been celibate for six months. Why? I just went back into therapy—don't know—I can't seem to meet people I like. That's probably just a cop-out."

87 percent of women say that it is hard to meet men they admire and respect:

"It's quite difficult for me to meet someone I am attracted to and have respect for. I am attracted to many men, but respect few of them. This is the hardest part of my life at this time, trying to find someone whom I can like and respect and have him feel the same toward me. If I can't date the right type of man for me, then I prefer to stay at home."

"It is easy to find someone I like and am attracted to—just not someone I respect."

"I have many interests and friends, but often feel the lifestyles of the males I date are not as interesting or varied—I find myself giving up activities or not engaging in them."

"I like to be with men who are gentle, kind, considerate, attentive. I enjoy sex, so I would like to be with someone who also enjoys sex. Men that have similar interests to mine would certainly be desirable. My dating has been very low-keyed, because I can't find men like this."

"It is extremely difficult to find someone whom you like and are attracted to. Perhaps I'm being too picky, but I've settled for less than what I've wanted in the past, with negative results. I hate bars. Did all that running around after my first divorce in my middle twenties. I've gone to churches, but the few men that are interesting are already married. It's hard for me to get involved in strictly 'singles' activities and clubs because it seems people are 'looking' for someone. There are a lot of 'available' people out there, but finding someone attractive, sensitive, intelligent, etc., etc., is impossible."

As one woman (representing many others) says, when asked if she "picks the wrong men," "what are the choices?"

"An objective observer might say that I select men who are unavailable for long-term commitment. There may be some truth to that. But then one might say all men lack something important. There are so many variables—white men do not tend to date black women—so the pool of available men is lessened. Quality black men are often those who are less available. Single, uninvolved black men who might like to date me tend to be a lot younger (which is O.K. except they also tend to act their own age—if they acted older, it would be O.K.). Or they tend not to be quality people—they don't share my values or they are not about anything in their lives except mundane day-by-day things. Then, quality men who are in a similar age group and single tend to want only marginal, uncommitted, disconnected, see-you-when-I-can kinds of relationships—and I'd rather have a somewhat greater sense of connectedness, even if it is with someone not totally available to me. So—who can say? Do I pick the wrong men? What are the choices?"

Another wonders how many men there are "out there" with the emotional and psychological capability of having more than casual emotional relationships:

"I always assumed that men's relationships with each other were their most important relationships. I was shocked to read men's own statements in *The Hite Report* [on men] saying they found these relationships shallow. It's no wonder I've had so few 'meaningful' relationships—there just isn't that potential out there. And to think I had (partially) bought the line that I was making the wrong choices time after time. I experienced incredible pain at the hands of all these men whom society has hacked at unmercifully to make sure there's nobody there."

Many women seek therapy, analysis, or counseling to deal with these problems; sometimes counseling is helpful:

"The sessions were helpful in getting me more in touch with my goals, ambitions, etc. But nothing was resolved or solved. I feel that I've made significant progress personally but didn't really experience any epiphanies."

But some types of therapy and psychoanalytic theory merely reflect the values of the general society—and assume that there is something wrong with the woman if she is "having problems" in relationships—that she may be too "demanding," "clinging," "insecure"—or, alternately, too "hard," too "cold";

a therapist, without realizing it, can apply these stereotypes (seemingly justified by elaborate academic theory) to the woman being seen: *

"It seems that in the past I always ended up with someone who I thought was inferior to me. I saw a shrink about this once, and was told that I had some unknown desire to destroy my relationships, and that is why I usually went with people that I really didn't like. I don't think this is true—I think I just needed to develop a lot more self-confidence—which I now have."

If so many women answer yes when asked, "Do you sometimes think you pick the wrong men?" this means either that the majority of women in this country have some kind of "neurosis," and don't think they are worth something better, or else that the majority of men—whether erratic geniuses, businessmen, or construction workers—are not treating women very well in their private relationships.

In fact, it confirms what women have said in Part I of this book: that the majority of men hold anti-woman stereotypes and practice harassing ways of treating women in relationships. In other words, women are not "picking the wrong men": the problem is that almost all men hold stereotypes about women that create problems. The majority of men, according to women here, have barely begun to realize the depths of their view of women as "other," nor have they begun the enormous job of reexamining their own philosophy, redesigning their own psychology.

Great Loves, Painful Love Affairs

Sometimes women describe very deep feelings of ecstatic love, obsession even—but for a man who is hurting them terribly. This is somewhat different from "picking the wrong man," since in these cases, there is an especially intense feeling.

How can it be that such deep love and pain can go together? How can a woman be deeply in love, when she is so unhappy at the same time? Crave someone who is hurting her? What does this mean?

---

*Two-thirds of all those in therapy in the United States are women. See *Women and Madness* by Phyllis Chesler (New York: Avon Books, 1973), a classic book which is still relevant today, and Naomi Weisstein's "Psychology Constructs the Female: Or, the Fantasy Life of the Male Psychologist (with some attention to the fantasies of his friends, the male biologist and the male anthropologist)" in *Social Education* (April 1971), pp. 363–73.

*One woman sent a copy of a heartrending letter she wrote to her lover,
explaining how much she loves him, but why she has to leave:*

"I love you so much. Our problem has nothing to do with my friends, as
you claim. You are so proud and try to make me feel so lousy that I don't want
to share them with you. You want me to be just like Jean, someone who
grimaces when asked if she is still with Jim—someone who allows for so much
hurt and being walked on so much—you think that's a wonderful woman.
Well, that is a wonderful woman (there are many things I like about her), but
that's a stupid woman too. If you think that's what a relationship should be,
then we have very different ideas about that.

"I tried every way I know to be everything I wanted to be for you, and
it hasn't been enough. I have a body and a brain many men would love to have
as their own, but you reject it time and time again, while lusting after or making
passes at God knows who (plus one of my dearest friends). I feel many conflicting emotions about it, but mostly, WHY? I've always been there for you, loving
you, loving your brain, loving your cock, caring and trying to help you and
myself be the best we can be together. Trying to hold the team together. But
I can't do it alone. I can't live with you, knowing things go on, like your
making a play for Laura after I've gone to work. I mean, what's the *reason*? I
have been trying to fulfill you for eighteen months and feel like I'm bruised
and battered from being for our team all alone and beating my head against a
brick wall.

"I can't live with the knowledge that you are thinking of and possibly
actually fucking others behind my back. That you would/could try and brain-
wash me into believing that that was just a one-time thing, then Hope comes
up, then Robin comes up—God knows who else was with you—is incredible
to me. That you could lie to me is incredible. But what's really incredible is
that you should *want* that. I have found myself craving sexual and emotional
attention from men a whole hell of a lot lately, but I know that I only feel it
because I don't have it from you. I want it so much from you—but you are
not there for me (really, or consistently), so I look for it in others, at least the
possibility of it anyway. But for you? Why you need others is something I find
hard to comprehend. The line about your French blood is the stupidest thing
I have ever heard, so I'm not even going to go into that.

"I have to survive this—I can't go down with you. It doesn't make you or
me feel any better to lie and cheat, but if you can't stop yourself from making
yourself feel bad, then I have to do what I can, namely—go. If I absent myself
from you, then perhaps you will feel better knowing you are not hurting me
or cheating on me—and so will I. I don't know.

"I love you desperately, but there is nothing I can do anymore except
drown with you, or take some action. I need to be loved, wanted, to know
someone really thinks I'm gorgeous sometimes, who gives me his undivided

attention sometimes. I've lost all that feeling with you, and I need it desperately. You must realize how you need it too, and then see how I do. You require so much sexual attention that having a woman (whom others would want) living with you and delighting so excessively in your boner isn't even enough for you! You require so much emotional attention that your friends have to make up for all the love and attention you seem to need from me and don't think you're getting! Christ! Then I am chastised for crying in the mornings and dreaming of evenings with you when you ravage me and we eat dinner and completely lose ourselves in each other? How can you reprimand me for wanting that? My God, are you a fool? That is THE BEST! Don't you remember?

"There is no law written that that has to end. And there's no reason why I should be told that I'm a pessimist and a fatalist if I say I don't think it will ever come again. Because I *do* believe it should but I don't believe you can right now. Or you won't.

"So let me go—love me enough to set me free from this thing and live while you work it out. I love you and want to feel that that is something you treasure again. Until then, I have to keep it inside because I can't give it to you anymore. Not until you really want it—in the right way—and are willing and able to grab it by the balls with me and do it."

Another young woman fell very much in love with a musician who is also a drug addict:

"A year and a half ago I fell in love with James. My blood fell to my toes when I first saw him—I swooned, I thought of nothing but him. All my energies were directed toward my love. Even my daily work I did for him. I thought of nothing else. I think love is a feeling you have right from the beginning for no known reason—and it isn't simply lust.

"It was grand for a time, but slowly it became miserable as he became the dominant one and introduced me to heavy drugs and ended up beating me after six months—a little sock at first, then a whole black-and-blue side. But when it was good it was wonderful. James and I lived together, cooked dinner, and took baths—played house. I paid all the rent and bills, including his $200 phone bills.

"Breaking up with him was the worst thing in the world. Although I still loved him, he was destroying me. He was/is addicted to heroin and refuses to admit it. He would spend money like water—and always ask me for more. It turns out he spent $3,000 of his parents' money in one month, plus about $400 of mine. I guess it's a typical junkie story, one is much like another. But when the person you love becomes a junkie—a common personality, that is—well, a musician by occupation—it's hard to accept. I mean, I'm twenty-five, went to all the best schools, both here and in London, etc. At first, heroin was supposed to be artistic—anyway things got dreadful and I finally had to keep him out. He got mad at me, thrashed around, said he was never coming back, and that time I took him up on it. Called a friend to come over and keep him out. The next day I changed the locks, packed up his things and put them in storage. It was just awful. He'd come bash on my door, send me love letters and hate letters.

"About a week later I let him stay with me because of the worst blizzard in twenty years, and then we saw each other on and off for five months—and finally quit. He still hit me and shouted at me, I finally ran away one day, I was at his new apartment. We haven't really seen each other since. I passed him once on the street. It's awful. It hurts and these new dates are not my James. But he was bad to me. I still cry. I only hated him for about a day.

"When he hit me, I would sometimes yell back. The last time I yelled, it got the attention of a neighbor who asked if I needed help. I said, 'Yes!' James said, 'I didn't hit her.' The neighbor called the police, who finally arrived after James had left. I suggested counseling but James refused. He definitely loved me, but he was impossible. He would not allow me to have my own life. I could never see my friends. He made them feel unwelcome. When they called on the phone, he'd play his trumpet so I couldn't hear them. He expected me promptly home from work every night. He got me drugged on heroin often, something we could do together—great.

"The biggest fight we had was after a going-away party for my friend Sue, one of the few friends of mine that James liked. We must have sniffed heroin, because though we were supposed to have stopped I think that week we did—anyway, this party was near my alma mater and included a lot of my old friends James didn't know, but we went with another mutual friend, Martha, so he wasn't alone. Well, I had fun at the party and he was uncomfortable and sullen and didn't even try to meet or talk to anyone, though I would introduce him and try to engage him in conversation. He just wanted to leave. Finally we did—he yelled at me and dragged me out the door.

"I was furious—he humiliated me in front of friends. Even though he'd treated me that way before often enough, I didn't want my friends to know. We got in the car and he yelled and yelled at me. I'd just say low bitter replies and since I wouldn't be forgiving he started hitting me. He even pulled over to the side of the road to bash me a little. By the time we got home there were bruises the pattern of the weave of my coat all over my left arm and shoulder. I went to work the next day.

"James seemed serious, but then he really wasn't. Why would he tell other men that he slept around on the road, though assuring me he didn't? Why couldn't he admit fidelity to other men? He always won through violence. We never resolved any of our problems. He treated me as an inferior. But if asked, I think he would say he supports the women's movement—because he thinks he should be progressive. In fact, he's a good ole boy at heart and wants a stupid, pretty girl to simply adore him. Which I did—but I'm not stupid.

"To get over it, I talked with friends. Read a lot. Worked hard. I'm still getting over it. I lie around in bed reading the paper. I go to bookstores and buy lots of novels even when I'm broke. I cook soup. I stare into space and just think. I have no sex life right now but I'm enjoying it. There is no one I want to have sex with. After one and a half years with one man it's hard to think of exposing myself to a virtual stranger. I've changed a lot in my views toward casual sex—it's rarely casual. I am even a little scared at the prospect.

"It's easy to meet people, but not mate material. I'm good-looking, fun, have a Bachelor of Fine Arts degree, I'm bright—but . . . Luckily I've got a good bunch of friends, so I'm not alone. But it's hard to find a nice boyfriend. I don't really respect these men I'm dating. How can you respect men who are just dying to jump into bed and just want their *idea* of me, not me? These guys say from the start that they are afraid of marriage! In fact, they are more than happy to announce that they 'don't want any commitments.' I let these boys take me out and then I sit back and observe them.

"And even if a few boys I am dating now are nice, I don't want to spend my time getting to know them really. There was nothing 'chemical' from the start. I went out with them for dinner and to meet them, but don't really care to spend any more time with them. They generally want to spend all their time with me until I tell them I have no plans to sleep with them in the near future. Then they disappear, which is fine, but a bit disconcerting. I find myself not wanting to answer the phone. Still, the companionship is important and I get a free meal and movie here and there which I otherwise wouldn't. Even though these boys don't hit me or do heroin, they still don't measure up. I miss the good James so much.

"So I watch late-night movies by myself on TV, or read. My all-time favorite love story is *Orlando* by Virginia Woolf. And I like the stories of Colette. Movies? *Ninotchka* with Greta Garbo. And Claudette Colbert movies. I like the women to be as smart as the men.

"Where am I going from here? I don't know. I had a successful show of my artwork when I left school. But I never (yet) did anything with it, I have no real achievement that I consider great. I'm working as a free-lance fashion assistant on photo shootings now. I guess what I want is to express myself, feel like I'm living, learning things, help people have fun, mean something to others, make a mark, make a splash. Be old and wise. Be in love again."

Another woman, although what she feels is not such intense love, is staying in a very unsatisfying relationship, being the "other girlfriend"—and asking herself why:

"I'm attractive, thin, got blond hair, seemingly independent—God, that sounds vain. The guy I like plays in a rock band. Every time his band comes to the East Coast, I spend a lot of time, energy, and money going to as many of his tours as I can. I realize even saying this how embarrassing it is. Not only does he live in another state, millions of miles away, he is very much involved with another woman.

"We used to have a lot of good times together, but when I started to want more, wanted some of my needs met, he got more and more distant—not because he's a bad person, but because he is involved with somebody else and it started to bother him—so the more he kind of started to avoid me, the more I ran after him. Finally, the last chance I got to see him, I confronted him, even though it was unnecessary, and all along his behavior and things he was saying, like things were going really well with his girlfriend, should have been enough, but they weren't—so I confronted him and he told me that we could be friends, but right now things are going really well with her and that he doesn't want to sleep with me anymore. I felt so dumb and stupid standing there, not much I can do . . .

"I'm not angry at him, because he was honest with me all along, I still like him for that, but I'm really angry at myself, for setting myself up. You could say, well, maybe I have a fear of intimacy because I go after people that obviously can't give it to me, or I go after people who are unattainable basically, kind of like a love junkie who can go after people who are involved with somebody or who have a million problems and think that well, you can save them or change them or that everything will be wonderful, and it never happens, so it's more of a fantasy. Because I never saw him that often, the relationship was a lot more to me than it was to him. I was just a diversion when he was on the road and it was lonely and dull. I fed his ego because I would go around looking for him. For me the relationship was just basically in my head, when I wasn't even around him. That's pretty sad, it's really sad.

"I'm in therapy now trying to work some of these things out. I was an obsessive shopper also. I guess I was trying to fill up my life. Those possessions don't make you any happier, but I love clothes to the point that it's an obsession. I spend too much time on shopping, overspending, just too much. Probably again because you kind of feel your life's out of control, you'll go and spend money because that's the one control you do have, you know, your credit card.

"My current state is kind of like well, yeah, I want to be loved, but I don't know how to love. I don't even know if I'm capable of it at this point. I've just had so many bad relationships, I don't think they've had anything to do with love at all, more of an obsession or trying to fill a void, nothing to do with two people sharing and caring about each other.

"The relationship that I've been involved with for the past three years, the one with the rock star singer, is just so horrendous. It is basically sexual and the sex with him is really not that good, it's predictable. He is very dominant. He's really into being in control all the time and it shows in bed. Why do I continue to tolerate it when the sex isn't even that gratifying? . . . That's why I'm in therapy now, I'm trying to figure it out.

"It's really not difficult for me to meet men because I work in an airport and I'm constantly around men that are attractive and that I would respect, but I'm just oblivious to it, I'm just not looking. My sex life is basically nonexistent.

"I look around at the men I went to high school and college with, most of them are married, you know, thirty, and it's like time and they got married and all of a sudden I woke up and I was single. I thought yeah, maybe I did miss the boat. But it probably ties in to the fact that my parents had such an unhappy marriage, that I might have made some unconscious decision not to put myself through that, so here I am.

"When I was younger, I had all these ideals and expectations. When you get older, you realize you're never going to reach them, so there's some kind of a letdown between the fantasy and reality of it. But I'm working on something better for me now."

How much unhappiness do women put up with, and why? Why do women stay in difficult relationships?

Sometimes a woman can deeply love a person who is not stable, cannot form a lasting day-to-day working relationship, or does not want to—but the relationship can still be deeply moving and important. Love, after all, is not just a knee-jerk response to someone who is "nice" to you.

The epithet "masochist" is often used to label women who are in unhappy love relationships, or relationships that are not "working out," with the undertone that "She probably needs a therapist," or "Isn't it a shame that so many women get themselves into these things?"

As noted before, women (but not men) are apt to be judged most strongly by the society in terms of "love" and their private lives—i.e., whether or not a man loves them, and whether they are married and (hopefully) have children. All relationships are seen (hopefully, again) as lead-ups to that "happy state." Relationships are tryouts for marriage, and if they "don't work" or are unhappy, they are "failures"—and a woman is a "masochist" if she stays in one. If a woman, on some particularly lonely and unhappy day, should say to someone who is not very open-minded, "My life is in turmoil!" she is likely to be met with the spoken or unspoken comment: "Oh, gee, can't she get it together? What's the matter with her?!" There is great pressure on women to be "successful" in personal life, to fit into what society expects—i.e., to find a nice man and settle down and be stable.

Are unhappy relationships "proof" that women are "masochists"? Too "loyal" and "supportive" for their own good? "Obsessive"? Do women get "hooked" into relationships, unable to leave?

The idea that women are "masochistic" if they are with someone who treats them badly fails to take into account the probability that the other person did act lovingly in the beginning, and still does at times. Sometimes, such relationships start out with very intense attraction and involvement, so that when the person doesn't turn out to have basic living skills, doesn't know how to share, or is incapable of being close, it causes a great state of turmoil in the woman, who loves the "good part" of the man, and hopes the "bad part" will change.

She can't bring herself to leave as readily as she might if she hadn't had those initial deep and ecstatic feelings.

One woman analyzes what happens this way: "The essence of male chauvinism as it is mixed with sexual desire is that first the man makes you mad with desire for him, sexually and physically, emotionally, by stroking you verbally and physically, telling you you are beautiful, wonderful, interesting, etc. Then he has you—and you have him. Then he begins to mix his love with condescending remarks, downgrading your interests and abilities, calling irregularly, showing his disrespect—until you are left still feeling 'in love' with him, desiring him, but now having to take him, have sex with him, on the basis of accepting your lowered status, feeling humiliated. After a while, you can lose your sex drive for such a man, but for a while (and this can be a year or two), passion may continue simultaneously with the shame and humiliation at this treatment. How to handle this psychologically? S/M fantasies? How to handle the fact that one is in love with someone who doesn't quite respect/see one as full a human being as himself, his best male friends, the President, etc.???"

The influence of the traditional "male" ideology directing women's behavior is obviously at work here too: if a woman is supposed to give love to the man, doesn't he need it even more if he is "troubled" and "confused"? Her assigned "role" does not encourage her to be angry or leave, she "must" stay and try to understand. But usually the situation (and his treatment of her) gets worse.

There are many cases in which it is clearly imperative that the woman leave—situations that amount to a form of constant psychological or emotional violence. Usually there is no one incident which in itself would tell a woman she is in a "burning building"; but good indicators are a series of incidents, or a constant feeling of being emotionally in suspense, a painful up-and-down, that makes for a great deal of anxiety and unhappiness.

In these cases, it is very difficult for a woman to weigh her love against the actual situation. How important are "happiness," stability, and "normality" anyway? How far can one go, getting emotionally "strung out" with the psychological demands of another? Such relationships take their toll gradually, so that one can lose contact with how much it really is costing to continue—or how much one has really changed.

Most women do leave unhappy and exploitative relationships*

Most women's reactions to unhappy or non-working relationships here do not bear out at all the popular idea that women love to be tortured, love pain, love

*Also, most of the divorces in the United States are initiated by women. However, women are once again in a no-win situation: if they leave their husbands, they are put down for being frivolous, not taking marriage and their responsibilities seriously, being "selfish"; if they stay and try to keep making it work, they are called "masochistic"! (See Part III.)

being emotionally humiliated. They may stay and "try to work it out" longer than men might—and this can be praised as loyalty, or ridiculed as "masochism"—but eventually they do leave.

74 percent of women have left relationships that made them unhappy:

"In college, I went out with an alcoholic. At first, I tried to help him, but learned that some people are too far gone and need pros. Then I wanted to stop seeing him, but if I brought it up he'd go into a rage. He'd shove me around and hit me. I was terrified. It fits the classic battered-woman thing— he'd say, 'Why do *you* do these things?' It's very spooky how easily manipulated I was into feeling that *I* had done something wrong. I finally saw his therapist and she set me on track and I went into hiding until he finally gave up."

"I was most deeply in love with a very immature, incompetent young man that I lived with and supported before I met my husband. He was very selfish and cruel to me, and yet we had an emotional intimacy that I have never experienced with my husband. I was never truly happy, except sexually (he was a very creative lover and really seemed to love my body and caused me to have powerful orgasms). But afterwards I would feel depressed because I could see the hopelessness of our situation, plus I was ashamed in front of my family and friends that I was involved with such an irresponsible person. Eventually I broke off with him."

Usually there are parts of the man the woman truly loves, in addition to the parts that make the relationship difficult, causing the decision to leave or break up to be extremely difficult:

"The man I had the most dislike for was one that could not keep his word to me, anyone else, or to anything. Parts of his personality I liked very much but I couldn't live with his constantly breaking his word. Because of that, he wasn't enough for me. I had to let him go."

"The most painful and confusing breakup happened with a man I loved sexually and found a lack of common interest with intellectually. Our lovemaking was wonderful. To this day I'd love to sleep with him."

"After my latest lover totally acted like a jerk—stood me up several times, told me he slept with someone he didn't know while on a job interview in New York, and in general behaved like a bastard—I still thought he was the sexiest guy I knew. I think I'm the type who sees a burning building and is stupid enough to think the flames would stop once I walk in—so to speak."

Just as with divorce (see Chapter 12), more often it is women who do the breaking up in a bad relationship; * *however, they usually feel that, emotionally, they have little choice:*

"I usually do the breaking up because of something the guy did. I'm hurt, and it takes a while to get over it. But I refuse to go with any guy who appears to be using me in one way or another, or who takes me for granted, thinks he's got me, shows me no respect by standing me up or something similar."

"I have been the one to initiate the breakup many times. I have always felt a terrible sadness, some guilt, but also a great sense of relief when I've broken away from an unsatisfactory relationship. The slow dying of the feeling of love has been the hardest to bear."

"I broke up with my last lover of two years—last year—after he hit me (no one hits me). He was jealous—I didn't care, 'cause he hurt me, so I figured he was not worth it. I felt dumb for wasting all that time."

Many women agree that even after breaking up with someone, no matter how bad the relationship, if the love was strong some of it still survives:

"Sometimes, despite my desire to hate and despise my ex-boyfriend, I think I still love him. I can't get those feelings out of my heart."

It is hardest to give up a relationship with a man—even though he is making you miserable or at least not happy—if he keeps insisting he adores you:

"About the divorce—he played around, said he didn't want a divorce, just 'freedom.' After three and a half years I was very thin and friends took me to a divorce lawyer. I knew I'd had enough of suffering through his affairs, so I started the divorce. He signed it, all the time saying, 'No, I love you.' He still says this! He's married to another woman, but he says he doesn't like her and that I am his only wife! He no longer interests me, though he tries to buy me back with his job retirement money—it would be worthwhile—but NO. At the time I cried a lot, although I was relieved that I could start living again. I did and did not want to break up. I entered therapy to help me let go of the relationship. It did help, but not totally. I loved my husband, still do although he hurt me deeply, in spite of what happened and in spite of my desire not to."

---

*Just as more women, statistically, initiate divorces than do men, women are also more often the ones to initiate a breakup, but they usually feel it is a "cleanup job," after the man has made the relationship impossible.

According to most women, the best way to get over someone is to stop seeing him entirely:

"In some ways, I'll really never get over my first love and our breakup. What makes it hard is that he pops up whenever he has time off from the Navy. He gives no warning. If he wouldn't show up I'd be much better off."

Or think frequently of his bad points:

"Every time I would miss the sound of his voice, or the phone would ring, and suddenly my stomach would clutch and I'd hope, hope, hope it would be him—I'd stop and think, no, wait a minute—he's a goon. Remember the time he locked you in the bathroom because he said you were being impossible when you wouldn't come out soon enough? Or how he always used to stomp out when you complained he wasn't listening? You don't want to go through all that again, do you? NO!!! It works."

Or have a replacement:

"To force myself to stay away from him, I'd leave my apartment early in the morning and wouldn't come back until late at night. My roommates told me he called constantly and came and sat around the apartment for hours waiting for me. He never caught me until about six weeks later and by then I was dating another man, so I was able to say no."

Most single women in the midst of breakups feel great relief and pleasure along with the pain:

"I wanted it. I wanted *me* back. I got me back. It was great. It was also hard and lonely. I felt strong, I gave up a lot for my freedom."

But 14 percent of women felt only pain:

"I hated being rejected, I felt like dirt no one wanted. A man I was deeply in love with found another woman. I felt like a failure, that she, the other woman, was able to give him something I could not. I went through a period of intense jealousy. I just couldn't stop thinking about the two of them in bed together. Initially, the thing I missed the most was the sex, and our closeness. I missed sleeping with him. Then after a while, I missed being with him in the day-to-day events. There was a time when I hated him and loved him at the same time—the division between the two is a fine one. It took me a good year to get over him, to get to the point where I wasn't thinking obsessively about him, and her. Talking to close friends seemed to help the most, especially friends who had gone through similar experiences. I remember talking with a male friend until three a.m. at a local diner, and feeling sooo much better afterwards. That seemed to be the turning point."

Breaking up a relationship is much more difficult if there is no "closure," no agreed ending, no discussion; talking things out is usually the best way to get a feeling of an ending:

"It was evident after a year of not acknowledging what was really going on in the relationship that it had to be ended. I waited until it caused me so much pain that I couldn't hold back anything I needed to say. I said everything that I *ever* needed to tell him and let my grief disappear through that instead of holding on to it so it could internalize in me."

Is it worth having a less intense relationship, just to avoid the pain of volatile ups and downs?

Often women who go into therapy to try to figure out why their love lives aren't working decide to rid themselves of a desire for romantic love, to make themselves more "rational," stifle so-called unrealistic expectations, and concentrate on more stable and friendly day-to-day relationships.

One woman, after having had a rather disastrous experience of being "in love" and dependent on a man she was living with, now, in the midst of therapy, is developing a low-key relationship with a man she feels will be stable and with whom she can work it out:

"In the last three years, I have finally started to grow in a positive way (although it doesn't always feel this way). The first major change involved removing myself from a self-destructive relationship. The man I lived with wouldn't marry me, always accused me of not really liking his daughter (who lived with us, or should I say, I lived with them). I constantly cleaned up after her, took care of her, talked to her after school, fed her, etc. Once he even hit me because she said I had been mean to her while he was out. Part of the time I lived there, I wasn't working, so I was financially dependent, and this was demeaning too. I mean, I felt like a real Cinderella. But I was crazy about him, I always liked sex with him, he was very sexy. It took me ages to leave. Even after I had gotten a degree, I still wanted to be with him, and also by that time, I was pretty low, so it was hard to get up enough belief in myself to make the move.

"Perhaps my biggest achievement so far has been to enter analysis to try to change. I have self-destructive ideas that were imprinted on me as a child. I am working to change these ideas, but sometimes I feel discouraged and depressed, like I'll never be able to straighten out anything in my life.

"My relationship now is with a wonderful man. We say that we are special friends, we enjoy a wonderful sex life together. We have both had terrible hurts in the past and are afraid of getting hurt again. We have different ways of running away from each other or denying that there is much love involved. In me, there is a constant battle between my desire to love, my fear of intimacy, and my fear of rejection. I am closest to my lover and my analyst—and to myself. My lover is very understanding and my analyst is wonderful—intelligent, perceptive, and human.

"The most difficult part is my fears. He is emotionally supportive in a crunch, although I seem to want it more than I should. I have to learn to ask for explanations if I can see that I am interpreting things in a different way than intended. My habit is to take everything said about myself negatively, so I am trying to relearn how to hear things about myself. I am learning to see his behavior in this light too, to recognize fear of failure on his part. Both of us are afraid to make commitments again—to trust another person fully. The worst thing he does/did is to occasionally stand me up when we first met, but I was able to express my anger (for the first time with anyone) and I think he realizes that he is repeating patterns now due to his being afraid of love.

"What makes me the maddest about him are indications of stereotypical male attitudes about money and power that occasionally surface. I talk to him about this—trying to present alternative ways of thinking, in a positive, supportive way. I have to be careful not to 'kill the love' because that's one of the ways I have to avoid intimacy or to avoid being loved. Sometimes it is easier to destroy it yourself before the other person destroys it.

"I consider myself a feminist. I think the women's movement helped me feel like I am less alone with my problems. I am still raging at the double messages in society, at discrimination, at sexism, at churches that cripple people sexually, etc. Mostly, I rage now at people who treat me like dirt. I think it's all right to rage, but I also want to learn to love—myself and everyone else."

Practicality Versus the Soul: Must Every Relationship End with the "Perfectly Adjusted Heterosexual Couple"?

Is "happiness" always the goal in a love relationship? There is a case to be made for not having to have every love fit into some socially approved scheme of the perfect household and the Perfectly Adjusted Heterosexual Couple. All relationships are not tryouts for "marriage"!

Sometimes women decide to stay because no matter how great the pain, their love is real, and feeling it, expressing it, gives them more pleasure, more of a feeling of being themselves, alive, than being stable and "normal." As one woman says, "I would go out of my way for my boyfriend, and love makes it seem not out of the way. This is the first time that I have felt like this. My two previous boyfriends loved me more than I loved them. I felt guilty when they would talk about our future together with happiness in their eyes and I felt doubt."

Instead of being called "masochists," why aren't women admired for their loyalty?

Women in unhappy love relationships are often courageous in trying to see a bad relationship through, trying to help the one they love, remaining loyal even when the other person is difficult, but this behavior is almost never seen as heroic. Instead women are often put down or called "masochists" ("clinging," "too needy," or "despicable females who only want something") for staying. Would men be admired for the same behavior? Or are men, like Lord Byron, or Rod Stewart, perhaps, seen as great romantic heroes when love is unrequited or doesn't work out?

This is an example of how what women do is frequently seen as inferior to what men do: women are rarely characterized as gallant and brave for questing after love; woman as the love hero and seeker is almost never glorified. She is seen as a victim—or stupid, perhaps.

Women also, in some of these relationships, are making a positive statement, in that they are not *reacting* to what the man does, but expressing their *own* view of the potential and relevance of the relationship, their *own* feelings. *They* are defining the situation.

A love affair that is non-stable is not a failure, necessarily, if it gives us poetry and beauty: this may be what we want. It may not be that we are "picking the wrong men." But in these situations, we are usually made to feel bad by society. ("It didn't work out! She can't get her life in order!") Society has penalized women severely when they do not form permanent alliances with men.

Women in this study *do* make themselves leave men they love, even while still loving them—if they need to. But sometimes there is a real reason for staying—for a while. What if we pledge our souls, and then are "betrayed," hurt, or the person we love changes? This does not mean we should not have pledged our souls, should not have loved. Isn't it better at least to make what we feel real for the time it is real—even if it breaks up? It is good to have the capacity to believe in the reality of another's love.

Is following an impractical "great love" a mistake?*

What is a good relationship? Is it getting along? Companionship? Feeling great passion? Closeness? Being there? Actually, a relationship can be very unstable, or even unhappy, and still provide a kind of nourishment for the soul, or somehow open up doors in one's mind that didn't exist before.

As one woman puts it, "He is the one I want to love. Some other relationships might be easier, or more talkative, but I don't *love* them. I love him for the unique person he is—I love a person, not a relationship. I'm not looking for a person to give me the best relationship there is, I'm looking for a person I feel connected to."

Being "obsessed" with love has at times been labeled "neurotic" behavior, as if only "rationality" is acceptable; and yet, even the Greeks accepted "divine madness" as a good. And, not even thinking in these extremes, it is undoubtedly true that people at times feel a connection beyond words.

But are women too prone to seek after the "great love," too easily led by their feelings, too likely to continue loving when it is not "rational"? And is this thirst for love somehow reflective of our thirst for approval and love, nurturance, from a society which hardly welcomed our birth as it did those of our brothers—a society which does not give much approval or encouragement to women, except in the secondary role of helping males?

Love as a Passion of the Soul

Or perhaps our quest for love is also a hidden form of love for ourselves—*we* are not supposed to love ourselves, so we hunger to find a *man* who can, to certify that love—to get the love we feel we cannot give ourselves. In a way, perhaps our quest for love is a sublimation of the spiritual ecstasy of the self, being one with that self. Is this why we may find it so hard to leave a man with whom we are "in love," even if the relationship becomes more negative?

Is love our emancipator or our oppressor? Love is, after all, the prescribed lifestyle for women, *the* lifestyle for women. "Love" can be very oppressive and manipulative and drain women incredibly—although it should not be like this—which has led many feminists to say that as women we should "throw off our chains," and "stop having sex with our oppressors," give up romance with men. But *feeling* love is not the culprit, *we* are not "weak," "masochistic," and "silly"—rather, it is the cultural context, the genderizing of society, that makes love "wrong," makes it such a problem. And women get the worst end of it, because women's love for men is/has been tied in with issues of financial

*See also Chapter 14.

need and social status. But to *feel* such deep love is a great gift, refreshing to the spirit.

A *series* of difficult relationships is not good. But, given the cultural problems, is it not possible that most women may have to go through many difficult relationships in order to find someone they can love and who also sees them as an equal, makes them happy—to "find one of the 'good ones' out there"?

Bad relationships can eventually be "toxic"; as one woman puts it, "Too much giving and you'll lose your soul." But, of course, living in a relationship where there is no deep love, just comfortableness (with love perhaps pretended, even to oneself), can also be damaging. The key is not staying too long— allowing yourself to discover what it is in yourself, in the relationship, in the other person, that unlocks something for you—and then, if the relationship is destructive for you, to leave.

Is There a "True Masochism"? Unanswered Questions About Passion

One woman describes her feeling more sexual when she finds a man who dominates her emotionally—or who she wants to dominate her:

"Usually I feel I can call the shots too easily. Maybe G. is superior to me, he controls the relationship emotionally—and that's what appeals to me? I don't want to call the shots with him. I want him to understand me but I don't want to dominate him. At the same time I feel like in some deep way he will take care of me. This is probably very unliberated and very bad—I know I should be more 'liberated' but I like him to take care of me, even to dominate me. Maybe it's just a question of respect, I respect him as being at least as intelligent as I am, and more successful, etc. And I am more sexually aroused with him. I really want him."

Is this an example of a woman surrendering power in a relationship—or a woman offering love and vulnerability, and the man playing by the rules of competition and "winning," being arrogant in return?

Yet the questions remain: why, for some women and men, does being insulted and humiliated only lead to a more intense desire for sex? Why doesn't it automatically kill love or desire? This is true of some men too—that the worse a woman treats a man, the more "hot" he will be for her. Is it "masochistic" to want sex with someone like this? "Craving someone who doesn't treat you right" is a subject not often talked about. Even one's friends tend to put one down for confessing such feelings.

Other women describe it this way:

"I have a real fascination, attraction, for the kind of person you shouldn't go out with. Like that song 'Uptown Girl'—it's stupid, but something like a 'bad boy' is very appealing, a tough guy, mean and direct, Elvis Presley, James Dean—you know. Nothing I've ever hurt myself over—but why is there this feeling???"

"My loves so far have ended unhappily. I seem to pick ones that are bad for me. Dangerous boys."

"I accepted a lot of things, such as his seeing other girls, just accepting a fairly low priority in his life, in order to keep him, to be a good, 'hip,' non-possessive girlfriend. There were a lot of painful things, like my giving him rides and him leaving me in the car while he did errands or had long chats. I was desperate for his love, very hot for him. This went on for months. Finally we were undressing to make love one evening and he got a phone call from a girl he'd already told me he wanted, and he went off to meet her. That was the end."

It is definitely possible to feel sexually attracted to someone whom one does not respect:

"The most passionate I've ever been was with a man I was in love with, but sometimes didn't respect a lot. He's long gone, but I still have the hots for him."

Another woman says fights (and all they imply) seem to make sex more exciting:

"There seems to be a strange correlation: when a man *talks* to a woman as his confidante, tells her his secrets, he's not really in love, or at least there's no hot sex. Also, when I get along too well with a man, when I can predict his every move, the passionate, 'in love' feeling goes away. I may still love him, but sex isn't as exciting. Am I perverse?"

"Masochistic love" has been the theme of countless "torch songs," especially earlier in the century, such as the one made famous by Helen Morgan with the refrain: "Oh, my man, I love him so— He'll never know— All my life is just despair, but I don't care . . . He may treat me mean, but when he takes me in his arms, everything is fine . . ."

The theme of the intertwining of sexual feelings and fear is explored by

Marcia Westkott in an essay, "The Sexualization of Fear."* According to Westkott, who also cites Karen Horney, fear becomes eroticized (as in the horror-film genre) for women during the years when girls are learning their secondary social status and relative powerlessness but also constantly having their sexuality pointed out to them. Horney, the famous rival of Freud earlier in the century, produced important works on the development of female psychology, in which this connection is brought out.

Another classic study is described by a woman who talks about a bad relationship in her past: "In a crazy way, the hatefulness made me more dependent on him. Researchers have done studies on baby monkeys who are given surrogate mothers that have sharp, metal spikes inside of them, and the researchers can push a button and make the spikes come out, and that throws the monkeys into an awful panic—but when the spikes are withdrawn, they cling more desperately to the mothers that just stuck them, because that is their only source of protection.† I was like one of those poor baby monkeys. Anyway, it was a terrible experience and I did not transform him with my love (my intention). It was one of those situations that I call a 'learning experience' because, of course, I did learn a lot—a lot!—it's just too bad that it took such a long, long time."‡

Sexual passion: a desire for "submission"?

Is there at times, in a passionate moment of love making, a feeling of wanting to submit to the other person, to be their "slave," to be owned, kept? Is this a legitimate feeling or a psychological malady? Is it part of passion or of brainwashing—falling abjectly subject to the "female" role? Can sexual desire sometimes feel like a desire to be subjugated, a desire for submission? Today, these feelings are almost always painted in the colors of pornography. Yet, some of the same feelings are found in the behavior of both men and women in the past.

When Romeo bends his knee and kisses Juliet's hand or the hem of her skirt, he is showing his love and also his submission, respect, his "fealty."§ Women in the Middle Ages‖ have been quoted as referring to their husbands as "my liege," meaning "my lord," a term having the same overtones as Romeo's gesture. If the mystique of faithfulness for either sex could be combined with real respect—not *forced* submission, but submitting oneself at that moment as

---

*Marcia Westkott, *The Feminist Legacy of Karen Horney* (New Haven: Yale University Press, 1986).
†Harry F. Harlow and Clara Mears, *The Human Model: Primate Perspectives* (New York: Halsted Press, 1979).
‡See pages 363–72.
§This gesture was also choreographed by Leonid Labrovsky into the famous 1940 Prokofiev ballet of *Romeo and Juliet* with Galina Ulanova and Konstantin Sergueyev.
‖A minority of upper-class women, to be sure.

a sign of great love, *choosing* to make the gesture—this would be very appealing. However, when women were (are?) legally, economically, and psychologically forced to submit themselves to their husbands, there is no romance involved, only paternalism or abuse.

As one woman says, "I must be brainwashed, but sometimes during sex, and only now that I am so in love with my love, I feel like saying to him, 'I want you to be mean to me, I want you to dominate me. I like it when you dominate me. I want to be owned by you, to be pregnant by you—my body imprisoned by what grows inside me, what you put there. I want to be submissive . . . even I want you to 'teach me who's boss.' Why do I feel all this? It's very deep, the feeling. I want him to fuck me as hard as he can. I would never admit this to any of my friends—I barely dare to hint at some of these ideas to him. I try not to worry too much about why I have them."

Are acts of domination and submission, even sadomasochism, satisfying emotionally in some cases? Does having these extreme feelings—a woman or man wanting to "hurt" or be hurt by a lover—mean that he or she is psychologically unbalanced?

Perhaps a desire for extreme states of being "in love" or feeling passion is related to a personal quest for states of spiritual ecstasy or enlightenment, a desire for intense feeling which is not allowed any other outlet, not even a religious one, in the present society. Being "in love" can serve as one form of enlightenment, self-knowledge, seeing things more clearly. Love is nourishment for the soul, the validation of the reality of the soul, the identity beyond "personality" and "social functioning"—and can keep one in touch with a non-verbal truth, an inner knowledge.

Are these thoughts incompatible with "feminism"? Not in any idealistic sense, as feminism is a developing philosophy. As B. Hooks remarks in *The Women's Review of Books*, "Feminism has the power to transform in a meaningful way all our lives. It is a philosophy, a new world view—not a lifestyle nor a ready-made identity or role one can step into."

But the subject of sexual desire and "submission" is too important to be dealt with as quickly as we are doing here, and should be the subject of more thorough investigation and analysis. In any case, these physical-emotional feelings are shared equally by women and men; they are not what is referred to by the cliché "women are masochists." We have seen clearly that, far from being masochists (i.e., people who love pain), women are admirable in that they are trying to love in an almost impossible situation—that is, to create an enclave of equality and respect with those whom the society declares to be superior, to have more rights. Perhaps women will give up trying and turn to other parts of life for satisfaction—but the society should start to appreciate women for their positive outlook, and stop scapegoating them. The villain or "idiot" is not women, but a society based on a hierarchical gender system, making men "superior" to women.

Single Women Debate Whether to Marry

Pressures on Women to Marry—Still

*"Sometimes I think even if I were a new Mozart,
it still wouldn't be enough. All my friends and family
would still be saying, 'And when are you getting married? Are you seeing anybody?'"*

Why does all of society seem to be implying that women who are independent,
never marrying, cannot still have complete lives—be accepted into the mainstream of society? Most women here who are single after age thirty say they
often feel they are not being seen as "who they are," but are constantly asked
"if they are getting married," or if there is "anybody."

Do women have the freedom *not* to marry?

Hovering over the whole subject of being "single" is the assumption that the
state of being single is a transient one: surely all women will marry eventually—
wouldn't they *want* to??? Isn't it just younger women who are "single"? Or
older women who are divorced or "undesirable"?! The younger women, it is
thought, will marry eventually if they are "lucky"; marriage is less likely for
the older, never-married, or divorced women, "of course." In sum, being
married is presented as the norm, *necessary,* and being single as a temporary way

of life—*and,* especially for women over age twenty-five, undesirable. ("What's the matter with her if she's not married?")

Many men, including well-known men, are "single" all their lives, and serve as heads of corporations, as statesmen, are sought after as famous artists, and so on. Rarely is their marital status an issue. In the case of some "world leaders," one is never quite sure (without doing research) whether they are married or not. For example, one never saw Leonid Brezhnev on television with his wife; she was only seen at his funeral. Was Charles de Gaulle married? Talleyrand? Beethoven? These are questions one doesn't even think of often— men are men, first and foremost. They are of substance in and of themselves, above and beyond marital status.

It is much more difficult for women to be perceived in the same way. For example, the news media frequently referred to Golda Meir as a grandmother, and the marital status of almost every other famous woman is a matter of frequent media comment.

While it is easy to think of famous men in the twentieth century who never married, it is almost impossible to think of famous women who never did. Simone de Beauvoir was not officially married, but "everyone" knew of her alliance with Sartre, thus a "marriage" of sorts. Garbo in fact never married. Katharine Hepburn was married only briefly, then remained "single" for forty years, but did have a close alliance with Spencer Tracy. In earlier centuries, however, there were famous women such as Elizabeth I of England, Jane Austen, Emily Brontë, Emily Dickinson, and Florence Nightingale—not to mention Joan of Arc, who remained single.

One's "chances" of getting married . . .

Patriarchal society challenges women to "prove" themselves by getting married. Even in the late 1980s the news media blew out of all proportion the results of a small study which calculated women's "chances" for marriage. (It did not calculate men's "chances.") Headlines such as "A woman who is not married by the time she is 25 only has a 5% chance of ever getting married!" were blared out, and the story raised a public furor, reaching the cover of *Newsweek* magazine—and making many women angry.*

The way this story was handled by most of the media revealed an incredibly

---

*A similar occurence in the media was the appearance from 1986 to 1987 of stories of "career women" who "gave it all up"—thus "proving" (with handfuls of women) that "real women" prefer the home. The same point was "proven" over and over in films of the thirties, forties, and fifties which showed successful career women offering to "give it all up" for men. Examples include Katharine Hepburn in *Woman of the Year,* Bette Davis in *June Bride,* and Ingrid Bergman in *Spellbound.* This "new woman" has become a stock character in plays, television, and movies—and yet, the trend of women "leaving the home" for work, rather than leaving work for home, continues, stronger than ever.

strong cultural bias: the "male" culture/media seemed to see nothing wrong with running a story on women's "chances"—but was not at all concerned about *men's* "chances."* The story fit in with the cultural bias that women must be married, must be concerned with whether they have a "chance." There was no discussion of how many "chances" a man has by the time he is such and such an age because it is assumed that men do the choosing and deciding, that they are always "a catch," and that all women "want a man." Women are, as one woman says, seen as "fish in a fishbowl, the prettiest waiting to be taken home."

And yet, though we may have lurking fears about these issues, the fact is that the majority of women now really do think differently about their lives— even if the press would rather pander to a spot the culture has made touchy for women than speak to who we as women have become.

As one woman says, "All of this focus society forces us to have about who is married and who isn't is crazy and makes us feel defensive needlessly. We are who we are. Why isn't that enough?"

Most women are not married for large parts of their lives: being single is "normal"

But now, in fact, the majority of women over fifteen in the United States are *single*: 20 percent have never married; 33 percent are divorced or widowed.† If the majority, 53 percent, of women (and men) are single, why is this presented, then, as "abnormal"?

Additionally, most women are married for less than half their adult lives. Including the years before marriage and years being divorced or widowed (now that the divorce rate has reached 50 percent, even given the high remarriage rate), the total number of years women on average spend married in their lives is less than half the total number of years they may expect to live as an adult.‡ For example, if a woman lives to be seventy, and is married twice for ten years each time, she will be married a total of twenty years—leaving a total of thirty-two adult years of being "single."§

*However, as columnist Ellen Goodman reported in the International *Herald Tribune*, September 29, 1986, on what she wittily calles The Study, "The Harvard-Yale people got into this whole catastrophe as an experiment, and for the first time used something called a parametric model . . . regarded as risky for such projections. The Census Bureau people used the standard model" and found much more moderate results.

†White, Yankelovich, Skelly Consulting Group Statistics in conjunction with a study done for *Women's Day* magazine, 1985.

‡Based on the average expected lifespan of women born between 1950–1970.

§The increase in the number of years people (especially women, who live longer) may spend being "single" is often seen as alarming, a threat to the family. However, family patterns are historically not as solid as our sentimental hindsight makes them seem. In fact, historians are now uncovering large

But despite the large number of years most women are single, "being married" seems to remain the ideological norm: we are told over and over that being single is a transitory state—in fact an undesirable state, especially for a woman over thirty, who is (still!) assumed to be "just waiting to get married."

A note on language (and Greta Garbo's reply)

Greta Garbo, in the film *Queen Christina,* made in the 1930s, when asked why she wouldn't marry the man the court had picked out for her (whom she didn't love)—and taunted with "You don't want to be an old maid, do you? A spinster? What do you plan to do?"—answered, "Be a bachelor!"

Why have the words used to describe older unmarried men and women been different—"bachelor" and "spinster"? (Is she sitting at home and spinning yarn?) A "bachelor," presumably, is out on the town enjoying himself when not working; a "spinster" is sitting at home "rejected."

Similarly, why are there two forms of address for women, depending on whether they are married or not, and only one for men? Although "Ms." is, thankfully, used by many people, many others still use Mrs. and Miss to distinguish women's "marital status," while men are simply Mr., no matter what their marital status. Why this discrepancy? Because men's marital status is/has been deemed to be less crucial to their identity than women's. Women's status has depended on being attached to a man.

What should we "name" women who are not married? Women "on their own"? "Single" seems to imply "one" or "solitary," with a slight discriminatory implication of aloneness: "one" should be "two." Perhaps "bachelor" is a better term because it, more than "single," implies that it is a state one has chosen, it is a "thing"—not "nothingness," a state one may be waiting to be "rescued" from. On the other hand, "bachelor" can sound lascivious.

So what should we call women who never marry—although they may have lovers—or women who are married less than one-fourth of their adult lives? Should we call some "single" and others "divorced"? Or are they all "bachelors"?

Life as women have come to know it now is larger than marital status, or being labeled by these old terms, with their various connotations. In fact, there is no adequate vocabulary to describe single women's lives now, and it is time we renamed all these stages and expressions of our lives.

amounts of demographic data which are changing our picture of the "standard" family in Western history. See Bibliography.

Mixed Feelings About Marriage

The great majority of single, never-married women have ambiguous feelings, are not quite sure how they feel about marriage—as one woman describes:

"It's lousy being single. A single woman has no status. She is prey to every creep who comes along. She has no way of knowing if a man is 'just shopping,' until she has begun to like him, and then finds out it was 'just sex' or another conquest for him—or that he has a terminal fear of commitments and forgot to mention it. Did parents watch out for men who would take advantage of their daughters in the past? Anyway, now there are no social sanctions or social judgments that the man has to face when he acts loving and pushes for sex and then walks out.

"On the other hand, being single and free and happy with one's friends may be better than being put down every day by your husband . . . I don't know.

"The idea of a family and love and holidays together sounds just great and I've been waiting so long, I would like to try it. But what if I don't like marriage? Will I be able to get rid of him? Or will he hurt me? I knew two men in the past I would have married but they weren't ready for marriage. I never wanted to marry someone if I didn't really love them, if I wasn't in love—other men who wanted to marry me, I just didn't want to be that intimate with—so here I am. Maybe I just think now I should get married because 'everyone else is doing it.'

"But the word 'married' to me sounds synonymous with being adored, being accepted. I guess I would love to be able to say, 'I'm married.' "

Many others similarly have mixed feelings:

"I enjoyed being single up to about age twenty-five. There were good times and freedom, but loneliness too—feeling left out when friends married, wishing I had someone to be with and talk to before drifting off to sleep."

"I still think that what I want most out of life is a "happy ever after"—but I can now accept the notion that it might never happen. I did expect that men would support me, in the past. I would move in with them, but then I hated the way they lived, their messy lives—and I still worked anyway. Where's the support and where's the protection? The idea that I will have to plan a retirement fund for myself in my old age is startling: who ever thought I would have to do *that?*"

"I guess I love Harold. But do I love him enough to want to have a child with him? I don't know. But if I don't have one now, if we don't get married this year, I really wonder if it will be too late. He's not bad; why don't I just go ahead and do it??? But the idea of having a child with him sounds like an effort. With Jerry, who I was crazy about, I loved the idea and I thought I would be happy every minute the baby was inside me, and it would be a joy to push it out. There it would be in the world, shiny and new. But I don't have that enthusiasm with Harold, even though it's a really good relationship for me and for where I am in my life now. But I have to decide whether I'm going to have children or not, and I have to decide now. I just can't."

"Over the last two years I've gone for long stretches without sexual relationships, and the ones I've tried have been less than satisfactory. I guess I haven't met anyone yet that I could be really close to. I think I am attracted to inappropriate men. I seem to choose strong men and then spend lots of time trying to bring them down to size. I'm not even sure I could stand to be married, but I've been happiest in a close relationship with someone. What do I need from a man? I'm not sure. There is a sheltering effect with a man, yet this is often not a reality but a perception that is comforting. I have many good women friends, ten- and fifteen-year friendships, but even though I love them deeply, the feeling or bonding isn't the same."

"I don't know if it is my brainwashing, but I was always raised that 'normal' women get married. But I know marriage is terrible for most women and seems to make them either weak and submissive or bossy. On the other hand, I am really tired of being a guy's 'girlfriend' (i.e., read 'doormat'), with everyone I'm introduced to looking at me with a slight leer, meaning: 'We know you both go to bed together and it isn't quite right but . . . etc.' And I never know if he, no matter how much he swears his eternal love, will be here tomorrow. Still, wouldn't I look funny just announcing to every date or guy I get to know that I am looking for marriage, not 'relationships'? They would all run like hell, I imagine."

Why not just "live together"? Living together, being an unmarried couple, has advantages and disadvantages; it is easier to leave a non-formalized relationship than a marriage, but there is frequently a feeling in the air of "What's going to happen?"—plus the idea that, since life is temporary, maybe this isn't real. As one woman says, "Maybe we're both not really *being* here—it's just a temporary stopping place. I'm disposable."

This lifestyle is not gaining rapidly in popularity, statistically, as a long-term arrangement. According to the 1985 U.S. population survey, only 2 percent of the population are living together as unmarried couples. In this study 6 percent of women have been living with a lover for more than one year.

41 percent are not sure if they really want marriage, or if there are just great pressures on them to get married:

"I am a little nervous about getting older and not ever having a child or settling down. I don't want to spend all my life alone. They say the greatest happiness there is is still being married to the right person. As my mother keeps telling me, 'Everything else is so much sawdust when the lights are out.' "

"Intellectually, I realize that people can be single all their lives. I have some role models (women) who were single, and so I feel that I would have some support for a decision that I might remain single. However, emotionally, I seem conditioned toward marriage. Some part of me does not want to be single forever."

"Love?? I'm in a state of confusion now. I've been involved with different men often enough to realize that I could never have been happy being married to any of them. But I feel the need to have a permanent man. Do I really need it or is it just something we women have been reared to believe—that we need to have a man to make our lives complete? My career is challenging, but it's important to me to do something where I can have a real impact on people. I'm twenty-four, I've got a degree and am making a good living, but not feeling satisfied. I'm independent and living alone in a neat apartment but I still feel a deep need to explore, change, and become 'adult'—which I guess I define as being at peace, or satisfied with yourself."

Women Who Don't Want to Marry

26 percent of single, never-married women between the ages of twenty and thirty* say they are not interested in marriage:

"The idea of marriage scares me right now. I am sure in time the fear will subside and I will see a different side to it. I think it is important for some individuals, but not all. I do not think I am monogamous by nature!"

"We are compatible on all levels—we laugh, we cry, we share many things, the same activities, and we are politically alike—conservative. I can tell my lover anything, and usually do! I am extremely happy, and so is he. But as to the future—we are too young to be looking at a lifelong commitment."

"Marriage seems overrated—people reaching for a type of security that just doesn't exist anymore. It is based on assumptions that aren't realistic. As a contract, it's very unfair and inequitable. I hope I never get married."

"Do I like being single? Well, I rarely think about it, I just *am*. I have plans for my life, and if I happen to find someone along the way whom I want to share my life with and who wants to share his life with me, that's fine. Sometimes I wonder if I'd be happier just living with close friends. What I want most is a rewarding career. A family filled with love would be wonderful, but my prime concern is my career. I think women are too dependent on men. Also, I hate the games involved in seeing them. I also believe that, in the last analysis,

---

*Excluding gay women.

an individual is always alone. I don't think this should make us feel lonely, because we are capable of having extremely intimate relationships with others, but rather secure, since we can rely on ourselves when all else fails."

"In a relationship, a lot of one's energy is directed away from oneself, to one's partner. The most valuable aspect of being single is that I get to know myself and enjoy my own company. I don't want to end this, at least for now."

"I like being single and not married . . . free to do what I want—see other people, have 'affairs.' But I still like having one or two people I can always go to. I like having some security—although I don't feel like I have to get married to get it."

"I like being single because I'm selfish. I spend a lot of time on myself, and it amazes me how someone could split that time up between a partner, a husband, and children. I don't know if I could ever do it; maybe that's an immature attitude, but that's how I feel."

"After being in a relationship for seven years, now that I am free I enjoy being able to go out and do what I want rather than having to decide as a couple—being able to come and go. You only have to answer to yourself and worry and care for yourself. I get more rest and privacy and take better care of myself when single. The only thing I miss is sex."

"Sometimes I feel pressured by parents and some friends to be married, but I have no need now to be a couple. I have more of a need to be a mother, and would like to have a baby, even without a partner. But part of me says that a baby should be brought into the world with two parents, still another part says that it's better to have one caring, loving parent than none."

18 percent of never-married women * *between the ages of thirty and fifty say they are not interested in getting married:*

"I am forty-eight. I like being single. It is nicer to be yourself than less than a person with someone else. The men I have seen, and still see on occasion, all tend to treat women traditionally . . . as less than equals. I would rather be the fifth wheel with other couples and content alone than be part of a couple and discontent a lot of the time."

"I believe in loving as intensely as possible whenever it happens to you, whomever you find to love—for as long as it lasts. I do not believe in finding the 'one' and considering that that is the end of loving anyone else. This would deaden the original choice also."

"I am thirty-eight. I have not come this far along to give up now and get married, just for the sake of the thing. I am too proud of my life. I have put too much into it. As I've become older, I have a stronger sense of myself. I'm less and less willing to settle for an inadequate love relationship. I'm glad I have finally reached this stage. Like too many women (and maybe men too), I used

*Excluding gay women.

to settle for men that used me for their own sexual purposes just to gain a little affection. The rewards weren't worth the grief."

46 percent of women who are divorced (and 59 percent who are widowed) do not want to marry again—at least any time soon:

"I am alone by choice. I am trying to sort my feelings out, get to know what it is that I really want in life and in a partner before I get involved again. I'm going to school, enjoying time with my children, seeing movies, reading, and living the way I want to live. I don't have the time right now to devote the energy a relationship takes."

"I have been divorced for three years. I ended the marriage by walking out on my husband. I received very little emotional support and sexual satisfaction from him, and acted and felt like a real slave. My life and career centered around him, and he put himself above all else. At this point I have no regrets, and I don't think I'll get married again."

"I thought, after my husband died, that I would like to get married again, but now I find I enjoy being single and living by myself. I like the freedom— the chance to come and go as I please without being accountable to anyone. I enjoy going to parties by myself. It is difficult to find someone I like enough to prefer being with them—part of the problem is that there aren't as many men around who have as good an education as I have, and intellectual conversation is something I care for a great deal."

"I like raising my children without any interference. I do miss someone to give me a break from the kids, someone to talk to—but I talk to my kids, so that isn't a biggie. My friends don't envy me, because they know what being a single parent on a limited income is like."

"I am a thirty-four-year-old secretary. I am separated and have two children, ages nine and seven. This was my second marriage, which lasted ten years. From now on, I prefer to live my future without marriage, as I tend to allow myself to be dominated. I am not in control of my actions and true feelings because of demands and pressures exerted on me by another individual, my husband, and this is not good for me *or* my children.

"Now, my children, my freedom, and my peace of mind make me happiest. My biggest achievement to date has been to begin shaking the idea that I must succeed in keeping everyone happy at all times. I feel that women need to learn to be in charge of their own lives. Not necessarily through any particular movement or organization, but by themselves—although the women's movement has made me realize how much advantage has been taken of me over the past thirty-four years. I am a giving person—but I want to establish new rules for myself where I really enjoy doing for people instead of feeling obligated. It is extremely difficult to shake off the old rules and strike out in one's own direction. I am still trying, but I feel I will make it, and when I do—I hope those around me will benefit also from my attitude and personality."

Women Who Do Want to Marry: What Are Their Reasons?

Loving one person: emotional security

After experiencing various relationships, many women want a longer, more committed relationship with one person; they want to love without fear:

"I want to marry because I don't want to split my love up. I have been in love in the past, and later we fell out of love, and then I went through that whole cycle again, and I don't want to anymore. I want to marry a man I fall in love with, and give him my love and be faithful to him and only him. This would be very satisfying to me."

"It would make me very happy to give all my love to one person and share my life with him. But I don't want to give my heart and then have it given back to me later. If we are not married, this might happen, so I am not secure enough to give all my love if we are just in a relationship and not married. Not being able to give all my love lessens my happiness and keeps me from being fully satisfied. I want to love completely."

Many never-married women look to marriage with the hope that it will provide the closeness and intimacy that seem so elusive and fleeting in non-married relationships. (See Chapters 5 and 6.)

Wanting children

Some women, 31 percent, say they married because they wanted to have children; *the following women married within the last five years:*

"I was in my twenties, working, when I fell in love, deeply, with my present husband. I remember that first year, I was so sexually passionate with

---

*Statistically, surprisingly few women cite this as having been their major reason for marriage, whether during the current decade or whether married during the fifties, sixties, or seventies. Related reasons are often cited, such as "wanting to be a family," but this is often earmarked as "in a permanent couple," "belonging somewhere"—not "wanting to have children."

him, and in all other ways too, that I would often feel, especially when we were making love, 'Oh, I want to get pregnant with you, I want to feel "you" growing inside me.' We officially married then because I did want to have a child. We married and I had those children, and it has been wonderful. I don't know if I would have had that strong desire for children if I hadn't fallen in love as I did with Richard. It just seemed inevitable."

"I married my husband, who is ten years older than I am, because I wanted to settle down and start a family. This was six years ago. I thought I was supposed to want a career, that this should fulfill me, but at a certain point, I just started thinking about babies, having babies. I can't even explain it. I was thirty-two at the time."

"I used to have 'executive lust.' One morning, on my way to work, I just thought, 'What am I doing? Is this how I am going to spend my life?' I was 'on my way,' too—really moving up in my job. But I realized I didn't think of this as 'life' anymore. I became overpowered by 'baby lust.' I was astonished at my own transformation."

Very few currently single, never-married women give children as a reason for wanting to get married, unless it is in connection with their age, knowing that this is an issue they will have to decide soon. Instead, women are much more likely to cite hoped-for intimacy and closeness, and/or social pressures.

Not all women want to have children; recent figures* have shown that twice as many couples as ten years ago have decided not to have children:

"I have no desire to have children. Frankly, I can't understand why any woman would, in the usual situation where she is working and also has to do most of the child rearing herself."

"Kids would obliterate my very fragile sense of identity, which is always in a state of just-about-to-crumble."

On the other hand, wanting to have children is not always connected in women's minds with getting married: women can have children alone now, after all, and many women who are married when they have a child find that

---

*According to *Newsweek* magazine (September 1, 1986), the number of couples in the United States who have decided not to have children has increased substantially in the last five years. Also, women now can have children without being married, and so a desire for children would not necessarily impel a woman to get married. The number of single, never-married women with children is 2 percent of the United States female population; U.S. Census figures show that in 1985 there were 7.7 million female single heads of households with children between one and seventeen years of age. See Current Population Reports, series P20-411 and P20-410, March 1985, U.S. Bureau of the Census.

they wind up raising the child alone anyway. Aside from frequent financial difficulties, many women and children do not find that this is an unhappy way of life at all.

Social pressure: "Why aren't you married yet?"

> *"The pressure to get married or find a life partner is great now, mostly internal. I feel that if I don't become involved soon there is something wrong with me. But I don't want to make a big deal about it, or I'll feel like the 'typical' picture of a desperate female trying to drag some poor unsuspecting male up the aisle."*

There is still enormous social pressure that says, "a woman is nothing without a man." Many women who suffer deep emotional anguish in a marriage or relationship will still stay because of this social atmosphere. As one woman puts it, "I clung to one fellow through physical and mental humiliation because I didn't want to be without a boyfriend. I was too emotionally dependent, and he took advantage of this to have his cake and eat it too—to date around and sexually abuse me because he knew I would be crying for him to come back and be loving again. Finally he went too far—he walked out at the intermission of a play I was in. I have not spoken to him since."

In fact, the most frequently cited reason single, never-married women give for thinking about getting married (unless they are "in love" with a particular man) is social pressure. The pressures on women to marry are still very powerful. As one man was heard to put this prejudice, "There's no mystery to why women get married. They just marry the first man who asks them."

Only a minority of women (14 percent) accept without question the idea that a woman's identity and status is tied up in having a relationship with a man:

"If a woman can truly make contact with one man, then I believe that is a link to all the men in the world, a most valuable link to have. I get a feeling of being truly grounded and in harmony with God's plan, a completion."

"I felt relieved after getting married. I didn't have to work at being attractive anymore. I had accomplished a goal which my upbringing taught me was my number one concern—to get a husband. I was relieved that the wedding was over and that my husband and I could go back to our real life again."

"Most out of life, I want to belong to a man."

As 49 percent of women point out, a man loving a woman is more than one human loving another; unfortunately this love also conveys the stamp of approval of society, carries with it the certification that the woman is an acceptable member of society. Some of these women are grappling with the hold this idea has on their minds—but others accept it as reality, the way things are, the way of the world:

"About a year ago, I at last came to the understanding that there's a chunk of my self-esteem that's tied up with being appreciated by a man. When I realized this I got very mad that I wasn't able to escape that particular conditioning."

"The problem with being single as a woman is that society does not respect you—you are expected to be with a man, this gives you worth."

"If women seem to want to marry more than men do, this is not because of a nesting instinct—but because (painful as it may be to recognize) the 'out' group always wants the 'in' group more than vice versa."

One young woman in high school knows this syndrome all too well:

"A lot of the girls I go to school with constantly need to be involved with someone. They end one relationship and start another within a week or two. They feel insecure and unwanted if they do not have a boyfriend."

The society (parents, television, etc.) is still breeding inferiority complexes into women and girls:

"I worry too much about my clothes, how I look, my face. I always feel ugly (even though I'm not—just ordinary). In some ways femininity involves not liking yourself, never being O.K."

"I start looking at myself and wondering why I could even aspire to this person when I have all these myriad things wrong with me, and he could see so many others better than myself."

But women/girls also often believe that their fear of not "having a man," or not being "perfect" enough, is created by some particular quirk of their personality or some deep lack of love in their childhood—a __personal__ insecurity:

"I think I have an extra need for affection and attention. That might come from the lack of them from my father—but I also think I do tie down men. I'm starting to let that go."

"I seem to pick men who haven't reached their full human potential. I have this belief that I can help them. It always drains me, and then I get mad at myself. I guess that won't ever change—I'm forty-seven."

"I pick men who tell me how unworthy I am and then say they love me anyway. I can remember letting one man in particular tell me how unworthy I was of his love and my not knowing what to do about it. That pattern, that some guy tells me how unworthy I am but that he loves me anyway, was started by my father."

As seen earlier, the belief that men have the ability (right?) to decide our value can make women very uncomfortable:

"I feel insecure and doubtful when I am in love—actually I feel insecure a lot of the time I am with men, regardless of the situation."

Thirty and not married: the terror . . .

88 percent of women say there begins to be a great deal of social pressure on them to be married after ages twenty-nine or thirty; one of the ways women experience this is as prejudice (fear?) against them in social situations—although people are sometimes envious at the same time:

"I can't shake the feeling that to be unmarried is still to be considered a 'reject,' to look like a 'reject'—everybody is wondering what's the matter with you. ('You're such a pretty girl, why hasn't some nice young man grabbed you up?')"

"I definitely have the impression people think there is something wrong with me for not being in a relationship—almost as if they feel pity. The envy they feel is much harder to get in touch with and is camouflaged by keeping their distance."

"Everywhere I go it seems I go alone, or with my daughter. I'm seldom seen with a man, so in society's eyes I'm somewhat of a failure. Incomplete. I do think people think there's something wrong with me for not being in a relationship. Sometimes I think so myself."

"In our society, even today when so many people are choosing to remain single, being single is somewhat like being a special-class citizen. I find this is especially true for women. If one is a woman alone, and especially a woman alone with children, there is the attitude that there really should be a man around to look after us all. My friends are, with few exceptions, women who are also single. Far from envying me, women who are in relationships tend to regard me with suspicion, as if, by the fact that I have no partner, I must be interested in theirs!"

"I've often felt that part of the reason I'm not invited certain places is that I'm 'unescorted' and that this makes people in a 'couple' uncomfortable, like, 'What do we do with the fifth wheel?' Conversely, acquaintances who are locked into unhappy relationships think I'm really fortunate. One woman I know feels very envious of my not having to hassle about child-rearing policies with anyone and that I only have to arrange for a sitter (no easy task sometimes) to be able to go out. Being lonely within a relationship must be really awful. When I'm lonely it's usually because there's no one there to share my feelings and thoughts with at that instant—not because whoever is there won't listen or hear what I say."

Many women say that married women still have more status than single women; single women are still not valued or sought after by society after their early twenties, as are single men. In a way, they are kept out of "mainstream society":

"To be an unmarried female is still, to many people, to be abnormal, unwanted, a 'reject.' "

"It's difficult to meet people of any worth as a single woman. Single women in this society are not valued—we're not sought after, we're just superfluous."

Also, although there is lip service to the contrary, there is still enormous pressure on women to be married, rather than just "living with" or "sleeping with" a man:

"We got married because I wanted to go to bed with him, and to have self-respect, I had to be married. Even though we were only married three years ago, and these are the 1980s, I don't know why, I just felt like men don't respect you unless you're married. Or maybe I don't respect myself unless I'm married. Anyway, something inside of me felt this to be true. So after the wedding I felt relieved. We wouldn't be judged by anyone anymore about whether we should be having sex or not."

"I married to get everyone off my back. I was tired of people looking down their noses because I was living with someone. I felt committed to him, but it was nice to make a public gesture to that effect."

"The problem with being single as a woman is that society does not give you a place of your own—eventually you are seen as a 'tramp' if you are not married."

"I didn't get married until I was thirty-two, three years ago. I was a hairdresser for twelve years. I loved dating and having men attracted to me. But I always felt guilty making out, like dirty or cheap because I did. I felt I should be married."

Although since the 1960s, women in their twenties have been told that there will not be pressure on them later to be married, that they are free of such "old restrictions," in fact, the amount of pressure by the age of thirty-five has not lessened. So many women, although they are fighting violently against these ideas, still feel (and hate themselves for feeling) that they must get married before thirty-nine or they will never "get anybody" or "fit in" to society. The epithet "man-hater" for unmarried women is a new version of "loser" (and both terms are ludicrous).

"What if I never get married?"

Quite a few women who have never married and are in their thirties are beginning to think seriously about the possibility that they will never marry:

"Why am I single? Oh, basically because I always have this attitude, kind of like a Jackson Browne song, that I always figured I was going to meet somebody automatically, and never worked at it, never went around like some of my friends do now, never looked for places to meet men. I just never bothered and all of a sudden I woke up and realized most of my friends are married and then, gee, is there something wrong with me, am I going to be single forever? I'm starting to think I'm going to be, starting to cope with that. You wonder what's going to happen when you're older and that kind of stuff. It's a little scary, but I don't really think I'm ever going to get married. And that's dumb because that's like saying, well, can't you take care of yourself?

"I have never entered therapy although I considered it seriously last year. I was depressed a lot. I approached my family doctor for a good therapist and he told me to get busy and stop dwelling on myself for a while. So after a week, I didn't feel as desperate, so I didn't call him back. I stay at home when I can and—this is something I hide from everyone—read trashy romantic novels! Really like Harlequin. Boy, that is hard to admit. I'm not sure I can explain why I read them. They're a total escape, predictable pure fantasy and always happy. I'm ashamed, I should read the classics!"

One never-married woman describes having gone through this feeling of crisis—coming out happy on the other side:

"I'm an unmarried woman of thirty-two years of age, averagely attractive. I derive a great deal of satisfaction from my job, despite the fact that it is demanding, tiring, and consumes much of my 'free' time. My greatest achievement is having gained an Honors Degree.

"My biggest emotional upset in life so far took place when I had to come to terms with the fact that I had lost (through my actions) a man I loved deeply.

I also about that time began to feel I couldn't continue to drift along with life, that I (I thought) had to 'find someone' and settle down. It was a very bad time for me. I was severely depressed. Flinging myself into a long, unsuitable affair with one man, and then into other brief affairs, I desperately thrashed around looking for a husband.

"I was miserably unhappy. When I wasn't out looking for 'my man' I spent hours in my nightclothes, unwashed, hair unbrushed, lying on the floor in the dark listening to sad, romantic music. In retrospect I find it amusing that another aspect of this dark period—closely tied, of course, with my anxieties about remaining unmarried—was that I felt I was getting old. I could not accept aging at all and quite seriously thought I would kill myself if I wasn't married when I reached thirty! I am sure I would have understood myself and my situation and come through it more quickly if I had had proper friendships at that time with women who were aware and self-assured. As it was, then my women friends were either married or similar in outlook to myself. Furthermore, in those days I did not take friendship between women seriously at all, the 'capture' of a man commanded all my attention and emotion. Friendship was seriously neglected.

"Looking back, I now realize I had grown up never even questioning that one fell in love (perhaps several times, but sooner or later married 'the one') and set up home with 'your man.' When it seemed that this might not happen, I could not really cope for a while, until it gradually dawned on me that I actually questioned these assumptions—whether they are right for everyone, and for me in particular. Indeed, I woke up one morning (quite literally) and suddenly understood with clarity that all along I had been enjoying my life, but that I had allowed the assumptions and beliefs of others to act as a distorting filter on my mind. Thereafter, I was free to allow my essential self to develop, and to work with my own ideas about how my life should be."

What are women who *never* marry like?

What are women who have never married like? Do they sit around the house all day in rumpled bathrobes with their hair in curlers? Or are they "femmes fatales," "hot dishes" with a new lover every week? And when they are old?

To some extent, society can accept women who are divorced or widowed, even if they then remain single for most of their adult lives, but it seems much harder for society to accept as serious and "O.K." women who *never* marry. It is extremely important, at this time in history, that women claim this right— the right to be respected and accepted for who we are, rather than for our attachment to a man. As one woman says, "I am extremely proud of my singlehood."

Family pressures

Women still get pressure from their families to marry. The following are replies from women in their twenties:

"My mother used to phone him up and ask him when he was going to marry me! She would also phone me and tell me that the only thing to do in life was to marry a rich man. My father asks me now when I'm going to settle down. I tell him that I'm *too* settled; I want to live!"

"My mother keeps telling me, 'Why don't you go out and *meet* somebody?' It's gotten to the point I'm afraid to tell her if I stay home to read a book. She's making me nervous."

One woman sent the note her friend wrote her, in which she apologizes for having put pressure on her:

"When we talked on the telephone today, after we hung up I was worried it might have sounded like I was pressuring you to get married somehow. This week's *People* cover has a photo of Madonna and Sean Penn and it says, 'Can Madonna get Sean Penn to the altar?' How pervasive all this stupid pressure is! At least they put it up front on the cover verbally, not trying to even imply that he would be the one 'trying to get *her*' to the altar: 'women want marriage, men don't' is still the message they give every reader! A desirable man is one who avoids being 'caught,' or some such drivel. Forgive me if I have added to this horrendous pressure from all around! You are right, a relationship can be good, married or not married."

Reproductive time pressures

There is also great pressure on women to decide about having children (and therefore about being married?*) before it is biologically "too late":

"I am sick of being single. I am single because there has not been a man whom I want to marry that also wants to marry me. I do not like realizing that I am each year losing another year during which I am of childbearing age. I

---

*See pages 323–24.

want children and do not have them. That is the only part of aging that saddens me, that kind of time is running out. I sense a strong nurturer and care giver in me that wants expression in being a wife and mother. I am tired of growing up and getting a formal education, and I am ready to settle down. A job, a hearth, a baby, and a committed lover/friend/roommate/comrade (alias husband) are what I want."

"They tell me as long as I'm still having cramps with my period I'm probably still ovulating. I am happy without children, and not sure whether I could handle the responsibility of a child, but everyone seems to love theirs even though it's a hassle. They say they wouldn't miss it for the world. So I guess I should hurry up and decide. But the men in my life have been so non-helpful to me, I wonder how they would be, trying to cope with a baby. I feel like I still have to baby *them*—never mind me being babied. Who would baby us all??? But I hope it isn't too late."

"I sometimes feel that I have been cheated—that deciding to remain single was a mistake. All the couples I see seem happy, though I know there are a great many miserable married people. My career is exciting, but it takes all my time. I wonder if I'm too old to have children."

"I used to think I did not want to have children. Now I think this might be possible, as long as I work out my feelings beforehand. The problem is that, with children, I would feel I had to and should spend a lot of time with them in their early years, and would feel some resentment if I felt separated from my work because of them. Therefore, I would not have children until I was sure that I had it worked out better in my head. I wouldn't want to pass on the resentment I might feel to them."

Some gynecologists and obstetricians* now are reporting an influx of women in their middle to late thirties who concentrated on their careers earlier, and didn't have children, who are now wondering if they made a mistake. Several of the women in this section are feeling this way. This is nothing to belittle; having to decide about the rest of one's life—whether or not one will have children—before one's life is half over, is a difficult and important decision which women have to make, and men do not face.

However, speaking of "desperate women in their thirties" is another example of how the society tends to see whatever women do as overly emotional and "hysterical." If men had this choice forced on them by biology, their facing it and struggling to make a decision would doubtless be considered a noble dilemma, worthy of Shakespearean drama, serious plays and films—a testing

---

*These statements were made to me at a meeting of the American College of Obstetricians and Gynecologists, where I lectured in 1984. Dr. Beatrice Troyden, an M.D. with ACOG in Philadelphia, in particular shared some valuable insights on this subject.

ground for a man's worth and courage! But, in women's case, it is often
ridiculed and trivialized.

*Finally, in addition to biological pressures relating to whether to have children,
there are also fears relating to aging—of being "thirty" and "not married" and
supposedly "losing one's looks," etc.:*

"What is going to happen to me when I get older if I am not married? I'm
already thirty-one. I'm enjoying my life now, but will I be left out and all alone
when I'm older if I don't marry now?"

"I was so depressed last year about turning thirty-two (noticed wrinkles).
My friends and ex-lovers are all starting to look old. It shocks me. I don't look
that old, no one can tell how old I am at college. They're usually shocked when
they find out. I guess I am a little nervous about getting older and not ever
having a child or settling down. I think I'd like to couple up with someone in
a year or so—I don't want to spend all my life alone."

Struggling Against the Stereotypes

With all these pressures on women to marry, it is a wonder that we are still
so often able to think clearly and rationally about the topic.

*One woman describes a valiant struggle against the hold these ideas have on
her; she is determined not to give up her self-esteem, power, and identity to the
approval of a man, or to let her self-esteem rise or fall on the opinions of
another person:*

"Owned. My parents owned me as a child, the way most parents own their
children. I hate this feeling. Really, it is the problem of giving your power away
to another person rather than them taking it away from you. You become
accustomed to the state of being owned as a child and tend to repeat this
relationship with others as an adult. I wish to move away from this—the
childhood things should stay in the past.

"I don't think I have unhealthy cravings for love but have to learn to love
myself more. I fear that I might have an unhealthy tendency to get dependent
on others. People who in the past (like my family) told me that I expected too
much affection were pushing me away because they had an inability to give
affection . . . so I felt my needs were babyish and bad. Now that I am learning
more about myself and about people, I realize that I have a normal need for
affection. Everyone could probably use more love."

46 percent of women have faced a similar struggle; many are still engaged in a daily, interior battle over this issue:

"I used to accept any man, just to have one, and then be desperate to keep him, swallowing my needs in order to be the sort of woman he would stay with. But that was too painful. During those years, when I had to be someone else to try to please a man, it was painful to do and I felt angry and disgusted when the relationship ended and I realized what I was doing. I'd feel like I had to be exactly what he wanted, or he'd leave for someone better. Even worse, I was accepting a relationship without commitment, even though I wanted and needed a commitment, 'cause I didn't want to drive the guy away—I'd just believe his assertion that I had a problem if I needed commitment. Now with my husband, I am pretty much free to be myself—it's wonderful. At the loneliest moments of all this I felt no connection to anyone or anything or to myself—it was just awful."

"Until I spent a long period on my own between two boyfriends, I had a tendency to 'fall in love' with any male person who offered himself. This was a problem. It took a big chunk of singlehood to learn that I don't need a boyfriend to be a person."

"I have come to terms with myself so that if a man wants me in his life—what a great bonus! But if I remain single, I won't die. I can fly solo or with a partner. I have many possibilities to choose from."

"Is it fair to say that I would prefer a man's love? I've been sexually attracted to women (not as strongly as to men, but this could be psychological) but never thought about falling in love with one. I suppose I have a lot more liberating to do of my own sexuality before I could do this and still feel confident in myself as a competent sexual women. I don't think I could give up men permanently. It's not the sex that would be lacking with women—that would be great, I'm sure. It's the symbol of male presence, the heterosexual couple which is so deified in our tradition that life becomes difficult if you're not part of it."

"The loneliest I have ever been is during adolescence when I felt I had to have a man to make me happy. Thank God I outgrew that! Now I realize the key to happiness is loving myself."

Another woman describes the stages she went through in weaning herself away from these feelings—not from being able to love, but from feeling constantly the potential for rejection—and created a new self:

"The suicide gesture seems to have been a turning point. I did kill the old, desperately dependent self, who was right in thinking she couldn't stand to live any longer. I guess I scared myself into changing. I realized that I still loved the gay man, but accepted our friendship the way it was.

But I kept my distance from him and didn't get close again till my marriage was well established—I had to get away and not spend my life just wishing things could be different with us. I spent a lot of time quietly at home during this emotional 'recovery,' quilting, drinking hot chocolate, listening to the local jazz radio program, just learning how to be alone and feeling all the feelings of loss I had to go through.

"It was lonely, but I couldn't have got to here without passing through that time. By knowing what I wanted, I think it let me recognize my husband for who he was when I did meet him. Without a time alone I might have stumbled, in desperation, into another bad relationship."

And many women speak with great pride of their hard-won independence and strength:

"If I always had to beg a man and plead for some time together, for a hug, for an encouraging word (or any word), forget it. I'm less lonely when I'm alone with my books."

"If I feel I have to keep my lover turned on by looking beautiful and seductive, then I'm not interested in him. I prefer more emotional substance. If I enjoy dressing up, and I please my boyfriend in that way, it's one thing. But I would not want to dress up only to keep him in my life as a 'boyfriend.' I don't need that."

"If a lover wants to leave, fine. He has to like me for what I am, and if he doesn't, I'm not going to keep him. I've grown up in this respect. I'm not going to play games to keep a man from leaving. I know I can survive without him."

Is It Better to Marry the "Wrong" Man or to Stay "Single Forever"?

What if a woman doesn't find a man she loves whom she wants to marry and who wants to marry her (the "right man")? Should she "settle" and marry "just someone nice"?

"I keep thinking—if I don't marry this one, I may never marry anyone else. Maybe he's the best I can find."

"All these pressures . . . He's such a nice guy, but, I don't know, there's a lack of enthusiasm I feel, maybe he has a lack of enthusiasm about life, maybe I want too much, maybe I'm a romance junkie at heart, waiting for Prince Charming or something like that. But why do I have to marry someone I'm not crazy about? On the other hand, I may never find anyone else. Will I be sorry later?"

One married woman, looking back, comments:

"It would be much more fun being single if you could *know* what would happen eventually—you could relax and enjoy it! But you wonder, will I meet someone 'better for me' in the future, or should I settle down with *this* one, no matter how many problems we seem to have?"

Only a minority of women stress that they would remain bachelors "forever" rather than marry the "wrong man." However, if it came to that:

"If I can't find the right kind of man, I find that I prefer to stay alone than to settle for less."

"I tell my friends, now, that I would rather have a good relationship with a new man every five years than stay in a bad relationship just for the sake of what 'society' will think. I applaud people such as Liz Taylor who continue to try to find happiness rather than give up."

———————————

What if the person a woman loves does not want to marry, or to marry her? Should she stay "single forever" if necessary, if she doesn't find someone whom she truly admires and loves? Perhaps, theoretically, yes. But the world has made this almost impossible for women, although with more women working outside the home, this will become an increasing choice. Nevertheless, the social and interior psychological pressure is still there. Will it diminish?

Feeling Embarrassed to Admit You Want Marriage: the New Pressure to Be "Independent"

"It's hard to admit I really want a man, I really want a marriage. No matter what I know politically, no matter how impossible or stupid it seems . . . I still want it. But I feel a great deal of pressure not to be preoccupied with love or romantic feelings, not to get carried away by a love affair."

Many women feel very conflicted and ambivalent over whether they want to be "independent" or, really would prefer a man to "take care of them":

"While I was single, I had perhaps an illusory feeling that the stable thing in my life would always be myself, my own strength—I had a sense of regaining a powerful self that had been subjugated in my former relationship. Then with my second lover, I felt very strong in the beginning—then I began to doubt his love and commitment at a certain point, and also became afraid to leave. Why? I had really liked being on my own before. Will I always revert, given half the chance, to go on trying to find the center of the universe in someone else? Am I weak?"

"Sometimes I have this urge to have a man put his arms around me and say, 'It's O.K., babe, I'll protect you from it all!' (I think his name is Mr. Knight in Shining Armor.) Very unhealthy, unrealistic, and utterly humorous!"

"I would like the man to dominate me for a change. I wouldn't want him to be overbearing or think of himself as superior. But once in a while I like someone to tell me what to do. I guess this shows a weakness in myself."

Being ideologically "correct"

Do women always want "equality"? What we get from love, from feeling loving, impassioned, is very hard to put into words: it sometimes involves deep hungers, which another person, for some reason, may awaken in us. Or sometimes a person we are in love with makes us experience a part of ourselves which had been asleep, dormant. Love or a feeling of affinity is not always explicable; and some of the feelings may not always be so clearly "doing what is right for you" on the surface, or "feeling what one should."

On another, more practical level, are these statements incompatible with women's independence? Or can women and men depend on each other sometimes and at other times be independent and still have a relationship? As one woman puts it, "I think my partner and I are both fairly independent and both fairly dependent . . . as I think most stable relationships are. But how can a relationship be happy and stable if only *one* partner is depended on all the time? How can *one* person always bear the weight, never changing off and leaning on the other?"

There is no such thing, of course, as being "equal" all the time. Relationships go up and down, now one way, now the other. Men—when they can afford to let themselves, when they feel safe enough—also enjoy being dominated at times, taken care of.

It is not that "dependency" is "wrong" but that women have *had* to be dependent for centuries, have had little or no status, and have found that the quality of their lives suffered because of this—even that, at times, they were in danger. "Independence" became a value for women, a battle cry in the 1970s (and earlier), because as financial "dependents" women were finding that if their situation was bad, they could not leave it. (See Chapter 11.)

Do women still have the "right" to be financially "dependent"?

Some women resent the ideology that says the only way to have a "real" self is to work outside the home, that staying in the home means remaining "underdeveloped." Aren't home-oriented skills at least as rewarding as working in an office or on an assembly line? Why shouldn't women work at home?

Some never-married women in their twenties feel guilty about not really wanting to choose "independence," preferring the idea of being (economically dependent) homemakers and mothers:

"I'd like to be dependent, but I'm afraid. After all women have fought through to grant me my independence, I'd feel, like, guilty if I regressed to a traditional domestic lifestyle."

"I wouldn't feel like I amounted to much if I just got married and had kids and that's all."

One young woman (living with a man and their child, financially dependent) questions this guilt and the value of "independence": *

"I used to have this belief about women working, that it was important that women were able to define themselves through their jobs and do important work. Now I wonder how I could have possibly believed that, because I never had a job that was valuable, a job that reflected any of my ideas. Once I was a bartender, once I filled out claims for insurance companies. I had stupid jobs, women's jobs, and yet I had this very bourgeois, *Ms.* magazine type of mentality that said somehow that was supposed to be important. And that *is* important for a small number of women, but it's not important for me and for most women. We don't find fulfillment through our jobs.

"But anyway, what the home is and the function of the home and the influence of the home have changed. Separating the world into public spheres and private spheres, putting all the emphasis on the public and having the home be this little isolated unproductive box where nothing is done but just to rest in order to go back out into the work sphere, is ridiculous and very straight, very patriarchal. I like the home to be a place where there is life and there is activity and productivity and things are really happening, an important place.

"I feel like I have to struggle a lot of times with this conflicting attitude within myself, that what happens here within my house isn't as valid as what

---

*See pages 346–50 for the rest of her reply.

happens outside in the world or as what happens at his workplace. That's an attitude that not only I have but also my friends have."

"Women are fed up with having 'equal rights'—it means you have to do everything!"

17 percent of women say that it is a step backward, not forward, that men are no longer being expected to support women:

"I regret the necessity for women's liberation. I feel women should have careers if they like and be paid equally for their work and not be relegated to typing, nursing, teaching, and hairdressing. But if a man and woman make the decision to have her stay home with the house and babies, then it should not be so easy for him to change his mind and leave her with a $900 mortgage payment, no real way of making much more than $15,000 a year, a fifteen-year-old habit of living on $75,000 a year, and no real training or prospects at age forty-five to do much else but be a corporate wife. I am opposed to divorce for moral reasons, but I also oppose it for economic reasons. The women's movement is about our only defense against being left. I regret that my daughters will be pretty much forced to choose lucrative careers and prove themselves in those careers just to protect themselves financially."

And one woman sums up what many believe—that even if women are "dependent," they are certainly not "less"; in fact, they are contributing at least as much to society by maintaining the well-being of the family as they would be by simply going out and performing a "job" every day:

"What have we as women contributed to society? I'm not sure. But I'm not uncomfortable with the idea of 'only' contributing softness and warmth and not discovering the cure for the common cold. I feel women provide the glue which holds American family life together. That takes some doing, sometimes against bad odds—when they have 'impossible' husbands for one reason or another, little money, not much interest in homemaking. Yet they rise to the challenge consistently. I feel I've done a fair job of doing this, and I feel real pride."

Quite a few women, as we have just seen, defend their right to stay home and be homemakers, not having to be "career women" to prove their "independence" or validity. They are right: feminism wanted to make a world of choice for women, and if women, having all the options, choose to stay home and develop children and family, this is a valid choice for them.

But there is a counterargument, an insistent undercurrent of thought, which asks whether a large element of pressure from society, or internalized pressure, might still be operating here—i.e., the belief that a woman is not a "real woman" if she is not married with children. Do some women's protests that it is legitimate or economically necessary to be dependent on a man cover over the belief that women, still, can only have real status in society by "having a man"?

"Independence" and "dependence" are much more individual matters than earlier analyses might suggest. In fact, one of the underlying questions of the debate between "conservatives" and "radicals" over the nature of the family is: is women's independence important and necessary for women themselves, or is it just necessary because men do not respect and support women who are mothers as they should? One woman remarks, "We need a new education for men on masculinity and what it is—including fatherhood. I was brought up by my mother to be independent and forget about being married. But being pregnant really changed my ideas about that—and about what a man should be. I didn't know what a good man was, that he *should* take financial responsibility—and that I could find one."

But another woman reminds us of the down side in old-style gender relationships: "Several men I know who are either married or involved in stable relationships say they believe that men have a duty to women, that women need men and a real man is responsible and provides for a woman. It's not surprising to me that women need men, but the idea that it isn't mutual bothers me. Noblesse oblige leaves you vulnerable."

The major trend by far for women today is to prefer financial independence; most women do not like being financially dependent or told what to do;* many feel a great deal of anger over their years at home with no choices:

"I am a forty-six-year-old woman in the middle of a long (over two years), bitter divorce. I went back to college; my children are grown and don't need me and I am sick of being sweet and patient. Those attributes didn't get me anything. They prevented me from having my own identity and from having fun."

23 percent of single, never-married women in their twenties, now working, say that they would give up their work or career for a marriage and family:

"I have been on my own for ten years. My work used to be the main thing—at least I expected it to make me happy. It satisfies a lot of needs in me, but not the real need for love. Although I have had various jobs and have

*See Chapter 11.

completed several levels of education, I don't regard these things as real successes. I'd give up a career for a great relationship, although with regrets."

"I love my work. I'm one of the few assignment editors at an affiliated
station in my state and I've been promoted three times in a year. But I feel my
life really hasn't taken off yet. That there's so much more out there ahead of
me—at least I hope so. I hate to say that I'm unhappy right now, because I have
a nice family, good job, friends. I know how lucky I am. But what I want most
in life is a man who loves and needs me, a couple of kids, and a cute little
dog—your basic old-fashioned dream."

"If I had children, my priorities would be: (1) my marriage, (2) my children,
(3) my career. I know that I am capable of fighting my way up the ladder in
the rat race, but love is by far more important."

"People think I'm very career-oriented, but I'd drop it all in a minute if the
right man came along and the choice was there. I love my work, but I've been
working and going to school now full-time since I was sixteen and I'm tired—
not burnt out really, just tired. I'd like to meet a man and settle down."

"Everyone keeps asking me, 'Got a job yet?' God, that pisses me off! I don't
want a job! I want to get married and have babies. Period! And usually the ones
asking me are people like mothers of my friends, women forty-five to fifty.
They never worked. I should say, 'No, I don't have a job yet. Do you?' "

*32 percent of women mention economic insecurities and worries as a problem
with being single—a fear of being economically alone all their lives:*

"I have been single many years. Getting to know one's self is very important, standing on your own two feet. But deep down inside, a big question I
have is, what if I lost my job or got sick? Who would help with the financial
part? And could I really afford to have children on my own??"

"I just can't believe I'm going through life alone. I don't want to. But if the
alternative is to go to bed with married men, or men who disrespect you and
hurt you, then I'll be celibate, I guess. Also, there's an economic part. Can I
really take care of myself for the rest of my life, all alone, with no one to fall
back on?"

But most women, in fact, do not think of marriage as a complete economic
support: most women are working outside the home, and most women realize
that they will probably support themselves and any children (and maybe even
their husbands) for long periods of their lives.

*19 percent of women in their twenties say they will "never get married." It is
interesting to note that for at least the last three generations, some women in
their early twenties have been saying they would never marry, that the*

pressures to get married were for the "older generation"—but these pressures still seem to mount as a woman reaches thirty; each generation of women in their twenties registers surprise that such "outdated" pressures haven't disappeared yet:

"I would have thought there'd be less social pressure nowadays, but my sister is going through this right now—and she was never like that before (you know, 'desperate for a man,' etc.). It's not funny, I feel sorry for her. Also, it makes me wonder if I will feel that way soon."

U.S. statistics (and statistics for almost all other countries) show that most women do marry (or will have been married and divorced) by the age of twenty-seven. What happens to women who say they will "never" marry? Do they marry because they fall in love/want to have a family, and this is "natural"? Because of enormous social pressure which only descends on a woman when she is about thirty? Because of "biological clock" pressures? The same question can be asked of men, who also have claimed since the 1960s that they are against marriage and plan to remain single "forever"—and yet, statistically, the majority of men in the United States are also married by the time they are twenty-seven.

The media during the mid-80s "reported" on women's supposed "disillusionment" with work/career life. Women's doubts were mistakenly interpreted to mean, "See, women are really mothers at heart, not cut out for the world of men and competition, where you have to be tough!" In fact, women *have* found the work world lacking, but do not feel the solution is to "give it all up." (More women than ever are working outside the home every year, and most women say this is because they *want* to.) What is happening is not a return to the 1950s; most women believe there must be a third (at least) alternative to either joining the world as men have made it, or staying home and being in charge of the family. Women are trying to create this third alternative.

But most women in their twenties (56 percent) say they could never really choose between work and family/marriage and want both:

"I want to be a loving, caring mother, but feel I am not the superwoman who can cope with having these two lives together. It is going to be difficult to find a perfect partner who will share the household chores and looking after the children. This is my biggest dilemma. If I had to choose, I think I would choose children, but would have them as late as possible so I can have a fulfilled life before."

"I have no intention of having to 'choose.' Hypothetically, if someone was to put a gun to my head and say, 'Career or husband, choose,' I would naturally choose both career and husband, in that order."

Many women point out with annoyance that men don't have to choose, that most men still are not sharing the initial stay-at-home time with young children:

"If there were more men willing to do their fair share around the home in raising a family, or forgoing their own careers temporarily, there would not be so much pressure for women to choose one or the other. As it is, it seems if a woman wants a career (and not just a job to make ends meet) she has to do double duty, or she has to postpone her family."

"Being a single parent, sometimes I relish the idea of just staying home being a mom, because mostly I dislike my job. If I had something stimulating that I loved going to each day, I would probably feel differently. After being around children every day, I'd like to try five-year stretches of both full-time. Men don't have to choose, so what it boils down to is that if they don't have to choose or do double duty, neither should we."

"It's downright sexist. No one ever is concerned that men might be 'unable' to balance career and family. If men took more responsibility for their children, women would not be in such a vicious double bind. Like my father, men (a lot of them) still, incredibly, think that their responsibility to their children is fulfilled when they bring home a paycheck. I'm heartened by the increase in men who want to be fathers in the fullest sense of the word. Obviously, our system is only superficially committed to the full emancipation of women, because good, cheap day-care programs remain a luxury. It's a great way to keep women in the home, dependent and powerless."

What does it mean to be "independent"?

Does being "independent" mean being not married? Or thinking independently within marriage? Being able to earn a living? What it really means is having a *choice*—and many women who are in the process of having children and enjoying it (see Part III) are part of a new generation who have truly chosen this.

Originally, it should be pointed out, the women's movement stressed women's right to jobs not only because of the sense of satisfaction with one's work that is possible, but because of the desperate need for financial independence that many women felt. Far from a pastime, work was encouraged as a means to avoid some of the most virulent forms of male domination felt at home—and women still complain about this.

Economic independence remains the basis for women having a choice. Although outside work may no longer be the only "badge of freedom," what we have now, women's somewhat increased status, rests on this economic base, women's ability to be financially independent. That is why it is so important to fight for. The right to have jobs and careers is symbolic of women's right to have a life outside of home.

Being Unattached and Independent: Calling Your Life Your Own

In Celebration of Life on Our Own

Why women like being single

"Every woman should have a chance to live at least part of her adult life alone!"

93 percent of single, never-married women say, no matter what the problems, they love the freedom and independence of being on their own, the fun of meeting and knowing different people, calling their lives their own: *

"I enjoy the idea of being single, especially at my age. I have the whole world to explore."

"I love doing what I want, when I want—and it forces me to reach out to others."

"Traveling and going places on my own, unencumbered by a partner—I enjoy it. I am free to go about as I please without having to defend my actions, or report to anyone. I have the option of doing all kinds of things! I haven't yet found anyone I love and respect enough to commit the rest of my life to."

*This does not mean that many of these same women do not also feel pressure to get married, or anxiety over their relationships, as we have seen in Part II.

"It's great to be responsible for no one but yourself. I love being able to flirt with anyone I please, not being tied down, having an apartment exactly the way I want it, not having to answer to anyone."

"I like being single—I like to check out the merchandise."

"I love being single—but not alone. That's probably why I have two men instead of one. The best thing I like about being single is there are no commitments. I come and go as I please."

"I like meeting and being with different guys. Even though it may not work out, it's still a good experience. I like getting attention from various men. Disadvantages? Days like Valentine's when all your roommates have boyfriends and you aren't seeing anyone, or if you haven't slept with anyone in a while."

Most women who become single after a divorce also love being on their own, independent:

"It's heaven to be single. No matter what problems the day brings, I look back, and by comparison the day is a fantastic success!"

"How do I feel? Good! I like to feel free, not tied down emotionally, because it always seems to engulf me. I never thought I could survive on my own, but I now realize I can spread my love among many people and have many fulfilling relationships."

"After living with my husband for four years, I discovered that I couldn't ever again stand the thought of living for a long time with another grown-up person. They sooner or later try to boss me, or I become the boss, and I can't bear it. Children (I have two) don't boss you around, and besides they grow and want to have homes and lives of their own. But a husband—to make him move you must start a catastrophe! Also, when I was married, I felt unwanted by everybody: men, employment managers, and working female friends."

"I definitely prefer being single to being a part of an even moderately unhappy couple! Sometimes I miss having someone I can count on to do things with, but marriage never provided that anyway."

"The great advantages all involve freedom—I love eating alone, shopping alone. I think the world travels in couples, though, and is mystified by individuality, especially in a woman. The great disadvantage is the huge number of married men hustling you if you are divorced. And the more independent and aloof you are, the more they fantasize about you—the macho challenge."

"If I want to cook dinner at seven or nine, or not at all, then I can. If I don't do the laundry for two weeks, I am the only one to complain. If I want to read in bed half the night, I can. And if on Saturday I look like a witch, and don't get dressed all day, it's my choice. I like being responsible for myself and knowing that I can make it on my own, that I am the only one I have to depend on. The disadvantages are not having that someone special who understands me and loves me, not being able to give all the love I have. But my sex life is great. I have three or four men whom I see occasionally and I thoroughly enjoy it."

"Being single has only one disadvantage: not having regular, consistent companionship and sex. Other than that, life is much better for me as a single woman. I can choose my friends, plan my social life, plan my private life, do and say what I please at home, make my home MINE (reflective of me), and I don't have to answer to anyone or explain my actions to anyone. Isn't it funny how long it takes to find out that freedom feels so good? Why do we rush into marriage like we do? Or is it just my age that makes me feel having my freedom has more advantages than marriage or commitment? I've had commitment, so now I don't miss it? I don't want to press any of my prejudices on my daughters—it will be hard to watch them and just let them go their own ways."

"I'm open for a love relationship to happen but it's just not that important to me right now. My own self, work, and friends are numero uno. I love being single. I'm celibate. I don't seem to find it necessary to be involved. I'm in school with a stipend; it's invigorating and exciting. Independence! I'm free! I love going alone to parties, restaurants, shopping, movies. Sometimes I feel like going with others, so I go with friends, but sometimes I just need to be alone, and since this is something I didn't have in my marriage, I'm still relishing it. Sometimes others try to make me feel as if there is something terribly wrong with me for being alone, but it's their problem."

Most women enjoy life alone, on their own, at every age—whether this means they like to sit at home alone with a book or a television program and a cup of hot coffee, or whether it means they have an enormously crowded social life, give dinner parties, go to plays and restaurants, have more friends than they can keep in touch with and as many lovers as they want—or both.

Only a handful of women don't like anything about being single:

"The first year I was single was sheer agony, the worst year of my life. Gradually, I've come to be more comfortable, but even now I'm lonely. Driving home from a party or from work, I wish I could have someone to talk to about the experiences."

"I liked the freedom once I got used to it, but found myself fair game for men on the make. Also, I found myself limited to 'women's' functions—I only met men in business relationships. Once I began dating one certain man, it was better."

"I didn't like being single. No emotional security, no stability, no financial security, no companionship, no closeness, no love or sharing, etc. . . . . I don't enjoy going out alone and never did, and my sex life when I was single was nil."

Having Children on Your Own: Woman/Child as a Family Unit

What if a woman wants children and is single and in her mid-thirties: should she take the option of being a single parent?

"Single mother" families, rather than being sad and depressed—as often referred to in stereotypes—are usually happy, content, and working quite well:

"Even though for weeks I'd thought and wondered and talked to my tummy, when the woman at my doctor's office said, 'The test is positive,' a surge of energy rushed through me! I remember feeling stinging tears in my eyes and a warmth, a full warmth all through, when I thought, 'Wow, there's really a baby in there!' I suppose there's been a give-and-take to having chosen to have my child. (I'm not married, never have been.) I chose to give up my job to be with my baby (no big sacrifice) so that my son can have my attention and so his first so important time won't be spent with sitters—I didn't have him so someone else (a sitter) would raise him. Whatever I've given up has been replaced.

"Having someone else to consider and plan for has helped me toward better treatment for myself. Seeing how dependent children are on their care givers has brought my horrendous childhood back from my subconscious and I'm now in the midst of therapy to help reverse all these feelings. Having a child that I love, really love, has let me see that I am capable of such strong emotion that I can take a risk and really care, and I can accept someone else's strong caring for me—it's not the same as a love relationship with an adult, but it's an eye-opener."

"I really get all I need from my job and from having children. Do you know how wonderfully close and affectionate it is to have children to sit in your lap and nestle next to you in bed, just leaning against you while you read them a story, or kiss them good night? I wouldn't have time to sit and play with them and talk on the edge of their beds before they go to sleep if I were married. From what I remember when I lived with someone, he was always demanding my attention, and I'm sure he would be now too—I'd feel guilty staying with the children that long, and from what I hear from other women, he would be rushing me, he'd want to be sure there was time for sex—and after all, between working, taking care of them, and having a few minutes for myself, how much time is there in the day anyway? So I find this a wonderfully relaxing way to raise children—comparatively."

However, one woman fears she has no right to raise children without a man:

"My only regret is that I had to raise them alone. They have missed out seeing what a relationship between a man and a woman could be like. But while they haven't had a chance to witness the positives, they haven't had to endure the negatives either. Whether or not that will be healthy for them, only time will tell."

But others remind us that many mothers who are married have found that, in effect, they are "single mothers" anyway:

"The best part of marriage is children. In the forties, a single parent was a problem for a child. But if I were doing it today, I'd have my children alone. My husband was a salary, not a father to them. I truly enjoyed all three of my sons—and their wives say I raised good husbands. But the children separated my husband and me because he wouldn't get involved—his excuse was work. I ran the home and worked full-time (after they were in school) and still put their needs first. Their father was rarely involved or around."

"Look at it this way, being a single mother, you only have one child! One person demanding your attention. Being married, you may work and still have to arrange for day care. A lot of why women feel so drained is not just 'overwork,' which is real, but the constant emotional drain of the man's needs, which are totally on the woman, and his harassment of her on top of everything else, instead of helping with the children, and so she feels constantly guilty that she is not dealing with, meeting his needs—for more sex, more attention, etc."

How many women who work and have children *prefer* not to have a man around?

One woman explains how being single for her, as a single parent, is part of a network of family, friends, and work which supports her life:

"I am single, black, and thirty-five. I am a parent and 'young career executive.' I have a twelve-year-old son living at home with me. I adopted after my husband and I separated. What I gained from my son has been tremendously helpful. He has reinforced my belief that loving is not ownership. He is his own person; I am mostly a guide, and provide warmth and support. I have fun with him and his friends, and he with me and mine. His friends' parents say that he is one of the most loving, creative people they know. I didn't 'make' him this way, he is as he is on his own.

"The most permanent things in my life are my family and a few special friends. Family being Mama and my three sisters, of course my son, and also my niece and two brothers-in-law. They are my base of support and freedom to be me. We are very close, and love relationships have taken on lesser importance than they did in my 'youth' (smile!)."

Interestingly, according to this research, children who grow up with only their mothers generally do quite well, both in careers and personal relationships. According to *The Hite Report* on men, boys who spend most of their child-hoods with only their mothers have a tendency to have better relationships with women later, are more verbal and less competitive in personal relationships than boys who grew up with both parents.

Establishing inheritance through women?

According to a cover story in *Newsweek* in 1986, "The Single Parent," by 1990 half of all households may well be headed by single parents—and most of these will be women. Certainly, then, women should have the right to enjoy the advantages of descendancy, inheritance, and family history that men have claimed as their exclusive right for so long.

Can women sustain social power (as men do) if there is no inheritance, legally, through women as there has always been through men? This includes names, money (some states' laws make it impossible for women to pass on property only to their daughters if their daughters are married!*)—and values. As a thirty-three-year-old woman in this study says, "Why I'm not married? Because I believe in and want to have descent through women—through my children, with my name and my values."

"Older" Single Women: Happy or Alone?†

Are some women afraid not to marry in part because of the stereotypes equat-ing being "old and alone" with being old and single—the idea that "no one wants an old woman"? What *are* the lives of older women like?

The stereotypes that portray older single women as "unhappy" are not

---

*One such state is Missouri.
†Further, single women of any age are not more "unhappy," as they rate themselves, than married women: single women on average rate themselves two points higher on the scale.

based on investigations of how women *themselves* feel. Here, we find that most of the single women over sixty in this study are *not* "unhappy"—certainly no more so than other women. Sixty-seven percent rate themselves over six on a scale of ten when asked, "How happy are you?"*

One seventy-year-old woman is single and enjoying it:

"I am a seventy-year-old grandma who lives alone, and is very alive. I have two dogs. Love to study and love kids, especially my grandchildren. Right now I'm happy. Tomorrow, who knows? I'm happiest doing things—riding, studying, hiking, dancing, going to Maine to see my two youngest grandkids.

"My lover died this spring. I miss him. But in a way I am relieved! I don't miss the put-downs. Since he died, I pass time reading dime novels. My goals? To write a little, fish, to design. Face death with humor!

"I'm not close to anyone, really. I had a roommate whom I've met again and still like. I feel loneliest when I'm around couples in love. But I guess I've just had too much pain and am scared of getting near anyone. Love is ambivalent yet all-encompassing, all-important—but I'm glad to be out of it.

"Right now I'm enjoying being single. Usually everyone else—when I'm not single—is more important than I am. Now *I'm* important and enjoying it! Except I'm here for my fourth daughter if she needs me! I always looked for love till now. Now all I've got is me, but I don't mind, I like it. Being single, you can do what you want. Don't have to do anything. I can study (I'm interested in history). It's O.K. being single when you are busy—but it's hard to contemplate dying alone and no one caring. And sometimes I like companionship. I don't like to go out alone, so I don't go. I'm too busy right now anyway. My sex life is nil except masturbation.

"I was the most in love in my last relationship. He was older (and very bright and attractive). We were happy at times. I liked feeling wanted, needed, and at home. It lasted till he died, holding my hand. I felt closest when I was being held, not necessarily fucked. Also, we would just be sitting in front of a fire talking, 'Oh, my dear,' he would say. But mostly, older men think feelings are nuts.

"I was married twenty-eight years (split twelve). There was a letdown after the honeymoon, yet I've no regrets. It was pretty awful when we were first married, we came to blows. I liked having my kids (five), but they could get me down. Having the first three was hell, then it got better. The marriage was difficult—he was a real chauvinist! But maybe I worked harder with my kids than with my husband.

"I had relationships outside of marriage. I felt awful about it. It was mainly a sexual attraction. (I wish I had one now—but nothing too overwhelming.)

*Sociologist Jesse Bernard also found in the early 1970s that single women were happier than married women; see *The Future of Marriage* (New Haven: Yale University Press, 1972).

"The divorce was hard, I felt like a failure. I broke it up. It just came apart—I had had it. I felt regrets, a failure, yet I was freer. I was really a walking nervous breakdown. A therapist helped me get out of it, get the feelings out. I learned you can never get in adult life what you never got as a child! Feeling this, and getting the pain out, saved my life. The therapists did not try to give me what I never got. They gave me my pain. In a way, I cried over it for ten years—for all the losses of my life. But I'm O.K. now—I'm happily scarred.

"Passion dims the trivia in life, and I like that. Not having an orgasm is not too important. I come easiest via masturbation. I first masturbated at fourteen. Later I learned also to orgasm with penetration, me on top. I started out with oral sex at sixteen! Most men like it. I have even wondered about exploring a woman's body. I feel part desire and part disgust. I think I prefer vaginal penetration of all of it—feel a bit embarrassed by others giving me oral sex. And I don't orgasm that way.

"My mother, am I like her? She played the violin. She used to hang her skirts on a tree and climb up in her bloomers! Early 1900s, of course. I'm like her, who else could I be like? I have four daughters, and three granddaughters. I never discussed sex with them.

"I admire women who can get up and go. Sally Shelton, Gloria Steinem, Eleanor Roosevelt, Indira Gandhi, Margaret Thatcher, Margaret Mead, Jackie Onassis, Elizabeth Cady Stanton. I believe in the women's movement. I'm a feminist. It made me realize what I missed. Although I am a nurse, I should have been a lawyer.

"I enjoy looking glamorous. Femininity means being sexually pleasing to men, yet firm in one's own ideas. I still shudder at masculine women. I enjoy beautiful clothing—although I live in jeans on a farm. I feed the horses, but can look well when dressed. I don't wear makeup (like Ma). Half the time I look a sight, so I'm not very feminine. Have fun, though. If you ask me how I look at seventy, I'd say—truthfully—awful!

"To women today I say: Love your kids and encourage them. Then do your own thing. With regard to love, don't worry about happy endings, life doesn't have them! But you can enjoy it meanwhile."

Do "older" women have a problem "finding" men? While some middle-aged or divorcing women mention feeling "invisible" or self-conscious in general, according to this study, women of all ages do find new lovers and new relationships, though many, it turns out, are not interested in marriage and prefer to remain single.*

---

*Statistically, reports usually assume that the higher number of unmarried older women means that they are unmarried because nobody wants *them*, they couldn't "find" anybody—never that they might *prefer* to be single.

31 percent of single women over fifty-five say they are dating or living with and enjoying significantly younger men, like the following woman:

"I feel good about the way I look. I feel my personality as vivacious, my energy as 'ready,' and I love the fact that I attract interesting people. I do not spend much time on my hair and makeup. I work in a department store.

"It is easy to meet someone I like and am attracted to, and whom I respect. They are usually much younger. I'm sixty-three and they are usually thirty-four to forty-five. I feel my sexual desires are damn healthy and best be enjoyed—I wish men my age had more like desires and needs.

"I have sex every six months or so. I know that is not good, but I do sometimes enjoy periods of no sex with another person. But I have loved my strong desire and physical activity. I resent that I'm not as active, or that my body has aged. I enjoy verbal exchanges, as well as the touching, kissing, and handling.

"If I could say just one thing to women today, it would be: 'Enjoy yourself, be interested, go more, do things you like.' "

Another woman, age sixty-five, certainly dispels any illusions that all older women not happily married are sitting home knitting:

"I am a retired nurse, two days after retirement. I loved to work as an R.N. on the maternity ward. I am sixty-five years old, have four grown children.

"I share my love with a seventy-two-year-old man who wants to marry me when I am through with my divorce (my second marriage, thirty-eight years). My favorite way to waste time is to go shopping and drive around in the car with him.

"We are happy and content—together almost two years. Since I am retired, we live together at his place. Gradually I take my belongings over to his. We plan to marry in July. We are too old to have children, but he often said he wished I could give him a child. I would not mind either.

"The most important part in this relationship is sexual intimacy, daily companionship, working together, cleaning up, feeding the farm animals, attending the garden. Growing plans to make an herb garden, buy some sheep, pigs. Having a gas well dug.

"I like best in this relationship being loved and cared for. I like least his jealousy, his thinking I am seeing other men on the side. He loves me more than I love him. I would say I *like* him very much and respect him. I think we need each other, we are lonely without the other. I feel loved. What I have to give will last longer than mere love.

"My partner tells me often he loves me. On birthdays, Christmas—he writes it down. He also loves me when my teeth are not complete (I have one tooth on a plate) or when my hair is not combed. I feel good and wanted. He said he would love me just the same if I would lose a breast to cancer. Or if we would not have sex altogether in case of poor health.

"He criticizes how I look at or act with other men. Once he was very mad because I turned around and answered a man's beckoning when leaving a party. I criticize his mistakes in grammar and at meals when he puts the knife in his mouth and that in bed he wears his underwear and does not change for nightwear.

"His jealousy is quite a problem. It is completely unfounded. But he has 'seen it with his own eyes.' I wish he would trust me eventually. The worst thing he ever did was tear out pages from my address book, under the letters R and W, because he thought they contained the addresses of a former or current lover. He cannot know me very well, since he would know then that there are no other men in my life. He does not want me to visit my sister in Indiana, he thinks a lover is waiting there for me. He does not know that one man (he) is enough for me, but I keep telling him this.

"I think men, especially older men, need a lot of love. If they lost their wives through death or divorce, they are very responsive to love and affection. My relationship with my lover is very important to me. I try to overlook what irritates me about him—his overweight. I want our relationship to go smoothly without argument. He talks more than I do. When I listen to what he is saying, I would not think it worthwhile to say the same. I find he is not attentive enough to what I am saying, he misses much, says his hearing is bad. He is weary when I tell him my problems. He wants a wife that has no problems and is smiling and in best humor all the time. I tell him I am a human being with ups and downs and he better accept that.

"I enjoy cooking together, having sex together, going places in the car, planting the garden, being together, reading—daily life together. The work load is done jointly. He does the heavy work like splitting wood and fueling the stove. I plan to bring order into his bachelor household. He never can find anything he looks for. I think he secretly suspects me if he cannot find an item!

"I expect from my future husband that he provide free shelter and food for me; in exchange I work for him and am his companion and sex partner. I plan to pay for my own car, insurance, repairs, gas, my dental bills, my clothing, my shoes, my trips if I go without him, one-half of our common trips. We will have our own separate bank accounts. These are the same arrangements I have presently with my husband. Being regarded as an equal partner in the marital union is important—being consulted on all important matters.

"For me sex plays a very important part in our relationship. Sex and intimacy is what was lacking in my marriage for twenty-two years. (For seventeen years of the thirty-eight we had a very nice sex life, my husband got me very excited. When he had his second climax I had my first. This was never boring.)

"Sex with my lover is enjoyable. Usually he stimulates me by hand to orgasm. When we are not together I masturbate. I orgasm easiest through masturbation, but if I do not catch one very soon, I give up and let go without. But most of the time it works. I find estrogen injections, which I take every half year for menopausal symptoms, improve my sex life considerably for a while. *The Hite Report* on female sexuality, the part that made it clear that very few women orgasm under 'in and out' but need clitoral stimulation, was nothing but the truth as far as I was concerned. I used to fake orgasm, not anymore.

"My lover had a prostate operation seven years ago. He has sexual feeling but not always an erection. He does not ejaculate, the semen at a climax enters his urinary bladder. He takes medication for his high blood pressure which also affects his erections. It is no use for me to show my passion, because if there is no erection, there is no sex for me either. Should I change this? I think I should."

Only 24 percent of single women over sixty are discontented with their situation:

"I am seventy-three years old. My husband passed away two years ago. I do not like being single. It's very difficult at my time in life to meet someone. Even though he was ill for practically a year before he passed away, I was desolate. I miss doing things together terribly."

"I am sixty, a teacher. I hate being single. I just ended an eight-year relationship, we lived together for six years. Saturday nights are devastating and times like New Year's Eve. I don't believe anyone envies my single state. I do have sex with my boyfriend about once every two weeks. It is difficult at my age to meet a man I respect, and I believe single men today want to avoid commitment. I was devastated when my boyfriend wanted to break up. He had other women.

"Earlier in my life, I felt wonderful when I married my husband at age nineteen. I was in love with him and it was wonderful. We were married for thirty years, but then divorced. I felt most passionate in my thirties. Recently, I reentered therapy to try to resolve my problems related to relationships. I'm still hurting over the breakup—he said he didn't like the way I kept my home. The conclusion of therapy so far is that I don't have enough self-esteem."

Of course, ageist remarks are made to women all the time:

"On the issue of aging, at fifty I find men quite able to seriously say to me, 'You look good for your age,' etc."

"Now that I divorced my husband, the attitude I get from all my friends (ex-friends?) is 'Oh, poor Nancy, she is all alone now . . .' And men—even my friends' husbands—all think I'm available for sex! They proposition me, and don't expect me to tell their wives because they are my friends. It's true—how can I? But it makes me mad."

One "homeless woman" took the time to write:

"I am age fifty-seven, attractive. I got married when I was sixteen. My father was starting to come on to me when he was drunk. Then my husband was violent all the time and used to threaten me with his hunting rifle when he was drunk. My mother died the first year of my marriage, so I had no other family.

"I stayed married a long time, eventually got divorced. I left men alone for a while, then I had a boyfriend. My boyfriend and I broke up two years ago because he was eleven years younger and I was the first woman he had known outside of his ex-wife and we were not sure if we were in love or just dependent on each other and scared to try and date others. I cried a lot. Took off from work, ill a lot.

"If I had not had to take care of my mother's dog I would have probably 'hung it up.' It was like being cast into a void where no one cared if you lived or died. In fact, I could have died, and no one would have known until I started smelling or my dog did something to attract attention.

"I think my having to keep working to eat or else find a garage I knew would be empty long enough for me to sleep in is what has kept me going. I had lots of good friends but they have their lives and family, so what the hell. I'm still trying to get over my relationship. I haven't circulated much recently.

"I'm worried for my future. My income this year was $6,000. This all goes to pay for food and the places I sleep. I'm not sure what will be coming next."

Another woman, age sixty-two, describes how after leaving her marriage, the only job she could get was in a photocopy shop for minimum wage, with a young, "snotty" male boss—but she is still glad of her decision, and proud:

"My first job after I became single was in a quick-copy shop at just over minimum wage. When I asked for a ten-cent raise after three months, the owner/boss kept me for two hours going over all my defects—while through a plate-glass window we could see his wife waiting to pick him up and probably not knowing what the hell the conversation was about. He made me wait another month for my ten-cent raise. I was about fifty-six at the time. I'd like to kill him.

"Nevertheless, I don't have a vocabulary to tell the pleasure of sleeping alone after sharing a bed with the same man for thirty years. It was heaven. It took months to get used to the sheer joyous ecstasy. I realized when he left that whenever I approached my home while he lived there, a tension of fear would build up. He's been gone about ten years and I still approach home late at night feeling an exultation that I no longer feel fear when I approach my house, but just pleasure. I exult daily in having won.

"The disadvantage of blessed singleness is that I live in what I call Noah's Ark. It used to be called a 'bedroom town,' a place for commuting husbands to keep their wives and children, but now is a corporate headquarters town. It used to be that I could walk downtown alone or with my kids any time of day and not see any men except the shopkeepers. Now you go downtown at noon and the streets are crawling with squads of men in their dull business suits who practically knock you into the gutter in their arrogance.

"Between being a suburb of families and patriarchal corporate headquarters, there is little social life for a single old woman. (I'm sixty-two now.) I have few friends. But I'm not lonely or unhappy. For the most part, I feel contented—that is, when I am not driven because I'm not accomplishing. What, I'm not sure.

"After taking the drastic, terrifying step of no longer kowtowing to my husband, I recognized him as a brutalizing monster. But at the time, he seemed better than most and everyone said to me, 'You're so lucky.' Romantic 'love' is a myth conjured up in our society to keep women enslaved—always looking for a mate in order to feel 'human.' The concept is enforced by Hollywood patriarchal moguls, admen, and the like—the male brotherhood.

"For my second job, the YWCA job counselor tore up my paper when she saw my only credentials outside of housework were the past ten years of volunteer work. No matter how I'd couch it, it would come out the same. So I typed like hell and tried apprenticing as a typesetter, but just wasn't the 'type' in shops, so finally just went temping as a secretary.

"Eventually, I had to get a renter to keep afloat. This turned out to be the biggest break for me. He moved in with his computer, and soon began teaching me with infinite patience to use it—so well that I am now doing a free-lance indexing paid job. I am enjoying this experience the most of anything since 1978. I keep thinking I should learn faster and do more. I don't know any woman with as sophisticated equipment as this, or with the knowledge that he and his friends have. It's fun knowing him.

"After raising five children to adulthood and independence, I entered the job market for the first time at fifty-six and I am surviving—'making it'! I need most now instances, occurrences, in which my intelligence is reaffirmed. My goals are to retain my home, remain financially independent, and start making enough money to do things like go to shows and concerts, travel and take vacations. I can see it's all within my grasp now—in just a year or two, I will have it all—and I can be proud of having done it myself."

The stereotype of being "old and alone" is basically inaccurate: in this study, 81 percent of single women over sixty-five like their lives very much (even if they could use a little more money): most enjoy their friends, their work, their gardens, lovers, in fact all facets of life. In fact, many women say they feel *happier* when "old and alone."

Why do negative stereotypes about older single women persist? Perhaps the evidence here will begin to change them.

Our Right to Ourselves

"I find that being single is a time I take quantum leaps in self-development. It seems to release a surge of creative energy in me. I think I am a better person for the time I spend alone."

Most women love to spend time alone

Although living alone is supposed to be lonely, most women love to spend time alone, have time to themselves. Many women can be themselves when alone in a more complete way than at any other time.

More women mention feeling lonely inside a non-close relationship than they ever do being single (almost no women mention feeling alone because of being single; see Chapter 1). Women say, over and over, that they have many good women friends, sometimes friends of a lifetime, and that their communication with them is the closest of their lives. Being single and trying out different relationships can be "lonely" because of the ups and downs, the lack of stability, and the constant "starting over." While breaking up or being in a bad relationship can be depressing, actually being "alone" is not, according to women here.

Most women in this study, single or married, say they would like to have *more* time alone. When asked, "What is your favorite activity for yourself, your favorite way to waste time?" the overwhelming majority of women chose activities that were solitary—such as taking a bath, reading a book, going for a long walk, perhaps with their dogs, having time to just sit and have a cup of tea, etc.

When asked, "What is your favorite way to waste time? Please yourself?" 92 percent of women mention activities they do alone:

"I love to play music and dance. I love to read, I read a lot, and I love movies. I love to sit around by myself and space out, I call it. That kind of time is very important, very, very important to me. It's not following any particular line of thought or concentrating on anything—it's just zooming around the cosmos in my head. I need that time to relax, to cool out. It seems to be sort of like a deep well from which the inspiration comes—whatever it is, I need it to go on with my life and my love relationships too. I guess it's being with myself, renewing my relationship to myself, and discovering who I have become lately. Reminds me to love myself and have fun with *my* life. Be *me.*"

"I like walking in the country during the early morning, being near the ocean, riding horses, and visiting museums—by myself, just free to see whatever I see."

"My favorite way to 'waste time' is to walk around—anywhere—and stop wherever I please, usually by myself."

"I love to go through old letters, rearrange and throw out books, read old writings of mine, including dreams."

"My favorite way to 'waste time' is to do absolutely nothing at all. I sit in the living room staring at the wall or turning the pages in a magazine or petting a cat—or masturbating! Alternatively, I do useless things at my computer, such as practice typing. I also read, but I don't consider that wasting time."

———————————————————

Being "alone" is not "sad" and "bad," but often very refreshing, restoring the spirit, allowing feelings to come to the surface, a recentering in oneself. It also allows time for creativity and planning/dreaming future thoughts. However, being single rarely means "living alone"; in fact, it means living *less* alone for many women.

One woman states memorably the case for being single:

"Being single, you have the opportunity to, in fact, change the world—as male thinking patterns are quite stuck and it is difficult to debrief yourself while involved with them. You have no one controlling or discounting you as a single (hopefully, anyway). Your life is more flexible. The disadvantages to being single I think mainly rest largely in one's security and affirmation needs. At our present stage of development, women are more defined by love relationships than men. Women want to be substantiated because this is an area of poverty for women—they don't usually substantiate themselves adequately, so they look for men to do it—and put themselves in jeopardy thereby. I think women are desperate for affirmation from the power group. But we don't have to be."

And another, who was married for twenty-five years, and now wouldn't trade her independence for anything, sums it all up:

"I was a wife and mother for twenty-five years, my work was basically homemaking. My greatest achievement is my four years of college. I didn't graduate, but I still see it as my greatest achievement, beyond mothering, beyond wifing, beyond anything else. Also—my divorce and entry into the world, because I don't feel like I was in the world or in any way in charge of my own life until I got divorced. I've been divorced for nine years. I prefer it.

"The best job I could get when I left the marriage was as a cleaning woman—that's my experience, what I did for twenty-five years. It's worth it to be on my own. Being in control of my life. Independence! Absolute independence. I love doing what I want to do, being with whom I want to be with, staying out as late as I want, changing my mind if I want, living the way I want, listening to the music I want.

"The divorce was like death and rebirth. I never had any regrets. I felt relieved that I could start living again. I still feel that relief nine years later. It took me six years to come out of my divorce, six years of emotional turmoil. I talked to my friends, and went to college in those years, which was very, very helpful.

"I remember crying over problems with my husband. Why? Because I could never reach him, I could never really communicate with him, never share with him. I had two semi-nervous-breakdowns during my marriage and felt very low immediately following my divorce. But I was the loneliest when I was married and my husband didn't share my life. I was lonelier married, when he was with me but I couldn't reach him emotionally. That made me feel very, very lonely.

"Was there a time that I gave up on love as not being very important? Oh, definitely. Relationships are still not very important to me. People always say, don't give up, don't give up. I don't see it as giving up, I see it as a preference.

"What is my sex life like? Oh, boy. Sometimes there is no sex life. I have nothing on a regular basis. But I enjoy periods of either no sex or being sexual with just myself. Taking care of my own needs. I was very shy when I married my husband. I relate more aggressively the older I get. I have branched out. I used to be strictly heterosexual, now I get a great deal of pleasure making love to women occasionally too. What I like best about sex with women is that women give, women are touchers, there is much more touching and caressing with a woman. They just don't go for 'the act' of sex. What do I like best about making love to men? I guess I like feeling feminine or like a woman maybe.

"When was I the happiest with someone? I'm trying to think—in a relationship recently, in the last two years—I only saw him under certain circumstances, we just got together and went out and danced and had a few drinks, went to a café or something. I was happiest when I was sharing with him, doing something, dancing. I don't know that I was ever deliriously happy about being in love.

"My most important relationship with a woman in my life has been my relationship with my daughter. She is my best friend. She is a ray of light in my life. I love her dearly, dearly, dearly, she is a beautiful human being. Have I talked to her about menstruation? Oh yes, years ago, she's older now. I told her that she was a human and her body was hers and that she should always take pleasure in her body and never feel guilty about it, and she thanked me profoundly, she still thanks me, she still remembers that.

"I'm white, ethnic Italian. Schooling—high school and four years of college. The approximate total income in my household—hold on—about $5,000. What kind of work do I do? As I said, I do cleaning work, it was what I did for twenty-five years, it's my best expertise. I obtained this questionnaire at my church.

"To women I say—you can be who you want to be. Look how I've changed! I've revised, I'm like T. S. Eliot. There will be time for a hundred more revisions. Oh, a thousand revisions."

7

Marriage and the Nature of Love

The Beauty of Marriage

"Take my heart, and I shall have it all the more."
—*Edmond Rostand,* CYRANO DE BERGERAC

"Marriage is a brush with eternity. That moment you stand there and promise to love until death, to plan to have a new generation together, you think of your own death—and what will come after."

The spiritual *idea* of "marriage," beyond patriarchal conceptions of male ownership of women and children, is beautiful. One person, recently married and in love, said with surprise, "Why do they say marriage is 'the end,' it will tie you down? Marriage is just the beginning. Love is a holy feeling, including during sex. Why has the world turned it into a thing that is joked about?"

What is "marriage" anyway? Another emotional world, or a patriarchal institution? A spiritual pledge, or legal domination of one by another?

One woman sent some notes from her diary, relating her feelings around the time of her wedding, beautiful feelings of love for her husband:

"Darling, now everything is enchanted. I woke up and you were lying there. I smelled your hair and rubbed my face against it—I also told you things. I thought, this is the first day of my life. I am new, everything is so new. I feel so open.

"It is mysterious. I want to be one—why do I feel that? It goes beyond any sexual feeling. I want to merge souls with you. There is an overwhelming urge to be one, to be unified. As you said today, I want to be able to see what you see, taste what you taste, hear what you hear.

"And once before, you said with astonishment, 'Is this what it's all about, just being with the one you love—is this the reason for everything?' Nothing else seems important now . . . it's a feeling of 'I am where I should be.'

"When you were away, I wanted to go embrace the chairs where you/we had sat—walk the places we had walked—and run away at the same time, not to be sad, so sad I would think only of why I couldn't put myself in motion to be with you, to go where you are."

The Feminist Critique of Marriage

Feminists have raised a cry against the many injustices of marriage— exploitation of women financially, physically, sexually, and emotionally. This outcry has been just and accurate—although many feminists are themselves married.

The psychological structure of most marriages—as we will see here—is indeed a hangover from the time, just about a hundred years ago, when women were still legally owned by their husbands. (The legal status of slaves in the United States in the eighteenth century was derived from the legal status of women vis-à-vis their husbands, as John Stuart Mill explained.) Even now, in some states in the U.S. today, and in many other countries, a woman cannot sell her property without also having her husband sign that he consents to her sale of it—thus, in effect, making him joint owner.* In France, banking custom was that married women could not have their own bank accounts without their husband's signature until only ten years ago, and so on.

If the analysis of marriage as unfair to women has been accurate for the most part, why haven't more women (although half *do* divorce) decided to "give marriage up"—especially now that most women work outside the home and have an income (if minimal) of their own?

It is not being "hopeless romantics," "love junkies," or "masochists" that makes women return to marriage as a way of life, even after divorcing. Marriage is not disappearing as a way of life because the idea of marriage still holds out the *hope*, the *promise* of the greatest intimacy and trust, the deepest human relationship possible. There *is* no other such institution, and until a woman has tried it, she will believe that: being single may be rough, but surely a man in *marriage* will be different. We are drawn to the hope, the promise, that there is an intimacy possible in life which includes connecting physically, holding someone inside you in the deepest recesses of your body, having that person

---

*For example, Missouri state law provides that if a woman inherits property, then decides to sell it, she cannot do so without her husband's signature (thus his permission).

know you and be accepting—close and in touch, verbally, emotionally, physically. Having children. Having it all. It is a physical and spiritual craving at the same time—not to be alone in one's most personal ecstatic moments.

Are women finding what they search for in marriage, in their relationships with their husbands?

How do women see marriage now?

The world has changed—and changed fundamentally in just the last seven years. The basic difference in marriages today is that now an average of 70 percent of married women (and 78 percent of married women of working age with no children at home) have full-time jobs outside the home.* Women are providing a large part of the financial support for the home for the first time in the twentieth century.†

What does this mean for marriage? Are women seeing marriage differently? This is a confusing time, full of mixed feelings and conflicting points of view for almost everyone—and great longings and disappointments too. What do they mean? Which way is marriage going?

*See U.S. Bureau of Labor Statistics, "Current Population Survey Data," March 1986, U.S. Department of Labor.

†However, the idea that women never before did this is inaccurate. In twentieth-century American culture, it is true that women's work outside the home has newly become a majority activity, whereas it was not earlier in the century; but in almost all previous centuries, especially before the Industrial Revolution, when the "lower class" was the largest class, most women were working at least as hard as men, and not only at "domestic chores": first, the basic center of all work/production was the home, not the "factory"; and second, most women took in extra work—i.e., washing, sewing, weaving, nursing others' children, and lodging boarders.

Ten Women Describe
Their Marriages

The women in this chapter represent the more than 2,000 married women participating in this study.* Their responses were chosen because they represent well the thoughts and feelings of other married women. Analysis of all the replies—a statistical and conceptual analysis of all the married women in this study—is to be found in the succeeding chapters.

1

I never in one million years saw myself not working and raising a child "alone" while my husband worked. He and I had agreed that he would take a paternity leave, but he didn't. Still, although my daughter takes up all my time, if you ask me if I am in love, I want to answer yes, with my daughter! More love than I ever thought possible and so easy to express. She's so smart and creative and pretty and good. She's only two, and you should just hear her singsonging a whole new string of sentences.

My current life has been full of crises: losing both grandmothers, the storm before my parents' divorce (and their each using me as a confidante), leaving work, finding out that my husband was going to take a promotion instead of paternity leave, loss of my old body image and self-image as a liberated married woman sharing work, chores, and ideals with hubby.

*Women living together with a man for over five years are also included in this chapter; they comprise 4 percent of the study population.

I am a professional psychotherapist, a hiker and biker (more in heart than in practice lately), an artist of sorts, and a feminist. I am proud of my graduate degree.

In our current setup we are straining to maintain equality and balance in an unbalanced situation: me with baby full-time, private practice part-time, him working full-time, caring for baby part-time. Sometimes I have faith it will all work out. He's a bit happier than me. It's unfortunate that he wasn't willing to share child rearing as we planned, thus forcing us into this situation. But providing money is now the least he can do since he is dependent upon me for practically everything else. I also feel it's a temporary situation which we are handling as well as possible. Naturally it affects the relationship—it points out to us dramatically how unbalanced our roles are.

My goal for years was to become a psychotherapist. Now that I finally *am* one, I hardly have time to keep it up.

Despite these problems, I'm still most in love with my husband (aside from my daughter, as I said!). My love for him makes me happy. It's like knowing you have someone to count on, to satisfy your sexual needs, to enjoy and to share everything you want with. It's lasted five years, really more. I've felt the most passionate in my life with him.

Our relationship isn't the center of my life but it's an important addition to my relationship with myself, my daughter, and my work. With my husband, I feel cherished, secure, and open with my own feelings. Our love has brought great pleasure and contentment, but it can lead to the greatest frustration and anger I've ever known because you're committed to the love—and when it seems you've reached a stalemate, what are you committed to? You yearn to reach resolution.

I gave birth at the maternity center where low-risk women and their partners can be educated and take control of their labor and delivery. It was the hardest thing I've ever faced and it took all my intellectual control to get through labor and relax. My husband and I were an exceptional team (as my nurse-midwife pointed out). I took a walk to Central Park with my brother and husband three hours before the birth, to ease the pain, to help bring the baby's head down, and to "speed" labor. My mother and brother were with us in the homelike labor room, as was the nurse-midwife (who had little to do and gave us privacy whenever we wanted it). My husband and I showered together about an hour before the birth, with the midwife right outside the bathroom door calling out advice when I felt the baby move down dramatically while showering! It was fine and we stayed in the shower, then went into the delivery room. My brother and Mom stayed by the door, and my husband had tea in the kitchenette between the labor and delivery rooms right near the end, but aside from that was with me the whole time. I was in a semi-sitting position on a regular bed in a cozy, well-equipped room with dim lights. We used Leboyer's method of welcoming a baby into this world and invited my mom and brother to watch the bath.

We had champagne and the best hamburgers I ever ate right on the clean delivery bed with brother, Mom, and midwife. We took pictures (discreet and treasured) throughout the labor and delivery and Mom kept a diary. It was a supportive and beautiful event, though very painful. I went home after another shower, last-minute instructions, and an appointment for a checkup one week later. The visiting nurse came the next day and we went to our own pediatrician on the baby's third day of life. My husband stayed home for two weeks (thank God) and Mom visited every day with food and gifts, as did other close relatives.

My husband cried (to think it was the end of "us" as we knew it) and was very excited and happy that we were to become a trio. We were both really in awe when she was born, almost shocked, and felt very sober and responsible when we drove her home three hours later. But right after the birth the awe was a high with silly-loving-exuberance which we extended to everyone there.

Without my child, life would be different. I would be working for $, etc., and not be in a quandary over how to work and raise her effectively and according to my heart. I would be free to eat, make love, shower, socialize, etc., when I wanted to, not when it was feasible according to her needs. My child comes first in my life now (since I left working to care for her), as a family is more important than any other loyalty—except loyalty to oneself.

Currently I crave most of all peace and quiet and time alone. I feel happiest when I'm able to engage in any activity fully and without having to think about my child or be interrupted by duties related to her care. However, when she and I are having a meaningful encounter, with minimal stress, I feel as alive and happy as I ever have.

My husband says he supports women's equality and believes it. I guess he does as much as he could with our society being the place he was raised. He is more liberated than any man I know. I feel there are times he treats me as an inferior. He doesn't leave me out of decisions, but he may act superior— sometimes when it's justified, some when it's not. The only way he treats me as an inferior is by not respecting my job of child raising and house/family management as much as he should. The truth is, most men are afraid to say they think the women's movement is stupid, but they act like it's aggressive, non-feminine, and overreactionary.

I cook, so he does the dishes. We share all other aspects of caring for the house, the baby, and social arrangements, but in a 90-10 not a 50-50 setup. I do all the budgeting, banking, bill paying, and care for the baby full-time (so I naturally do more of everything for her and some things that he hardly ever does). My time away from the family has to be arranged; his is built into the system—including driving home alone from work and walking around freely without baby bag, child, or other paraphernalia (groceries, cleaning).

By mutual consent I handle the $ now—because I do it better and because since I don't earn much now (very small private practice part-time) I want that involvement with $. When it becomes burdensome he shares and I always share information records and problems or decisions of major import with him. It affects our relationship positively, as it allows for mutual respect—I for his earning, he for my managing. It works so smoothly that financial matters are not a source of stress. I buy most of the groceries (unfortunately) to avoid weekend madness.

His complaints? He doesn't like my "foul language," my meticulous attention to planning for guests, and my comments on sexism he thinks are too constant and sometimes too harsh. I complain about his lack of initiative in house/family-related responsibilities, his sloppiness (and careless arrangement of things), and how he spends his free time. And yes, I've had some screaming, hitting fights with my husband.

Sex is usually tender, fun, and rewarding. I enjoy it and always orgasm—during foreplay, not intercourse. It's over too soon and not usually preceded by time together doing something which might stir our desire to get together sexually. I don't mean foreplay—I mean play or work or some adventure before foreplay. The best thing is the intimacy it engenders.

When I told my husband most women don't have orgasm simply from intercourse, he was surprised—couldn't believe it was that common, but began to believe it. I was glad he wasn't acting with any false ideas anymore . . . even though he'd always satisfied me manually and orally. I wasn't embarrassed because I wanted him to know the truth about the big "I" (intercourse). I like giving oral sex, but not being ejaculated into my mouth, so I don't allow that. Most men I've known were not uncomfortable with giving oral sex. My husband loves it, but it took him some time before marriage and after to get used to enjoying me doing it to him. Now he loves that too. His hand on my clitoris feels super. I rarely guide his hand, as he knows me so well, but sometimes if I want it to last longer or not be so powerful, so quick that there's no peak, I'll ease him up a bit, or slow him down, or speed him up.

I consider myself a feminist in all I do (including mothering and paying taxes). I have deep feelings about fairness and speaking up for my rights against adversity. Some of this reflects on how I saw my mom. She was a full-time mom and home manager. I'm like her in some ways—the big ones: (1) I can't concentrate on my own pleasures until I clear the table, so to speak—get duties out of the way; (2) feel I have to help everyone (less than she does); (3) management skills.

Also in my life, I have a close friend who is very important to me. She makes me a cup of tea and provides a neat, pleasant, relaxing environment for me in her home. We get together near the end of the day on Fridays, usually with the kids or during my free time on weekends, alone. With the kids we talk in her house, or take the kids to the park or other fun places for them; alone we go out to eat or drink or shop or to a movie or just to talk. We've helped each other through difficult times indirectly by being available and offering an oasis of no stress. With her, I feel relaxed, understood, comfortable, happy.

I'm beginning to feel that I've lived a long time and accomplished very little (I'm thirty). I'm looking forward to age forty—a time when, supposedly, there is stability as far as major life changes, and you have confidence and mastery over your situation.

2

Saddled with four children, one of whom is nineteen months old, I really need my husband right now. I have hopes of being more independent later on, as I have many interests. I can't be sure if my husband really loves me or just needs a woman, but I think he loves me.

Our biggest problem is money. I was highly worried after we married because of the financial pressures. He disclosed to me that he was several thousand dollars in debt just before we married. I had never known such things. He also had to pay a hefty amount of alimony and child support to his previous wife. I had been on welfare and had to go off it once I was married. Our income now is $15,000 for the six of us.

The worst thing he's ever done is called me fatso. I finally yelled and screamed, but he instigated it. We never fought before we moved to this house last year. I hate it here, and we fight over it. I am no longer so attractive since I got fat after the fourth baby. He has told me I am sexually desirable. Of course, I loved hearing that. Right now I am suffering from exhaustion, but my husband refuses to acknowledge this or help when I am extremely tired and I can't sleep or rest because the baby needs constant watching.

We've been together eight years and had never had a real fight until we moved to this house. We disagree and fight all the time about moving out of here. He likes it and I don't, although he says he will move if we find another place. However, I wanted him to borrow money so we would have the rent and security money ready when a new place turns up; and he refuses to do so. We are fighting over that all the time. I tried to borrow money on my own from Household Finance and was turned down. I'll be upset if something turns up and he makes some half-assed excuse why we can't take it. He's already suggested we go away over the Thanksgiving weekend and stay overnight; and after thinking about it, I realized he'd be spending money we should be saving for the move, especially since he won't borrow it. I am very angry. This house has no storage space, it has bad wiring, it is old and a lot of things go wrong and the landlord is too cheap to fix them, our rent has been increased by $100, etc.

We also fight about the fact that I am tied down with the baby, who is now nineteen months old. I point out to him that I am tantamount to a disabled person, and he refuses to believe it. He refuses to believe that housework is work, and refuses to lift a finger around here unless he has to. We used to get along better, but having the baby, who is very active and into everything, puts a big strain on me. I am prevented from earning money I could be earning (I still do typing work at home). I believe the baby has to come first, but I am upset about being stuck.

None of the arguments get resolved. They get ended because he tells me not to talk anymore; I'm giving him a headache; he'll talk about it later. He isn't interested in listening to me at all, but I have to listen to him, although I point out to him that I want to have my say also.

I expect the problems to be resolved once my children are older and I can earn more money. If he doesn't like the fact that I intend to be more independent and drive around and attend meetings, etc., he's going to have to figure on a divorce. Once I'm not tied down with the baby anymore, I'm doing as I please.

He's more interested in doing the talking than in listening to what I have to say, especially lately. I would say he talks more, though he would deny that and make a remark about how I talk too much. I would like the quality of our conversations to improve but wouldn't bank on it. Instead I hope to find other people to carry on conversations with, eventually. I am not interested in an extramarital affair, however.

The practical arrangements, ha. I do the dishes, cooking, and as many household chores as time allows. He seldom helps and only if he has to. He *has* to if we are expecting someone. Then he may help straighten up. I don't have time between the baby and typing work to keep the house very neat and can't even spare the time if I know someone is coming a month in advance. So occasionally he does help do that. He takes the clothes to the laundromat now, but that's the only way we can get them done. I don't have a working washing machine and can't get out myself.

I take care of the children, primarily. He does help out with them and occasionally with the baby, although even to get him to help me with her for five or ten minutes so I can get dinner on the table is a hassle.

What I like least in our situation: not being able to loaf. If he's working, he doesn't like to see me sitting around. He'll find something for me to do.

We have slept in the same bed off and on. The reason we don't now is I believe strongly in breast feeding and nurse my babies two or three years, almost always lying down, so I sleep with them and there's no room. We have "the family bed" out of practicality. I'd rather sleep by myself, personally.

We share the money. We each have a separate account. He has a business account, and I am a signatory on that, and I have my own NOW account. That came about when his ex-wife sued us and the court gave her almost our entire income. I wanted to prove that a lot of the income in our household was mine, so I started my own account. Of course, no one in the court or so-called justice system here cared about that. I found I liked keeping my own checkbook because I was used to it, having been single so long, and he was crabby about how I made entries in his book.

But even with my own account, if we need money to pay something and he doesn't have it, I pay it if I have the money, and vice versa. Last month he paid the rent, this month it looks as if I will have to pay most of it. He usually buys groceries, but if necessary, I pay for them. I usually pay the back bills to credit companies and Visa, but if I don't have the money, he pays them. We get help from my parents and his mother too.

I'm content with the financial arrangements. I feel it necessary to be equal in deciding what to do with the money, but we haven't had much to spare since we've been married. As a matter of fact, we owe more than our income allows us to pay.

I was quite relieved when I knew I was pregnant the first time. I was not married, age twenty-eight, and I had been trying for seven months and thought perhaps I had fertility problems. My lover reacted casually, as it was a casual affair to him. He was not there after the child was born and only saw her once because I made him. He abandoned me when I was six months pregnant. He later denied fathering her and we've never gotten a penny from him (I didn't ask him for money), and wants nothing to do with us.

When I was pregnant the first time, I made a conscious decision to choose having the baby over using the money for a down payment on a house I had picked out. I would have had enough money for the down payment, but I did want the child more. I do miss having the house, but I have no regrets about my decision. It seems unfair that women are always having to choose between having children and working.

I guess *I* decided to get married to my current husband; he really didn't want to. I was renting an apartment, and he rented a room across the hall in the same house. (I originally met him through the personals—"The Selling Post.") Before we legally wed, I would go across the hall and visit him in his room when my daughter, age three, was sleeping. He did actually live with us, though, eating with us, etc.

When we had been living together for a few months, he was still legally married to his first wife. I didn't know when I met him he wasn't divorced yet; I was dating quite a few men at the time. When the divorce came through— suddenly and unexpectedly, by the way—he claimed he wanted to be "single" for a week, which I let him.

I knew I wanted to be legally married, and if I had continued just living together I would have felt I was being cheated out of something. He did not propose, and neither did I. But I know it came from me. We were planning on it becoming legal after his divorce, and I became pregnant while we were living together. I guess I lived for so many years with this tremendous fear of never marrying that I knew I wanted it to be. It wasn't a hard decision, but I did have my misgivings about it.

Why did I decide to marry him? Mainly to have more children. Also for a sex life. Economic pressures for sure—I hated living in apartments and figured I could at least afford to rent a house with his help. And having someone to go out with to see shows, etc. I think his primary needs were sex and companionship.

My husband definitely does not see me as an equal. He almost always tries to treat me as an inferior, and I fight it all the time. He pretends to ask me for a decision but it is already a foregone conclusion what the decisions will be. If I go against what he wants, there is trouble. This is getting more pronounced as time goes by. He acts superior and supercilious, not only to me but to everybody else too.

I have never acted violently. Though lately my husband's behavior has gotten me very upset and I've screamed and dented the big stainless-steel bowl by throwing it. I never did anything like that before and feel he incited it.

I want to have us get along, but I won't work to keep him with me. He's free to leave anytime.

As far as I know, he's been faithful to me, though he wasn't to his ex-wife, obviously. He was more or less separated from her when he met me, however. Of course, I want him to be monogamous, and he'd be better off not telling me if he's not. No extramarital affairs for me either. I believe in monogamy.

I like having children, exasperating as they can be. Mine are all very active. Giving birth was rather easy. All four were born at home, the last three with no one attending at all but myself and my husband. I would never consider it a sexy or orgasmic experience, as some do, but it was easier, safer, and better than a hospital delivery. I've never had an episiotomy, never mind a cesarean. My husband was around for the three deliveries, though reluctantly. He "caught" two babies. One was born before he could get into the room. He is not thrilled about the birth process, and I prefer laboring alone, with him nearby if I need him.

With all the big claims about how it's great to have your husband there, I find having a baby is like making, and I don't like doing that in front of my husband. It's a mess. I don't like him to see me like that; though it was helpful to have him catch the baby, especially the last one, because the cord was over her shoulder. I think by now he's convinced that it's better and that the doctors are fooling people, but he's not crazy about being involved in it.

I was a feminist all my life, always knew I was just as good as any man. I do see where my "consciousness has been raised." For instance, when I was dating my first boyfriend, both his mother and father worked in the state hospital where I did. Occasionally I would have dinner there, and his mother would come home from work and scurry around preparing dinner, etc. His father would light up his pipe, sit down with the newspaper, with his feet up. I never questioned that idea. Now I am indignant about it. Of course, why get her dissatisfied if she accepted that? I guess I would be more satisfied with life if I just accepted the status quo, like the slaves did before Lincoln freed them, but I can't do that. I have to fight it, because my integrity depends upon it.

3

On the surface, I am an attractive, intelligent, cooperative, kind, sympathetic, understanding fifty-eight-year-old woman who has been privileged in many ways, spared many potential disasters common to women. Underneath I am the child who stifled herself rather than inconvenience or upset her family and who learned early not to ask to be held or ask (or expect) anyone to consider her feelings as important.

I am in love but my husband is succeeding in strangling that love through starvation. I am closest to my psychotherapist and a couple of women friends. But even with my therapist, I follow my pattern of not wanting to upset the therapist by a too disturbing sharing of feelings! In my relationships, I usually practice a pattern of observation and accommodation: I watch to see how they feel and what they think, and then I align myself accordingly.

My happiness rating has normally been low. Whenever I deviated from playacting, I was on the verge of tears. Crying was unacceptable to my parents, my husband, and my children, so playacting at happiness was my solution. After moving twenty-seven times during marriage (military), I am at last reveling in close, sharing friendships with women, in a form of volunteer work which teaches me something and gives me a real "high," a new academic and artistic association that brings me more pleasure than anything in my life.

When I was about thirty-five, being very busy being the adequate home manager, mother, and supportive wife of a career naval officer in his first commanding officer role, I was still very busy denying that my husband—although he had made all the provisions for our financial security and gave us some of his superficial attention when convenient—really had no interest in us as persons. This, even though several years before he had told me he couldn't be a hypocrite and say he loved me. Since he had never said anything to bolster or reinforce my self-esteem, I took that blow in stride. Since my own capacity for expressing myself had always been so repressed, I was more comfortable with a less than exuberant marriage. Steady and secure but no highs.

I married because I thought being married was the most acceptable role, and he was attractive and had the potential for success. I had known him all my life—the lifestyle we would have was familiar to me. (My father was also an officer.) I thought intimacy would surely develop.

I plan to stay married. I do not intend to sacrifice my investment in the marriage. After thirty-four years, it has its advantages—security, belonging somewhere. The worst part is being less than a whole autonomous person.

At the time of marriage I didn't mind using my husband's name, but now I feel using his name contributes to loss of identity. But I am not comfortable (and never have been) with any of the names (and there is nothing difficult or odd about any of them). I just don't feel they refer to me.

I am glad to have children now but at the time I did not like having them. They have become responsible, independent adults, but I was not able to give them the real affection and emotional support every baby should have. I was a "responsible" mother but I didn't get any joy from motherhood. However, I doubt if I would have stayed married without them because my husband was married to his career right from the start.

We are doing better because he rarely is rude now. However, he rarely listens. I've found I need intimate talk, so I have found others who will exchange such talk.

The worst thing he has done to me has been to lack the courage to be honest with me and not to apply his considerable talents at brainstorming and problem solving to our personal relationship. The worst I have done is not to have told him years ago how devastated I was by his put-downs, caustic remarks, and insensitive rudeness. It was a mistake to let him think that behavior was acceptable to me. I shouldn't have harbored my anger all those years.

He criticizes physical attributes over which I have no control and the fact that I don't snap back "yes" or "no" answers to questions that I consider need some thought and elaboration; that I don't "explode" sexually. I criticize most that he talks too much about things that have happened to him; that he interrupts frequently; that he politely asks questions which he obviously isn't interested in having answered since he changes the subject before the answer is given.

I have not had any affairs, but I would like to have one if I knew an unattached man who attracted me and appreciated me and made me feel good about myself. My husband? Maybe experiences with other women would help him sort out his own handicaps with his sexuality and, even more, his emotional sterility.

I came closest to an affair once years ago when I met a naval officer for whom I felt an immediate affinity. After frequent social contacts when we always had plenty to talk about, we both realized simultaneously that it was a lot more than friendship. We felt a very strong physical attraction for each other but did nothing more than steal a couple of exquisitely satisfying kisses (something my husband is incapable of—at least with me).

We talked a lot about our love but never really considered doing anything about it. He was in a very sensitive position and could not have survived a scandal professionally. He went home to his family, and after one letter telling me his time with us would never be forgotten, we had no further contact. Years later we heard he had lung cancer and my husband and I sent him a note—no response. I still remember how great it felt to be admired, desired, and appreciated for all of me. But it hurt my self-esteem that he could give it all up—even though I think he took his cue from me.

Presently sex with my husband is nonexistent because he has a lack of desire. I still would enjoy it because I need touching and closeness, even though full orgasm is usually impossible. Sex with him is rarely emotionally satisfying. It was always unemotional, "by the book." There was rarely any desire displayed on his part beyond genital craving. He was patient and persistent but deaf to suggestion. Usually silent unless to complain of something—he never shared his feelings with me.

I hate his pretense that all he does is for me, yet he is not able to listen or to understand my needs.

The money is in our joint control. I do most of the banking, etc.; he does most of the investing. Both of us are prudent and fairly good managers and neither feels required to ask permission to spend money. He has earned the actual income but I feel I contributed an equal amount in labor and sacrifice and commitment and responsible managing. I feel I have earned my half of every penny he made.

We don't fight and differences are never resolved, partly because I don't allow myself to express anger. I have tried very hard to find out what is inside of him but I'm sure my perceptions are somewhat faulty, because he is rarely self-disclosing. I am most angry when he cuts me down either by words or actions—even when I suspect it's the classic bully's way of trying to build up his own esteem by hurting someone else. The same old conflicts seem to remain with us. I've quit trying to do anything about it. When I try to discuss a difference I feel strongly about, he refuses. I withdraw from arguments.

However, last week we had to go into town for something and he suggested going to a very nice restaurant (more my taste in food than his) and we had a lot of good self-disclosing, sharing conversation. He didn't seem threatened by sharing with me and seemed to listen to my disclosures. He has withheld all touching and affection for many months but at least that night I felt the warmth of friendship.

I don't think I am good at giving love. Love to my parents was financial provision and society's mandate to love God and country, parents and all the old distant relatives and family friends—and especially don't upset anyone or be an embarrassment. I was forty-eight before I met a woman who showed me the value of warmth and caring, and I've been coming along slowly since then.

It makes me lonely to think of the terrible waste of my femininity and sexuality. I have become very despairing of ever achieving a good satisfying sexual relationship with anyone or ever achieving satisfaction with myself. Well, there just isn't any joy anywhere in my life to date.

The women's movement helped to make me realize my own strength and value and to accept men's inability to break out of their destructive mind-sets right away. It made me feel cheated by being born too soon. I could have profited a lot from modern therapy when I was five instead of having to suffer so much pain for fifty years before anyone recognized my need for help. I always appeared the strong, competent, calm, accommodating, reliable, and helpful person—and I was still scared, repressed, depressed, and had no joy under the façade.

I have made some good close friendships now, but only in the last few years when I've been able to stop putting husband and family's needs first. One friend (that I mentioned) persisted for many years until I could allow myself to accept her warmth and caring. Now we are close and she listens to me, really cares and encourages me to take care of myself. I also have a relatively new friend with whom I have a lot in common. We hike together weekly and act as sounding boards for each other's dilemmas. I have discussed most things with her, but not my sexual dilemma. Earlier in my life, I didn't even know how to be friends.

I have a daughter who is talented, highly intelligent, and liked by her peers—but has suffered from my repression and rigidity; only now, at ages thirty-three and fifty-eight, are we learning to communicate honestly and caringly.

I admire women who are independent thinkers and doers. I dislike women who unhappily wish they were as above yet don't even take "baby steps" to achieve it. I am a different woman now from the one so influenced, hurt, lied to, repressed, and depressed by men. I don't think I can "ungrow" and fall into any of the old traps. I will give my remaining life a better chance.

4

I am forty-four. I was a single working mother for ten years, have been divorced and remarried. Am too heavy (size 16) and too old to suit me, but my husband, who is six years younger and slender as well as sexy, likes me this size and still finds me arousing, so I guess I can't holler too much. I am still considered very pretty (used to be always known as one of the most beautiful girls in town—Grace Kelly type). I'm one of the lucky ones who found the kind of mate that I only used to fantasize about and never dreamed really existed. We've been married fourteen years.

With my present husband, I'm terribly happy. It was like all the things lovers always say. As though you were the only two people in the world, sitting on cloud nine, and in this case, the certain knowledge that, of all the people in the world, this was my mate. I knew we belonged together and that without him I was incomplete. Having a successful career no longer mattered. All that mattered was being where he was so that I could be with him for the rest of my life if possible, or for however long was possible. I packed up three kids and moved a thousand miles away from a career and family and friends to be with him and I'd do the same thing today.

Oh, my Lord, when we met we were incredibly passionate! I had always *felt* extremely passionate, but this was the first time in my life I had been able to let go and *be* passionate. I could just do and say anything I wanted and could have all the sex I wanted for the first time in my life, plus he did all the things I had ever dreamed of a man doing (and some I hadn't thought of), so I really pigged out on sex. He used to joke that I only loved him for his body and, for a while, he wasn't far off. Keep in mind that I was thirty-one, with three kids, and had never had good sex even after one husband and several lovers. Imagine how starved I was!

We have three grown children from my first marriage, three "homemade" children, one adopted, and are working at adopting another, plus a seven-year-old granddaughter lives with us a lot of the time. There were many times of great intensity and happiness for us—during the pregnancies for our three children, when they were born, when our one and only boy was born, most times of all after making deep and extra satisfying love, many other times too numerous to mention.

Most of all, I want to be with him. He is what makes life worthwhile. With him, I thoroughly enjoy living; even the hard parts and the sad parts are bearable with him. Also, he is still darned good in bed and can always rise to the occasion, bless him. Sharing all the children with him is another of the good things, especially since he doesn't differentiate between "mine" and ours. He's right there along with me when there's a problem with one of the older kids. Having had a husband who didn't like his kids the first time around and abused them, I really appreciate having a husband who is a good father. Also, we enjoy talking, having sex, sharing our big old (one hundred ten years) house and the work on it, all the kids, reading the same books, watching *Hill Street Blues*, sharing our two dogs, playing cards, going out to dinner (when we can)—just our regular existence, which is always busy and usually hectic. (As I'm writing this, I have five kids and two dogs swarming around me!)

Wishes? I wish I had more time, more energy, and a tad bit more money. He says he's happy and sure seems to be. If I could change anything, I would have him let go more when he's angry. He tends to hold things in too much.

He tells me he loves me at odd times during the day or after we make love. During lovemaking it depends on the mood we're in. Sometimes we "talk dirty"; other times it's just tender talk, like "Do you like this and this?" and "I love to see you excited," things like that . . . He never did tell me in words that he thought I was beautiful or very desirable, but he always showed it in his eyes and the way he acted. I never had to wonder. And he has always, from the beginning, told me he loved me over and over and most emphatically. I respond sexually to him when he talks to me in erotic tones or words, not so much as to what he says, but the tone of voice he says it in, sometimes to something specific but usually it's his tone of voice.

I felt "right" with him from the very first, a feeling of belonging. He proposed ten days after we began dating. When he asked me to marry him, at that time I thought I never wanted to be married again, ever. But I also knew

I did not want to be without him, so I agreed. We'd known each other for over a year. We'd been apart for three months and it had been sheer hell for both of us, so even though we were both very leery of getting married, being apart was worse. At that time, I had three daughters, aged sixteen, fourteen, and eight, so living together was out of the question. And his boss would also have thrown a fit. Personally, I wouldn't have cared, but with the girls and his job, there was no choice except marriage.

We were elated after we got married. Our feelings increased and things got better for us as we relaxed and got to know each other better. Not sexually. Sex had been great from the very first time. Emotionally, I mean. He got even sweeter and more attentive after we were married. I felt the same at the beginning as I do now, except it's deeper now. I am aware that it is *not* always like that, but for us, that's the way it was.

The best things about marriage are: Being together so much. Not having to get up and get dressed and go home. Having sex when we're horny instead of waiting for a chance to be together. Living with each other. There is no worst. After being so unhappily married the first time, I didn't expect it to last and be so good. I figured the bloom would wear off eventually and I'd get bored. I never dreamed it would be so good and get better. I love the term "wife" because it's been his pet name for me ever since we got married. And I am very proud to use his name.

I think feeling passionate is the best feeling there is. I get very passionate when I haven't had sex for a while, or right before my period, or after reading an erotically arousing book. I get a feeling of intense pressure inside my vagina, my breasts feel swollen and very sensitive to the touch, I can't hardly stop thinking about it and respond to the slightest thing my husband does.

Sex is *good*. Sometimes it's *GOOD* but it's always at least *good*. I always enjoy it and sometimes I *love* it so much I wish we could have a rerun or save it like a souvenir to enjoy all over again. There isn't really a worst thing about sex with him. Sometimes I wish he'd be a little more "caveman" but that's all. The best? Oh, when we're both very hungry and we have an "orgy," draw it out, make it last a long, long time, tease each other, get both of us very aroused and stay that way as long as we can stand it. I get very uninhibited then and so does he and it's just tremendous. He has great control and can hold back such a nice long time.

When I'm very horny, almost anything will make me come. Otherwise, if I'm not very hungry . . . with a vibrator; somewhat hungry . . . clitoral stimulation by hand by my partner; pretty hungry . . . oral sex; very hungry . . . oral sex, clitoral touching, intercourse, sometimes even just going down on my husband or having him suck my nipples will do it. I told my husband that sometimes I don't come, and most of the time, if I don't, it's perfectly all right with me. He didn't use to believe me, but now he does, and if I need to finish, he takes care of it for me. When I first admitted to him I masturbated, I felt ashamed and embarrassed. He reassured me that it was all right and normal and that he found it exciting in me.

Most men do not know how to make love or don't care about it. They don't offer clitoral stimulation—at least not once they get you into bed. When they are trying to convince you to let them in, they do lots of stimulating, but once they can have intercourse, they figure that's all that's needed.

That's why I was so thrilled to find this husband because he loves all of it and is rarely *ever* in a hurry. He loves the feeling of being aroused and likes to stay that way as long as he can stand it. He's also found that it increases the intensity and the length of his orgasm. It also often brings on "instant replay," which usually doesn't last long but is fun.

I'd like to see sex be a little less open in our society in general—I mean, publicly. However, in the family, my daughters and I do talk about sex, and sex with our husbands—frequency of it, normalcy of oral sex, having sex during pregnancy—and I've also told them that if their husbands want to suck their breasts while they are a nursing mother, there's nothing wrong with it, just make sure they feed the baby first. I found it highly stimulating when my husband sucked me until it was gone. It was a fantastic experience with all three kids, and I wish I could get pregnant again so we could have that experience again. It was great!

Pregnancy with this husband was grand. I got even more horny during pregnancy and he finds me very exciting while pregnant as well as while I'm a nursing mother. We were also very excited about the baby coming. He was there with me for the last two births, and he was as thrilled as I was, the tears were rolling down his face the same as mine at the joy of our babies. When my girls started menstruation I always hugged them and told them congratulations, and got a little teary-eyed—it's a special time for us.

I think the biggest and only real fight we ever had was nine years ago when he had kissed someone else at a party and lied about it. I threw a drink in his face. And the rat wouldn't help me clean up the broken glass either. He yelled a little and glared a lot and after a while we made up.

But really we don't fight. We occasionally snap at each other and then later feel terrible about it, but if one of us is angry with the other, we just talk it over and work it out. No one wins or loses and we always feel bad if one of us has been hurt or offended or whatever. We both will apologize when there's been a problem.

We don't criticize each other. I think because we both recognized at the very beginning that each of us was extremely sensitive and vulnerable and because we each had highly critical parents. What works best is talking things over quietly and telling the other when something has upset you, without being angry at the time. Just saying nicely, "You know, you really made me angry for a few minutes," or even "You know, I'm angry with you," only saying it quietly.

I do the housework, but he helps with the kids, the dogs, the trash, anything heavy, the yard. We each do our share and try to help each other. When I was working, he did a lot more. We've always shared the same bed. Good Lord, I haven't had sex with anyone else. I believe in monogamy, but that's not what keeps me faithful. I'm faithful because I love him. I would be crushed if he was unfaithful. I wouldn't want him to tell me.

After many, many years of being the wage earner and budget runner, I was delighted to let him have this responsibility when we got married. I can do it, but I am perfectly happy not to. I really think we share the financial control. We have no problems over money. Just don't have enough. (Does anyone?)

If I hadn't met him, I would have gone on to have a business career, hopefully successfully. At the time we married, I had reached a crossroads and had three excellent offers, all of which I wanted, and was trying to decide which to take. I would not change anything now. I have tried to have a career along with all the kids and my husband and have found that in order to be the kind of wife and mother I want to be, it is necessary to stay home and find my creative outlet in other ways. My husband is most important to me, then my children. And, at times, I do feel torn because quite often my energies are used up by the kids and my mother's care, leaving my husband shortchanged. I wish I could give the kids and my mother less and give him more. As they all get older, this pressure has lessened considerably.

But I have five kids to take care of, plus a twelve-room house, a big yard, a husband, two dogs, three cats, two kittens (even baby goats one time), plus grown kids who like some attention too, and I make most of the clothes for me and my little girls, plus wedding gowns and then maternity clothes for the grown girls, as well as dolls and Barbie clothes for the little ones. That doesn't include doing all my mother's wash and mending and heavy cleaning.

It is a great way of life, and sharing it with my husband makes it perfect—I love sharing all the family things. Like, we had a tense time when our favorite grown daughter was safely delivered of a much-wanted baby girl after an earlier miscarriage and a previous very dangerous birth. This is less than a week ago, and was most joyous to us because we were so worried about her and fearful for the baby's safety. Our daughter had a very quick and easy delivery and a one hundred percent healthy baby and we were just walking on air. That same day, we got a *big* package from another daughter, who is in Turkey with her husband, full of just wonderful presents for all of us, and we agreed that some days are so full of happiness that you just can't hold it all. We were able to be at the hospital together and see the new baby and mommy together and this was very much a thrill for us. So I wouldn't change a thing about my life—just the excitement of doing all this together is what I want, what I want my life to be.

5

I am seventy-one and live with my husband. The relationship has lasted forty-seven years as of now. While I care for him as a person, I am not "in love." My husband and I view so many things differently. He is deeply religious; I am agnostic. He is very traditional in male/female roles; I am a feminist. There is no sex in the relationship. I plan to spend the rest of my life in it because of lack of options. I care about his welfare and his happiness because he is a fine person.

I would like him to change philosophies. When we were first married, I too was very traditional. He is fond of telling me, "You are not the girl I married." Incidentally, a lot of our money goes to the church and related activities. We live in Salt Lake City, Utah. I criticize his seeming inability to grow—I was going to say, change—but he is changing by becoming more and more steeped in religion, and developing a consuming interest in spectator sports.

I truly object to his opposition to feminism. I have felt it as an attack on my core being. I suppose the worst thing I have done to him was becoming disillusioned with religion and inactive in the church. He criticizes my lack of religious belief and blames it on feminism's goals. But I have to be true to myself. Is this really something I have "done to" him? Don't I have as much right to my beliefs as he does?

Although he is traditional, he will fix himself meals if I am not at home. I am a retired school supervisor, and I have to have some independence—to see my friends, etc. We are both retired from paid employment, so he will some-times do household chores now, on a very limited basis.

He controls his money, I control mine. We have separate checking ac-counts, because when I started earning a wage and put it in a joint account, I finally became angry at his accusations of incompetency with a checkbook, and opened my own account at a different bank. He generally buys the grocer-ies and pays the household bills (we have had arguments over this) because I tell him he should live by the church's precepts (in which he believes) and support his wife. He doesn't support me, of course—such things as clothing, medical bills, gas for the car, entertainment, etc., I pay for myself.

I remember the feeling of exultation with my first paycheck after going back to paid employment. I had been housewife/mother/wife for sixteen years, and now I was working as a substitute teacher. (I had been fired from teaching when I married—it was district policy.)

I had one affair with brief and widely spaced encounters over a couple of years. The man lived in another state. I am not sure what it gave me. It was and is not known to my partner. Probably part of it was nostalgia, I suppose, because I had loved him in college. I prefer my husband to be monogamous, but would not want to know if he were not. We sleep in twin beds.

I was the happiest with my husband before marriage. I was romantically in love. We had known each other several years—perhaps, as I look back now, in a superficial way. But then, marriage was the only thing for a female. Otherwise you were a failure. Why do I stay now? Of course, I love him in a certain way, or I wouldn't stay. But it is difficult to evaluate how important this is because of my lack of other options. If I had adequate economic independence, and if I knew myself well enough to know I could be reasonably content to live alone, I would leave.

As I said, we used to argue about religion, and now it is feminism. I decided it was futile to discuss religion, and I am rapidly coming to the same conclusion about women's issues. No winner. We both end up with hurt feelings. Nothing gets resolved. I am usually the one to say I'm sorry. He tells me that feminism is wrong—in some aspects, *immoral.* He is bitter about it, and has told me more than once he doesn't want to hear about it again. But I think religion has victimized women. It says that women are to be used.

My best woman friend and I are philosophically similar. We take classes together, go to movies, lunch, shopping. We have a good time and share interests in each other's families (she is a widow). We are both feminists, mothers, and agnostic liberals politically. We talk on the phone, and do many things together. We have much more in common (outside of the family) than my husband and I do.

For myself, I enjoy reading, seeing the beauties of nature, stimulating conversation, learning. I enjoy beauty in everything. I would feel better with some reassurance about the political stability of the world, for the future as well as the present. I am sad that I won't live to see the changes I hope for. To younger women, I say: Become aware, then become active. Make changes!

6

I am a twenty-eight-year-old woman, a bohemian-type mother of one who is up at six a.m. to type this while her baby sleeps.

A few years ago, the thing that made me feel best was to drink whiskey with my sweetheart and dance all night long. Now my pleasures are more subtle: sitting in the rocking chair with my child, taking walks in the woods with her and her father, taking her to the park to see the squirrels.

All I want from life is to be alive—to be awake and feeling, thinking, and alive in all my senses—in every bit of my body and spirit and mind. And not to die in a nuclear war.

I am in love with my sweetheart, John. He is also my best friend, the person that I am closest to. Of course, I am also close—closer?—to my daughter. She is so familiar and intimate to me that she is almost some aspect of myself in a new, raw, pure form—is that too esoteric? I tell my lover my secrets, but my daughter already knows them.

When I was younger, I was very self-destructive—I was into heavy drug use, including shooting up—and bad relationships. I am not anti-drug now, but when I use drugs anymore it is—as Yoko Ono said—out of celebration and not from boredom or unhappiness. I hung out in crowded barrooms most of the time and fucked men that I didn't especially like and smoked cigarettes and waited for something to happen. My biggest accomplishment is the fact that I am healthy now, that I don't do things to hurt myself, that I have found that calm, alert place that is in each of us, and most days I feel myself living and acting out of that place.

When I first hooked up with John, I was breaking up with a boyfriend whom I had lived with for about a year. I was trying to save money to go to Europe and I needed a cheap place to live. John and his girlfriend had opened up their relationship after almost five years and they were buying a house with her other boyfriend. They are anarchists, they believed that anything was possible. I had known them for about six years, but had gotten closer to John because he hung out in the bar where I worked. I used to talk to him during my breaks and one night he brought me a copy of a book by Ivan Illich. I was working at a rock-and-roll bar and no men ever talked to me about ideas or culture or postindustrial society. I was very touched by his gift and a little romantic feeling was planted.

So when he and his girlfriend and her other boyfriend offered to let me move in with them, I thought that I should tell her (the girlfriend) about my feeling, which I defined as a "small crush." She encouraged me to ask him out and I did, and we fell madly in love and they broke up. His girlfriend and I then used to get together for dinners and talk about what was happening. We could never eat a thing. I tried to be sympathetic, supportive, etc. . . . but nothing is as selfish as new love, so I guess I was basically false. I was imbued with the optimism and egocentricity of young love: I was certain that everything was going to be wonderful. She wanted to be able to fall in love with other people, but she didn't want for him to. Put like that, it sounds unfair, but that's the way I feel too. Not that I was ever jealous of her. I was excited by the idea of living with all of them and being a family and having kids and sleeping together and growing gardens and eating wholesome food and sitting on the porch together in the summertime. Sometimes I still feel disappointed that it didn't work.

On one of our first nights together, John brought a folder full of papers for me. They included some mimeographed stories that he liked, an article that he had written, some pictures of himself when he was younger. He would bring me favorite albums to listen to and books—he continued to share his favorite books with me. He really shared himself with me, and when I talked, he listened closely to what I said. We were both very interested in each other, very curious and interested.

Now I am very happy and very unhappy about our relationship. For the past three years, we have been living for the future, in a sense. We are saving money to buy land and a boat so that we can sail around the world. Two years ago, we bought a business and John works there seven days a week and many nights too. I do all the domestic work. We have a very traditional role structure right now, which is fine with me. I would much rather play with my baby and cook rice than work in an insurance office, which is what I was doing before. I just wish that John had more energy for me and that he was doing something that we value, and that he didn't have to cut his hair and wear tailored pants— that symbolic stuff really bothers me. Being in love with a revolutionary was a lot more romantic than being in love with a businessman, but there you have it.

We hardly have intimate moments anymore. I miss them. Ever since I've been pregnant or nursing, I don't have my sex drive. When we were sexual, my sweetheart was pretty verbal—would tell me that he loved me and that I am beautiful, things like that, and sometimes he would describe what we were doing a little bit while we fucked. I liked that.

Lately I have been feeling more and more alone. Some days he comes home for dinner and we eat with nothing to say to each other. At night he lies in bed watching the news on the TV and I feel like we are on different planets. It is chilling. I remember so clearly the way we used to be together—how immediate he felt to me, how completely accessible and how excited he made me feel about being alive. I like merging with another, if it is the right person. Sometimes I fantasize about having a new lover, but it is always him; it is always John, the way he used to be at the beginning.

. . .

Daily life? John goes to work in the morning while I am getting up. I spend the day cleaning, cooking, caring for our child, shopping, traditional women's things. I like it. I have a group of friends who have children my daughter's age and we visit regularly and exchange child care. Our rule is that whenever someone else is taking care of your child, you can't do laundry or wash the floor or any of that kind of thing—you have to take a walk or write a letter, something *fun*—but it is a hard rule to follow.

John comes home at 5 p.m. and we eat dinner. Then he goes back to work until 7 or 8, while I hang out with the baby. Then he usually watches the news until 10:30 p.m. while I read and the girl plays. He says that I shouldn't disparage watching the news, but it's all TV to me. We all hang out in the bedroom on the mattress. We go to sleep, all of us, about 10:30 p.m. We all sleep together. It sounds rather dreary, spelled out like that. Some nights I go to math class and some nights I volunteer at our neighborhood women's health clinic. Every now and then we might go to a movie, or camp in the woods, or visit a friend, but the vast percentage of our time is predictable and routine. It gives new meaning to the concept of oppression—but it is only temporary.

I think I was most disappointed with John during the first months of my pregnancy because he was pretty distant. I was introspective and quiet—I liked to go for walks or lie in the backyard underneath the trees. I felt magical. For him it was business as usual. John is a strong, assertive personality, he is an initiator, very resourceful and self-confident. I am indecisive, more passive, not so sure of myself.

My favorite thing is talking with him. He is sensitive and authentic and always makes absolute sense to me. If I could change things, I would just add enough money for a little piece of land and a sailboat. The material plane does matter! Then John and I and our child could be together and have energy and travel and have adventures, and still have a garden and a compost pile too.

I love having a child—I want three or four of them—although the nuclear [family] arrangement is not suited for it. Mothers and children should not spend most of the day alone together. It is a crazy way to have kids! One of my best friends and her baby moved downstairs from me recently. Having someone there to watch my child while I run to the co-op or do laundry makes a tremendous difference to the quality of my daily life. The psychological benefit is important too: we share recipes and advice and feelings. Two women talking over the clothesline—it is not an image that I once would have related to or respected, but I like it just fine. It suits me.

Her birth was wonderful. I used the Bradley method, which is simply relaxation and deep breathing. I was surprised at how painful childbirth was—somehow I thought that if I just relaxed enough, I would give birth nonchalantly, like a cat in a closet, but I didn't. It hurt very much, but it wasn't a bad or scary kind of pain—it stretched me to my limit. I had to give myself up to it, let it overwhelm me, and when it was over everything seemed sharp and very, very clear. I think that it is a therapeutic pain, although that idea would have infuriated me at the time.

John was with me. It was very special seeing him hold our new baby. He carried her around the room and she stopped crying, became very quiet, looking at us with startled, new eyes. I felt overwhelmed by love for both of them.

Now is the only celibate time I've spent since I was a teenager and it's interesting. A lot of my identity is tied up with myself as a sexual person. I really value people being sexually attracted to me—it's weird, I know. It's crazy, because at the same time, on one hand, I want for people to be attracted to me, but on the other hand, whenever men show me that they're attracted to me, in the ways that they traditionally do, I resent it, I hate it, I'm very uncomfortable with it. Things are just not always consistent.

This current period of no sex drive is good for me, it's interesting because I don't respond to people sexually and people don't respond to me sexually. On the rare occasions that they do, I'm surprised, but mostly they don't. I went to a party the other night. I used to get into being flirtatious and having little encounters that would have sexual overtones, even though nothing would happen. It was fun to do that, but this time a man was trying to do that with me and I didn't like it, I felt uncomfortable with it, it wasn't fun and it just felt sort of phony, kind of awkward. It's been liberating to me in some ways to have this sexual thing on hold for a while, not to have my sexuality so strong. My ego has not crumpled.

My favorite part of being in love is the beginning. I like those passionate, intense beginnings. It was hard for me when this relationship moved into a more mellow phase. I still can't accept the first part as being gone for good. Sometimes I think that if our relationship was "opened up" it would feel new again.

. . . .

I never liked being single. Since I was nineteen, I've only spent about six months not living with a boyfriend. I regret that. Both times I left my long-term boyfriends I felt excited about being on my own and I planned to spend a lot of time at home, reading and writing and doing yoga. It's so awful and oppressive to live with someone you don't like. I was also excited by the idea of being able to have lots of lovers, but each time I broke up I didn't stay at home doing neat, creative things. I felt disoriented at home, I couldn't relax, I was restless, so I spent all my time in bars instead. I went dancing almost every night. I didn't enjoy my promiscuity. It was disappointing, boring, phony, and no orgasms. Having a boyfriend is nice because then most other men will leave you alone, you don't have to deal with the sexuality bullshit scene.

I've been thinking too about the idea of independence. In our culture we really value it. Especially now for women, independence is a quality that is highly valued and it's something I've begun to reevaluate, because I've always felt kind of bad because I'm not independent. But then why is that valuable, why is it valuable to be able to be autonomous and be able to live your own life and not really be connected up with people and depend on other people and have people depend on you? So I'm feeling better about that, about my dependence, although I wish that I had lived alone more.

I lived with two men when I was younger—one was when I was nineteen, for over three years. Actually, my biggest emotional upset so far in life was living with this man, because he was violent. At first he was merely critical of me. Over time I cut myself off from my friends—I only saw him and *his* friends, who were biker types mostly. My self-concept became fuzzier and fuzzier—really very bad, pitiful—so that by the time he hit me it wasn't unthinkable. I had become a person who could be hit. I was a feminist—I considered myself a feminist anyway—so it was especially hard for me to admit what was happening. I didn't tell anyone until it was over.

Most of the time we lived together, we lived alone in an apartment. I don't know what would have happened to me if we hadn't had to move. We moved into a farmhouse with a group of other people. I had become very insecure, I couldn't *say* anything anymore. I was afraid to say what I thought. I didn't talk in front of people. I was afraid to go to the grocery store. Something awful had happened to me. I couldn't understand what I read, I couldn't follow themes when I went to a movie. If I read a book *now* that I read during that time period, I don't remember it—it's as if I never read it. I don't know what happened to me.

He would do things like hit me because I pulled the covers off him at night. If I didn't fill up the ice-cube trays all the way or if I didn't wash all the towels when I did the laundry, he would scream at me. He would burst through the laundromat doors, holding the offending towel and screaming, "You dumb cunt!" while the other ladies opened their mouths in surprise. I was cautious with him because there was always this thing that might happen, this violence, and so I tiptoed through conflict most of the time.

In a crazy way, the hatefulness made me more dependent on him. Researchers have done studies on baby monkeys in which they are given surrogate mothers that have sharp metal spikes inside of them and the researchers can push a button and make the spikes come out and that throws the monkeys into an awful panic—but when the spikes are withdrawn, they cling more desperately to the mothers that just stuck them, because that is their only source of protection.* I was like one of those poor baby monkeys. Anyway, it was a terrible experience and I did not transform him with my love (my intention). It was one of those situations that I call a "learning experience," because, of course, I did learn a lot—a lot! It's just too bad that it took such a long, long time.

The first night that I told him that I wanted to leave him, which was about two years before I finally did leave him, we were sitting in the living room. After I told him, he ran into the bedroom. I could hear him rummaging around his dresser and his top drawer, and I knew that he kept his pistol, his loaded pistol in there, and I thought that he was going to shoot me. I can remember very clearly sitting on the couch thinking: "Now he's going to shoot me." I knew I didn't have time to escape, and I just sat there. But he was only looking for a match to light a cigarette, so that was that.

I regret that it took me so long to break up. I spent half of the four years breaking up. I kept thinking that there would come a time when it would be easy and he would accept it. But that time didn't come, of course. When I finally got away, I expected to feel sad and miss him, but I didn't. The first night I spent alone I stretched out on my bed so that I filled the whole thing up and I put my arms behind my head and I lay there, smiling and smiling, so happy—I was so happy to be rid of him at last. It was one of the most wonderful moments of my life.

---

*Harry F. Harlow and Clara Mears, *The Human Model: Primate Perspectives* (New York: Halsted Press, 1979).

I was sort of financially dependent on the second man that I lived with. I worked part-time at a bar, but he brought home most of the money. But we still didn't have enough to pay bills; our electricity was always being shut off and we could never pay our rent. I did household jobs and sometimes we had to borrow money so that we could buy groceries. We were always borrowing money from people, but on the other hand, we were wildly extravagant. We would spend our last cent at a Chinese restaurant, and then we would buy cocaine—one time I remember we spent $100 for a gram of cocaine and we didn't even have a dollar bill to use to snort it with.

He had his own unsuccessful business, working with bands. Mostly he'd hang out and smoke cigarettes and drink beer and smoke pot in his little office. I worked hard, I worked in our garden and worked nights in the bar, so I worked harder than he, actually, I think. Our rap was that you couldn't separate the work I did for us and the work that he did, that it was all the same and there wasn't any distinction between mine and his, but one night we had an argument, and he told me that I should leave, that I should go someplace else and live. But he said, "Where can you go? You don't have anything, you don't have a real job and you don't have any money, and you don't have any way to take care of yourself." So that was the bottom line, I saw. That was a turning point in our relationship.

At one point, we agreed to have a so-called open relationship. He fucked other women a couple of times, but when I wanted to fuck someone, he decided that we should be monogamous. I left him.

I made the same mistake when I broke up with him as with my first boyfriend, trying to do it in a nice way. I kept thinking that after a while it would get easy and he would accept it and we would be friends. Then one night he got violent with me, so I never saw him again. I was very upset: I figured that one violent boyfriend could be bad luck, but I felt like two in a row was statistically unlikely, and I was afraid that I was attracted to violence or maybe brought out violence in people.

Also when I was twenty-two, and had just busted out of my relationship with the violent man, I was attacked in the bar where I worked. I didn't know where to go, so I went to the house of that same old fascist first boyfriend. I ended up spending the night with him and, oddly enough, it was not a good place to go after a sexual assault! He tried to be sympathetic but he just couldn't understand why I didn't want to fuck him that night. I finally gave him a blow job so that he would shut up and leave me alone. When I walked out of that house, that was the turning point in my feelings about myself and my body. As I walked out of his house, I knew that I was never going to be back with him, ever, that I was never going to fuck this man I didn't like anymore, that I was not going to be raped again, that I wasn't going to be coerced or bribed or intimidated into sex again. From that point on, something changed, and it was a profound change in my sexuality and the way that I see myself as a sexual being. My sexuality has been my own after that.

· · ·

Maybe I started disrespecting myself enough to let these situations happen because of an event that occurred in my childhood. When I was ten, I had been sexually assaulted by a neighbor man. After that, I didn't hug or kiss my parents anymore and I always wore a dress with shorts underneath it because I wanted to be modest. The man who molested me, the neighbor, was my father's friend and a friend of my family's. He was a colonel in the Air Force. I told my mother and she spent a lot of time with me for a while afterwards, but she also said some damaging, unthinking things. First, she told me to take a bath, then she told me not to tell anyone—she said that this could ruin his whole career!

She told me about a similar experience that she had had when she was a girl, but without trying to help me understand the context, without showing me that it wasn't my fault, or trying to make me feel safe. It just seemed like a bizarre episode. It didn't make any sense to me, and I couldn't tell anyone, so it became something that was horrible and unspeakable. It grew in my mind and the significance of it grew. It could have been deflated if she had handled it differently.

I think she should have let me tell the police, even if they would have been terrible to me. I don't think they would have been, but they wouldn't have been more terrible than I was to myself.

It was painful and infuriating that nothing changed for anyone else. I saw his car; his daughter had been my best friend but I couldn't stand to be near her anymore, I thought somehow that it was her fault too. They went to our church. Every week after mass, my mother and my sister and I would go to the officers' club, where my sister and I would get milk shakes. On warm days we would sit outside there on the patio. But now, since he went there too, I would have to say, every Sunday, that I didn't feel like going, and I would walk home instead.

My parents continued to socialize with them, and one night my mother came home and said, "Guess who I danced with tonight," and she told me that she danced with him, and yes, she'd slow-danced with him. I was stunned and I still cannot imagine why she said that to me, but I can never ask her. I can talk about it to anyone else, it doesn't bother me at all, but not with her.

I was depressed for a long time after that—I was Catholic and felt I had committed a mortal sin. Everything around me told me that it was my fault. I couldn't bring myself to confess it; I couldn't tell a priest what had happened. Eventually, we moved away. I had nightmares for about five years, and when I was sixteen, I finally told my best friend. Once the assault was out of the realm of the unspeakable, I could deal with it. But it would have been much easier and much less damaging if someone had been there when I was ten years old.

Sometimes I think about finding him now and writing to him, or exposing him, but I don't know, he's gone, he's far away, he's old, he's very old now.

· · ·

My mother is very much into the concept of having a daughter to pal around with. I resent that because it seems to me that all she is interested in is that some kind of *form* is adhered to—it doesn't matter at all what the substance is. She talks constantly, incessantly! about any detail of her life: what she ate for breakfast, what she said to the waitress, what shoes she was wearing, how she feels about her boyfriend biting his fingernails, the pants that he wears—but when I start to tell her about some land I am looking at to buy, she says, "O.K., well, I've got to go now."

I was a teenager before I discovered any faults in my mother. Now she drives me crazy. She is insecure, critical, submissive, and bitchy. She doesn't stand up for what she believes in. She will do anything to avoid confrontation and she has taught me all of that, all of those awful traits, and I will probably always struggle with them. The thing that I like about her is her kindheartedness. She is typical of lots of Americans, I think, in that her politics are conservative and nationalistic, but whenever she is faced with an individual who is suffering, she is human and generous and loving. She just can't make the conceptual leap between her politics and daily life.

I'm trying to accept the fact that our relationship will always be limited and flawed, but it makes me sad. I used to be resentful: I resented her like you resent an old lover who has disappointed you by being human.

There is a tremendous amount of tension in the air whenever we are together, but if I refer to it—if I say, "I wish that we could get along better"— she looks at me with a blank face. She cannot recognize it. Recently, as I've become more removed, I try to sympathize with her. She's very critical of other people, to make herself feel better. (She's not very intellectual, and she feels the deficiency.) Very common, I do it too. But finally, I have to accept the fact that my relationship with her is limited, will always be limited. I guess I'm disappointed that we can't really be close, that we don't really have anything to say to each other.

My sweetheart's mother, on the other hand, is someone I can sit down and really talk to. She's smart, she's a feminist, she's involved and interested in the world around her and what's happening. It's fun. So that's filled in the gap for me. I'm lucky in that way, although in some way, it just throws up the futility and sadness of the relationship with my mother all the more.

· · ·

I don't like getting older. I'm almost thirty years old; I find that I'm changing, my body is changing. I don't have that robust pink twenty-year-old look anymore and I don't like that, I don't like it at all. I didn't expect it to bother me so much and I'm hoping maybe it's just because I'm twenty-nine and that it's a transition that I can get used to and age gracefully, but so far I'm not handling it too well.

I remember when my mother first started menopause, all of a sudden within a few years she started looking older. I was in high school at that time and one day I was home for lunch and she was in the bathroom and she was standing in front of the mirror and pulling the skin of her face back toward her ears and peering at herself very critically and muttering about how she was getting wrinkles and saying, "If only I could tape it, I think I could get it to stay back." I thought that was pretty sad, and have always remembered that scene. I can empathize with it and her. In fact, I find as I get older, the idea of plastic surgery doesn't seem so disgusting to me anymore. I wouldn't admit that to very many people.

I think, of course, part of the problem is that we don't have any images of older women that we can look up to in our society. What I'm trying to do for myself is to pay attention to women I admire, like Doris Lessing, who are older women, to focus on them and see how they have aged.

The things I admire most about women are our ability to nurture, our empathy, our sense of connectiveness. I consider myself a feminist, although I don't relate to any of the official women's groups. I used to, but found myself thinking that there were certain ways I was "supposed" to act that were correct or certain ways that I should dress or certain things that I should say, and it became oppressive.

The most important thing to me now is freedom. I think feminism had an important role in leading me to that point, kind of a jumping-off point. I now see that it's been an evolutionary thing—feminism, the idea of freedom, change, social change—but my combined belief system isn't stagnant, my values are always changing and evolving.

For instance, I used to have this belief about women working, that it was important that women were able to define themselves through their jobs and do important work. Now I wonder how I could have possibly believed that, because I never had a job that was valuable, a job that reflected any of my ideals. I was a bartender, once I filled out claims for insurance companies, stupid jobs, women's jobs, and yet I had this very bourgeois "*Ms.* magazine" type of mentality that said somehow that was supposed to be important. That *is* important for a small number of women, but it's not important for me and for most women. We don't find fulfillment through our jobs.

Another thing is that always, before I had a child, I was very much pro the day-care system and believed women should go on with their lives and carry on after they had children just as they had before. But now I believe very much that someone should be home with the child, some important person, not someone who is being paid, but some important person who is there because they have a commitment and because they love that child. I think generally that's the mother because of just the breast-feeding function of nursing, although I don't see any problem with the father doing it, and ideally it should be more than just one parent. But anyway, my whole belief about what the home is and the function of the home and the influence of the home has changed. Our separating the world into public spheres and private spheres, putting all the emphasis on the public and having the home be this little isolated unproductive box where nothing is done but just to rest in order to get back out into the work sphere, is ridiculous and very straight, very patriarchal. I like the home to be a place where there is life and activity and productivity and things are really happening, an important place.

I feel like I have to struggle a lot of times with this attitude within myself that what happens here within my house isn't as valid as what happens there outside in the world, like what happens at John's workplace, and that's an attitude that not only I have but my friends too, it's all around me.

I guess that if you looked at my life in a superficial way you could say that I am right now, anyway, very traditional, but the kind of feeling I have about myself and the kind of possibilities that I see for myself are different than they would have been if there was no women's movement. The women's movement has helped me to love myself, probably the most important thing, the most profound thing one could ask.

7

I am a black woman, thirty-two, intelligent, college-educated, humorous, loving, kind, generous, fun, responsible, sensitive, honest, cautious, capable of hurting, ambitious, determined, stubborn, sarcastic, defensive, friendly, sexy, sensual, and loyal! I am presently overweight, but working on it—for *me*.

I want most to fulfill the potential that I have. I want to look in the mirror and say, "You're all right, woman. You've set goals. You've accomplished some and you're actively working toward the others. You're O.K.!" (I hate my present job—I'm not using my abilities, or making the money I'm worth, no chance for promotion.)

My greatest achievement so far is being able to help hold my marriage of five years together—working and growing (slowly) in spite of great setbacks and obstacles. We still love each other, even with the difficulties—and looking at this world and the people we know, that's saying a lot! My greatest crisis was having to have my baby aborted because it was in my tubes. I was four months pregnant and it was a boy. We already had his name. I wanted to give up active participation in life—not commit suicide, just stop living.

Now we live in a juvenile facility with six male juveniles as our charges. We have full responsibility for their day-to-day well-being. Therefore, I am a domestic (ugh) and he does the errands (doctor's extracurricular, meetings with probation officers, school entries, etc.).

Our salary is paid to us on a 50-50 basis (equal pay works here, since the house mothers complained a year ago about the 75-25 split set up originally). My husband spends more than I (he gets to get out of the house more and this is where he becomes self-centered and undisciplined). He spends his money and part of mine because he does not budget and stick to it. It has adversely affected our relationship in that I paid bills and he made bills, but did not pay them. Our credit has been damaged. We have recently agreed to a new arrangement where I will get all the money, pay him a weekly amount plus gas, and be responsible for all bill paying and savings.

I consider him my best friend. The worst part of marriage is that one has to always consider the other. I can't just decide to go out with the girls and go. I feel obligated to call my husband and say I'm going such and such a place and I'll be home around such and such time. Not because I have to, but to keep him from worrying and keep him informed.

At home, we have shared all household chores, although I tend to take "territorial rights" over the kitchen because I enjoy that area of the house. He takes "territorial rights" over furniture rearranging in all rooms.

We originally agreed to get married because we were expecting a baby and we were living together, so we agreed to legally tie the knot (sounds like a trap, shouldn't have written that)! However, we lost the baby before we married. I guess we decided we might as well go on. I don't know if I'd do it again, I didn't mind just living together. But I plan to stay married, because I take commitments very seriously and there is no reason not to stay married to my wonderful man. He may not be the best, but he's the best I've found.

I have never had sex with any other man since I've been married, nor do I plan to. He has only had one affair that I am aware of to a certainty, because he told me after it was over, although I suspect he has had others. For the most part it does not upset me because I don't worry about it. It becomes an issue for me only if I start feeling he is taking me for granted or neglecting me.

Having grown up meeting my father's mistresses, I never had any illusions or expectations that my husband would relate sexually to me only. It would be nice if he had sex with me and me alone, but I wouldn't be surprised if he went to bed with another woman. I was close to my father, and he shared his secrets (infidelities) with me. I was the shield he used to get out of the house away from my stepmother when he was "stepping out" with his lady friends. The places he took me were to his mother's and his many different "women's" houses. I loved him, but with the mistresses using me, I did not respect him.

Anyway, I learned at the age of twenty-two to forgive my parents for their faults and to accept them as the imperfect human beings they are. I hope all children learn to forgive their parents for not being everything we children wish they (parents) were.

． ． ．

I was happiest with my husband and closest on our honeymoon. It lasted four days and it was fantastic! But I was most deeply in love when I was twenty-five with another man. It felt like heaven and hell. He was complicated. He was emotional, adventurous, hardworking, determined, inexperienced in committed relationships, immature in being caring, trusting, non-jealous, achievement-oriented, open to new ideas, and searching and experimenting with who he was and who he wanted to become.

He wanted to search for greener pastures and put me on hold just in case he didn't find any. I wouldn't degrade myself this way after having declared my total commitment to him. We had lived together for a year, but he wasn't satisfied with me. It took me a year to get him out of my heart. To forget him, I worked as a volunteer to befriend an ex-offender, was a Big Sister, set up a series of workshops for college students on various subjects, joined a spa and attended three nights a week, fasted for six weeks, jogged a mile every day, and took graduate classes in the evening. I can't remember the last time I felt so fulfilled and proud of myself! Then I met my present husband and he offered me the emotional security I wanted from a man. But that was the last time I loved without reservation, without holding back, and so freely.

I also had one other devastating breakup during college. My boyfriend then just came up to me at a party and said he wanted to split up because I was too fat. I wanted to crawl in a hole and die. I still had to work with him every day all summer long. He even started dating my ex-roommate and they had the nerve to ask me "if I would mind them dating"—as if it mattered how I felt. I was the model of composure at school and work (they both worked where I worked) but when I went home I cried myself sick. On the weekends, it was even worse. I thought my heart would bust from pain sometimes, but I learned that even though I felt like dying, a broken heart doesn't necessarily kill.

Men place too much importance on weight. I've always been overweight or big. I'm a big woman. I was big when they met me, but it seems the deeper the involvement, the greater my weight becomes a problem for them. My husband is the only man who I knew up front didn't like fat women, but he married me, and he's been patient, though no less vocal. He sees it as a problem I must conquer by myself, with little or no help or support from him.

After being five and a half years with my husband, I'm just now beginning to expose myself sexually. Two years ago I told him I masturbated. Five months ago I masturbated simultaneously with him. Two months ago I clitorally stimulated myself during intercourse. But I haven't yet told him in detail what to do to please me, or asked him to finish me off after he's through. That takes a lot of guts. Booze helps me open my mouth but the next day I can't believe what I told him. Like, I can't believe I told him that I had orgasms in the bathtub under the faucet. When he asked me, I said, "So what, I'm not the only one," and I showed him the Hite Report on other women who did. He was astonished, to say the least. I was totally red, super embarrassed.

I like sex as often as the mood hits me, which changes from day to day. Sex is important, but not a panacea. It doesn't make up for lack of money, abusive behavior, lack of common goals, etc.

My most recent fight with my husband had to do with him playing head games. He was telling me that our things in storage were in jeopardy because the place they were stored had been broken into. I asked him what he had done about it, and he said he didn't care about that junk anyway. I went crazy because he had recently been on a spending, going-out, socializing spree leaving me to take full responsibility for everything. I got very angry and told him he was treating me like a pair of comfortable old shoes. He then went to the car and brought in about six or seven boxes.

Then I *really* flew off the handle, because it became clear he was just testing me. I told him to find some bitch in the street to play dumb games with but not to ever test me for my reactions by being nonchalant about the things we have worked hard and sacrificed for. He was surprised at my vehemence and my revelation of feeling neglected and asked how long I had been holding that in. I told him he had been too busy to allow me a chance to express my feelings. He listened, though. I even got through to him so that we were able to discuss and change our finances so that I would manage the family money. It was worth the few minutes of yelling.

But talking is depressing when I am not getting through. In general, when I try to talk to my husband, he doesn't take the time to really hear and understand what I mean. He uses information that I give him about things that disturb me about myself or are a problem for me and throws it back in my face during an argument to best me.

My friendships with women are not like this at all. We generally let our hair down and say exactly what we think and can share ourselves and know we have each other's ear. We communicate. It is harder to talk to my lover because of egos, pride, being called too sensitive, being turned off when something critical is said. My friendships have been the most enduring parts of my life.

Giving love is easier for me now than when I was younger, because I've learned to love and respect myself more now. I've learned to like my husband in spite of the things about him that I don't like, and to love him for who he is. I love his smiles (he's stingy with them), his aggressiveness, his gentleness. My favorite love story is *Their Eyes Were Watching God*, by Zora Neale Hurston. It is a book written by a black woman who created it during the "Harlem Renaissance" era. It's the first black love story I ever read—about black people living, loving, being strong, being hurt, survival, caring and feeling.

I like the perseverance of our relationship through many ups and downs, our ability to work very well together when we get past our pettiness, and I like our intimacy—emotional, spiritual, and mental. I'm happy except for some things; I'm unhappy with my husband's interest in cocaine (not hooked, but loves it) and his tendency to be chauvinistic. He is unhappy with my weight, as I said, but overall he is happy with me as a person except for my occasional sarcasm and defensiveness.

Our biggest problem is financial. It can be better if my husband would recognize that I am the more competent financial manager in the family and allow me to be in charge of the money flow, with his status being more as a consultant in terms of making decisions. I was financially dependent on my husband for two months once and it was a miserable experience. I hope never to experience it again. It did affect my relationship because I didn't feel free to ask for money (my reservation). When I couldn't stand it any longer, I got dressed and told him to take me to the employment office. We found a job as a couple and started working the following week.

I'm a feminist but still feel the women's movement excludes black women in a fundamental way. White women have an agenda that is different from black women's in that it has as priority those things which are not necessarily priority to many black women. We share commonalities but our starting places are different. I grew up in a female household, so the women's movement was always a part of me.

I love my femininity. I define it as being a predilection to combine intelligence and emotion to its finest. Being feminine means being able to cry for the starving, the homeless, the poor, and the pleasure of being able to see a beautiful sunset. It also means working to relieve poor social conditions without expecting gratitude. It means combining the frivolous, the unimportant with the building of great buildings or the creation of great art forms. It's the complexity of a woman who is a successful businesswoman and a great friend. I enjoy beautiful things. I agonize over what shade of lipstick and nail color to wear. I don't spend as much time as I need to on my looks right now; my clothes are disgraceful, but I'm losing weight, which is pepping me up.

I have loved my husband most. I have learned to cope with things in our marriage I swore I would never put up with. I am truly committed in a way I never thought I would be. Although not all the things I've looked for in relationships or all the kinds of love I want have come yet, I'm still hopeful and working on it.

8

I picked for a husband a man who was, frankly, a dummy, because in him I could instill knowledge about me, my needs and desires, as writing onto a blank page unspoiled by misinformation. I chose a man with a good steady job, and a distaste for cheating developed in a previous marriage—his wife had the other man's child less than four months after the divorce. I warned him if he ever hit me I'd leave him, because it's like with dogs biting (once they learn they can physically do it, they'll do it again . . . someday), and his reaction told me he didn't believe men had a right to strike—even if the woman hit first, and hit hard.

My husband is not stupid, but he is naïve. He's slow to catch on, and his life revolves to a great extent around his penis—that's all right. He's honest and true blue, as faithful as a groundhog, endlessly patient and kind, and lets me do as I want. I took advantage of him, and he was glad for the crumbs I gave him, never complained and never so much as raised his voice against me, let alone struck me. I was so endeared by his unfailing devotion, and so impressed by his character and strength and determination, I fell in love with him. He's a much better person than I am, and for that I bring all my know-how to bear to solve his problems, without seeming to (so that he won't feel inadequate), I protect him and keep him safe as best I can from actual physical dangers and from illness and tooth decay, and I try to teach him how to better communicate with people and understand what makes them "tick." I do everything I can for him, and I would never intentionally hurt him. I would never betray him. Even though he wouldn't know, maybe, I would know. He deserves the best, and so I'm the best I can be.

I believe in monogamy, and I have never had sex—not so much as held hands—with another since I started dating my husband. Life is complex enough, and either you are married or you aren't. To make a marriage work, you need fidelity. More so today, in a world of somewhat relaxed morals, you need to know you can turn your back and nothing "funny" is going to go on behind it. We know we can trust each other. I want him to be monogamous, because you know things about each other no one else in the world knows. However, I must look elsewhere for someone to meet the needs of my mind, my curious spirit which seeks to know all things knowable, learn all things. I enjoy and need to have long involved discussions on a variety of complex subjects, and my husband just isn't up to that.

I have been married almost five years. I'm twenty-four. We have no children—neither of us wants any—and we are quite happy. I have been called sophisticated, "obviously expensive, but properly understated." I am educated—not just from books and about *things,* but from life and about people. I am quite independent and strong-willed. My love, my husband, is steady as a rock. *Friends,* I've found, are not dependable. They can declare unending loyalty, and drop you like a hot potato.

I am satisfied by the way he loves me, and charmed by it as well—his devotion is unquestioning and his admiration of me inspires me to be, as much as I can, as good and wonderful and true as he believes in his heart that I am. He makes me feel good about myself. That is feeling loved, surely! We tell each other we love each other in the way we say "good morning," "good night," "see you when you get back," "I see you're 'down' and want you to know you are loved, in the hope the reminder will help," "it's a lovely day, isn't it?" Tone of voice and expression of face, context, denote what is meant. I have come to accept it, and I feel very maternal, protective. I love him passionately and reverently now.

I try to be as beautiful and seductive—i.e., desiring of my husband—as I can be as my contribution to the building up of my husband's ego. I do it for him, as a gift, and I do it for myself, as a boost because I like the way he looks at me. I don't feel, however, that I *have to.*

Right now, he works forty hours a week and brings home the entire paycheck and I give him an allowance. I have complete control of the money—and therefore the responsibility for our financial condition and progress in investments. We have a dishwasher, and more often than not he loads and unloads it; I cook—he doesn't know how, though I'm teaching him little by little because no one, in my view, should be so helpless! "What if something happened to me?" I said. "You'd starve, or be forced to eat out constantly."

Every once in a while I like to pick up a few extra dollars ghost writing, proofreading, and editing, and when I'm working I insist on some help around the house. At first it was a struggle, but he is getting better at it and is even taking an interest in the condition of the house as something *he* can personally do something about, not just as something that *somebody* (me) ought to take care of. I am also taking a class or two out at the college—that's the main way I feed my hungry mind—and so I am never "idle."

What I like best is that I can depend on him; he's there, both physically and mentally/emotionally. It seems unkind to say it, as I am well compensated for this lack in other areas, but he does not meet my intellectual needs. I *can* talk with him about anything, but many subjects which interest me and/or which I may be somewhat of an authority on are frankly over his head and uninteresting to him. He listens as politely as possible for as long as he can stand it when I speak of things beyond his scope of interest and comprehension. He also talks about the things which interest him—a lot of which bore me, alas. But when we get on the subject of sex, people, life, animals, or food, we get along wonderfully and can communicate freely and endlessly. This is enough. I have never heard of, or seen, a better love than this one. We are both happy with each other—not hysterically happy, just *happy.*

Basically, our daily schedule is like this: he gets up and goes to work—his clothes are coordinated by me the night before so he always looks his best—comes home and has dinner. I get up in the morning, dress—I coordinate my own clothes after doing his—on to class, or study at home, exercise and dance, start dinner, and he comes home and we eat together. We seldom watch the news—too depressing. I write, read, watch TV, and he listens to his radio, and maybe watches a little TV with me. I study, and he cleans up the kitchen, and we clean the birdcage. (We have a parakeet.) We do the laundry together once a week, shop for food together, and set aside two evenings per week for making love. The schedule is not rigid, it is flexible, but it serves as a base and keeps things organized. He irons his clothes and I iron mine. I sew on the occasional button, and he takes out the trash, gets the mail, and checks the oil. Daily life is comfortable, peaceful, often fun—sometimes we go window shopping and sometimes we take long drives in the country.

Any money that is his or mine is *ours,* the money goes into a joint account. I control the money, and therefore am responsible for our financial situation at any given time. Although he has the legal right to spend our money, he never does without asking if we can afford X amount. *Together* we pay *our* bills—I am the one who actually writes the checks—and we save a little. If we want something and there's enough left to buy it, we buy it—or if he wants some-thing, or if I want something, it may be bought from our common fund. This is fine with me, and the only way I could stand it. I could not stand not knowing our exact financial situation, and not having control of it. I could not stand to be given an allowance by a man who controlled and managed the money.

I could, in fairness, stand a situation in which we together sat down and did the "book work," but I'm glad my husband isn't interested, so that I don't have to consult him or even explain anything to him because it's simpler and easier to just do it myself and be done with it. I know what I'm doing and where everything is, and I can breeze through it—if I had to do it with him, or explain to him what I was doing or had done, it would be time-consuming and difficult because he doesn't understand many things about finances. Before we got married he had to have a business manager and an accountant. I'm guilty, with my husband, of what I've criticized men for, withholding important informa-tion—i.e., when I take a financial loss in an investment, I don't tell him about it.

This is going to sound like a fairy tale, but we've never fought. I've berated him once or twice, when he said he'd cleaned the bathroom and I went in and found the trash hadn't been emptied and there were curly hairs in the sink. (Don't fuckin' tell me it's clean when it's not! And if you can't bring yourself to do the job *right*, say so and be done with it!) He has never so much as raised his voice to me. He doesn't argue. He listens and thinks, and we talk things out with love and humor.

He seems to think I'm an encyclopedia, however, and that gets annoying when we have a fine reference library—my collection, which he is free to use and which I've shown him how to use. How would you like to be balancing the checkbook and have someone come in and want to know if cockroaches sleep?

When I had been married about two years, I suddenly realized what the creeping feeling I'd been having for, oh, several months was: I would rather die, literally, than hurt my husband, his pain was my pain, his life was my life, his welfare was more important than my own, his health, his happiness, every-thing about him mattered so much that he was—and still is—the most impor-tant person, the most important thing in my life. I was always a "me first" person until then, scratching and digging my way up, absolutely ruthless—not violent, but cunning and unscrupulous—and at first I was mad at myself for allowing myself to fall in love with my husband, a man I'd married because he could provide me with a good living—and I wouldn't, don't, have to work—and because he seemed easily enough manipulated, controllable, "trainable."

Women, in this society, still need financial support. Nowhere that I know of does a women make as much as a man, even for the same job when she has the same skills and/or qualifications, and despite all the lip service to "equal pay for equal work." I don't make enough money with what I do to support myself—I mean the basics of food, clothing, and shelter—and I have no medical insurance except through him, which comes through his company and his job, so there is no way I could keep my part of it if we broke up. I try not to think too much about this, because it makes me nervous. I'm taking a gamble that he will stay with me "unto death," and if he does not, I may be—depending on when and whether or not I make a lot of money in the meantime— desperately broke.

It certainly affects the relationship. I don't dare take him for granted now, or cheat, or fail to watch him closely for signs of discontent. He has a hammer over my head, though I don't believe he is consciously aware of it yet, and it keeps me "in line"—in addition to love, which I feel for him and which makes me *want* to make him happy.

. . .

Before I got married, I loathed sex; I felt it was something a woman had to put up with. Now, I'm hopelessly addicted—I love it! With my husband. (It's true, what they say, that it is the "quiet ones" you've got to watch out for!) During sex, he is reverent, and then bold and says exactly what he wants, and then back to reverent, and then bold again. I always orgasm, unless I choose not to—which I sometimes do for the purpose of concentrating fully on his pleasure, as a pure gift. I orgasm with his penis inside my vagina—because he likes to feel the contractions, and the presence and pressure of his penis inside me adds depth to the orgasm—by using my fingers at my clitoris, rubbing it gently on one side and then the other, with little up-and-down motions.

I hesitate to put the word "worst" in the same sentence with any statement about my sex life, but if there would be anything that could improve it would be his assertiveness in bed. The best thing about sex with my husband is his lack of macho. He isn't afraid his "manhood" will be somehow damaged if I get on top—in fact, he rather likes this position (with me sitting on him) because he can feel and tease my breasts that way.

I found sex a big disappointment when I first started having it and up until I got to know my husband really well—about one and half years after we were married. It was boring, silly, and sometimes even revolting. But, with my husband, I began to see that my pleasure truly excited him. So I moved and participated instead of just lying there quietly, letting him "do as he wanted"— and this made him feel good and worthwhile as a person, and as a husband. The sights and sounds and smells of a live person taking pleasure in *him* excited him tremendously. The men I slept with before were woefully ignorant of how to please a woman, female anatomy.

The first time I had an orgasm with another person, it was with my husband, with him sucking and nibbling gently on my nipples and me stimulating my clitoris by hand. It was after we'd been married for about a year and a half. One day he said he wanted to know why I disliked sex so much. He was sincerely interested in doing something about it. I was surprised and pleased by his reaction, and we began with the basics, my showing him, lights on, what was really down there, and what I did to it to make that feeling happen.

Now I usually orgasm by my own masturbation during intercourse. It was hard to do the first time after a lifetime of conditioning that (1) masturbation is "self-abuse" and (2) it was saying the man wasn't good enough. But I enjoyed it, and so did he, so we figured, being consenting adults, we could, would, and should do whatever feels good and works for us. So much for the training of childhood.

Besides sex, I *love* to be hugged in bed. I lie on my right side and he is behind me, also on his right side, with his left arm holding me. We do this a lot.

. . .

As a child I was dressed in navy-blue skirts and white blouses and sensible shoes. I had buckteeth and straight hair. I felt ugly, and the other children always made fun of me. I was an A student. I didn't have any friends, so I had lots of time to study. But when I grew up, I studied the art of makeup and hairstyling, and developed a style of dress that was conservative, respectable, and dignified—I wear cream-colored linen suits, silk blouses, and four-inch heels (I have great legs!). I had my teeth fixed.

I was not close to either parent—my grandmother was the one who held me. My mother had troubles of her own so consuming she hadn't the time or strength to devote herself to me. My father was repulsive (he belched, broke wind, and was generally obnoxious). He didn't know me, I hardly knew him. He never touched me except to beat my backside and legs with his belt when my mother told him I'd been "bad."

He also told me if I ever "did it" he'd disown me, after beating me for "it." My mother told me, when my periods began, that I could "get into trouble," so never let the boys "touch me." What did all this mean? Father (translation): If you are not a virgin when you marry, you will disgrace me, yourself, and this family, and I'd kill you for it if I could, but since I cannot do that I will beat you, forget you were ever born, cast you out of my life forever. Mother (translation): Boys will try to have pleasure with you, *use* you, and if you get pregnant, you will be disgraced, no man will want you. Don't let them do that to you! Make one of them *marry* you to get sex!

I left home at fifteen, got my own place, a job, and severed all contacts with my parents. My adventures included: The milkman who gave me herpes (or, that is, I found out later I had herpes). Then I was lunchtime amusement for a man who lived alone but was "married" in his mind or heart or somewhere to a married woman who was waiting for kids to grow up to divorce her husband. Also, when I was fifteen, I had a "one-night stand" with a fellow who was having problems at the time with his live-in girlfriend.

I believed in my late teens there was no such thing as love, and that men and women got married and cheated on each other and gave lip service to love and caring when they couldn't feel anything. I was lonely, and I grew cold. Paul Simon's song "I Am a Rock" was "my song," because it says exactly how I felt. I didn't believe there was any real love in the world—just people using people—and I didn't want to live like that.

I found in dating that the man would take love seriously at first, but then move on to the next expectation: women are property, women are for sex, and there are lots of women. Love is idealized in the beginning, and then cauterized.

. . . .

Now, I am in love with my husband. He is my best friend, my lover, my companion, my heart and soul. He is a part of me, and I am a part of him. He is the most important person in the world to me. Still, he is not the center of my life. It's a paradox. I don't know how to explain it.

I love being in love with him. It gives me a reason to live, someone to share with. Love is pleasure, comfort, peace, warmth, security, truth—noble. It's the only thing in life worth doing, at the base of it. Love, unlike hate, or even indifference, is limitless, positive, and worthwhile.

Our differences? They're not so important. My husband isn't an intellectual, and I am one. We have a relationship in which he defers to me without being subservient. Sometimes I think it would be nice to have a man my intellectual equal or better, until I remember that because of culture and that very knowledge he would possess, such a man would be a pain to live with because he would feel the need to dominate me.

Now, looking around—as a matter of curiosity only, as to just what is in the "market" now—I see some men that if I were single I would like to get to know more about. They are all, like my husband, older than I am, established with careers, dark, trim, and neat, but not skinny. Unlike my husband, they are intellectuals, more my mental equals (in some cases, superiors). I wouldn't really want to marry one of them, however, as I fear they would try to "own" me and tell me what to think.

I like things as they are. We are alike and we are different. My husband has "horse sense," and he functions in daily life well enough. We are fantastically and wonderfully close emotionally and enjoy a tremendous sexual life. With him, I can be relaxed and just give and give and give. It seems like the more I give him, the more love I want to give.

9

I am a forty-five-year-old homemaker. I have one child at home, a boy age fourteen with problems including hyperactivity and learning disabilities. My husband and I have been married almost twenty-five years. My stepdaughter is twenty-nine, married. I'm also a stepmother of two boys. I hate housework!

I have worked outside the home, but not in fifteen years. I was an assistant advertising manager at our local weekly newspaper. I would love to get back into newspapers again. I am also a college dropout. When younger, I had many more friends than I have now. At times, I feel very isolated. I have a quick temper and anger easily.

Somehow I am trapped in my own house. How did that happen to me? When I became pregnant a few years after being married, I had just reached the freedom of not needing a babysitter for my thirteen-year-old stepdaughter anymore. I knew that having a baby would mean less freedom for me. I gave up my job on the paper that I loved. Maybe with it I gave up—as it turned out—my chance to have independence for the rest (?) of my life. Financially, I gave up a lot. How would my life have been different? Wow! No one can ever know, but I'm quite sure I would no longer be married to this man. I gained mainly economic security and a great number of material things, such as color TV, a kitchen TV, dishwasher, electric dryer, new appliances, etc. These do not make me happy—just more comfortable and spoiled to the point where I'd find it very hard now to live without these material things. My therapist is helping me to build up a small savings of my own.

I do not plan to stay married, but I have no time frame as to when it'll be over, except when my son is no longer living at home. He is now almost fifteen but is so immature I can't say how long he'll live at home. I hope to be free by the time he is eighteen. What I'm trying to say is that sometimes the stress of having such a child overwhelms me.

Still, last fall my son was suddenly hospitalized sixty-five miles north of our home. During the first two weeks, I wrote in my journal that I felt I'd lost my role—as a mother. That was the primary way I'd defined myself for fourteen years. Suddenly with my son no longer at home, without even his dirty laundry to wash, I was like a ship without a rudder. Never mind that many times I had felt overwhelmed by dirty laundry—I do even now. The loss of my "job" caught me off guard. I could barely get out of bed in the morning, and when I did I felt I had nothing purposeful to do.

My husband and I fight most about sex and our son. I frequently lose control and become unreasonable, sometimes during the fight I feel out of control, depending on how upset I get. When the fight is about sex, it usually ends with my husband saying "forget it," and he goes to sleep and I go do my dishes or whatever. Sometimes I don't know the next day if the fight is still on or not. He can go to bed mad and sleep fine, and since he goes to work before I'm up, we don't see each other in the a.m. Sometimes my husband will yell, during a fight, that he wants me and/or my son out of the house by the time he comes home from work the next day. I never believe him and carry on with my day's scheduled activities. Usually my husband will apologize, either with an a.m. phone call or at night after work. If I feel I've been wrong, I'll also apologize.

My husband every so often says, "It's all mine—everything here—I earn all the money." This used to hurt me very much until I mentioned it to a therapist who told me it was a very stupid thing for my husband to say. He thought my husband should realize "it's a partnership—that the wife provides services that can be counted in as . . ." (I forgot the rest.) I tried this out on my husband tonight as he discussed divorce settlements of his two divorcing nephews. I think maybe the partnership idea may have sunk in. This part of the financial agreement definitely affects our relationship.

I'm trying to look at it in a different way so as not to feel as if I'm the subservient one. I have begun saving leftover money from groceries, then my father gave me $500 for a birthday gift, and I put it in an account as an "escape hatch." My husband was furious when he found out, but I paid for his fiftieth birthday party (dinner for twelve friends and relatives at a restaurant) and $218 for his gift—a flight to Florida, with all the family.

I handle all the money. My husband comes home every Thursday, hands me the paycheck, and I give him back forty dollars for his allowance. I write all the checks. Even so, my husband does not see me as an equal. He leaves me out of almost all the decisions. I often learn of "our" vacation plans when he tells someone else in my presence.

The practical arrangements—I do the dishes, I also make the beds, cook the meals. I take care of our one child at least 85 percent of the time. What my husband does with him is mainly recreational or disciplinary. The few times I've gone out to a meeting at night and left my son home with my husband, I've come home to find my husband asleep on the couch in front of the TV. He was supposed to remind our son to make his sandwich for school the next day. So I always come home before the boy's bedtime. If the sandwich hasn't been made and I ask my husband about it, he is very hostile to me. At other times it is to my son's credit that he has remembered to make his sandwich.

If my husband tells me, "That was a good meal," somehow I don't feel very elated at the praise. Maybe it's because I really hate to cook—it's almost an effort for me, one that I must perform daily for at least six days a week. (We usually eat out Saturday nights.) Maybe it's my relationship with my husband—not a very good one. Pleasing him is not my goal in life. However, if he criticized my cooking (adversely), I used to get very hurt. Or if there's a bad family argument and no one eats the meal, I'm very upset because I think, "Here I slaved cooking this meal, and here's the thanks I get—no one eats it." This doesn't happen too often anymore.

Occasionally my husband will clean the living room—dust and vacuum. I first thought he was trying to embarrass me, since if the room was dirty, obviously I hadn't cleaned it. But soon I changed my attitude, possibly due to someone I heard on the radio, probably a feminist. It's his house too, and if the dirt bothers him, he can clean it. I don't say to him, "Thank you for doing 'my' cleaning"—because I don't think of it as my cleaning! My husband had tried shaming me into cleaning. He'd make comments on how dusty the coffee table was. I didn't react at all. But the next day I got out the furniture polish and cleaned the living room so everything shone. He never said a word of appreciation to show he even noticed.

I cleaned house thoroughly again recently because a Respite care worker for my son was due to meet with us at our home. Again my husband said nothing. I'm not the first wife to observe that families say nothing when wives do things right. It's only the bad things that get comments. This has led me to my present attitude toward housework: No one really appreciates it, so why break my neck? My house is pretty clean and we all have clean clothes when we need them and food for our bellies, but I don't enjoy housework and I'm sure I never will.

I'm also good with mechanical things. About two months ago my automatic washer stopped spinning during the spin-dry cycle. Faced with two foam pillows soaking in a nearby tub, I was pretty angry that the spin cycle refused to work. I banged the door a few times, as that had helped once before, but not this time. I called my father to ask if he had any ideas for fixing it. I did not ask him to come and fix it. He told me to check for a nail or a pin lodged at the bottom of the washtub. I checked and no nails. So I lifted up the heavy, awkward washer top and looked at the area where I thought the problem was. It looked as if a bracket holding wires had fallen off the hinge. I replaced it and *voilà!* My washer was back to spinning again! What a proud sense of accomplishment I felt. It's not often in my role as homemaker that I can get that feeling. There are few rewards to homemaking. I sure hope someday we homemakers get social security credit for our time spent at home working.

. . .

I believe in monogamy probably because of my upbringing. But I am not monogamous—and if you'd told me twenty years ago that I'd say that now, I wouldn't have believed you. There is a man I have loved for over fifteen years. My husband does not know of this affair at all. It began as a flirtation, with him as the aggressor. He'd always kidded the women in our little social group, a public service volunteer group consisting of his wife, my husband, and some others. One night after an evening out, we two couples returned to our house. We were always swapping dancing partners, so I danced with him, my husband and his wife dancing together. We were in the kitchen; they were in the living room, dancing to records.

Soon Jim decided to shut off all the light in the kitchen and his hands began to wander, and I guess he made what is called a "pass." He had had a very large amount of liquor and was quite inebriated, but not silly or disgusting—just passionate. I too had had a few drinks. I made no loud protestations to his wandering hands; it felt good. I did try to act a bit demure, whispering things like "Be careful, they'll come in from the other room and catch us!" He said, "How do you know they aren't doing the same thing?"

After that night Jim called me at home and said he'd like to come see me sometime. I hesitated, but finally let him come and see me at my house. He worked nights; my husband worked days. Jim made love to me in a way I never knew was possible. He was anatomically very different from the only other man I'd ever known intimately (my husband) and I was overwhelmed. He was always very tender, never "talked dirty" to me, though I knew he could. He never forced me to do anything I didn't want to do, but he was very persuasive and could always convince me of a reason for trying something new.

At the present time I still love him very much, but we no longer see each other weekly. The intervals have been as long as one year (he just didn't call me and I couldn't reach him). It is now anywhere from three weeks to maybe two or three months. Lately, I've done more calling of him.

At one point, he called me to tell me he was getting divorced and moving in with a woman. I asked, "Where does that leave me?" He answered, "I don't know, but you always knew there was no future in our relationship." I said, "I see," and hung up the phone. Then I cried and cried. My heart was broken, I was devastated. I put on the radio talk shows to try to get him out of my mind. (I was all alone in my house, as usual, with my son and husband at school and work.) The radio didn't help. I had difficulty sleeping, and when I was alone, I'd take naps and try to forget, but I could not sleep. Of course, I could tell no one. I began telling myself: "Forget him!" Every time he came into my mind I'd say the same thing. My husband heard via the "grapevine" that Jim had gotten a divorce and was living with another woman. I made some appropriate remark, greeting the news as if it were truly new to me, then went down in the cellar to my laundry room and cried again.

After three months I was just about getting over him when he called and asked if I'd be home that noon, as if nothing had ever happened. I told him how upset I'd been, but nevertheless I let him back into my heart and house again. I know I'm probably a fool, but I love him and whenever he wants me, I'm his. He's not staying away from me anymore, so we're right back where we always were. He did tell me he was very sorry he hurt me so.

Why can't I give him up? He makes me feel good about myself, he's good for my self-esteem. He accepts me totally, never making any derogatory comments about my body. I guess I am dependent on him for sexual satisfaction and emotional fulfillment, as well as the fact that he is about my only real friend that I can talk to. But I do try to play down any of my idiosyncrasies because, years ago, he said, "I could never live with you; you'd drive me crazy." That hurt me more than he ever knew.

I hope someday I'll have another relationship that will have a "future" in it for me. But for now this is it.

I'm still very unsure of myself sexually. Jim actually does call most of the shots, such as position. I tried once to position myself in such a way that I got more pleasure, but I was so awkward that I felt very uncomfortable and never tried it again. But I know I still like that position and once in a while he happens to use it and I enjoy it. But it's a variation of the one I tried that first awkward time. I guess this ties into a "feminist" question—do I have the assertiveness to ask for what I want in my sexual relationship? The answer is still no, unfortunately. I don't know why, chances are he wouldn't object if I made my views known as to what pleasures me. We are bound by a time limit now (his lunch hour) which rather limits time for experimentation. But as I write this, I'm convincing myself it's O.K. to ask for what I want, and maybe I will, the next time I see him.

. . .

Emotionally I worry that I am becoming as antisocial as my mother became in her later years. She actually would say, "Oh no, not more company, what are those people doing here?" My present therapist has asked me about my isolation and lack of friends, and I'm trying to do something about it. I don't make friends easily, especially in my present community. Some of my best friends of the past years have disappeared. They're my college friends and they've stopped writing to me. (I tried to get one girl to resume our writing friendship. I sent her a "fill in the blank," stamped, self-addressed postcard—she returned it with only the words "busy, busy, busy" scrawled on it, plus "good luck with your college course.") I need more local contacts. Even when I join classes or groups, I'm still a loner.

About two and a half years ago, I decided to go back to school (community college) and take a few courses with a view toward preparing for a job. I found I could not juggle housework, studying, child care, and personal life. The college-level work was quite grueling. It was a total change from being an eighteen-year-old college kid, unmarried and responsible only for my own personal needs. Now that I had a family, I found it very hard to schedule time for studying.

Somehow I did manage to write papers that got plaudits for my writing and I got a B for the course. But it was not a practical course aimed at the job market. On top of this, the teacher was a stickler for details, and suggested that next I take an English composition course to learn modern grammar and punctuation rules. So another fall found me registered for still another college course, and with no job in sight. I attended about five sessions of the class, wrote one or two papers, got the plaudits for my writing from the very dynamic, interesting, and oh so young instructor (male). Then he began talking about the research paper due December 1. I viewed this as totally irrelevant to my life and goals. I needed to get on with other, more practical courses—or not to take any more courses!

On the night just previous to the class I finally made my decision. I told my family I decided to quit. My husband did not say much, as usual. (I was paying for college with my own money, my small bank account, so he couldn't even say his usual "How much is this going to cost me?")

That night, after my family went to bed, I was all alone as usual, a time I usually value. It's the time I get my chores done—loading the dishwasher with supper dishes and washing my son's thermos bottles and lunch box. I always do this work with either the radio or the TV on, usually starting at 11:30 p.m. and Johnny Carson's show.

But this night all I could do was cry. I cried through Johnny's monologue, I cried through his whole show and on through the next show. Somehow I managed to get dishes in the dishwasher and the other chores done, but I was thoroughly miserable. All I could think of was that I was a failure. Finally, before this long night was over, I took a deep breath and resolved to get on with my life, even though it meant postponing thoughts of a career indefinitely. So this is where I'm at right now.

. . .

P.S. I've done the largest chunk of this writing on a night my son spent on a field trip with his class. In other words, when my son is not at home, I'm free to "do my own thing." I can be more myself. I wrote this tonight from 1 a.m. to 4:30 a.m. I guess I feel freer too when my husband is asleep.

10

My greatest achievement has been to complete all of my high school education, a goal I set myself when I became pregnant at fifteen and had to drop out of school. It was a personal goal that I was obsessed with, even though for years I held a good job working in telecommunications with electronics, making a great paycheck. I have even more educational goals now.

I was sixteen when I separated from my first husband. My family supported me, and my mother wanted me to stay with her, even with the baby. She welcomed me with open arms, she was very comforting. But I felt shame at such an embarrassing situation. I was fortunate enough to have a boyfriend, my husband now, who helped me out. It was still scary to leave home with a baby in tow, on your own at seventeen.

Our relationship was one of dependence on my part because of my situation. I felt that I owed him everything for taking on a child-woman with a child. I was not mature and did not choose my second husband well as a woman would do the second time around. I admired his qualities of being a good worker, strength (my dad was strong), and he was not a person who would treat you unfairly in money matters or non-support. I did not know that he would be a wife beater, because I'd never seen that in anyone. I thought that I deserved it, that I was bad and deserved all those beatings and verbal abuse. It wasn't until I was well into my twenties that I woke up.

My husband beat me off and on, up to almost two years ago. I hated my husband when he beat me. I told only two or three of my friends in the ten years of marriage. I loathed my husband for his cruel streaks. I have gotten revenge by taking a lover, but that was not my intent. I wanted to have someone to tide me over the feelings I'd lost for my husband, the respect was gone. I would never end the marriage, but he could and now it won't hurt as much.

I started completing my education through correspondence because I'd always held down a full-time job. I started to take a few night courses, when I worked steady days for a while, and I started to set goals. I also made my feelings known that I wouldn't accept any more beatings. (His father used to beat his mother.) I became a more independent person when I started to like myself more. I won a beauty contest and that made me more confident that all those people I worked with would vote for me. I was well liked and it made me think that I could certainly do better than this. I was determined to improve my marriage. He was worse when he drank, so I didn't ever discuss anything with him when he was drinking. He went to a shrink for a few months but he didn't like the answers that were coming back to him. He could not see his faults.

I believe in monogamy even though I have a lover outside my marriage. It is going on two years that I have been having this sexual relationship. The reason is simple. After my husband beat me for years and accused me of having affairs and then got involved with some friends of his, smoking pot, which he knew I was totally dead against, and kept going on fishing trips which enabled him to do this, I became more used to him away and started to find I didn't miss him.

One day, in spring, he went into one of his rages and ripped a whole handful of hair out of the back of my head. Luckily I have long thick hair and no one knew. I was already being "staked out" by a detective in the city who'd met me just once and taken quite a fancy to me. He was calling and talking to me under the pretense of business (I was a witness in a trial) and we became telephone friends. One day, he came over to the house and we just looked at each other, like two kids, and that was that. We were in each other's arms. He had more class than to seduce me in my house, so he said we'd better think about this more before we got involved. The next day, he took me to a motel and made the best love to me that I've ever experienced.

The affair hurts me because I can't be with my lover enough to see how we'd be other than in bed. I hate the deceptions, the fear of being found out, the fear that if I was with him, would he do it to me? I guess we'd never trust each other. I fell in love with my lover, and he didn't want to, but he fell in love with me too. He says he's scared of his feelings, and so am I. We're scared to hurt all these people, we just keep hurting each other instead. I feel exciting and confident thanks to my lover, and on the same level, I feel like nothing because he doesn't want me. I pretended not to love my lover when he said, "We weren't supposed to fall in love." What were we supposed to do?

My husband expects me to understand he is from a rotten home, but I don't understand why our home has to be a replay of his. He thinks it's an excuse to beat his wife, throw things, or abuse his home because that's left from his parents' home. We argue about my rights as a person to the same privileges as he expects as a man. I have the right to choose a career of my choice, and excel by means of courses, and as long as I pay my way, I don't see the problem. He says, "No wife of mine is going to work in an all-male environment ever." He thinks I'm a slut or something or he feels that insecure about himself.

My husband knows the necessity of my working, but he is always making sexist remarks like "When our mortgage is paid you could quit work." As if my job isn't important to me, which it is, extremely important to me. He thinks women are still in the days when they couldn't vote.

Our biggest problem is his feeling of disdain for women and that includes me. He finds women are stepping out of line when they do police work, high-technology jobs, or muscle jobs. He calls them cows or sluts on the road if they are driving and dare cross his path. He yelled and cursed me twice at work in front of people I work with because I was working in a man's environment one day.

I long for a relationship where each would feel equal respect for the other's career and personal goals. That trust would be great enough to allow friends of both sexes and no suspicions to creep into the relationship. I would like a feeling of friendship to be there and encouragement. I want praise and compliments and hugs and kisses.

We each keep our paychecks, and he pays the bills, I buy the food and save huge amounts for the mortgage and paying off the vehicle loans or any big purchases. One thing I like with my husband is running (five miles), skiing, and I like fishing with him, then sex, then dinners out or any holidays, trips, or drives. Anything that excludes conversation.

I like my husband's and my relationship when we are alone together, or on holidays. The worst is when he's working and I'm on swing shift. He is incredibly intolerable and nagging. He hates it because he can't control me as much when I'm opposite shift.

I hate his moods of depression, which I know are a mental problem. I fear his hostility in our arguments and his childish paths of destruction when I'm not doing everything the way he wants or if I've set a goal and he is dead against it. His jealousies and chauvinistic feelings against women, even in sports, are what would kill us, not my lover, or my job. My husband is a person who is jealous and possessive, even jealous of my goals, my course, anything that doesn't include him. My lover I can talk to and he compliments me, encourages my goals, and makes equal love to me.

I doubt I'll stay married, the odds are against it. Still, I feel my son prevents me from changing the course of my life now because I always have to consider the outcome with regard to his well-being. I've always had to think for two, not one.

I love my son, but he has no initiative in school or in his private life. I felt love for him as a baby and vowed to protect him and take good care of him. I made a point of reading to him every night for a little while, a half hour at least, until he was about eleven years old. Then we got him involved in sports until he was fourteen, when he lost interest. Still, he kept up his guitar and he has some satisfaction in that, but does not respond to anything his teachers say. He doesn't have the courtesy to call and ignores curfews and rules set up by this house.

*

I'm in better physical condition than I've ever been in. I'm only thirty-one and I feel young and sexy. I look at more men now, wondering what they'd be like in bed. Mostly cops, because of my lover, and also because of their mustaches, which turn me on. Sexually, my husband tells me what to do to his body to give him the most enjoyment. He does not tell me he loves me, that he finds me beautiful or desirable, or try to please me . . . but it's O.K. because my lover does.

My husband isn't interested in my orgasms, only his pleasure. I could perform fellatio and he was not at all enthusiastic about cunnilingus. I felt like I was boring him if I took too long to climax, so there I'd be masturbating in the bathroom, after or the next day. When I tried to discuss it with him, he became insulted: "Don't blame me because you've got a problem."

My husband satisfies himself as a rule and only lately (I have complained loud and clear) thinks I might like to orgasm, if only once a month. I enjoy sex fully and participate in it readily, eagerly. He says it excites him to see me masturbate in front of him, but he doesn't know I masturbate a lot because of him. I orgasm if I'm on top or in a position like 44 where I have contact with a certain spot with the tip of his penis. He doesn't like this. The worst thing about sex with him is that he is finished in five minutes flat and that's on a good night. My lover has the right touch, my husband's "arm gets tired," as does his tongue.

I have masturbated in front of my husband and he was turned on, and relieved he didn't have to exert himself. I resent his attitude totally. My lover is a big turn-on and I masturbate thinking of him, even when I'm with my husband.

I was loneliest when my lover got married. He didn't even tell me for two weeks and continued a sexual relationship with me. I felt the loneliest because I couldn't tell anyone. Just my best girlfriend and she had seen it coming. I felt betrayed, I felt that I'd not only lost my lover but my friend. I felt used. I wanted to die, but wouldn't.

My lover claims to love his girlfriend-turned-wife and yet he wants me forever. Maybe he has set aside a special place of pleasure for me, outside his life with his wife? I don't trust love anymore.

Sometimes, when I'm away from my lover, I think, why isn't my lover happy with the wife he took only one year ago? I just don't understand but I feel powerless to stop. Our relationship is sex, and excitement, and telephone sessions. We keep each other alive when everything else is falling down around our ears.

. . .

I would have loved high school if I'd been more secure. I was so afraid of the other kids. I didn't have a good enough home, so I felt beneath the other kids. I like writing, and got good marks. It was a great pressure to me to dress like them. We just didn't spend money on things like that. Living in the country, I couldn't join sports because of no ride back home if you missed the bus and nobody to come and get me.

I felt out of it, and that was one reason I got pregnant. A baby to love and me to be somebody special to. I guess children don't see life the way it really is. We think of immediate solutions. But I showed everybody that I could look after myself and my baby. That's a form of strength that won my father's respect and even my pessimistic brother-in-law's admiration.

Today, my mother and I can talk about anything in the world, she is so straightforward and honest with her feelings. We share poetry and stories and hurts and happiness. We had our clashes when I was growing up, I was not to be bossed. But when I ended up pregnant, my mom never deserted me, she stood by me as only another woman would do. I carry total woman-woman respect for her. She has always maintained that we are welcome to come home if our marriages failed, perhaps because she was lonely without my father. I respect her and I understand her.

My best woman friend is honest and makes me feel warm. I tell her my most intimate feelings and doings. I trust her totally. She would never tell and she would help me if I needed her. She is honest enough to tell me she hates what I'm doing (the cheating) and she fears for my life should my husband find out. She says that I should end my marriage if I want to sleep with someone else. She says she couldn't live with my husband. She hates my lover for causing me pain. She sees the tears sometimes and knows what I'm going through. We work together twice a week at a restaurant. I feel relaxed and happy with her. She is divorced and hasn't got a man at the moment. When she's not in a relationship, she can be very cold about my two relationships. That is annoying.

I admire the way women are taking the lead in jobs and in their future. I see them sticking up for each other and not settling for sexist remarks in the workplace or anyplace.

Men don't respect women enough. They treat us as if we are asses, tits, cunts, and legs, not even joined together! I hate it when they refer to us as dolls or broads, and I hate the way they lump us together as stupid. I like the way they open doors, those who still do, and I like feeling, sensitive men, strong and soft at the same time. But most of the time, a woman feels alternately loved, used, needed, and abused in sexual relationships.

I have picked violent men and male chauvinists before, but my lover is not like that. Or is he? He likes to have one woman for sex and excitement and then another woman he keeps for his wife. Neither of my relationships now fills an empty space inside me. I guess there is no one who could do that. It's been vacant too long.

I had to work very hard to overcome the problems of my marriage and keep the relationship going. Somewhere along the line I gave up. I kept myself together with other interests and have resigned myself to the fact that my husband will leave me if (1) I change jobs to a career on a male-oriented level, (2) I wear sexy clothes, (3) I make male friends.

Now, at thirty-one, I strive for an advanced education, higher goals. I study everything in sight and even though I still feel confident in my looks, I glow at praise from teachers' remarks on papers I've done. A 90–95 percent average is suddenly as all-important as "You could pass for twenty-one!"

I feel at the mercy of no one now. I accept myself and I am proud of myself in most areas. I'm not proud that I live with a man who's beaten me for so long, or that I sleep with a married cop who loves his wife. I'm proud that I can handle it.

Extramarital Sex and Affairs

Are Most Women Monogamous?

70 percent of women married more than five years are having sex outside of marriage—although almost all also believe in monogamy:

"I am happy with my husband. He is the solid, stable person I need, although seldom very passionate. Our relationship built up very slowly. It took me time to realize I did love him and could be happy with him. But the most passionate I have ever felt is in my relationship with my lover. This is a very physical love affair and we can never be with each other for long without wanting to make love."

"I had a fifteen-year affair that was intense and passionate. I was serious, he was too; we never considered breaking up our individual families, it was strictly 'extracurricular.' At first, I idealized him; now I am merely very fond of him, seeing him a little more realistically. He is lusty, uninhibited, and very stimulating in bed, besides which we have done lots of little things my husband was never interested in—driving around the countryside, dancing, ski club, working together. I guess he was sort of a hobby with me, it was fun and challenging to keep him aroused, interested, etc.!!! My husband has, I believe, never been 'unfaithful' to me. Knowing his lack of interest in sex, I would be astonished to find out he had ever indulged himself elsewhere. I would hate to be married to a promiscuous man; however, at this point, if my husband had a nice lover that provided him pleasure, I would not have any emotional objection. It would not upset our particular status quo."

"Strange, I believe in monogamy, but I am not monogamous. I have had extramarital affairs—one lover was with me for ten years. Right now there are three I see on and off. Nothing serious or heavy. Even a friend's husband, once, but too much guilt. Why? I need the variety. Sex with one man becomes boring. God forbid my husband should know! He is faithful, although he travels quite a bit, so I'm not one hundred percent sure. (It's not fair of me to wish he were faithful. Who am I to talk?)"

"It was all-encompassing. The person showed me how wonderful sex could be. He was caring and sensitive, then became demanding of my time. I gave it to him. My marriage fell apart because of this affair. It is still going on, but his marriage is back together again."

"Monogamy is a combination of all the things that love should include—respect, trust, honesty, love. But last year I had an affair. It was just sex. He was a guy we had gone to school with, who lived next door to us with his wife, and we did things together with them all the time. My husband worked, his wife worked. I stayed home with the kids, who were tiny, and he was unemployed. He liked me. I considered him a pest before our affair started, even though he made me laugh and we had good times together. I didn't get much out of the affair, maybe excitement. Sometimes revulsion. I think my husband is 'faithful' to me. He may have done his share of looking, and he was seen with a girl in the car with him when I was home with the baby, but I don't think he ever was sexually unfaithful."

"I have had extramarital sex and it was terrific. I didn't feel guilty at all, I was too busy enjoying it. If my husband suspected, he said nothing to me. The affair confirmed my sexuality and attractiveness to me. My husband is from the old school of thought when it comes to sexual relations. He does not perform manual or oral stimulation of my clitoris. I'm tired of being unfulfilled sexually. Many times I told him I wasn't satisfied, but he felt it was my problem, not his. So I did something about it. The affair was not serious emotionally but very heavy sexually, we really had a good time together."

Why Do Women Have Affairs?

The majority of women having affairs say they feel alienated, emotionally closed out, or harassed in their marriages; for 60 percent, having an affair is a way of enjoying oneself, reasserting one's identity, having one person appreciate you in a way that another doesn't:

"I had sex outside my marriage. I found a man who loved me and respected me. I had felt the same way about him for a long time, and never dreamed he felt anything but friendship for me. It was very short-lived but very serious. It made me feel lovable at a time when my self-confidence was at an all-time low."

"The affair is not something I am proud of. But I was close to this man—I got an affirmation from him that I was not able to get from my husband."

"The affair made me feel free to be me for the first time. It was exciting. I felt like he was my salvation. He truly cared if I enjoyed sex, not just his own satisfaction. I got high blood pressure out of it, but I also gained an inner feeling about myself—I could really express myself with him."

"In my outside relationships, I get real companionship, someone who doesn't care if the ironing is done or not, someone I can be a real person with."

"I have had several affairs—but only one for any duration. It lasted more than four years. I felt so unappreciated at home and was given 'love' and appreciation in the relationship. The effect on me personally was to build me up, support me, and help me to cope with my marriage."

"Believe in monogamy? What is it, a religion? A scientific theory? Monogamy is one of the ways a relationship can be lived. I have had sex outside our relationship, at a time when I was severely depressed, alienated from my husband, numb. I wanted to touch something alive that would touch me back, see if I could feel. It was that or lie down in a snowstorm and let it cover me."

"When I was married I had an affair, about the last two years. It was wonderful. It made me realize that I could be treated as a person with intelligence and as an equal. My ex-husband did not make me feel this way. The person I had an affair with was also a wonderful lover. It is now eight years or so later and we still keep in touch."

"I am a homemaker, raising two children, going back to school at fifty-five. Do I believe in monogamy? Yes, but I am not monogamous. The reason for my affair for three years now has been hunger for affection. I told my husband several times I could not live without affection. But I plan to stay married.

"I am financially dependent and it is a problem, I resent my husband controlling all the finances and keeping them secret from me. I am not a full partner in our marriage. I do all the housework, grocery shopping, cooking, laundry, etc. My husband controls everything, pays the mortgage, pays for groceries, makes money available to me. He even controls my love relationship. I have his approval to have a lover, but even though I have his approval, when our daughter came home from school two days early and I had a dinner date, he made a big scene, brought our daughter to the same restaurant, and locked me out of our bedroom and was furious for three days.

"The affair is fun. We are both married to other partners. I do not feel guilty and I don't believe he does either. Neither of us is contemplating divorce, only enjoying a relationship that makes life more fun. The time recently I was the happiest was on an overnight trip with my lover. He had me laughing hysterically at least three times in one day. Something that almost never happens to me."

"My husband chose to ignore me for years . . . and years . . . Eventually I started having affairs. My first affair was exploratory, full of learning, intense, satisfying. I grew as a person, I learned that I could be responsive and damned good in bed too, when treated with enthusiasm instead of apathy. It was very serious and very secret. My lover was tender, considerate, and loving. I wondered why I had waited thirty-nine years before I had my 'Growing-Up Experience.' We remain friends. Now we just meet on our anniversary date to discuss our lives and have a drink.

"I had three affairs while living with my husband. The one just mentioned lasted eight years, two others lasted three years each. The effect of all this was to make a deteriorated marriage worth staying with, while I developed my sense of self, and prepared myself for life alone. The kids were finally grown up enough to be reasonably responsible. The effect on me was positive—my self-esteem grew enormously.

"My husband and I argued until we both decided that to ignore each other was easier. Most of the arguments were over the kids. I was to blame for *everything*. I returned to college, obtained a degree, studied, developed myself, waiting until I could leave. I was loneliest just before I left.

"I did need some therapy before I could move out of the family home. I had never been alone in my entire life, and couldn't make decisions. I learned the decision-making process and finally was able to realize that alone is great. Now I'm a different person—a new person. What do I do in my private moments, moments just for myself? I like to daydream, watch the breeze blow through the leaves, remember past moments of happiness. Wish for yet unspoken dreams."

"I was very happy with my husband and felt very close to him through much of our marriage of twenty-five years. When I realized he didn't really love me anymore, I spent two years crying and drinking, then I took a lover.

"I have had a lover now for three years. He is married and has children and grandchildren. I love him because he gives me some sexual and emotional things I need. I am no longer *in* love with either him or my husband—I'm not now in love with anyone. Perhaps with one of my daughters. I like my lover's admiration and acceptance of me. He likes my body and he likes to watch himself make love to me. He accepts those things about my body which are not as lovely as they once were, and just talks about what he does like.

"Our religious values tell us this is wrong and yet he calls me daily and he means it when he says he wants to be with me. He smiles at me with approval, desire, and appreciation. He cooks for me and takes time to show me new things and to fantasize with me about what we would do if things were different. Just being alone together talking, sharing, complaining, and making love is wonderful."

One woman, married forty-five years, relates the history of her life within her marriage, the enormous alienation and distance she has felt for years, and talks about her lovers:

"I am a northeastern WASP, age sixty-one, high school education, housewife, 5'6", overweight, pretty, strong opinions and appetites. I am married to my husband since 1941. We live together, no children. The basis of this relationship was first being in love, then learning to live for the long-term companionship through the years. I like the constancy, the sharing of goals. I love my husband as a friend, almost as a brother.

"My husband and my relationship might have been better if he had been more interested in me sexually—although there certainly were other problems. In fact, we are arguing more now than we did in the first half of our marriage because he traveled then and was away often; now he is home 365 days a year and there is greater opportunity to disagree.

"The most recent fights I've had with my husband are always for the same reason—he fails to cooperate when the activity or circumstance requires two. It is always about something trivial—holding the garbage bag open while I fill it with contents of the garbage pail, wastebaskets, etc. We always fight about his lack of cooperation and his lack of thoughtfulness. The fights end because I grow silent and say nothing more—he is usually unresponsive or if he's overtired he will become enraged and shout, 'Oh yes, you are always perfect.' I recognize that as a sign of futility and walk away from him and say nothing more on the subject. No one can win in this situation. I feel angry, repressed, frustrated, upset, and depressed.

"Arguments end when he leaves the room. If they are protracted, and even if I am speaking logically but in anger, he will leave the room and go into the bathroom and shut the door and stay there for ten to fifteen minutes. The problem is not discussed, no one ever says they are sorry, the fight is pushed aside, and we resume a normal, peaceful household. I tried to talk over problems, but he never responded, so I stopped trying, many, many years ago. My husband doesn't try to find out what's inside of me—he is incapable of verbalizing or showing any indication that he is concerned about my viewpoint. When he was scheduling business trips here and abroad I was *never* invited along. He always treated me in many ways as an inferior, letting me manage all kinds of unpleasant situations on my own.

"Until 1975 I was financially dependent upon him. I didn't feel badly about it—I did my share of work and gave my share of effort to the marriage in every other way. In fact, in my marriage, the dependency seemed to work just the other way: he seemed to need me as a child needs his mother. When the relationship developed this way, I withdrew certain aspects of love (sexual, for instance) to seek a balance in which to continue the relationship without my chafing against it. He has never complained that I do not love him. I don't know how much my husband loves me—he needs me, and is dependent upon me. I need to be needed, and in this way I find some satisfaction.

"I don't believe in monogamy now. I have had extramarital affairs, twelve of them. One for two months, one for three months, one for one year, three for two years, two for three years, one for five years, one for fifteen years, one for eighteen years, and one for thirty-three years. Many were concurrent; only two were exclusive. The reason was that I required love and sex—both together, when possible. I could not have survived had I not fulfilled these needs, so it enriched my life and helped me to seek a good platonic relationship in my marriage, which actually saved the marriage. My husband did not know.

"Most of the affairs were exciting, fulfilling, educational, socially broadening, spiritually enriching, and satisfying. Four were very serious. Of the four that were serious, I loved my lovers completely, admired each and treasured every moment I was with him, needed him sexually and his physical presence. I don't know or care if my husband has been faithful to me.

"I plan to stay married. I prefer to face old age with a companion I already know. But now I am 'single' in that I don't have any affair at the moment. My more recent lovers are happily married or dead, or we've lost track of each other, or they are too old now—in their late seventies and eighties—and it is difficult to find or meet someone I like and am attracted to. I'd rarely have respect for the 'new' man. But because of this, I often feel empty, unwhole, aggravated and stressful, unloved.

"I fell the most deeply in love with a man who had just returned from World War II. I was overwhelmed with joy, passion and pleasure, as if I had met my other half. He was tall, strong, opinionated, loving, and very sexual. We were so much in love it was dangerous—by that I mean we were obsessed by one another and spent twelve to fourteen hours making love each day, for nineteen days. Three years later he found me again and we enjoyed each other whenever possible off and on for a period of two years. He was married but separated from his wife. He was an alcoholic, and when I discovered that, I told him never to see me again. He tried through mutual friends to arrange meetings with me, but I never consented.

"That was the happiest I ever was with someone, and the closest. I liked being in love, for it is sheer pleasure—it is learning and enriching, it is joy, and at the end, it can be excruciatingly painful.

"Then when I was fifty-four I took an inventory of my life, the credits and debits of emotional stress, and decided to retire from sexual activity. Now I would like (at times) to be more active again, but I'm not willing to spend the effort.

"Friendships are more enduring because one demands less of friends than one does of lovers. Friends can lie if they wish, be untidy, unclean, disorderly, secretive, but lovers should be truthful 90 percent of the time, practice tidiness and cleanliness, live an orderly life, not withhold too many secrets, and not pursue gambling, drugs, alcohol, cults, etc.—otherwise it interferes with the love affair.

"The most important relationship with a woman in my life was the friendship I had with my best woman friend. She had wit, similar interests to mine, a broad-mindedness about sex and all aspects of living, talent. We went to the theater and to movies and art exhibits and walked and talked together. Once we even shared a lover. I no longer see her and no longer talk to her by telephone. She became senile and has no memory.

"My ideas and feelings about the women's movement affected my life—*not* the *present* women's movement, the early one when women became suffragettes, etc. I read about them, knew some of them, agreed with their ideas and always tried to apply these ideas to my own behavior and lifestyle. Certainly these ideas affected my choice of women friends and confidantes, my attitudes about professional women, and the women in my own family circle. And my feelings about women's liberation definitely affected my relationships with men—I felt free to enjoy them as friends and lovers, and this was *not* common in my economic, social, ethnic group.

"In closing I must add that I have often wondered if sexual needs force us into relationships, or if one could find gratification in a celibate life. In other words, do we need sex in our lives, or not having had it, could we live full lives without it? I shall never resolve this question! But I do believe that sex offers the greatest pleasure in life. Still, I have settled for a good companionship with my husband. Facing old age, with no other family, we can have an agreeable and quiet life together—with the same interests and goals.

"I found this questionnaire excellent and well rounded. It gave me an opportunity to take inventory of my youth, middle age, and coming old age, something I had not taken time to ponder over for twenty years. Many thanks."

6 percent of women who have very good marriages emotionally still have affairs, as one woman describes:

"I am currently happily married to a wonderful man, four years. We have no children. I am twenty-nine. He and I are so close that we almost seem to be part of each other. I trust him completely, and I know I can turn to him with my problems. I love my husband now more deeply than I have ever loved anyone. It is a love that has grown over the years. We have been through many rough times in our relationship, but the love has always endured. Actually, I didn't believe myself capable of loving another human being as much as I love him.

"The happiest I have ever been was with my husband when we moved into our first house. We had only been married a short time and I remember feeling like everything was finally coming together for me and working out right.

Other happy times are unexpected times, like maybe we will be shopping or doing the laundry together, and we'll embrace. I just suddenly feel overwhelmed with a feeling of love and devotion. I get these overwhelming feelings of love for him and I have to hold him and tell him how much I love him. The same thing happens to him. Sometimes we just sit and hold each other and smile. Nothing special, just sharing life together.

"My husband goes above and beyond the call of duty when it comes to showing me how much he loves me. He gives me flowers, calls me, sends cards to me at work. He also fixes my lunch for me every morning and calls me at work every day at noon with "the day's joke." He even does this when he has to be out of town on business, I used to think men like this only existed in books. Not so—I have one of them! He is not a perfect human being, but he does everything he possibly can to make me feel loved. He also says that I make him feel loved. I try to do little things for him that he appreciates. I cut out articles for him that I think he will enjoy.

"Another example: I am in the process of starting my own business. The night I finished painting and began moving furniture into the office, my husband helped me. I know he has no idea how much his happiness and excitement meant to me.

"The thing I like least about our relationship is our sex life. There is a vast difference in our sex drives. He is satisfied with sex once or twice a month, whereas I would prefer three to four times a week. If I could, I would make my husband less inhibited and also bestow upon him the sex drive he possessed when we first met.

"Monogamy can work, I believe, but it is not right for me. Even before we were married, while we were living together, I had two affairs. The first was short-lived—two months maybe. The second lasted three years and ended only when my lover moved to another state. I am still in contact with him, and when he is in town, we still see each other—sometimes for sex, sometimes not. We are very close friends and share a special love for one another. He, too, is married.

"These relationships have caused strong emotions in me always—sometimes happiness and sometimes sadness. It can be very frustrating finding the time and place to see someone that you desire. Overall, though, I think the effects have been emotionally harmful, because there is no way to carry the relationship through to a happy ending. It must always end sadly. There is always hurt. But there hasn't been any effect on my marriage. My husband is unaware of my sexual relationships with these people, although he knows that I am friends with them.

"I believe that my husband has been faithful to me, and I like him being faithful to me. I would be afraid that he might find someone that he loved more than me. I always make clear to other men in my life that my husband comes first—they come second. It may sound like I have double standards, and I probably do."

Another woman is not quite sure why she and her husband do not have sex much anymore—and why she has a lover:

"The question of monogamy presents me with a terrible conflict. I do believe in monogamy, but even though I have determined that infidelity is always destructive and that I should remain faithful, I do, from time to time, have affairs. Sometimes they are very brief (one-night stands), sometimes longer. I am currently having an affair that has been going on for nearly a year.

"Sex is the most important part of my relationship with my lover and actually the lack of sex in my marriage worries me. My husband and I have very little sex. I'm not sure why. We were very active sexually when we first met. We had sex every day, three or four times a day. While some cooling off was expected, our marriage has become a sexual desert. We now have sex once every two months. At first I pursued him, he would complain of fatigue. Our sex life was also pretty free. We were verbal, adventurous. In the past few years our sex has become perfunctory. I have tried to find out what turns him on. I've asked him directly, tried different things to see what his reaction would be. If I had to say what turns him on I'd be compelled to say, NOTHING!

"I still enjoy my husband's company and it has not made me unresponsive to him. This affair is definitely sexual in nature. I have no desire to be married to my lover or even to spend lots of time with him, unless it is in bed. What do I get out of it? My lover has an insatiable desire for me, to know my body, my mind, my every little twist and turn.

"I have been married for three years. I am thirty-eight, married for the second time, two children. I also have a job that I love, giving me the opportunity to travel. My marriage is good. I cannot honestly remember the last fight we had. I was most recently angry with him for coming home late when we were expecting dinner guests. He refused to entertain my outburst and kept joking around with me until I came around.

"Having someone I can depend on is the best thing about my marriage. I need his stability. I feel very loved. It makes me feel guilty that I don't love him as well as he loves me. I think he unconsciously knows that my love is a sometime thing. He knows of one affair I had. He was inconsolable. Given his basic nature to bury things, he has outwardly gotten over it, but I'm sure he still bears the wounds inside. I believe my husband has been faithful to me. It is not in his nature to do otherwise.

"I do not usually come to orgasm with my husband. Most often I masturbate after he has rolled over and gone to sleep. I don't know if he knows I masturbate. We don't discuss it. Sex with my lover is fun. He thoroughly enjoys a woman's body, has apparently paid attention when making love and knows where to touch, how to touch, and will ask if this feels good, or where his hand or finger should be. I am not used to this. Also, my lover not only knows I masturbate but insists on my doing it while with him, either mutually or while he watches. At first, he just plain asked me when the last time was that

I masturbated. His assumption that I did made it easy to say 'two days ago.' He then took my hand, put it between my legs, and said, 'Let me see you do it.' Between his encouragement and his watching me, I was nearly wild. It has become a regular part of our lovemaking.

"I still feel passion for my husband and find myself wanting him when I look at him or think about him. But I feel the same way, only a bit stronger, for my lover."

21 percent of women give lack of sex or poor sex at home as their main reason for having affairs:

"I believe that monogamy is the healthiest way to live. But because my marriage is so unsatisfying in the physical sense, I have had four extramarital affairs, ranging from a couple of stupid but intense flings of several months to an involved and mutually satisfying relationship of five years. If my husband ever suspected, he never let on and probably repressed it for the good of all concerned."

"I am very close to my husband but I must admit not 100 percent. I cannot climax with him and I would give most anything to be able to. Then perhaps I would not need my lover. Obviously my husband does not know I see my lover. I feel almost closer to my lover at times because he is the most totally intimate man I have ever met. It is his nature. I wish I could share everything with my husband."

Especially for women who were virgins at marriage, affairs are appealing as sexual experimentation:

"I had never slept with anyone but my husband. I was sixteen when I started to go out with him and was a virgin. When I was twenty-nine I wanted to experience some of life. I wanted to know what sex was like with someone else. I had to try for about one year before I found a man who was willing to have an affair. It was my experience that men are much shyer than they appear to be. When I tried to get someone to bed, three times three different guys backed out. Didn't help my ego much."

"I know it would hurt him if he felt that my sexual needs have not been satisfied by him. But I have had other sex twice—both within two days. I had been a virgin bride. Twenty-one years later I wondered what another sex partner would be like, wondered if I had been missing something. I felt that this might be my last chance to find out. I felt guilty and depressed, ashamed of myself. I didn't tell anyone about it. It made me realize how terrific my husband and marriage is. Although it was a Zipless Fuck, certainly not serious, I thought he was sexy. I didn't get anything out of it, not even an orgasm! I think my husband has been faithful to me, and I'm grateful. It makes me feel that I'm meeting all his needs in that area, that I still turn him on, that I'm sexy."

A surprisingly low 7 percent of women have affairs because their husbands had one first and they are furious, or devastated:

"I discovered he had a long-term affair and occasional one-night stands. Having been devastated by his unfaithfulness, I looked to other men for positive feedback. In the process, I found a unique and wonderful man and fell in love."

"I learned of my husband's unfaithfulness after twenty-seven years of marriage. The first twenty-seven years were very peaceful. An argument was a very rare happening in our home. Since becoming aware of my husband's infidelity we have had more arguments in six years than in the previous twenty-seven. My affair had the effect of making me feel sexy and beautiful. It was also a way of getting even with my husband."

Most affairs do not begin because a woman falls in love: * *however, 19 percent of women do fall in love with the men they are having affairs with:*

"I had a sexual relationship outside my marriage that gave me sexual fulfillment of the quality I had always dreamed of. It made me feel desirable. He made me come alive when I was near him. I became very serious about the relationship, very much in love. He kept cautioning me about getting too serious. Now, it's rather ironic that for the last year he has wanted me to run off with him. He says that he loves me more than ever; he thinks of me always. That may be, but while I do love him, I'm not in love anymore, although sex with him is still the most fantastic thing."

"During the last eight years, I was deeply in love with my married lover. Much more so than with my husband of twelve years. I was happy, but frustrated and angry much of the time. In fact, the frustration and anger far outweighed the happiness. My lover would never consider leaving his family, but did not want to leave me either. I honestly feel that if he had lived to be ninety, I would still be waiting by the phone for his call. While he was still enjoying good health, I never experienced such intense passion in my life."

One woman is quite in love with her lover:

"My love for this man is intense and overpowering. He is always with me—if not physically, in a spiritual sort of way. I have never felt anything like this for any other person. I am probably closest to my husband, because I still spend most time with him, but the underlying feeling is very different. My love lives in my heart, so to speak. I think of him often (all the time). I love his attributes and his faults. It's unconditional, the real thing.

---

*This was also true of men in the previous study: but even fewer men were ever "in love" with the women with whom they were having affairs. Most men prefer to have affairs with women with whom they are friends. See *The Hite Report on Male Sexuality,* Chapter 2.

"I am so happy when I am with him. Being able to express my love for him has been like capturing a piece of heaven. I have loved him for some twelve years, admitted to myself a little over a year ago, told him seven months ago, and finally made love with him four months ago. He guessed I was in love with him the first time we kissed, nearly a year ago, although I wouldn't admit it to him, how silly. I have felt very passionate with him, although I think it is frightening for him, so I have to restrain myself a little.

"My husband says he doesn't love me and I believe him. We both love the children and we get along. He just doesn't seem to care about much else but work. I don't hate him, he's just not very lovable. I care for him, I care about him, have sex with him, but I ache for my lover. I don't ache for my husband.

"During pregnancy my husband wasn't especially turned on by my growing belly. I had to masturbate a lot (not too good a substitute, however!). During the first birth, I had a large episiotomy on the side, which didn't heal for about nine months following delivery. Intercourse was extremely painful and my husband was not patient with me at all. If he had been more affectionate, if I could have been more sexually responsive, the list goes on, perhaps things could change. But now we go day to day, hoping for the best.

"When my lover said he wanted me, I thought I was hearing things. My husband just does not relate this way. I love to be talked to during tactile loving. When my lover talks tenderly to me, then uses real horny talk, it drives me wild. He has a wonderful sensuous way of kissing. Sometimes he seems like he is going to suck me inside of him. Other times he is soft and very tender. He is delighted that he can still get milk from my breasts. (My husband wants nothing to do with this.) It is only a drop or so but he loves the taste and pays a lot of attention to my breasts for a little sweet taste. This is very arousing for me. We don't always have time for intercourse, and I have come to enjoy the times we are together only with foreplay.

"Sex with my husband is usually intercourse with some foreplay. I would like him to handle me and talk to me, but he doesn't. I have to remind him to remove his glasses. I can orgasm, and ask him to help me, but he usually interprets it as a demand and won't do it. He knows I don't come during intercourse. He claims that his mistresses were orgasmic during intercourse. I think it is more probable that they were faking, or he gave them more stimulation.

"My lover stimulates my clitoris without my asking him. He has freely masturbated in front of me. (My husband has never done this; only recently did he admit that he's done it in private.) It was hard for me to believe that he was thirty years old when he got his first blow job, but I was delighted to be the first one to give him one. I thought everyone did this, at least sometimes. He was so tired the first time he orgasmed this way and so surprised that I swallowed the semen. It was a sheer pleasure to see him so happy and contented.

"I would leave my husband today if my lover were free, and take the children with me. My husband earns the money, and so the financial arrangements have unfortunately caused me to stay put, but I feel I belong with my children anyway. He feels he is somehow superior for earning money. This irks me, because *he* couldn't care for a family and home in the right way.

"My lover's wife is an alcoholic and is ill off and on. Because she would be unable to care for the children alone, he cannot leave her. Of course, I'd love it if he divorced, but he loves his children very much.

"I would like to plan a future with someone, but right now I have my own dreams and my own future which I must worry about and deal with. At this point, I don't think my husband will be a part of it."

For 17 percent of women, an affair is part of the alienation process that leads to a divorce:

"I have had one affair which lasted about a year—of which six months were heaven. 'It just happened'—we both had needs to be met—we lived with spouses who would have us believing we were crazy—we needed to prove we were sane, that affection and kindness still existed—that our beliefs and ideals about relationships weren't totally off base—and to relax and laugh a lot. It ruined the marriage—I was no longer committed—I left it physically and emotionally. My affair gave me a taste of what life could be like—so much better—I could be human and alive.

"The affair was rapid. We went out for a drink after work. By 8 p.m. that night we were into it all—it was as if we'd known each other for years. It was very serious—we reached the point of looking for a house. I was crazy about him. I still love him, but I don't think we could live together. We needed each other at that point in our lives. Not now."

————————————

But most affairs do not lead to divorce. In fact, as seen, many women continue extramarital relationships as a stable way of life for years. The average number of years for affairs that are not one- or two-time meetings, is, surprisingly, four years.

But, interestingly, most women opt to stay in a marriage even when the love in the affair is deeper; women who divorce their husbands usually do so because of what is lacking in their marriage, not because they are in love with someone else:

"I was most deeply in love in my extramarital relationship. I was more passionate with him in a sexual encounter than I had ever been with my husband. But I stayed in the marriage."

"I stayed with my husband, we are happy. But it was important for me to love again so intensely."

If extramarital affairs are making a marriage livable, propping up an inadequate marriage, is this always a good thing? One woman wonders:

"I had sex outside of my first marriage. The outside relationships gave me many of the things missing from my marriage. But they kept me in a bad marriage longer than I should have stayed. In my present marriage I have been monogamous and will continue to be. When I feel the need for other relationships, I now think that I will get a divorce."

Finally, 12 percent of women say their affairs are simply a form of fun and excitement:

"Each affair is different. Almost all are playful and sexy. I like them usually much less than my 'true love'—my husband—but they have a pretty good sexual spark!"

"My affairs are a diversion, like going to a movie. I find it very easy to meet and talk to people—in fact, this is a little hobby of mine. However, men (both married and single) still find it awkward when they meet an outgoing and available married woman (me) and are often unsure initially. I help them get over this."

"After three months of working with him, I began socializing with him. One evening while my husband was out of town, I invited him and his roommate over for dinner. While the roommate was downstairs listening to the stereo, we went upstairs and made love on the bathroom floor. I seduced him. He was surprised, but this encounter led to three more before he decided that what we were doing was wrong. About seven months after that we went out to lunch together (not uncommon). We ended up at his apartment, though, and in bed. I sure was surprised. I thought that we might start seeing each other again, but it was a one-time thing. He never mentioned it again and neither did I. We still work together, and he and his girlfriend socialize with me and my husband. No one knows, and we always act professionally at the office. I really like this guy, and I hope we can continue to be friends. He could still have me anytime he wanted!"

Surprisingly, like men, * *the overwhelming majority of women do not feel guilty for their affairs; only a few do:*

"My greatest problem with my lover is my guilt. Sometimes it tears me apart. I would love to be able to totally commit myself to my husband without needing this other man in my life."

"The affair was cheap, it wasn't serious. I liked the man, but his wife and I are best friends. I wish I hadn't done it."

*See The Hite Report on Male Sexuality, Chapter 2.

It is notable that 89 percent of women keep their affairs secret, they are never "found out." Here, and in *The Hite Report on Male Sexuality*, most women and men seem to feel—aside from being afraid of the other's reaction—that it is more civilized, more polite, simply to keep their extra relationship secret and save their spouse's feelings.

Double lives: What do they mean?

Do affairs imply that there is something profoundly wrong with a marriage? If one wants a marriage which is emotionally close, yes. If one wants a marriage for a "stable home base" but expects little emotionally (see Chapter 12), this is another matter.

Most women in this study are having affairs because they are looking for emotional closeness and support, a way to have a more real relationship. The basic cause of women's search for love and enjoyment outside of marriage has to do with women's emotionally alienated state within marriage. The condescension and lack of emotional closeness women are experiencing in their marriages (see Part I) is having a disastrous effect on women's ability to survive emotionally while staying completely within a marriage. Thus, for many women, having an outside relationship is one of the few ways to stay in the marriage. Having an affair can put new love and humanity into one's world, enabling one to go on living.

Women are not looking for affairs basically for "more sex" or "sexual variety," as men often say men are (but is it true of men either?)—although some women do want more excitement and romance. Women often feel more powerful emotionally in outside relationships (they are), because they cannot be taken for granted, they must at least be listened to, so that they won't leave.

The chronology of alienation

While only 13 percent of women married less than two years are having outside sex, the rate after five years jumps to 70 percent for women (and 75 percent for men), but does not increase much after that. The likelihood of a man having an affair also does not increase precipitously after five, ten, or twenty years of marriage, but only after the first two years.

The likelihood of a woman having an affair increases precipitously after five years of marriage. Why does it increase? Not simply because time has passed, or "sexual boredom" has set in. Perhaps it is because all those years of a man's emotional distancing and challenging behaviors, subliminal harassment, finally begin to take their toll.

Perhaps at the two-year point, when men begin to have extramarital sex, the woman is doing the greatest amount of "bringing up the issues," hoping things will change. Maybe—and the time factor here can only be guessed at—it is at about five years that most women finally give up trying to "get through." In short, the "male" ideology's unequal (and unspoken, half-conscious) emotional contract has a devastating effect, a chilling effect, and is the cause of the loss of most of the closeness in relationships and affairs.

Do women have more extramarital sex today?

Is this much extramarital sex among women a new phenomenon? In 1953, Alfred Kinsey found that 26 percent of women were having sex outside of their marriages. In this study, 70 percent of women married five years or more are having sex outside their marriages. This *is* an enormous increase. Women's rate of extramarital sex has almost tripled in thirty-five years; it is almost equal to that of men (75 percent after five years of marriage).*

Does this reflect a growing "equality" on the part of women, or a growing discontent on the part of women and men with the essential state of their relationship? Does it predict the splitting up of our society into millions of atavistic individuals? Certainly it represents a transition to something—and the nature of the home is the issue being discussed.

Has this increase come about gradually, over the years, or precipitously during the peak years of the "sexual revolution"—that time when "sex" was considered to be a "normal, natural, healthy expression" of one's body, and monogamy a "neurotic" repression of "natural behaviors"?† (Will the fear of AIDS coming to the general population deflate these figures on extramarital sex? This is possible, but not probable, since most women's affairs are not with "casual" partners, but are long-lasting relationships.) But perhaps most women have been having affairs from time immemorial,‡ and Kinsey's figures were just rather low because he was conducting face to face interviews, often with a husband one day and a wife the next—with relevant facts written down for his records. This may have inhibited reporting on the part of some inter-

---

*Men's rate of extramarital sex has also increased (doubled) during the same period.

†Of course, the "sexual revolution" should not be confused with the women's movement; the "sexual revolution" wanted to make sex acceptable before marriage for women; the women's movement had a much deeper and broader agenda, focusing on women's legal, educational, and financial rights. Some women agreed with the "sexual revolution"; others didn't. But the "sexual revolution" was generally begun and discussed by male novelists, male-oriented magazines, and so on.

‡Unfortunately, we have very few figures on extramarital activity on the part of the majority of people in previous centuries. For the nineteenth century, one can look at the work of Peter Gay and others; for earlier centuries, important historians include Lawrence Stone and Natalie Davis; Stone and others are currently working on newly released divorce court records in England in the Middle Ages, and this may provide new information.

viewees. The present study is based on anonymous questionnaires, so that women would have had no reason to conceal anything.

But in all probability, these figures do represent an increase.

Who is more likely to have an affair?

Some people may be quick to jump to the conclusion that the increase in extramarital sex is a "career woman" phenomenon—that more and more women are having affairs because more women are working outside the home now. But statistically, this is not borne out by this study: the difference is very slight between the extramarital rate of women working inside the home and that of the women working outside—and almost all women do work outside the home now, in any case. In fact, women in the home (without outside jobs) have a slightly higher rate of extramarital sex, in this study.

At least as many women who are financially dependent in their marriages are having affairs as women with jobs or careers. The likelihood of a woman having an affair does not increase because a woman has her own money. Thus not only is this not a "new woman" or "career woman" phenomenon; in fact, just the opposite may be true: women who are economically dependent may feel more frustration about their lives, and, not having an outside job, an affair may be one of the few outlets (besides children) a woman can turn to in an emotionally unfulfilling marriage. Of course, many women also look to their women friends for close emotional relationships, but an affair holds the possibility of physical affection too. But women with jobs may be more intent on focusing their energy on work and friends at work than an additional lover.

In other words, while women may like sex and adventures with men at times, many may now be finding more diverse interests in their lives, so that having a lover may not be the focus or the only "out" it once was in an unsatisfying marriage. Today even a lover might be getting less emotional investment from a woman.

One group has a much lower rate of extramarital affairs: women who are "in love" with their husbands, as opposed to "loving" them (see Chapter 12), are much more likely to be monogamous. Ninety-eight percent of women who say they are currently "in love," as opposed to "loving" their husbands, are monogamous.

But other than that, women who are monogamous are not statistically older or younger, do not have more or fewer children, may or may not work outside of the home, and may or may not be more or less religious: the rates of extramarital sex vary only minimally for these groups. After the first five years, during which the overwhelming majority of women are trying hard to make it work, only women who have "made it work," basically, remain completely monogamous.

It might also be interesting to ask, is women's thinking about their right to love and a real relationship new? Have women's expectations of close emotional contact increased since the recent women's movement? Perhaps women now put a greater value on what they are giving to men emotionally, so that this makes them notice more acutely when men do not give back. Women now—with their increased economic and other power, achieved during the last twenty years—are less likely to believe or accept the ideas women expressed so often as recently as the 1950s: "That is just the way men are," "You just have to accept it." Women want to have a real life with someone now—emotionally, psychologically, intellectually, and physically.

How Do Women Feel About Their Husbands' Affairs?

Seventy-nine percent of the women in this study say that they do not believe their husbands or lovers are having affairs; only 15 percent express doubt; only 19 percent say they know that they are or were in the past. Do women who have affairs tend to suspect their husbands more? No; most state, without hesitation, that their husbands are "faithful."

82 percent of women state they believe that their husbands are "faithful":

"I firmly believe he is not having sex with other women. He is just not that type. He finds that when you're in love you simply don't just have sex with everybody."

"I am quite sure that my present husband is and will be monogamous. As long as we are married, I hope he will be."

Not only their husbands, but also their lovers!

"My husband was, to my knowledge, faithful to me. My lover was faithful. I believe the man in my current relationship is not sleeping with other women. I would like to be able to say that as long as my partner was satisfying me he could screw someone else—but I'm not that secure!"

According to *The Hite Report* on men, 72 percent of men married more than two years are not monogamous. Who is right? Are these extremely different populations? Or are women fooling themselves?

Although most wives think their husbands are "faithful," are they? Many replies mention incidents like these:

"A couple of times he's stayed out all night working or visiting with friends, and he hasn't called me or anything."

"He has never had sex with anyone else, and I feel very good about this. I'm not sure if I would want to know. One time I thought he was making out with another woman while I was in the same room. I was furious with him. I grabbed him by the chin and screamed, 'You creep!!! You creep!!!' Turns out they were doing an erotic dance, but his cock wasn't even hard. Boy, was he shocked when I started screaming and calling him a creep!"

"My husband was entrapped into a 'soliciting a prostitute' charge (which was later dropped and for which he sued and won a decision on the grounds of entrapment and false arrest). Anyhow, we were both so bummed out by the whole thing, both so depressed, both so supportive of each other, that when we made love I actually wept; for the first time in my life I wept during sex. I truly felt loved, cherished. That was two years ago."

———————

In fact, most wives seem unaware of their husbands' possible extramarital relationships. While the great majority certainly believe their husbands are not seeing other women, based on the statistical discrepancy just mentioned, probably some of them are.

Many single women remark that they know very few men who are monogamous:

"I honestly believe I could seduce my best friend's father if I wanted to—some fidelity these guys have. My disillusionment began a few months after I left my husband, when my husband's best friend (who was married and assured me it was fine with his wife) told me I was the only woman he wanted to go to bed with. Then a married judge tried to get me in bed, a married accountant, a married jewelry salesman, etc., etc."

"I do not get involved with or date, nor have I ever even been attracted sexually to, a friend's husband, boyfriend, or date. But I sure have had my friends' husbands, boyfriends, dates, and friends try and go with me—in fact, most of them. Usually when the guy makes a pass, I think, 'What more does he want?' It seems many men are seeking newness, which they equate with passion. Newness meaning lots of women."

"Since I have been divorced I have been astounded at the number of married men who have expressed interest in me—the first was my ex-husband's best friend, whom I regarded as a brother. I still can't believe the crassness of some men—how easily they disregard a sense of loyalty to their wives. Wives, I have a message for you—your husband is out hustling women. Those of us with self-respect are disgusted by him, and you should be too. Divorce him and get some self-respect! I am thirty-eight, currently living with a male who is my best friend (for the past two years), but before that I lived for nine years of marriage with a sexist man until I found out what was going on."

Women who know of their husbands' affairs are usually hurt and angry:

"I still love my husband very much, even though this other relationship he is involved in is hurting me deeply. I have never had a desire not to love him. I really don't think I could stop loving him."

"My husband has not been faithful to me. How do I feel? Mad as hell. I am angry and it hurts. It is like having some kind of sickness that is slowly eating away at me. I cannot just turn off my feelings and just stop loving him like I was turning off a light. I want my husband to be monogamous. I don't think I am expecting or asking for anything more than he is asking and expecting of me."

"The worst thing that he has ever done is sleep in another woman's bed when he should have been home with me in our bed. He may have someone else. I'm glad I don't know."

"I know he is seeing someone. I feel depressed, jealous, at a great loss. My ego is suffering."

"Each time my husband has been with another woman, or even when he goes to a strip joint, I get less interested in love."

"He does not satisfy me sexually because I have this constant competition with his other woman on my mind. 'I'm probably not as good as she is.' 'My body is not as nice as hers.' 'What am I not doing that causes him to go seek out others?' To try and help the situation we started trying new things: exotic lingerie, vibrators, positions, locations, etc. This was fine until he then started frequenting strip joints. Now I feel degraded and am not interested in that sort of thing anymore. I am not in love with my husband, but having lived with someone for thirty-one years, you just can't discard all the feelings you have for him. I still love him, but not as much as I did."

"I don't think he was ever faithful. I tried not to think about it. I wanted him to be faithful. He always insisted he was, even when it was obvious that he wasn't. He had an affair with the same woman for five years. It didn't seem to bother him. I was too afraid of him to push him on the matter. I would not have sex outside the relationship, and if I did, I certainly would not tell him about it. He'd kill me. He almost did just because he thought that I had."

"I have suspicions that my husband was probably unfaithful. He did become seriously involved with a twenty-year-old divorcée when he was thirty-five and was planning to leave pregnant me to marry her. However, he claimed that he had not had sex with her. Preposterous! . . . To my mind it didn't substantially matter, as I felt he had erred in the most serious way by deceiving me and becoming so emotionally involved—the withholding of his true feelings about me and then going behind my back to solve them I thought was gross immaturity. I felt horribly betrayed."

One woman is going through a lot of turmoil:

"I am so unhappy. I have to force myself to keep going. The children are close but cannot understand what I'm going through. Two years ago, I thought I was a happily married mother of three. My husband had a good job, we had a lovely home in a happy community. I devoted myself to raising my family and helping my husband in his career, keeping the house clean and tidy, making friends with neighbors, and going to church regularly.

"But underneath, there was turmoil. Over a period of ten years, my husband had been unfaithful. We had gone through several crises, all over one woman, and with the help of marriage counselors, ministers, relatives, and friends, *I* had come through. Of a forgiving nature anyway—'soft'—I wanted the children to have a *united* family atmosphere to grow up in. I believed my husband would grow out of his 'yearning' for another and accept his responsibilities to our family. He didn't. In the end there was a complete breakdown. He started disappearing literally overnight 'just to sort things out.' I was 'only trying to help' and he was 'sorting things out.' In the end I couldn't take any more.

"My husband was always telling me that I didn't seem to need him as the other woman did. What he meant was that I managed without him—I had to—it wasn't that I wanted to.

"He still keeps in touch with the children but his other woman has moved in with him now and I am getting a divorce. I stopped wearing his ring.

"I did have an 'affair' with a dear man who helped me through one of my marriage crises. Our relationship was very precious to me. Given the right conditions, we might have made a life together, but I chose to stay with my husband and keep the family together. It was the wrong decision. I could never anymore give anyone advice on the lines of 'stay for the sake of the children.' The children survive a crisis remarkably well so long as they are cared for and kept in their usual routine.

"I do not like being single but prefer it to the anguish of staying in a cold partnership. I have long periods of celibacy which I do not enjoy. That was one aspect of my married life which stayed enjoyable on the whole. Sex was not a problem with us. Still, it is difficult to feel and act passionately when you have an eight-year-old who could walk into the bedroom at any minute. Time must be made for weekends away, thought given to ways of keeping passion alive! My husband had pornographic magazines hidden. He was a great man for his 'boobs.'

"Now, my friends are keeping me going. It is very important to be able to talk to people. I did cry a lot in private and my son still offers occasionally to 'get a bucket.' But you really have to rely on your own willpower or inner strength to get through. People can be very kind but tend to give conflicting advice—'Get him to talk!' or 'For goodness' sake, leave it alone now, let it be forgotten about.'

"I spend a lot of time daydreaming, trying to work out my problems in my own mind. I would like not to be independent, if I could depend on a man to look after me and my three children (two still at home)—but I can't, so I am independent. I guess it will take getting used to."

It is interesting that almost no women phrase their feelings as anger at the "other woman," competition—as stereotype says women used to, and as this woman does:

"I hated Dorothy. She kept making a play for John. I asked her a million times to leave him alone. She said she'd do what she wanted. They eventually had an affair, even though her husband told her he'd leave her if she had another one. I met her one night and told her I wanted to tell her husband, I was so mad. She said, 'You're not gonna do any such thing.' I hauled off and hit her and we had a real fight. I won—but it did not stop the affair. I have to remember it was as much John's fault as hers."

Some women begin to think about having their own affairs:

"My husband seemed to like me staying home, caring for the family, but meanwhile, I learned he was out having affairs with career women. I first noticed a change in him when he said that he thought that a local parenting organization was discriminatory because a mother employed outside her home during her child's infancy could not assume an important position. I tried to explain to him that this seemed right to me, that babies need mostly Mommy during their early years.

"Although he knew I was doing what I felt was right, the women's liberation ideas starting working on him (ideas of his mistresses, no doubt!). He started putting me down in subtle and not so subtle ways. I was confused because at the time I didn't know he was having affairs. I couldn't understand what had happened to my supportive husband. On the other hand, I mentioned going to work recently and I could see this was threatening to him too.

"I see my main occupation as homemaker and mother. I am a support person and caretaker to those who immediately surround me—my children, my husband. I like helping other people. I like being a mother. I also have a little craft business which I operate—*very* part-time—out of my home. I am an average person, thirty-two years old, a high school graduate. But I am a social being—a human being with gifts to give and needs that have to be filled by other people. I'm beginning to think of looking outside our marriage for some of my affectionate needs."

"I think that if I do start seeing other people it will give me bargaining power, which I'm lacking. Many times I feel like he has all the power—makes most of the decisions and I just comply—which infuriates me."

But 14 percent of married women have rather positive attitudes toward their husbands' affairs or potential affairs:

"I think he should experiment a little; he'd learn what a good thing he has and maybe become a better lover."

"I felt free after he had slept with a friend."

"My husband says he has been faithful in our entire marriage. I believe him. I'd like him to have an affair, perhaps it would open his eyes to what the 'woman of the eighties' wants in a sexual partner."

"My husband did have sex with one of his college students after he learned of my affair. I don't know how I feel about it. I think I'd feel better if he did it out of love rather than just for physical experience, as he claims I should."

"It's up to him. I don't need to know."

"If my husband was unfaithful, I hope he would be as good at covering it up as I am. But, knowing him, he would let it slip. I would never divorce him over unfaithfulness, I believe it is a part of life. I would expect, however, to always be first."

"For me what has been a conflict at one stage of my life is no longer a conflict. Thinking about my husband and other women literally drove me crazy. I no longer think about it or am bothered by it."

"I'm sure my partner is not having sex with anyone else now, although he has in the past a few times. That has been perfectly fine with me. I think it's kind of nice, really; I'm glad that he feels free to express his affection for other people. I don't have to worry about his lying to me, since he seems compelled to tell me as soon as anything happens (Catholic guilt?) and since he has no reason to lie. Besides, maybe he'll pick up some new tricks."

Men's Reactions to Their Wives' Affairs

40 percent of men react stormily to their wives' affairs when found out: *

"I cheated on my husband after he shattered my world by cheating on me. I did it for revenge and also to be told I was pretty and wonderful, etc.—the romance. I felt terribly guilty afterwards and only truly loved my husband. I forgave him but he never truly forgave me. It had a damaging effect on our relationship, things were never the same."

"The affair was physically and emotionally draining, mainly because my husband found out about us and forced the issue. He came to the place we were and confronted us. I hated myself and cried for days."

---

*However, only about one-fourth of women having affairs had ever had their husbands find out about them. In fact, most affairs (74 percent) are never discovered or openly recognized either here or in the previous Hite Report.

One woman recounts the upsetting changes in her life that came about when her affair was discovered:

"Several years ago, I fell irrationally in love, and emotionally I was stretched beyond my capacity. Within a period of two months, the conflict between my floundering marriage and my affair came crashing down on me. My husband left me and my affair became public knowledge. I lost every friend I had made in the previous ten years, my children were not welcome in the parochial school they were attending, nor were their friends allowed to invite them to birthday parties, sleep-overs, etc. I was told that 'I was dead to the community,' and in fact I came to believe that I was.

"The man I was having the affair with swore to his wife and our friends that he would never attempt to contact me again in any way and would report to them if I tried to contact him. (I did once, and he did 'report' me.) I began seeing a therapist for some 'first aid,' but did not recover enough to feel well again until about a year later. Even now, I have not completely recovered. I still have periods of depression, a terrible sense of loss, dreams, and a longing to 'go back' and try to undo the damage inflicted on my family, friends, and myself."

However, the overwhelming majority of women in this study do not find their lives "ruined" when an affair is found out—whether it is their own affair or their husband's. Rather, it seems to provide an opportunity for the two either to sit down and really talk and work out a new basis for their relationship—or, sometimes, to split up.

But surprisingly, 60 percent of men's reactions to their wives' affairs are very low-key, sometimes even relaxed, compared to stereotypes of male behavior; is this because many men (72 percent according to The Hite Report *on men) are also having secret extramarital sex and feel relieved when they discover they are not the only ones?:*

"My husband found out I'd been having an affair with a close friend of ours, and it had been ongoing for several years. He was angry but it was a controlled anger. Now he has shown me over the course of the last seven years what love really means. He didn't beat me up or throw me out or do any of the usual things men are said to do. He held me—he told me that he loved me, he ultimately forgave me and has (much more than I might be able to do in the same circumstances) forgotten it and begun to trust me again. I have never (after the initial emotional upset) felt so loved and at peace with a man."

"I have had three affairs in the course of my marriage. He knows vaguely, but won't address it."

"I had a serious and very emotional affair with a friend of ours. My husband encouraged the affair partly as a way of keeping me. He knew I had deep emotional needs which were not met by our relationship, and he chose to let me find satisfaction elsewhere rather than to try to fill them—a way out for himself."

"Two and a half years ago, I had a six-month affair. A couple of weeks after the last incidence of lovemaking, with great trepidation, I told my husband about it. He knew the fellow and I thought he might respond with ridicule: 'Him? Couldn't you have picked someone better than that?' I also thought he might respond with anger: 'Didn't you value our relationship more than that?' Actually, he did not respond either way. He was somewhat shocked and wanted to know how serious I thought it was. I said I promised him that I wouldn't have a regular sexual relationship with this fellow. He said he was glad. From then on, he completely respected my privacy in this matter. The only way he even knows it is over is that during the summer the man moved away.

"I rather expected my husband to regard me coldly, knowing full well my lust might not be occasioned by himself, but by having recently seen my lover. But not so; he was as warm and loving as if we'd never had our conversation. Maybe more so! I suppose it does make a spouse look twice at the level of emotional response he/she's been putting forth, when a bomb like that is dropped.

"The affair was wonderful for me emotionally. He was so powerfully attracted to me, thought I was beautiful. It was wonderful to hear that, because I've never felt good about the way I looked. He used to really flatter me by finding out where I was and going out of his way to seek me out. He memorized my schedule, and used to walk by the door where I worked just to check and be sure I was there that day.

"Sexually, physically, the affair was pretty sorry. The conditions we operated under were terrible, which allowed us to dream of being snowbound and having one glorious night to spend together in the comfort of an actual bed and with plenty of time. As it was, he 'came' almost immediately, which was shocking for me. I never climaxed until the very last day I was with him.

"Though he never once said even a halfway critical thing about his wife, I did gather and could believe that he was in search of sex more often than she. He was probably in need of sexual shoring up as much as I was in need of hearing how he couldn't keep his eyes off me. However, I'm sure I did nothing for his sexual self-image, because he knew he was not satisfying me. He had never had an affair before.

"He did not tell his wife about it. I felt terrible about that. Occasionally I have had a dream about her calling me up in horrible anger (I know her slightly). He told me at the time, 'She doesn't want to know.' 'How would she handle it if she did know?' 'I don't know, but I can tell you this. She'd handle

it a lot better than I'd handle it if it was her having the affair.' But he had no
intention of allowing her to have one. The irony of it did not pass him by. He
couldn't justify it. He could only say what was fact."

*One woman found that it was not her husband but her lover who put her down
for having an affair:*

"Finally after years of just making love with my husband I was alone with
P. and for the first time in my marriage I let myself drift with what was
happening and we made love on my birthday, after a beautiful celebration. I
felt good about it, until, that is, he said, cuttingly, 'You do this often, do you?
You ought to channel your excess sexual energy into something more creative,
you know.' GAAAAAA!"

*Only a few marriages (5 percent) have "open marriage" agreements; one of the
rare "open" relationships that seems to be working is that of a young high
school teacher:*

"I'm a thirty-one-year-old high school teacher, living in a small town with
my husband and daughter. I feel most alive doing sensual physical things—
swimming, dancing to rock music, and particularly making love. Making love
in a 'swinging' situation with one other couple, or by myself with my lover,
as well as with my husband, is a very affirmative 'high.'

"I'm in love with the man who is my husband and with whom I've lived
for almost fifteen years. I also love (in the sense of 'being crazy about') Jim, who
is my lover and a few years younger than I. Then my daughter, who is now
seven. The very closest I have ever felt to another person would be several times
with my husband, after he or I had seen another lover. Lots of emotional
tension, plus the demands and release of transferring a lot into our relationship
together, make those times very intense.

"The sense of having a family, the security of focusing around the three of
us, building a home, is the most important part of our relationship. Also, having
a sexual partner available so frequently. I think we love each other pretty much
'equally.' Of the two of us, I'm the one to whom outside relationships mean
the most. He enjoys the freedom of 'being able to if . . .' I've done a good deal
more.

"My marriage comes closer than anything I'd ever dreamed of to filling my
'deepest needs for closeness with another person.' But nobody can be everything, fill every part of you. The parts I can't share with my husband—wild,
more impulsive, dramatic, and intense—right now I share with my lover. Illicit
lovemaking in a pickup truck, an evening under a full moon by a pond, a night
when I didn't leave until 3:30 in the morning—all these are things I have with
my lover, over about three years, which I certainly treasure and don't want to

lose. I'm hoping he will eventually find a woman who will understand his relationship with me and not stand in his way. I'm afraid chances are pretty slim, so right now I'm just trying to take what we have and enjoy it while it lasts. Bringing it back to my marriage, the ability to share part of my reactions (not all) with my husband has deepened our sense of closeness and awareness of each other as individuals—besides leading to some fantastic lovemaking.

"My family relationships are the most important single aspect of my life. Our daughter was not planned, and my first reaction when I found out I was pregnant was to set up plans for an abortion (I have never told her that and never will). The craziness of paying more for an abortion than for a delivery of a living baby, and my (totally unexpected) shock and horror at the idea of aborting *my* child that was already living inside me, backed by my husband, who was the first to suggest that perhaps we should actually have the baby, and keep it—led to a decision to have her after all. We took the money we'd borrowed for the abortion and went on a joyful antique-buying trip through New England, and never regretted it for a second.

"My husband gradually did more of the day-to-day care for her as she got older. By the time she was three, she was spending many hours a day more with him than with me, and it showed in the way she started turning to him when she would fall and hurt herself, or make something in preschool that she wanted to show us, etc. We used to think that there was 'something special about Mommy,' a close bond from the physical birth and nursing, that made her turn to me more—but then realized it was a matter of who was spending the most time with her, and it became 'something special about Daddy' because of the time they were together.

"I feel great about my 'affair,' though sensitive to its disturbing implications to my husband and to my lover (who does not want to be 'tied down' by any too emotional expectations on my part). My husband knew about it from the first time we had sex.

"As far as 'swinging,' my husband and I were both interested in sexual variety (my husband more than I, as I was the only woman he had slept with). We discovered, unexpectedly, that the emotional sharing and intimacy were at least as important in the swinging experience as the sexual part. Sharing the experience together also makes us more responsive to each other—and more appreciative. We're the opposite of bored with each other after fifteen years, which seems pretty exciting.

"I really find the word 'faithful,' used to describe monogamy, distasteful. My husband has had sex with another woman he feels a great deal for (she is now married and lives in Texas), as well as in swinging. It is very hard—anguishing—to be alone while the person one loves and is married to is out with someone else and probably having sex—but I feel very deeply that it is worth it for the involvement, freedom, and added dimensions of experience. The most surprising thing was finding out several years ago that my husband had had a sexual relationship with a male friend almost as long as his relationship with me. He was very ambivalent (hadn't told me about it for years) and felt that he had been 'seduced' really against his own wishes. The three of us now have a 'threesome' going when we can get together.

"My lover is certainly wary of a 'deep commitment' to a woman, of marriage, and of pressure to have children. As an already married woman and mother, I seem to provide him with a 'safe' romantic relationship.

"I am conscious of getting older—getting gray hair has been bringing it home to me—and certainly conscious that physical beauty does not increase with age. I am trying to get my body into better shape and keep more physically active, and I am also very happy about sensing myself maturing emotionally and intellectually, so I feel quite desirable. Though I am not walking around afraid that my husband will stop loving me, I certainly want to do all I can to preclude the possibility.

"I'm trying to broaden my friendships with women too. I don't really have a 'best woman friend' right now. There are several women whom I see in family contexts (playing cards, having dinner together), which include our husbands and children, whom I would like to get to know better, but that's as far as it goes."

But many more women who have tried open marriage are "open-marriage dropouts"* than like it:

"It started as 'group sex' with him and his wife—both of our families had lost their incomes during the mid-age crisis. We wanted to grab at something wild—we were rebelling and perhaps saying, 'Doing things the traditional way doesn't work. You were wrong, parents.'

"After lots of figuring we decided it wasn't worth all the agony, that these sexual relationships were not enhancing our lives at all but building a sense of confusion and unease, and that there was no need to explore other people's bodies in order to be close friends. I don't believe that monogamy is best for everyone, but honestly, I can't see what good it does me to go to bed with different people, with strangers."

"Basically I believe monogamy is the best philosophy for me, and from what I've observed, for most people. When I was in my mid-twenties (about ten years ago) my first husband and I experimented with 'open marriage.' He was the one that originated the idea, he'd fallen in love with a friend of mine and wanted to sleep with her. He wanted to be 'totally honest' with me. At first I was shocked, but when I thought about it, I felt it was 'good for us.' Besides, I had been attracted to other guys for some time myself.

*Women feel this way above and beyond any fear of sexually transmitted diseases, such as AIDS or herpes.

"At first, we found a new lifestyle and were like converts to a new religion. This was the perfect life for everyone, and anyone who didn't like it did not have a 'mature' relationship. My husband, and all of the other men I met who tried open relationships, were the ones to instigate them, but couldn't handle it in reality. The idea of 'their woman' (the one they were publicly identified with) being screwed by another guy was unacceptable to them. By this time, however, I had had several affairs.

"Eventually we were divorced. I continued having affairs for two years longer, always spouting the philosophy. In the end I met my present husband. I explained that I didn't believe in monogamy. He said that was fine for me, but he thought it was nuts and said goodbye. I thought about it after he'd left and realized I was giving up the perfect man for a crazy philosophy. I saw that none of the other relationships could ever develop beyond the infatuation stage because we could never trust each other. We had to protect ourselves from being hurt, so we never got close enough to be hurt. I went to him and told him I'd accept monogamy (but I had reservations).

"At the present time I could not conceive of risking all we have developed for a temporary, limited relationship. The four or five friends I had that were experimenting with open relationships came to similar conclusions. Some patched up their original relationship, some formed new, permanent relationships, but none of the women (or the men) feel that open relationships really work. As for secret affairs—I think sometimes it is necessary to 'prove' yourself for some personal reason. It's risky because the excitement of affairs tends to dull the original relationship, but I feel they can be constructive if kept secret. The real danger comes in damaging your partner's ego and in breaking the trust which is the basis of a good relationship. I am so careful to protect this ego/trust balance in my present relationship that I will not even express attraction for someone, even on TV. My husband does the same for me. Consequently I feel I am the most desirable woman in the world to him. And he is the most desirable man in the world to me."

Being "The Other Woman"

52 percent of single women say it is wrong and/or impractical to go out with married men, and do not do it:

"It is a sin to have sex outside of marriage, or to even 'just go out with' a married person."

"I've been tempted but thought it would be a destructive situation, and there are other fish in the sea."

Some mention their desire to be loyal to other women:

"I refuse to see a man who is married, regardless of the circumstances. I'd feel it to be a deception on my own womanhood. Women have been screwed over by the establishment and have allowed it to happen too long. Among the numerous changes I have effected in my life as I have grown in the feminist movement, one is that no matter how desperate I feel for sex or attention, I won't take it and deceive another woman at the same time."

"I went out with a married man who didn't tell me he was married. As soon as I found out, I immediately stopped. I will not be a third party in someone else's relationship. I don't need the hassle and I'm sure his wife doesn't. It's more important to me to support women than men, even if I don't know them. If he (the husband) is sleeping around, there's probably already trouble in their marriage and I won't become part of that trouble."

"I think far too much of women to go with one's husband. At about twenty I flirted with a married man who told me how bad his marriage/wife was. Something might have happened but I met his wife—she was a beautiful, nice mother of four with a jerk for a husband."

But a surprising 45 percent of single women are remarkably blasé about seeing married men:

"When I was single I had affairs with married men. One long-term. It felt sneaky—yet exciting."

"I have gone with several married men. We got along quite well. I never insisted they leave their wives, though in one relationship I would have preferred him to."

"I did it both when I was single and after I was married—it was doubly terrifying and yet exciting because of the extra dose of danger connected with it."

"I am going with a married man right now. It is not as difficult to handle as I expected. In fact, it's pretty easy. We have a good relationship without a lot of expectations."

"I once had an affair with a married man. Experienced my first orgasm. We are great friends to this day. Having platonic dinner with him tonight."

"I dated a lot of married men. They are just like all people—some of them I liked, some of them I didn't."

"I'm only seventeen, but I think it would be fun someday to try that. I know some men right now who'd be fun to go with."

"At times I have enjoyed seeing men married and living with someone else. It means they have their principal needs met by other than me and we can share good quality time. At times, I need someone to be more primary to me and then I do not enjoy married men."

"I've dated many married men. I didn't mind that they were married. That made the relationship more inviting to me. I was not looking for anything serious or long-term at the time. I didn't give his wife much thought. At this time in my life I was very male-centered. I didn't think about the wife as a sister or even another woman. I didn't see her as an important person to consider. I used to say, 'Hey, I'm fucking him, not his wife.'"

Frequently, as seen, these relationships sound surprisingly "normal" and enjoyable:

"I most enjoy talking and laughing with him. He is such a relaxing person to be with. And he is very tender in intimate moments. He doesn't say much, but his actions show how he feels. He holds me and we'll talk about anything. When he kisses me before he leaves, I get the feeling that he desperately doesn't want to go. I feel so good with him. I just wish he could overcome the guilt that pops up now and then."

One woman thinks it is particularly flattering being wanted by a married man:

"It is exciting to think that a man finds you desirable when he has a woman whom he obviously found desirable at some time waiting at home. Still, a married man is an enigma because there is always the suspicion that he may be playing along."

But other women say they cannot respect married men who have affairs; one who became briefly involved says she decided he was a "wimp" to stay in a marriage he didn't like:

"I was infatuated with a married man for a short while my first year in college. I came to see him as a real wimp for limping along in his relationship with his wife and decided to save myself all this bother and hassle by breaking off with him. We never did sleep together a second time. He was a nice guy, and an extraordinary artist, but he just didn't have enough character. I would never consider an affair with a married man now, I don't think."

Although most women do not agree, 22 percent say that being involved with a married man is a lonely or emotionally wrenching, painful experience:

"It was hell. There was no emotional support at bad times—no holidays together. Lots of heartache—not worth it."

"It was like always having a wall between us, or a little piece of him was always somewhere else, never quite totally with me."

"It can hurt a lot and can be very lonely. One constant heartache—unless you like triangles."

"When my married lover broke up with me, I hated him and myself for several months afterward. I couldn't really start living again until I'd gotten him back, gotten him to leave his wife, and then I broke up with him."

"My first love and sexual experience was with an older, married man. That has to be the loneliest existence for anyone. Waiting for him to call you, spend time with you, etc. Even when you're together it's lonely, because you know he will leave you all alone. I cried myself to sleep at night many more nights than I care to remember."

"Things were very closed and secretive. I never even knew where he lived, never met any of his friends and mine never met him. It was as though I was leading two distinct lives. I spent a lot of time waiting, hoping, and not knowing when or if he'd show up. I also woke up alone every morning regardless of how close our sexual relationship had made us feel; it was always only momentary because he had to leave and I always knew it was going to end—I wonder if we ever really gave ourselves as completely as we would have if his wife had not been (figuratively) in bed with us. I don't think my experience of 'the man calling all the shots' is unlike many other women's and it would be great to see a study done on the emotional makeup of both parties that lets or helps create these situations."

Some say being clandestine makes them feel cheap or uncomfortable:

"I once dated a married man briefly and I really did not like it. I felt very much like I was playing second fiddle. I hated all the hiding and not seeing each other on weekends."

"I once had a relationship with a married man. It was profoundly painful for me because I felt like an accomplice to his infidelity. After three unsuccessful tries I finally ended it, but I worshipped the man. He called all the shots. I had been divorced two years when I met him—it seems ironic that my marriage had no infidelity, but my single life did. I do not recommend it—I believe that the single person is manipulated by the married person, who does not have the courage to get out of a bad marriage. I wound up feeling that I served as his entertainment—his unpaid whore."

—Or guilty:

"I felt very sorry for his wife and two children. In fact, I thought about calling her up and telling her about it, which I also told him. He did not care, as he proclaimed that his love for her was dead, and she knew it. He planned on getting a divorce from her and marrying me. I liked her far too much and had a lot of 'guilt' feelings. I finally told him that I didn't want anything further to do with him until he did get a divorce (which I knew was not my fault—about him divorcing her for me—but I had 'guilt' about 'sneaking' around). He asked me if I could wait one year. I told him that I didn't know for sure. In the meantime, I did a lot of thinking and could not get the thought of myself as a marriage wrecker out of my mind. I met someone else. He is still with his wife, as it should be. Besides, if he did marry me what would have stopped him from 'cheating' on me, just like he did with her?"

Most women prefer not to think about whether their lover is having sex with his wife also:

"It is difficult for him to be faithful to me since he is married. I knew he had a wife and it was something I had to face. It doesn't bother me knowing he is in bed with his wife, for I know I have him even though I'm not there. I must, for I am having an affair with him!"

"My lover is 'faithful' to me. I know him too well. He has sex with his wife but I don't consider that being unfaithful to me. I know that I would be upset if he found someone else, but his wife is an accepted part of our relationship. I do not think she knows about me."

"As for my lover, I know I am not the only woman in his life. I don't like it but there's nothing I can do about it."

Some like the limitations on commitment—a "safety zone":

"I'm seeing a married man. He's great and has no control or ties on me but yet I still have him."

"The fact that he was married was not a problem to me. It was more like a 'safe zone.' I could be sure that he would not push for marriage between us."

"The only reason I got into this relationship was because he is married. It protects me from getting too emotionally involved with him. It keeps my feet firmly planted on the ground."

Women who are married often find they can establish a good or working relationship with another married person; does this mean they are still "the other woman"? Yes:

"My lover is married. I don't mind his being married now but when I was single it upset me terribly. Since I am now happy in my marriage I don't really care if my lover is married or not."

"My second affair was with a married man. Actually, I think it was the best. They are far less demanding on your time—if you are married also. For a while I was living by myself, and I hated always waiting on him. It helps me to understand a little more how the single men in my life must have felt. If you understand from the start that a married man isn't going to leave his wife, you can probably have a pretty decent affair. Don't ever expect him to leave, though. Even if he did, you would never trust him if you were married to him."

Single women with married lovers are likely to take these relationships more seriously than married women: *

"I like being in love. Our frustration is the fact that he is married to another. He loves her and his small children very much and will not leave them. I understand that and it is acceptable but I do wish we had more time together. Perhaps that's why we don't take each other for granted. Our time together is so very precious. It is like nothing I've ever known. I am very happy when we are together and even when we aren't together."

"I am very much in love with my man. I think our feelings for each other are shared equally. I love him for being him. I accept him just as he is. He is honest and open with me about his 'other life.' He doesn't have to impress me. I hurt when he hurts. I hurt when I see him struggling with guilt. I love him enough to let go if it gets to be too much for him. I am a better person for loving him, and if I ever have to let go, we both will have known a very special love."

"We are free in our thoughts, actions, and speech when together. And friends, true and blue—in public. But we aren't free to marry. Happy? Yes, for we have each other—no matter what. He would like to take me home as his own—and sometimes he cries because he can't. A big strong beautiful man and he sheds tears because I'm not his to do more for!"

"Our time together is very precious to both of us. I feel I give him so much and add to his life. What he gives me in return is fantastic. I feel so much love it hurts. I am not sorry I got involved. We both separately tried to break this off, but neither one of us can.

"I can't contact him except to call his accountant and leave a message. I don't really worry, for he is very good about calling. Our relationship is not only sex: we do not go to bed together every time we are together; in fact, we have gone three months without going to bed. We have lunch together at least once a week.

"He told me last week he was going to have me one way or the other even if it killed him. I feel the same way, but I have known from the beginning that I could not pressure him. I know he will leave his wife. It will all take time. He has a lot to lose, for he is a big businessman, has worked hard all his life and has property, business, money, etc. I have told him not to do anything stupid, for he has worked very hard. We have excellent communication. There isn't anything we can't talk about. We are very honest with each other. He makes me so happy, I feel like a complete woman and very satisfied. One thing that really intrigues me is that I always felt a man had an affair for the sex part of it, but it is not true in our case. He has sex with his wife also.

*And single women in love with their married lovers are more likely to be monogamous.

"We do so many things together. We meet in intriguing places, haul dirt to a house he is building, sell cattle, sit under a rack and drink wine, or he does plumbing for my girlfriend. It feels so good to be with him. I enjoy every minute of it. I wish he were single."

"I love him so much and know I can never give him up even if I never can have him all the time. The only way I can give him up is by death. I know as time goes by we are liable to get caught in this affair by his wife. I don't want to hurt her, I don't know her, but there is more to being a wife than spending money, social activities, and saying you are Mrs. Such-and-such. As long as I make him happy and he makes me happy, we will continue. He wants me to find someone and get married and be happy, but he has said he would be hurt and it would make his life miserable."

One woman in her fifties describes the hurt she feels at being suddenly dropped when her lover returned to his wife—as she had taken the relationship seriously:

"I am fifty-five, divorced after twenty-five years of marriage, mother of three, grandmother of two. I have been working in a full-time secretarial job for twenty years, plus I sell Tupperware. I am Christian and very involved in church. I do not feel my age and probably don't act it.

"I had an affair for the last year that just ended. This relationship brought me a number of things—love, passion, sexual intimacy, self-confidence. But I was not happy because he was not yet divorced. I struggled with this constantly except when we were together; then I just enjoyed being with him. We enjoyed sex, talking, being affectionate. But we didn't go out because he was still married.

"Eventually he told me he loved me and had for a long, long time, but he also said he was not in a position to marry me. But he didn't say anything about breaking up. Then I didn't hear from him for about two weeks and I called and he did not return the call. The next week I called again and he did not return the call until the end of the week. In the course of conversation, I said that he really sounded good and he said yes, things were going very good at home and they had decided to give it a try for three months. He asked me to have lunch with him the next day, but he did not show up, and I have not heard from him since.

"I was very hurt that he just left without a word, because I thought we had a very deep friendship and we should have been able to talk about it. I thought he knew me well enough to know I would not create a scene. He was my first real love and everything was so good. I almost went to pieces. It has taken me a long time to put myself back together, to accept the fact that I will never see him again. He was the center of my life. So much of what I did and the plans I made were flexible in case we had a chance to be together.

"After eight months I have finally accepted our breakup. No one knew of the affair, so I could not talk to anyone about it. It has been very difficult. I pray a lot. Until I accepted what happened, he was on my mind constantly. I could not put him out. I can finally try and do that. I am not always successful. My heart still leaps when something reminds me of him. But I know it is over."

Whatever happened to "the other man"?

Finally, there is the phenomenon of "the other man"—i.e., a single man whom a married woman is having an extramarital affair with; why is it that this is not a term heard, equivalent to "the other woman"? Certainly, this is a common enough practice to deserve a name; could it be that "the other woman" is such a common term because, once again, language is used to enforce the society's dominant ideology: a term is created for women, who are singled out, so that the double standard punishes women who have "illicit" sex but does not punish men in the same way. This is another example of how our language is permeated with vocabulary that judges women differently from men—negatively. In this case, the stereotype harks back to the prototype of the evil woman, Eve the Temptress, for which there is no male equivalent.

Finances and Housework

Finances: Who Earns the Money and How Is It Split?

70 percent of women now earn money: What is the effect on marriage?

The biggest change in marriage in this century has happened in the last seven years: now, for the first time, the majority of married women have an income of their own. No matter how small this income is, it is the difference between choice and no choice.

It is often said that women are working in such large numbers now because of financial necessity: keeping up a "middle-class" standard of living (or saving for college educations for the children, etc.) requires the work of two people instead of just one. However, contrary to this "explanation" (which suits the needs of an ideology that doesn't want to believe women are changing), women here say they work because they like to have a life of their own. Many have experienced being financially dependent and found that they were treated like children or bossed around; others have always worked and don't want to give up the skill they are proud of, reputations they have worked to build up. Of course, women also cite financial need of the family, and complain about work, as men always have: sometimes it is exhausting, boring, and one dreams of a perpetual holiday. But 86 percent of women here, whether they say they are working for the money *because of the independence money brings,* or because they feel more complete when they participate in the "outside" world, agree they don't want to go back to the days when women didn't have the opportunity to have jobs and careers. They like working, and they like financial independence—even though they may want to share with someone.

How do women feel about being financially dependent on their husbands?

87 percent of women who are or have been financially dependent feel uncomfortable and unhappy in this situation:

"I am financially dependent on my husband. What I have is what I've chosen: not working, being home with the children. I don't feel as independent as I did when I was working before I married. I very rarely spend money on myself. I just feel unfair spending someone else's money on myself. But my husband would hate it if I worked. He wants to feel he's head of the family, the real provider."

"I've worked outside on and off—but he pays the bills. Without my own income, I am nothing but a slave—my years of work, raising children, and keeping house have been taken for granted and expected. And I am made to feel guilty for not having done (or now doing) more!"

"It still is a problem that I'm working on—I'm going to school—but I want to fill my kids' needs also—so it's a tightrope and there is only so much time and health. I feel inferior to him as a result of the financial dependence—and he feels superior as a result."

"I felt guilty asking for any money and I wouldn't ask unless it was for groceries."

"I was dependent on my husband. At the time, all seemed very right and normal to me, but when he left, one of the things he said was 'You only need me for my money.' "

"I felt being dependent took away a great deal of my independence. I felt like a poorly paid or unpaid servant."

"I felt like an employee most of the time: 'Could I please have an extra five dollars this week?' I hated it and still do."

"This was a problem in my marriage—I felt like a whore the last three years when I was unemployed and in law school. Now, although I am presently financially dependent on my lover, it doesn't matter—because only a few months ago he was financially dependent on me. (We alternate on money earning.)"

"I felt I had to continue the relationship even if it was not going well because I could not afford to do otherwise."

"I am financially dependent on my husband. It can be a problem at times. I am not too crazy about it. I feel funny buying gifts for him and using *his* money."

"I was financially dependent on a man I was married to. I felt guilty spending his money. He started cheating on me and I felt bad about it until I realized that then I didn't need to feel guilty spending his money anymore. I could see it as 'revenge.' I couldn't talk about all this to him, I couldn't talk about it to anybody."

"I was financially dependent on my husband. I felt like a parasite. Because the money was his, I felt that if it ever came to the bottom line, I would have no say in how the money was spent. Fortunately, he was considerate of my feelings and needs and the matter never came to a head."

"I am now financially dependent on the man I live with. I don't like it but I am not able to work now to support myself, so I consider myself very lucky to have someone to support me. When my husband holds it over my head—like I should be eternally grateful to him—I don't like it."

"He controls saving and spending. I hate it. I have to ask for money to buy clothes, etc. It is degrading because I work just as hard as he does, yet I'm like a lowly servant."

"When I lived with my husband, and the children were small, I could not have a job of my own. I had to ask my husband for money—which made me feel like an idiot; dumb, poor, and helpless."

"I was financially dependent when I was married. I felt guilty spending money on myself, even if it was something I needed. I felt that only after the rest of the family was taken care of completely, then and only then would I buy something for myself. Now we both work at careers. We split everything down the middle. We have separate accounts. We like it this way. It solves a lot of conflicts. One person is not bearing the burden of another. I treat myself to luxury, take pride in wearing nice clothes, and enjoy myself without feeling guilty."

But sometimes financial dependency does not seem to be a problem; in fact, for 13 percent of women, it seems to be accepted as a part of a good relationship:

"I was financially dependent on my ex. It didn't bother me a bit. I'd been independent and working for many years prior to the marriage. I'm thankful I was able to stay home with my kids during their early years. The fact he was bringing in all the money didn't seem to affect the relationship. Had I needed to work for us to stay financially able, well, then I would've felt compelled to, but we were able to live on his income fairly comfortably."

"My husband is a fireman. I no longer work since our daughter was born, but I do babysit another child. We could use more money but it is more important to be home with our daughter."

"I was financially dependent on my husband when the children were young and generally I didn't mind since I had been reared to believe this was the way it was supposed to be."

"My husband enjoys my being home. He likes to provide financially for us (a modest, but adequate, income). When I did work outside the home, my husband was very supportive and encouraged me to do what I wanted in regard to work and career. Having experienced both, we prefer our lifestyle now. I love the freedom and the leisure. He loves the fact that I am happy and have more to offer him in a supportive sense."

Do these women have more self-esteem and so value their homemaking services more highly than some other women? Or do women who insist on making their own money have more pride?

These women have a very clear sense that they work as hard inside the home as the man does at his job—that they provide essential services and therefore are just as entitled to the money as he is:

"I felt guilty about not being able to contribute financially, but then I realized that he had maid, chauffeur, chef, etc. privileges plus the title to the house! He contributed money, I labor."

"He has earned the actual income, but I feel I have contributed an equal amount in labor and sacrifice and commitment."

"I was financially dependent on my husband during the ten years I was home with the children. However, we had had three years of experience in dual-paycheck living prior to that. I always felt the money was as much mine as his. I worked as hard at home as he did at work; he was dependent on me to care for the house and the children."

"I was totally financially dependent on my husband until just a couple of weeks ago (at the time of the sale of the house). I never felt wrong, apologetic, or concerned about it. I always felt I worked hard enough at being wife, mother, housekeeper, hostess, etc. to deserve that financial security. However, at the moment of holding a check for several thousands of dollars in my hand and knowing it was mine and it would keep me independent for quite a while, I felt something new and unexpectedly wonderful. As if I'd rounded an unexpected bend in the road and discovered a new road, an unexpected vision before me. I immediately found financial counsel and determined to become knowledgeable about investments. I think, in that moment, I sprouted leaves that had only been buds for a long, chilly spring."

But others are not so sure:

"I can't figure out what I am doing that is equivalent in the relationship. This could be because I don't give enough value to myself. The situation with money has in the past affected the relationship. I always felt badly accepting money and/or gifts from a man. I am trying to unlearn the bad parts of my childhood experiences that made me end up like this. At the same time, I would like to hold on to my sense of pride in my own accomplishments and ability to take care of myself."

"Should" we value ourselves more and not feel uncomfortable being financially "dependent"? Is it our financial dependency or men's attitudes toward us when we are economically dependent which make us uncomfortable? Are we "brainwashed" to feel we are worth too little?

In the United Kingdom and other countries, there is a movement, "Wages for Housework," which advocates the idea that the husband should pay the wife for her services within the house—especially if she works full-time at home, doing the child rearing and cooking, cleaning, etc. Only in this way, it is argued, can the woman have the dignity of independence that will make it possible for her to stay in the marriage out of choice. In the United States, while this would be a wrenching economic adjustment, there is no question that it would improve the status of women—and women's respect for men.

Even if a woman is comfortable being financially dependent on a man, still there may be insidious psychological effects, as one woman describes:

"I think many women 'fall in love' and get locked into a dependent relationship. The mere fact of dependency on the part of an adult usually brings on feelings of inferiority on her part and his too. I wish I had a dime for every man I've heard say that his wife 'does nothing but housework and child rearing,' who say, 'I support her very well,' 'She's always spending my money,' etc., and my favorite (or least favorite, as a member of the female gender) is: 'I'll keep the marriage together, that way I'll always have my laundry done, my home clean, my meals ready, and I'll know when I'm older where my next fuck is coming from, and there will be someone there to push my wheelchair if I need it.' Is that all that woman is once he supports her? A housekeeper, cook, prostitute, and nurse? If women could maintain independence and equality in a relationship this shouldn't happen—but even the best intentions don't seem to work once she depends on him."

Women who "only" work at home do not receive pensions or social security benefits:

"I have always been financially dependent. I did not work when my children were young. My earnings now are significantly less than my husband's. Now that I am older I have a problem related to retirement. Since I will not receive a pension when I stop working, I will no longer have an independent income. I am reluctant to go back to asking for personal funds."

Even earning a small amount, or keeping one's job skills up to date, seems to take the pressure off:

"He earns more than I do, and we depend on his salary to live. But I like having earning power. I like when I make enough so I never have to ask for any money. I like that feeling of independence. I used to be sole breadwinner when he was in school."

"About twelve years of our thirty I worked full-time. And I still work half-time and plan to continue to do so until I'm forced to retire unless something happens that necessitates my going to work full-time. It has been a problem only when I feel too dependent. Seems our god MONEY has gotten to me and it symbolizes independence. And, of course, since it affected me and my decisions, it affected the relationship."

"Currently I am substitute teaching and this gives me a sense of contributing to the economic unit, because my husband respects this more than he does any caring for the children, etc., and since he provides the child care when I do this, he has a new respect for how much work that is (your basic role-changing thing). He is very good-natured about this—not 'ashamed' to tell his male friends, etc."

—Or Having a Small Bank Account of One's Own:

"Since I worked before marriage, I do have my own money and keep it in my own personal account. It gives me a certain amount of independence which both my husband and I are aware of."

If leaving a man is not a viable financial alternative for a woman, she can never be really sure she is staying because she wants to or because she has to; and women who want to divorce can suddenly realize they are without resources or funds:

"I'm staying in a relationship I would rather have left years ago. Can't afford to leave. I'm fifty and don't know what kind of a job I could get."

"The reason I gave myself originally for getting married was the glamour of the war (World War II) and seeking romance and mutual security. It was torturous for me to finally admit to myself during the 1970s that I married him for money. I stayed in the marriage because of the kids and he was a good provider. I thought there was no way I could ever make money. My self-image was that the only job I was qualified for was that of dishwasher in a basement. That's the image he reinforced through years and years of marriage."

"At fifty-eight, when you want out of a marriage, you haven't worked in thirty years, damn right, money affects everything. He closed the checking account. Before that he always gave me an allowance like a child. The reason we took so long with our separation and mediation was that he was going to cut me off without a cent except for six months to train for a job. And he was not acknowledging any responsibility for our daughter, who just couldn't make it on her own."

Although the situation for most women is better than ten years ago, the impact of economics and especially economic dependence on women should not be considered "a thing of the past," as one woman's situation forcefully illustrates:

"I'm a twenty-five-year-old black woman. I'm loving, caring, intelligent, and fun. I've got lots of potential, but I'm not particularly happy. I guess I am 'young,' but I don't feel it. I'm afraid of getting older, if I continue to be poor. I don't want to be a shopping-bag lady.

"My biggest problem right now is having to depend on a man to survive. He's a thirty-three-year-old musician, we've lived together more than five years. Economics is the basis of the relationship. I'm broke and he's putting up with me. Regular sex is the best aspect for him. Food and shelter for me. The most difficult part is that he doesn't want me here. I don't love him, I've never been in love, but I do care about him a great deal. I don't feel loved by him either.

"I want financial independence. My own car, apartment, job, money. My own choices. I go to college part-time and am trying to get a career, but at this point in time it looks so far away. Being with my friends, who like me without qualification, makes me happy.

"We had a big fight over his supporting me the other day. He feels trapped. I feel trapped too. After all, I've been trying my best to find a job for more than two years. There are just no jobs here. Unemployment in Detroit is 25 percent. He insisted that I wasn't trying hard enough. I suggested that he look in the want ads and see 'all those wonderful job opportunities available to me.' He compared me to 'all the other women who wanted to fuck up his life,' including his mother. I walked away from him. He grabbed me by the shoulders and shook me. I went to my room and lay down and read. A couple of hours later he apologized for shaking me and calmly explained why he was right. He doesn't normally get physical. Once he raised his arm as if to hit me. Sometimes he pokes me with his fingers to make his points. He always feels bad about it afterwards.

"We fight about money most frequently. Nobody wins. I feel as though I have stomach flu during the fight. Sometimes I even have diarrhea. These arguments never get resolved. Sometimes they go on and on until I fall asleep, or sometimes he just stops when he realizes that he's getting into the same argument he always has. He usually says he's sorry, and that's when I get to hear the story of his miserable life again. We don't really make up. He thinks it's my fault.

"I was happiest with him when I was working days and he was working nights and we both had our own money and cars and friends. Whenever we got together we enjoyed each other. That was only two years out of our five living together.

"He usually doesn't treat me with much affection and respect now. He's not emotionally supportive. In intimate moments, he doesn't tell me he loves me, or that I'm wonderful or beautiful. He doesn't tell me that I make him want sex with me, or talk tenderly. He told me he didn't want to sleep in the same bed with me anymore, and made me get my own bed. He says I'm fat and ugly. He says I'm a leech.

"He doesn't know me very well. He talks a lot about himself, but when I try to share about myself, he doesn't want it. When I do have the apartment to myself, I spend a lot of time reading, listening to the music that I like, soaking in the tub with my herbal concoctions and masturbating. This gives me some time to 'talk to' myself. My women friends are easier to talk to anyway. I don't have to explain my meanings to women like I have to with men. My women friends understand what I say right away.

"I guess now what I'd really like is a career I can depend on. I don't have any great expectations about love."

More and more women are finding that they basically support themselves all through life, whether married or not:

"I have never been totally financially dependent on a man. My husband was not financially responsible, I carried the financial load. Later when I lived with a man for about two years, he shared equally in joint financial things. This was a new experience for me—having someone carry their share of the load. Otherwise I have, as an adult, taken care of myself."

82 percent of women under twenty-five stress that they never want to be financially dependent:

"Never was dependent except on my father. It was a problem even with my father and I don't ever want to be financially dependent on a man again."

"I've never been, and if I can help it, never will be. I like being part of his life, but not slapping him with the money burden. I don't and never will like people spending money on me. I feel guilty."

"I don't like to be financially dependent on anyone. It would upset my balance in the relationship."

One woman describes how her marriage has changed since she became the major wage earner:

"Money is a great issue in our marriage because my husband always had a good income, whereas I was struggling with my business and he was constantly reminding me that he supported both me and the business—even though he used it to his benefit as a substantial tax write-off. He had little or no compassion about my financial situation until he became involved in a traumatic business deal and soon after that was unemployed.

"Since my husband has been unemployed and I have gone to work and school, he has been much more helpful with housework and child care. He also has a new humility about his once infallible 'earning power' and admits that he may never have full-time work again.

"But the idea that work makes a woman multi-dimensional or that work is somehow intellectually challenging is a bunch of bull doodoo. I think women with fulfilling, upwardly mobile careers tend to forget that most women who work do so out of economic necessity and do whatever they can stand to do for money. I am fortunate that I have had fairly stimulating careers, but I also know that not all women, or men for that matter, share that experience."

Another tells how happy she feels now, earning half the household income and sometimes more:

"I have been financially dependent on my husband for about four years, and it was a major problem in how I viewed myself and my contributions to our relationship. I have felt much better about myself since earning my share, and sometimes more than my share, of our household expenses. I would NEVER want to go back to a time of not having my own independent source of income. I feel much more assertive in all realms when I know I am capable of supporting myself financially, having the work experiences, work friends, and so forth, so I am not too dependent on my family. I very much enjoy being the one who brings in more money—and for personal selfish reasons, I hope it continues for quite a while! Though the more money we have, the more we've had time to go out and do entertainment-type fun things together, which has been great."

One woman, married twenty-six years and the major wage earner for much of that time, doesn't seem to see her situation as unusual:

"I am fifty-two years old, upper-middle-class, wife, mother, college graduate, career woman. Married at twenty-six and still happy. Except for the year my daughter was born, I have worked full-time since I graduated from college—the last twenty-two years. I am the major wage earner in our household. My husband is self-employed—a wonderful person, but a terrible businessman.

"Since we both work, for the most part I do all the household things, and he does the cellar, garage, cars, outside-type things. Occasionally he helps with the dishes, laundry, cleaning, etc. Previously I took care of my daughter for the first year, my husband for the next nine months, then we had sitters. We'd take turns staying home when she was sick.

"As I'm the major wage earner, I pay most of the bills (mortgage, food, property taxes, etc.). My husband, who works very hard and earns little, pays his business expenses, pet bills, all house repairs, remodeling, garden, outside expenses, etc. We both have our own checking accounts. Over the years I've learned to accept the fact that I'm in a business that pays well and he's in an unreliable one.

"The best part of being married is that in a way I feel independent. Nice to have someone to share life with. I am a 'scheduled' person, which sometimes drives my family nuts, but to accomplish all I have to do I have to schedule my time carefully. I wish my husband were a bit more assertive and a better businessman, but perhaps if he were, he would not be so easy to live with."

What percentage of women are still supported by men? For how long? The meaning of work to women

There are some women who want to be "dependent," especially while having children and while the children are young. This is a choice that should be open to a woman or a man, without any social stigma. But only 17 percent of women in this study say they want to stay home for more than two years with young children and be totally dependent; most want to have a family and to work too, as men do, after the initial years of raising children.

Women staying home today for more than two years are in such a minority that they often feel defensive:

"What I want my husband and lover to realize is that it was *my choice* to stay home and raise the children. Babies are only little for a very short time. I didn't want to miss out on all this for all the money and exciting career in the world. It's once in a lifetime. My lover seems to understand this the best. When I told him I wanted to be home until my children were in school, he said, 'At least that long.' He understands how important it is to children to have a parent available to them. The women's movement should emphasize choice, but it hasn't. It seems to be saying more: 'Compete with men,' 'Day care is just as good as Mommy.' It's really not liberating at all."

One woman, however, says, "shamelessly":

"I've been married nineteen years. The best thing about it? I don't have to work! (The worst? Not much freedom to be me.)"

————————————

Approximately 29 percent of women still believe theoretically that men should give women financial support in return for keeping a home and rearing children. But although even more women may not have objections to this exchange in theory, almost all agree that it involves real problems in practice—since a man's earning all the money seems to make most men act superior.

Therefore, most women in this study are much more comfortable with having jobs than with being dependent: 92 percent of those who have had an independent income never want to go back to being without. Only 12 percent of women in this study who are now dependent wish to remain so; the others, of every age group (there is no wide discrepancy between older and younger women), want to have a family *and* work too. They want to be out in the world, have the status and prestige that this brings, the fun of being in contact with many people, and the financial rewards. Even though women agree that most outside work is drudgery, just as housework is drudgery, the consensus is that housework is a greater drudgery, and in the end, one has no salary to show for it.

Are women often uncomfortable when they are dependent on a man because this is a "natural" feeling or because of most men's attitude—i.e., a woman's being financially dependent makes many men act superior? Perhaps for both reasons. But no matter what the theoretical answers here, the practical reality is that, for the overwhelming majority of women now, having a job is a ticket to autonomy, independence, ability to determine one's own future, and broader interests in life.*

Some women, however, question the new "equality" system in which women are expected to "pay their own way," while men still do not reciprocate by giving equally in other areas, such as housework and emotional support:

"I've really been fucked over by feminism. I mean, I went with this well-off man and that one, and I never got married, never took a thing—and here I am,

*On the other hand, is it that outside work is so fulfilling that everyone wants to escape from the home, men too; or, is home the stable harbor that one can always run to after a hard day in a ruthless, competitive work world? Which is more the prison?

fifty, without a cent, in a world where men have money and women don't. Sure, I work, I have an enviable job, but I really don't have any money. I could have had a house, etc. Why didn't I take them? My pride. But I guess if I had it to do all over, I'd still do the same things."

Some women here and in other studies (such as one done by *Woman's Day* in 1985–86) feel resentful at now having to earn money "too," since they are still doing most of the work at home—both emotional and physical work. They may say, "Now men have it all," that men have been the "big gainers" in the last ten years (as *Woman's Day* puts it). Men now have less economic pressure on them since women are contributing money, working outside the home, while most men are still expecting/enjoying housekeeping services, a mothering service for the children, sexual service (a definition of sex which always guarantees him an orgasm and access to her body or else an "explanation"), and a woman striving for general social graces, probably working on her appearance, doing her hair, etc. So women feel men have many fewer responsibilities, while women have less and less time for themselves. In fact, some conservative women's groups have argued that women "had it made" when men supported women—that women had *more* prestige when it was thought "only right" that men support women—and that now women have less power and status.

But most women, even those who resent men's "having it all," like the independence that comes with having jobs. Seventy-six percent of the women in this study, women of all ages, of all marital and economic backgrounds, do not want to go back to being financially dependent on a man. They want men to change their attitudes instead.

Women manage the money in most families

It is amazing to see how many women are managing the entire family finances—in the face of the stereotypes about how incapable women are and how poor women are at math. Ninety-one percent of the women in this study, whether or not they work outside the home, have the responsibility for balancing the books and paying the bills.

What does it mean to be "in charge of all the money"? Is this just another form of housework, or is it a position of power?

82 percent of women replying to this study say they are "in charge" of the family money, even if the husband is the only outside wage earner:

"I do not work outside the home. My husband hands me his paycheck, does not even sign his own name. I then handle all the finances. I prefer it this way but wish he would take some interest and at least know what our finances are."

"He is the only one working outside the home. He keeps what he will need for the week out of his pay and the rest goes in the bank. I make sure the bills are paid when they are due."

"He gives me the money and I pay the bills. He abdicates all financial things to me. I don't mind, I've been doing it for seventeen years, so I guess it's a habit. He resents when we're broke, but doesn't care to know why, it just depresses him."

Many women, as seen, also say that their husbands are not reliable or especially good at handling the family budget:

"After a year or so of problems, the financial duties were eventually settled by putting his salary in a joint account. I withdrew a certain amount to run the house on. I paid all the bills (out of the joint account)."

"We both worked. I had always been a good money manager, had good credit, paid my bills on time. He never paid his bills on time, had bill collectors after him, water shut off, electricity shut off (it should have been a good indicator to his character, but I was blind to all the negatives), rent always late. So it was agreed upon before we married that I would handle the money. We would have a joint account. All the necessary bills would be paid out of one pot, and within a year's time, we hoped, our credit-type bills would be paid off, even though it meant doing without during the meantime."

One couple switches financial control every couple of years, with good results:

"We have taken turns controlling the money, and it works out well for one person to be in charge but switching over every year or two. He's doing the money stuff now, especially the bills, but I do the shopping. He just tells me how much I can spend without breaking us in the budget."

Money-sharing arrangements of those with double incomes

With couples who both work outside the home, three basic money- and expense-sharing methods are widely used.

1 (32 percent)

Each person has a prearranged responsibility for paying certain items every month:

"We both work and have a regular income. I pay for the food, utilities, clothing, and household items. He pays the mortgage and the heat. He usually pays the property taxes, though I paid them this year because he was short of funds."

"I buy the groceries, household and personal items, items for my son, and gifts. My husband pays for rent, heating, our vehicle, our nights out, parties, and insurance. Whatever is left over from our check is the 'spending money'—no questions asked. We never argue about money."

"My husband pays all the bills in regard to the house. I pay for anything that has to be done to the house as upkeep, even building, plumbing, etc. I pay for most of his clothes and I pay for our annual vacation—usually in the area of $2,000 or $3,000 to go out of the country! I buy the groceries. I think he spends too much money on entertaining his friends but he doesn't like being questioned in this regard."

"We both work. He pays most of the bills because he is running a business and can claim many expenses under his business. I pay the mortgage. I resent that he can afford to buy a major item occasionally but I only buy things like clothes. But I have enough money left to go to plays or the ballet, which is very important to me. I go with my sister or women friends and he does not object to this."

"We alternate mortgage payments. He pays insurance and electricity. I pay MasterCard, telephone, and my school loans. We have one joint savings account from which to pay large and one-time bills. We take turns buying groceries. Feels equal."

"We both work and we keep our money entirely separate. Because he makes twice as much as I do, we split the utilities one-third (me) and two-thirds (him). The mortgage is split down the middle (as I want 50 percent financial equity in the property). The groceries are split 60-40 except when his daughter is staying with us, then he picks up an additional 10 percent, and the split is 70-30. I pay all my own expenses—medical, dental, car, etc.—and he does likewise. Every two weeks we settle up our accounts and I pay him or he pays me what each of us owes the other. We generally split 50-50 on household items. If one of us wants something that the other doesn't, then the one that wants it has to buy it himself. We share all our possessions, but we do know what is mine, his, and ours. I believe the reason for all these 'rules' is that we were both financially burned in our first marriages. We both love this arrangement, and it works very well for both of us. It gives us each a great deal of independence without putting all the financial responsibility on just one person."

2 (36 percent)

All money is put into one account; control of the account is sometimes joint, or sometimes one or the other has the responsibility for writing checks and balancing the budget:

"We both work. All of the money goes in together. I control it because he couldn't be bothered to do it right. We discuss major purchases. He has an account of his own for moonlighting money, which he spends on his Jaguar. I think he sometimes feels he has to ask for money. But it is because he is too disorganized to remember to go to the bank."

"He and I both put our earnings in the same account. Most of our holdings are in both our names. I manage the money, though, in spending for most things, in keeping the accounts, etc. I pay the mortgage. I buy the groceries. I like the financial arrangements. I am better at doing those things than he is, so I do it. This does not affect the relationship."

"We split the money, after all the rents, debts, bills are paid. Not a lot left. It's very businesslike."

"We share it. Everyone gets an allowance and there is a budget. Sharing money makes it 'closer.' Money is not an issue in our marriage."

"All our money is pooled. It always has been since things have loosened up financially for us. We both feel free to spend a certain amount without checking with each other. It works out well, we are both responsible. There is no blame. There is a mutual rejoicing when we find out we have an extra $100!!!"

3 (28 percent)

Another way of doing it is to split expenses 50-50, usually with separate bank accounts:

"We used to spend my check and save his for purchases—we would put mine in my checking account and his in his savings account—it didn't work. Now we keep our money separate and split things 50-50. It works much better and I feel the independence to spend my money as I please. We both work, though he makes much more than I."

"We both work. We split everything down the middle. We have separate accounts. We like it this way. It solves a lot of conflicts. One person is not bearing the burden of another."

"Everything half and half. We both teach part-time. He makes a bit more than I do. I support myself and my child. He supports himself. We both feel best this way."

But this method works less well if one (generally the woman) makes less money than the other, even though both are working full-time:

"We both worked. He made more than I. Money left over was ours to spend. In my case, there was none left over. Obviously the money arrangement was unfair, but he still had a hard time holding on to enough money to make the car payment, much less rent, groceries, etc. I didn't like the finances and that helped end our relationship."

———————————

Sharing expenses 50-50, or deciding just how to split the expenses, can be a problem when the woman makes significantly less money from her job than the man; since this is the case for most women in the United States, this is a common problem; however, some couples think in terms of dividing expenses based on proportionate earnings, as in types 1 and sometimes 2.

Some women feel very uncomfortable about the discrepancy; but should the woman pay half if she makes less?

"I've always tried to pay half of everything, but he makes $25,000 a year and I make $4,000. So I feel very inferior, guilty, etc."*

"I make no more than $7,000 per year as a secretary and a voice teacher. Our money is all lumped together, but since he makes more, he obviously is paying for almost everything. I often wish that I hadn't married right after college so that I could have had the chance to make and spend my own money without feeling guilty."

On the other hand, 12 percent of the women answering make more or all of the money,† which can bring up different problems or feelings:

"So far I have assumed at least half the burden financially. This is against my upbringing, in which men paid for everything."

"I have never been financially dependent on a man. However, I have been in the reverse situation where a man who was living with me was at times financially dependent on me. It put a strain on our relationship because he didn't want to do anything that would upset me because he knew that he depended on me."

"Money is not an issue, mainly because I make as much or more than he does, so I never feel financially dependent upon him. I pay all the bills, his money gets all the extras."

*This is also a question in "dating" situations; but as one woman says, "Who wants to stop and take out a slide rule?"
†How does this compare with U.S. Census figures? Is this figure increasing?

"I was originally attracted to my husband because of his financial sol-vency—often having supported a former lover off and on for two years. I felt very uncomfortable and used in this former relationship with a man who could not hold a job, pay for his share of things, and had no ambition to be responsi-ble. Consequently, I was very impressed when I met my husband, that he had a good job, owned property, could balance his checkbook, etc. In fact, his financial prowess at the time may have clouded my perception of him—and I was so attracted to his being able to pay for things that I think I overlooked other problems in our relationship."

————————————————

This has been a particularly touchy and difficult issue for black women, be-cause, since so many more black women are able to get jobs than black men, the women are often accused of "robbing the men of their masculinity." The woman can be working very hard and supporting the house, and also taking the criticism. See Michele Wallace, *Black Macho.*

One younger woman, married six months, is not sure she is comfortable financially supporting her husband:

"I've been married for six months, and I like it. The best parts of being married are the moments of very deep feeling for the other person. The worst part of being married is the fear that it may not last.

"The biggest problem in our relationship is up until a month ago, my husband was unemployed and we lived exclusively on my salary. Financial freedom for me was a wonderful accomplishment at as early an age as sixteen. Being able to earn a good living, by my own standards, has always done a lot for my feelings of self-worth and independence.

"When all of a sudden money became tighter—when we got married it became something I had to worry about—I had to struggle a bit with my feelings. Having your own private money means that you can spend it on yourself when you have a mind to. When you are responsible for someone else and the money is both of yours, you don't always have this luxury. I didn't like the feeling that the money was no longer mine, even though I was earning it. We now both work, although my husband earns less by about half. I pretty much keep track of the money and make sure the bills are paid, the rent, etc. Does this money situation affect our relationship? Yes. It's good in the sense that I cannot ever be in a position of financial dependence. But perhaps this undermines what could be a total sense of trust in my mate. This world has made me untrusting and extremely defensive.

"The happiest I ever was with anyone has probably been during these first few months with my husband. I have felt very close, and discussed with him things about me which I fear to be my deepest failures and which I have never revealed to anyone. But I would like more intimate talk. I find I am practically always the initiator. When I am unhappy about something, I will eventually express it in as honest a way as I can manage. This usually is productive and leaves me feeling better afterwards. I hate confrontation, but hate not being understood more. My husband will more often than not end up understanding what is going on. I feel very close when we resolve something.

"The most recent fight was concerning what I perceived as a lack of respect in his treatment of me when he was helping me unload my long-awaited etching press. I needed help, but still wanted to be in command of the situation. He and my brother, however, tended to view 'helping me' as doing it 'for me.' This was very upsetting, as this kind of occurrence makes me feel as if I can't ask for help without risking my control of the situation. I find this attitude particularly distressing when it comes from someone I want very much to trust.

"I am usually treated with respect and affection. When I'm not, it really sticks out and hurts. When I am occasionally made to feel silly, I resent it bitterly.

"He has never, I don't believe, told me he loves me. On occasion he has told me I'm beautiful. His non-verbal treatment of me in intimate moments is usually clearly loving; however he plays games with my sensitivity to my weight at times. I take this more seriously than he does. Also, whatever his intentions, I do not like to hear him joke about other women (with respect to him)—how they like him, want him, etc.

"Work is split right down the middle: we alternate days cooking, weeks cleaning, share the gardening, the bread baking, always *both* cook when we entertain, he does all the laundry and empties the kitty litter always, but I do other little things which compensate. This sharing of responsibilities enriches our life together *tremendously,* it makes us feel very responsible for our partici-pation. Daily life is fairly smooth. I fight sex roles very hard.

"I lived alone for eight years, during which time I would go for as long as almost a year without sexual relationships. When I would seek them out, it was more for the affection than for any real sex or male companionship. I loved my freedom and independence, and for the most part found men to be very disappointing. But then, watching all of my friends and acquaintances become parts of couples, I began finding it hard to feel normal about being single.

"Now I maintain a lot of my singleness in our relationship, perhaps because of those years of solitude. I have a need for space to myself—I need time alone at home, and we have integrated this into the scheme of things. It is sometimes a simple matter of knowing what you want and feeling you have the right to ask for it. Unfortunately there are no provisions in this society for the woman who wants it all: a good home life, children, a rewarding career, financial security, a multitude of interests in which she delights so it is normal to feel torn. I *try,* nonetheless, to arrange my life so that these things are not in competition. This could very well be impossible.

"Although I'm closest emotionally to my husband, I do have an extremely intimate female friend with whom I have a deep intellectual involvement. I feel good after seeing her, she is a very inspiring person. She also understands me in a very thorough way. I love her sense of wit, her support of me, her truth to her own values, and her loyalty to the pursuit of good art. What I like least about her? Perhaps her wimpiness in the face of society at large.

"My friendships have been similar to my love relationships except that in my friendships I have perhaps treated myself better. My friendships, which are always good, have been closer. Generally speaking, my friendships have been more rewarding, enduring and intimate, there has been more real sharing. I tend to have more trust in women. Women search, they are creative in their problem solving. They try to improve things. They are more sensitive toward others, as a general rule. I like women a lot. Women make the world a better place to live."

Even when a woman makes more money, provides the basic income for the couple, she may still be demeaned and condescended to, have to fight for her rights (and even be made to feel guilty for wounding her husband's "masculinity"!)—as the previous young woman's marriage shows. Status doesn't automatically come with money.

Housework: Are Women Still Doing the Housework? Even Though Most Women Now Work Outside the Home?

"When I have just worked all day on four hours' sleep, am running through the rain up the driveway with six bags of groceries, the phone is ringing (no one is answering it although both my husband and my son are home)—my husband is yelling for clean underwear and my son is complaining he is hungry—I finally get dinner ready and after that they both collapse on their beds in front of the TV while I am stuck with all the dishes and running the sweeper as well as feeding the dog and taking out the garbage—what can I say?"

"Chairman Mao to the contrary, women have held up more than half the sky. Anyone who doesn't think so can just try doing housework for a whole family."

"I feel it is a personal insult to me, his attitude about the house. He says I am 'obsessed' with cleanliness, but he could let the whole house go until cockroaches run over the piles of his dirty underwear by the bed, and then look up at me and say, 'What's the matter?'!"

"Men don't help with housework—or they take out the trash and stand around waiting for the applause and the tearful hugs and 'I love you! You're so wonderful! You're such an understanding man, so good and so modern!' "

"First he expects dinner, then he wants to make love, he says I can wash dishes 'tomorrow' (never mind that I have to go to work tomorrow too), but somehow they should magically be done. There is just never enough time, I have to cook dinner, maybe he will 'help,' then if I don't want to make love I am accused of not loving him. So you can't win."

Most women still do most of the housework. A recent study found that for every two hours a man puts in on domestic chores, a woman puts in five. How do women feel about this? Aren't concepts of sharing work at home changing, especially since only thirty percent of married women now do *not* work outside the home? Almost all married women are working at full-time jobs, and also doing most of the work at home, and this includes women with small children.

Women in our society are becoming more and more overworked; if one adds to this the emotional services women feel they must provide (and men feel that women must provide), as seen in Part I, it is clear that there is an unfair situation going on here regarding who is putting in more hours per day. If some men might say that the solution is for women to give up their outside work (if financially possible), women might answer that it is not fair for men to be able to choose which work they will do, and automatically assume that domestic work is "woman's work."

76 percent of households in which the woman works full-time outside the home and/or has children at home under twelve do not seem to have yet worked out any concrete domestic work-sharing arrangement—the assumption being the woman will do it (and maybe the men will "help"):

"Our household system is all-American and old-fashioned. We could star in *Leave It to Beaver* if I didn't have to work for financial reasons. I don't seem to have as much fun running the house as June Cleaver did, though."

"What are the practical arrangements? I do it all plus a full-time job. Who does the dishes, makes the bed? Me. Cooking, taking care of the children? Me. What is daily life like? Drudgery."

"I do dishes, make beds, cook, care for kids. I work part-time (staff physician at three nursing homes), pick up my fourteen-year-old at school at 3:30, make dinner, do paperwork, go to bed."

"Who does the housework? Takes care of the children? I do, I do, I do, I do. My husband does not do 'women's work.' "

"When I was working full-time we shared the cooking, dishes, etc. Now that I'm laid off, everyone thinks good ole Mom should do it all."

"I do the dishes (occasionally he will), he makes the bed one-third of the time. I do all the cooking, caring for the children, paying bills, garbage, insurance filing, etc., and cleaning up after him and the children (yes, some anger there)."

"The kids share the dishes. I make the beds, work, and take care of the kids (this is mostly keeping track of them now, as they are teenagers). I make sure everything runs smoothly. If something needs to be done I have to tell him. But mostly I do it. Including garbage, fixing things, mowing the lawn, and car maintenance."

"Raising the children takes from my marriage not only money, privacy, and space, but some days I swear they also take my sanity. How can I be a loving, adoring, caring wife when I'm being den mother, PTA chairman, holding a job, keeping house, disciplining children, and cooking dinner? My husband has only recently taken part in household chores and child raising. He's much more helpful than he used to be since I work full-time. But he's not as helpful as he could be. I think we'll both be happier when the kids are grown."

"Practical arrangements, in one word . . . ME."

"Me! Me! Boring! Boring!"

"I sometimes feel as though I am suffocating. When I am in difficulty with my husband, and coincidentally my daughter starts crowding me, and, maybe, at the same time my responsibilities are piling up at work, I will have what is known as a night of terror, in which during sleep I will actually be suffocating. This has happened three times in the past year and it is the most frightening thing that has ever happened to me. I wake up at the last minute gasping for breath."

In 54 percent of cases, the concept that if both work outside the home, or there are small children, then the housework should be shared is at least in *principle* accepted; however, the idea that if a woman has small children at home, this is more than equivalent to a full-time job outside the home, and therefore housework should be *equally* shared, is less accepted.

Most women say sharing of housework and child care, going to the cleaners, etc., is something more accepted in theory than in practice: 80 percent of women in marriages where it is "supposed to be" shared say they still wind up doing most of it:

"The most recent fight was over sharing the household duties. We both work and had agreed to share everything. I felt I was doing three-fourths."

"While we were happy, we took turns with doing dishes, cooking, making beds, etc. That was part of my admiration for him. He was willing to do his part; he scrubbed floors, toilets, vacuumed, ironed, and did so willingly. When things started to go bad, all that was a source of conflict. He wouldn't put in his equal time with the children. He started going to a gym several days a week while I was stuck at home all the time with the kids, never any time to go out myself. It was a totally unhealthy situation. I was trying to play a 'wife' role, working full-time, taking care of the children, etc., so that I could also make time to be alone with my husband. No other outlets of any kind. With all the frustrations of our priorities, money, kids, role playing, church pressures—everything—became unbearable."

"When he's home in the evening, we're supposed to take turns at getting our son to bed. But I definitely feel the onus of all this falls on me. If I let up for a minute he slides easily back to a position of doing no housework. He has not internalized his responsibility. The toilet bowl gets filthy. Finally I clean it. But to share all duties, whether it is 50-50 or not, is important to make a relationship work. This way each person feels competent and responsible, not put upon or overburdened. Respect is propagated along with self-reliance."

"Daily life seems to present some of our greatest problems. When he comes in the house and strews his clothing across the floor, flings the papers around, and has total disregard for the house, I take it as his discounting my needs. . . . We have sat down at times to figure out who does what, but those arrangements have never worked. It is still freestyle and not working well. He has a motel mentality."

And in most cases of "sharing," women say they are the organizers, delegating tasks to the other family members (husband and sometimes children), who are the "helpers":

"We share housework—I am the organizer, but he'll 'help' whenever I ask."

"Practical arrangements are basically my role. I have taught my family to share in the responsibilities, but I'm still the one to dole out the roles. No one else would wash clothes if they weren't sorted and put in front of the washer. I resent my role at times. I constantly work to make everyone pitch in. My husband and the kids always have to be reminded to do something. It's occasionally a big source of aggravation for me. I really don't relish being elected the maid, cook, chauffeur—somehow that just happened. Slowly as I work to break those roles, I hear resentments from my husband. He may preach ERA, but in his heart he liked it better when he was supreme being with someone waiting on him. Who wouldn't? I find most men I know sharing similar attitudes to this. It burns me up!"

"On the weekends, we are supposed to share. Lest this sounds too idyllic, I am generally the one who knows what has to be done. My partner can relate to the fact that meals have to be made and the kitchen has to be cleaned;

however, the rest of the house could be knee-deep in rubbish and he wouldn't notice. We have a large lot, an enormous garden, and chickens, so there is a lot of outside work to do. This is shared, although here, too, I am usually the one who directs what has to be done and when."

Where there is a concept of equal sharing, most women still find themselves often in a position of having to "remind" the man—making the woman feel like an unpleasant disciplinarian, as well as frustrated that she has had to be the one to start the action:

"My husband will do anything I ask—but he sees nothing to do by himself."

"I take care of the house and children. He helps when I ask—once in a while, he'll do the dishes on his own. He knows now not to ask, 'Shall I do the dishes for you?' as I have often said they are not solely my dishes and he can do the dishes for us."

In 48 percent of marriages women refer to their husbands' "help"; once again, this implies the woman has the primary responsibility:

"The chores are primarily mine, though my husband does help a lot. More than a lot of men I know."

"I do most of the housework, but my husband will do things if I am sick or anything."

"I do most of the household chores. He will help if asked but does not take initiative to get anything done. He is messier than I am and I have to pick up after him continually. I don't think he is this way consciously, however."

Women who are responsible for all the housework and child care and do not work outside the home often say they wind up feeling isolated and lonely:

"I always felt very isolated in the house. He goes, he comes, I'm always here. He gets dressed in a suit, there is a reason why his shirts have to be very white and crisp. It doesn't matter quite as much if I look my best, because I'm going to be cleaning, etc., and probably getting my clothes dirty anyway. I guess this is demoralizing."

"I was lonely within the family when I was cleaning and they were playing games. I had learned in every fiber of my being what was proper for a wife and mother, and I did my damnedest to follow every rule and one-up all who had gone before me. My home and my husband and my children would have been given the Good Housekeeping Seal of Approval."

Even in marriages in which only the woman works outside the home, housework is still "shared"; it is almost never considered the man's responsibility—although it would be the woman's if she were not working:

"My husband and me share all housework inside and out, also taking care of our daughter, since he's been laid off and I'm working."

"Because he's unemployed at the moment, he plays the role of house husband. Dishes are half and half, he makes the bed, he often helps me with meals, and we share equally in other major weekly chores, i.e., vacuuming, cleaning windows, etc. I do the laundry. We both go shopping."

"We split most of the household chores. Since I work and my husband is home now, he willingly does much of the cleaning and errand running. I grocery shop, cook, and wash."

Also, when a woman has a small business or "outside" work she does in the home, she almost always also does the housework, answers the phone, cares for the children, and so on:

"I do all the usual housewife work because I am at home. Of course, I do my writing at home. I compromise by not keeping an immaculate house. The whole family helps clean at times. My husband is neat and my son takes care of his room. In the morning everyone gets their own breakfast. I make dinner. My husband makes breakfast on the weekends."

Relationships with teenage children also represent "work" which gets "automatically" directed toward the woman in most families—i.e., keeping track emotionally, "being there" for crises, etc.:

"My daughter is now seventeen; I think the early years of night feeding, diapering, chasing toddlers, childhood illnesses, etc., were not nearly as trying as the teen years. It is so many-faceted, the raising of a teenager; keeping open communication lines between me and her is very important."

"I do the child care—my children are teenagers, and it takes a great deal of effort to keep communication lines open—I am the one who does this. If a counselor at school needs to be called or if the kids need money for anything, I am responsible. My son stole a pair of shoes this winter and I was the one who marched him back to the store—my husband chose to ignore the situation."

But there is a lot of authentic sharing starting to take place; 23 percent of couples have reached successful sharing arrangements, and are enjoying them:

"I wash the dishes, he unstacks the dishes. I clean the house, he does all the clothes. Everyone makes whatever beds they want, I don't care. We both help with the meals equally. I take care of the kids during the day. In the evening he's very willing to take care of the kids and put them to bed while I visit a friend or go to a movie. He would want me to tell you that he gets the kids up and off in the a.m. while I sleep—then I get coffee in bed as they walk out the door. I usually stay up very late doing my work (I have a small business). Even when I don't ask, he's done the washing, cleaning, made the beds, washed the dishes, and taken complete care of the kids. Anything I can do, so can he. I've surprised him by mowing the yard a few times."

"We help each other out in most every routine thing. He is by far the better cook; however, I always get stuck doing the dishes (he dries them). I wash the clothes, take out the garbage, and make the beds."

"The housework is shared more or less on an equal basis. I do laundry, he empties trash. I cook three nights a week, he cooks three nights a week. I feed the cats in the afternoon, he does it in the morning. I wash dishes (actually, the dishwasher washes the dishes). He pays the bills. I clean half the rooms, he cleans the other half. It's all written down and all agreed to. The system works with varying success depending on whatever else we're doing. He's a student. During finals he's very lax about the housework, as am I when I'm writing on a deadline."

"I doubt that there is another couple in America that has the 'practical arrangements' mapped out as specifically as we do. Because we both work, we try very hard to share the household responsibilities. And we have tried to make it so that we each do the things that we do best or mind doing the least."

"He makes the bed every morning and keeps the house picked up. He puts my things on a table for me to put away later (when he puts them away, he forgets where he put them). He also picks up my dirty clothes from the floor and puts them in the laundry. I do all the cooking and he cleans up the dishes afterwards. He runs the dishwasher. The items that don't go into the dishwasher (pans, Tupperware, knives, etc.) are stacked and it is my responsibility to wash these by hand. He takes out the garbage and cleans the cat litter. I feed the cats and make sure they have clean water. I also am in charge of their general grooming—brushing and bathing. I vacuum and dust the upstairs and he does the downstairs. I sort and wash and dry the laundry and he folds it and hangs it up. I scrub all the bathroom fixtures, change the towels, and put new sheets on the bed. He waters the plants and feeds the fish. I feed the turtles and frog. I wax the floors when they need it and keep the kitchen fixtures clean. We have a garden, in which we share responsibilities. He does the heavy work. We each take care of our own cars (washing, changing oil, routine maintenance) and bicycles. We generally go grocery shopping together, but I make the list and pick out the foods at the store. He puts the groceries away when we get home. I do all the sewing. He is very fair-minded, and when I do his work for him, he takes me out to dinner or to a movie, or does some of my work for me."

Who does the "housework" in non-married relationships?

"We don't live together but when he spends the night I do the household chores—all of them."

"We take turns at being at each other's houses—a bit more at his house. We share cooking and pots and expenses for food and going out. I'm mostly responsible for my child and babysitting arrangements. But he spends a lot of time with both of us, shares the expenses when we go out, and buys her shoes and presents for her sporadically. He also babysits one evening a week while I teach in the evenings."

"It's always at his apartment, since I am married. He is a good cook too and is self-sufficient concerning housework—one of the things I like about him—as opposed to my male chauvinist pig husband, who is lazy and dependent."

And in 2 percent of cases, the husband does more housework:

"We each cook and clean up after ourselves. My husband does more housework than I do. He cleans up the bathroom and bedroom weekly. I straighten up and occasionally do the kitchen floor."

"Until a year ago, I did it all, *and* put in a fourteen-hour day—then I walked out. Now, except for evenings and weekends, he does most of it."

"My husband was a bachelor until he married me at age thirty-five. He has always taken care of himself, maintained a home, decorated it, cleaned it, done his own laundry, cooking, shopping, etc. Now, if the hamper is full, whoever sees it does it first. My husband is a wonderful cook, loves to do it, and does it whenever he can. He is in business for himself and is home most evenings before me and makes dinner. We each care for the children. He can do everything as well as or better than I can."

Many men's motel mentality

Most men, as described by women here, still have—as one woman picturesquely puts it—a "motel mentality" around the house. The philosophy of sharing is gaining acceptance, but reality is slow to follow.

Most women have a similar experience—that is, they "see" dust and chores to be done around the house, while men will walk on by a dirty glass that needs to be taken to the kitchen (since one is going that way anyway), etc., not "seeing" it. This makes many women very frustrated, and most women, after a period of "nagging" a man to do something, whatever it is, just give up and do it themselves or leave it undone, because trying to get someone else to do something eventually takes more time and is more upsetting than if one does it oneself. But this leaves a fermenting residue of anger just below the surface, a feeling of being exploited and not respected.

Are Changing Finances Changing the Shape of Marriage?

As seen in Part I of this book, and in Chapter 9, the emotional contract in most marriages is not equal, nor what most women would consider emotionally satisfying. Obviously, the economic self-sufficiency women have just achieved, and all that it can imply, filtered into men's consciousness—or perhaps economics alone will not bring equality. Or, perhaps most men have no idea how to develop the skills of emotional nurturing that most women are asking them for.

Similarly, women's working outside the home does not seem to automatically mean that men now do their share of housework. But changing finances are definitely changing the shape of marriage: *women* feel different. Women working outside the home no longer feel men can talk down to them—although men still do. This makes most women even more irritated when they are not respected, when men revert to unconscious stereotypes, seeing them as "service" people or emotional "pushovers" who, for a few words of flattery and a little lovemaking, will do almost anything.

On the other hand, since most women do not make as much money as men do, most being ghettoized into lower-paying "women's" jobs, many women still feel a man's financial support is necessary, at least as a backdrop. Though as we shall see in Chapter 12, many women (even those with very low salaries, even women with children) are now choosing to leave unsatisfying marriages. If economic self-sufficiency has only begun to change the emotional interior of marriage, it has at least made it possible for women to leave marriages. Although the media now—as they did in the late 1940s after World War II, when society wanted women to leave wartime jobs and let men returning home have the jobs (also with the end of war production there were fewer jobs available)—run propaganda stories about women who "give it all up" for a suburban backyard, these stories are based on only handfuls of women.* Despite these stories, and despite women's exhaustion with the labels ("women's lib," "women's movement," "new women," etc.), the ideals of dignity, independence, self-definition, and pride live in women everywhere—as we are seeing here.

Women are threading their way through the morass of being told "what to do" on every side—by magazines, their husbands/men, some branches of feminism, psychology, fashion magazines, all of it—and making very interest-

---

*Similarly, beginning with the Civil War, the media have run stories almost punctually every ten years, declaring that "the women's rights movement is dead"—implying that women can't "keep it together," "real women" don't really want "all that," and so on.

ing choices, creating new categories of living for which there are really no terms yet.

Over and over, women say they love their freedom; it could almost be a theme song for this book. But as much as women want freedom, they also want love, and they cannot understand why the two should be contradictory. Women are choosing to continue believing in nurturing and being kind, not judgmental, as their values—but are also refusing to continue to "take it" from men. Based on women's value system, women's way of "not taking it" in marriage—after arguing and bickering for a few years trying to get the relationship to change—means leaving. Women, defying categorization as either "feminist" or "traditional," have as their goal making love relationships work, but making them work by different, radically different, emotional arrangements.

12

Women's Feelings About Divorce

Women Initiate Most Divorces

It is most often women who are deciding on and asking for divorces. Ninety-one percent of women who have divorced say *they* made the decision to divorce, not their husbands. This is quite surprising, since it so completely contradicts the popular view that it is the woman who is usually "left," that women are more "security-oriented" than men, etc.

Most women say they tried for several years to improve their relationship before deciding to leave. And most, again contrary to expectations, ask for and get divorces, not because the man is being "unfaithful" (even though he may be—and also she may be), and not because of "poor sex" (most women feel that this can be either worked out or lived with, by getting another lover outside the marriage), but because of their loneliness and emotional isolation within the marriage.

What Are Divorces Like for Women?

Most women's statements here are remarkable for the sense of relief and well-being expressed after deciding on a divorce, although the woman may have been upset and felt guilty during and right up to the decision:

"It was the clearest decision of my life. I wanted the divorce. My ex-husband had abandoned the family, not supported us for years, had a drug habit and was physically abusive. I felt wonderful after I made the decision. I felt like a failure living in such a sick relationship. I felt successful for having made the decision. It has been almost a year since I left. I cried for ten years. I don't cry about it now. My friends were tremendous supports to me."

"I wanted the divorce because I was very unhappy. I got it when I finally realized that I was O.K. but the relationship was horrible. I felt like a failure anyway, even though I knew I was not—emotions are strange and hard to separate from facts. I felt free for the first time in my life. I was relieved to be on my own."

"I was married nine years. I left my husband—I felt I could not be *me* in that marriage. Leaving was very difficult. I was married in the Catholic Church and felt tremendously guilty. It took me five years to get up the courage. The day I left, I cried without stopping for many hours, the entire time I was packing, saying goodbye to him. I felt so sad—so sad that we couldn't turn the clock back and erase all the years of non-communication. But after I left, I felt free, alone, like I was reborn. I have no regrets about leaving, only staying so long."

Most women say they felt that no matter how hard they tried to make it work, their husband remained psychologically inaccessible, often condescending:

"It was very hard for me to break up my marriage. I was married for eleven years and miserable through most of it. But I kept trying to make it work. He made me feel like a non-person. Nothing I did was ever right for him, so I would do more and try harder and he would keep shooting me down until I felt totally empty and hopeless. I had to leave to gain my self-respect back, live my life and be happy and healthy. It was hard for me to do because I had so many doubts that I'd never make it on my own. I felt only relief after he moved out, never once did I regret it. I felt much freer, I never felt like a failure. (I would have been a failure had I stayed with the marriage.) I talked a lot to my friends and couldn't have made it without their support."

"What triggered the whole thing was we were coming up on our twenty-fifth anniversary and the kids were making plans for a big party. The thought of spending another twenty-five years like the past twenty-five, I could not handle. He drank, gambled, went out with other women. Had affairs. Was never any help with the kids, never participated in any activities with them. We did very few things as a family. We had no communication whatsoever. Sex was always when he wanted it, and toward the end that was never. We went out on my birthday and our anniversary, usually combined, as they are only two days apart. I couldn't really devote myself to church work because I never knew when or what he would be doing, and I had to wait for him to say what he was going to do before I could make plans for myself. I had no self-worth. Even my kids had more sense than I did, they couldn't understand why I stayed married for so long."

"I wanted to break up and initiated it, because after seven years of trying alone to do something with my marriage, I decided it was useless. We both were living totally separate lives and only connected in bed. My husband saw many women (right from the beginning he was rarely home), broke engagements with me by simply not appearing, and did not share equitably in financial obligations, causing tremendously horrible money problems.

"Breaking up with him is right up there with the top ten best things I have ever done in my life. First, I felt like a failure, but then I experienced a freedom not to be believed! I hated him and then stopped. Hating requires too much energy. My life became beautiful, wonderful. It was a period in which I could focus on my own growth and really reassess what I wanted and expected to have in a relationship with a man."

The majority of women express that somehow, during the marriage, they felt taken out of life, not more connected to life:

"I'm glad it'll soon be over. I want the divorce because of his constant use of 'power' to have me be what he wants, instead of who I am. I felt at first that that was how life was, then sad, then happy when I made the decision to end it."

"We got married too young, had children too fast, and assumed too many financial responsibilities. From the time I got pregnant until the day I left, I felt like my life was on hold or it was happening to another person. I am the one who left and who wanted the divorce. When I left, I felt free and happy. I felt some hate toward him, but I didn't cry a lot. I mainly got back into the swing of things—dating, finding a job, and enrolling in school. I didn't do any housework, laundry, or cooking for over a year!"

The great majority also say that their personality came back to life quickly after the divorce:

"I wanted to break up. He still sits waiting for me to come home ('to wake up and come to my senses'). It was hard, but I am glad. The regret was for waiting so long. I felt freer. I knew I could start living again, and I had friends that would listen and cheer me. I started to shine."

"I felt as though a heavy burden had been lifted when he left the house and the divorce became final. A whole new personality came over me, as I had had to live in his shadow for almost fifteen years. It was like being born again, I felt a tremendous sense of freedom."

"I knew deep inside that I was doing the best thing for me. I felt relieved and like I could start living again without all the strain this relationship had placed on me—always wondering if he really cared for me or not. It was like I found myself again."

"Getting my divorce was the most difficult thing I have ever done in my life, but also the most wonderful. I wanted my divorce. I no longer wanted to be with my ex-husband. Not only did I not love him (I'm not sure I ever did), I did not like him! I never hated him. I even feel bad for him. He'll never see life as I do, and I think he is missing out.

"I did my crying before I got my divorce. Having the children made this transition very difficult, but I certainly have started living again. I have another chance at life and I am going to take it. I lost a lot of friends in this process. He made me out to be the real bad guy and they bought this. I have made new friends that are really friends, and no longer feel bad about the ones that are still his friends. It was a very hard road but well worth it!"

One woman threw parties for her divorcing friends:

"When I lived in the suburbs, I used to have open house Wednesdays for my women friends and their kids. One Wednesday morning, a friend came over all broken up, she had decided to get a divorce. As I was shopping later for that afternoon's get-together, on a whim I stopped in the liquor store and bought a bottle of champagne, announcing it was to celebrate a divorce—which obviously unwound the dealer! I came home and we all drank to her success and new life. Well, word spread like wildfire! It was built up for the next week into a bash with fireworks—so successful that when another friend got a divorce, we did it again! Finally, it was written into most of our town's divorce agreements that there were to be no public celebrations!"

While 71 percent of women, including women of every age and economic status, express relief and well-being, 24 percent of women have mixed feelings about getting a divorce and find it harder to recover:

"Divorce was horrible, even though it was the best and only solution—we both wanted it because we'd reached a point where there was too much damage to repair; we lived separate lives and were totally incompatible. Still, I felt like a rug had been pulled out from under me. I couldn't regain my balance. It's taken over a year to feel normal again. I still need to talk about it, but to rehash it makes me angry all over again. I am beginning to be able to laugh at the lunacy of the whole marriage. I still feel both elation and despair—a roller-coaster effect."

"I had been in therapy for two years and was really in touch with how rotten the relationship was. I issued the ultimatum of either he invest in the relationship—get counseling or something—or leave. He left. I felt and still feel at times all sorts of things—guilt, regrets, anger. I hid, cried, screamed, laughed, felt relief and sorrow. I talked a lot with friends, which helped the most. Each time the sadness comes it goes away a little sooner and you know that you can survive it. Everyone encouraged my leaving, but they were scared to hear my rawest feelings."

"It took me seven years to get to the point of asking for a divorce. I almost had a nervous breakdown. I went into therapy, struggled for a long time to come to terms with myself and my life. I also did a lot of praying. Finally I made the decision. Even after that, since I did not believe in divorce, I had a lot of guilt. Even after two years, I still feel guilt."

One woman explains the tremendous confusion she felt when she left:

"When I left my husband and moved in with another man, all of a sudden my husband decided he wanted me back. He called me constantly—to the point where I just let the phone ring and ring. I was so confused. I started seeing a shrink. It took me nearly a year to file for a divorce. I felt very cut off from the rest of the world. Everyone in my family was upset with me. My father threatened to disown me, I didn't speak to him for nearly a year. My mother lived out of state, but let me know she wasn't happy. My best friend severed our relationship. I couldn't decide what I wanted to do, life just seemed to be caving in all around me and there was no way out. I was desperately looking for someone to make the decision for me, so that if things didn't work out, it wouldn't be my responsibility. Looking back, I wonder how I ever managed to get through that part of my life. Everyone was mad at me. The reason they felt like they did was because John put on such a good front for everyone. They all thought he was so perfect, and it was me who was all messed up.

"I was so lonely when I was married. He was very wrapped up in work and paid little attention to me. I was miserable, and he didn't seem to care. He was happy to just let things go as they were. If he had at least tried to change, maybe I would have stayed longer. I really don't think that it ever would have worked out, though. He was just too self-centered.

"Even though I was the one that got the divorce, initiating the breakup was by far the hardest thing I have ever done. I was confused and disoriented. I was never sure it was what I really wanted to do, I just couldn't see any other way. I did not want to spend the rest of my life unhappy. It took me a couple of years to really get over him. Moving in with my present husband helped me more than anything. He was the one who told me to be true to my heart, and said I had the strength to get through the whole thing. He did wonders for my self-esteem on my road to recovery."

A small number of women (4 percent) express feeling terribly sad and hurt—usually these women had not decided on the divorce themselves, but "were divorced" and thus not in control of the decision:

"I was extremely depressed over a situation I had no control over. My husband left me when I was twenty. I spent two months in the hospital then because of depression. I found it very difficult to cope with the breakup. I had a lot of feelings to sort out—sadness, anger, relief, anxiety. I had to go through a mourning period as if a close loved one had died. It took me two years to feel good about living again."

"I was divorced. It was very hard, very painful, mostly because I lost custody of my child because I am a lesbian."

"I was twenty-two with two kids. He got off scot-free. I didn't see my friends for weeks. Some days I stayed in all day, not getting dressed and keeping the drapes drawn."

"My husband wants this divorce—it is the hardest thing I have ever faced. I cry a lot. I feel alone and afraid. I'm working and fighting desperately to keep my marriage together. It is all one-sided on my part. I've been in therapy for ten months—I hope I am getting stronger. This is from a thirty-six-year-old, pensive, caring, confused woman."

Some women, a minority (7 percent), are still friends with their ex-husbands and like them very much:

"I feel good with no regrets. We both have started new lives. We both still love each other! Have the same friends except the new ones. We just couldn't live together as husband and wife."

"Actually I feel I had a successful marriage for about thirteen years, a successful separation (little friction and relatively little trauma for the children), and have just effected a successful divorce—we remain cordial and have no real disagreements, even over money. Dividing furniture these last few weeks has been strange but not really wrenching. I've been rather happy to see objects we both care about go to him when I knew I couldn't move them to a small apartment. I did not cry a lot over the end of the marriage—I was too into the affair at the time. I had a good friend to talk to and many other friends slightly less close who understood and accepted—were never accusatory and often very supportive. There was never a matter of friends 'choosing sides,' for we did not battle. In my life it seems that everything except the affair has happened in a slow-paced way, so that there has been time to adjust to each change and be ready for the next one when it came. Time has always been the healer—and psychiatry in the one instance when time wasn't the cure-all."

The process of divorce and the courts

The process of divorce, the legal proceedings, according to many women, are ugly—the experience is made more difficult by the courts:

"The system is terrible to force people to wait so long and make it all so bitter. You begin with a friend, make him a lover, then a husband, then all the love dies, a lot of it because of the divorce process—obviously love had died anyway and you'd given up a husband, but now you not only lost a lover and friend along the way but now have an enemy."

"Divorce sucks! No way around it. When people say they got a friendly divorce I don't believe them. My first husband and I decided mutually to get a divorce—but during the divorce we lost love and respect for each other. It ended up shitty. Now he doesn't and has never kept up child support."

"The inequity of divorce laws for women is embittering. I had one good judgment just once, when there was a woman judge on the bench. I got the house and two years of 'rehabilitative' alimony after thirty-eight years of marriage because even after the bastard left, I still had kids in high school using my car and eating and having all kinds of problems. He was married four months later, went to California, and never paid alimony after five months. I have never known any woman who didn't get screwed by the divorce court. The whole thing sucks.

"And my damn female lawyer, when I went back to get my alimony, did what every damn female professional does when you need them—just like the boys always say—she was having a baby to cement her second marriage and prove herself a female, with two sons by her first marriage, which should have been enough. Meanwhile, my ex took his pills and had women fixing him dinners and solacing him and had money for the best damned lawyers in Connecticut. I had to sell my wedding and engagement rings to get a retainer to get a lawyer. My lawyer acted pissed that I didn't behave like a 'good sport.' I wanted to kill him and his fucking lawyer—and my own fucking female attorney."

One woman offers her advice for the divorce proceedings:

"It's not only smart to get a transcript afterwards, but more important to go down to the courthouse before the trial and look over your file.

"In my case, at one point I went back to court solely to present a document my ex had written and notarized (some financial promises that a previous lawyer had not presented). When the hearing went against me and I was demoralized, I went back to look at my file (feeling like a thief in the night, Cinderella complex script). It turned out that 'the lawyer's secretary' had accidentally forgotten to put in the paper the whole hearing was to be about, which of course meant the judge had not even seen the document!

"Divorce is, altogether, quite a trip. Here's my advice for other women—just some random ideas:

A. Possible problems with lawyers to watch out for:
   1. Did they tell you what to bring to the first meeting?
   2. Was a complete questionnaire filled out for or by the client (you) and a copy given to her?
   3. Were good questions asked to clarify the situation?
   4. Did he or she tell the client her different options—pros and cons?
   5. Cost?
   6. Did they tell the client which judge they were using and why?
   7. She or he should attempt to negotiate all decisions outside court.
B. Possible problems in court:
   1. Is the judge prejudiced against or for your lawyer?
   2. Is there enough time for the client (you) to speak and have your side presented?
   3. Did your lawyer ask for everything he said he would?
   4. Did the judge make clear decisions, enforceable decisions, so you won't have to go back to the court later to define or enforce them?
   5. Did the judge make decisions based on facts and not assumptions? (I went back to court to ask for my share of my ex's retirement, which the former lawyer had forgotten to ask for. After lengthy presentation on both sides, the judge said I was not to get any of the retirement funds because the former judge 'must have taken it into consideration.' Ironically, the former settlement said I was to get 'all the community property' and a 'whole life' insurance policy—neither of which I got part of, much less 'all.')
C. Division of assets:
   1. Community property: __ percent wife, __ percent husband.
   2. Homemaker's lost earning power—did she receive equalizing compensation in alimony, equalizing to his salary or her value? How long will it continue? What is her total lost earning power? This should be awarded in enforceable, lump sums instead of monthly income over many years.
   3. What would she get if he dies?
D. Child support: This is an issue commonly discussed. Isn't it only 40 percent of husbands who pay child support, and then only for four years?

"If you have difficulty, report your lawyer to the Bar Association. I reported one of my lawyers, but I was not allowed to attend the hearing, nor was I assured by the lawyer appointed to represent me that he would read my statement, nor did I get an accounting of what did happen at the hearing or the results. This whole system is really a can of worms. It should be exposed."

Counseling, in the sense of talking through decisions or difficult periods with someone, can be helpful in making a break-up less destructive:

"Both my ex-husband and I went to a marriage counselor together for a year and a half before I actually left. When I first brought up the idea of a divorce, he asked that we see a counselor. I gradually clarified the fact that I no longer wanted to live with him."

"I was in counseling for a short time after my divorce, since I had moved and did not want to bother others by long distance. Therapy provided the listening care I needed 'til I established new friends."

"When someone said sympathetically, 'Divorce is rough,' I responded, 'Compared to what?' Worse is continuing a marriage which needs to end. In becoming single now, I feel like I am in the right place at the right time. We went to this counselor for two months to try to hash out whether to separate. When my husband decided he wanted a divorce, I went to the counselor alone to work through my tendency to keep 'taking care of' my estranged husband. I am not in a relationship now and in fact am celibate. I am enjoying living."

The economics of divorce and the "feminization of poverty": facing poverty but leaving anyway

Many women are afraid to divorce because of economics, but do so anyway:

"I divorced my husband because of his drinking and cheating. I felt guilty because he really loved and needed me and the children, but I felt very lonely, especially at night. Also, I was afraid that I couldn't support the kids on my own. It was really hard not to take the 'easy way out' and just go back with him."

"I wanted the split, but I felt a terrible sense of personal failure, and fear that I could not literally survive—feed myself, pay the bills, etc. I felt very scared. I really was alone. My parents were no help. My mother 'didn't want to interfere'—wouldn't talk about it. It was very nearly the most traumatic time in my life. I did what I had to do to survive: I worked at my job, paid the bills. I also made many women friends, close friends. I learned that I could live without him and that marriage isn't the only success a woman can make of her life."

Women do face definite economic hardships after divorce, as compared to men. According to the U.S. Department of Labor, two-thirds of women who divorce lower their standard of living.* For one thing, while the fact that most women now have their own income is doubtless making it *possible* for them to leave, that income is usually considerably smaller than their husband's. Furthermore, only 14 percent of women are awarded alimony, and 58 percent child support, and even fewer, 4 percent, actually *receive* any alimony (and 14 percent *receive* the child support they were awarded); most courts have not found adequate ways of enforcing their decisions. Men frequently move to other states where the court's stipulations do not apply; when their salaries are garnished, they often take jobs which do not involve W-2 forms. Alimony and child support are not paid in two-thirds of all divorces, and even in over one-half of all the cases in which it is awarded, according to U.S. Department of Labor statistics.†

Nevertheless, women, *knowing full well that this will be the case,* are initiating the vast majority of divorces. Indeed, most divorced women in this study with annual incomes of less than $7,000 say they are happier now, facing problems with making ends meet, than they ever were when more comfortably off but being put down at home. (See Chapters 11 and 12) Thus the "feminization of poverty" is a powerful indication‡ of women's emotional alienation within marriage—as is the strong sense of emotional well-being, the feeling expressed by so many women here that now they have a new chance at life.

*See also Chapter 11. Statistics show that the standard of living usually drops for a woman, whereas it rises for a man after divorce.
†See Current Population Reports, series P-23, No. 148: "Child Support and Alimony, 1933" (Supplemental Report), U.S. Bureau of the Census.
‡Is the increasing rate of single, never-married, female heads of households, especially teenagers, also an example of women choosing single motherhood, even if poor, not women "being deserted"? Are teenaged mothers single by choice, or are they "deserted"? Most girls could have gotten abortions but did not. In cases of unmarried pregnancy, studies have shown that for women at the poverty level, many look forward to having a child as a way of establishing a home of their own, as they will now receive not only love but also sometimes financial support, however meager, according to one study (Planned Parenthood) in the southern United States.

As real as the "feminization of poverty" is, and as reprehensible as it is for a society such as ours, it is a misunderstanding of the phenomenon to assume that women would always accept having a husband's or a man's assistance, if he would only be willing to provide it.

What Is the Purpose
of Being Married,
According to Married Women

The Basic Pleasures and Benefits Women
Find in Marriage

Companionship, "belonging somewhere," and security

Almost always, women who are married mention (sometimes along with other things) that they like the feeling—real or hoped for—of stability, security, a shared past and future together—"belonging somewhere": *

"The main basis of our marriage is just the pleasure, the security, of daily companionship, working together toward common goals, a sense of knowing the other is there when needed, a genuine caring about the welfare of each other."

"The best part is being able to have him there when I need him to love (I don't like the hours he works because he's always tired). We are both happy."

"Knowing you don't have to face life alone is the best part."

"Security, mutual respect. Each of us knowing the other is always there."

"Married fifteen years. I like the family unit being together—it makes you feel secure and content. (Sometimes it's nice to just have the house to myself,

---

*84 percent mention companionship or having a home as their principal reason for liking marriage—even though they wish they could change the emotional relationship with their husband, as they describe it in Part I, and may have a high level of dissatisfaction.

and be alone for a while.) Before I was married I was searching for something in my life. Now I feel I've found it. I like the term 'wife,' it makes me feel as though I belong to my husband. The best part is snuggling up to him and having him hold me when I really need it."

"I have been married for twelve years. The best part of marriage is feeling that it is my haven, my retreat from the world. I can simply be an extension of my husband when outside pressures get me down. I like being his 'wife.' My reasons for getting married were security and insulation from being hurt in a love affair again."

"I think I married him to replace my father, to have a rock to anchor on. When he came along, he was so steadfast, so decent and honest and uncomplicated and all man, yet kind and caring and so much in love with me, I just couldn't let him go. Even though I went through a couple of years of tortured indecision about marrying him, he waited for me to say yes. And he has remained that steady rock, faithful, loving, dependable."

As seen in Chapter 3, many describe this in terms of being needed:

"The most important part of this relationship is love, sexual intimacy, our spiritual unity (Christianity), our new family, and companionship. I like best the feeling of needing and being needed."

And on some level, being married means being number one to someone, being important to them:

"He tells me he loves me, that I look great, that I turn him on, that I'm the only one for him. I love him to tell me these things. It makes me feel great and adequate, that I'm first to him, I matter, I'm really important."

"We'll celebrate our twenty-fifth anniversary in a few months. The best part is the intimacy of knowing you are the most important person in the world to someone."

Some have completely unromantic marriages but do not seem to mind, still liking marriage for its companionship:

"I like the daily routine, just having a body there in the house moving around. Someone you know will be there. Our sex is satisfying. I get what I want and he gets what he wants. There really isn't a whole lot of romance or talk, just being there."

"The best part is the companionship—available and likable companionship—whether it's in sex or eating or going places."

"The best part of being married (twenty-five years), I guess, is the sharing of interests and concerns and the dependability of having my husband around all the time."

"I like the best about it that he's always there, no matter what I say or do."

"We are together not only because of the importance of our children and family but also because I just don't like being alone."

Even women with very unsatisfying or frustrating marriages say they enjoy the daily companionship:

"What I like about my marriage is the economic security and daily companionship. Travel is easier together too. For my husband to give me a divorce, he would have to admit defeat—he can't do this—he never makes a mistake! And I like having a dinner partner—even a silent one is better than none. Least I like intercourse with him (about once a month). Am I happy? Yes. My partner? Don't know."

"Consider this: We don't talk much except perhaps in the car on a trip and then mostly about what to do when he retires. We haven't even considered or discussed sex for at least sixteen years. We are not openly affectionate. Our children are independent and cause us no worry. We have no hobbies that we share, except traveling, and that's not very often. We do go out to dinner occasionally but I object to the expense. So what do I enjoy? I guess mostly we must be enjoying muddling along through daily life together, watching a little TV, looking out for each other's interest in small ways."

Only 2 percent of women say they value their marriages for the growth and spiritedness they find in them—rather than "belonging":

"When we are together I feel full and content, free to express whatever it is I'm feeling—anger, sex, silliness, humor, anxiety, general values, and sensitivity to a situation. We learn from each other—*listen* to one another, and *accept* one another. On top of it all, I get excited when I see him! I guess that is really love!"

Although most women seem to value companionship so much, one woman comments that, for her, it is just the opposite:

"The worst thing about marriage? Having a person around all the time!"

Sometimes the "belonging" women refer to can have a negative edge; one younger woman, although not very happy, plans to stay married because the alternative—being single—is so unappealing to her:

"I am twenty-five, married four years. Sometimes I work as a clerk-typist, but when employed, I prefer switchboard work. I don't know if I'm in love, but I care for my husband. We have a son almost three.

"I would like a closer relationship with my husband. I have had to work hard to keep the marriage functioning smoothly. The basis we are operating on now is that we like each other, we love our son, we don't think that we could find anything better, also we'd go broke if we split up. What is the problem? Everything, mostly.

"We really don't have many heart-to-heart talks, since he goes to bed early and I stay up late a lot. He mumbles when I try to talk to him at night and I do the same thing when he tries in the morning. I talk more than he does, and it's very hard to draw him out on some things. He doesn't hardly ever get excited about things. I would like more intimate talk. In that respect, we do better by letter, or on the phone. For a long time we thought we were doing so well on communication, but we were only saying what the other person wanted to hear.

"I am currently financially dependent on my husband. I don't feel bad about it. If something happened to me or if we split and he retained custody, he would pay an awful lot of money to get the services that I provide. At times I feel guilty, but he quickly doesn't let me think that for long. When I worked for a while, my husband was glad, because although the money was not a prime consideration, he knew that I needed to get out of the house and be around other people.

"I do most of the housework, but my husband will do things if I am sick or anything, especially after a trying day with my son and one baby girl that I take care of. She drives me crazy. My son is very neat now that he's almost three—he's lots of fun to be around and go places with. Sometimes we have the same tastes in entertainment, like movies and amusement parks and such.

"I was only married five weeks when I tested pregnant. When I first started puking (crude but true) and thought I might be pregnant, my reaction was: 'It's too soon!' Then it hurt a lot when, after I was pregnant so soon after marriage, my husband decided he wouldn't do anything with me sexually, because he was afraid of injuring the baby, even though I tried to convince him that he couldn't hurt it at this stage. After the birth, we only had intercourse twice before he was sent on a year's unaccompanied tour in Japan. (He's in the Marines.) Worse, I had to stay with my mother. I saw a counselor for six months while my husband was overseas because I was very reluctant, as the time grew near, to go back to him.

"When he came back, we went to two counseling sessions together, but we have never really gotten close. Our sex life is almost nonexistent. It is a problem that we know has to be resolved, but we are willing to give it the time it needs. Well, my husband would have made a great celibate priest or monk.

"When I was single, I was slick. Although I never have orgasm during intercourse, I let all of my lovers, all but one (well, two), *think* that they were the one to accomplish that for me! I never talked about it honestly until my husband. He knows that I masturbate, and says he is glad, because I only found out that I *could* have orgasm through masturbation, which I only tried after a lot of reading, mostly *The Hite Report*. The worst thing about sex is that it often seems like all that work is for nothing except his orgasm. So far masturbation is the only way for me to orgasm. I only learned this about four months ago, I was twenty-six. I was very pleased to find that I was normal, since I had been afraid that I was one of the two percent that never achieved orgasm. One day I talked to Jeannie, a neighbor of mine—I told her that I did not orgasm. She was sympathetic, and gave me her copy of *The Hite Report* to read. She has since moved away. My upstairs neighbor is a friend, she uses my phone and we visit a lot, but nothing like an exceptionally close friend like Jeannie.

"I do plan to stay married. In most aspects, I am better off married than not. I faced the alternative to being married all of my life—being single—and it's very lonely. My relationships fell into a few categories: where I loved the man and he didn't know I was alive; or he used me for sex; or where we liked each other a lot but circumstances interfered. Except for my husband, I was usually miserable because I did not have a relationship with the other person, or I knew they were using me.

"Sometimes I think I fell in love with my husband *because* he was in love with me. Also, I have often thought that since my childhood seemed barren of love, I have gone searching for it in almost any way I could think of. There was also social pressure to get married, especially young adults of my church were expected to get married. Also, getting married, economically we could do more together than alone. His job has much more upward mobility than mine ever did. Sexually, I had been celibate for two years and didn't care for it. (How some things change!) Would I marry him again? Yes, but not so soon. I think that I married too young, at twenty-two.

"He makes me feel content, but some of the aliveness, the great joy, is not there. I don't think I could ask for more, but I often would like to. I feel much better to have talked about all of this. Six months of counseling helped very little. I'd like to figure out something on this earth that I'd really like to do that's within reach, and go for it. Impossible dream: I'd like to be a crew member on the first or even the second interstellar starship. Sometimes I don't like it here very much."

Economic cooperation

While the majority of married women now work outside the home, still, since women make less money than men, and know they are usually "last to be hired, first to be fired," many continue to feel financially in need of men as a backup in their lives:

"I have not yet been totally or really financially dependent on anyone, but I have felt *psychologically* dependent because I always knew that if I lost my job or went broke, he would be there—at least I thought he would be there. I don't like to feel financially dependent because then I think I am prostituting myself—like the man owns me or is taking care of me."

For many women, unfortunately, economics are still a necessary part of their decision to marry and/or stay married:

"My marriage is not the world to me. I can live without it, but for the economic reasons, I'll stay put. I have a good job and a nice home to which I have greatly contributed over the years; in fact, I have put more into it than necessary. I'll stay where I am now because at this point in time I don't think I want to start finding new roots."

"I have been married nearly seven years. I like the companionship and the additional financial support. I was married eighteen years to another man who contributed little financial support. I do not like to be confined or to have the feeling that someone else has control over me. But I got married the second time for financial aid in supporting a household. I also felt lustful toward this man!"

"Now, with both of us unemployed, the lack of money is definitely a contributing factor to our staying together."

"Habit. I'm used to him and he's used to me. Also economics enter the picture here. We're both out of jobs, and money's tight. It's easier financially together than apart. Also, I just hate living alone. Too much work. He helps with the housework, which makes my life easier."

"I've almost always had an income but I could not support the family myself. There were always financial problems. But my ex-husband didn't like me working because it made him feel insecure; however, he liked the money. Then when I worked anyway (nights) and he was home, he shirked his responsibilities and left the children home alone."

"The best part of marriage is the kids; the worst, fighting mentally to develop self-esteem against someone who doesn't like me. I wouldn't marry him again, but I'll stay married until I can't take it anymore, because I can't support the kids. But I am going to school to gain needed job skills so I can."

Many more women today are willing and able to leave marriages, despite possible economic hardship, if they find themselves in demeaning, spiritually oppressive relationships. In fact, 90 percent of divorces are brought by women, not men (contrary to popular stereotype), as we have seen; the increasing "feminization of poverty" (usually interpreted as men deserting women) in fact shows that many women are choosing to leave bad relationships and be poor (whether this means taking a low-paying, marginal job and/or also getting support from the government) rather than stay in demeaning situations.

In short, many women are deciding to change their situation, even when they have small children, despite the economic consequences—i.e., they know they may live with their children below the poverty level. The vast increase in the number of single heads of household consists of women with children; the "feminization of poverty" statistic is in large part formed of these families and of older single women living alone. The popular public assumption that these women are "left" or "deserted" by their husbands is out of date. In fact, many choose to leave their husbands, or even never get married, feeling they can provide a better home and psychological environment for their children and themselves alone.

Another popular conception that has mostly gone by the board: fewer women than ever before are marrying to find "economic support" or a "good provider"—although women and men are both, of course, at times attracted to the upscale lifestyle of a prospective partner. But women generally, now, expect work and look forward to working most of their lives. Most assume they will often be their own major or sole support—and many like it that way, as seen in Chapter 8.

The physical warmth of marriage—for some

Many women also love the physical warmth and affection they feel while lying close together in bed, embracing, sometimes talking. Although only 44 percent of women say they have this in their marriages on a regular basis, this is one of the most beautiful sections of this book:

"I like so many things about our relationship . . . the honesty, the quiet whisperings late at night, the affection, the times we are goofy and laugh ourselves silly, our love life, our projects we share around the house, and the way we sit around on days off and plan for the future. It's all very basic, but it's wonderful. Or when my partner unexpectedly comes to me and gently talks and touches me. He says I make him happy and that I add beauty to his life. He has a miraculous way of making our bodies melt—it's a mixture between love and lust. It makes me feel sooo good, so loved and at one."

"When my husband and I are lying in bed together, talking and holding each other, it is the finest feeling in the world."

"He is so charming. What I love best about him is when we are together, lying in bed, talking and holding each other. I feel wonderful . . ."

"This morning we had sex and cuddled close for a while. It's Sunday, so we had time. I felt the warmth of our love as we talked about our oldest daughter."

"We enjoy falling asleep together arm in arm more than anything."

"Last night he had been upset with one of his friends and I waited up for him until late, so I could talk to him about it and hold him until he fell asleep."

"I enjoy sitting with him and just talking about world events, work, old times. The evenings we spend at home alone are some of the best. He is always very tender and loving, tells me how beautiful I am (even though I'm not). He always sleeps with his arms around me. It makes me feel very secure and loved."

"The most intimate times we spend together are lying on the bed naked, just touching, enjoying each other's company. We will be quiet mostly, talk a little, then be quiet again—it's neat."

"In intimate moments my husband is very gentle and he has love in his eyes, he tells me he loves me . . ."

"Although he is dead now, the things I liked best were the degree of how he loved me and his children and his smile and the times we lay in bed all wrapped up in one another."

Other happy and affectionate times are while away on vacation—or just alone together with no one around:

"When we go for long walks on the beach at sunset we talk about anything and everything. I feel so happy when we're together like that."

"I am the happiest when we can toss away everyday tasks and just go out and do something frivolous or fun for a day. There is nothing to concentrate on but each other and our feelings."

"On weekends when we went to the hills, just the two of us with no one around, we were so happy."

"We go to an island in the Gulf of Mexico for two or three days now and then. There we are so happy. We shed our jobs, our kids, our money problems, our daily lives. We live very intimately. We stay in a small room. We shop and watch birds and visit galleries, and enjoy being together. I love him and it's a little piece of heaven. There is no phone, no kids knocking on the door, no neighbors, no one we know. It holds our marriage together. Going there now and then is stronger than cement. I discover him all over again."

"The happiest I ever was was while I was pregnant the first time, during the last months. We went on vacation during my seventh month and just spent time alone together, in the Virgin Islands. I think we made love more than we did on our honeymoon."

Many of these intimate times are connected to sex, before sex; in fact, a majority of women say that their husbands act very tender and loving before sex and during intimate moments; these can be the very same women who at other times are having the problems of alienation and male distancing discussed earlier:

"He talks very tenderly to me. He is always telling me that I am beautiful and sexually exciting. I feel so good about myself when we are together like that."

"He says 'I love you' all the time. During intimate moments, he often just holds me with extreme tenderness. In more superficial times, he makes a big thing about how horny I make him."

"He is very loving and tender. He often tells me he loves me and that I am wonderful. This makes me feel really good about our relationship and myself."

"He's very emotional. He often tells me why he loves me and that he is happy. He talks about how he wants to have sex with me and why. While we make love, he tells me how he feels. These are usually the most emotional times in our relationship, when we can stop and be affectionate and loving."

"He is so sweet and tender, always wanting to please me. He tells me he loves me, that I have the nicest body he's ever seen, that he's never been this happy, he's so glad he found me. I feel like I am in heaven."

"I love looking into his deep eyes and feeling the warmth of his body next to mine. He always tries to please me, he is gentle, the most considerate lover that I have ever had. The most orgasms I have ever had have been with my husband."

"He is very sensitive and gentle. He caresses and softly touches me. He says he loves me, and tells me how he thinks I look beautiful—more than ever. He compliments my figure. He is very tender. It makes me happy. We can say anything to each other in intimate moments. Sometimes it's tender talk, other times it's like 'Do you like this and this?' or 'I love to see you excited,' things like that. And he has always, from the beginning, told me he loved me over and over and most emphatically."

"He tells me he loves me about two or four times a day, at the very least. He touches me and kisses me whenever we see each other, in public or at home. We usually spend time holding each other every day whether we make love or not, and he calls me 'cute stuff' and 'beautiful' and says he likes being with me. It makes me feel so good every time he shows me or tells me he cares for me or that he was thinking about me that day. I don't know why he cares, for he loves me more than I love myself at times. I'm just so glad that he does. It keeps me going."

33 percent say their husbands are not so loving:

"Sometimes he says he loves me. I can't remember the last time."

"In subtle ways, through Hallmark, he tells me, or through compliments given by a second party."

"During intimate moments my partner seldom talks. I often feel that I am servicing him. He is passive in his lovemaking. I think it is embarrassment. I long to have him hold me and be romantic. Sometimes I just need to be held and I have to ask him to hold me."

"Last year I bought a teddy—something cool to sleep in and much more sexy than I ever had the courage to wear in front of him. He laughed and laughed when he saw me in it, although, as a man, he might think it was sexy and attractive on me. Oh, how I hurt after that. I was humiliated. I'm not overweight—135 pounds, 5'6", and other people tell me I'm attractive. I still feel hurt."

Although most women value and want an active sex life, sex *itself* is cited as only number five in what women find important in their marriages. However, the state of sex between women and men has improved in marriage from what it was ten years ago.

Having children

Most women who have children say that this is one of the most important aspects of marriage; * *even if they have mixed feelings about their marriage, if it is not happy, 74 percent are very happy about having had their children:*

"I was in shock the first month of my pregnancy. We'd just sold our house, given up a job, and my husband was a full-time student in grad school. But I gained a richness of experience I would never have dreamed possible."

"I gained a lot by having children. I have always been very interested in who they were at their various stages; how they observed the world was fascinating to me (and still is) and had a great influence on how I thought about things. The pure and totally accepting love of a small child is one of the most beautiful things in life. (It is good to enjoy it at the time, as they get quite critical when older.) A baby sucking at one's breast gives feelings of the utmost warmth and contentment. Having these children, watching them grow, has been a great delight for me."

"I was thrilled when I knew I was going to have my husband's child. I was on cloud nine. I was giving him something that no one else could. Sure, another woman could have his child, but it would not be the same child that we had created. I gave up working outside the home to be married and have children. Both my husband and I believe that it is important for children to have the parent-child relationship, with as few babysitters as possible, when they are newborns and very young children. If I didn't have children, I would probably be working and I don't even know if I would be married. I have gained, just

---

*Of course, women do not "need" to be married to have children—although economically it may help, and emotionally most women prefer it. But women, even if not married, are quite able to enjoy the pleasures of having children, and some prefer it that way. See Conclusion to Part II.

being able to bring a life into this world. To be able to leave a little bit of myself and my husband when we are gone."

"I thoroughly enjoy having children. I am amazed that I live with such interesting good people. I can barely comprehend the fact that they come from me. When I first became pregnant I felt again the way I felt at the onset of my menstrual cycle—I am here on earth, part of it, I am it. This is life. I want to feel it all, good or bad.

"It was a bad time to become pregnant because we were newly married, had no money, but I let it happen. It was like carving a private space out of time. The immediate future became known—I would have a child, I would do the things people do when they have children. I'm not sure that I gave up anything when I married and had children. It's possible that I could have gone to a career at an early age, but if I'd had the courage to do that, I wouldn't have gotten married. I am married now and have children now and I also have gotten up courage along the way."

Some women point out the feelings of physical warmth and sensuality they receive through being close with their children:

"There is a great physical satisfaction in cuddling one's children—especially when they are so little and tender. I cherish this. It is wonderful to hold a child in your arms and feel that closeness that has often been denied. My children have given me a sensual nourishment that I have never quite known before. There is nothing like it."

—or during pregnancy or childbirth: *

"Having my daughter was one of the most profound and maturing experiences of my life so far. I loved my body getting larger and larger, loved feeling her hopping around inside me, and really got into the intensity of the delivery, which happened undrugged, totally conscious, very quickly, and with a need for more oxygen to get to her (I had to breathe into an oxygen mask to raise her heartbeat rate just before she was born). All the pain, pushing, helpful people around, and the happiness of her finally being born and crying and waving her little hands and feet—unbelievably moving! I felt really in touch with elemental nature—life—and my own body."

---

*As one woman says, "I think many researchers have neglected the importance of this period in a woman's life, and underestimate its power to affect her personality and orientation to herself, her relationships with others, her community and world. The negative aspects are the ones emphasized . . . the moods, the postpartum depressions, the physical discomfort . . . but not the joy, the pleasure, the excitement, the participation in a miraculous event."

Almost all women are ecstatic and excited when they first receive news they are pregnant:

"I felt like I was a queen, the most important person going."

"I was happy, happy, happy, happy when I got pregnant! I resigned from a super-professional neat-o job to stay home (high school counselor). I like being at home with our child."

"I felt excited and scared when I found out I was pregnant. My husband was also excited and scared. Everything was great when she was born. I fell in love with her. I would do it all over again."

"When I first received the news I was pregnant, I was elated, elated. My husband also. He is a wonderful father to our daughter—tender, caring, and always on her side in life. I love having children and it is great having them."

Obviously, not all women feel so ecstatic about pregnancy or having children; here we are documenting the positive feelings women have in marriage, and for many women, a large part of these positive feelings revolve around having children.

Of course, not all childbirths are like this; many women experience a great deal of pain and discomfort:

"I had extremely painful deliveries—and unlike popular wisdom says, I have not forgotten. My husband was in the hospital waiting room. It was not what one might call a scintillating experience. I like having children, but they should develop another way of having them."

Women also like *not* having children

Interestingly, although most women who have children say it was and is a peak experience, 92 percent of the married women who decided not to have children also say they never regretted it, that in fact they are very happy about their choice:

"I am thirty-nine and have been married two years. Neither my husband nor I want children—he says he wants to have more time with me. I have never wanted to 'grow up and have children,' and do not have any longing for them. Even when we visit friends with children—or especially then—I am glad we don't have any. I love our life together, and we can always adopt some later if we change our mind."

"I have never had any children. I just never felt the maternal urge to do so. I also knew that the sole responsibility for raising them would have rested on my shoulders (my husband's only interest was his work and he said that whether we had children or not was up to me). I had my own life and career to consider. There were social pressures to have children ('You're selfish'; 'You're not a real woman'; 'You're unfeminine'), but I got around that by telling my detractors that it 'just hadn't happened.' This response provoked sympathy from some, envy from others, especially from women whose own careers had been stunted by their decision to stay home to raise their families (as was the norm in the fifties) or who were juggling the roles of mother and career woman. To this day, I have never regretted my decision not to have children."

"When I was a young wife, I felt pressure to have children. Some of my peers were having careers *and* raising children; others chose to be housewives and mothers, and a few years later confided their regrets to me for not having continued to work outside the home. I had always known that I did not have the energy to do both, and I chose a career, though I sometimes worried that perhaps I *should* have a child.

"Societal pressure to have children was great then, and I was frequently told that I was selfish for not having children, not a 'real woman,' I was 'unfeminine.' So I resorted to the lie: 'It just hasn't happened.' The reaction to that was generally one of pity. But I would make exactly the same choice again: I have never regretted the lack of children; my career rewards have been great in terms of the satisfaction they have brought me and the help I've been able to give others."

43 percent of women, even though they love their children, speak with regret of not being able to keep up active jobs and careers at the same time:

"I have tried to have a career along with all the kids, but I have found that in order to be the kind of wife and mother I want to be, it is necessary to stay home and find my creative outlet in other ways."

"I love kids, so I put my career in the back seat for the first ten years and really played mommy. It's too bad I didn't know you could do both. It's a hard struggle for me now."

19 percent of women who have children have mixed feelings about having had them, and 37 percent worry about their negative effect on their relationship with their husbands:

"When I found out I was pregnant, I was not pleased. After I realized it was a given fact, I adjusted to it. I liked having them, and I liked being pregnant, but I wish the decision had been a conscious one. Even though I truly love being a mother, I really don't know if I would have had them. I liked what I was doing before and saw myself as more career-oriented."

"Did it change my relationship with my husband? Our sex life has decreased. I'm a nursing mother, and am often tired. The baby sleeps with us too."

"I wanted a child and felt great when I knew I was pregnant. I think my husband initially thought I was like a child with a toy. His response to our newborn was minimal. Over a period of years he showed so little interest in the kids that I lost my respect for him because of it."

"I love my son dearly, but I had to give up about 99 percent of my time when he was born, and even now I have almost no time to myself. I was pretty unstable when my son was born with all the demands that a baby makes. Now that he's getting a personality of his own, it's a lot easier. The first two years were miserable for me."

"One month my period was five days late. I couldn't believe it, as we had always used precautions. We went through several uncertain weeks waiting for the positive pregnancy test. We certainly did not want to terminate the pregnancy, but we both really hated the idea that something so major was now going to take control and we weren't ready for it. I treasured each day from then until the birth, knowing my days of such freedom from care were numbered."

"I have two children. They're O.K. Sometimes I wish there was just the two of us to consider. Although I wanted my first baby, I felt overwhelmed by the anticipated responsibilities. I gave up my job. We'd travel more if we didn't have children. But we wouldn't have shared many joys, worries, triumphs, disappointments. To my husband, children were a far more important part of marriage than they were to me. I had ambivalent feelings about it, but overall, in retrospect, I'm glad I had them because he makes me feel that I've given him a very precious gift."

"Basically I like having children. They are a trial at times and at times I wish I didn't have to be responsible for them—that I could be free to do what I want. But they are also fun. Given it all to do over again, I would still have them, but I would have waited a few more years and done a bit more traveling and saved more money. After the children, our relationship definitely changed. But it is hard to tell what was caused by the children and what was caused by time. Mainly we both have to hold down different parts of the child-rearing job, leaving us much less time for each other. The noise the kids make makes it hard for us to talk. We go out without them to regain our sanity and we insist (I insist) on ten minutes after dinner without them each night. This helps."

Many women say teenagers can add even more stresses to a marriage:

"My mate was very critical of how I handled my son in his thirteenth year (when, with a rush of hormones, he became a monster overnight). The basic disagreement as to how to deal with a hostile, troubled child (he thought I was too lenient) was a real test for the survival of our relationship. However, we, and my son, came through it."

"Although I loved having children and was ecstatic when I first knew I was pregnant, actually our relationship has become more comfortable and easy since the kids have left home. We seem to be more relaxed, and things have changed for the better. Perhaps having three teenagers around was not the most conducive way to maintain our peace of mind."

68 percent of women, happy or not, comment that children take away time that they and their husbands used to spend alone together—and change the atmosphere:

"Having children cut down our time together and my energy. We don't make love as often as we would like to, and naturally it cut down on our privacy, so that we can't do it on the spur of the moment."

"After becoming a mother, I guess I became more strict. My husband said I was not as much fun."

"We were never as close after. He always seemed intimidated by my need to care for the kids."

"I guess having children did change our relationship. We used to do things together at times. When the children came he just went out by himself."

"Having children changed my relationship with my husband. I was busier and always tired, since I also worked full-time outside of the home. I really resented him for having all that free time—especially in the evenings."

8 percent of women even imply that having children ruined their marriages:

"Having children caused my husband and me a lot of hassling—it has been expensive and took my attention from him. You might say it finished us. All the personality conflicts and needs have left irreparable scars."

"I don't particularly like having children. Giving birth wasn't bad at all, but raising them was hell. I'd never do it again if I could do it over. Raising three children so close together was hectic. Children took time away from my husband and we disagreed so much on how to treat them. It was hitting and yelling all the time—he didn't know how to treat his own children. He alienated them and therefore put me on the defensive."

Stepchildren in second marriages can create other sets of problems:

"After the children were born in my first marriage, he no longer received all the attention and he didn't like it. Then in my second marriage, we each had two children already. Blending families and stepparentry is very difficult— but also very rewarding. In our case, I felt uncomfortable suddenly having sons, whereas before my children were both girls, and the boys could at times be a little macho even at their tender ages. I think his boys and my girls getting to know each other really had a tremendous impact for the better on both of them understanding the other sex more. But it kept my husband and me busy mediating the disputes and mediating our own perceptions too."

"I did live with a man and the children from his previous marriage. I think that having the children there put great stress on the relationship because roles and rights were never clearly defined."

"Stepchildren are very powerful and they know it. They can destroy the new couple's home by making the parent choose between the new spouse and the old (well-loved) children."

But 38 percent feel, even if it changed the atmosphere, having children brought them closer to their husbands:

"My husband 'caught' both our babies. Giving birth together will be among our peak experiences. Rarely have we felt so strong a bond, so much a team. Both of our pregnancies were planned. We were both happy, excited, scared. Now that we have the children, we are even happier, sometimes more scared (it's an awesome responsibility), and incredibly tired much of the time. Having children is infinitely more joyful than we imagined and much, much more work than we expected."

"I think we each gained appreciation and respect for each other; you go through a lot with children and it teaches you a lot about each other. The home study process for adoption did that too. We hassled the bureaucracy together and felt like warriors in successful battle. Promotes camaraderie and intimacy."

Social acceptability/social approval

As seen in Chapter 8, there is enormous pressure on single women after their middle or late twenties to be married, to "fit in," be part of "society," and also to have children. Although it is popular to say that this pressure has gone away or is "much less strong now," in fact more women marry in the United States today than ever did in the nineteenth century, and 81 percent of women today speak about social pressure to marry or remain married as being one of the main reasons they feel more comfortable married.

Women, as seen in many parts of this book, often remark on how keenly they feel the difference in the way the society perceives them, depending on their marital status:

"After twelve years of marriage, I found he was having affairs and I was left with the choice of taking the kids and leaving him or staying and making the best of it. I decided to stay, because, among other reasons, being married meant being treated more respectfully in my daily life—i.e., to shop clerks, authorities, I was a 'Mrs. Somebody,' not a 'Miss Nobody' with two children."

"I sure as hell like the term 'wife' a lot better than the term 'girlfriend.' "

"I am forty-three, a widow. It was important to me to be in a good marriage to a good, solid citizen in the community. I would like to be in another marriage like this."

"One reason I agreed to stay married to him, despite the lack of love and the generally unsatisfactory relationship, was to have a partner for dinner, dance, and travel. It means a lot."

And sometimes, women's descriptions of the pleasures of having children have a tinge of this feeling of gaining social approval, "fitting in," too:

"I felt more 'womanly' . . . more feminine, more whole when I was pregnant . . . I did not like labor and delivery, but it seemed like a small price to pay."

"I was delighted when I was carrying my first child. I feel that I gained the greatest thing in life—motherhood and a whole new concept of love and caring."

Love: What kind of love do most women want in their marriages?

What percentage of women say they remain married "for love"—and for what kind of love?

As seen in Chapter 3, most women say that they feel loved by their husbands in the sense of being "needed" more than being "seen" for themselves. Relatively few mention feeling really understood or valued for their own unique characteristics. In a sense, some women seem to feel that the man's "being there" is a kind of tribute—something the woman gets from the man. Most women say the kind of love they have in their marriages is not based on in-depth two-way emotional support. Women who can communicate with their husbands on this level are extremely happy about it, but also extremely rare (see Part I).

Only 6 percent of those responding list equal emotional support as one of the main pleasures of their marriages:

"Communicating always feels good and is the basis of our relationship. I also have more fun with my husband than anyone else."

"I love sitting around in a dark living room and talking about our future together."

"He bends over backwards to give me the time and support I need. He enjoys my silliness and takes my rages without trying to change me."

"I love being married to this man. I married him because of his fun, sense of humor, sensuousness, sincerity, honesty, and trustworthiness—and so we could share dreams and fantasies. He picks me up when I am down, and vice versa."

"He loves me the way I am at any given time. When I complain about the condition of my body (after a baby like) he's very honest and helpful, yet very flattering and supportive. He's very gentle."

Are most women "in love" with their husbands?

Given the assumption in our society that one grows up, falls in love, and gets married, it is surprising how few women say they are "in love" with their husbands and how acceptable this seems to be to them.

Of those married more than two years, only 13 percent say they are "in love" with their husbands; 82 percent of women say they love their husbands, but define that love as caring and/or companionship.

One woman's statement points out starkly the difference for her between being "in love" with her husband, and loving him:

"Being 'in love' is a high, irrational feeling where anything goes. It's unpredictable. Taking risks is easy. It's like feeling immortal. But really loving is an earthy thing. It's putting up with dirty clothes on the floor, cleaning up the bathroom after he's been sick in there, coming back when you're still really mad at him, sitting by his side night after night as he watches TV programs you hate. It's also worrying when he's late from work, realizing how much you take him for granted when he's out of town on business. It's seeing his loving face looking down on your baby. It's the weeks and months without sex because you're too exhausted from child care to have any desire. It's the memories you share. It's walking hand in hand and talking on a summer evening. It's all the day-to-day things that build up into a rich tapestry of caring for one another.

"At this time I love him more than I ever did before. Last year, I would have said the same thing. And I guess that a year from now I will love him even more, though it's hard to imagine how I possibly could. After eleven years, we are very happy together. This love we have is gentle and quiet and unassuming. It's security and stability. It's constant and supportive. It's forgiving. That's the biggest thing about it. No matter what, our love for one another is forgiving—accepting each other's faults and shrugging them off, then moving on."

82 percent of married women define the love in their marriages as caring:

"I've been married eight years. The best part is the security. I find it difficult to separate love and companionship as reasons for wanting this relationship. I know they are both important to me. A long-term relationship allows me to feel safe in expressing myself sexually. I think I enjoy having someone to count on in our daily life most of all. I am generally happy in the sense that I don't look for satisfaction from outside the marriage from other men. I feel very secure and safe. It may sound dull put this way, but compared to the rest of my experience, it is like heaven. There is genuine caring, which I didn't expect to share with a man. I can visualize living with him until death."

"You love a total personality after you have shared many years and moments with them; it's hard to separate any one reason why I stay married. My husband is a good lover and reads me very well, is patient with my changing sexual likes and dislikes. He is very closed concerning companionship—he is very hard to get to open up and talk about things that are really important to him, his feelings, etc. . . . so although I'm happy in most ways, I'm also unhappy."

"You can form an immediate feeling of affinity and attraction to a person, but I do not see how this could be classified as 'love.' Real caring is most substantially built in small increments over time, tested and built of trust. The test takes time."

As seen here, women are not marrying "for love" as much as for a whole complex of reasons related to "home": companionship (even if more emotionally distant than most women would like), "security" (real or imagined, as most women would say), having children, feeling "loved" and/or approved of by the society; feeling "special" or number one to someone, at least officially. How valid are most women finding these purposes for marriage? Fifty percent of women are divorcing, with most of those divorces brought by women. Many remarry, continuing to hope for, look for the "home" and warmth of human society which the word "marriage," on some level, promises.

But is what we want "out there," waiting to be found? Or is it, perhaps, waiting to be designed; i.e., is "home" a concept we must make—a new democratized family in which there will be much more chance for "home" to be all the things we hope for?

14

What Is Love—
Passion or Caring?

Women, Both Single and Married, Debate
the Nature of Love

**"How would you define love? Is love the thing you work at
in a relationship over a long period of time, or is it the
strong feeling you feel for someone right from the
beginning, for no known reason?"***

*Most women clearly identify two different feelings: one is being passionately "in
love," and the other is loving, learning to care for another person over time:*

"Daily life with a partner versus the passion and excitement of a new or
brief encounter is the saddest part of 'being in love.' There have been times
when I have wept bitterly because I knew a man I 'wanted' would never 'stick
around'—and I have also wept because a man I really loved and cherished as
a friend was no longer exciting sexually. I think my husband is very attractive,

---

*A few women object to the term "in love" or "falling in love"—e.g., "Love to me is a choice I
consciously make toward another and is something different from 'falling in love.'" One writer, Dorothy
Tennov, has referred to being "in love" as a state of "limerance." See Dorothy Tennov, *Love and
Limerence: The Experience of Being in Love* (New York: Stein and Day, 1981). Also see Elaine Hatfield
and Richard L. Rapson, "Passionate Love—Sexual Desire," *Archives of Sexual Behavior*, Vol. 16, No. 3
(New York: Plenum Press, 1987).

but I do not have the desperate desire for him that I once did—and I swore I would never lose that feeling. However, he has a dearness that I cherish, and I try to focus on this when I feel that the electricity is gone."

"In the beginning of a relationship there is infatuation, butterflies in the stomach, etc. Your heart beats wildly and you feel elated because he's entered the room! But this is not the love you have after thirty years of marriage. My love for my husband is real—not the heart-pounding sort but the kind I'll live with forever. I've learned to respect him. I value his opinion. I seek his comfort when I'm sad or upset. I care about him and how he is. That's the best love."

"For me being in love caused more pain and anguish than pleasure. The frantic quality of being in love carries with it exquisite pain. My happiest times have been with my husband, with whom I don't think I have ever been *in* love but whom I love very much and who has shared many of my most important moments."

"Our relationship is of a 'loving' nature—comfortable, more than excited. I probably have felt more 'passionate' for a lover, but I am passionate about our relationship and wanting to keep it, so I guess I'm passionate about my husband too. Passion doesn't stay alive so much in familiarity."

"I care very much about my husband and his happiness and unhappiness. When I love, my thoughts are not sexual; I just care about the other person. I wish there could be both loving and being in love in a marriage. When I'm in love I can't think rationally and I'm very antsy, agitated, with extreme bouts of happiness and unhappiness."

How Does It Feel to Be Passionately "In Love"?

Women describe being "in love" as a very intense feeling:

"I am so in love with my husband! He's beautiful and intelligent, rarely criticizes people. He knows how to appreciate life and character. I absolutely adore him and believe that after eight years together, I am still infatuated with him. I feel such a deep affection for him it almost hurts."

"I was eighteen when I fell madly in love. He was sensitive, kind, gentle, soft-spoken, with an inner strength. I married him and it's the best thing that ever happened to me. He makes me feel loved, sexually exciting, protected from hurt, etc. If possible, I love him more today than I ever did."

"The first time I went to bed with him, I felt as though the world had stopped and I was a shooting star sending out enough light to illuminate the blackest of black holes. Both in bed and out, it was an overpowering sensation and I couldn't get enough of him."

"I want to be with him every second. I want to hold and be held by him, make love and see the love in his eyes when he watches me."

"When I first saw him I felt a lurch, a leap, and then a kind of internal sigh, an 'At last. Where have you been for so long?' A deep sense of recognition and a 'relaxed excitement.' It also felt scary as hell. He was like everyone I'd ever been in love with before in some small way and then himself, more so. He is beautiful to look at, astoundingly intelligent, very warm and beautifully sensual (but only in bed, almost never in public), his voice makes my ears feel good and my chest and spine, he has very penetrating eyes, his sense of humor is delightful, he can do or figure out almost anything, and he's maddening, frustrating, infuriating, invigorating, unpredictable, uncontrollable, and nice. I do not know how to describe what he is like. He is himself, and I like the way he is. I have known him for eight years."

"Every time I see him my heart fills with joy. His face refreshes me, rejuvenates my spirit, my soul. He fills all my needs, intellectually, emotionally, spiritually, and physically. He is the one and only person I have ever been passionate about or with."

"His touch on me is always just captivating me, no matter how far my thoughts are from sex. It is the quality of his skin and the uninhibited, simple way with which he might close his hand over mine. He never seems to move in a pattern, he always seems to approach me as if the idea had just sprung from his most inner impulse. Even on point of penetration he seems to have ideas that express themselves on me and through me as if each moment was the essence of living, not a sexual prowess or manly exertion, just being. Wonderful."

Others say that, although it is over, being passionately "in love" was one of the deepest, most profound experiences of their lives:

"At my deepest I felt like if he left the room I thought I would die. The person was shy around people. It lasted one year. He moved away and we lost touch. I lost my virginity to him and a part of me would love to see him today."

"It was the most devastating feeling ever, hot, cold, the greatest high, happy, sad, very insecure, Not In Control. He was the sun, the moon, the stars, could do no wrong (even though he does). Very likable, good looks, sexy and lovable, good at giving. There was always a feeling of a deeper inside relationship, kind of an unspoken understanding between us."

"Both times I have been in love I've known it at once. The usual chatter that goes on in your head—which you more or less think of as yourself—suddenly seems much fainter and smaller, and underneath is something larger, quieter, more sure of itself, definitely you but also tuned to the other person.

When I'm in love, I don't ever feel quite alone. Something of the other person is always in my mind."

"I fell the most deeply in love with the man I later married. It felt wonderful and terrible. I loved him with the very core of my being. He was everything to me, my best friend, my lover, my intellectual soul mate. He was highly intelligent, full of fire and enthusiasm, a radical in his ideas, a lot of fun. The relationship lasted for ten years, seven of those in marriage. It was a union of extremes, we alternately passionately loved one another and hated one another. We were neurotics together, we discovered from the other what was missing in ourselves. It was vital to both, and through it, we grew, reached out—but perhaps too much of our energy was focused either toward or against each other.

"Eventually the powerful chemistry between us, which was once sparkling and positive, became ugly and negative. And we parted. As we share two children and he loves them as much as I do, the relationship has never really ended; it is now a different entity. We have different mates, but a part of me will always love him. I see him every day in the faces of my children and he is still the most intellectually stimulating person I have ever known."

———————

Perhaps falling in love is one of the ways we get in touch with our spiritual essence, our real feelings—as, being in love, we feel free to express all of our thoughts, we see more clearly our lives and the world.

Many Women* Don't Like—or No Longer Trust—Their Passionate Feelings

Being "in love" is impractical and painful

No matter how wonderful it can feel to be "in love," 69 percent of married women and 47 percent of single women say they have decided they do not like, or no longer trust, being "in love"; it is too volatile, too dangerous:

"Being in love can give pleasure, even joy, but most of the time it's painful, unreal, and uncertain. It took a long time to learn anything from it, and most

---

*In *The Hite Report* on men, most men too say that they did *not* marry the women they had most deeply, passionately loved; most men also say they do not trust passionate love. But men, unlike women, are taught to downplay emotional feelings, while women are more encouraged to experiment with them, express them. These women have more painful experiences than most men before deciding to give up on this kind of love; men try to avoid these experiences from the beginning—or, at least, always keep them as low-key as possible.

of what I learned is that I should avoid it. But unfortunately, for me sexual passion seems to be stuck in being in love. I wish I could take those feelings, bring them to marriage, and use them here."

"I do not like being in love. I feel too vulnerable. I have a bad pattern of being too skeptical and cautious at first, then I lay myself wide open and am taken advantage of. I would rather be with someone I feel comfortable and safe with than to be in love."

"Being in love has its moments. The excitement is incomparable. But I do not like the hysteria, longing, and inability to function. I need to be in control of myself and my environment."

"The time I fell in love most deeply was a horrible experience. I was nineteen and gave everything of myself to him. The more I gave, the less challenging I was. I hurt and tried more. A year later, I married someone else, all for the wrong reason. He called me on my wedding day with 'I'll always love you.' We went back together again after my divorce. Stupid me with all the same open feelings. He left me six months later."

"My first relationship was the deepest in love for me, and the most horrifying. She gave me my first job. She was head of the department; she was my excuse to move out of the house. (For my parents' sake we 'shared' her apartment for four years.) I loved her very much. I worshipped her; I still do. The first two years we were very happy, very sexual. But I wasn't 'feminine' enough for her. She gradually began dating other girls, and after four years, found a little educated thing, younger than I at the time, invited her to move in with the two of us, and six months later 'asked' me to leave. When I refused, she fired me. As much as I hate her now, I still love her."

But even after they have left or are no longer together, many women say it is hard to stop loving someone; love, once felt, for many women never ends:

"I loved my first husband deeply (and hated him at the same time for going off and marrying someone else and having another baby with her) and still feel a connection to him after all these years (like he's the only one who knew the real inside me). Now it's kind of a happy-sad love for him, mixed with ambivalence because I don't think I ever could forget the hurt I felt during our separation and divorce. Every time he brings his child from the other wife along to pick up my kids, I get a stab that reminds me of all the pain. I try to be adult about it and realize what is, is, but it still is a reminder of the rejection."

"I was in love with a man who was eight years older than me, one of my brother's friends. I was twenty-five. He was strong and domineering and very intelligent. I tended to feel a little afraid of him. We went out together for more than a year, and then I took my courage into my hands and asked him if he planned to get married to anyone. When he said no, it was terribly painful. I couldn't sleep for weeks, and I even dreamt about him for years, even after I married someone else."

"I am still very much in love with my deceased lover. I still think of him most of the day and miss him terribly."

"*Splendor in the Grass* (a movie with Natalie Wood) has been my favorite love story since junior high. I identify with it. The story in *Splendor* is where the love was so strong, and the parental and societal pressures so great, the couple was forced to break up—she going to a mental institution and later each of them to marry others. Natalie Wood goes to see Warren Beatty (her love) in the end, when they are both married to someone else. He asks her if she's happy and she says she doesn't know, she doesn't ask herself that question much anymore. She asks him if he's happy and he says that, like her, he doesn't ask himself that much anymore. He says it's funny how things turn out, but what's the use, you take what you get. Later her girlfriends ask her if she still loves him and she just thinks the words of Wordsworth's poem, something like 'no, nothing can bring back the hour of splendor in the grass, glory in the flower, we will grieve not, but find comfort in what remains.' (Probably slaughtered the poem—but the message is clear.)"

It can also be difficult to stay away from a destructive lover; the deep feelings are hard to give up, and the period of withdrawal can seem empty:

"I care for a lover that I should hate. He's treated me bad and has little respect or understanding of who I've become, yet I want him. Why? I don't know and it takes all my strength to stay out of his life. I've got to let him go. It's destructive to me, to my self-worth and self-esteem."

"Love has nothing to do with its object. What they do may cause you such harm that you have to leave—but you can still feel love for them."

Does being involved with the "wrong man" mean a woman is psychologically "messed up"? Or are there very special aspects of the loved one's personality worth treasuring, despite bad points? Or attributes that are particularly meaningful to a woman at a certain stage in her life, so that part of her feels that this sense of "being alive" is more important than the "normality" of achieving a "successful" relationship? How can a woman tell when this is the case or when she is not valuing herself enough? See Chapter 7.

Women sometimes harden themselves after being hurt in love, fighting against being so vulnerable in the future:

"I was most deeply in love with my first love. It was so strong and sudden, I adored him, but didn't let it show for fear of losing him. It was a marvelous feeling to be with him—I still regret the games I played out of fears. I would have liked to be authentic. When it ended six months later, I was so horribly torn apart that I decided I would never love so much again but find someone that would love me more than I did them, in order not to suffer."

"I drive past his parents' house almost every day to my exercise class. I still think of him. I'm thirty now. I will never let myself be hurt again like that."

But despite all this, 53 percent of women say they are determined not to close off this part of themselves, even though they may be quite fearful of gut attraction and where it may lead:

"I feel most alive when I'm in love. It is both pleasure and pain. It is terrifying, risky, exhilarating. It is dangerous, but it is worth it."

"Although the only affinity we had was physical, he was a turning point in my ability to go along with my desire for someone instead of fighting it, so I'm deeply grateful for the relationship, even with all its flak."

While being passionately "in love" is an important experience, to make it a positive addition to one's life is difficult—almost an art:

"How can love be honest? Or transformative? Falling in love is crucial, but falling in a pool doesn't guarantee you'll learn how to swim."

"Deep emotional relationships are really a problem, almost impossible. Most of us are so inexperienced at dealing with real emotion in someone else that we simply don't know what to do at any given outburst on the part of the other. Even if we do know, we would have to have a lightning-action coping technique, sandwiched in between work, evening meetings, social events that have been planned far in advance (and are very hard to change because everyone is so busy), and whatever it takes to support life for you and the people you live with. There's just no time, space, or energy to cope with overly emotionally involved people, at least in the environment I live in."

One problem with passionate love, which makes stability difficult, is that every little thing matters so much; this can make one feel vulnerable and touchy, leading to potential arguments or withdrawals of affection:

"Do I like passionate love? I'm in a relationship like this now. Things get too big easily. My feelings are too close to the surface for comfort. I am afraid of feeling this way, afraid of losing myself in her, of loving her more than me. I have a great deal of ambivalence. But I am learning a lot about myself, and there is also joy."

"I feel very threatened by people I'm attracted to. I'm much more at ease around people I dislike or scorn or feel smarter or prettier than."

Being deeply attracted to and "in love" with someone can make a relationship tend to be less stable, simply because each partner cares so much about what the other does. What if any given angry statement means one's partner is leaving? Losing interest? This is why being "in love" tends to be so tumultuous.

54 percent of women give stability as their reason for preferring loving, caring feelings over being passionately in love:

"I prefer the more stable contentment of an ongoing and reciprocal relationship. I want my 'I love you' to be answered by 'I love you too,' not 'Thanks.' "

"I am now married and have maintained a happier state over a period of time than I ever have had. I can share feelings with my husband that I have not been able to do with my mother, my father, or former lovers. It is less electric, more rewarding."

"At times I get lonely and dispirited enough to think I would like someone to be in love with me. I feel joy when I'm in love. Nevertheless, it's not a state of mind that's compatible with everyday life. If you really want to give yourself up to love, you have to forget the idea of a career, an extensive social life, any sort of day-to-day, how-can-I-survive way of thinking. I think being in love is very important. It is the only thing that teaches people to see out of someone else's eyes. But it doesn't provide practical solutions or teach you to take care of yourself."

59 percent say passionate love cannot last:

"Being 'in love' is that magic first time together, when you want her and she wants you. Loving someone, I assume to be a continuous, perpetual relationship, which I have longed for but never seem to find."

"Intense, erotic love is temporary—loving is attachment, commitment, and respect."

"A time of excitement and pain—too intense to prolong."

But 22 percent of women say that if you work at it, passionate love will last; it is fragile but one can create an environment in which it can flourish in a pure and intense form:

"My husband and I have been married for three and a half years. I am in love with him and love him, I think about him constantly. My heart still goes pit-a-pat. He takes my breath away, and gives me that wonderful aching between my legs. I can firmly state that I love him more now than I did when we first married (which was quite a lot then). I believe love is a commitment, a dedication to someone with whom you can go through anything and come out on the other side."

"I like being in love today because of the person with whom I am in love. We respect each other and are very kind to one another. I am amazed to have a male best friend for whom I feel strong sexual passion—I am convinced this is very rare. We have had all the feelings—pleasure, pain, learning, enlightenment, frustration, joy. I feel a lot of joy in my life because of him, and a sense of emancipation. We have worked hard for this. Of course, I am thirty-eight—it's about time I felt such happiness."

But if forced to choose between passion and stability, 58 percent of women say they would pick a relationship that runs smoothly:

"Between my last lover and my husband—I must be crazy not to want a nice, solid, stable husband and children. What else is there?"

"Hopefully, women who find themselves going through 'excessive emotional trips' with a man would reassess things and determine whether or not they really need this man in their lives! I mean, does he enhance a sense of calm and serenity that we want in our lives? When the two are together, is it like 'coming home'? A haven? If not, I am confused as to why women would allow themselves to experience ongoing emotional trips when they have the option not to do so. Particularly if they are married."

"It is not the intense love which is all-consuming, but at this time in our marriage our more mature feelings are right for both of us. Our love relationship is based on respect, endurance, and maturity. Quite boring, but it does work since we cannot hurt one another to any great degree as other loves have in the past."

"Love develops in a feeling of respect and sensitivity for another person. It grows as values and experiences are shared. If both parties have a genuine self-respect, the love can be developed. The more I hear of arranged marriages in other cultures, the more I am convinced that they, too, have something going for them. As one Pakistani woman (M.A. Home Ec.) recently said to me, 'What's so special about sex? Poof! A few minutes and it's over. There are more important things in marriage.' "

Is being "in love" a delusion, a psychological problem? just lust?

17 percent of women do not take being "in love" seriously; they say it represents an unbalanced mental state:

"Being 'in love' is a neurosis."

"How would I define love? Oh, gracious . . . I would define it as the only socially acceptable psychosis. The in-love person is in this state of socially acceptable psychosis, and people in love can rattle me more than anybody I know because what they see in the person they love and what that person is really like are just two totally different things. Being in love, you're mentally off balance, you're not perceiving the person or the world around you in a state of reality. I think loving someone is caring about that person and being able to see that person in the light of reality."

"Many people 'fall in love' out of their desperate neediness."

—or simple infatuation, somewhat "childish":

"That was infatuation. It was just silliness when we were kids."

Other women say passionate love is a delusion, an illusion:

"I think of being 'in love' as movie-like. The romantic Hollywood myth, lots of gooey-eyed giving and thinking everything will be perfect forever. I suppose I'm being cynical. Times when I feel like I'm in love, I always think it's a lot of fun and don't care if I'm being silly, but I'm still aware of it as temporary."

"Love must be worked at, says me, the perfect Calvinist. What you feel right off the bat is projection. It's not real. 'Love at first sight' is bullshit, you don't even know the person. It's about a figment of your imagination that the 'beloved' just happens to fit."

And yet, one of the women who agrees with this point of view—

"Being 'in love' is a fallacy or at best a disease created on the movie screen, but *loving* another human being is always a pleasure, learning, enlightening, giving, and a joyful experience."

—is also the woman who wrote:

"It was while I was married I was the loneliest."

And this is not an atypical contradiction. Are women really so "happy" with the "loving" they describe? Or are they happy giving love, but sometimes feel lonely because they do not get enough love in return?

28 percent of women say that being "in love" is just lust—purely sexual: *

"I think it is simple lust in disguise, or an excuse to feel better about sex."

"I don't think I loved my husband the minute we first met. I think we were 'in heat.' We couldn't get enough of each other."

"Falling in love is superficial lust without emotions. Selfish desire."

"Lust is the strong feeling from the beginning that causes your heart to race and your body to melt. Love grows from sharing hopes and dreams and goals, his being there to pick up the pieces of your deepest hurts."

"I do not believe in 'love at first sight,' even though that feeling happened to me on several occasions. I think now that it was more lust and passion, plus an intense curiosity of the unknown. After the curiousness wears off, a person gets down to the true meaning of love—two people relating to each other on an equal basis and as a team."

However, a few women argue that even if one's feelings are "just lust," this is no reason to discount them:

"Feeling passionate is very important for me. The exhilaration carries one through the day, making the petty frustrations of work easier to bear."

But 41 percent of women refuse to make a separation between "lust" and being "in love," feeling this is all part of one larger emotion:†

"I usually feel the closest after we make love because it is an expression of all of the wonderful feelings I have toward her. When we make love I feel as though we are a total entity—I can't tell where she leaves off and I begin. It seems to be a 'complete' feeling capturing my emotions, my intellect, and my physical awareness."

"Perhaps most people believe sex is physical and love is emotional. Sex for me was synonymous with love always. I could not separate the two. My belief was that we were 'of one flesh.' Sex often is reverence when one or both persons have suffered a great loss—job, bereavement, etc."

One woman thinks these unexplainable feelings might be more real than "rationally" learning to understand a person, and defining that as love—but questions her own wisdom:

"When I am in love, I feel they are real, I can express my real self with them, time is real time. But maybe I am projecting, maybe I have a story in my head of what my life is about, and I meet them and decide they are the character in

---

*How many women find that they don't feel really "turned on" with men they have friendly relationships with? That they are more turned on to men they fight with? See Chapter 7.
†See also the conclusion to Chapter 5.

my story, the one that can understand the deeper me. But if I can feel and express things I otherwise don't, isn't that a deeper form of reality? Or is it only inviting them into *my* story—not being involved in theirs?"

What Is Passionate Love? How Does It Fit into Life?

"Desire leads you straight out of security, to a place where there are no rules . . ."
—Professor Elizabeth Petroff, reflecting on Hadjewich of Brabant, a Flemish beguine of the twelfth century

Is being passionately "in love" a "neurosis"? Sappho felt it, the Roman poet Catullus felt it—it must be ancient. Ezra Pound translated ancient Egyptian poems which show that the mysterious feelings of love are not a product of "bourgeois mentality":*

Tranquil our paths
When your hand rests in mine in joy,

When you embrace me
So bright is the light that shines from you
I need balm for my eyes.

The whole world shines . . .
I wish we could go on sleeping together,
Like this, to the end of eternity.

However, the incorporation of "love"—especially passionate love—into family structure as we know it may be a somewhat late development in human history. Recent archaeological studies of human groupings in pre-history have not proven that the first families were father-mother-children; in fact, the earliest families were probably mothers and infants, or clans, with "fathers" being a later concept.† Did love between lovers in the earliest human groupings

*From "Conversations and Courtship," in *Love Poems of Ancient Egypt*, by Ezra Pound (New York: New Directions, 1962). Another famous artistic expression of combined physical and spiritual passion is in Richard Wagner's opera *Tristan und Isolde*, in which the lovers sing to each other a very moving duet, with words expressing their spiritual unity as they stand embracing: "Thus might we die, ever one, without end, never waking, never fearing . . . In the heaving swell, in the resounding echoes, in the universal stream of the world-breath, to drown, to founder—unconscious—utmost rapture!"
†See symposium presented at the annual meeting of the American Association for the Advancement of Science, 1985, Shere Hite/Robert Carneiro, "Controversies over the Nature of the Early Family."

contain long-term caring, what we might call "familial love"? Or only, as is often assumed, "short-term" passion? And are physical and spiritual passion as easily separable as our culture tries to make them?

Some women (12 percent) say they have never experienced being "in love" or ecstatic feelings. Why do some women report feeling these so much more frequently than others? Are the women who do, women who somehow are especially "needy" for love, or those who enjoy peak experiences? Are they women who want to work through some interior unanswered feelings—or are they women who want to connect with something larger than themselves, larger feelings? Are they, even, longing for a kind of religious experience? On the other hand, are those who don't have such intense feelings closed off to life, "blocking their feelings," overly practical and out of touch with deeper parts of themselves? One woman describes her desire to strive for "something more," a great love, this way: "I crave an absolute. Love that comes before all else, love that is deep and cannot be explained is that absolute."

Sometimes it would seem that a desire for "romantic love"—for more spiritual closeness, a lack of aloneness—is in part a longing for the impossible, a longing to end the solitariness of the soul, a longing for the completing of the soul. Is the desire to have children with someone when "in love" a feeling of the soul's desire for unity—or a biological trick on women triggered by the mechanics of sexual arousal?

"If I can't have passion, I'd rather not bother." Are single women more likely to prefer being "in love"?

"If I can't have passion in a relationship, I'd rather not bother at all with it. It seems to me all that stuff about learning to care, putting up with endless doldrums, is just made up to make women 'do their duty' and take care of a family and a man. By passion, I mean that feeling of excitement you have about another person—getting to know them, sharing things with them, feeling a sense of wonder, and, of course, physically wanting to have sex with them too. It may not last forever, but you can be friends after, and I'd rather keep my life alive this way, not turn into a robot like I've seen so many people do, by having to be in a situation and insist that I love the person, when you are really just there out of habit (or fear of leaving). Of course, you *do* love those people, you always will. But that is not the kind of love I want to *live* with someone. I want to grow, be excited about them and have a sense of adventure, of marvel—to be fully *alive.*"

73 percent of currently single, never-married women say that companionship would not be enough for them, that they want to feel "in love," a passionate desire and commitment:

"I do not like being part of a couple if I'm not in love with the other person. I greatly prefer being celibate over sharing sex with someone that I don't really care for. Sex is meaningless and depressing otherwise."

Most single women now in their twenties say they want more than security and companionship in marriage: when they marry, they want to be "in love." Is this what women of most generations would have said before they married, only modifying their views later? Or is this a change in ideology for women— i.e., is feeling "in love" now more important to women than finding stable companionship or a "good provider"? It may be that the more financially and psychologically independent women become, the more they can afford to look for passionate love. But many women today also decline to choose "romantic love," preferring to focus their energies on work and a broader spectrum of friends and activities.

Women Who Believe in Love as Caring

Still, the large majority of married women in this study (82 percent) say that real love means loving over time—not feeling "in love," passionate, but learning to know and care for the other person:

"Most of all, love is a condition of companionship and closeness which is very important—liking them for what they are and the way they are. Not trying to change them. Doing many things together. It takes a long time to get to know someone like that."

And there is a consensus among the married women who define love as caring that early feelings of being "in love" generally grow into a deeper love, defined as caring and understanding—if the relationship continues:

"I grow less and less 'in love' with my husband as time goes on, but the regular love grows stronger as we learn to respect each other more, and I learn to understand his feelings more. I like the inner glow and strength this gives me—it's just as valuable as those first intense rushes of excitement."

Some say that this kind of love is the best because it leads to growth, it is inspiring:

"Loving someone besides yourself seems to make you better than you would be. Love allows or insists that you look away from yourself and toward someone else; their happiness, fears, frustrations, become important to you."

"Love should make you feel capable of great feats. As my daughters have become more secure with my love for them, they seem to try more and more difficult feats for themselves. As other people join in their lives adding more love, they climb even higher. This is what my husband and I feel about our love: love gives us the security to stretch ourselves, to try out new things, to let go of fears and insecurities. Love is nurturing in a very broad sense."

One woman gives a more in-depth version of what this love is, how she defines it, and how it has fit into her life and changed over thirty-eight years:

"I like being a housewife. I like making my world neat and tidy (though I can let it all go too). I love to cook and would resent it if he tried to take over *my* kitchen. I don't have a lot of quarrel with the traditional male/female roles, as long as it does not involve dominance. None of these traditional roles came about by accident. I like men who are protective of women, who are gentlemen in the finest sense of the word. The traditional qualities of males appeal to me. Take charge, take care of females. I enjoy all that.

"When we got married, he handled the money, he handled our lives, he was the leader. Now, I handle most of the money, I am generally the leader. It is all into one big pot, well managed, allowing an early retirement for him and a partial retirement for me. I don't think it is possible for me to not work ever again. Damn right I believe in equal pay for equal work. If I were a young single mother who needed a secure income, I'd go after a traditional male job with a union backing me. But I adore being feminine.

"I do like making money too. But accomplishment, more than money, is what matters. And frankly, him being the main wage earner has allowed me to explore, has allowed me time to learn. And during the years I have made more money than he did, it was fine with him. He thought it was wonderful. He has totally supported my design business, even to the point of pasting the layouts himself when I couldn't afford to hire anyone. He has never come on 'macho' and tried to hold me back. I guess I've known for a long time that I am bright and creative, though for too many of my adult years, I felt inadequate, sometimes stupid, socially inferior, neurotic.

"I think I have what I want. I've been in this marriage thirty years and even though divorce has been considered, some part of me in those worst times knew I'd be in more pain without than with him. And I believe in happy endings.

"My husband, I adore this man who often annoys me. At various periods throughout childhood and adulthood I've loved him with deep intensity. In truth he is spoiled rotten with small lavish touches. I don't go as far as to cut up the meat on his plate, but almost. Love is getting yourself out of the way and supporting that other person one hundred percent. I have put myself aside many times and he has put himself aside. We trust each other with money, our lives, everything. Love is all there is. Nothing else we do in this world can matter as much as loving people and being loved.

"Making love relationships work . . . well, some of it is simply hanging in there. And also I've always had the knowledge that whatever was going on, no matter how bad, it would be worse without him. I believe in happy endings and guess what . . . I get happy endings. All problems can be solved. The most important thing I am getting out of this relationship is security—the security of having someone there at all times. Trust. Safety.

"I also believe in monogamy. Why? Because I've tried it the other way. One day when my husband was away on business (we had been married about twelve years, and he had recently been transferred from one state to another by his company), a letter arrived (typed address, no return) forwarded from his old company address to our new home address. I opened it as I opened all bills and junk mail, etc. It was from a woman. Reading that was worse than experiencing the death of a loved one. For days I considered everything from suicide to divorce. I felt totally destroyed, betrayed, unloved, tricked, and I guess most of all I felt there was something wrong with me, that I could not keep him satisfied. (What ego to take total responsibility for the actions of another! And to assume there was something wrong with me, not him.)

"When he came home, a few days later, in desperation, frustration, and being middle-aged crazy at thirty-six, I asked for an open marriage, and got it. Then I became depressed—then highly attracted to a slightly younger man who represented all the rebel things I had never done. (I resented never getting to be twenty-one and a hippie!)

"The first affair was serious on my part. I adored this guy. The problem was he worked for and highly respected my husband. Made it tough on him. Me, I just wanted to get him into the nearest bed as often as possible, and he was dealing with heavy guilt. He and my husband eventually cleaned it all up between them and he wouldn't see me again. I yearned for him for a long time afterward and dreamed of him in my sleep, daydreamed about him when I was awake. I was 'in love' but I did not love him enough to leave my husband.

"Then, over the course of the next four or five years, I had several one-night stands. Frankly, there is nothing in the world as great as something 'strange' on the side. It made my life very exciting, provided a lot of insights. Meanwhile, my husband was having miscellaneous sexual adventures.

"At one point, we went through extensive and intense therapy together, bared our souls, sometimes I learned more about him than I cared to know. It was passionate, loving, sad, joyous, freeing. Everything it should have been. Now, knowing there is nothing we can't tell each other—I value this honesty highly. (But once he told me he had had a homosexual encounter. On some level I knew it, but I really would have been happier not knowing it for sure. Just like I could have lived out my life quite happily without knowing that little mite parasites live around the roots of our eyelashes.)

"Then there came a time when I'd experienced all those things, and I was through. Back to monogamy. It was what I basically believe in, yet without the open marriage, we probably would have ended up divorced. So maybe there is a time and place for all things. It would have terrified me when I was young if my husband had gone and stayed with somebody else. Now I know he'll come home. He always did come home, and if he should have another affair, he will come home.

"After thirty years of marriage, I think we know everything we can about each other, positive and negative, and we stay together, do things together, enjoy some things separately, we are secure together. I was jealous for years until I figured out it was my own insecurity and that he wasn't going anywhere, or at least not very far away. We are not 'in love'—I equate that with the high passions of a teenager.

"Am I satisfied? Not one hundred percent. I would like more affection, but I also recognize that I am not open to affection on his terms all the time. I get caught up in my own business. At the moment, sex is in something of a rut. I am overworked and tired and go to bed and to sleep very early. But circumstances will change shortly and we'll get out of this rut and back to more exploring of sexuality.

"I feel I am a loving, giving human being. I care deeply about the people in my life. I love my daughter a lot—and my parents. Pets—I had a cat who was a companion for so many years, he was a part of me and my life. After two years I still think of him and miss him and grieve a little. But my husband is my life. What we have together can never be replaced. I'm so glad I hung in there and waited until we got to this place. I love him very much."

Some married women, like the previous woman, seem to be saying that there can be another kind of passion involved in long-term relationships:

"I think sexual passion can go out of a long relationship, but I don't think passion for each *other* or each other's heads or for love needs to lessen at all; in fact, it may become greater with time. If passion equals chaos, as it has for me in the past, I think passion does have to move over in terms of a more stable relationship."

A few married women say that the feeling of being "in love" is reborn again and again in a good marriage; it comes and goes:

"It is important to be 'in love' and to love someone in order to marry them. Without both feelings the marriage will die. Being 'in love' means rediscovery, keeping the relationship fresh and new no matter how many years you have spent together. Loving means the other person satisfies you mentally, physically, spiritually, and emotionally. In order to be involved with a person in the first place, there must be a mutual feeling of respect and admiration for him or her."

"I'm not 'in love' with him. I can be, and drift in and out of that feeling. So does he. He's told me at times he falls in love with me—although he always loves me."

"I think that sometimes I am 'in love' with him, other times it is just that I love him—I'll look at his face and be overcome with love for him. Other times, I can't believe I married him. My—what fickleness!"

"Love comes in waves, sometimes strong, sometimes it fades, other times it's overwhelming, times you don't know if it was love at all."

*Others imply that women should stop pushing for "the great love"—
intensity—and enjoy the simple things and daily companionship
that are, finally, the best that a relationship has to offer:*

"We enjoy so much traveling—we bought a small motor home about ten years ago and found that we liked the freedom of it, and when he retired we bought a better one and I resigned from teaching and we hit the road, coming home only a couple of months at a time before taking off again. We love that life. But when we moved here a few years ago, to be near my mother and because we liked the mountains, we spent time fixing up a little house, and recently my mother's health has kept us home. But I think our happiest times are away in some wilderness campground, off the beaten path, walking, enjoying a campfire, birding, reading, soaking up the beauty of it all. That we share."

*14 percent of married women say that neither romantic love nor even loving is
necessary as long as needs are met and a certain polite and good treatment of
each other is maintained:*

"I don't think he loves me, but he treats me the way I want and need to be treated. He's funny and makes me laugh and he's very affectionate."

"I have come to believe that what I really want in a relationship is not so much passion as a sort of British politeness. Wasn't it Kurt Vonnegut who asked for 'a little more common decency' in relationships? I agree. Common decency and politeness can go a long way."

"I thought I was 'in love' with my husband, but I am not sure now we ever did love each other, and now we definitely do not love each other. We show an unusual degree of consideration and decency and concern for the other's welfare—but this is much more a function of how I want to live in the world, what kind of a person I value being, than a special feeling of attachment for him."

Does the emotional contract make it necessary for women to "play it safe" in relationships?

It is possible that the reason many women in this study prefer giving love to being "in love," is because they have found that men frequently display such hostility in superficial encounters (see Parts I and II) that they have learned to tread very gingerly, to get to know a man very carefully, to make sure he is not like this, full of inner hostility, before trying to have a relationship. If most women prefer, over the long term, an understanding based on mutual companionship and even friendship, then this may be partially because of an unequal gender system (the emotional contract) which makes it necessary to build a framework with a man over time—and not because falling "in love" is by nature "adolescent" or "immature."

Perhaps, also, people at times ridicule the feeling of being "in love" because they want to deny how important it really is. "Perhaps it is too sad to admit its importance when it is gone, or when one can't live with what one really wants (or once had)," according to Dr. Shirley Zussman, past president of the American Association of Sex Educators, Counselors and Therapists. People can then, with reason, say, "It doesn't last" or "It's too dangerous and volatile," etc., as a way of denying its reality and beauty. "But everyone must," she continues, "know in their hearts how important it is, and recognize its meaning. Even if it *is* at times transitory, it is still one of the most important experiences of life."

Is caring always "love" or is it sometimes just "liking"? Is there anything wrong with this?

In some of the answers we have seen, women seem to "like" their husbands more than "love" them. They seem more "used to" them than any kind of stronger feelings; they care, but more in a friendly or brotherly-sisterly family sense.

Only a few women feel free enough to discuss whether they "love" their husbands or simply like them, feel accustomed to living with them:

"I am not in love with my husband, although I find this hard to say and certainly would not say it to him or any of my friends. I feel a great deal of affection and fondness for him, but is it really friendship or love? Does it matter?"

"I believe real love is the strong feeling you feel for someone right from the beginning for no known reason—even though people will tell me I'm overly romantic. I don't believe in being in a long routine relationship, although that's what I'm in. I'd like something more passionate and romantic. I know all couples have their problems, nothing's ideal, but there *is* real love, and even if you only have it a few times in your life, still you *know* that what you feel is different, special."

"Sometimes I think worked-at love is an invention of people and not real. True love is exhilarating, hard to describe—a feeling that 'This is right, very right.' You can't find it easily."

"I used to think that love was something you could cultivate. I still think it can be cultivated but I believe now that we do have special great loves in our lives, and for me, they involve a strong feeling right from the start. However, I refused to accept my strong feelings, and meanwhile tried the cultivating type with my husband. I do care for my husband, but it's not great love."

"People get so lonely, an emotional relationship can make you *believe* you are in love. Some people find it hard to accept a relationship as a 'friendship' instead of a serious love. I was deeply involved in an affair that was more of a friendship. It was nice, but I don't think I would ever have fallen in love with him, even though we were compatible in all respects."

Some women (15 percent) do in fact say they married men with whom they knew they were not "in love" nor even "loved"; these marriages are sometimes quite happy:

"With the man I loved the most, we fought, and when I tried to call him, to help him, be with him, he was depressed, wouldn't let me reach him. He joined the Army and I never heard from him again. That was about six months after I'd dropped out of school. Two months later I married a nice guy I'd known for five months. I wasn't in love, but it was comfortable. We're still married, ten years later."

"The biggest problem is I don't know if I love him or if I'm using him for his money, his car, his material possessions."

"I was never sure if I was 'in love' with my husband, or just enjoyed the attention given to me."

21 percent regret not having married someone with whom they were "in love": *

"I like having someone around, a moving body. The worst part of marriage is the ironing. I plan to remain married for convenience' sake (married thirty-one years). But it would have been lovely to have been in love."

"I don't love my husband. I feel disappointed because I think I'm capable of loving someone passionately. I thought of leaving him at one point, but I

---

*This does not mean that 79 percent of women *were* "in love" when they married.

don't feel secure enough to take that risk, even though I earn ample money. I just don't feel I could cope with it all, the single world. I couldn't compete. I'm forty-five. I find my gratification in my work. It partially compensates, but I feel I missed something in life."

"I divorced my ex-husband because our marriage was on the surface. I didn't really love him, although I cared about him."

For how many women was a more low-key, "loving" marriage the kind of marriage they wanted, and for how many was it simply the only kind they could find at the time?

Hostile emotional relationships

Sometimes one can be heavily involved emotionally in a relationship or marriage—but it is anger and not love or even liking that is holding the relationship together. This kind of struggle can continue over many years.

Most women agree that, in the abstract, "it is quite possible to be in a heavy emotional relationship with someone you are not in love with": *

"I married for many reasons that were not love, but it was a very heavy emotional relationship. I never, even now, could figure it out totally. It was very hard to disengage myself from."

"A lot of people go along in heavy emotional relationships that cause them a lot of turmoil, but I don't think it is really love. They are caught in situations which developed from earlier choices and have little to do with 'love' or caring. They have just made a life together."

Twenty-three percent of women (married and single) in this study report quite negative attachments, two people somehow locked in a competitive struggle, each trying to get love but also angry.

One-way giving and caring

Some women who define "real love" as being understanding and caring more than "passionate" also emphasize the importance of giving unselfishly to the

*Phrase taken from one of the questions asked.

other person without expecting anything (even emotional support?) in return—
a sort of "service" definition of love:

"Love is giving without expecting any reward or compensation for your caring. It is being honest and showing yourself without reservation. Putting your mate's feelings and situation equal to or before your own. Being in love transcends descriptions or words; you can't touch it or explain it, an attempt to define it degrades the emotions which you feel."

"Love is long-suffering and kind, is not jealous, does not get puffed up, does not brag, does not behave indecently, does not look for its own interests, love never fails."

"Love is when you'd willingly give up one of your kidneys, and not think about right or wrong, just about what the one you love needs and you have and so you give. Love is forever, a bond that holds you together. Love comes from the heart—it either exists or it doesn't."

"Love is absolute self-denial in favor of another person's needs—unselfishness, giving to the other as much and often as possible that which you know makes her happy without strings attached."

"Love is genuinely valuing another's happiness and well-being more than your own. Consideration of another person, doing for that person selflessly, being available for whatever that person needs."

"Love is true understanding and compassion. I care that he eats properly, stays healthy, try not to upset him, keep the house reasonably quiet, etc."

"I love him by taking care of him when he is sick and depressed. I stand by him when times are bad."

One woman describes love as an "act of will":

"Love is an act of your will. You can 'love' anyone if you want to. You simply 'do' it. You care for them, you put their feelings above your own, you do what is best for them and not for yourself. If you treated your worst enemy in this manner, you would be loving them."

———————

Are women being misled by gender stereotypes about what a "nice girl" should be, or what a "good wife" is like, so that they feel at times they must continue "loving" no matter what they are experiencing?

The love that has been emphasized to most of us as "real love," especially for women, is "spiritual," giving love, the love of Mary, the mother, ever caring for her child—a love which does not involve (female?) passion or physical desire. Eve, the other archetypal model of womanhood, illustrates the "evils" of female intellectual curiosity and sexual desire, "selfishness"—she is not "giving" and supposedly does not represent "real love."

Which of these loves is "real love"—passion or giving? Of course, neither and both—and many other loves too. But one of the most important problems for our culture is the taboo against combining these types of love; why are the spiritual and physical so inevitably (at least verbally) at odds? And why is love with a strong physical component, passion, so often disparaged, trivialized, downgraded?

When is "caring" just following social pressures to "take care of others"?

The question of what love is for women is a particularly important one, since the society has for so long tried to define women in terms of "love." The dominant ideology has defined men in terms of what kind of work they do (and told them *not* to be defined by love); it still tends to define women first in terms of whether or not they are married, have a family, and whether a man loves them. As one woman who agrees with this puts it, "A woman, to be a real woman, should love someone—and also have children to love!"

But most women now are asking themselves *why* they are with the men they are with, why they are in the relationships they are in. Women are in the process of redefining for themselves whom they love and why, resisting being forced by social and economic pressures into "loving" someone simply because that is "what women do."

"Is the Normal Course of Relationships That Passion Just Dies After a While?"

"I believe there is a contradiction between sexual passion and a long-term relationship in a marriage. Sexual passion is very emotional, causing imbalances in daily life. A long-term stable relationship calls for tranquillity, composure, and steadfastness. A truly passionate relationship includes frenzy, rapture, hunger—none of which make for a very tranquil arrangement. But a long-term love relationship can be passionate if one does not *live* with the partner."

———————

Can sexual passion, being "in love," live in a marriage? Most women who were "in love" when married say that if two people stay together, the "in love" feeling subsides into a "loving" or caring feeling after a year or two, as part of the "natural" development of things.

Is this an inevitable progression? Or is it the injuries seen in Part I, built into the smallest everyday interactions of the two by a culture which puts men and women at odds—"genderizes" them—do these unnecessarily adversarial situations destroy intensity?

One woman wonders whether her growing sexual disinterest in the man she lives with is "natural," or the result of various things she is angry with him about:

"I hope there is no general contradiction between passion and stability, but for me the daily living, working, and conflicting with the man I'm living with does seem to cool the passion. Like, he usually treats me with respect, but sometimes makes me feel silly or stupid. If I swear, he will say, 'Watch your language!' in a rude manner. This makes me angry. Still, he is emotionally supportive on some things.

"Or I wonder if I believe (perhaps unconsciously) that I should not feel sexual passion for a good, stable, hardworking type (which he is)? (Perhaps because my father was one, and he and my mother never were physically close, as far as I could see?) On the other hand, it would be O.K. to be 'corrupt' or passionate with a 'playboy' type man because he is already 'no good'?!!?

"But I have been extremely angry with him for real reasons. The most was when he refused to take care of me as I needed when I was very ill for a few days last summer. I realize men aren't taught how to do this, but he should have been able to fill my requests, which were not so demanding. He seemed to get angry when I'd ask for a drink or a blanket. This after I had waited on him damn well not so much earlier when he was ill. I also sometimes resent that he has trouble relating to and understanding my work, and sometimes devalues it."

The checkmate pattern: male emotional distance/harassment, followed by female sexual lack of interest

Why do women become alienated sexually? Does passion die automatically— or is it killed? Does sex with the same partner become boring over time, or does the subtle process of alienation, often created by male-dominant attitudes, gradually drive the woman away? Make her feel "passive" and "uninterested"?

Several women describe succinctly the pattern in their relationships of gradually being turned off by a subtle alienation, a subtle discrimination emanating from the man:

"One thing that has always amazed me is how a man can ignore you or treat you shabbily and then expect you to respond to him with love when he wants sex. It seems that the quality (or lack of it) of the relationship is not important to men, only the sex. This is not true for me; if the relationship is not good, neither is the sex."

"The actual happiness shared with another person I felt most clearly and keenly with the friend I had an 'affair' with. I can be with him scrambling over stones to cross a river or clambering up some beach cliffs and feel totally at peace with him and with myself and with the world around me. I can feel how he is in the same trance of peace and contentment in the way he notices with loving interest little happenings in the water or amongst the grass. That peace and happiness used to be also in our lovemaking. However, since, I have discovered areas of total lack of communication in both directions, and they make me want to remove myself out of the circle of his intimacy; rather than that I have come to the point where I just do not find him to be the possible carrier of such happiness for me anymore. I no longer want to be beguiled, even though he can easily beguile me."

"In the beginning, sex was excellent. He would talk very tenderly and intimately to me—in Italian—very romantic, exciting, and sexy. I loved it. Toward the end, we just began going through the motions and sex wasn't as fulfilling anymore. We became so different from how we had been. It just got to the point that I didn't care to have sex anymore, since I wasn't emotionally satisfied. Then he'd criticize me for not being loving and affectionate, and I'd criticize him for always being horny and wanting sex and not fully understanding how I felt. In the beginning, we enjoyed working together, helping each other do the dishes, cook, fix the garden, do handy work around the house. Then it just all disintegrated."

"We lead independent lives away from each other, not much togetherness, children are the most we have in common. I can always tell when he wants sex: at these times I can't do anything wrong! This turns me off! Also, he criticizes my weight! The more he criticizes, the more I eat!"

The emotional alienation created by the distancing and harassing behaviors seen in Chapter 1 can make a woman withdraw emotionally from a relationship—even though she may still act "giving" and stay physically in it. But she may put her real feelings and self "underground," eventually wanting sex less and less, acting less enthusiastic, being less emotionally involved in the relationship—perhaps focusing on children more for her emotional fulfillment. Often at this point, the man starts complaining that there is not enough sex, and frequently begins looking outside the relationship for "sex." This leads to further distance and alienation while the woman struggles for a while to break through but after a while tries less and less to make a real relationship, perhaps taking a lover herself. The relationship degenerates into "being there," with varying degrees of warmth.

Another woman describes this pattern in a marriage of eighteen years; toward the end of her reply she becomes so sad that she is unable to continue:

"He says I don't appreciate him. I don't criticize him anymore because of his explosive temper. If I did, I'd talk about what I need and what I don't seem to be getting. I'd also talk about me doing for him all the time—and not much coming back, especially in sharing the housework.

"I'm willing to talk about anything—if he'd listen and not fall asleep or get uncomfortable and move away. But he's very insecure talking about himself and his feelings. I tried a long time—and finally don't do it anymore.

"Fill my deepest needs? Are you kidding? My deepest needs are completely unfilled by this relationship. I would share every part of me if someone would just listen and accept what he'd heard, but my husband does not.

"This relationship is peripheral to my life, even though it takes most of my time. I am forty, married eighteen years, one child age thirteen, and one, twelve. In my life, I want to make a difference, to be somebody for someone, to be loved. I am a teacher.

"Why do I stay in the marriage? Because of the security, and because my husband is a pretty good lover. I also feel the children need a stable family environment to grow up in. I am also a Christian. Also, I've always felt that my husband loves me—well, needs me. I feel more unloved than loved. He's afraid I'll leave him and that he won't be able to cope. I could leave any day and get along O.K.

"Still, I think my husband is more happy than I am. Why not? He gets what he wants—some sex, a square meal, someone to do his laundry, yell at the kids, run errands—why not? But I enjoy the security, even though I feel like I give a lot without receiving much in return. I would be happier with someone who would understand me, love me, appreciate me, and who would be willing to dialogue (not monologue) about anything going on in life. I seldom have this.

"I've had sex outside my marriage. I don't believe my husband knew about it. I was looking for many things, but never found much—mainly one-night stands here and there. Just seemed to happen. I always hoped to find a great lover or my ideal man—but one doesn't find such things in today's men. I wanted to be wanted, I guess, and for a short time I was.

"I believe my husband has been entirely faithful all this time—not that he hasn't had the opportunity to do differently, 'cause I know of several women who've invited him to transgress a bit. He is too insecure. But if he's unfaithful, that's his situation. I don't want to know.

"I was most in love during the first two years my husband-to-be and I went together in college. We didn't have intercourse until the wedding night, when I was twenty-two. Sex was a dud for me and I wondered what all the hullabaloo had been to get married. He, of course, loved having sex available all the time—and never seemed to be satisfied—but I got nothing from it and so began putting him off almost immediately.

"I gave up my job as a high school teacher to have my daughter. I'm not sad about that except that I've never been able to get back into that field since. I didn't mind staying home with the young kids but now I'm teaching college part-time and my responsibilities are pulling me many different ways.

"The best way to make this relationship work is for me to do what needs to be done to keep us together, and he lets me. I wish it were different, but this is the reality of my situation. If I would change things, I'd make my husband grow up—become more sensitive, more open, more willing to communicate and not be afraid of his feelings, of me, or anyone.

"Our best times come when we do things together, like go shopping, make something together (build a fence, bake a pie, etc.), take a class the same night so we have something to talk about.

"When our children were small I was financially dependent on my husband, and even now I continue to be, even though I work part-time. I've said to myself that I wouldn't leave or break up this relationship unless I could support myself. Since I'm not in that position now, I have this subconscious 'out'—a cop-out, I know. My husband thinks it's O.K. that I work part-time and he always says he wishes I'd get a really good job so I could support him, and he'd stay home. Since he does not share the housework at all, I have the feeling I'd still be doing it even if he did stay home.

"The most recent altercation came just a week ago when my husband threw my cat off the bed and against a wall, saying the animal got more affection than he did. I was so surprised—there was no warning at all that he felt this way—so I couldn't think of a thing to say except to think later that again his insecurity couldn't take even the competition (?) of a cat.

"Our fights are generally about little things. I'll ask him to go get some milk—and he blows up because he thinks I should've done it, etc. No one wins; wait—he wins because I don't bring 'it' up again; I just do it, whatever it was, rather than bring up something that stirs up conflict. You can see I'm a real peacemaker and will put down my own self and feelings rather than open up another can of worms. I always feel after a fight that he's won one more round.

"No one says they're sorry. No making up—just get off by oneself and eventually the anger disappears and we go on again.

"I think men take love and falling in love with women only seriously enough to get the woman to marry them, and then when they have it made, they let out the worst. Having just heard about the Peter Pan Syndrome in men, I really think the guy who came up with the theory is right on; most men are just grown-up boys who cannot be mature in love and relationships of any kind.

"In my relationships with men, I've settled, I've put up with men who weren't worth it just because I wanted to be needed in any way. It made me feel shoddy after. I try to be honest with men, but when I see that most are afraid of honesty, I'll use anything I can to get what I want. Now I say, if they're afraid of me (us women), then fuck them.

"I think most men, underneath the surface, are more emotionally dependent than women are, but they use their macho and chauvinistic tendencies to disparage the whole idea. They are afraid that showing tender emotions will make them look weak, particularly if other men see them. I think it'd show a strong man but that's not the way they see it.

"I'm getting so depressed writing this, I can't go further. My relationship with my husband seems so less than ideal that I am beginning to feel very badly. Good luck to you all."

Married Women Who *Are* in Love with Their Husbands

One woman, married over nine years, having made some significant changes in her relationship, describes now being very much in love with her husband:

"I am so much in love with my husband that this love doesn't compare to anything else in my life. He is my friend, my soul mate, my heart. I've been in love with him since we met. I want this to last not only till the end of my life but for eternity! If I'm reincarnated, I want to come back with him! I love him so much that it can't be measured. He feels the same. He says that when he met me, he felt that the reason why he was born was to be with me and love me and take care of me. I feel that my capacity for joy came alive when I met him.

"We've been married for nine years, lived together a year before. We have one child, a boy who is three. This is an incredible love. It's impossible to say who loves who more—the love just keeps growing and getting better all the time. We could be alone for the rest of our lives and be totally filled up and happy—of course, I'd need some books too!

"I think what makes me happiest is being able to make plans. I like being able to say, 'In five years, let's have a baby,' or 'In six months, let's buy venetian blinds.' Knowing that we'll be together. The permanence and commitment is a joy. I love being in love. I don't find it painful or frustrating at all. Having someone to share a life is the best situation.

"Love is the strong feeling right at the beginning and the thing you work at. It's certainly the chemistry but it's also building a history together. It's knowing each other so well you can finish the other's sentence but being surprised at how much more there's still to learn about each other and cherish. He's definitely the one who makes me feel most passionate. I like and dislike the intensity—it brings enormous pleasure and security but it can also be exhausting.

"We like to be alone. We like to lie in bed and talk and touch each other. We have a million jokes, talking about things that have happened to us, silly expressions, etc. Sometimes in the middle of making love, we just say something funny, and laugh and can't finish having sex.

"How we act during sex depends on the mood. He always makes me feel good about myself. He's very receptive to my mood and that seems to set the tone for our intimate moments.

"We like to be together sharing the little details of our life—being with our child, walking our dogs, going to the supermarket—we like doing anything as long as we're together.

"He used to have a hard time expressing himself, but over the years he began to let his feelings out. That used to be our big problem. Now it's never an issue. We only criticize each other when we feel the other has been thoughtless or selfish. When we used to fight, I'd say, 'Do you want to end the marriage?' He'd say, 'Don't say that unless you really mean it,' to which I'd reply, 'Do you want to end the marriage?' Needless to say, this became a pattern that was used in every argument and escalated our minor skirmishes into major battles. It took a long time to break out of that routine, but we finally realized that it wasn't necessary to go that far in order to demonstrate the intensity of our feelings.

"I never thought there'd be someone, I never thought it was possible to have a love like this. I share all of myself—there's nothing we hold back, nothing that we keep apart from the other. We talk about everything. I used to drive him nuts and not let him go to sleep so we would have more time to stay up and talk. This is the best relationship I've ever seen. Nothing I've seen in friends' or relatives' relationships even comes close.

"We are not the best housekeepers. He does the heavy cleaning. (He shares the housework—if he didn't, this place would be condemned!) We eat simply. Generally, we do (mostly him) some cooking on the weekends so we'll have some goodies during the week. When money is flush, we eat out a lot. I take care of our child, but evenings and weekends, he kind of takes on that role. He does laundry and I do entertainment, I mean I pick the movies and restaurants and think of ways to keep having fun. We sleep in the same bed, used to take showers together all the time, but now our child likes to shower with my husband. Daily life is great—we can't wait for weekends. We never get enough of each other. Once we had a month-long vacation and we were together twenty-four hours a day. It still wasn't enough—when work resumed, we felt like we still hadn't had enough time.

"This relationship is more important to me than anything else in my life."

And one very poor young couple, together three years, is managing—despite
very precarious circumstances, absolute poverty—to sustain an intense and
passionate love for each other:

"I'm married, no children, one cat. I'm bright, witty, fun, bitchy, good-looking, overweight, and devoted, drive toward my goals, twenty-two, crave achievement and success. I make a surprisingly good wife.

"I am ridiculously in love. I'm still afraid that my husband will disappear at any moment. The relationship seems so good—even the struggles work well. I'm afraid of the dependence I feel that I swore I would never develop. I love him madly—spiritually, mentally, playfully, sexually, admiringly, respectfully, emotionally. He turns me inside out with joy. I can feel my soul. Love is great. And scary. I'm afraid it'll evaporate because I don't feel I deserve this joy and security. The happiest times are the secure times. The little daily rituals are precious, the morning's first coffee in total frump together.

"In the beginning, we were so dead broke we were living in the back seat of his car, had no jobs, and were moving from city to city in search of a place to survive. Now we are living with his grandparents, still due to money problems. Economics are the worst—we're trying to work the world of arts-entertainment. But being in his arms each night, each morning, makes living worthwhile. Sex is a little limited in his grandparents' house! But we are generally O.K. about locked doors, no yelling, more 'scheduled' discreet time. Basically, I'm happy within my own discontentment with career. I am happy with love.

"We've been married nearly a year, after two years of living together off and on. The best is having him there when I need him, bringing morning coffee, and especially holding me when I go to sleep. I cannot sleep without him—that's part of the worst. I thought I would hate marriage, that I'd feel trapped, that he'd leave me, hurt me. 'Wife' does not feel suited to what I would call myself. It sounds so strange, as does 'husband.' He's just Paul. And I am so proud to wear his name.

"Once entangled with Paul after lovemaking, we, at the same time, said, 'Do you feel married?' (We were living together at the time.) The combination of warm sex, the child's game of 'jinx,' the coincidence of identical thoughts, was a brief delightful mind/spirit/heart union beyond intercourse. I think that's when we actually decided we would eventually marry. My cynical side says yes, I'll be alone—death. My hopeful side, which grows stronger daily, believes that strong love spans all ranges and survives into reincarnations.

"Before him, I had spent two and a half years with man after man and I enjoyed only the temporary holding. When I met him—and he easily gave me my first male-induced orgasm—I married him! Monogamy was a surprise. I never thought I could be satisfied. I desire sex with no one but him. I think this means I'm heart and soul monogamous. Or I got it 'out of my system' before the marriage with the endless parade of strange dicks. He has been completely faithful. I cannot believe it.

"I am always afraid that all my happiness now will dissolve before my very eyes. We both grew up watching our parents rip one another to pieces, and that leaves a permanent insecurity in me. Quite honestly, I don't know how hard I work at marriage. Sometimes I'm conscious of it. Sometimes I catch myself working against it, out of fear.

"Sometimes I get scared, for no real reason, and try to run; I build walls. I'm still so afraid of the commitment and I try to hide myself, thinking he can't hurt me, but I know he knows me too well already. Even when I'm playing games, he will humor me until I'm straightened out with myself. I think it's insecurity from the constant 'iffy' days I survived with my nutty parents.

"I hate to admit it, but Paul is the center of my life. I feel so weak writing that. But he brings me life itself. I am horrified that he will grow tired/bored with me, that someone new, prettier, smarter, kinder, will catch his eye. I am very afraid of the forties—when he might need younger women to bolster his ego, etc., because I've heard it from the other side already. I was 'the other woman' before, and although I never stole any love, I took sex, and I feel that someday I'll pay for those 'transgressions' with the loss of my own husband. Sound ridiculous?

"He was the only man who ever worried whether or not I enjoyed sex and orgasm. I did feel embarrassed when he realized that he had given me my first orgasm. It was almost like having my virginity, it was so new and exciting. When he asked to see how I masturbated, it was tough at first. I made him close his eyes. But he was the one who suggested it for my enjoyment, so that gradually eased my nervousness and embarrassment.

"We would be friends, even without sex. I think we would love one another even if we were, say, physically incapable of sex. But the sex is so tied to the love and day-to-day basic life that I really can't imagine it.

"He has terrific stamina, will not quit until I'm satisfied. I love sex with him. It's exciting, I want him so much I ache (all over, not just vaginal). A general pattern is cuddle, play tickle a little, kiss, rub, kiss, I lick or suck him a little, he licks my genitals until I am nearly there, then he enters me, sucking my nipples, kissing me, holding me so tight! I 'help out' with clitoral masturbation. And I come first, unless he's out of control—a rare thing. It isn't complete until I feel his orgasm. I need to feel him release and relax before I can be satisfied. It's best with him in me, I'll masturbate my clitoris, and he's locked on that nipple. That is great.

"The fact that he worries more about contraception than I do eases my mind for pleasure. I don't have to hold back. I can trust him to deal with his limits. And he is incredibly tender. I feel safe, loved, trusting—a little girl in a warm, safe, right place.

"Our sex life is like the ocean's tides. One week will be hot fuck after hot fuck, then we'll have clumsy times, crabby-bitchy times, off times, but we just ride it as it comes. The bad doesn't get too bad, and the good just gets better. It rides from cool-comfortable to real passion. Constant passion is only in books—it is cartoons. Passion grows from strong love, but it is like an explosion: there's a boom. It cannot boom constantly. One long scream would be boring. Our passion is real and always there is an undercurrent. I want to live with him always, to die tangled in his arms, asleep, gray-haired, and still wet from his lovemaking."

Which Kinds of Love Work Best in Marriage?

A classic question or decision women and men have had to contemplate is whether they want to—or can—marry someone with whom they are "in love," or whether they think it is better to choose someone who seems to provide safe, stable companionship with less volatility, less of the vulnerability they may feel with someone with whom they are "in love." Surprisingly, there have been no large-scale studies which attempted to statistically correlate the results of type of love with how many marriages and relationships actually work out.* Statistics related to these correlations here may be found in the appendixes.

Women often debate within themselves the meanings of these feelings: What is "falling in love"? Is it just sexual? Is caring, learning to understand someone over time, more "real," more "mature"? In fact, 82 percent of the women in this study are asking themselves why they are in the relationships they are in, what kind of love it is they feel—whether it is the "right" kind.

When women think about getting married, or when a marriage or relationship isn't going well, they wonder if it is their fault—whether they have made a mistake: on the one hand, if they are in an "in love" relationship, they can think perhaps they are "messed up," not being "rational" and "mature"; on the other hand, if they are in a "reasonable," low-key relationship, but "still not satisfied," they may blame themselves for wanting "security" too much, being "too dependent."

Are the stereotypes and assumptions about what kind of love works in relationships accurate? One theory holds that falling "in love" is "unreal," one is "projecting" onto the other person; that the only "real love" is getting to know a person over time. Others believe that a more low-key or steady love is not love at all but merely "taking care of" someone, a security-oriented definition of love, formulated to prove one can "make a relationship work."

*Schwartz and Blumstein correlate other factors. See Pepper Schwarz and Philip Blumstein, *American Couples: Money, Work, Sex* (New York: Morrow, 1983). Also see the essay on methodology in the appendixes.

According to the first theory, falling in love does not work for long-term relationships because it is "juvenile" (the two people don't really "know" one another, and therefore mature love is not possible). And yet just the opposite case could be made—that it does not work because the two people care *too* much, and so their feelings are too easily wounded, and this is what creates the tension, leading to flare-ups and explosions. On the other hand, countering *this* argument, it could be said that while it is true that passionate "infatuation" makes people susceptible to easily hurt feelings, it also makes them care about overcoming lapses in communication, and makes them want to try to scale any barriers to reach each other.

If the intense feelings of first love *are* transitory, why is this so? One theory is that falling in love really shuts out the world for a time; when the world forces itself back in, this is when the "in love" feeling dies a little. Do some couples find a way of keeping the outside world out, building islands of time and space apart for only each other and their innermost thoughts? Times to re-create closeness? Or, as many people believe, does the so-called love-yearning expressed so well by Mahler end or change when fulfillment or togetherness is achieved?

Most of the women in this study do not marry the men they have most deeply loved. This was also true of men in *The Hite Report* on men: most men did not marry the women they had most passionately loved. But this did not make their relationships "happy," as we have seen. Women, as seen here, hope that by avoiding the highs and lows of being "in love," they can make a relationship more secure, if not inspired, and a better setting for living and raising children.*

The constantly heard assumption that "in love" marriages don't last and that more low-key love relationships are more stable and do last has no basis in statistical fact, as demonstrated here. Further, in marriages that *do* last, there still remains the question of level of happiness within the marriage. As we have seen, even a quiet love, a supposed "safe haven," can turn out to be filled with arguments (or silences). While the turbulence associated with being "in love" can be difficult, the daily problems seen in most relationships in Part I (which are mostly "loving" relationships) demonstrate that most typical "loving" marriages also contain the unequal emotional contract, which is condescending to women, harasses women while also putting great emotional demands on them, expecting them to provide love and support. Of course, such relationships can

---

*But, most women (as opposed to men, who often don't even *like* feeling "in love," because they feel "out of control") do like being in love. However, as one woman puts her final thoughts on the matter, "Being in love to me is thrilling, exciting, it's magic—but it can also turn your life upside down, and put you in a confused state of mind. It can be extremely painful and heartbreaking. I don't regret ever having been in love—but who would want to *live* with it???" Women, as opposed to men, however, do not generally pride themselves on their "rationality" and "objectivity" in making their choice of marriage partner. For men it is often a matter of pride not to have picked someone with whom they were "in love" for marriage, since, according to men, the decision for marriage should be based on more "rational," "objective" considerations.

easily lead to eventual alienation and frequently finally to a kind of emotional death.

In other words, the supposition that if contentment replaces passion, the marriage will be more stable is not borne out by the research of this study. Here most women say their marriages are not based on being passionately in love, and yet their satisfaction levels remain low. Therefore it is logically impossible to say that passion is the cause of instability in relationships.

What this study shows is that the dynamics that kill love basically involve inequalities in the emotional contract. The emotional contract itself must be changed before relationships can be stable *and* happy—whether based on "loving" or being "in love."

Statistically, in this study, marriages and relationships are most likely to break up when the man refuses to discuss issues and problems which the woman finds to be important, and this goes on over a period of time, so that alienation grows. As the emotional distance widens, most women restructure the emotional relationship inside the marriage and the nature of their feelings. We do not know, for the most part, how relationships (whether "in love" or "loving") would fare without the interference of the unequal emotional contract.

New emotional arrangements within marriage

There are myriad types of emotional arrangements within marriages, but there are three basic new models of what the psychological arrangements should be: (1) the emotional intimacy model (most women would prefer this type, if they could achieve more equality and closeness with their husbands); (2) the "home base" model, usually emotionally distanced, but working on the level of "being there"; and (3) the teamwork model, in which the partners actually work together and their work/business is the focus of their life together; this third type of marriage is still quite rare.

In other words, first, there is the marriage in which intimacy, emotional and psychological, is the primary goal. This is the emotional arrangement most women are trying to get their husbands to adopt in Chapters 1 and 2—and the way of life most women would prefer. (And they do it with their women friends; see Part V.)

Then there is the marriage that provides a "home base" for the rest of one's life: "being there" is all that is really required. The traditional marriage, still so prevalent, as seen, is not the same as the new "home base" marriage because in the traditional arrangement, the woman is providing a stable base for the husband and children to go out from and live their lives, but the woman herself has little room or time for her own life; the marriage is not a stable base for her; she *is* the home base for others. It is not a backdrop for her life, it *is* her life. In the "home-base" marriage, the emotional contract remains intact, with male distancing and harassment of women continuing—but usually the woman doesn't care so much anymore, as she has placed her primary emotional interest elsewhere.

Finally, one woman describes the team concept of marriage: "Last winter we had saved up enough money so that we had the freedom to concentrate on our own work without having to worry about money. We worked in the studio until very early hours. Working together, with our dreams, free to use our true abilities, was wonderful." Other women are starting small businesses with their husbands as partners, and find these team marriages very exciting.

Why do so many women have "home-base" marriages?

"My relationship with my husband is the center of my life because it allows me the freedom to move outside of it but to return for sustenance. It gives the children a space to grow up in. It provides a solid economic base, companionship. It allows me to pursue my career without abandoning my children (my husband is there)."

———————

Although this woman sounds as though she has ultimately made a practical choice about how to organize her life, most women in home-base marriages have developed them after giving up on creating a more emotionally intimate marriage.

The promised emotional intimacy of marriage is a phantom for most women at a time in history when men are taught more than ever to deny their emotional lives, to be "rational," "scientific," and "objective" above all else. Men are constantly downgrading the importance and validity of emotions, so that for women to be constantly trying to bring men back to a level of more emotional openness becomes an endless occupation, overwhelmingly involving—i.e., a great deal of emotional work. Therefore, many women who remain married are now making a sort of new arrangement by developing the home-base or distanced marriage: in a way, they are making marriage *their* home base now, as so many men have always done—taking their freedom to go outside of it as much as they want, for work, friends, and lovers, while still using it. This is a workable way of life for a woman, as long as she does not care "too much" and is not longing for a deeper emotional contact with her husband.

Is it possible to love and not love totally?

What is the meaning of love after all? Feeling a deep connection to another person, to friends or family, letting one's soul feel alive—also, when we are alone, those moments when everything seems real and our awareness of the beauty of life is heightened—also the memory we have of long-ago times we spent with those we loved and love still—aren't these moments the times we feel most ourselves? Is this "love"?

There is no complete language for the emotions—very few of the nuances have been named.* This makes love more difficult to think or write about. Women certainly have not created the vocabulary about love, even though society tends to define women by whether they are "loving," and so on. But men alive today have hardly created the language either: although "men" through history have been the guardians of "learning" and "writing," men too are now born into a culture in which certain words, concepts, are given to them as "reality." One tries to fit one's inner feelings into these words one has inherited and yet, are the concepts the best, fullest possible? Or are they suffocating us?

As one person puts it: "It is difficult to explain, but there is something in this society that is constantly teaching you what you are supposed to feel. The feelings you are told *not* to have, you eventually, from frustration, learn not to express and finally not even to feel at all. ('Told' can also mean that there is just no name for them, no recognition of their existence.) This constant indoctrination into how-one-is-supposed-to-feel often leads people, finally, to not know how they really *do* feel." Therefore, love in a way is a lost concept— one vague word to cover a multitude of feelings and experiences. Which ones are the "real" experiences?

What is love? As one woman paraphrases Tennessee Williams' character Stanley Kowalski (in *Streetcar Named Desire*), "I believe in the colored lights. Which is reality—the levels you can reach, touching another person with the colored lights? Or daily life?" Each of us can make our own choice—or a different choice at different points in our life—but the consequences seem to be enormous, both for us as individuals, and now also for the culture.

---

*The Greeks in classical times debated the topic of love with three (some say four) words in place of our one. Most other languages have more terms than ours.

Marriage— A Promise of Home

Are Married Women Happy, Or Not Going After Their Dreams?

"I am not really happy but I am not unhappy either."

Are married women "happy"? Can we even ask this question? What does it mean? As one woman puts it, "Life has its ups and downs and you just have to go on living." And another, "I don't look at life in terms of 'happy.' How 'happy' I am can refer to what a certain situation or person makes me feel, but cannot be talked of in general. Life is too double-edged and complicated to be 'happy.'" Another echoes, "Happy is an odd word, ill-defined in this society. I am filled with a sense of well-being and contentment at certain times."

In a way, one could say that some marriage relationships in this study are working on the level of the old model of predictable roles which at least provide stability in some people's lives. But, basically, what we have seen here is that women are not staying married for the most part because they are happy but because there seems to be no place else to go. They are not emotionally supported or even basically now financially supported—although they like the feeling that there *is* some financial backup in their lives, and they like the idea of "belonging somewhere," having children with someone, plus the social acceptability of marriage. However, 50 percent do *not* stay married.

The feeling is inescapable, as we have seen throughout all of these chapters on marriage, that love relationships as a whole could be so much better:

"In my marriage, I can be a homemaker, have kids. I can still live my own life. He ignores me, so I make the best of it. My husband is happier than I am, only because I leave him alone and don't nag him. I still feel frustrated."

"We've been married twenty-three years. The best part of being married is the physical warmth and comfort. The worst is the frequent anger I feel. Marriage is more drudgery than I thought—I mean the housework involved. We married because we hated being apart and wanted to be together. I'd do it again and plan on staying married because I love having my children."

Here is a very typical answer from a woman as to why she likes her marriage and plans to stay there; it is very general and really doesn't explain anything, but it is exactly the kind of answer most women give:

"I like just spending time with my husband. Whether it's vacationing or working in the yard, going out to dinner, cooking together, lying in bed, reading, even talking (if the subject is not too sensitive or controversial). My husband tells me he loves me often. He does not tell me I'm beautiful, desirable, or wonderful—I wish he would. I would like more intimate talk. I have not shared most of myself with my husband nor has he shared himself with me. He has said that feelings and emotions are private and need not be shared with anyone."

In a nutshell, women's most usual reasons for "liking" and "disliking" marriage come down to such things as the following: *

"The best part of being married is the companionship and being together. The worst part is having a job *plus* the job of running the house—my husband refuses to help. We have been married two years."

"The best part of being married is having a companion to go places with you. Perhaps the financial security is even better. I'm just out of school and it's tough."

"I like the companionship but loathe the bossiness, always having to consider the other person in social plans, and I dislike losing my credit at banks or businesses because I'm the wife. It is unfair to assume the woman automatically takes a back seat to her husband."

If these are the bottom-line reasons for being married, the reasons half of women are staying in their marriages (the other half are divorcing, although

*Statistics show that married men are healthier and live longer than single men, but these statistics do not hold up for women.

they often try another marriage), it is easy to understand why many women sound somewhat resigned, and give themselves only a "five" or so when asked to rate their happiness on a scale of one to ten.

Double Lives: Leaving a Marriage Emotionally

Women are deserting marriage in droves, either through divorce,* or emotionally, leaving with a large part of their hearts.

As we hear married women talk about their lives here, we see that almost 90 percent are putting their primary emotional focus elsewhere. Most women, as seen in Chapter 3, have begun to give up on creating the amount of emotional closeness and intimacy, the equal partnership, that they had wanted in their marriages. Most, after an initial period of trying, have gone on to find other places to invest their emotional lives. Woman after woman, after the initial years of "trying to get through" gives up and begins to disengage quietly, gradually, perhaps even unnoticeably.

Is this what women really want? No, not at first, at least—but many women come to feel they have no choice: "How I have come to handle it is, I just don't focus so much on it anymore. Then if I am disappointed, it doesn't matter so much. I roll with the punches. Maybe the love will build back up over a period of time. If not, it's better to have other parts of my life I am involved in. Then everything goes smoother."

Most women separate themselves emotionally in these cases without really even trying; it just happens. They find themselves drifting away, no longer able to relate to the other "person" in the relationship, who does not seem to see them or what is happening, and who remains withdrawn, "unknowable," distant.

One woman describes the stages like this: "At first, I pretended I didn't care about my husband as a bitter response to his own uncaring attitude. Eventually, for my own sanity, I stopped pretending and I really didn't care. I was worrying myself *sick* over him, and I decided I had to worry about me!" But she, like many others, did not actually leave; she chose to stay but to move her emotional focus, her inner life, elsewhere. As seen, most of the 50 percent of women who stay married eventually use their marriages as a sort of "home base" (see Chapter 13); they are not staying because they have the emotional relationship they want.

This 50/50 division is striking—almost as if women are poised at a turning point, at the moment of deciding their future. Women ask themselves: Should

---

*90 percent of divorces are brought by women, not men.

we adapt marriage to our lives, using a "male" model, that is, using it as a relatively non-emotional home base, as many men seem to do—or will some better way be created out of our thoughts, a more perfect vision of what relationships can be?

The situation is complex: women often think of leaving marriage . . . but to leave marriage is to go—where? While women may be frustrated with trying to create love, openness, and intimacy with men who don't return them, or do so only sporadically—after which a woman has to start the "opening up" process all over again—when women do "give up on love," and turn away, as nearly half do, many still come back to try again, remarry, always torn, always asking: Why is it like this anyway? Why is it so difficult?

The injustice of the larger society is reflected in the basic assumptions of the traditional emotional contract in marriage, and yet there often seems to be no other place to turn for warmth and love. As seen in Part II, the "singles world" of dating and relationships is certainly no better. Women have marvelous relationships of emotional closeness with their women friends, but most women do not want to look to women for physical intimacy. Classically, women have often turned much of their emotional focus toward their children, to share emotional warmth with them, and many still do so, but this is not complete.

The seeming lack of anyplace else to turn, and sometimes the lack of hope of finding a better relationship with someone else, are what make many women stay in their marriages and try for a compromise, even if they are emotionally alienated. Even if a woman does not find emotional closeness, she can use the relationship for physical affection, general companionship (someone to have dinner with, if not talk to . . .), and someone to have children with. ("This can be distracting for several years, anyway," as one woman puts it, "because they make a lot of noise!")

Facing this impasse, women—whether they decide to stay or to leave—frequently ask themselves if their expectations are too high; "What is the best one can expect out of life/love relationships?":

"It's like life just offers you quicksand all around you. I feel sorry for the ones that just sink. I was in a very destructive relationship for two years. When I left the last time, I still cried every day, I missed him so much. But I knew I was doing the right thing, and eventually I felt better. Now I am really glad I left."

"Do all relationships end up this way? There you are, after ten years, just putting up with the other's faults? And sex is boring, the hurts of the past make you sarcastic and mean, etc.? There's a lot of mediocre love in the world. Or are most of us just scared of living?"

So, women often go through stages in their relationships: first, there may be bickering, "bringing up the issues," a woman trying to stand up for her rights to keep the emotional channels open; next, if a woman decides to give up on trying for emotional intimacy but doesn't want to leave home (after all, it is a place to belong, perhaps the place where she and her children form a unit with their father), she may, like many women at that point, design another life for herself, a separate life, a life outside the home.

In fact, the majority of married women are leading double lives: 90 percent of women married more than four years say that their relationship with their husband is not the main source of their emotional gratification—or expectations. Double lives are important for women, and necessary; one might say that for many women, they are the only way to live with a man and love both him and themselves at the same time.

The British film, *The Red Shoes* (1949), in which the main character is forced to give up her career as a ballerina by the men who "love" her, is a moving portrayal of the many pressures on a woman to choose between self-expression and marriage. To force a woman to choose is really to put her in an impossible situation—indeed, a life-threatening situation.* But the truth (not depicted in the movie, but true nevertheless, as seen countless times here) is that even if a woman does *not* choose a double life, does choose to put her marriage before her "life"; by the very fact of her feeling pressured to choose, making ongoing choices (against herself, in favor of loyalty), she becomes alienated from the one she wants to love, the one she has made the choice in favor of. Why should such a choice be necessary? Why are women supposed to "prove" love in this way? And paradoxically, having chosen to remain "loyal," she may find herself lonelier than ever, because she cannot reach him and she has no other outlets: the harder she may try to reach the one she loves, the further away he may seem to be.

What kinds of "second" double lives are there? First, jobs, careers, and going back to school are many women's preferred new "second" identity. As one woman puts it, and she represents many, many more, "My greatest achievement, even though I'm married, is my work and my ability to support myself. I gain recognition for what I do in life. My salary (!) shows that I am considered somebody, worth something to the world. I love my children and my husband too, but my work is what makes me feel like getting up and getting going in the morning."

Despite the popularity in the media of stories of women who "give it all up" and return to twenty-four-hour-a-day homemaking, the trend statistically

---

*Even if this is "only" her emotional life—or her identity, her self-expression.

is the reverse: the number of women working outside the home is steadily increasing—and most women like it, according to this study. While some younger, never-married or just married women do find the idea of staying home with babies for two or three years appealing, most discover that after that, they want to "go back out to work into the world." They often worry that they will have trouble reinstating themselves.

Although the pressure of being torn between work and home for women is often portrayed as simply a problem of too little time (and there *is* too little time, if women continue to do most of the "housework" as well as "outside" work), the pressure comes also in great part for women from the emotional strain of feeling depleted by being asked to give too much, with not enough emotional support for one's own "starring" role. (See Chapter 3.)

Another vitally important type of "second" life for the great majority of women is women's close friendships with other women. In fact, the primary emotional support of most married women is their best woman friend. Women describe these friendships in Part V, as in the following: "I love talking to my best friend. She is so much easier to talk to than my husband. He gets silent or seems to feel threatened if I really open up and start talking about things. She just listens and I can tell by the way she reacts she is interested and understands. She always seems to know the right thing to say."

Traditionally, as noted, many married women have also turned much of their emotional focus toward their children. Women have been alternately ridiculed for doing this (called "smothering"), or put down for *not* doing it—not being "loving enough," not devoting themselves to their families sufficiently, working outside the home, and so on. Even after children are grown, the closeness often remains, as here: "My relationships with my adult children are more satisfying than what I have with my husband—even though we still live together, and I spend all my time with him."

Still another way many women have found to have second lives is through therapy or psychological counseling. Since their relationship with their counselor is private, secret even, women can express another part of themselves, create a different life in this setting, apart from the world. They can, with a good persona, explore any thoughts, no matter how "forbidden." In this way, perhaps the fact that so many women are in therapy (a disproportionately large number compared to men) can be seen as positive: that is, while the medical establishment may see "therapy" as "treatment" of a woman with "problems," women may often see it as creating a new life, a new philosophy—a way of making clear and visible their own inner reality, the way they see things which seems to find no validation or recognition in the outside "real"/unreal world.

Finally, a classic way women have separate lives is through extramarital affairs. As we have seen, 70 percent of women married five years or more have affairs—and the average length of these affairs is four years. This is a clear indication that these women have two separate and different lives going on side by side, and are not just involved in "sexual flings" (even though they usually are not "in love" either). Many women seem to feel that in an affair they somehow have more equality—maybe because they are not "owned" or maybe because the man does not think so much in terms of gender stereotypes—for example, does not assume (as in the singles world) that the woman is looking for marriage.

Are "home-base" marriages the answer?

"Home-base" marriages are an improvement which women have created for themselves over the traditional marriage in which the woman provided the "home base" for the man and children, but herself *had* no individual life: she *was* the home base. Still, can women be happy over the long term living with such an emotionally alienated situation at "home"? Even if they are finding emotional fulfillment elsewhere?

One woman describes this type of marriage in her own life, but with an undertone of frustration: "I got a job and have really started enjoying it, especially the time out on my own and having my own money. But my life with my husband is no different than it has been. It is still a matter of two unlike people on two opposing paths attempting to live a semblance of parallelism. He lives his life, and I live mine."

Most women, ideally, would desire a different emotional structure in their marriages (even though they would like to continue working and making money independently). However, they find that their partners resist the emotional restructuring required. So women go along struggling, often bisecting themselves emotionally (if they stay in the relationship)—trying to become accustomed to the arrangement. While they believe that the purpose of a marriage should be emotional intimacy, they decide, finally, that if one cannot have such intimacy, marriage can at least produce a base from which to live one's life. For the moment, for some women, this may be a workable solution. At the same time, however, this new "home base" marriage also represents women *leaving* marriage—emotionally and psychologically, with their hopes and dreams.

More and more women resent having to bisect themselves like this. Where will this lead?

Redefining marriage: progress or cop-out? Does "liberation" mean rejecting marriage?

Various theorists have made the case that, since marriage generally exploits women, requiring more domestic services (cooking and cleaning) than single life, as well as loss of various legal and financial rights, if women were truly "liberated," they would give up marriage. Since most women have continued to marry, it is implied (often by the media) that they are "uninterested in liberation," backsliders, "traditionally oriented"—just proving what women's fundamental "nature" is, after all. But this argument leaves out the important factor that no matter how "liberated," "independent," or "self-defining" women become, women/people will still want to make a "home," belong somewhere—and the institution said to be equivalent to home in this sense in our society so far is "marriage."

Men too, with their vociferous denial of interest in "commitment," have been rebelling against marriage as a way of life (at least, verbally rebelling) for at least half a century, complaining that they feel restricted in it. As one man writes, "Marriage seems so impractical. It cuts off one's interaction with a lot of the world. Even getting into 'a relationship' is so demanding—and how long can one be expected to pour so much energy into just one person?" One of the first manifestations of men's alienation from marriage in the twentieth century was James Thurber's cartoon putting down a giant, possessive wife (whose body took over the whole house); then later the "playboy philosophy" and then the "sexual revolution" with its single male movie heroes and rock star idols. However, it often seems that the media approve of men's tendency to denigrate the idea of marriage, since men are "questing" after Meaning, Themselves—but look down on women who are against marriage as "unnatural," "man-haters."

It has been said for twenty years that "marriage is dead." Now people often say they marry "because of children." But the real reason for the continuing popularity of marriage, for both women and men, is that almost uniquely in our society, "marriage" holds out the promise of not being left alone in a very cold and competitive world, where it often seems that individuals don't matter very much. What we need is a new "home," a new concept of what "home" is and where to find it—those feelings of happiness and peace we long for.

Was There Marriage Before Patriarchy?

Is marriage a "natural" institution? Or was it invented? Would people "naturally" want to marry—even without the current social structure? Was there marriage before patriarchy?*

The problem with general discussions in the media of "family" issues—i.e., the cry "the family is dying"—is the assumption that only with the nuclear family can we have a "civilized" world, because it has "always been this way," "even in the Paleolithic caves."

But is this true? *Was* there "marriage" before patriarchy, that social order

*Some gay couples express the desire to "marry"; is this because of the cultural atmosphere around them—or an impulse to make a public ceremony of those feelings?

in which women were declared to be the possessions of first, fathers, and later, husbands—the aim of which was to produce children who would "belong to" the father and take his name? or were the earliest families, in fact, mothers and children? And did inheritance and name go through the mothers, as some paleoanthropologists and archeologists now believe?*

"Marriage" as we have known it for centuries has been legally defined in terms of property and inheritance.† Were there ceremonies celebrating personal romantic love in pre-patriarchal times? No one knows—and yet, surely people have always wanted to mark the passages of life in some public way; one can only speculate on what the nature and meaning of those celebrations—if any—may have been.

Just so, we cannot yet imagine, perhaps, what our future (post-patriarchal?) institutions and celebrations may be. But we can say that "marriage," even a reinvented marriage, should not be pushed on people as the only real way to "real happiness" or involvement with the world. Many women in this study are quite happy in other ways. We can have great self-expression and love through our work, our friendships, our children, our love for many things: the earth, plants, flowers, the animals who share the planet with us—and our "pets." Depth of feeling, investing oneself passionately in *something* seems to be what matters to be happy.

Marriage as longing for home—

Marriage, despite the high divorce rate (and the unhappiness rate), remains an important institution in our society.

Why do women return to marriage? Even after the pain and turmoil of various relationships, the emotional ups and downs, many women still come back to look for something—what?

What *is* marriage in our society? The repository of all the hopes each one of us has to be not alone, to have affection and warmth and stability and meaning in life. To be seen as someone special, real, important beyond being "productive" in the society, someone understood and valued as a human being, not just a production unit. There are no similar alternative institutions, none even close (although there should be)—and so no matter how bad things are,

---

*There is no evidence to suggest that the patriarchal family has always existed; in fact, much evidence exists to the contrary, that indeed the earliest families were women with children/clans. See the work of Richard Potts of the Smithsonian or David Pilbeam of Harvard University.

†Various Marxist theorists have of late tried to define marriage in terms of labor, as a way of giving women's work a measurable value in the system. Even sex has been considered a form of production, labor, in order to be placed within the theoretical analytical system. But rather than making women's activities at home fit into a labor-analysis, this wage-production framework for conceptualizing political reality should be transcended and a new analysis developed. See Joan Kelly, "The Doubled Vision of Feminist Theory," in *Women, History and Theory: The Essays of Joan Kelly* (Chicago: University of Chicago Press, 1984), part of the Women in Culture and Society Series edited by Catharine R. Stimpson.

we keep regravitating to marriage as we know it, trying to reinvent it. But there is a lot to be said for living "alone," with a network of friends—even though the mythology, the magical aura surrounding "marriage" is not there yet for other ways of life.

We have asked, "Are women happy in marriage, or not going after their dreams?" Women may be answering softly that perhaps now their dreams lie elsewhere. The promise, the hope, the desire is still there—for the perfect, great, intimate love that will last and be happy and lead to a family—all of it. But it is doubtful that women will ever again see love in the same way.

Is the "Age of the Family" Over?

If women are alienated from men, and beginning not to see marriage as their primary emotional support or definition, what will this mean for the society? If women leave marriage, emotionally or physically, does this mean that the age of the "home" and "family" is over? Would the end of this "home" be good or bad? What *is* home, after all?

"The family is the basis of our society; without it, the society will crumble."

Would the dissolution of home as we know it be a disaster? Or would it be a good moment, a time of reorganization, rethinking, a chance for recreation of a basic social institution along better lines—a good basic social reorganization, shifting the values of the overall society? If men no longer find there can be a hierarchical family, could this influence for the better their view of how the rest of the world is shaped?

The current assumption—correct in many ways—is that the nuclear family is the linchpin of our whole system, and that without it, the society as we know it will be in jeopardy. It would indeed be in for a big change. But would this be a bad thing? Are we, in fact, in the midst of a transition back to the mother-child family? Statistics on female single heads-of-households certainly make a strong case for this.

Thus, it is mostly a male fear that without the nuclear family, the system would collapse; all that would be left of the society would be a market economy, with millions of isolated individuals jockeying for position. Many men wonder,* would there be no place one could go for relief? for an atmosphere of trust?

This brings out an interesting point: has the society been counting on

*In newspapers and the popular media, and in the previous Hite Report.

marriage (i.e., on women) to counteract the harshness of the "outside world" with its competitive "male" system/values to make that world bearable for men? In that case, the system—that hard, "rational" system—has been running on women's spiritual energy (or, as others might say, "off women's backs"), and this in turn would explain the fear *men* have that if women are no longer there to fulfill the "home" role . . . what will we have? An atavistic mass, with no one feeling very valued in life. Of course, if the dominant value system changed by taking on some of "women's" values, one might not have only one's "nest" to rely on for comfort, because the "outside" world would not be so violent.

But if, under the "male" ideological system (perhaps especially in its present, winner-take-all market manifestation), individuals have no one to "come home to" who values them and shows appreciation, understanding, "sees them," can this lead, in a hierarchical society like our own, in which only the ones "on top" really count, to an escalation of the social violence already present? This at least is the nightmare.

In fact, a case could be made that "home" values are preindustrial values that survived because they were tucked away from the world in the "home" and that these values became an "anachronism" when most work began to be done in factories (and not the home) during the Industrial Revolution. They were values in a "time capsule," waiting to be rediscovered.

In any case, now that the main action is not in the "home," women too live increasingly outside it, and the market system has caused the prestige accorded things made and done at home to decline—home life and work life are being penetrated by the same values. Women are under pressure to take on the values of the dominant workplace, the dominant society, the "male" ideology.

Now, therefore, is a good time to scrutinize those values, as well as the values of "women's" culture or *Weltanschauung*, to see which parts of them, i.e., the stress on cooperation and teamwork, might be helpful in solving some of our current problems. Somehow, what we need is a new vision, a more valid framework, for redefining our relationship with work, with each other, and with the planet that supports us.

B. F. Skinner has asked, in a recent issue of the *American Psychologist*, "What is wrong with daily life in the Western world today?" His answers are less than profound, but the question goes to the heart of things, for it is not only our manufacturing units that are in trouble, and our fiscal policy, and our international relations, and our natural environment, but our very daily lives, our relations with each other. Similar worries have been focused on the "home" in the popular media, i.e., why are there so many divorces? Why don't couples get along? Why is there incest and violence between spouses—and so on. In fact, the entire value system must go under review to discover what it is that is making people—especially men—behave in such violent and aggressive ways, whether the reference is to sullen "workers" or angry husbands or aggressive drivers. And this is a large part of what the dialogue among women here in this book is about, what women are asking themselves and each other and the world.

"The family would lose its central personality— the mother . . ."*

Women have been the centerpiece—some would say "altarpiece"—of the home for a very long time. Although women have not always been very happy, nevertheless, the continuance of this institution did seem—for a while at least— to represent a world of permanence, an eternal order of things. Strangely, it was women, the less powerful of the genders, who were the basis of this aura of stability—the place men always "came home to"†—like Ulysses to Penelope: the end of the journey was to be admired and appreciated by a woman.

Even if women have been coerced into presiding over the home (by such means as economic and legal subjugation and the pressures of public opinion) still, it is amazing to think that by leaving the home, as women are doing (whether physically, through divorce, or emotionally, by simply ceasing to care), the linchpin of society is slipping—or at least some people feel it to be slipping. "Women" (or the idea of "woman") were, in Western "male" ideology, the most permanent of realities, fixed in the role of retiring, devoted, selfless motherhood—a symbol. That symbol was ideologically powerful, even though women themselves as individuals have had very little power.

Some right-wing theorists warned in the 1970s that if women left the home, left their "place," they would lose what power they had, and still not gain a position of equality in the "outside" world. Others, feminist theorists, have worried that if reproductive technology becomes more and more advanced, men will make babies in tubes and therefore not need women anymore, leaving women even more powerless, redundant. Both analyses are based on seeing women's reproductive/creative powers as our basic means of status in the society. Would we be foolish not to rely on our traditional "stronghold" in the future? Or is it eroding anyway? Have we decided we cannot live this way anymore, with our choices so circumscribed? Do we also see the perilous position the larger society is in at the moment, the precariousness of all our futures in these times, because of the ideology the society is operating on, and does this add to our feeling that we want to be, must be, involved in solving the problems?

Here is another choice women are facing, then: should we continue to base our "power" on our capacity to re-create life? (If men have re-created life in the test tube—admittedly with our eggs—have they finally become the

---

*Chafe, William H. *The American Woman: Her Changing Social, Economic, and Political Roles, 1920–1970* (Oxford: Oxford University Press, 1972).
†Is this also the function of Mary in the Catholic religion?

"equals" of women, that is, they can now create life too?) Or should we turn to the larger society and insist on our claim to equal "ownership" of the system, an equal right to design and name the means of production, the philosophy, the art and culture, all of it?

Longing for Love

What is home? Where is it? How many people have at one time or another found themselves standing in the middle of their own living rooms, but being unhappy, shouting, "I want to go home!"? And how many people living in apartments, instead of houses, feel "This is not really a home, this is an apartment"? Shouldn't a "home" be physically permanent? Now at the end of the twentieth century, it is so rarely permanent: we move frequently, and we divorce frequently.

Much as we try, and much as statistics tell us that the stable-for-a-lifetime nuclear family is not the "norm" anymore, something in us still feels that we want "it"—and that we have failed, we are "wrong" if we do not "make it work," have that particular home. And yet, as seen, many women inside that kind of "home" do not feel nourished or cared for—or even connected. Many feel tremendously lonely and angry. And men, as seen in *The Hite Report*, are often angry with it too.*

Home is a state of mind; home in an emotional sense tends to creep up on one. It takes a while for affection to grow, increments of trust and counting on someone or a place or a certain situation—until one day, "it" really *is* home. And this is what women are trying to get to, in a way, in Part I when they "complain" that men won't get close to them: because, then, there is no "home."

Can we reorganize the home and family so that it is more than, as some have called it recently, just "the feeding and sexual gratification of two production units"? Yes, heterosexual love relationships can become much better, but there is no reason why they alone should be taken seriously, counted on as "home." Each person knows in fact where her or his heart lies, where she or he would go this minute if they could—where home is. It should be seen as positive that now we have the choice of creating "home" where we find it—not having to make ourselves fit into the "right grouping of people," in the proper "box" for living.

If "home is where the heart is"—where one feels loved, "seen," and we remember this, it will help us to stop thinking that a "home" must consist of one man, one woman, and 2.3 children. Recreating home will take more than

---

*Even while the world was changing all around them, becoming industrial or now post-industrial, and men were frequently having to learn new jobs, men could always return "home to a woman."

men "helping" women with the dishes; men will have to re-create themselves—respiritualize themselves, be able to believe in women, stop worrying about dominating. Women, having been in the home for so long, may not want to put so much effort into it again so soon. It may take women a while to begin to trust men again.

We need a new concept for the basic structure we call "home," as part of the reevaluation of the purposes of the society in general. What *is* our social philosophy today, the overall purpose of the society? Economic production? Stable families? To provide a place guaranteeing the individual's right to a search after meaning or the "pursuit of happiness"? To rescue the planet and change our relationship to nature, while the planet will still support us?

It is clear that women's great inner questioning is part of large cultural change—one that women are playing a central role in, as those with another perspective to offer, alternative possible solutions to current problems. The society needs a new infusion of idealism and dreams—a redefinition of goals. As women think through their personal lives, try to understand them and the men they love, they are critiquing this world, and envisioning a new one. Women are going through a revolution, and they are taking the culture with them.

PART FOUR

Women Loving Women

Listening on Another Frequency

"The conversations with Anne-Marie would be so complete and involved—like 'Oh, this dinner we're going to, I have really mixed feelings about it. How do you feel about it?' And then we would speculate on our thoughts, talk about it. Or if we were having a fight, one of us would say, 'You're really taking advantage of me,' and then the other would say, 'Tell me why—explain to me how you feel about that—tell me what you mean, in depth,' and then she would listen to me for five or ten minutes—she might complain about what I said, but still she would listen. That's the relationship I had with her.

"With a woman in a relationship, nothing's taken for granted—whereas men sometimes have the attitude: we'll just cruise along here and everything will be O.K. With women, there's always a discussion, always, and the direction of the relationship is constantly up for revision. At least, it was like that with us. And I carried this on into my current relationship. I'm afraid that, really, my current partner can't deal with so much analyzing of feelings, there is too much intensity and focus on the relationship for her. . . .

"But I think that your identity develops through these discussions. Even though when you have two women together who are extremely introspective and always examining what's going on, always questioning, it can be really too much, the constant questioning—still, it's great."

Is love between women different? More equal? Do women get along better together than female/male lovers? Or is this the wrong way to put it: is what we are looking at here a different culture, of which we should ask different questions?

One woman remarks, "I think this is a window on a world that most women have no conception of whatsoever—an all-woman culture."

A note on statistics

Eleven percent of the women in this study have love relationships only with other women. An additional 7 percent sometimes have relationships with women. One of the most surprising findings is the number of women over forty, most of whom were in heterosexual marriages earlier in their lives, now in love relationships with women for the first time. Sixteen percent of women over forty have love relationships only with other women, and 61 percent percent of women over forty now living with another woman, as lovers, were previously married. Of the total "gay" population, 31 percent are in relationships, 52 percent are living together, and 17 percent are single.

15

Seven Women Describe
Loving Women

1

In all truth, I probably loved my first lover more than I have ever loved any woman—it was with sheer naïveté and abandon that I loved her and held nothing back. She was intelligent, sensitive to me, always gentle. She encouraged me to try new things, teased me in sweet ways, taught me how to be supportive, and always looked at the positive sides of other people. She was attractive—taller than I by about three inches, had long auburn hair and hazel eyes like my own. She is a brilliant woman, and very quiet—too quiet. She often brought me small surprises. She was very giving.

She hit me twice. Once when we were "courting" and she was drunk—which wasn't normal for her. And once when we were quarreling she put her hands to my throat because she wanted me to shut up. I rarely experience passionate rage—but anger flared through my body like a violent storm and I told her to never lay a hand on me again. She didn't. I forgave her, but I never will forget the experience.

She was the *first* relationship of my life. I am more cautious now. I would never abandon myself that much again to anyone: my relationship today is far more healthy than that one. But every emotion I have ever discovered was tied up in that first relationship, and it was all-consuming for me.

I cried myself to sleep in it, as it was ending and after it ended. I was the loneliest at the conclusion. I was so unable to deal with the thoughts of my lover having another lover that I cloistered myself in my apartment for fear of seeing "them" together. Ultimately, I took a job in another part of the country so that

I could free myself—a smaller city where I knew no one. I suffered miserable loneliness until I got established. I missed not only my lover but the friendship I had with her, and my other friends whom I left.

In the end, I like to think that I chose to end the relationship; at the time I felt as though I had no choice. My lover got involved with someone else while I was out of town. There were no warning signs. We were supposedly a "model" couple in the lesbian community, after six years of a lovely relationship.

During years three and four we cared for her terminally ill mother. I was the only one who worked full-time and contributed to both of their support. Her mother, not being well mentally as well as physically, constantly tried to manipulate my lover to choose between myself and her. My lover wasn't a very strong woman in that regard. In a nutshell, I believe that it was that experience that ultimately destroyed our relationship.

Her mother became so unbearable that I finally moved to a separate apartment and after a few months insisted that my lover decide to live with me or not. She moved back in with me, but never forgave herself or me for the guilt she felt for not taking care of her mother on a live-in basis. Her mother finally got settled in an apartment for the disabled while we still cared for her needs on a daily basis—even though she had quit speaking to me. Though her mother didn't die until a year and a half after we split up, it created an insoluble wedge between us.

Her getting involved with a woman who had been heterosexual up until that point was somewhat out of character. But at the end of our sixth year, that's what occurred. For a while she convinced me that it would pass, that she would get over this passing interest. Neither of us had been inseparable before, we each had made social plans both separately and together, but were always monogamous, we always came home at night. She quit coming home, quit letting me know she would/wouldn't be home, etc. I hung in for two months and couldn't take it anymore and told her she had to move out.

Once she moved out we merely had things on hold. She continued this other relationship, refused to choose between the new lover and me, and seemed happy to have both. Ultimately I had to choose not to see her at all because I was so devastated by the experience. I quit going out to socialize, quit seeing friends, cried incessantly, and in general wallowed. I was sure if I ran into them my heart would fall on the ground and break in two.

Our sexual life had long diminished to perhaps three or four times a year. Since my lover refused to discuss anything that might be interpreted as a conflict, and sex was one of those, she would not discuss over the years our lack of sexual activity and persuaded me it was such a private matter that it ought not be discussed by me with one of my close friends. Since it was my first relationship, I could believe that sex simply declined. I had no other experience to prove otherwise. I was amazed that she had found some sexual interest with someone else.

We had had a very deep love, and I thought, because of my Catholic upbringing, that that was the only one I would ever have. I was prepared to make it work, but there was little left of me by way of self-respect.

I didn't even begin to get over it until I quit seeing her or talking to her at all. I couldn't free myself. I would create fantasies. If we were going to spend the day together I would wait for her to beg my forgiveness, tell me it was all over, etc., etc. Instead, she'd take a nap and dream of the other lover. I allowed myself to be a total victim.

Finally a very close friend had to tell me that for my own sake I had to not see her for a while. It was the best advice I received. I took a job three thousand miles away in a city where I knew no one so that I could pull myself together and start again. My career was the one thing that was going well in my life, so I grabbed on to that. I wish that I could have pulled myself together and stayed in the same town at least with some friends—who are like "family" to me—but I wouldn't allow myself to "live" while I was there. Also, I was embarrassed—felt like everyone knew there was something wrong with me for failing in a relationship. I resented her taking her new lover to meet my closest friends. Then I *really* didn't want to see them, because I was afraid of being compared to the new lover. Leaving was the best thing I could have done for myself to get myself living sanely and normally again. It took two years. I felt like an utter failure and was willing for the longest time to place all the blame for the whole thing on my own shoulders.

We have since remained friends. She has suffered greatly for the "way" that our relationship ended, and apologized. Since we are so far apart we rarely see each other, but we correspond. I miss her now and then, though less and less as time passes. We have little in common now. I still have never met the "other" woman and, frankly, never care to. I realize that my rage should be directed at my ex-lover, but there were times when it all centered on the "other" woman.

My parents, of course, had no idea what was occurring and were nursing my brother through a divorce at the time. I resented the fact that he could so easily have their support and that it wasn't available to me because my family didn't know the facts or the situation. People at work didn't know my lifestyle either and many commented that a terrible change had come over me because I no longer smiled.

After the breakup and the subsequent move, I believed that I had "blown" my one chance at love. I didn't think I was entitled to another chance!

. . . .

Today I would describe myself as a thirty-seven-year-old single feminist who happens to be a lesbian involved in a committed relationship. I have a profession and enjoy my work and my friends.

I am happy in the relationship I am involved in now. Our relationship is two years old. "In love"? I prefer loving—it's more rational and has far more potential for growth. The most important part of our relationship is the day-to-day joy in the love we share. Sex is an expression of that. She is aggressive, intelligent, humorous, self-possessed, and open-minded. I respect her a great deal. Although I love her more than being "in love," I have experienced great passion with her. I am intent on making this relationship the best, deepest long-term friendship I have ever had.

She thinks she loves me more than I love her, but I think it is equal. One thing critical to each of us is that neither be "caretakers." I feel very loved, but she is not sentimental or gushy—I'm the sentimental one! The time most recently that I was the happiest with my lover was after a party we had with a few of our close friends. It was a simple occasion, the joy just had to do with our enjoyment of each other. I especially like being with her with others, but most of all, going home with her after we've been out.

The biggest fight we had was shortly after we were living together and her ex-lover's parents were in town. She is good friends with the ex and her family. We were invited for a holiday dinner and I hit the roof at the thought of going. I didn't want to spend "my" holiday with an ex-lover's family. Though, I admit, I had it out of proportion—it was only in terms of friendship—but I was feeling sensitive. We didn't go.

Our practical arrangements for the housekeeping are as follows: Until recently we had one evening a week for housecleaning, but she has more time at home, so she has started doing that. (I don't feel like I'm pulling my load— the purpose in her doing it is to give us more quality time together.) I do the ironing because it is mostly my clothes that get ironed. It is her own home, and she enjoys being outside (I don't), so she maintains the yard. Often I prepare dinner the night before and she has it ready when I get home from work. We pool money for groceries. I pay rent. We each pay the cost of our own phone calls, which are mostly long-distance to respective families. We do not pool our money otherwise—she is far more wealthy than I.

If anything goes wrong with the house, it is her financial responsibility. If we acquire new furniture or want to change things that we could move with us if we moved, we split the expense. Financially she is helping me to find ways to invest my money so that I can become more financially independent. We each have authority to act on the other's behalf in medical emergencies. If anything happened to her, I would have the house. We're planning on buying a new car together.

Marriage may be old-fashioned, but I like old-fashioned things. I happen to be a person who operates best in a monogamous relationship. I haven't had any extramarital affairs, and I would not; nor is my lover having another relationship; I don't believe she has since we have been serious about being together. When I was single I did a lot of sexual experimenting and recall vividly a period of nearly a month when I didn't spent one night alone—I had three different partners. Ultimately I decided that it wasn't worth it anymore.

My first orgasm was with my first lover. She kept insisting that I always stopped too soon, and that was why I didn't orgasm. So I kept on, and I had one! I dug out the Christmas tree lights (in July) and hung them around the bed to celebrate.

Now I have multiple orgasms in one session of making love and I feel much less inhibited. We sometimes use a dildo and are able to orgasm simultaneously by using it and rubbing our bodies together. Those are the best orgasms—when they are simultaneous. I also love to be stimulated anally—I become uncontrollably aroused. But this is a taboo with my partner—she doesn't know that I have experienced it! I'll have to tell her and perhaps persuade her to try it.

I usually feel the closest after we make love because it is an expression of all of the wonderful feelings I have toward her. When we make love I feel as though we are a total entity—I can't tell where she leaves off and where I begin. It is a "complete" feeling.

I was raised working-class Irish Catholic. My parents have been married for forty-two years. My mother's greatest disappointment in me is that I never married and have no children. She doesn't know about my lifestyle—and would be unable to discuss it if I told her. I was very devout in my religion in the past, but now, although I still practice my religion in the church, and still define myself as a Catholic, I have a very strong belief structure that is personal and my own.

Absolutely I am a feminist. The women's movement affects most of what I do. I work with people who are like-minded, and who understand that women need to exert all the power they have. Women relationships are the most important in my life.

2

I am sleeping with my first lover again after two years apart. We once lived together for eleven years, and have known each other for fourteen. Before we were lovers, we were best friends in high school. I was most deeply in love with her when I was fifteen. We spent every minute we could together. We wrote science fiction stories and lived in a world of fantasy all our own. We wrote notes to each other every night and talked on the phone. On weekends, we went for trips together. It was joyful. (When I wasn't joyful, I was thoroughly miserable!) Then we became lovers when I was eighteen (my first). It was my first year at college and her last year of high school.

We have broken up three times. All three times it was awful. I lost my appetite, my period was delayed, nothing seemed real. I couldn't talk about her without crying. After long enough, the second two times, however, I felt freer, and really *was* freer. I made deeper friendships with other people. She said the same thing.

Now I feel ambivalent about being with her again. I don't think I am *in* love with her, but I realize she loves me and always has. When I was in love with her, I had a great need to be affirmed by her, for her to demonstrate her loyalty, behave as part of a couple, know and accept everything about me. After having other relationships I realize this was unrealistic and destructive. I am no longer so demanding. I can see the strength of her feeling, which was always hidden from me before. I don't want my life to revolve around her as it once did, but there is still a lot of affection and real caring between us. I think of being in love as a window that's open for a while, and then closes again.

The most devastating time in our relationship was when I was twenty-five, and learned that she, to whom I'd been completely faithful, was having an affair with her (male) employer. I still loved her, but after that, *I* had an affair with my (male) business partner. I've always accepted it as inevitable that I would lose love; after all, my mother changed toward me, my analyst stopped being accessible when the analysis was finished, and so on. The only relationships that have lasted have been the ones I didn't depend on, and the less dependent I've been, the better they've been. When I am dependent, I am always sure that sooner or later the other person will be off down the road. So I never told my business partner (my only male lover), for instance, that I loved him. I sometimes think he might have liked to know, but I could never figure out how to say it in any way that wouldn't have been some form of claim on his time or sympathy. Perhaps he wouldn't have minded that. But the risk was too great.

Years ago I was extremely jealous, but I don't believe in monogamy anymore. Still, I want to be careful not to cause any harm. Since I stopped being monogamous, I've become more sexually experimental. I like having sex with many different women. Their different styles fascinate me. My lover also says that I'm much better at making love now, and her response is much stronger than it was before I had slept with other women. I love exploring every part of a woman's body, especially her breasts, clitoris, and anus.

· · ·

My first lover (the one I'm with again now) used to enjoy acting out fantasies of being captured. In fact, she first became close to me by telling me how she had had another woman act out a beating scene with her. I was flattered by her frankness. When we became lovers, I sometimes acted out scenes with her, but I refused to beat her. I told her that if she had had a disciplinarian mother like mine, she would know what it was like to see someone beat people and animals and wouldn't be so keen on the idea. But as time went on, I began to realize that forcing her to have my kind of sex wasn't any different from her forcing me to have a kind of sex I didn't like. I began to feel I was arrogant in assuming she wasn't normal, whatever that means.

So I tied her up and beat her with a piece of rope, and then we had sex. All her inhibitions disappeared. She was like someone who was transformed. Her face as she came had an expression of real beauty—I don't know how to describe it. We kept on having S/M sex. I felt like a pervert but at the same time I was happy because she was happy. After I became a feminist activist I felt real conflicts about it and in the end I left her. This was as much because I felt I was leading a double life as anything else.

Eventually S/M became topical in the women's movement, and when I was asked for my views, I felt I had to be honest. At the same time, as a result of my experiences on the scene, I began to understand why my lover had felt the way she did. I think that she actually felt safer having S/M sex because it let her express her sexual fear, rather than forcing her to conceal it. Ordinary sexual encounters aren't too different from any other social situation. You are supposed to be pleasant, polite, not do anything without explanation. You certainly aren't supposed to get angry or show fear. In some ways it has a lot in common with visiting the doctor. By expressing her fear, my lover could overcome it. When I slept with other women, later, the atmosphere was thick with fear. But mentioning it was against the rules. The only way to take the pressure off was to withdraw suddenly or act very cold and callous. This hurt the other person much more than a beating. (I never hit my lover hard, because I couldn't stand to.)

Most of my feminist friends refused to listen to this. (I also feel very strange writing about it.) When I found that my point of view was dismissed, and my personal experience made no difference to women I had called my friends and known for years, I became depressed, got mononucleosis, and thought about suicide. I couldn't face the fact that feminists could behave the way the ruling clique in my fifth-grade class behaved, and that I'd given up my relationship out of loyalty to something that turned out to be so hollow.

Two years later, she and I started sleeping together again. I didn't want this to happen, partly because of the shreds of feminist identity I still had left. But it was impossible to miss the fact that she really did love me and wanted to sleep with me. So I decided that as long as I was the notorious sadomasochist in the local women's community, I might as well put some heart into it. I became a very creative sadist and acted the part to the hilt. Since I hate inflicting pain, I thought up punishments like washing the dishes. I realized that the suspense was everything. There is a lot more in this kind of creativity than in gifts of material things or extravagant avowals of love. Both of those are binding but creativity is just as rewarding for the giver, and doesn't foster such a sense of debt. Whatever the truth to this, my lover has begun to change her attitude so completely that I think she may someday stop being dependent on S/M. She now seems just as moved by non–S/M as she only was by S/M sex before.

I think that "rough" sex is a separate category from rape fantasies, which I used to have when I was a teenager. I thought that men raped the women they found most fascinating and desirable (the way they do in gothic novels). Now I have many fantasies and invent new ones all the time—my fantasy life seems to focus on anything and everything. The basic situation, though, is always the same: Because of who I am and where I am (a queen ordering her slaves to make love to her, a prostitute's client, a wildly attractive woman or man), sex becomes allowable and indulgence is all right. Everyone has a good time and is passionate and affectionate and carried away. One of my longest-running fantasies was about seducing a very cold, withholding businesswoman in a spartan sort of hotel. Without saying a word, we both suddenly fall onto the bed in our tight skirts, stockings, and heels (I am another businesswoman) and start kissing, hugging, and removing enough clothing to masturbate each other, panting and groaning in a very abandoned way.

Before I knew how to masturbate, I made up "bad stories" in order to feel turned on. Recently I tried masturbating after reading an erotic story by a lesbian. The experience was much more intense than usual. In Susan Griffin's book *Pornography and Silence,* I read about violent pornography such as snuff flicks. These sound horrifying, and I can't imagine how they could be titillating in the same way as my own pictures and stories. The women in commercially produced pornography are so passive and characterless that they seem to be intended to turn people on in some other universe.

I wear the ordinary lesbian feminist uniform most of the time, but I have long dresses and would wear Elizabethan women's clothes if I could wear anything—except I'm sure they'd be uncomfortable. I'm not sure how much my love of beautiful clothing doesn't stem from the fact that the world around you, except the feminist world, reinforces you massively when you "look after your appearance."

I used to admire women's sensitivity, tolerance, and especially their ability to listen to others. I felt men were incapable of interest in others, and only wanted to use them. Since becoming a feminist I have realized that women are just as capable of insensitivity as men, and though they usually know more about others, they don't use their knowledge any more wisely than men might. Being a feminist has made me much more pessimistic about women, but more realistic.

. . .

Deep emotional relationships are really a problem, almost impossible. Most of us are so inexperienced at dealing with real emotion in someone else that we simply don't know what to do at any given outburst on the part of the other. Even if we do know, we would have to have a lightning-action coping technique, sandwiched in between work, evening meetings, social events that have been planned far in advance (and are very hard to change because everyone is so busy), and whatever it takes to support life for you and the people you live with. There's just no time, space, or energy to cope with emotionally dependent people, at least in the environment I live in.

The women's movement is going through a difficult period just now. I miss the support it gave in the early seventies. The movement itself over the last few years has changed so greatly. It isn't so much about everyday life anymore, so you can no longer tell men they can start by doing the dishes and go on to more advanced lessons later. Some men I know have made major changes in their lives (income-sharing schemes, for instance) in order to express their solidarity with women.

Writing this questionnaire has made me realize how profoundly the women's movement has affected my life and how the loss of my unquestioning loyalty to feminism—which I'd formed long before I ever met any feminists—has left a very large gap. The thing that made me believe in feminism was that it was about listening—and respecting each woman's point of view. The "real" feminists weren't the leaders, but the ordinary women in c.r. groups—"feminism" was a flow from them to the writers, commentators, and organizers. If I could find something to replace or revive this picture, I would be able to move on.

3

I'm gay, age 53, been gay all my life, have many friends and ex-lovers who are friends, and a large circle of women I am close to.

I have always loved being gay. Being accepted as an equal among equals. I think women are wonderful, I just love women, I always have. Most of my life, I have been in long relationships. I went with one woman for ten years, and another for seven. Those were the longest, but it was always four years, three years—things like that. I was always going with somebody.

I was deeply in love twice. The first time was with the first lover I ever had, the first woman I slept with. (She was also my boss!) She was twenty years older than I, and moved me out of my family and my oncoming marriage—which I had felt was inescapable. She handled all that. She was terrific. She had electric blue eyes and a wonderful way of looking stern and loving at the same time.

Strangely, although I had many long-term love affairs after that, I never had anything that intense again, until two years ago. Then there was a woman I really loved—she was very, very good-looking and rich (maybe not too bright). We had a strong sexual alliance—the physical relationship was just sublime. I melted when I saw her, I forgot where I was and who I was in her arms. I floated away to some other world—it only lasted those three months.

But on the other hand, I think I spent all my life in relationships—I never had time off, in a way. I was *always* in a relationship, I had tons of relationships, tons and tons. It seemed like I couldn't even stay single. And when I was in a relationship, I didn't play around or anything. Now I'm tired of the whole thing, tired of the inevitable compromising, working it out, reporting in . . . No matter how in love you are, you're still two different personalities who are not going to mesh in everything, so you are going to have conflicts, you're going to have arguments. I'm tired of relationships.

. . .

This year things have changed quite a bit for me because I had a mastectomy. That's another reason I guess I'm not sexually interested. I never thought I would get cancer—*me!* But I also never knew how much support there would be in the gay community for me either. I felt very loved, very supported.

Nancy was the last woman I had an affair with before the mastectomy. What is really ironic is that Nancy—I had already stopped seeing her sexually when I got the news that I had a lump—had had a mastectomy twenty years before—a radical mastectomy in the days when they took out everything. So when she heard, even though we were by then "just friends," she was very concerned. In fact, the night before, I went out to dinner with my friends as usual—and she was there, and all the time we were having this ongoing argument because she insisted on going to the hospital with me the next morning and I insisted on her not going. It meant a two-hour trip for her from the suburbs, three subway trains, and I had already broken up with her anyway. I didn't want to be indebted, to incur an obligation. I said, don't come.

Anyway, she showed up, unexpectedly, the next morning to go to the hospital with me. Thank goodness she came, as it turned out. I went in at about noon. I had a local anesthesia. When you have a local, there's nothing, no pain, you go and come home the same night.

During the lumpectomy, they found out immediately that it was malignant. I was even conscious, I heard all the bells ringing. (When there is a positive cancer test in the lab they start ringing the bells and yelling for you to come up there right away.) I asked the doctor, "How is it?" He said, "It's positive, but don't worry, we got it in time." I figured he meant the lumpectomy was it, even though there was the positive ding-dinging in the surgery. He was teaching somebody at the same time he was working on me, explaining everything—so I heard everything.

I put on my clothes and went into the waiting room. Nancy was waiting there. When the doctor came out to speak to us, even though I was a little shaky, I thought I was fine. But he said, "I suggest we make an appointment for the mastectomy as soon as possible." I said, "What do you mean! Do you mean I have to have a mastectomy? You mean I have to have a mastectomy?" All of a sudden, it felt very hot in there, and I fainted.

The doctor had thought I knew—since I was conscious during the operation. But I didn't know he had meant that once we took the *whole breast* off, I would be perfectly well. He meant that I wouldn't die of cancer because he had caught it so soon. So, when he told me, I was so alarmed that I got very nauseous and started to perspire, then I got very dizzy—that's when I fainted.

I was very upset, to put it mildly. Nancy came home with me and actually moved into my apartment for a week. She went to work during the day, but came back every night and stayed there. I wanted to have the next operation right away, but my insurance policy doesn't pay unless you get a second opinion, so I had to delay the operation for two weeks. The waiting was awful.

During all that time, I was terrified. I wouldn't let Nancy out of my sight, except when she went to work. She slept in bed with me. She didn't demand sex or anything. I was just terrified—terrified, absolutely frightened. I felt comforted that there was someone there. She's a sensational cook anyway. That's part of the way she took care of me.

Actually it was Christmas vacation and I was due back at work on January 2. Everybody expected me back, I hadn't told anybody. I waited until the last possible minute to tell them I wasn't coming in, and why. I called them the morning before—the woman I drive with and my boss (another woman). Later I found out there was a lot of commotion at work—people crying and getting upset. Another friend of mine drove me to the hospital. (I had stored my car.) She had also had a mastectomy—there are an awful lot of women out there who have had mastectomies, you just never hear about them. I think lesbians are more open about it. Maybe heterosexual women need to keep it more secret.

I remember, when I was wheeled back to my room, I was furious because I felt so terrible. I was retching, trying to throw up, and hadn't eaten in twenty-four hours, so there was nothing to throw up. Horrible nausea and so dizzy. Just horribly sick. No pain, but my feeling was anger at all this. I learned subsequently that I got hepatitis from the blood transfusion. But I didn't know that then.

When I came back to my room, there were three women there, like the three wise witches. First there was my friend Anne, then the woman I drive with to work, and another friend. The three of them were all there! They didn't know that I had hired private nurses, and they were expecting to stay with me through all this illness. Wasn't that marvelous? Three such different types of women. I mean, not all gay, only one gay woman, they were just three very caring, great women who never even knew each other. They met there. None of the three of them knew the other was coming, each had come thinking she alone would be doing it.

Fortunately, because of all the information I had gotten from my friends, I had hired three shifts of private nurses. Because you can imagine, there was no way I could have gotten to a buzzer. And besides, they don't pay attention to you. They have other people around too. I was violently ill.

I had asked that nobody come to the hospital room. It's a good thing I said that, or I would have been deluged. As it was, I had a phone, and everybody in the world called. It seemed like thousands. And dozens of visitors. When I got out (faster than anyone you ever heard of—three days), Anne came to take me home. It was like a big social event. The doorman kept getting all this stuff, flowers all over the place. And then different people would come—friends bringing food—every day. And the place looked like a funeral parlor—plants and flowers, there wasn't enough room for them. Other friends of mine came and took care of the flowers. And I got my cat back immediately, my friends brought my cat back.

I was so well taken care of I hardly had a minute's rest. I mean, I had to get up immediately and straighten up the place and straighten me up because of the next surge of guests, the next crowd coming. But at least I didn't feel lonely. I felt very cared for. It takes your mind off it when you're dealing with the immediate people coming and bringing you gifts.

The support was just amazing—I mean, I have never seen anything like it. All the women I knew were calling, taking me to the hospital, bringing food over, watching my pets, moving my car, etc. It was really amazing. I never knew there was so much support out there.

A friend of mine remarked that it sounded like I got more support than most heterosexual women, who would rely on perhaps their husbands, who are not really equipped or used to being in a taking-care-of role. I was really very well taken care of. Ours is more of a community, a lesbian community, than hetero-sexuals have. Also, I think the fact that I was not in a relationship accounted for a lot of the concern. People have a tendency to think that when you're with somebody, the somebody is taking care of you. But a lot of it is just simply a closer-knit community—I think lesbians are more of an extended family.

And too, I think women identify more with other women who are having a mastectomy than with any other illness—it's sort of a crippling of one's self-image that everybody recognizes. So it's very nice. I certainly was glad I wasn't a straight woman then. But I've been glad about that for thirty years.

The people at work were shocked. I mean, I had danced out of there, before Christmas, doing flip-flops—and the next thing they hear is I'm not coming back because I'm having a mastectomy. People don't usually find out and do it that fast. So they were very shocked. Also, they were shocked that I talked about it. Women are "supposed" to be ashamed of mastectomies. It's as if they've done something wrong, they don't blatantly state it. They asked me if I minded them putting a notice up on the board, and I said no. Usually they put euphemisms: "She's in the hospital for surgery." I said no, state exactly what it is. I think that shocked them.

Actually, my chest doesn't look too bad. It's just a little shocking. But you get used to it. There are no real scars. I've seen my sister's radical mastectomy, which was a disgusting mess. The scar tissue was a horror. I have nothing but one little skinny scar that goes vertically. And—what else can I say about it? Nothing.

The happy thing was when I didn't need any chemotherapy. I had a party! I remember Shirley—she bought some great champagne. And she tells the liquor man that she needs a great bottle of champagne because her friend has healthy nodes!

. . . .

Now, I've had a drastic non-sexual change in my life. I haven't been going out with anybody. I go out with friends, but I have not been seeing anybody with an eye to any sort of relationship. I don't want any. I'm not interested in sleeping with women. I feel I may not be attractive.

I stand in front of the mirror and look and try to decide how it would, you know, strike somebody. Objectively, how do I look? I know better, because Nancy had had a mastectomy and it didn't bother me one bit, one iota. I knew it before I slept with her, of course. Lesbians who have mastectomies make sure that everybody knows about it. I never had the least feeling about hers—i.e., would I or would I not find her attractive? It never even entered my mind. So I know that other lesbians are just as sensible and smart as I am, right?

But it doesn't make any difference. It's in my mind. It's me. I can't exactly explain it. People have even come on to me, who certainly know everything about me. It doesn't matter to them. It's what's in *my* mind. That I am not physically attractive. Or I don't feel physically attractive.

My friends are sort of nudging me—the ones who are involved, particularly, and the ones who are looking (and all of my friends fall into one of those two categories). There isn't anybody like me around, except one person—but even she says vaguely that she hasn't given up hope, that somewhere there is this perfect relationship. Of course, I scoff. I don't know why she even says this, she really knows better. But she is not doing anything about it either. She's had eighty-five relationships already in her life.

So my friends have kind of given up on trying to force me into a mated situation, because they see a lot of people come on to me and I just haven't responded. Usually, after parties and things, someone will just hang around after everybody else leaves—you know, wait them all out. This is the usual thing. They'll wait everybody out, then the last couple of people will nervously say goodbye, because they see what's going on.

Other people have been blunt. One woman, very cute—I really liked her—said, "I only need one breast to play with." She actually said that to me. She perceived that this was what I was worrying about. But I'm not really worrying about that—it's hard to explain. And my other ex-lover keeps bothering me constantly.

This doesn't mean I'm not as crazy about women as ever. If I could generalize in the abstract—women are more caring. Of course, I'm a woman, so it's easier for me to relate to women. I think they're nicer people. Besides, I like dealing with equals, with peers. I like people who are like me. Women—I like the way women look and smell. And feel. They feel and smell and look so much better than men do. They even sound better. I like everything they do better.

But now that I haven't got any sex drive after the mastectomy, I'm not bothered sexually with the lack of a relationship, whereas I used to be before. And I feel liberated not having to *always* be looking for some sexual alliance. I can be more at ease with my friends. There isn't any of that possible what-may-happen-in-the-future type of thing. Or: "Is this an eligible woman?" I make it very clear that I'm not looking, that I'm not available. I don't tell them why, I don't have to justify it.

. . .

I'm very social, I go to parties—I simply go by myself, and I like it. Lots of women who are single seem to need a companion to make them feel more secure walking in and out of the door, and I refuse to play that game.

Also, I think I'm going through a process of subtle reshifting. I'm different than I was before. People have said to me that I should go into therapy, but I know I shouldn't. There isn't any point in my going into therapy because I don't want to change. I was in therapy before for eight years, and it did me a world of good, but this is different. The only reason for going into therapy is to change something in oneself. They want me to be like I was before. (And also to be more like them. It validates their experiences and desires.) Now there's something, to them, amiss with me, because I don't want a relationship. I haven't got any sexual desire. To them, that is incorrect, even unhealthy, they might say, making value judgments. They feel the situation should be corrected.

I've gotten to like being alone a great deal, even though I'm a very social person. I love living alone, sleeping alone. I never used to before. Actually, all my life I didn't basically sleep alone. But now if I'm not interested in sex, it's more comfortable to sleep alone, having the privacy and independence to wake up at three in the morning and make any kind of racket or do anything I want. Whereas before, you always had to be considerate about your bed companion, you know. Tiptoeing around, not making noise. It's very nice to do whatever you want at any hour and any time.

What I love especially, I love not having to tell anybody where I am. Not having to report. I get such a kick out of this! It's a relief after a thirty-year habit of doing this. For example, nobody knows where I am right now. Isn't that delightful? I may have vaguely mentioned it to somebody, but I'm sure they're not thinking about it. It's such a childish thing and yet I get such a kick out of it!

On the other hand, of course, I miss the thrill and the excitement of that first marvelous flush of sexual attraction. The first consummation—I think that's really almost one of the best things in life, you know, when you come together with someone that you're very sexually attracted to, who is sexually attracted to you, and it first begins. Those beginning first few days are one of the best things about being alive. And I do miss that. But I don't have it. I don't know if it will ever come back. Everybody assures me that it is a phase I'm going through. But I don't know. My sister used to say that to me all my life. Everything is a phase I was going through.

But the bad things in relationships make me tired. If I seem to be a burnt-out case, it started to happen even before the mastectomy. I just have had enough of all these relationships. I guess what I'm saying is, I love women, but I'm expressing disgust with the whole coupling process. The whole two-by-two thing. I want to get off of Noah's Ark. No relationship is perfect, but with women the ones that endure, what happens is that you accept what's wrong with it, and deal with it on that basis. I'm not willing to do that anymore. It isn't worth it to me.

In my ten-year relationship, we were mature enough to realize that you can fight and still have a relationship—which is the only way you last for ten years anyway. You fight all the time, but you last for ten years. The real reason I left that relationship was I realized that I could not depend upon her in an emergency. Little minor things, but whenever I was in trouble, I realized I was on my own. She was not there for me. And I thought, what's the point in having a relationship with somebody if you cannot count on them when you are in trouble? You need some emotional support. And she was never there.

I was willing to go on arguing, even being miserable now and then, but when I really realized that about her, I figured I'd better not stay any longer. It's better to either find someone you can count on or not have anyone. It took me a long time to realize that about her, because I really couldn't believe it. I had had signs of it all along, but I had never had that experience from a woman before. Other women in other relationships were always able to be there—the ones I took seriously, the ones where I thought I might stay with them for the rest of my life. And I could even see this in the ones that weren't serious, that they were there for me, somebody like L. and other people.

I have a big social circle—a huge network of friends—so that I am really more inundated than isolated. I think that most lesbians do have a lot of friends, if they are at all political or social. It's not only that, it is also time: as you get older, you have developed stable relationships with friends over the years. Especially if you don't move too much, you build up this real heavy network of . . . it's more than friends, it's an extended family.

We worry about each other. Thanksgiving and Christmas, I worry about them. Especially single women. It's just as solid as any other kind of family. But people generally think to go for the traditional kind, they think they'll have more security, and I don't think that's necessarily true.

My friends do not say to me, my lesbian friends, "What are you going to do when you're older?" They know better than that. They know there is no guarantee that if you're in a relationship or married, you will have someone to "depend on" when you're older. And it seems to me anyway, in the end, everybody dies alone. And even if people want to, what can they do for you?

Maybe it's preferable to die alone—not, you know, as in a horrible loneliness, but basically, in the end, none of your friends will ever want you to die anyway. And so therefore when you are in the midst of a kind of a serious reconciling with yourself, they all will be trying to get you to be who you were before. And it's just not possible. So very few people might understand that, and let you go through it.

· · ·

Most of all, since the mastectomy, I realize more than ever that I love being alive. I love—I just love living. I like what I do. I like socializing. I love going to the movies. I love reading books. I love being alone. I love watching my

VCR. I love going to parties. I love dancing. I love walking my dog. I love the beach. I get a lot of pleasure out of life. I just love the things I do.

What I have learned to change is to get rid of a lot of the stuff I don't like. The obligatory stuff. Even relationships I don't like, obligatory people. Sometimes I still feel too obligated, but I am conscious of it, and make every effort to get myself to get rid of the stuff I really don't like that I don't have to do. And just do what I really like. Whenever possible.

I also spend more money now than I used to. I don't worry about saving it. I've become sort of yuppie-ish, if you want to call it that! If there's something I see that I want, if I have enough money for it, I buy it, and don't count the cost. Like my $2,000 bed. Did I tell you about that?

4

I'm twenty-one now, just graduated from college. I finally have time to read, write, play guitar, and wander around, meet people. Without question, my love and roommate is most important to me, and my favorite "waste" (no waste!) of time is to be in bed with her reading, sleeping, making love. I'm pretty happy, yep.

We've been together for eight months. We figure on being together indefinitely, or a couple of years. Her dad still wants her to marry some nice boy, and that might be inevitable. Nothing lasts forever. Also, we'd both like children, and it's possible but difficult for gay couples to raise kids—legal hassles, school systems, peer problems for the kid, and so on.

It's hard to say what's the most important part of our relationship—how well we get along, how much we love each other and take care of each other, how happy I am just to be with her. We definitely have the best sex, the most fun in bed, that either of us have ever had. I read a notice of a lecture being given a couple of weeks ago called "Lesbian Relationships: Bonding or Fusion?"! The speaker was observing that lesbians tend to fuse, to try to meld together into one entity, rather than remain two separate entities with a bond between them. This has become somewhat of a joke between us. I think a little less fusing and a little more "separate-entitying" would be better. But I don't really mind—people will always be separate, that's how we're born and that's how we die, one at a time, one per body, alone. Being alone is one thing you can always count on.

Our two-person household is run like the communal house we lived in at school—grocery purchases go on a list, along with bills and rent, and every month the list gets balanced, each paying her share. I'm more concerned with order and cleanliness, and also spend more time at home, so I do more cleaning, sweeping, and dishes. We both like to cook, and eat together every night. She goes to work, I go to the co-op to work or to the library, or downtown, or just stay at home, reading, writing, and playing guitar.

My lover is a bit taller than me, and quite beautiful—sort of foreign, a lit. major. She looks at things very naïvely sometimes and is often just fascinated with people, and children, toys, clouds, and the sound of traffic. She holds my hand when I cry, and lets me talk, listens to me, and ends up crying too. So I cheer up.

We were both real "cool" when this started, you know, met at a drinking party, did a lot of posturing, pretending it was all just sex, all very modern and adult. Then we started getting attached, confessing that we'd each had an eye on the other. Suddenly I was caring more about seeing her than anyone else, and being unaccountably happy whenever she was around. We resigned ourselves, admitted we were in love, but pretended to our housemates that we were really cool and adult and not emotionally involved.

She has never hurt me, ever, but I hurt her once, quite badly, when we first started talking about ourselves. She told me she'd had a happy childhood, that nothing really bothered her, she had certainly never considered suicide, and suddenly I saw insurmountable walls, irreconcilable differences. "I can't live with you, you're too happy!" And of course, she started crying. She'd been lying, being cool still, so I wouldn't reject her. What could I do? She was crying, and I loved her. I hugged her and held her, and told her how sorry I was, and how wrong. That was seven or eight months ago.

My own experience in high school was that I hated it. I was popular enough, wore "in" clothing until I was bored with it, had a cool boyfriend who liked music, camping, and pot, and an older boyfriend who joined the Air Force and was a jerk. I liked kissing my cool boyfriend, especially if we were stoned, but the other boyfriend always made me nervous, and I never really liked anything physical with him, although I did like the idea of having an older boyfriend who had a car and picked me up after school.

Underneath it all, I was so lonely. I even thought about suicide one particular year. Nobody understood me, I was too "smart" and "weird," and I thought I might be a lesbian and I would never be normal. My friends were very nice, but we just couldn't talk.

When I first thought I might be lesbian—I spent the summer with an incredible unrequited crush on a girl I worked with—I asked my friends at school if they would still love me if I was gay. They said, "Of course," and "Don't be silly," and one woman who worked with a lot of gay men said, "People fall in love with people." I find it hard to imagine falling in love with men. They seem a bit more closed with their emotions—as if they all came from the East Coast and women from the West—and many of them are more interested in pure mechanical sex than the average woman. With some of the men (boys, really) I went out with, it was always a bit difficult—I was uncomfortably more intelligent—we never really could talk, and I always felt that it was wrong and unlucky of me to be so smart.

My parents are really great, they're the one thing I never hated in high school. I was sorry to leave to go to college. As a child, I remember Dad holding me upside down, while I held on to his ankles and we "funny-walked." Once we went to England and Dad had to drive on the wrong side of the road. My brother was two years older than me, and I wanted to do everything he did—ride to the end of the street, go to nursery school, be a paleontologist.

Away from them, at school, I wasn't so happy. I got into a relationship right away—then, after a while, we weren't in love anymore, just addicted. Oh, sometimes, when the light was soft and just right, she'd be so beautiful, just like it used to be. But mostly it wasn't. We quarreled, cried, never wanted to have sex, but we were terrified at the thought of breaking up, being alone and having no one to sleep with. That was bad. Finally, I said I was so jealous of a boy she'd slept with that I had to break up with her or lose my stomach lining. She cried and felt terrible and said we'd work something out. Finally she broke up with me. We just couldn't get along anymore. We promised always to be best friends, and always to stay close. I cried, didn't sleep, was behind in my schoolwork.

One day it was my birthday, so I took some MDA to "cheer up." What a mistake! I walked into the coffee shop at school, and one of my friends came over and said, "What's the matter? You look kind of down." And I started crying. Three of my male acquaintances sat up with me all night hugging me and letting me babble and cry and babble. That was a turning point. Soon after that, I made some new friends and felt more relieved and happy than I'd been in months. It was fun being single! It was so surprisingly pleasant, I kicked myself for not breaking up months ago.

My relationship now is probably the most important thing in my life, for the time being. We are as close and as comfortable as two people can ever be. She's grouchy and annoying and playful when she comes back from work, and I am sometimes weepy and sympathetic, sometimes buoyant and energetic, depending, I think, on the weather. Whoever's higher cheers the other up. I can't imagine anything better . . . well, maybe if I liked rock and roll and reggae, and she liked politics and camping.

We tried being apart for a while—I had to graduate and visit my parents and go to a wedding in California—and we concluded (each of us): "I could live without her, but I'd rather not." It's hard to say what will happen in the fall when she goes back to school and I get a job. Am I in love now, forever? I don't know. I like being alone, walking around, meeting people in museums and stores and buses, and parties! But after a while you meet everyone you're going to in the bars, and it gets dull.

Right now I'm really concerned with what kind of career I will have. This summer, I'm a carpenter, do odd jobs; this fall, I hope to get a job in electronics and/or computers (my major). But I also feel a need to help improve the human condition—tending at the moment to Marxist feminism (the world is in bad shape, wars, starvation, pollution, competitive not cooperative living, but so far in recent history only men have been in control). I don't know how I can be involved in this with my job! But I still have a lot of time to work it out.

5

It is very hard for me to let people know I'm gay. I'm shy. My usual way of relating to people, including most "friends," is to try to please them, be who they want me to be. To tell these people (my friends) that I am gay—something that would not please them, they being straight—well, this is extremely difficult. Being who I am is easy for me to do alone but next to impossible among most people.

I'm not in love or in a relationship now. I'm thirty. My best friend is a man with whom I have a brother-sister relationship. He says I'm the best friend he's ever had—I feel pretty much the same about him—he's straight, but has difficulty with sexual relationships with women.

When you're single for a long time, the things you do to make life bearable turn out to be things that perpetuate singlehood. For example, I get great solace and entertainment from reading. But staying home reading keeps me from meeting people, and walking around with earphones on makes people not inclined to have contact with me.

If I meet someone I like, I'm scared to death of them and either flee or say deliberately mean or snotty things around them. I feel very threatened by people I'm attracted to. I'm much more at ease around people I dislike or scorn or feel smarter or prettier than.

Sex life: I masturbate about once a week or so. I haven't had many sexual encounters with women, and the most times I've ever made love to the same one was three times. I've been cosmically delirious in a woman's arms like nothing I've ever had with men—it's absolutely amazing.

Before I consciously knew I was gay, I was in love with several straight women. The first was my roommate in college. She enchanted me. I would drop everything for her. Although my greatest fear is of forfeiting myself, losing my ego and my sense of myself, I lost myself to Joyce, gladly. This was very unhealthy but so what.

I started therapy a year ago to deal with my final admission that I'm gay. I had shut that out for a long, long time. Since "coming out" and admitting to myself that I am a lesbian, I've gotten more involved in the women's community here, working on projects like the Women's Music Concert, etc., where I feel more that I fit in—that who I am is more accepted—and I'm starting to have a few friends.

6

I was in a relationship with a woman for two years. I really loved her. I put myself through every possible emotion with her. I took everything that I possibly could with her, every amount of happiness, growth, pain and anguish—I let myself experience all of it, enjoy and suffer every ounce of it, until I got to a point where I just could not take any more, and that was it. I couldn't feel anything. I was relieved to not be with her. It was like I was numb. Even when I got to the point where I couldn't take any more, it still took a long time for me to leave.

For the first year, it was very intense and very monogamous. Especially the first three months of living together were incredibly intense and passionate. Then it started to have a certain chaotic quality to it. Personal, emotional traumas, like she felt totally torn apart by the relationship, by her family, her past life. Her family did not know she was gay, they didn't know she was living with a woman, and they wanted her to come home to marry her ex-boyfriend. That was giving her a lot of pressure, including *inside* of herself, so she began to have this identity crisis of who she was. That created a lot of trauma, but at the same time, the relationship was still really hot and passionate, worth every moment. Because every moment, we were *together*, we felt like we were progressing through something *together*.

Then after the first six months, we began an intense work project together. It became completely insane. She felt a great time pressure to *do* something with her life. This constant pressure eventually led to my having a great deal of anxiety too. From that point on, the relationship was always traumatic. Also, she was really into work, while I had just left working every single minute for the last five years, not having one vacation. I didn't want to focus on work. (How do you get two people to go in the same cycle at the same time? I mean, it even gets down to menstrual syndrome, pre-, post-, and during! If you're not on the same menstrual cycle, then you won't even have one week out of the month where everybody will be normal. I may be trashed out by feminists for saying that, but I truly believe in pre-menstrual syndrome, I experience it myself.)

We had arguments—*wow*, did we ever! The typical pattern would be—for example, we'd be driving down the highway, like one time she was driving and I was reading a map. I was sitting there with a flashlight, inside the car, trying to read the map, and she was screaming at me because I can't read it properly. No matter what I do, I don't do it good enough. Or I don't do it the way that she wants it done. So she begins to get frantic and yell at me, and I begin to freak out. Sometimes I would just sit there and take it, or try to be real rational and logical, and say, "Calm down. Why are you getting so upset? Let's relax, pull over. Let's stop at a restaurant and look at this thing." But she would always feel the constant pressure of time—we've got to do this *now*. And I would be saying, "Let's relax!" And she would flip out.

I remember this one drive with her constantly screaming about something that I was doing wrong. We drove three hours like that, I was calm the whole way, calm and logical and passive. Then we got to where we were going, and the last straw hit. She said one more thing, I think it was something about dropping something. And that was it. I just grabbed her by the throat and began to strangulate her and screamed, "If you say one more fucking word, I'm going to kill you." And that was it.

She was constantly telling me how to do my work, so it got to a point where I was completely inhibited in it. I couldn't do well because I knew I was going to be told I was doing it wrong. It wasn't her advice that was wrong, it was the way she gave it. She would blurt everything out in this hypertension kind of way. My head was spinning around all the time. It destroyed the respect that we had between each other.

But in spite of all the torment, it was worth all of it. Spiritually, emotionally, mentally, she brought me into a whole other area, she expanded me in a way I couldn't have imagined before. We worked together, lived together, and shared every part of our lives.

. . .

We were monogamous for almost two years. Then gradually she began questioning the idea of monogamy within a relationship. This happened in discussions among friends, always in a philosophical sense; never like her saying to me, "*I want to have an affair.*" Always done in a sense of "exploring oneself as a woman." I always voiced my opinions, very much against it, saying I feel like it's difficult enough to maintain a relationship without having outside forces. You can only deal with so many things in life. You have your individual self, and your relationship with another human being. And if you choose to share your life with that person, having a house together, maintaining living quarters, a social life—plus still seeing your friends, and you also need time to spend on your own—then it's impossible to be having several different love relationships at once.

It's also absolutely, completely impossible in a live-in situation. No matter what, somebody's going to get hurt. I don't believe that anybody is going to feel great when their lover doesn't come home and sleep with them at night— and they know that they're out sleeping with somebody else.

But at some point, she began having an affair with this other woman, who was a mutual friend of ours. I didn't know about it until it had been going on for a while. Actually, I was working with this woman at the time, and didn't know the affair was going on. A good portion of what I was doing, career-wise, relied on my relationship with this woman. We were working together.

What ended up happening is that once when my lover went away for a weekend, supposedly to do some work, while she was away I sort of had this uneasy feeling. Meanwhile, I was trying to reach the woman I worked with because I wanted to work on the project while my lover was away. I couldn't contact the woman, but never really put it together. But then when Evelyn didn't phone to tell me she was on her way home (she had someone else— another mutual friend—phone me and say, "Oh, she's on her way home, she's going to get in a little late"), something just clicked inside of my head. Why couldn't she call me herself, why couldn't she talk to me? And I immediately knew that she was having an affair. So when she got home the next day—like six in the morning—I woke up, she said hi, and I just looked at her, and the first words out of my mouth were "Are you having an affair?" And she was just like "What? You know?" And I said, "Look, I have to go to work in an hour, and I have to *know*. Are you having an affair?" And she said no, and denied the whole thing from the start. I said, "I don't believe you. I think that you're lying to me. And if you're lying to protect me, or whatever, I just want to know. I have to know." And then she said yes, that she was having an affair.

I went through the whole realm of with whom, and she didn't want to tell me with whom, and I mentioned several names, and that woman's name was one of them. And she denied it, and said, "I can't tell you, I won't tell you." So I let that go. And then about two months later, I knew that this was still going on, and we were trying to, like, iron out things in our relationship—but we absolutely couldn't talk about it. She said she still loved me, but "that's just life." She needed some "outside sources" right now. "If we're going to stay together, I need this," she said—acting as though it was really better for our relationship. I said that it's impossible for it to be better for our relationship, 'cause all it's going to do is hurt me. And so, with that, I went to work.

About a month later, I figured out who it was. I was supposed to have dinner with the woman I was working with that night, to talk about work. It was a vital talk. I don't know what tipped me off, but it was something like Evelyn didn't come home the night before, or something weird happened to make me keep thinking and thinking about it. And all of a sudden it just clicked, and I called Evelyn from work. I said, "Are you having an affair with [so-and-so]? Is that who you're seeing?" And she said, "No." And I said, "Don't bullshit me. I know you are. Tell me, is this who you're having an affair with? I have to know now." And finally, she said, "Yes." And so I just said, "O.K., that's all I want to know."

She said, "I couldn't tell you because I knew it would ruin everything that you're planning to do," and I said, "That's right. It just did ruin everything." And that was it. I hung up with her, immediately called the other woman and said, "Look, do not call me, do not come over, forget about the meeting, I know what's going on now, and I just can't deal with you." And this woman's response was: "Oh, I'm really sorry. I wanted to tell you the truth all along, but it wasn't for me to say. I know what you're going through." And I just said, "You have no fucking idea, you could not have any fucking idea of what I'm going through." And I hung up, and that was it.

Then this affair went on for quite a while while Evelyn and I were still living together. We still went on. I kept thinking that it was going to stop eventually. She would spend whole nights away about one night out of a week, and maybe another evening. My feeling during the whole time was just completely cheated. I had to live with her and deal with all the bullshit that went on in our relationship, the cleaning of the house, the financing, all those aggravating things we had to deal with together, to the point of where we weren't having any fun. There wasn't a day out of the week where we spent our quiet moments together just lying around in bed or listening to music or reading poetry or something like that. And that's the time that she was spending with this other woman. That's what all new relationships are based on, that kind of sharing thing. I mean, you're not immediately dealing with each other's financial problems. So I felt like, how can I possibly compete with that initial feeling?

It went on like this for a while, she couldn't just come out and say to me, "That's it, I'm leaving you and going on my own." She's not very strong. In part, she couldn't bear to hurt me, but also she was afraid to leave me for *herself*, for her own reasons.

Eventually, I said to her, "I think you have to move out, I can't deal with this, I can't function—I can't live like this, with this other relationship." She said, "Don't give me an ultimatum, don't give me a choice to make." And I said, "I'm not giving you a choice. You have no choice. I don't want you to stay with me and stop seeing this woman, then have you resent it for the rest of your days. I'm just telling you that we can't live together anymore, and you know that." And she's saying, "I know, but I couldn't say it." I was upset. I mean, I worked really hard to bring myself up to say it. There was no time during all that that I could ever have a discussion without crying. And to this day, sometimes I have a difficult time with her.

So she moved out, within a month's time she moved out—but then we still saw each other all the time. She lived in one house, I lived in another, ten minutes away from each other. We were constantly together. Either I stayed at her house or she stayed at mine. And whether we were having sex or not was a very small part of it. At that point, that had sort of really died out, an occasional sort of thing.

At the same time, if we *were* having sex, I would think about her having sex with somebody else. I wasn't able to forget it. I was always sad. It gradually made sex even worse and worse—but I was freaked out if she *didn't* want to make love. I can remember her saying at one point, "I don't want to stop making love with you, I don't want to feel like we have to stop making love."

That went on for a long time, us going back and forth, her still seeing this other woman, and us still spending tremendous amounts of time together, and then her saying, "Oh, I have to go now," or "Oh, you better not stay tonight," or something—or me finding something belonging to this other woman at her house, you know, like her Calvin Klein underwear, or some kind of shit like this, and just sort of trying to overlook it, but at the same time always being in a constant state of anxiety, knowing that she's seeing this other person, because I was still so much in love with her. Even though she was gone, and we had made that decision, I was still completely in love with her, and she was still sort of bound to me. She was, like, caught, emotionally caught. I don't know that she was *in* love with me, but she had been in love with me for a long time, though.

She is essentially a good person—loyal and loving, caring. It was harder for her to break away because of that, to differentiate between loving me and being in love with me. I sympathized with this completely, because of the difficulties I had had leaving my male lover.

But on the other hand, sometimes I didn't feel sympathetic, I felt angry—I feel angry now. I feel very jerked around by her. At the end, there were certain times when she just didn't want to hear anything about how I felt (about her lover), she couldn't bear to hear anything, she couldn't care. She would be really cold with me, she would say, "This is the way it is, take it or leave it—I don't give a shit what you think!" She probably said those things more to convince herself than to convince me. Or maybe to shock me—she wanted me to hate her, because if I hated her, then she could pull out a lot easier. But I didn't hate her. I never did.

Then there was a time when I started going out with someone new. Evelyn's immediate reaction was to be extremely jealous. One time when I was on my way out the door to go and meet this other woman, she attempted to make love with me, saying, "I don't want you to go, stay here with me." And my response was just to laugh in this very cynical way, and say, "This is what I have to do to turn you on? I have to go out and be involved with somebody else? This is pathetic." And I got up and left. I was repulsed. I thought the whole thing was really demented, perverse.

So anyway, I went ahead with my new crush, which was fun for a while, but didn't go anywhere because she was leaving the country.

This was a very intense period where we were all hanging out together, all working together. There was a lot of tension. Even though I really liked her, I was in a very bad state. Eventually, Evelyn became involved with someone new (a mutual friend) who was also going away. Even though I still had unresolved feelings, I liked Evelyn's new lover and didn't feel betrayed, because Evelyn and I had already broken up.

After her new lover left, I spent ten straight days with her, staying over-night at her house, sleeping with her every night, discussing her feelings about her new lover. We didn't have sex—just spending the night together, staying together, doing everything together like we normally did. And dealing with this whole thing of whether or not she should join her lover, what should she do. I don't think this could ever happen with a man after a love relationship is over, still being able to share things on such a deep level. I think in relation-ships with women, if you are honest about your feelings, the love is never really over. You always have a bond between you, an infinity, because you were able to love on such a deep level.

It was very hard but I put myself through it. I made myself stay. It killed me, but I made myself stay, because I wanted to cut myself off emotionally. I didn't want to have any illusions about her still wanting to be with me, and all of that. I wanted to kill all possible illusions.

I succeeded. When she got on the plane and she left, I was free. That's when

I really felt free. I was just, like, relieved. But on the other hand, tears streamed down my face.

Why? Just because I miss her. Now, a year later, I depend on her still, in certain ways. And she depends on me. We're impossible together, sometimes her lover would like to strangle both of us, because we fight. We argue like we used to argue, like lovers. And then we have "our" certain things that we both know about, and both pick up on. That's the kind of intimacy that we have. People always comment on that. They say, "I can't believe the two of you are still so close."

And I still love her. I think I'll always love her, but, I mean, I recognize the fact that we cannot be together. And that's what she recognized early on, I think. It wasn't only the affair, but the feelings in general, the whole thing of recognizing that we really should not be together. It was too destructive for one another. We lost ourselves in the relationship somewhere.

Now she stays in my mind like a person that I love very much, not as a person that I'm obsessed with. We talk on the phone, we get together. And she calls my lover, and tells her she'd better take good care of me. I still tell her everything in my life. I get on the phone, and say, "Well, my girlfriend's being a bitch, and I don't know what to do." She says, "You do know—and I want you to be happy."

7

I used to be a lesbian, and although becoming one was frightening because of the label, it's the most comforting identity I've had since I was a cheerleader in junior high school.

I am now with a man I don't really love, and yet feel guilty about. I love him in the human sense, as if we've been married for twenty years—and if I were ready for resignation and peace, I'd love him decently and do my needlepoint. So that is a constant drag. I'm afraid of being alone, but I suspect I'd feel much freer and happier if I told him it was over. I'm not in love. I don't have the feeling of closeness with him that I had with my woman lover.

I was most deeply in love with her—but then, in some ways my current male lover has awakened more fantasies of total, self-centered happiness. In both cases, I was happy, but knew instinctively that too much closeness would destroy the relationship by destroying me. I wish I'd had the courage to fight for those boundaries of self, because both loves were ruined, although I'm still with my male lover. Being in love was indistinguishable from passion; it was more than sex; we wanted to smash together like cars, exchange engines. I had endless, constant, incredible sex with my woman lover, and endless sex with my male lover, which hurt me physically, so that I grew angry, and which didn't always lead to great pleasure, another source of anger. In both cases, though, my weakness in giving in to their demands, not preserving an outside life and using some of that joy for myself, led to a growing, stifled hostility in me and a passivity, a lack of active, responsible loving of them and myself, that destroyed/is destroying the relationships. I'm twenty-six.

The loneliest I've ever felt was when I was leaving her. It was like realizing again that I could not have my mother's love, like losing a part of myself. I got drunk by myself a lot. Somehow, though, the feeling of being completely alone gave me strength and made me realize I wanted to live—that I couldn't survive yet by myself, but I wanted to learn how to.

I cried for a long time when I was leaving. I was losing a whole identity and world of women's love, my friends, good sex, emotional closeness. She, my lover, had changed my life, made me capable of loving other people openly. She was smart and aggressive and shy; she didn't think she was beautiful, she was also a manipulator and a bit crazy. Depressed and confused. Sometimes I wish we'd just been friends so that we could be friends now. We seemed to have a similarity of perception and ease of communication that I've never had with anyone else. Even our lies were known ones. Nothing needed to be spelled out, but the part we spelled out was a mutual world. My lover told me that I was beautiful until I believed it.

At first I was glad to be free of her demands, but as my current relationship turned out to be ambivalent, I missed her more and more. I didn't have that closeness and wasn't free either, since I'd gotten right into something as involved as the first one. I was angry at her for getting involved immediately with one of our friends, thus cutting me off from that woman and in some ways from the whole group we'd been seeing. Also, being straight cut me off from them. I felt as though I'd lost the only person I would ever completely love. I was on the edge, emotionally. I didn't have enough resources of my own to survive.

Also, although we had a great emotional understanding, she had a bad temper and would pinch or hit me in small ways, like an angry child. She was a bully, and when our relationship ended, when I got involved with someone else and told her I was going to leave, she tried to hit me. I hit her back and kicked her, and she caved in. At this point, I felt very sorry. But I left.

I still feel a lot for her when I see her and she still feels it for me. I've never had as wonderful sex as with her, probably because I've never felt that closeness. Sometimes I still think my former lover is what I want—the woman I was with—but I can see that I didn't have enough strength in that relationship.

. . .

Now I've had one lover, a man, for almost two years. We lived together for one year. He would like to marry me, but I am not sure that I want to, so we are living apart and trying to solve various questions of career, schooling, and my doubts. When I fell in love with him, I wanted to be cared for economically, given children, protected from the world, fucked, the whole gothic romantic womanly complex. Now I realize that I never want to be economically dependent on one person, that I'd go crazy being sole caretaker of a household of children and dirty clothing.

These days, about the only thing I like doing with him is being with other people who bring out the best in him. The humor and joy of living is lost in our wrangling and tension. Talking is a bust. We aren't able to sort out problems and we aren't able to just chat enjoyably about everyday life. I would like to be listened to more, challenged less about areas that I do know better than he does. I can never be the expert, the teacher. He has to know better. When I do gain authority it obviously undermines him completely, shakes his faith in himself.

We struggle constantly over questions of sex and independence, mostly sex. As it is now, I can't imagine spending the rest of my life with him. He's not happy either, but he says he wants to marry me. I'm being told I'm loved, but who I really am is not getting a fair hearing.

But I feel guilty about wanting to leave him; I want security and am afraid of being alone in the world. The threat of poverty is a huge weight on the fear side that tells me not to leave him. And I feel guilty for being afraid.

He tells me he loves me, strokes my head. Or that he likes my breasts and pussy (his word), my bottom, a sort of dismembering kind of appreciation. He criticizes my depression and dependence, though if I wake up and go out with friends or do things on my own, he starts to undermine it. He wants me to be more feminine, though he isn't openly critical. I criticize his crudeness and emotional weakness. Other problems? My intellectual interests are a threat, instead of an inspiration. My problems are something to be hammered out with a crowbar, not understood. I can't say that I'm any more accepting of him. I don't think you can be completely open with another person without shaking some of that faith they need, that someone carries a bit of infallibility. But at the same time I wish he could bring out more of me, accept the contradictions, just let me express myself (a worn-out phrase, but accurate) in talking and living.

I want non-invasive love that can watch from a distance and ask the right questions. When he needs to tell me how he feels it's never just that—self-expression. He saves it for some enormous demand and describes it in terms of my inadequacy. Feelings are never the common bread of life, but a special force to be hauled out with great effort when performance no longer suffices. So the relationship demands too much energy; I resent the time spent arguing questions instead of living. At the same time, my relationship with myself and my work is far from gratifying. If it were, I'd leave this man. Or I'd marry him and be happy. Freedom either way.

We live apart. When we lived together, housework was always an area of conflict. He would do it, but it had to be a special, big cleanup after days of squalor, while I like the sort of efficient, constant small things that make a house more than a dumping ground. And regarding the big operations, he would never "submit to" being told when to work.

Oh boy—money. When we lived together we had about the same income— but he was always buying records and clothes, while I seemed to spend most of my money on the house. My way with money is to buy food and necessities, and splurge only once in a while. His style is to spend a lot on luxuries. He resented organizing shared expenses and was very angry when I expected him to pay for my car he had wrecked—the idea of lovers owing each other bothered him.

We slept in the same bed, but I would have liked another bedroom for nights when I was angry at him or wanted to stay up and read or write. If I live with someone again, or him, we'll have rules about work. I don't want to have to spend all my time negotiating.

In both my relationships I've become far too involved in making the relationship work—they should have worked on their own, or I should have let them go down the drain. I have trouble doing anything good or useful for myself, which affects all my relationships with other people. In college, I began to learn to take care of myself and work harder, and it was in some ways the most happy time of my life so far. There's some sort of barrier that prevents me from doing what I want, or even knowing what I want.

Our worst problem is sex—the way we want to have it seems totally different. He just can't seem to get used to seeing anything but intercourse as "real sex"—I can't come that way, and he seems to think clitoral stimulation is for "before" or "after" or some such thing. Also, I would like to be dominating in sex, but I haven't worked out dominance of a man; it seems he always wins—what's the use of arousing someone who'll get it one way or the other? I like to make active love; I have trouble being the passive partner. Lack of motion, however, isn't passivity. I can make active love to him with my vagina, but I don't always move.

I'd like to know how other heterosexual women feel and what they do. The only woman I've talked to is my sister, who is the original incorrigible heterosexual. You couldn't get her off men with a sledgehammer. She didn't come at all with men for ten years, so I suppose we have different priorities.

Then again, sometimes I think that if I felt better about him, these problems would seem unimportant and fucking would be better. There is a tremendous emotional component to fucking for a woman, the more so because her orgasmic response isn't tied automatically into vaginal stimulation.

Dreamy sex with women—I think what I miss about sex with a woman is the sensual touching, the realization that sex is a feeling of intimacy and a pattern of sexual motion, not a penis in a vagina (or a vagina around a penis). Sex with someone else should involve the subtle rhythms which communicate desire. Only occasionally have I felt that sort of rhythm in my male lover's touching, whether by hand or mouth or penis. I think he doesn't realize that they are all sex to me and none of them is primary. He always touches me too hard, too quickly, too jittery—irregularly. His body is hard and he often moves me around like a doll—I have to say no or yes all the time—the resistance or cooperation of my body isn't sufficient information.

I feel as though women are natural sexual partners. I like women's bodies. Breasts are beautiful, all is beautiful. I like women's soft skin and softer feeling of muscles with fat over them, finer fingers, smaller joints. Because I had a woman lover (and because I'm a woman), I recognize more parts of a woman's genitalia than clitoris, vagina, and vulva—I know and love intimately every fold, every texture and variation of sensation. I often masturbated (we wouldn't have even called it that) with my woman lover. We just did what felt best, and if one of us couldn't make the other come, she'd take over while the one who'd been rubbing or eating touched some other part, kissed her breast or lay close and pressed against her. Often I'd rub my own clitoris while she fucked me with her fingers. (Of course, the other way around too.)

In the sense that I went from a female to a male lover in the last couple of years, my style has changed. But in the sense that I've always let my lover shape the form of our sexual experiences, I haven't changed at all. With my woman lover there was never any question that the clitoris was the seat of sensations, although we did many other things with our bodies, but I gradually became the servant and withdrew further and further from what I wanted in bed.

I want a monogamous relationship. I've never had sex outside of my relationships, I'm not the sort of person who could carry it off—both my lovers have been watchful and intervened at any dangerous point. Maybe because of my guilt I signaled to them to intervene. I think that sex outside of those relationships would have helped me resolve feelings of being trapped, of being subjugated. I think I'd feel more powerful and independent if I had sex outside my relationship.

The worst thing he's done to me is to pick up a woman in a bar (or she picked him up) and sleep with her because my sexual problems made him feel impotent. We had a big fight when I saw the woman he'd slept with a week before, and he admitted that he'd slept with her (before, he'd told me that he backed out before intercourse). It wasn't really a fight, because I just screamed and hit him without resistance on his part.

. . .

I feel that I should break up—but I don't want to go through the pain. He complains that I don't love him enough; he feels that I have more power in the relationship (because I am less satisfied with him than he is with me), so occasionally he strikes out. But interestingly, he won't believe that his angry body language, striking out, intimidates me and makes it harder for me to get openly angry at him. I feel such a threat of his superior strength that I just want to withdraw when he gets angry.

We usually argue about sex and how to spend time. He usually wins in the sense that we do what he wants to do, keep sleeping together, stay together.

We never fight openly and with a clear conflict of wills. I'm almost never angry in a glad-to-be-pissed-off kind of way. It seems he's either lecturing me or I'm sort of nibbling at his corners. We never really resolve anything. He usually initiates the making-up process while I haven't even begun to say what's bothering me, or I have but he's shot down everything I have to say. I go along with the peace initiative but not with joy or energy.

I saw two therapists to solve the problem of going from a gay relationship to a straight one. One therapist was a straight woman, one a gay man. I didn't feel that either of them was able to understand that my problems with sex are separate from the issue of whether I want to be with this man or not. Both of them decided that I just don't like him. Sometimes I don't, but I don't want to be restricted to women—I'd like to marry and have children.

I have finally decided (for now) that I am just too vulnerable to give up a man who cares for me, that it is too threatening to feel like a failure, like someone who'd never have a normal relationship with a man. I have real ambivalence about this particular man, but can't stand to feel so alone. I rejected the therapists' advice to leave him.

16

Are Love Relationships
Between Women Different?

Another Way of Life

Is there a difference in the way women in gay relationships define love, compared with the types of love we have seen so far?

This *is* a separate culture, and yet it is also, inevitably, influenced by the culture at large. Speaking of this, one woman in her twenties asks, "*Are women better?* There are women I meet who are like 'soul sisters'—and then there are those who are just like most men—cold, distant, unable to communicate, using people, not taking other people's feelings into consideration. Have a lot of us been co-opted by male views of power—power as necessary to make a relationship attractive? We don't have many alternate models. Still, intense and maybe over-analyzed as they have been, I think my relationships with women have been closer and more rewarding than any relationship I have ever had with a man. Maybe we're not perfect, but we're definitely onto something."

Another woman, in her fifties: "People in the women's movement said the problem with relationships is that men are so macho—i.e., they never apologize and they don't ask about feelings. So gay relationships should be a lot better, because both women have the same basic equality. Is it easier to get along? I would say yes. The best types of relationships are same-sex relationships, especially between women. They have the best chance in the world: they are more equal, and time together is much better quality. But even with all this going for them, there is no way that disputes won't come up. What you learn is to negotiate those disputes, and try to remain a team anyway. Women understand this better, the team concept. I could never have a relationship with anyone except a woman. I think that's the best way in the world to go."

What is love?

"How do I love her, now after ten years? I love her mind, her body, her abilities. She's very brave and strong, exceptionally brilliant, and a beautiful woman."

"Our love feels like a stream that flows on and on, growing ever stronger and deeper, giving me a sense of peace and center. Her sense of humor always makes me laugh; her constancy and the knowledge that she is eminently dependable give me strength; the wonderful sparkle of my passion for her—the sense of joy in her just being there—is a daily joy for me. We live near each other, we sleep together, bathe together, wash each other's hair, and rub suntan lotion on each other. I love the warmth and intimacy of that. We sort of roughly share money, whoever has some shares—we're both poor. We generally tell each other everything—intimate things, memories, dreams. We are monogamous."

"When we make love, she makes me feel as though I'm the most beautiful woman in the world. She plays with my long hair and tells me how sexy she thinks it is. She tells me she loves the shape of my breasts. I especially love it when she whispers, 'You are so soft.' "

"My lover is the one I live with twenty-four hours a day and go on holiday with. She is a spark strange to me. Close, but from far, far off, like no light I've ever seen. A sound that constantly catches my ear, and sets my mind reeling. I am in love with her comfortably, vigorously, and for a long term. I love her too. She is my lover, my soul mate; the one I think about when I see a certain smile, when my heart sings—a sister I have known from centuries ago. We were together once, and it was easier or more difficult than it is now—but someday, some life, it will not be hard; it will be as natural as it feels. I'm in love with her *depth*, her sparkle. It makes me secure to know I'm deeply loved."

"My lover is beautiful, courteous, intelligent, well read, and attentive. Her political and spiritual views are important to her and similar to mine. I feel happy when we are together, we have a lot of exciting adventures. For example, she had an idea of how we could start a business and get rich, and we are working on that now and have a good chance of succeeding. We live together and have a pleasant lifestyle. We don't fight but we do argue sometimes. As time passes things are working out. Our biggest difference is opposite tastes in silverware design—that and a few more serious issues! I have a greater fear of intimacy, which is slowly diminishing. I work too many hours. I neglect her sometimes and she suffers in silence. She is developing her assertiveness, and I am becoming more attentive. We share very well."

39 percent of gay women in relationships are currently "in love" with their lovers—as is the following woman:

"I am twenty-five years old, black—in love with a thirty-two-year-old woman. She's all I think about, I can't sleep, can't think straight, she's just constantly on my mind. I would like to settle down with her and be comfortable, also financially. My lover feels the same for me. When she first kissed me and told me she wanted me too, I was so happy. Being in love with her is a challenge—it's joy, pain, frustration, hurt, learning, happiness all rolled into one. My favorite love story is my own.

"I've been in this relationship for two years. I have one nineteen-month-old daughter from a previous relationship. She has one child from her ex-husband. The most important part of our relationship is communication, passion, love, and sexual intimacy, in that order. Worst is we lack time together. She lives with her relatives. If I could change things, I'd move into my own place and invite her to come with me. I love and adore her.

"I broke up with a man I used to date before I became gay. He's the father of my child. One day he just took off. I went through a lot of changes, but after a while I came to the conclusion it's his loss, not mine. I came out of it O.K. I was good to him and there was no appreciation for it. To me women are more sensitive, lovable, affectionate, better to get along with, and more faithful. I feel more emotional commitment when I have sex with a woman. This feels better to me.

"My lover is the woman I have loved the most and hated the most. She's sweet, loving, generous, kind, stubborn, selfish, good lover, confused. Not really sure what she wants out of life. We see each other often, we go shopping, to movies, out to lunch, events, etc. We talk on the phone about everything. We have a good time most of the time—except when she likes to make me jealous. I guess she likes to see how I react and if I care.

"I feel a lot of passion usually when we are out to dinner or a movie and we start teasing each other. My passions go wild. I like to explore all parts of her body, especially breasts and vagina and clitoris. The taste and smell really turn me on. Usually I orgasm the best with oral sex. Sex with someone I love is much more fulfilling.

"My woman feels it's not necessary to have a man or a lover or a baby to be a whole, complete woman. I agree. You can be a woman without any of these. A lot of women feel you must have a baby and a man in your life to be whole. I don't. You can just be yourself."

Gay women discuss as often as heterosexual women the differences between "passion" and "caring,"* musing over the choices:

"Being in love is a short-lived state. Loving someone is something which lasts."

"Being in love is basically selfish. While it seems to enfold the beloved, it's only one's joy at finding someone you think you won't have to work on. Loving over time means finding out what feels good to *them*, and learning to give it. Between and among those states are so many other ones. Maternal/paternal love, seeing another person as a child to be nurtured. Sometimes it seems more important to like someone than to love her. But being *in* love is a time of bonding that can't be replaced by logical manipulation."

"Love stories? I like Jane Austen, her vision of love as a mutually respectful state which grows out of friendship. But I think she missed the complications of sex—that is, she splits passion from respect. The problem is that people have to find both, at least if they're going to be monogamous."

"I think sexual passion suffers with life. Passion cannot be a constant because nothing else is. Illness changes passion. Death changes passion. Fear changes it, as do anger, poverty, drugs, pain, a phone call from the folks. That's life. Passion can return just like the return of wellness, hopefulness, money . . ."

"Often my passions have not meshed well with the rest of my life—or rather, the object of my passion has not been the sort of person I want to live with."

"I know that when I felt the most passionate, that fit all my 'pictures' of being in love. But if I look at it in a detached way, I can see that it was mostly about sex. I am open emotionally—I must have some feeling for the person I'm having sex with, but I tend to confuse passion with love. I always thought being 'in love' would include that blinding passion, the need to tear at someone's clothes and make love constantly. And yet the person I had this feeling with is extremely screwed up, very immature emotionally, and not someone I could really have a healthy relationship with on a day-to-day basis. It's disconcerting to realize that my ideas about love have not been very realistic. I suppose that's not uncommon, but it makes for confusion."

"*In love* is explosive, obsessive, irrational, wonderful, heady, dreamy. *Loving* is long work, trust, communication, commitment, pain, pleasure."

"We have a lot of respect for each other's creative silence, for each other's interior life. We would feel totally lost without each other but it isn't a blind, confused desperation—because fundamentally we love and respect ourselves. But life would be less challenging, less inspiring without each other. Simpler, perhaps, but less rich."

"My current relationship is the first, for me, of its kind. It began in friend-

*See Chapter 14.

ship, and it exists for me as a steady, sustaining sweetness of love, like happiness! I sometimes miss the heavy passion of a former relationship (a touch of masochism, perhaps) but I don't for a moment miss the panics, gnawings, or emotional scrapings of these earlier lovers. I love her less madly than earlier lovers, but far better, more deeply. The biggest problem between us is unsatisfying or perhaps unexciting sex. In some way, I suspect the failures here are related to the nature of the love, and that lust and mad passion aren't the core of our being together. That is brand-new for me. I haven't yet learned, perhaps I won't ever, how to translate the deep caring love and affection I feel for her into sexual excitement such as I'm accustomed to. I need to learn and I'm trying to. But I have more fun with my current lover than I've ever had. We talk, go to movies, play tennis, work out, travel, even work together sometimes. I love being with her."

"I think 'in love' feelings are a peak experience of contacting a higher point of ourselves and the universe, projected onto the other. But it's more important to *love* someone you are going to live with."

"I enjoy being in love, but wouldn't want it to be a lifelong feeling or state of being, it's basically frustrating for me. I think to live with someone, to love them, is vitally more important than to be in love with them. Love is the day-to-day strength needed to exist. To be 'in love' is like a drug, a euphoria, a hypnotic state where I take leave of my more responsible self and act like a kid again. Real love is trust, concern, caring, empathy. I usually can sense people I will love at the first or second meeting."

While 43 percent of gay women say they would "risk it all" for a relationship, more disagree: 57 percent of gay women say passionate love, being "in love," is too volatile to work. Still, the percentage of gay women who like *living* with a passionate relationship is significantly higher than among heterosexual women.

Here, as in "straight" replies, confusion and contradictions are frequent:

"I still desire that big passion though I know it doesn't last."

"Actually, I don't really know about working at love for a long period of time—it just hasn't worked for me."

But one woman says both passion and stability are possible:

"You do not have to choose between passion and stability. Sex grows much better. Daily details are a turn-on too. There is an ebb and flow to it—it sparks at times."

Sometimes love transcends a simple definition; one woman, age twenty-nine, describes suffering deeply when her lover died, still loving her:

"My lover died four years ago. Initially I had a lot of physical reactions: I felt sick, I was cold all the time (it was summer), I felt hollowed out, I couldn't sleep or eat. I felt bodiless, was amazed to look and see that my arms and legs were still there and still seemed to be attached to something. After that was a feeling that the world was going to explode, that it was the end of the world and I was witnessing it. It was terrifying. I was baffled by the way no one seemed to be very concerned about it. In particular I remember watching one friend ironing a shirt. 'Well,' I thought, 'she wouldn't be doing that if the world were coming to an end.' But I wasn't very convinced. These sensations seemed external to the event of my lover's death.

"Then I was afraid to be alone, empty, had a sickened feeling most of the time. On the advice of friends, I wore an armband for a time, and that helped considerably: outward manifestation of inner pain made me feel less alone, and I couldn't that way collude with those who couldn't deal with me and so pretend I was O.K. Pretending I was O.K. was the most horrible sensation and I did whatever I could to avoid it. I felt if I didn't I'd lose my mind.

"Fortunately, I *was* granted a place of honor and given lots of attention throughout all the rituals of grieving by her family.

"No part of me wasn't sorry. *Every* part of me was sorry, including some parts I was surprised were sorry, like the parts that were driven crazy by her, the part that needed more space, the part that was convinced we just weren't suited. *Now* I sometimes will think: 'I'm almost glad she died before we had to deal with *that*'—some painful or difficult or you-gotta-be-here-now-for-this issue. But I honestly can't say that even the part of me that just wants to sleep on into eternity isn't sorry.

"I was also furious! And I was afraid to be, especially at first, when I still had the idea that she was hiding or that it was all a mistake or on a trip or something and would maybe come back. I was afraid being angry would keep her away. I think I'm still afraid to be angry. It feels as if I don't want to admit that the loss of someone could affect me this much.

"As part of the initial reaction, I felt that now that I had lost the most important thing, I was invincible, nothing could hurt me. I went to sections of the city I normally avoided, I took risks. After that, though, came a long period of feeling that *everything* could hurt me, especially when I saw that I was going to go ahead and form attachments to others and open myself up to more loss.

"What I miss most about her is the way she would try. She wouldn't throw in the towel, she kept coming back for more even if what I was currently dealing out wasn't too appetizing, in the hope? belief? that it would change. It was a consistency, an essential there-ness, that I find now is rare. I felt that, as long as I too kept trying, she would never say, 'Oh, hell, I give up.' I can never replace her."

Pleasures of Relationships: What Are the Parts of Love Relationships Between Women That Women Most Enjoy?

86 percent of women say that talking, often being affectionate at the same time, is a number one pleasure in their relationships:

"Talking, affection, daily life, visiting friends."

"Swimming, talking, having sex, dining, being affectionate. Daily life together."

"Talking, laughing, cuddling, doing things together, going to the country. Affection."

"Making love, hugging, holding, talking, having sex, being affectionate, talking some more—daily life together. And—playing music together, reading out loud to each other, hiking and bicycling together, holding each other and being intimately non-sexual."

"Talking. Seeing movies, plays, talking about them and being affectionate."

"Walking and talking on the beach. The relationship is very important to me. I feel very peaceful in it and I know that I perform better in work and in play because of the stability and satisfaction I feel from it."

"I was very happy last week when we spent an entire day together without planning a thing ahead of time. The spontaneity was wonderful. I felt the most carefree I had in months. In general, I love to share and talk about all the little things happening in my life, every day. It is important to me."

"I enjoy talking with her the most. I look forward to telling her all the little things that happen in my life and hearing what has happened in hers. Being able to talk about anything and everything. Also socializing with her."

82 percent of women say their love relationships with other women (and their friendships) are excellent in that they are able to talk easily and intimately:

"It is very easy to talk. I feel very close."

"Talk is sublime. All sorts of good talk—we both do it."

"When we talk, it's long and deep and revealing. We are accepting and understanding."

"It's usually very easy to talk. She'll talk often about feelings, ideas, reactions, etc., and we encourage each other to continue this. It's a very new relationship. I do feel that I need friends to share a separate life with too. There are parts of me that I still keep to myself, secrets or fears that aren't ready to go public. She understands that too."

"She and I could not survive in a relationship unless we communicated feelings and ideas. For instance, she can say to me, 'You're being too clingy,' or I can say to her, 'You're being too distant.' And then we talk it over."

Gay women's descriptions of their happiest times are very appealing:

"I love just being with her! Sometimes when we're together we spend time reading. We are each in a separate world, yet we are together. I also like cuddling and being affectionate. Sex is definitely a top priority!"

"I am as happy as possible right now. We have a few rough spots to go through yet. I'm very inspired by her, I love our easy feeling of intimacy. I guess what I like least is I never really know how she feels at any given moment, as she finds it very hard to talk."

"I was truly happiest when I fell in love, when I was being held by my first lover, within her arms in bed at night."

"Laughing, talking, drinking, eating, discussing—we make love through all of it. We're passionate in different ways all day. It's wonderful and fun being together."

"I *love* cuddling up and watching TV movies together. We love intimate conversations. Making love is fantastic. (We don't say 'having sex'—it's too cold.) We are both very affectionate. Even in public we aren't really intimidated by stares and smirks, we just ignore them. We think of our openness as a way of desensitizing people to homosexuality."

And, atypically:

"Fooling around—sex, drugs, and rock and roll!"

The second most frequently mentioned pleasure in women's relationships, listed by 81 percent of women, is sex; most women say sex with another woman is highly enjoyable:

"Sex with my partner is great. Do I enjoy it? Yum. Usually orgasm? Yes! The best thing is the playfulness and that sex between us is a metaphor for our closeness emotionally."

"Sex is wonderful. I love it, almost always orgasm. The worst thing is when it ends. Sometimes I roll around the bed with sheets and pillows and blankets, caressing and rubbing my body against them and grinding. These things are incorporated into our lovemaking. The great thing about being with her is I feel perfectly fine doing *whatever* I want to during sex."

"I love everything about my lover's body—her breasts, clitoris, vulva, vagina, anus, oral sex. I love to taste and smell her, and I think I look and smell delightful to my lover. She knows brilliantly how to stimulate me, though she does very little direct touching of the clitoris. I never have to guide her, though I did the first few times, and now, can she make me come! I have all kinds of fantasies—aggressive, brutal, loving, exhibitionist, sadistic, masochistic, rape, heterosexual, bisexual, animalism, sodomy, pedophilia; I cast myself in all different roles, male, female, child, animal, multiple people. My lover has been everything under the sun and whole groups of people—all kinds of situations. I tell her before, during, and after what the fantasy was, or sometimes I don't tell at all. And frequently there is no fantasy—just us."

"Sex with my current partner is very good. I enjoy it and almost always orgasm. I like oral sex, but prefer to orgasm manually. I feel the freest I've ever been with her. We talk during lovemaking, and I have watched my lover masturbate and this helps me bring her to orgasm. I feel most passionate when the feeling between my lover and me is very close and intimate. It's as if I know where I'm going and am sure I'm going to get there. When I am most passionate, I get off on pleasing her and feeling her excitement. Sometimes I wonder what pleases me more, having an orgasm or feeling her have an orgasm."

Women describe why they prefer sex with women:

"The softness, the affection, the gentleness, and the mystery."

"*Everything* is soft—soft bodies, *breasts*, smooth faces, wet crotches . . ."

"I love women. Their warmth and sensitivity. I love to please them."

"When I was nineteen and in love, I just found it so warm and sharing and exciting. There's a bond between us that my experience with men could never compare to."

"I like women's ways, bodies, passions, gentleness/power. I like the lack of violence and hostility."

"Sex with men is not loving and caring as it is with women (and gentle). Everything is more humane."

"Sex with women is much more satisfying than with men, especially the loving closeness and equality of power."

"Women are much better lovers than men, and are more concerned with their partner's feelings."

"Initially sex was very good, much better than with my male lovers. Reasons: with her I had no preconceived angers or resentments, or few of them, and we had no need to use the vagina except for what felt good to the possessor of it."

"I have never felt pressured to have sex by a woman. I was *always* pressured by men. I had not one date that didn't pressure me. I had several dates that got physically violent, and I usually felt pressured into pretending to like being mauled while at the same time trying to sweetly put a stop to it. There is still pressure, on the street, in conversation, to respond with interest to men's sexual advances."

Sex between women can be extremely tender:

"She's always tender with me. As far as sex *talk* is concerned, she's not used to it, as I am her first lover. But she likes it when I talk to her like that."

"She is a very tender and caring lover. She has never really told me she loves me yet, but I know she cares a great deal for me. She says I'm beautiful but I really don't think of myself that way. She loves my body and thinks it's sexy. That, she never hesitates in telling me."

"I feel desired when she makes love to me. I also feel she recognizes my vulnerability and is treating me gently."

Or sex between women can contain very racy elements:

"Sex with my current lover has been better than at any time in my life (and that's saying something). We quickly discovered that our fantasies run in surprisingly similar directions, and have been able to be open about our needs and desires in new ways. We are both very passionate and almost always orgasm. We especially like to fuck, with fingers or dildos, in every position we can dream up. We like being restrained and sometimes tie each other up (one at a time, of course!) or hold each other down. We like rough sex, squeezing hard, biting, pulling hair, occasional whipping. I also love to eat her cunt, which drives her crazy. She doesn't like to do it to me so much, which wouldn't have been O.K. in previous relationships (it was a real bone of contention in my last one), but is O.K. here because sex is so good in every other way."

"S/M has a very important place in my sex life. The feelings that are let out through some of our practices have yet to be expressed as well in any other way. The trust, first of all, must exist on a very deep level. Once trust is established, letting go is easy. The bad press S/M has gotten has had an effect on my acting out in fantasy. With my lover, I have found a bonding in trust, love and openness that surpasses any I have experienced in the past."

"I like rough, passionate sex because it goes beyond the barriers of 'niceness' that so many women build around themselves. There's no feeling of holding back, as there so often is with politically correct gentle sex—'S&L,' as one of my friends has dubbed it (sweetness and light, that is). My current lover and I have experimented some with S/M and bondage and found it very exciting and sexy. Everything we've done has been totally consensual and the 'bottom' (who it is varies) always has control, along with the illusion of being out of control. We've included things like spanking, whipping, hair pulling, and biting, never to the point of injury or even marking. What makes it so good is the feeling of completely letting go."

Many women, both straight and gay, point out that there is a difference between what they may fantasize and what they may want in actuality:

"Both my lover and I fantasize prolifically about S/M, rough sex, and rape, some bondage. Though I've experimented with lovers, I find I hate these things in actuality. They are only delirious in fantasy. Sometimes in the heat of passion we spank, bite, strain against one another and penetrate each other, kiss hard, but none of these things with any roughness, pain, or force, especially not force."

While some women (of all ages) feel very free, 32 percent of women (of all ages) are very shy:

"Masturbating in front of my lover—I've wanted to do it with her, and I've talked her into doing it in front of me a few times, but she doesn't like the idea at all."

"I don't like penetrating a woman's vagina, probably because I don't like having it done to me, but I've learned to do it and some women really like it. I've only penetrated a woman's anus once—what I like to do is rub the outside of it, which is very sensitive."

And while sex itself is very good for 76 percent of gay women,* 29 percent also report problems:

"I have genital herpes, so I've been masturbating with lovers for years and years. I don't remember ever feeling bad about touching myself, although I don't like having to be on the alert lest my partner come in contact with the lesion. My lovers have mostly accepted this very well. I especially like it if they caress me and kiss me while I do it. My current lover is very turned on by seeing me touch myself, and I can really get into putting on a show for her."

"Some women have tried to pressure me into sex. I gave in to one in particular: she had decided we were having a 'relationship' because we had slept together a few times. I liked her as a person and felt extremely guilty about the fact that I didn't return the intensity of her feelings. I hated every minute of sleeping with her on those occasions. I gritted my teeth with anger whenever she couldn't see my face."

"It's a sad fact—or not so sad, depending on how you look at it—that

*See *The Hite Report* on women, Chapter 7.

women don't push as hard for sex as men, and that other women don't feel as guilty about saying no to women as they do to men. I don't think it means women want sex less than men—either the ones who ask or the ones who refuse. But they feel more guilty about sex—especially lesbian sex."

Younger women especially can sometimes be shy and have difficulty having orgasm—even with themselves:

"I just started having orgasms for the first time in my life one and a half years ago. I never masturbated as a child. I tried it as an adult because I knew my friends had or did, but became frustrated because I didn't get stimulated clitorally easily. Then I went to a sex therapist. I resented having to learn it at my age. I was angry that I hadn't done it as a child. I started to get into it a little bit after a while, though, once I developed some patience with myself. Now that I orgasm, I enjoy masturbation very much!"

"I am a twenty-two-year-old lesbian, living with my lover, in college. Sometimes we are both self-conscious during sex, and have a hard time breaking through that. We sometimes can. That makes me feel wonderful, strong, and passionate. When we can't it is always a letdown and I feel embarrassed, a failure. Neither of us has orgasms—that is a barrier we cannot break. I don't masturbate. All this is something I want to change. A couple of years ago, I had no desire to look at my own sexual blocks. I now do."

"Many of my friends know that I don't orgasm, period. They give me books on masturbation, personal tips, etc. Some of them have even volunteered to help me out (directly). One friend suggested that when I finally do have an orgasm, I should send out announcements (ha)."

"Even with women, I often feel like I *should* like sex or have sex, but I don't always. Generally, I feel aloof in bed, more of a performer, and have a hard time relaxing. I never have an orgasm with a partner. I feel like something's wrong with me that I don't particularly enjoy sex. The way I orgasm is with a vibrator directly stimulating my clitoris. I've tried masturbating with a lover and am feeling more comfortable with it, but I don't like to tell her she can't give me an orgasm. I have a vibrator on me but I'm shy about showing someone how to masturbate me—I feel like I shouldn't do so. I wind up being more active and dominant during sex because I feel more confident about myself that way than I do the other way around."

———————————

But in general, women together have a much higher percentage of orgasms than during heterosexual sex, according to *The Hite Report* on female sexuality and other studies.

Single gay women now also worry in particular about having sex with new partners. With the possibility of AIDS, as one woman puts it, "I worry because if a gay woman is going to sleep with a man once in a while, it will probably be a gay man. And gay men have the highest risk of AIDS. So if a woman I sleep with has slept with a gay man, this puts *me* at great risk! Especially for having casual sex—or *any* sex. Wow!"

Problems Between Women in Love Relationships

"Having a relationship with a woman you are in love with isn't all peaches and cream."

Two women point out what 93 percent of gay women would agree with—that women together are not immune to problems:

"We used to say that women together would have perfect love, it was just men who were messing things up, didn't know how to love. But in gay relationships a lot of the same things can go on, like one is more distant, or one decides their independence comes before everything else, and so on—which is very disillusioning. Love between women isn't automatic heaven."

"There are also power struggles with women, unfortunately. Like financially—one person being dependent on the other, one being better off than the other—leaving one feeling lesser, if she's financially dependent. And also from the standpoint of needing someone, there's a constant kind of thing that goes back and forth about who needs who so much, who's more dependent, who is less dependent. If I'm too dependent, she gets paranoid; when she's dependent, I get paranoid; but at the same time, if she's *not* dependent, I get paranoid!"

The most typical problems reported by women include:

"We have difficulty letting the other person have their own 'space.' Acting as individuals yet still being a couple."

"We are quite different intellectually. She wants simpler things in life. I wish she would read more, my being in school is very hard. I wish I had more time and energy for us, but there's so much studying, balancing is tough."

"The problems grow out of things we let pass—they come up later on, usually with anger or frustration."

"Instability. I wish we could legalize our gay marriage and be treated like straight marriage by society."

"We are two of the strongest-willed women on earth. I hope we can end our struggles without going through a breakup."

"My mood swings, crankiness, and desire for isolation when I'm under pressure at work are a problem. I should relax and enjoy her more."

"Not enough time together. Too many other commitments: family, career."

"Probably my unsociability. I would change *that* about *myself*. But I'd much rather have her accept me the way I am."

"Old patterns from old relationships. We are using counseling to clarify all this to each other."

"I don't like her social competitiveness—her preoccupation with trivial things, like what people will think."

"She picked a big fight after my grandmother's funeral, and then again on my first day at my new job."

"She criticizes me about being a 'grumble,' and I criticize that she doesn't talk enough in front of other people—though I don't harp on it. She's rather shy. She criticizes my abrupt way of saying things."

"She publicly humiliated me in our community. So I had an affair right under her nose. I paid her back for mind-fucking me."

"Our biggest problem is her lack of spontaneous affection, her tendency to withdraw, shut me out. Be in a rage instead of talking."

"Not taking my feelings into account, or acknowledging them, is what she does that hurts me most. I guess my worst action toward her has been to be too possessive."

"She says I am too nurturing and give too much to others."

"Our biggest problem? My violence, her silence."

"I become cold and distant at times. But she has always said something to trigger this."

"She leaves me hurting sometimes. It is not always easy to talk. We have often and frequently attained the level of closeness I desire, and I believe we can continue to stay close and open. But it's hard sometimes to do this."

Practical arrangements of living are usually not problems; 95 percent of couples living together describe good working arrangements:

"I cook. She does dishes. We always slept together when we lived together, though we maintained two bedrooms. She's tidier."

"Somehow, we're naturally, instinctively synchronized with each other. We both do everything and love doing it for each other. Especially cooking. We cook every day."

"I'm usually at her apartment. We eat out. Never make her bed. Of course, we sleep in it together."

"We both cook, clean up, make beds, do laundry, wash the car, plant the flowers, paint and repair. I'm better at visualizing things, she is better at actualizing them. We sleep together and bathe and shower together."

Women with children have special problems to deal with—although children, as seen, can add complications in heterosexual relationships, too.

One woman broke up with her lover because of her lover's child:

"I had a seven-year relationship which I left because of her child, to tell you the truth. To put it frankly, I could not stand the competition. I don't like sharing. Which is probably why I have monogamous relationships. I didn't want to share my lover with her daughter. Although most people won't admit that, that was the reason. And your daughter is your daughter forever. There's no divorce, no getting rid of, no nothing, and she's going to outlive her mother, you know. Not even death. And I cannot cope with that. I simply can't.

"Also, the daughter didn't know that she was gay, so that we had to be hiding it all the time. That was a terrible pressure. I didn't know if I would have felt differently if the daughter had known. But on the holidays, for example, when we all get together, it was 'phony.' But I never wished that she should tell her daughter. You can't wish that. The daughter was too young.

"I don't think children can deal with that. I lived with her when her daughter was between seven and fourteen. Children these ages, who are concerned with their peer group, who want to be just like everybody else in the world, can't cope with the fact that their mother tells them they're a lesbian. That's too way-out for them.

"When they are a little more grown-up, and they can be a little bit different than everybody else, then that's O.K. But not between seven and fourteen. They should be seventeen at least. Out of high school. In high school, you have to go lockstep.

"Of course, there are gay mothers who disagree with this. And that's a big debate within the women's movement, with single mothers who are gay. I've known some who have told their children they don't want to give up their lives. That's why they're doing it. Or they say it's like bringing them up in a Santa Claus world and then finding out that reality is something different. Whereas if you grow up knowing the reality, if it's a happy family it's a happy family, even if you are different. Maybe it's getting easier for kids now. I mean, if you look at the statistics, something like half of kids can expect to grow up in homes with only one parent, usually the mother. So nobody is like anybody anymore anyway maybe.

"But my lover never did acknowledge—she and her daughter have never acknowledged her sexuality, although it is quite clear, now that her daughter is older, that she knows it just as well as I do. She's very bright. But they never discuss it openly, and apparently that's more comfortable for both of them, that's why they do this. Yes, her daughter is straight. She's twenty-four and totally into dating, everything."

Coming out to one's children can be even harder than coming out to one's parents:

"I wish I could talk to my daughter more openly about my sexuality. My twenty-year-old understands to some extent and is supportive, but my seventeen-year-old refuses to hear. And so I can talk with them only about their feelings, expressions, fears, and hesitancies about heterosexual sex. This they discuss with me, but not my present life. A shame."

Is love between women more equal? Do women treat each other with more respect? Is emotional giving and sharing more reciprocal?

96 percent of women say they do feel loved equally, or in a satisfying way, by their women partners—with daily ups and downs, of course:

"We love and need each other equally. I feel loved and satisfied. She is respectfully attentive, she pays attention to me when I need it, and I do to her. I'm more likely to state my desires, but I encourage her to do what she wants and say whatever she feels."

"I love her—possibly a little less. I think she needs me more. I feel loved. I'm satisfied."

"Sometimes I feel loved less, but not much. It seems that she needs me more, but in fact I don't think that's true."

"We both think that we love each other more than we're loved. Sometimes she *thinks* she needs me more."

"I feel her love and it warms me and feeds me. We both express need for each other, although I think she expresses it more easily."

But 74 percent of women together also have their share of the standard daily insecurities of love:

"I am always questioning whether she really loves me, or if I love her more. I don't enjoy feeling that way because, by projecting into the future like that, I affect the present with my paranoid mood."

"Sometimes I feel loved, other times ignored. Am I satisfied? No."

"I feel more needy than I think she does. I feel loved, but I am somewhat insecure. I want her to want me more. Yet, I would dislike it greatly if she depended too much on me or drained me."

"I feel loved and satisfied at this point and I think our feelings are quite equal. But before, part of the problem was my feeling I needed her more than she needed me. If there were any feelings or needs that were different from mine, my insecurity (in myself) caused me to feel very threatened—which is not exclusive to my love relationship either. I would project my insecurities and desires onto her. I depended on her to make decisions for me. My unwillingness to be responsible for my own needs has made it necessary for us to be separate. I want to learn how to trust myself to take care of my own needs and only go into a love relationship out of a genuine desire to be with the person, to share with them, not out of a need to attach myself."

"Our most recent 'fight' wasn't really a fight at all, but rather a conflict of needs. It involved a misunderstanding. My lover and I had planned to spend Saturday night together and she called Saturday afternoon and expressed that she was tired and drained and needed some time alone. I took that to mean she didn't plan on spending the evening with me. What she had meant was that she needed time alone then, but not the entire evening. At the time, I felt hurt and angry that she didn't want to spend time with me. We did spend time together later and talked things out and the evening was very pleasant."

"The relationship wasn't all so smooth from the beginning. At first, she didn't feel the way I did toward her, and when she told me this, I hated her. I was so angry. I pretended to care less than I did, to see what would happen. It worked. When I wasn't paying much attention to her, she started attaching herself to me. Now I never let her know how much I need and desire her because I never want her to feel smothered. I am very emotionally dependent on her, but will not let her know it."

"I think I love her more, but only because I will permit myself to fully feel and experience my feelings. I think I am less afraid of the vulnerability. She can't/won't—for many reasons—open up. So this relationship isn't very satisfying to me right now."

"Things are pretty balanced between us. I might not want to admit I need her as much as she needs me. I have always felt that being needed more put you in a stronger position—a position I've had a hard time maintaining in a past relationship. I feel loved by her. Sometimes I wish she were more demonstrative. Of course, in public it's hard, but also with friends, she could be more demonstrative. She could give me little gifts, things that would make me feel special. I'd love the attention. She's not too adventuresome, but I enjoy what I do get. That's part of being involved with a woman in her first relationship, I guess. The pluses and minuses weigh out evenly."

29 percent of women in gay relationships express similar feelings of insecurity and emotional "neediness" as those expressed by women in heterosexual relationships in Chapter 3 ("The Emotional Contract"); they sometimes feel dependent and less than desirable:

"I've always been too emotionally dependent—afraid of being deserted, even when I wasn't sure I wanted a relationship. Just being deserted is a failure.

The 'sickness' in my loves has always been a result of the fact that I didn't have enough resources outside the relationship."

"When things are good between us, I feel somewhat loved. I may require more than what's usually acceptable."

"Ultimately, I've found that I am very afraid of intimacy. I used to choose almost exclusively people who were emotionally unavailable. I think the aspect of that pursuit was 'exciting' on a 'romantic' level. It's also about being a victim, not deserving, etc. It also keeps the focus on others and off me. Therapy has been tremendously helpful. It comes down to a matter of me accepting and loving myself and not looking to others to do it for me."

"I tried to keep Jennifer with me (my lover of three years), tried to please her, give her 'time,' 'space.' I was terrified of losing her, but hardly spoke of what was actually going on in the relationship—i.e., that it was going downhill. I often felt not loved enough."

"At twenty-seven, I feel very distressed and lost, I'm trying to work out of it. That's why this relationship is important to me. It centers me, gives me reason for continuing. I think my partner now loves me more than I love her. I'm more or less her first love. However, I will leave it when the time is right. I am the biggest problem in any relationship. Because it's not easy for me to talk to anyone, especially about inner thoughts, feelings, etc. I hate wasting time, I have a great fear of time running out on me. What I want most from life is freedom and peace of mind. On a scale of 1 to 10, I would have to rate my happiness as a 2, a 1 would be death."

"When I lived with my lover, I have to admit I actually encouraged her dependence. She wanted someone to lean on and who understood train schedules and could balance a checkbook, and I never did anything to make her feel she could do those things quite well for herself. This was very satisfying after years of being told by my mother that I was unbelievably helpless, dependent, childish, etc. (However, I shouldn't be blaming either her or my lover.)"

"I can be aloof when I start feeling too close—I withdraw or cool off emotionally, physically, and in other respects. I need affection but don't easily let myself have it when it's accessible. I know this comes from growing up in an alcoholic family. It shows my lack of trust, insecurity, low self-esteem, my own pride. I'm aware of this and only *very slowly* changing."

Most gay women (58 percent) also say they do not want "overdependency" emotionally from their lovers, which makes them feel uncomfortable:

"If she seems too dependent on my approval, always wanting to be to-gether, I feel uncomfortable, smothered!"

"Drained. It's not fair. I don't want to be someone's mother."

"If it's too much, I run like hell."

"Suffocated."

"I feel uncomfortable when someone's very emotionally dependent on me—like I'm expected to reciprocate. It's funny because I help them get there."

"Confined, angry."

"Trapped."

"It's never really happened, but I think I'd run for the hills if it did. It's not anything I want, and perhaps I choose women who are not very dependent."

"I feel restricted, tied up, restrained, made accountable. I hate it."

But 42 percent say they enjoy providing reassurance; insecurity seems to be accepted between women, and meets with a more supportive reaction, even from women who feel uncomfortable with it, than the reaction often found in men: *

"I'm always very clinging and emotionally dependent upon lovers, as they are with me—we'll tell each other how much the other is cherished dozens of times a day. Yet we can be strong and independent when the situation calls for it. I need constant reassurance, and provide it for my lover, who needs it too. Any lover I've ever had suffered these fears and needed them assuaged. I love to smooth them and build their confidence in the relationship daily, even when the relationship is of long standing."

"I would feel glad if someone was very emotionally dependent on me. If they needed me more, I would be there for them. I've never felt suffocated or owned in a relationship."

Generally, there is much more concept of mutual responsibility for the other's emotional well-being between women:

"If someone does seem very dependent on me, I can't just dismiss her demands without feeling guilty and inadequate."

"When she is angry with me, I want to stay with her until she tells me all her feelings, no matter what they are—because this will hurt me less than not remaining close, and if she begins to silently resent me, we will not be close."

"We try to talk things out on the spot."

Fighting

Of course there are fights between lovers, just as in heterosexual relationships— only throughout, the tone in these women's descriptions sounds less alienated than the tone of those in Chapter 2:

"Our biggest fight would have to have been when Sharon was so depressed she felt no one could pull her out. She tried to get me to stop seeing her, to

---

*See Chapter 3.

leave her alone to let her fall into a deeper depression and wallow in her own misery. I told her no, I wasn't gonna let her do that to me, her, or us. We went through a big wrestling match which let out some of the anger she had against herself."

"Biggest fight? She was a bitch because my corn on the cob was not immediately ready for her meat dish when we were entertaining. Seriously, we almost never fight."

"What do we fight about? She says I shout at her. Does not like me to have any contact with my past lover. Also, she thinks I am too still—I don't always *do* things—am too often content to *be*. I criticize her not letting me always be the Number One Boss, Cat, Beeootiful and Million-Dollar Chickie and sometimes I have to be number two or three. She is also fond of using tea towels as all-purpose wipes."

"The most recent problem occurred over holding hands. I was in an affectionate mood and wanted to touch her constantly. She was moody and didn't feel like being close. I got angry at her unresponsiveness and she was mad at me for not respecting her need for space. She said, 'Lovers don't always have to hold hands.' We fought in whispers because we were with other friends, and I cried. We made up the next day."

"We fight about what I feel are cases of not taking responsibility on her part. We fight about me changing my mind, we fight about the limitations we've put on our relationship, what's expected, how much is made-up, how much is real and mutual. We try to work things out totally before we go on to something else, so resentments don't build. I am just in these past three months allowing myself to loosen my control of my emotions."

A large number of fights (48 percent) are about jealousy and outside lovers:

"This past weekend, we had a big fight. After two days of being very close—bad weather and so we remained indoors—during the early evening she received a phone call. She spoke in front of me and I could tell that the person on the other end was upset about something. When the call terminated, I asked who was that, immediately feeling guilty about invading her privacy. She shot me a look but did not answer. I thought that she would explain after the TV show we were involved with was over, but she said nothing. I was dismayed. I went home earlier than usual.

"We met for dinner (at her request) the next night. She wanted to *know* why I was acting cold and annoyed. I told her. She said she would have told me at a later time. The call was from a young woman who about five to six weeks ago came on to her. She told her she was with someone—but this person has called my lover several times—visited her at work—always angry about a bad relationship she is having with her girlfriend. I knew nothing of this. She knew I'd be angry and didn't know how to tell me. I feel she's been dishonest and not seeing that this person is trying another route to get her."

Are there more breakups over sexual attraction to others than in heterosexual relationships? See pages 597–604.

87 percent of women in couples report being able talk through problems—even if that "talking" is at a rather high pitch:

"Usually we get problems out before they are *real* problems. This means having long, serious emotional talks, which are usually resolved. Usually, we both feel good about them—but when I was drinking too much, I would get defensive and we had a few screamers. It's okay now, though."

But for 14 percent conversation and important talking are still not easy:

"If she's willing to open up, it's O.K., but she is very self-protective sometimes. But right now is also a very hard time for her, she has to deal with a lot, things like her abuse as a child. Still, it's very hard for me, being so shut out. Other times, it's so easy, we're close and so warm."

"Sometimes I don't listen when she is telling me something that is hard for her to express. I only hear how it affects me, not what she's saying about her feelings. And she's not able to talk things through once she's upset, while I want to keep after it until the subject is worked through completely."

"I am not really a good talker. I am a better writer. My thoughts and feelings get clogged between my mind and my mouth. I still usually talk more than she does. I would like more intimate talk, but I don't want to push it. It will come with time. We love making future plans together. But as much as I love her and love talking together, I guess there will always be parts of me I can't share."

"It's fairly easy to talk, but I talk more about feelings and the relationship. It's hard for me to criticize her, because she gets defensive very easily. And I get preachy!"

"Our biggest problem is that both of us are bad at bringing up issues. I am, at the moment, going through lots of feelings that need to be aired. Sexual moments are when the communication flows more freely."

One couple is in the midst of working this out:

"There's a lot of bickering. For example, when she gets uptight about her work, then she gets whiny, cranky, nervous, and starts complaining. My initial reaction is—aggression: "If you want to give me shit, then I'm going to give you shit." I tell her things like "You're pompous," "You're impossible," etc., feeding the fire. I have a tendency to do that. If somebody gives me a lot of grief, I throw it right back. So I have to grab on to that irra-

tional, very immature side of myself, and say, "Wait a minute, I'm not arguing with my mom!" Which is also the way she deals with me, like she's
arguing with her mother. It took me a while to recognize this in myself. I
just sat there and looked at the way she argued with me, and then I realized
that that's the way I argue with my mother. That's the way she argues with
her mother, bitching and moaning and griping about everything. But now I
am learning sometimes to say, "O.K., wait a minute, just remember everything you've learned, sit there and be calm, deal with this in an intellectual
way." But it's a fine line, I have to control myself. So far what's doing it is
two days a week of therapy at eighty dollars a week. That's what keeps me
from going over the edge.

"Taking a very calm, logical approach does work. When she becomes
irrational and whining, I just sit back and say something very rational, intelligent, and adult, like "Please, do you have to be so hurtful?" Or try to find
something to say that can sort of strike her, slow her down a little bit. Or I'll
say, "I'm really trying my best. I've tried my best to make everything work—to
give you everything that I possibly could. And this is the best that I can do,
so I feel like you shouldn't complain so much. Then she'll usually quiet down
and really try."

15 percent of women say there is <u>too much</u> talking and analyzing:

"Some women, I think, over-analyze their relationships. For example, in
my recent personal experience, being lovers with a social worker, it sometimes
seemed to me that she viewed our affair as an extended psychotherapy session.
I resisted her attempts to do therapy on me and to force me to talk about things
sooner and in more detail than I felt comfortable with. Don't get me wrong,
I'm not opposed to therapy, which has helped me a lot in the past. But it belongs
in the therapist's office, not in my bedroom."

"In my current relationship, when something needs to be talked over, I'm
usually the one who brings it up. This is a reversal of the pattern in my previous
relationship, in which my then lover analyzed *everything.* "

*One woman says she has found this—or that there is a lot of talking that is at
once draining, intense, <u>and</u> great—a sort of total introspection:*

"Definitely, relationships with women have been a lot more traumatizing
than any relationship I ever had with a man—because of all the introspective
shit you go through. I mean, in my relationship with Frank for five years, I
was introspective, but he wasn't. Strangely, it's *more* traumatic if both people
are. I had always thought it would be less, because if you're doing it by yourself,
it's alienating. But you gain a lot more by both people doing it, in the long run.

It's painful, it's agonizing, but you gain a more solid connection. I can still completely relate to everything my lover (ex-lover) says, whereas I can't relate to what Frank says, even though we are still friends."

There is also some physical violence between women—in 18 percent of couples, especially younger couples:

"I was never hit by a lover but one did have a record of having physical fights with her ex. When she was upset and screamed, she'd clench her fist or grab me. I told her if she ever hit me, she'd never see me again. She didn't, but I left anyway eventually. (She was an alcoholic.)"

"We had a huge fight over nonsense. I calmed down. She wouldn't. She berated me. I begged her to stop. I felt humiliated. She hit me. I slapped her across the face and told her I hated her. I meant it."

"My ex-lover beat me up and I felt terrible, I felt meaningless and abused and thrown away."

"I've had a few fights with one of the lovers I used to see. We would hit each other. I was the one who would start them. Sometimes when I get angry I want to hit something."

"My first lover hit me in the last stages, while I was breaking up with her. She was angry. I let her. However, one day I threw her against the wall and knocked her out. Then I decided never to try violence again."

One woman describes the final stages of breaking up in her relationship, and how angry and ambivalent she feels about it:

"I'm twenty-four. With my present lover, I am happy and unhappy. We have been together for almost two years—the most passionate relationship of my life. But now we are in the process of changing our relationship, at my insistence. I don't know how it will turn out. We are to move separately at the end of the month.

"I like most our communication and sex, and the least, feelings of inequality. I feel loved but at times not appreciated enough for exactly who I am. Our problem from her end is that she doesn't tell me negative things she feels soon enough. She also says I don't tell others how I truly feel, trying to avoid conflict. But she's not tactful, she is vengeful, petty, and at times mean! She is also very affectionate, loving, and sexy, and I love her—even when we fight.

"I always felt I was dangerously losing my individuality the further I immersed myself in a relationship. Now I feel as though I'm breaking new ground. I want to be a lot less wishy-washy about my lovers' demands in the future. I am just now allowing myself to loosen my control of my emotions. I even yell, scream, and curse at times. Alas, we are just learning to walk away with residue from anger. Before, we had to sit and process it all until it had totally evaporated. Then we discovered you can't always do that—sometimes it takes time to see the other's point of view, or maybe uncover what it was you were really angry about. Oftentimes, the issue you fight over is a vent for something else, something you didn't know how to bring up. I do this a lot.

"Usually after fighting, we would make love. It used to be: she would cry and I'd hold her. It's been a long time since we did that, it seems.

"We are trying to work things out. We go to a counselor every other week. I've cried a lot. I hate her at times so intensely. I also love her more than anyone. I have lots of mixed feelings about what I want and how to proceed. So I am throwing myself into work. I can work twelve to fifteen hours a day with no trouble. I have also turned to my friends. My family has been very supportive of both of us—especially my mom.

"But I don't know if I'll ever be in another committed relationship. I guess I just don't know what I want. I don't go out with other women, I still feel like I should consult with her before making plans, sometimes I feel I should do things with her that I'd rather not, 'cause she might not have anyone else to do it with. Most of these feelings I make up, she doesn't say anything to make me think this and probably doesn't even realize I feel that way.

"Neither of us had extramarital affairs (that I know of). We go back and forth on the issue of monogamy. My mind can handle it, it's my heart and pride that have difficulties with it. I am too insecure to feel O.K. if she were to go out and bed other women. I would truly like to be able to feel good—O.K.—in a non-monogamous arrangement. I guess I'd rather know—before, I didn't want to know. But that entails too many lies, omissions—then distrust. Yuck. I the past I've gone to bed with married women. Now that I've been on the other end, I promised myself never again to be that selfish and inconsiderate. I liked being with unavailable women in the past, they weren't going to heap a ton of expectations on me.

"Our sex life is great! Super exciting—I could ask anything of her. I always orgasm. The best part is the excitement and the feeling of intimacy. I worry that I will never find as fun and fine a lover as she. Passion is very important to me. I would never be with a woman in a primary relationship if there wasn't much passion between us. I like the way passionate women embrace life, it's not just a sexual characteristic, it's a way of living your life.

"Love to me means putting another woman's welfare before all others, caring, being interested in what happens to her inside and out. Love changes—in the beginning there is flirtation and game playing, excitement, trying to impress her. I guess I'm just in a stage of asking questions now. I have all of life before me, to make it whatever I want. If I only knew what that was."

Are Women in Gay Relationships Monogamous?

While 94 percent of women in lesbian relationships believe in monogamy, one-third have had or are having sex outside their relationships:

"I was having an affair with another woman while I was with my present lover. The affair grew to be very serious and I started to feel love for her. But I was, and still am, very much in love with my present lover. I was very confused and felt guilty. But still my feelings grew for the other woman. Eventually, my lover found out and we almost broke up. I still have strong feelings for the other woman, but we are not having an affair anymore. I think it's better that way because I still have the one I really love."

"I have had sex outside of my relationships, every one. My partners usually knew about it. I felt O.K., never guilty or secretive. The effect on the relationships varied, depending on how secure each of us felt. I believe in monogamy but not to the point of denying myself satisfaction or experience, and not to the point of holding my lover responsible for my sexual gratification."

"I was intensely attracted to a woman. I was not in love; I was in lust. It had nothing to do with my lover. The other woman and I were very attracted, knew what we were doing, what the limitations were, and we did it. It was fine. Fun. Non-involving in any sense of long-term."

"I love women. I love to flirt. I love the seduction. I've never slept with other women when I wasn't sleeping with my primary relationship. That doesn't seem at all sporting."

"When I was younger, I cheated occasionally, but I do not like feeling deceitful. I think monogamy is preferable if you have a close relationship with one person."

"The affair is/was not serious. It was with a close mutual friend. It fulfilled a need in me for adventure and passion, but this need is not as important as my need for my more comfortable primary relationships. The sex outside my relationships was/is basically fun and is not something that is absolutely necessary."

"I've had sex outside the relationship and knowingly to my partner. I feel good about it. Neither of us believes in monogamy. We do believe in a primary relationship that comes first and foremost."

"I was nine years younger than she was and felt I needed new experiences. A couple of times I started to love one of them, but I never had a mental affair or spent time with these women. It was only *sex*. A few times here and there."

"I was seeing someone, but finally I stopped. It made me sad. It was with a man I had been seeing before my relationship with the woman began. The affair was not serious. It was the revival of a long-ago connection. It had more to do with sex and more to do with youth and the past."

26 percent of gay women say their lovers have had or are having sex outside the relationship now:

"The biggest problem in our relationship is that Kris is involved with a man at the same time. This causes me pain because I want her exclusively. It is also difficult working out the mechanics of the relationship (i.e., when I feel I need to be with her, it is sometimes impossible because she already has planned to spend time with him)."

"First, I was bugged by her fidelity (suffocated)—and then I was bugged by her infidelity (betrayed)."

"I felt bad—badly used. I want her to level with me."

The percentage of gay women involved in sex outside their relationships is much lower than that of married women or women in long relationships with men; another difference here is that almost always the other woman knows—or finds out very quickly—that something is going on. More gay women know about their lovers' affair than do heterosexual women. This is probably due to the more intense and emotionally close or verbally sharing types of relationships between women, as opposed to the more distant relationships most women speak about in Chapter 1.

Is the possibility of contracting AIDS now changing the patterns of monogamy or casual sex in lesbian relationships? While gay women, as other women, discuss AIDS, there is no lessening of sexual activity because of this possibility, the principal reason being that the incidence of AIDS is so low in the lesbian community. While the male homosexual community has been specifically touched by this disease, the gay female community has not. And since few lesbian women have sex with men, it is even more difficult for the disease to be transmitted. It is most likely perhaps when a woman is menstruating, and for this reason, many gay women have had themselves tested.

Most women, finding out about their lover's affair(s), are very upset:

"My last lover was a woman of forty-one with two children. I went out with her for two years. I took the relationship seriously, and fully expected it to continue until eventually we would live together. I felt totally dedicated to her, in a way that surprised even me with my non-monogamous leanings! She, however, mistrusted my feelings, and began playing all sorts of mind games with me. Seeing how far she could go with me, what she could get away with. Of course, I let her, explaining it all away to myself as: It's something she needs to do, it's important that I let her follow her needs, etc. And she did. Took the ball and ran with it. Going out with others, trying to make me jealous. I rationalized it away. It eventually got quite terrible, and we broke up with a gigantic fight."

"The *first* time I broke up with my girlfriend was spectacularly draining. She is very important to me. I'm definitely the closest to her of anyone, but I'm not sure I'm in love anymore. This is why I just moved out. I love her but I don't think I'm 'in love' anymore. I don't think she's happy either.

"She is a horrible philanderer and always has been. I put up with it for three years. We lived together two years. I finally decided I didn't need that bullshit, so I moved out. I still see her and sleep with her, but I sleep with other women too. After all that time of watching her go out with others, I decided to try it too—now I like it and I'm not sure I'm basically monogamous anymore either.

"I think I wanted to see what my lover liked about it so much and maybe to get back at her—not get back, but catch up. Feel even. I was terribly angry and she was away a lot. Being with another woman in another city, I did it once—I liked it, did it again, had some one-night affairs, and I'm now on my third 'relationship' outside the relationship. None have been serious, but the one I'm having now may become so.

"I started therapy because of the awful time I had dealing with my breakup with her. It helped immensely. I was horribly jealous when she was cheating on me and I wasn't. She constantly lied about the other women. I read her diary. Now I don't give a shit. I'm very independent. I went on with her when I shouldn't have. But breaking up is awful. It's as bad as divorce, of course. I try to get over it now by having lots of sex and plenty of fun.

"It's odd, I've had the best sex of my life with her—definitely. But this woman I see on the side is also a delight in bed. I'm afraid I'm going to lose even that sex link with my girlfriend. We have great sex. Very physical, very verbal. She talks dirty to me. She tells me how excited she is, she tells me what I look like. We moan, we coo, etc.

"So, my relationship has become peripheral. I want to leave it. I think we'd make better friends and that's what I want. I've hated her at times. I've had violent fights where I've *hit* her and been hit—over some lover or other of hers. She has done things to me I never thought I'd swallow, but I did come back for more abuse. I had to work my tail off to keep this thing going for three years, and now I want out. In fact, I am out."

The agonies of being jealous are universal, and can happen to anyone in love, as this woman's story shows:

"We were out at a disco. I got jealous about the amount of women who went up and talked to my girlfriend. I was feeling insecure because she seemed very happy to talk to people, and I didn't see her half the night.

"The next day, I felt really bad about it, and I started to think, 'Why am I acting this way? What's wrong with me? I have to get a handle on this.' I wanted to explain to her, and say, 'Look, I'm really sorry, it's just my own insecurity.' So I talked to her on the phone, and she said, 'Listen, I've got to get out of the house tonight, let's go to a movie or something.' And I said, 'O.K., O.K., great, let's go have dinner—we'll talk, and then we can go see a film,' and she says, 'O.K.'

"So I get home from work, and she's in there putting her makeup on, and she says, 'Let's go out to the bar.' And I said, 'To a bar?! I don't want to go to a bar. I really want to talk to you, we need time together. I don't want to go to a bar again, O.K.?' She was very insistent. 'Let's just go for a while.' Finally, I said, 'Look, I really feel like we have to talk.' I'm freaking out, and she's saying, 'I just want to go out to a bar. I don't want to talk, talk, talk, being heavy all the time, being so serious all the time! You don't want to have fun!'

"Then my response became: 'O.K., all right. You want to go out? We're going to go out. Boy, are we going to go out!' I decided to go out with the idea of getting totally obliterated-drunk. That was the way I had to deal with it. I didn't feel strong enough emotionally to say, 'Well, you go out and I'm staying home'—although I do that now. I knew that I was wrong, essentially, the night before, so I didn't want to create a whole other compounded issue on all this.

"It started out, we were hanging out together, kind of moping, 'cause we were still annoyed. Then we started hanging out with other people. I ran into this girl I knew and started talking to her, so this made my girlfriend very happy, 'cause then she can just go and do what she wants. She stayed outside, talking to the people outside the door. Then she comes running over to me and says, 'Isn't this wonderful? We both are having a great time at different parts, and we're still together. We can still have other friends and meet new people and still be together. Isn't this like a mature relationship, right?'

"So I'm saying, 'Yeah, yeah, yeah,' and meanwhile I'm drinking rum. We ended up hanging out till I don't know how late it was, and I just kept on drinking. I got completely drunk, got like thrown into a cab, taken home, put into bed. I mean, I don't even know how I got home. It was one of those nights where the next day you're told everything that happened to you, everything that you did.

"The next day, I woke up in a complete panic, because I woke up and she wasn't there. She was not in the bed. I started to flip out. I'm thinking, 'Did I come home with her last night? I can't remember.' So I get up and she's not in the house. I panic. Then she calls and I say, 'Were you home last night? Did you sleep with me last night?' And she's really pissed off, saying, 'I slept with you.' Now, I become a complete lunatic at this point, right? An utter fool, drunken, crazy, insane, a schizophrenic person, all due to insecurity from previous relationships. She had left the house at seven in the morning. She couldn't sleep and she was upset from the night before because all I kept talking about in my drunken state was responsibility and finances and 'somebody has to do the laundry.' All my resentments were coming out.

"I went through four days where I was totally sick to my stomach, couldn't eat, couldn't function, couldn't do anything, and that's when I ran to see my therapist. My feeling was that I'm not going through this all over again. I'm going to work it out."

10 percent are more philosophical about whether a relationship is monogamous or not:

"I don't think my lover is sleeping with anyone else right now, mostly because of lack of energy. I would prefer monogamy but I don't require that of her in order to stay in the relationship. Mostly I'm concerned with what she gives me. If that's O.K., then I don't worry much about what else she does. Of course, I want to know what's going on."

"In her past she's been pretty innocent. She only got into some heavy petting with one boy. How do I feel? Everybody goes through it. I'd like her to be monogamous but I'm not possessive enough to try to force her to be that way if she doesn't want to."

"I know she has. It's O.K. with me. I don't believe in monogamy."

Arguments may not be over affairs, but over flirtations or perceived flirtations—some real, some the simple attractions of acquaintances, enthusiasms of friendships:

"The worst thing she ever did to me happened on a recent vacation, when she flirted with me all evening and then wouldn't come to bed with me. Instead, she stayed up late talking to a friend of mine who'd come along with us, telling my friend she was attracted to her. She completely ignored my needs to be with her and to know what was going on. I was very hurt and my friend was surprised and freaked out. We talked this one out, and things have smoothed over. But it illustrates her occasional obliviousness to what's going on outside of herself.

"During this recent situation when my lover stayed up late telling my friend that she was attracted to her, I was in bed in the next room feeling miserable, not really sure what was going on. My friend says my lover wanted to go to bed with her, but my lover denies it, so I don't know exactly what the truth is. The worst part of it for me was that she 'tuned me out' during the whole incident. When we first talked about it later she was very defensive, but afterwards she apologized and we've since made up."

One young woman says there is too much intermixing of affairs among friends in her group, possibly because of the relatively small size of the gay community in her area:

"This kind of stuff goes on all the time in women's groups. The groups become really incestuous, one person sleeping with one person's ex-lover and then the other one, and everybody knows what everybody else is doing. If we had affairs with strangers no one knew, that would make it easier, probably—but the gay community is such a close-knit group and the numbers are not that big—so you wind up sleeping with lovers of ex-lovers and mutual friends, and it's very painful sometimes. That goes on continuously and there are no scruples. Nobody has any morals about anything, it seems.

"I think that this has to do with women subconsciously thinking that we obviously have no morals to begin with, to be having a gay relationship in the first place. Therefore, why should we put any confinements or restrictions on ourselves? Also, if you're gay, then you're living an 'alternate life,' and why should you conform to what society says is morally right? We're not conforming in any other way, so why are we supposed to conform in this way, to monogamy? Monogamy is something that's been institutionalized, set up.

"That seems to be a lot of the mentality. Although the ones who talk about it in an existential way have generally ended up being the ones who are screaming the most when their girlfriend is screwing somebody else. They say that this is all right, this is the way things are, and then when it happens to them it's a whole other story. I watched that happen with two friends, who sat there and told me and my girlfriend, 'Oh, yeah, well, it's O.K. to have affairs. We handle these exterior affairs. I have mine, and my girlfriend has hers. We just cope with these things, because they're inevitable, and it's going to happen.' *Then,* when it actually ended up happening inside *their* relationship, the one who had been talking the most about how they could handle it was totally losing her mind!

"Meanwhile, listening to them, my girlfriend gets the idea that this all could work out, that this could be O.K."

Lesbian extrarelationship sex tends to turn into friendship or a long-term affair; "casual sex" is usually harder to have with another woman than with a man, as one woman explains:

"I found it much easier to have casual sex with men than I do with women—in fact, I find it almost impossible to have the kind of 'fun' but essentially impersonal sexual encounters with women that I used to have with men. There is no way you don't get to know the other woman in the process—

there is a lot more talking, more affection—you become friends, at the very least."

Being the "other woman" in a gay relationship is eventually traumatic, according to most women:

"My present lover was in a monogamous relationship when we met. We had a 'stormy' affair for one and a half years before she finally broke up with her. It was *hell*. I wanted her to leave, we had periods of not seeing each other for weeks or months at a time, then we'd get back together when we couldn't stand it anymore."

"I was in a relationship with a married woman for two and a half years. I minded that she was married but I was getting out of my masochistic phase and put up with her stuff."

"I was in love with her. It was painful. I knew she needed me but I knew I couldn't give her the day-to-day stability that her lover gave her. Our affair inspired her, gave her something she needed, gave her strength. Her own relationship grew from it. I was never resentful, because I wanted the best for her and I knew we could never live together."

"My first relationship was with a married woman. I was twenty-one years old and didn't know what I was getting into. She had cheated on him before. I did want her to get divorced, but not for my sake—for herself. Unfortunately, she did move in with me and it was the worst hell (one of them) of my life."

61 percent of gay women are and always have been monogamous: *

"I'm fifty-four. I'm basically monogamous by nature, have almost never had sex with someone else when I've been involved with a lover. I believe in monogamy for me as most closely fitting my emotional realities. I would *much* rather prefer my lover to be monogamous. But I don't think it's necessarily the only solution for everyone."

"The relationship is monogamous. I find it difficult, in an emotional sense, to maintain more than one sexual relationship. I would like to be able to handle more than one affair at a time because I think I would grow from it and I like to experience new feelings. It is possible that I would have sex outside of the relationship in the future and I would tell of my intentions before the affair started. I know my partner is not having sex with anyone else. I trust her and would not want her to be monogamous. It is very important to me that my

---

*Particularly, women over thirty in gay relationships tend to be more monogamous. This is just the reverse of the trend among heterosexual women in marriages: Women over thirty who have been married over five years *increase* their rate of extramarital sex.

partner and I communicate to each our feelings about monogamy. We are currently at the same place in our feelings but that could change in the future."

"I would not have sex with anyone else while involved with her—there is absolutely no reason to. Yes, I want her to be monogamous and I want her to tell me if she is not."

"It was a terrible weakness in her to go after women. You can find your friends charming, but why do you have to act on it? There are women that I'm extremely attracted to, but I have different kinds of relationships with them, because I've channeled it into another way."

"We're wife and wife"

31 percent of gay women have been or consider themselves currently married, in a woman-to-woman marriage:

"I like to be married. The best part is the constant love, and the worst is the fights. We're wife and wife. We got married. It was originally her idea. She proposed. We decided to get married because we were terribly attracted. It wasn't a hard decision—it took me one night of thinking. I felt very good, elated, and my feelings for her didn't change. Her actions toward me didn't till after six years of marriage."

"I was married to a woman for many, many years. Being married is very secure and I like that. Being 'safe' in the institution it represents. It happened when I finally stopped denying that I would be with her 'tomorrow.' I gave up orthodox religion and family when I did it. The worst thing was discovering how phony the 'institution' is and how unsafe. I expected it to be exactly like promised in America, and it was very, very different. One marries a stranger and divorces an alien."

Fear of Non-Lasting Relationships

Do gay relationships last? Does gay marriage work?

The most pronounced problem for gay women/couples—aside from lack of public acceptance and oppression, being forced to hide their lives—is perhaps the increased difficulty involved in establishing gay relationships as permanent relationships. If the possibility of permanence is increased by an institution which accepts, makes public, and glorifies heterosexual love (legal marriage), gay women do not have access to this or a similar weighty institution.

Many gay women express a fear that all their lives they will go from one relationship to another—and even if "one" lasts ten years or so, imply that this is not satisfying or does not feel very secure:

"I'm happy now, though I wonder how long our relationship will last. Even though I trust her and know I can count on her, and feel she loves me and my body—still, what happens if the love dies?"

"Is it 'normal' in relationships that the passion dies after a while? And what do you do then? Do you stay, out of commitment, but live a dull humdrum life together? Or just drift from one partner to another every few years, as you fall in and out of love? I really wonder what happens when you are older."

"I feel kind of depressed right now. I don't think I will ever be in a relationship more than three years. Will I go on just working things out with different women all my life? It's different from my picture of life—I think things should be more permanent. Maybe relationships come and go no matter how hot. I'm getting cynical in my old age! But when I am in love I am very energized and turned on to the whole world."

Thirty-nine percent of gay women in this study had been or were in relationships of more than ten years (of women over thirty); 46 percent of women over forty had been in such relationships.

In fact, the average length of gay relationships of women over age twenty-nine is not too much different from the average length of relationships and marriages (averaged together) of heterosexual women over twenty-nine; and the average length of gay relationships of women over twenty-nine is *longer* than the average length of non-married heterosexual relationships.

Breaking up: Is it harder for gay women?

Since there is no institutionalized public acknowledgment of gay relationships, * i.e., "marriage," breaking up is more of an emotional test for gay women, more of an emotional ordeal; it brings up all the questioning about the possibility of permanent or lasting relationships—and in many cases, the pain must be hidden, endured alone:

"I felt my first great love at eighteen. When we broke up I was really confused. I wondered if I was really a lesbian or if she was the only woman

---

*And even small public acknowledgments are off limits, as one woman explains: "It bothers me when we, as lesbians, can't have small affectionate interchanges in public—like kissing when I come home if someone who is not gay is there. I'm not talking grand passion here—just the daily niceties." As some consolation, the very secrecy involved can at times mean that the lesbian community is a much more close-knit, almost extended-family kind of group, providing more support for its members.

I would love. I felt really alone and isolated. Because I wasn't close to my parents, I couldn't tell them. I had no outlet for my feelings and I suffered a terrible detachment from everything. I was in my first year of undergrad and it was a miracle I didn't fail. For many of my lesbian friends, it was the same, the first breakup was devastating because it opened up everything for questioning again. You have to decide then: Is this a life choice or just her? It was so painful but really pivotal in my own coming out. I wept stronger and deeper than I ever have before or since."

"The biggest emotional upset I've faced is coping with the breakup and subsequent loss of a three-year love relationship with a woman I'd lived with and hoped to be with for many years to come. She is now a friend, and in fact my closest friend. Our 'lovership' ended a couple of years ago. I am still partly in love with her. I was happy in the middle period—after I'd stopped fighting falling in love, accepted being loved, and before I feared losing her love. When I lost her, I felt the love in a piercing way. I cried myself to sleep because I couldn't make her love me and need me and want me. I was probably the loneliest in my life at that point, was destructive to myself in other ways."

"My second lover absolutely broke my heart when she left me. I felt totally alone. I loved her very much. I relived the loneliest period of my life when my father and mother separated and I felt estranged from the world. It took about a year and a half to feel whole again and feel that I could deal with her again as a person, although after maybe eight weeks I was functional and often cheerful."

"When I ended a long-term relationship (my first) it was dreadful. Even though it was mutual, and I knew she couldn't give me what I needed, the pain was awful. It was a long time till I could sleep without the TV on—and I just cried and cried for what seemed like forever. I've never been married or divorced, but pain is pain. I didn't have any legal stuff to deal with, so maybe that is worse, but many lesbian couples would—they own houses together, etc."

"The worst was ten or eleven years ago, when a lover I lived with and whom I loved deeply left me without much warning. First she blew hot and cold for about a month: 'We don't spend enough time together' followed by 'I need more space.' She'd fallen in love with a woman with whom she'd had a two-day affair on a recent trip to Europe, and I made the mistake of not feeling jealous. I thought my lover would realize that this other woman was thousands of miles away while I was here for her. She didn't. Perhaps she wanted me to make a big scene or something—I really don't know, never figured it out. Or perhaps she was just bored and dissatisfied with her life in real-world New York, which wasn't as exciting as a European vacation, and her relationship with stable, ordinary me, as opposed to her Swiss girlfriend, who, apparently, was on the verge of suicide for reasons totally unrelated to my lover. Shortly after she left me, my lover proceeded to drop almost all her friends for reasons none of them ever discerned. The breakup was intensely traumatic for me; it was seven years before I was able to fall in love again, although I did have relationships in that time. I moved into a small room in an apartment with two straight women near school, started eating compulsively and thinking about suicide. Fortunately, I went into therapy and didn't kill myself."

"When I left her, I thought my life was over. It's been two years now and it still hurts. Even after two years we've never really 'settled' or 'finished' things between us. We are fairly good friends, see each other two or three times a month, but the subject of 'us' and our past is carefully avoided. Whenever she needs help, financial or moral support, etc., it seems I'm the first one she turns to. At first, when I left, I worked harder, engaged in extensive self-abuse, and drank a lot. I felt nothing was solid or permanent and still have that view today."

"Not counting my present relationship, the past lover I loved the most was the one I lived with when I was twenty-four. I was extremely happy in this relationship, which I thought would last for the rest of our lives. I saw it as the cornerstone of my life, something that would be a solid foundation for me, something to come back to to renew my energies. We had an active, satisfying sex life, but this was not when I felt the most passionate. The relationship ended suddenly (in my view, at least), after fifteen years, at her initiative. I was wrenchingly lonely and unhappy. . . . When she broke up with me (over the telephone), I cried for three days. I thought I would never stop crying."

"Even if I want to break up too, I find it devastating. Worse than divorce. A woman lover becomes so many people to you—you end everything."

"It took fully five years before I had completely recovered from this first affair. It was very intense for me. I made more concessions and compromises than I had ever done before, and worked very hard on the relationship. After three and a half years, she left one day, which really shocked me. That was three years ago, and I still have a lot of anger, and I don't talk to her now. The first year of this last breakup was extremely difficult—I used friends a lot more than I ever had before."

"The hardest breakup was with my lover of three years. Her decision to end the relationship was due to the fact that she had gotten involved with someone else. We tried to work it out in a rational way, opting for a shot at non-monogamy. We tried for a while, but it soon became too difficult for either of us, and her new lover also. It was what a divorce must be like. We tried to be friends, but again realized this situation wouldn't work because I was still in love with her. She moved out about four months later, and I began to wake up to reality.

"It was incredibly difficult for me—I didn't accept it at first. We were still living together after breaking up, and hearing my ex and her new lover making love in the next room was absolute torture. I started going to therapy and later joined a group for lesbians who had just broken up. (Where I established contact with a woman who later became my lover.) It helped minimally—for

I was angry and felt totally rejected and couldn't understand why *she* had done this to *me*. It took me almost a year to really accept the situation, to be able to think and talk about it without getting hysterical. I felt then that if I could live through that, I could live through anything. I felt as though I'd hardened, lost a part of myself after the end of the relationship.

"I threw myself into my schoolwork and job. They were the most permanent things in my life. They were the connections to sanity."

"I'm not completely over the breakup after two years, but am mostly so. At least, I can see that we weren't/aren't 'meant' for each other. I never stopped seeing her, I couldn't do that because being away from her was harder than being with her. I talked about her but after a while tried not to and resented that I was still in love. I sometimes had a hard time concentrating on work but took solace in it. The most stable thing in my life during the breakup was definitely not my family, they didn't understand, didn't ask. Friends? *She* was my best friend. Work—it had its ups and downs. So, without any real support, for the first time in my life I felt I was losing my own strength.

"Now I'm cautious, somewhat untrusting, and doubtful about my ability to fall in love. I entered therapy around the time of the breakup. Therapy helped because I needed permission to talk about my feelings, and because I was able to see why and how holding on was related to neglected aspects of my life. I concluded that there is no 'cure,' except for trusting myself more. And stopping picking the wrong lovers, alcoholics, drug abusers, emotional abusers. I'm getting 'better.' Someone I'm currently 'seeing' is someone whom I respect but I'm not that attracted to her! Still, now that I'm more aware of my tendencies, it helps."

One older woman sees the changing of relationships over a lifetime in a different, more positive, way:

"I've been gay for thirty years. I've had long relationships, so have my friends, but almost nobody stays together 'for life.' We used to worry about this—we thought heterosexuals seemed to stay together far more than gay couples did. The obvious answer, we said, was, well, we had less problems leaving each other than heterosexuals did, because we didn't have to cope with a divorce, the legality of it. And we mostly didn't have children. And very rarely did any of us have enough money to have property in common as we do now. It was easier. Also married women may not have left because they were not working and so they couldn't, financially. Even despite what they say about alimony, it really wasn't happening, so therefore there were a lot of economic pressures, whereas with lesbians there wasn't any economic problem.

"Gay men stay together longer, and always have, for years and years, because sexual monogamy is not important to them. They stay together because, if it's a compatible relationship, they all mostly let each other go out and screw with other people, having no problems. What keeps the relationship together is, you go home to your good old buddy that you're used to living with, whereas most women cannot do that emotionally. The whole mind-set and psychology of women is different."

Another woman points out the instability that may be built into gay relationships by their non-acceptability, which also necessitates their completely individually designed shape: *

"A non-conventional relationship, with no rules, is much more difficult. In a marriage, in the traditional sense, if just by chance the roles that people are taught happen to fit two individuals, then that's a pretty good arrangement— they know exactly where their circumscribed areas are, what they're supposed to do. That's probably reassuring. But for most of us in gay relationships or marriages or whatever, *now*, there aren't any rules, really, so you're kind of making up your own as you go along. It's this constant thing of trying to figure out how it works. I sometimes wonder if a lot of the problem gay relationships have is trying to make them fit into the stereotypical relationship (straight) that we have been brought up to know and accept as being 'the way' to have a lover. On the other hand, during the 1960s when everybody was saying, we want to get out of the traditional marriage, it's unhip to be monogamous, etc., it led everybody to believe that they had no right to put their foot down at *any* stage, and that didn't work either."

But eventually, many gay women realize that "breaking up" is not to fail somehow in life, if one has had rich relationships:

" 'Breaking up' is a horrible expression. It should be banned. You build something *unbreakable* when you really love. Some of the most gratifying moments in my life have involved realizing that the three people (two women, one man) I have *really* loved are still very close to me. I feel they are my three true friends. One woman I know would do anything for me. And the romance is still there with all three. It's beautiful. It isn't about living life together. It is great affection and respect. I am richer and stronger because I've known them and vice versa. The separation is difficult. I hide in my work. I don't talk to my friends about it. I write. I sleep. I miss the smell of the person most. Suddenly, the bed is empty. The spaces, places we've shared, become a part of our histories. I usually make a total separation by moving across the Atlantic. It is later, much later, that the beautiful friend-ships have begun. It takes a while to get to know oneself again, to find one's internal equilibrium, to get perspective."

*Some single women in non-married, heterosexual relationships also speak of this problem; see Chapter 6.

And not all breakups are so painful:

"I've had several breakups with lovers—they were all pretty traumatic— except for the last one, which happened after being together four years. It was a mutual decision—but she was the one who brought it up. It was just time we went our separate ways. I was shocked it was so easy—it probably was because the distance between us had been growing for so long . . . I knew for a long while things were not right."

"It was difficult but ultimately liberating. I wanted to break up. It was an unhealthy relationship, too dependent."

"I had no regrets about the breakup. It didn't make the pain less, but she couldn't give me what I needed, the commitment I wanted, and it just couldn't work out. I did not feel like a failure—then or in other breakups—that's not what it's all about. Sometimes things just can't work—so you hurt, and then you heal, and then you try to find someone else."

An amazing 64 percent of gay women remain long-term friends with their most serious lovers: *

"Admittedly, neither one of us is clear as to where our relationship is going. She said she didn't want pressure, I said I wasn't pressuring, but maybe I had to pull back to protect myself and basically we started a verbal struggle, with me trying to throw the responsibility to her in terms of making the choice of how often or if we'd see each other. We both got very contracted and extreme. We decided we couldn't see each other at all, we had to break up, couldn't talk on the phone, etc.

"Finally, we realized the futility of what we were doing, and realized that we couldn't lose touch with one another, it just wouldn't work. We may not be lovers anymore, but we love each other, love spending time together, and will have to see what unfolds. The important thing is still to enjoy each other, when we can. I have prayed a lot, gone back into therapy, talked to friends, and tried to love myself and be as positive as I can."

One woman talks about her frustration—and what she longs for:

"Sometimes I get tired of going through life negotiating relationships and working it out. Like, will I ever arrive at some kind of plateau where I finally get the results of my labors? Once you've run the last mile, they may still leave you for a younger, or more intelligent, or older, or whatever woman—or a man! You've got to worry about whether your lover is fucking somebody else, or *will* find somebody else—whether they still like you today, or if they like

*See also pages 544–67.

the way your hair looks, or *something*. Shit that I really can't be bothered with. And whether or not I'm intellectually up to par.

"I guess what I would want in a relationship is—like a marriage. Somehow, when I look at having relationships with women, I don't see that as ever being possible, or lasting for a long period of time. (You know, first you get "the house," etc., etc.) Maybe there would be more security in a relationship with a woman who has children, who is used to responsibilities. Maybe I could have a more solid relationship with a woman who is older than I am—who has already gone through all the responsibilities I know how to handle too. I've been taking care of myself and other members of my family for all these goddamn years (even though I'm still in my twenties). But the women I know my age in the gay scene haven't had the same experience with responsibilities.

"Solid relationships seem hard to find. Even my friends who had solid relationships, although they don't break up, are all having extramarital affairs. So what do you go for? Do you go for the security of a loving, caring relationship or do you go constantly for passion? And if that passion drops off, do you then run out and do something else? I don't know. But if I'm going to be in a relationship where I'm going to give it everything I've got and build my life around it, then I want a solid relationship with somebody who shares the responsibility, who would go all the way, try to build a life together too."

Gay Women and Money

How do most gay women handle finances in their relationships? share money and expenses?

Finances and economic dominance or dependency are generally not a big problem in gay relationships—although it is common for one woman to make more than the other, and 21 percent of women are supporting the other in a couple.

Here are typical ways women share expenses:

"I've got more money, but I give her as much as she wants (which is not very much). We've got a common financial goal. I'm willing to work hard to set us up for life so we can do other things, such as pursue careers in fields that don't pay, like politics (honest type) or the arts."

"Financial arrangements do not affect this relationship. We are both working and pay our own obligations. I make more money than she does, so I offer to pay for social activities most of the time."

"We both work as professionals. We share all the finances equally. We each control our own money. My friend/lover owns the house and I pay her rent."

"She pays a certain amount each month toward rent. I pay the mortgage. We both buy groceries. Most important for the relationship is to keep the channels of communication open and to be understanding."

"We split the expenses but I supported her for one year or so. I usually paid the bills (I wrote the check, that is) and she paid me back when she was making money. I've always made more money, so it's been mostly a function of who had what."

"I control the money, pay the rent, buy the groceries. Temporarily I must take on more responsibilities until she gets her degree. She is a full-time student with little income."

"We have separate incomes and do not combine or share money. We spend freely and equally on each other. We maintain separate residences. We are in comparable income brackets and our finances have no bearing on the relationship."

"We keep it separate. Keeping track is hard, but we prefer having our money separate—especially at times when our incomes are different."

"Our money isn't shared. She fills in my shortfalls in money needs, or helps me use mine more wisely."

"We share our money. Virtually all expenses are split in half. We each contribute x number of dollars to our joint account, rent, groceries, entertainment, dinners out, movies, gas bills, telephone, etc.—all comes out of the joint account. We both work. I made more last year. We'll make about the same next year. She handles paying the bills. I don't always have a true picture of just what we have. She keeps saying no to extra expenses I suggest. I have had similar financial arrangements in my last two relationships. I feel it works very well. It does not have a negative effect on our relationship."

But total dependence can obviously be a problem:

"She pays the rent and I buy the groceries. It's O.K., but if things are not emotionally going well, it feels like a problem. Money can certainly affect a relationship. I think it intimidates me."

One woman whose lover was recently financially dependent on her is questioning her own motives in the relationship:

"I ask myself, 'Why did I pick her, knowing it would be an insecure relationship?' I picked her because at that time I *needed* someone who was going to be dependent on me. I initiated this relationship because I wanted someone to be dependent on me, grateful for what I could do for her, who would therefore stay with me. I needed someone to love me and need me and desire me. Especially sexually. And so, I took this on. But at the same time, I was giving her these quick 'grow up' lines, like you've got to realize this and you've got to realize that, about earning a living, etc. Actually, she *did* go out and get a great job. I didn't expect her to be so self-sufficient so quickly! I thought this was going to drag out for a while, at least I'd have her there for a while before she took off.

"But it happened so quickly—it freaked me out. For all I know, this could turn out to be the best, healthiest relationship I've ever had, because I am strong-willed, and she is strong-willed. Just the same way I wouldn't want someone to manipulate me in those terms, she didn't want someone to manipulate her. I really respect her for this. She immediately said, 'I'm going to go out and get a job, and I'm going to support myself.' She didn't just say it, she went out and did it. She has been working ever since, and makes money now. I have to respect that, even if it means she has to pull away from me in order to be able to get herself to do it."

One couple, very poor at the moment, is struggling not to let this interfere with their love:

"Now, money is short, and we live inside this little square-box room. She wasn't working for a while, and would say she felt completely dependent, and didn't want to feel dependent on somebody. It made her feel lousy, out of control, too emotionally dependent. She would say, 'How do you think your supporting me makes me feel! Me being so emotionally dependent on you, and economically dependent on you. What if something went wrong? Then where am I going to be? What if we have a fight? Where do I go?'

"I understood her reaction completely, but at the same time, I wished she wouldn't have those feelings—I was still in a passionate dream world. And I am very idealistic: in work, I deal with the realities of things, but love-wise, emotionally, I am just from the heart. I felt like, we'll work all these things out, don't worry! I didn't say that haphazardly, but knowing that I would have to put in endless hours of effort to work it out. But I know it'll stay a problem if we don't do something about it."

Do gay women have money—or are most poor?

One woman gives a surprising description of her gay community:

"There's a kind of cliché about gays not having money because on TV they're out there on the street in kind of rough clothes holding up protest signs. And so people get the idea that they are usually poor—certainly never rich! Well, many lesbians and gay men have pots of money. Gay men may, in fact, be one of the wealthiest sectors of the population.

"There is a community near New York which is probably where most lesbians are concentrated. They have all these houses and cars—the women out there are monied. Of course, they are not as monied as the gay men. But for women, as a group, they have money. They own businesses and houses and expensive toys, clothes—all that.

"These women also have money because they have been working all their lives. It isn't like they just came out of a marriage and had to start learning how to earn a living. They've been doing it all their lives. The average age is about fifty. So they've had time to really build up a savings and get used to running their financial lives. There are a lot of wealthy women out there.

"What's interesting is the philosophical change it has brought to the locale. I mean, naturally, even though there are a lot of gay people there, it's primarily heterosexual, as all communities are. But the people who live there have gotten to respect women more because of us. They don't generally walk around seeing a woman entrepreneur as "a lesbian," but they know that an awful lot of women own property there, and run an awful lot of businesses. I don't know if they think whether they're lesbians or just women, but there is a much healthier respect for women there than I've seen in other areas of the country. (Especially in New York City.) There's a woman mayor too, which isn't too common.

See appendixes for a statistical breakdown of the income brackets of gay women.

Being Single and Gay

Do gay women like being single?

62 percent of lesbian women like being single, but usually not as a permanent way of life: *

"I like being single because I have more time for friends and feel less lonely. There are less struggles and complaints."

"I have learned a lot about myself being single. It is wonderful not to have to answer to anyone."

"I enjoy being single, going to restaurants, bars, or parties—this way I can

---

*Statistically, fewer gay women are "single" at any given time than heterosexual women. Is this due to women's liking of relationships, and men's difficulties with relationships (mixed feelings about whether they like/want them?), or women's greater annoyance with men not trusting them as equals—or other factors?

flirt and sometimes end up with a date. Some people are jealous that dating for me is easy. It can be fun but after a while a pain in the ass—the extremes of loneliness are no fun either."

"I need to be on my own right now—for self-inquiry, self-acceptance, self-reliance. I also like the freedom to date several people if that presents itself. I am not looking for a full-time love relationship so that I can focus on really taking care of myself now. But I fear being alone 'ultimately' (which is a total projection)."

One young woman describes mixed feelings that many younger gay women have about being "single":

"I'm a student, age nineteen, also a waitress. I'm introspective, I like to read books about women or literary figures (Virginia Woolf, etc.). I'm left politically. I'm gay, unattached, and relatively happy. I haven't achieved anything wonderful as yet. I haven't had any big, long-lasting love relationships yet either. I was most in love with my girlfriend when I was sixteen (it was non-sexual), and earlier this year I had a lot of passionate feelings for a longtime close friend.

"The hardest part of being gay is to meet women that I find attractive, interesting, and who have values similar to mine. I don't go to women's bars much, and of course it's hard to find such women in non-gay places. Being single gets lonely. I wish I had more good friends. I'm very happy when I'm with a group of friends or relatives and we all have a good time together.

"I've only been able to keep my sanity during this current isolation because I live in a large city and can go to feminist bookstores and see very good, creative plays by gay playwrights and go to nice bars—not the smoky, dirty, dark kinds that make you feel like a degenerate. These kinds of support systems are very good for the spirit. What the rest of the people in other, more backward parts of the country and the world go through, I hate to visualize."

And an "older" woman who likes being single explains that she thinks love relationships are overly emphasized:

"Friendship with women has been my basic support system. Without women it would be a desolate, lonely life. I've had long-lasting relationships with many women. I find women easier to share with and relate to—much more so than men. Now I am sixty-four, currently single. I prefer the intimacy and love of women. Although relationships with others are important (we cannot live totally without love and companionship) I don't see that as the aim of life. Once you find out and discover your own goal, you then can seek someone to share it, if that is your choice. But too many women become trapped in a relationship to the detriment of life's other gifts."

Surprisingly, 14 percent of gay women who do have a regular lover still consider themselves "single":

"The advantage of being single, for me, is a kind of freedom. I can get the best of both worlds—have a lover, but still be able to see friends alone, etc."

"Despite my relationship, I consider myself single. I like being single because I feel free to do whatever I want, no one makes demands on me or my time. I come and go as I please. I like shopping alone, or seeing my friends. Some things I just don't like to share with a lover. But I do enjoy being with a lover while seeing a movie or eating in a restaurant."

One woman has a unique reason for disliking being single—it's a hassle:

"I always liked having a relationship because it saved a lot of time. You didn't have to go out and date other people and concern yourself with whether you were going to sleep with this one or that one. There was always a lot of that commotion and I was always glad to get rid of it. Even though it's fun, there's a lot of time consumed in this whole thing. And then, in a relationship there's always somebody to do whatever you want to with. You have someone to go to the ballet with, to movies and parties, and that's nice too. It's always nice to have a partner. And someone to go on vacations and play with, etc. A relationship is nice."

21 percent of gay women, of all ages, feel they would like more time not being committed to a relationship, as one woman describes:

"The way I've been seeing relationships lately is that they are constantly traumatizing and constantly drag me away from what I should be focusing on. I mean, I've definitely gotten good things too, but a lot of traumatic aspects seem to go along with love. It becomes debilitating. In fact, I'm not sure it's worth the trouble to have a really intense relationship!"

56 percent complain that they have difficulty at times finding someone who is "right" for them:

"It is very difficult the older I get. I can't find someone I really have things in common with."

"It's very difficult if you just go to bars. The best thing is to go to places where a lot of members would be gay, so that you have such a large circle of friends that that's how you meet people. You meet people mostly from friends that you know."

"My profession deals almost entirely with women, but I don't like to have love affairs with people I work with. So it's difficult to meet women, since I live in a medium-sized town, and there is only one bar—which I don't like anyway."

Coming Out Is Hard to Do—But Most Women Sound Very Happy About It

Women just coming out can be very shy:

"I am eighteen years old, blond hair, blue eyes, medium build, and am very creative with the way I think and act. I'm in love right now with a very beautiful woman, but I don't have the guts to ask her how she feels about me, which leaves me pretty much confused. If I get up the courage to talk to her about the way I feel for her (even though I think she knows already), I hope we can come to some agreement on a relationship (we've been to bed together already once). I don't have sex as much as I want to, which is a lot. My mom still thinks I'm a virgin. This whole affair with this woman I'm in love with is very frustrating but exciting. I can feel the orgasms pent up inside of me waiting to come out with her. The hardest part is letting her know how I feel."

"Just recently, I have begun to include women in my choice of sexual partners. My relationship with my friend has grown much more important. We have made love. When we made love, she stared into my eyes and whispered my name. We masturbated each other. With her I loved sex. This is especially significant because, in the past few years, I have not enjoyed sex very much. I love to touch her body. It is so thrilling."

Most women under twenty-five who have recently come out feel good about their lives, but often are told by others they are "doing something wrong," "making a big mistake":

"I am twenty-two years old. I recently informed my mother that I am lesbian. She took the news horribly!! She believes the only way I can be happy is if I marry and have children. This really shocks me, as she is very miserable with her life. Although she is usually quite understanding about most things, she could not deal with the fact that I was a lesbian at all; to her that represents total failure!"

Or women themselves feel they have "wrong thoughts" and desires:

"On the one hand I feel that I have certain bisexual tendencies, but on the other hand I don't. I love making love with a man but I just have this curiosity about women. There, that's it. It doesn't sound like that much of a problem, but it bugs me. I have alluded to this 'problem' with my fiancé but we really haven't talked about it. I feel I am accepted and understood by him, I guess, but I still can't reveal a few thoughts and feelings to him because of my own insecurities.

"I began to tell him something a while ago . . . but I couldn't. I hinted. The reason it's weird is because it has to do with sexuality and we both are open about that. But this specific aspect of myself cannot be shared unless I am comfortable with it myself. I guess I'm not. It's not that he wouldn't accept that aspect of me—or understand it—*I* don't accept it or really understand it myself. (How's that for being vague!)"

The period before coming out is often filled with agony, inner doubts, and a feeling of loneliness, caused by trying to make oneself "fit in" to heterosexual "norms":

"I wasn't gay in high school and knew no one who was. I should say, I didn't *know* in high school that I was gay. I didn't like high school. I was lonely, never felt like I fit in, didn't date. I felt like being intelligent was boring and lonely. I started dating boys in senior year in high school, had a few sexual experiences, and then came out to myself at nineteen—so my heterosexual career was short-lived. (I have, however, had a few heterosexual 'interludes' since.) I wanted to be with boys so I would feel normal, but still didn't feel normal—the sex I had was to be tolerated and rarely 'fun.' It was much better with girls (at twenty and later). But even then, even with girls, it took me a while to become really sexual—the excitement was still unusual for me and transitory for a long time."

"In high school I became aware of my attraction to other women, but I quickly forced it out of my mind, telling myself, 'Everybody has these feelings, it's O.K. if you don't do anything about it!' I never considered that I might actually be a lesbian, since lesbians were obviously sick and deviant and I was neither. I remember seeing an ad for *The Ladder* and being very curious to see it, but too scared to subscribe. I discussed these feelings with no one."

"High school was rough for me. With boys, I was nervous, I liked them, even liked kissing some, but found them very aggressive and not very attractive physically. Being with a girl was ecstatic. Although I was gay, I didn't really know what to do with it, so I was pretty much in the closet. I didn't like feeling abnormal. I was loneliest my whole life before I came out. My parents never knew I had sex at fifteen, but I came out to them as soon as I came out to myself. My mother was more upset than my father, who accepted me regardless.

"I felt love right at the beginning of my first affair—an incredible over-whelming desire to know her, a feeling I could share everything with her and not be hurt. We lived off the energy that was created between us. After three years, we broke up. We were still living together when she decided to get involved with someone she worked with. I had thought this woman and I might hit it off as friends. Anyway, they hit it off instead. It was a very bitter time, as I went on trying to salvage the relationship. Eventually, she moved in with her new lover, we tried being friends, it failed miserably. We haven't been in touch for two years."

"When I was in high school (five years ago), I felt ugly, fat, left out, and weird. I think it was related to my emerging lesbian sexuality and my realization I was not about to fit in. I then transferred to an alternative, open-concept school where most of the kids were outsiders—super smart, gay, or from unusual parents, etc. I felt happier—like I fit in most of the time—but still I had problems. My mother was stricter and I had an earlier curfew than my friends. They all laughed at me. I was always between things—my mother's wrath if I arrived home late or my peers' laughter.

"I dated boys from fourteen to sixteen. I felt it was a social necessity, but it always made me feel sad and alienated because I knew I was gay. (I fell in love with another girl at age twelve and we shared some physical affection. I was unable to admit to myself at sixteen that I loved her far more than any boy.) My first straight sex was at eighteen, and my first lesbian sex too. But my parents were proud when I dated boys. They never noticed my women lovers. I felt awful about that because I knew I was a fake.

"Leaving home was splendid. I wanted nothing more than to live freely and openly as a lesbian and explore all the other wonders of life. And that's what I'm doing!"

———————————

But when the decision to "come out" is made, the picture changes almost immediately; the amount of enthusiasm and pride expressed by almost all lesbian women is remarkable: 94 percent feel only positive about their decision to "come out."

86 percent of women describe their first love as important, serious, beautiful—whether they have been "out" for one year or twenty:

"I 'fell in love' in my last year of college with a classmate. I was floored when I realized what was happening to me emotionally. I said to myself, 'You're in love with another woman, you are!' I was shocked, surprised, and very pleased to *at last* have 'fallen in love.' I was shocked because I knew that falling in love with another woman was not considered normal, surprised that I was doing something considered abnormal by society, since I'd always been a very popular girl, dated the star basketball player in high school, a summa cum laude in college. But with those boys I had not fallen in love, and very in love

I was with my Jane. She was my first *love*. I always liked sex, but after Jane I preferred women and sought them out, while men sought me out. I wonder if my aloofness from them, untouched emotionally, increased their pursuit; if it did, that didn't impress me."

"I came to be a lesbian when I was about twenty. I kind of knew all along as an adolescent that I had homosexual feelings, but chose to date boys to cover up my feelings. When I was sixteen, I had a terrible crush on a cheerleader that I worked with in a restaurant. After a time, we became friends, and about four years later, lovers. The entire relationship lasted nine years and was very intense and passionate.

"Sex with women is much more of an emotional feeling and a closeness that I just haven't found with men. It's much more than a different physical touch, it's an inner intensity that can't be equaled. There are no rules or expected sexual behaviors involved. It is the freest kind of love I know.

"By the way, my mother thinks my lesbian lifestyle is great! I like my mother very much, I admire and respect her and think she is one in a million. I can't think of too many seventy-year-old mothers who think their daughter's lesbianism is great and support her lifestyle. I think I am very much like her—enthusiastic about life and always running in high gear. I like my mother's enthusiasm for life and her open-mindedness."

Still, 46 percent of gay women in this study are secretly gay, "in the closet":

"I really had no one to talk to then—and now, even at thirty-six, my parents still don't know—the family would be scandalized, it's just not worth it. I take most of my courage from the personal lives of women I know who are engaged in long-term lesbian relationships."

A married woman who is terrified of what she has felt for another woman tells a quite different story:

"I used to work for a woman and her family, I was a domestic help for them. It grew very emotional, into something so powerful and intense that I couldn't wait to see her each week. The way she spoke, her walk, her whole being was magic to me. She made me happy just being with her. Nothing improper ever took place. She knew the way I felt about her. I couldn't stand the torment I was going through and I also had a husband and children. I loved them so much, yet at the same time I felt so much for her.

"I terminated my employment with her. I deeply regretted making this decision, but I couldn't see any other way out of it all. Seven months have now passed, I have never seen her since, not even passing in her car. I still feel so much for her, I ache to be with her. I feel confused and unhappy sometimes, but I know my duty lies with my husband and children.

"The future frightens me, as I fear I could fall deeply in love with other women. I'm going to night school, and taking an interest in voluntary work to get myself mixing with people of both sexes. I find it hard to come to terms with my bisexuality. I try very hard to curb these feelings for women, but it's painful at times."

One woman remembers what it was like coming out in the 1950s:

"Coming out and being gay was like joining a mysterious underground group—very sub rosa. The big thing then was the bars, and they would often be raided. I've literally known women who have spent nights in jail. It was terrible, a horrendous situation. The authorities couldn't keep them, but they used to terrorize them, terrify them to death with strip searches, intimidation, things like that. I remember going into a bar and checking out where the back exit was, so in case there was a raid I could get out very quickly.

"And you would half expect it. You'd hear some place was raided the night before and so on—so we were all very closeted and surreptitious and there was a lot of pretense and false identities. I used to make up past marriages for people at my jobs. I had used my sister's married name—and made up other past histories. Also, you were stuck with the Monday-morning pronoun: people would ask you what you did over the weekend; you'd tell them, but change all the pronouns.

"Also, in the fifties, in bars a lot of women were wearing sort of butch/fem things. But I was always—for some reason or other—very contemptuous of that. And my crowd was never like that. So if someone came up and asked me, I would take a fast educated guess as to what they wanted, and then that was always what I used to claim. Whatever it was the person wanted was what I would be!

"I remember the first time I saw a whole roomful of women dancing at a bar—it was a breathtaking moment. I'll never forget it. It was at the Bagatelle—the most popular place in New York. Some of the other very famous ones were the Grapevine and the Wind Song. Those places were all Mafia-owned. They used to have a woman front them, a woman running it, but she never owned it. The first self-owned place was the Sahara."

Women over Forty: Becoming Gay for the First Time

One of the most surprising findings in this study is the number of divorced women in their forties and fifties who are having love relationships with women and finding this a comfortable, in fact, excellent, way of life.

Amazingly, 24 percent of the gay women in this study were having a lesbian relationship for the first time after age forty; this represents a definite departure from past statistics. The following woman, previously married and with children, describes this change in her life:

"Throughout my life, my women friends have been strong, courageous, beautiful people whose friendship has meant more than nearly anything else. But never in all of my forty years had it occurred to me that I might love a woman in a sexual way. I have hugged and kissed woman friends, we have wept and laughed together, struggled through our respective marriages and divorces together, worked together. But never did I realize that I would feel physically attracted to a woman. It did not occur to me that I might have the ability to love a woman. I have engaged in conversations in which I espoused the theory that human beings would be bisexual if social barriers had not restricted their thinking, etc. But those conversations were intellectualizing on my part.

"Now suddenly, a new world has opened up to me. I've asked a thousand questions, with dozens yet unasked. I have learned and experienced so much joy and dazzling pleasure that I find it difficult to understand why I didn't discover it before.

"Two years ago, I moved to this state to take on a new job. Since I was here, I had been celibate the entire time. My job was so time-consuming and full of pressure, I had little time for myself. My daughters are older and require attention from me in the evenings. After weeks also of evening meetings and late nights at the office, I preferred to be at home with them, rather than looking about for men. I masturbated occasionally, but even that lost its allure. The responsibilities of my job and my children seemed to drain every ounce of my energy and I spent little time worrying about my own needs. Then one night about a year ago, I lay in bed and masturbated and as soon as I reached orgasm, I began weeping with horrendous, racking sobs over the desolation and loneliness I felt. I felt engulfed with a sea of need—needing to be touched, fondled, caressed, hugged, and kissed. I wanted someone to love me again.

"About this time, through some gay friends of mine, I happened to meet a very special woman. In the beginning, I had no intentions of looking for anything other than female companionship with her—we had mutual interests and would share records. This turned out to be the most wonderful relationship of my life so far. It has literally revived me, and brought me back into the world of feelings, happiness, relaxation—intimacy and love. My daughters think we are just friends—that is all I am prepared to cope with with them right now.

"I still think of myself as single, and probably always will. I treasure my singlehood almost as much as I treasure my self-identity. I love being single. The happiest times in my adult life have been when I was single. My lover wants for us to live together and make a long-term commitment, but I am not interested in giving up my freedom. I doubt I'll ever give it up.

"Sex with my lover is so pleasurable—sometimes warm and nurturing, sometimes passionately heated and overpowering, sometimes fun and games. I enjoy it immensely. I nearly always orgasm (through clitoral stimulation). With my husband, orgasm was an on-again, off-again thing. I was not always sure why I couldn't get there on occasions when I didn't. With my woman lover, I get there nearly every time, just as I do when I masturbate. I have several different levels of orgasm and I just can't seem to control which one or ones I'll have each time. Occasionally, in the past few weeks, I have orgasmed without even trying to do so.

"Having spent twenty-two years of my life preferring sex with men because that was all I knew, now after six months with a woman I can say that sex with her is preferable to any of the men I have known. Her desires and needs for touching, holding, kissing, caressing are much the same as mine. I don't need to 'train' her to know 'how I like it.' With her, I can so much more easily enjoy her pleasure because I know how she feels. I am far more turned on by her clitoris, vulva, and vagina than I am by a penis and testicles. Her orgasm is more powerful to me, a 'sympathetic vibration.'

"All of her touching excites me. My breast and nipples are the most sensitive, and she can bring me the closest to orgasm this way. But it is the clitoris which holds the magic. I'm tempted to say that orgasm is the best part of our sex. However, I did orgasm with my husband and it was not as exquisite as it is with my lover. It is the quantity and quality of holding and affectionate touch which I share with my lover that makes it all so different, so wonderful."

Another woman, age forty-two, describes the "magical quality" of her life now—in contrast to life with her ex-husband:

"I'm a relatively well-adjusted, happy, healthy, loving middle-aged woman, deeply in love, probably for the first time, and closest to my lover—another forty-two-year-old woman.

"There's a glow—a magical quality—to being 'in love' which gives all of life's experiences more joy and delight. It may not be necessary for everyone, but I wouldn't have missed it. We have compatibility on every level—physical, mental, emotional, and spiritual—which has been the key. In the past when I loved someone, my husband and two other men, we only connected at one or two levels.

"My love and I have lived together for two years, and we had known each other at work for four years before. We went on a weekend camping trip together—and fell in love. My son is twenty-two and lives in another city with his girlfriend of seven years. He and other family members are not aware of the totality of our 'relationship,' only that we are housemates. Companionship, total intimacy (including exquisite sex), and economics, all are considerations in our partnership. We've been able to save money, make major purchases jointly, and share our house while renting the second. We have taken all our vacations together, including a study tour of Europe and trips to visit relatives and friends. Our physical intimacy and passion is more tender and gentle, slower but deeper and more powerful. We fall asleep every night with arms and legs intertwined.

"For the first time, the loving seems equal—I have always felt that I gave far more than I received. Now I feel totally loved and secure—and so does she. We enjoy everything about our life together—cooking, dishes, garbage—are all easy and effortless—not the power struggle of my married years. Going to bed at night or for an afternoon nap is our favorite activity—just for the snuggling, holding, and sweet talking.

"Talking is relatively easy and equal. She's learning to ask for what she needs—knowing that it's finally O.K. to ask—that happiness is not related to total self-sufficiency as she had thought. We are both sharing all parts of ourselves—without withholding, judging, or criticizing. Years of therapy and growth experiences before we met had prepared us for a close and deep relationship—but we hadn't found a partner with the same background and expectations until now.

"Next to my relationship to God or self, this relationship is central to my life and happiness—only death would make me leave it.

"Our household chores are shared—the last one up makes the bed. She gardens and does yard work while I do most of the cooking. We both share the dishes and garbage and major cleaning. Laundry is shared—started by whoever has a bigger load. Occasionally we take long baths together with candlelight, champagne, and strawberries.

"We have separate checking and savings accounts and keep track of shared expenses. She pays the mortgage when we're living at her house. I pay utilities since I'm home more. We share groceries, entertainment, phone, etc. There's been no negative effect on the relationship because of finances.

"I can't imagine wanting to have sex with anyone but my partner, but if I ever did, I would not tell. It would only create pain for her.

"A recent especially joyous day was last weekend when we slept late (a rare treat), made love in the morning (our favorite time), fixed a wonderful brunch, and then got all dressed up for a friend's wedding. The service was beautiful—it was like we were being married—or renewing our vows—just to be attending. Then we walked barefoot on the beach at sunset.

.   .   .

"My sex life now is happy, joyful, and fulfilling—actual sexual play to orgasm happens only about once a week, but the touching, snuggling, and holding is at least as important and that's every day. Sex is like dessert—a treat when we have the time and are in the mood—wonderful, but not the core of our love.

"Needless to say, my sexuality has changed dramatically in recent years—from a relatively monogamous marriage—to dating several men—to a committed partnership with a woman. I've become much more experimental and playful. My easiest orgasms are (1) oral sex, (2) vibrator, (3) clitoral stimulation by partner's hand. My first orgasm was at about twenty-eight, after four or five years of marriage! I had reached plateaus frequently, and finally 'went over the edge'—at last—with manual clitoral stimulation for a long time. I had read about masturbation by then and finally knew what it was supposed to feel like. Then I tried fingers, running water, and vibrator—all worked.

"I was vaguely aware of homosexuality as a teenager, but never felt any attraction to girls or women. After my divorce, I dated several men. Some were excellent lovers, but not ready for commitment. Sleeping with my friend on our camping trip ended my search.

"She had already had an affair with a woman—and was much more prepared for the experience than I was. What I prefer about sex with her is the intensity of sensation with the gentlest touch—our bodies match—and we can anticipate exactly what the other wants or needs to bring endless orgasms.

"When I was married, sex became routine, boring, and predictable. Oral sex was a rare (once or twice a year) treat for me, which he obviously did not enjoy. Later, in dating, few men seemed to enjoy giving (all enjoyed receiving) oral sex. Now it's an easy, natural, and reciprocal form of loving—and I don't miss penetration or a thrusting penis at all. Sex merely reflects the state of the total relationship, and seems to grow and enrich, or become boring and routine, depending on all parts of the relationship.

"Passion and stability seem to grow together for us. We are more free to express passion as our commitment deepens.

"I love oral sex—giving and receiving. With a woman partner, it is an incredible chance to 'make love to yourself.' I've always liked the musky smell of sexual arousal in a freshly showered partner and hoped he/she liked my smell too. I don't like S/M and other hurting forms of sex—they are the result of the very immature development of those who participate. Pornography reduces women's power and authority over their own bodies. One date showed me a few magazines and I was shocked and disgusted. I did not get turned on.

"I enjoy anal stimulation—with a finger or small penis. When my vagina was very stretched out from childbirth and before my tubes were tied and my vagina tightened, anal penetration was very stimulating.

. . . .

"When I got married in 1961 at eighteen it was because I hated dating and living at the dorm or at home. I found a sweet, sensitive, sophisticated man and decided I'd do better if I were married. Although we eventually divorced, I believe that my choice was good—I have yet to meet a man with his strengths and qualities.

"Yet later, when my son was an infant and my marriage was very unsatisfying, I cried myself to sleep frequently. I didn't see divorce as a possibility because I took the vows 'deadly' seriously. I was the loneliest when my son was young and we lived in the mountains with no neighbors and I commuted forty miles to a job with no kindred souls.

"For most of our marriage I was the primary wage earner and it was a problem for his ego. The decision making was 'equal' but the earning wasn't and I was always reluctant to veto his wishes—not wanting to 'emasculate' him with money. We always lived on the edge of financial disaster—we overspent and had no savings.

"Most men forty and over are very threatened by the women's movement—feeling that if women gain something, men will have to give up something. My husband had very mixed feelings. Intellectually he supported women's issues in church, school, and work settings—but at home he was hostile about helping with housework, cooking, and other 'women's work.' His head and his heart were not together.

"At two points during my twenty-year marriage I experimented with affairs. One was with a friend's husband (they had just separated). But the sex was no better and he was no more capable of intimacy than my husband.

"We first separated for a month about seven years before the divorce—at his wish. At the time I didn't know that he was dating his secretary—and planned to marry her. He filed for a divorce then—and only hours before it was final we decided to move to California and try again. It was very painful for both of us—we both cried a lot.

"The second time—after seven more years of trying and some therapy—I resolved to end it because the same issues and problems still existed—unresolved. It was not easy. He was angry but unwilling to do therapy alone or together. I had a list of 'needs' regarding the relationship—and a six-month time line. When four months had drifted by with no changes, I set a moving date—and he decided to move. I helped him find an apartment, arranged for a friend's truck, and helped him move. That time I felt very relieved—and knew that it was really over—and that I could start my life anew. I had many friends who helped me through the hard times—and I put much more time and energy into work.

"Being a large woman, over forty, with a Ph.D., makes it almost impossible to meet men to whom I am attracted, and even more difficult to meet one whom I respect. I have always been (or tried to be) honest and forthright with men—not manipulative—and discovered that most of them prefer to be manipulated. They know how that dynamite works and are not comfortable with 'straight talk.' Having long been identified with feminist ideals and causes, I have dealt with men at home, at work, and while dating who were nervous and uncomfortable about women's issues.

. . .

"My current partner is the most important relationship I've had. This is the happiest and closest I have ever been. It's almost too good to be true—beyond any dream or fantasy I ever had of marriage or life with a man. It's the first relationship that does not require 'working at'—it's been effortless for two years. In addition, I've had several deep and lasting (ten-plus years) friendships with women.

"I admire women's ability to endure—to survive and make a good life for themselves and their children despite the political and/or personal climate that men have created. Eleanor Roosevelt and Margaret Mead were early role models. More recently, I admire Shirley MacLaine and Gloria Steinem— would like to be like them in ten years. All four have made real contributions.

"I am very grateful to the women's movement for giving a political and historical perspective to the feelings of powerlessness and desperation that we all experience privately—thinking something was wrong with me—I didn't fit into the mold.

"To women today I say: love yourself first and don't eliminate women as possible partners in life!"

And another woman, living in Texas, describes her life now with her lover:

"I have been in a gay relationship for the past year with my lover. She's a thirty-six-year-old divorced schoolteacher. She is wonderful—she shows un-conditional acceptance of others, especially me. She has helped me through some of my most desperately emotional times. I didn't know I could love this much. I love her just as much as my sister, whom I have loved all my life.

"I am forty-five, born in central Texas. I moved in with my childhood sweetheart at twelve and married him when I was eighteen. We were married twenty-four years, had three children, then separated a little over three years ago. I have two years of college education. In my marriage, we were happy until my husband was unfaithful. I felt devastated. This was probably one of the most emotionally trying experiences I've ever had. I asked for a separation and then left the family. He began dating a nurse and decided to file for divorce.

"I had always been financially dependent on him, it always felt like 'his' $. I thought he wanted it that way. Today I feel glad I've had these three years to grow and know I can depend on myself—even though at times I'm still scared about that. My sadness was about the loss of someone to love and who loved me in return. But I also felt much freer and exuberant! I definitely started living again.

"But, being so eager to seek myself, I wasn't prepared for a deep depression which I had in the beginning—it seemed hard to know who I was as an individual, single and without a male counterpart. Before I met my woman lover, I was frustrated, lonely, and touch-hungry—glad for strong friendships with other women. Being 'single' was important to me as a way of knowing who I really am rather than the roles I've always filled. I tended to follow my mother's role while married.

"So the last year has been a big change for me. First, accepting myself as gay was hard, and then my ex-husband broke confidence about my gay relationship and told some of my favorite relatives. I was unable to handle all of this for a while, but now I am better. Women's liberation is a fantastic process. I would not have been able to make all these changes without it, and I support the movement. I am just against the idea of using anger to convince the opposition to a feminist viewpoint."

Once Gay, Always Gay?*
Once Straight, Always Straight?

11 percent of women express a feeling of freedom about changing their sexual/romantic orientation; some do not want to have to "label" themselves one way or the other:

"I am getting pressure from her to decide whether I am gay or not."

"I felt this pressure to label myself once I had had sex with another woman. And the fact that I 'experimented' with sex with women is always with me now, I carry it around like a shadow—although *I'm* not ashamed."

12 percent of women now between twenty and thirty who do not consider themselves "gay" have "experimented" with lesbianism, as has this woman:

"Although I am not a lesbian, I guess I can be labeled 'bisexual' because of my one experience with another woman. I have never told my boyfriend because he would probably think I was doped up or weird (this incident happened while we were just starting our relationship).

"At first I thought it was 'sick,' but I was wrong. It's just like being heterosexual, only women prefer sex with women. Anyway, I was on my way home when this woman I knew sat next to me (whom I had not seen in a long time—three months) and suggested I come over for a drink. Nothing was ever planned, but as soon as she sat next to me and put her hand on my thigh, I started to get wet. Electricity flew all over my body. Then noticing I didn't say a word (I guess I was pretty surprised), she moved her hand up to my breasts, which sent currents to my brain. Then she started unbuttoning my blouse, skirt, panties, etc., until I was nude. She was wearing a red silk kimono which emphasized her beautiful full breasts. Then she started to massage my neck, my heavy breasts, sucked them like a baby, touched me all over, going downwards until she reached my pussy.

---

*As Alfred Kinsey pointed out, there are not two discrete groups, one heterosexual and one homosexual: "The living world [including the animal kingdom] is a continuum" and heterosexuality and homosexuality are only the extreme types sitting at the poles of this "rich and varied continuum."

"Even though I had never experienced this, I didn't stop her. In fact, I practically begged her to fuck me, but she only smiled and brought me over to her water bed. Then she went to my pussy again and started blowing my pubic hairs apart. She licked me there. Darted her tongue for what had to be at least half an hour until I started to orgasm. Then she thrust three fingers up my pussy like a penis and pumped them in and out. I seemed to feel more pleasure and comfort than from a man. Anyway, she did this until I started to come again and quickly took off her red robe and gently mounted me. I started to suck her breasts while she practically squashed her pussy on mine.

"After that happened, I avoided seeing her at first, but then we became good friends, although we never fucked again. Sometimes I now dream that she's doing it to me with a dildo or with a banana. In short, I just want to tell everyone and every woman that it is not sick to make love (at least once) to another woman. In fact, it's an enrichment to everyone!"

6 percent of girls who are not "gay" later do express physical affection/sexual feelings with other girls in grade school and high school:

"When I was in junior high school, I had encounters of touching and kissing and sucking parts of other girls' bodies at slumber parties—the same was done to me too."

But most girls in high school and earlier do not have sexual relations with other girls—as opposed to boys, who, gay or not, frequently do have sex with other boys during high school.*

23 percent of lesbian women in their twenties or younger do not seem to expect always to be gay:

"I like being single because I'm young and I don't believe in settling down (with a man) until I'm older. I only date women now because I find them much more reliable, lovable, sensitive, respectful, etc. (I've been gay for two years.)"

"Three years ago I fell in love with my best friend—a roommate. It felt wonderful, beautiful, I was completely happy, my sexuality felt wonderful for the first time in my life. She was beautiful—beautiful face—beautiful eyes. The

*In fact, both the Kinsey study and *The Hite Report* on men showed that the percentage is about one-third of boys. On the other hand, girls do start masturbating to orgasm significantly earlier than boys, who almost always start only at the onset of puberty—perhaps a year or a few months before they have the ability to ejaculate, at about age eleven or twelve.

relationship lasted two years and ended by her choice to have a man—the ending was the worst thing in my life."

"I've always been attracted to women, though lately I've had some attraction for men come up. I've only had sex with two men and would like to try it again. I love sex with women because it's so connected on so many levels; I love their bodies, their hearts, their minds—always have. I love the equality of making love with women, the possibilities, the varieties. But I want to know men too."

"She's very interested in finding a nice guy and settling down. So am I! But meanwhile, we'd rather be together. We're very happy. We're in college and have a lot of friends we hang out with—no need to make a decision right away."

This can be very upsetting to women who love these women; one woman describes how another woman's not taking her as seriously as a man she was seeing hurt her—and influenced her to decide to take men more seriously than women herself:

"When my boyfriend Craig first started working so much, I was very lonely. I started having a romance with a woman friend. She was very forward with me sexually, but she wouldn't talk about what was going on and she wanted it to be a secret. I resented that. I was infatuated with her: bought her little gifts, wrote love poems to her, all that. I daydreamed about her all day long at my desk. One night when we were making love, I asked her what she thought about our relationship when we weren't together, and she said that she tried not to think about it. That hurt.

"After a year, she started romancing my boyfriend's brother. When all of us were together, she made it clear that her relationship with him was more valid than ours, although she would tell me privately that our relationship was more important: 'I always have these kinds of relationships with men.'

"I had a turning point one night, not only in terms of my relationship with her but also regarding my relationship with Craig. The four of us were supposed to spend a weekend together. After a night of watching them be a heterosexual couple together—his brother asserting his heterosexual privilege—I was a mess. I hated her and him and I hated Craig. I lay on the bed, with a blanket over my head. We didn't have a car, but Craig borrowed one and took me away. He took me to a lake up north, in the country, and we spent the night in a friend's guesthouse. When I woke up in the morning, I felt happy and clear with my emotions for the first time in a long time. I had lost my feeling for the woman and I had gained a new appreciation and respect for Craig. I'll never forget his gentleness and consideration for me during that time. He was a real friend to me. I married him."

*While most women who become "gay" after being "straight" remain gay, 8 percent of gay women return to heterosexual relationships; the most frequent reason given is a desire to fit in with society:**

"I am twenty-seven years old, have identified myself as a lesbian for eight years but recently became sexually involved with a man. At this point, I still feel lesbian.

"Being involved with a man after eight years of being lesbian-identified brings up a lot of confusion and rethinking. I think he is happy but he is somewhat frustrated with his own life predicament. I love him more than I'm 'in love' with him. Perhaps I am being more wary and cautious. I don't mind that he's a man, but I do prefer women's bodies in being sexual and sexually attracted. I guess if he was a woman that would help or if I was more attracted to the male body. But he is very warm and tender, very loving.

"I prefer at this point to not share all parts of myself with him because I have other close women friends who fulfill some of these needs. He does feel a bit jealous about my close friendships with women but he accepts it. Our relationship is as important as my relationship with my close friends. I am also very physically affectionate with an ex-lover. My partner knows about the kind of relationship we have. I feel good about it—it feels healthy and nurturing to have a woman friend I can be physically affectionate with.

"I feel like she listens to me and we are honest with each other. We get together to talk, eat, sleep, lots of hugs, about three times a week. I have a good time with her and love her very much."

Remarkably, 32 percent of gay women in this study were married (heterosexually) before; their reasons for leaving their marriages were the same as those given by women in other chapters of this book:

"I have been married. I liked the idea of permanence and the dailyness, but I found it hard to combat society's view of me as a 'wife.' Also, my husband and I had somewhat different ideas about life, it turned out."

"I was married. I mostly did not like it. The best part was the security and the worst part the brutality."

"I was married. I didn't like it. None is the best part of being married. Everything is the worst. I expected it to be different. I thought it would end my loneliness."

"I was married for ten years. It was O.K. The worst was feeling like Mrs. So-and-so, dependent, the lack of communication verbally and emotionally.

---

*It is actually more common to go from straight to gay than vice versa. Of course, there is a larger "straight" population to begin with, but this cannot totally account for the difference.

The best part was we were good friends, had good sex, had fun together, and traveled a lot. I gave up an independent self-image. We made decisions jointly, but his career took precedence regarding where we moved, because I didn't have a career. I like my life now so much better."

As seen, an amazing 24 percent of gay women first fell in love with another woman after they were forty; most were married before, but now prefer a love relationship with another woman—as this woman describes: *

"Who I am is a divorced woman who has happily attained the age of fifty-three, an information specialist by vocation, a Quaker by 'convincement,' and many other things, such as mother of four mostly grown-up daughters, grandmother of two, handywoman, coper with household emergencies, and perpetual seeker after 'there must be a better way.'

"What I want is more time than I have. As a woman working full-time and balancing care of house, daughter, dog, two cats, and lover (not necessarily in that order), I don't have much! I would like time to take more vacations, travel, and sit by an ocean shore and hear the waves pounding in. I like hearing music I love—a Rachmaninoff concerto, or a verse of some wonderful hymn.

"My greatest achievement to date? Having the courage to finally, finally get out of a destructive relationship and risk getting into another, deeper, incredibly more meaningful one. The divorce from my husband of thirty-one years was really terrible, and I was scared out of my mind a lot of the time. I started the legalities in 1979, backed out, then started everything again with a better lawyer in 1981. The final settlement took until mid-1983. Today, the thing I'm most proud of is that I've managed to get as far as I have past a redneck, WASP, bigoted background and at least partly into the light.

"I am in love with a woman I met in 1979. She is the first woman I've ever had a physical relationship with—though I have had many very close relationships with other women. It is hard for me to think of myself as lesbian, but it is even harder for me to think of myself in a relationship with a man. This is the deepest relationship of my life; the one that has caused me the greatest pain and given me the most joy; the one that has most forced me to grow.

"I am very much in love. Falling in love with her was the most remarkable experience I have ever had in my life. Until that time, I had given up believing in the 'storybook' experience. When I met her, I realized that everything I had ever read about falling in love was true, and I've had it all with her.

"To live with someone, it is important to have fallen in love first—it is such a wonderful, idiotic, incredible thing to share later on when the relationship has matured into a less exciting, more permanent entity. And the remembering

*See pages 622–28.

helps when the problems come along and have to be worked out. Love is also hanging in there when things really get terrible and the adjustments seem too difficult and the sacrifices too costly—hanging in there and getting help and working out the problems.

"Our relationship has gone on for almost five years. We met in 1979, she ran away, and we met again in 1981 and have been together ever since. We only live together on weekends. We don't have children because we are both women—but even if one of us was male, we wouldn't have. She is child enough for me and I for her.

"For me, the most important part of this relationship is to know that I belong to her and she belongs to me in ways that neither of us knew before. I am happy in the relationship—I am often inspired, and have written poetry and long letters about it.

"When we fell in love, we couldn't touch each other without falling in bed together, and once spent eight hours making love, at the end of which we were both so exhausted we could hardly make it to the restaurant to have dinner. I believe falling in love is wonderful—it is definitely one of the three most important experiences in life. Now is when I am the happiest and most close with anyone—I have someone to share my life with in a way it has never been shared before. I no longer feel like a loner, or an oddity, or someone that doesn't belong.

"What I like most is this belonging, the physical touching, and the stimulation of minds meeting. What I like the least is that we can't right now live together, so we sometimes spend time when we're together getting over the time we spend apart. She is as happy with me as I am with her—a little more nervous about the relationship than I, but very happy.

"We enjoy walking by the lake, talking, having sex, lying in bed together and watching TV or reading, going to movies, dancing, having friends over for parties, playing games like Trivial Pursuit, marveling over the English language, touching.

. . .

"She most often criticizes my leniency with my seventeen-year-old daughter, especially my allowing her to use my car so much. I most often criticize her for her leniency with her cats, and for taking her problems out on me by being touchy. The biggest problem in our relationship is alcoholism and my reaction to it. This worries me for when we do live together—I hope I will be creative in taking care of myself during the episodes. I think the worst thing she ever did was to get totally, completely out-of-control drunk. This has happened on a few occasions; we usually have a terrible fight which lingers in our relationship for several days and is difficult for both of us to get over.

"It is easy for us to talk, about everything. We both have our times of talking, and probably on the whole she talks a little more than I do. We both have our times of 'babbling'—hers is when she has had a fair amount to drink; mine is when I'm feeling ill at ease in the relationship, such as when we've been apart for some time (physically) and are just getting together again.

"There's nothing I can't share with her, or at least I haven't found anything I can't share. I feel very accepted and understood, I've waited a long time to be able to share so much of myself! As I found out when we came close to breaking up after one disastrous vacation, *nothing* is more important than this relationship, and no sacrifice too much to make. Nothing would make me leave it.

"I do the dishes, washing, some of the cooking, most of the housekeeping (both of us have cleaning people) when we are together, regardless of whose house we are at. We sleep in the same bed, have separate working spaces in whichever house we are at. We both enjoy working in our places when we are together—we tend to have entirely different ways to go at almost anything, so we usually are very careful about projects such as joint house repairs or making anything together.

"Each of us takes care of our own finances, and I take care of joint ventures, keeping a simple cash-flow book, which usually ends up even unless I'm spending a long time at her house or vice versa. We find that it is easier for the person in whose house we are to do the paying, and then accounts are squared after the 'long time.' When we actually are able to live together, some of this may change, but I feel confident that we can work it out.

"I think the best and only way a relationship can work is for both the people in it to be completely committed to it, and willing to discuss and work out the problems. We have a really wonderful therapist that we have joint sessions with when we run into something really hard to handle; so far this has worked very well. We try to keep little mottoes in mind, such as 'What is *really* important to me?' and also that we want to be on the other person's 'side' against whatever comes. These things were missing in my thirty-one-year marriage—we were never able to get past our own needs and desires long enough to make any concessions to the relationship.

. . .

"I feel married to her. In my 'real' marriage, I liked all the things we did together when the children were small. I liked knowing I never needed to be alone, that I had someone to be there and to fix things, to pay the bills, and to give me financial security. The worst thing was his terrible insecurity and jealousy.

"I think it was my idea to get married—and a big part of that was knowing that in my family, for generations, women got married and left home when they were out of high school, and men enlisted in the service when they were out of high school. Parental responsibility was until the child was eighteen, period. So parental pressure plus social pressure equaled marriage. Most of the women in my graduating class got married out of high school and had a child by the end of the first year of marriage. So, at first I felt elated—now I was 'grown-up' and doing what 'grown-up' people did.

"I was excited when I found out that I was pregnant. I quit my job almost immediately and stayed home to keep house. I think my husband was very scared when he found out I was pregnant—the financial responsibility for a wife and child—but then he also got over that and enjoyed them. He took a large part in the child rearing, and was especially good with them when they were little—he had endless patience with them.

"The relationship didn't begin to change until the children were a little older—he went back to college after the first child was born, and we were so busy just trying to make it financially (and scholastically, for him) that we just went from one day to the next as well as we could manage it.

"I'm not sure my life would have been different if I hadn't got married. I think I might have managed to develop into the same person if I'd had a career instead of a marriage and children. I'm really glad my life turned out as it did—it's nice to have the best of both worlds—or *all* worlds, children and now this fulfilling love. Speaking of my present relationship, I do sometimes feel torn between my lover and my child—but not as much as I used to. My child is now seventeen, and is developing her own life—so I exercise my right to have *my* own life."

Being gay: a political choice, or a biological given?

Is being gay "biological"? 54 percent of gay women say that, for them, it is:

"I prefer sex with women because I want to be made love to by them, and make love to them. With men, I only wanted to be made love to. I love women's bodies, particularly their breasts, and I love to caress and kiss them. I have no such feelings about men's bodies. I believe that I have always felt this way, but that, through part of my life, I repressed these feelings because I wanted to be able to feel toward men the same way that I feel toward women."

"For me, there was no question of a choice. Once I embraced this lifestyle, I embraced it completely. I never considered for a fraction of an instant changing. It wasn't like people around me were pressuring me (they wouldn't have thought me 'disloyal' in the 1950s—there was no political pressure), it was just that I was happy. I felt that I had come home."

"Presently my lover is a woman. I've always loved women. Occasionally I would date a guy, but I never got anything out of it. Women are so loving and understanding. They are soft and I like the way they smell. Women are beautiful and they were meant for each other. I just wish society would understand that and stop putting it down and saying we are mentally ill."

"I used to think that being gay was a matter of choice, but I don't anymore. I am becoming more and more convinced that much of it is genetic. I do know that men have never attracted me, and the sexual encounters I had with the one male I dated were not in the least arousing to me—at the time I understood why women always talked about doing their 'duty'—there certainly was no enjoyment in it. Women, on the other hand, are gentle and soft and caring, more psychically in tune with me and more aware of what feels good. Women are very affectionate.

"I believe that heterosexual women may feel as good about sex with egalitarian male partners, but for me, the only worthwhile sex is with my lover, who is a woman. When I first became gay I privately thought of myself as bisexual—that it was only important to love someone and it didn't matter if it be male or female—after a few years I came to realize that I was woman-identified and that I was a lesbian—and happy for it."

It seems probable, on the basis of replies to this study and the previous two studies, that some individuals feel a definite biological inclination toward sexual interest in members of the same sex, while others decide that this is a way of life they *prefer.**

On the other hand, 46 percent feel their being gay is a choice on their part—and half of those feel this choice is political, as explained by the following woman:

"The reason I prefer women is not just sex. I'm more concerned about putting my energies into women. I've always had stronger emotional attachments with women—with my sister, my childhood and later friendships. When I was younger and seeing guys, always—in the back of my mind—I was waiting until I was 'ready' for a relationship with a woman.

"Men in most relationships I have seen always want to control things or at least feel their own power—it seeps in no matter how subtle their attitude is. Negative attitudes about being gay are the worst, though. It can be tedious and troublesome to remember that everyone else is wrong about a very important part of your nature—sort of like keeping the ghosts out by locking the back door and then finding they still go in through the cracks.

"I would like to see more of the myths about lesbianism driven from the earth. I feel I am a very normal, healthy, attractive person (at least people

*See Alan P. Bell, Martin S. Weinberg, and Sue Kiefer Hammersmith, *Sexual Preference: Its Development in Men and Women* (Bloomington, IN: Indiana University Press, 1981).

always tell me I am, when I remark otherwise on my 'down' days). I want to have a healthy, loving, productive relationship like everyone else, and I want to bypass many of the problems I see in relationships with men—even good relationships.

"Feminism? Well, of course, each woman has her own definition of what it is and is not. For me it basically means that the fundamental relationships we have between men and women, adults and children, women and women, men and men, don't work, they're unhealthy and don't make people happy. And they need to be changed, and I want to be one of the people experimenting with my own life in order to change them."

Is gay love more "politically correct" love? more chic? (Is there such a thing as "heterosexual oppression"?)

It might be natural for any oppressed group to turn on those oppressing them and declare their own superiority. Actually, however, in a way relationships between women *are* superior. Still, it cannot be dictated to women that they *"should"* cease being "heterosexual" and become gay. Unfortunately, in some gay circles, there has been a holier-than-thou attitude directed by gay women at straight women.

This attitude of "follow the correct political line if you want to be one of us" has also been reflected in a strict dress code (and even a behavior code). Quite a few gay women remark on the pressures surrounding dress and clothing. As one woman puts it, "In dating women I am far more appearance-conscious than I ever was with men—not to be classically 'feminine.'" Another worries, "Makeup. I miss makeup a lot—and a certain kind of dressing I did when I was straight—getting done up for an evening. So sometimes I still tend to do myself up more like a straight woman than a typical gay woman."

One woman is rebelling against all of this pressure: "I like sensual fabrics, so I guess I have a 'femme' appearance. I feel lesbian women tend to stifle their physical aesthetics too much in terms of both clothes and taking care of their bodies." And for many women, all this is not a problem: "I do not dye my hair even though it is graying since I want to convey the message visually that I am mature and have experience that you can count on. In other words, I use my ageing to my advantage."

And gay women, unfortunately, can be "macho" too:

"For a while, my lover worked as a waitress in a gay place, and she was constantly harassed by women. They would actually come up and put a hand on her ass. Constantly saying things to her, like 'Oh, you're gorgeous, come home with me.' And she would say, 'Why don't they just keep their problems to themselves? I'm working, I don't want to be bothered.' She would come home practically in tears, just feeling like she had been raped all night long, feeling completely disillusioned with women. (At the same time, though, if a really attractive woman came up and said that, she'd be really up for hearing it. That's the other side of it.)"

Most gay women as seen here, at least half, indicate that one of the most important parts of their lesbianism is making women the basic focus of their lives, giving the full measure of their support to women. Almost all lesbian women in this study say they are very proud of being woman-identified.

Loving Women: Does This "Make" You Gay?

Where is the dividing line between gay and straight affection for a friend?

"I was closest to my college roommate. It was pre-women's movement. She was humanistic, loyal, tender. Funny. She was one of the most 'together' people (hackneyed, but it describes her) I've ever met. She and I were inseparable. I sketched her in the nude and even had some sexual thoughts, but didn't take them very seriously. Men were the object of the day. She and I have lost touch. She got involved in community work in a large city and I moved to the country. We met a few times but she was way ahead of me. She was a role model to me—very human and didn't look down on me in the least. We were partners in all kinds of 'crime.' Nice craziness!"

"At one time I thought I was 'in love' with my roommate and I talked to her about this. She said it was normal to have those feelings, especially after coming from the bad situation I did at home. We tried lesbian love at one time but it wasn't for us. Whenever we date it's with a group of friends—we're always double- or triple-dating or with three or five people—it's good to have a lot of people to relate to. I love my roommate because she embodies the values I feel inside. Because of my upbringing and the powerful influence my father had on me, my inability to love or show it or to put other people's feelings first, I'm a contradiction. I feel one way, but I act another. If I keep this up I'll never get it together."

Gay women describe their love for their best friends

Some gay women have close women friends who do not know that they are gay—but many more have close women friends who of course know, but continue long platonic friendships together.

"I am in love again at present—but I am not closest to my lover. My new relationship only started about two months ago. I am closest to my best friend. I am not afraid to show her *any* side of me."

"We are fellow professionals and interested in the same things—everything! We travel, sail, talk, work. Get together at least several hours a week."

"I don't have a best woman friend, I have four! I love their sense of humor, openness. We go to the movies or dinner, once or twice a week. They listen to me and they like me."

"My best woman friend is something else. She is twenty-five, eight years younger than myself. She's a hard worker, very reliable in work and interpersonal relationships, self-reliant, but sociable. She's a natural leader of people, and when there's something that needs to be done, she'll organize it and do it. Always willing to go on the line for something she believes in, also mature enough to give it some hard thought before precipitating action. She wants to learn, sees her flaws, recognizes her ability to hurt people, as well as her ability to give joy, pleasure. She's a lot of fun to be with, full of life, exuberant, striving always to succeed and never taking no for an answer. We exercise together. We eat together. We drink together. We sometimes go to the movies together. We pick raspberries. We watched the tall ships on the Hudson. Mainly we talk together. Sometimes I give her a back rub. We spend quite a lot of time together, and she's helped me through some really tough times."

"My best friend is intuitive, intelligent, and very sensitive. She is not a very strong woman emotionally, but is supportive and nurturing. I like the fact that I feel comfortable enough with her to show her any side of me."

One woman tells a story of extreme love and loyalty from her best friend:

"I have an extremely important relationship with my best woman friend, who is also a psychologist. She has been my teacher, therapist, 'boss,' mentor. She is bright, articulate, extremely competent. I admire her for her high standards, her reserve, her emotional control, and a seriocomic way she has of relating, especially to my lesbianism. (I'm really rather butch, and long ago when I used to be uncertain and ambivalent about being a 'dyke,' she was the one who said it's O.K. My straight married friend!)

"We have an unusual friendship. She buys me jewelry from Tiffany's and clothes from Bergdorf's, and I give her autographed Meg Christian records and the latest novel by Rita Mae Brown. What do we do together? We try to get together at least once a week for a drink, dinner, sometimes take courses together in art, go to museums, and on a few occasions we've gone away together.

"When I had only known her about a year, I was involved in an accident wherein I was hit by a car and my left leg nearly torn off. The police asked who to call and I told them to call her. She found me in the emergency room. God knows what I looked like while they were working on me, but despite however difficult bearing with all the blood was, she stayed with me five hours while they cleaned and scraped. I screamed, cried, held on to her, and told her how much I loved her. (Pain and Demerol had taken away any thought to restrain expression—besides, there was a real chance that I would die and I wanted her to know.)

"The next morning when I came to in the intensive care unit—she was there. And for the ten weeks I spent in the hospital she visited as often as she could, we talked on the phone. I was studying for graduate school and she got me books and articles and registered me for school. I got out of the hospital three days before school started. I was in a cast to my hip and didn't have the strength to walk half a block. I did go to work—as an administrator, so I didn't have to move—and took three courses. She did all my library 'footwork,' at least for most of that semester.

"Well—we developed a bond. Mostly non-verbal. As I said, she is very reserved. On only one occasion did she acknowledge verbally that she loved me too—with the same implications of intimacy and intensity. But it doesn't have to be spoken. Our ongoing friendship is a loving relationship—lived. I feel 'high' with her when we're together, also sometimes relaxed. We also spend a lot of time working together—ordinary time, when it's just pleasant working companionship. Perhaps the only aspect of a relationship that we have not shared is that we have never been lovers.

"I like the least that when she's in trouble or has problems, she withdraws. It took me a long time to recognize this—because she'd just suddenly turn off. Now that I know I can draw her out and get her to open up and let down that perpetual guard, we're even closer because we have found a way to communicate through these times."

And, of course, as seen, many gay women describe their lovers as their best friends:

"My closest woman friend is my lover. She is beautiful. Beautiful light green eyes. We spend all of our time together whenever possible. Before we were lovers, we would ride around in my convertible Corvette, go on picnics, walk in the woods, go swimming. I always felt excited over our friendship— nervously excited when I was going to see her. Her kindness, her beauty I liked the best—her irresponsible 'loose' behavior I liked least. She has always been there for me."

"My closest woman friend is my lover. She is the most beautiful woman in the world! I never spend enough time with her, but when we are together we spend long times talking, or reading, or going out dancing or to eat. We also go to group meetings, go walking with no purpose or destination, and make love."

A remarkable 62 percent of gay women remain close friends with their important ex-lovers:

"The deepest I have loved someone is the person from whom I am now separated. We still see each other as friends. I have been happier with her than with anyone by far—the happiest period of my life was during the time I was with her. I'm glad that we're still friends."

"We are ex-lovers and have lived together for ten years since the relationship ended. We are 'family.' "

"The most important relationship with a woman in my life was the woman I was involved with for nine years. We were lovers and thought of our relationship as a marriage. This was when I was sixteen to twenty-five years old. Part of the person I am today is wrapped around the interaction between me and her in our relationship. I love this woman. Now we are friends. She is talented, intelligent, creative, very sensitive, and childlike. We have never been out of touch for more than a week."

"My previous lover of three years is now my business partner, remains my best friend, is with me almost every day, spends the night, is affectionate, etc. We broke up because of differences in sexual appetite, physical ability, and some small differences in lifestyle and personality. It was mutual and it was not difficult—more like a reevaluation and entrance into a new stage of our relationship. I love her more now—we make excellent friends. We mourned the passing of our exclusive coupledom and yet both felt freer."

"I love her as my best friend. We see each other almost daily and talk on the phone several times a day. We do many things together and have helped each other many times. Often she is my soul support. We have a great time together, laugh, giggle, get silly. We have great political discussions, discuss our most intimate thoughts."

When is love for another woman "gay," and when is it friendship?

Where is the "borderline" between being "in love with" one's friends and loving them—and does it matter?

"My best friend and I have hiked together, traveled, read philosophy, Zen, and holistic health books together, worked, talked, played together for six years, and developed a deep (but non-sexual) love for each other which we were sure would last forever. I had never loved anyone so intensely. We spent most of our time together though I was married (she was alone). She is very intelligent, funny, beautiful, and we went through so much pain and pleasure together. My relationship with my current lover ultimately destroyed our friendship, which had begun to become sexual only in the last two months before it broke down. It would have broken down even if it hadn't become sexual: we were always 'lovers' in a sense, and the intrusion of another woman was too much. The loss of that friendship was/is like a death to me."

"My best friend is the reason I answered this questionnaire. I love her so much and I don't understand it. She's helped me through some of the lowest points of my life. She's encouraged me to be the whole person I am today. We probably had an affair without sex. We saw each other several times a week, talked on the phone every day for hours, shopped together. She bought me things I needed but couldn't afford. She took me to the movies and plays and the zoo. She loved my kids and took them out and bought them stuff. She convinced me to dress better, color my hair, wear more makeup. To be happy. She made me so happy. She taught me to put up with things I was drowning in. She encouraged me to get a job. I can't ever say how much of the happy, healthy me of today I owe to her. She helped me to find out what I want and who I am. When I'm with her things are great. We enjoy each other. I love her the most of any woman in my life."

"As I've grown up I've had many crushes on women—some of which have turned into good friendships (nothing sexual). I believe women can be attracted to women sexually as they are to men. This doesn't mean you're gay—it's merely a physical attraction. Usually I find this physical attraction dies as soon as I get to know the person well and become friends."

"My best woman friend and I are so compatible and feel very comfortable around each other. She is very honest and open, very accepting, and doesn't try to change me. She lets me be. We communicate so well. Our love for each other has been very strengthening. We have both helped each other deal with difficult situations to make major moves in our lives. The only thing in the past that used to bother me was her passivity. Now, though, she is not nearly as passive in dealing with people.

"We also have been sexually attracted to each other, but decided not to act upon it. We have used it to become closer emotionally. I love her and hope that we remain close throughout the years. We have even talked about being the 'life mates' of each other. Why do people have to be married or lovers to spend their lives together? I feel that two friends can make that commitment."

Fear of loving and desiring another woman: Do some heterosexual women love their women friends more than they love men?

Women often feel emotionally closer to other women than they do to men, as seen earlier. 89 percent say they wish they could talk to the men they love in the same intimate and easy way they can talk to their best friends. Descriptions women give of their best friends contain a remarkably happy and loving tone of voice, as seen in Chapter 18.

On the other hand, most women feel that they are basically "heterosexual"—i.e., they do not feel "attracted" to women physically, sexually, but see them as basically psychologically accessible, or possibly soul mates. If one took away women's remaining economic dependence on men, and men's dominance in the larger society, would women still feel that they "should" be "heterosexual"? Or are women getting another kind of closeness, a non-verbal closeness, in their sexual relationships with men? On the other hand, are some simply psychologically attracted to the power men have, feeling themselves powerless without a man to "help" them in society?

This is not to imply that "all women are gay underneath it all" but to point out that women can reexamine their preconceptions about what a long-term gay lifestyle means, and whether or not one can find security and happiness there.

Being woman-identified: a valid alternative

> *"There are a lot of qualities women assume they can
> get only from men that they can get from a woman too,
> if they just tried it."*

Perhaps women don't feel they can find permanent security with another woman, as with a man; if so, this may be a false idea. Of course, being gay doesn't have the status of being heterosexual, or being part of a nuclear family—whatever the shape of that nuclear family psychologically. But women, as we see here, *are* giving each other a great deal of emotional and even financial security (economic cooperation). It is quite possible for a woman to live her entire life in this woman-to-woman culture. Indeed, 92 percent of women over thirty-five who are doing so say that this is providing them with an excellent base for their lives.

Women sum up the pleasures and importance of loving other women:

"Falling in love is not as important as not falling out of love. These relationships I share with women with whom I am forever in love—with or, probably, without sex—are the relationships I value above all others. The lovers who are closer than friends; friends deeper and more multifaceted than lovers. The ones I will always meet up with again, and know they are somewhere out there in the world; not forgetting our love; using it to strengthen them."

"My experience has been that women are more caring and more honest in relationships than men are. They are much more satisfying. As the Alix Dobkin song goes, 'You can't find home cooking in a can, or clean air in a traffic jam, You can't find a woman's love in a man. Never in a million years.' Love between women is much different for me than with men. There is no comparison! Sex is also much different—much softer, sweeter, and real."

"I believe a love relationship between two women is far more serious than one between a man and a woman. Women run on a higher emotional level than men will let themselves, and they get to deeper levels with each other."

Another world, another culture

Women's lives together have a rich texture at once all their own, and at the same time, filled with many of the same human problems heterosexual women face. And yet, there is a feeling here of looking in on a special culture, another way of life, breathing a different air. The existence of this world is a great cultural resource: it provides a place of strength and beauty to draw on, opening up for all the pleasure of diversity and new ways of seeing things, being together.

Why should anyone have to defend lesbianism as a way of life? In fact, as historian Carroll Smith-Rosenberg has written in her study of women in nineteenth-century America, one can see things just the other way: in fact, "to see heterosexuality as an artificial construct imposed upon humanity [would be] a revolutionary concept."* Who is to say which is more "natural": to love the opposite or one's own sex? Greek men of ancient times would certainly have been hard-pressed to give an answer. Perhaps it is even more important here to ask why it has become so taboo for women to hold hands even in friendship, or to demonstrate physical affection as they did in Victorian times. Once again, as stated in Chapter 5, it seems imperative for us to review our entire concept of sensuality—as well as our priorities in terms of friendships/feelings for other women.

*Carroll Smith-Rosenberg, *Disorderly Conduct* (New York: Alfred A. Knopf, 1985).

Many, many women here have expressed the deepest feelings of love, joy, passion, and sorrow for the women they love. A passage by the poet Judy Grahn says something about the deepest longings of all our hearts, describing intense feelings of closeness for her lover, feelings which transcend death.

a funeral: for my first lover and longtime friend
Yvonne Mary Robinson, b. Oct. 20, 1939; d. Nov. 1974
*for ritual use only**

wherever I go to, you will arrive
whatever you have been, I will come back to
wherever I leave off, you will inherit . . .
whatever we resurrect, we shall have it

we shall have it, we have right

you have left, what is left.

I will take your part now, to do your daring . . .
lots belong to those who do the sharing.
I will be your fight now, to do your winning
as the bond between women is beginning
In the middle at the end
my first beloved, present friend
if I would die like the next rain
I'd call you by your mountain name
And rain on you

want of my want, I am your lust
wave of my wave, I am your crest
earth of my earth, I am your crust
may of my may, I am your must
kind of my kind, I am your best

tallest mountain, least mouse
least mountain, tallest mouse

you have put your very breath upon mine
i shall wrap my entire fist around you
i can touch any woman's lips to remember

we are together in my motion
you have wished us a bonded life

*Judy Grahn, *The Work of a Common Woman* (Trumansburg, Pa.: The Crossing Press, 1978), pp. 102–103.

PART FIVE

To Transform the Culture
with Our Values

The Other Transformed

Forty years ago, Simone de Beauvoir aptly described women as the "Other"—as defined by men and men's view of the world. Now, women have taken that position as Other and transformed it, turned it around, making of it a new vantage point from which to analyze and define society. No longer are women an "other" knocking on the door to be let into the society. Women now have gone beyond this point, reaching a stage where they no longer want to integrate themselves into "men's" world so much as to reshape the world, make it something better. From "outside," we are in an advantaged position to do just this: we can understand and interpret the system we are distanced from more clearly than those at its center.

We are like astronauts now, watching the earth recede ever farther into the distance, becoming smaller and smaller—seeing the "male" ideology ever more clearly—now as only one historical world view among others, no longer all of reality. New points of view, ideas, and perspectives are taking shape swiftly, as we gain ever more distance from the way things have been. This is the process of revolution we are all creating.

Women's thinking about relationships is causing them to question the whole system

What is going on right now in the minds of women is a large-scale cultural revolution. Women everywhere are asking themselves serious questions about their personal lives. These questions are growing initially out of their desire to have closer, more satisfying relationships with the men they are with. As their frustration with these relationships increases, many begin to ask deeper and deeper questions—finally, not only about love, but about the entire system.

As woman after woman lies in bed at night wondering, "Why did so and so not call?" or "Why doesn't my husband turn over and talk to me about this thing that he knows is on my mind, or at least that I told him is on my mind?" she begins thinking, analyzing all the possible answers. First, she may wonder, "Is it *me?* Is there something wrong with me?" Next, she may try to figure out the psychological makeup of the man she is with, his individual psychological background. Then, to understand this, she often begins to look at *his* parents' family structure—and then next at the overall social patterns that made *them* that way—until finally, in her searching, she comes face to face with the whole system, and asks herself how *it* got the way it is.

In other words, the pain in many women's personal lives, or the built-up frustration as women try to figure out a relationship (or deal with the loneliness inside it), leads women to a series of deeper questions about *why* love is so difficult—why men behave as they do, why a man can be sometimes loving, sometimes cold and distant—*why?* This *"why?"* echoes down through almost all the pages of this book. And the question, "Does it have to be this way?" Pondering these questions, women are developing a rather clear-cut and detailed idea of what it is they really want out of relationships—what they think are the right bases for human relationships and for the society as a whole. This is what the reflections we are listening to throughout this book really mean.

Women's dissatisfaction: driving social change

As women think through these questions, they are causing everything to change. Recognizing the problems, thinking through the issues, women are becoming different from what they are analyzing. Having to analyze a thing so deeply removes one from it, and so women begin to feel removed from the current system, things as they are. It is impossible to ask these questions and not change, to stop the process inside oneself: seeing the situation, a new level of understanding and awareness takes place which cannot be undone, and so one is—whether one wants to be or not—transformed—changed forever.

The feelings of alienation women are describing here in their personal lives are leading to the formulation of a new set of political goals and philosophical beliefs, a new philosophy, based on women's traditional point of view, modified by the changes women have made during the last twenty years.

Women are in a struggle with the dominant ideological structure of the culture. As women see their relationships and their lives differently—*become* different—many are no longer content to live biculturally. And wrestling with themselves on many issues, they also discuss these matters with their women friends—comparing relationships, asking what is the best one can expect out of life, and how to interpret men's actions. These discussions between women are part of a very important process of creating and maintaining a specific value system.

Finally, these changes in thinking are all happening in conjunction with women's new economic situation which, as noted, has been called "the quiet revolution."* Within the last ten years, the number of women with jobs and businesses has increased so markedly that in fact women as a group are no longer essentially economically dependent on men. This is a startling development—and one whose implications have only barely begun to take hold. Although many women receive extremely low salaries (and day care is expensive), more women than ever have enough resources to make it on their own, if they have to—even with children, and even if only minimally. The 50 percent divorce rate, mostly initiated by women, and the "feminization of poverty" mean that women today would rather leave a relationship than stay and put up with a negative situation.† (See Parts I and III.)

"I don't just want equality—I want something better"

Women's reevaluation of themselves and of the culture is part of a process that has been going on for some time, for over a century.‡ During the last twenty years, this change, which could be called a revolution in women's definition of themselves and of society, has been occurring in stages.§ Stage one began with women "demanding equal rights." Stage two was women trying to take a place in, join, the "male" world. And stage three, now, is women consolidating their own value system, examining and discussing the society as we know it, accepting some values of the dominant culture, discarding others—leading to the cultural struggle currently in progress.‖ The fourth stage of revolution would be to change the culture.

The stage of women "demanding equal rights" was superseded by the

---

*So referred to by Elizabeth Dole, and later by *The Economist*.

†The "feminization of poverty" is a phenomenon that has been misinterpreted: it is caused not so much by men leaving women as by women choosing (now that they have an alternative) to leave men, even if they have to be poor. A large number of women are refusing to stay in bad situations any longer. See Parts I and III.

‡The feminist tradition in France has been traced back five centuries to Christine de Pisan, a French writer who defended women in the 1500s. See Joan Kelly's *Women, History and Theory* (Chicago: University of Chicago Press, 1984).

§These do not refer to Lenin's or Trotsky's or Betty Friedan's stages.

‖Women's reexamination of our situation began with "equal rights" but has evolved into much more than this. As Evelyn Fox Keller has commented, "We began by asking a few simple questions about equality, and it was like unraveling a ball of knitting; the more we looked for the beginning, the more we unraveled, until finally we are undoing the whole thing." Thus, questions women have raised about "equality" have led to discussions, examinations, and reconceptions of the nature of methodology in the sciences/social sciences, the philosophical understanding of "truth," the various definitions of "science," and so on.

current stage when women discovered that "equal rights" would mean integrating themselves into the "male" value system. Women, as we have seen, are under great pressure to give up their traditional (even if newly redefined) values and take on "male" values (such as giving up relating sex to feelings so much, etc.). But many women feel they cannot do this and be true to their own beliefs; for example, most women do not want to be competitive and continually relate to others in terms of one-upmanship.

As one woman put it, "Women can only have 'equal rights' if they adopt the whole male value system. But most women cannot do this and maintain their own integrity; women would have to compromise themselves." "We are not trying to say anymore that we want to be just like men," another woman states. "We are women, not a cloned version of 'men' or the society's version of who we are! We refuse to accept these terms."

The result is that women are faced with having to redesign the whole system. Many, as seen, solve the problem (temporarily?) by living double lives—bisecting themselves to keep things going. But, while many women are in fact trying to make decisions about combining their culture with the "male" culture, trying to see which values are workable in both systems, most men are not trying to fit in with women's "ideology." Nor do they see why they should. They feel women are supposed to adapt to *their* ideology.

Women as a force in history*

Women's thinking is revolutionary: redesigning their personal lives and the nature of relationships, women are deciding what they do and do not want life to be, clarifying their own philosophy. Where we are going is still unclear—but that is one of the exciting things about what we are seeing here—that there are so many individuals participating in this reformulating of what is going on, so many points of view.

Of course, in any value system there will always be debate, as, for example, in the "male" system there are "democratic," "conservative," and "liberal" points of view, and so on; it is not that we have to pin down exactly what every woman would think or do were she to run the government, or what she thinks and believes now. However, one thing *is* clear, and that is that the spectrum of women's thought represents a different cultural outlook from that represented by men in *The Hite Report* on men and in other works.

Cultural change, then, is something we are all in together now, as at night when we go home and try to accommodate our needs to his *but* still insist that he meet us halfway; or when we talk to our friends; or when we work at a standard job but try to do it our own way. In this manner we are all changing society,

*As Mary Beard put it so aptly in her 1927 work.

developing a new consensus of what is valid philosophically as a way to live.

There is nothing that can stop this process—it is the mental development of each and every one of us every day. Why at this time in history are *women* so important to this process—in fact, the driving force behind change? Perhaps because of the economic independence we have just achieved—but really, who can say? Historically, there may be many reasons, but history is also funny like that: a cause or an idea may lie dormant—as "freedom" and "individuality" did within the Christian tradition for centuries, all of a sudden to blossom during the eighteenth century as the Enlightenment—whose philosophical and political concepts within only fifty years became so widely held that they completely overturned the old order. The new watchwords became "liberty, equality, fraternity," and "the rights of man."

We are in another one of those times—a time of fundamental change. Only this time the "revolution" is coming from women. It is such a sea change in consciousness—whether women consider themselves individually "conservative" or "liberal" in the old sense—that it has already progressed beyond the possibility of return or forgetting.

We are living through history. We have a chance to be dynamic actors and we are doing this—both well-known women and "unknown" women everywhere. We are taking our place on the stage, and history will judge us for the progress we make—both for ourselves and for the world.

Loving Men at This Time in History

Where Is Love?

Strangely, hauntingly, most women in this study—whether married, single, or divorced, of all ages—say they have not yet found the love they are looking for, that they hope their greatest love is yet to come:

"My family, it is O.K. But I think I will never find what I truly want in love. My greatest love was too unstable, too much hurt. I am still looking for the love I need to share in my life and I hope I have time for it to come later."

"I have not found what I need in love and family. This gives me a desperate feeling in the pit of my stomach. I am losing faith and hope of realizing it in my lifetime."

"I have not as yet been able to give the love I would like to give, neither have I received it. Since I come from a broken home, maybe I don't know how. I would like to have a love that is openly expressed without fear of rejection."

Most women, no matter how frustrating their relationships or how clearly they see the difficulty of coming to a real, mutual recognition with a man they love, still hope for, long for, love. As one woman says, love keeps returning to us, resurfacing perhaps as some kind of key: "In some way which I cannot find the words for yet, romantic love contains the key toward my identity—toward discovering myself, my inner being." Many women feel this way. Why? Perhaps women are right to come back, to try again and again to make love work or understand why it does not.

And yet, most women want not just "love," but the kind of real love they are talking about. And so it is no surprise that women who are in relationships so often still talk about a "deeper love" to come, have a hidden part of themselves that believes that there is more, more to life somehow . . . And indeed, shouldn't there be?

One memorable woman, very pensive, in therapy, muses over these thoughts, trying to sort out what her life means, asking herself where to find love, which kinds are "right," whether she is making the correct choices—asking herself if she should stop taking love so seriously:

"The most deeply I fell in love was with my husband in my junior year in high school. I felt happy, fulfilled, excited, funny, wondrous—every blissful adjective one can describe. He was handsome, serious, adventurous, rebellious, fun, a good dancer, honest, trustworthy, and my friend as well as lover. The relationship lasted through many ups and downs, and eventually a marriage and children. We have now been divorced for eight years. He's as good a father as he can be, the children love him, and although so many things have happened during the intermittent years, I still have warm and sometimes longing feelings for the way it used to be. Realistically, we are now so different. I was forced into years on my own of self-discovery and exploration, responsibility for the children, happiness and unhappiness, and I'm still learning.

"Upon our divorce, he immediately remarried. I never saw him for three years after their child was born. More than three years. I cried all the time. I wanted to die. I wanted to sleep all the time so I wouldn't have to think about anything.

"I had always believed that no matter what happened, no matter who we were with, we would always get back together. Three years later, when he separated from his wife, by that time my hatred had subsided because I had been involved with (and was broken up from) a love I had lived with for two years.

"At that point, I quit my job, took some time off to be with my kids, and decide what I wanted to do, think, get involved in a hobby, and generally just relax. It was a really good time for me—not necessarily 'happy,' but a good break. I was off work for about nine months, and it was one of the best times of my life.

"I married a second time, but now we have been separated almost two years, and the divorce should be final in a month. I thought I was being more practical when I married him. I loved him (though I was not 'in love') because he was interesting, knew a lot about different things, had more experiences, seemed more 'in tune' with life, shared some of the same interests I did. I wanted to have another child, thought it would be easier financially with two people working, it would lighten the load of me doing everything myself (taking care of the children, running a house, and working too), and I would feel more comfortable about sex.

"Although we were married two and a half years, we were only together six months. Why? I was trying to play a 'wife' role, working, taking care of the children, etc., so that I could make time to be alone with my husband. No other outlets of any kind. We never had enough time to develop a relationship that could have been healthy, because all the frustrations of our priorities, money, kids, role playing, church pressures—everything became unbearable. The thing I liked best was the companionship—having someone there all the time, in bed, someone to do things with, share my life. But I was not happy— neither of us was.

"Maybe part of the problem was that I was trying to juggle the importance of my children's needs with those of the relationship, instead of it being the total family as the important unit. He also had wanted his children from a previous marriage with us.

"Sex was glorious until the relationship started having problems. I always enjoyed it, even when things were going bad, except for the mental pain. When the reasons for doing it (as an expression of love and joy) weren't there so much anymore, it became all for the physical pleasure of it, which added confusion. I usually had an orgasm, but there was a lack of mental intimacy after it was over, and the time of cuddling became less and less as we had more and more problems.

"There were so many 'worst things' it's hard to remember which thing was worst. If I named them off I would sound stupid for ever putting up with them or him. Our arguments never seemed to get resolved or ended. They just cropped up again later. I would usually end up saying I was sorry just to keep the peace, but only after a period of anger. If we tried to talk the problem over it usually ended up in another fight. The last straw was his taking a Sunday to go skiing with another woman, who was a platonic friend (I knew her), when I had planned to be with him because my kids were spending the day with their dad. He expected me to stay home with his daughter while he went with this other woman skiing. Regardless of my wishes, he was going to go do what he pleased.

.   .   .

"I'm not in a relationship now, nor am I in love. I am thirty-four years old, a mother, a student in college, a concerned citizen, a traveler, sometime realist and sometime idealist. I don't have one person that I am closest to. There is always at least one part of my life that is left out of my relationships with everyone I know, be it my children, my psychologist, my friends. Probably I am closest to my children, although they are too young to care about the things I care about most deeply, or to really see my pains, hopes, and dreams.

"But—considering all this—strangely, I feel better than I have in a long time. While I prefer to have an intimate relationship with someone, I am alone now by choice. I am trying to sort my feelings out, get to know what it is that I really want in life before I get involved again. I'm going to school, which I really enjoy. I'm enjoying my children, going to movies, reading, and living the way I want to live. I don't have time right now to devote the energy it takes to work at a relationship, because I fear it would interfere with my plans to continue school, which takes a lot of concentration. If I want to be a slob, not wash the dishes or clean the house, I can be a slob. I don't feel like trying to impress anyone right now. I just want to be left alone. I miss the sex, but that's not enough.

"I want more, but I'm not sure what, so I'm taking my time to learn. It would be nice to be able to have someone to go places with, but I go by myself. All my friends are involved with someone and don't have time for girlfriends, or they are married. Why is that? I'm trying to cultivate new interests and friends too. Wondering what it is I have in common with people who put their friends after their boyfriends or lovers. I think there's room for both.

"After breaking up with my first husband, I went crazy for a while, got involved seriously with a couple of different guys, and went out with a lot more. After my boyfriend, I went out, but didn't really get involved. Never fell 'in love' again. After the breakup of my present marriage, I have not gone out at all. I had one 'date' about two years ago and that has been it. I have shied away from any dating or involvement completely. I don't trust my judgment, don't trust men, and really don't want to get involved any more until I know what it is I want. I've missed out a lot because I've wrapped myself up too much in my love life.

"I felt secure when I was in love, but now that I can look back at my relationships, they were always self-doubtful. I think that is why I am afraid to get into another one. I would feel warm and content, secure, loved and accepted, which improved my self-confidence, but it also made me emotionally dependent on that other person for those feelings.

"I always felt I tried harder to work at getting to the real issues that were causing problems. I felt that my partners weren't doing their part in trying. So I usually broke up relationships first, if only to make them see how serious the problems were and to try to fix what it was. I hoped they would see this and come back and work it out with a counselor or whatever. But they usually ended it permanently, not wishing to come back and work it through.

"I'm afraid to feel truly in love again because it seems the bottom always drops out. Now it's 'nothing gained, nothing lost.' I know that's not healthy thinking either and I hope I'll get over it with the help of continued counseling, but I've immersed myself so completely in the past in these relationships, maybe I don't know what healthy security in a relationship is like. I see it, but I don't know how to choose the type that would be good for me on a continuing basis.

"I feel confident by myself, don't have to worry about acceptance or rejection, and am comfortable with my children. I don't want to put them through anything more at this sensitive age that could reflect on their own lives later. I want to be sure I know what I'm getting into before subjecting them. I want to set an example for them so they have some kind of model to use in their own future relationships.

"I can't say that there is any particular thing I like best about men at this point in time. Any good qualities they have, women have twofold. The only thing nice is that they have different bodies. What I like least about them is their unwillingness to change and make their lives happier. To get to the basis of a problem and work it out (mental problems). To be sensitive to the needs of other people. (Of course, *all* men are not like this.) I hate the types that are stuck in the macho roles, unbending Reagan-Falwell types, who feel the need to impose their beliefs on others, and refuse to look at alternatives to life that may work better than their views. They don't want to *learn*.

"Women just seem to *care* more about *everything*. You can get understanding, sensitivity, equality, encouragement, admiration, love, tenderness, friendship, partnership, loyalty, trust, cooperation, consideration, honesty, nurturing, and sex from women, but as far as the sex is concerned, I prefer exclusively men. Since we have to share the planet with the other 50 percent being male, it would be nice if we could receive all the above from them as well as from our own sex. (I don't mean all women, but on the whole.) Men seem to have something missing.

"I used to be against the women's movement because of the draft, because of the tactics of the originators of the movement, but either the rest of the women are changing their tactics and becoming more convincing or I am changing. I think it's a little of both. I am in favor of the women's movement, and am not against any of the issues I have learned about, thus far. I think the women's liberation movement is the only hope for things to change. For us to be able to share in the decisions of the world, and to become truly equal human beings. Mostly I believe in *human* liberation from all the stifling, rigid images and policies we've been raised with over the generations. Those that affect *people* all over the world. I believe that women's liberation is the answer to men's need for liberation from their stagnant roles.

"*Most* men seem to feel the women's movement is stupid and radical. They believe in the equal-pay-for-equal-work concept, but don't really believe that women are capable of or suited to the same types of work as they are. That is the only issue most men will come even close to agreeing with. *Most* are still traditionalists, raised in the stereotypical male view that moms are supposed to stay home with their children, while dads are the breadwinners. That the husband has the final say. That women are scatterbrained when it comes right down to it. That men should be the ones to fight the wars (it never occurred to them that if women were to share in political power, aggressions around the world might be altered drastically), run the country, the businesses, be the protectors. That an unborn child's right to life is so precious because *they* don't have to be in a position, which most women are in financially (and societally), to worry whether that child, once born, will be able to eat and live a healthy physical and emotional life with the love and support of two able parents who can give it the nurturance it needs. Most men ignore the *facts* and rely on their male view as *right* and give no room for change and growth. They don't have to face facts, because they are still in control. If they ever learn to share their power (whether through law or whatever means), they will finally become real human beings.

"I think there are more and more men who are realizing that their wives need to work (whether through want or need), and slowly, slowly changing their attitudes. These men are in a minority, but they are a positive example to other men around them, and to their own children.

. . .

"I have not yet found what I'm looking for in love or family. I feel the older I get, the less my chances are of finding someone with whom I will be compatible for a lasting relationship. I still hope that the kinds of love and relationships I want are yet to come. Sometimes I'm cynical, sometimes skeptical, but I have so much love to give, I hope there will be someone I can share my life with, some one person who shares my ideas, hopes, joys, love, and adventures."

Can Women Change Relationships?

Many, many women are living in situations with men that are making them think deeply; they question themselves daily, asking themselves why relationships are so difficult, why men so often resist their attempts to change things, wondering how some men can ridicule or turn a blank stare to women's pleas for more emotional empathy, and for less challenging, distancing behavior. As women think about all of this—first asking themselves if there is something wrong with them, then trying to decipher the personal history of the man they love, asking themselves about his childhood, his family, why he is silent, why he behaves the way he does—while women are asking themselves these things, they frequently go on to question the whole system that has made relationships the way they are, and ask, "Why does it have to be this way?"

At least 88 percent of the women in this study, whether married or single, are now asking themselves these questions on a more or less daily basis. Women are attaining a philosophical frame of mind—and the more women stand back mentally from their situation and analyze it, the more women are also, unavoidably, changing who they are—and the more distant they are (ironically) becoming from the very men they want to be closer to—the men with whom they can't even discuss these questions.

In fact, the emotional infrastructure of most relationships, the emotional contract, creates a pattern of diminishing affections, as we have seen in Part I. Can this basic infrastructure be changed?

This is a difficult philosophical question: *How does one remake one's life, one's world?* More belief and trust must be possible, less cynicism and more true communication than we have seen in many of the marriages and relationships in this study so far. But *how?*

Old-style relationships

Throughout this book we have seen many examples of old-style relationships and marriages—i.e.:

"The relationship works when I do what I'm supposed to, have enough social activity to keep him interested, and listen to his problems."

"We lead independent lives away from each other, not much togetherness, children are the most we have in common. My husband seems content, though, and I love him being a good provider and father."

17 percent of women don't think equal communication with men is possible; they believe in submerging their feelings and thoughts—"not making waves": *

"Don't make waves—just go along and let things that are not important, or you feel he won't think are important, be forgotten."

"How to make it work? Avoid areas of conflict. I'm not saying that I like it that way, but that's what works best."

"The only time this relationship worked was when I conformed to his life plan—a wife who works part-time, does cooking, cleaning, child care, and likes to camp and boat and have sex three to four times per week."

"Feel from your heart. There are times I feel like saying something or making a point, but my heart wants to hold and love him."

"Not to express my dissatisfactions. I'm fearful of making him angry."

"If he is in a bad mood, never take it personally, don't bug him about it. When you sense the time is right, ask him about it gently and find out what is going on with him and help him through it."

Some women describe this in their mothers' marriages:

"Success? That depends on one's definition of success. My parents have a 'successful' marriage because my mother lets my dad do her thinking for her. Is that success? I don't know that I've ever really seen a successful heterosexual

*Substantially fewer younger women say this.

relationship. I would define one as a relationship in which no one had to give up who she is (or, in rare cases, who he is) to keep the other person."

A wife in a retired couple describes her marriage, saying she and her husband were never close, but after thirty-five years she has come to accept it:

"My relationship with my husband does not fill my deepest needs for closeness with another person. It never has. Even after thirty-five years together, I don't feel he really knows me, knows deeply the person I am, what is most important to me, what is most necessary for me. I wonder if he has the capacity to know, the sensitivity to be aware, to hear what I'm saying beyond the words I say. It isn't a matter of telling, and I doubt if he would know if I told him. But I would prefer to share completely with him if that were possible; that to me would be the ideal—a communion of body, soul, and mind. Ha! I really don't believe that is possible between man and woman—too many other things get in the way. And perhaps it is, after all, the best.

"I am a fifty-five-year-old white married woman with two grown sons. I'm an intelligent, sensitive, emotional, rather insecure person whose life seems to go in peaks and valleys, good times and bad. I can't be pigeonholed or stereotyped. I like many things (rock music, hiking, flying kites) which don't fit the image of a fourth-grade teacher, which I was for twelve years, until my husband had to take early retirement. I love life and all it offers. I'm loyal to friends and family, like things to go smoothly and pleasantly, have maintained close friendships for many years, yet I'm a loner, a private person, don't need much social life.

"We bought a small motor home about ten years ago and found that we liked the freedom of it. When he retired we bought a better one. I resigned from teaching and we hit the road, coming home only a couple of months at a time before taking off again. We love that life. Recently my mother's health has kept us home, but I think our happiest times are away in some wilderness campground off the beaten path, walking, enjoying the campfire, birding, reading, soaking up the beauty of it all. That we share.

"The long-running conflict between us over the past thirty-five years has been basically his jealousy—of other men, my friends, even our children. I've come to realize this is due to his insecurity, his rather weak self-image, and that there is really little I can do about it. But it has led to some bad scenes, rough arguments, long days of hurt and resentment. But, at last, in the past two or three years, there has been a gradual mellowing out of this problem, he has really tried to deal with it. Just his trying has helped me. So this conflict has been eased. We argued more when we were both working, had two teenage sons plus his mother at home, and I was after all those years just finding my wings, getting some confidence in myself, reaching out a bit. His insecurity couldn't take my budding independence.

"There have been good times and better times with sex over our thirty-five-year marriage, but really no bad times. Except for his wanting sex more often usually than I do. We enjoy lying close together and stroking each other, touching and talking, and take delight still in each other's body, sex or no sex. Oral sex is sort of one-sided; I like to take his penis in my mouth sometimes, but he has never gone down on me, never asked me if I would like him to.

"I read *The Hite Report,* and was overjoyed to find that I'm not the only woman who does not orgasm from intercourse! I had my husband read some of it too, as I felt, though he had never really complained, he believed something was missing, that most women surely did. He read it willingly and we talked about it, and both feel better about it. I orgasm easiest by clitoral stimulation from my husband, with his hand.

"The main basis of our marriage is just the pleasure, the security, of daily companionship, working together toward common goals, a sense of knowing the other is there when needed, a genuine caring about the welfare of each other—call all this love, I don't know. There is also good sex, sharing of joy and sorrow. We are two rather different people and personalities, yet somehow it all meshes, in spite of rough times, arguments, different attitudes, jealousy, and much more.

"I've often wondered, if I had to do it all over again, would I marry him? I honestly can't say."

In other words, the "old model" refers not to whether a woman works inside or outside the home (or whether the man does, for that matter), but to an attitude of emotional inequality within a relationship. Most women want to receive the same emotional support and interest they have been giving. They want to talk, to listen and be listened to, to feel the same energy and enthusiasm coming back that they are giving—to talk with intimacy and pleasure about each others' perceptions, childhoods, plans and dreams, hopes for the future, questions about people and life. Be a team. Have fun together, make life an adventure. Many mention wanting trust and respect—and an end to competition or need on the part of men to put them down, make them feel "less."

What we are concerned with here is not the division of labor (cooking, child rearing, financial support) but the emotional contract, that unwritten part of the marriage institution documented in Part I. It has become generally accepted during the last fifteen years that women should not be limited to choosing only child rearing as their careers. There has been heated debate about whether women working outside the home, or having an independent income, would make for happier marriages. As it turns out, having a *choice* of staying home or going out to work is what makes the marriage "more equal," not just the particular role one chooses at any given time. But this must be a real choice, with real options, not just the best of very poor alternatives.

Sometimes, as we have seen, women are happy in marriages in which they stay at home and have children and their husbands go out and work; others are miserable in these marriages. The deciding factor is usually the amount of equality of attitude present—equality in terms of respect, two-way communication, and mutual emotional support—and the amount of choice available to the woman, whether she has other choices or "outs" (for example, economic outs) if she wants to take them, so that staying is her own choice, what she *wants* to be doing.

In "old-style" traditional marriages, the man lived in one sphere and the woman in another. Emotional intimacy was not the primary goal. Now, with women trying for equality in the emotional/psychological realm, most women are finding it painful that men are not ready to go as far in reaching them, to reach out to them emotionally, as women are. Should women, therefore, to avoid pain, care less? Or should women keep on trying to change a man they love, to draw him out and make things closer—even if this process has to be begun anew every day, day after day?

Some "conservative" groups in this country—since the women's movement has brought up the subject of inequality—have put forth the idea that women and men can be equal in the "traditional marriage," because even though the woman may stay home with the children and have no money of her "own," the man earning all the money outside the home, there is equal respect for both roles.

Sometimes the traditional marriage does seem to contain equality of respect. As one woman describes, in an atypical answer, "My parents have always been very affectionate, openly, with each other. They never seemed to argue. My mother seems the epitome of the decorative professional's wife. She does everything around his life and his goals. He is the master of the house. My father, though master, is not a tyrant. He listens to her, shares with her, gives her many gifts, fun surprises, treats her special, and is very care-giving."

But as we have seen and as the divorce rate shows, the great majority of marriages have not fared well under this system. The "traditional but equal" philosophy can also be a cover for the undercurrent that says a "good woman" *must want* to stay home and raise children.

Lest we develop too nostalgic or idealistic a picture of marriages featuring the "male leader" or even "leaders with different roles" (she is the leader inside the house, he outside), it is important to remember that these relationships can be terrifying, with one person in final control all the time—as one woman remembers her mother's marriage:

"My parents argued often. It was a tense place to grow up. My father was convinced of the traditional roles for men and women. He was a professor, she a 'wife.' He decided his responsibilities as a husband went only as far as earning regular pay. All the rest was up to her. For a while, he tried to keep her in line with '*Other* wives do this, *other* wives do that.' My mother, the intrepid survivor that she is, developed defenses of her own. Her very 'aliveness' broke through constantly, she was/is involved deeply with every sphere of life. She worked far harder at the marriage than he did, trying to change destructive patterns. We had family counseling and Dad wouldn't participate. He punished her in psychological ways, wouldn't speak to her for weeks, withheld sex (this Mom told me), and so on.

"One day, at the low point of their marriage, he tried to drag her up the stairs by her wrists, saying, 'It's time for bed. It's time for bed.' This terrifying episode happened on Father's Day when I was eleven and I wonder now if he had a 'lesson rape' in mind for her when he got her upstairs. She wore wrist braces for several years after that, and coupled with the rickets she suffered as a child, faces the risk of prematurely crippled hands. Writing this brings tears to my eyes and I wonder if my writing it will be of any use to you. Perhaps it will put my devils to rest. My mother has beautiful, gnarled workman's hands. She has found work using her hands, and beautiful things come from them. This one act of cruelty from my father pains me more than I was aware of."

"New model" relationships: changing the emotional contract*

Twenty-one percent of women have managed to change non-communicative relationships into communicative ones. As one woman says, "I like the openness we have now—the baring of ourselves to one another. It took a few years to be able to do this—he couldn't feel enough trust to be so vulnerable, but once he saw I wouldn't hurt him or use it against him later somehow, he opened up and was always 'there' for me . . . now we are both very happy."

What women think is important to make a relationship work, the new emotional model, is clear. Although many do not have all these qualities in their relationships, the characteristics they want are equality, dignity, and close two-way communication:

"It's practically gospel that good relationships have good communication. Then *both* partners should have an equal hand in their decisions, responsibilities, plans, child raising, drudgery, etc."

"When we discuss things that one of us doesn't understand, we keep talking

---

*Actually, what women want is to democratize the family. As one woman puts it, "Everybody's always talking about democracy. But they just want to apply it selectively. I keep thinking of Reagan—he is one of the ones always saying democracy is so great. But he only applies it to *some* institutions: to government, but not religion or the family! Men are always in charge there!"

and asking questions, it's always enjoyable—and our relationship is too important to have misunderstandings between us."

Of course, "new model" relationships and marriages are not perfect, and include fights and difficult moments too, but they are generally nothing like the violence just described; talking things over is too easy and much more fun.

To get a relationship to change can be difficult, because it is, in essence, to challenge the whole system, ask men to mesh their values in with ours—accept the validity of the "female" philosophical debate. A woman who calls her friend on the phone in distress, saying, "He doesn't love me anymore, what can I do?" Or, "This is what he said, what does it mean?"—is, in a way, fighting the entire system, trying to see how she can keep her integrity and still have a relationship.

Couples involved in change (20 percent succeed)

The road from a relationship based on role expectations to an equal, workable individual arrangement can be very rocky:

"Men and women seem to live in different worlds. My present relationship is very difficult, not very rewarding, but I'm very emotionally attached to my lover. We've been through two years of tearing each other to bits and putting us back together again. I don't think we're through yet. It certainly doesn't work as I was led to believe it was supposed to work. It's only from tearing ourselves away from illusions about what is 'supposed' to happen that we've even begun to find ourselves and each other in the wreckage we've created."

28 percent of women in marriages of over twenty years are taking steps to consciously restructure their marriages even after all this time; sometimes this coincides with when the children leave home:

"I have been most deeply in love with my husband. We have been married more than thirty years. Our relationship comes and has come first—is primary—for both of us throughout the years. We have changed our style of relating with different stages in life. The most important recent change took place about ten years ago when our youngest child left for college. We consciously reviewed our relationship and decided how we wanted to restructure our lives and live as two mid-life adults. There were times when I cried myself to sleep—there was pain as well as pleasure working at our relationship. We became more honest with each other. We tried to allow for individual freedom as well as joint expressions of our love."

One of these women, married thirty years, speaks very candidly about the rough—and good—times she and her husband are going through, in the process of trying to make the relationship more equal and emotionally reciprocal:

"I am and have been deeply in love with my husband. I've been both happy and unhappy with him. The unhappy parts have to do with roles and not being peers. That's being worked on. But parts of our thirty years have been very happy and the relationship has lasted all this time and is still going, though at times I wasn't sure it would continue—and I would never place bets on it yet!

"I feel ambivalent about marriage. I like it—but it sure needs some bugs worked out. For instance, the 'roles' that people assume in it without discussion or questioning. I'm working with my husband, and we are trying (after thirty years) to restructure and rework our marriage to be much more satisfying than it has been. We have a counselor helping us.

"After thirty years of marriage, he sees me as an equal—peer—for the most part. There are occasions when it is evident that the old male cultural values surface. But he wants to be rid of them and tries hard when they are pointed out in a reasonable way. He sometimes treats me like I am his child, but I'm quick to let him know these occasions when I feel that. So he tries to stop and the times are fewer and fewer. I'm rarely left out of major decisions. On a rare occasion, he will not consult me if he knows I will absolutely disagree. But when he has left me out, the consequences have been pretty bad, so it's (I hope) a thing of the past. There is, of course, no guarantee. But on the couple of things where I feel most strongly—perhaps I should say one thing, extramarital acting out—I think he's aware the consequences are 'no marriage.' So, as we are trying to work out the aftermath of that, I hope it won't happen again. He doesn't really 'act superior'—no—that's not really his style.

"We fought over the way he said something to me—*telling* me how I was behaving instead of telling me what he wanted and how he felt. He doesn't have to tell me how I am behaving and feeling—I know! He can ask—but not *tell* me about me.

"He doesn't realize—perhaps even now—that he needs to spend time and thought and energy on the relationship. He realizes that to some degree but not sufficiently, I think. It's always left up to the woman—still is, too much of the time. I think men generally take falling in love seriously, but it doesn't play as strong a part in their lives as in a woman's. Men's work plays such a strong part in theirs—and themselves. They are conditioned to consider themselves more, I believe.

"The man I have actually hated the most is, I suppose, my husband. But it's only been the concomitant of love and frustration with differences. I remained angry over some issues for years—especially the issue of his not treating me as a peer—an equal. But I've given up my anger as he progresses and as

I progress in working out these things. And I was and have been depressed at times—sometimes badly.

"I have been loneliest in my life when my husband and I have had deep problems between us and there looked like little way to make it better, different. But somehow we always did make it better or different. Probably the worst thing I have done to him is to help maintain his inadequacies by stepping in and doing things for him—in a sense, perform as his mother rather than his wife. I suppose I most criticize him for not telling me what he wants, how he feels, or denying that he feels things when his non-verbals indicate he does feel them.

"What I have always liked best about being married is the cuddling after the alarm rings in the morning!

"If I could change one thing, it would be to get him to be more expressive of his emotions, his wants, needs. But that's coming."

Another woman, married twenty-nine years, after a year in which her husband has been away in another country and she has been on her own, realizes how unequal their relationship has been and plans to change it on his return:

"I am forty-six years old, happily married, with two children. I am equally happy about my work and other interests—ballet, watching football, and knitting.

"When I was seventeen I fell in love with my husband. It was intense, to the point of suffocation, and sweet. I loved having and raising my children and was lucky enough to be able to stay home with them until the youngest was twelve. Even so—if I had it to do again I would have waited until later. Doing it the way I did doesn't give a woman a chance to know herself—she falls into the mold of being just wife and 'mommy.'

"At this stage in my life I am finally becoming me, but in the past I found it difficult to express this to my husband. He still expects me to do all the wifely duties concerning keeping the home, work full-time, and conform to his ideas. He has been on a foreign assignment for a year, working. Now he is coming home. I have *enjoyed* this separation, my life is my own, I needn't worry about being home at five to prepare dinner, can clean at ridiculous hours, watch my TV programs or not watch at all. After twenty-seven years of marriage, I think this separation has done us, and particularly him, a lot of good. I am hoping he will appreciate our life more.

"When he comes home, I hope to make changes, and explain myself to him. I like being part of us, but dislike not being me. My husband stifles me. I cannot really be myself when I am with him. I am very careful about what I do and say. Our biggest problem is not being able to talk. He talks *at* me, and what he says is law. I don't seem to be allowed an opinion. I am rebell-

ing, though, and plan to take a stand! He makes me feel stupid and inadequate. He plays the man of the family, in the old-fashioned sense. He has an
arrogant countenance in every aspect. He is happier than I am with the relationship, but I'm sure I'll stay married—it's just that I'm going to make
some improvements!"

*Another woman went to extreme lengths to get her husband to see how he was
using the relationship—with good results after a long period of struggle:*

"I got to a point where I was ready to confront my husband with the fact
that he was preventing me from enjoying life with his casual attitude toward
holding up his end of our marriage. He did as he pleased, came and went as
he felt like, always managed to find an excuse when I needed him. I had to do
everything. Every once in a while he would drop by to tell me what I should
do, or what I should have done about something. I finally got the nerve to tell
him that he could do some things himself if he wanted them done in a certain
way; if he wants to contribute I'd be glad to accept, to confer with him, it would
make a nice change from nothing, from being the family all by myself. He
backed off. No, he was too busy doing as he pleased to help out, and he
clammed up. I left, going to work, slammed the door, but stood in the stairwell
stock-still for fifteen minutes. I was stunned, I couldn't take a step. The situation was intolerable. I had to hit him hard somehow.

"O.K., I said to myself, this is it. I had kept a journal of all his sins for over
a year. When he treated me a certain way, I was always nonplussed, I couldn't
believe he was doing whatever he was doing and was unable to respond on the
spot. Later, in the journal, I could dissect his behavior, my feelings, what
consequences his behavior had for me, and decide what to do about it. I
watched myself in my journal. Standing in the stairwell, I said, O.K., verbally
he can always respond in a patronizing, scornful way to me, but I'm not going
to talk, he's going to read. I walked in, he didn't even look at me. I got my
journal, threw it on the table next to him, said something, I don't remember
what, and walked out.

"I stood in the stairwell again. I was drained. I was all done, I had tried
everything. He would know now, or he would never know. I was surprised
to realize that I was beginning to feel calm. He called me at work later, and
said he wanted to talk, he was sorry. It was my turn to be nonplussed again.
HIM wanting to TALK? We did and he understood what he'd done wrong,
but it took him years to change his behavior. I'd tell him what I needed or how
I felt and he'd say, 'Bullshit!' before I'd finished the sentence. It got worse
before it got better. I began to cut myself off from my needs and feelings in
order to escape his telling me they were meaningless. That's when I had the
affair."

Another says that after several years of being "really militant," she now has an equal and wonderful marriage:

"I have been married ten years, and I can tell you it is fantastic—now. In the beginning, he wouldn't do anything to help me around the house, he was just arrogant like most men, he expected me to do everything, so I had to make a big thing of making him see my point. I just refused, for about a year, to move even a dish if he didn't also move a dish. If there were dirty dishes on the table, or dirty ashtrays, or phone calls to be made, I just didn't make any, unless we stood right there together and he made just as many as I did. When he stopped, I stopped.

"Now it is wonderful—he is so supportive and understanding, he helped me have a way to go back to work with the children here and he really takes a part in all the household. My sisters have both been married twice, it never lasts more than two years or three. I keep saying, 'Wait, wait! If you keep on trying, eventually you will have something great. Don't give up! Be really militant—*really*.' It is a shame that women have to do this to make men see, but it's worth it when you become a team and have that closeness."

———————————

Sixty-two percent of the happiest couples in this study (of those together more than five years) have been in counseling together. Perhaps this indicates the ability of therapists to help, by providing a framework in which a couple can air out problems; or perhaps it indicates that these special couples care more, have more openness toward trying various means of keeping open the channels of communication—or both. In any case, while many people think that talking things over with a third party is a mark of shame or failure, in fact just the opposite is true: it is the mark of a growing relationship, one which has a chance to transcend the culture's unfortunate limits, one which can be better than all the rest.

72 percent of women in their twenties who are just beginning marriage are also taking steps to redefine marriage, * to make it more personal and individual (although appallingly few are successful as yet):

"I feel responsible for my marriage, for what it is and will be. I have trust in my husband's responsibility toward this also. I feel we are making our marriage what it needs to be for *us.*"

"The best way to make a marriage work is for both of you to have a clear idea of what you want—not to feel that it must conform to some ideal image outside, but only to what really feels good and works for you yourselves."

———————————

*See also Part III for more of those just starting out and dealing with these issues.

"Our relationship is only six years old. However, now my husband and I have created a marriage which suits *our* needs—we have been very careful to define it in our own terms. I was very apprehensive about marriage in the past, not realizing I had this power. I was not interested in serving anyone. That's not a problem now."

There is really no "definition" of marriage to follow, if one wants to avoid the types of marriages all too many people have wound up with in the past. Each couple has every opportunity to make something uniquely theirs.

One woman in a new marriage is quite consciously trying to keep her "single" or "primary" self in marriage, to maintain her personal integrity:

"I am thirty-four, married for a year and a half, first marriage, no kids. I make art (no money out of it); art is my process of self-transformation. I hope it affects other people also, helps them transform themselves. The other thing that makes me real happy is my love relationship with my husband. I love him more than I have ever loved anyone in my life.

"The combination of getting married and trying to maintain my career has been the biggest crisis of my life so far. Before marrying, I had thought being able to have a working, viable marriage and continuing my career would be in conflict. I was convinced on a sort of unconscious level that these two things were mutually exclusive. During the early stages of our marriage, it almost turned out to be true. At that time, I wasn't bringing in much money, I was working part-time. My husband was working full-time and he and I were expecting me to do most of the housework and errands. I did them but I resented it. After about nine months, I went into a very deep depression. To try to resolve this, I took a trip and was away for two and a half months. This gave me some space—and time for what was going to surface to come out.

"After I came back we had many discussions and decided the solution was to separate ourselves financially. Now we both contribute a percentage of our incomes to a household budget, and the rest of our incomes we spend as we please. This allows me to feel that my free time is my own and that I can use it in my artistic pursuits and not feel guilty. We also split the housework and the errands; we wrote them all down in a book, we divided them up, we rotate who does what, month to month. This has relieved the tension and the impossible feeling I was having before.

"My husband's real supportive, although he has outcroppings occasionally of resentment, or what I think is unconscious sabotage from him. Sometimes I get complaints that I'm not spending enough time on him or complaints about my share of the housework. Sometimes I get pissed off and we have a real good fight. On some deep level he has fixed beliefs about the roles of women and men that he hasn't been able to overcome yet. I do too. Sometimes, on an unconscious level, he wants a traditional wife, he wants somebody who puts him first, who puts his career first, who will sacrifice time she might spend on herself and her own career for keeping the house, doing things for him, doing something that might help his career, etc. And I'll get a resentful comment from him or an action that sabotages things going on in my life. But that's not mostly what I get. Mostly what I get is support, interest, love, and kindness."

Many women—whether just married or married for thirty years—find that marriage works better if they can retain a kind of single stance, mentally:

"My husband is great, but unless I maintain my single frame of mind, it doesn't work at all. I have to assert my rights on an active basis, not just lie back until he (unconsciously) challenges them, and then argue with him about them. I have to take space myself, painful as it is for me, but as I want to be with him so much, I do it. But it's even more painful when I don't assert my life (almost 'forgetting him') and suddenly he, without noticing, has taken it all and I don't have any space left and we fight. Then we are even further apart."

"The biggest fights that I have with my husband are about my need for 'time out' now and then. We do agree as to the ways to deal with my teenagers. I need to get away for a few hours once in a while. Go shopping, to a concert or the like. He has begun to understand this."

One woman who is extraordinarily happy now in her second marriage tells how she got there:

"I am so 'in love' with my husband. I'm in love with him because he's such fun to be with; I trust him implicitly; he adores and respects me; supports my ego; makes wondrous love with me; shares the same interests—photography, philosophy, astronomy, business, etc., etc.

"I loved my ex-husband but I don't believe I was ever 'in love' with him—his very nature could not allow that honesty which seems to be the key element in being 'in love.' For me being 'in love' is by far the more satisfying. Within this relationship I have opened myself totally to everything life has to offer. This 'in love' business based on honesty has dynamic power behind it—the power to make you believe in your own human potential—all because somehow you know you can trust the person. It takes time to test out the honesty.

"I'm so deeply in love now, so happy. We eat three meals a day together—I carry a picnic basket covered with an embroidered cloth to his store nearly every day for lunch. We are always affectionate—even in his store. We fight when things get hard or we are growing too fast or have to make a big change (like now) in our life. We've worked through the horror of insecurity (what if he/she leaves me). Our fights are verbal frustration. We live far from our families, are too tired from starting a business or becoming an administrator to have much of a social life (until now). We rarely watch TV. We talk incessantly to one another (our favorite sport), live in a rural, isolated, harsh environment—a great stress for people loving sun and outdoor life. In spite of this it's a great love affair. We are the most passionate now after ten years together.

"Love should make you feel capable of great feats. As my daughters have become more secure with my love for them, they seem to try more and more difficult feats for themselves. As other people join in their lives, adding more love, they climb even higher. This is what my husband and I feel about our love: love gives us the security to stretch ourselves, to try out new things, to let go of fears and insecurities. Love is nurturing in a very broad sense. You can have strong feelings right from the beginning but then the real work begins . . . spending your life together.

"This relationship is important to me because of the capacity for understanding—here's a person to whom I can say anything. I can ask him any question and he will answer with candor. He listens and cares about what I think, feel, and do. All the rest is a result of interaction. I know this because I lived with another man for eighteen years who never heard, cared, or felt anything about my innermost thoughts. The more intimately we relate on an intellectual and emotional level, the more intense the passion and sexual intimacy becomes on a physical level. We don't have children together, but he is close to my daughters.

"Talking is our great joy. We often choose that over social gatherings. Talking has contributed to both our successes. Our daily life consists of putting into practice our talks. He talked incessantly while starting his new business. Sometimes it drove me crazy. We are talked about in our community. We are known as 'the talkers.' We celebrate the good times and fight through the hard times, talking all the while. We talk ourselves into entirely new lifestyles. We would never have grown so much together had we not used this formula.

"We cook breakfast and usually dinner together. When we both worked full-time, we shared all the household chores. He's a great ironer! And then when he started the business and I still worked, he was unable to help at home. It was really difficult. We hired a cleaning lady and I began to dread cooking, walked more so I wouldn't have to deal with car upkeep, etc., etc. It was a horrible time for us. After two and a half years I made the decision to stop working so I could devote full time to his needs at the store, two houses, two cars, etc. It's been a real financial strain to prepare for, begin, and operate a new business at a time in my life when I expected to have good earning capacity between us. It's meant we've not been able to eat out a lot, buy things: clothes, new furniture, and what I consider essentials. But I took a risk and bloomed as an administrator, we both took a risk to quit a well-paying job to begin a new business. Three and a half years later it's a roaring success and he's quite a different person; secure, confident, never ill. Our flat was recently featured in a news tabloid home section featuring 'How to Decorate with Thrift Store Savvy.' The trick is to live your life ever open to change and acceptance.

"I like being married a lot, I'm pretty much a one-man woman. Even when I was single (after my divorce) I never enjoyed the mating rituals. I feel great pride in being the wife of such a wonderful man. (I also know the feeling of shame in being wife to another, not so wonderful man.)

"How did we get married? A friend in Mexico lived in a house with an old chapel—the idea began there as an ideal wedding spot—it was actually our friend's idea. He and I talked it over and I guess it was me who asked. He was very afraid of marriage. We'd known each other about two years and had been living together eight months. I knew my daughters had a hard time with their mother living with a man. We were also madly in love and became a glimmer of hope for several hundred people in a place where everyone had stopped believing in long-term anything. It became a challenge for our own emotional security.

"We were elated and euphoric for four years. People used to stop us on the street because of the glow around us. My feelings grew deeper and deeper. His actions toward me continue to grow more loving.

"Having sex is the celebration of our daily life together. During sex, he's incredibly loving and more open than at any other time of the day. He lets go of everything but us for the time being. He tells me all kinds of wonderful things. We had to practice for a long time before our bodies and minds could grasp the simplicity of 'letting go,' especially when the business was getting started. If there's nothing on your minds but each other—the experiences can't help but be fruitful. My body gets real excited after all the day's chores are finished and I know we have time together. We sleep very close together. We were very shy and modest at first, afraid of giving too much of ourselves for fear it might suddenly end.

. . .

"I love having my children. The first child was born when I was nineteen. It was a difficult birth (thirty-six hours of labor). The second—no problems with the birth, but I was traumatized by my husband's behavior (drinking and not coming home). Both births were done completely alone—I was dropped off at the hospital and left to fend for myself.

"I married young because I thought being single was a drag (this was in the 1950s). I gave up freedom to do what I wanted, which was be on my own—go to school. My parents couldn't bear the thought of my being alone. They convinced me on some level that I would become promiscuous and didn't have the brains to make it on my own. Marriage seemed the only alternative.

"I was financially dependent on him for fourteen years and it didn't bother me a bit—I expected it to be that way—until I began making money on my own. Suddenly I began seeing things differently. For one thing, there was more of it and other possibilities began opening—like freedom! I eventually left him because part of me was convinced I could support myself.

"I left after eighteen years of marriage. He had a secret life of honky-tonk bar women, gambling, and drinking, and I finally found the courage to leave. I hated him for cheating and lying. It made me feel crazy. He had that 'Mr. Nice Guy' image and people often thought me a bitch to live with. I tried to leave a couple of times, but somehow I always thought *I* was the cause and thus tried harder. I became mentally inert and depressed as years went by. I waited to get out of debt (worked three jobs) and finally left. I never want to see him again. I feel deep pity, but I'm still angry at the damage to my ego, and my own stupidity for putting up with it for so long.

"When I left, I felt triumphant on the one hand and like a complete failure on the other. I did hate him—*had* to hate him in order to leave. It was awful and I became hysterical once right after I left. The relief was so great I lost ten years in appearance immediately and plunged headfirst into life. My doctor and close friend had helped me with permission to leave—he felt I would die if I didn't get out—in spite of the money. Most of my acquaintances thought I was out of my mind.

"My parents had told me when I divorced that my daughters would grow up to become whores and prostitutes—that I was warped and sick for not staying where they could watch over me since I didn't have a brain in my head. Eight years earlier they had told me I must be such a bitch to live with, no wonder he drank and never came home, etc.

"At the time of the divorce, I had to leave two teenage daughters behind with their father. I left with $400, moved to a different state, was disowned by my parents and a number of friends, but supported emotionally by my daughters . . . they helped me succeed! I left the state, setting out with my $400 to begin a new life. I 'fell into' a small southwestern university as a full-time student, with a part-time job, apartment within walking distance—all the things I needed in order to survive. Then my sixteen-year-old daughter joined me and she and I lived on $117 a month plus food stamps while I pursued an education. I worked very hard at school and began to see my own potential.

"The next year, my daughter returned to Oregon to finish school with her friends. I worked even harder at school after that, then I bought a one-way ticket to Mexico to attend an American art school there. I needed to get even further away from everyone in order to become more myself. I received a B.F.A. My daughters helped me tremendously during this time—as though their own futures depended on my success . . . and indeed they did. I also whooped it up, dancing in the streets and being crazy part of that time. I needed that kind of fling in my life.

. . .

"Now I've been with my husband ten years. We both want to do and be a lot of things. Our backgrounds haven't made that easy. I'm hypersensitive and extremely emotional about most of life. When frustration becomes unbearable I'll pick a fight so I can rant and rave a while (usually not more than a few hours!). This doesn't occur too often. He is the same way—we usually know it's coming in advance. The pressure of selling a business and moving to a remote place is hard and once in a while we fight because we know we have to live with it.

"About six years ago, my husband began dealing with a lot of insecurity. Once he went into a rage and leaped up from the dinner table, throwing dishes against the wall. He stalked through the house breaking pottery he had made. He was totally 'out of control' and I let him rage a while and then held him and told him how glad I was he finally 'let go.' His biggest fear was that I really didn't like him. He always said that first when we fought through these conflicts. I was really overwhelmed, scared and angry, but on some level knew he had to get a lot of stuff out.

"Since starting the business, every now and then he becomes a bit of a tyrant. Even though I know it's temporary, it freaks me out. He resists advice or criticism (but then I do that too). My problem is that when he complains about things, I offer advice when the timing is off. It bothers me too if he doesn't help enough when I really need it. We use the weekend retreat ten miles from where we live as a personal haven during fights.

"We know the conflicts will be resolved just because we're fighting—that's how we've overcome our terrible insecurities. Being so much in love gives us the assurance that the fight will be resolved. We've made sure that sex never becomes an issue during these times. In fact, our sex life seems to make quantum leaps as a result. We sort of take turns making up—we both initiate talking since that's our favorite thing to do. If it's particularly bad I'll telephone from a booth and we seem to make progress due to the distance. We've never stayed mad more than a few hours.

"I've been in therapy many times adjusting within our relationship. When the business was started I was having my own success. It was exhilarating, then suddenly interrupted by my wonderful, quiet husband, who decided to grow at the same time. We clashed head-on. His personality changed, as did mine, and we were often at war. Our whole world changed and it took all kinds of help to keep it balanced. Therapy helped a great deal. We became more trusting, more independent, more accepting, more adaptable, and quicker to change our actions.

"From the beginning I knew this relationship would require a lot of work, but I also knew it would be worth it. I felt great fear for at least the first seven years that he would tire of me and leave. He had the same fears. We kept working on that and now do not have that fear. We are more excited with each other now than at the beginning of our relationship. He's very excited by me right now, especially because I'm getting older and freer. I'm much more open sexually and find it great fun being adored by my man.

"It used to be that if we fought he would be afraid to make love. I felt sex had nothing to do with whatever problem we were working on. He loved sex and was willing to work on that theory. Gradually we began noticing our sex was getting freer and more uninhibited. It continues feeling better and better as we solve more and more problems that come up in our everyday lives. We probably spend more time together than most couples and it does not make the passion less. In fact, we have much more sexual passion now.

"I'm not a beautiful woman at all, yet this man makes me feel so and as a result I feel more beautiful and other people reflect that back to me. I know what feeling seductive can elicit from even a shy, quiet man. I'm astounded that other men tell me and my husband what a sexy woman I am.

"A couple times a month I feel an overwhelming passion. It feels wonderful, a craving. I can't keep my hands off him. I feel more aggressive, I love exploring his body—especially his genitals. My man has a wonderfully formed body, slight in stature and very firm. I have penetrated his anus and I like what it does to him. I also like oral sex a lot. He loves having that done to him—I do like oral sex for myself sometimes but my husband is not comfortable with the taste. I feel fine about myself *and* the fact that it bothers him; we have enough going for us so that it's not an issue. All I wish is we could make more time for sex—hopefully that's what we are heading toward in our new life.

"I've never had an extramarital affair—even when I knew my previous husband was cheating. I felt so destroyed as a woman by his behavior I could *never* do that to another person. I believe in absolute monogamy, as does my husband.

. . .

"My daughters and I talk openly about sex—we have talked about masturbation and each know that the other does this sometimes. We talk about problem areas. I send articles and information and my daughter who is a nurse keeps us informed as well. She confided in my husband and me that she once had sex with two men at once. That shocked me a bit, but it was good to talk about it between us. My husband is as open as we are too.

"My younger daughter was recently married and my husband 'gave her away.' The ceremony was extra special in that he (who has never had children) became a father, father-in-law, and grandfather officially on that day. He helped me deal with my last shred of guilt for being a divorced mom during this event. I wanted to give my daughter something special for this day—my husband suggested my gift: 'to have the best time I've ever had in my entire life.' Something clicked and I felt permission to 'let go.' I danced the feet out of my rose-colored glitter panty hose. I have never felt such joy—and she understood. He and I celebrated the gift later at a motel and I believe we were the closest ever.

"My latest more important relationship has been with my older daughter. We are each other's dearest friend. I recently spent ten days at her house and we hardly did anything except hang out together. We read together, watched tons of TV movies—a rarity for me. One night we laughed so hard watching the tube I rolled off the couch and nearly threw up. We talked together, walked on the beach, roller-skated, and went on rides at the Boardwalk. She is twenty-seven, single, an R.N. who struggled through school and all sorts of traumas, mostly alone. She is adored by everyone who knows her, incredibly competent, a joy to know. Her values are an inspiration to all her friends and co-workers. Lots of wonderful things happen to her as a result of her personality. She can be bossy, but it's fun watching her become more sure and secure. I feel comfortable chiding her. I can talk to her about drinking too much (her, not me). She can talk to me about being neurotic (me, not her), etc., etc. I feel truly blessed by this child. Her sister is much the same.

"I most admire women's ability to adapt. They have to maintain such flexibility, with children changing so rapidly and juggling all the activities within a family. Men seem much more resistant to that much change. We wouldn't have a social life if it weren't for me, he just doesn't think about those things. I also admire women's openness. Men in general are much more reserved with their emotions. I most admire women who continue growing while raising the children. I truly admire women who fight for the rights of woman-kind. I've never considered myself a feminist, though many people think of me that way.

"Women also have a right to their own time. In the last few days, I've been thinking I need some. Since my daughter just got through nursing school and my husband has been involved with his new business, I've given a lot of energy to them. I loved working but feel a need to stop for refueling. I've supported all these people financially and emotionally for the past six years and now feel the need to give something to myself.

"I love being feminine. My life has become an art form. I create environments in which to live, art to hang on my walls, healthy food to satisfy my hunger, poetry for my soul, exercise for my health, innovation to excite my husband, and most of all I create challenge to keep my spirit alive.

"To women I say: Find something creative to do with your time. Laugh a lot, love a lot, and have the best time you can possibly have—*all* the time. I was never a bored housewife—every day was a challenge for me to create something wonderful: a story, a joke, a meal, a dress, a painting, a garden, a friendship. My daughters treasure their childhoods yet I lived with a man I could barely stand. It was not a waste—it was an education for all of us. My daughters and I went forward, their father went backward. We all make those choices."

Marriage and living with "younger men"

Fourteen percent of the women in this study are married to or live with men ten years or more younger than themselves. These marriages often work quite well. However, age is no guarantee of equality in a relationship; good attitudes are a function of individuals, not generations, according to both this study and *The Hite Report* on men, and can occur at any age.

The following woman, living with a man thirteen years younger, describes her very happy life:

"I am a young middle-aged woman who loves life. I love taking my two dogs for a walk in the woods. Their exuberance and love of running and playing makes me feel almost high. My boyfriend, with whom I live (for two and a half years), also makes me very happy. He is non-demanding and tends to be very happy to have me as I am, not as he would change me to be (like men in my past). I love being with him, working with him, making love to him. It's a real satisfied, peaceful feeling. I'm more passionate and at ease with sex with him than I have ever been. He is thirteen years younger and I see a potential there for problems, but I will deal with that when and if the time comes. I do imagine spending the rest of my life with him, but if that does not happen, I'm sure I will love someone new.

"My philosophy of relationships? I tell my friends that I would rather have a good relationship with a new man every five years than stay in a bad relationship just for the sake of what 'society' will think. I applaud people such as Liz Taylor who continue to try to find happiness rather than give up and become bitter old women.

"My greatest achievement personally has to be the fact that after twenty years of marriage to a bigoted man, I finally realized that I was O.K., contrary to what he had always told me, and could one way or another make it on my own, and have a relationship because I wanted to, not because I had to. I went on to get a divorce and discovered that I was so happy without him that I had only one regret, and that was that I had not divorced the drunk nineteen years sooner, when after one year of marriage I knew in my heart it had been a mistake. But, 'as we all know,' nice girls do not get divorces just because their husbands are bastards, they do not risk the gossip at work, they do not deprive their child of having a father. Of course, I know all this is untrue now, but it took many years to gain this wisdom and to have enough confidence in myself to go forth on my own. I did not work then and did not have anyone in the world I could talk to. I felt completely trapped, helpless, and lonely. Many of these feelings were self-inflicted, but at the time I could not sort that out.

"My lover and I are both happy, and talk about the future with ease because neither of us demands a permanent commitment from the other. We enjoy sex, daily life, hobbies, going out, etc. He tells me he loves me, he says how much he loves to make love to me. Sex is wonderful.

"The biggest area for concern (not presently a problem) is our age difference. I am afraid that one day I will be too old for him. The only time I felt a difference in our ages that was a problem was during the first year when he left me home alone on our first Christmas together to go to a family dinner at his parents' house. I was terribly hurt. But we worked it out after that, now we always spend holidays together.

"The other day we were doing some canning of preserves together in the kitchen, and I said I was going to start dyeing my hair, some gray was beginning to show up. He showed minor interest, saying of course it was my hair, but he thought it was great the way it was, maybe streaked it would be nice, and then we went on to discuss whether to use paraffin in the tops of the bottles this year. I am very happy with him, and I believe he is with me. It's a quiet and wonderful feeling of being together."

And another, now in her second marriage, this time to a man ten years younger than she is, sounds extraordinarily happy:

"I'm forty-one years old, a middle-income high school teacher with two children. After over nineteen years of marriage I finally realized the only things that made me happy were totally unrelated to my husband. The entire marriage had been filled with fighting and verbal abuse—but I stayed because of the kids and my own poor self-image, which I later realized he had fostered all along. I was never truly satisfied either sexually or emotionally, but I blamed it on my own inadequacies. After my separation, thanks to two female friends I began to see myself in a new light. I lost a lot of weight and felt for the first time in my life like a special, self-reliant woman.

"The cocktail scene introduced me to a wide variety of men, from caring, sensitive lawyers to insecure pilots and back to demanding, self-centered men.

"After three years of separation, I remarried and have found all the happiness and sexual and emotional fulfillment that I wanted but felt I was incapable of having. My present husband and I carried on an active sexual relationship for over a year before we married, helped each other through very hard emotional times. His kindness, caring, and loving were always steady. However, he had been hurt so badly in his first marriage, he was reluctant to put complete trust in me. Now, after ten months, we both have the love and the kind of relationship we both longed for. We are friends and lovers. We rely on and need each other in many ways.

"I am probably a '9 1/2' in happiness (with '10' tops). I derive pleasure from so very many things. My love relationship is warm and satisfying and I am always anxious to come home to my husband's warm, loving arms. My job is fulfilling, especially when students return to visit you or when a special ed. student learns some self-assurance. I have horses and the love they give is warm and exciting. Riding in the woods and feeling the warm breezes or seeing the glories of nature is a high beyond words.

"Life without my husband would be very empty, even with the same things. Before we married, time without him, time on my hands (as Elton John sings) was the blues. Now it's 'laughin' like children, livin' like lovers, rollin' like thunder under the covers!' The song is very descriptive of love. I think no matter what my husband would do or what might befall him, I'd be beside him.

"The first time I met him, he impressed me so with his kindness and concern that he was on my mind a lot and I finally decided if I ever saw him again I'd make the first move and tell him how much I appreciated his conversation and how I felt he was a very special person. Now that we are married we both are working for a successful continuing relationship. We don't have 'problems,' it's just things that affect us as a unit that we have to try to work at or tackle together—i.e., my ex, his ex, his being a stepfather, or not getting enough 'alone time,' etc.

"Believe it or not, this man shares the work willingly without my asking! I usually cook and clean up, but he'll often clear the table—cook, if I ask. We make the bed together 90 percent of the time. We sleep in a king-sized bed but it might just as well be a single because we like to feel the soft warmth of each other. Every morning he loves to cuddle, and our mornings always begin with warm skin-to-skin hugs and kisses under the covers.

"I'm the happiest I've ever been now (and I'm no spring chicken). Because my husband is ten years younger than I, I really hope Mother Nature is kind to me in the 'looks' department. I try harder to look good for him because I feel he's very handsome. Growing old won't bother me if we can do it together. Many things are important to me, so I don't like to take too much time with my hair or makeup but, even in coveralls and mud boots cleaning out a barn, I'm feminine. I don't have to look like a model all the time.

"We both work. I wish there were a good way to handle money as a couple. I'm not entirely satisfied and neither is he, but it's better than we both had it in our first marriages. I am definitely passionate. I'm sure my first husband, especially at the end, felt like I was a cold fish. Even *I* thought I was frigid. But with my current husband, sex is exciting, warm, loving, explosive. In twenty years of marriage with my first husband I practically never had an orgasm. Still, sometimes I don't think my genitals are pretty and I am concerned about how I smell. Monogamy? I believe if a relationship is all-around right, sex outside a marriage isn't necessary or even something one wants. I am monogamous and I want him to be also.

"We fight rarely, usually about my son's actions. He usually says he's sorry first. We both hurt inside and feel terrible during. After? We are sad and even more loving. We usually talk things out. My son, age ten, who lives with us, is good but can get on your nerves. My husband also feels bad that he's raising the son of a man whom he hates (for all the things he did to me in my marriage and the things he's done to me and the boy recently). And now, when he cannot have his own boy with us and do for him the things he's doing for his stepson, he feels even worse. I wish we could have met earlier and that the children could have been ours.

"What we have in love, passion, sex, and daily companionship is beyond compare. We want to grow old, retire, and spend all our years together. I feel very loved."

Men's Resistance to Change

Most women are unable to get their relationships to change

*"Tell me, are many women finding that it is possi-
ble to change a man, to make things work better?"*

The majority of women have not been able to produce significant change in their relationships by asking for it or "working at it." Seventy-one percent of women, although they are standing up for themselves by "bringing up the issues," are doing so without success, and/or must continuously keep on doing so.

In other words, the great majority of women, no matter how they scream, plead, or reason with men they love, have not been able to bring about the kind of change they want. Those who have, have often done so in couple counseling, as seen. Many women describe feeling shocked and surprised that it is so difficult to change the condescending attitudes of men they love and who love them.

Of course, there is no real change at all if the woman has to keep "bringing the man out," "encouraging him" emotionally, etc., incessantly. As one woman remarks, "It's like housework—women's work is never done!" Change only occurs if the man is willing to take on some "female" values in the relationship too—draw the woman out, worry about her emotional condition that day, and so on. And some men do do this.

Some men are clearly trying to understand the changes women are asking for:

"The men most important to me have honestly tried to understand the women's movement, although most have never quite comprehended some of the issues. They have, however, tried to accommodate their thinking to the new image of women and, on the whole, succeeded. It is discouraging to me, though, that so many men think that because things have improved somewhat, everything is fine now. They are surprised when I tell them that we still have a long way to go."

"He thinks I shouldn't get too angry at society, or at little slights, etc. But he keeps trying to understand what it is that's bothering me. He read *The Bleeding Heart* (Marilyn French) for me. It made him very angry."

She went on to say that this attitude of his, his *trying* to understand, makes her very happy. However, many men (according to both *The Hite Report* on men and women's responses to this study) seem only to realize that there is "something wrong" when there begins to be "not enough sex" at home.

But 83 percent of women believe most men do not yet understand the basic issues involved in making intimate relationships work, as women discuss in Part I:

"Most men do not want to love a woman—they want to control her. The problem lies in their dishonesty or disregard for their own feelings."

"Love is a problem for those of us who seem to be biochemically hetero. Men are not taught the skills and attitudes of sensitivity that make a good spouse, mate, lover, or (by my definition) friend."

"He doesn't realize—perhaps even now—that he needs to spend time and thought and energy on the relationship. He realizes it to some degree now but not sufficiently, I think. It's always left up to the woman."

"He always tries to see ulterior motives as to why I am doing such and such, rather than accepting or receiving an expression of my love to him. He distrusts love."

―――――――――――

The overwhelming majority of women say they wish that men would learn more of the "female" skills of expressing warmth and closeness—how to pick up on the subtle cues from another person, how to be more giving and involved. In short, women want men to learn to love, not only sexually, but as equals.

Values and attitudes women would like men to take on in relationships include the following:

"Be more open—honest—talk a lot, work on it. If only for the time you're together, be there one hundred percent."

"Be able to identify the reason why you are feeling a certain way. Be able to unconditionally listen, to put yourself in the other person's place as much as possible."

"Never put up a wall or hold the other person at arm's length. Be interested, and always talk things out. Have arguments by all means, but talk it over quickly, and make up—why be unhappy?"

"Qualities of love I admire: acknowledging the other when they have just done a thoughtful or positive thing, being able to put the other at ease, like sensing the other's needs without them having to always say what the need is, etc. These are good qualities, but I don't have them in my relationship. They would save me a lot of anxiety."

On the other hand, some women point out that if women would take on more aggressive characteristics, be "more like men," this could "solve" the problem too; at least, women would not be taken advantage of:

"Women are not forceful enough to get what pleases them in relationships. They let themselves be pushed around and don't stand up for themselves."

"Women don't know what they want and/or don't know how to get it and/or are afraid of losing it and/or don't feel entitled to it and/or don't see that most men are emotional retards."

But another man's letter in response to <u>The Hite Report</u> *on men displays, with vituperative eloquence, many men's disparaging attitude to what women are saying they want in relationships:*

"I guess there are marvelous rules of sensitivity and consciousness in women's culture which are definitely to be admired. But they should not be taken to extremes—nor should men be expected to comply with them.

"Men may be too alienated and too respectful of each other's privacy, and see barriers all around—we all know what's wrong with that. BUT. On the other hand, the idea that process is all, relationships are all—usually involving a *lot* of talking, some crying, intense discussion of sisterly insecurities and other feelings, what I call 'girl anguish'—is all a little too much.

"I guess the rules of the game (the female culture game) involve things like you have to be there for the other at all times, and especially at the time of need—even if you are involved with an important 'real world' activity, such as work. You must express abject penance if you cannot come to the rescue, listen to a problem, on the spot. You should have been there, always ready, always available. All of this involves a lot of talking on the phone. A real premium, a positive value, is always placed on expression of feelings. In fact, it is considered the essence of being female to be intensely preoccupied with these things. Certainly, I do believe that compared to 'male culture,' emotional openness and closeness are all to the good, and to be desired—but . . .

"I feel that this is a childish pattern. There is something to be said for male patterns of a certain amount of privacy and distance. Is the world inside one's head—or is it 'out there'? Males operate excessively on the notion that it's 'out there.' But sometimes women operate excessively on the notion that it's 'in there'—i.e., in the relationships and feelings. Most conversations I have heard are marked by frequent affirmations of love of each other—and indeed, an underlying theme of almost all conversations between women seems to be a need for support and affirmation. I get so tired of it—the intense discussion of the details of one's life and what one thought about it.

"I find the pressure from women to resolve everything through total discussion at the moment, of anything that is bothering them, coercive and productive of conflict. Male sulking is a terrible thing, it's true, but it *is* coercive if a woman says that, if there is a hint of friction, everything *must* be resolved then and there—'or else!' (I am aware that women would say that theirs is a positive characteristic, and that men's desire to 'stick their head in the sand' at any seeming conflict rather than face it and resolve it is a product of *our* polluted upbringing; they may be right . . .) But I don't like it. I just don't like this way of life being held up as a standard for behavior (especially my behavior)."

Few men have, even now, truly questioned their personal definitions of relationships with women. Most resist changing these relationships to a deep extent. Have most men begun to realize, even dimly, the possible connections between "male" distancing techniques and a desire to keep power and control?

The need for men to rethink, change their attitudes toward love relationships, is a large social problem which most men have hardly begun to address as yet. Will men change? And, coincidental with this, do most men understand the changes women are aiming for in new-type relationships? Probably most do not understand at all what women have in mind as yet. As we have seen, most women say that men they know are generally not trying as hard as they are to make the relationship work—work in the way women mean, with emotional equality, more respect for human dignity. Women do not want to be denigrated anymore. Women want to create a new emotional contract with men. But most men are playing by different rules. Perhaps most men really have no idea what it is they should/could be doing; women, as we recall, frequently say that their husbands do not seem to be aware that there is something they are not doing, something they should be trying, in fact something missing.

67 percent of women say they encounter many conflicts when they try to make the relationship into an equal one:

"We argue about my rights as a person to the same privileges as he expects as a man. I believe I have the right to choose a career of my choice, and excel by means of my college courses, as long as I pay my way. But he says, 'No wife of mine is going to work in an all-male environment—ever.'"

"Arguments and disagreements were frequent during the first few months of our marriage and toward the end—the theme being that of asserting myself or trying to work as a couple, not as two opposing individuals. The major conflict during seven years was my husband's need for power—as reflected in one of his statements: 'The women aren't taking shit anymore.'"

From replies in both *The Hite Report* on men and women's replies here, it seems that individual men change their idea of themselves and relationships much faster as a result of large or traumatic personal experiences—whether these experiences come from an unusually strong love relationship with its ups and downs, which may gradually make a man reevaluate himself, or whether they come from events such as job changes.

Change also occurs in men when women as a group confront the policies of "male" culture. This has already had some very good effects—i.e., by working as a group, the "women's movement," women have been able to get equal credit for women from banks, more job openings for women, the reform of some marriage laws, the right in theory for women to own their own bodies and also to define their own sexuality (still in progress), and so on. Perhaps, too, in the emotional sphere, paradoxically, women will gain more change in their personal relationships by making a public front, "complaining" publicly about men's frequent lack of emotional support and disrespect in personal, "private" relationships.

The basic problem is that most men still don't see women as their equals *(even though they often think they do)*—and until they do, these slights, this distance, will continue. This is extremely unfortunate. It is not fair to make a woman fight for her rights in a relationship, and even worse, this constant forcing of a woman to defend her self-esteem frequently turns love into disillusionment, ashes. Sexism degrades the whole experience of deep love, but does this so subtly that everyone asks, even as the process is occurring, "What is happening? Why is it happening?"

Men's injustice to women: a lack of integrity

Will men change without being forced to? Or will men change only as part of a larger social change? Do most men believe non-hierarchical, equal relationships are possible? Do men *want* them with women? As discussed in Part I, one of the most basic beliefs of the "male" ideological system is that life is "naturally" hierarchical, that men (especially) just "naturally" compete for dominance and status. If, in the "male" ideology, all life is seen as hierarchical, and competition for "dominance" is seen as a law of "nature," then equality is not really possible, only temporary truces. In fact, in their love relationships, many men still fear that "equality" means they will be "dominated." So the system of men's distancing and condescension continues, with women "bringing up the issues," leading to men's silent withdrawal, claiming that women are the ones "making trouble"—not seeing that their own built-in assumption that "women are trying to dominate" is a large part of the problem.

If a woman is not treated equally in a relationship, and still wants to stay in it, how can she "force" equality into the relationship? Not by *making* herself "equal," since women already *are* equal. Are women going to have to wrest power and respect from men by *taking* it? Force men to acknowledge them by aggressively working to change society? Or will men eventually perceive revising the "male" ideology to be in their own best interest?

Do men believe that lack of equality is resented by women? That their own feeling of superiority is as strong as it actually is? And that this lack of equality is one of the biggest dangers to the happiness and success of their relationships? No, according to most women in this study.

Men need to create a new style of relationships with women. Right now, men's idea of the "male" way of life as heroic and courageous is in direct conflict with their treatment of women, their frequent lack of emotional development in personal relationships, disinterest in equal sharing with women, and the pain they often inflict on others and themselves. How can men reconcile their pride in the "male" virtues of courage, strength, and heroism with the domination and condescension so often shown in their behavior toward women?

Why is it so hard for men to change?

Men, to remain in the "male" club, must observe very rigid rules of behavior, wear a very limited repertoire of clothing, have a very limited range of emotional expression in daily speech, and show a profound respect for the patterns and rituals of male hierarchy. And part of showing loyalty to the "male" club is ridiculing the "out group"—i.e., women. Of course, this ideology hurts men too, dehumanizing them by telling them to glory in their lack of humanity— because the meaner, rougher, tougher you can be, the more of a "real man" you are.

How do women respond to this attitude? As one woman says, regarding why she decided to "fight back," " 'Assertive,' 'demanding' women may be put down and caricatured as 'bitchy'—but have you ever noticed that women who stick to what they want often come out on top? Whereas a woman who just keeps on giving, with the man usually oblivious to her feelings, just winds up burned out and unhappy?"

What should a woman do if a man won't change the relationship?

The stereotypes which tell us to just keep on being "loving" and "giving" no matter what—aren't they to everyone's disadvantage? Being loving and giving is good when a situation is not exploitative; unfortunately, with most men at this point in time, this is usually not the case.

But, "Nice women don't get angry," as one woman reminds us: "My sister and I probably both could have done with a bit more give-him-a-kick-in-the-ass energy toward men in our makeup." One of the things that may keep women where they are is that they often try to keep from acting on anger, and so become more and more immobilized, even paralyzed. Turning anger in on oneself can make one more and more vulnerable and depressed, less and less able to act.

On a personal level, if we find that men aren't treating us with much respect, we can stop treating them with so much respect, also. We might in addition begin to expect them to overtly work for women's rights in some way—i.e., support a women's rights organization, contribute money, etc. Do we really respect men? After all, we may respect some things they do, but do we respect their overall attitude toward us?

To appease men or confront them: a political question

How to deal with male aggression is one of the most difficult questions facing women every day now, both as individuals and as a group trying to change our status in the world, and the values of the culture along with it.

How to handle aggression was also an issue for France during World War II: whether to appease the German government or fight back. Then, of course, it was considered an important political question. It is just as serious for women, although rarely acknowledged as such. Women's discussion of possible choices/courses of action in the face of male aggression—i.e., whether to appease the aggressor or fight back openly—is one of the most important matters before women now, but mentioning it is almost taboo.

If women are angry, where should we put our disgust and dissatisfaction? Into action? (As one woman puts it, "De-tranquilize yourself and start a revolution!") There are thousands of ways to do this, little ways and big ways, every day. It doesn't mean leaving a man you love (necessarily, unless that is what you want), but it may mean confronting the whole system, supporting women and men who are "not like that," emphasizing new values, values we believe in, refusing to buy products that advertise in ways that emphasize competition and ridiculing of people, that pollute the environment; it can mean taking nature and animals seriously, reevaluating our spiritual lives, our relationship to the universe. We can stop to see how, with our daily supermarket purchases and other uses of money, we support those whose values we disagree with.

How many women find it necessary to leave, or be prepared to leave, to make their demands for change heard?

In many cases, women cannot get the men in their lives to consider changing things until they are seriously prepared to leave. One woman, who did not actually get a divorce, still feels that saying she *wanted* to leave helped the relationship improve, got her some breathing space: "I tried to get a divorce, he didn't agree, and asked me to stay. I did, but on *my* terms. Often I'm sorry I didn't leave—but the decision to divorce is like facing the death of a loved one or losing a limb. Anyway, I like me better now that I declared—I am a person."

Is it better to stay and make relationships change—if one can? Perhaps yes, perhaps no: it all depends on how much energy one wants to put into relationships, instead of into other parts of one's life, one's self. Maybe the ideology which tells us we must love and put other people before ourselves keeps us going back long past the point when we should. Or perhaps our frequent lack of financial power keeps us where we should not be in terms of freedom of the spirit.

Is it our responsibility to change a relationship? If we are already suffering from it, "should" we just walk away and let the other side invest the time, energy, and work to save it—if it is worth it to them? How good is our "bargaining power" as long as we are determined to stay?

Risking Losing All Love by Insisting on Real Love

Most women have to fight for their rights in personal relationships—even with men who love them, even if it is depressing and alienating to have to do so. This may not be fair, but this is the way it is for most women.

If one is going to stay and try to make it work, fighting back, if faced with the gender stereotypes seen in Parts I and II, is essential. One must bring the assumptions and stereotypical beliefs out into the open. Also, professional counseling or a third party can help, using someone else to change the tone of the problem, put it into another context. Don't be a "silent victim" of gender violence, whether emotional or physical. These dynamics are keeping many women in a depressed state spiritually, and silent in the larger society, when the fact is that their voices are important and valid and need to be heard.

One woman believes that for a man to work through these inequality and distance problems, being deeply in love with a woman is often the best way for him to really discover *himself:* "I don't think most men really do understand the problems a woman faces, or what a relationship can be—how great it can be. They have to live through all these stages with a woman that they love, then they can really grow and expand."

More and more men today find themselves attending counseling or therapy sessions to learn the increased emotional relating expected of them in a relationship—the broadening of the emotional spectrum that is necessary for men to sustain an in-depth relationship with a woman. This should be very rewarding for men in their relationships with themselves and each other also, since it represents an expansion above and beyond what the "male" role in life would have told them is appropriate.

But should women have to put so much effort into working on a relationship? Should women have to help men change? Or is this just one more example of women doing more supporting of men emotionally, the same old traditional one-way helping role?

Is It *Women's* Responsibility to Help Men Change?

*"Can things be changed? The question is, will men
bother? It's like, everyone comes home after work, and
asks the woman (who just came home too), 'What's for
dinner?' And she says, 'What did you cook?' "*

Is the price women pay for marriage and relationships too high? How many compromises can a woman make before loss of self-respect and identity creep in?

Most women say they feel they are trying harder, working more at relationships than men. Why aren't most men working as hard to change relationships? Men are complaining constantly that they don't like the nature of relationships—women "nag" at them, etc. Don't they want to find out what is wrong? Especially since they seem to want these relationships anyway: after all, statistically, most men do marry by their mid-twenties, and most single men continue to date women and have relationships.

After all, men's identities are being eroded too if they are in relationships that are non-expressive and emotionally repressed. Living this way is emotionally numbing—almost non-real. Isn't this what men are really complaining about? Men's psychological identity can be eroded too in non-valid relationships; however, many men may not be aware of this, as they are not used to dealing with psychological, introspective issues, and also don't think of their emotional identity as their primary identity—until perhaps later in life, or until it is too late. (Many men think that if they are functioning at work, everything is O.K.; women should just stop "complaining.")

The onus should not be on women to "fix" relationships. If a relationship is forcing a woman to be half of herself, making her feel "needy," she has the right to leave. If the changes she is asking for are not understood, as so many women say—i.e., the man doesn't perceive what kind of relationship it is the woman is working for, just hears "complaints," should the woman put more of her energy into trying to "work out the relationship," absorbing the hurts and slights she feels? Putting so much of ourselves into changing relationships and marriages might cause us to neglect great novels and symphonies we might write instead. And probably history will never reward *us* for the achievement of changing relationships or marriages! (But maybe it will, if women write more of the history books.)* And so we have the right to just leave this whole area of "work"—and decide that this is not "who we are." Perhaps, as many women are now thinking, the only way to get what we want in love is to "forget love," transcend the choices we now have, make a new reality.

In other words, changing a relationship may take a lot of work, and unfair work at that, because it involves changing not only ourselves but also men—who should be doing the "emotional housework" of changing themselves, not making us push them into it. If a woman doesn't want to do this, that is a perfectly valid choice.

How many men can overcome their own fear of "losing masculinity" by dismantling the stereotypes they have been brought up with—enough to make a relationship work? Men face a difficult Catch-22: to question the value of domination is the only way to change masculinity—but to lose dominance is to be considered "unmasculine."

That is why, although women sometimes have some success creating a workable private relationship with a man, this private relationship usually doesn't carry over into larger changes. Changing the system one to one often means a man will change when with a woman some of the time, especially when alone, but will not oppose "male" attitudes and values in a group of men—and therefore, nothing really changes because very little is passed on to other men or to the next generation of men as new attitudes or behavior patterns. Thus it may be necessary to change the whole culture in order to change love relationships.

Or can *you* beat the system? (I hope so!)

Who wants to wait for long-term social changes? They may be a good idea, but life is *now*, and doesn't everyone want to grab what happiness and love she can? Why bother being mad at men? Why not just find "one of the good ones" out there and get on with your life? Of course, if this were so easy, we would not be seeing what we are seeing in this book. But if *you* are one of the exceptions, enjoy it. Even if you are not, by using some of the themes in this

*As psychologist Beatrice M. Hinkle stated early in the century, "Throughout human history, women's individuality, personality and creative potential have been sacrificed to male psychological needs. This is a violation of [women's] personality." From a paper presented by Kate Wittenstein at the Berkshire Conference of Women Historians, June 19, 1987.

book, you may be able to create a relatively unique situation, or change your relationship, or find something better.

But it is still important and definitely worth it to try for the Big Change, stick up for other women and for a better system.

Should Women Take a Mass Vacation from Trying to Understand Men?

> *"I sit here in this argument, discussion, thinking to myself, surely you will say what I need to hear next, or give an opinion on this, your feelings about this . . . and yet you don't. And no matter for how many hours or days or years you don't, I can never stop listening, never stop hoping, waiting for, hearing your reply in my mind. And sometimes I think the frustration of waiting to hear your opinion, what you think, really think, will drive me mad."*

One woman, at a very trying time in her life, wrote the following:

"Single women should boycott men—have a national strike! All these games are so demeaning to women! Barbaric on the part of the men and pathetic on the part of the women. They plot, 'Should I do this or that, how can I get him,' etc., etc., etc. Men's attitude, even with AIDS, is: 'New York is a candy store.' I think women should live together and raise children together—period. Men have a way of approach and avoidance (distancing)—you know, first, romantic seduction and candlelight, the chase—but then, to *live* with a woman? How? Why? Who cares? New York is a candy store—and women are the candies, treats for men—not people.

"Even very nice men are full of stereotypes and dangerous preconceptions that can injure a woman's basic sense of self. Think of the nastiest names you can to call a man and they all relate to women—i.e., 'pussy-whipped,' 'dominated by a woman,' 'he's a momma's boy,' 'son of a bitch,' 'fuck off,' and so on.* Men's attitudes are so bad, so impaired, and they don't even realize how negative to women they are. They think they *love* women! It will take some massive action to make them start realizing, start thinking about all of this—like a national strike, or a boycott, a new version of *Lysistrata*. But women (any woman who is) should stop humiliating themselves—and married women too—just to 'have a man'! It's holding us all back!"

*See Dr. Janet L. Wolfe, "Women," in A. Ellis and M. Bernard, eds., *Clinical Applications of Rational-Emotive Therapy* (New York: Plenum, 1985).

The gradual wearing down of an identity: a betrayal of yourself?

"Women haven't yet begun to fight for their rights in personal relationships"

"If you're giving all and getting nothing . . . get out."

In fact, some would say that women should stay away from love affairs with men until we can change this emotionally draining system. The reason: if women are brought up with "love as their destiny" (i.e., to think that love is the most important goal in life), and men are not—*and* if women believe in love as giving, and men do not—then the system itself, with its two ideologies of "male" and "female" behavior, supports men in "starring" in relationships and in the outside world, with women supporting them emotionally and domestically.

Does this system make women angry? Yes—but often this anger is stymied because "women have no right to anger": a "good" woman is loving and giving, not "nagging" and "demanding." How can a woman be "loving" and change her situation at the same time? Will she have to give up her image of herself as a caring, understanding person, and worry that she is "bitchy" or unpleasant if she "insists" or "complains" to a man that she wants to change the relationship, or tells him that he has to change?

One woman expresses doubt as to whether it can all really work right now:

"A lot of women I know have a growing pessimism, a feeling like 'I don't trust men.' They are making it by depending on their women friends. We just don't have the power to make men change. But it's hard to give up the idea of being loved by a man—being cherished, a cherished woman, a desired sex object—a needed, treasured sex object. And it's hard to come to terms with being the principal breadwinner for your children. Men like us because we can make them feel like cherished children too—with our training to be good, soft, responsive. We are great for men—we provide them with the only kind of emotional openness since their mothers. But they are so ungrateful about what we give. I wonder about my son—how can I bring up a non-sexist child who won't fit in? Do I have the right to make him not conform? So I guess I'm kind of pessimistic."

A Long Goodbye to the "Male"* Ideology

"I want to love him and be close to him, but I just can't, the way I used to be. He can't understand what I'm talking about half the time, it seems, and when I try to insist or explain it more to him, he gets irritated. So I have to just let it go—let go of him, my dreams, love him for who he is, even if he can't understand a lot of who I am. I feel I see him clearly, who he is and how his life became what it is—but he doesn't know me the same way."

Can one be as close as one dreams one can be? What's "out there" in contemporary society? Is it an atmosphere conducive to letting love relationships develop? If society separates the two genders so decisively that it impedes love—a kind of supracultural version of Romeo and Juliet, the two genders made to promise to believe in different ways of life and to distrust one another—what is an individual to do about it?

It is not that women think men are the enemy—but many women do think that men who live by the "male" ideology are the enemy. In a way, this book, besides being a redefinition by women of who they are, what reality is, is a massive plea from women for men to stop living by their current rules and rethink what they are doing to themselves, to women, and to the planet.

If men could only see how their belief system is hurting them too, how it is possible to lead a different life, they might—they probably would. In a way, most of them do understand on some level: the majority of men in *The Hite Report* on men say that after high school their best friends are their wives, or the women they know—because they find it impossible to really talk to other men. This is a clear indication that men *do* understand that no one can live with the "male" system alone—an indictment by men of their own system.

How alienated *are* women from a system based on the "male" ideology (in which women in the United States are not even considered for the office of President, and receive so much less money and status for their work)? How far has this process gone in women's minds? Are women so dissatisfied that this is the reason for the high divorce rate—are more women than ever now leaving marriages because they refuse to live any longer with a man or a system that classifies them as less, less important, less intellectual, less rational?

As individual women go through this process of struggling to understand what is making love so difficult, they often find themselves gradually and painfully saying goodbye—with deep regret and sadness—to a belief in the possibility of the kind of love they had wanted with men. Also, many find they have suddenly lost faith in the entire "male" cultural system itself.

This process of leave-taking usually happens in stages. First women bargain

*Here, as elsewhere in this work, "male" of course refers to a cultural rather than a biological condition.

with themselves: "O.K., so I won't ask him to do the laundry or pick up the kids anymore—it's not worth it. I love him, he's a man and you just can't expect all this overnight, but I love him and I can enjoy him—and where else could I find a better lover, or a man who loves me as well?" When even this bargain doesn't really work, next to go is a woman's belief that she is loved "well." Still, she stays, because "I still love how well we know each other, what we have built up over time, and I hope he believes in this too . . ." and so on. With each bargaining chip, in this interior dialogue, a woman gives up one more emotional tie to the man until she realizes, finally, that she *is* in fact *alone*, living by herself, emotionally.

As women struggle with this inner dilemma, questioning themselves daily about the same issue, the feeling often is: "I am giving more than he is emotionally, trying harder to make it work. Why doesn't he try harder, seem to want to meet me halfway? Does he even understand that he is not? Will the relationship ever be better? Am I a fool to continue it? Should I keep on struggling? Give less energy to it? Should I *leave?*"

This state of inner questioning, alienation, and frustration many women are experiencing—whether they stay in their relationships or leave—represents a long goodbye not only to the man in question but also to "male" culture and to our allegiance to that culture's hold on us. In the process of leaving a man, whether emotionally or physically, so many women, as we have seen, go through layers of self-questioning about the meaning of love, relationships, life, the nature of family, work, what life is all about—all the basic philosophical questions one has to confront to make major decisions. And as women's thoughts about these inner questions seem to raise more and more questions, women are piece by piece analyzing and seeing "male" culture for the first time. Through this independent thought, women are shifting their allegiance from the frame of reference that has for so long dominated everything.

It seems that women today are already moving into a different frame of reference. While most are doggedly trying to get men they love to change, they are relying more and more on their women friends as major supports and primary relationships. Many are turning away from expecting too much from men and love—even though they still love men very much, and still would want this love to come first in their lives if it would be first for the man, too.

One woman comments on the transformation she sees in her own mind, having gone through all these emotions in relationships:

"I think the solution is that we have to mentally transcend the whole thing. It's not a question of to be with men or without them. The real solution is when you reach a stage where somehow or another it's just not the biggest worry in your life—it's a different way that you see the world. You live in another sphere, which is to become whatever your interests are, and maybe men are part of it and maybe not, but it is not *the* feature. Female friendships are definitely a part of it—I don't mean that now women should give up men and live only with women and follow some feminist party line, that's not it . . . I mean you live somewhere else emotionally—love can be there and become more or less important in your life—but you don't get your identity through a man."

Although a large number of women in this study say they want to "give up" on love in the sense of not taking *men* so seriously (as seen in Part III), this by no means is to say they want to give up their values, their belief in life as potentially kind, filled with close relationships, based on a loving way of approaching other human beings and animals, rather than a competitive or judgmental stance. Most women want relationships based on a team concept of work and "going ahead together."

One woman describes this shift in her own life: "Actually, I have far less need for overt 'affection' since I have found so many other things that make me feel good, including the esteem of both friends and strangers, personal experiences of music and nature. It is not that I don't need love, but that romantic love does not seem a great necessity."

"Masculinity": a heroic tradition?

Glorious, heroic images of masculinity abound in history—mythic figures who sail out to find their destiny, rescue their countries, create great science and art. These heroic efforts seem to imply no negative attitudes toward women— except, of course, women were not allowed on any of these expeditions. The heroic quest has been a male preserve.*

To be "male" seems to have two traditions: masculinity as being coura- geous, brave, and noble—and masculinity as being macho with women, aggres- sive and competitive with others, "conquering nature," justified as "natural behavior," "human nature." Which is the "real" masculinity?

How can such a tradition as the noble male—going into space, building mathematical systems, discovering the laws of the universe—exist side by side with the lowly tradition of oppressing women—keeping women out of educa- tional institutions, excluding women from power in governments, and gener- ally treating women as second-class, often less than fully human?† How is one

---

*There are also, it must be said, a few noble images of women contained in standard history books, those of women ruling their countries—Catherine of Russia, Empress Maria Theresa of the Holy Roman Empire, and Queen Elizabeth I of England, to name those best known. But generally, when not born to it, the role of hero has been reserved for men. When Jeanne d'Arc lived a heroic life on her own initiative, and in male terms, she was eventually inquisitioned and killed.

†Early Christian "scholars" debated whether women had souls, just as in the Freudian tradition "analysts" now wonder whether women are "masochists." In fact, the American Psychiatric Association, in 1986, designated a new category of disease (there being only fourteen categories altogether), "masochism." While women in the field have protested this, it has been basically adopted by the all-male board of review.

to reconcile in one's mind that a great tradition could also contain the least noble of traditions?

Historically, the classical Greek state, which is so admired for its balanced ideas of government and philosophy, was, we must remember, *not* balanced: it was a male democracy—excluding women and slaves from free speech and government, already containing the stereotypes of the "talkative" woman (Socrates' wife was said to "nag" him), the only philosophical women or women of letters being categorized as "mistresses." (Does this mean they had lovers? That they were not married? That famous men were attracted to them, and they allowed these men to make love with them? Men who have lovers are not categorized by history as "lovers," and yet women are frequently presented by the history books as no more than "mistresses," "harlots," or "courtesans.")

Has there always been this split in the culture's choice of possibilities offered to men? Or is the "macho" side of being male* more with us today? Gore Vidal once quipped, on being asked what he thought about "masculinity": "Oh, masculinity—I hear they had a bad outbreak of it down near Tampa, but I think now they're getting it under control."

The "Male" Ideology and the Psychology of a Culture

What is the "male" system, and how does it affect men? Why do men think and behave as they do?

The "male" ideology is the dominant frame of reference for Western civilization. In fact, it is the basic building block of almost all current societies, no matter of which religion or state system—Eastern, Western, or non-aligned; Islamic, Christian, or "atheist." And so, the "male" ideology is, in a way, everyone's ideology, although women live biculturally, also knowing the rules of their own belief system. Racism, gender prejudice, and class divisions may all be different varieties of this basic "male" ideology, which is essentially an ideology of hierarchy.†

Now, the question is: is this ideology biological, "natural" (because "women have children" and because "when men compete, some are stronger

---

*Are "lower-class" men more "macho," as has often been said, because they cannot be "men" any other way, by having money and power, etc.? This seems a condescending point of view: surely there are idealistic men who are poor, in at least as great a quantity as there are idealistic men who are educated or well-to-do. On the other hand, idealists such as Rousseau never realized they were prejudiced against women, of course. Often, growing up with a single mother, according to the findings in *The Hite Report on Male Sexuality*, is the most likely way in which men/boys lose their stereotypes about women.

†See pages 139–40. Does the noble part of this tradition—the positive, outward, socially interested side of the masculine—have to include the anti-woman ideology? Can a group only define itself by making itself "special" and excluding others?

and smarter"), or is it part of a historical cultural system spread by a warlike group (the Indo-Europeans) which expanded out of the East in succeeding waves, between approximately 15,000 and 5,000 years ago? *Have* women always and everywhere been "dominated"? Were women, through the centuries, the "weaker" class? If we begin to consider prehistory (history before written language), which is at least ten times as long as what we call "history," we may find a quite different picture of social attitudes and family structure.

Hierarchy: "human nature" or an ideological construction?

Is a hierarchical social structure necessary, or is it antiquated and out of place in an age of democracy? Do hierarchy and inequality keep popping up in all kinds of societies because they are "human"—or is this behavior exaggerated by a "male"-hierarchical ideology?

As noted earlier, one of the most important ways through which the hierarchical system of unquestioning obedience to authority (or "what is") is transmitted to Jews and Christians alike is through the biblical tale of Abraham taking his son Isaac up on a mountain where God had commanded that he kill or "sacrifice" the boy. Abraham is given no reason other than that the Lord commanded it, and that therefore it was "right." From this, Abraham learns that he must obey the system and not ask why the rules are the rules. He must show his loyalty by not questioning authority. This system rewards men, especially "upper class" men, with elevated status.

Today, this elevated status continues to be reinforced in men by the daily use in the English language of the pronoun "he," the adjective "his," and the generic term "man" to refer to all humans. Further, as noted, men are reminded in "nature" specials on television (and popular biology textbooks) that they have a "natural" tendency (therefore "right"?) to be "dominant," to "rule"— that "competition for dominance" is "part of their natural behavior." But even if this were true in some species of animals, it is certainly not true in all, and who is to say which is the "model" for *our* species? And even if it were "natural," would this make it "right"?

Applying democracy to the family

Most men, while they would probably say they believe in democratic government, have not stopped to think that they have not applied the same principles to the family. Many seem to assume that women are not capable of being equal, and that men/husbands know what is best for women.

But, in fact, with the promulgation of the idea of equality and democratic government during the Enlightenment, the idea of man as Automatically-Head-of-Society-and-the-Family became an irrational part of the system, i.e., if power was not derived from the authority of God and the scriptures, but now rested on the innate ability of each individual in a democratic system—on what did male authority in the family rest?

Since belief in gender superiority went so deep in the ancient "male" ideology, this glaring inconsistency was not widely questioned until relatively recently,* beginning in the nineteenth century—and then, for the most part by women. Indeed, rather than men recognizing the error of their ways, in the nineteenth century many men "found" support for the idea of male superiority in "science" (or popularized science).† The Darwinian,‡ nineteenth-century version of "male domination" succeeded the old idea of the God-given inherited right of kings (and men) to rule, in the following way: humans, it was said, had come to dominate other animals as we evolved, because we were superior; similarly, within our species, it was claimed, males "naturally" competed with females and each other for "dominance"; therefore, if we have a social structure in which men are dominant, this is clearly proof that males were and are "naturally" superior, i.e., stronger, "smarter,"§ and so on. (Similarly, adherents of slavery in the eighteenth and nineteenth centuries argued that blacks were slaves because their "natures" were to be lazy and dependent, and that they were happy that way, etc.) Darwinian competition was also used to "justify" sharp divisions between social classes in the nineteenth century, and continues today as the framework for theories of "free competition in the marketplace."

All this is not to say that competition, such as in games, normal trading, etc., is not part of life, but that cooperation has been left quite underemphasized. Many biologists and primatologists and even economists are now trying to make up for this by showing how important the cooperative forces of nature and society are.

In any case, the competition theme is a central point in the "male" ideology: "real" men "naturally" compete for a spot in the hierarchy, *must* compete (or they are "cowards" and "wimps"!). This is one of the most important credos of "masculinity." In fact, without a belief in competition as a ruling force of "nature," men would not be able to continue their hierarchies, including looking down on women, and still feel morally righteous about them.

And there is an underside to all of this for men too: by having to close off one side of themselves to women's equal humanity, blind parts of themselves

---

*Although as early as 1776, Abigail Adams asked her husband, working on the new American Constitution, "not to forget the ladies" (in a letter); he declined to comply. And, even earlier, such women as Christine de Pisan had written of women's rights in the fifteenth century.

†And in new psychological theory. See Chapter 3, and also Shulamith Firestone, *The Dialectic of Sex*.

‡Or, Darwinism in its popularized form.

§For part of the nineteenth century, it was commonly assumed by the scientific community that the brains of males were larger than the brains of females. However, when the opposite turned out to be the case, this "fact" could no longer be used to justify male authority, and so the issue was quietly dropped.

to their inhumanity to women through the general social system, not "see," in order to be loyal to the men's hierarchy, men coarsen themselves—deaden their sense of justice.

Men live with the interior knowledge, conscious or not, that by ruling, they are dominating someone, i.e., women. Since they live with/have to look at those they have more privilege than everyday, they must develop a way of not really "seeing" them. Men know on some level that they are not superior, and they know that this gender division is unjust—so the question becomes, how to live with it? The answer is, learn not to really "see" it.

Research from *The Hite Report* on men shows that most boys, between the ages of eight and fourteen, go through a stage of learning which involves forcing themselves to disassociate from, stop identifying with, their mothers. They are forced by the culture to "choose," to identify henceforth only with things "male," not to retain any "female" ways about them, for this would "ruin their chances" in life. This is a period of great stress for boys, who often feel guilty and disloyal for thus "leaving" the mother; many never recover fully.* And so, boys go through a stage of first, identifying with their mother, then next, having to break with that identification and learn to keep a distance, disassociate themselves, ridicule women/their mother, dominate them/her, and finally, reach the stage where they can rule, dominate with no qualms. *This* is the psychology of men which should be studied. But it is not; instead, the questioning is focused on women: "explanations" are sought for the so-called "problems of women."

Finally, this learning process, living with this knowledge of injustice built into the system, means that gradually men lose their ability to *see* injustice, and also to be just, to recognize justice and expect it of themselves—because they have been so carefully educated by the "male" culture to turn a blind eye to injustice on a massive scale. Living with this forced blindness leads to cynicism: idealism about life is impossible in such a situation. Thus, the "male" ideology breeds negativity toward life, finally becoming a blight on the culture.

How big a part of the "male" ideology is seeing women as second-class?

If part of the "male" ideological system is the assertion that men are "better" than women—smarter, more "rational," that they are more important, more capable of running corporations, launching campaigns, building things, being philosophers (because they are more "rational" and "scientific"), and so on—

---

*A large part of teenage boys' "mean and nasty" crazes are attempts by them to deal with their culturally imposed guilt; i.e., if one is "bad" already, one might as well glorify being an outlaw, being really tough and cruel, etc. Thus, the glorification of being mean and nasty as being "really male" (for example, as frequently seen on MTV and in children's monster or war toy commercials) comes because men (by definition) can never be "good."

how big an investment do men have in seeing women as "less," second best? Obviously, quite a substantial one. But is it logically necessary to the overall ideology? Is being "anti-woman" making men continue to try to keep women subservient, and thus the deeper definition of the "male" ideology—or is seeing aggression as "natural"?

Which came first: the "aggressive belief in competition for dominance" side of the "male" ideology—or owning women? Some say that the idea of some "owning" others came about when men first wanted to control female sexuality and thus "own" their offspring, be sure the children were "theirs." Perhaps this is true: the "male" ideology is obsessed with keeping the genders separate. This may be in part because men would lose control of inheritance and reproduction if women had choices of other family systems and were not forced to be so focused on men, or so loyal to "male" institutions.

What is "male pride"?

To play devil's advocate for a moment, why shouldn't men look down on women? Men have built the bridges, the mathematical systems, the rockets, and so on. Do men feel that, since they have built all this—the universities, great music, etc.—they have every right to be proud of what "they" have done?*

But does a twenty-year-old male have a right to "male pride"—as he personally had nothing to do with all these achievements? Isn't his "male pride" just a matter of taking advantage of "class" privilege? Is most "male pride" a cover for the ideology of men as dominant? Men as having the right to "possess" all they see?† Man is the sun, with the world and women as his province, which revolves around him at his bidding? "Male pride" essentially means: do not challenge a man, do not challenge what he says or does, or you are challenging the male world, and all the power behind it.

Women also have the right to take and build on the good parts of "male" culture, because, after all, young men don't start with "nothing" either; they build on the cultures before them. And women have contributed substantially to what has been built; also, in a profound sense, women may have built much of the pre-patriarchal tradition which merged with later patriarchal cultures. For example, the idea of "justice" of the classical Greeks (portrayed by the figure of a woman) was not pulled out of thin air, but undoubtedly harked back

*Perhaps some men look at women's position the way the victors looked at the Germans after World War I: women cannot be admired, have no right to be proud and independent, because they are/have been owned, captured, defeated. As one woman answers this "men have done it all" point of view: "Sure, they have been nurtured and made comfortable by women—it helped them be all they could."

†Did communism, as an idealistic system in theory of "give to all according to need," try to do away with the "taking" aspect of the "male" ideology? Even earlier, Christianity emphasized a turn-the-other-cheek, love-thy-neighbor point of view, especially in Jesus' teachings, downplaying the earlier idea of a wrathful God to whom "men" owed blind obedience. Thus humanism, the "Rights of Man," and even communism as an ideal can all be seen as outgrowths of Judeo-Christian *ideals*.

to a long and rich tradition of debates over what "justice" is and how society should operate.

When looked at more closely, in practice "male pride," more often than being related to courage and bravery, means that men should not be "challenged"—i.e., assertions of "male pride" are really usually a demand for dominance. "Male pride" is considered a supreme value, which must not be tampered with. What we are looking at here is not "human nature," as it is so conveniently called by those who would like to justify the status quo, that is, men dominating society because they are superior, but an endlessly repeating ideology, created by a certain group/groups at a certain time in history. Beliefs teach rules which dictate their own logic. But this does not mean they *are* logical or right.

Shakespeare's *The Taming of the Shrew* illustrates the "it's all biological" school of "masculinity." It and similar stories should, if used in high school English classes at all, be noted as examples of psychological problems growing out of a particular culture, a specific ideological point of view. Classes should not be led to believe that these characters represent "human nature." If so, the story in fact eggs boys on to make just such things as "taming the woman" the "test of their dominance" or "masculinity"—which they are told is a "biological urge," an urge they have a "right" to feel and act on, that they "can't help" but display.

Men's fear of being "in love"

What does the ideology of "masculinity" tell men about how to deal with love in an ongoing, *mutual* relationship? Nothing. It only tells men to be dominant, to dominate relationships, and to make sure the woman doesn't "dominate" them. This explains many men's fear of being "in love" and displeasure when "overcome" with feelings for a woman. A "real man" must separate himself; assert his "pride" and "dominance" before all else.

Thus, the opposite side of the coin of a "masculinity" defined as being "tough," "able to take it," is that most men also are afraid to express emotions or be too close to women, lest they seem "weak." To put it another way, the split between love and reason in classical Western thought (with "love" decreed to be "feminine," and "reason" "masculine") makes it difficult for many men to love without inner conflict.*

---

*Where did this particular dichotomy come from historically? To assume it sprang out of "nature" would be to stay within the parameters of the current ideologically defined "reality." It would be interesting to explore, historically, the various strands of this mind/body division in other Indo-European societies, compared with *pre*–Indo-European thought and culture—although what we know of these societies is as yet fragmentary. Quite a few languages of these earlier societies (what languages or signs are known) have yet to be deciphered (such as Linear A on Crete).

Men, most men in *The Hite Report on Male Sexuality*, were seen to have enormous inner conflicts over their love relationships—but few doubts that they were doing the "right thing" when they chose in favor of "reason" and against "irrational" feelings of love and attraction, whether physical and/or emotional and spiritual. Most men were proud of their ability to resist their feelings. At the same time, there is a logical contradiction in this denial of emotion: men may hold demeaning attitudes to women's "emotionality," but most still rely on women's emotional support to get them through.*

Change is a Catch-22 for men

While many men are extremely sensitive to ethical and moral issues, the closest many have come to developing an "ethical" position for themselves vis-à-vis woman has been to believe men should take care of women. While it is praiseworthy for men, or anyone, to take care of others, this does not resolve the basic issue. If men are to be fair-minded, they must look at the overall system and completely overhaul its idea of what an ethical relationship between men and women would be.

But change is a problem for men, because to give up "dominance" may mean being seen as "unmasculine"—but to question the value of domination is the only way to improve "masculinity," or society. How can men, given this no-win situation, change their ideology? (And besides, as has often been said, who wants to give up "power" if they don't have to/aren't forced to?) The first step is for men to look inside themselves and understand their lives and their philosophy better.

The current state of world affairs: the connection between "male pride," a hierarchical social structure, and international terrorism

One could make the statement—seemingly exaggerated at first glance—that political terrorism for "independence" and some men's terroristic attitudes toward women are all part of proving "masculinity"—as unfortunately defined by patriarchal cultures around the world.†

---

*Men's emotionality is encouraged in such events as the Superbowl, which is all—male, a glorification of the male, and one of the rare times men are really allowed and encouraged to be emotional; many women feel they become "overly emotional" about it.

†This could be seen as a male version of the feminist precept, "The personal is political."

The "male" ideology in its current phase, with its acceptance of the increasing amount of violence in the world and toward the natural environment, and its seeming lack of emotional concern for individuals, its focus on power and "dominance," is allowing aggression and terrorism to run riot. If the "male" ideology prescribes that competition is "natural," why *shouldn't* anyone use any means at hand to "win" in the competition for "dominance"—since power and winning are all that are respected in the final analysis anyway? In the current political situation, terrorism is a built-in consequence, a logical outcome of the "male" ideology with its focus on hierarchy.

As the feeling intensifies through increased media communications that the world is small, that we are a global village, the belief increases that one individual doesn't really matter very much, that we are expendable. Every day, as television shows us so many parts of the world, we cannot help but realize how "small" we are as individuals—that some nations and some individuals are very rich and powerful, while others are very poor. The poor and powerless can *see* the others, the rich and powerful, day after day on television, and in newspapers. This reminds them/us forcefully of their/our position, reminds us that the dominant ideology only respects power—and this knowledge increases aggression, as aggression seems to be the only way to be heard. And in a very terrible way, this is true. Disruptive acts are almost the only way for a small state or individual to get its/his(?) voice heard, or for a small state to make a point, in a hierarchical world system.

Within the system now (whether the world/state system or the "male" system as individual women encounter it with men) other alternatives are limited or closed off. A new system should be devised in which small countries and/or women are not driven to such desperate states of mind, to a feeling there is no other alternative than to fight or remain powerless, because those in power (or the man in the relationship) won't listen.

It is significant that terrorists are mostly male: is this a sign of the poverty of the "male" psyche (as created by the "male" ideology) in which men can't talk out their troubles (which would be "weak"), or can't facilitate cooperation with those around them (because they are taught to judge and compete)—or is this a sign of the "powerless" ("power is wrong") mentality of women, who would be afraid to show anger, be "unloving" or "aggressive"? Here we have our dilemma again, seen in Part I: which system is "right"? Without stopping to analyze all the possible answers here (as we have done already in many sections of this book), it can definitely be said, at least, that it is a weakness and a failure of the "male" system not to deal with all the possibilities and complexities of a very diverse world—instead insisting on dominating and trying to control the diversity which could be so productive and so harmonious. Valuing people and their feelings is perhaps the basis of democracy in government; why can't men now begin to apply this idea, valuing each individual equally, to their own personal lives and political opinions?

Origins of "male" domination

Did the "male" ideology have a historical beginning, was there a time and place when this social system with its hierarchical ideology and religious structure (as differentiated from the more egalitarian pantheon of the Greeks, the Egyptians, probably the pre-Greeks, and others) became established? Or is "male" domination a "normal" function of male hormones—i.e., testosterone levels make men restless, "aching for a fight," loving a good battle? Haven't these hormonal influences been exaggerated by those who would wish to rationalize aggressive masculinity as "natural"; to say that "male" "human nature" as we know it is "natural," and therefore "male" dominance in the social structure is also "natural?" Almost all the academic and scientific disciplines are currently involved in exploring these arguments, finding pieces of evidence.

Others argue that "male" domination originates not from "male hormones" but from the "biological" nature of the family; that is, as we have heard (ad nauseam), women "have" to stay home to take care of their children, leaving men to go out and defend them, get food. However, it has been shown that in gathering-hunting societies women do most of the gathering, and also that the majority of the food is gathered; therefore, women in some societies in prehistory probably provided most of the food. Also, there is a current debate in anthropology regarding whether the rest of the food was hunted or scavenged.*

On the other hand, perhaps male domination is not biological at all but the result of a historical accident—certain tribes with this ideology winning key battles, battles won in fact *because* of their having this ideology: an extremely competitive, combative, and warlike group could easily be the victor over less militaristic, more peaceful societies.

We do not know enough about prehistory (the time before writing, or writing that has not been deciphered or was perishable) to trace the various strands of philosophical thought back much further than 3000 B.C.† But we know that high forms of art and culture existed at least as long ago as 35,000 years, as the Ice Age art exhibit appearing at the Museum of Natural History in New York, and featured as the cover story of *Newsweek* in the fall of 1986 demonstrates.

---

*Richard Potts, paper delivered before the American Anthropological Association annual meeing, 1985.
†The original Hebrew God was pictured as being wrathful and aggressive in the earliest parts of the Old Testament. However, one historian has questioned the male role offered to men by Adam; in *The New York Times Book Review,* John Boswell of Yale University has written that Adam is really a kind of non-person, a passive being who doesn't really do much except succumb to Eve's temptations, she being the major actor. This is an interesting viewpoint, and might corroborate the belief of some that in earlier history (or prehistory) women were held supreme and were those in charge of society.

The Old Testament of the Bible makes an important point of repeating, in stanza after stanza, the lineage of certain people, *because it wants to establish the tradition of descent through fathers,* not through mothers. What does this imply? That *maternal* descent may have been traditional for preceding millennia, as suggested by lists of female names found on clay tablets in Crete and elsewhere. The Old Testament also inveighs against the worship of female gods (who were popular in Canaan* and elsewhere)—thus also implying the existence of a possible important status for women, at least in religion, in competing ideological systems of the time.

Primatologists and fossil paleoanthropologists (those who study bone fragments of primates and humans one to two million years old) now believe that the "first families" were almost certainly mothers and children living in a clan grouping—the father being a later addition.† What contribution did pre-state societies in which women may have had a more important or even the leading role in "governance," the making of rules, weighing justice, have in forming the tradition of states seen later in history? How did "chiefdoms" become a male-dominant system?

Archaeologists studying pre–Indo-European culture have added many more questions to the puzzle: Crete probably was not a patriarchy, and indeed, many of the civilizations around the Mediterranean basin in prehistory had long traditions of holding sacred female creation figures, or "goddesses." Archaeological sites such as Çatal Hüyük in Anatolia (Turkey, near the Mediterranean) had no walls around the city for defense: therefore, was the point of view of these societies less warlike?‡ If so, this could disprove the "male" ideology's position today that "aggression" is a large and "natural part" of (biologically ordained) "human nature." In fact, contemporary society is urging men on a daily basis to be aggressive and competitive, not "soft"—deemed to be the two basic "natural" opposites of human behavior. Another spectrum is not seen as possible, nor another composition of "human nature"—either in the past, as having once existed, or for the future.§

---

*Ba'al, referred to only by name in the Bible, was in fact a female deity.

†Roundtable discussion, Institute for Human Origins, University of California, Berkeley, November 1986.

‡Is classical Greece one of the crossover points, culturally, between earlier goddess-centered, less martial "states," such as Crete, and the warlike trend of the tradition? No one is sure; some scholars speak of invading Indo-European tribes with a warlike ideology who had invaded northern India two centuries earlier, coming then into Greece and later Italy, pushing the indigenous populations to the south, where they continued their traditions of goddess worship (usually with many deities) up until the historical period of the Roman Empire and even later. Of course, a supremely hierarchical system must not be a multi-deity system, but a "one god above all" system—the point which the Hebrews made so much of. For a discussion of the changeover in Greek mythology, see Jane Harrison, *Prolegomena to the Study of Greek Religion* (United Kingdom: Merlin Press, 1981).

§See S. Hite and Robert Carneiro, abstracts, 1985 annual meeting of the American Anthropological Association.

How Angry Could Women Get?

Do almost all women feel generalized repressed anger at men and "male" society for dominating them?

How do women feel coming up against this "male" code of behavior, with its wall of hierarchy?

Do most women feel some form of generalized anger at men, for being in control of the society, the home, their lives, everything—having more power, more status, more influence? And is this independent of how they are or are not treated as individuals by the individual men in their lives? This would be only logical, after all; women would have to be cone-heads as a group not to have some of these feelings. Undoubtedly, this makes even the slightest remark which seems condescending maddening to a woman who has to fight this in every aspect of her life—and worst of all, at home too.

Why shouldn't women be mad at all of history for keeping them out? Can we really celebrate the Declaration of Independence with the same glee that men do? Is it really ours? And how happy can we be, enjoying Richard Strauss's music, when we know he had such misogynistic views? Is history really *ours*? Or is our history only really beginning—even though there were great women during all periods, known and unknown, remembered and forgotten?

Would women ever spontaneously just become so angry that there would be an unstoppable expression of centuries of pent-up feeling, a dam bursting?*

Such things do happen suddenly, to the puzzlement of historians, who ask, why *then*, when the conditions had been there all the time? Why the French Revolution *then?* Or why the revolt *now* in South Africa, when the situation has been discriminatory to blacks for a long time? Why the solidarity and show of strength now?

Would women ever reach such a point of frustration that they would become even more politically active, even violent? Could the situation be anything like the situation in South Africa, with women ready to fight for their rights and for their belief in how the society should be run, their right to a complete part in the government? Or is our policy of non-violent resistance better?

In a way, the position women are in is the same as that of some terrorists: some have been explaining their situation for years, trying to talk, etc. Finally, they become so frustrated that they begin to say, "Well, I'll make some trouble and then they'll *have* to listen." It's a phenomenon similar to somebody in a family who's not getting through, a child maybe, who starts throwing his or

---

*Do women really feel this much dissatisfaction? As a reporter for National Public Radio commented with regard to a *1986 Women's Day* study of married women: "If we saw this much dissatisfaction in any other sector of the population, we'd be talking about revolution."

her plate on the floor during dinner. When you can't get through, after a long enough period of time, out of frustration, either you take it out on yourself and become suicidal, self-destructive, or you challenge the society—and one way is to become "terroristic."

Many women's anger is seen coming to the surface here. Do women have the right to "revolution"? Or, if "women can't be angry," "it's not ladylike," would this be impossible? Many women today feel like they don't fit in anymore, either "at home" or at work. At home, they feel guilty and "unprogressive" for being "at home"; while at work, a woman has to prove she is "just as good as a man," but still does not receive equal pay or equal opportunity. This makes women somewhat like a group without a home, without a place to be—a large displaced population, a people without a country.

If women don't fit in anymore, and are a majority of the population—as in fact they are—wouldn't this make women a potential revolutionary segment of the population?

"Kept waiting for too long?"

An editorial in the London newspaper *The Guardian* (reported in the *International Herald Tribune* on August 31, 1986), while speaking of the mental state of blacks in South Africa who are waiting and striving for equality in their country, applies in some rather startling ways to women's quest for equal rights:

"South Africa [is] in an unstable equilibrium. The massively discontented Africans lack the unity and strength to overthrow apartheid, with its overwhelming apparatus of repression. But the power of the security machine is not so great that it can go where it likes without meeting resistance stiff enough to exact a steady toll on the human (mostly black) instruments of white domination. Such a stalemate could last for years or decades.

"The answer to the overriding question as to what kind of South Africa will emerge in the end becomes clearer the more the blacks are made to wait before they come into their inheritance. The bitterness in the townships is piling up even as more and more whites tell the opinion pollsters that they recognize majority rule as inevitable.

"The nature of the African government that emerges on that day will be directly related to what it has to endure and overcome to achieve power. If the outcome displeases the whites and their supporters in the West, they have only themselves, and President Botha and his ilk, to blame. Black resistance to apartheid is no longer just a law-and-order problem, if it ever was."

The injustices, making for instability, are clear. As the United Nations Decade for Women Conference in Nairobi in 1985 declared: "Women do almost all of the world's domestic work, which combined with additional work outside the home means that many women work a double day. Women grow about half of the world's food, but own hardly any land. They are concentrated in the lowest-paid occupations and are more vulnerable to unemployment than men. In the area of health, women provide more health care than all the health services put together. Women perform two-thirds of the world's work, receive one-tenth of its income and own less than one-hundredth of its property."

The conference called for recognition of the value of women's unpaid labor, by asking governments to invest in services to women in the ratio to which they make a contribution to the national economy. This is estimated at 30 to 85 percent of the GNP, depending on the country.

There are interesting echoes here of women's assertions in Part I. Here too, many men seem to have a tendency to let things get to a crisis stage by walking away (from a "complaining woman" or a "complaining people") until the group is so alienated that the government/man is faced with a catastrophic, black-and-white situation; people/women are forced to choose either to use force to gain equality, or to leave the person or the country altogether.

One woman correctly reminds us that we are still in the midst of a revolutionary process that is not over:

"Women are magnificent, resourceful, strong, brave, creative. Sensitive, warm, intelligent, and they communicate on altogether a different, more fluent and intuitive level than men. They are more self-sacrificing and nurturing, and if anyone will ensure the survival of this planet and this species, they are the ones. They are the backbone of this world economy. The ones whose un-recompensed, unceasing labor has made a decent standard of living available to so many.

"I'm a radical feminist at the cutting edge of the women's movement which is just beginning and which will create the most fabulous global revolution you've ever seen, 53 percent of the population, rising against patriarchal-hierarchical thought. My advice to women? Rise up! Take power! Don't be afraid! Listen to women."

———————————

Or, as Christabel Pankhurst, the English suffragist (1880–1956) tells us, "Remember the dignity of your womanhood. Do not appeal. Do not beg. Do not grovel. Take courage. Join hands, stand beside us, fight with us . . ."

Friendships Between Women: Another Culture, Another Way of Life

Women describe their friendships with other women as some of the happiest, most fulfilling parts of their lives. Eighty-seven percent of married women have their deepest emotional relationship with a woman friend, as do 95 percent of single women. These relationships are extremely important—a frequently "unseen" backdrop to women's lives that is nevertheless as solidly "there" for them as the air. Women rely on each other, knowing they can, in moments of crisis, or just for daily emotional nourishment and fun—being alternately children, mothers, sisters, and pals to each other, sometimes all on the same day. There are moments of letdown, even betrayal, but these are the exception, not the rule. And yet it is expected that women will consider their friendships to be much less important than love relationships with men or, especially, marriage.

Women Love Their Friendships with Other Women

94 percent of women speak of very close and important friendships with other women:

"I have lots of wonderful women friends. After I broke up with Dave, I threw a 'Girls' Club Party' for girls only, with champagne, pastries, and all kinds of beauty aids—facials, henna, manicures, everything. It was to thank all the great girls in the world."

"Women are the most important people in my life. My close relationships with women have kept me going where all else failed."

"She was my first true love, and my most important. Knowing her helped me find myself."

"I think close friendships turn you into a higher being. You want to excel, live up to others' expectations, develop higher expectations of yourself. The worst thing that somebody can do to me is not to give me credit for what I can do (be non-supportive) or bore me. That is something that my closest friends never do."

Women's descriptions of their friends brim over with warmth, admiration, and affection; the overwhelming majority of women, when they describe their friends, express feelings of great enthusiasm and happiness:

"We do a lot of talking and laughing. I like her honesty, and sense of the humor and irony of life. She's non-judgmental. She has helped me through difficult times, just by being there for me to talk to, by listening and caring. With her, I feel like myself. I have an identity that feels right."

"My best friend listens but does not condemn, accepts me as I am. Usually what we do together is meet for lunch or dinner, drinks, talk for hours at her house or mine. I feel her presence, comfort without words, total understanding even if I don't understand, miss her when we don't get together. Her faults? She's always complaining she's fat when she's just right. Also, she complains about her kinky hair, which looks divine."

"She is my age, we are in an all-women's college. She is very supportive and a very good listener—not at all selfish, very funny and attractive. She is Catholic, in a way that I would describe as the best way to be Catholic—in her dealings with others and outlook toward the world—but she makes her own choices on issues. We go out for coffee, just sit and talk—or we choose some really different place to go and just do it. She is very spontaneous, and we share a lot of laughs. I always feel thrilled to see her—of all my friends, I love and respect her the most and no matter what different paths we take—we always have things to say to each other. She isn't as easy to talk with about sex as other friends—mostly because she has not had a lot of experience. Still, I like to confide in her almost more because it seems like her opinion is more level-headed and steady—while never judgmental of me."

"My best woman friend is someone who I know would operate in my best interests, and support my point of view in my absence. Together we enjoy everyday life, talking, mostly, or rehashing our views as to the nature of this existence. We have made a pact that regardless of whether we are in a relationship with a man, we will always have time for each other. On rereading this it sounds rather schoolgirlish, but I do believe women's friendships are eternal. I feel valued when I am with her—none of the game playing around the house (if the wash needs doing, it gets done)—and we are able to criticize each other with affection and not need the emotional 'charge' of a row to come out with the truth. The thing she does that I like least? If we go to a party, she gets too drunk. I can't stand other people judging her superficially when there is so much more."

"I've known my best woman friend for fifteen years now. I like (love) her because I can be completely open and honest with her and she does not judge me for how I am feeling. I have shared so much of my life with her and she with me, she probably knows me better than anyone. We do all sorts of things together—everything from shopping to going on vacations together (and occasionally with our lovers). She has helped me through childbirth, divorce, depression, every time I've needed a helping hand she has been there. We spend (try to) at least one day a week just catching up and we talk on the average of four times a week on the telephone—sometimes more. Once in a while we see each other every day if it's possible."

"She's twenty-two years old, married, with a five-month-old baby. We have been friends since first grade and are still very close. She's very pretty—naturally wavy brunet hair, very well groomed and honest. We don't spend as much time as we should because she has a family to take care of. She's given me advice when I have asked for her help on some problem, but I really can't tell her about my gay lifestyle, she'd be hurt in her own way!"

"My best woman friend is like a candle that always burns. We see each other two or three times a week, because we are both busy with work and other circles of people. She is a constant source of energy and inspiration for me, and she says I am the same for her. We have gone through a lot together. I have other good women friends, but there is no one I love and trust and admire more than her. We always understand what the other is feeling."

"We went to high school together and now, seven years later, we are still friends. She has very average features but when she is talking or laughing it is so animated and expressive. I always feel great after I see her because we talk about everything so easily. She has helped me through innumerable difficult times and I love her very much."

"My best woman friend is my age, very beautiful and very strong, both emotionally and physically. We are at different schools now, and we don't call each other because it is too expensive, but we write. She is serene, insightful, strong, not dependent. She has goals and will not give them up for any man. We hug and touch often while we visit together (usually we just talk). She was strong for me when I thought I was pregnant and didn't know what to do about it. She is also incredibly gentle and she picks up on the emotions of people around her very easily. I have even written poetry about her. We have been friends for six to seven years. I can't think of anything about her I like least."

"We have been friends for thirteen years. She's smart, but not academically educated. She knows me like a book, I can never fool her. She makes me aware of things about myself I don't even realize, she makes me think but won't solve my problems for me. When we are together we talk for hours. When we are together for the first time after a long while, I feel like there is a strong bond between us, yet there are also many things that have changed."

"My best woman friend is vivacious, talented, humorous, full of energy, insightful, aggressive, and interested in my well-being. We see each other less now that she has a baby, but we still make a point of talking several times a week. She and her husband helped me get through a very bad time when I left a man I was living with. I was without a place to live and they housed me for a week, helped me to move, etc. They couldn't have been better."

"She's helped me through many crises and is the first person I turn to for support and/or advice. She is the woman I've loved the most. When we spend time together, I usually hang out at her home so we can enjoy all our kids together (she has four daughters). We also make a point to spend time alone, without kids—we'll take a day and just take off—go out for lunch, shop a little, walk around town checking out art shops and talking—mostly talking. That's what's best about it all. We're able to talk about anything and everything. I have friends here where I live with whom I feel very intimate. I could discuss any of the same issues I'd discuss with my best friend, but what's different is that she knows me far better than any of these others. We have both helped each other through difficult times. We have wonderful meaningful times together."

"We have been friends for twenty-nine years. She is the mother of two daughters and stepmother to two more, plus she has a career (finance). She progressed from being just another paper pusher to being head of her own department. What I like most about her is her willingness to listen when others talk. Although she has her own opinions, she hears the other person out first, before offering her viewpoint. Together we share a love of animals, especially horses and dogs. We ride horses together as often as possible. We also just like one another's company and it is not necessary to 'do' things when we are together. She has been there to help me through difficult times, not so much through what she has said to me, but just by being there when I needed her. How do I feel when I am with her? Usually peaceful, joyful, and alive. We talk to each other almost every day on the phone and get together usually one to two days a week. She and her husband have a farm that they go to on weekends and we usually are there with them part of every weekend. The thing I like least about her is her addiction to shopping. She shops as entertainment! We cannot go past any kind of store without her stopping and looking to see what they have."

"We've always been able to confide in each other. We could talk for hours about anything. I've always felt that when I'm with her I could say or do anything. She loves me for who I am. We like to go to the beach or outdoors, we both enjoy nature, good times, food, and fun. From each other we've learned good communication skills. We get to the meat of a matter. We both enjoy going down to a deep, emotional level."

"My best friend and I met when we were working as waitresses. We were the best-looking, the silliest, and the flirtiest. One of the things I like best about her is that she can talk about her feelings and isn't afraid of what I'll think. That makes it so that I can do the same thing with just as much comfort. We probably talk about once or twice a week, either on the phone or at one of our houses. She has helped me get over a lot of breakups, and can always cheer me up when I'm depressed."

"She is a very compassionate person, not just for my problems, but for the human race. She doesn't pass opinions or take sides. She has been a tremendous help to me by just listening. The only thing I don't like about her is that she can't handle her finances and is always in debt."

"She's unique. She's got long, beautiful red hair. She dresses a little differently than the rest of the women I know. I do too! She's got a thin, great body. She's capable, intelligent, fun-loving, deep, caring, and friendly. Sometimes she functions from a negative standpoint. That's definitely a turnoff at times, but I understand. She has a great sense of humor about herself."

"She has a marvelous sense of humor and is the only person I know that when I leave her home or hang up after a telephone conversation I am invariably smiling."

"My best woman friend has a sweet face and a look one can trust. What I like above all in her is the sweetness with which she sees the world, a spirit of goodwill and goodness, and yet, with a great intelligence, she doesn't fool herself or others, but always tries to make things work for the best. Together we share mostly our feelings and visions and life, we analyze our actions and reactions toward each other and other people, and when we meet, we talk endlessly and time always flies. One hour is a minute and we never get tired of exchanging. We try to see each other as much as we can, but it's never enough, since we don't live in the same city, but we keep in touch with two phone calls a week.

"She is my most precious ally through bad and good times. When I am with her, I feel happy, elated, trusting. The only thing that I do not like in her is sometimes a lack of courage in dealing with difficult issues, her tendency to avoid problems which might be important or essential, but it's mostly a past regret because nowadays she has made great progress on that issue. Another little defect is a little tendency to get oversatisfied with herself or to want to present a permanent happy image—to the outside world, not in our relationship. To me, it's a very fulfilling relationship."

Friendships between women are carried on even from great distances:

"I see her every eighteen months or so when we visit, and then spend a rather frantic twenty-four hours a day together with a lot of social doings. She phones occasionally and writes long informative and supportive letters. She listens to me, really cares and encourages me to take care of myself. The thing I like the least is that she takes on much more than she can physically and emotionally handle and doesn't nurture herself enough."

"My best friend—we met the first day of college—twenty-eight years ago. We have an indestructible bond, even though our lives are quite different, and we haven't lived in the same city for fifteen years. Neither of us has married or had children. When we're together I feel complete. (Of course, we only see each other maybe once a year and for only a few days to a few weeks.) We write to each other and occasionally call if we have hot news or a problem (we're 3,000 miles apart). She's a very quiet person, in contrast to my sometimes rowdy demeanor. We go out to eat, to movies (which we talk about for hours afterwards). We take trips together and I guess you could say we 'pal around.' None of the above sounds remarkable, but there's something indescribable about our friendship."

Many women have had the same women friends since high school or even grade school; sometimes women remember their childhood and girlhood friends as being the closest of their lives, even later:

"One special friend and I were very close in junior college. We worked together. It was the first time in my life that I felt free and encouraged to 'open up' and express my thoughts, my feelings, my ideas. I'll be continually indebted to her for taking the time to help and being so interested in and concerned with me. She was also the person I have been closest to. We would laugh and 'go crazy' and have a good time. I felt very relaxed and comfortable around her. I could speak my mind and my feelings. She was very smart, insightful, and perceptive."

"My best friend all through elementary school was a smart, 'weird' kid like me, and was rejected by the other kids, like me, but she didn't let it upset her like I did. Since no one else would play with us, we played together at recess a lot, and went to each other's houses too. We'd usually play out an imaginative situation—we had a whole stable of imaginary horses, plus a couple of dinosaurs, all with names and personalities, and we'd ride them and take care of them. In first grade we were in an advanced reading group together by ourselves. My mother didn't approve of her because her mother was a messy housekeeper and she had a lot of pets. Sometimes we would hug and once another girl called us 'queers'—we didn't even know what that was. But maybe that's what my mother was worried about! But there was nothing sexual between us. The most sexual thing that passed between us was that I offered to play 'look and show' and she graciously declined."

Women often support each other emotionally through difficult times in relationships with men, through marriages, or through breakups and divorces:

"I love my best friend so much. She's helped me through some of the lowest points of my life. She's encouraged me to be the person I am today."

"During the roughest time in my life so far—our business was going bankrupt, creditors were calling us, I was working two dead-end minimum-wage jobs (about a sixty-hour week) and had no time for my daughter, who was two years old; my marriage was falling apart under all the strains and blames, and I cried all the way to and from work while driving the car. This went on every day for about two months (the car was the only place I had privacy), until I felt I couldn't take it anymore. I was thinking of just taking the car and some money and taking off and not coming back, but it was impossible for me to really do that, and I felt totally trapped. I called up a friend and said I really had to see her. She sensed how desperate I was and saw me despite being in the middle of packing for a vacation trip the next day. I sat in her car and cried with my head in her lap. After this incredibly reassuring experience—the first time in my life I ever made such a demand on someone, and the person 'came through'—things got better little by little."

Why Are Women So Happy with Their Women Friends?

Emotional Empathy and Subtle Communication Between Women

"We always know what the other one is feeling."

92 percent of women say it is easier to talk to other women than to most men:

"Women feel a common bond for each other and relate better to each other's problems. My husband takes everything like a personal threat to his security. I couldn't tell him anything I tell my best friend."

"It is easier to talk to women than to men. (Some women, and some men.) On the whole, women understand more, can relate more, and aren't squeamish about details. We offer help to each other because we can talk more easily, and the encouragement often makes us stronger individuals. We care more and love more, and aren't afraid to show it to our women friends. Men can be good friends too, but they just don't seem to understand the *human* side of feelings by putting themselves in the other person's shoes like women do. I think the statement is both sad and true. It's healthy to have a close female friend that one can talk to about anything, but your husband should be your best friend too, someone you can share anything with. It seems those couples whose marriages last and are happy are the ones who are each other's best friends."

"I find it easier to talk to women because men hide behind logic when an emotional response is what is needed. We all need someone to laugh with us, feel happy with us, and cry with us. If I could talk to my husband and he to me as my best woman friend does, we would have a super-hot thing."

"It is easier to get through to women. It is easier to reveal your emotions to women. Men are not close to their own feelings, so they have difficulty when it comes to interacting with women who have their guards down."

"The thing I like best about Jane is that I can talk to her about absolutely anything under the sun. Nothing shocks or surprises her. Jane's listened to me talk through tons of difficult times, fights with my folks, my separation from Keith—his stay in the hospital. I've helped her think through a long-drawn-out divorce, her relationship (now two years old) with her subsequent lover, and the recent death of her father. We always have a good time when we're together. We're free to be ourselves no matter how good or bad we may feel, and then all of our problems don't seem so bad."

"Last year I needed to make a decision about whether to stay with my fiancé or start seeing another guy I was crazy to go out with. I wanted a totally unbiased point of view. A woman I hardly knew at school sat down and listened to me in the coffee shop for hours on end, letting me get everything straight in my head—then finally she told me that she couldn't tell me what to do but she thought I could make a good decision. The best advice I got from anyone. I think that women are basically more in tune with other people than men are. Women also tend to look at life more as a whole than men do. They see things as part of an interrelated larger picture rather than reducing the world to mechanical, isolated pieces."

Women have developed among themselves a way of relating that makes it possible to have intensely close relationships, to share intricate inner thoughts, and to have a large repertoire of feelings expressed and understood. How women talk together is different from how women and men talk together, in most cases. Women have a special communication with each other which is more detailed, more involved in searching out, listening for and hearing the other's inner thoughts—working together to explore the feelings one is trying to express.

One woman, who has been in love relationships with both a man and several women, describes the differences she finds in communication; not only the tone but the quality and depth of the conversations are different:

"The conversations with Anne-Marie would be so complete and involved—like 'Oh, this dinner we're going to, I have really mixed feelings about it. How do you feel about it?' And then we would speculate on our thoughts, talk about it. Or if we are having a fight, one of us will say, 'You're really taking advantage of me' (for example), and then the other will say, 'Tell me why—explain to me how you feel about that—tell me what you mean, in depth,' then she would listen to me for five or ten minutes— she might complain about what I said, but still she would listen. That's the relationship I had with her.

"With a woman in a relationship, nothing's taken for granted—whereas men sometimes have the attitude: we'll just cruise along here, and everything will be O.K. With women, there's always a discussion, always, and the direction of the relationship is constantly up for revision. At least, it is like that with us.

"Whereas, before, in an argument or a discussion with John, my ex-boyfriend, I would get—nothing. It would just be totally disregarded. Or if I pushed, he would say, 'You're crazy, I just refuse to discuss this.' And that would be the end of the conversation. I would rant and rave, on and on, without him listening, without him paying a bit of attention to me—he would usually start doing something else at the same time, like cleaning his desk or something. And then after I got done ranting and raving, he would say, 'See what I mean? You're a complete lunatic.' And he'd walk away and not say anything else.

"I definitely get more response from my woman lover. Talking with her is completely different. (Of course, it depends on how patient we are that day with each other.) But more often than not, when I bring up something, or drop a remark, I get a response—like 'What do you mean? How can you say that?' or 'Tell me more about what you mean by that.' On the other hand, sometimes with my previous woman lover it all became such a complex psychological interaction—it became top-heavy. So that anything you do, you know thousands of interpretations on the other side, and to discuss it becomes like this massive thing. During one of these discussions, in fact, my previous girlfriend just told me to fuck off. I'm afraid that, really, she just couldn't deal with so much analyzing of feelings, there was too much intensity and focus on the relationship for her.

"Of course, it's true, to a degree, when you have two women who are telling each other all their inner thoughts, both very intense, it can get really turned inward—but still, it's great. I think that your identity develops through these discussions. It's a real process of discovery for me—both of me and of her. It's a great experience."

Most women point out that they feel they can talk freely to their friends without being judged:

"She is fun, open, warm, sharing, non-judgmental. This is probably the most important for me. I can tell her anything without fear of 'what she will think.' "

"I'm especially close to my sister. We can bare our souls to each other and it is O.K.—no judgment is forthcoming, only support."

"I only have one close friend with whom I discuss my sex life. Nothing shocks us and we discuss everything together openly. We've been friends for fourteen years. She understands me better than anyone (even my husband) and we can discuss anything. She often doesn't realize what a valuable person she is—this is her only lacking quality."

"No matter how long it's been since I've seen my women friends, we click and can talk about anything. They're non-judgmental, supportive, and I know if I need them they'll be there. My secrets are safe with them and they'll be honest with me."

"I always feel great after I see her because we talk about everything so easily. She has helped me through innumerable difficult times and I love her very much."

The majority of women also appreciate the quality of genuine interest shown to them by their friends, who frequently draw them out to talk:

"What do I like about her? She never puts me down—she listens and is INTERESTED."

"The woman friend I am closest to right now . . . compassionate, HONEST (I feel whatever feedback, advice, comment I get from her is not 'what I want to hear' but her sincere feelings). She is witty and can always make me laugh (almost always). She never laughs *at* me or puts me down for what I feel or say. She cares and would do anything for me that I asked— she also knows that I respect and care enough for her not to make any unreasonable demands on our friendship. She does not 'take care of me,' she nurtures my confidence in myself and gives me support. I have been going through some difficult times of late and have been seeing her more often than usual—what a great help!"

"My two closest friends *take me seriously,* understand my feelings, and give me sympathy, love, and warmth when I need it. I appreciate their insights, perceptions, and intelligence."

While this support which women show each other, their interest in each other's thoughts and feelings, is something women also give to the men in their lives (see Part I), the difference women find here is that the emotional support and interest are returned:

"I love the intimacy that develops with my women friends, the freedom to really 'compare notes' together."

"She's wonderful. Charming, bright, witty, beautiful both physically and intellectually. She's self-assured and unafraid. In the course of day-to-day life, we console and congratulate each other, and bounce ideas back and forth. We both come away happier because of sharing our lives."

"My relationships with women have in general been more intimate, there has been more real sharing. Women are trustworthy, you can talk to them— they search to help you think of solutions, they are creative in their problem solving. They try to improve things."

The Importance of Women's Friendships

Women speak more freely with each other

Women's free expression of themselves when together makes further expression flourish, facilitating a good exchange of ideas. In fact, this increased dialogue among women in recent years may have led in part to the current renaissance of women's writing and creativity in the arts, politics, scholarship, and science.

However, although women exchange ideas and understand each other easily and find there is no credibility gap, women say that a man may (even unconsciously) doubt or mentally override what a woman is saying in favor of his own version of the "truth," judging what she says—trying to dominate her mentally, in fact. Feeling this inhibits many women, even prevents them from speaking.

Girls learn early on that they live in two cultures, and they adopt dual personalities: when they are around men, their behavior "must" change and they "must" become less assertive, less talkative, listen attentively to men, give men more time to express themselves, defer to them. As one woman expressed it earlier, "Things I kept finding myself doing/feeling around men: feeling like they were the important ones. Feeling too big, in all ways: too tall, too large, said too much, felt too much, occupied more space than I had a right to." Women do not generally feel these ways around other women.

Friendship is thus a valuable key for women—a society into which women can tap and in which they can feel free to talk openly and express themselves. It is vital to have women's friendships, groups, and even communities, or just time for women to spend together, be friends, because in this way women can be themselves, think their own thoughts, say them—and in sharing come up with new insights, ideas, and possibilities.

Women's friendships: often emotionally closer than love relationships with men

Over and over, women say that their friendships with other women are more open and spontaneous, that it is easier to talk, that women are rarely judgmental, are good at listening and giving feedback, and that this is helpful in thinking through problems and ideas. When women describe these friendships, their tone of voice changes, lightens up and sounds freer.

Women are each other's basic support systems, whether single or married. Throughout their work, their achievements, their major decisions, difficult times, and changing relationships, women are being cheered on, encouraged, and believed in by their friends.

Here the dynamics of women's caring and giving work to women's advantage: women do not wind up feeling drained, since the support is mutual. The giving is not taken advantage of, considered "soft" or "weak." The idea of any given conversation is to understand and help draw out the other person, not (as in some "male" interpersonal patterns) to "judge," decide if the other person is "right," or win the point. Most women are more receptive and give more "acknowledging" feedback: "I heard you and understand what you are saying."

Is it harder to "talk to" a male lover because there is more vulnerability in a love relationship than a friendship? Or is it easier to talk to women because women are less competitive, prefer to be supportive? While it is true that love relationships are more intense and demanding—"I think the quality of love I give this man I am in love with is much more selfish and demanding than that I give to women," as one woman says—the fact that women believe that the basic role of a friend or lover is to listen and understand, not dominate or judge, goes much further in explaining why more men also say women are their best friends, rarely other men. In fact, most married men say that their wives are their best friends—but most married women, as just seen, say they only *wish* their husbands could be their best friends.

Most men, as they explain in *The Hite Report* on men, when they need someone to talk to, turn to women as friends, not to men. Ninety-three percent of men in *The Hite Report* say that after school they do not have a close male friend; 89 percent of those over age twenty-five say that their best friend is a woman, or, in fact, their wife. Men rarely turn to other men for friendship—to have close friends they can talk to. This clearly indicates that women's way of relating is preferred by both women and men when they want a close companion to trust, talk to, and be open with.

Why, then, is so much fun made of women's being enthusiastic, non-combative, talking with their friends? Why are women put on the defensive, their conversations referred to as "gabbing away" and "girl talk"? This is merely the dominant ideology proclaiming itself superior—when in fact the dominant ideology relies on this very talk and enthusiasm *from* women, counting on women to be non-aggressive, "loving," and caring—to give men emotional support.

Women, as seen in Part I, believe listening and supporting the other person is one of the basic ways in which love is shown; they feel it is inappropriate to be competitive, distant, or not tuned in emotionally (mentally absent?) in a personal relationship. Many women have developed skills in observing and tuning in to the inner thoughts, wavelengths of others, whether male or female. This skill is one of the great cultural resources of our society. However, this skill can be very dangerous for women individually when used in a non-equal relationship—one in which they are not getting their emotional or intellectual needs met in return, i.e., the man is "starring" in the relationship, with the woman as the non-listened-to supporting cast.

Women say their friendships with each other do not leave them feeling drained, as do so many of women's relationships with men, even when quite emotionally involved. Women's ideology works well when it is in contact with other women, because, while women's "giving" is met in many men with a "men have the right to take" attitude, in a relationship with another woman the two "givings" work to mutual advantage. In other words, "giving" to other women works, because women are "giving" back.

Even class or "marital status" differences among women are not as difficult to overcome as gender divisions: women say they can still talk to other women with more ease and feeling of acceptance, being "heard," than they can to most men, including the men they love/who love them the most.

This style of listening without judgment, "being there" emotionally, registering having "heard" and understood another person, can serve as a new model for men's relationships with women, and with each other. Just as women have made major shifts in their lives in the last ten years, men too can with great benefit make shifts in their personal lives by learning these new attitudes.

Talking about men: are women "using" their friends, or trying to understand another culture?

While most women enjoy telling and hearing from their friends about what is going on in their love relationships, 22 percent complain that their friends talk "too much" about their love lives or "boyfriend":

"What I've always disliked about women friends is their constantly talking about their involvements with men. It bothered me that we didn't talk enough about our *own* plans and problems."

"I like women who are not centered on men or kids and can discuss ideas and don't go on complaining year after year about personal situations that are not under control. If a woman is having a problem, I like to see her examine it and solve it, not just complain about it and be afraid to do anything about it. I don't have a lot of emotional needs or personal problems to dump on people anymore."

"I find women boring because they only talk about hair, makeup, and men."

"I hate women that let themselves get the raw end of a deal—who aren't in control of their lives—and want to tell me endlessly about it."

"Probably one of the most tiring parts of my being with women friends is that so many of them are continually talking about men. I get tired of discussing whether 'there are any good men here.' There is more to single life than finding a man! I tell them, 'Who cares?'"

"I've disliked women friends who constantly talked about their relationships with men; *we* talked about what they should have been talking to the *man* about."

Is spending a lot of time talking with women friends about problems in love relationships with men "using" women (or "gossiping")? Or is it part of working out our philosophy of life? Women often do support their friends emotionally during relationships with men; most friends like to be there for their friends at such moments.

But there is more to this subject: these conversations between women also have the important function of enabling women to discuss their own value system, to reaffirm it, as it is being challenged on a daily basis by the dominant "male" value system and culture, and, especially, by the men they are involved with. In other words, these conversations are an important way in which women compare their own value system with the dominant culture's ideas of who they are and what is going on. In these conversations, women are often trying to come to grips with, understand, how the two systems come together, and the meaning of men's actions—which are culturally "other," and often seem aggressive and inexplicable. Women are developing their own analysis, independent of the dominant culture's version of "the relationship" and what it means.

In discussing such questions as how to deal with/understand/acknowledge various slights and subtle unjust or harsh treatment from men—whether to appease a man or "make an issue" out of it—women are in fact dealing with philosophical dilemmas central to our social structure. Women want to hear how their friends react in similar situations, to gauge their own reactions (since there is no support for them in the "dominant" culture), and to know how their friends are managing or if they are not.

These are important debates necessary for thinking through and defining their own value system, naming what is going on, as opposed to what the "male" culture says is happening, and who it tells us we "are."

Breaking Up with a Friend

Some women tell sad stories of breaking up with a friend they loved:

"I had a very close friend in high school and most of my college years. We grew up together from about age thirteen, experimenting with pot, talking about sex, media stars, and everything we saw and experienced. She got addicted to some heavy drugs, including heroin, and I helped her cold-turkey one time but it didn't last. I don't know why the friendship ended. I suspect our respective male relationships had something to do with it. I remember being puzzled about why she didn't answer my letters or return phone calls or want to get together as often as we had. Then she didn't come to my wedding or even call or write saying why. I saw her a couple of times after that, but I guess I was tired of being put off and I eventually stopped calling or writing. I still occasionally have dreams about meeting her again and having her act as if nothing had ever gone wrong between us. I feel guilty about it and rejected. I haven't been quite so close to a woman since."

"My best friend and I are kind of drifting apart right now. She wants to be a dancer and she is doing some kind of exotic dancing. Now, I've never seen her do it but I have an idea what this is like. She is not totally nude but she doesn't wear a whole lot and she just basically dances in these bars and she gets paid pretty well for it. She likes this dancing and she knows I disapprove of it. It's really changed our relationship. I find the whole thing absolutely nauseating, the fact that men just sit there and watch her, not because she has good dancing technique, but because of the fact that she is using her sexuality to get their attention."

"This topic is a little difficult because the best female friend I ever had fell in love and got married about a year ago, after which she lost her grip and decided she couldn't support two major relationships. Hence, despite the discussions of our mutual friends and (God bless him) her husband, she has hardly spoken to me for the last six months. I haven't replaced her yet. She was a bright, tough, sensitive, witty, creative single parent who put herself through college in her thirties. For several years we saw each other every day, went to films and plays together, proofed each other's writing, traveled, spent holidays, traded aesthetic opinions, borrowed each other's clothes, laughed and cried and cursed and perpetrated revenge, shared possessions both useful and frivolous, educated the kids, talked till indecent hours, read exciting passages aloud over the phone, cooked together, ate together, got high together (but contrary to popular opinion, did not sleep together).

"When I was with her, and this may be the thing I miss the most, I walked taller and felt invincible because I had somebody who'd fight back to back with me. She helped me through some difficult times indeed, and I hope I did the same for her. To tell the truth, I thought that with her I had beaten the system, but I should have known the goddam system would beat me in the end. And what I always liked least, come to think of it, was the way my own life and habits would get revamped according to what was happening with her previous man."

One woman speaks of a disintegrating friendship between herself, a divorced working woman, and her friend, who has remarried and devoted herself to her family:

"My best friend is currently sinking into a quagmire of wifedom and stepmotherhood—she is playing this role to the hilt and it is tremendously disturbing to me. When I met her seven years ago, we were both newly divorced—she was thirty-two and I was thirty-one. We really talked then, even took weekend vacations together. God, how I loved her—her honest humor, spirituality, everything. Now she seems a shadow of herself. She was only divorced for one year when she married again—a man she only knew three months. She tells me she still doesn't know why she married him. (I think she has accepted her parents' standard that to be whole, a woman must be married and have children.) She has previously talked about divorce from time to time, but I doubt if she will do it, at least not until her fourteen-year-old stepdaughter is grown. She admits she envies me—I have stayed single these seven years— she has seen me through a number of men. I think she also envies the fact that I have found a man I love and respect, live with, but will not marry.

"I seldom see her now that she is married, unless I go to her business office. She never calls me from her home—she says she is too tired after cooking three meals, running her business, and keeping books for her husband's business too—she also says she has no privacy in her own home, even her bathroom. This is the same person who, as a single person, so treasured her privacy that even I did not 'drop in'—I called first. Our paths are diverging—in truth, I think she is regressing into the role of wife and mother—sort of a live-in servant to her family. Meanwhile, I am becoming a radical feminist. I don't know how much longer I can attempt to keep this friendship alive."

Is this split between "single women" and "married women," or homemakers and career mothers, inevitable? In fact, most married women's best friends are also married, and most single women's best friends are also single. But wouldn't this be "normal," just as people's friends may often be in the same age range, or in the same type of work? Or is this a form of the double standard—"wives" vs. "single women" (or competition)? Does "marital status" represent such a wide gulf in "status" (?) or world view or place in the world that it is hard for the two to relate—for all kinds of reasons?

Others report similar splits between married and non-married friends:

"I think the most important relationship I've had was with a girlfriend I had for six years. She and I grew up together as teenagers and did everything together. I loved her a lot. She got married last year and has since changed. We have become less and less close."

"I have one really good girlfriend, but as we have gotten older, she is more interested in her children and her husband than she is in me."

"As I'm out of college a couple of years, all my friends around me are getting married. I watch friend after friend getting engaged, and I'm starting to feel soon I won't have any friends, they'll all be too busy with their husbands and their families. I'm starting to feel like 'If you can't beat them, join them.' "

Some married women feel very cut off from having any friends at all:

"Most of my friends are also women who work and have husbands and families and have very little available time for friendship. There isn't enough time to just sit and talk. A lunch or an evening together once in a while isn't enough for a deep friendship. We women are split in too many directions."

"I liked one of my college roommates a lot. She was very intellectual and open. She lives far away now and we rarely see each other anymore. It's been very hard to develop new relationships with women since I've been married."

Do some married women feel they must keep their relationships with women friend(s) secondary, lest their husbands become angry?

"I have made some good close friendships but only in the last few years since I've been able to stop putting the needs of my husband and family first."

"Presently, I have no one particular friend. The few I have are objective and discreet. They have helped me through difficult times and would always. I cannot be closer because of my husband."

Sometimes women feel they want or need different friends after marriage or a divorce; one woman, in the midst of changing from being married and financially dependent to being independent and self-supporting, is also in the midst of changing her friends:

"I am changing what I think of my women friends. I try to be understanding and just listen, hoping *they* will see the folly of some of the things they are doing with their men, jobs, whatever. They are still my friends, but I feel differently about most of them. Maybe less respect for them. I am impatient with the 'all talk, no action' type of 'liberated' mentality in some of them. Sometimes I wonder if I really know any of them at all anymore. I still love them, and want them for my friends, but I feel I have to move away from them. With men, I'm beginning to notice things more than I used to. So many are still so caught up in the 'male' way of thinking—yet thinking at the same time that they are 'allowing' their spouses/girlfriends to be liberated. Sometimes I feel sorrier for the men than I do for the women. The losers (both sexes) are the ones who hang desperately on to the old traditional values (some of which are good, of course) of male-female roles. If only because they fail to allow themselves to *learn.*"

———————

Of course, there are many more ambivalences and interesting dynamics, difficulties and jealousies, between women friends than there is space to discuss here; see the special issue of Women's Studies International Forum, "Rethinking Sisterhood: Unity in Diversity," edited by Renate Duelli Klein, vol. 8, no. 1 (Oxford: Pergamon Press, 1985), and Janice Raymond, *A Passion for Friends: Toward a Philosophy of Female Affection* (Boston: Beacon Press, 1986).

Women and Power

We may love our women friends, but do we take them seriously?

*"I've never spent much time hating any woman for
long (except my mother for periods). I am easier with
women. Does that mean that along with the rest of the
world, I don't take them seriously enough?"*

Do we think women are as important as men? as powerful?

*Sometimes women say they feel hurt if their friends take the men in their lives
more seriously—or put men first, just because they are "men":*

"I'd never do what my friends do to me: plan something with me weeks in advance, but if their boyfriend asks them somewhere, break our plans. For instance, my one friend who is married, she planned to go to a show with me two weeks in advance. Two nights before the show I called her and asked her what night for sure she wanted to go, Friday or Saturday. She nonchalantly says, 'Oh, me and my husband are going to that show Friday.' No mention of me at all. I was left out in the cold. I know he's her husband and that's great, but the least she could have done was ask me to join them. She didn't. Before she was married she wanted to go to a show with me, and he wouldn't *let* her! That's too possessive."

"She always waits for me to call, and makes no plans for us to spend time together anymore. I think she thinks that once you have a guy or are married, everything is different."

"She has a boyfriend, so we don't do anything together. All my friends are married or have boyfriends, so I don't do much of anything with any of them anymore except talk on the phone once in a while."

"There are times when I get irritated at her because she wraps herself so entirely in her men. Why do her reasons for doing things have to be a reaction to what her boyfriends do or don't like her to do?"

"I really hate to say this (or I should say, I feel guilty about saying this) but I can't stand a woman who wants nothing out of life except to find a man who'll sweep her off her feet to servility and baby making. What's strange about this is that one of my closest friends is this way. We've been friends since sixth grade, before feminism was part of my vocabulary."

83 percent of women complain that their mothers and fathers brought them up to think less of themselves than of the men around them, to mentally serve and wait on men:

"My mother certainly did show me how to be 'feminine': don't be tough, don't be strong, be 'nice,' polite, passive, assume you are wrong and everyone else is right. Always put others' needs before your own. Oh, and it's an absolute duty to be as pretty as possible."

"I felt from as long as I can remember that my brother was treated more generously, lovingly, and unequivocally than I. While I remained the class honor student, he was not penalized for getting C's (although his IQ was tested as the same as mine). The rules he had to keep were more relaxed. He was given money for 'owning' pigs and cows, which was a kind of pay for his hours spent in the fields with my father (and he *did* truly work). But I worked also, just as many hours! During those years my mother worked outside the home, I did the majority of the housework and often cooked midday dinners for as many as a dozen farm helpers at harvesting times (I was twelve and thirteen). My work was not rewarded with the ownership of animals: I had no money. I deeply resented my brother and always felt my mother did not understand that. My mother did not think that my daydreams could come true. Her lack of faith in me and amused (not exactly cruel) attitude toward my ambitions made me very angry. I often had fits of shouting about it and consoled myself in my bedroom listening to the radio."

"My mother is much more loving and kind to my brother than she ever was to me. She prefers him. Many times she won't send me a birthday or Christmas present because she says she wants to get him something really special. She's got a blind spot where he's concerned. I just always knew that boys were more special."

Most women hate it when they see women giving men more respect than other women:

"I admire women who can love other women and not be ingratiating with men. I hate women who have split personalities—one for their women friends and one for their men friends. I admire a woman who loves who she is and doesn't try to live up to someone else's expectations."

"Women contribute many things to society—I'm thinking of women lawyers, women physicians, women writers, women photographers, etc. I hate it when they are too dependent on men and relationships. Some of the biggest talkers on freedom and being career women have married the first man they met after graduation, and spend all their time taking care of him. I hate that."

"The problem is, so many men think so much of themselves as if they are so much better than women. Many men are spoiled, especially by women who are being condescending to themselves and to other women by treating men as if they are gods. I believe women are much stronger than men emotionally and spiritually. I believe women have more endurance and stamina. I dislike the fact that women feel they have to have a man and that the male figure is catered to and given the utmost respect as the dominant sex. I hate it when women subordinate themselves to men."

Fear of the power of the "male" system

"I really think something has to be said about this. This has to be stopped—I mean, women's trashing of each other when they feel they have to choose between hanging on to a man's shirtails and ditching their women friends and women they work with. We are afraid of men. We are afraid that they will hurt us, fire us, say bad things about us—or if it's personal, not love us, call us names, and so on. But why should we apply a double standard to men?—we let them trash us and then we treat them nice, but with women, we would never do that.

We are sucking up to men's power when we do this, not standing up for ourselves. It's only natural to be afraid of power that can hurt you—but it's something we've got to fight. We've got to be brave. We can beat this system if we just stand up to it—and love each other, be loyal, don't ever let each other down if we are right."

Most women's only real complaint about their women friends, whom they frequently admire in every other way, is that they can be "wimps" in the face of possible male disapproval:

"My friend is great—except sometimes in the face of male authority."

"What my friend does that I like the least is not to be frank about her feelings if she thinks they'll be offensive or negative to men."

"My best friend—I love her sense of wit, her truth to her own values, and her loyalty. She's just, unfortunately, wimpy in the face of men when we're together in groups."

"Women love, they suffer without blame, they are patient to a fault. But I dislike their lack of self-esteem and their belief that they are not at least equal if not superior to men. Through this belief they are taught early to play games, and use sex to get what they need. However, they deserve it without having to do this."

"What I like least is her complaining about the injustices in society to women. I would prefer that she change these complaints into action, complain to *men*, and get involved with other women working to change things."

"I dislike some women's willingness to accept the status quo—they are afraid to go out and shake up the world."

"I grew up with a girl who was very similar to me, we were best friends through grade school. I hate her now, she became a kiss-ass to men and men's rules and society."

"What I like least about my best friend is her wimpiness in the face of society at large."

Fifty-eight percent of women say that they sometimes find their friends afraid to "challenge" or openly disagree with men's ideas or anti-woman remarks in public—or find that their friends are afraid to take the lead in conversation, state forcefully their opinions, etc., in groups. In other words, many women are still hesitant to act in a non-subservient manner in public situations—i.e., "challenge" male "dominance" (being in charge) publicly. (And women have testified amply to their often well-justified reasons, i.e., men's reactions, in Part I.)

Noble thoughts and extreme transcendence—men only?

Do we take women's and our own intellectuality seriously? As one woman says, meaning to praise her friend, "I find her wise and strong. She likes to talk about deep things." What does this mean? In a man, would "deep thinking" be considered a philosophical-intellectual personality? But in a woman, does it somehow have the flavor of an "earth mother" connection—i.e., related to a biological "nature" or "inner wisdom"—rather than the "pure intellectuality" of men?

Standing in for male power: are we strong enough yet?

Are we strong enough economically and socially now to stand in for male "power figures" with each other? Can we trust our power yet?

As one woman puts it, "I'm twenty-three. Women my age have taken to assimilating male behaviors because we basically think they are better. We've been raised to look up to men and naturally try to 'mirror' them. Like, I repeat how I want to be single and on my own, I act like I am emotionally 'in control' most of the time—but do I really feel that way? Or am I just watching football because it makes me look uncool not to like it?"

If women try to join "male" culture—since it has the prestige and is the dominant one ("if you can't lick 'em, join 'em")—will this solve our problem, get us status? No, because we will still not be men, we will only be ratifying the "male" system by our behavior. (Therefore, do we have to "win," "dominate" with *our* culture, just to get "equality"?)

Since men have more economic and political power than we do, don't we still have to keep our ties with this system, no matter how we are treated? As Connie Ashton-Myers puts it, "Can any woman seriously question an assertion that her status ultimately depends on her pleasing, in one way or another, a male or set of males in control of some social institution, from the multinational corporation to the smallest nuclear family? And this arrangement has been perpetually nurtured and reinforced within the patriarchal family."*

There is such a thing as a legitimate fear of male power. Can we separate understanding men from copping out, fearing them—and save our integrity, our dignity, our value system? The challenge is to continue our valid feelings of love and still devise a way of facing down the system.

*She continues: "How has [patriarchy] persisted? It functions with the cooperation of women themselves who today strike bargains similar to those struck in prehistoric times . . ." Connie Ashton-Myers, reviewing Gerda Lerner's *The Origins of Patriarchy* (New York: Oxford University Press, 1986), in Coordinating Committee for Women in the Historical Profession newsletter, vol. 17, no. 1 (February 1986).

Are we afraid to challenge male power?

*"Every little girl is told to be a good girl!! Be nice!
Don't make waves!!! That is what it means basically."**

We may not be afraid anymore to live our own way, by our own rules. But do we still fear challenging "male" dominance in the society? This would not be surprising; we may fear confronting men or male power directly—with good reason. However, in the past hundred years, when we did work together, we *did* win such things as the right to vote, equal employment legislation, and we were almost able to pass the Equal Rights Amendment to the Constitution, which may now be won in the 1990s.

Solidarity Among Women

Can women be power centers in society now? Can we trust each other enough? Will we stand up for each other?

Do we take our relationships with other women seriously enough now to use them as a power base, a form of solidarity?† This is a question which affects all of our futures, and the status of women for generations to come—because if we can't take each other as seriously as we take men, then we will not have the solidarity to change things. Respecting each other, we will be much more powerful.

But if we can't count on our friends in public, if we see them bow to "male" power in public, how can we respect them? And we may feel we too must hide our thinking, continue existing on two levels, knowing the dominant "reality" and also knowing our interior thoughts about it, but rarely voicing those thoughts or doing anything to change the system. Because, beneath it all, we feel we have to continue to respect/fear men who run the system too much.

As one woman describes this feeling in herself, and coming out of it, "I used

---

*In Russia, girls are given a similar message; girls who show overly "independent" or rowdy behavior may find themselves sent for a stay in a labor camp for girls with "wayward" behavior (Desmond Smith, *Smith's Moscow* [New York: Knopf, 1976]).

†As a woman in the documentary film *Bread and Roses* put it, after organizing women garment workers in the 1920s, "We weren't just nice girls anymore; we were vigorous people who wanted to change society."

to feel like I had to be 'nice' all the time (I hate to admit it, but especially to men) until one day I caught a glimpse of myself in a mirror, being kind of obsequious and fawning. From that moment on, I decided to be me, even knowing full well that I would not be as attractive—or 'non-threatening'—to men. But I just didn't have a choice, and still be able to live with myself."

The "male" ideology has tried to breed in us a form of passivity, especially in public situations. For example, if we voice an opinion, we may be seen as trying to "dominate" the situation, or the men present. (However, if we are silent, we may be seen as "wimpy"!) It may be hard for us to speak out and make our thoughts part of the world when we are taught that men's thoughts are more "profound." We are frequently discouraged by men from stating our views, told not to "challenge" the status quo in even the smallest way, by being reminded how men hate "ballsy," "aggressive" women. We become, unconsciously, "man pleasers," and change our behavior around men so as not to be "outspoken," or seem to challenge them—i.e., so the man can be (or seem to be) the leader, dominant.

Most of the time we tell ourselves, what does it matter anyway? I can get my way, or get my point across, another way. (And so, women are "rewarded" by being called "manipulative.") In other situations, we go along with the system because it can be fun—i.e., in a "dating" situation, going out to dinner, letting the man invite us, take us, etc.

Another reason for our reticence, in addition to male pressure not to be "aggressive," "strident," or "nagging" (!), is that many women have a fundamental desire for more grace in life, less hostility and competition. If the only way to have that, part of us says, is not to speak up around men, not to "challenge" men's touchy "dominance," so be it. But this brings us back to the philosophical dilemma of how to handle aggression without being overrun.

We have seen that women are fighting for their values in personal relationships; however, the less aggressive patterns of the "female" philosophy may not be automatically suited to "win" against an aggressive ideology such as the "male" system. This has been a persistent problem for women, or indeed for any society which is more peace-loving, or does not at times have the capacity to defend itself. For example, Poland, which refused to maintain a great standing army although the other countries of Europe were building theirs, was, as a result, partitioned three ways in the late eighteenth century.

How much "aggression" is good as a personal quality? Do we want to change this part of our value system? Women, especially women "at home," or "mothers," have been called "wimpy," but this is in part a "male" ideological view of the "peacemaker" role women have had—in fact, the role women often see as part of their idealism, their honor. Most women in this study believe women's interpersonal values of nurturing, listening, sharing enthusiasm, non-aggression, and caring should be preserved. And that this is quite different from being "wimpy," even in the face of "male" power. If Gandhi and Martin Luther King could practice non-violent resistance, so women feel that they can too—in fact, feel that they have been doing so for far longer. What forms of resistance are appropriate for us in our situation? See Chapter 19.

Being Proud of Each Other and Supporting Each Other: The Key to Changing Our Status

When asked the most important advice they could give other women now, women frequently say to love and respect each other and ourselves:

"My advice to women? Love yourself and each other, the rest will come."

"Open your eyes. Value your women friends, love yourself and each other first. Don't be afraid to be strong and define *yourself*. We are great!"

"Love yourself, be active to help this world become a place in which you want to live. But enjoy the means of doing so, don't just live anticipating the future."

"Make sure you always have a support group of women. Women are bright and strong and emotionally expressive, loving and motivated. They have a fullness men lack."

"If I could give any advice to other women, it would be to clear out your life of the things that make you unhappy. Don't stick with ugly jobs or ugly relationships because of some future thing you're hoping for. Don't suffer now in anticipation that it will be better in the future. Spend more time on the things that do make you happy. And love other women—don't let the system get you! You are great and you can make it!"

"Women! Be happy! Hear your own song, dream your own dreams and put them first, have the birds sing for you, sing with them. Love other women, have many friends. Go out and do things—don't be afraid anymore!"

Do we take our women friends seriously enough to write them into our wills? One woman, at least, takes a female relative this seriously:

"The most important relationship with a woman in my life is with my youngest sister. She is the beneficiary of my will and I feel she will give my possessions the most thoughtful consideration in disposal."

Others say that women must help other women professionally:

"I had a mentor relationship with a woman who chose me as her successor as a Symphony Guild president. She spent great amounts of time grooming me for the position, and at the same time she had in me someone with whom to share her frustrations. I continue to feel great warmth toward her and feel that she truly cares about me as an individual. Because she is very busy with her job and with a difficult family situation, we have lunch only a couple of times a year now. Still, I have enormous gratitude toward her for believing I had the potential for leadership at a time I did not know it, and she partly did it by expressing her own self-doubts to me and seeking my advice—treating me as an equal before I actually felt equal. Eventually, she and I and a couple of other women who were equally willing to accept major responsibilities in the volunteer sector (leading to major business positions) became a kind of elite group in our small city. We are not intimate friends but have great respect for one another and feel a closeness and concern about one another's continued self-realization (including in emotional ways)."

"I talk about women's situation with friends and such. Tell them that we have to stick together, not let ourselves be divided and conquered. And act on it. I give more to a lot of women than I would naturally, I give them time and support when I might rather get on with my own thing. I try to be pretty up-front about it, someone for anyone to argue with if they need to take on a feminist. I am a Ph.D. research scientist at a top-notch institution in a man's field and I can do all of this and not feel like a hardened, masculinized, embittered witch. I owe the women's movement the debt of my work life."

But other women complain that, while women are good as friends, they generally don't have enough knowledge of the world to give practical advice, or offer "connections"—therefore women can't be taken as seriously:

"What's missing in my women friends is that I have no mentor. I don't need a role model, I make my own role, but there is no one that has similar experience, there is no one who has done what I've done and can clue me in or encourage me, or give me ideas. All my friends are younger—much different, or at earlier stages of their lives. They have sympathy, empathy, but no concrete help."

One woman puts down women who have these negative attitudes to women, who do not support other women, and calls them "male-identified":

"Some women don't bond with each other, or worry about women's issues—they want to be 'smart,' and compete in 'serious,' traditional 'men's' areas, the 'real world' . . . they are brainwashed. They are male-identified. They don't see that the point is to make/reveal the larger world—that women's thoughts are just as valid."

Women now *do* support each other, more and more, as we have seen here: over 80 percent of all women have their closest emotional relationship with another woman.

This is not to say, of course, that all the women we know are perfect, that *we* are perfect, that all the women we know are our friends, or that all the women we meet have all the wonderful, nurturant qualities described here. And yet, even with women who can snap and be condescending, we have much more in common than we might wish; the shared experience of being a woman in a gender-oriented society creates a strong underlying bond—if not always respect. Many women are still male-identified in their thinking about other women, and may take out their general frustrations on women as the weakest, most convenient target, the safest, the least threatening group to be aggressive against.

One woman describes this commonality she shares with her mother through all the ambiguity, "I identify more with my father because he has always had a job and I do too; I want to be more like him than I want to be like my mother. But my mother I can talk to in a way I never could my father. She is always there for me—not on every level, but for bottom line survival, I *know* she is there. She is the one I turn to when I've got to be *sure*."

We offer each other a great reservoir of strength for all kinds of purposes in our lives. We must not be ashamed of the love we bear for one another. By respecting each other, putting each other first, recognizing who we are, we will change our status.

To Make a World in Which More Love Can Flourish

A Renaissance of Human Nature and the Spirit

"This is about 'women's rights,' yes—but what we are after even more is human dignity, the redefinition of the soul."

We are in the midst of a profound upheaval—one of those sudden and major changes that is a long time building but that finally, just when everyone thinks it will never happen, is there, like the French Revolution. And so for women it is now: women have stopped bowing to the ideology of many centuries—ideology built into sociology, psychology, and religion.

Enormous changes happen suddenly—a revolution that takes twenty or one hundred and twenty years, after all these centuries, is amazingly short, historically speaking. And yet the change that women have made in just the last ten years is phenomenal, the ramifications everywhere and growing.

As women, we are different. We have become space-time travelers; we have moved into another world, another century, another reality—leaving behind psychological allegiance to "the way it used to be," to "male" ways of doing things, the "male" ideology.

Like astronauts, we are moving ever farther away from the planet, now discerning the outlines of the system more clearly, seeing it for the first time as merely an ideological system, a set of beliefs with no right to define us*—and so we no longer accept the definition of our "place" by this ideology. We are self-naming and indeed beginning to "name" the rest of the culture, including "male psychology"—and this in the midst of a dominant culture that still tells us we "can't do this," that we are wrong.

The twenty-first century—now?

It is said that the nineteenth century began in 1789 with the French Revolution, and lasted until the twentieth century was ushered in with the 1920s' era of "modernism." What we may be witnessing now is the beginning of the twenty-first century, a little early: suddenly we find ourselves faced with a changed world, with new concerns, ideas and choices pressed on us unexpectedly, before we can fully comprehend them—before we even have words to describe them.

We feel that the "old order" is crumbling: everything that seemed permanent, that was taken for granted, is now under question—our systems of industrial production, finances, marriage and "home," even our relationship with nature as we become more and more aware of the damage we are doing to our environment, the dwindling of the natural resources, and now the threat of nuclear annihilation. Nothing seems to work "as it should" anymore—"the times are out of joint."†

The homeless on our streets—everyone wonders when they will "go away." And yet everyone knows somehow that their numbers will increase. There is a secret fear that they will surround "us" and engulf "us": is nowhere "safe"?‡ And the fact is that nowhere *is* safe, because the "world," that is, the

---

*As historian and feminist theorist Joan Kelly writes, ". . . the fact that we have such a view indicates that we are in a new social and political position with regard to patriarchy. It has been a strength of patriarchy in all its historic forms to assimilate itself so perfectly to socioeconomic, political and cultural structures as to be virtually invisible." Now, we *see* it—and not just some women, but many, many women. (See Joan Kelly, p. 225.)

†As B. F. Skinner asked in the May 1986 issue of the *American Psychologist*, "What Is Wrong with Daily Life in the Western World?" Needless to say, he did not mention the patriarchal-hierarchical value system.

‡For example, an editorial in *The New York Times* in May of 1987, by A. M. Rosenthal, describes "a whole new class of Americans: abused, abandoned . . . (children), often homeless and wandering, the antithesis of the country's concept of itself . . . In (New York) alone, 40 percent of the children live below the poverty line, a way of saying usually undernourished." Often the implication of such statements is that women/mothers should "go back home" and "take some responsibility" for these children. But as we have seen here, what the children (and mothers) may be fleeing is the emotional violence and insistence on dominating that many men are displaying in their relationships with women. Of course, this "wandering, homeless, out of place underclass" is not only children, but many adults, unemployed (many not even listed in the U.S. unemployment figures, since they are workers who have "given up," as the category reads). The alienation described in detail in this book is a large part of the reason for the spiritual loss or "giving up" of many people, female and male.

"underprivileged" or "underdeveloped" world, *is* growing and will swallow "us" up. The moral imperative is for more justice: for those who can to *do* something, to comprehend the situation and think through what is going on, so that it becomes possible to channel the changes that are taking place in a positive way. Indeed, we must embrace those "others" in order to redefine the direction we both will go. We are like swimmers caught up in a tide who suddenly meet in a cross current, our destinies entwined: we will sink or swim together. In other words, a democratic society cannot work without all its members involved and working together somehow; the educational and legal systems must make this possible, keep on making this possible.

What is wrong with the society is not money or lack of it (although these things matter), but the injustice that exists on a global scale—and people's knowledge that the global situation is unjust.

This is a knowledge that cannot be taken back. Perhaps it was inevitable—after the rise of rationalism and science in the seventeenth century, and the decline of the type of religion which said there is no way to change the world, and that one's reward for suffering (or being poor) would come in the afterlife*—perhaps it was inevitable that with democracy, the coming of the belief in the possibility of change, that perpetual revolution would become our modus vivendi.† With this, we took on a profound optimism and plan for change about the world and society. The American Revolution and the Communist Manifesto alike grew out of this promise. But with this optimism has also come frustration, and in some quarters, profound disillusionment, as the injustices of the system continue, and the plans and promises are not yet implemented.

There is a call for justice in the air, a feeling of anger that traditional power relationships have not ended, that the ideals of the last two centuries,

---

*The values relating to the need for justice in *this* world were stated, for example, in Pope Pius XI's Quadregisimo Anno statement in 1931: "In our days, not only is wealth accumulated, but immense power and despotic economic domination are concentrated in the hands of a few, a natural result of limitless free competition . . . permit[ting] the survival of those who pay the least heed to the dictates of conscience."

†When the center pin of divine right/church authority came loose from Western society in the eighteenth century, a process begun with the emergence of science and rationalism in the seventeenth, one of the greatest social transformations of all time was set in motion—one which will most probably lead to the undoing of patriarchy and its hierarchical assumptions. Strangely, all these currents of thought can be seen as growing originally out of Christianity itself, through its belief in the equality of all individuals before God (even though women were not included for a long period, and animals never were).

The first blossoming of this undercurrent was seen perhaps with Luther, emphasizing that all men's souls were equal, rich or poor, and that money should not be a part of access to heaven or the benefits of the church. Later, in the eighteenth century, it was seen that class privilege was unjust: all "men" were created equal and all should have the "rights of man." When racism became an issue in the nineteenth-century U.S., slavery was determined by many to be undemocratic and against the basic principles of a just society. Now in the twentieth century, beginning also in the nineteenth, the domination of men over women, by whatever slogan—whether "protection," "different but equal," or so on, is also seen as unjust and a practice which should be ended.

democratic ideals of equality of opportunity and respect, not to mention economic equality, are being implemented too slowly—having to be fought for too hard.

The lack of chances for many, the knowledge that the situation into which you are born makes all the difference—is creating a seething, almost directionless, hostility in many societies. All over the world now people believe that all people, not only the rich or privileged, should have dignity, opportunities, the right to personhood. This is, after all, what we say we believe. Conditions globally will surely continue to be unstable until ideals and conditions are more in alignment.

Put most simply, we can say that the reason for our instability is our lack of justice. There is too great a difference between our stated beliefs in equality and humanity and the realities of the society. Our chaos and terror are caused by the unhappiness of millions of people—women and men.

In the face of these unsettling conditions, we often as a society turn to the non-working but beloved ideas of the past. For example, in economics, we say "competition" will save us: "competition" must be right for the economy if it has been right for the last hundred years (and never mind if it has not always been right—during the depressions of the 1890s and 1930s, for example—or if, without everyone starting out from the same equal footing, it doesn't quite fit in with democratic ideals). Others, seeing the industrial base eroding and realizing that "pure competition" is not solving the problem, have begun to speak of trying the opposite, i.e., more cooperation between "workers" and employers.* But, it is interesting to note, cooperation is one of the primary values of the "female" system we have been discussing.†

In family and personal life, a "return to traditional values," it is said, will save us—women should stay in the home, be "the mother," while the man goes "out" and "provides for" the family. But most women do not want to give up their jobs, no matter how boring, because they mean access to the outside world and some degree of autonomy, in addition to financial benefits. (See Chapter 11.)

Ironically, many women too would like a return to "traditional values," but by this, women mean something different. Women mean more love, more dignity, justice and equality in that love; they no longer want relationships based on one-way giving, with the man the recipient, "on top," able to go out and be as competitive as he wants, because the woman is always there at home,

---

*See, for example, Robert B. Reich, *Tales of a New America* (New York: Times Books, 1987), and Tom Peters, *Thriving on Chaos* (New York: Knopf, 1987).
†Though neither women nor even all white males were included in the provisions of the constitution, it is perhaps not insignificant that the ideals of the framers were more linked to cooperation for the common good than to "individualism" or individual competition, which they considered selfish or negative.

ready to absorb the alienation and violence—a form of battle fatigue—he may feel when he returns, ready to comfort and restore him. Women say *men* should learn the "traditional values" of emotional support, connection and nurturing.

Meanwhile, as women grow less and less willing to provide emotional nurturing and support when they do not get it in return, it is no wonder that many men feel the family is collapsing and they "can't go home again."* For them ("the society"), there is no more "Mother" to turn to. (Women, of course, are used to not having a "Mother" to turn to, someone always there to understand, "hear" and comfort them—although fortunately we do have close friendships with each other.)

So—as we find ourselves as a society with no clear plan for the future that seems to offer hope, we stand in confusion and can only regret that the values of the late, great nineteenth century have been undone while the twentieth century with its modernism did not prove satisfying. We feel paralyzed, every new idea seems only to jeopardize even more of what it was that once was "home"—our precious hold on what we keep hoping might still give us some sense of protection, some of what we feel we have lost,† what we long for— what is it? Warmth? Stability? Peace of mind? Enough to eat? Absence of fear? Love?

The nineteenth century was beautiful in many ways—certainly its art and culture and standard of living for the growing middle class, even the houses it built, were warm, beautiful, glorious. This way of life with its family and work structures was envisioned as eternal, lasting forever. Looking back from what we have now, it is understandable that we mourn its passing and long for some of its beauty. But its beauty (and its terrible failures, such as the poverty of large numbers of people, and the oppression of women and some races) does not mean that we cannot create something yet more beautiful: a society which is based on a true equality, with even broader democratic principles—one which will endure for the coming centuries, even more stable and productive, with a better quality of life.

This is clearly a time of an "old order" dying—but it is also the beginning of the new. The challenge for us is to identify out of the seeming chaos those elements that will serve to make a better, more democratic system than we have ever had, a society whose values in actual daily practice are more like the ideals in which we believe, a society based more on justice than on hierarchy.

---

*Most women, on the other hand, have never *been* "home," since they are not really getting emotional support from men; they do not regret what was, but rather what might have been.
†See also the conclusion to Part III. Thus, for example, we have become preoccupied with the 1940s film "It's a Wonderful Life" and are setting it up as the model of what we have lost—even though most women today would hardly see it as domestic bliss.

Could the Values of "Female" Culture Serve as a Framework for a Revolutionary Philosophical Transformation?

"How much, if ever, have institutions corresponded to the imaginative ideals that women created, love as women have imagined it? How much have women really imagined what all the possibilities are?"

—ELIZABETH PETROFF*

This study states many women's philosophical case for a new organization of human relationships—and therefore, of the society.† Women here are questioning the human condition, saying it can be better than it is.

Equality and interaction as a social framework are not just idealistic dreams. Cooperation and teamwork are viable ways of organizing society. Nevertheless, it is often heard that women are "too emotional" to run governments, that "women's" "soft-hearted," cooperative ideals would not work on a global level in government or international relations. And yet, how can a system which has brought us to the brink of nuclear war and ecological disaster call another system unworkable or impractical?

If the "male" value system has brought us to the edge of annihilation, whether by nuclear war or destruction of the equilibrium of nature, it is time to look at other possible social organizations. In large part it is the interpersonal patterns of the "male" ideology, with its constant encouragement for men to use competition for dominance as the means of "resolving" disputes, that has lead the world to the situation in which it now finds itself, with total destruction possible.

"Women's" philosophy truly does contain other ways of resolving disputes, or preventing them before they arise, i.e., the subtle negotiating process described earlier. In the midst of the very real problems with which society is now faced—problems the current system does not seem to be able to address adequately—it is time to take a serious look at "women's" alternative philosophy.‡

---

*S. Hite and E. Petroff, "Controversies over the Nature of Love," American Philosophical Association, annual meeting, 1986.

†Indeed, how people make relationships is the basis of the social structure; or, "the personal is political," the social structure in microcosm.

‡Of course, not all women are "just" and "kind," while many men are; it is not one's biology that creates these characteristics. However, women's shared experiences do tend to create certain understandings and ways of relating to the culture, just as do men's.

One woman states clearly what the debate is all about:

"I wonder where it's all leading. Now women are more integrated into society, and groups such as NOW, women's business networks, and the like are gaining more influence. Still, I don't think women feel entirely comfortable with the business world or professional schools. For me, it's not even the problem of discrimination—I'd almost welcome an up-front problem of that sort. It's just the feeling that the institutions of society, based on power and built by men, are organized and led all wrong, are shooting galleries.

"Competition and the exploitation of underlings competing against each other for the favor of a few powerful people are stupid ways of getting the world's business done. Men seem more disposed to handle reality as a game of ego-presentation individual combat. Women seem more naturally inclined toward more subtle ways of establishing cooperation.

"I'm really torn between the idea that women are more subtle social creatures and need a society built for and by them, and the theory that women are just as competitive as men and need only to begin to show it, to move into the world and play the game as men do. But at the top of that game is the bomb, the ax. National competition. Who wants that?!"

"Women's" Culture: A Different Tradition

Women have a culture and value system with a different spirit, a different orientation to life as discussed in Part I—a system with a complex and subtle history. This philosophy has grown out of women's historical involvement with the family, and is based on how to relate to other human beings, hear them, create more interpersonal understanding.

Women have often been put down for staying home, being "non-intellectual"; however, while women were "just at home," they were also developing this very important and ingenious culture. The fact that "women's" philosophy has grown out of personal and family relationships does not make it any less serious or politically profound than the "male" system.

While almost all women know how to operate in the "male" world, and are living bi-culturally, most men seem hardly aware that there is a distinguished belief system which women have carried on for centuries that deserves philosophical discussion and respect—although men often react with anger and fear when it seems that women will stop being "loving"—i.e., stop carrying on some of the traditions of their "sub"culture.

On the other hand, this set of values can also be held by men, and is not always held by all women, as one woman pointed out in Part IV: "I used to admire women's sensitivity, tolerance, and especially their ability to listen to others. I felt men were incapable of interest in others. . . [but] since, I have realized that women are just as capable of insensitivity as men, and though they usually know more about others, they don't always use their knowledge any more wisely than men might."

Women describe the qualities of "women's" culture they find in women as a whole: *

"Women seem to be more sensitive and caring as *people* than most men are. They seem to be more in tune with the things in life that are really important. Most women are more affectionate and warm than men. You can talk about just about anything with a woman (most), and feel a real kinship, an unspoken understanding. Most men are too surface, women like to get to the real meat of things."

"I think women in general are more 'sensitive' than men—more concerned about what is happening around them and how others are feeling and what will be the effect of their actions on others. They have a less compartmentalized view of things than men. Women also survive the most difficult life events— more so than many men, who have women to handle the emotional stuff for them."

"Women seem able to be closer, opener with other women, they can share in a way that is very hard for a man. They are perhaps better able to accept their own flaws (they are used to being considered imperfect, I guess). Maybe we are more able to really say that we're sorry. Also, so many women seem to have to work so hard. If you haven't gotten married, then you have to work awfully hard to get and maintain a decent job, a decent wage. The superwoman is something else. Makes the rest of us feel small. But that doesn't mean I don't admire them."

"I admire women's attitudes toward life, their strength, intuition, adaptability, and warmth—their emotional availability—their soft and beautiful bodies, their intelligence. They are sensitive; easier to be with. Great women? I think of Simone de Beauvoir, Eleanor Roosevelt."

And, as one woman put it earlier:

"I admire the quiet work of women, their defense of interpersonal peace— doing decent things when they don't get much credit for doing anything. I want to see women move into the world and rebuild the bridge between private

---

*Most men would probably not disagree with this description (see The Hite Report on men); however, many men seem simultaneously to want women to hold these values, and at the same time be able to enjoy disparaging women for having these values, i.e., thinking them "weak" and calling women "too sensitive," and so on.

spheres and public works, which was destroyed by industrialization. How about the hundreds of women going to graduate school in chemistry? Right on! I'd like to see private morality extended to the earth; I hope that women retain some of the knowledge they gained raising children and shoring up civilized human relationships when they are out in the dogfight."

A complex vocabulary of feeling

"Women's" system has developed elaborate forms of communication and a special style of conversation which emphasizes mutuality, listening with empathy, demonstrations of reciprocal understanding, giving of signs of recognition and feedback.

These kinds of unnamed, small, caring gestures and also intellectual responses that facilitate dialogue are extremely important to the "female" system. They comprise a large part of what we have seen women asking from men in their relationships in Part I—and what we have seen women demonstrating with their friends in Chapter 18. For example, when having a conversation with someone, women display more signs of active listening and hearing, interest, encouraging the other person to continue talking, indications of recognizing and understanding what the other person is saying. This leads the person speaking to feel they are "heard," "seen," and creates/generates a great deal of positive energy. If this interactive way of relating could be translated into the culture at large, it would lead to a much more positive attitude in society.

People have often derogatorily called women "manipulative" or "intuitive"; the nugget of truth here is that women indeed "see dust," whether it is physical or emotional; women want to make things around them go well and can easily tell when someone's feelings are "out of whack"—whereas disharmonies "in the atmosphere" do not seem to bother most men to the same degree, nor do they feel compelled to try to straighten them out. Women frequently see the subtle signs of people's emotional states, and want to "say the right thing," help the person along. Another way to put this is, women often have a heightened perception of "intangibles": they are more sensitively attuned to small details of behavior or expression of feelings.

Thus, if the central focus of the "male" ideology has to do with hierarchy and maintaining rank within that hierarchy, complying with (or rebelling against) the rules and regulations of "masculinity" (individual thought being allowed only so far in the system*), "women's" philosophy is basically

---

*The fact that men are allowed so little leeway in forms of dress—they must wear pants, with a jacket and shirt; while women can wear all kinds of things—shows the value that men and the "male" system place on conformity, showing membership in the "male" group, because only through abiding by the rules of conformity can one prove one is part of the "male" club, or the official ruling elite. That is why men adhere so strongly and with such pride to these forms. Who would ever catch a man wearing a skirt, no matter how "liberal"?

centered on the importance of treating other people with respect and dignity. It is less hierarchically structured, less concerned with following rules and authority than with bringing out the best in individuals, valuing each.

In addition, the "female" system's belief in non-aggressivity and nurturing makes for a built-in self-criticism or introspection in most women in times of stress, conflict, or when being attacked. Men, on the other hand—encouraged to believe they are "right" (especially if "challenged" by a woman), taught to attack when under stress, always to assert dominance over women, and never to take a "backseat" even in conversation—do not have this same tendency to scrutinize themselves psychologically. This can make dialogue about problems nearly impossible.

On the other hand, the importance of relationships in "women's" value system does not mean that one has to always be in a relationship or be preoccupied with the emotional status of one. This can limit one's ability to relate fully to the larger society, as one woman describes: "I would like to think that having relationships with people is the most important part of life. But you just get exhausted. I feel like there's other contributions that I need to make, that I can't do because I spend so much time on individuals. I value those individual relationships as the most important thing in my personal life. But when I think of what I want to do within society, what I would like to be able to contribute, then that's much bigger and greater than anything individually." In other words, "nurturing," as women have discussed, can refer to a way of life, not only to a way of being in individual relationships.

Finally, in women's remarks throughout this book there has been a feeling of shock or outrage at the basic injustice with which many men have treated women in relationships—a sense of being judged unfairly and "thrown away," often without even the dignity of an explanation or a graceful departure. Women, through these comments and through their comments on their friendships with other women, seem to be implying a basic substratum of a belief in fairness, in an essential justice or ethical sense which surely everyone must have—but do men utilize it in their relationships with women? Or do they believe that the idea is to "get away with" whatever one can? (And yet, women would answer, how can you build something with another person, something like trust, when you are tricking them, "getting away with" something?)

In summary, from wherever it comes, women seem to have a cultural framework of their own, which includes a highly developed ethical system and a rich, subtle style of sophisticated interpersonal relationships.

As Jim Berry describes it, quoting from *The Spiritual Dimension of Green Politics*, by Charlene Spratnek: "Patriarchy, so repellent to a growing number of women, ought to be just as repellent to men. Spratnek finds that the term 'patriarchal culture' connotes not only injustice toward women but also the accompanying cultural traits: love of hierarchical structure and competition, love of dominance-or-submission modes of relating, alienation from nature, suppression of empathy and other emotions, and haunting insecurity about all these matters. These traits usually show up in anyone, male or female, who opts to play by the rules of patriarchal culture." (From *Amieus Journal*, June-July 1987)

A new relationship with nature

These values are also linked to a view of "nature" as something to be nurtured and lived with on an equal basis, not "dominated." Ecologically, our world is in danger; much of our planet could die.*

According to the World Wildlife Fund: "Without firing a shot, we may kill one fifth of all species of life on this planet in the next twenty years. . . . Years ago, rain forests circled the earth in abundance from South America to Africa, Malaysia, and Indonesia. Yet in the time it takes you to read this sentence, another eight acres of rain forest will have been bulldozed and burned off the face of the earth. . . . Not only do [these forests] provide food and shelter to at least half the world's species of wildlife, these tropical forests also generate about 50 percent of our own rainfall as they return moisture to the air. . . . Commercial exploitation and growing population demands will speed destruction of rain forests as well as oceans, grasslands, lakes and wetlands. . . . We are in a breakneck race against time."†

And the international group Greenpeace states: "Our goal is a more civilized attitude by humans towards other species. . . . With every week that passes another unique and irreplaceable species becomes extinct. At this very moment, a few hundred more pounds of nuclear waste are being created . . . toxic and chemical wastes are being dumped into the oceans or discharged in fragile rivers. . . . *It is not enough to treat the threats to our environment as abstract, it requires personal intervention* . . . a few people founded Greenpeace because they'd finally decided they had had enough of just standing by and watching the world be desecrated. . . . [These individuals have taken personal action such as] looked over their shoulders at a harpooner trying vainly to kill the whale they were protecting with their bodies. And they've looked back into the angry eyes of sealers unable to club the defenseless newborn animals these people were shielding from the hunter's club . . ."

Some people find this kind of idealism ridiculous—and especially ridicule it in women. As one woman objects, "Women like to be kind to everybody, but we are laughed at. What is wrong with kindness to animals? It is usually men who are hunters—how many women take out hunting licenses? On the other hand, women wear fur coats. If they could see the animals murdered, I'm sure they wouldn't." Hunting for the fun of "sport," killing not for food, is strange. It is hardly "sport," since the stakes aren't equal—deer and quail don't have guns to shoot back with. So what kind of "sport" is it? Sport means equal

---

*See, for example, Rachel Carson, *Silent Spring* (Boston: Houghton Mifflin, 1962); Jeremy Rifkin, *Entropy: A New World View* (New York: Viking Press, 1980), and Jacques-Yves Cousteau and Y. Paccalet, *La mer blessée* (Paris: Edition l'Odyssee-Flammarion, 1987).
†World Wildlife Fund, August 1986. Many of our medicines are also made from the plants found in these dying forests.

stakes, but this is just violence, a way for men to feel they are hunters exercising their caveman or killer instincts.

A particularly chilling example of this attitude is related by a boy telling of an experience he had in childhood:* "I used to go hunting with my dad during my boyhood. Unfortunately, I have always been a very poor marksman (my hands shake too much). I gave up hunting after an incident in which my dad and I were duck hunting in a boat with some other men. I had just brought down a duck, and we paddled the boat over to pick it up. As we reached it, I was astonished and delighted to find it still alive and looking well. It seemed so cute and attractive, I envisioned taking it home with me, nursing it back to health, and keeping it for a pet. One of the men picked it up and proceeded to beat its brains out over the side of the boat."

Idealism and enthusiasm for life

What many people want to see in the world now is a more idealistic spirit, almost a reverence for life, a sacred feeling about each other, a sense of wonder and curiosity—in place of the cynicism that passes for sophistication and verges on hostility much of the time. These elements were, in a way, represented in an earlier, more religious view of life in the sense that then, at least, people acknowledged that life was a mystery; the current popular view that all of life is ours to own through "science" is a part of the smug cynicism that many women would decry (as Einstein did, when he said that the more science tells us, the more mysterious life becomes). Reverence for life is a spiritual quality that is part of the different orientation to life being considered here.

This issue has been explored by a number of modern philosophers, especially Heidegger. As Joseph Fell reminds us, "It is in Heidegger that one finds the philosophically most important expression of this new/old attitude in all of twentieth-century thought. No one has explored the deep historical roots of Western violence to nature more penetratingly." This is most clear, perhaps, in Heidegger's *The Question Concerning Technology.*

Other new currents of thought relating to idealism and social justice are being seen in the work, already cited, by Robert Reich and Tom Peters. Reich, for example, believes that the only way American business can survive is to empower the individual worker (such as was done by Federal Express). The Marxist dialectic "has not worked," and so what is necessary now is "the empowering of *all* the members of the organization who work together for the common goal." In other words, the way to compete successfully now is to cooperate. But, it should be noted, this is traditional anti-hierarchical "women's" philosophy in corporate language.

* *The Hite Report on Male Sexuality* (New York: Alfred A. Knopf, 1981), page 5.

Even more strikingly, an article in Barron's, Feb. 16 and 23, 1987, by Benjamin Stein, discussed the problems of Wall Street in terms of too much aggression, describing the six "main points" of the "male world" with its "strict pecking order" as part of the problem.

General statements about nurturing others and cooperative values can be ridiculed. But how is the concept of "nurturing" a society different from the statement by John F. Kennedy: "Ask not what your country can do for you; ask what you can do for your country"? And yet, somehow, it would seem "unmanly" to ask men to "nurture" their country. Once again we see how the subtle meanings of words, and the specialized vocabularies for the two genders, filter our view of what we are looking at. (See Chapter I.)

In "women's" value system, a certain idealism about love and a belief in nurturing others consistently reappears. Women tend to see these behaviors as "only just"—to feel these behaviors are basic to any system of justice, and, in fact, one of the most important aspects of how a human being behaves in her/his society.

Women's traditional idealism and involvement with "underdog" causes is well known. Women have been associated with idealistic movements throughout history: Harriet Beecher Stowe's *Uncle Tom's Cabin* had great influence during the nineteenth-century anti-slavery movement, and many women were deeply involved in the various abolitionist societies of the times, out of which the early feminist movement grew.* And of course, it was Rosa Parks in 1955 who first refused to sit in the back of the bus in Montgomery, Alabama. Thus began the modern black protests against segregation, eventually involving hundreds of black schoolgirls going to jail in the South. Women have always been, as well, the backbone of church relief services of all denominations, collecting clothing, sewing, and mailing blankets. It was also women who collected schoolchildren's baby teeth so that tests for strontium 90 could be made, leading to the treaties between the U.S. and the USSR banning nuclear weapons testing in the atmosphere. And women were deeply involved in the One World movement which led to the founding of the League of Nations, the predecessor to the United Nations.

Theoretical Debates over "Women's" Culture

Readers should not confuse this discussion of the differences between "men's" and "women's" cultures as referring to or implying biologically ordained "separate spheres." As Rosalind Rosenberg points out,† certain branches of nine-

*See historian Ellen DuBois's, *Feminism and Suffrage: The Emergence of an Independent Women's Movement in America* (Ithaca, N.Y.: Cornell University Press, 1978.)
†Rosalind Rosenberg, *Beyond Separate Spheres: Intellectual Roots of Modern Feminism* (New Haven, Conn.: Yale University Press, 1982).

teenth-century feminism did indeed believe for a time in women's "superior ethical insight and nurturant qualities" that they seemed frequently to attach to biology. However, other feminists never agreed with this point of view, and early in this century, feminist scholars made it a point to show that the vast majority of observable sex differences could be traced to cultural condition-ing—although "Victorian science had a bedrock belief in the primacy of biol-ogy over culture."

These two schools of thought became known, in later twentieth-century scholarship, as "egalitarian feminism" (differences are caused by cultural condi-tioning), and "separate spheres" feminism (women's "distinctiveness"). How-ever, what is being discussed here are precisely the cultural differences that make for two different cultures: there are no biological differences that make one gender or the other "better," smarter, or wiser, but there *are* two separate historical traditions, which are all mixed together into the ideology we see poured out at us every day from television programs and commercials, so that even small children show the dictated traits before we believe they can even comprehend what is being said. Both cultures have had good and bad points, but what we are focusing on here is a part of the "male" culture that the "female" culture cannot rival: the way in which the "male" system has declared itself better and kept women out of schools, out of running the government, owning property, and everything else it could for a very long time. If this were not the case, we would hardly have to discuss "two cultures" here.

Is "women's" system "superior"?

By stressing the positive, nurturing qualities that many women believe in, and that they are asking men to consider taking on, are we falling into the trap of saying that women's moral sense is superior to men's? We are not saying that women are innately superior, or that women have been perfect "saints" who love everybody, without a vicious bone in their bodies. However, the nurturing qualities that women have developed may be more appropriate, in fact, the needed antidote for the emphasis on aggression that has come to characterize the dominant "male" system.

Still, does the point of view that women have a "nurturant philosophy" of life contain within it the belief that "female" values are more morally righteous? Are we saying women's (or anyone's) being loving and giving in relationships or in politics is "morally superior"?

This is one of the issues at stake here: *is* loving-giving, whether in personal life or in politics, a value we wish to hold central in our society? As seen in Part III, many women will not continue this tradition of nurturing for men if men are not going to take on these values too, at least in relationships. Is "nurturing" also necessary to keep the larger society running? In a sense, caring for the system so that the conditions of democratic opportunity and freedom are safeguarded is a form of "nurturing"—the same kind of daily attention to detail that it takes to keep a home running, or to keep a relationship emotionally alive. One way of not having to "nurture" society is to have a society in which human relationships and education/jobs are all based on a "free market value" system, in which survival depends on ability to compete "freely"—no matter how poor you are (too poor for education? too hungry to go to school? to think straight?) or of what color or gender. This kind of society at least needs no tending, no "nurturing," no bothering with. But will it work? Will it be stable, or will it come apart at the seams, just as ours is doing, because of the injustice and desperation felt by many—and subsequent demoralization?

The fact that it may be women who now have the more relevant value system is a historical phenomenon—not a matter of superiority. Also, although it is most often women who hold these beliefs—that competition and dominance are not particularly productive or graceful ways of running life, and that nurturing is a valuable characteristic for humans to cultivate in their relationships with one another, or for countries to cultivate in *theirs*, both women and men can hold this value system. And indeed, many men are involved in trying to create a more just, less combative society*—and it is hoped that many more men will join in the debate women are having in this book and elsewhere, over what our values should be and where our society is going.

Is it only a reaction to male domination?

Is "women's" culture a sign of oppression—or a creative way women have shaped their historical situation? Some would ask, Is "women's" belief in "nurturing" noble, or merely a rip-off of women? Since women have been forced to believe they should be "nice," are women being "dumb," in "falling for it"? If women are "nurturing," is this no more than the way women have been forced to behave, a reaction to their powerlessness?

In other words, are we looking at a "real" culture—or are women's nurturing and loving qualities simply the result of women's oppression? Are our "understanding" and "giving" qualities merely the tactics developed by those who had to try to survive in a world in which they had to please and depend on those in power (men)? Indeed, it is sometimes said that "women's" value system is not a culture created by women; rather, women's "loving" and "helpful" mannerisms are simply the necessary strategies of any oppressed group which has to monitor people's attitudes toward it closely—develop antennae to survive.

But recent historiography based on the study of many groups has concluded that people have responded in different ways to their historical circumstances, interacting and changing situations, no matter how difficult, putting their own

*And, as one woman bluntly puts it, "Women can be just as macho and nasty as any guy."

particular stamp on them.* Women could have reacted quite differently to their circumstances than they did and could have developed much more "paranoid" and less positive ways of handling their "role." Who is to say that another group would have created an equally strong system under such conditions?†

Therefore, should we value what women have been doing, the culture they have been building? Or believe that if women hadn't been "oppressed," they would have done what men did—i.e., joined armies, built governments, and formed the economic system as we now know it? But would men have built armies if *they* hadn't grown up under the ideological system they did?

Finally, even if "women's" culture had grown up in response to historical oppression or biological impulse, would this make it any less valuable today? Especially now? In the long run, it does not matter whether this "nurturing," non-violent tradition is the result of a secondary historical status, or of a biological "nature" (hormonally designed to nurture children), or whether it is something women created over time, through their history—or even an expression of their soul. The point now is that this is a valuable cultural resource that should not be overlooked or discarded.

Biologically ordained?

On the other hand, if women's basic philosophy is not simply a product of oppression, are women *biologically* ordained to be nurturing?‡ Is our culture still not something *we* have made, we can be proud of? According to the "male" ideology, it is more "natural" for women to want to nurture and love/support people, because they bear children and can breast-feed, and therefore their hormonal systems are different from men's; this is what makes women "naturally" nurturers and "nest builders," or so the hypothesis goes.§ While men and women do have a different hormonal balance, there is no biological evidence that female hormones make women "loving" (although it has been shown that testosterone, basically a male hormone, may increase aggressiveness).‖ Thus,

*Those who have particularly contributed to this theoretical perspective include historians Jesse Lemisch, Herbert Gutman, and Eric Foner.
†Is this also true of the Jewish cultural heritage, especially as developed over the last three centuries?
‡This question is also addressed in Part I.
§Which has led some to suggest that this is as much a problem as "PMS" and should also be treated hormonally!
‖As to animal and primate studies, there are no clear-cut conclusions to be drawn from either. The primates are all quite different from each other and from us. And there are as many animal species which are organized cooperatively as there are species which are organized competitively. The variety of social organization among animals is enormous. In one of the best and most concise accounts of this controversy, Professor R.C. Lewontin sums up and refutes all the basic biological arguments for personality determination by gender in a letter to the *New York Review of Books*, Oct. 24, 1985, pp. 54–55.

See also the substantial modern philosophical literature on the extent to which human thought is capable of—in fact, can't avoid—suspending "automatic" natural or biological determination of attitudes and behavior; e.g., Edmund Husserl, *Ideas: General Introduction to Pure Phenomenology and a Phenomenological Philosophy* (Boston: Kluwer/Nihoff, 1983); Martin Heidegger, *Being and Time* (New York: Harper women's "characteristic" of being nurturing is most probably part of a histori-cal-cultural tradition, not a simple biological given. There is a great deal of proof that the "male" cultural system puts enormous pressure on men to make them aggressive and challenging, and puts pressure on women to keep them from "threatening" "male" dominance, etc. (See Chapter 3.) Surely, there is a place for competition in the world, but its role for men has been greatly overemphasized and encouraged by the culture.

Other discussions of women's "separate voice"

Documentation of "women's" system, or "sub" culture, is becoming more and more voluminous. As early as 1923, psychologist Beatrice M. Hinkle wrote that the same theories could not be applied to the psychology of both men and women, since the conditions under which men and women develop are markedly different. Karen Horney, Jessie Bernard, and Simone de Beauvoir all noted this issue before 1950. (De Beauvoir referred ironically to "the culture of men as the culture of all.")

Beginning in the early 1970s and continuing until the present, such feminist journals as *Signs, Off Our Backs, Feminist Studies,* and, *Frontiers,* as well as *Women's Studies International Forum,* published in London, have run numer-ous articles discussing women's culture and art, often with debate about whether it represents a different culture. Carol Gilligan's recent work, *In a Different Voice,* argues that "Among the most pressing items on the agenda for research on adult development is the need to delineate *in women's own terms* the experience of their adult life."[*]

Carroll Smith-Rosenberg, historian of nineteenth-century America, argues in *Disorderly Conduct* that women's friendships in the nineteenth century clearly illustrate a separate culture, as seen in the letters these women write to each other and their diaries. The finding of a "female" voice, the naming of reality by women, is also something Mary Daly has written about. Linda Gordon has brought up this issue by questioning whether the "female tradi-tion" is the same as a feminist tradition (see her essay, "What's New in Women's History?"). Elizabeth Petroff, among a growing number of scholars of medieval and early modern times who are looking at this subject, has docu-mented a similar uniqueness in the writings of medieval women saints and visionaries.

While none of these perspectives or theorists agrees totally with any other—and there is certainly no intention here to present this work as in

---

and Row, 1962); Jean-Paul Sartre, *The Emotions: Outline of a Theory* (Secaucus, N.J.: Citadel Press, 1971) and *Being and Nothingness* (New York: Washington Square Press, 1965); Rollo May, ed., *Existential Psychology* (New York: Random House, 1961).
[*]See Carol Gilligan, *In a Different Voice* (Cambridge: Harvard University Press, 1982), pp. 172–3.

"blanket agreement" with all the above, since the theory in the present study must stand on its own—still, that two different cultural structures do exist and live side by side is a fact which has been noted by not a few scholars.

And still more controversy

One commentator criticizes this discussion of "female culture," saying she believes that "female"* values are being praised now as virtues only because women are losing the battle for "real equality." But did the "black pride" theme of the Civil Rights movement presage the demise of that movement—or was it an important element of the ongoing re-evaluation of the situation of Afro-Americans? The latter is more accurate. However, according to this commentator, "exalting" the "female" system is simply a "natural" response to "not winning" (what is "not winning"?)—i.e.: "The alternative to an unwinnable struggle is to emphasize difference rather than equality or freedom, asserting ideals like kindness and cooperation as feminine, and exalting them over their male counterparts . . . cooperative ideals are put forward as feminine, while [the achievements of competition] tend to be brushed aside; the huge joint effort from both sides that would be needed if we were really to revalue all these values is not forthcoming."†

But this huge effort to reevaluate both cultures is exactly what we are doing here, and what women everywhere, as documented here, are struggling in their lives to do now. Indeed, the elicitation of men's views in *The Hite Report* on men, along with this volume, is potentially a major step toward comparing and beginning a dialogue between the two systems.

There is no sense in trying to act as if these two cultures do not exist—and are not in fact in conflict. They are probably on their way to forming one, more unified, culture for both genders. But what that culture will be like is a very important question.

In fact, it is imperative to investigate (as we are doing here) what kind of "equality" we will have. Many women are saying now that they want not so much to "join" society as they do to change it, make it better. As historian Joan Kelly puts it, "Current political goals . . . are neither to participate as equals in man's world, nor to restore to women's realm and values their dignity and worth. Conceptions such as these are superseded in the present will to extirpate gender and sex hierarchy altogether, and with them all forms of domination. To aim at this . . . is a program that penetrates both to the core of self and to

---

*Here, as always, we are talking about a cultural, not biological, attribute.
†Mary Midgley, "Crisis in the Movement," a critique of three books on contemporary feminist thought, *The New York Times Book Review,* summer 1985.

the heart . . . of the male domain, for it will require a restructuring of all social institutions."* This is the point of view presented here.

To investigate the two value systems is not to create more distance between women and men, but to face reality, to analyze it and resolve it—in a way that mere simplistic demands for "an equal piece of the pie" can never do. This is not "running away" into "better-ism," but contributing to a more realistic, solid analysis.

How Would This Transformation in Culture Occur? How Does Change Happen?

Are revolutions about changing thinking, or taking power?

What if we *did* take seriously what we feel we know? What if we did try to establish generally what seems to us to be a better way of doing things? Remembering that women *are* a majority of the country, and that there are many men too who believe in the values of caring, fine-tuning relationships both at home and in business or global politics, keeping situations working for all parties involved before crisis situations develop, surely, with the majority of women and many men believing in these principles, we could make quite a try at it.

Why don't we? Why do we let the situation continue as it is? Because it is the way things have "always" been, with the "male" ideology dominant, a star fixed permanently in its heaven? How hard *would* it be to change? If women would support each other, as individuals and in economic and political alliances with each other, it could be fairly easy. If women would decide to cooperate on common goals, we could do anything.

On the other hand, do we have to "do" anything? If a large percentage of the population knows something is wrong with the ruling system, that it is unfair, and understands the antiquated ideology (the "male" ideology) behind it, this is already an enormous psychological change that cannot but have a tremendous impact—especially in combination with women's rapidly accelerating economic independence. Simply by thinking this way—not seeing men as more powerful, not feeling pressure to "get a man," not giving in to "male" power in the system, whether it is in a personal emotional relationship or at a bank with a male executive—each such woman is making change happen now: if a large part of our population is inwardly critiquing the overall system,

*Joan Kelly, "The Doubled Vision of Feminist Theory," *Feminist Studies* 5:1 (Spring 1979), p. 223.

separating themselves mentally from it, then that new mental life *is* a new culture. Or is this too simple?

Another theory of change is that revolution happens when the beliefs of some infiltrate or convert the beliefs of the many: "We have to convert them—show them our system is superior." By trying to change men in our personal relationships, will women change the larger society?

Sometimes the reverse happens. To make an analogy with politics: in what was known during World War II as the "Stockholm syndrome," referring to Sweden's attitude to Germany, a group often gradually comes to love and identify with its captor. On the other hand, sometimes a culture that is dominated by another politically and militarily *does* still manage to have its culture become dominant eventually. For example, the Romans were "civilized" by the Greeks (but the Greeks had more prestige than women do). Christianity was adopted by the Romans through an imperial decree—but did the imperial decree come about because of Christianity's underground popularity? Would it have eventually died out, even with its popularity, without the imperial decree? Traditions in Germany were changed by Christianity, but many of the old traditions survived simply because of their popularity and the strength of people's belief in them. Perhaps there has never been an example quite like our own.

There is tremendous pressure, as we go into new areas, to take on "male" colors, "male" beliefs, downgrade ourselves and our own way of life. Perhaps we ourselves fear trying out our own "sub"culture on the larger system, especially on a political level. But the "female" system, with its storehouse of humanistic values emphasizing mutuality and cooperation, is a cultural treasure. And we have not thrown out "male" values in a wholesale way: over the last twenty years of large-scale and historically important questioning of our values and identity, we have taken from the "male" system whatever was of value to mesh with the "female" system.

Some say we can best fight for our rights by electing political candidates: if "power only respects power," the more women become members of political groups, the more likely it is that we will see women candidates selected by the parties for major political office. And if we vote for them, we will see them elected. Others suggest that we form an alternative party. After all, the Green Party was started in Germany quite recently by a woman, Petra Kelly, and has had a great effect on German politics. The Green Party deals especially with issues of ecology and nuclear war. In Iceland, where women have been much more active than in the U.S., a feminist party won 10 percent of the vote and six seats in Parliament. In Norway, half the parliament has recently become female, due to women's organizing. And, as Corazon Aquino, in a speech at Harvard University on September 21, 1986, stated, "Women led the change of power in the Philippines, by using non-violent protests."

On the other hand, something in the political system in the U.S. and elsewhere seems to create a tendency to select women who are as "tough as the guys"—which is what "women's" philosophy is trying to examine and change. So the political system, as it is, can contain a built-in contradiction for many women who do not like fighting for power. Still, many people do believe that women in general would be more idealistic in the running of government than men tend to be—better suited to office, in fact. As one man wrote *The New York Times* on Sunday, March 8, 1987, "Would women be as corrupt, aggressive and exclusive as men [in recent politics] if given the opportunity? I think not . . . men are unwilling or unable to give up a role, a way of behaving, that was once necessary . . . [which] creates conflict with other men . . . [Women's] preference for negotiation over fighting, their abhorrence of violence, their inclination to compassion . . . are the qualities needed for leadership in the twenty-first century."

The principles of mutuality in relationships, such as women use with each other, are the essence of good diplomatic skills, which could be well used in government. The United States and now other countries seem constantly to find themselves in situations with "third world" countries in which they must choose either supporting non-humanitarian "right-wing" dictators or seeing the government "fall" to a "left-wing," supposedly egalitarian philosophy (communism) which, however, often leads also to a violent, non-humanitarian "left-wing" dictatorship. But why do these situations reach such an extreme point?

These confrontational situations in the world are remarkably similar to those seen in Parts I and II in women's private lives with men. "Sticking his head in the sand," as one woman describes her boyfriend's reaction to her discussions about their relationship; so some governments refuse to listen to the "demands" of disenfranchised women or small countries, thinking the problems will all just "go away" (that the really smart people are the ruling elite of men around the world). These attitudes lead to more and more seething resentment, until it is too late to resolve things productively, whether in the world political situation or in the home.

But old-style politics, running for office, may not be enough. What about creating a new, nonaligned coalition—a *philosophically* non-aligned coalition? Should we start a different kind of organization—combining politics, economic boycotts, and ecology issues? In a way, "women's" revolution is not so much aimed at politics or the political system (although we would like to have half of the Congress women) as it is at economics, ideology, and philosophy.*

Women have a great deal of economic power—collectively, an enormous amount. Women now would be financially able to form a network to support

---

*One of the goals of this new coalition could be the "de-violentizing" of America's media culture that is sent around the world.

other women and women's projects/corporations, etc. Could we form collective corporations, go into business with each other?

Other theorists, going in an entirely different direction, say women can force change by paying most attention to the politics of private life. Some women (sometimes called "feminist separatists") call on women to boycott men, that is, stop having relationships with men, remove their emotional support from men who have not changed—in other words, remove their energies from men entirely, stop supporting the "male" system in all areas, including emotionally—in work, in love, and any other way possible.* This is a tactic that could clearly have a profound effect if large numbers of women did it.

In fact, while most women would not think of themselves as "separatists," the high divorce rate, with most of those divorces being initiated by women, and women's emotional "leaving" of many marriages, even if staying physically in them, does resemble this actual position.

Will non-violent resistance work?

All of these strategies we have been looking at are forms of non-violent, peaceful resistance. Will they really work, or are we fooling ourselves?

Is it so simple as to say that since we are 51 percent of the population, if we begin to see ourselves as forming the core of society, the center of history and philosophy—as men have done for centuries—then this will automatically change things? Or must we face male power, enter into a real confrontation, force men to stop dominating us and to share power?

After all, for centuries, women have been half the population and have lived with a "sub"culture of separate values, expressed more or less overtly in different times and places—but this alone did not change women's second-class status. History shows us that simply being a majority—even with the heightened sensibility we have today—is no guarantee: for example, even though women got the vote earlier in the century, our status did not change—certainly not sufficiently.

Can we change women's status by "convincing" men to "give" us our rights? Or are we just kidding ourselves, taking the easy way out? With the French Revolution and others, it was finally necessary for people to show strength, to actually take power to change things, because those in power wouldn't listen, wouldn't *hear*—exactly as women have described men in Chapter 1.

---

*Within feminist circles, the separatist call at times had the unfortunate consequence of causing women who did fall in love or were married to feel somehow ashamed; and so, as if it were not enough to have the "male" culture calling women "masochists" for loving "too much," now some feminists seemed to be calling others "masochists" or implying that they needed their consciousness raised if they were with a man.

At times in history, peaceful or less militaristic movements have triumphed over larger forces. For example, Gandhi was able to found a movement which eventually, along with other factors, ended British rule in India. The Bible speaks of David and Goliath—although David used the same means as Goliath—namely, force (he was smaller and with less power, but did win). The non-violent protests of the civil rights movement are of more relevance; however, while they have "raised consciousnesses" of both blacks and whites, the concrete factors in the lives of most blacks have not changed sufficiently; most blacks still have lower income, higher unemployment, less education, higher infant mortality rates, and no blacks are chosen as candidates for President by major parties.

According to historian Michael Howard and others for centuries before him (Clausewitz, for example), arming oneself, being ready for a fight, is the only way to "enforce peace," to keep from being taken over. Of course, if we could live with a basic ideology different from the currently dominant "male" ideology, this might not be true of "human nature"—we might not all need to have the arm-or-be-eaten psychology. However, living as we do in the current situation where hierarchy is a way of life and competition and aggression are rewarded, how does this affect the strategy women must use to change the situation?

Are we pacifists by choice—or are we *afraid* to fight?

If women have been dominated by men for centuries, the question goes, "Why have women stood for it?" "Why haven't women revolted?" Women have accepted their own oppression, men say, and this is used to "prove" women's basic "passive" character, women's supposed lack of leadership ability, women's innate recognition that men should lead! Therefore, this is a question we should consider seriously: Should we fight? Do we make it easy for men to continue, not change, because we don't frighten them, i.e., they believe they can count on our "peaceful" beliefs to keep us from making a revolution or taking power?

Another way of changing the culture, then, is to have the kind of revolution that men usually make to take power, to force men/the culture to change. Bruno Bettelheim showed in his concentration camp studies how quickly a person's orientation and view of life can change when the circumstances and power dynamics around her/him change radically; women in power, boycotting men, would have this effect on men immediately. And it would change forever our perception of ourselves and our power. We would never ever again think of ourselves as powerless.

As Janet Sayers has put the issue in "Feminism and Science,"* "Feminism can no more secure equal power and status for women with men in . . . society solely through drawing attention to the unreasonableness and injustice of present power imbalances between the sexes than was the eighteenth century French bourgeoisie able to secure its rights simply through demonstrating the irrationality of aristocratic rule and privilege. . . . The bourgeoisie only secured the rights of the men of its class through revolutionary overthrow of the physical and ideological forces whereby the aristocracy held power. It remains to be seen whether feminism can only secure equal status for women with men in society through revolution."

A militaristic strategy?

If women did assume militaristic tactics toward attaining their rights, would this change women's basic ideology of non-aggression—and therefore defeat the whole purpose? Or is this only the argument used by those who would encourage women to stay in their place, trying to scare us off by saying "power corrupts"?

These kinds of decisions are always hard, whether faced by nations or by individuals. How does one deal with aggression, keep a place of respect and dignity in the world? There do seem to be times when one has to fight, even if one doesn't want to.

In his analysis of the position of women in the twentieth century, written in 1972, historian William Chafe† describes in detail the patterns of "women's liberation" from the 1920s to the 1950s—and at the end of his argument, seems to be saying that the *ideology* of "women's place is in the home" (woman as second, not supposed to lead) has so far been too strong to be overcome. While Chafe is far from a radical, he (without intending to make this implication, perhaps) states over and over that only the "substantial upheaval" of World War II, and not any "propagandizing" by "feminists," changed women's basic situation—i.e., World War II brought significant numbers of women out of the home and into the work force, giving them an independent income—and this included women of all ages, not just, as before, mainly women who worked when they were single before they married. This financial independence, Chafe implies, brought them a certain amount of general independence and thus "liberation." But according to his analysis,‡ it was only "compulsion" or "substantial upheaval" that forced change for women on the society.

---

* *Women's Studies International Forum* 10 (2).
† William Chafe, *Women and Equality: Changing Patterns in American Culture* (New York: Oxford University Press, 1977).
‡ And that of others, such as Alice Kessler-Harris and Ruth Milkman.

In this assertion, then, he is (without meaning to, probably) calling for revolution on the part of women—i.e., his study would imply that women are fooling themselves by believing that any amount of talk or "consciousness changing" will create lasting, fundamental change in women's status. He has argued that our patterns are repeating themselves, that evolutionary change in such a fundamentally embedded ideology is impossible, especially with a vested interest—i.e., the "male" ideology (not Chafe's terminology)—consistently working against it.

Women's Honor—Our Own Code

Women are now of a revolutionary spirit, but we are non-violent by "training" and/or belief and disposition. Most women don't want to fight militarily—and are not convinced it would work anyway. Women in power, it is quite possible, would be "just like men"—although this is not necessarily true, as the nature of our consciousness could change this. But the worry is that a "political revolution" might only repeat the patterns we have, replacing one hierarchical structure with another.

Political change, without ideological change, seems only to create the same hierarchical power structures it means to eradicate. For example, capitalism and communism both turn out in practice to create hierarchical states, because the underlying assumptions are those of the "male" ideology with its basis in hierarchy, defense of turf or dominance, focus on status.*

A non-violent philosophical framework

How can we change the dominant ideology, and our status now, if our system dislikes aggression? Perhaps we should take a cue from a black civil-rights song that proclaims: "I know one thing we did right, was the day we started to fight." The question for us is, what kind of fighting will really work?

First, the fight has already begun, as women everywhere are now fighting being owned, fighting for a different way of life in thousands of ways—in legal suits for jobs, asking why not about jobs and positions that are dominated by men, and in the millions of personal struggles with men, asserting their dignity. To know all of this is crucial for women now, for everything one of us does has an impact on women we never saw and who never saw us.

---

*Freud reached the conclusion (which he did not want to reach) that this system is inevitable, because (he believed) there is a human aggression instinct. Marx held that aggression is just a function of economic modes of production in history and thus not inevitable. The position of this work is that aggression and competition are not inevitable, not because they are merely a function of economics, but rather because they are part of an entrenched and very ancient ideological system, as described in Chapter 17 and in other parts of this book.

There is no one way of fighting that is right; finally, *all* ways are right—being reflective, introspective, thinking, fighting, voting, running for office, boycotting products—as long as somehow one's voice is heard, one's opinion is registered. We must act with courage. Those who do nothing are inviting repression; those who act boldly will see the results of their work. Even just among one's friends, to make what you think, really think and believe, known and clear means a lot.

We have something valuable to give the world now—our belief system, our philosophy. Our knowledge of how to give, how to love, is a richness we can diffuse throughout the whole culture.

Ideological revolution

"Women of the world, unite! You all know what's wrong—but it's wrong not only with your personal life, it's wrong in the entire system."

So, if it is not (not only?) "power" we want, but major philosophical change, then the rethinking we are doing, and the devising of a clearly articulated alternative is the kind of fighting that will make a lasting difference—along with all the rest.

Struggles for hierarchy and dominance won't stop being perceived as the most basic form of behavior, or be replaced by cooperation, without a revolution in consciousness, a revolution in what is known as "personality structure" (which is essentially the spectrum of possible personalities created by any given social structure). We badly need a revolution in thought and behavior patterns on every level, an important change in consciousness.

Some feminist philosophers have been working on questioning the values of the "male" system, analyzing possible alternative world views, trying to think beyond Western philosophy or patriarchal philosophy as we know it, with its parameters so narrowly limited by classical Greek thought and the Judeo-Christian tradition's tightly patriarchal values. Other female scholars are working in anthropology and archaeology in order to increase our knowledge of possible, alternative social systems*—counterarguments to the idea that "all societies are male-dominant" and that all we see in front of us is the result of "human nature" rather than certain ingrained philosophical and cultural positions, behavior created by society. Women are researching new information,

*See, for example, Alison Jaggar, *Feminist Politics and Human Nature* (Totowa, N.J.: Held, 1983); Sandra Harding and Merill B. Hentikka, eds., *Discovering Reality: Feminist Perspectives on Epistemology, Metaphysics, Methodology and Philosophy of Science* (Boston: D. Reidel, 1983).

rather than saying, "Well, women have always and everywhere been dominated—so maybe they like it that way," which has been the position of more
than one major academic school of thought.

In fact, now, after twenty years of work and rethinking in various fields,
women have formulated new ways of viewing almost all fields of thought,
including psychology, biology, philosophy, history, primatology, and anthropology—and this process is ongoing. There has been a cultural revolution, a
revolution in thinking, which has caused a renaissance in almost all the disciplines, and which is still going on—perhaps has hardly begun.*

Still, while women in most academic disciplines and many feminist writers
have done great work in critiquing "male" culture, women's building of a new
way of looking at things, reformulating their philosophy, can be said to be most
importantly taking place now in the thoughts and actions of women everywhere—as seen in this study.

The interesting and important thing about this revolution is that it is not just
being made by an isolated group of people; it is women and some men everywhere who are thinking these thoughts. For women these issues are pressing,
since many women meet the "system" every day in the faces of men they love:
the exquisite pain and contradiction women experience receiving men's double
messages lifts many beyond the daily to the highest plateaus of thought and
reflection. Thus, as we have seen, it is in large part the behaviors of men they
love which has led to the crystallization of the level of awareness women are
now expressing—an awareness which cannot be removed from the history of
consciousness.

The current statistics on marriage and divorce confirm these findings—and are
strangely symbolic of the moment we are in: 50 percent of women leave their
marriages, 50 percent stay, even if not emotionally satisfied. We are clearly at
a turning point, half in and half out of a new time. The picture is striking—
almost as if women were pausing, stopping a moment for reflection, half way
out of a door, still turning to look back, bidding goodbye to the past, before
setting out on a journey.

This journey in consciousness is further impelled by women's new economic situation—which in turn was/is being created by women's new view of
things: the great majority of women are now financially independent for the
first time in history. Seventy-five percent of women now have jobs, earning just
enough money to be independent (although not well off, by any means; women
still make only 66 percent of what men make, according to U.S. Bureau of
Labor Statistics). This independence, in addition to our belief in our own
worth and importance, means that we are at a new time and place in history.

*See the bibliography for some of the classics women have produced.

And we have created this situation for ourselves: women have pioneered the jobs and the ideas.

A New Philosophy

"I think women are really re-designing the world.
The next century is ours—mentally and in every other
way."

This philosophical revolution, which Jessie Bernard has named the Feminist Enlightenment,* is the biggest realignment of thought in two centuries or more. It is extending democratic ideas and a different sensibility into love relationships, science, and politics.

This is not only a "female revolution" but a general revolution: to fight for women's rights and dignity is to fight for an entirely different ordering of the social structure, based on a different understanding of personal relationships.

Just as the Enlightenment built upon older structures, transcended them, adding new dimensions to the philosophical framework of the society and the understanding of "human nature" (out of which grew the idea of democratic government), so in the same way what women are doing now is enabling society to take another philosophical step forward.

This new philosophical questioning applies not only to Western society: it is a critique of hierarchical social systems that exclude women (and others) and the thought patterns created out of these systems all over the world. Women are creating, on an international scale, a global critique of "male" ideology. Women are questioning how social organizations and governments are formed, how "leadership" is decided on, and want to change the belief systems behind those choices.†

In fact, gender may be the basic, original split that needs to be healed to alter society,‡ to lessen aggression as a way of life. Women are re-integrating "female" identity, leaving behind the double-standard split that began at the beginning of patriarchy, with Eve, followed by Mary as her opposite—and beyond this, trying to end/overcome the opposition between "male" and "female" emphasized by our culture. And this questioning of gender hierarchy leads to a questioning of all kinds of hierarchies, such as those based on race and class, not just gender.

*Jessie Bernard, *The Feminist Enlightenment*, work in progress.
†See the bibliography for feminist magazines founded by women in "non-Western" countries.
‡See also Chapter 5.

Not "the human condition"—not forever . . .

Would it be too simplistic to blame all our problems on the "male" ideology, with its hierarchical and aggressive motifs?

What *is* the cause of human brutality and injustice? Communism says it is the system of "capitalism," the West says it is the system of "communism," Islam says it is Western materialism, feminism says it is the ideology of "patriarchy"—and others say it is just "human nature," that evil tendencies are always there, that there is an ongoing fight between good and evil.

Of course, there *are* people in every system who are "not like that," everyone agrees—people who are multi-sided, generous, open, thoughtful, idealistic, and honest.

It is tempting to say—or at least it should be pointed out—that patriarchy, the "male" ideology especially as it has been developed over the last 2,500 years, may be a very large part of the problem, because it may be *the* system underlying all the other systems. If the system we now have is "human nature," and not an ideology, if the system as we now know it is something growing out of our very biological natures, and not a historical system which, once entrenched, becomes hard to dislodge—"reality" seems to mean living with an increasing amount of violence, massive inequity in global food distribution, in health and educational opportunities—and a grating friction in people's personal lives, plus destruction of the natural environment, not to mention destruction of each other in hurtful psychological games.

If all this is true, then there is nothing to be done except for each person to retreat to her or his own mountaintop and hope for the best. But we do not have to believe this.

Many people (both women *and* men) do hope for, have a longing for, a different way of life—for more politeness, more civility, more warmth—less hostility and aggressiveness. It is a challenge for us to somehow rise above the "natural" hostility and triviality of daily life at the moment, given the current psychologies created by the dominant culture as we know it.

Another world (or perhaps several) is possible, another landscape, full of fauna and flora, both in nature and in the human imagination—positive mental constructs not yet discernible to our "human nature as competitive" belief system. If hierarchy is the basis of all our institutions now—from religion to the state,* to the family, and to love relationships—this need not last forever. It is just that our view of what is possible is temporarily obstructed.

---

*The U.S. Constitution was an attempt to balance a government, rather than structure it hierarchically—one of the few lasting examples in history.

A new spirit: the "other" now as seer

"Feminism didn't work? My god, it hasn't even started! We are Luther posting the statements on the cathedral door, we are Jeanne d'Arc with our army to defend ourselves. We no longer believe in the male gods; their power over us has ended."

This is the resistance, the beginning of the change—when the Other describes the dominant society, its ideology, for the first time, names truly what was before taken to be "human nature" and inevitable. Now, it is named as a belief-system, and so it is possible for new beliefs and reflections of reality to spring forth.

What is it, finally, that we hope for? A way of seeing things that would value each individual, recognize each individual's unique contributions, empower each individual—ending the psychological circle of hierarchy and competition. A new social contract not only with each other but also with the planet and the other creatures who share the earth.

This alternative system, with its new spirit and aura, is still in the process of formation. Like a star, twinkling with light and motion, it is radiating out waves of energy to all around it, particles of light and illumination. This is the third step of the process that has been building for so long, and one that will continue far into the future.

Appendixes

Essay on the Methodology of
the Hite Reports

New Trends in the Social Sciences

*The Hite Reports are part of an international trend in the social sciences express-
ing dissatisfaction with the adequacy of simple quantitative methods as a way of
exploring people's attitudes. More and more the social sciences are turning to various
qualitative methods, attempting to find out what people are thinking in a more
complex way than projecting into their minds on the basis of preconceived categories.
Hite elicits from the populations she studies not only reliable scientific data, but also
a wide spectrum of attitudes and beliefs about sex, love and who people are.*

JESSE LEMISCH
Professor, Department of History
SUNY, Buffalo

*The research methods of the Hite Reports pioneered many current research trends,
including the mixing of quantitative and qualitative data. Originally criticized,
these techniques are now widely copied by many in the field not only in the U.S.
but abroad.*

TORE HAAKINSON
Wenner-Gren Center, Stockholm

There is a growing and highly sophisticated literature critiquing social science
methodology, and in fact, Western philosophical concepts of "knowing." Part
of this critique is growing out of sociology itself, as predictive models have
failed to materialize; and part of it grows out of feminist rethinking of the

philosophical assumptions behind various disciplines. Two ground-breaking anthologies of feminist scholarship in this area are: *Discovering Reality: Feminist Perspectives on Epistemology, Metaphysics, Methodology, and Philosophy of Science* (edited by Sandra Harding and Merrill B. Hintikka);* and *Theories of Women's Studies* (edited by Gloria Bowles and Renate Duelli Klein).†

The issues are brought out in the following excerpts from a fascinating article by Gloria Bowles, University of California, at Berkeley:

"On The Uses of Hermeneutics For Feminist Scholarship"‡

> ... *the one discovery of the decade which enables us to understand and to move beyond the tension between discursive inheritance of Western thought and the feminist perspective [is that] what counts as knowledge must be grounded on experience.*
>
> SANDRA HARDING AND MERRILL B. HINTIKKA (1983)

> *Thinking begins only when we come to know that reason, glorified for centuries, is the most stiff-necked adversary of thought.*
>
> MARTIN HEIDEGGER (1977)

... The scientistic world view, which sits atop the university and defines the social sciences and reaches even into the humanities, has as its goal the so-called "objective knowledge" of mathematics and the physical sciences. Only now are literary criticism, and many other disciplines, wresting themselves from "objective" analysis, whose primary result is a divorce of objective knowledge from evaluation. It is not that the Humanities are merely rebelling against their place on the bottom rung under the Sciences in twentieth century intellectual history. It is rather that the Humanities are realizing that their subject matter is so thick with personal and interpersonal experience, with moral and evaluative judgments, that the "impersonal" and "value-free" methodological strategies of the Sciences are at best irrelevant and at worst a distortion of the subject matter itself. This critique of scientism/logocentrism in the Humanities, while not inclined to throw all objective analysis out of the window, has been primarily a "negative" critique which has analyzed the limits of this borrowed methodology. Feminist scholarship has not only stood critical in a "negative" sense of traditional concep-

*D. Reidel Publishing Company, London, 1983.
†Routledge & Kegan Paul, London, 1983.
‡*Women's Studies International Forum*, December 1984.

tual assumptions, but has made the positive move of putting forth alternative epistemologies which use experience, intuition and evaluation (both of women as individuals and of women as a "class") as modes of knowing. Further, women *qua* women seem to stand in a sort of privileged position in regard to the formulation of such new orientations of thinking. A critique of scientistic thought is not so difficult for women, since we have always used ways of knowing in addition to reason. Throughout male recorded history, men have been the "takers," while women have assumed (or have been forced to assume) the role of "caretakers." Women live in a world where little is impersonal and much is personal, where little is fixed or certain and much is ambiguous and volatile, and where little is value-free and much requires an evaluative response. We have long lived our lives in the intimately personal and non-objective context of the daily needs and concerns of other human beings. We bring all this experience, these skills and perceptions, to our scholarly work and into the academic community. Here we are confronted by the modern form of traditionalism in the scientific mentality and its dictatorial regulations.

In the contemporary academic community, due in part to the recently emerged and broadly based critique of scientism and to the accomplishments of feminist scholarship, this scientistic mentality has become increasingly difficult for traditional scholars to justify. . . . [It is in] the hermeneutic or interpretive tradition where one finds the critique of logocentrism in a powerful form. I am using the most inclusive term, hermeneutics (*Hermeneutik* simply means "interpretation" in German), to designate a constellation of methodologies which stand critical of the objectivism and scientism of the white male tradition. These are the loosely defined movements which have emerged in the post-war years in Continental thinking under the nomenclatures of "phenomenology," "post-structuralism," "hermeneutics" and, most recently, "deconstructionism."

One need not devote one's life to a reading of Heidegger and Foucault and Feyerabend and Derrida (nor do I think Women's Studies scholars should) to see that these writers are saying what we as feminists have been saying all along—that there is something profoundly wrong with the tradition. . . .

For there are common points of interest in the ideas of hermeneuticists and feminists. The "hermeneutical circle," although it has different connotations for different thinkers, means essentially that there is no such thing as a "detached," "neutral" or "objective" place to stand when we know something. We are always speaking from a "prejudiced" (in the sense of pre-judgment) and "interested" and "evaluative" posture. This is the circle, that we are intimately (personally, socially, historically) involved with what we claim to know. This is Heidegger on the nature of hermeneutical thinking:

> But if we sense this circle as a vicious one and look out for ways of
> avoiding it, even if we just "sense" it as an inevitable imperfection, then
> the act of understanding has been misunderstood from the ground up
> . . . What is decisive is not to get out of the circle but to come into it
> in the right way. . . . (Hoy, 1982)

Traditional thought claims to be able to leap out of the hermeneutical/
interpretive circle and to speak of so-called "value-free," "disinterested,"
"objective," and "ethically neutral" knowledge. Thus, the hermeneutical/
interpretive tradition says all efforts to deny the "circular" and "interested" and "evaluative" nature of thinking are conceptually confused or
dishonest. Feminist thought, precisely because it acknowledges and asserts
its "prejudices," must, from the hermeneutical perspective, be judged as
one of the only available theoretical postures which holds good claim to
intellectual integrity and sophistication.

Heidegger contends that the Western tradition does not know how to
think; he speaks of openness, receptivity and listening. Both he and Derrida
say that truth is to be found in absence or in the spaces between words, a
theme common to French literature. Many Women's Studies scholars had
our original training in literature; for us, there is both irony and gratification
in the "news" that the new model for understanding is the expressive language of the text. Many scholars—not only literary critics but anthropologists and philosophers as well—are talking about the literary text which
should replace the machine model as the locus of analysis. For example,
feminist biologists have been questioning this model and now some prestigious men in the field are making the same point. *It is crucial to realize that
the literary text, in its paradigmatic form, is an imaginative narrative of those
personal interrelations which have long formed the life-world and the existential
reality of women.* [Hite's emphasis] Those who have proposed the literary
text as the interpretive model have not recognized any special affinity between the literary narrative and the feminist perspective and women's life
experience.

However, many white male thinkers are uncomfortable with the hermeneutic circle—and engage in endless discussions of it—because for them
it raises the specter of total relativity, the fear that we will never be able to
know anything in an absolutely objective and certain way. Male thought,
with its linear habits, would thrust itself out of the circle. It is difficult for
men to make the critiques of logocentrism; the few who are trying, from
within the tradition, find it hard to embrace intuition and experience as viable
ways of knowing. The struggle to affirm what they have been taught to
denigrate is enormous. . . . As women, we are not so attached to old ways
of thinking since we have been discovering our own. Thus it is that the
critique of logocentrism in *Theories of Women's Studies* and other feminist
works is more directed and unmediated—feels less cumbersome—than many

contemporary male critiques. These feminist essays contrast, for example, with the introduction to a very fine book, *Interpretive Social Science: A Reader,* edited by Paul Rabinow and William M. Sullivan. It painfully and painstakingly elaborates "The Interpretive Turn: Emergence of an Approach," the only way out of a failed social science: "As long as there has been a social science, the expectation has been that it would turn from its humanistic infancy to the maturity of hard science, thereby leaving behind its dependence on value, judgment, and individual insight" (Rabinow and Sullivan, 1979). The authors mock that polarity, the "hard" and "soft" sciences. Through science, one moves out of the softness and the world of the mother into hardness, which is mature; one leaves a world of dependence, the proper sphere of value and insight. For these writers, it is not easy to say, many pages later: "We propose a return to this human world in all its lack of clarity, its alienation, and its depth, as an alternative to the continuing search for a formal deductive paradigm in the social sciences." . . . Significantly, what they do not say, these male writers, is that they are leaving behind a world of male thought to enter the province of female thought. A growing number of them have been able to make the critique of logocentrism; but so far none of them has been able to analyze their own sexism—and I mean sexism in its many guises, from the denigration of women in prose and in public to a complete ignorance or an appropriation of the enormous advances of feminist scholarship. Moreover, the bulk of male scholarship of the hermeneutic/phenomenological persuasion has been unable to move beyond the preliminary effort of a negative critique of the limitations and irrelevancies of the traditional scientistic methodology. When asked by traditional critics for their alternative ways of knowing, they have little to offer beyond interesting generalities. Some of these thinkers have said explicitly that it is not up to them, it is beyond their capacities, to offer positive alternatives. The problem, and the promise, is that they have not realized that these alternatives will come from us—feminist women scholars who stand removed enough from the tradition to see things differently.

Explication of scientific method as used in research for the Hite Report trilogy

The main concerns of this research were described in the abstract of a paper presented at the American Association for the Advancement of Science annual meeting in May, 1985,* entitled "Devising a new methodological framework for analysis and presentation of data in mixed qualitative/quantitative research: The Hite Report Trilogy, 1972–1986":

*See published proceedings, statistical abstracts, annual meeting, American Association for the Advancement of Science, May 1985, Washington, D.C.

There were unique challenges to be faced in devising the methodology for the Hite Reports, which comprise a 3-vol. study of over 15,000 women and men in the U.S., 1972–86. First, although quantification was necessary as part of the final result, a simple multiple-choice questionnaire could not be used, since the theoretical concept for the project stated that "most women have never been asked how they feel about sex" and "most research has been done by men": therefore, it was important not to assume predetermined categories, but to design an essay-type questionnaire which would be open-ended. Also, the data-gathering was designed to protect the anonymity of the respondent. Secondly, compilation of data from essay questions is very difficult, if the data are to be carefully and rigorously treated. . . . Finally, and almost as labor-intensive as compilation and categorization of data, presentation of findings was planned to serve more than an informative function; rather than simply giving readers statistics plus the author's theoretical analysis of data, the aim was to create an inner dialogue within the reader, as s/he mentally conversed with those quoted. Therefore, large parts of text comprise first-person statements from those participating. The format of presentation shows how these fit into intricate categories of social patterns.

The Four Stages of Research

I.
QUESTIONNAIRE DESIGN

One of the most important elements in the design of *Women and Love* was that the participants be anonymous, because in this way a completely free and uninhibited discussion could be ensured. For this reason, a questionnaire format, rather than face-to-face interviews, was chosen, with respondents specifically asked not to sign their names, although other demographic data were taken. That this anonymity was in fact an aid to communication with participants was verified in statements by respondents in each study, such as the following:

I would find it very hard to say all these things to another person, and I'm sure many women would feel the same as I. I am sick of reading various "advice" columns about what I should be feeling, but I have not found another forum for saying what I think myself, taking my own time, rethinking, not feeling any pressure to be perfect or "in" or anything. I am saving my answers; they have been very important to me.

The second choice to be made regarding format related to how the questions would be asked. In the sensitive realm of personal attitudes, a multiple-choice questionnaire was out of the question, because it would have implied preconceived categories of response, and thus, in a sense, would also have "told" the respondent what the "allowable" or "normal" answers would be. Although a multiple-choice questionnaire is much easier for the researcher to work with, it would have given a subtle signal to the participant that the research categories were equated with "reality," or "allowable reality," whereas the intention here was to permit women's own voices to emerge, for women to say whatever they might feel on the deepest level to be the truth of their situation, with nothing to intervene or make them censor themselves.

Also, the development of the questions in this study has always been an interactive process with the participants. (In a way, this was true of the Kinsey questionnaires as well, since Kinsey developed several questionnaires over his period of research.) In this study, questionnaires were refined and modified at the suggestion of those responding, so that, for *Women and Love*, there were four basic versions of the questionnaire used over several years.

Coming from an academic background with a strong awareness of the ideological elements in the definition of culture, and with a background in the women's movement which gave further emphasis to this idea, it was a constant matter for concern that questions are not simple questions, but always have several layers of meaning. For this reason, the methodology used here was designed to pay special attention to this issue.*

Many people hold the mistaken belief that multiple-choice questionnaires represent the height of scientific objectivity, in that they can be quantified and need no "interpretation." Nothing could be further from the truth. All researchers, no matter how careful or aware/unaware of their own biases, *do* have a point of view, a way of seeing the world, reflecting the cultural milieu in which they were brought up, and so on—and these assumptions are subtly filtered into categories and questions chosen. (Philosophically speaking, we are all/all life is "biased" and subjective; it is only by combining a mass of subjectivities—all of our "seeing," if you will—that we find, through collective sharing of perception, a "fact"; in other words, for example, we only "know" the sun will come up tomorrow because we have seen it come up every day, and we all agree that the probability is that it will come up again tomorrow.)

Thus, to design the categories of response for a multiple-choice questionnaire is a political act, unavoidably filled with subjective bias, whether consciously or unconsciously so, and whether the researcher considers him/herself to be "neutral" or "apolitical" and so on.† If a study wishes to find out what's "out there," it cannot impose prior categories on that "out there"; it needs to develop its research instrument through an exchange with "them," the participants, before proceeding. This was done in the current study by listening to

---

*Points presented at a speech to the National Women's Studies convention, University of Kansas, 1978.
†As both Elie Wiesel and John F. Kennedy have pointed out, to be "neutral" or "apolitical" is, in fact, to be highly political, because one is endorsing the status quo.

respondents' suggestions and, indeed, eliciting comment from them as to their feelings about the questionnaire. In other words, there was an ongoing interactive process of sequential refinement in designing the questionnaires for this project. Less meticulous care for research design may mean that a researcher only reifies his or her pre-existing expectations as to the content of the opinions/answers "discovered."*

The difficulty of studying the emotions

As Judith Long Laws has said, "Most social scientists still avoid the study of feelings and attitudes, because of the difficulty in quantifying such studies, and the belief that this is the 'best' kind of social science. This is not always true; quantification is not always the best way to arrive at understanding. ... The Hite Report was the first large scale set of data where women talked about their own experiences in their own voices."

For this reason, essay questionnaires—which are not less "scientific" than multiple-choice, and in fact are recommended for use whenever possible by methodology textbooks—were the research tool of choice. The goal of this study was to hear women's deepest reflections on the nature of love, and to learn how they see love relationships now in relation to the whole spectrum of their lives. The method was important also in that it enabled participants to communicate directly with readers, sharing myriad points of view—in essence debating with each other throughout the text.

II.

DISTRIBUTION OF QUESTIONNAIRES
AND COMPOSITION OF SAMPLE

The questionnaire following this essay and similar versions were distributed to women all over the country beginning in 1980. Their purpose was to discover how women/we view ourselves and our relationships with men and the world now, how we define "reality."

*In the case of *The Hite Report* on female sexuality, for example, the point of view was woman-oriented, in that it let women define sex as they saw it, rather than assuming that the male definition of sex which had been predominant for so long was the only possible "correct" definition. For this, the work was described by some as having a "feminist bias." In fact, much of the previous research into female sexuality had been less than "scientific": rather than taking the information that most women could orgasm more easily during masturbation or direct clitoral/vulval stimulation than during coitus, and concluding that therefore this is "normal," previous studies had started with the assumption that if women did not orgasm during coitus, there must be something wrong with them—that they were somehow defective, "dysfunctional," psychologically or physically abnormal. Research was often geared to finding out what the cause of this "defect" might be. This was a non-scientific approach, not an objective way of looking at female sexuality.

In short, no study is free of bias, or a point of view; the important thing is to recognize this fact, and to clarify, insofar as possible, just what that point of view is.

Distribution of the questionnaires was extremely widespread and painstakingly done, in order to reach as many kinds of women with as many varied points of view as possible. In order to ensure anonymity, it was thought best to send questionnaires to organizations rather than to individuals, so that any member who wanted might be able to answer with complete assurance that her name was not on any list or on file anywhere. Clubs and organizations through which questionnaires were distributed included church groups in thirty-four states, women's voting and political groups in nine states, women's rights organizations in thirty-nine states, professional women's groups in twenty-two states, counseling and walk-in centers for women or families in forty-three states, and a wide range of other organizations, such as senior citizens' homes and disabled people's organizations, in various states.

In addition, individual women did write for copies of the questionnaire, using both the address given in my previous works and an address given by interview programs on television and in the press. However, if an individual woman did write for a questionnaire, whether she returned it or not was her own decision, therefore assuring her complete anonymity, as her reply was unsigned and bore the postmark and demographic information requested, such as age, income and education, but not name or address. All in all, one hundred thousand questionnaires were distributed, and four thousand five hundred were returned. This is almost twice as high as the standard rate of return for this kind of questionnaire distribution, which is estimated at 2.5 to 3 percent. A probability method of sampling might have yielded a higher rate of return, but then an essay questionnaire would not have been possible; the purpose here was to elicit in-depth statements of feelings and attitudes, and multiple-choice questions would have closed down dialogue with the participants.

Finally, sufficient effort was put into the various forms of distribution that the final statistical breakdown of those participating according to age, occupation, religion, and other variables known for the U.S. population at large in most cases quite closely mirrors that of the U.S. female population. See charts in the Statistical Data.

Could the study have been done using random sampling methods?

"There are many forms of scientific methodology besides the random sample; those of us in the field know that there is no such thing as a random sample in sex research, but this does not make the work unscientific if, as in the Hite Reports, the study population is carefully matched to the demographics of the population at large."

THEODORE M. MCILVENNA
Institute for Sex Research

Almost no major research using essay questions today is done with the use of random samples. As Dr. Gladys Engel Lang has explained at the beginning of this work, most survey research now tries to match its samples demographically to the general population in other ways; for example, by weighting responses to conform to the population profile, somewhat similarly to the methods used here. But an even more important reason for not using random sampling methods for this study is that a random sample cannot be anonymous; the individuals chosen clearly understand that their names and addresses are on file.

Does research that is not based on a probability or random sample give one the right to generalize from the results of the study to the population at large? If a study is large enough and the sample broad enough, and if one generalizes carefully, yes; in fact, the Nielsen television studies, and national political polls generalize on the basis of small, select, non-random samples all the time. However, in a larger sense, no one can generalize from their findings, even if one were to somehow miraculously obtain a completely random sample—the reason being that variables such as psychological state, degree of religious or political fervor and so on are not measured; thus there is no guarantee that those picked in a random sample, although they might represent the population at large in terms of age and income, would also represent the population in terms of psychological make-up.

III.
ANALYSIS OF REPLIES:
MEASURING AND UNDERSTANDING
ATTITUDES AND EMOTIONS

To go from essay statements to mixed quantitative/qualitative data is a long and intricate process.* Of course, some portions of the replies received are already in quantifiable form, i.e., questions answered with a "yes" or "no." But the majority of questions were not so phrased, since the intention, as discussed, was to open dialogue rather than to close it.

There is an ongoing and abstruse discussion in the field of methodology as to how best to study emotions, belief systems, and attitudes—not to mention how to quantify them. For example, not only is the question, "How do you love the person in your current relationship? What kind of love is it?" a difficult one to answer, but also the answer is every bit as difficult to analyze and compare with other answers received, and in some cases build into statistical findings. Nevertheless, it is possible to do this, if such statistics are attached for

---

*Thus, in this study, there were over 40,000 woman-hours involved in analyzing the answers, plus at least 20,000 put in by the women who answered the questionnaire. This of course does not include the time and effort needed to turn the resulting compilation of data into a book.

thè reader to numerous examples of definition by the participants, such as is done in this study.

Specifically, the information was analyzed in this way: first, a large chart was made for each question asked. Each person's answer to the question being analyzed was then transferred onto that chart (usually many pages long), next to its individual identification number. The many months required for this procedure were actually very valuable in that they provided extensive time for reflecting on the answers.

Once the charts had been prepared, the next step was to discover the patterns and "categories" existing in the answers. Usually patterns had begun to stand out during the making of the charts, so that the categories more or less formed themselves. Then statistical figures were prepared by totaling the number of women in each category, following which representative quotes were selected. This procedure was followed for each of the 180 questions.

In addition, one main chart was kept onto which much of the information from other charts was coded for each individual woman, so that composite portraits could be drawn and compared. Any attempt at condensation or computerization at an early stage of the analysis would have defeated the purposes of the study: to find the more subtle meanings lying beneath the more easily quantifiable parts of the replies, and to keep intact each individual's voice so that participants would remain in direct communication with readers, thus reinforcing the integrity of the study. After all the replies had been charted, and the process of identifying categories completed, with representative quotes selected, statistical computation was possible.

Analyzing data from essay-type questionnaires, then, is a complex endeavor, but there is no way, if one cares about accuracy and detail or wants to search out and understand the deepest levels of the replies, that lengthy testimonies such as these can be understood quickly—and it is precisely the possibility of reaching these deeper levels that makes the essay questionnaire more valuable for this purpose than multiple-choice. Although multiple-choice questions make the researcher's job easier, only through listening to an individual's complete and free response, speaking in her own way and with her own design, without restriction, can more profound realities be reached.

IV.

PRESENTATION OF FINDINGS:
A NEW INTERACTIVE FRAMEWORK

In lectures, Hite's approach is a kind of Socratic dialogue wherein participants are able to question their own prejudices and ignorance, thus learning by thinking through a logical idea for themselves—instead of being simply presented with a "fact." Her method in the Hite Reports is similar. Essentially she carries on an intense dialogue with her readers, making them question assumptions and sharpen their own thinking and critical faculties through identifying with the dialogue she is having with the printed responses. Her readers are thus stimulated to a process of independent thinking and evaluation.

LAWRENCE A. HORNE

American Philosophical Institute, New York

As theorists have pointed out, simple presentation of people's statements is not a rigorous approach to documenting "reality"; people's statements do not "speak for themselves"; there are assumptions and things left unsaid. True analysis requires a complex presentation of subjective data—not just, "people say this, and so that's how it is." For example, in the study of male sexuality, if most men said they have extramarital sex and that it keeps their relationship/marriage working, while it does not bother them—must the researcher conclude simply that since the majority say this, this is "how men are"? It would be simplistic to draw this conclusion. There are many elements in every decision, and it is the researcher's job to search out all the variables.

As it was explained by Janice Green, "In standard social science projects, one researcher's unstated and often unexamined or unconscious point of view is projected onto a research design, and then later also onto the presentation and interpretation of findings, in a rather undigested way. In oral history, at the other extreme (such as that by Studs Terkel), [each bit of] data is allowed to 'speak for itself'—but there is still no clarification of assumptions, biases or other hidden factors."

Dialogue between participants and researcher

Most basic to the methodology of the Hite Reports is the separation of "findings" from analysis and interpretation. This is done by choice of research design, questions, and method of analysis, and, in particular, the style of presentation of the final analysis—that is, separating the interpretation of what people say from what they do say. At times, in the text, participants debate with each other, in their own words; at other times, analysis of what people are saying can bring out several possible sides of a point; researcher and participants can agree or debate at different places in the text. In this way, the metaphysical dilemma of how much of what participants express is ideology can also be addressed. As Janet Wolfe, director of the Institute for Rational Therapy, has explained, "This complex approach has confused some general media reviewers, especially as Hite's work is accessible to a wide audience. But this many-layered structure is another part of Hite's overall methodology, in that she means to involve as many people as possible in this dialogue (not presenting closed "norms")—since it is, after all, a dialogue about social change."

The issue of class as related to presentation of data

Much of the important work of the last few years in women's history and sociology has focused on class and economics as the major point for analysis; however, the purpose here is somewhat different.

Although it is important to write about women in terms of class and race, and not to see "all women" as "the same," the focus of this study is not class but gender and gender ideology, that is, the experiences women have in common because of their gender. Also, this book is not built around comparisons of the attitudes of women in the various traditional socioeconomic groups for the simple reason that differences in behavior and attitude are not the major dividing line between women on these issues that some have theorized they might be. But even more importantly, the intention here was not to focus on class differences between women and what should be done about them, but on men's attitudes to women and what should be done to change them, strategies women have devised for developing their own lives while still dealing with the overall society's view of them—and to find the similarities and dissimilarities in women's current definitions and redefinitions of their relationship with men and society.

Nevertheless, women in this study include a vast cross-section of American women from different socioeconomic groups and "classes." Great care was taken to ensure that statements by women from all classes are well represented throughout every portion of this book. Women's backgrounds will probably emerge to some extent through their manner of speaking/writing. However, perhaps unfortunately, some grammar and spelling was "corrected" so that answers could be more easily read. While some replies were very appealing when their original spelling reflected a personal style or regional accent, it seemed that in print these misspellings sometimes looked demeaning to the writer, or might be seen as trivializing that respondent. It is hoped, however, that enough of the original syntax in the replies is intact so that readers will get a feeling of the wide diversity among the respondents.

Finally, it does seem that based on this research, there are large areas of commonality among all women. While clearly the experience of a poor woman is different from that of a wealthy woman, and so on, in fact, the emotional expectations placed on "women" as a group by the society seem to be much the same. From the statistical charts and from women's statements here, it is clear that, with regard to gender relationships, variables such as "class," income, education, and race are not nearly as influential as the overall experience of being female.

Note on the use of "many," "most" and "some" in the text

For ease of reading, not every statement in the text is given with its related statistic; therefore, as a guideline for the reader, it will be useful to know that "most" refers to more than 55%, "many" to any number between 40% and 65%; "some" indicates any number between 11% and 33%; while "a few" will mean a number between 2% and 11%. In addition, tables giving a complete breakdown for all the major findings (of which there are 120) can be found in the statistical appendixes below. This is the largest amount of precise data given in any study since Kinsey; certainly Freud never attempted any such large sample. The Schwartz/Blumstein data, while covering relationships, contained less intricate and less numerically coded data relating to the emotions, although this was an excellent study.

Even though, for ease of reading, these general terms are at times used, it is felt that the context makes their meaning clear; in addition the extensive statistical appendixes include the precise data.

The media and the Hite Reports: reactions by scholars in the field

In the general popular media, there seems to be a widespread misunderstanding of the types and validity of methodologies available in the social sciences—not to mention the subtle debates discussed earlier in these appendixes. For example, even an important medical writer for *The New York Times* in 1976 opened a story on the first Hite Report with, "In a new, non-scientific survey of female sexuality . . ." The press has often made the mistake of equating "scientific" with "representative," and although both criteria are met by these studies, the press has at times insisted on the "non-scientific" nature of the work.*

Many commentators in the scholarly community have tried to inform popular writers of their mistake:

Mary Steichen Calderone, M.D., MPH; Founder, Sex Education and Information Council of the U.S. (SEICUS):

The subject of human sexuality is one that closes many minds to any objective approach to it, so much so that panic and anxiety often cause people who

---

*In addition, "hard science" is still considered by many to be truly the province of the "male," as Evelyn Fox Keller points out in her article "Gender and Science": "The historically pervasive association between masculine and objective, more specifically between masculine and scientific, is a topic which academic critics resist taking seriously. Why? . . . How is it that formal criticism in the philosophy and sociology of science has failed to see here a topic requiring analysis? The virtual silence of at least the non-feminist academic community on this subject suggests that the association of masculinity with scientific thought has the status of a myth which either cannot or should not be examined seriously." (From Sandra Harding and Merrill B. Hintikka [eds.], *Discovering Reality*, pp. 187–205, Copyright 1978 by Psychoanalysis and Contemporary Science, Inc.)

have only marginal scientific information to repudiate such an approach to its examination. Hite's has been such an approach. Her studies have given ordinary women and men opportunity to verbalize their long-suffered panics and sexual anxieties, thus making it possible for other researchers and educators in this new field of sexology to understand better what has been going on in human minds, through the centuries, about a part of life that is universal and central to every human being born. We have an enormous store of information about the human reproductive system and its functioning, most of it gained in the past fifty years. . . . Hite's research, as with all research dealing with thoughts and feelings, cannot be expected to be analyzed with the same techniques as those that tell us what doses of what drugs give what results in what kinds of patients. . . . We are a scientifically illiterate people, and honest scientists such as Hite are bound to suffer as a result.

Robert M. Emerson, Ph.D., Professor of Sociology, UCLA; Editor, *Urban Life: A Journal of Ethnographic Research:*

Statistical representativeness is only one criterion for assessing the adequacy of empirical data . . . other criteria are particularly pertinent when looking at qualitative data. This is primarily the situation with Hite's research, [in which the] . . . goal can be pursued independently of issues of representativeness, or rather, even demands a logic that is at variance with that of statistical representativeness. The logic is that of maximizing kinds of or variations in sexual experiences, so that the whole range of such experiences can be described; the frequency of any such experiences is another matter, one that is linked to the logic of representativeness.

Much of Hite's work seeks to organize qualitative comments in ways that do not involve an exhaustive set of categories, but again directly convey the more significant themes or patterns, in ways that also identify and explore variations in and from these patterns. Here again, range, breadth, and variation are more important than strict statistical representativeness. . . .

John L. Sullivan, Ph.D., Professor of Political Science, University of Minnesota; Co-editor, *American Journal of Political Science,* and editor, *Quantitative Applications in the Social Sciences,* Sage University Papers series:

The great value of Hite's work is to show how people are thinking, to let people talk without rigid a priori categories—and to make all this accessible to the reader. Hite has many different purposes than simply stating population generalizations based on a probability sample. Therefore questions of sampling are not necessarily the central questions to discuss about her work. Rather, it is a matter of discovering the diversity of behaviors and points of view. Hite has certainly adequately achieved this kind of analysis. If she had done a perfectly representative random sample, she would not have discovered any less diversity in points of view and behaviors than she has discovered.

Her purpose was clear: to let her respondents speak for themselves, which is very valid. . . . What purpose would it have served to do a random sample, given the aims of Hite's work? None—except for generalizing from percentages. But Hite has not generalized in a non-scholarly way. Many of the natural sciences worry a lot less about random samples, because their work is to test hypotheses. And most of the work in the social sciences is not based on random samples either; in fact, many if not most of the articles in psychology journals are based on data from college students, and then generalized. Interestingly, they are not criticized in the same way Hite has been.

In short, Hite has used a kind of intensive analysis method, but not of individuals—of attitudes and feelings. One might say she is trying to put a whole society on the couch. Hers are works with many different purposes, and scholars and readers can use them in many different ways.

Gerald M. Phillips, Ph.D., Pennsylvania State University; Editor, *Communications Quarterly Journal:*

The Hite studies are important. They represent "good" science, a model for future studies of natural human experience. . . . There have always been serious problems for social scientists involved with studying human emotions . . . they cannot be catalogued and specified . . . the most advanced specialists have difficulty finding and specifying vocabulary suitable for objective discussion of human emotions and their impacts on individuals and societies. . . . Hite has acquitted herself of this task remarkably well.

The major share of published studies in the social sciences are done numerically under the assumption that similar methodology produced truth or reliable generalizations for the hard sciences. . . . What social scientists obsessed with "objective scientificity" do not seem to understand is that the hardest of scientists, physicists, for example, must engage in argument at the onset of their experiments *and* at the presentation of their data. . . . The problem with numeric measurement in the social sciences is, in the first instance, it works well only when the things being measured behave like numbers. Human data rarely stands still for measurement. . . . A major issue with which social scientists must cope in the future is how to describe and compare ephemeral numbers. . . . It is also the practice of contemporary social scientists to [unnecessarily] obscure their methodologies in complex mathematical formulae . . . [it would be better to give] a statement of what was discovered, presented as simply and succinctly as possible . . . a clear discussion of the theoretical basis for the study . . . and a clear description of the people studied [as in] the Hite model. Hite is a serious, reliable scholar and a first-rate intelligence.

Robert L. Carneiro, Ph.D.; Curator of Anthropology, The American Museum of Natural History, New York:

> Hite's work can definitely be seen as anthropological in nature. The hallmark of anthropological field method lies in working intensively with individual informants. And though Hite used questionnaires, they were questionnaires that invited long and detailed replies rather than brief, easily codable ones. . . . And from these responses, presented in rich, raw detail, deep truths emerge—truths which, in many cases were probably never revealed to anyone else before . . . for every question she presents a broad spectrum of responses. . . . One comes away from Hite's books with a feeling that an important subject has been plumbed to great depths . . . of inestimable value.

Questionnaire*

The purpose of this questionnaire is to hear women's points of view on questions that were unanswered in the original *Hite Report* on female sexuality. For example, how women feel about love, relationships, marriage, and monogamy were not covered, due to lack of funds. We would very much like to hear your thoughts and opinions on these subjects now, as well as anything else you would like to add. The results will be published as a large-scale discussion of what was said, with many quotes.

The questionnaire is anonymous, so do not sign it. *It is not necessary to answer every question!* There are seven headings; feel free to skip around and answer only those sections or questions you choose. Also, you may answer on a tape cassette, if you prefer. Use as much additional paper as you need.

Send your answers to Shere Hite, P.O. Box 5282, F.D.R. Station, New York, N.Y. 10022

HELLO!

1. Who are you? What is your own description of yourself?

2. What makes you feel happiest, the most alive? Your work? Your love relationship? A hobby or second career? Music? Going places (travel,

*This is one of four versions of the questionnaire distributed over a period of seven years.

concerts, dinner with friends)? Your children? Family? How happy are you, on a scale of one to ten?

3. What do you want most from life?

4. What was your greatest achievement personally to date?

5. What was the biggest emotional upset or disturbance you ever had to face—the greatest crisis, the thing you needed the most courage to get through?

6. Are you in love? Who is the person you are closest to?

7. What is your favorite way to "waste time"?

GROWING UP FEMALE

8. As a child, were you close to your mother? Your father? Did they love you? What did you like most and least about them?

9. Was your mother affectionate with you? Did she speak sweetly to you? Sing to you? Bathe you and do your hair? Were there any clashes between you? When was she angriest? What do you think of her today? Do you like to spend time with her?

10. Was your father affectionate? How? Did you talk? Go places together? Did you like him? Fear him? Respect him? What did you argue about? What do you think of him today?

11. Were your parents affectionate together in front of you? Did they argue? What did you learn from your father was the proper attitude toward your mother? What did you learn from your mother was the proper attitude toward your father?

12. Did your mother show you how to be "feminine"—act like a girl or a "lady"? Did you and your mother do things your brothers or father did not do, and vice versa? How would you define femininity?

13. Were you (are you) a "tomboy"? Was it fun? Were you warned against acting too rough, playing "boys'" games, not acting "ladylike"? Were you urged to be a "good girl"? Were you rebellious?

14. Did you masturbate as a child? How old were you when you started? Did your parents know? Your friends?

15. What did/do you like and dislike about high school? Was/is there a lot of pressure to conform, be like everyone else? Dress a certain way? Be popular? To be a virgin, or to have had sex?

16. Did/do you have a best friend? Did you spend the night at each other's houses? Talk on the phone? What about? Go out together? Are you still in touch?

17. How did you feel when you started dating? When you first kissed? Made out? Had sex? Did you discuss any of this with your parents? Friends?

FALLING IN LOVE

18. Are you "in love" now? How can you tell?

19. How would you define love? Is love the thing you work at in a relationship over a period of time, or is it the strong feeling you feel right from the beginning, for no known reason?

20. To live with someone, is it more important to be "in love" or to love them? What is the difference between being "in love" and loving someone?

21. When, with whom, were you most deeply in love? Were you happy? What was it like? Did the relationship last? Was this when you felt the most passionate?

22. Did you ever cry yourself to sleep because of problems with someone you loved? Why? Contemplate suicide? When were you the loneliest?

23. When were you the happiest with someone?

24. Do you like being in love? Is it a condition of pleasure or pain? Learning? Enlightenment? Joy? Ambivalent feelings? Frustration? How important is it?

25. What are your favorite love stories, in books or films?

YOUR CURRENT RELATIONSHIP

26. Are you in a relationship now? For how long? Do you live together? Are you married? Do you have children?

27. What is the most important part of this relationship, the reason you want it? Is it love, passion, sexual intimacy, economics, daily companionship, or the long-term value of a family relationship? Other?

28. Are you happy with the relationship? Inspired? What do you like most and least about it? Can you imagine spending the rest of your life in it? Is your partner happy?

29. Are you "in love"? Or do you love them, more than being "in love"? What kind of love do you feel?

30. Do you love your partner as much as s/he loves you? More? Does one of you need the other more? Do you feel loved?

31. What is the biggest problem in your relationship? How would you like to change things, if you could?

32. What do you enjoy doing together the most? Talking? Having sex? Being affectionate? Daily life? Sharing children? Hobbies? Going out? Other?

33. How does your partner act toward you in intimate moments? Does your partner tell you s/he loves you? That you are wonderful and beautiful? Very sexually desirable? Talk tenderly to you? Use baby talk? Sex talk? How do you feel?

34. What things does your partner most often criticize about you? What do you most often criticize about him/her?

35. What is the worst thing your partner has ever done to you? The worst thing you have ever done to him/her?

36. Is it easy to talk? Who talks more? Would you like more intimate talk—about feelings, reactions, and problems? Future plans and dreams?

37. Does the relationship fill your deepest needs for closeness with another person? Or are there some parts of yourself that you can't share? That aren't accepted or understood? Or do you prefer not to share every part of yourself?

38. Is the kind of love you are giving and receiving now the kind you most want? Have you seen another type in a friend's relationship or a movie or novel that you would find more satisfying?

39. Is this relationship important to you? How important? The center of your life? An important addition to your relationship with yourself and/or your work? Or merely peripheral—pleasant, but lacking somehow? What would make you leave it?

40. What are the practical arrangements? Who does the dishes? Makes the beds? Does the cooking? Takes care of the children? What is daily life like? Do you sleep in the same bed? Take baths or showers together?

41. Do you share the money? Who controls the money? Do you both work outside the home? Who pays the rent or mortgage? Buys the groceries? How do you feel about the financial arrangements? Do they affect the relationship?

42. What is the best way you have found to make a relationship work?

43. If you are married, how long have you been married? Do you like it? What is the best part of being married? The worst? Before you got married, did you expect it to be like it is?

44. Why did you decide to get married? Because of love? Sex? Social pressures? Economic pressures? Pregnancy? Companionship? To have children? A home life? Emotional security? Was it a hard decision? Whose idea was it? How long had you known each other?

45. How did you feel immediately after you got married? Elated? Worried? Did your feelings for him change? His actions toward you?

46. If you have children, do you like having them? What was having your children like? Was your husband there?

47. How did you feel when you first knew you were pregnant? How did your lover/husband react? After the child was born? Does he take as much part in child rearing as you?

48. Would your life have been different if you had not had children? How? Would you do it over again?

49. Which is more important: Your job? Your love relationship? Your children? Yourself, having time for yourself?

50. Do you believe in monogamy? Have you/are you having sex outside the relationship? Known to your partner? How do you feel about it? What is it/was it giving you?

51. What was your original reason? Were you in love? Was there a lack of understanding or closeness at home? A desire to experiment sexually? Anger? Long absence? Other? Is/was the affair serious?

52. Do you think your partner is having sex with anyone else now? In the past? How do you feel about this? Do you want your partner to be monogamous? Do you want to know if s/he is not?

53. Would you have sex outside the relationship in the future? Tell your partner?

54. Have you ever dated someone married? Did you mind that s/he was married? Did you want them to get divorced, and marry you?

55. Describe the biggest (or most recent) fight you had with your husband or lover.

56. What do you most frequently fight about? Who usually wins (if anybody)? How do you feel during? After?

57. How do conflicts or arguments usually get resolved—or at least ended? Who usually says they're sorry first after a fight? Who initiates talking over the problem? Making up?

58. Describe the time recently you were most happy with your lover, most joyous.

BEING SINGLE

59. Do you like being "single"—whether you are single now or were in the past? Why are you single?

60. What are the advantages of being single? Disadvantages? Do you like going out alone, to a party, restaurant, or shopping, etc.? Or do you sometimes get the impression people think there is something wrong with you when you are not in a couple? Do some people envy you for being single?

61. What is your sex life like? Do you enjoy periods of no sex with another person?

62. Is it easy or difficult to meet someone you like and are attracted to, and whom you respect?

63. Do you think most men today want to be married? Do single men find it difficult to accept the idea of marriage at first? Do they tend to avoid commitment? Do you think men today are less committed?

BREAKING UP/GETTING A DIVORCE

64. If you have ever gotten divorced, or broken up with someone important, what was it like? Who wanted to break up—you or the other person? Why?

65. Were you glad or did you have regrets? Did you feel like a failure, or did you feel freer—or both? Did you hate the other person? Cry a lot? Or feel relieved, that now you could start living again?

66. How did you get over it, if you didn't want to break up? How long did it take? Did you talk to friends? Hide from them? Work harder?

67. While breaking up, what did you feel was the most permanent, solid thing in your life? Your parents or relatives? Friends? Children? Your work? Yourself?

68. Was there a time at which you gave up on love relationships as not being very important? You preferred to put more energy into work or children? You revised your definitions of what kind of love was important? Or have you always put love relationships first in your life?

69. Have you ever lost a loved one through death? What do you miss most about the person? Was a part of you not sorry? Did you feel deserted? Free? Did you grieve?

SPECIAL PROBLEMS IN RELATIONSHIPS

70. Did you ever enter therapy to try to solve personal problems related to your love relationships? What were they? Did therapy help? What were your conclusions?

71. Do you sometimes think you pick the "wrong" lovers? What kinds of lovers do you pick?

72. Are you jealous? Of friendships? Career? Other women? Men?

73. Did you ever grow to hate a lover? Act violently? Scream? Hit them? Did a lover ever strike you, or beat you? What were the circumstances?

74. Have you ever loved someone who hurt you deeply, in spite of what had happened, and in spite of your desire not to love them any longer?

75. Who usually breaks up the relationship first—you or the other person?

76. Do you sometimes find you have to employ a "streak of manipulative coldness"—keep your distance, keep things "cool"?

77. Have you ever pretended you cared less than you did? That s/he was less important than they were? Put up a front? Did it work?

78. Are you afraid of clinging? Making someone feel tied down, "unfree"? Did you ever feel you were too emotionally dependent? Are men afraid of women's dependency? If you tell a man you love him, will he feel tied down?

79. Did you ever have a nagging fear of losing someone's love, or being deserted? That the other person would grow tired of you?

80. Do you ever feel you have "unhealthy" needs and cravings for love and affection? As one woman put it, "My love has usually been too blind, too desperate."

81. How do you feel if someone is very emotionally dependent on *you* in a relationship? Needs you more? Complains that you don't love him enough?

82. Have you ever felt that you were "owned" or suffocated, held down, in a relationship, so that you wanted out?

83. Do you think men take love and falling in love as seriously as women do—if they do? What part does it play in men's lives? Are men more emotionally dependent, or women?

84. Were you ever financially dependent on a man you lived with? Was this a problem? How did/do you feel about it? Did/does it affect the relationship?

85. How do you think men feel about women working outside the home? If you work, and are married/living with someone, how does he feel about it? Does he share the housework?

86. Does your husband/lover see you as an equal? Or are there times when he seems to treat you as an inferior? Leave you out of the decisions? Act superior?

87. How do most men you know feel about the women's movement? How does your husband/lover feel about it?

SEXUALITY

88. What is sex with your partner (or in general) usually like? Do you enjoy it? Do you usually orgasm? During which activity? What is the worst thing about sex? The best?

89. Has your sexuality, or your style of relating sexually, changed over the last few years? In what way?

90. Have you read *The Hite Report* on female sexuality? Which ideas do you most agree with? Disagree?

91. Which is the easiest way for you to orgasm: Through masturbation? Clitoral stimulation by hand from your partner? Oral sex? Intercourse (vaginal penetration)? With a vibrator?

92. If you orgasm during vaginal penetration, how do you usually do it? (a) By added clitoral stimulation from your partner? Please explain. (b) By your own clitoral stimulation/masturbation during penetration? (c) By being on top and rubbing against your partner? (d) Friction of the penis inside the vagina, without other stimulation? (e) Other? Please describe.

93. When did you first orgasm—during sex with a partner, or masturbation? (a) Did you discover masturbation on your own, or did you read about it? How old were you? How did you feel? Did your parents know about it? Friends? (b) When you had your first orgasm with another person, which activity was it during? Did you learn to make it happen, or did it happen without trying?

94. Have you ever masturbated with a partner? During intercourse? During general caresses? Was it hard to do the first time? How did you feel? What

was his/her reaction? Do you have to have your legs together or apart for orgasm?

95. Have you told a woman friend you don't orgasm from intercourse (if you don't)? Explained your sex life in any detail to her? What did you say? How did she react?

96. Have you told a man you don't orgasm from intercourse (if you don't)? What did he say? Did you tell him most women don't? How did you feel?

97. Have you talked with your mother, sister, or daughters about some of these things? Do they know if you masturbate? Do you know if they do? What else have you talked about? What would you like to talk about?

98. If you prefer sex with women, how did you come to this point of view? If you prefer sex with men, how did you come to this point of view? Have you always felt this way? What do you like best about sex with women/men?

99. Does sex with the same partner change over the years? Does it become boring, or more pleasurable? Or does it depend on how the relationship goes?

100. Is there a contradiction between sexual passion and a more long-term, stable relationship? Do you have to choose? Do the daily details of living conflict with, or make difficult, feelings of passion?

101. When do you feel most passionate? How does it feel? Craving? Do you become more aggressive? Or want to be taken?

102. Do you usually like to be more passive or active, dominant, during sex?

103. Do you like exploring a man's body? His chest? Penis and testicles? Anus and buttocks? Have you ever penetrated a man's anus with your finger? How did you feel about this? How do you feel about giving him oral sex? Do most men/does he like you to do this—or is he shy and uncomfortable?

104. Do you like, or would you like to try, exploring a woman's body? Her breasts? Her clitoris? Her vulva? Vagina? Anus and buttocks? How do

you feel about giving her oral sex? Do you like the taste and smell? Do most women like you to do this, or feel shy and uncomfortable? Do you like penetrating a woman's vagina? Anus?

105. Do you like to be stimulated vaginally? Penetrated? By a finger? Penis? Dildo? What do you like and dislike about it?

106. Do you like to be stimulated/penetrated anally? By a finger? Penis? Dildo? How does it feel, and why do you like or dislike it?

107. Do you like oral sex to be done to you? What do you think about how you look and smell? What does the other person usually seem to think? How about during menstruation? Do you orgasm this way?

108. Can your partner stimulate you with his/her hand or finger on your clitoris? To orgasm? How does it feel? Do you have to guide his/her hand?

109. Have you shown someone how to masturbate you—that is, how to stimulate you to orgasm with their hand? Do most men offer clitoral stimulation by hand or mouth for orgasm, without being asked?

110. Do you use fantasies to help you orgasm? During sex? During masturbation? Which fantasies?

111. Do you ever feel pressured into sex? Into liking sex? Why? To be loving? To be "hip"? Have you ever been raped? Was this an important experience? How did you feel? Whom did you tell?

112. Do you like rough sex? What do you think of bondage-discipline? Spanking? Sadomasochism? Have you ever experienced them? Fantasized about them? Had rape fantasies? What were they like?

113. What do you think of pornography? Do you look at it? How did you feel when you first saw it? What does pornography tell you about what it means to be a woman?

114. Does your partner look at pornography? What kind? Men's magazines? Videotapes? How do you feel about this?

115. Do you use birth control? Which kind? What are its advantages and disadvantages? Do you think men should be involved in birth control?

116. Have you ever had an abortion? Why did you decide to have it? How did you feel after you had it?

FRIENDSHIPS BETWEEN WOMEN

117. What is or has been your most important relationship with a woman in your life? Describe the woman you have loved the most. Hated the most.

118. What do you like about your closest woman friend? What do you do together? When do you see each other? Has she helped you through difficult times, and vice versa? How do you feel when you are together— do you have a good time? How much time do you spend together, or talking on the telephone? What does she do that you like least?

119. Were you close to your mother? Did she work outside the home, or was she a full-time mother and homemaker? Did you like her? Admire her? How did you feel about her taste in clothing? Are you like her?

120. Do you have a daughter? How do you feel about her? Have you talked to her about menstruation and sexuality? What did you say? What did she say?

121. What things about women in general do you admire? Which well-known women have contributed most to our society?

122. What do you think about the women's movement? Do you consider yourself a feminist, or in favor of the women's movement?

123. Have your feelings about the women's movement and its ideas affected your life?

124. Do you enjoy being "feminine"? How would you define "femininity"? Do you enjoy beautiful clothing? Dresses and lingerie? Do you spend time on your hair and makeup? How do you feel about the way you look? How "feminine" are you?

125. How do you feel about getting older?

126. If you could say just one thing to other women today, what would you tell them?

127. What do you think is the biggest problem in the United States today?

THANK YOU

Please give the following statistical information:

a. What is your age? b. What is your racial background? Ethnic? c. What is your total amount of schooling? d. What was the approximate total income of your household before taxes in the past year? e. What kind of work do you do (inside or outside the home)? f. Where did you obtain this questionnaire?

Statistical Data

Composition of Study Population as Compared to U.S. Female Population

Following are statistics presenting variables about the respondents, including geographical location, age, educational background, occupation, marital status, and other information. Also presented are statistical figures for the general female population of the United States. In most categories, the breakdown of the female population of the United States and the population of this study correspond closely.

Category	Study population %	U.S. female population %
AGE*		
under 18	4 %	25 %
18–29 years	23.5%	19.5%
30–39 years	19 %	15.5%
40–49 years	14 %	10.5%
50–59 years	11.5%	8 %
60–64 years	8 %	4 %
65–84 years	14.5%	12.5%
85 years and over	2.5%	1.5%
EDUCATION†		
Up to high school graduate	55.5%	67.2%
Some college	23 %	16.7%
College graduate or more	21.5%	16.1%
INCOME‡		
under $2,000	19 %	18.3%
$2,000–$4,000	12 %	13.2%
$4,000–$6,000	12.5%	12.2%
$6,000–$8,000	10 %	9.7%
$8,000–$10,000	7 %	7.4%
$10,000–$12,500	8 %	8.8%
$12,500–$15,000	5 %	6.2%
$15,000–$20,000	10 %	9.8%
$20,000–$25,000	8 %	6.4%
$25,000 and over	8.5%	8.2%
RACE/ETHNICITY§		
White	82.5%	83
Black	13 %	12 %
Hispanic	1.8%	1.5%
Asian	1.8%	2 %
Middle-Eastern	.3%	.5%
American Indian/Eskimo	.9%	1 %
TYPE OF AREA|		
large city/urban	60 %	62 %
rural	27 %	26 %
small town	13 %	12 %

*Based on Current Population Reports, July 1986, U.S. Department of the Census.
†Based on Current Population Survey, March 1986, U.S. Bureau of the Census.
‡Based on Current Population Reports, March 1986, Consumer Income Series P60 no. 154, U.S. Department of the Census.
§Based on Current Population Reports, U.S. Department of the Census.
|Based on Current Population Reports, U.S. Department of the Census.

Category	Study population %	U.S. female population %
GEOGRAPHIC REGION*		
Northeast	21 %	22 %
North Central	27 %	26 %
South	31 %	33 %
West	21 %	19 %
HOMOSEXUAL/LESBIAN		
lesbian	11 %	
bisexual	7 %	
MARRIED/SINGLE†		
single: never married	24 %	22.7%
single: divorced, separated, or widowed	27 %	23.6%
married	49 %	53.6%
1–3 years	18 %	14.5%
3–6 years	26 %	23.3%
7–20 years	34 %	no figure
with children under 18	46 %	48.1%
WOMEN IN THE LABOR FORCE‡	72.3%	70.8%
married women	70.2%	66.3%
divorced women	89.0%	85.2%
married women with children		
under age 6	53.5%	56.2%
children ages 6–17	72.2%	71.3%
women with no children	81.0%	78.3%
POLITICAL AFFILIATION§		
Democrat	46 %	44 %
Republican	28.5%	30 %
Independent	24 %	21 %
Conservative	.5%	3 %
Radical	1 %	2 %

*Based on General Population Characteristics, April 1, 1980, U.S. Department of Commerce.
†Based on Current Population Reports, July 1986, U.S. Department of the Census. See also Part II for Skelly, Yankelovich, and White figures. Varying projections result from the multitude of choices and assumptions made by statisticians, for example, regarding life expectancy tables; choice of base year is also very significant, as well as projected divorce rate. See also National Center for Health, Marriage and Divorce Statistics branch.
‡See Current Population Survey, May 1987, U.S. Department of Labor, and Current Population Survey, March 1986 supplement, U.S. Bureau of Labor Statistics.
§Based on CBS News poll, May 1987, distributed by the Eagleton Foundation, New Jersey.

Statistical Breakdown of Findings

The percentage recorded in each of the major findings is an average of the percentages in the statistical breakdown for that finding. Throughout these tables, blank categories are those to which the question is not applicable.

CHAPTER 1

Basic dissatisfactions with the current emotional contract

84% of women are not satisfied emotionally with their relationships.

AGE		EDUCATION	
—%	under 18	86%	up to high school graduate
86%	18–34	85%	some college
85%	35–50	84%	college graduate
84%	51–70		
81%	71 and over		OCCUPATION/EMPLOYMENT
		89%	homemaker and/or mother (full-time)
INCOME: annual		75%	full-time employment
89%	under $5,000	84%	part-time employment
89%	$6,000–$14,000	88%	unemployed/student
82%	$15,000–$39,000		
84%	$40,000–$74,000		MARRIED/SINGLE
76%	over $75,000	92%	single, never married
		86%	divorced, separated, or widowed
RACE/ETHNICITY		74%	married
84%	White	70%	1–5 years
85%	Black	79%	6–15 years
84%	Hispanic	75%	16–25 years
82%	Middle Eastern	72%	over 25 years
83%	Asian-American	74%	
84%	other		

16% of women have the emotional closeness they want in their relationships.

	AGE			EDUCATION
—%	under 18		14%	up to high school graduate
14%	18–34		15%	some college
15%	35–50		16%	college graduate
16%	51–70			
19%	71 and over			OCCUPATION/EMPLOYMENT
			11%	homemaker and/or mother (full-time)
	INCOME: annual		25%	full-time employment
11%	under $5,000		16%	part-time employment
11%	$6,000–$14,000		12%	unemployed/student
18%	$15,000–$39,000			
16%	$40,000–$74,000			MARRIED/SINGLE
24%	over $75,000		8%	single, never married
			14%	divorced, separated, or widowed
	RACE/ETHNICITY		26%	married
16%	White		30%	1–5 years
15%	Black		21%	6–15 years
16%	Hispanic		25%	16–25 years
16%	Middle Eastern		28%	over 25 years
17%	Asian-American			
16%	other			

88% of women say they want more equal emotional relationships with the men they love; they do not want men to put them on the defensive.

	AGE			EDUCATION
86%	under 18		86%	up to high school graduate
89%	18–34		88%	some college
90%	35–50		90%	college graduate
87%	51–70			
88%	71 and over			OCCUPATION/EMPLOYMENT
			92%	homemaker and/or mother (full-time)
	INCOME: annual		84%	full-time employment
89%	under $5,000		87%	part-time employment
88%	$6,000–$14,000		89%	unemployed/student
90%	$15,000–$39,000			
86%	$40,000–$74,000			MARRIED/SINGLE
85%	over $75,000		89%	single, never married
			89%	divorced, separated, or widowed
	RACE/ETHNICITY		86%	married
88%	White		84%	1–5 years
88%	Black		88%	6–15 years
90%	Hispanic		88%	16–25 years
86%	Middle Eastern		84%	over 25 years
87%	Asian-American			
85%	other			

96% of women believe they are giving more emotional support than they are getting (empathic, non-judgmental listening and understanding, careful and thoughtful feedback, and general emotional support).

	AGE		EDUCATION
—%	under 18	94%	up to high school graduate
95%	18–34	97%	some college
97%	35–50	97%	college graduate
96%	51–70		
96%	71 and over		OCCUPATION/EMPLOYMENT
		98%	homemaker and/or mother (full-time)
	INCOME: annual	97%	full-time employment
97%	under $5,000	94%	part-time employment
95%	$6,000–$14,000	95%	unemployed/student
96%	$15,000–$39,000		
94%	$40,000–$74,000		MARRIED/SINGLE
98%	over $75,000	96%	single, never married
		94%	divorced, separated, or widowed
	RACE/ETHNICITY	98%	married
94%	White	98%	1–5 years
97%	Black	98%	6–15 years
97%	Hispanic	97%	16–25 years
96%	Middle Eastern	98%	over 25 years
96%	Asian-American		
96%	other		

98% of women say they would like their husband or lover to talk more about his feelings, thoughts, and dreams, and to ask them more about their own.

	AGE		EDUCATION
—%	under 18	97%	up to high school graduate
97%	18–34	98%	some college
98%	35–50	98%	college graduate
99%	51–70		
98%	71 and over		OCCUPATION/EMPLOYMENT
		98%	homemaker and/or mother (full-time)
	INCOME: annual	97%	full-time employment
96%	under $5,000	98%	part-time employment
97%	$6,000–$14,000	98%	unemployed/student
98%	$15,000–$39,000		
99%	$40,000–$74,000		MARRIED/SINGLE
99%	over $75,000	98%	single, never married
		97%	divorced, separated, or widowed
	RACE/ETHNICITY	98%	married
98%	White	97%	1–5 years
97%	Black	98%	6–15 years
98%	Hispanic	99%	16–25 years
99%	Middle Eastern	97%	over 25 years
98%	Asian-American		
98%	other		

83% say they initiate most deep talks in relationships with men:*

	AGE		EDUCATION
79%	under 18	81%	up to high school graduate
89%	18–34	85%	some college
83%	35–50	83%	college graduate
82%	51–70		
81%	71 and over		OCCUPATION/EMPLOYMENT
		82%	homemaker and/or mother (full-time)
	INCOME: annual	85%	full-time employment
82%	under $5,000	83%	part-time employment
84%	$6,000–$14,000	81%	unemployed/student
85%	$15,000–$39,000		
83%	$40,000–$74,000		MARRIED/SINGLE
81%	over $75,000	86%	single, never married
		81%	divorced, separated, or widowed
	RACE/ETHNICITY	84%	married
84%	White	84%	1–5 years
82%	Black	82%	6–15 years
82%	Hispanic	86%	16–25 years
83%	Middle Eastern	85%	over 25 years
83%	Asian-American		
84%	other		

*The majority of the remaining 17% say that talks are initiated equally, or that they themselves do not enjoy serious discussions.

64% say the man they are involved with responds minimally to these attempts at deeper discussion.

	AGE		EDUCATION
56%	under 18	65%	up to high school graduate
59%	18–34	63%	some college
69%	35–50	64%	college graduate
72%	51–70		
64%	71 and over		OCCUPATION/EMPLOYMENT
		66%	homemaker and/or mother (full-time)
	INCOME: annual	62%	full-time employment
68%	under $5,000	63%	part-time employment
68%	$6,000–$14,000	65%	unemployed/student
61%	$15,000–$39,000		
62%	$40,000–$74,000		MARRIED/SINGLE
61%	over $75,000	65%	single, never married
		63%	divorced, separated, or widowed
	RACE/ETHNICITY	64%	married
63%	White	60%	1–5 years
64%	Black	61%	6–15 years
62%	Hispanic	68%	16–25 years
64%	Middle Eastern	67%	over 25 years
65%	Asian-American		
65%	other		

76% say the men in their relationships rarely try to draw them out or get them to speak about their thoughts and feelings.

	AGE		EDUCATION
70%	under 18	78%	up to high school graduate
71%	18–34	74%	some college
80%	35–50	76%	college graduate
81%	51–70		
78%	71 and over		OCCUPATION/EMPLOYMENT
		78%	homemaker and/or mother (full-time)
	INCOME: annual	79%	full-time employment
74%	under $5,000	74%	part-time employment
75%	$6,000–$14,000	73%	unemployed/student
77%	$15,000–$39,000		
78%	$40,000–$74,000		MARRIED/SINGLE
76%	over $75,000	77%	single, never married
		75%	divorced, separated, or widowed
	RACE/ETHNICITY	76%	married
77%	White	73%	1–5 years
76%	Black	75%	6–15 years
75%	Hispanic	79%	16–25 years
76%	Middle Eastern	77%	over 25 years
75%	Asian-American		
76%	other		

81% say they would like for men to listen with more interest in what they are saying, to take their thoughts more seriously, and give more intelligent feedback.

	AGE		EDUCATION
88%	under 18	80%	up to high school graduate
85%	18–34	82%	some college
77%	35–50	81%	college graduate
79%	51–70		
76%	71 and over		OCCUPATION/EMPLOYMENT
		85%	homemaker and/or mother (full-time)
	INCOME: annual	78%	full-time employment
91%	under $5,000	79%	part-time employment
82%	$6,000–$14,000	82%	unemployed/student
75%	$15,000–$39,000		
76%	$40,000–$74,000		MARRIED/SINGLE
81%	over $75,000	85%	single, never married
		79%	divorced, separated, or widowed
	RACE/ETHNICITY	79%	married
82%	White	76%	1–5 years
83%	Black	79%	6–15 years
80%	Hispanic	81%	16–25 years
80%	Middle Eastern	80%	over 25 years
81%	Asian-American		
81%	other		

41% of women say that men sometimes tell them or imply to them that they should not feel what they are feeling, or should not express it.

	AGE		EDUCATION
40%	under 18	40%	up to high school graduate
42%	18–34	44%	some college
41%	35–50	39%	college graduate
40%	51–70		
42%	71 and over		OCCUPATION/EMPLOYMENT
		42%	homemaker and/or mother (full-time)
	INCOME: annual	40%	full-time employment
43%	under $5,000	40%	part-time employment
40%	$6,000–$14,000	42%	unemployed/student
40%	$15,000–$39,000		
40%	$40,000–$74,000		MARRIED/SINGLE
41%	over $75,000	42%	single, never married
		40%	divorced, separated, or widowed
	RACE/ETHNICITY	41%	married
43%	White	40%	1–5 years
40%	Black	39%	6–15 years
39%	Hispanic	43%	16–25 years
41%	Middle Eastern	41%	over 25 years
42%	Asian-American		
40%	other		

84% say men frequently respond to things they say with an attitude of ridicule or condescension, often expressing this through intonation.

	AGE		EDUCATION
82%	under 18	90%	up to high school graduate
86%	18–34	81%	some college
87%	35–50	81%	college graduate
83%	51–70		
84%	71 and over		OCCUPATION/EMPLOYMENT
		87%	homemaker and/or mother (full-time)
	INCOME: annual	82%	full-time employment
87%	under $5,000	81%	part-time employment
86%	$6,000–$14,000	84%	unemployed/student
84%	$15,000–$39,000		
81%	$40,000–$74,000		MARRIED/SINGLE
81%	over $75,000	82%	single, never married
		81%	divorced, separated, or widowed
	RACE/ETHNICITY	89%	married
84%	White	86%	1–5 years
85%	Black	87%	6–15 years
83%	Hispanic	91%	16–25 years
82%	Middle Eastern	92%	over 25 years
84%	Asian-American		
89%	other		

95% of women report forms of emotional and psychological harassment from men with whom they are in love relationships.

AGE		EDUCATION	
96%	under 18	94%	up to high school graduate
95%	18–34	95%	some college
94%	35–50	96%	college graduate
95%	51–70		
96%	71 and over		OCCUPATION/EMPLOYMENT
		96%	homemaker and/or mother (full-time)
	INCOME: annual	94%	full-time employment
96%	under $5,000	95%	part-time employment
96%	$6,000–$14,000	95%	unemployed/student
94%	$15,000–$39,000		
95%	$40,000–$74,000		MARRIED/SINGLE
94%	over $75,000	94%	single, never married
		95%	divorced, separated, or widowed
	RACE/ETHNICITY	96%	married
95%	White	97%	1–5 years
94%	Black	96%	6–15 years
95%	Hispanic	94%	16–25 years
95%	Middle Eastern	95%	over 25 years
96%	Asian-American		
95%	other		

91% of women report hearing, as part of their daily lives, "loaded terms," which are used especially for women and which diminish or demean their words or actions; these include "insecure," "needy," "irrational," "she's got her period," "demanding," "complaining," "bitchy," and "hysterical."

AGE		EDUCATION	
90%	under 18	94%	up to high school graduate
91%	18–34	90%	some college
92%	35–50	89%	college graduate
93%	51–70		
89%	71 and over		OCCUPATION/EMPLOYMENT
		91%	homemaker and/or mother (full-time)
	INCOME: annual	92%	full-time employment
92%	under $5,000	90%	part-time employment
90%	$6,000–$14,000	91%	unemployed/student
91%	$15,000–$39,000		
89%	$40,000–$74,000		MARRIED/SINGLE
93%	over $75,000	92%	single, never married
		91%	divorced, separated, or widowed
	RACE/ETHNICITY	90%	married
92%	White	88%	1–5 years
90%	Black	89%	6–15 years
91%	Hispanic	90%	16–25 years
89%	Middle Eastern	91%	over 25 years
93%	Asian-American		
91%	other		

55% report that men often negate or make fun of the feelings they express, putting them on the defensive, and refuse to acknowledge their right to name their own feelings—insisting that their own interpretation is more correct.

	AGE			EDUCATION
49%	under 18		56%	up to high school graduate
54%	18–34		54%	some college
60%	35–50		55%	college graduate
57%	51–70			
56%	71 and over			OCCUPATION/EMPLOYMENT
			57%	homemaker and/or mother (full-time)
	INCOME: annual		56%	full-time employment
62%	under $5,000		55%	part-time employment
55%	$6,000–$14,000		53%	unemployed/student
54%	$15,000–$39,000			
49%	$40,000–$74,000			MARRIED/SINGLE
55%	over $75,000		54%	single, never married
			53%	divorced, separated, or widowed
	RACE/ETHNICITY		55%	married
55%	White		54%	1–5 years
54%	Black		55%	6–15 years
59%	Hispanic		56%	16–25 years
52%	Middle Eastern		55%	over 25 years
55%	Asian-American			
54%	other			

56% of women cite experiences of being undermined or sabotaged psychologically by their husbands and lovers.

	AGE			EDUCATION
54%	under 18		57%	up to high school graduate
55%	18–34		56%	some college
56%	35–50		55%	college graduate
58%	51–70			
56%	71 and over			OCCUPATION/EMPLOYMENT
			58%	homemaker and/or mother (full-time)
	INCOME: annual		57%	full-time employment
55%	under $5,000		55%	part-time employment
56%	$6,000–$14,000		55%	unemployed/student
52%	$15,000–$39,000			
59%	$40,000–$74,000			MARRIED/SINGLE
57%	over $75,000		57%	single, never married
			56%	divorced, separated, or widowed
	RACE/ETHNICITY		56%	married
57%	White		52%	1–5 years
55%	Black		59%	6–15 years
56%	Hispanic		57%	16–25 years
54%	Middle Eastern		56%	over 25 years
55%	Asian-American			
55%	other			

37% say that in mixed groups men often "take sides" with each other, if put in a position to choose between bonding with another man and loyalty to a woman.

	AGE			EDUCATION
—%	under 18		36%	up to high school graduate
32%	18–34		38%	some college
34%	35–50		37%	college graduate
39%	51–70			
43%	71 and over			OCCUPATION/EMPLOYMENT
			40%	homemaker and/or mother (full-time)
	INCOME: annual		35%	full-time employment
39%	under $5,000		36%	part-time employment
36%	$6,000–$14,000		37%	unemployed/student
36%	$15,000–$39,000			
37%	$40,000–$74,000			MARRIED/SINGLE
37%	over $75,000		35%	single, never married
			39%	divorced, separated, or widowed
	RACE/ETHNICITY		37%	married
36%	White		35%	1–5 years
38%	Black		36%	6–15 years
38%	Hispanic		37%	16–25 years
37%	Middle Eastern		38%	over 25 years
36%	Asian-American			
36%	other			

87% of women say they feel they are not really "seen" by the men they are with.

	AGE			EDUCATION
88%	under 18		88%	up to high school graduate
90%	18–34		89%	some college
86%	35–50		84%	college graduate
85%	51–70			
88%	71 and over			OCCUPATION/EMPLOYMENT
			92%	homemaker and/or mother (full-time)
	INCOME: annual		85%	full-time employment
88%	under $5,000		85%	part-time employment
85%	$6,000–$14,000		86%	unemployed/student
86%	$15,000–$39,000			
87%	$40,000–$74,000			MARRIED/SINGLE
89%	over $75,000		89%	single, never married
			87%	divorced, separated, or widowed
	RACE/ETHNICITY		85%	married
89%	White		84%	1–5 years
85%	Black		83%	6–15 years
86%	Hispanic		86%	16–25 years
87%	Middle Eastern		86%	over 25 years
87%	Asian-American			
87%	other			

78% of women say they are treated as equals in their relationships with men only sporadically; that frequently they have to fight for their rights and respect.

	AGE			EDUCATION
71%	under 18		78%	up to high school graduate
84%	18–34		78%	some college
78%	35–50		78%	college graduate
80%	51–70			
79%	71 and over			OCCUPATION/EMPLOYMENT
			82%	homemaker and/or mother (full-time)
	INCOME: annual		79%	full-time employment
79%	under $5,000		74%	part-time employment
80%	$6,000–$14,000		76%	unemployed/student
78%	$15,000–$39,000			
77%	$40,000–$74,000			MARRIED/SINGLE
76%	over $75,000		78%	single, never married
			77%	divorced, separated, or widowed
	RACE/ETHNICITY		78%	married
80%	White		78%	1–5 years
79%	Black		77%	6–15 years
78%	Hispanic		79%	16–25 years
77%	Middle Eastern		78%	over 25 years
76%	Asian-American			
76%	other			

19% of women do feel they have equal emotional and intellectual interactions with the men they love.

	AGE			EDUCATION
—%	under 18		19%	up to high school graduate
24%	18–34		19%	some college
19%	35–50		20%	college graduate
18%	51–70			
14%	71 and over			OCCUPATION/EMPLOYMENT
			20%	homemaker and/or mother (full-time)
	INCOME: annual		18%	full-time employment
18%	under $5,000		18%	part-time employment
19%	$6,000–$14,000		19%	unemployed/student
20%	$15,000–$39,000			
18%	$40,000–$74,000			MARRIED/SINGLE
19%	over $75,000		17%	single, never married
			20%	divorced, separated, or widowed
	RACE/ETHNICITY		20%	married
17%	White		19%	1–5 years
18%	Black		20%	6–15 years
19%	Hispanic		18%	16–25 years
20%	Middle Eastern		19%	over 25 years
19%	Asian-American			
21%	other			

CHAPTER 2

Patterns in arguments and fights in love relationships

79% of arguments and fights in marriages and relationships of from one to five years are caused by women fighting back against ("complaining about") unequal or unsatisfying emotional treatment.

	AGE			EDUCATION
—%	under 18		80%	up to high school graduate
79%	18–34		79%	some college
80%	35–50		79%	college graduate
80%	51–70			
79%	71 and over			OCCUPATION/EMPLOYMENT
			80%	homemaker and/or mother (full-time)
	INCOME: annual		81%	full-time employment
78%	under $5,000		79%	part-time employment
79%	$6,000–$14,000		78%	unemployed/student
79%	$15,000–$39,000			
80%	$40,000–$74,000			MARRIED/SINGLE
78%	over $75,000		80%	single, never married
			79%	divorced, separated, or widowed
	RACE/ETHNICITY		79%	married
80%	White		78%	1–5 years
79%	Black		77%	6–15 years
80%	Hispanic		81%	16–25 years
78%	Middle Eastern		79%	over 25 years
79%	Asian-American			
79%	other			

72% of women say they are usually the ones to "bring up the issues" that are causing emotional distance, in the hope of talking them out.

	AGE			EDUCATION
—%	under 18		73%	up to high school graduate
74%	18–34		72%	some college
73%	35–50		71%	college graduate
70%	51–70			
72%	71 and over			OCCUPATION/EMPLOYMENT
			74%	homemaker and/or mother (full-time)
	INCOME: annual		70%	full-time employment
72%	under $5,000		71%	part-time employment
74%	$6,000–$14,000		72%	unemployed/student
73%	$15,000–$39,000			
72%	$40,000–$74,000			MARRIED/SINGLE
70%	over $75,000		72%	single, never married
			72%	divorced, separated, or widowed
	RACE/ETHNICITY		73%	married
73%	White		72%	1–5 years
71%	Black		70%	6–15 years
72%	Hispanic		72%	16–25 years
72%	Middle Eastern		75%	over 25 years
72%	Asian-American			
72%	other			

88% of women say the men in their lives prefer to avoid "talking things over" and that insistence can lead to an argument.

	AGE			EDUCATION
—%	under 18		90%	up to high school graduate
87%	18–34		88%	some college
88%	35–50		87%	college graduate
89%	51–70			
88%	71 and over			OCCUPATION/EMPLOYMENT
			87%	homemaker and/or mother (full-time)
	INCOME: annual		89%	full-time employment
88%	under $5,000		88%	part-time employment
88%	$6,000–$14,000		88%	unemployed/student
89%	$15,000–$39,000			
88%	$40,000–$74,000			MARRIED/SINGLE
88%	over $75,000		92%	single, never married
			89%	divorced, separated, or widowed
	RACE/ETHNICITY		84%	married
89%	White		84%	1–5 years
89%	Black		83%	6–15 years
87%	Hispanic		82%	16–25 years
87%	Middle Eastern		86%	over 25 years
88%	Asian-American			
88%	other			

76% say men rarely take the initiative in bringing up problems in the relationship for discussion.

	AGE			EDUCATION
—%	under 18		78%	up to high school graduate
76%	18–34		75%	some college
77%	35–50		75%	college graduate
76%	51–70			
76%	71 and over			OCCUPATION/EMPLOYMENT
			76%	homemaker and/or mother (full-time)
	INCOME: annual		76%	full-time employment
77%	under $5,000		75%	part-time employment
76%	$6,000–$14,000		76%	unemployed/student
78%	$15,000–$39,000			
75%	$40,000–$74,000			MARRIED/SINGLE
76%	over $75,000		75%	single, never married
			74%	divorced, separated, or widowed
			78%	married
	RACE/ETHNICITY		78%	1–5 years
77%	White		79%	6–15 years
77%	Black		77%	16–25 years
75%	Hispanic		78%	over 25 years
74%	Middle Eastern			
76%	Asian-American			
76%	other			

81% feel guilty for arguing or "bringing up issues" which "break the peace," and yet will do so when they see no other way to resolve them.

	AGE			EDUCATION
80%	under 18		81%	up to high school graduate
81%	18–34		81%	some college
82%	35–50		80%	college graduate
81%	51–70			
81%	71 and over			OCCUPATION/EMPLOYMENT
			82%	homemaker and/or mother (full-time)
	INCOME: annual		81%	full-time employment
83%	under $5,000		81%	part-time employment
82%	$6,000–$14,000		81%	unemployed/student
81%	$15,000–$39,000			
81%	$40,000–$74,000			MARRIED/SINGLE
80%	over $75,000		80%	single, never married
			80%	divorced, separated, or widowed
			83%	married
	RACE/ETHNICITY		82%	1–5 years
83%	White		83%	6–15 years
82%	Black		83%	16–25 years
81%	Hispanic		84%	over 25 years
80%	Middle Eastern			
80%	Asian-American			
80%	other			

61% say that "bringing up the issues" does not lead to a resolution of those issues.

	AGE			EDUCATION
—%	under 18		60%	up to high school graduate
61%	18–34		61%	some college
62%	35–50		61%	college graduate
60%	51–70			
61%	71 and over			OCCUPATION/EMPLOYMENT
			62%	homemaker and/or mother (full-time)
	INCOME: annual		61%	full-time employment
62%	under $5,000		60%	part-time employment
62%	$6,000–$14,000		60%	unemployed/student
61%	$15,000–$39,000			
60%	$40,000–$74,000			MARRIED/SINGLE
61%	over $75,000		61%	single, never married
			61%	divorced, separated, or widowed
	RACE/ETHNICITY		61%	married
62%	White		62%	1–5 years
64%	Black		62%	6–15 years
60%	Hispanic		60%	16–25 years
60%	Middle Eastern		61%	over 25 years
61%	Asian-American			
61%	other			

48% say that men frequently become competitive during fights and refuse to listen to another point of view.

	AGE			EDUCATION
49%	under 18		47%	up to high school graduate
48%	18–34		47%	some college
48%	35–50		49%	college graduate
47%	51–70			
48%	71 and over			OCCUPATION/EMPLOYMENT
			49%	homemaker and/or mother (full-time)
	INCOME: annual		48%	full-time employment
48%	under $5,000		48%	part-time employment
49%	$6,000–$14,000		48%	unemployed/student
50%	$15,000–$39,000			
47%	$40,000–$74,000			MARRIED/SINGLE
47%	over $75,000		47%	single, never married
			48%	divorced, separated, or widowed
	RACE/ETHNICITY		48%	married
47%	White		48%	1–5 years
48%	Black		48%	6–15 years
49%	Hispanic		49%	16–25 years
48%	Middle Eastern		48%	over 25 years
47%	Asian-American			
48%	other			

51% say that during fights men become silent and/or arrogant and seem not to hear anything being said, sometimes leaving the room or the house.

	AGE			EDUCATION
49%	under 18		50%	up to high school graduate
50%	18–34		52%	some college
51%	35–50		50%	college graduate
52%	51–70			
51%	71 and over			OCCUPATION/EMPLOYMENT
			51%	homemaker and/or mother (full-time)
	INCOME: annual		52%	full-time employment
51%	under $5,000		51%	part-time employment
50%	$6,000–$14,000		51%	unemployed/student
50%	$15,000–$39,000			
52%	$40,000–$74,000			MARRIED/SINGLE
51%	over $75,000		51%	single, never married
			51%	divorced, separated, or widowed
	RACE/ETHNICITY		52%	married
52%	White		51%	1–5 years
51%	Black		52%	6–15 years
51%	Hispanic		52%	16–25 years
49%	Middle Eastern		53%	over 25 years
51%	Asian-American			
52%	other			

29% say that even though "bringing up the issues" may lead to an argument or unpleasantness, eventually there is real talking and the issue is clarified and/or resolved.

	AGE			EDUCATION
25%	under 18		29%	up to high school graduate
22%	18–34		29%	some college
30%	35–50		29%	college graduate
29%	51–70			
29%	71 and over			OCCUPATION/EMPLOYMENT
			28%	homemaker and/or mother (full-time)
	INCOME: annual		27%	full-time employment
29%	under $5,000		29%	part-time employment
28%	$6,000–$14,000		29%	unemployed/student
30%	$15,000–$39,000			
29%	$40,000–$74,000			MARRIED/SINGLE
30%	over $75,000		29%	single, never married
			28%	divorced, separated, or widowed
	RACE/ETHNICITY		29%	married
28%	White		29%	1–5 years
27%	Black		30%	6–15 years
30%	Hispanic		30%	16–25 years
30%	Middle Eastern		28%	over 25 years
29%	Asian-American			
29%	other			

10% of women say that discussions are easy, even with difficult matters.

	AGE			EDUCATION
8%	under 18		10%	up to high school graduate
9%	18–34		11%	some college
10%	35–50		10%	college graduate
10%	51–70			
10%	71 and over			OCCUPATION/EMPLOYMENT
			9%	homemaker and/or mother (full-time)
	INCOME: annual		10%	full-time employment
9%	under $5,000		11%	part-time employment
10%	$6,000–$14,000		10%	unemployed/student
10%	$15,000–$39,000			
11%	$40,000–$74,000			MARRIED/SINGLE
10%	over $75,000		10%	single, never married
			11%	divorced, separated, or widowed
	RACE/ETHNICITY		10%	married
11%	White		9%	1–5 years
11%	Black		10%	6–15 years
9%	Hispanic		10%	16–25 years
8%	Middle Eastern		10%	over 25 years
9%	Asian-American			
10%	other			

73% of women say that they are usually the first to initiate verbal rapprochement or say "I'm sorry," while men will more frequently touch or kiss as a way of making up.*

	AGE			EDUCATION
—%	under 18		72%	up to high school graduate
72%	18–34		73%	some college
71%	35–50		73%	college graduate
73%	51–70			
73%	71 and over			OCCUPATION/EMPLOYMENT
			73%	homemaker and/or mother (full-time)
	INCOME: annual		72%	full-time employment
74%	under $5,000		72%	part-time employment
72%	$6,000–$14,000		73%	unemployed/student
74%	$15,000–$39,000			
73%	$40,000–$74,000			MARRIED/SINGLE
73%	over $75,000		74%	single, never married
			73%	divorced, separated, or widowed
	RACE/ETHNICITY		73%	married
71%	White		71%	1–5 years
75%	Black		75%	6–15 years
76%	Hispanic		72%	16–25 years
73%	Middle Eastern		74%	over 25 years
72%	Asian-American			
73%	other			

*37% of women say they resent this form of "making up" and want to hear that the man is "sorry" too; they want to discuss the problem, and regard physical affection as a way of merely plastering things over, rather than solving the problem.

53% of women say that no talking takes place and the issues are dropped, as if they do not exist.

	AGE			EDUCATION
57%	under 18		52%	up to high school graduate
53%	18–34		51%	some college
52%	35–50		55%	college graduate
52%	51–70			
52%	71 and over			OCCUPATION/EMPLOYMENT
			53%	homemaker and/or mother (full-time)
	INCOME: annual		52%	full-time employment
53%	under $5,000		54%	part-time employment
52%	$6,000–$14,000		53%	unemployed/student
50%	$15,000–$39,000			
57%	$40,000–$74,000			MARRIED/SINGLE
54%	over $75,000		55%	single, never married
			50%	divorced, separated, or widowed
	RACE/ETHNICITY		53%	married
53%	White		52%	1–5 years
54%	Black		52%	6–15 years
52%	Hispanic		54%	16–25 years
53%	Middle Eastern		54%	over 25 years
53%	Asian-American			
52%	other			

63% of women say men seem to see having sex as a preferred way of ending an argument, whereas they would prefer to have sex only after resolving the issue and do not see sex itself as a resolution.

	AGE			EDUCATION
—%	under 18		63%	up to high school graduate
65%	18–34		63%	some college
64%	35–50		62%	college graduate
64%	51–70			
62%	71 and over			OCCUPATION/EMPLOYMENT
			60%	homemaker and/or mother (full-time)
	INCOME: annual		65%	full-time employment
63%	under $5,000		64%	part-time employment
63%	$6,000–$14,000		63%	unemployed/student
62%	$15,000–$39,000			
62%	$40,000–$74,000			MARRIED/SINGLE
64%	over $75,000		63%	single, never married
			63%	divorced, separated, or widowed
	RACE/ETHNICITY		63%	married
64%	White		63%	1–5 years
65%	Black		64%	6–15 years
65%	Hispanic		63%	16–25 years
62%	Middle Eastern		62%	over 25 years
62%	Asian-American			
62%	other			

16% of women say they have good types of fights with their husbands/lovers, clearing the air: both end with understanding the other's point of view.

	AGE			EDUCATION
18%	under 18		15%	up to high school graduate
16%	18–34		15%	some college
15%	35–50		17%	college graduate
16%	51–70			
13%	71 and over			OCCUPATION/EMPLOYMENT
			17%	homemaker and/or mother (full-time)
	INCOME: annual		18%	full-time employment
15%	under $5,000		14%	part-time employment
15%	$6,000–$14,000		15%	unemployed/student
16%	$15,000–$39,000			
17%	$40,000–$74,000			MARRIED/SINGLE
16%	over $75,000		15%	single, never married
			14%	divorced, separated, or widowed
	RACE/ETHNICITY		17%	married
17%	White			17%	1–5 years
17%	Black			18%	6–15 years
16%	Hispanic			16%	16–25 years
15%	Middle Eastern			17%	over 25 years
16%	Asian-American			
16%	other			

39% of women have been struck or beaten by a husband/lover.

	AGE			EDUCATION
28%	under 18		38%	up to high school graduate
41%	18–34		37%	some college
36%	35–50		42%	college graduate
51%	51–70			
39%	71 and over			OCCUPATION/EMPLOYMENT
			42%	homemaker and/or mother (full-time)
	INCOME: annual		40%	full-time employment
38%	under $5,000		37%	part-time employment
37%	$6,000–$14,000		38%	unemployed/student
40%	$15,000–$39,000			
41%	$40,000–$74,000			MARRIED/SINGLE
39%	over $75,000		39%	single, never married
			40%	divorced, separated, or widowed
	RACE/ETHNICITY		39%	married
39%	White			39%	1–5 years
38%	Black			38%	6–15 years
39%	Hispanic			38%	16–25 years
40%	Middle Eastern			39%	over 25 years
39%	Asian-American			
39%	other			

CHAPTER 3

Women's reactions to emotional inequality in relationships—seen both individually and as provocative new cultural patterns

93% of women say they believe they are trying harder to make their relationships work than men, initiating much more emotional outreach.

	AGE
89%	under 18
93%	18–34
95%	35–50
95%	51–70
93%	71 and over

	INCOME: annual
92%	under $5,000
94%	$6,000–$14,000
93%	$15,000–$39,000
93%	$40,000–$74,000
93%	over $75,000

	RACE/ETHNICITY
95%	White
90%	Black
92%	Hispanic
94%	Middle Eastern
94%	Asian-American
93%	other

	EDUCATION
93%	up to high school graduate
92%	some college
93%	college graduate

	OCCUPATION/EMPLOYMENT
94%	homemaker and/or mother (full-time)
93%	full-time employment
93%	part-time employment
93%	unemployed/student

	MARRIED/SINGLE	
94%	single, never married	
94%	divorced, separated, or widowed	
90%	married	
	89%	1–5 years
	89%	6–15 years
	91%	16–25 years
	91%	over 25 years

84% of women say they believe that having loving relationships is one of the first priorities in life, but that most men do not have the same priorities.

	AGE			EDUCATION
89%	under 18		89%	up to high school graduate
94%	18–34		93%	some college
79%	35–50		80%	college graduate
74%	51–70			
84%	71 and over			OCCUPATION/EMPLOYMENT
			86%	homemaker and/or mother (full-time)
	INCOME: annual		82%	full-time employment
83%	under $5,000		84%	part-time employment
82%	$6,000–$14,000		84%	unemployed/student
83%	$15,000–$39,000			
84%	$40,000–$74,000			MARRIED/SINGLE
85%	over $75,000		84%	single, never married
			84%	divorced, separated, or widowed
	RACE/ETHNICITY		84%	married
85%	White		83%	1–5 years
80%	Black		85%	6–15 years
88%	Hispanic		85%	16–25 years
84%	Middle Eastern		84%	over 25 years
84%	Asian-American			
84%	other			

95% of women say men assume they will take first place psychologically in a relationship.

	AGE			EDUCATION
95%	under 18		94%	up to high school graduate
94%	18–34		95%	some college
93%	35–50		95%	college graduate
96%	51–70			
96%	71 and over			OCCUPATION/EMPLOYMENT
			95%	homemaker and/or mother (full-time)
	INCOME: annual		93%	full-time employment
95%	under $5,000		96%	part-time employment
92%	$6,000–$14,000		96%	unemployed/student
97%	$15,000–$39,000			
96%	$40,000–$74,000			MARRIED/SINGLE
96%	over $75,000		96%	single, never married
			94%	divorced, separated, or widowed
	RACE/ETHNICITY		95%	married
95%	White		93%	1–5 years
94%	Black		97%	6–15 years
94%	Hispanic		96%	16–25 years
95%	Middle Eastern		96%	over 25 years
95%	Asian-American			
95%	other			

84% of women in relationships of more than one year describe the kind of love they are receiving from men as being needed.

	AGE		EDUCATION
—%	under 18	81%	up to high school graduate
83%	18–34	87%	some college
82%	35–50	84%	college graduate
82%	51–70		
87%	71 and over		OCCUPATION/EMPLOYMENT
		84%	homemaker and/or mother (full-time)
	INCOME: annual	83%	full-time employment
84%	under $5,000	82%	part-time employment
83%	$6,000–$14,000	85%	unemployed/student
85%	$15,000–$39,000		
84%	$40,000–$74,000		MARRIED/SINGLE
84%	over $75,000	84%	single, never married
		84%	divorced, separated, or widowed
	RACE/ETHNICITY	84%	married
82%	White	83%	1–5 years
86%	Black	84%	6–15 years
85%	Hispanic	85%	16–25 years
84%	Middle Eastern	84%	over 25 years
84%	Asian-American		
84%	other		

64% of women say the love they receive is not satisfying to them.

	AGE		EDUCATION
—%	under 18	64%	up to high school graduate
61%	18–34	62%	some college
60%	35–50	65%	college graduate
69%	51–70		
66%	71 and over		OCCUPATION/EMPLOYMENT
		64%	homemaker and/or mother (full-time)
	INCOME: annual	64%	full-time employment
64%	under $5,000	63%	part-time employment
63%	$6,000–$14,000	64%	unemployed/student
63%	$15,000–$39,000		
64%	$40,000–$74,000		MARRIED/SINGLE
65%	over $75,000	63%	single, never married
		62%	divorced, separated, or widowed
	RACE/ETHNICITY	66%	married
65%	White	65%	1–5 years
66%	Black	66%	6–15 years
60%	Hispanic	67%	16–25 years
61%	Middle Eastern	67%	over 25 years
66%	Asian-American		
65%	other		

87% of women say they think men are more emotionally dependent on women than women on men after the first few months of a relationship or marriage.

AGE			EDUCATION	
78%	under 18		86%	up to high school graduate
88%	18–34		87%	some college
89%	35–50		87%	college graduate
93%	51–70			
87%	71 and over			OCCUPATION/EMPLOYMENT
			87%	homemaker and/or mother (full-time)
	INCOME: annual		85%	full-time employment
86%	under $5,000		86%	part-time employment
88%	$6,000–$14,000		86%	unemployed/student
88%	$15,000–$39,000			
87%	$40,000–$74,000			MARRIED/SINGLE
87%	over $75,000		85%	single, never married
			85%	divorced, separated, or widowed
	RACE/ETHNICITY		90%	married
85%	White		91%	1–5 years
86%	Black		92%	6–15 years
88%	Hispanic		89%	16–25 years
88%	Middle Eastern		89%	over 25 years
87%	Asian-American			
87%	other			

69% of women say that men seem confused by falling in love.

AGE			EDUCATION	
63%	under 18		60%	up to high school graduate
60%	18–34		60%	some college
57%	35–50		58%	college graduate
57%	51–70			
57%	71 and over			OCCUPATION/EMPLOYMENT
			59%	homemaker and/or mother (full-time)
	INCOME: annual		58%	full-time employment
58%	under $5,000		57%	part-time employment
59%	$6,000–$14,000		57%	unemployed/student
60%	$15,000–$39,000			
57%	$40,000–$74,000			MARRIED/SINGLE
57%	over $75,000		65%	single, never married
			58%	divorced, separated, or widowed
	RACE/ETHNICITY		54%	married
58%	White		53%	1–5 years
59%	Black		52%	6–15 years
61%	Hispanic		55%	16–25 years
60%	Middle Eastern		56%	over 25 years
57%	Asian-American			
58%	other			

79% of women are questioning whether they should put so much energy into love relationships.

AGE		EDUCATION	
72%	under 18	76%	up to high school graduate
82%	18–34	79%	some college
81%	35–50	82%	college graduate
81%	51–70		
79%	71 and over		OCCUPATION/EMPLOYMENT
		71%	homemaker and/or mother (full-time)
	INCOME: annual	85%	full-time employment
80%	under $5,000	81%	part-time employment
79%	$6,000–$14,000	79%	unemployed/student
78%	$15,000–$39,000		
78%	$40,000–$74,000		MARRIED/SINGLE
79%	over $75,000	79%	single, never married
		78%	divorced, separated, or widowed
	RACE/ETHNICITY	79%	married
80%	White	80%	1–5 years
79%	Black	79%	6–15 years
78%	Hispanic	78%	16–25 years
78%	Middle Eastern	79%	over 25 years
79%	Asian-American		
78%	other		

89% feel torn between men's demands for love, their "duty" to be giving and supportive of others, and their need to have time for their own thoughts and ideas.

AGE		EDUCATION	
90%	under 18	89%	up to high school graduate
92%	18–34	88%	some college
89%	35–50	88%	college graduate
87%	51–70		
86%	71 and over		OCCUPATION/EMPLOYMENT
		89%	homemaker and/or mother (full-time)
	INCOME: annual	88%	full-time employment
89%	under $5,000	89%	part-time employment
90%	$6,000–$14,000	90%	unemployed/student
88%	$15,000–$39,000		
89%	$40,000–$74,000		MARRIED/SINGLE
89%	over $75,000	88%	single, never married
		89%	divorced, separated, or widowed
	RACE/ETHNICITY	90%	married
89%	White	91%	1–5 years
88%	Black	90%	6–15 years
89%	Hispanic	89%	16–25 years
90%	Middle Eastern	88%	over 25 years
91%	Asian-American		
90%	other		

How important are love relationships to women?
The current debate

34% of women believe women should become less "emotional," less focused on love as a basic means of fulfillment—i.e., "not care so much."

	AGE			EDUCATION
37%	under 18		28%	up to high school graduate
38%	18–34		36%	some college
30%	35–50		38%	college graduate
31%	51–70			
34%	71 and over			OCCUPATION/EMPLOYMENT
			30%	homemaker and/or mother (full-time)
	INCOME: annual		36%	full-time employment
34%	under $5,000		36%	part-time employment
35%	$6,000–$14,000		33%	unemployed/student
33%	$15,000–$39,000			
33%	$40,000–$74,000			MARRIED/SINGLE
34%	over $75,000		35%	single, never married
			37%	divorced, separated, or widowed
	RACE/ETHNICITY		30%	married
34%	White		28%	1–5 years
37%	Black		30%	6–15 years
31%	Hispanic		32%	16–25 years
34%	Middle Eastern		30%	over 25 years
33%	Asian-American			
34%	other			

81% of women say men tell them or imply to them that there is "something wrong with them" when they are not "loving" and "giving."

	AGE			EDUCATION
84%	under 18	85%		up to high school graduate
81%	18–34	81%		some college
80%	35–50	78%		college graduate
80%	51–70			
80%	71 and over			OCCUPATION/EMPLOYMENT
		80%		homemaker and/or mother (full-time)
	INCOME: annual	82%		full-time employment
81%	under $5,000	81%		part-time employment
82%	$6,000–$14,000	81%		unemployed/student
84%	$15,000–$39,000			
79%	$40,000–$74,000			MARRIED/SINGLE
80%	over $75,000	81%		single, never married
		81%		divorced, separated, or widowed
	RACE/ETHNICITY	81%		married
83%	White		80%	1–5 years
79%	Black		81%	6–15 years
80%	Hispanic		82%	16–25 years
81%	Middle Eastern		81%	over 25 years
81%	Asian-American			
81%	other			

62% of women describe their reaction to men's emotional harassment and aggression—mixed at the same time with men's demand for love and nurturing—as emotional confusion.

	AGE			EDUCATION
64%	under 18	62%		up to high school graduate
63%	18–34	62%		some college
62%	35–50	62%		college graduate
61%	51–70			
61%	71 and over			OCCUPATION/EMPLOYMENT
		60%		homemaker and/or mother (full-time)
	INCOME: annual	59%		full-time employment
62%	under $5,000	64%		part-time employment
63%	$6,000–$14,000	64%		unemployed/student
63%	$15,000–$39,000			
61%	$40,000–$74,000			MARRIED/SINGLE
61%	over $75,000	65%		single, never married
		60%		divorced, separated, or widowed
	RACE/ETHNICITY	61%		married
62%	White		60%	1–5 years
63%	Black		59%	6–15 years
62%	Hispanic		60%	16–25 years
61%	Middle Eastern		63%	over 25 years
61%	Asian-American			
62%	other			

27% report becoming angry and losing respect for men under these conditions.

	AGE		EDUCATION
27%	under 18	27%	up to high school graduate
28%	18–34	26%	some college
29%	35–50	27%	college graduate
25%	51–70		
27%	71 and over		OCCUPATION/EMPLOYMENT
		27%	homemaker and/or mother (full-time)
	INCOME: annual	25%	full-time employment
28%	under $5,000	28%	part-time employment
27%	$6,000–$14,000	28%	unemployed/student
27%	$15,000–$39,000		
28%	$40,000–$74,000		MARRIED/SINGLE
26%	over $75,000	27%	single, never married
		28%	divorced, separated, or widowed
	RACE/ETHNICITY	27%	married
26%	White	29%	1–5 years
29%	Black	25%	6–15 years
26%	Hispanic	26%	16–25 years
26%	Middle Eastern	27%	over 25 years
27%	Asian-American		
27%	other		

40% of women faced with these unequal patterns in the emotional contract eventually leave such relationships.

	AGE		EDUCATION
—%	under 18	39%	up to high school graduate
44%	18–34	40%	some college
40%	35–50	42%	college graduate
39%	51–70		
37%	71 and over		OCCUPATION/EMPLOYMENT
		42%	homemaker and/or mother (full-time)
	INCOME: annual	40%	full-time employment
36%	under $5,000	58%	part-time employment
40%	$6,000–$14,000	39%	unemployed/student
42%	$15,000–$39,000		
42%	$40,000–$74,000		MARRIED/SINGLE
40%	over $75,000	—%	single, never married
		—%	divorced, separated, or widowed
	RACE/ETHNICITY	—%	married
41%	White	—%	1–5 years
39%	Black	—%	6–15 years
40%	Hispanic	—%	16–25 years
40%	Middle Eastern	—%	over 25 years
40%	Asian-American		
41%	other		

42% of women in this situation create a double life for themselves, finding another primary relationship, whether it be with work, a lover, children, or friends.*

	AGE			EDUCATION
—%	under 18		44%	up to high school graduate
45%	18–34		43%	some college
41%	35–50		40%	college graduate
41%	51–70			
41%	71 and over			OCCUPATION/EMPLOYMENT
			42%	homemaker and/or mother (full-time)
	INCOME: annual		43%	full-time employment
42%	under $5,000		41%	part-time employment
43%	$6,000–$14,000		42%	unemployed/student
44%	$15,000–$39,000			
40%	$40,000–$74,000			MARRIED/SINGLE
42%	over $75,000		—%	single, never married
			43%	divorced, separated, or widowed
	RACE/ETHNICITY		42%	married
43%	White		30%	1–5 years
42%	Black		42%	6–15 years
41%	Hispanic		49%	16–25 years
41%	Middle Eastern		47%	over 25 years
42%	Asian-American			
42%	other			

*See also statistical appendixes, Part III.

34% of women say they no longer believe that love relationships need be "number one" in order to have a happy life.

	AGE			EDUCATION
29%	under 18		33%	up to high school graduate
31%	18–34		34%	some college
34%	35–50		34%	college graduate
39%	51–70			
37%	71 and over			OCCUPATION/EMPLOYMENT
			28%	homemaker and/or mother (full-time)
	INCOME: annual		38%	full-time employment
34%	under $5,000		36%	part-time employment
33%	$6,000–$14,000		34%	unemployed/student
33%	$15,000–$39,000			
35%	$40,000–$74,000			MARRIED/SINGLE
34%	over $75,000		31%	single, never married
			36%	divorced, separated, or widowed
	RACE/ETHNICITY		35%	married
36%	White		35%	1–5 years
35%	Black		35%	6–15 years
31%	Hispanic		34%	16–25 years
30%	Middle Eastern		35%	over 25 years
34%	Asian-American			
31%	other			

26% of women say they believe in looking at other parts of life with more interest, rather than focusing so strongly on men and relationships with men.

	AGE			EDUCATION
22%	under 18		27%	up to high school graduate
28%	18–34		26%	some college
30%	35–50		26%	college graduate
26%	51–70			
24%	71 and over			OCCUPATION/EMPLOYMENT
			25%	homemaker and/or mother (full-time)
	INCOME: annual		26%	full-time employment
27%	under $5,000		27%	part-time employment
26%	$6,000–$14,000		26%	unemployed/student
26%	$15,000–$39,000			
25%	$40,000–$74,000			MARRIED/SINGLE
26%	over $75,000		25%	single, never married
			26%	divorced, separated, or widowed
	RACE/ETHNICITY		26%	married
26%	White		25%	1–5 years
26%	Black		26%	6–15 years
26%	Hispanic		26%	16–25 years
26%	Middle Eastern		26%	over 25 years
27%	Asian-American			
26%	other			

14% are against making a relationship with a man the center of their life, as a matter of principle.

	AGE			EDUCATION
19%	under 18		13%	up to high school graduate
18%	18–34		14%	some college
13%	35–50		15%	college graduate
11%	51–70			
19%	71 and over			OCCUPATION/EMPLOYMENT
			15%	homemaker and/or mother (full-time)
	INCOME: annual		14%	full-time employment
14%	under $5,000		14%	part-time employment
13%	$6,000–$14,000		13%	unemployed/student
13%	$15,000–$39,000			
15%	$40,000–$74,000			MARRIED/SINGLE
14%	over $75,000		12%	single, never married
			14%	divorced, separated, or widowed
	RACE/ETHNICITY		15%	married
14%	White		10%	1–5 years
13%	Black		15%	6–15 years
12%	Hispanic		19%	16–25 years
14%	Middle Eastern		16%	over 25 years
14%	Asian-American			
14%	other			

59% of women are now struggling against the cultural belief that equates a woman being loved by a man with a woman's acceptability and status in the society.

	AGE		EDUCATION
60%	under 18	59%	up to high school graduate
62%	18–34	60%	some college
60%	35–50	59%	college graduate
56%	51–70		
57%	71 and over		OCCUPATION/EMPLOYMENT
		58%	homemaker and/or mother (full-time)
	INCOME: annual	59%	full-time employment
59%	under $5,000	59%	part-time employment
60%	$6,000–$14,000	60%	unemployed/student
59%	$15,000–$39,000		
58%	$40,000–$74,000		MARRIED/SINGLE
58%	over $75,000	59%	single, never married
		58%	divorced, separated, or widowed
		59%	married
	RACE/ETHNICITY	60%	1–5 years
59%	White	62%	6–15 years
60%	Black	57%	16–25 years
58%	Hispanic	58%	over 25 years
59%	Middle Eastern		
59%	Asian-American		
58%	other		

CHAPTER 5

Single women's feelings about sex in the post–sexual revolution years

89% of single, never-married women in their teens and twenties say they find men's attitudes toward sex and forming relationships confusing.

	AGE		EDUCATION
—%	under 18	91%	up to high school graduate
—%	18–34	89%	some college
—%	35–50	88%	college graduate
—%	51–70		
—%	71 and over		

	INCOME: annual
88%	under $5,000
89%	$6,000–$14,000
90%	$15,000–$39,000
89%	$40,000–$74,000
88%	over $75,000

	RACE/ETHNICITY
89%	White
90%	Black
88%	Hispanic
89%	Middle Eastern
88%	Asian-American
89%	other

92% of the single women in this study are irritated that the game/sport for men of "trying to get a girl" just for the "score" of it is still going on (i.e., the double standard).

	AGE			EDUCATION
93%	under 18		92%	up to high school graduate
92%	18–34		93%	some college
92%	35–50		91%	college graduate
91%	51–70			
92%	71 and over			

	INCOME: annual
94%	under $5,000
92%	$6,000–$14,000
91%	$15,000–$39,000
91%	$40,000–$74,000
92%	over $75,000

	RACE/ETHNICITY
92%	White
92%	Black
91%	Hispanic
91%	Middle Eastern
92%	Asian-American
92%	other

85% of single women in their teens and twenties say most men still see sex as a sport or have a "shopping" attitude toward women.

	AGE			EDUCATION
—%	under 18		85%	up to high school graduate
—%	18–34		84%	some college
—%	35–50		84%	college graduate
—%	51–70			
—%	71 and over			

	INCOME: annual
84%	under $5,000
85%	$6,000–$14,000
86%	$15,000–$39,000
85%	$40,000–$74,000
85%	over $75,000

	RACE/ETHNICITY
85%	White
85%	Black
86%	Hispanic
86%	Middle Eastern
86%	Asian-American
85%	other

76% of single women say they frequently have sex on their "first date" or time together—although most would rather wait, even if they are physically excited.

	AGE		EDUCATION
79%	under 18	76%	up to high school graduate
84%	18–34	75%	some college
75%	35–50	77%	college graduate
66%	51–70		
—%	71 and over		

	INCOME: annual
78%	under $5,000
77%	$6,000–$14,000
75%	$15,000–$39,000
75%	$40,000–$74,000
76%	over $75,000

	RACE/ETHNICITY
76%	White
76%	Black
75%	Hispanic
75%	Middle Eastern
76%	Asian-American
76%	other

41% of women married during the last ten years cite one of their reasons for marriage as exhaustion and depression at having to be wary of being "taken" when single, treated without respect.

	AGE		EDUCATION
—%	under 18	42%	up to high school graduate
41%	18–34	40%	some college
42%	35–50	41%	college graduate
43%	51–70		
40%	71 and over		OCCUPATION/EMPLOYMENT
		41%	homemaker and/or mother (full-time)
	INCOME: annual	40%	full-time employment
42%	under $5,000	42%	part-time employment
41%	$6,000–$14,000	41%	unemployed/student
41%	$15,000–$39,000		
41%	$40,000–$74,000		
40%	over $75,000		

	RACE/ETHNICITY
40%	White
42%	Black
41%	Hispanic
41%	Middle Eastern
40%	Asian-American
41%	other

94% of single women say the situation before knowing if a relationship *is* a "relationship" is the time they feel most vulnerable.

	AGE			EDUCATION
92%	under 18		94%	up to high school graduate
95%	18–34		93%	some college
95%	35–50		94%	college graduate
94%	51–70			
95%	71 and over			

INCOME: annual
92%	under $5,000
94%	$6,000–$14,000
95%	$15,000–$39,000
95%	$40,000–$74,000
94%	over $75,000

RACE/ETHNICITY
94%	White
95%	Black
94%	Hispanic
93%	Middle Eastern
93%	Asian-American
94%	other

83% of women say they prefer sex in the context of emotional involvement, sex with feelings, rather than "casual sex."*

	AGE		EDUCATION
84%	under 18	84%	up to high school graduate
83%	18–34	82%	some college
84%	35–50	83%	college graduate
83%	51–70		
83%	71 and over		OCCUPATION/EMPLOYMENT
		83%	homemaker and/or mother (full-time)
	INCOME: annual	83%	full-time employment
83%	under $5,000	82%	part-time employment
82%	$6,000–$14,000	83%	unemployed/student
83%	$15,000–$39,000		
84%	$40,000–$74,000		MARRIED/SINGLE
83%	over $75,000	84%	single, never married
		82%	divorced, separated, or widowed
	RACE/ETHNICITY	83%	married
82%	White	81%	1–5 years
83%	Black	85%	6–15 years
84%	Hispanic	84%	16–25 years
83%	Middle Eastern	83%	over 25 years
83%	Asian-American		
83%	other		

*It is unclear how many of them feel this way because of the unpleasant attitudes they have encountered after sex on the part of some men, and how many simply think sex is only pleasurable when connected to feelings. Of course now, fear of AIDS makes everyone, at least theoretically, prefer sex in a relationship; however, unless the relationship is several years long, this is no guarantee.

27% of single women now date infrequently, after earlier periods of much more active sex lives, because they do not like many men's "trashing" attitudes and prefer to remain emotionally stable.

	AGE		EDUCATION
—%	under 18	28%	up to high school graduate
27%	18–34	27%	some college
28%	35–50	26%	college graduate
29%	51–70		
25%	71 and over		

	INCOME: annual
27%	under $5,000
26%	$6,000–$14,000
27%	$15,000–$39,000
28%	$40,000–$74,000
27%	over $75,000

	RACE/ETHNICITY
27%	White
28%	Black
27%	Hispanic
29%	Middle Eastern
28%	Asian-American
27%	other

53% of women fantasize at times about a very free sexual life; most also fear these thoughts and worry about becoming "too sexual."

	AGE		EDUCATION
55%	under 18	53%	up to high school graduate
54%	18–34	52%	some college
52%	35–50	53%	college graduate
53%	51–70		
53%	71 and over		OCCUPATION/EMPLOYMENT
		54%	homemaker and/or mother (full-time)
	INCOME: annual	53%	full-time employment
54%	under $5,000	53%	part-time employment
54%	$6,000–$14,000	52%	unemployed/student
52%	$15,000–$39,000		
52%	$40,000–$74,000		MARRIED/SINGLE
53%	over $75,000	54%	single, never married
		53%	divorced, separated, or widowed
	RACE/ETHNICITY	53%	married
53%	White	52%	1–5 years
52%	Black	52%	6–15 years
53%	Hispanic	54%	16–25 years
54%	Middle Eastern	54%	over 25 years
53%	Asian-American		
53%	other		

13% of single women say they like casual sex, or even one-night stands, for adventure and excitement.

	AGE		EDUCATION
7%	under 18	12%	up to high school graduate
19%	18–34	11%	some college
14%	35–50	14%	college graduate
12%	51–70		
—%	71 and over		

INCOME: annual
13%	under $5,000
14%	$6,000–$14,000
14%	$15,000–$39,000
13%	$40,000–$74,000
13%	over $75,000

RACE/ETHNICITY
14%	White
14%	Black
13%	Hispanic
10%	Middle Eastern
11%	Asian-American
12%	other

CHAPTER 6

Inside dating relationships: an unequal balance

92% of single women in relationships say they spend a large part of their time trying to figure out the relationship they are in.

	AGE			EDUCATION
90%	under 18		92%	up to high school graduate
94%	18–34		92%	some college
92%	35–50		93%	college graduate
92%	51–70			
92%	71 and over			

	INCOME: annual
93%	under $5,000
92%	$6,000–$14,000
91%	$15,000–$39,000
90%	$40,000–$74,000
93%	over $75,000

	RACE/ETHNICITY
92%	White
92%	Black
91%	Hispanic
91%	Middle Eastern
92%	Asian-American
92%	other

73% of single women in relationships describe vague or ambivalent behavior on the part of the man.

	AGE		EDUCATION
75%	under 18	72%	up to high school graduate
74%	18–34	71%	some college
73%	35–50	74%	college graduate
72%	51–70		
70%	71 and over		

	INCOME: annual
73%	under $5,000
72%	$6,000–$14,000
73%	$15,000–$39,000
74%	$40,000–$74,000
73%	over $75,000

	RACE/ETHNICITY
73%	White
72%	Black
74%	Hispanic
73%	Middle Eastern
73%	Asian-American
73%	other

76% of single women in relationships say they want to trust the man they are with, but his behavior makes them wary; yet when they look for "reassurance," they are put down for being too "insecure" and "clingy."

	AGE		EDUCATION
77%	under 18	76%	up to high school graduate
76%	18–34	76%	some college
75%	35–50	75%	college graduate
74%	51–70		
76%	71 and over		

	INCOME: annual
76%	under $5,000
75%	$6,000–$14,000
76%	$15,000–$39,000
77%	$40,000–$74,000
76%	over $75,000

	RACE/ETHNICITY
77%	White
76%	Black
77%	Hispanic
76%	Middle Eastern
75%	Asian-American
76%	other

79% of women say they are afraid of "clinging" or making someone feel "tied down."

	AGE			EDUCATION
79%	under 18		78%	up to high school graduate
80%	18–34		79%	some college
81%	35–50		79%	college graduate
80%	51–70			
79%	71 and over			OCCUPATION/EMPLOYMENT
			77%	homemaker and/or mother (full-time)
	INCOME: annual		80%	full-time employment
79%	under $5,000		81%	part-time employment
79%	$6,000–$14,000		79%	unemployed/student
78%	$15,000–$39,000			
80%	$40,000–$74,000			MARRIED/SINGLE
79%	over $75,000		83%	single, never married
			80%	divorced, separated, or widowed
	RACE/ETHNICITY		75%	married
79%	White			76%	1–5 years
78%	Black			79%	6–15 years
80%	Hispanic			75%	16–25 years
79%	Middle Eastern			71%	over 25 years
80%	Asian-American			
79%	other			

82% of single women say that most of the men they know seem to want to avoid commitments.

	AGE			EDUCATION
83%	under 18		81%	up to high school graduate
82%	18–34		82%	some college
81%	35–50		83%	college graduate
82%	51–70			
82%	71 and over			
	INCOME: annual			
82%	under $5,000			
84%	$6,000–$14,000			
80%	$15,000–$39,000			
83%	$40,000–$74,000			
82%	over $75,000			
	RACE/ETHNICITY			
82%	White			
83%	Black			
82%	Hispanic			
82%	Middle Eastern			
81%	Asian-American			
81%	other			

88% of single women wonder if they are picking "the wrong men."

	AGE			EDUCATION
88%	under 18		87%	up to high school graduate
87%	18–34		88%	some college
86%	35–50		89%	college graduate
88%	51–70			
87%	71 and over			

INCOME: annual

87%	under $5,000
88%	$6,000–$14,000
88%	$15,000–$39,000
89%	$40,000–$74,000
88%	over $75,000

RACE/ETHNICITY

87%	White
88%	Black
89%	Hispanic
88%	Middle Eastern
88%	Asian-American
87%	other

87% of all women say it is difficult to meet men they admire and respect.

	AGE			EDUCATION
88%	under 18		87%	up to high school graduate
87%	18–34		87%	some college
88%	35–50		87%	college graduate
88%	51–70			
87%	71 and over			OCCUPATION/EMPLOYMENT
			86%	homemaker and/or mother (full-time)
	INCOME: annual		87%	full-time employment
87%	under $5,000		88%	part-time employment
86%	$6,000–$14,000		87%	unemployed/student
88%	$15,000–$39,000			
86%	$40,000–$74,000			MARRIED/SINGLE
86%	over $75,000		87%	single, never married
			88%	divorced, separated, or widowed
			87%	married
	RACE/ETHNICITY		89%	1–5 years
87%	White		85%	6–15 years
87%	Black		86%	16–25 years
86%	Hispanic		87%	over 25 years
85%	Middle Eastern			
86%	Asian-American			
87%	other			

77% of single women in relationships of three months or longer are monogamous.*

	AGE			EDUCATION
—%	under 18		78%	up to high school graduate
77%	18–34		77%	some college
78%	35–50		77%	college graduate
77%	51–70			
76%	71 and over			

INCOME: annual
77%	under $5,000
76%	$6,000–$14,000
76%	$15,000–$39,000
75%	$40,000–$74,000
78%	over $75,000

RACE/ETHNICITY
78%	White
77%	Black
76%	Hispanic
77%	Middle Eastern
77%	Asian-American
77%	other

*The average length of single relationships lasting longer than two months is seven months.

43% of single women say men they date are not monogamous.

	AGE			EDUCATION
38%	under 18		43%	up to high school graduate
45%	18–34		42%	some college
45%	35–50		43%	college graduate
44%	51–70			
43%	71 and over			

INCOME: annual
43%	under $5,000
42%	$6,000–$14,000
43%	$15,000–$39,000
44%	$40,000–$74,000
43%	over $75,000

RACE/ETHNICITY
43%	White
44%	Black
45%	Hispanic
41%	Middle Eastern
42%	Asian-American
42%	other

23% of single women in relationships do not believe in monogamy.*

	AGE		EDUCATION
—%	under 18	24%	up to high school graduate
22%	18–34	23%	some college
23%	35–50	23%	college graduate
24%	51–70		
23%	71 and over		

INCOME: annual

24%	under $5,000
23%	$6,000–$14,000
22%	$15,000–$39,000
23%	$40,000–$74,000
23%	over $75,000

RACE/ETHNICITY

23%	White
24%	Black
24%	Hispanic
23%	Middle Eastern
23%	Asian-American
23%	other

*4% of single women in relationships have "open relationships"; but it is more common, when seeing more than one man, not to bring it up.

CHAPTER 7

What to make of one unhappy relationship after another: women and "masochism"

87% of women have had, at one time or another, relationships that were painful or draining.

	AGE		EDUCATION
84%	under 18	89%	up to high school graduate
89%	18–34	86%	some college
89%	35–50	86%	college graduate
88%	51–70		
87%	71 and over		OCCUPATION/EMPLOYMENT
		89%	homemaker and/or mother (full-time)
	INCOME: annual	88%	full-time employment
87%	under $5,000	86%	part-time employment
86%	$6,000–$14,000	86%	unemployed/student
87%	$15,000–$39,000		
87%	$40,000–$74,000		MARRIED/SINGLE
85%	over $75,000	87%	single, never married
		88%	divorced, separated, or widowed
	RACE/ETHNICITY	87%	married
86%	White	87%	1–5 years
87%	Black	86%	6–15 years
86%	Hispanic	87%	16–25 years
88%	Middle Eastern	86%	over 25 years
87%	Asian-American		
87%	other		

74% of women have left relationships that made them unhappy.

	AGE		EDUCATION
73%	under 18	74%	up to high school graduate
74%	18–34	74%	some college
75%	35–50	75%	college graduate
74%	51–70		
74%	71 and over		OCCUPATION/EMPLOYMENT
		75%	homemaker and/or mother (full-time)
	INCOME: annual	74%	full-time employment
72%	under $5,000	74%	part-time employment
76%	$6,000–$14,000	73%	unemployed/student
75%	$15,000–$39,000		
74%	$40,000–$74,000		MARRIED/SINGLE
74%	over $75,000	75%	single, never married
		74%	divorced, separated, or widowed
	RACE/ETHNICITY	74%	married
74%	White	73%	1–5 years
73%	Black	74%	6–15 years
74%	Hispanic	74%	16–25 years
75%	Middle Eastern	75%	over 25 years
74%	Asian-American		
74%	other		

CHAPTER 8

Single women's thoughts about the advantages and disadvantages of marriage

41% of single women have mixed feelings about marriage.

	AGE			EDUCATION
42%	under 18		41%	up to high school graduate
41%	18–34		42%	some college
41%	35–50		41%	college graduate
40%	51–70			
41%	71 and over			

INCOME: annual

41%	under $5,000
41%	$6,000–$14,000
42%	$15,000–$39,000
43%	$40,000–$74,000
42%	over $75,000

RACE/ETHNICITY

41%	White
41%	Black
41%	Hispanic
40%	Middle Eastern
40%	Asian-American
41%	other

26% of single, never-married women between the ages of 20 and 30 are not interested in marriage.

	AGE			EDUCATION
—%	under 18		26%	up to high school graduate
—%	18–34		27%	some college
—%	35–50		26%	college graduate
—%	51–70			
—%	71 and over			

INCOME: annual
25%	under $5,000
26%	$6,000–$14,000
27%	$15,000–$39,000
26%	$40,000–$74,000
26%	over $75,000

RACE/ETHNICITY
26%	White
24%	Black
25%	Hispanic
27%	Middle Eastern
26%	Asian-American
26%	other

18% of single women who have never married (excluding gay women), now between 30 and 50, say they are not interested in marriage.

	AGE			EDUCATION
—%	under 18		17%	up to high school graduate
—%	18–34		18%	some college
—%	35–50		18%	college graduate
—%	51–70			
—%	71 and over			

INCOME: annual
19%	under $5,000
18%	$6,000–$14,000
17%	$15,000–$39,000
18%	$40,000–$74,000
17%	over $75,000

RACE/ETHNICITY
17%	White
17%	Black
18%	Hispanic
18%	Middle Eastern
18%	Asian-American
18%	other

46% of divorced women do not want to marry again—at least in the near future.

	AGE			EDUCATION
—%	under 18		47%	up to high school graduate
42%	18–34		46%	some college
46%	35–50		46%	college graduate
49%	51–70			
—%	71 and over			OCCUPATION/EMPLOYMENT
			46%	homemaker and/or mother (full-time)
	INCOME: annual		45%	full-time employment
46%	under $5,000		45%	part-time employment
47%	$6,000–$14,000		46%	unemployed/student
46%	$15,000–$39,000			
45%	$40,000–$74,000			
46%	over $75,000			
	RACE/ETHNICITY			
46%	White			
47%	Black			
46%	Hispanic			
46%	Middle Eastern			
45%	Asian-American			
46%	other			

43% of single, never-married women do want to marry eventually, seeing marriage as an emotional haven, a promise of warmth and intimacy, stability.

	AGE			EDUCATION
46%	under 18		41%	up to high school graduate
40%	18–34		45%	some college
43%	35–50		43%	college graduate
—%	51–70			
—%	71 and over			
	INCOME: annual			
42%	under $5,000			
44%	$6,000–$14,000			
44%	$15,000–$39,000			
42%	$40,000–$74,000			
43%	over $75,000			
	RACE/ETHNICITY			
42%	White			
43%	Black			
44%	Hispanic			
44%	Middle Eastern			
43%	Asian-American			
43%	other			

33% of single, never-married women want to marry because they are beginning to feel strong social pressure.

	AGE		EDUCATION
21%	under 18	33%	up to high school graduate
45%	18–34	34%	some college
34%	35–50	33%	college graduate
—%	51–70		
—%	71 and over		

	INCOME: annual
33%	under $5,000
34%	$6,000–$14,000
33%	$15,000–$39,000
32%	$40,000–$74,000
32%	over $75,000

	RACE/ETHNICITY
33%	White
34%	Black
35%	Hispanic
32%	Middle Eastern
33%	Asian-American
33%	other

52% of divorced women would like to marry again, to share companionship, responsibilities, and children.

	AGE		EDUCATION
—%	under 18	52%	up to high school graduate
51%	18–34	53%	some college
52%	35–50	52%	college graduate
54%	51–70		
52%	71 and over		OCCUPATION/EMPLOYMENT
		53%	homemaker and/or mother (full-time)
	INCOME: annual	57%	full-time employment
53%	under $5,000	50%	part-time employment
52%	$6,000–$14,000	52%	unemployed/student
52%	$15,000–$39,000		
51%	$40,000–$74,000		
51%	over $75,000		

	RACE/ETHNICITY
52%	White
54%	Black
51%	Hispanic
50%	Middle Eastern
50%	Asian-American
57%	other

32% of single women mention economic insecurities as a problem with remaining single over the long term.

	AGE			EDUCATION
—%	under 18		32%	up to high school graduate
32%	18–34		30%	some college
34%	35–50		34%	college graduate
30%	51–70			
32%	71 and over			

INCOME: annual

32%	under $5,000
33%	$6,000–$14,000
32%	$15,000–$39,000
31%	$40,000–$74,000
32%	over $75,000

RACE/ETHNICITY

32%	White
32%	Black
33%	Hispanic
32%	Middle Eastern
32%	Asian-American
32%	other

46% of single women are waging a conscious struggle against the hold stereotypes that say "you must have a man" have on parts of their minds.

	AGE			EDUCATION
44%	under 18		46%	up to high school graduate
45%	18–34		47%	some college
47%	35–50		47%	college graduate
47%	51–70			
46%	71 and over			

INCOME: annual

46%	under $5,000
47%	$6,000–$14,000
46%	$15,000–$39,000
45%	$40,000–$74,000
45%	over $75,000

RACE/ETHNICITY

46%	White
46%	Black
47%	Hispanic
46%	Middle Eastern
45%	Asian-American
45%	other

56% of single, never-married women in their twenties say that they do not want to choose between work and marriage/family; they want both.

	AGE			EDUCATION
—%	under 18		58%	up to high school graduate
—%	18–34		54%	some college
—%	35–50		56%	college graduate
—%	51–70			
—%	71 and over			

INCOME: annual

57%	under $5,000
56%	$6,000–$14,000
56%	$15,000–$39,000
55%	$40,000–$74,000
54%	over $75,000

RACE/ETHNICITY

56%	White
56%	Black
57%	Hispanic
55%	Middle Eastern
56%	Asian-American
56%	other

23% of single, never-married women in their twenties, now working, say that they would give up their work or career for marriage/family if it seemed appropriate.

	AGE			EDUCATION
—%	under 18		24%	up to high school graduate
—%	18–34		23%	some college
—%	35–50		23%	college graduate
—%	51–70			
—%	71 and over			

INCOME: annual

24%	under $5,000
25%	$6,000–$14,000
23%	$15,000–$39,000
23%	$40,000–$74,000
23%	over $75,000

RACE/ETHNICITY

22%	White
23%	Black
22%	Hispanic
21%	Middle Eastern
23%	Asian-American
23%	other

92% of all women—when asked, "What is your favorite way to waste time? Please yourself?"—mention activities they do alone.

AGE

89%	under 18
94%	18–34
95%	35–50
92%	51–70
92%	71 and over

INCOME: annual

91%	under $5,000
92%	$6,000–$14,000
93%	$15,000–$39,000
95%	$40,000–$74,000
90%	over $75,000

RACE/ETHNICITY

90%	White
94%	Black
92%	Hispanic
91%	Middle Eastern
91%	Asian-American
92%	other

EDUCATION

92%	up to high school graduate
93%	some college
92%	college graduate

OCCUPATION/EMPLOYMENT

90%	homemaker and/or mother (full-time)
94%	full-time employment
95%	part-time employment
90%	unemployed/student

MARRIED/SINGLE

92%	single, never married
93%	divorced, separated, or widowed
92%	married
91%	1–5 years
92%	6–15 years
93%	16–25 years
92%	over 25 years

CHAPTER 10

Sex and love affairs outside of marriage

83% of women believe in monogamy as an ideal way of life.

	AGE		EDUCATION
82%	under 18	81%	up to high school graduate
83%	18–34	85%	some college
84%	35–50	83%	college graduate
83%	51–70		
84%	71 and over		OCCUPATION/EMPLOYMENT
		81%	homemaker and/or mother (full-time)
	INCOME: annual	80%	full-time employment
85%	under $5,000	85%	part-time employment
81%	$6,000–$14,000	85%	unemployed/student
82%	$15,000–$39,000		
83%	$40,000–$74,000		MARRIED/SINGLE
83%	over $75,000	87%	single, never married
		80%	divorced, separated, or widowed
	RACE/ETHNICITY	83%	married
83%	White	85%	1–5 years
82%	Black	84%	6–15 years
83%	Hispanic	81%	16–25 years
82%	Middle Eastern	81%	over 25 years
83%	Asian-American		
83%	other		

70% of women married five years or more are having sex outside of their marriages.

	AGE			EDUCATION
—%	under 18		71%	up to high school graduate
65%	18–34		70%	some college
75%	35–50		69%	college graduate
71%	51–70			
—%	71 and over			OCCUPATION/EMPLOYMENT
			72%	homemaker and/or mother (full-time)
	INCOME: annual		68%	full-time employment
71%	under $5,000		69%	part-time employment
72%	$6,000–$14,000		70%	unemployed/student
68%	$15,000–$39,000			
69%	$40,000–$74,000			
70%	over $75,000			

RACE/ETHNICITY

70%	White
71%	Black
70%	Hispanic
69%	Middle Eastern
70%	Asian-American
70%	other

Patterns of extramarital sex of women who have affairs

Length of affairs:

12% casual sex or one- or two-time meetings
9% 1–11 months
14% 1–2 years
23% 3–5 years
4% 6–10 years
2% 11 years or more
6% intermittent with same person

Number of affairs:

Married 2–4 years:

one affair: 17%
two affairs: 13%
several: 5%

Married 5–10 years:

one affair: 14%
two affairs: 26%
three affairs: 22%
several: 8%

Married over 10 years:

one affair: 7%
two affairs: 21%
three affairs: 25%
four–five: 18%
six–ten: 9%
more than ten: 4%
49% one regular lover
15% more than one lover simultaneously

76% of married women having affairs say that their main reason is alienation from their husbands.

	AGE		EDUCATION
—%	under 18	77%	up to high school graduate
75%	18–34	78%	some college
78%	35–50	74%	college graduate
76%	51–70		
76%	71 and over		OCCUPATION/EMPLOYMENT
		75%	homemaker and/or mother (full-time)
	INCOME: annual	76%	full-time employment
74%	under $5,000	76%	part-time employment
75%	$6,000–$14,000	77%	unemployed/student
76%	$15,000–$39,000		
76%	$40,000–$74,000		
76%	over $75,000		

	RACE/ETHNICITY
76%	White
76%	Black
75%	Hispanic
76%	Middle Eastern
76%	Asian-American
75%	other

92% of married women go through a stage of fighting back against harassing and intimidating behaviors, lasting from two to four years, before many decide that another solution to the situation is an additional relationship.

	AGE		EDUCATION
—%	under 18	93%	up to high school graduate
94%	18–34	93%	some college
91%	35–50	92%	college graduate
91%	51–70		
92%	71 and over		OCCUPATION/EMPLOYMENT
		91%	homemaker and/or mother (full-time)
	INCOME: annual	92%	full-time employment
93%	under $5,000	92%	part-time employment
92%	$6,000–$14,000	93%	unemployed/student
92%	$15,000–$39,000		
91%	$40,000–$74,000		
91%	over $75,000		

	RACE/ETHNICITY
92%	White
93%	Black
92%	Hispanic
92%	Middle Eastern
92%	Asian-American
92%	other

12% of married women having affairs have only "casual sex" or one- or two-time encounters.

	AGE			EDUCATION
—%	under 18		11%	up to high school graduate
11%	18–34		12%	some college
12%	35–50		12%	college graduate
13%	51–70			
12%	71 and over			OCCUPATION/EMPLOYMENT
			13%	homemaker and/or mother (full-time)
	INCOME: annual		12%	full-time employment
13%	under $5,000		12%	part-time employment
13%	$6,000–$14,000		11%	unemployed/student
11%	$15,000–$39,000			
11%	$40,000–$74,000			
12%	over $75,000			

	RACE/ETHNICITY
12%	White
11%	Black
10%	Hispanic
14%	Middle Eastern
12%	Asian-American
12%	other

21% of married women having affairs say that one of their main reasons for having affairs is lack of sex or poor sex at home.

	AGE			EDUCATION
—%	under 18		22%	up to high school graduate
22%	18–34		20%	some college
21%	35–50		21%	college graduate
20%	51–70			
21%	71 and over			OCCUPATION/EMPLOYMENT
			21%	homemaker and/or mother (full-time)
	INCOME: annual		20%	full-time employment
21%	under $5,000		19%	part-time employment
21%	$6,000–$14,000		23%	unemployed/student
25%	$15,000–$39,000			
20%	$40,000–$74,000			
20%	over $75,000			

	RACE/ETHNICITY
22%	White
20%	Black
21%	Hispanic
21%	Middle Eastern
21%	Asian-American
20%	other

Statistical Data

6% of married women have affairs even though they have good emotional relationships with their husbands, and equal interaction.

	AGE		EDUCATION
—%	under 18	6%	up to high school graduate
5%	18–34	7%	some college
6%	35–50	6%	college graduate
7%	51–70		
6%	71 and over		OCCUPATION/EMPLOYMENT
		6%	homemaker and/or mother (full-time)
	INCOME: annual	6%	full-time employment
6%	under $5,000	5%	part-time employment
6%	$6,000–$14,000	6%	unemployed/student
8%	$15,000–$39,000		
6%	$40,000–$74,000		
5%	over $75,000		

	RACE/ETHNICITY
6%	White
7%	Black
5%	Hispanic
6%	Middle Eastern
6%	Asian-American
6%	other

12% of married women say the reason for their affairs is to add simple fun and excitement to their lives.

	AGE		EDUCATION
—%	under 18	12%	up to high school graduate
11%	18–34	13%	some college
12%	35–50	12%	college graduate
13%	51–70		
13%	71 and over		OCCUPATION/EMPLOYMENT
		14%	homemaker and/or mother (full-time)
	INCOME: annual	10%	full-time employment
12%	under $5,000	11%	part-time employment
12%	$6,000–$14,000	12%	unemployed/student
12%	$15,000–$39,000		
13%	$40,000–$74,000		
12%	over $75,000		

	RACE/ETHNICITY
13%	White
11%	Black
12%	Hispanic
12%	Middle Eastern
12%	Asian-American
11%	other

77% of married women never "fall in love" with the men they are having affairs with.*

	AGE			EDUCATION
—%	under 18		77%	up to high school graduate
78%	18–34		78%	some college
77%	35–50		77%	college graduate
76%	51–70			
77%	71 and over			OCCUPATION/EMPLOYMENT
			78%	homemaker and/or mother (full-time)
	INCOME: annual		77%	full-time employment
79%	under $5,000		75%	part-time employment
76%	$6,000–$14,000		77%	unemployed/student
76%	$15,000–$39,000			
75%	$40,000–$74,000			
77%	over $75,000			
	RACE/ETHNICITY			
77%	White			
78%	Black			
77%	Hispanic			
77%	Middle Eastern			
77%	Asian-American			
76%	other			

*This statistic is quite similar to that of men having affairs: the great majority of men also do not have affairs because they "fall in love," and they also do not "fall in love" with their lover during the affair—although they usually feel quite fond of her. See *The Hite Report on Male Sexuality*, Chapter 2.

89% of married women keep their affairs secret and/or are never "found out" (or at least never confronted by their husbands).

	AGE			EDUCATION
—%	under 18		89%	up to high school graduate
89%	18–34		88%	some college
90%	35–50		89%	college graduate
88%	51–70			
89%	71 and over			OCCUPATION/EMPLOYMENT
			88%	homemaker and/or mother (full-time)
	INCOME: annual		89%	full-time employment
89%	under $5,000		89%	part-time employment
90%	$6,000–$14,000		90%	unemployed/student
89%	$15,000–$39,000			
88%	$40,000–$74,000			
89%	over $75,000			
	RACE/ETHNICITY			
89%	White			
88%	Black			
89%	Hispanic			
89%	Middle Eastern			
90%	Asian-American			
89%	other			

76% of married women having affairs are rather matter-of-fact about their double lives and do not feel guilty.*

	AGE			EDUCATION
78%	under 18		75%	up to high school graduate
74%	18–34		76%	some college
76%	35–50		76%	college graduate
75%	51–70			
76%	71 and over			OCCUPATION/EMPLOYMENT
			76%	homemaker and/or mother (full-time)
	INCOME: annual		75%	full-time employment
76%	under $5,000		75%	part-time employment
76%	$6,000–$14,000		76%	unemployed/student
77%	$15,000–$39,000			
76%	$40,000–$74,000			
75%	over $75,000			

	RACE/ETHNICITY
76%	White
77%	Black
76%	Hispanic
76%	Middle Eastern
75%	Asian-American
76%	other

*Once again, this is similar to men's stated feelings about their affairs: 92% of men having affairs do not feel guilty for having them. See *The Hite Report on Male Sexuality*, Chapter 2.

91% of married women not having affairs describe themselves as "in love with" their husbands (as opposed to loving them) or describe a close and satisfying, emotionally equal relationship.

	AGE			EDUCATION
—%	under 18		91%	up to high school graduate
91%	18–34		90%	some college
92%	35–50		91%	college graduate
90%	51–70			
91%	71 and over			OCCUPATION/EMPLOYMENT
			90%	homemaker and/or mother (full-time)
	INCOME: annual		93%	full-time employment
91%	under $5,000		91%	part-time employment
90%	$6,000–$14,000		91%	unemployed/student
89%	$15,000–$39,000			
89%	$40,000–$74,000			
93%	over $75,000			

	RACE/ETHNICITY
91%	White
92%	Black
90%	Hispanic
91%	Middle Eastern
91%	Asian-American
91%	other

87% of married women having affairs say they believe their husbands are "faithful."*

	AGE			EDUCATION
—%	under 18		87%	up to high school graduate
88%	18–34		87%	some college
87%	35–50		86%	college graduate
87%	51–70			
86%	71 and over			OCCUPATION/EMPLOYMENT
			87%	homemaker and/or mother (full-time)
	INCOME: annual		87%	full-time employment
85%	under $5,000		87%	part-time employment
87%	$6,000–$14,000		86%	unemployed/student
90%	$15,000–$39,000			
89%	$40,000–$74,000			
89%	over $75,000			

	RACE/ETHNICITY
87%	White
88%	Black
89%	Hispanic
88%	Middle Eastern
87%	Asian-American
87%	other

*According to *The Hite Report on Male Sexuality*, 72% of men married more than two years are having sex outside of marriage, mostly unknown to their wives.

47% believe their lovers are "faithful."

	AGE			EDUCATION
—%	under 18		47%	up to high school graduate
48%	18–34		48%	some college
49%	35–50		47%	college graduate
45%	51–70			
46%	71 and over			OCCUPATION/EMPLOYMENT
			46%	homemaker and/or mother (full-time)
	INCOME: annual		47%	full-time employment
49%	under $5,000		48%	part-time employment
50%	$6,000–$14,000		47%	unemployed/student
45%	$15,000–$39,000			
45%	$40,000–$74,000			
46%	over $75,000			

	RACE/ETHNICITY
47%	White
48%	Black
47%	Hispanic
46%	Middle Eastern
47%	Asian-American
47%	other

79% of married women having affairs are having them with men who are married, not with single men.

	AGE			EDUCATION
—%	under 18		79%	up to high school graduate
80%	18–34		80%	some college
81%	35–50		79%	college graduate
77%	51–70			
78%	71 and over			OCCUPATION/EMPLOYMENT
			84%	homemaker and/or mother (full-time)
	INCOME: annual		76%	full-time employment
79%	under $5,000		77%	part-time employment
80%	$6,000–$14,000		78%	unemployed/student
81%	$15,000–$39,000			
78%	$40,000–$74,000			
78%	over $75,000			

	RACE/ETHNICITY
79%	White
79%	Black
80%	Hispanic
78%	Middle Eastern
79%	Asian-American
79%	other

14% of married women having affairs say they think an affair on the part of their husbands would be beneficial.

	AGE			EDUCATION
—%	under 18		14%	up to high school graduate
13%	18–34		13%	some college
14%	35–50		14%	college graduate
14%	51–70			
15%	71 and over			OCCUPATION/EMPLOYMENT
			14%	homemaker and/or mother (full-time)
	INCOME: annual		13%	full-time employment
14%	under $5,000		14%	part-time employment
14%	$6,000–$14,000		14%	unemployed/student
15%	$15,000–$39,000			
16%	$40,000–$74,000			
14%	over $75,000			

	RACE/ETHNICITY
14%	White
15%	Black
15%	Hispanic
14%	Middle Eastern
14%	Asian-American
14%	other

40% of men react stormily to their wives' affairs when found out (although most are never found out).

	AGE		EDUCATION
—%	under 18	41%	up to high school graduate
41%	18–34	40%	some college
42%	35–50	40%	college graduate
39%	51–70		
39%	71 and over		OCCUPATION/EMPLOYMENT
		40%	homemaker and/or mother (full-time)
	INCOME: annual	41%	full-time employment
38%	under $5,000	40%	part-time employment
39%	$6,000–$14,000	39%	unemployed/student
42%	$15,000–$39,000		
41%	$40,000–$74,000		
40%	over $75,000		

	RACE/ETHNICITY
40%	White
41%	Black
39%	Hispanic
40%	Middle Eastern
41%	Asian-American
40%	other

60% of men's reactions to their wives' affairs are low-key.

	AGE		EDUCATION
—%	under 18	60%	up to high school graduate
61%	18–34	61%	some college
60%	35–50	60%	college graduate
59%	51–70		
60%	71 and over		OCCUPATION/EMPLOYMENT
		59%	homemaker and/or mother (full-time)
	INCOME: annual	59%	full-time employment
61%	under $5,000	60%	part-time employment
60%	$6,000–$14,000	61%	unemployed/student
60%	$15,000–$39,000		
59%	$40,000–$74,000		
60%	over $75,000		

	RACE/ETHNICITY
60%	White
59%	Black
59%	Hispanic
60%	Middle Eastern
61%	Asian-American
60%	other

Statistical Data

48% of single women say they are or have been at times the "other woman" to a married man.

	AGE			EDUCATION
28%	under 18		48%	up to high school graduate
57%	18–34		47%	some college
49%	35–50		48%	college graduate
58%	51–70			
—%	71 and over			OCCUPATION/EMPLOYMENT
			48%	homemaker and/or mother (full-time)
	INCOME: annual		49%	full-time employment
49%	under $5,000		48%	part-time employment
50%	$6,000–$14,000		48%	unemployed/student
47%	$15,000–$39,000			
47%	$40,000–$74,000			
47%	over $75,000			

	RACE/ETHNICITY
48%	White
49%	Black
48%	Hispanic
48%	Middle Eastern
48%	Asian-American
49%	other

52% of single women say extramarital sex with married men is wrong or impractical, and they do not do it.

	AGE			EDUCATION
51%	under 18		51%	up to high school graduate
52%	18–34		53%	some college
54%	35–50		52%	college graduate
52%	51–70			
52%	71 and over			OCCUPATION/EMPLOYMENT
			52%	homemaker and/or mother (full-time)
	INCOME: annual		51%	full-time employment
52%	under $5,000		51%	part-time employment
53%	$6,000–$14,000		52%	unemployed/student
50%	$15,000–$39,000			
51%	$40,000–$74,000			
52%	over $75,000			

	RACE/ETHNICITY
52%	White
53%	Black
50%	Hispanic
52%	Middle Eastern
51%	Asian-American
52%	other

CHAPTER 11

Are the financial and domestic structures of marriage changing?

86% of married women who work say they like working outside the home, and prefer not to go back to the days when they did not have this choice.

	AGE		EDUCATION
—%	under 18	86%	up to high school graduate
86%	18–34	87%	some college
87%	35–50	86%	college graduate
87%	51–70		
86%	71 and over		

	INCOME: annual
86%	under $5,000
85%	$6,000–$14,000
85%	$15,000–$39,000
87%	$40,000–$74,000
86%	over $75,000

	RACE/ETHNICITY
86%	White
85%	Black
86%	Hispanic
86%	Middle Eastern
85%	Asian-American
86%	other

75% of married women who work outside the home say the reason they like it is the economic independence (or at least, in some cases, semi-independence) it brings.

	AGE		EDUCATION
—%	under 18	75%	up to high school graduate
75%	18–34	74%	some college
74%	35–50	75%	college graduate
74%	51–70		
74%	71 and over		

	INCOME: annual
74%	under $5,000
75%	$6,000–$14,000
75%	$15,000–$39,000
76%	$40,000–$74,000
75%	over $75,000

	RACE/ETHNICITY
75%	White
74%	Black
75%	Hispanic
76%	Middle Eastern
75%	Asian-American
75%	other

87% of married women who are or have been financially dependent on their husbands express feelings of discomfort in this situation, describing how they dislike asking for or using "someone else's" money, especially for themselves.

	AGE		EDUCATION
—%	under 18	87%	up to high school graduate
87%	18–34	88%	some college
88%	35–50	87%	college graduate
87%	51–70		
88%	71 and over		OCCUPATION/EMPLOYMENT
		88%	homemaker and/or mother (full-time)
	INCOME: annual	87%	full-time employment
90%	under $5,000	86%	part-time employment
85%	$6,000–$14,000	87%	unemployed/student
86%	$15,000–$39,000		
87%	$40,000–$74,000		
87%	over $75,000		

	RACE/ETHNICITY
86%	White
87%	Black
87%	Hispanic
88%	Middle Eastern
87%	Asian-American
87%	other

82% of single women under 25 years old stress that they do not want to be financially dependent in marriage.

	AGE			EDUCATION
—%	under 18		75%	up to high school graduate
—%	18–34		81%	some college
—%	35–50		79%	college graduate
—%	51–70			
—%	71 and over			

	INCOME: annual
76%	under $5,000
79%	$6,000–$14,000
85%	$15,000–$39,000
88%	$40,000–$74,000
—%	over $75,000

	RACE/ETHNICITY
82%	White
81%	Black
82%	Hispanic
82%	Middle Eastern
81%	Asian-American
82%	other

91% of married women are the family "bankers" and have the responsibility for balancing the books and paying bills.

	AGE			EDUCATION
—%	under 18		91%	up to high school graduate
90%	18–34		92%	some college
91%	35–50		91%	college graduate
92%	51–70			
91%	71 and over			OCCUPATION/EMPLOYMENT
			92%	homemaker and/or mother (full-time)
	INCOME: annual		90%	full-time employment
91%	under $5,000		91%	part-time employment
92%	$6,000–$14,000		91%	unemployed/student
92%	$15,000–$39,000			
91%	$40,000–$74,000			
91%	over $75,000			

	RACE/ETHNICITY
91%	White
92%	Black
91%	Hispanic
90%	Middle Eastern
91%	Asian-American
91%	other

76% of households in which the woman works full-time outside the home and/or has children under 12 to care for do not have concrete, equal work-sharing domestic arrangements.*

	AGE			EDUCATION
—%	under 18		76%	up to high school graduate
77%	18–34		75%	some college
76%	35–50		76%	college graduate
75%	51–70			
76%	71 and over			OCCUPATION/EMPLOYMENT
			79%	homemaker and/or mother (full-time)
	INCOME: annual		74%	full-time employment
77%	under $5,000		75%	part-time employment
76%	$6,000–$14,000		75%	unemployed/student
75%	$15,000–$39,000			
76%	$40,000–$74,000			
76%	over $75,000			

	RACE/ETHNICITY
75%	White
76%	Black
76%	Hispanic
77%	Middle Eastern
76%	Asian-American
76%	other

*Typically, concrete, equal divisions of work are not discussed; rather, it is stated that the man will "help out." Since women are used to doing housework and men are not, this usually means that the woman continues doing most of it, with the man frequently not noticing what needs to be done.

80% of women say they do most of the housework and are also the organizers and reminders for others of their part of the housework.

	AGE			EDUCATION
—%	under 18		81%	up to high school graduate
80%	18–34		80%	some college
81%	35–50		80%	college graduate
82%	51–70			
80%	71 and over			OCCUPATION/EMPLOYMENT
			82%	homemaker and/or mother (full-time)
	INCOME: annual		78%	full-time employment
80%	under $5,000		79%	part-time employment
79%	$6,000–$14,000		80%	unemployed/student
80%	$15,000–$39,000			
81%	$40,000–$74,000			
80%	over $75,000			
	RACE/ETHNICITY			
81%	White			
80%	Black			
79%	Hispanic			
80%	Middle Eastern			
80%	Asian-American			
81%	other			

23% of married women say they have reached successful and equal sharing arrangements with their husbands.

	AGE			EDUCATION
—%	under 18		23%	up to high school graduate
22%	18–34		24%	some college
23%	35–50		22%	college graduate
24%	51–70			
22%	71 and over			OCCUPATION/EMPLOYMENT
			20%	homemaker and/or mother (full-time)
	INCOME: annual		25%	full-time employment
23%	under $5,000		24%	part-time employment
25%	$6,000–$14,000		23%	unemployed/student
24%	$15,000–$39,000			
21%	$40,000–$74,000			
22%	over $75,000			
	RACE/ETHNICITY			
23%	White			
22%	Black			
20%	Hispanic			
24%	Middle Eastern			
25%	Asian-American			
25%	other			

CHAPTER 12

Women's feelings about divorce

91% of divorces are initiated by women.

	AGE		**EDUCATION**
—%	under 18	90%	up to high school graduate
93%	18–34	92%	some college
91%	35–50	91%	college graduate
89%	51–70		
—%	71 and over		**OCCUPATION/EMPLOYMENT**
		—%	homemaker and/or mother (full-time)
	INCOME: annual	91%	full-time employment
90%	under $5,000	91%	part-time employment
90%	$6,000–$14,000	91%	unemployed/student
93%	$15,000–$39,000		
91%	$40,000–$74,000		
91%	over $75,000		

	RACE/ETHNICITY
91%	White
92%	Black
91%	Hispanic
91%	Middle Eastern
90%	Asian-American
91%	other

89% of women who are separated or divorced say that they were lonelier in marriage than at any other time of their lives.

	AGE			EDUCATION
—%	under 18		90%	up to high school graduate
86%	18–34		91%	some college
89%	35–50		87%	college graduate
91%	51–70			
90%	71 and over			OCCUPATION/EMPLOYMENT
			—%	homemaker and/or mother (full-time)
	INCOME: annual		88%	full-time employment
88%	under $5,000		89%	part-time employment
89%	$6,000–$14,000		90%	unemployed/student
89%	$15,000–$39,000			
89%	$40,000–$74,000			
88%	over $75,000			
	RACE/ETHNICITY			
89%	White			
88%	Black			
87%	Hispanic			
88%	Middle Eastern			
89%	Asian-American			
89%	other			

71% of women express relief and well-being after a divorce.

	AGE			EDUCATION
—%	under 18		72%	up to high school graduate
75%	18–34		71%	some college
73%	35–50		71%	college graduate
70%	51–70			
67%	71 and over			
	INCOME: annual			
70%	under $5,000			
71%	$6,000–$14,000			
72%	$15,000–$39,000			
73%	$40,000–$74,000			
70%	over $75,000			
	RACE/ETHNICITY			
70%	White			
71%	Black			
72%	Hispanic			
71%	Middle Eastern			
71%	Asian-American			
70%	other			

24% have mixed feelings and find it hard to recover after a divorce.

	AGE			EDUCATION
—%	under 18		24%	up to high school graduate
22%	18–34		23%	some college
24%	35–50		24%	college graduate
23%	51–70			
25%	71 and over			

INCOME: annual

24%	under $5,000
22%	$6,000–$14,000
20%	$15,000–$39,000
26%	$40,000–$74,000
27%	over $75,000

RACE/ETHNICITY

24%	White
24%	Black
23%	Hispanic
24%	Middle Eastern
24%	Asian-American
24%	other

CHAPTER 13

Why do married women like being married and/or stay married?

72% of women married over three years say they appreciate most in marriage the feelings of "belonging somewhere," companionship, and security.

AGE

—%	under 18
70%	18–34
72%	35–50
74%	51–70
72%	71 and over

INCOME: annual

72%	under $5,000
73%	$6,000–$14,000
74%	$15,000–$39,000
70%	$40,000–$74,000
71%	over $75,000

RACE/ETHNICITY

72%	White
72%	Black
71%	Hispanic
71%	Middle Eastern
72%	Asian-American
73%	other

EDUCATION

72%	up to high school graduate
73%	some college
72%	college graduate

OCCUPATION/EMPLOYMENT

72%	homemaker and/or mother (full-time)
70%	full-time employment
71%	part-time employment
73%	unemployed/student

41% of women specifically mention the security that economic cooperation (not being the sole wage earner for a family) gives them.

	AGE			EDUCATION
—%	under 18		41%	up to high school graduate
41%	18–34		40%	some college
41%	35–50		41%	college graduate
42%	51–70			
41%	71 and over			OCCUPATION/EMPLOYMENT
			43%	homemaker and/or mother (full-time)
	INCOME: annual		39%	full-time employment
45%	under $5,000		40%	part-time employment
43%	$6,000–$14,000		41%	unemployed/student
40%	$15,000–$39,000			
38%	$40,000–$74,000			
39%	over $75,000			

	RACE/ETHNICITY
41%	White
41%	Black
42%	Hispanic
41%	Middle Eastern
42%	Asian-American
41%	other

82% of women married over three years say that the physical warmth, affection, and body presence of the other person is the part of marriage they most cherish, although they don't always have it consistently.

	AGE			EDUCATION
—%	under 18		82%	up to high school graduate
82%	18–34		83%	some college
83%	35–50		82%	college graduate
81%	51–70			
82%	71 and over			OCCUPATION/EMPLOYMENT
			82%	homemaker and/or mother (full-time)
	INCOME: annual		81%	full-time employment
85%	under $5,000		81%	part-time employment
80%	$6,000–$14,000		82%	unemployed/student
81%	$15,000–$39,000			
82%	$40,000–$74,000			
82%	over $75,000			

	RACE/ETHNICITY
82%	White
81%	Black
81%	Hispanic
82%	Middle Eastern
83%	Asian-American
82%	other

44% of married women say they *can* count on close physical affection on a regular basis.

	AGE		EDUCATION
—%	under 18	42%	up to high school graduate
48%	18–34	44%	some college
46%	35–50	46%	college graduate
44%	51–70		
39%	71 and over		OCCUPATION/EMPLOYMENT
		41%	homemaker and/or mother (full-time)
	INCOME: annual	46%	full-time employment
44%	under $5,000	45%	part-time employment
45%	$6,000–$14,000	44%	unemployed/student
44%	$15,000–$39,000		
43%	$40,000–$74,000		
44%	over $75,000		
	RACE/ETHNICITY		
43%	White		
44%	Black		
44%	Hispanic		
45%	Middle Eastern		
44%	Asian-American		
44%	other		

74% of married women with children say they are very happy they have their children, although this is stated separately from reasons given for liking marriage in most cases.

	AGE		EDUCATION
—%	under 18	75%	up to high school graduate
75%	18–34	74%	some college
74%	35–50	73%	college graduate
73%	51–70		
74%	71 and over		OCCUPATION/EMPLOYMENT
		76%	homemaker and/or mother (full-time)
	INCOME: annual	75%	full-time employment
71%	under $5,000	74%	part-time employment
75%	$6,000–$14,000	71%	unemployed/student
77%	$15,000–$39,000		
74%	$40,000–$74,000		
74%	over $75,000		
	RACE/ETHNICITY		
76%	White		
74%	Black		
75%	Hispanic		
74%	Middle Eastern		
74%	Asian-American		
74%	other		

19% of married women with children say having children has had a mixed effect on their relationship with their husband.

	AGE			EDUCATION
18%	under 18		19%	up to high school graduate
19%	18–34		19%	some college
20%	35–50		19%	college graduate
21%	51–70			
18%	71 and over			OCCUPATION/EMPLOYMENT
			19%	homemaker and/or mother (full-time)
	INCOME: annual		18%	full-time employment
21%	under $5,000		18%	part-time employment
19%	$6,000–$14,000		19%	unemployed/student
17%	$15,000–$39,000			
16%	$40,000–$74,000			
19%	over $75,000			
	RACE/ETHNICITY			
19%	White			
18%	Black			
19%	Hispanic			
19%	Middle Eastern			
19%	Asian-American			
20%	other			

31% of married women say having children brought them closer to their husbands.

	AGE			EDUCATION
—%	under 18		31%	up to high school graduate
30%	18–34		32%	some college
31%	35–50		31%	college graduate
30%	51–70			
32%	71 and over			OCCUPATION/EMPLOYMENT
			30%	homemaker and/or mother (full-time)
	INCOME: annual		31%	full-time employment
31%	under $5,000		32%	part-time employment
32%	$6,000–$14,000		31%	unemployed/student
32%	$15,000–$39,000			
31%	$40,000–$74,000			
31%	over $75,000			
	RACE/ETHNICITY			
31%	White			
31%	Black			
32%	Hispanic			
32%	Middle Eastern			
31%	Asian-American			
31%	other			

93% of married women over age 40 who decided not to have children say they are very happy about their decision.

	AGE		EDUCATION
—%	under 18	93%	up to high school graduate
—%	18–34	92%	some college
—%	35–50	94%	college graduate
—%	51–70		
—%	71 and over		OCCUPATION/EMPLOYMENT
		—%	homemaker and/or mother (full-time)
	INCOME: annual	92%	full-time employment
91%	under $5,000	93%	part-time employment
93%	$6,000–$14,000	93%	unemployed/student
95%	$15,000–$39,000		
93%	$40,000–$74,000		
93%	over $75,000		

	RACE/ETHNICITY
93%	White
94%	Black
93%	Hispanic
93%	Middle Eastern
92%	Asian-American
92%	other

56% of women married more than three years say they also enjoy the feeling of social acceptability of being married, fitting into a recognized social category.

	AGE		EDUCATION
—%	under 18	56%	up to high school graduate
57%	18–34	57%	some college
58%	35–50	56%	college graduate
53%	51–70		
56%	71 and over		OCCUPATION/EMPLOYMENT
		60%	homemaker and/or mother (full-time)
	INCOME: annual	53%	full-time employment
55%	under $5,000	55%	part-time employment
54%	$6,000–$14,000	56%	unemployed/student
56%	$15,000–$39,000		
58%	$40,000–$74,000		
57%	over $75,000		

	RACE/ETHNICITY
56%	White
57%	Black
56%	Hispanic
56%	Middle Eastern
55%	Asian-American
56%	other

CHAPTER 14

Is love passion or caring?

13% of women married more than two years say they are "in love" with their husbands.*

	AGE
—%	under 18
13%	18–34
12%	35–50
13%	51–70
12%	71 and over

	INCOME: annual
12%	under $5,000
14%	$6,000–$14,000
13%	$15,000–$39,000
12%	$40,000–$74,000
13%	over $75,000

	RACE/ETHNICITY
14%	White
12%	Black
13%	Hispanic
13%	Middle Eastern
13%	Asian-American
13%	other

	EDUCATION
13%	up to high school graduate
12%	some college
13%	college graduate

	OCCUPATION/EMPLOYMENT
14%	homemaker and/or mother (full-time)
13%	full-time employment
12%	part-time employment
13%	unemployed/student

*See Chapter 14 for women's differentiation between "loving" and being "in love."

82% of women married more than two years say they "love" their husbands, but are not "in love"; they love them more in a friendly than a passionate way.*

	AGE		EDUCATION
—%	under 18	82%	up to high school graduate
82%	18–34	80%	some college
83%	35–50	84%	college graduate
82%	51–70		
81%	71 and over		OCCUPATION/EMPLOYMENT
		86%	homemaker and/or mother (full-time)
	INCOME: annual	78%	full-time employment
81%	under $5,000	81%	part-time employment
82%	$6,000–$14,000	82%	unemployed/student
84%	$15,000–$39,000		
80%	$40,000–$74,000		
82%	over $75,000		
	RACE/ETHNICITY		
82%	White		
81%	Black		
82%	Hispanic		
83%	Middle Eastern		
82%	Asian-American		
82%	other		

*These women are usually the same women who describe the basic benefits of marriage as "belonging somewhere," companionship, and security.

69% of married women say they do not trust being "in love."

	AGE		EDUCATION
—%	under 18	70%	up to high school graduate
68%	18–34	69%	some college
69%	35–50	69%	college graduate
70%	51–70		
69%	71 and over		OCCUPATION/EMPLOYMENT
		71%	homemaker and/or mother (full-time)
	INCOME: annual	70%	full-time employment
69%	under $5,000	67%	part-time employment
67%	$6,000–$14,000	68%	unemployed/student
68%	$15,000–$39,000		
71%	$40,000–$74,000		
69%	over $75,000		
	RACE/ETHNICITY		
69%	White		
69%	Black		
70%	Hispanic		
70%	Middle Eastern		
69%	Asian-American		
69%	other		

47% of single women also say they do not trust being "in love."

	AGE			EDUCATION
39%	under 18		48%	up to high school graduate
49%	18–34		47%	some college
53%	35–50		46%	college graduate
48%	51–70			
47%	71 and over			OCCUPATION/EMPLOYMENT
			46%	homemaker and/or mother (full-time)
	INCOME: annual		48%	full-time employment
48%	under $5,000		47%	part-time employment
47%	$6,000–$14,000		47%	unemployed/student
47%	$15,000–$39,000			
46%	$40,000–$74,000			
47%	over $75,000			

	RACE/ETHNICITY
47%	White
48%	Black
47%	Hispanic
47%	Middle Eastern
48%	Asian-American
47%	other

54% of all women, married and single, say that stability is their basic reason for preferring "loving," defined not as passionate love but as caring.

	AGE			EDUCATION
49%	under 18		54%	up to high school graduate
53%	18–34		55%	some college
59%	35–50		54%	college graduate
54%	51–70			
54%	71 and over			OCCUPATION/EMPLOYMENT
			54%	homemaker and/or mother (full-time)
	INCOME: annual		55%	full-time employment
54%	under $5,000		53%	part-time employment
53%	$6,000–$14,000		54%	unemployed/student
53%	$15,000–$39,000			
54%	$40,000–$74,000			MARRIED/SINGLE
54%	over $75,000		48%	single, never married
			57%	divorced, separated, or widowed
	RACE/ETHNICITY		57%	married
54%	White		51%	1–5 years
53%	Black		60%	6–15 years
54%	Hispanic		55%	16–25 years
54%	Middle Eastern		62%	over 25 years
55%	Asian-American			
54%	other			

CHAPTER 16

Feelings between women: is love different?

79% of women in gay relationships say the most pleasurable part of the relationship is the combination of talking together and being physically affectionate during special intimate moments.

	AGE		EDUCATION
78%	under 18	79%	up to high school graduate
79%	18–34	80%	some college
77%	35–50	79%	college graduate
80%	51–70		
79%	71 and over		

	INCOME: annual
79%	under $5,000
78%	$6,000–$14,000
79%	$15,000–$39,000
80%	$40,000–$74,000
79%	over $75,000

	RACE/ETHNICITY
79%	White
80%	Black
79%	Hispanic
78%	Middle Eastern
79%	Asian-American
79%	other

75% of women in gay relationships say the second most pleasurable part of their relationship is sex and sensuality with another woman.

	AGE			EDUCATION
74%	under 18		73%	up to high school graduate
79%	18–34		77%	some college
77%	35–50		76%	college graduate
71%	51–70			
74%	71 and over			

INCOME: annual

74%	under $5,000
76%	$6,000–$14,000
76%	$15,000–$39,000
75%	$40,000–$74,000
75%	over $75,000

RACE/ETHNICITY

75%	White
74%	Black
76%	Hispanic
75%	Middle Eastern
75%	Asian-American
76%	other

96% of women in gay relationships say they feel loved in a satisfying way by their lover, and that their lover treats them and sees them as an equal.

	AGE			EDUCATION
97%	under 18		96%	up to high school graduate
96%	18–34		97%	some college
95%	35–50		96%	college graduate
96%	51–70			
—%	71 and over			

INCOME: annual

98%	under $5,000
94%	$6,000–$14,000
96%	$15,000–$39,000
94%	$40,000–$74,000
98%	over $75,000

RACE/ETHNICITY

95%	White
97%	Black
96%	Hispanic
96%	Middle Eastern
95%	Asian-American
96%	other

76% of women in gay relationships also mention feeling the small daily insecurities of a love relationship: "Does she love me as much as I love her?"

	AGE			EDUCATION
80%	under 18		76%	up to high school graduate
80%	18–34		75%	some college
76%	35–50		77%	college graduate
72%	51–70			
72%	71 and over			

	INCOME: annual
75%	under $5,000
76%	$6,000–$14,000
75%	$15,000–$39,000
76%	$40,000–$74,000
75%	over $75,000

	RACE/ETHNICITY
76%	White
77%	Black
76%	Hispanic
75%	Middle Eastern
75%	Asian-American
76%	other

82% of women in gay relationships say that they can talk easily and intimately with their women lovers.

	AGE			EDUCATION
83%	under 18		81%	up to high school graduate
85%	18–34		82%	some college
80%	35–50		83%	college graduate
80%	51–70			
82%	71 and over			

	INCOME: annual
82%	under $5,000
81%	$6,000–$14,000
81%	$15,000–$39,000
82%	$40,000–$74,000
83%	over $75,000

	RACE/ETHNICITY
82%	White
81%	Black
82%	Hispanic
82%	Middle Eastern
83%	Asian-American
82%	other

14% say that important talks with their lovers are not easy.

	AGE		EDUCATION
17%	under 18	14%	up to high school graduate
14%	18–34	15%	some college
10%	35–50	14%	college graduate
12%	51–70		
17%	71 and over		

	INCOME: annual
14%	under $5,000
12%	$6,000–$14,000
16%	$15,000–$39,000
13%	$40,000–$74,000
14%	over $75,000

	RACE/ETHNICITY
15%	White
14%	Black
13%	Hispanic
14%	Middle Eastern
14%	Asian-American
14%	other

15% of women in gay relationships say there is *too much* talking and analyzing of feelings.

	AGE		EDUCATION
14%	under 18	15%	up to high school graduate
15%	18–34	14%	some college
12%	35–50	16%	college graduate
18%	51–70		
—%	71 and over		

	INCOME: annual
15%	under $5,000
14%	$6,000–$14,000
16%	$15,000–$39,000
15%	$40,000–$74,000
15%	over $75,000

	RACE/ETHNICITY
15%	White
16%	Black
15%	Hispanic
16%	Middle Eastern
16%	Asian-American
15%	other

78% of women in gay relationships report fights.

	AGE			EDUCATION
76%	under 18		78%	up to high school graduate
78%	18–34		77%	some college
80%	35–50		78%	college graduate
81%	51–70			
77%	71 and over			

INCOME: annual

78%	under $5,000
77%	$6,000–$14,000
78%	$15,000–$39,000
79%	$40,000–$74,000
78%	over $75,000

RACE/ETHNICITY

78%	White
77%	Black
78%	Hispanic
78%	Middle Eastern
77%	Asian-American
78%	other

28% of women in gay relationships say their fights are alienating and left unresolved.

	AGE			EDUCATION
29%	under 18		29%	up to high school graduate
28%	18–34		28%	some college
27%	35–50		28%	college graduate
28%	51–70			
29%	71 and over			

INCOME: annual

28%	under $5,000
35%	$6,000–$14,000
28%	$15,000–$39,000
24%	$40,000–$74,000
25%	over $75,000

RACE/ETHNICITY

28%	White
29%	Black
28%	Hispanic
28%	Middle Eastern
27%	Asian-American
28%	other

72% who have fights say those fights can be intense, but usually lead to an airing of important issues, and a resolution.

	AGE			EDUCATION
71%	under 18		70%	up to high school graduate
74%	18–34		73%	some college
71%	35–50		74%	college graduate
72%	51–70			
72%	71 and over			

	INCOME: annual
72%	under $5,000
73%	$6,000–$14,000
72%	$15,000–$39,000
71%	$40,000–$74,000
72%	over $75,000

	RACE/ETHNICITY
74%	White
72%	Black
73%	Hispanic
72%	Middle Eastern
71%	Asian-American
71%	other

5% report physical violence, such as shoving and pushing, during a fight.

	AGE			EDUCATION
4%	under 18		6%	up to high school graduate
5%	18–34		5%	some college
6%	35–50		5%	college graduate
6%	51–70			
5%	71 and over			

	INCOME: annual
5%	under $5,000
6%	$6,000–$14,000
5%	$15,000–$39,000
4%	$40,000–$74,000
5%	over $75,000

	RACE/ETHNICITY
5%	White
4%	Black
5%	Hispanic
6%	Middle Eastern
5%	Asian-American
4%	other

33% of arguments are about outside lovers.

	AGE			EDUCATION
32%	under 18		34%	up to high school graduate
34%	18–34		33%	some college
34%	35–50		33%	college graduate
32%	51–70			
33%	71 and over			

	INCOME: annual
33%	under $5,000
35%	$6,000–$14,000
31%	$15,000–$39,000
32%	$40,000–$74,000
33%	over $75,000

	RACE/ETHNICITY
32%	White
34%	Black
33%	Hispanic
33%	Middle Eastern
33%	Asian-American
33%	other

87% of gay women say they believe in monogamy in love relationships.

	AGE			EDUCATION
89%	under 18		87%	up to high school graduate
85%	18–34		86%	some college
87%	35–50		86%	college graduate
87%	51–70			
87%	71 and over			

	INCOME: annual
86%	under $5,000
87%	$6,000–$14,000
87%	$15,000–$39,000
86%	$40,000–$74,000
86%	over $75,000

	RACE/ETHNICITY
87%	White
88%	Black
89%	Hispanic
87%	Middle Eastern
85%	Asian-American
86%	other

33% of gay women have had or are having sex outside their relationships.

	AGE			EDUCATION
34%	under 18		33%	up to high school graduate
33%	18–34		32%	some college
32%	35–50		34%	college graduate
33%	51–70			
34%	71 and over			

	INCOME: annual
33%	under $5,000
34%	$6,000–$14,000
33%	$15,000–$39,000
32%	$40,000–$74,000
33%	over $75,000

	RACE/ETHNICITY
31%	White
32%	Black
34%	Hispanic
36%	Middle Eastern
32%	Asian-American
33%	other

Half of gay women's affairs are known to their partners, although rarely accepted with equanimity.*

	AGE			EDUCATION
57%	under 18		52%	up to high school graduate
51%	18–34		50%	some college
46%	35–50		48%	college graduate
46%	51–70			
—%	71 and over			

	INCOME: annual
52%	under $5,000
50%	$6,000–$14,000
49%	$15,000–$39,000
48%	$40,000–$74,000
51%	over $75,000

	RACE/ETHNICITY
51%	White
50%	Black
49%	Hispanic
50%	Middle Eastern
50%	Asian-American
51%	other

*Gay women in couples are much more likely to know of each other's affairs than those in heterosexual relationships, especially marriages. Perhaps one reason is that most gay women talk so freely with each other, that it is not quite in character to hide this; also, the gay community in most cities is rather small and close-knit.

39% of gay women say they enjoy "casual sex" with other women.

	AGE			EDUCATION
45%	under 18		41%	up to high school graduate
40%	18–34		37%	some college
37%	35–50		39%	college graduate
34%	51–70			
—%	71 and over			

	INCOME: annual
39%	under $5,000
40%	$6,000–$14,000
41%	$15,000–$39,000
38%	$40,000–$74,000
38%	over $75,000

	RACE/ETHNICITY
39%	White
40%	Black
39%	Hispanic
39%	Middle Eastern
38%	Asian-American
39%	other

61% of gay women have been monogamous through all of their important relationships.

	AGE			EDUCATION
—%	under 18		63%	up to high school graduate
62%	18–34		60%	some college
61%	35–50		60%	college graduate
60%	51–70			
61%	71 and over			

	INCOME: annual
63%	under $5,000
60%	$6,000–$14,000
60%	$15,000–$39,000
60%	$40,000–$74,000
61%	over $75,000

	RACE/ETHNICITY
61%	White
62%	Black
61%	Hispanic
62%	Middle Eastern
61%	Asian-American
61%	other

31% of gay women have been or consider themselves currently married, in a "woman-to-woman marriage."

AGE		EDUCATION	
—%	under 18	30%	up to high school graduate
32%	18–34	31%	some college
30%	35–50	30%	college graduate
31%	51–70		
—%	71 and over		

INCOME: annual	
31%	under $5,000
32%	$6,000–$14,000
34%	$15,000–$39,000
30%	$40,000–$74,000
30%	over $75,000

RACE/ETHNICITY	
31%	White
32%	Black
31%	Hispanic
30%	Middle Eastern
31%	Asian-American
30%	other

46% of gay women over 40 are or have been in love relationships of ten years or more.

AGE		EDUCATION	
—%	under 18	75%	up to high school graduate
—%	18–34	76%	some college
—%	35–50	76%	college graduate
—%	51–70		
—%	71 and over		

INCOME: annual	
75%	under $5,000
75%	$6,000–$14,000
77%	$15,000–$39,000
76%	$40,000–$74,000
77%	over $75,000

RACE/ETHNICITY	
76%	White
75%	Black
76%	Hispanic
77%	Middle Eastern
77%	Asian-American
76%	other

64% of gay women remain long-term friends with their most serious lovers.

	AGE			EDUCATION
—%	under 18		64%	up to high school graduate
65%	18–34		64%	some college
66%	35–50		63%	college graduate
62%	51–70			
64%	71 and over			

	INCOME: annual
63%	under $5,000
64%	$6,000–$14,000
64%	$15,000–$39,000
65%	$40,000–$74,000
64%	over $75,000

	RACE/ETHNICITY
65%	White
64%	Black
63%	Hispanic
64%	Middle Eastern
64%	Asian-American
65%	other

64% of gay women who are financially dependent or partially financially dependent in their relationships say that they feel uncomfortable about this and would like to change it.

	AGE			EDUCATION
66%	under 18		64%	up to high school graduate
65%	18–34		65%	some college
64%	35–50		65%	college graduate
64%	51–70			
61%	71 and over			

	INCOME: annual
64%	under $5,000
61%	$6,000–$14,000
68%	$15,000–$39,000
64%	$40,000–$74,000
65%	over $75,000

	RACE/ETHNICITY
65%	White
64%	Black
64%	Hispanic
63%	Middle Eastern
64%	Asian-American
63%	other

24% of gay women have tried a lesbian relationship for the first time after age 40.

	AGE			EDUCATION
—%	under 18		24%	up to high school graduate
—%	18–34		26%	some college
—%	35–50		24%	college graduate
—%	51–70			
—%	71 and over			

INCOME: annual

23%	under $5,000
22%	$6,000–$14,000
24%	$15,000–$39,000
26%	$40,000–$74,000
25%	over $75,000

RACE/ETHNICITY

25%	White
23%	Black
24%	Hispanic
24%	Middle Eastern
24%	Asian-American
23%	other

32% of women now in gay relationships were married heterosexually before.

	AGE			EDUCATION
—%	under 18		31%	up to high school graduate
31%	18–34		32%	some college
33%	35–50		32%	college graduate
33%	51–70			
32%	71 and over			

INCOME: annual

30%	under $5,000
34%	$6,000–$14,000
34%	$15,000–$39,000
32%	$40,000–$74,000
32%	over $75,000

RACE/ETHNICITY

32%	White
31%	Black
31%	Hispanic
30%	Middle Eastern
33%	Asian-American
32%	other

19% of women have changed either from a heterosexual to a homosexual relationship or vice versa, and say they would consider doing so again (changing back).

	AGE			EDUCATION
—%	under 18		19%	up to high school graduate
18%	18–34		18%	some college
17%	35–50		18%	college graduate
20%	51–70			
20%	71 and over			

	INCOME: annual
21%	under $5,000
19%	$6,000–$14,000
18%	$15,000–$39,000
18%	$40,000–$74,000
19%	over $75,000

	RACE/ETHNICITY
19%	White
18%	Black
18%	Hispanic
19%	Middle Eastern
20%	Asian-American
21%	other

54% of gay women say that being gay for them is biological, that they "always knew."

	AGE			EDUCATION
57%	under 18		56%	up to high school graduate
54%	18–34		52%	some college
50%	35–50		54%	college graduate
55%	51–70			
54%	71 and over			

	INCOME: annual
55%	under $5,000
54%	$6,000–$14,000
53%	$15,000–$39,000
55%	$40,000–$74,000
54%	over $75,000

	RACE/ETHNICITY
55%	White
54%	Black
55%	Hispanic
55%	Middle Eastern
54%	Asian-American
55%	other

46% say that their being gay was a choice.

	AGE			EDUCATION
45%	under 18		45%	up to high school graduate
44%	18–34		46%	some college
48%	35–50		45%	college graduate
47%	51–70			
46%	71 and over			

INCOME: annual

46%	under $5,000
46%	$6,000–$14,000
46%	$15,000–$39,000
45%	$40,000–$74,000
46%	over $75,000

RACE/ETHNICITY

45%	White
47%	Black
48%	Hispanic
44%	Middle Eastern
45%	Asian-American
46%	other

67% of gay women state that they are very proud of being gay.

	AGE			EDUCATION
61%	under 18		67%	up to high school graduate
72%	18–34		68%	some college
68%	35–50		67%	college graduate
70%	51–70			
64%	71 and over			

INCOME: annual

66%	under $5,000
67%	$6,000–$14,000
69%	$15,000–$39,000
68%	$40,000–$74,000
67%	over $75,000

RACE/ETHNICITY

67%	White
67%	Black
68%	Hispanic
67%	Middle Eastern
66%	Asian-American
66%	other

CHAPTER 17

Women's struggle to change the whole aura and understanding of relationships with men

83% of women say they do not believe most men understand the basic issues involved in making intimate relationships work.

	AGE		EDUCATION
81%	under 18	84%	up to high school graduate
83%	18–34	83%	some college
85%	35–50	83%	college graduate
84%	51–70		
83%	71 and over		OCCUPATION/EMPLOYMENT
		79%	homemaker and/or mother (full-time)
	INCOME: annual	85%	full-time employment
80%	under $5,000	85%	part-time employment
84%	$6,000–$14,000	83%	unemployed/student
86%	$15,000–$39,000		
82%	$40,000–$74,000		MARRIED/SINGLE
83%	over $75,000	84%	single, never married
		83%	divorced, separated, or widowed
	RACE/ETHNICITY	82%	married
82%	White	80%	1–5 years
83%	Black	82%	6–15 years
83%	Hispanic	85%	16–25 years
82%	Middle Eastern	82%	over 25 years
81%	Asian-American		
83%	other		

71% of women in marriages and relationships of more than two years have not been able to produce significant change in their relationships by asking for it, "bringing up the issues," or "working at it."*

	AGE			EDUCATION
—%	under 18		70%	up to high school graduate
71%	18–34		72%	some college
72%	35–50		71%	college graduate
72%	51–70			
71%	71 and over			OCCUPATION/EMPLOYMENT
			71%	homemaker and/or mother (full-time)
	INCOME: annual		71%	full-time employment
70%	under $5,000		71%	part-time employment
72%	$6,000–$14,000		71%	unemployed/student
72%	$15,000–$39,000			
70%	$40,000–$74,000			
71%	over $75,000			
	RACE/ETHNICITY			
71%	White			
73%	Black			
72%	Hispanic			
71%	Middle Eastern			
71%	Asian-American			
71%	other			

*However, 32% were able to bring about change by leaving, ceasing to provide emotional services, while waiting for the man to see what kind of closeness the woman had withdrawn so that he could develop his skills in returning it, becoming empathic.

21% of women have changed non-communicative relationships into equal and interactive relationships, often by going to counseling sessions with the man.

	AGE		EDUCATION
—%	under 18	22%	up to high school graduate
20%	18–34	19%	some college
21%	35–50	22%	college graduate
22%	51–70		
21%	71 and over		OCCUPATION/EMPLOYMENT
		23%	homemaker and/or mother (full-time)
	INCOME: annual	21%	full-time employment
21%	under $5,000	20%	part-time employment
22%	$6,000–$14,000	20%	unemployed/student
24%	$15,000–$39,000		
20%	$40,000–$74,000		MARRIED/SINGLE
20%	over $75,000	20%	single, never married
		20%	divorced, separated, or widowed
	RACE/ETHNICITY	23%	married
24%	White	21%	1–5 years
20%	Black	24%	6–15 years
19%	Hispanic	24%	16–25 years
21%	Middle Eastern	23%	over 25 years
21%	Asian-American		
21%	other		

17% of women believe change is impossible: "this is the way men are."

	AGE		EDUCATION
13%	under 18	17%	up to high school graduate
11%	18–34	18%	some college
17%	35–50	16%	college graduate
21%	51–70		
25%	71 and over		OCCUPATION/EMPLOYMENT
		16%	homemaker and/or mother (full-time)
	INCOME: annual	19%	full-time employment
17%	under $5,000	18%	part-time employment
18%	$6,000–$14,000	18%	unemployed/student
17%	$15,000–$39,000		
18%	$40,000–$74,000		MARRIED/SINGLE
17%	over $75,000	15%	single, never married
		19%	divorced, separated, or widowed
	RACE/ETHNICITY	17%	married
17%	White	16%	1–5 years
19%	Black	16%	6–15 years
18%	Hispanic	18%	16–25 years
17%	Middle Eastern	18%	over 25 years
17%	Asian-American		
17%	other		

88% of women, single and married, have begun to ask themselves deeper questions about men and men's behavior in relationships, wondering why the culture has created so much confusion in men about expressing their feelings and being comfortable being equal with women.

	AGE		EDUCATION
89%	under 18	87%	up to high school graduate
88%	18–34	88%	some college
87%	35–50	88%	college graduate
88%	51–70		
89%	71 and over		OCCUPATION/EMPLOYMENT
		87%	homemaker and/or mother (full-time)
	INCOME: annual	88%	full-time employment
88%	under $5,000	88%	part-time employment
86%	$6,000–$14,000	87%	unemployed/student
89%	$15,000–$39,000		
89%	$40,000–$74,000		MARRIED/SINGLE
87%	over $75,000	89%	single, never married
		90%	divorced, separated, or widowed
	RACE/ETHNICITY	86%	married
87%	White	85%	1–5 years
88%	Black	86%	6–15 years
88%	Hispanic	87%	16–25 years
86%	Middle Eastern	87%	over 25 years
87%	Asian-American		
87%	other		

CHAPTER 18

Women's friendships: a different cultural system in action

94% of women describe very close, important, and enjoyable friendships with other women.

	AGE			EDUCATION
96%	under 18		94%	up to high school graduate
94%	18–34		93%	some college
95%	35–50		93%	college graduate
94%	51–70			
92%	71 and over			OCCUPATION/EMPLOYMENT
			92%	homemaker and/or mother (full-time)
	INCOME: annual		96%	full-time employment
94%	under $5,000		94%	part-time employment
98%	$6,000–$14,000		93%	unemployed/student
91%	$15,000–$39,000			
93%	$40,000–$74,000			MARRIED/SINGLE
94%	over $75,000		94%	single, never married
			95%	divorced, separated, or widowed
	RACE/ETHNICITY		94%	married
94%	White			93% 1–5 years
93%	Black			94% 6–15 years
93%	Hispanic			95% 16–25 years
95%	Middle Eastern			94% over 25 years
95%	Asian-American			
94%	other			

85% say the most wonderful quality of their friendships with women is the ability to talk freely and openly without being judged, to be truly listened to.

	AGE			EDUCATION
84%	under 18		84%	up to high school graduate
83%	18–34		85%	some college
82%	35–50		86%	college graduate
85%	51–70			
86%	71 and over			OCCUPATION/EMPLOYMENT
			87%	homemaker and/or mother (full-time)
	INCOME: annual		85%	full-time employment
85%	under $5,000		83%	part-time employment
84%	$6,000–$14,000		85%	unemployed/student
86%	$15,000–$39,000			
86%	$40,000–$74,000			MARRIED/SINGLE
85%	over $75,000		85%	single, never married
			84%	divorced, separated, or widowed
	RACE/ETHNICITY		86%	married
85%	White		85%	1–5 years
84%	Black		86%	6–15 years
86%	Hispanic		87%	16–25 years
85%	Middle Eastern		86%	over 25 years
85%	Asian-American			
85%	other			

87% of women say that their friendships with other women are emotionally closer than their love relationships with men.

	AGE			EDUCATION
88%	under 18		87%	up to high school graduate
89%	18–34		86%	some college
85%	35–50		87%	college graduate
86%	51–70			
87%	71 and over			OCCUPATION/EMPLOYMENT
			87%	homemaker and/or mother (full-time)
	INCOME: annual		87%	full-time employment
87%	under $5,000		85%	part-time employment
90%	$6,000–$14,000		86%	unemployed/student
85%	$15,000–$39,000			
86%	$40,000–$74,000			MARRIED/SINGLE
87%	over $75,000		89%	single, never married
			88%	divorced, separated, or widowed
	RACE/ETHNICITY		84%	married
87%	White		83%	1–5 years
88%	Black		84%	6–15 years
89%	Hispanic		84%	16–25 years
88%	Middle Eastern		85%	over 25 years
87%	Asian-American			
87%	other			

89% of women emphasize that they want to make their relationships with men as close, happy, and equal as their relationships with their women friends.

	AGE		EDUCATION
90%	under 18	90%	up to high school graduate
89%	18–34	89%	some college
88%	35–50	88%	college graduate
89%	51–70		
89%	71 and over		OCCUPATION/EMPLOYMENT
		88%	homemaker and/or mother (full-time)
	INCOME: annual	89%	full-time employment
88%	under $5,000	90%	part-time employment
89%	$6,000–$14,000	90%	unemployed/student
86%	$15,000–$39,000		
90%	$40,000–$74,000		MARRIED/SINGLE
89%	over $75,000	87%	single, never married
		88%	divorced, separated, or widowed
	RACE/ETHNICITY	92%	married
90%	White	94%	1–5 years
90%	Black	92%	6–15 years
89%	Hispanic	90%	16–25 years
89%	Middle Eastern	91%	over 25 years
89%	Asian-American		
89%	other		

Bibliography and Additional Reading

Following is a partial bibliography of some of the important works relevant to this book, including many of the classics produced by women during the last ten years, as described in Chapter 19. It is inevitable that many significant works are not included here, as the amount of scholarship produced is so vast—the outpouring of what Jessie Bernard has termed "The Feminist Enlightenment."

ACKERONI, FRANCESCO. *Innamoramento E Amore.* Rome: Garzani Editore s.p.a., 1979.

ALEXANDER, JEFFREY C. *Theoretical Logic in Sociology:* Vol. 3, The Classical Attempt at Theoretical Synthesis: Max Weber. London: Routledge & Kegan Paul, 1984.

ALIC, MARGARET. *Hypatia's Heritage: A History of Women in Science from Antiquity to the Late Nineteenth Century.* Boston: Beacon Press, 1986.

ALLAN, GRAHAM. *Family Life: Domestic Roles and Social Organization.* New York: Basil Blackwell, 1985.

ALLGEIER, ELIZABETH RICE, and NAOMI MCCORMICK, eds. *Changing Boundaries.* Gloversville, N.Y.: Mayfield, 1982.

ARENDT, HANNAH. *The Origin of Totalitarianism.* New York: Harcourt Brace Jovanovich, 1951.

ARIÈS, PHILIPPE. *Centuries of Childhood: A Social History of Family Life,* trans. Robert Baldick. New York: Alfred A. Knopf, 1962.

———, and ANDRÉ BEJIN. *Western Sexuality: Practice and Precept in Past and Present Times,* trans. Anthony Forster. New York: Basil Blackwell, 1983.

ARIÈS, PHILIPPE, and PAUL VEYNE, eds. *History of Private Life: From Pagan Rome to Byzantium,* Vol. 1. Cambridge: Harvard University Press, 1987.

ARON, ARTHUR, and ELAINE ARON. *Love and the Expansion of Self.* New York: Hemisphere, 1985.

ASHWORTH, GEORGINA, ed. *Women's Studies International Forum.* Vol. 8, No. 2: "The U.N. Decade for Women, An International Evaluation." Oxford: Pergamon Press, 1985.

BACHOFEN, J. J. *Myth, Religion and Mother Right.* Princeton: Princeton University Press, 1967.

BACON, MARGARET HOPE. *Mothers of Feminism: The Story of Quaker Women in America.* New York: Harper & Row, 1987.

BARBACK, CONNIE. *For Each Other.* New York: Signet/New American Library, 1985.

BARDWICK, JUDITH. *Readings on the Psychology of Women.* New York: Harper & Row, 1971.

BARON, DENNIS. *Grammar and Gender.* New Haven: Yale University Press, 1986.

BARRY, KATHLEEN. *Female Sexual Slavery.* New York: New York University Press, 1984.

BART, PAULINE. *Stopping Rape.* New York: Pergamon Press, 1985.

BAZIN, GERMAINE. *The Louvre.* New York: Abrams, 1958.

BEARD, MARY R. *Women as Force in History.* New York: Macmillan, 1946.

BEAUVOIR, SIMONE DE. *After "The Second Sex" (Conversations with Simone de Beauvoir and Alice Schwarzer).* New York: Pantheon, 1986.

———. *La Ceremonie des adieux; suis de Entretiens avec Jean-Paul Sartre.* Paris: Gallimard, 1981.

———. *When Things of the Spirit Come First,* trans. Patrick O'Brian. New York: Pantheon, 1982.

———. *The Second Sex.* New York: Alfred A. Knopf, 1953.

———. *The Woman Destroyed,* trans. Patrick O'Brian. New York: Putnam, 1969.

BELL, SUSAN G., and KAREN M. OFFEN. *Women, the Family and Freedom: The Debate in Documents.* Vol. 1: 1750–1880. Stanford: Stanford University Press, 1982.

BELLAH, ROBERT N., et al. *Habits of the Heart: Individualism and Commitment in American Life.* New York: Harper & Row, 1985.

BENEVENTO, NICOLE, ed. *Building Feminist Theory: Essays from Quest, A Feminist Quarterly.* New York: Longman, 1981.

BENSON-VON DER OHE, ELIZABETH, and VALMARI M. MASON. *An Annotated Bibliography of U.S. Scholarship on the History of the Family.* (Preliminary draft.) Munich: U.S. Family History Project, 1984.

BENVENUTO, BICE, and ROGER KENNEDY. *The Works of Jacques Lacan.* New York: St. Martin's Press, 1986.

BERGMANN, BARBARA. *The Economic Emergence of Women.* New York: Basic Books, 1986.

BERKIN, CAROL RUTH, and MARY BETH NORTON. *Women of American History.* Boston: Houghton Mifflin, 1979.

BERNARD, JESSIE S. *American Family Behavior.* New York: Harper & Row, 1942.

———. *The Female World.* New York: Free Press, 1981.

———. *The Future of Marriage.* New Haven: Yale University Press, 1972.

———. *The Future of Motherhood.* New York: Dial Press, 1974.

BETTELHEIM, BRUNO. *Surviving and Other Essays.* New York: Alfred A. Knopf, 1979.

BINGEN, HILDEGARD of. *Scivias/Know the Ways.* Santa Fe, N.M.: Bear & Company, 1986.

BIRD, CAROLINE. *The Two-Paycheck Marriage.* New York: Rawson, Wade, 1979.

BLEIER, RUTH. *Science and Gender: A Critique of Biology and Its Theories Of Women.* New York: Pergamon Press, 1984.

BLUMSTEIN, PHILIP, and PEPPER SCHWARTZ. *American Couples: Money, Work, Sex.* New York: William Morrow & Co., 1983.

BONFIELD, LLOYD, RICHARD SMITH, and KEITH WRIGHTSON, eds. *The World We Have Gained: Histories of Population and Social Structure.* New York: Basil Blackwell, 1986.

BOON, JAMES A. *Other Tribes, Other Scribes: Symbolic Anthropology in the Comparative Study of Cultures, Histories, Religions and Texts,* New York: Cambridge University Press, 1983.

BOSWELL, JOHN. *Christianity, Social Tolerance, and Homosexuality: Gay People in Western Europe from the Beginning of the Christian Era to the Fourteenth Century.* Chicago: University of Chicago Press, 1976.

BOWERS, JANE, and JUDITH TICK, eds. *Women Making Music: The Western Art Tradition, 1150–1950.* Champaign, Ill.: University of Illinois Press, 1987.

BOWLES, GLORIA, and RENATE DUELLI KLEIN, eds. *Theories of Women's Studies.* London: Routledge and Kegan Paul, 1983.

BRADLEY, MICHAEL, et al. *Unbecoming Men.* Washington, N.J.: Times Change Press, 1971.

BRIDENTHAL, RENATE, and CLAUDIA KOOZ, eds. *Becoming Visible: Women in European History.* Boston: Houghton Mifflin, 1977.

BRONER, E. M. *A Weave of Women.* Bloomington, Ind.: Indiana University Press, 1985.

BRONNER, LEAH. *Biblical Personalities and Archeaology.* Jerusalem, Israel: Keter Publishing House Jerusalem Ltd., 1974.

BROWN, JUDITH C. *Immodest Acts: The Life of a Lesbian Nun in Renaissance Italy.* New York: Oxford University Press, 1986.

BROWN, JUDITH K., and VIRGINIA KERNS, eds. *In Her Prime: A New View of Middle-Aged Women.* South Hadley, Mass.: Bergin and Garvey, 1985.

BROWNMILLER, SUSAN. *Against Our Will.* New York: Simon & Schuster, 1975.

———. *Femininity.* New York: Simon & Schuster, 1984.

BRUUN, GEOFFREY. *Nineteenth-Century European Civilization: 1815–1914.* New York: Oxford University Press, 1957.

BULLOUGH, VERN L. *Sexual Variance in Society and History.* Chicago: University of Chicago Press, 1980.

———, and BONNIE BULLOUGH. *The Subordinate Sex: A History of Attitudes Towards Women.* Champaign, Ill.: University of Illinois Press, 1973.

BULMER, MARTIN. *The Chicago School of Sociology: Institutionalization, Diversity and the Rise of Sociological Research.* Chicago: University of Chicago Press, 1984.

———. *Theory and Understanding: A Critique of Interpretive Social Science.* Oxford: Basil Blackwell, 1986.

BUNCH, CHARLOTTE. *Feminism in the '80s . . . Books 1, 2 & 3.* Denver: Antelope Publications, 1983.

———, et al., eds. *Building Feminist Theory . . . Essays From Quest, A Feminist Quarterly.* New York: Longman, 1981.

BURCKHARDT, JACOB. *The Civilization of the Renaissance in Italy.* Oxford: Phaidon Press, 1945.

BYNUM, CAROLINE WALKER. *Jesus as Mother: Studies in the Spirituality of the High Middle Ages.* Berkeley: University of California Press, 1982.

CALHOUN, CHESHIRE, and ROBERT C. SOLOMON, eds. *What Is an Emotion? Classic Readings in Philosophical Psychiatry.* New York: Oxford University Press, 1984.

CAMBRIDGE WOMEN'S STUDY GROUP. *Women in Society: Interdisciplinary Essays.* New York: Virago Press/Merrimack, 1983.

CAMPBELL, ELAINE. *The Childless Marriage, An Exploratory Study of Couples Who Do Not Want Children.* New York: Tavistock/Methuen, 1986.

CAPLAN, PAULA J. *The Myth of Woman's Masochism.* New York: Dutton, 1985.

CAPRA, FRITJOF, CHARLENE SPRETNAK, and RUDIGER LUTZ. *Green Politics.* New York: Dutton, 1984.

CARDLAND, DOUGLAS K., JOSEPH P. FELL, et al. *Emotion.* Belmont, Mass.: Wadsworth Publishing Company, 1977.

CARNE, MARCEL. *Children of Paradise.* New York: Simon & Schuster, 1967.

CARSON, RACHEL. *Silent Spring.* New York: Houghton Mifflin, 1962.

CHABROL, CLAUDE. *Le Recit Feminin: Contribution a L'Analyse Semiologique Du Courrier Du Coeur et . . . Dans La Presse Feminine Actuelle* (Approaches to Semiotics Series, no. 15). Hawthorne, N.Y.: Mouton, 1971.

CHADWICK, JOHN. *The Mycenaean World.* New York: Cambridge University Press, 1976.

CHAFE, WILLIAM H. *The American Woman: Her Changing Social, Economic, and Political Roles, 1920–1970.* New York: Oxford University Press, 1972.

———. *Women and Equality: Changing Patterns in American Culture.* New York: Oxford University Press, 1977.

CHAFETZ, JANET SALTZMAN. *Sex and Advantage: A Comparative, Macro-Structural Theory of Sex Stratification.* Totowa, N.J.: Rowman & Allanheld, 1984.

CHAMBERS-SCHILLER, VIRGINIA LEE. *Liberty, A Better Husband: Single Women in America, The Generations of 1780–1840.* New Haven: Yale University Press, 1984.

CHASE, KAREN. *Eros & Psyche: The Representation of Personality in Charlotte Brontë, Charles Dickens, George Eliot.* New York: Methuen, 1982.

CHERLIN, ANDREW J. *Marriage, Divorce, Remarriage.* Cambridge: Harvard University Press, 1981.

CHESLER, PHYLLIS. *Mothers on Trial.* New York: McGraw-Hill, 1986.

———. *Women and Madness.* New York: Avon, 1973.

CHICAGO, JUDY. *The Complete Dinner Party.* New York: Anchor Press/Doubleday, 1981.

CLARK, ALICE. *Working Life of Women in the 17th Century.* New York: Methuen, 1982.

CLARK, CHERYL. *Living as a Lesbian.* Ithaca, N.Y.: Firebrand, 1986.

CLAVIERE, MAUDE LA, and MARIE ALPHONSE DE RENE. *The Women of the Renaissance.* Norwood, Pa.: Norwood Editions, 1980.

CLIERI, PRES. *Considering Parenthood.* San Francisco: Spinsters Ink, 1985.

COREA, GENE. *The Mother Machine.* New York: Harper & Row, 1985.

———, R. DUELLI-KLEIN, J. HANNER, et al. *Hutchinson Education in Association with the Explorations in Feminism Collective.* London: Pergamon Press, 1986.

CORNWELL, ANITA. *Black Lesbian in White America.* Tallahassee: Naiad Press, 1983.

COTT, NANCY F. *The Bonds of Womanhood: "Woman's Sphere" in New England, 1780–1835.* New Haven: Yale University Press, 1977.

———, and ELIZABETH PLECK. *A Heritage of Her Own: Families, Work and Feminism in America.* New York: Simon & Schuster, 1980.

————, eds. *A Heritage of Her Own: Toward a New Social History of American Women.* New York: Simon & Schuster, 1979.

Courage Magazine, Germany.

COWAN, RUTH SCHWARTZ. *More Work for Mother: The Ironies of Household Technology from the Open Hearth to the Microwave.* New York: Basic Books, 1983.

CRAWFORD, LINDA, and LEE LANNING. *Loving: Women Talk About their Love Relationships.* Minneapolis: Midwest Health Center for Women, 1981.

CURTIN, MARY E. *Symposium on Love.* New York: Human Science Press, 1973.

DALY, MARY. *Beyond God the Father: Toward a Philosophy of Women's Liberation.* Boston: Beacon Press, 1985.

————. *Gyn-Ecology: The Metaethics of Radical Feminism.* Boston: Beacon Press, 1979.

————. *Pure Lust: Elemental Feminist Philosophy.* Boston: Beacon Press, 1984.

DARNTON, ROBERT. *The Great Cat Massacre and Other Episodes in French Cultural History.* New York: Random House, 1984.

DARWIN, CHARLES. *The Origin of the Species and the Descent of Man.* New York: Random House/Modern Library.

DAVIS, DAVID BRION. *The Problem of Slavery in the Age of Revolution, 1770–1823.* Ithaca, N.Y.: Cornell University Press, 1983.

DAVIS, NATALIE ZEMON. *The Return of Martin Guerre.* Cambridge: Harvard University Press, 1983.

————. *Society and Culture in Early Modern France.* Stanford: Stanford University Press, 1965.

————, and JOAN WALLACH SCOTT. *Women's History as Women's Education.* Northampton, Mass. Sophia Smith Collection of Smith College, 1985.

DEGLER, CARL N. *At Odds: Women and the Family in America from the Revolution to the Present.* New York: Oxford University Press, 1980.

DeKOVEN, MARIANNE. *Gertrude's Granddaughters.* New York: New Feminist Library, 1986.

DE WAAL, FRANS. *Chimpanzee Politics: Power and Sex Among Apes.* New York: Harper & Row, 1983.

DINER, HELEN. *Mothers and Amazons: The First Feminine History of Culture.* Garden City, N.Y.: Anchor Press/Doubleday, 1965.

DREYFUS, HUBERT L., and PAUL RABINOW. *Michel Foucault: Beyond Structuralism and Hermeneutics.* Chicago: University of Chicago Press, 1982.

DuBOIS, ELLEN C. *Feminism and Suffrage: The Emergence of an Independent Women's Movement in America 1848–1869.* Ithaca: Cornell University Press, 1978.

————, et al. *Feminist Scholarship: Kindling Groves of Academe.* Champaign, Ill.: University of Illinois Press, 1978.

DWORKIN, ANDREA. *Ice and Fire.* London: Secker and Warburg, 1986.

————. *Right Wing Women: The Politics of Domesticated Women.* New York: Putnam, 1983.

ERKHARDT, ANKE A. and JOHN MONEY. *Man & Woman, Boy & Girl: Differentiation and Dimorphism of Gender Identity from Conception to Maturity.* Baltimore: Johns Hopkins University Press, 1972.

EHRENREICH, BARBARA. *The Hearts of Men: American Dreams and the Flight from Commitment.* New York: Anchor Press/Doubleday, 1983.

————, ELIZABETH HESS, and GLORIA JACOBS. *Remaking Love: The Feminization of Sex.* New York: Anchor Press/Doubleday, 1986.

EICHENBAUM, LUISE, and SUSIE ORBACH. *What do women want? Exploding the Myth of Female Dependency.* New York: Coward, McCann, & Geoghegan, 1983.

EICHLER, MARGRIT. *The Double Standard: A Feminist Critique of Feminist Social Science.* New York: St. Martin's Press, 1980.

ELIAS, NORBERT. *The History of Manners.* New York: Pantheon, 1978.

ELLIS, ALBERT, PH.D. *How to Live With—and Without—Anger.* New York: Reader's Digest Press, 1977.

————. *Overcoming Resistance: Rational-Emotive Therapy With Difficult Clients.* New York: Springer Publishing Co., 1985.

EMERSON, ROBERT M. *Contemporary Field Research.* Boston: Little, Brown, 1983.

FADERMAN, LILLIAN. *Surpassing the Love of Men: Romantic Friendship and Love Between Women From the Renaissance to the Present.* New York: William Morrow & Co., 1981.

FASS, PAULA S. *The Damned and the Beautiful: American Youth in the 1920's.* New York: Oxford University Press, 1977.

FAUSTO-STERLING, ANNE. *Myths of Gender: Biological Theories About Women and Men.* New York: Basic Books, 1986.

FEDERATION OF FEMINIST WOMEN'S HEALTH CENTERS. *A New View of a Woman's Body.* New York: Simon & Schuster, 1981.

————. *Woman-Centered Pregnancy and Birth.* Pittsburgh: A Women's Publishing Company/Cleis Press, 1984.

FELL, JOSEPH. *Heidegger & Sartre: An Essay on Being & Place.* New York: Columbia University Press, 1983.

Feminist Studies. College Park, Md.

FERGUSON, KATHY E. *The Feminist Case Against Bureaucracy.* Philadelphia: Temple University Press, 1985.

FIGES, EVA. *Waking.* New York: Pantheon, 1982.

FINE, REUBEN. *The Meaning of Love in Human Experience.* New York: John Wiley & Sons, 1985.

FINKELHOR, DAVID, and YLLO KERSTI. *License to Rape: Sexual Abuse of Wives.* New York: Holt, Rinehart and Winston, 1986.

FINLEY, M. I. *Aspects of Antiquity: Discoveries and Controversies.* Harmondsworth, England: Penguin Books, 1960.

FIRESTONE, SHULAMITH. *The Dialectic of Sex,* rev. ed. New York: Bantam, 1971.

FONER, ERIC. *Tom Paine and the American Revolution.* New York: Oxford University Press, 1976.

————. *Politics and Ideology in the Age of the Civil War.* New York: Oxford University Press, 1980.

FORSTER, MARGARET. *Significant Sisters: The Grassroots of Active Feminism, 1839–1939.* New York: Alfred A. Knopf, 1985.

FORSYTH, ILENE H. *The Throne of Wisdom: Wood Sculptures of the Madonna in Romanesque France.* Princeton: Princeton University Press, 1972.

FORWARD, SUSAN, and JOAN TORRES. *Men Who Hate Women and the Women Who Love Them.* New York: Bantam, 1985.

FOUCAULT, MICHEL. *The Care of the Self.* New York: Pantheon, 1987.

————. *The History of Sexuality.* Vol. 1: *An Introduction,* trans. Robert Hurley. New York: Pantheon, 1978.

————. *The History of Sexuality.* Vol. 2: *The Uses of Pleasure,* trans. Robert Hurley. New York: Pantheon, 1985.

FRANCISKA, B. *Love, A Symposium.* Black Mountain, N.C.: New Age Press, 1976.

FRASER, ANTONIA. *The Weaker Vessel: Women's Lot in Seventeenth-Century England.* London: Weidenfeld & Nicolson, 1984.

FRAZER, SIR JAMES GEORGE, F.R.S., F.B.A. *The Golden Bough: A Study in Magic and Religion.* Vol. 1. New York: Macmillan, 1922.

FREEMAN, Jo. *The Politics of Women's Liberation.* White Plains, N.Y.: Longman, 1975.

FRIEDAN, BETTY. *The Feminine Mystique.* New York: Norton, 1963.

FROMM, ERICH. *The Art of Loving.* New York: Harper & Row, 1974.

Frontiers: A Journal of Women's Studies. Women's Studies Program, University of Colorado.

GALLOP, JANE. *Reading Lacan.* Ithaca, N.Y.: Cornell University Press, 1985.

GAY, PETER. *The Bourgeois Experience: Victoria to Freud,* Vols. 1 and 2. New York: Oxford University Press, 1984.

————. *The Enlightenment: An Interpretation.* Vol 1: *The Rise of Modern Paganism;* Vol. 2, *The Science of Freedom.* New York: Alfred A. Knopf, 1969.

GIDDENS, ANTHONY. *The Constitution of Society: Outline of the Theory of Structuration.* Berkeley: University of California Press, 1985.

GIDDINGS, PAMELA. *When and Where I Enter: The Impact of Black Woman on Race and Sex in America.* New York: William Morrow & Co., 1984.

GILBERT, V. F., and D. S. TATLA, eds. *Women's Studies: A Bibliography of Dissertations, 1870–1982.* Oxford and New York: Basil Blackwell, 1985.

GILLIGAN, CAROL. *In A Different Voice: Psychological Theory and Women's Development.* Cambridge: Harvard University Press, 1982.

GILMAN, CHARLOTTE PERKINS. *Herland: A Lost Feminist Utopian Novel.* New York: Pantheon, 1979.

GIMBUTAS, MARIJA. *The Goddesses and Gods of Old Europe: Myths and Cult Images.* Berkeley and Los Angeles: University of California Press, 1974.

GOODICH, MICHAEL. *The Unmentionable Vice: Homosexuality in the Later Medieval Period.* Santa Barbara, Cal.: ABC-Clio, 1979.

GORDON, LINDA. *Woman's Body, Woman's Right: A Social History of Birth Control in America.* New York: Viking, 1976.

GOTTLIEB, RHONDA. "The Political Economy of Sexuality" in *Review of Radical Political Economics,* Vol. 16(1): 143–165 (1984).

GRAHN, JUDY. *The Work of a Common Woman—Collected Poetry* (1964–1977). Trumansburg, N.Y.: Crossing Press, 1984.

GREEN, RICHARD, M.D., ed. *Archives of Sexual Behavior.* New York: Plenum, 1987.

GRIFFIN, SUSAN. *Pornography and Silence: Culture's Revenge Against Nature.* New York: Harper & Row, 1981.

————. *Woman and Nature: The Roaring Inside Her.* New York: Harper & Row, 1978.

GROSZ, GEORGE. *Love Above All.* New York: Schocken Books, 1985.

GUITTON, JEAN. *Human Love.* Chicago: Franciscan Herald Press, 1966.

GUTMAN, HERBERT G. *Work, Culture and Society in Industrializing America.* New York: Random House, 1977.

HAFEH, ELVIN. *Culture and Morality: The Relativity of Values in Anthropology.* New York: Columbia University Press, 1983.

HALLERT, JUDITH P. *Women and Daughters in Roman Society: Women and the Elite Family.* Guildford, England: Princeton University Press, 1985.

HAMANN, BRIGITTE. *The Reluctant Empress: A Biography of Empress Elizabeth of Austria.* New York: Alfred A. Knopf, 1986.

HAMILTON, EDITH. *Mythology.* New York: New American Library, 1940.

HAMILTON, ROBERTA. *The Liberation of Women: A Study of Patriarchy and Capitalism.* Winchester, Mass.: Allen & Unwin, 1978.

HAMMER, SIGNE. *Passionate Attachments.* New York: Rawson Associates, 1982.

HARDING, SANDRA, and MERRILL B. HINTIKKA, eds. *Discovering Reality: Feminist Perspectives on Epistemology, Metaphysics, Methodology and Philosophy of Science.* Holland: D. Reidel Publishing, 1983.

HARLOW, HARRY F., and CLARA MEARS. *The Human Model: Primate Perspectives.* New York: Halsted Press, 1979.

HARRAGAN, BETTY LEHAN. *Games Mother Never Taught You: Corporate Gamesmanship for Women.* New York: Warner Books/Rawson Associates, 1977.

HARRISON, JANE. *Prolegomena to the Study of Greek Religion.* United Kingdom: Merlin Press, 1981.

HARTMAN, SUSAN M. *The Home Front and Beyond: American Women in the 1940's.* Boston: Twayne, 1982.

HARTSOCK, NANCY C. *Money, Sex and Power: Toward a Feminist Historical Materialism.* Boston: Northeastern University Press, 1985.

HAWKES, JACQUETTA. *Dawn of the Gods: Minoan and Mycenaean Origins of Greece.* New York: Random House, 1968.

———. *Prehistory.* New York: New American Library, 1963.

HAYDEN, DOLORES. *The Grand Domestic Revolution: A History of Feminist Designs for American Homes, Neighborhoods and Cities.* Cambridge: MIT Press, 1981.

HAYZER, NOELEEN. *Working Women in South-East Asia: Development, Subordination and Emancipation.* United Kingdom: Open University Press, 1986.

HEIDEGGER, MARTIN. *The Basic Problems of Phenomenology.* Bloomington, Ind.: Indiana University Press, 1982.

———. *Being and Time.* New York: Harper & Row, 1962.

———. *The Question Concerning Technology and Other Essays.* New York: Harper & Row, 1977.

HEIDEL, ALEXANDER. *The Gilgamesh Epic and Old Testament Parallels.* Chicago: University of Chicago Press, 1946.

HIGHAM, JOHN, and PAUL K. CONKIN, eds. *New Directions in American Intellectual History.* Baltimore: Johns Hopkins University Press, 1979.

HINKLE, ROSCOE E. *Founding Theory of American Sociology.* Boston: Routledge & Kegan Paul, 1980.

HITE, SHERE. *The Hite Report.* New York: Macmillan, 1976.

———. *The Hite Report on Male Sexuality.* New York: Alfred A. Knopf, 1981.

HOAGE, R. J., ed. *Animal Extinctions, What Everyone Should Know.* Baltimore: Smithsonian Institution Press, 1985.

———, and LARRY GOLDMAN, eds. *Animal Intelligence, Insights into the Animal Mind.* Baltimore, Smithsonian Institution Press, 1986.

HOCHSCHILD, ARLIE RUSSELL. *The Managed Heart: Commercialization of Human Feeling.* Berkeley: University of California Press, 1983.

HOLCOMBE, LEE. *Wives and Property: Reform of the Married Women's Property Law in Nineteenth-Century England.* Oxford: Martin Robertson, 1982.

HOLLISTER, C. WARREN. *Medieval Europe: A Short History.* New York: John Wiley & Sons, 1964.

HOPE, LAURA LEE. *The Bobbsey Twins in Eskimo Land.* New York: Grosset & Dunlap, 1936.

HORNEY, KAREN, M.D. *Feminine Psychology.* New York: Norton, 1967.

————. *Neurosis and Human Growth: The Struggle Toward Self-Realization.* New York: Norton, 1950.

HOSKEN, FRAN P. *Female Sexual Mutilations: The Facts and Proposals for Action.* Lexington, Mass.: WIN News, 1980.

HOWARD, MICHAEL. *The Causes of Wars.* Cambridge: Harvard University Press, 1984.

HUGHES, JUDITH, and MARY MIDGELEY. *Women's Choices: Philosophical Problems Facing Feminism.* New York: Weidenfeld & Nicolson, 1984.

HUIZINGA, J. *The Waning of the Middle Ages.* New York: St. Martin's Press, 1924.

HUNT, MORTON M. *The Natural History of Love.* New York: Alfred A. Knopf, 1959.

HUSSERL, EDMUND. *Ideas: General Introduction to Pure Phenomenology and a Phenomenological Philosophy.* Boston: Kluwer/Nihoff, 1983.

HUXLEY, ALDOUS. *The Human Situation.* New York: Harper & Row, 1977.

Hypatia, A Journal of Feminist Philosophy. Edwardsville, Illinois.

ILLICH, IVAN. *Gender.* New York: Pantheon, 1983.

INGHAM, MARY. *Man: The Male Myth Exposed.* Century, 1985.

INTERNATIONAL CONFERENCE ON LOVE AND ATTRACTION. *Love and Attraction.* New York: Oxford University Press, 1979.

IRIGARAY, LUCE. *This Sex Which Is Not One.* Ithaca, N.Y.: Cornell University Press, 1985.

JACOBY, SUSAN. *The Possible She.* New York: Farrar, Straus & Giroux, 1979.

JAGGAR, A. M. *Feminist Politics and Human Nature.* Totowa, N.J.: Rowman & Allanheld, 1983.

————. *Learning Our Way.* Trumansburg, N.Y.: Crossing Press, 1983.

————, and P. ROTHENBERG. *Feminist Frameworks: Alternative Theoretical Accounts of the Relations Between Men and Women.* New York: McGraw-Hill, 1984.

JANSSEN-JURREIT, MARIE LOUISE. *Sexism: The Male Monopoly on History and Thought.* New York: Farrar, Straus & Giroux, 1976.

JAY, KARLA, and ALLEN YOUNG, eds. *The Gay Report.* New York: Simon & Schuster, 1977.

JEFFREYS, SHEILA. *The Spinster and Her Enemies: Feminism and Sexuality 1880–1930.* London and Boston: Pandora Press/Routledge & Kegan Paul, 1982.

Journal of Interdisciplinary History. MIT.

Journal of Marriage and the Family. St. Paul, Minn.: National Council of Family Relations.

JULLION, JEANNIE. *Long Way Home: The Odyssey of a Lesbian Mother and Her Children.* San Francisco and Pittsburgh: Cleis Press, 1985.

JUNG, C. G. *Aspects of the Feminine.* Princeton: Princeton University Press, 1982.

KAMEN, MARTIN D. *Radiant Science, Dark Politics: A Memoir of the Nuclear Age.* Berkeley: University of California Press, 1985.

KANT, IMMANUEL. *Foundations of the Metaphysics of Morals and What Is Enlightenment?* Indianapolis: The Bobbs-Merrill Company, Inc., 1959.

KEATS, JOHN. *You Might As Well Live; The Life and Times of Dorothy Parker.* New York: Paragon House, 1986.

KEEGAN, JOHN. *The Face of Battle: A Study of Agincourt, Waterloo and the Somme.* Harmondsworth, England: Penguin Books, 1978.

KELLER, EVELYN FOX. *Reflections on Gender and Science.* New Haven: Yale University Press, 1985.

KELLY, AMY. *Eleanor of Aquitaine and the Four Kings.* Cambridge: Harvard University Press, 1950.

KELLY, JOAN. *Women, History and Theory: The Essays of Joan Kelly.* Chicago: University of Chicago Press, 1984.

KEMPER, THEODORE. *A Social Interactional Theory of Emotions.* New York: John Wiley & Sons, 1978.

KENNEDY, SUSAN ESTABROOK. *If All We Did Was to Weep at Home: A History of White Working Class Women in America.* Bloomington, Ind.: Indiana University Press, 1980.

KEOHANE, NANNERL, MICHELLE Z. ROSALDO, and BARBARA C. GELPI. *Feminist Theory: A Critique of Ideology.* Chicago: University of Chicago Press, 1981.

KINGSTON, MAXINE HONG. *The Woman Warrior: Memoirs of a Girlhood Among Ghosts.* New York: Alfred A. Knopf, 1976.

KINSEY, ALFRED C., et al. *Sexual Behavior in the Human Female.* Philadelphia: W.B. Saunders Company, 1953.

KITTO, H. D. F. *The Greeks.* Harmondsworth, England: Penguin Books, 1951.

KLEIN, RICHARD G., and KATHRYN CRUZ-URIBE. *The Analysis of Animal Bones from Archaeological Sites.* Chicago: University of Chicago Press, 1984.

KLOTMAN, PHYLLIS R., and WILMER H. BATZ. *The Black Family, the Black Woman: A Bibliography.* Salem, N.H.: Ayer Co., 1978.

KRAFT, WILLIAM F. *Sexual Dimensions of the Celibate Life.* Kansas City, Kans.: Andrews & McMeel, 1979.

KRIEGER, S. *The Mirror Dance.* Philadelphia: Temple University Press, 1983.

LADURIE, EMMANUEL LE ROY. *The Peasants of Languedoc,* trans. John Day. Champaign, Ill.: University of Illinois Press, 1974.

LANCASTER, OSBERT. *Classical Landscape with Figures.* London: Redwood Burm Ltd., 1947.

LANG, GLADYS E., and KURT LANG. *The Battle for Public Opinion: The President, the Press and the Polls During Watergate.* New York: Columbia University Press, 1983.

LaROUCHE, JANICE, and REGINA RYAN. *Strategies for Women at Work.* New York: Avon Books/The Hearst Corporation, 1984.

LASKETT, BARBARA, ed. *Contemporary Sociology* 15(5), September 1986.

LASLETT, PETER. *The World We Have Lost: England Before the Industrial Age.* New York: Scribner, 1965.

LAVIGNAC, ALBERT. *The Musical Dramas of Richard Wagner and His Festival Theatre in Bayreuth.* New York: Dodd, Mead, 1898.

LEANDER, BERGITTA. *Women—From Witch-Hunt to Politics.* New York: The United Nations Educational, Scientific and Cultural Organization, 1985.

LEBSOCK, SUZANNE. *The Free Women of Petersburg: Status and Culture in a Southern Town 1784–1860.* New York: Norton, 1984.

LEMISCH, L. JESSE, ed. *Benjamin Franklin: The Autobiography and Other Writings.* New York: New American Library, 1961.

LENZ, CAROLYN R., et al. *The Woman's Part: Feminist Criticism of Shakespeare.* Champaign, Ill.: University of Illinois Press, 1984.

LERNER, GERDA. *The Creation of Patriarchy.* New York: Oxford University Press, 1986.

———. *The Female Experience: An American Documentary.* New York: Macmillan, 1979.

LESSING, DORIS MAY. *Documents Relating to the Sentimental Agents in the Volyen Empire.* New York: Alfred A. Knopf, 1983.

LEVITAN, SAR R., and RICHARD S. BERNS. *What's Happening to the American Family?* Baltimore: Johns Hopkins University Press, 1981.

LEWONTIN, R. C., STEVEN ROSE, and LEON J. KARIN. *Not in Our Genes: Biology, Ideology and Human Nature.* New York: Pantheon, 1984.

LINDEN, RUTH ROBIN, et al., eds. *Against Sadomasochism: A Radical Feminist Analysis.* San Francisco: Frog in Well, 1981.

LINDSEY, KAREN. *Friends As Family.* Boston: Beacon Press, 1982.

LLOYD, GENEVIEVE. *The Man of Reason: "Male" and "Female" in Western Philosophy.* Minneapolis, Minn.: University of Minnesota, 1985.

LOREZ, GUDULA. *Wo Die Nacht Den Tag Umarmt: Erotische Phantasien und Geschichten von Frauen.* Berlin: Verlag Gudula Lorez, 1979.

MALCOLM, JANET. *In the Freud Archives: Psychoanalysis and the Impossible Profession.* New York: Alfred A. Knopf, 1984.

Manushi, Indian Women's Magazine.

MARGOLIES, EVA. *The Best of Friends, the Worst of Enemies: Women's Hidden Power Over Women.* New York: Dial Press, 1985.

MARKS, ELAINE, and ISABELLE DE COURTIVRON, ed. *New French Feminisms: An Anthology.* New York: Schocken Books, 1981.

MARX, KARL, et al. *The Woman Question.* New York: International Press, 1951.

MAY, ROLLO, ed. *Existential Psychology.* New York: Random House, 1961.

McAULAY, ALASTAIR. *Women's Work and Wages in the Soviet Union.* Winchester, Mass.: Allen & Unwin, 1981.

McDERMOTT, DIANE, ed. *National Women's Studies Association Newsletter* 2:2 (1984).

McNAMARA, JOANN. *A New Song: Celibate Men/Women in the First Three Christian Centuries.* New York: Harrington Park, 1985.

MIDGLEY, MARY. *Beast and Man: The Roots of Human Nature.* Ithaca, N.Y.: Cornell University Press, 1978.

MILLER, ALICE. *For Your Own Good: Hidden Cruelty in Child Rearing and the Roots of Violence.* New York: Farrar, Straus & Giroux, 1983.

———. *Thou Shalt Not Be Aware! Society's Betrayal of the Child.* New York: New American Library, 1986.

MILLETT, KATE. *Sexual Politics.* New York: Doubleday, 1970.

———. *Sita.* New York: Farrar, Straus & Giroux, 1977.

MITCHELL, JULIET. *Women: The Longest Revolution.* New York: Pantheon, 1984.

MITFORD, NANCY. *The Sun King: Louis XIV at Versailles.* London: Hamish Hamilton, 1966.

MITTER, SWASTI. *Common Fate, Common Bond: Women in the Global Economy.* London: Allison and Busby, 1986.

MONEY, JOHN. *Love and Love Sickness: The Sciences of Sex, Gender Differences, Pair Bonding.* Baltimore: Johns Hopkins University Press, 1980.

MORGAN, ROBIN. *The Anatomy of Freedom.* New York: Anchor/Doubleday, 1982.

———, ed. *Sisterhood Is Global: The First Anthology of Writings from the International Women's Movement.* New York: Anchor/Doubleday, 1984.

MORREAU, JACQUELINE, and SARAH KENT. *Women's Images of Men.* New York: Writers and Readers, 1985.

MOSES, CLAIRE G. *French Feminism in the Nineteenth Century.* Albany, N.Y.: State University of New York Press, 1984.

———, ed. *Feminist Studies* 10:1 (1984).

MOSSIKER, FRANCES. *Madame de Sévigné: A Life and Letters.* New York: Alfred A. Knopf, 1983.

MOTHERSILL, MARY. *Beauty Restored.* Oxford: Clarendon Press/Oxford University Press, 1984.

MOUNT, FERDINAND. *The Subversive Family: An Alternative History of Love and Marriage.* Winchester, Mass.: Allen & Unwin, 1983.

McDERMOTT, DIANE, ed. *National Women's Studies Association Newsletter* 2:2 (1984).

NICHOLSON, LINDA J. *Gender and History: The Limits of Social Theory in the Age of the Family.* New York: Columbia University Press, 1986.

NIETZSCHE, FRIEDRICH. *Thus Spake Zarathustra: A Book for Everyone and No One.* New York: Penguin Books, 1961.

Nouvelle F, French women's magazine.

NUSS, SHIRLEY. "Female Representation in Political Life: Global Process and Prospects for the Future," in *International Journal of Sociology of the Family* 16:1 (Spring, 1986): 1–18.

O'BARR, JEAN F., ed. *Signs: A Journal of Women in Culture and Society* 11:3 (1986).

O'FLAHERTY, WENDY DONIGER. *Dreams, Illusions and Other Realities.* Chicago: University of Chicago Press, 1984.

OLDS, SHARON. *The Dead and the Living.* New York: Alfred A. Knopf, 1984.

———. *The Gold Cell.* New York: Alfred A. Knopf, 1987.

O'LEARY, VIRGINIA, RHODA K. UNGER, and BARBARA S. WALLSTON, eds. *Women, Gender, and Social Psychology.* Hillsdale, N.J.: Laurence Erlbaum Associates, Inc., 1985.

ORBACH, SUSIE. *Hunger Strike: The Anorectic's Struggle as Metaphor for Our Age.* Winchester, Mass.: Faber & Faber, 1986.

O'REILLY, JANE. *The Girl I Left Behind: The Housewife's Moment of Truth and Other Ravings.* New York: Macmillan, 1980.

ORTNER, SHERRY B., and HARRIET WHITEHEAD. *Sexual Meanings: The Cultural Construction of Gender and Sexuality.* New York: Cambridge University Press, 1981.

OSBORNE, MARTHA LEE, ed. *Women in Western Thought.* New York: Random House, 1980.

OUTHWAITE, R. B., ed. *Marriage and Society: Studies in the Social History of Marriage.* Philadelphia: International Publications Service, 1981.

OUTHWAITE, WILLIAM. *Concept Formation in Social Science.* New York: Methuen, 1983.

OZMENT, STEVEN. *When Fathers Ruled: Family Life in Reformation Europe.* Cambridge: Harvard University Press, 1983.

PAGNOL, MARCEL. *Topaz.* Boston: D. C. Heath & Co., 1936.

PAIGE, KAREN ERICKSEN, and JEFFERY M. PAIGE. *The Politics of Reproductive Ritual.* Berkeley: University of California Press, 1981.

PAYNE, ROBERT. *The Life and Death of Lenin.* New York: Simon & Schuster, 1964.

PETERSON, DALE. *A Mad People's History of Madness.* Pittsburgh: University of Pittsburgh Press, 1981.

PETROFF, ELIZABETH ALVILDA. *Medieval Women's Visionary Literature.* New York: Oxford University Press, 1986.

PETROVSKA, MARIJA MEROPE. *The Dramatic Impact of a Myth.* American University Studies 3. Vol. 9. New York: Peter Lang Publishing Inc., 1984.

PHILLIPS, PATRICIA. *The Prehistory of Europe.* Bloomington, Ind.: Indiana University Press, 1985.

PHILLIPSON, DAVID W. *African Archaeology.* New York: Cambridge University Press, 1985.

PITKIN, HANNA F. *Fortune Is a Woman: Gender and Politics in the Thought of Niccolo Machiavelli.* Berkeley: University of California Press, 1984.

PLAKANS, ANDREJS. *Kinship in the Past: An Anthropology of European Family Life 1500–1900.* New York: Basil Blackwell, 1985.

POGREBIN, LETTY COTTIN. *Family Politics: Love and Power on an Intimate Frontier.* New York: McGraw-Hill, 1983.

POMEROY, SARAH B. *Women in Hellenistic Egypt from Alexander to Cleopatra.* New York: Schocken Books, 1984.

PRATT, VERNON. *The Philosophy of the Social Sciences.* New York: Methuen, 1978.

PROUST, MARCEL. *Un Amour de Swann.* Paris: Editions Gallimard, 1919.

———. *The Past Recaptured,* trans. Andreas Mayor. New York: Modern Library, 1932.

———. *Remembrance of Things Past.* Vol. 2, trans. C. Scott Moncrieff and Terence Kilmartin. New York: Random House, 1927.

Psychology of Women Quarterly. American Psychological Association.

RABINOW, PAUL, and WILLIAM SULLIVAN. *Interpretive Social Science: A Reader.* Berkeley: University of California Press, 1979.

RAGLAND-SULLIVAN, ELLIE. *Jacques Lacan and the Philosophy of Psychoanalysis.* Champaign, Ill.: University of Illinois Press, 1985.

RANSOM, ROGER L., and RICHARD SUTCH. *One Kind of Freedom: The Economic Consequences of Emancipation.* Cambridge: Cambridge University Press, 1977.

RAYMOND, JANICE G. *A Passion for Friends: Toward a Philosophy of Female Affection.* Boston: Beacon Press, 1986.

REIK, THEODOR. *The Need to Be Loved.* New York: Farrar, Straus & Giroux, 1963.

REITER, RAYNA R., ed. *Toward an Anthropology of Women.* New York: Monthly Review Press, 1975.

RENVOIZE, JEAN. *Going Solo: Single Mothers by Choice.* Boston/London: Routledge & Kegan Paul, 1985.

RICH, ADRIENNE. *Compulsory Heterosexuality and Lesbian Existence.* Denver: Antelope Publications, 1982.

———. *Of Woman Born: Motherhood as Experience and Institution.* New York: Norton, 1986.

RICHARDSON, LAUREL. *The Dynamics of Sex and Gender.* Boston: Houghton Mifflin, 1977.

RIFKIN, JEREMY. *Entropy: A New World View.* New York: Viking, 1980.

ROBERTS, ELIZABETH. *A Woman's Place: An Oral History of Working-Class Women 1890–
     1940.* Oxford, England: Basil Blackwell, 1984.

ROGERS, KATHERINE M. *Feminism in Eighteenth-Century England.* Champaign, Ill.: Uni-
     versity of Illinois Press, 1982.

RORTY, AMELIE OKSEMBERG, ed. *Explaining Emotions.* Berkeley: University of Califor-
     nia Press, 1980.

ROSENBERG, ALEXANDER. *Sociology and the Preemption of Social Science.* Oxford, England:
     Basil Blackwell, 1981.

ROSENBERG, ROSALIND. *Beyond Separate Spheres: Intellectual Roots of Modern Feminism.*
     New Haven: Yale University Press, 1982.

ROSSI, ALICE S., ed. *Gender and the Life Course.* New York: Aldine Publishing, 1985.

ROWBOTHAM, SHEILA. *Dreams and Dilemmas.* New York: Virago Press, 1984.

RUDDICK, SARA, and PAMELA DANIELS, eds. *Working It Out: 23 Women Writers, Artists,
     Scientists and Scholars Talk About Their Lives and Work.* New York: Pantheon,
     1978.

RUDE, GEORGE. *Europe in the Eighteenth Century: Aristocrats and the Bourgeois Challenge.*
     New York: Praeger Publishers, 1972.

RUETHER, ROSEMARY RADFORD. *Religion and Sexism: Images of Woman in the Jewish and
     Christian Traditions.* New York: Simon & Schuster, 1974.

RUSH, FLORENCE. *The Best Kept Secret: Sexual Abuse of Children.* New York: McGraw-
     Hill, 1980.

RUSSELL, DIANA E. H. *Rape in Marriage.* New York: Macmillan, 1982.

———. *Sexual Exploitation: Rape, Child Sexual Abuse and Workplace Harassment.* Bev-
     erly Hills, Cal.: Sage Publications, 1984.

———, and NICOLE VAN DE VEN, eds. *Crimes Against Women.* Proceedings of the
     International Tribunal. East Palo Alto, Cal.: Frog in the Well, 1984.

RUSSIANOFF, PENELOPE, PH.D. *Why Do I Think I Am Nothing Without A Man?* New
     York: Bantam Books, 1982.

SAID, LAILA. *A Bridge Through Time: A Memoir.* New York: Summit Books, 1985.

SARTRE, JEAN-PAUL. *Being and Nothingness.* New York: Philosophical Library, 1956.

———. *Emotions: Outline of a Theory.* Secaucus, N.J.: 1984.

SAVERS, JANET. *Sexual Contradictions: Psychology, Psychoanalysis, and Feminism.* London:
     Tavistock.

SCHAEF, ANNE WILSON. *Women's Reality: An Emerging Female System in a White Male
     Society.* Minneapolis, Minn.: Winston Press, 1987.

SCHAEFER, LEAH CAHAN. *Women and Sex.* New York: Pantheon, 1973.

SCHLIEMANN, DR. HENRY. *Mycenae: A Narrative of Researches and Discoveries of Mycenae
     and Tiryns.* New York: Aeno Press, 1967.

SCHULENBERG, JOY. *Gay Parenting: A Complete Guide for Gay Men and Lesbians With
     Children.* New York: Anchor Press/Doubleday, 1985.

SCHUR, EDWIN M. *Labeling Women Deviant: Gender, Stigma and Social Control.* New
     York: Random House, 1984.

SCHWARZER, ALICE. *After "The Second Sex."* See Beauvoir.

———. *Die Kleine Unterschied und Seine Grossen Folgen.* Frankfurt: Fischer Taschen-
     buch, 1975.

SEAMAN, BARBARA. *Free and Female: The New Sexual Role of Women.* New York: Fawcett Crest, 1972.

SHANGE, NTOZAKE. *Betsey Brown, A Novel.* New York: St. Martin's Press, 1985.

————. *For Colored Girls Who Have Considered Suicide When the Rainbow is Enuf.* New York: Bantam, 1980.

SHERFEY, MARY JANE, M.D. *The Nature and Evolution of Female Sexuality.* New York: Random House, 1966.

SHERMAN, JULIA. *On the Psychology of Women: A Survey of Cryptical Studies.* Springfield, Ill.: C.C. Thomas, 1975.

SHIPLEY, JOSEPH T. *Dictionary of Word Origins.* New York: Philosophical Library, 1945.

SHIRER, WILLIAM L. *The Collapse of the Third Republic: An Inquiry into the Fall of France in 1940.* New York: Simon & Schuster, 1969.

The Signs Reader. Chicago: University of Chicago Press, 1983.

SIMMEL, GEORG. *On Women, Sexuality and Love.* New Haven: Yale University Press, 1984.

SIMONS, MARGARET, ed. *Hypatia: A Journal of Feminist Philosophy* 1:1 (1986).

SINGER, IRVING. *Mozart and Beethoven: The Concept of Love in Their Operas.* Baltimore: Johns Hopkins University Press, 1977.

————. *The Nature of Love.* Vol. 1, *Plato to Luther.* Chicago: University of Chicago Press, 1985.

————. *The Nature of Love.* Vol. 2, *Courtly and Romantic.* Chicago: University of Chicago Press, 1985.

SINGER, JUNE. *Androgyny: Toward a New Theory of Sexuality.* New York: Anchor/Doubleday, 1976.

SINGER, PETER. *The Expanding Circle: Ethics and Sociobiology.* New York: Clarendon Press/Oxford University Press, 1982.

SKINNER, QUENTIN, ed. *The Return of Grand Theory in the Human Sciences.* Cambridge: Cambridge University Press, 1985.

SMITH, A. J. *Literary Love: The Role of Passion in English Poems and Plays of the Seventeenth Century.* London: Edward Arnold, 1983.

SMITH, BARBARA. *Towards a Black Feminist Criticism.* Out and Out: Out and Out Pamphlet Series.

SMITH-ROSENBERG, CARROLL. *Disorderly Conduct: Visions of Gender in Victorian America.* New York: Alfred A. Knopf, 1985.

SOMMERS, FRANK G., M.D., and TANA DINEEN, PH.D. *Curing Nuclear Madness: A New Age Prescription for Personal Action.* Toronto: Methuen, 1984.

SPENCE, GERRY. *Trial by Fire: The True Story of a Woman's Ordeal at the Hands of the Law.* New York: William Morrow & Co., 1986.

SPENDER, DALE. *Man Made Language.* London: Routledge & Kegan Paul, 1985.

————. *Personal Chronicles: Women's Autobiographical Writings.* Women's Studies International Forum, Vol. 10, No. 1. Oxford: Pergamon Press, 1987.

————. *Women of Ideas and What Men Have Done to Them: From Aphra Behn to Adrienne Rich.* London: Routledge & Kegan Paul, 1982.

————, ed. *Feminist Theorists: Three Centuries of Key Women Thinkers.* New York: Pantheon, 1986.

SPENDER, LYNNE. *Intruders on the Rights of Men.* New York: Pandora, 1983.

Spengler, Oswald. *The Decline of the West.* Abridged edition. New York: Alfred A. Knopf, 1962.

Spretnak, Charlene. *Lost Goddesses of Early Greece.* Boston: Beacon Press, 1978.

———. *The Spiritual Dimension of Green Politics.* New York: Bear & Co., 1987.

Stavrianos, L. S. *The Balkans Since 1453.* New York: Holt, Rinehart and Winston, 1953.

Steinem, Gloria. *Outrageous Acts and Everyday Rebellions.* New York: Holt, Rinehart and Winston, 1983.

Stern, Fritz, ed. *The Varieties of History.* New York: Random House, 1956.

Steuber, Charles Herbert. *Sexual Racism: The Emotional Barrier to an Integrated Society.* New York: Harper & Row, 1976.

Stewart, James Brewer. *Holy Warriors: The Abolitionists and American Slavery.* New York: Hill and Wang, 1976.

Stimpson, Catherine R., and Ethel Spector Person, eds. *Women: Sex and Sexuality.* Chicago: University of Chicago Press, 1980.

Stolz, Barbara Ann. *Still Struggling: America's Low-Income Working Woman Confronting the 1980s.* Lexington, Mass.: D.C. Heath, 1985.

Stone, Lawrence. *The Family, Sex, and Marriage.* New York: Harper & Row, 1977.

Stone, Merlin. *Ancient Mirrors of Womanhood.* Vol. 1, *Our Goddess and Heroine Heritage.* New York: Sibylline Books, 1979.

Strasser, Susan. *Never Done: A History of American Housework.* New York: Pantheon, 1982.

Sturrock, John, ed. *Structuralism and Since: From Levi-Strauss to Derrida.* Oxford: Oxford University Press, 1979.

Suleiman, Susan Rubin. *The Female Body in Western Culture: Contemporary Perspectives.* Cambridge, Mass.: Harvard University Press, 1986.

Sullivan, John L., ed. *Qualitative Applications in the Social Sciences.* Beverly Hills, Cal.: Sage Publications Inc., 1979.

Sundquist, James L. "Has America Lost Its Social Conscience—And How Will It Get It Back?" In *Political Science Quarterly* 101:4 (1986): 513–33.

Swerdlow, Amy, Renata Bridenthal, and Joan Phyllis Kelly. *Household and Kin: Families in Flux.* Old Westbury, N.Y.: Feminist Press, 1981.

Sylvan, David, and Barry Glossner. *A Rationalist Methodology for the Social Sciences.* Oxford: Basil Blackwell, 1985.

Symons, Donald. *The Evolution of Human Sexuality.* New York: Oxford University Press, 1979.

Tanner, Nancy. *On Becoming Human.* Cambridge, England: Cambridge University Press, 1981.

Taylor, Barbara. *Socialism and Feminism in the Nineteenth Century.* Manchester, N.H.: Virago, 1983.

Teilhard de Chardin, Pierre. *On Love.* New York: Harper & Row, 1972.

Tennov, Dorothy. *Love and Limerence: The Experience of Being in Love.* New York: Stein & Day, 1981.

Tentler, Leslie Woodcock. *Wage-Earning Women: Industrial Work and Family Life in the United States.* New York: Oxford University Press, 1980.

Thackray, Arnold, ed. *Isis: An International Review Devoted to the History of Science and Its Cultural Influences.* 1983.

Thomas, Keith. *Religion and the Decline of Magic.* New York: Scribner, 1971.

THOMPSON, E. P. *The Making of the English Working Class.* New York: Vintage, 1963.

TILLY, LOUISE A., and JOAN W. SCOTT. *Women, Work and Family.* New York: Holt, Rinehart and Winston, 1978.

TIRYAKIAN, EDWARD A. "Sociology's Great Leap Forward: The Challenge of Internationalization," *International Sociology* 1:2 (1986): 155–71.

TODD, JANET. *Women's Friendship in Literature.* New York: Columbia University Press, 1980.

TRUMBACK, RANDOLPH. *The Rise of the Egalitarian Family: Aristocratic Kinship and Domestic Relations in Eighteenth-Century England.* New York: Academic Press, 1978.

TUCHMAN, GAYE, ARLENE KAPLAN DANIELS, and JAMES BENET. *Hearth & Home: Images of Women in Mass Media.* New York: Oxford University Press, 1978.

ULRICH, LAUREL THATCHER. *Good Wives: Image and Reality in Northern New England 1650–1750.* New York: Oxford University Press, 1980.

VALE, JULIET. *Edward III and Chivalry: Chivalric Society and its Context 1270–1350.* Woodbridge, England: Boydell and Brewer, 1983.

VETTERUNG-BRAGGIN, MARY, ed. *Sexist Language: A Modern Philosophical Analysis.* Totowa, N.J.: Rowman & Allanheld, 1981.

VIDA, GINNY, ed. *Our Right to Love: A Lesbian Resource Book.* Englewood Cliffs, N.J.: Prentice-Hall, 1978.

VISURE, ELINA. *Poverty and Children: A Study of Family Planning.* Helsinki, Finland: The Academic Bookstore, 1969.

WALKLEY, CHRISTINA. *The Ghost in the Looking Glass: The Victorian Seamstress.* London: Peter Owen, 1981.

WALLACE, MICHELE. *Black Macho and the Myth of the Super Woman.* New York: Dial Press, 1978.

WARNER, MARINA. *Alone of All Her Sex: The Myth and the Cult of the Virgin Mary.* New York: Random House, 1976.

———. *Joan of Arc: The Image of Female Heroism.* New York: Alfred A. Knopf, 1981.

WATKINS, SUSAN COTTS, JANE A. MENKEN, and JOHN BONGAARTS, "Demographic Foundations of Family Change," *American Sociological Review* 52 (June 1987): 346–58.

WEBER, EUGEN. *Peasants into Frenchmen: The Modernization of Rural France, 1870–1914.* Stanford: Stanford University Press, 1976.

WEEKS, JEFFREY. *Sexuality and its Discontents: Meanings, Myths & Modern Sexuality.* London: Routledge & Kegan Paul, 1985.

WEISSTEIN, NAOMI. " 'Kinder, Kuche, Kirche' as Scientific Law: Psychology Creates the Female" in *Sisterhood is Powerful,* ed. Robin Morgan. New York: Random House, 1970.

WEISSTEIN, NAOMI, VIRGINIA BLAISDELL, and JESSE LEMISCH. *The Godfathers: Freudians, Marxists and the Scientific and Political Protection Societies.* New Haven: Belladonna Publishing, 1981.

WESTKOTT, MARCIA. *The Feminist Legacy of Karen Horney.* New Haven: Yale University Press, 1986.

WHITEHEAD, ALFRED NORTH. *Process and Reality: An Essay in Cosmology.* New York: Harper & Bros., 1929.

WHITMARSH, ANNE. *Simone de Beauvoir and the Limits of Commitment.* New York: Cambridge University Press, 1981.

WHYTE, MARTIN KING. *The Status of Women in Pre-Industrial Societies.* New Haven: Belladonna Publishing, 1981.

WIERZBICKA. "Human Emotions: Universal or Culture-Specific?" *American Anthropologist* 88 (1986).

WITTGENSTEIN, LUDWIG. *The Blue and Brown Books: Preliminary Studies for the Philosophical Investigations.* New York: Harper & Row, 1958.

WITTIG, MONIQUE. *Les Guerilleres.* Boston: Beacon Press, 1985.

Women's International Network News. Lexington, Mass.: WIN News, 1987.

The Women's Review of Books. Wellesley, Mass.: Wellesley College.

Women's Studies International Forum. Oxford: Pergamon Press.

ZURIFF, G. E. *Behaviorism: A Conceptual Reconstruction.* New York: Columbia University Press, 1985.

Please state your views

Shere Hite would very much like to hear from readers as to their thoughts about the issues raised in this volume. All discussions of the contents would be welcomed, as would personal experiences or reflections. Alternatively, those who would like to may answer the following specific questions:

1. With which parts of this book did you most agree? disagree? find most emotionally involving?

2. Do any experiences of your own coincide with those women have described in this book?

3. Do you feel women today, as reflected here, are generally angry, frustrated, or basically happy? Which are you?

4. What was your mood as you read this book—or what moods did you feel while reading different parts of the book?

5. How is your own personal life going? What is the best thing about it? the worst? Are you anticipating any changes, or have you made any changes recently?

6. Would you like to run for political office? Why or why not?

7. What gives you the most satisfaction? your work? someone you love? your spare time?

8. Please add anything else you would like to say.

Send your replies and other thoughts relating to this work to Shere Hite, Post Office Box 5282, F.D.R. Station, New York, New York 10022. Please include your age, occupation, and any other relevant information.

A NOTE ON THE TYPE

This book was set on the Linotype in Janson, a recutting made
direct from type cast from matrices long thought to have been
made by the Dutchman Anton Janson, who was a practicing
type founder in Leipzig during the years 1668–1687.
However, it has been conclusively demonstrated that these types
are actually the work of Nicholas Kis (1650–1702), a
Hungarian, who most probably learned his trade from the
master Dutch type founder Dirk Voskens. The type is an
excellent example of the influential and sturdy Dutch types that
prevailed in England up to the time William Caslon
(1692–1766) developed his own incomparable designs
from them.

Composed by The Haddon Craftsmen Inc.,
Scranton, Pennsylvania

Printed and bound by R. R. Donnelley & Sons,
Harrisonburg, Virginia

Designed by Marysarah Quinn